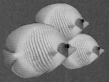

Organisational Behaviour

on the Pacific Rim | 2e

The McGraw·Hill Companies

McGraw-Hill
Irwin

National Library of Australia Cataloguing-in-Publication Data

McShane, Steven Lattimore.
    Organisational behaviour on the Pacific rim.

    2nd ed.
    Includes index.
    For tertiary students.
    ISBN 0 07 471658 1.

    1. Organizational behavior—Pacific Area. I. Travaglione,
    A. II. Title.

302.35

Published in Australia by
McGraw-Hill Australia Pty Ltd
Level 2, 82 Waterloo Road, North Ryde, NSW 2113, Australia
Publisher: Ailsa Brackley du Bois
Developmental Editors: Lucie Stevens, Georgia McElvaney
Publishing Services Manager: Jo Munnelly
Marketing Manager: Jennifer Lim
Editor: Felicity McKenzie
Designer and Typesetter: Tricia McCallum
Illustrator: Kim Webber
Permissions Editor: Leanne Poll
Proofreader: Tim Learner
Indexer: Di Harriman
Printed on 65gsm matt art in China by CTPS

Organisational Behaviour
on the Pacific Rim | 2e

Steven McShane
Graduate School of Management
University of Western Australia

Tony Travaglione
Asia Pacific Graduate School of Management
Charles Sturt University

McGraw-Hill
Irwin

Boston   Burr Ridge, IL   Dubuque, IA   Madison, WI   New York
San Francisco   St. Louis   Bangkok   Bogotá   Caracas   Kuala Lumpur
Lisbon   London   Madrid   Mexico City   Milan   Montreal   New Delhi
Santiago   Seoul   Singapore   Sydney   Taipei   Toronto

Welcome to McGraw-Hill's

It's all about flexibility. Today. You want to be able to teach your course, your way. McGraw-Hill offers you extensive choices in content selection and delivery backed by uncompromising service.

Your course: Connect your students with leading texts and study guides, websites, online readings, online cases, online course materials and revision programs. To assist you in teaching your course, McGraw-Hill provides you with cutting edge resources, including online testing and revision, instructor's manuals and guides, test banks, visual resources and PowerPoint slide shows. Your McGraw-Hill Academic Sales Consultant is trained to help match your course with our content, today.

Your way: Your McGraw-Hill Academic Sales Consultant, our instructional designer, and our E-learning team are trained to help you customise our content for your existing or new course. We carefully examine and match your course to our content and then discuss what, how, and when you would like it to be delivered — online or in print. It is that easy.

Your guarantee: Our programs are backed by our unique service guarantee. If you are a loyal McGraw-Hill customer, we will convert your course to our content each time your course changes — we use only qualified instructional designers or we consult with your own academic staff. Ask about our Course Conversion Program today!

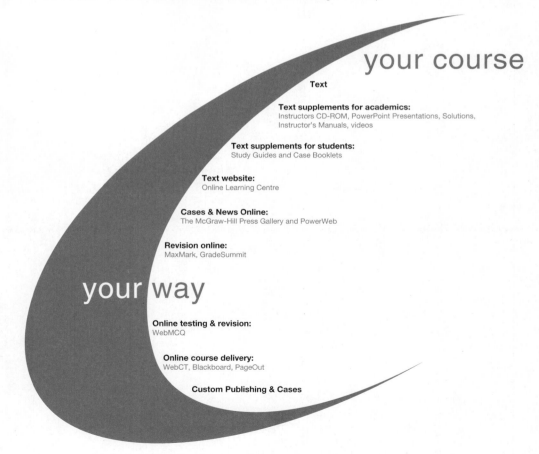

your course

Text

Text supplements for academics:
Instructors CD-ROM, PowerPoint Presentations, Solutions, Instructor's Manuals, videos

Text supplements for students:
Study Guides and Case Booklets

Text website:
Online Learning Centre

Cases & News Online:
The McGraw-Hill Press Gallery and PowerWeb

Revision online:
MaxMark, GradeSummit

your way

Online testing & revision:
WebMCQ

Online course delivery:
WebCT, Blackboard, PageOut

Custom Publishing & Cases

www.mcgraw-hill.com.au/contenttoday

About the authors

STEVEN McSHANE

STEVEN L. McSHANE is Professor of Management in the Graduate School of Management at the University of Western Australia, where he receives high teaching ratings from students in Perth, Singapore, and other cities where UWA offers its programs. He is also an Honourary Professor at Universiti Tunku Abdul Rahman (UTAR) in Malaysia and previously taught in the business faculties at Simon Fraser University and Queen's University in Canada. He is a past president of the Administrative Sciences Association of Canada. Steve earned his PhD from Michigan State University, a Master of Industrial Relations from the University of Toronto, and an undergraduate degree from Queen's University in Canada.

Steve has conducted executive seminars with Nokia throughout Asia, the Australian Healthcare Association, Wesfarmers Group, Peters Brownes Group, ALCOA World Alumina Australia, Vasse Felix Wines, Clough Engineering, Healthcare Association of Western Australia, the Conference Board of Canada, and many other organisations. He is also a popular visiting speaker, having given four-dozen talks to faculty and students in almost a dozen countries over the past three years.

Along with co-authoring *Organisational Behaviour on the Pacific Rim*, Steve co-authors (with Mary Ann von Glinow at Florida International University) *Organizational Behavior: Emerging Realities for the Workplace Revolution*, 3rd edition (2005) and *Organizational Behavior: Essentials* (2007). He is also the sole author of Canadian *Organizational Behaviour*, 6th edition (2006). Steve has also published several dozen articles and conference papers on diverse topics, including knowledge management, the socialisation of new employees, gender bias in job evaluation, wrongful dismissal, media bias in business magazines, and labour union participation.

Aside from teaching and writing, Steve enjoys spending his leisure time swimming, body board surfing, canoeing, skiing and travelling with his wife and two daughters.

Steven McShane (left) and Tony Travaglione teaching in Singapore.
Photo courtesy of Richard Ang.

TONY TRAVAGLIONE

TONY TRAVAGLIONE is Professor of Management and Sub Dean Corporate Relations at Charles Sturt University. Over the course of his career, Tony has held a number of senior leadership roles including Professor and Dean of the Adelaide Graduate School of Business and Professor and Head of the Newcastle Graduate School of Business. He has also held the position of Visiting Professor at the Stanford University Graduate School of Business.

Tony holds a Doctor of Philosophy degree from the University of Western Australia. He is recognised internationally as an expert in the area of leadership. He has developed numerous leadership development programs for both public and private sector organisations. He is skilled in the delivery and feedback of a number of assessment instruments, ranging from staff attitudes to leadership style inventories. Tony is currently working on an Australian Research Council (ARC) grant in collaboration with Main Roads Western Australia on developing a new approach to values driven leadership.

Tony has been active in the area of consulting in Australia and overseas. In Australia, his clients have included the ANZ Bank, QANTAS, Main Roads Western Australia, Westrail, Hunter Area Health and Centrelink. His consultancy work has appeared in prestigious and rigorously refereed international journals including the *International Journal of Human Resource Management* (UK), *Personnel Review* (UK), *Journal of Managerial Psychology* (USA), *Journal of Strategic Change* (UK) and the *Journal of Business and Leadership* (USA).

Tony has always enjoyed his spare time by the beach and walking. In more recent years he developed a keen interest in cooking traditional Italian and Greek dishes.

Preface

WELCOME TO A NEW ERA OF ORGANISATIONAL BEHAVIOUR! Knowledge is replacing infrastructure. Values and self-leadership are superseding command-and-control 'management'. Networks are replacing hierarchies. Virtual teams are replacing committees. Companies are looking for employees with emotional intelligence, not just technical smarts. Globalisation has become the mantra of corporate survival. Co-workers aren't down the hall; they're at the other end of an Internet connection located somewhere else on the planet.

Organisational Behaviour on the Pacific Rim, 2nd edition, is written in the context of these emerging workplace realities. It prepares students for this new era by discussing the latest OB concepts, such as four-drive theory, resilience, emotional intelligence, virtual teams, social identity theory, and knowledge management. This book has also become respected for being the first to describe several contemporary issues and practices, such as employee engagement, corporate blogs and wikis, future search conferences, psychological harassment, bicultural audits, and appreciative inquiry.

Active learning, critical thinking, and outcomes-based teaching have become important foundations of classroom learning, and *Organisational Behaviour on the Pacific Rim* sets the standard of support by providing dozens of cases, team exercises, self-assessments, video programs, and online support materials. Dismissing the traditional model that OB is for managers alone, this book also pioneered the more realistic view that OB is for everyone who works in and around organisations.

Contents in brief

PART 1	INTRODUCTION	1
Chapter 1	Introduction to the field of organisational behaviour	2

PART 2	INDIVIDUAL BEHAVIOUR AND PROCESSES	33
Chapter 2	Individual behaviour, values and personality	34
Chapter 3	Perception and learning in organisations	68
Chapter 4	Workplace emotions and attitudes	104
Chapter 5	Motivation in the workplace	136
Chapter 6	Applied performance practices	170
Chapter 7	Work-related stress and stress management	200

PART 3	TEAM PROCESSES	231
Chapter 8	Decision making and creativity	232
Chapter 9	Foundations of team dynamics	264
Chapter 10	Developing high-performance teams	294
Chapter 11	Communicating in teams and organisations	324
Chapter 12	Power and influence in the workplace	354
Chapter 13	Conflict and negotiation in the workplace	384
Chapter 14	Leadership in organisational settings	412

PART 4	ORGANISATIONAL PROCESSES	443
Chapter 15	Organisational structure	444
Chapter 16	Organisational culture	474
Chapter 17	Organisational change	500

Additional cases		527
Appendix A	Theory building and systematic research methods	546
Appendix B	Scoring keys for self-assessment activities	556
Glossary		572
Index		580

Contents

About the authors v
Preface vi
Student CD-ROM xv
Text at a glance xvi

E-student xx
E-instructor xxii
About the book xxiv
Acknowledgments xxvi

PART 1   INTRODUCTION   1

CHAPTER 1   INTRODUCTION TO THE FIELD OF ORGANISATIONAL BEHAVIOUR   2

The field of organisational behaviour 4
Organisational behaviour trends 6
The five anchors of organisational behaviour 14
Knowledge management 19
The journey begins 22
Chapter summary 23
Key terms 24
Discussion questions 24

Learning objectives 2
Skill builder 1.1 Case study: Ancol Pty Ltd 24
Skill builder 1.2 Team exercise 25
Skill builder 1.3 Web exercise 26
Skill builder 1.4 Self-assessment 27
Skill builder 1.5 Self-assessment 28
Reality check 1.1 Attracting talent through work–life balance 11
Notes 28

PART 1 VIDEO CASE STUDY

New Belgium Brewery 32

PART 2   INDIVIDUAL BEHAVIOUR AND PROCESSES   33

CHAPTER 2   INDIVIDUAL BEHAVIOUR, VALUES AND PERSONALITY   34

MARS model of individual behaviour and results 36
Types of individual behaviour in organisations 39
Values in the workplace 42
Values across cultures 46
Ethical values and behaviour 49
Personality in organisations 52
Chapter summary 58
Key terms 59
Discussion questions 59

Learning objectives 34
Skill builder 2.1 Case study: Pushing paper can be fun 59
Skill builder 2.2 Team exercise 60
Skill builder 2.3 Team exercise 61
Skill builder 2.4 Self-assessment 62
Skill builder 2.5 Self-assessment 63
Skill builder 2.6 Self-assessment 63
Skill builder 2.7 Self-assessment 63
Skill builder 2.8 Self-assessment 63
Reality check 2.1 Company 'brand' attracts talent 41
Notes 64

CHAPTER 3   PERCEPTION AND LEARNING IN ORGANISATIONS   68

The perceptual process	70	Learning objectives	68
Social identity theory	73	**Skill builder 3.1** Case study: From Lippert-Johanson Inc.	
Stereotyping in organisational settings	75	to Fenway	94
Attribution theory	78	**Skill builder 3.2** Class exercise	96
Self-fulfilling prophecy	80	**Skill builder 3.3** Team exercise	97
Other perceptual errors	82	**Skill builder 3.4** Web exercise	98
Improving perceptions	83	**Skill builder 3.5** Self-assessment	99
Learning in organisations	84	**Skill builder 3.6** Self-assessment	100
Behaviour modification: learning through reinforcement	85	**Skill builder 3.7** Self-assessment	100
Social learning theory: learning by observing	87	**Reality check 3.1** Stereotyping and social identity	
Learning through experience	89	discourage women from entering engineering	76
Chapter summary	92	**Reality check 3.2** Reinforcing leading and lagging	
Key terms	94	indicators of workplace safety	88
Discussion questions	94	Notes	100

CHAPTER 4   WORKPLACE EMOTIONS AND ATTITUDES   104

Emotions in the workplace	106	Learning objectives	104
Managing emotions at work	111	**Skill builder 4.1** Case study: Fran Hayden joins	
Emotional intelligence	113	Dairy Engineering	125
Job satisfaction	116	**Skill builder 4.2** Class exercise	129
Organisational commitment	119	**Skill builder 4.3** Team exercise	129
Psychological contracts	121	**Skill builder 4.4** Self-assessment	130
Chapter summary	124	**Skill builder 4.5** Self-assessment	132
Key terms	125	**Reality check 4.1** Japan's freeters bring a new	
Discussion questions	125	psychological contract to the workplace	123
		Notes	132

CHAPTER 5   MOTIVATION IN THE WORKPLACE   136

Needs, drives and employee motivation	138	Learning objectives	136
Expectancy theory of motivation	145	**Skill builder 5.1** Case study: Buddy's	
Goal setting and feedback	149	Snack Company	161
Organisational justice	153	**Skill builder 5.2** Team exercise	163
Chapter summary	159	**Skill builder 5.3** Self-assessment	164
Key terms	161	**Skill builder 5.4** Self-assessment	165
Discussion questions	161	**Reality check 5.1** Protesting unfair 'fat cat' pay in the	
		United Kingdom	157
		Notes	165

Contents (continued)

CHAPTER 6   APPLIED PERFORMANCE PRACTICES   170

Financial reward practices	172	Learning objectives	170
Job design practices	179	**Skill builder 6.1** Case study: The Regency Grand Hotel	191
Empowerment practices	184	**Skill builder 6.2** Team exercise	193
Self-leadership practices	186	**Skill builder 6.3** Self-assessment	195
Chapter summary	190	**Skill builder 6.4** Self-assessment	196
Key terms	191	**Skill builder 6.5** Self-assessment	196
Discussion questions	191	**Reality check 6.1** When rewards go wrong	178
		Reality check 6.2 The empowerment of Semco	185
		Notes	197

CHAPTER 7   WORK-RELATED STRESS AND STRESS MANAGEMENT   200

What is stress?	202	Learning objectives	200
Stressors: the causes of stress	204	**Skill builder 7.1** Case study: A typical day for Joe Hansen, managing director	220
Individual differences in stress	210	**Skill builder 7.2** Team exercise	223
Consequences of distress	211	**Skill builder 7.3** Self-assessment	223
Managing work-related stress	213	**Skill builder 7.4** Self-assessment	224
Chapter summary	219	**Skill builder 7.5** Self-assessment	225
Key terms	220	**Skill builder 7.6** Self-assessment	225
Discussion questions	220	**Reality check 7.1** *Karoshi*: death by overwork continues to invade Asia	207
		Notes	225

PART 2 VIDEO CASE STUDIES

Employee loyalty	228
Pike Place fish market	228
Stress in Japan	229
The Container Store	229

PART 3 TEAM PROCESSES

CHAPTER 8 DECISION MAKING AND CREATIVITY 232

Rational choice paradigm of decision making	234	Learning objectives	232
Identifying problems and opportunities	235	Skill builder 8.1 Case study: Employee involvement cases	252
Evaluating and choosing alternatives	238	Skill builder 8.2 Class exercise	254
Evaluating decision outcomes	241	Skill builder 8.3 Team exercise	255
Employee involvement in decision making	244	Skill builder 8.4 Team exercise	257
Creativity	246	Skill builder 8.5 Class exercise	259
Chapter summary	251	Skill builder 8.6 Self-assessment	259
Key terms	252	Skill builder 8.7 Self-assessment	260
Discussion questions	252	Skill builder 8.8 Self-assessment	260
		Reality check 8.1 Famous missed opportunities	237
		Notes	260

CHAPTER 9 FOUNDATIONS OF TEAM DYNAMICS 264

Teams and groups	266	Learning objectives	264
A model of team effectiveness	269	Skill builder 9.1 Case study: Treetop Forest Products	286
Organisational and team environment	269	Skill builder 9.2 Team exercise	288
Team design features	271	Skill builder 9.3 Self-assessment	289
Team processes	274	Reality check 9.1 Elite New Zealand prison team's	
The trouble with teams	283	'culture of obedience'	278
Chapter summary	285	Notes	290
Key terms	286		
Discussion questions	286		

CHAPTER 10 DEVELOPING HIGH-PERFORMANCE TEAMS 294

Self-directed work teams	296	Learning objectives	294
Virtual teams	301	Skill builder 10.1 Case study: The shipping industry	
Team trust	304	accounting team	316
Team decision making	306	Skill builder 10.2 Team exercise	317
Team building	311	Skill builder 10.3 Self-assessment	318
Chapter summary	314	Skill builder 10.4 Self-assessment	319
Key terms	316	Reality check 10.1 Celestica's lean self-directed work teams	298
Discussion questions	316	Notes	319

Contents (continued)

CHAPTER 11 COMMUNICATING IN TEAMS AND ORGANISATIONS 324

A model of communication   326
Communication channels   327
Choosing the best communication channels   331
Communication barriers (noise)   333
Cross-cultural and gender communication   336
Improving interpersonal communication   338
Communicating in organisational hierarchies   340
Communicating through the grapevine   343
Chapter summary   344
Key terms   345
Discussion questions   345

Learning objectives   324
Skill builder 11.1 Case study: Bridging the two
    worlds—the organisational dilemma   345
Skill builder 11.2 Team exercise   347
Skill builder 11.3 Team exercise   347
Skill builder 11.4 Team exercise   349
Skill builder 11.5 Self-assessment   349
Reality check 11.1 British organisations ban email to
    rediscover the art of conversation   329
Reality check 11.2 Nonverbal gestures help crowd
    control during Iraq war   331
Notes   350

CHAPTER 12 POWER AND INFLUENCE IN THE WORKPLACE 354

The meaning of power   356
Sources of power in organisations   357
Contingencies of power   360
Influencing others   363
Influence tactics and organisational politics   369
Chapter summary   373
Key terms   374
Discussion questions   374

Learning objectives   354
Skill builder 12.1 Case study: Nirvana Art Gallery 374
Skill builder 12.2 Team exercise   377
Skill builder 12.3 Self-assessment   378
Skill builder 12.4 Self-assessment   379
Skill builder 12.5 Self-assessment   379
Skill builder 12.6 Self-assessment   380
Reality check 12.1 Politics at WorldCom lead to
    record-breaking accounting fraud   371
Notes   380

CHAPTER 13 CONFLICT AND NEGOTIATION IN THE WORKPLACE 384

The conflict process   386
Sources of conflict in organisations   389
Interpersonal conflict management styles   393
Structural approaches to conflict management   396
Resolving conflict through negotiation   399
Third-party conflict resolution   402
Chapter summary   405
Key terms   406
Discussion questions   406

Learning objectives   384
Skill builder 13.1 Case study: Conflict in close quarters 406
Skill builder 13.2 Team exercise   408
Skill builder 13.3 Self-assessment   409
Reality check 13.1 Arthur Andersen's fee feuding 392
Reality check 13.2 Telstra's new executive team
    tries a forcing conflict handling style   395
Notes   410

CHAPTER 14 LEADERSHIP IN ORGANISATIONAL SETTINGS · 412

Perspectives of leadership · 414
Competency (trait) perspective of leadership · 415
Behavioural perspective of leadership · 417
Contingency perspective of leadership · 418
Path–goal theory of leadership · 418
Other contingency theories · 422
Transformational perspective of leadership · 424
Implicit leadership perspective · 428
Cross-cultural and gender issues in leadership · 429
Chapter summary · 432
Key terms · 433
Discussion questions · 433

Learning objectives · 412
Skill builder 14.1 Case study: Josh Martin · 433
Skill builder 14.2 Team exercise · 435
Skill builder 14.3 Self-assessment · 435
Reality check 14.1 Procter & Gamble trades charisma for transformational substance · 425
Reality check 14.2 Leading through *ubuntu* values · 430
Notes · 436

PART 3 VIDEO CASE STUDIES

Bully Broads 440
Celebrity CEO charisma 441

PART 4   ORGANISATIONAL PROCESSES · 443

CHAPTER 15 ORGANISATIONAL STRUCTURE · 444

Division of labour and coordination · 446
Elements of organisational structure · 449
Forms of departmentalisation · 453
Contingencies of organisational design · 462
Chapter summary · 465
Key terms · 466
Discussion questions · 466

Learning objectives · 444
Skill builder 15.1 Case study: FTCA: Regional and headquarters relations · 466
Skill builder 15.2 Team exercise · 469
Skill builder 15.3 Self-assessment · 470
Reality check 15.1 The extreme team structure of W. L. Gore & Associates · 459
Notes · 471

Contents (continued)

CHAPTER 16 ORGANISATIONAL CULTURE 474

Elements of organisational culture 476
Deciphering organisational culture through artefacts 478
Organisational culture and performance 480
Merging organisational cultures 484
Changing and strengthening organisational culture 487
Organisational socialisation 489
Chapter summary 493
Key terms 494
Discussion questions 494

Learning objectives 474
Skill builder 16.1 Case study: Hillton's transformation 494
Skill builder 16.2 Web exercise 496
Skill builder 16.3 Team exercise 496
Skill builder 16.4 Self-assessment 496
Reality check 16.1 German advertising firm embraces a 'back to work' culture 482
Reality check 16.2 Schwab suffers the perils of clashing cultures 485
Notes 498

CHAPTER 17 ORGANISATIONAL CHANGE AND DEVELOPMENT 500

Lewin's force field analysis model 502
Unfreezing, changing and refreezing 505
Strategic visions, change agents and diffusing change 511
Three approaches to organisational change 512
Cross-cultural and ethical issues in organisational change 516
Personal change for the road ahead 517
Organisational behaviour: the journey continues 518
Chapter summary 519
Key terms 520
Discussion questions 520

Learning objectives 500
Skill builder 17.1 Case study: The excellent employee 520
Skill builder 17.2 Team exercise 521
Skill builder 17.3 Self-assessment 522
Reality check 17.1 Carlos Ghosn relies on high involvement to transform Nissan 509
Notes 524

PART 4 VIDEO CASE STUDIES

Childcare help 526
Home sweet home, work sweet work 526

ADDITIONAL CASES 527

CASE 1 Anchor Foods 528
CASE 2 Arctic Mining Consultants 530
CASE 3 Big Screen's big failure 532
CASE 4 High noon at Alpha Mills 537
CASE 5 Not all call centres are the workhorses of the twenty-first century 539
CASE 6 Perfect Pizzeria 541
CASE 7 Strategic change at Computarget 543

APPENDIX A THEORY BUILDING AND SYSTEMATIC RESEARCH METHODS 546

APPENDIX B SCORING KEYS FOR SELF-ASSESSMENT ACTIVITIES 556

GLOSSARY 572

INDEX 580

Student CD-ROM

VIDEO CLIPS

- Watch how the manager of Pike Place Fish Market turned his business around and made it renowned for employee motivation. Witness how coaching has helped female executives working in Silicon Valley labelled as 'aggressive' regain an appropriate amount of power and influence in the workplace. Learn how other theories of organisational behaviour are put into practice in a live workplace setting.
- Each clip is supported by a corresponding video case study that summarises the key concepts represented in the footage.
- Discussion questions challenge you to explore the issues raised in the video clips

FOR INSTRUCTORS

Video clips are available on DVD or VHS for qualified adopters of *Organisational Behaviour on the Pacific Rim*, for use in lecture theatres. Please contact your McGraw-Hill representative for more information.

SELF-ASSESSMENT EXERCISES

The CD-ROM includes nearly three dozen self-assessment exercises that reflect the concepts described throughout the text. These self-assessments support the active learning process that helps you to understand and absorb OB concepts.

Most self-assessments are scientifically developed, validated and documented in reputable sources such as *Educational and Psychological Measurement*, *Organisational Research Methods*, *Journal of Management*, *Personality and Individual Differences* and *Academy of Management Journal*.

These self-assessments capture the latest OB concepts, including workaholism, self-leadership, dispositional mood, self-efficacy, empowerment, telework disposition and creative personality.

FILL IN THE BLANKS

Nearly 200 fill-in-the-blanks questions help you learn OB terminology and concepts. They also offer you the opportunity to quickly revise key concepts.

YOUR NEW COPY OF *ORGANISATIONAL BEHAVIOUR ON THE PACIFIC RIM* IS PACKAGED WITH A FREE CD-ROM WHICH CONTAINS PROFESSIONALLY PRODUCED INTERNATIONAL VIDEO CLIPS, SELF-ASSESSMENT EXERCISES, AND FILL-IN-THE-BLANKS QUIZZES.

Text at a glance

ORGANISATIONAL BEHAVIOUR ON THE PACIFIC RIM 2E is a pedagogically rich learning resource. The features laid out on these pages are specifically designed to enhance your learning experience and help you gain a deeper understanding of the concepts this text examines.

CHAPTER MATERIAL

CHAPTER OPENERS WITH LEARNING OBJECTIVES

Every chapter opens with a series of learning objectives, outlining the skills that you should have attained upon completing each chapter. Each learning objective is repeated in the margin of the main text, where the relevant material is covered (see pp.324–5).

OPENING VIGNETTE

Each chapter opens with an introductory vignette. These stories will help you place the concepts covered in the chapter, into the context of a real organisation (see p.152).

Top spread (pp. 152–153)

leadership development of its senior executive group. As the name implies, multisource feedback is information about an employee's performance collected from a full circle of people. The Australian government managers receive feedback from their boss, four subordinates and two other people familiar with their work. These people anonymously complete the online survey, and managers receive the feedback as a report showing the combined results.

Research suggests that multisource feedback tends to provide more complete and accurate information than feedback from a supervisor alone. It is particularly useful when the supervisor is unable to observe the employee's behaviour or performance throughout the year. Lower-level employees also feel a greater sense of fairness and open communication when they are able to provide upward feedback about their boss's performance.

However, multisource feedback also creates challenges. Having several people review so many other people can be expensive and time-consuming. With multiple opinions, the 360-degree process can also produce ambiguous and conflicting feedback, so employees may require guidance to interpret the results. A third concern is that peers may provide inflated rather than accurate feedback to avoid conflicts over the forthcoming year. A final concern is that critical feedback from many people can create a stronger emotional reaction than if the critical judgment originates from just one person (your boss).

Executive coaching

executive coaching A helping relationship using behavioural methods to assist clients in identifying and achieving goals for their professional performance and personal satisfaction.

Another rapidly growing practice involving feedback and motivation is **executive coaching**, which uses a wide variety of behavioural methods to assist clients to identify and achieve goals for their performance and well-being. Executive coaching is usually conducted by an external consultant and involves one-on-one 'just-in-time' personal development using feedback and other techniques. Coaches do not provide answers to the employee's problems. Rather,

P&O Nedlloyd's Australian chief gets coached

Soon after his promotion to general manager of P&O Nedlloyd in Australia, Bob Kemp hired an executive coach to help him discover and repair his vulnerabilities. He was particularly keen to share up his self-awareness skills because, as the top executive, there was no one above him at the shipping and logistics firm to regularly monitor his interpersonal style as a leader. Over several sessions, the executive coach teased out Kemp's weak spots, such as his listening skills and being approachable. Before long, Kemp's colleagues and wife noticed a positive change. 'Very early in the process, people started telling me I was changing, and I started to feel more at ease in the new role,' Kemp recalls. He also noticed that people were 'walking out of my office with a slightly more positive attitude'.

they are 'thought partners' who offer accurate feedback, open dialogue and constructive encouragement to improve the client's performance and personal well-being.

The evidence so far is that executives who work with an executive coach perform better than those who do not. Coaching comes in many forms, so this positive result should be treated cautiously. Still, executive coaching has become a popular form of feedback and development for executives throughout the Pacific Rim. For instance, a few years ago Alison Clark was burning out from overwork, and her business, Tickles Child Care Centre in Te Puke, New Zealand, was suffering from high staff turnover. With the guidance of an executive coach, Clark discovered the leadership issues she needed to address in order to improve the business and her personal life. The ongoing coaching has had a demonstrable effect: Clark has recently earned New Zealand-wide awards for her entrepreneurship and team development.

Choosing feedback sources

With so many sources of feedback—executive coaching, multisource feedback, executive dashboards, customer surveys, equipment gauges, nonverbal communication from your boss, and so on—which one works best under which conditions? The preferred feedback source depends on the purpose of the information. To learn about their progress towards the accomplishment of a goal, employees usually prefer non-social feedback sources, such as computer printouts or feedback directly from the job. This is because information from non-social sources is considered more accurate than information from social sources. Corrective feedback from non-social sources is also less damaging to self-esteem. This is probably just as well, because social sources tend to delay negative information, leave some of it out, and distort the bad news in a positive way. When employees want to improve their self-image, they seek out positive feedback from social sources. It feels better to have co-workers say that you are performing the job well than to discover this from a computer printout.

EVALUATING GOAL SETTING AND FEEDBACK

A recent survey of organisational behaviour researchers recently identified goal setting as one of the top OB theories in terms of validity and usefulness. This high score is not surprising given the impressive research support and wide application of this concept in a variety of settings. In partnership with goal setting, feedback also has an excellent reputation for improving employee motivation and performance.

Nevertheless, both goal setting and feedback have a few limitations. One problem is that combining goals with monetary incentives can motivate employees to set up easy rather than difficult goals. In some cases, employees have negotiated goals with their supervisor that have already been completed! Another limitation is that goal setting potentially focuses employees on a narrow subset of measurable performance indicators while ignoring aspects of job performance that are difficult to measure. The saying 'What gets measured gets done' applies here. A third problem is that setting performance goals is effective in established jobs, but seems to interfere with the learning process in new, complex jobs. Thus, we need to be careful not to apply goal setting when an intense learning process is occurring.

ORGANISATIONAL JUSTICE

Taiwan has legislation guaranteeing gender equality in the workplace, but over half of the 4000 working women recently surveyed in that country say that men get paid more for doing the same work. 'It's unfair,' says Hsieh Hsuen-Hui, a senior trade specialist at an export company in Taipei. 'Monthly salaries that male colleagues receive are about NT$10 000 (A$415) higher than what I get, even though we are doing the same job.' Hsieh's boss believes that men should be paid higher wages since they are more flexible when it comes to overseas business travel. Some employers openly say that they pay men more because they have a greater need

Bottom spread (pp. 236–237)

markers (anger, caution, delight, etc.) to that information. These automatic emotional responses, together with logical analysis and the emotions triggered by that analysis, determine whether we perceive something as a problem, an opportunity or irrelevant.

Let's say that a worried-looking colleague tells you that the company's salesperson in Queensland has just quit. Your initial reaction (emotions generated upon hearing the news that the salesperson has quit) might be worry and frustration. Meanwhile, the rational part of your brain works through this information, recalling from memory the related knowledge that the Queensland salesperson's performance was mediocre and that an excellent salesperson at another company wants to join your firm in that state. Will initially felt like a problem was really an opportunity, based on your rational analysis of the situation. The initial emotions of worry or frustration might have been wrong in this situation, but sometimes your emotions provide a good indicator of problems or opportunities.

PROBLEMS WITH PROBLEM IDENTIFICATION

Several problems occur during the problem identification stage. One concern is that employees, clients and other stakeholders with vested interests try to influence the decision maker's perceptions of problems or opportunities. This persuasion 'frames' the person's view of the situation, which short-circuits a full assessment of the problem or opportunity. A second biasing effect is that under some conditions people block out negative information as a coping mechanism. Their brain refuses to see information that threatens their self-esteem. A third perceptual challenge is that mental models blind people from seeing opportunities that deviate from the status quo. If an idea doesn't fit the existing mental model of how things should work, the idea is dismissed as unworkable or undesirable. Reality Check 8.1 describes how narrow mental models are the source of several famous missed or near-missed opportunities.

A fourth barrier to effective problem identification is that decision makers often exhibit faulty diagnostic skills. One diagnostic flaw is that leaders are expected to be decisive, and this decisive image motivates them to zero in on a problem without sufficiently analysing the facts. Another diagnostic skill flaw is the tendency to define problems in terms of their solutions. Someone who says 'The problem is that we need more control over our suppliers' has fallen into this trap. Notice that this statement focuses on a solution (controlling suppliers), whereas proper diagnosis would determine the cause of the symptoms before jumping to solutions.

This focus on solutions occurs because it gives decision makers a sense of comforting clarity in ambiguous situations. People want to make sense of their immediate environment, so alternatives are unconsciously evaluated (tagged with emotions) as soon as they are identified, not just consciously evaluated later through logical analysis. Solutions that worked well in the past are typically viewed favourably, even though they were applied under different circumstances, because these known solutions increase closure and predictability. Some executives are known for cutting the workforce whenever they face problems; others introduce a new customer service program as their favourite solution to a variety of problems. The point here is that decision makers tend to look at problems from the perspective of the ready-made solutions that worked for them in the past.

IDENTIFYING PROBLEMS AND OPPORTUNITIES MORE EFFECTIVELY

Recognising problems and opportunities will always be a challenge, but the process can be improved through awareness of these perceptual and diagnostic limitations. By keeping in mind that mental models restrict a person's perspective of the world, decision makers are more motivated to consider other perspectives of reality. A second method of minimising perceptual and diagnostic weaknesses is to discuss the situation with colleagues. Decision makers discover blind spots in problem identification by hearing how others perceive certain information and diagnose problems. Opportunities also become apparent when outsiders explore this information from their different mental models. Third, leaders require willpower to resist appearing decisive when

8.1 REALITY CHECK

FAMOUS MISSED OPPORTUNITIES

Mental models create road maps that guide our decisions. Unfortunately, these maps also potentially block our ability to see emerging problems and opportunities. Here are a few famous examples.

Graphical user interfaces, mice, windows, pull-down menus, laser printing, distributed computing and Ethernet technologies weren't invented by Apple, Microsoft or IBM. These essential elements of contemporary personal computing originated in the 1970s from researchers at Xerox PARC. Unfortunately, Xerox executives were so focused on their photocopier business that they didn't bother to patent most of these inventions. Xerox has successfully applied some of its laser technology but lost the value of Xerox PARC's other computing discoveries is much larger than the entire photocopier industry today.

Nia Vardalos wrote a comedy screenplay based on incidents involving her Greek-Canadian family. None of Hollywood's literary agents were interested. 'They all said it's not good; it's not funny' said Vardalos, who honed her writing and acting skills at the Second City comedy group. Undeterred, Vardalos turned the script into a successful one-woman show in Los Angeles. None of Hollywood's talent agents accepted her invitation to see the show, but when actors Rita Wilson and Tom Hanks watched her skits, they immediately supported her in making a movie. Even with Hanks on board, Hollywood studios rejected the script, but HBO agreed to provide a paltry US$2.5 million as a favour to Hanks. With a budget of only US$5 million, *My Big Fat Greek Wedding* became one of the highest grossing independent films of all time. The screenplay that no one in Hollywood wanted was also nominated for an Oscar.

When the World Wide Web burst onto the cyberspace scene in the early 1990s, Bill Gates wondered what all the fuss was about. Even as late as 1996, the Microsoft founder signposted investors for their love-in with companies that made Internet products. However, Gates eventually realised the error in his mental model of computing. Making up for lost time, Microsoft bought Hotmail and other Web-savvy companies and added Internet support to its Windows operating system.

The best television commercial in history (as rated by *Advertising Age*) almost didn't see the light of day. The Apple Macintosh 'Why 1984 won't be like *1984*' clip features a female athlete hurling a sledgehammer at a giant TV screen of an Orwellian Big Brother, liberating thousands of subjugated followers. Apple initially rejected the ad agency's (Chiat-Day) now-memorable phrase in an Apple II newspaper ad, but agreed to use the theme to launch the Macintosh computer during the 1984 Superbowl. The Macintosh team and sales force were ecstatic with rough cuts of the ad, but every outside director on Apple's board despised it. One remarked that it was the worst commercial of all time; another insisted that Apple immediately change its ad agency. Based on the board's reaction, Apple CEO John Sculley asked Chiat-Day to cancel the Superbowl ad space. Fortunately, the agency claimed it could only sell off some of the time, so Apple had to show the commercial. The single sixty-second ad shown during the Superbowl had such a huge effect that it was featured on evening news over the next several days. A month later, Apple's board members applauded the Macintosh team for a successful launch and apologised for their misjudgment of the commercial.

Nia Vardalos's comedy screenplay about her Greek-Canadian family was rejected by Hollywood literary agents and studios, yet it eventually became the top-grossing independent film in history and was nominated for an Oscar.

Sidebar

Text at a glance (continued)

END-OF-CHAPTER MATERIAL

TEAM EXERCISES

The end-of-chapter material contains a broad range of exercises to help you further develop your skills. Enjoy working with your peers on the team exercise, which will not only help you understand the content of the chapter, but will also improve your communication skills (see pp.288–9).

SELF-ASSESSMENT EXERCISES

These exercises are designed with personal reflection in mind. Take the test and find out more about your attitudes and personality. You will find more of these exercises on the CD that accompanies the text.

DISCUSSION QUESTIONS

These short answer questions provide you with the opportunity to revisit and discuss concepts and scenarios which relate to the chapter you've just read (see pp.252–3).

END-OF-CHAPTER CASES

These cases bring to life key concepts which have been explored in the text. The questions that accompany them will help you develop the analytical skill that you will need in the workplace.

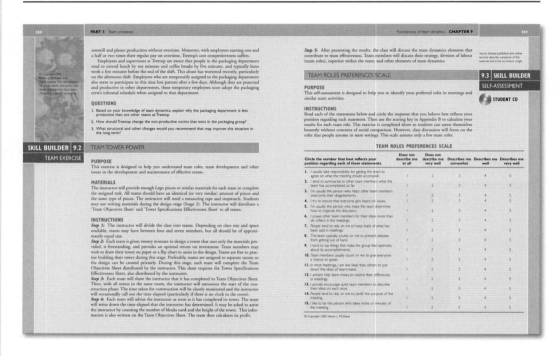

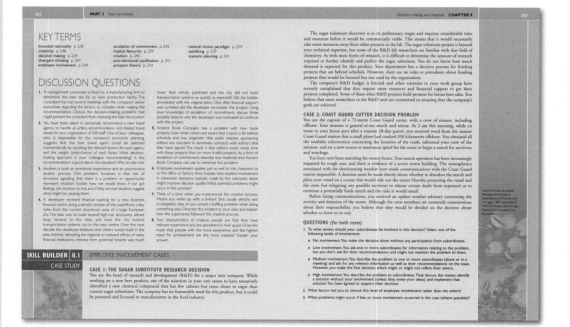

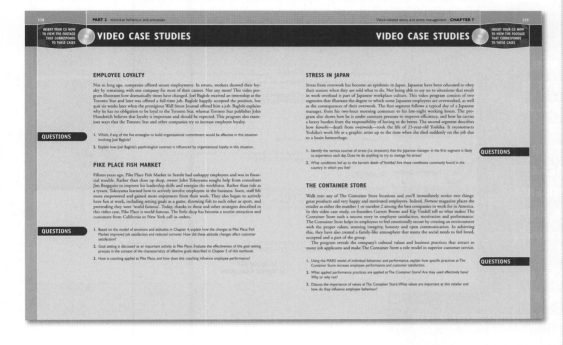

VIDEO CASE STUDIES

Video case studies are available for each part of the text. These case studies summarise the issues raised in the video footage, which you will find on the CD that comes with your text. The discussion questions which are included at the end of every case explore the themes and issues that related to each video clip (see p.228-9).

E-student

THE ONLINE LEARNING CENTRE
THAT ACCOMPANIES THIS TEXT IS
AN INTEGRATED ONLINE PRODUCT
DESIGNED TO ASSIST YOU IN
GETTING THE MOST FROM YOUR
COURSE. THIS TEXT PROVIDES A
POWERFUL LEARNING EXPERIENCE
BEYOND THE PRINTED PAGE. SIMPLY
VISIT www.mhhe.com/au/mcshane2e
TO ACCESS THE RESOURCES
AVAILABLE. EACH COMPONENT ON
THE ONLINE LEARNING CENTRE IS
DESCRIBED BELOW AND CAN BE FOUND BOTH IN THE
STUDENT EDITION AND INSTRUCTOR EDITION.

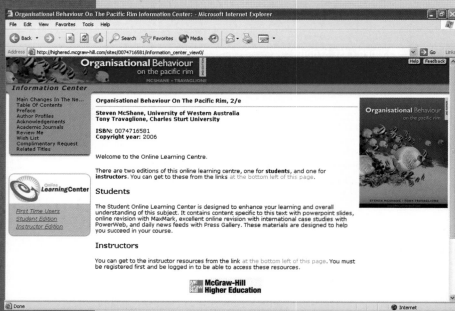

POWERPOINT® SLIDES

The student edition showcases a set of PowerPoint® slides
that distil the key concepts from each chapter in the book.

www.mhhe.com/au/mcshane2e

Maximise your marks with this unique online self-assessment tool, exclusive to McGraw-Hill Australia. MaxMark offers approximately 30 multiple choice questions per chapter for self-paced revision on each of the key concepts in the chapter. MaxMark also provides you with 'Feedback' and 'More' information from the text, to increase your understanding of the topics covered. You can randomise the questions and set yourself time limits, track your progress throughout the semester and thoroughly test your knowledge before exams. For access to MaxMark, see the registration card at the front of this book.

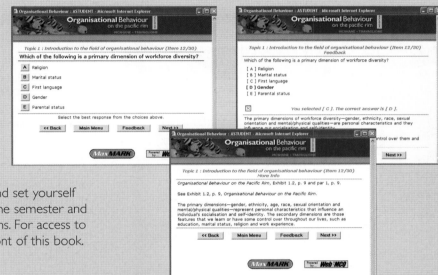

PowerWeb is unique to McGraw-Hill and provides you with full-text international articles that are published in international journals and magazines. These articles relate to key concepts from each chapter of the text and are updated annually. For access to PowerWeb, see the registration card at the front of this book.

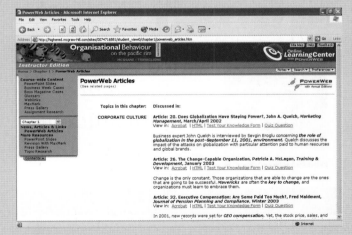

E-instructor

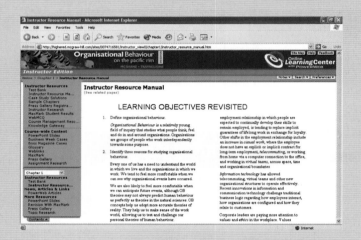

INSTRUCTOR RESOURCE MANUAL

The instructor resource manual has been authored by Steven McShane and features lecture outlines that correspond with PowerPoint® slides, teaching notes and solutions to discussion questions and case studies. It also provides additional cases and class exercises to enrich your learning program.

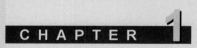

Introduction to the field of organisational behaviour

POWERPOINT® SLIDES

This text comes with a full suite of colour PowerPoint® slides that consolidate key concepts from each chapter of the book. Present these slides in lecture theatres to reinforce OB principles to your class, and distribute them as lecture notes.

www.mhhe.com/au/mcshane2e

TEST BANK

The test bank contains 50 multiple choice or true/false graded questions for every chapter. It is formatted for delivery in WebMCQ as well as WebCT or BlackBoard formats.

WEBMCQ

WebMCQ provides more than 2000 online questions, ranging from multiple-choice to essay style questions, which form a powerful tool for revisions and testing. It is capable of tracking and reporting, so that you can monitor the progress your students are making. This flexible resource has been authored by Steven McShane and is exclusive to McGraw-Hill; it is also available in WebCT or BlackBoard formats.

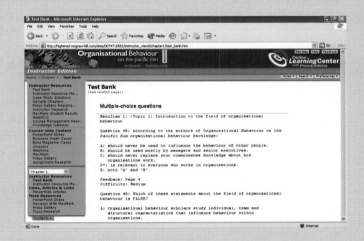

INSTRUCTOR RESOURCE CD

For ease of access, the instructor resource manual with case study solutions, PowerPoint® slides, Test bank and Artwork files are all available on CD.

COURSE MANAGEMENT SYSTEMS (CMSs)

Course management systems allow you to deliver and manage your course via the internet. McGraw-Hill can provide online material to accompany this text, formatted for your chosen CMS. See your McGraw-Hill representation for details.

PageOut is McGraw-Hill's exclusive tool for creating websites quickly and easily. It is designed for people with little or no HTML experience. PageOut allows you to create a website using your own materials and your choice on McGraw-Hill's online content.

About the book

ORGANISATIONAL BEHAVIOUR ON THE PACIFIC RIM, 2ND EDITION, is written around three important philosophies that we believe create a refreshing change in organisational behaviour reading: (1) Pacific Rim context; (2) contemporary issues and trends in OB; and (3) active learning. This book is also written with the view that OB is relevant for everyone in organisations, not just managers. Everyone who works in and around organisations needs to understand and make use of organisational behaviour knowledge. This book helps everyone to make sense of organisational behaviour, and provides the tools to work more effectively in the workplace.

PACIFIC RIM CONTEXT

Organisational Behaviour on the Pacific Rim, 2nd edition, is written completely in the Pacific Rim region by authors who live and work here. This Pacific Rim orientation is most apparent in the numerous real-life anecdotes spread throughout this book. For example, the book describes the creativity of employees at Rising Sun Pictures in Adelaide, how Pretoria Portland Cement has become one of the best places to work in South Africa, how a skunkworks team at GM Holden in Melbourne catapulted the car maker's reputation as a designer of new vehicles, how management at Kowloon Shangri-La Hotel in Hong Kong directly communicates with all staff, how Cocoplans in the Philippines strengthens employee performance through positive self-fulfilling prophecies, and how ASB Bank in New Zealand strengthened employee engagement to become one of the best-performing financial institutions in the region.

Without losing its Pacific Rim focus, *Organisational Behaviour on the Pacific Rim, 2nd edition*, also serves up plenty of examples from around the planet. For instance, readers will learn how Dubai's Department of Development identified its core values and taught employees how to apply those values at work, how Exxon Mobil's Fawley plant in the UK applied behaviour modification to improve safety, how Mayo Clinic in the United States brought in an anthropologist to decipher its corporate culture, why employees at Semco in Brazil have incredibly high levels of empowerment, and how Canadian Tire introduced appreciative inquiry to bring about positive change among its retail staff.

CONTEMPORARY CONCEPTS AND TRENDS IN OB

Every chapter of *Organisational Behaviour on the Pacific Rim, 2nd edition*, is built on dozens of articles, books, and other sources from diverse sources. You can see this in the references. The most recent literature receives solid coverage, resulting in what we believe is the most up-to-date organisational behaviour textbook available. These references also reveal that we reach out for emerging OB concepts in information systems, marketing, and other disciplines. At the same time, this textbook is written for students, not the scholars whose work is cited. So, while this book provides new knowledge and its practical implications, you won't find detailed summaries of specific research studies. Also, this textbook rarely names specific researchers and their university affiliations; instead, it focuses on organisational behaviour knowledge rather than 'who's-who' in the field.

Organisational Behaviour on the Pacific Rim, 2nd edition, also keeps students on the crest of knowledge by discussing several emerging workplace issues. For example, the previous edition of this book was the first to introduce social identity theory, appreciative inquiry, Schwartz's values model, the effects of job satisfaction on customer service, learning orientation, future search events, workaholism, bicultural audits, and several other groundbreaking topics. This edition continues its mandate to offer emerging OB knowledge by introducing new information on several topics, such as employee engagement, four-drive theory, resilience, communication blogs and wikis, psychological harassment, separating socioemotional conflict from constructive conflict, Goleman's emotional intelligence model, and the automaticity and emotionality of the perceptual process.

The role of emotions now dominates many organisational behaviour studies, and this emerging knowledge is integrated throughout *Organisational Behaviour on the Pacific Rim, 2nd edition*. In particular, readers will learn how emotions influence perceptions (Chapter 3), attitudes (Chapter 4), employee motivation (Chapter 5), decision making (Chapter 8) and conflict (Chapter 13). The effects of globalisation as well as the relevance of knowledge management in organisational behaviour are also highlighted throughout this book.

ACTIVE LEARNING

In this era of active learning, critical thinking, and outcomes-based teaching, *Organisational Behaviour on the Pacific Rim, 2nd edition*, offers valuable resources to aid student learning. Every chapter includes at least one short case that challenges students to diagnose issues and apply ideas from that chapter. Several comprehensive cases also appear at the end of the book. Several of these cases are written by instructors around the Pacific Rim and relate to companies in this region.

Along with case studies, *Organisational Behaviour on the Pacific Rim, 2nd edition*, supports active learning with one or two engaging team, web, or class activities in every chapter. Many of these learning activities are not available in other organisational behaviour textbooks, such as Where in the World are We? (Chapter 8) and the Cross-Cultural Communication Game (Chapter 11). This edition also has nearly three dozen self-assessments. Self-assessments personalise the meaning of several organisational behaviour concepts, such as resilience, self-leadership, *guanxi* orientation, empathy, creative disposition, and corporate culture preferences.

We also have a strong commitment to the philosophy of linking theory with practice, which is also essential for active learning. By connecting concepts with real-life examples, students are more likely to remember the content and see how it relates to the real world. And, quite frankly, including these examples makes the content even more interesting, thereby motivating students to read on. This engaging approach is further strengthened through several video segments which highlight specific organisations on a variety of organisational behaviour topics.

Acknowledgements

ORGANISATIONAL BEHAVIOUR ON THE PACIFIC RIM, 2ND EDITION, symbolises the power of teamwork. More correctly, it symbolises the power of a *virtual team* with Tony Travaglione in New South Wales, Steve McShane in Western Australia, and members of the editorial and design team located around Australia.

Superb virtual teams require equally superb team members and we were fortunate to have this in our favour. Publisher Ailsa Brackley du Bois led the way with unwavering support, along with the strong endorsement from McGraw-Hill Australia Managing Director Murray St Leger. We are grateful to Developmental Editors Lucie Stevens and Georgia McElvaney for maintaining the schedule and keeping track of the many pieces of this project. Publishing Services Manager, Jo Munnelly, maintained admirable poise and support while maintaining the tight production schedule involving many people around the country. The keen copy-editing skills of Felicity McKenzie made *Organisational Behaviour on the Pacific Rim, 2nd edition,* incredibly error free. Permissions Manager Jared Dunn and Photo Researcher Leanne Poll did a tremendous job of finding even the most challenging pictures that we had requested. We also extend a special thanks to Tricia McCallum, who designed this colourful second edition. Thanks to you all. This has been an exceptional team effort!

Several lecturers reviewed parts, or all, of *Organisational Behaviour on the Pacific Rim, 2nd edition.* Their compliments were energising and their suggestions significantly improved this edition. We extend our special thanks to:

- Julia Connell (The University of Newcastle)
- Elizabeth Creese (RMIT University)
- Andrew Noblett (Deakin University)
- Lucy Taksa (The University of New South Wales)
- Lesley Treleaven (University of Western Sydney)

We also thank more than 100 university and college lecturers in the United States and Canada who reviewed one or more chapters of the American and Canadian editions of this book over the past three years. Their suggestions also strengthened the quality of the Pacific Rim edition.

We would like to thank the following people who have in the past contributed reviews, cases and exercises that have helped to successfully shape *Organisational Behaviour on the Pacific Rim, 2nd edition*:

- Jeffrey Bagraim (University of Cape Town)
- Hazel Bothma (University of Cape Town)
- Maree Boyle (Griffith University
- Gail Broady (The University of Western Australia)
- Ian Brooks (University of Canterbury)
- David Brown (La Trobe University)
- Allan Bull (Macquarie University)
- Lorraine Carey (University of Canberra)
- Judith Chapman (University of Western Sydney)
- Julia Connell (University of Newcastle)
- Elizabeth Creese (RMIT University)
- Bernadette Cross (The University of Newcastle)
- Natalie Ferress (The University of Adelaide)
- John Gilbert (University of Waikato)
- Howard Harris (University of South Australia)
- Kate Hutchings (Monash University)
- Brad Jackson (Victoria University of Wellington)
- Peter Jordan (Griffith University)
- Alick Kay (University of South Australia)
- Peter Lok (The University of New South Wales)
- Gido Mapunda (University of South Australia)

- Aletta Odendaal (Technikon South Africa)
- Karl Pajo (Massey University)
- Tracy Potgieter (Eastern Cape University)
- Rod Salzman (Charles Darwin University)
- Brenda Scott-Ladd (Murdoch University)
- Michael Segon (RMIT University)
- Michael Sheehan (University of Glamorgan, Wales)
- Richard Sisley (Auckland University of Technology)
- Conrad Smidt (Rand Afrikaans University)
- Deb Stewart (Victoria University)
- Robert Thompson (Queensland University of Technology)
- Sally Townsend (Swinburne University of Technology)
- Lesley Treleaven (University of Western Sydney)
- Linda Twiname (University of Waikato)

Our special thanks extend to the following people who contributed cases and exercises to the 2nd edition:

- Hazel Bothma (University of Cape Town)
- Julia Connell (University of Newcastle)
- Arif Hassan (International Islamic University Malaysia)
- Christine Ho (The Univeristy of Adelaide)
- Glynn Jones (Univeristy of Waikato)
- Peter Lok (The University of New South Wales)
- Robert Ogulin (The University of Sydney)
- Jo Rhodes (Griffith University)
- Brenda Scott- Ladd (Murdoch University)

We are also much indebted to a number of Canadian and American companies that also contributed cases to the 2nd edition.

Along with the reviewers, contributors, and editorial team, Steve extends his gratitude to his students for sharing their learning experiences and assisting with the development of *Organisational Behaviour on the Pacific Rim*, as well as his American and Canadian editions of this book. He is also very grateful to colleagues at the Graduate School of Management who teach organisational behaviour, and related subjects. These wonderful people listen patiently to his ideas, diplomatically correct his wayward thoughts, and share their experiences using the Pacific Rim or American editions of this book in Perth, Jakarta, Manila and Singapore. Finally, Steve is forever indebted to his wife Donna McClement and to their wonderful daughters, Bryton and Madison. Their love and support give special meaning to his life.

Tony would like to thank all of his academic colleagues who have supported him over his 20-year career as an academic. Tony is especially grateful to Professor David Plowman from the University of Western Australia and Grant O'Neill from Charles Sturt University. A special thanks also to Antonia and his three fantastic daughters Natalie, Michelle and Annalise who have provided wonderful support to him over many years.

STEVE MCSHANE
University of Western Australia

TONY TRAVAGLIONE
Charles Sturt University

PART I

Introduction

CHAPTER I
Introduction to the field
of organisational
behaviour

VIDEO CASE STUDIES
● New Belgium Brewery

CHAPTER 1

Introduction to the field of organisational behaviour

LEARNING OBJECTIVES

After reading this chapter, you should be able to:

- define organisational behaviour and give three reasons for studying this field of inquiry

- discuss how globalisation influences organisational behaviour

- identify changes in the workforce in recent years

- describe employability and casual work

- summarise the apparent benefits and challenges of telecommuting

- explain why values have gained importance in organisations

- define corporate social responsibility and argue for or against its application in organisations

- identify the five anchors on which organisational behaviour is based

- diagram an organisation from an open systems view

- define knowledge management and intellectual capital

- identify specific ways that organisations acquire and share knowledge.

'We all get older—but at Westpac, that's not a barrier to getting a job.' So began Westpac Banking Corp's invitation for applicants at its new call centre in Brisbane. 'You've got the life experience—we've got the customers who want to talk to people like you.' Westpac created the unusual ad after discovering that its call centre employees were much younger than the customers they served. By reminding applicants of its fair employment policies, Westpac was able to hire more people over forty-five years of age, thereby better representing the population and serving clients more effectively.

A dozen years ago, Westpac was struggling with billion-dollar losses and lacklustre relations with staff and customers. Today, Australia's oldest bank is ranked as the world's top financial institution for corporate social responsibility. In addition to its ethical employment policies, Westpac achieved this global status for developing innovative climate initiatives, such as its specialised environmental markets group that trades both carbon credits and renewable energy certificates. The bank also receives kudos for helping low-income members of society improve their financial literacy and receive better access to banking services.

Along with its external stakeholder focus, Westpac pays attention to hiring and keeping the best employees. 'There is a war on for talent and we want to win it,' says Westpac executive Ilana Atlas. Twice each year, Westpac's chief executive, David Morgan, and his team of direct reports attend a series of half-day discussion forums around the country where they hear directly from 2000 employees about their views of the company and its leaders. Still, Westpac is far from perfect. Its New Zealand staff went on strike over ethical concerns when the bank introduced targets and performance measures to sell debt products to customers.

Westpac Banking Corporation has leveraged the power of organisational behaviour to become one of the most successful and respected companies around the Pacific Rim.

Employee turnover rates at its call centres are as much as 60 per cent annually, with some employees complaining that rotating shifts, constant monitoring and restricted toilet breaks make it unbearable to work in the centres.

In spite of these foibles, Westpac has won work–life balance awards and is trying to provide a more employee-friendly workplace on other fronts. For example, the bank doubled parental leave when a recent survey revealed that many Westpac staff planned to have children within the next couple of years.

Morgan explains that a disciplined focus on the needs of employees, customers and other stakeholders sustains the company's long-term success. '[It's all about] internal service, leadership, people, performance management, the productiveness of your culture feeding into your employee commitment, feeding into employee longevity, feeding into employee productivity, feeding into customer satisfaction and customer longevity, feeding into the breadth of the relationship and retention. It is executing each point of that better and better. And cumulatively, over a number of years, it is very powerful,' says Morgan.[1]

WESTPAC HAS BECOME A POWERHOUSE IN AUSTRALIA'S financial sector, but its real power comes from applying organisational behaviour theories and practices. More than ever, organisations are relying on organisational behaviour knowledge to remain competitive. For example, Westpac executives have developed a customer-focused culture. They actively communicate with employees, engage in various forms of corporate social responsibility, and take a disciplined approach to employee performance and well-being. The company also empowers employees through an 'ask once' policy, in which employees who are asked a question by a customer will do whatever it takes to find the answer themselves. These and many other organisational behaviour concepts and practices make a difference to the organisation's success and to employee well-being.

This book is about people working in organisations. Its main objective is to help readers understand behaviour in organisations and to work more effectively in organisational settings. While organisational behaviour knowledge is often presented for 'managers', this book takes the broader and more realistic view that organisational behaviour ideas are relevant and useful to anyone who works in and around organisations. This chapter introduces the field of organisational behaviour, outlines the main reasons why you should know more about it, highlights some of the trends influencing the study of organisational behaviour, describes the anchors supporting the study of organisations, and introduces the concept that organisations are knowledge and learning systems.

THE FIELD OF ORGANISATIONAL BEHAVIOUR

organisational behaviour (OB) The study of what people think, feel and do in and around organisations.

LEARNING OBJECTIVE

Define organisational behaviour and give three reasons for studying this field of inquiry.

Organisational behaviour (OB) is the study of what people think, feel and do in and around organisations. OB researchers systematically study individual, team and organisational-level characteristics that influence behaviour within work settings. By referring to organisational behaviour as a field of study, we mean that OB experts have been accumulating a distinct knowledge about behaviour within organisations—a knowledge base that is the foundation of this book.

By most estimates, OB emerged as a distinct field around the 1940s.[2] However, its origins can be traced much further back in time. The Greek philosopher Plato wrote about the essence of leadership. The writings of Chinese philosopher Confucius in 500 BC are beginning to influence contemporary thinking about ethics and leadership. In 1776 Adam Smith advocated a new form of organisational structure based on the division of labour. One hundred years later, German sociologist Max Weber wrote about rational organisations and initiated discussion of charismatic leadership. Soon after, Frederick Winslow Taylor introduced the systematic use of goal setting and rewards to motivate employees. In the 1920s Australian-born Harvard professor Elton Mayo and his colleagues discovered the importance of formal and informal group dynamics in the workplace, resulting in a dramatic shift towards the 'human relations' school of thought. As you can see, OB has been around for a long time; it just wasn't organised into a unified discipline until after World War II.

WHAT ARE ORGANISATIONS?

Organisations have existed for as long as people have worked together. Massive temples dating back to 3500 BC were constructed through the organised actions of many people. Craftspeople and merchants in ancient Rome formed guilds, complete with elected managers. And more than 1000 years ago, Chinese factories were producing 125 000 tonnes of iron a year.[3] There are equally impressive examples of contemporary organisations, ranging from the massive and highly complex oil and gas projects along Australia's northwest coast to the phenomenally successful Sydney Olympics of a few years ago.

So, what are **organisations**? They are groups of people who work interdependently towards some purpose.[4] Organisations are not buildings or government-registered entities. Rather, they consist of people who interact with each other to achieve a common purpose. 'A business is just a registered name on a piece of paper,' explains Grahame Maher, the Australian executive who revived Vodafone's operations in both New Zealand and Australia and now leads Vodafone Sweden. 'It's nothing more than that unless there's a group of people who care about a common purpose for why they are, where they are going, how they are going to be when they are there.'[5]

Some OB experts are sceptical about the relevance of goals in a definition of organisations.[6] They argue that an organisation's mission statement may be different from its true goals. Also, they question the assumption that all organisational members believe in the same goals. These points may be true, but imagine an organisation without goals: it would consist of a mass of people wandering around aimlessly without any sense of direction. Overall, as Vodafone's Grahame Maher stated, organisations consist of people with a collective sense of purpose. This purpose might not be fully understood or agreed upon, but it helps employees to engage in structured patterns of interaction. In other words, they expect each other to complete various tasks in a coordinated way—in an *organised* way.

organisations Groups of people who work interdependently towards some purpose.

WHY STUDY ORGANISATIONAL BEHAVIOUR?

Organisational behaviour seems to get more respect from people who have been in the workforce a while than from students who are just beginning their careers. Many of us specialise in accounting, marketing, information systems and other fields with corresponding job titles, so it's understandable that students focus on these career paths. After all, who ever heard of a career path leading to a 'vice-president of OB' or a 'chief OB officer'? Even if organisational behaviour doesn't have its own job title, most people eventually come to realise that the field is a potential gold-mine of valuable knowledge. The fact is, everyone in the workforce needs to understand, predict and influence behaviour (both their own and that of others) in organisational settings (see Exhibit 1.1). Marketing students learn marketing concepts and computer science students learn about circuitry and software code. But everyone benefits from organisational behaviour knowledge to address the people issues when trying to apply marketing, computer science and other fields of knowledge.

Reasons for studying organisational behaviour

EXHIBIT 1.1

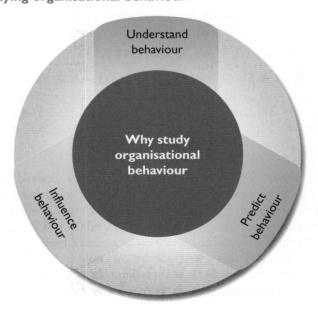

Understanding, predicting and influencing

Each one of us has an inherent need to understand and predict the world in which we live.[7] Since much of our time is spent working in or around organisations, OB theories are particularly helpful in satisfying this innate drive to make sense of the workplace. OB theories also give you the opportunity to question and rebuild your personal mental models that have developed through observation and experience.

While understanding and predicting are important, most of us need to influence the organisation in various ways. Whether you are trying to introduce a new marketing strategy, encourage staff to adopt new information technology, or negotiate more flexible work arrangements with your boss, you'll find that OB concepts play an important role in performing your job and working more effectively within organisations. This practical side of organisational behaviour is, according to some experts, a critical feature of the best OB theories.[8]

Organisational behaviour is for everyone

This book takes the view that organisational behaviour knowledge is for everyone—not just managers. We all need to understand organisational behaviour and to master the practices that influence organisational events. That's why you won't find very much emphasis in this book on 'management'. Yes, organisations will continue to have managers, but their roles have changed. More importantly, the rest of us are now expected to manage ourselves, particularly as companies remove layers of management and delegate more responsibilities. In the words of one forward-thinking organisational behaviour writer many years ago: 'Everyone is a manager'.[9]

OB and the bottom line

So far, the answer to the question 'Why study OB?' has focused on how OB knowledge benefits you as an individual. But organisational behaviour knowledge is just as important for the organisation's financial health. According to one estimate, firms that apply performance-based rewards, employee communication, work–life balance and other OB practices have three times the level of financial success as companies where these practices are absent. Another study concluded that companies that earn 'the best place to work' awards have significantly higher financial and long-term stock-market performance. Essentially, these firms leverage the power of OB practices, which translate into more favourable employee attitudes, decisions and performance. These findings are not new to Warren Buffett and other financial gurus, who consider the organisation's leadership and quality of employees as two of the best predictors of the firm's financial potential.[10]

ORGANISATIONAL BEHAVIOUR TRENDS

There has never been a better time to learn about organisational behaviour. The pace of change is accelerating, and most of the transformation is occurring in the workplace. Let's take a brief tour through five trends in the workplace: globalisation, the changing workforce, evolving employment relationships, virtual work, and workplace values and ethics.

GLOBALISATION

LEARNING OBJECTIVE

Discuss how globalisation influences organisational behaviour.

New Zealand Dairy Group, Kiwi Dairy Company and the New Zealand Dairy Board decided a few years ago to join forces as a global enterprise in order to compete more effectively against Nestlé, Danone, Unilever, Kraft Foods and other global giants. The merged company was so globally focused from the outset that it was temporarily called GlobalCo until the name Fonterra was chosen. The adjustment to a global operation was not easy. Executives were replaced as the company needed to adopt a different mind-set. 'A lot of people in the NZ Dairy Board were very New Zealand-centric and culturally did not understand the global challenges of the teams offshore and the different operating companies,' acknowledges a Fonterra executive.

Computershare's global advantage

It takes a lot of organisational savvy to become the world's largest (and only global) share registry company. That's what Melbourne-based Computershare has achieved over the past dozen years. From a small business serving a few Australian companies in the mid-1990s, Computershare today operates in twenty-one countries around the planet to keep track of share ownership and related services for stock exchanges and publicly traded companies. The company's rapid growth has occurred by acquiring smaller share registries in several countries, then acculturating employees to Computershare's values and standards. Today, Computershare's diverse workforce of 10 000 people (compared with just seventy people in the mid-1990s) manages 90 million shareholder accounts for more than 14 000 corporations around the world. 'We are about taking advantage of what we have got, which is a global company based on a global standard IT platform,' explains Computershare founder and chief executive Chris Morris (shown in photo).[12]

Courtesy of Computershare Ltd

Today, Fonterra is the world's largest and lowest-cost dairy ingredients company. It operates in 140 countries, employs 20 000 people, and represents 40 per cent of the global dairy trade. 'To think that a country of 4 million people could have created an organisation of this global scope, that is literally number one in the world at what it does, is very impressive,' says Fonterra chief executive Andrew Ferrier.[11]

Fonterra is a rich example of the globalisation of business over the past few decades. **Globalisation** refers to economic, social and cultural connectivity with people in other parts of the world. Fonterra and other organisations globalise when they actively participate in other countries and cultures. While organisations have operated across borders for more than two thousand years, the degree of globalisation today is unprecedented, because information technology and transportation systems allow a much more intense level of connectivity and interdependence around the planet.[13]

Experts continue to debate whether globalisation improves the financial and social development of poorer nations, but at least the issue has made executives more aware of the ethics of serving communities, not just shareholders. Meanwhile, globalisation has provided Fonterra and other firms with new markets and resources as well as a broader net to attract valuable knowledge and skills.[14] But globalisation is also criticised for increasing competitive pressures and market volatility. Globalisation is also linked to 'offshoring'—outsourcing work to lower-wage countries. Collectively, these events potentially reduce job security, increase work intensification, and demand more work flexibility from employees. Thus, globalisation

globalisation Economic, social and cultural connectivity (and interdependence) with people in other parts of the world.

might partly explain why many people now work longer hours, have heavier workloads and experience more work–family conflict than at any time in recent decades.[15]

Globalisation is now well entrenched, so rather than debate its merits the real issue is how corporate leaders and employees alike can lead and work effectively in this emerging reality.[16] OB researchers are turning their attention to this topic, such as determining how well OB theories and practices work across cultures. GLOBE Project, for instance, is a large consortium of OB experts studying leadership and organisational practices across dozens of countries. Globalisation also has important implications for how we learn about organisational behaviour. The best-performing companies may be in Helsinki, Singapore or Sao Paulo, not just in Melbourne or Wellington. That's why this book presents numerous examples from around the planet. It is important that you learn from the best, no matter where their headquarters are located.

THE CHANGING WORKFORCE

LEARNING OBJECTIVE

Identify changes in the workforce in recent years.

Walk into the country headquarters of HSBC Bank in Sydney, London or elsewhere and you might think you have entered a United Nations building. The London-based financial institution has dramatically embraced diversity over the past decade. 'In a world where homogeneity and standardisation dominate, HSBC is building a business in the belief that different people from different cultures and different walks of life create value,' says Darren Friedlander, HSBC Australia's head of marketing. Margaret Leung, located in Hong Kong as HSBC's global co-head of commercial banking, echoes this sentiment. 'We want to attract the best people and we want the best to rise to the top. The wider you cast the net, the better the chance of catching the top performers,' she says.[17]

HSBC Bank is a reflection of the increasing diversity of people in the workforce in many countries. Exhibit 1.2 identifies the primary and secondary dimensions of workforce diversity. The primary categories—gender, ethnicity, age, race, sexual orientation and mental/physical qualities—represent personal characteristics that influence an individual's socialisation and social identity. The secondary dimensions are those features that people learn or have some control over throughout their lives, such as education, marital status, religion and work experience. The Australian and New Zealand workforce has become more diverse along many of these primary and secondary dimensions, particularly in terms of race/ethnicity, gender and generation (age/work experience).

EXHIBIT 1.2

Primary and secondary dimensions of workforce diversity

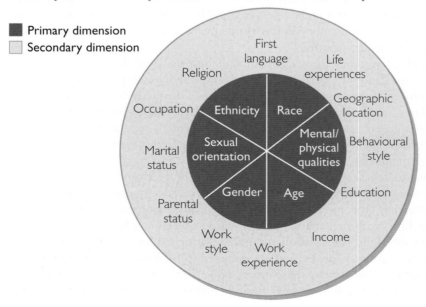

■ Primary dimension
☐ Secondary dimension

Sources: Adapted from M. Loden, *Implementing Diversity* (Chicago: Irwin, 1996); S. Bradford, 'Fourteen Dimensions of Diversity: Understanding and Appreciating Differences in the Workplace', in J. W. Pfeiffer, ed., *1996 Annual: Volume 2 Consulting* (San Diego: Pfeiffer and Associates, 1996), pp. 9–17.

Supporting diversity pays for Pak 'n Save

Mt Albert Pak 'n Save is a role model for cultural diversity. More than half of the supermarket's 300 employees were born outside of New Zealand, representing fourteen different cultures. Brian Carran, who owns the Pak 'n Save franchise, actively supports this diversity. Employees are encouraged to display their national flags on their name badges, making it easier for customers to find a staff member who speaks their language. The store has a Muslim prayer room and accommodates employee requirements during Ramadan. Employees can accumulate holiday leave for extended visits to their home country. The supermarket's training takes language and literacy issues into account. Due in part to its support for cultural diversity, Mt Albert Pak 'n Save has become the fifth largest supermarket in New Zealand (based on revenue) and enjoys a much lower employee turnover rate than other supermarkets.[19]

Courtesy of Pak 'n Save

Racial/ethnic diversity

Workforce diversity is partly due to nondiscriminatory immigration policies and employment practices in many countries. For example, over half of Australia's immigrants came from the United Kingdom and Ireland during the late 1960s. Today, these countries represent only 15 per cent of immigrants, and more than 25 per cent of immigrants are from various parts of Asia.[18] Even in countries with less diversity, globalisation puts employees in more contact with people from diverse backgrounds. Hong Kong is about 95 per cent Chinese, but many Hong Kong employees do business daily with suppliers and customers from every possible ethnic and cultural background elsewhere in the world.

Women in the workforce

Another form of diversity is the increasing representation of women in the workforce. Well over 50 per cent of Australian and New Zealand women participate in the paid workforce compared with only 20 per cent a few decades ago. Gender-based shifts continue to occur within many occupations. For example, women represent almost one-third of physicians in Australia and New Zealand, compared with less than 20 per cent in the early 1980s.[20]

Generational diversity

Another noticeable difference is the values and expectations of people in various generational cohorts.[21] Several writers suggest that *baby boomers*—people born between 1946 and 1964—tend to expect and desire more job security (at least, at this stage in their lives) and seem more intent on improving their economic and social status than do other generation groups. In contrast, *Generation-X* employees—those born between 1965 and 1979—are typically less loyal to one organisation and, in return, expect less job security. Instead, they are motivated more by workplace flexibility, the opportunity to learn (particularly new technology), and working in an egalitarian and 'fun' organisation. Meanwhile, some observers suggest that *Generation-Y* employees (those born after 1979) are noticeably self-confident, optimistic, multi-tasking and more independent than even Gen-X co-workers. These statements certainly don't apply to everyone in each cohort, but they do reflect the fact that different generations have different values and expectations.

Diversity presents both opportunities and challenges in organisations.[22] In some circumstances and to some degree, diversity can become a competitive advantage by improving decision making and team performance on complex tasks. For many businesses, a diverse workforce also provides better customer service in a diverse society. As the opening vignette to this chapter described, Westpac Banking Corporation actively recruited older job applicants for this reason. At the same time, workforce diversity presents new challenges, such as conflict, miscommunication and perceptual problems in organisations and society.[23] These diversity issues will be explored more closely under various topics throughout this book, such as stereotyping, team dynamics and conflict management.

EVOLVING EMPLOYMENT RELATIONSHIPS

Globalisation and the changing workforce have produced two contrasting changes in relationships between employers and employees: (1) aligning the workplace with emerging workforce expectations, and (2) increasing workforce flexibility to increase organisational competitiveness.

Aligning the workplace with emerging workforce expectations

work–life balance The minimisation of conflict between work and non-work demands.

Work–life balance—minimising conflict between work and non-work demands—was seldom mentioned a couple of decades ago. Most employees assumed that they would put in long hours to rise up through the corporate ladder. Asking the boss to accommodate non-work responsibilities and interests was almost a sign of betrayal.[24] But two-income families and Gen-X/Gen-Y expectations have made work–life balance a 'must-have' condition in today's employment relationship.

Westpac Banking Corporation, described at the beginning of this chapter, is a case in point. As one of Australia's top workplaces for work–life balance, Westpac offers part-time work, job sharing, home-based work, leave without pay, career break and carer's leave. Jody Welch benefited from Westpac's work–life balance arrangements. To help ease in her return to work after the birth of her first child, the Westpac employee in Brisbane was able to initially work one day a week, then a five-day fortnight, before re-entering her job full-time.[25] Reality Check 1.1 further illustrates how companies need to pay close attention to these work–life balance expectations or risk losing the war for talent.

Along with providing more work–life balance, companies are adjusting to emerging workforce expectations of a more egalitarian workplace by reducing hierarchy and replacing command-and-control management with facilitating and teacher-oriented leaders. Gen-X/Gen-Y employees also want to work in companies that make a difference, which may explain why Westpac and other employers are paying more attention to serving the community rather than just their shareholders, a trend that will be discussed in more detail later in the chapter.

Younger employees tend to view the workplace as a community where they spend a large part of their lives (even with work–life balance), so many expect opportunities for more social fulfilment and fun. Again, several companies are making this shift in the employment relationship. Google, the company that created the ubiquitous search engine, is a sparkling example. The company's Googleplex (headquarters) in Mountain View, California, 'resembles a glimmering playground for 20-somethings', says one observer. The building is outfitted with lava lamps, exercise balls, casual sofas, foosball, pool tables, workout rooms, video games, a restaurant with free gourmet meals, and a small pool where swimmers exercise against an artificial current. Beach volleyball matches are held in the courtyard, and roller hockey games are

ATTRACTING TALENT THROUGH WORK–LIFE BALANCE

Tony Bates had a high-flying career as head of private banking at Macquarie Bank, but he wanted a shorter workweek and was prepared to accept a proportionately lower pay. When Bates tried to discuss his need for work–life balance with the three executives above him—all baby boomers with no children—one replied: 'If you work your guts out for thirty years, you'll retire at fifty-five and get [work–life] balance in the last thirty years.'

That was enough for Bates, a Generation-Xer and father of three children. He started his own boutique financial planning business in Sydney, spacing his work across four days a week. 'I'm on about 60 per cent of the money I used to make, and working fewer hours,' says Bates. 'Just knowing I can pick up the kids after school takes out the stress, so I'm happier at home and happier at work.'

Experts warn that Generation-X and Generation-Y employees such as Tony Bates are bringing different expectations to the workplace, and that corporate leaders need to offer more work–life balance to attract and retain them. 'What do we do with a generation who refuse to be motivated by money or power?' asks Saatchi & Saatchi Australia advertising executive Sandra Yates. 'How terrifying, how ironic, that the levers that have served us so well in business all these years appear to have no sway at all with the twenty-something set.'

The importance of work–life balance isn't just anecdotal. One survey identified a lack of work–life balance as one of the three main reasons why New Zealand employees looked elsewhere for work. (The other two were a poor work relationship with the boss and feeling undervalued.) A poll conducted by the Institute of Chartered Accountants in Australia also found that providing employees with flexible work arrangements is the best way for employers to retain staff and provide them with greater levels of job satisfaction. When 1000 Canadians were asked to identify the 'top indicators of success in your own career', work–life balance was far ahead of salary level, challenging job, level of responsibility, or any other option listed.

Helen Melrose knows that offering work–life balance is a competitive advantage in the ongoing battle to recruit the best talent. 'We are a small firm but we are competing with the big companies for staff,' says Melrose, who co-founded Auckland law firm Burke Melrose a decade ago. 'Burke Melrose keeps work to between 8 am and 6 pm with no weekends and our clients understand our philosophy that we are lawyers who have real lives and commitments,' she says. 'Most of our staff have young children so we have to be flexible; they are a priority and no one grizzles if a child is sick and the parent has to stay home.'

Sources: Ipsos-Reid, 'What Are Canadians' Top Indicators of Career Success?', Ipsos-Reid news release (Toronto, 7 May 2003); F. Carruthers, 'Generation Xcluded', Australian Financial Review, 27 August 2004, 46; 'Legal Professor and Work/Life Balance Firm Share Top Rank', National Business Review, 26 August 2005; Z. Efrat, 'Get a Life', CFO Magazine, December 2005, 1; M. Story, 'One Size Doesn't Fit All', New Zealand Herald, 8 June 2005, E01; H. Trinca, 'Young on the Mark to Run Their Own Race', Australian Financial Review, 25 October 2005, 59.

played in the parking lot. Google executives had to remind some employees that making the Googleplex their permanent residence was against building-code regulations.[26]

Increasing workforce flexibility

As some companies are aligning employment practices with emerging workforce expectations, they are also demanding more flexibility from employees to remain responsive to globalisation and other sources of turbulence. This increased flexibility partly occurs through

LEARNING OBJECTIVE
Describe employability and casual work.

employability An employment relationship in which people are expected to continuously develop their skills in order to remain employed.

casual work Any job in which the individual does not have an explicit or implicit contract for long-term employment, or one in which the minimum hours of work can vary in a non-systematic way.

employability, in which employees are expected to manage their own careers by anticipating future organisational needs and developing new competencies that match those needs.[27] From this perspective, organisations are customers, and employees keep their jobs by continuously developing new competencies for the future and performing a variety of work activities over time. Furthermore, employability shifts the burden of this adaptability to employees rather than employers, although the latter are expected to offer the resources and opportunities to assist in the process. 'I think people are starting to understand the concept of lifetime employability rather than lifetime employment,' says Rich Hartnett, global staffing director at aerospace manufacturer Boeing. 'It's a good idea to stay current with what's out there and take personal responsibility for our own employability.'[28]

Casual work

Along with employability, companies are making more use of **casual work** (also called *contingent work*) to increase workforce flexibility. Casual work includes any job in which the individual does not have an explicit or implicit contract for long-term employment, or one in which the minimum hours of work can vary in a non-systematic way. This employment relationship includes anyone with temporary or seasonal employment, freelance contractors (sometimes called 'free agents') and temporary staffing agency workers.[29] The Australian Bureau of Statistics estimates that people without paid leave or any of the entitlements that permanents expect represent 28 per cent of the workforce, up from 15 per cent in the mid-1980s. This group represents only some forms of casual work, so the actual percentage of Australians in casual work would be higher.[30]

Why has casual work increased? One reason is that it allows companies to reduce costs by more closely matching employment levels and competencies with product or service demands. This is particularly apparent in service industries, where casual work is most common. It is also the preferred employment relationship for 'free agents' with high-demand skills and who enjoy a variety of interesting assignments. At the same time, research suggests that casual workers potentially have higher accident rates as well as lower performance and loyalty. However, these outcomes depend on the type of casual workers (e.g. 'free agent' contractors versus new hires on temporary status) as well as whether casual workers are separated from, or interact regularly with, permanent staff. Another concern is that permanent employees feel that it is an injustice if their employer treats casual workers as second-class citizens.[31]

VIRTUAL WORK

virtual work Work performed away from the traditional physical workplace using information technology.

Rush hour isn't much of a rush for Tan Swee Hoong. She enjoys breakfast with her three children, heads them off to school, then walks from the kitchen to her study. There, the Singapore-based Hewlett-Packard relocation manager checks her email and uses the telephone to connect with team-mates on her work projects. Tan Swee Hoong's daily routine is an example of **virtual work**, whereby employees use information technology to perform their jobs away from the traditional physical workplace. Tan's virtual work, called *teleworking* or *telecommuting*, involves working at home rather than commuting to the office. Virtual work also includes employees connected to the office while on the road or at clients' offices. For instance, at any given time 30 per cent of Deloitte's employees in Sydney are out of the office. Some of the accounting firm's staff members work from home, but many are at a client's workplace or on work-related travel.[32]

LEARNING OBJECTIVE

Summarise the apparent benefits and challenges of telecommuting.

Tan Swee Hoong is more of a pioneer than a typical employee in Singapore and most Asian countries. In spite of respectable broadband availability and increasing traffic congestion in Singapore, Hong Kong, Seoul and Taipei, telework is still relatively rare. It is somewhat more common in Japan, where 6 per cent of employees telework; the Japanese government wants to increase that figure to 20 per cent by 2010. Various surveys estimate that between 15 and 25 per cent of Australian employees (excluding owners and the self-employed) telework some of the time, and that two-thirds of large Australian companies offer eligible staff the opportunity to telework. American studies indicate that around 20 per cent of employees in that country work at home at least one day each month.[33]

Some research suggests that virtual work, particularly teleworking, potentially reduces employee stress by offering better work–life balance and dramatically reducing time lost through commuting to the office. Under some circumstances, it also increases productivity and job satisfaction. Nortel Networks reports that 71 per cent of its UK staff feel more empowered through virtual work arrangements. Others point out that virtual work reduces the cost of office space, and improves the environment through less pollution and traffic congestion.[34]

Against these potential benefits, virtual workers face a number of real or potential challenges.[35] Although telework is usually introduced to improve work–life balance, a large percentage of Australian teleworkers recently reported that teleworking actually made them work longer hours, took time away from their family, and increased pressure after normal work hours. Unfulfilled social needs is another common complaint, particularly among virtual workers who rarely visit the office. Managers at IBM Australia introduced ways to reduce this sense of isolation by motivating its teleworkers to visit the office once or twice each week. 'It is all about getting [teleworkers] back to the office, for social reasons, or encouraging people to come into the office and have those face-to-face meetings,' says IBM's manager of diversity in Australia.[36] Virtual work also requires employees to have some degree of technological savvy as well as to be self-motivated and organised. Also, it works better in organisations that evaluate employees by their performance outcomes rather than 'face time'.

Virtual teams

Another variation of virtual work occurs in **virtual teams**—cross-functional groups that operate across space, time and organisational boundaries with members who communicate mainly through information technology.[37] Virtual teams exist when some members telework, but also when team members are located on company premises at different sites around the country or world. Teams have varying degrees of virtualness, depending on how often and how many team members interact face-to-face or at a distance. There is currently a flurry of research activity studying the types of work best suited to virtual teams and the conditions that facilitate and hinder their effectiveness. As with telework, some people are better suited than others to virtual team dynamics. Chapter 10 will examine the issues surrounding virtual teams in detail.

virtual teams Teams whose members operate across space, time and organisational boundaries and who are linked through information technologies to achieve organisational goals.

WORKPLACE VALUES AND ETHICS

The opening story to this chapter described Westpac Banking Corporation's success as a corporate citizen. The financial institution began this journey in the late 1990s by rediscovering its underlying values. Vodafone Australia, ANZ Banking Group, Xerox, Dell Computer and a host of other organisations around the world have also re-examined the values that drive decisions and behaviour within their organisations. Xerox chief executive Anne Mulcahy claims that reaffirming the company's values 'helped save Xerox during the worst crisis in our history'.[38]

Values represent stable, long-lasting beliefs about what is important in a variety of situations. Values guide our decisions and actions. They are evaluative standards that help define what is right or wrong, or good or bad, in the world. Values dictate our priorities, our preferences and our desires. They influence our motivation and decisions.[40] Although leaders refer to the values of their companies, values actually exist only within individuals; they are *personal values*. However, groups of people might hold the same or similar values, so these *shared values* are ascribed to the team, department, organisation, profession or entire society.

values Stable long-lasting beliefs about what is important in a variety of situations.

Values-based leadership at Dubai's Department of Economic Development

The senior management team at the Department of Economic Development (DED) in the Emirate of Dubai recently devoted several months to identifying the agency's core values: accountability, teamwork and continuous improvement. Each of these three values is anchored with specific behaviour descriptions to ensure that employees and other stakeholders understand their meaning. DED also organised a series of workshops (shown in photo) in which employees participated in a 'Values Mystery' exercise to help them recognise values-consistent behaviours. To develop a values-based organisation, DED will also use these three values to evaluate employee performance, to assess employee competencies and to identify management potential.[39]

Courtesy of Dubai Department of Economic Development

ethics The study of moral principles or values that determine whether actions are right or wrong and outcomes are good or bad.

Importance of values in the workplace

Values are not new to organisational behaviour, but they have become the subject of several popular books, the mantra of corporate leaders and the foundation of many corporate transformations in recent years. Governments in Australia, New Zealand, the United Kingdom, Canada and several other countries have also made values the foundation of employee decisions and behaviour. As one New Zealand government report proclaimed: 'Values are essentially the link between the daily work of public servants and the broad aims of democratic governance.'[41]

Why have values become so important? One reason is that as today's workforce rejects 'command-and-control' supervision, leaders are turning to values as a more satisfactory approach to aligning employees' decisions and actions with corporate goals. Values represent the unseen magnet that pulls employees in the same direction.[42] A second reason is that globalisation has raised our awareness of and sensitivity to cultural differences in values and beliefs. Increasing cultural diversity also presents new challenges as organisations discover shared values acceptable to all employees.

The third reason why values have gained prominence is that organisations are under increasing pressure to engage in ethical practices and corporate social responsibility. **Ethics** refers to the study of moral principles or values that determine whether actions are right or wrong and outcomes are good or bad. People rely on their ethical values to determine 'the right thing to do'. Ethical behaviour is driven by the moral principles we use to make decisions. These moral principles represent fundamental values. Unfortunately, executives are receiving low grades on their ethics report cards these days, so ethics and values will continue to be an important topic in OB teaching.

Corporate social responsibility

Over thirty years ago, economist Milton Friedman pronounced that 'there is one and only one social responsibility of business—to use its resources and engage in activities designed to increase its profits'. Friedman is a respected scholar, but this argument was not one of his more popular—or accurate—statements. Today, any business that follows Friedman's advice will face considerable trouble in the marketplace. Four out of five Americans say that a company's commitment to a social issue is an important factor in deciding whether to work there and whether to buy its products or services. Another poll reported that 97 per cent of American and European MBA students would relinquish significant financial benefits to work for an organisation with a better reputation for ethics and corporate social responsibility. Almost 80 per cent of Canadians say that the company's record of corporate social responsibility has either a moderate or a great deal of influence on their decision about where to work.[43]

Corporate social responsibility (CSR) refers to an organisation's moral obligation towards all of its **stakeholders**. Stakeholders are the shareholders, customers, suppliers, governments and any other groups with a vested interest in the organisation.[44] This multiple stakeholder focus is apparent in the opening story to this chapter. Westpac is the top bank in the world for its CSR activities because, in addition to addressing shareholders' needs, it supports social and environmental issues in the community and tries to treat its employees with respect and fairness.

As part of corporate social responsibility, many companies have adopted the triple-bottom-line philosophy. This means that they try to support or 'earn positive returns' in the economic, social and environmental spheres of sustainability. Firms that adopt the triple bottom line aim to survive and be profitable in the marketplace (economic), but they also intend to maintain or improve conditions for society (social) as well as the physical environment. For instance, The Warehouse evaluates every one of its stores each month in terms of how little landfill waste it has created per $1 million of sales. New Zealand's largest retailer is also working towards minimising packaging and reducing the amount of transportation needed to move its inventory to each store.[45]

Corporate leaders seem to agree that corporate social responsibility is an important part of the organisation's obligations, yet many have difficulty translating these attitudes into meaningful behaviour. Wal-Mart, the world's largest retailer, claims that it monitors suppliers with one of the toughest codes of conduct in the industry, yet an undercover camera crew recently revealed child labour in some third-world factories that manufacture Wal-Mart products. For more than a decade, Interface, the world's largest floor-covering company, has tried to transform itself into an ecologically friendly manufacturer. It has made more progress than other firms in the industry, but critics point out that Interface has fallen short of its original well-publicised goals for sustainability and may have exaggerated a few of its achievements.[46] The point here is that CSR is receiving a lot of attention, but in many organisations the rhetoric runs well ahead of actions.

corporate social responsibility (CSR) An organisation's moral obligation towards its stakeholders.

stakeholders Shareholders, customers, suppliers, governments and any other groups with a vested interest in the organisation.

THE FIVE ANCHORS OF ORGANISATIONAL BEHAVIOUR

Globalisation, the changing workforce, evolving employment relationships, virtual work, and workplace values and ethics are just a few of the trends that will be explored in this textbook. To understand these and other topics, the field of organisational behaviour relies on a set of basic beliefs or knowledge structures (see Exhibit 1.3, overleaf). These conceptual anchors represent the way that OB researchers think about organisations and how they should be studied. Let's look at each of these five beliefs that anchor the study of organisational behaviour.

LEARNING OBJECTIVE

Identify the five anchors on which organisational behaviour is based.

THE MULTIDISCIPLINARY ANCHOR

Organisational behaviour is anchored around the idea that the field should develop from knowledge in other disciplines, not just from its own isolated research base. Some OB experts have recently argued that the field suffers from a 'trade deficit'—importing far more knowledge from other disciplines than is exported to other disciplines. While this is a possible concern, organisational behaviour has thrived as a result of its diversity of knowledge gained from other fields of study.[47]

EXHIBIT 1.3

Five philosophical anchors of organisational behaviour

Multidisciplinary anchor	OB should import knowledge from many disciplines
Systematic research anchor	OB should study organisations using systematic research methods
Contingency anchor	OB theory should recognise that the effects of actions often vary with the situation
Multiple levels of analysis anchor	OB knowledge should include three levels of analysis: individual, team, organisation
Open systems anchor	OB should view organisations as open systems that interact with their environment

The upper part of Exhibit 1.4 identifies the traditional disciplines from which organisational behaviour knowledge has developed. For instance, sociologists have contributed to our knowledge of team dynamics, organisational socialisation, organisational power, and other aspects of the social system. The field of psychology has aided our understanding of most issues relating to individual and interpersonal behaviour. Recently, the field of neuroscience has contributed new ideas about human drives and behaviour.[48]

The bottom part of Exhibit 1.4 identifies some of the emerging fields from which organisational behaviour knowledge is acquired. The communications field helps us to understand the dynamics of knowledge management, electronic mail, corporate culture and employee socialisation. Information systems scholars are exploring the effects of information technology on team dynamics, decision making and knowledge management. Marketing scholars have enhanced our understanding of job satisfaction and customer service, knowledge management and creativity. Women's studies scholars are studying perceptual biases and power relations between men and women in organisations.

THE SYSTEMATIC RESEARCH ANCHOR

scientific method A set of principles and procedures that help researchers to systematically understand previously unexplained events and conditions.

A second anchor for organisational behaviour researchers is their belief in the value of studying organisations through systematic research methods. Traditionally, scholars have relied on the **scientific method**, forming research questions, systematically collecting data, and testing hypotheses against those data. This approach typically uses quantitative data (numeric information) and statistical procedures to test hypotheses. The idea behind the scientific method is to minimise personal biases and distortions about organisational events.

grounded theory A process of developing theory through the constant interplay between data gathering and the development of theoretical concepts.

More recently, OB scholars have also adopted qualitative methods and, in particular, **grounded theory** to understand the workplace. Grounded theory is a process of developing a theory through the constant interplay between data gathering and the development of theoretical concepts. Through observation, interviews and other forms of data collection, researchers form concepts and theories. But as they return to gather more information each time, they also test the concepts and theory created up to that point in the research study.[49] Appendix A at the end of this book provides an overview of research design and methods commonly found in organisational behaviour studies.

Multidisciplinary anchor of organisational behaviour

EXHIBIT 1.4

Discipline	Relevant OB topics
Traditional disciplines	
Psychology	Drives, perception, attitudes, personality, job stress, emotions, leadership
Sociology	Team dynamics, roles, socialisation, communication patterns, organisational power, organisational structure
Anthropology	Corporate culture, organisational rituals, cross-cultural dynamics, organisational adaptation
Political science	Intergroup conflict, coalition formation, organisational power and politics, decision making, organisational environments
Economics	Decision making, negotiation, organisational power
Industrial engineering	Job design, productivity, work measurement
Emerging disciplines	
Communications	Knowledge management, electronic mail, corporate culture, employee socialisation
Information systems	Team dynamics, decision making, knowledge management
Marketing	Knowledge management, creativity, decision making
Women's studies	Organisational power, perceptions

THE CONTINGENCY ANCHOR

'It depends' is a phrase that OB scholars often use to answer a question about the best solution to an organisational problem. The statement may seem evasive, yet it reflects an important way of understanding and predicting organisational events, called the **contingency approach**. This anchor states that a particular action may have different consequences in different situations. In other words, no single solution is best in all circumstances.[50]

The contingency anchor explains why OB experts tend to be sceptical about sure-fire recommendations that are so common in the media and in popular press books. While the ideal situation is to identify universal theories—where the concepts and practices have equal success in every situation—the reality is that there are usually too many exceptions to make these 'one best way' theories useful. Even when a theory seems to work everywhere, OB scholars remain doubtful; an exception is somewhere around the corner. For example, Chapter 14 discusses how leaders should use one style (e.g. participation) in some situations and another style (e.g. direction) in other situations. Thus, when faced with a particular problem or opportunity, we need to understand and diagnose the situation and select the strategy most appropriate *under those conditions*.[51]

Although contingency-oriented theories are necessary in most areas of organisational behaviour, we should also be wary about carrying this anchor to an extreme. Some contingency models add more confusion than value when compared with universal ones. Consequently, we need to balance the sensitivity of contingency factors with the simplicity of universal theories.

THE MULTIPLE LEVELS OF ANALYSIS ANCHOR

This textbook divides organisational behaviour topics into three levels of analysis: individual, team and organisation. The individual level includes the characteristics and behaviours of

contingency approach The idea that a particular action may have different consequences in different situations.

employees as well as the thought processes that are attributed to them, such as motivation, perceptions, personalities, attitudes and values. The team level of analysis looks at the way people interact. This includes team dynamics, decisions, power, organisational politics, conflict and leadership. At the organisational level, the focus is on how people structure their working relationships and how organisations interact with their environments.

Although an OB topic is typically pegged into one level of analysis, it usually relates to multiple levels.[52] For instance, communication is located in this book as a team (interpersonal) process, but it is also recognised that it includes individual and organisational processes. Therefore, you should try to think about each OB topic at the individual, team and organisational levels, not just at one of these levels.

THE OPEN SYSTEMS ANCHOR

open systems Organisations that take their sustenance from the environment and, in turn, affect that environment through their output.

The **open systems** anchor of organisational behaviour refers to the notion that organisations need to interact effectively with the external environment. Organisations take their sustenance from the environment and, in turn, affect that environment through their output. Thus, a company's survival and success depend on how well employees sense environmental changes and alter their patterns of behaviour to fit those emerging conditions.[53] In contrast, a closed system has all the resources needed to survive without dependence on the external environment. Organisations are never completely closed systems, but monopolies come close because they operate in very stable environments and can ignore stakeholders for a fairly long time without adverse consequences.

LEARNING OBJECTIVE

Diagram an organisation from an open systems view.

As Exhibit 1.5 illustrates, organisations acquire resources from the external environment, including raw materials, employees, financial resources, information and equipment. Inside the organisation are numerous subsystems, such as processes (communication and reward systems), task activities (production, marketing) and social dynamics (informal groups, power dynamics). With the aid of technology (such as equipment, work methods and information), these subsystems transform inputs into various outputs. Some outputs (e.g. products and services) may be valued by the external environment, whereas other outputs (e.g. employee layoffs, pollution) have adverse effects. The organisation receives feedback from the external environment regarding the value of its outputs and the availability of future inputs. This process is cyclical and, ideally, self-sustaining, so that the organisation may continue to survive and prosper.

EXHIBIT 1.5   Open systems view of organisations

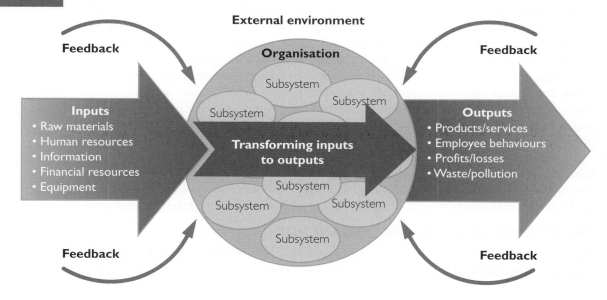

External environment and stakeholders

As open systems, successful organisations monitor their environments and are able to maintain a close fit with the changing conditions.[54] They do so by reconfiguring their outputs (e.g. new products and services, reducing waste) and transformational processes. At the same time, this dynamic capability must not be accelerated to the point where it depletes the organisation's resources or gets too far ahead of market demand. The point here is that organisations need to adapt to changing environments, but not so much that they overspend their resources or overshoot stakeholder needs.

Stakeholders represent a central part of the internal and external environment. As mentioned earlier, a stakeholder is any person or entity with a vested interest in the organisation. Stakeholders influence the firm's access to inputs and ability to discharge outputs. And unless they pay attention to the needs of all stakeholders, organisational leaders may find their business in trouble. For instance, leaders may put their organisation at risk if they pay attention only to shareholders and ignore the broader corporate social responsibility.[55] We see this stakeholder misalignment when job applicants avoid companies that ignore corporate social responsibility and when organisations fail to treat their employees and suppliers with respect.

Systems as interdependent parts

The open systems anchor states that organisations consist of many internal subsystems that need to be continuously aligned with each other. As companies grow, they develop more and more complex subsystems that must coordinate with each other in the process of transforming inputs to outputs.[56] These interdependencies can easily become so complex that a minor event in one subsystem may amplify into serious unintended consequences elsewhere in the organisation.

The open systems anchor is an important way of viewing organisations. However, it has traditionally focused on physical resources that enter the organisation and are processed into physical goods (outputs). This was representative of the industrial economy but not of the 'new economy', where the most valued input is knowledge.

KNOWLEDGE MANAGEMENT

Knowledge management is any structured activity that improves an organisation's capacity to acquire, share and use knowledge in ways that improve its survival and success.[57] The knowledge that resides in an organisation is called its **intellectual capital**, which is the sum of everything known in an organisation that gives it a competitive advantage, including its human capital, structural capital and relationship capital.[58]

- *Human capital.* This is the knowledge that employees possess and generate, including their skills, experience and creativity.
- *Structural capital.* This is the knowledge captured and retained in an organisation's systems and structures. It is the knowledge that remains after all the human capital has gone home.
- *Relationship capital.* This is the value derived from an organisation's relationships with customers, suppliers and other external stakeholders who provide added value for the organisation. For example, it includes customer loyalty, as well as mutual trust between the organisation and its suppliers.

KNOWLEDGE MANAGEMENT PROCESSES

Intellectual capital represents the *stock* of knowledge held by an organisation. This stock of knowledge is so important that some companies try to measure its value.[59] But knowledge management is much more than the organisation's stock of knowledge. It is a *process* that develops an organisation's capacity to acquire, share and use knowledge more effectively. This process is often called **organisational learning** because companies must continuously

LEARNING OBJECTIVE

Define knowledge management and intellectual capital.

knowledge management Any structured activity that improves an organisation's capacity to acquire, share and use knowledge in ways that improve its survival and success.

intellectual capital The sum of an organisation's human capital, structural capital and relationship capital.

organisational learning The knowledge management process in which organisations acquire, share and use knowledge to succeed.

learn about their various environments in order to survive and succeed through adaptation.[60] The 'capacity' to acquire, share and use knowledge means that companies have established systems, structures and organisational values that support the knowledge management process. Let's look more closely at some of the strategies companies use to acquire, share and use knowledge.

Knowledge acquisition

Knowledge acquisition includes the process of extracting information and ideas from the external environment as well as through insight. One of the fastest and most powerful ways to acquire knowledge is by hiring individuals or acquiring entire companies. Knowledge also enters the organisation when employees learn from external sources, such as discovering new resources from suppliers or becoming aware of new trends from clients. For instance, a team of employees at Amcor, one of the world's largest packaging companies, continuously searches around the world for intellectual property and patent-licensing opportunities. This knowledge acquisition process recently helped the Melbourne-based company to develop plastic packaging that prevented table grapes from falling off their stems. A third knowledge acquisition strategy is through experimentation. Companies receive knowledge through insight as a result of research and other creative processes.[61]

An important contingency with knowledge acquisition is that organisations must have enough **absorptive capacity** to acquire the knowledge. Absorptive capacity refers to the ability to recognise the value of new information, to assimilate it and to apply it to commercial ends. The absorptive capacity to acquire new knowledge depends on the company's existing store of knowledge. Without basic knowledge of plastics and package manufacturing processes, Amcor engineers could not have effectively applied outside knowledge to improve the packaging for table grapes. Thus, acquiring new knowledge from the environment requires an absorptive capacity, which depends on the organisation's existing foundation of knowledge. This absorptive capacity also applies to the ability of entire societies to develop.[62]

Knowledge sharing

Many organisations are reasonably good at acquiring knowledge, but they waste this resource by not effectively disseminating it. As several executives have lamented: 'I wish we knew what we know.'[63] Valuable ideas sit idly—rather like unused inventory—or remain hidden as 'silos of knowledge' throughout the organisation. Many organisations improve knowledge sharing by creating digital repositories of knowledge—computer intranets in which employees document and store new knowledge as it becomes available. While somewhat useful, these electronic storage systems can be expensive to maintain; they also overlook the fact that a lot of knowledge is difficult to document.[64]

An alternative strategy for knowledge sharing is to give employees more opportunities for informal online or face-to-face communication. One such approach is through **communities of practice**—groups bound together by shared expertise and a passion for a particular activity or interest.[65] One pioneer in communities of practice is Clarica Life Insurance Company. Realising that its sales agents possessed valuable knowledge which other agents might not have been aware of, the company created an online forum where knowledge can be actively shared among the sales agents.[66]

Knowledge use

Acquiring and sharing knowledge are wasted exercises unless the knowledge is effectively put to use. To do this, employees must realise that the knowledge is available and that they have the freedom to apply it. This requires a culture that supports experiential learning, which will be described in Chapter 3.

LEARNING OBJECTIVE

Identify specific ways that organisations acquire and share knowledge.

absorptive capacity The ability to recognise the value of new information, to assimilate it and to apply it to commercial ends.

communities of practice Informal groups bound together by shared expertise and a passion for a particular activity or interest.

Keeping the Sydney Olympics memory alive

Dallas Kilpoen/Fairfax Photos

The Sydney Olympics in 2000 was a massive challenge, made all the more difficult by the fact that previous Olympic organising committees had not documented how to run this type of event. 'You had a situation where every two years, a $2–4 billion Olympic event would be staged somewhere, and every time the organisers would start all over again— no historical data, no corporate knowledge,' explains Craig McLatchey, former secretary-general of the Australian Olympic Committee and board member of the Sydney Organising Committee for the Olympics Games (SOCOG). 'You would see SOCOG staff literally sitting in front of a blank sheet of paper, trying to work things out.' To create a more permanent organisational memory, SOCOG asked every division and functional area to complete an extensive 'how to' template based on their experiences in the Sydney Olympics. After the event, SOCOG had produced ninety manuals documenting each area's mission and objectives, key risks, key stakeholders, key interactions, operations plans, budget, organisational charts, multi-year staffing, key considerations, and key lessons and recommendations. This documented memory of the Sydney Olympics became a major resource for Athens and other Olympics. Future Olympics committees and applicants have also captured organisational memory by hiring McLatchey and other former Sydney Olympics executives.[68]

ORGANISATIONAL MEMORY

A few years ago Evercare decided to move its headquarters and manufacturing from Flint, Michigan, to Waynesboro, Georgia. The move nearly killed the manufacturer of household cleaning products because none of its production employees wanted to leave Flint. So when the company's executives arrived in Georgia to set up production, they struggled to rebuild the company's manufacturing and distribution systems from scratch. 'Nothing was documented,' recalls an Evercare executive. 'All of the knowledge, all of the practices were built in people's heads.'[67]

Evercare's experience is a reminder that intellectual capital can be lost as quickly as it is acquired.[69] Corporate leaders need to recognise that they are the keepers of an **organisational memory**. This unusual metaphor refers to the storage and preservation of intellectual capital.

organisational memory
The storage and preservation of intellectual capital.

It includes information that employees possess, as well as knowledge embedded in the organisation's systems and structures. It includes documents, objects and anything else that provides meaningful information about how the organisation should operate.

How do organisations retain intellectual capital? One way is by keeping good employees. Progressive companies are attracting and retaining high-quality staff by adopting employment practices that are compatible with emerging workforce expectations, including work–life balance, egalitarian hierarchy and a workplace that generates more fun. A second organisational memory strategy is to systematically transfer knowledge before employees leave. This occurs when new recruits apprentice with skilled employees, thereby acquiring knowledge that is not documented. A third strategy is to transfer knowledge into structural capital. This includes bringing out hidden knowledge, organising it and putting it in a form that can be available to others.

Before leaving the topic of organisational memory and knowledge management, you should know that successful companies also unlearn. Sometimes it is appropriate for organisations to selectively forget certain knowledge.[70] This means that they should cast off the routines and patterns of behaviour that are no longer appropriate. Employees need to rethink their perceptions, such as how they should interact with customers and which is the 'best way' to perform a task. As Chapter 17 will reveal, unlearning is essential for organisational change.

THE JOURNEY BEGINS

This chapter provides some background about the field of organisational behaviour. But it's only the beginning of the journey. Throughout this book, you will be challenged to learn new ways of thinking about how people work in and around organisations. The process begins in Chapter 2 with the presentation of a basic model of individual behaviour. The next six chapters introduce various stable and mercurial characteristics of individuals that relate to elements of the individual behaviour model. Next, the text moves to the team level of analysis. A model of team effectiveness is examined along with specific features of high-performance teams. The text also looks at decision making and creativity, communication, power and influence, conflict and negotiation, and leadership. Finally, the focus shifts to the organisational level of analysis, where the topics of organisational structure, organisational culture and organisational change are examined in detail.

CHAPTER SUMMARY

Organisational behaviour is the study of what people think, feel and do in and around organisations. Organisations are groups of people who work interdependently towards some purpose. OB concepts help us to predict and understand organisational events, adopt more accurate theories of reality, and influence organisational events. This field of knowledge also improves the organisation's financial health.

There are several trends in organisational behaviour. Globalisation requires corporate decision makers to be sensitive to cultural differences. Another trend is increasing racial/ethnic and generational diversity, as well as an increasing percentage of women in the workforce. Employment relations are also evolving as companies adapt workplace practices to support emerging workforce expectations, while also demanding more flexibility through employability and casual work.

Virtual work occurs when employees use information technology to perform their jobs away from the physical workplace. Virtual work includes teleworking as well as virtual teams. Virtual teams are cross-functional groups that operate across space, time and organisational boundaries with members who communicate mainly through information technology. Values and ethics represent another trend. In particular, companies are learning to apply values in a global environment, and they are under pressure to abide by ethical values and higher standards of corporate social responsibility.

Organisational behaviour scholars rely on a set of basic beliefs to study organisations. These anchors include beliefs that OB knowledge should be multidisciplinary and based on systematic research, that organisational events usually have contingencies, that organisational behaviour can be viewed from three levels of analysis (individual, team and organisation), and that organisations are open systems.

The open systems anchor suggests that organisations have interdependent parts that work together to continually monitor and transact with the external environment. They acquire resources from the environment, transform them through technology, and return outputs to the environment. The external environment consists of the natural and social conditions outside the organisation. External environments today are generally highly turbulent, so organisations must become adaptable and responsive.

Knowledge management develops an organisation's capacity to acquire, share and use knowledge in ways that improve its survival and success. Intellectual capital is knowledge that resides in an organisation, including its human capital, structural capital and relationship capital. Organisations acquire knowledge through various practices, including individual learning and experimentation. Knowledge sharing occurs mainly through various forms of communication, including communities of practice. Knowledge use occurs when employees realise that the knowledge is available and that they have enough freedom to apply it. Organisational memory refers to the storage and preservation of intellectual capital.

KEY TERMS

absorptive capacity p. 20
communities of practice p. 20
contingency approach p. 16
casual work p. 12
corporate social responsibility (CSR) p. 15
employability p. 12
ethics p. 14
globalisation p. 7

grounded theory p. 16
intellectual capital p. 19
knowledge management p. 19
open systems p. 18
organisational behaviour (OB) p. 4
organisational learning p. 19
organisational memory p. 21
organisations p. 5

scientific method p. 16
stakeholders p. 15
values p. 13
virtual teams p. 13
virtual work p. 12
work–life balance p. 10

DISCUSSION QUESTIONS

1. A friend suggests that organisational behaviour courses are useful only to people who will enter management careers. Discuss the accuracy of your friend's statement.

2. Look through the list of chapters in this textbook and discuss how globalisation could influence each organisational behaviour topic.

3. Corporate social responsibility (CSR) is one of the hottest issues in corporate boardrooms today, partly because it is becoming increasingly important to employees and other stakeholders. In your opinion, why have stakeholders given CSR more attention recently? Does abiding by CSR standards potentially cause companies to have objectives that conflict with those of some stakeholders in some situations?

4. 'Organisational theories should follow the contingency approach.' Comment on the accuracy of this statement.

5. A number of years ago, employees in a city water distribution department were put into teams and encouraged to find ways to improve efficiency. The teams boldly crossed departmental boundaries and areas of management discretion in search of problems. Employees working in other parts of the city began to complain about these intrusions. Moreover, when some team ideas were implemented, the city managers discovered that a dollar saved in the water distribution unit might have cost the organisation two dollars in higher costs elsewhere. Use the open systems anchor to explain what happened here.

6. After hearing a seminar on knowledge management, a mining company executive argues that this perspective ignores the fact that mining companies could not rely on knowledge alone to stay in business. They also need physical capital (such as digging and ore processing equipment) and land (where the minerals are located). In fact, these two may be more important than what employees carry around in their heads. Argue for or against the mining executive's comments.

7. At a recent seminar on information technology, you heard a consultant say that over 30 per cent of Asia's largest companies use software to manage documents and exchange information, whereas firms in Europe are just beginning to adopt this technology. Based on this, the consultant concluded that 'knowledge management in Europe is at its beginning stages'. In other words, few firms in Europe practise knowledge management. Comment on this consultant's statement.

8. BusNews Ltd is the leading stock-market and business news service. Over the past two years, BusNews has experienced increased competition from other news providers. These competitors have brought in Internet and other emerging computer technologies to link customers with information more quickly. There is little knowledge within BusNews about how to use these computer technologies. Based on the knowledge acquisition processes for knowledge management, explain how BusNews might gain the intellectual capital necessary to become more competitive in this respect.

SKILL BUILDER | 1.1   ANCOL PTY LTD

CASE STUDY

Paul Sims was delighted when Ancol Pty Ltd offered him the job of manager at its plant near Shepparton, Victoria. Sims was happy enough managing a small metal stamping plant with another company, but the executive recruiter's invitation to apply for the job of plant manager at a leading metal fabrication company was irresistible. Although the Shepparton plant was the smallest of Ancol's fifteen operations across Australia and New Zealand, the plant manager position was a valuable first step in a promising career.

One of Sims's first observations at Ancol's Shepparton plant was that relations between employees and management were strained. Taking a page from a recent executive seminar that he had attended on building trust in the workplace, Sims ordered the removal of all time clocks from the plant. Instead, the plant would assume that employees had put in their full shift. This symbolic gesture, he believed, would establish a new level of credibility and strengthen relations between management and employees at the site.

Initially, the 250 production employees at the Shepparton plant appreciated their new freedom. They felt respected and saw this gesture as a sign of positive change from the new plant manager. Two months later, however, problems started to appear. A few people began showing up late, leaving early, or take extended lunch breaks. Although this represented only about 5 per cent of the employees, others found the situation unfair. Moreover, the increased absenteeism levels were beginning to have a noticeable effect on plant productivity. The problem had to be managed.

Sims asked supervisors to observe and record when the employees came or went and to discuss attendance problems with those abusing their privileges. But the supervisors had no previous experience with keeping attendance records and many lacked the necessary interpersonal skills to discuss the matter with subordinates. Employees resented the reprimands, so relations with supervisors deteriorated. The additional responsibility of keeping track of attendance also made it difficult for supervisors to complete their other responsibilities. After just a few months, Ancol found it necessary to add another supervisor position and reduce the number of employees assigned to each supervisor.

But the problems did not end there. Without time clocks, the payroll department could not deduct pay for the amount of time that employees were late. Instead, a letter of reprimand was placed in the employee's personnel file. However, this required yet more time and additional skills from the supervisors. Employees did not want these letters to become a permanent record, so they filed grievances with their labour union. The number of grievances doubled over six months, which required even more time for both union officials and supervisors to handle these disputes.

Nine months after removing the time clocks, Paul Sims met with union officials, who agreed that it would be better to put the time clocks back in. Employee–management relations had deteriorated to below the level they had been when Sims had started. Supervisors were burnt out from overwork. Productivity had dropped due to poorer attendance records and increased administrative workloads.

A couple of months after the time clocks were put back in place, Sims attended an operations meeting at Ancol's headquarters in Melbourne. During lunch, Sims described the time clock incident to Liam Wu, Ancol's plant manager in Christchurch. Wu looked surprised, then chuckled. Wu explained that the previous Christchurch plant manager had done something similar, with similar consequences, six or seven years ago. The manager had left some time ago, but Wu had heard about the time clock incident from a supervisor during the supervisor's retirement party two months ago.

'I guess it's not quite like lightning striking in the same place twice,' said Sims to Wu. 'But it sure feels like it.'

QUESTIONS

1. Use the systems theory model to explain what happened when Ancol removed the time clocks.

2. What changes should occur to minimise the likelihood of these problems in the future?

HUMAN CHECKERS

1.2 | SKILL BUILDER

TEAM EXERCISE

PURPOSE

This exercise is designed to help students understand the importance and application of organisational behaviour concepts.

MATERIALS

None, but the instructor has more information about the team's task.

INSTRUCTIONS

Step 1: Form teams with six students. If possible, each team should have a private location where team members can plan and practise the required task without being observed or heard by other teams.

Step 2: All teams will receive special instructions in class about the team's assigned task. All teams have the same task and will have the same amount of time to plan and practise the task. At the end of this planning and practice, each team will be timed while completing the task in class. The team that completes the task in the least time wins.

Step 3: No special materials are required or allowed for this exercise. Although the task is not described here, students should learn the following rules for planning and implementing the task:

Rule 1: You cannot use any written form of communication or any props to assist in the planning or implementation of this task.

Rule 2: You may speak to other students in your team at any time during the planning and implementation of this task.

Rule 3: When performing the task, you must move only in the direction of your assigned destination. In other words, you can only move forward, not backward.

Rule 4: When performing the task, you can move forward to the next space, but only if it is vacant (see Exhibit 1).

Rule 5: When performing the task, you can move forward two spaces, if that space is vacant. In other words, you can move around a student who is one space in front of you to the next space if that space is vacant (see Exhibit 2).

Exhibit 1   **Exhibit 2**

Step 4: When all teams have completed their task, the class will discuss the implications of this exercise for organisational behaviour.

QUESTIONS

1. Identify organisational behaviour concepts that the team applied to complete this task.

2. What personal theories of people and work teams were applied to complete this task?

3. What organisational behaviour problems occurred and what actions were (or should have been) taken to solve them?

SKILL BUILDER | 1.3   DIAGNOSING ORGANISATIONAL STAKEHOLDERS

WEB EXERCISE

PURPOSE

This exercise is designed to help you understand how stakeholders influence organisations as part of the open systems anchor.

MATERIALS

Students need to select a company and, prior to class, retrieve and analyse publicly available information over the past year or two about that company. This may include annual reports, which are usually found on the websites of publicly traded companies. Where possible, students should also scan full-text newspaper and magazine databases for articles published over the previous year about the company.

INSTRUCTIONS

The instructor may have students work alone or in groups for this activity. Students will select a company and will investigate the relevance and influence of various stakeholder groups on the organisation. Stakeholders will be identified from annual reports, newspaper articles, website statements and other available sources. Stakeholders should be rank-ordered in terms of their perceived importance to the organisation.

Students should be prepared to present or discuss their organisation's rank-ordering of stakeholders, including evidence for this rank-ordering.

QUESTIONS

1. What are the main reasons that certain stakeholders are more important than others to this organisation?

2. Based on your knowledge of the organisation's environmental situation, is this rank-order of stakeholders in the organisation's best interest, or should specific other stakeholders be given higher priority?

3. What societal groups, if any, are not mentioned as stakeholders by the organisation? Does this lack of reference to these unmentioned groups make sense?

IT ALL MAKES SENSE

1.4 SKILL BUILDER

SELF-ASSESSMENT

 STUDENT CD

PURPOSE

This exercise is designed to help you understand how organisational behaviour knowledge can help you to understand life in organisations.

INSTRUCTIONS

(Note: This activity may be done as a self-assessment or as a team activity.) Read each of the statements below and circle whether each statement is true or false, in your opinion. The class will consider the answers to each question and discuss the implications for studying organisational behaviour.

Due to the nature of this activity, the instructor will provide the answers to the questions. There is no scoring key in Appendix B.

1.	❏ True	❏ False	A happy worker is a productive worker.
2.	❏ True	❏ False	Decision makers tend to continue supporting a course of action even though information suggests that the decision is ineffective.
3.	❏ True	❏ False	Organisations are more effective when they prevent conflict among employees.
4.	❏ True	❏ False	It is better to negotiate alone than as a team.
5.	❏ True	❏ False	Companies are more effective when they have a strong corporate culture.
6.	❏ True	❏ False	Employees perform better without stress.
7.	❏ True	❏ False	Effective organisational change always begins by pinpointing the source of its current problems.
8.	❏ True	❏ False	Female leaders involve employees in decisions to a greater degree than do male leaders.
9.	❏ True	❏ False	People in Japan value group harmony and duty to the group (high collectivism) more than do Australians (low collectivism).
10.	❏ True	❏ False	The best decisions are made without emotion.
11.	❏ True	❏ False	If employees feel that they are paid unfairly, nothing other than changing their pay will reduce their feelings of injustice.

SKILL BUILDER | 1.5 | TELEWORK DISPOSITION ASSESSMENT

SELF-ASSESSMENT

FULL EXERCISE ON
STUDENT CD

Some employees adapt better than others to telework (also called telecommuting) and other forms of virtual work. This self-assessment measures personal characteristics that seem to relate to teleworking, and therefore provides a rough indication of how well you would adapt to telework. The instrument asks you to indicate how much you agree or disagree with each of the statements provided. You need to be honest with yourself in order to obtain a reasonable estimate of your telework disposition. Please keep in mind that this scale considers only your personal characteristics. Other factors, such as organisational, family and technological systems support, must also be taken into account.

NOTES

1   F. Rotherman, 'Calling It Quits', *Unlimited*, September 2004; 'Westpac Enhances Its Package of Family Friendly Policies', *Asian Banker*, 15 March 2005; 'The Banker Awards 2005: Global Awards', *The Banker*, September 2005, 68; 'Bank Staff Strike Nationwide', *New Zealand Herald*, 20 December 2005; A. Cornell and J. Moullakas, 'Just How Great Is Gail Kelly?', *Australian Financial Review*, 7 May 2005, 20; A. Maitland, 'Old Hands Back in Demand in the Global Workforce', *Financial Times* (London), 6 July 2005, 13; E. Ross, 'Finishing School', *Business Review Weekly*, 24 February 2005, 64.

2   M. Warner, 'Organizational Behavior Revisited', *Human Relations* 47 (October 1994), 1151–66; R. Westwood and S. Clegg, 'The Discourse of Organization Studies: Dissensus, Politics, and Paradigms', in *Debating Organization: Point–Counterpoint in Organization Studies*, eds R. Westwood and S. Clegg (Malden, MA: Blackwood, 2003), 1–42. Some of the historical bases of OB mentioned in this paragraph are described in: J. A. Conger, 'Max Weber's Conceptualization of Charismatic Authority: Its Influence on Organizational Research', *The Leadership Quarterly* 4, no. 3–4 (1993), 277–88; R. Kanigel, *The One Best Way: Frederick Winslow Taylor and the Enigma of Efficiency* (New York: Viking, 1997); J. H. Smith, 'The Enduring Legacy of Elton Mayo', *Human Relations* 51, no. 3 (1998), 221–49; T. Takala, 'Plato on Leadership', *Journal of Business Ethics* 17 (May 1998), 785–98; J. A. Fernandez, 'The Gentleman's Code of Confucius: Leadership by Values', *Organizational Dynamics* 33, no. 1 (February 2004), 21–31.

3   J. Micklethwait and A. Wooldridge, *The Company: A Short History of a Revolutionary Idea* (New York: Random House, 2003).

4   D. Katz and R. L. Kahn, *The Social Psychology of Organizations* (New York: Wiley, 1966), chapter 2; R. N. Stern and S. R. Barley, 'Organizations as Social Systems: Organization Theory's Neglected Mandate', *Administrative Science Quarterly* 41 (1996), 146–62.

5   N. Hooper, 'Call Me Irresistible', *Australian Financial Review*, 5 December 2003, 38.

6   J. Pfeffer, *New Directions for Organization Theory* (New York: Oxford University Press, 1997), pp. 7–9.

7   P. R. Lawrence and N. Nohria, *Driven: How Human Nature Shapes Our Choices* (San Francisco: Jossey-Bass, 2002), chapter 6.

8   P. R. Lawrence, 'Historical Development of Organizational Behavior', in *Handbook of Organizational Behavior*, ed. L. W. Lorsch (Englewood Cliffs, NJ: Prentice Hall, 1987), 1–9; S. A. Mohrman, C. B. Gibson and A. M. Mohrman Jr, 'Doing Research That Is Useful to Practice: A Model and Empirical Exploration', *Academy of Management*

Journal 44 (April 2001), 357–75. For a contrary view, see A. P. Brief and J. M. Dukerich, 'Theory in Organizational Behavior: Can It Be Useful?', *Research in Organizational Behavior* 13 (1991), 327–52.

9   M. S. Myers, *Every Employee a Manager* (New York: McGraw-Hill, 1970).

10 D. Yankelovich, 'Got to Give to Get', *Mother Jones* 22 (July 1997), 60–63; D. MacDonald, 'Good Managers Key to Buffett's Acquisitions', *Montreal Gazette*, 16 November 2001. The two studies on OB and financial performance are: B. N. Pfau and I. T. Kay, *The Human Capital Edge* (New York: McGraw-Hill, 2002); and I. S. Fulmer, B. Gerhart and K. S. Scott, 'Are the 100 Best Better? An Empirical Investigation of the Relationship between Being a "Great Place to Work" and Firm Performance', *Personnel Psychology* 56, no. 4 (Winter 2003), 965–93.

11 '"Huge Responsibility" on Globalco to Perform', *New Zealand Herald*, 18 June 2001; 'A Major Player on the World Milk Stage', *Weekly Times* (Sydney), 8 September 2004, 91; K. Newman, 'Greener Pastures', *MIS New Zealand*, September 2004, 18; V. Marsh, 'A New Mood of Self-Assurance', *FT.com* (London), 18 March 2005, 1.

12 S. K. Witcher, 'Australia's Computershare Stays Nimble, Hoping to Lead Share-Registry Market', *Wall Street Journal*, 11 December 2000, B19A; R. Gottliebsen, 'New Spheres in Going Global', *Australian*, 29 November 2003, 28; 'Computershare on Track for Record Revenue', *Australian Associated Press*, 9 November 2005.

13 S. Fischer, 'Globalization and Its Challenges', *American Economic Review* (May 2003), 1–29. For a discussion of the diverse meanings of 'globalization', see M. F. Guillén, 'Is Globalization Civilizing, Destructive or Feeble? A Critique of Five Key Debates in the Social Science Literature', *Annual Review of Sociology* 27 (2001), 235–60.

14 The ongoing debate regarding the advantages and disadvantages of globalisation are discussed in: Guillén, 'Is Globalization Civilizing, Destructive or Feeble?'; D. Doane, 'Can Globalization Be Fixed?', *Business Strategy Review* 13, no. 2 (2002), 51–58; J. Bhagwati, *In Defense of Globalization* (New York: Oxford University Press, 2004); M. Wolf, *Why Globalization Works* (New Haven, CT: Yale University Press, 2004).

15 C. L. Cooper and R. J. Burke, *The New World of Work: Challenges and Opportunities* (Oxford: Blackwell, 2002); C. Higgins and L. Duxbury, *The 2001 National Work–Life Conflict Study: Report One, Final Report* (Ottawa: Health Canada, March 2002).

16 K. Ohmae, *The Next Global Stage* (Philadelphia: Wharton School Publishing, 2005).

17 R. Autherson, 'Embracing Diversity', *South China Morning Post* (Hong Kong), 12 March 2005, 10; HSBC Australia, 'HSBC's Largest Australian Advertising Campaign', HSBC Australia news release (Sydney, 13 October 2005).

18 Commonwealth of Australia, Department of Immigration and Multicultural and Indigenous Affairs, *Immigration Update 2004–2005* (Canberra: DIMIA, December 2005).

19 'Tapping into Cultural and Spiritual Diversity', *EEO Trust Work & Life Bulletin*, September 2005, 6–7.

20 P. Gavel, J. Evans and J. Young, *Who Are the Doctors of Tomorrow? Some Australian Perspectives and Thoughts* (Australian Medical Workforce Advisory Committee, 2005).

21 R. Zemke, C. Raines and B. Filipczak, *Generations at Work: Managing the Clash of Veterans, Boomers, Xers, and Nexters in Your Workplace* (New York: Amacom, 2000); C. Loughlin and J. Barling, 'Young Workers' Work Values, Attitudes, and Behaviours', *Journal of Occupational and Organizational Psychology* 74 (November 2001), 543–58; C. A. Martin and B. Tulgan, *Managing Generation Y* (Amherst, MA: HRD Press, 2001); M. R. Muetzel, *They're Not Aloof, Just Generation X* (Shreveport, LA: Steel Bay, 2003); S. H. Applebaum, M. Serena and B. T. Shapiro, 'Generation X and the Boomers: Organizational Myths and Literary Realities', *Management Research News* 27, no. 11/12 (2004), 1–28.

22 O. C. Richard, 'Racial Diversity, Business Strategy, and Firm Performance: A Resource-Based View', *Academy of Management Journal* 43 (2000), 164–77; D. D. Frink et al., 'Gender Demography and Organization Performance: A Two-Study Investigation with Convergence', *Group & Organization Management* 28 (March 2003), 127–47; T. Kochan et al., 'The Effects of Diversity on Business Performance: Report of the Diversity Research Network', *Human Resource Management* 42 (2003), 3–21.

23 R. J. Ely and D. A. Thomas, 'Cultural Diversity at Work: The Effects of Diversity Perspectives on Work Group Processes and Outcomes', *Administrative Science Quarterly* 46 (June 2001), 229–73; D. van Knippenberg and S. A. Haslam, 'Realizing the Diversity Dividend: Exploring the Subtle Interplay between Identity, Ideology and Reality', in *Social Identity at Work: Developing Theory for Organizational Practice*, ed. S. A. Haslam et al. (New York: Taylor and Francis, 2003), 61–80.

24 W. G. Bennis and R. J. Thomas, *Geeks and Geezers* (Boston: Harvard Business School Press, 2002), 74–79; E. D. Y. Greenblatt, 'Work/Life Balance: Wisdom or Whining', *Organizational Dynamics* 31, no. 2 (2002), 177–93.

25 S. McLean, 'Happy Employees a Work in Progress', *Courier-Mail* (Brisbane), 2 April 2005, L06.

26 R. Basch, 'Doing Well by Doing Good', *Searcher Magazine*, January 2005, 18–28; K. Coughlin, 'Goooood Move', *Star-Ledger* (Newark, NJ), 5 June 2005, 1.

27 M. V. Roehling et al., 'The Nature of the New Employment Relationship(s): A Content Analysis of the Practitioner and Academic Literatures', *Human Resource Management* 39 (2000), 305–20; W. R. Boswell et al., 'Responsibilities in the "New Employment Relationship": An Empirical Test of an Assumed Phenomenon', *Journal of Managerial Issues* 13 (Fall 2001), 307–27; M. Fugate, A. J. Kinicki and B. E. Ashforth, 'Employability: A Psycho-Social Construct, Its Dimensions, and Applications', *Journal of Vocational Behavior* 65, no. 1 (2004), 14–38.

28 M. Jenkins, 'Yours for the Taking', *Boeing Frontiers*, June 2004, http://www.boeing.com/news/frontiers/index.html.

29 A. E. Polivka, 'Contingent and Alternative Work Arrangements, Defined', *Monthly Labor Review* 119 (October 1996), 3–10;

D. H. Pink, *Free Agent Nation* (New York: Time Warner, 2002); C. E. Connelly and D. G. Gallagher, 'Emerging Trends in Contingent Work Research', *Journal of Management* 30, no. 6 (2004), 959–83.

30 I. Campbell, 'Casual Work and Casualisation: How Does Australia Compare?', *Labour & Industry* 15, no. 2 (December 2004), 85–111.

31 B. A. Lautsch, 'Uncovering and Explaining Variance in the Features and Outcomes of Contingent Work', *Industrial & Labor Relations Review* 56 (October 2002), 23–43; S. Ang, L. Van Dyne and T. M. Begley, 'The Employment Relationships of Foreign Workers Versus Local Employees: A Field Study of Organizational Justice, Job Satisfaction, Performance, and OCB', *Journal of Organizational Behavior* 24 (2003), 561–83; A. L. Kalleberg, 'Flexible Firms and Labor Market Segmentation', *Work and Occupations* 30, no. 2 (May 2003), 154–75; B. A. Lautsch, 'The Influence of Regular Work Systems on Compensation for Contingent Workers', *Industrial Relations* 42, no. 4 (October 2003), 565–88; Connelly and Gallagher, 'Emerging Trends in Contingent Work Research'; B. Pocock, J. Buchanan and I. Campbell, 'Meeting the Challenge of Casual Work in Australia: Evidence, Past Treatment and Future Policy', *Australian Bulletin of Labour* 30, no. 1 (March 2004), 16–32.

32 S. de Castro and Y.-C. Tham, 'Home Work', Digital Life, 8 February 2005; F. Smith, 'Teleworkers So Near and Yet So Far', *Australian Financial Review*, 6 September 2005, 58.

33 'Employees' Increasing Get Choices: Mercer', *WA Business News* (Perth), 17 November 2005; Australian Telework Advisory Committee (ATAC), *Telework—International Developments* (Paper III) (Canberra: Commonwealth of Australia, March 2005); Australian Telework Advisory Committee (ATAC), *Telework in Australia* (Paper II), (Canberra: Commonwealth of Australia, March 2005). These estimates exclude employees who bring work home from the office, because this practice isn't usually considered virtual work.

34 L. Duxbury and C. Higgins, 'Telecommute: A Primer for the Millennium Introduction', in *The New World of Work: Challenges and Opportunities*, ed. C. L. Cooper and R. J. Burke (Oxford: Blackwell, 2002), 157–99; V. Illegems and A. Verbeke, 'Telework: What Does It Mean for Management?', *Long Range Planning* 37 (2004), 319–34; S. Raghuram and B. Wiesenfeld, 'Work–Nonwork Conflict and Job Stress among Virtual Workers', *Human Resource Management* 43, no. 2/3 (Summer/Fall 2004), 259–77.

35 D. E. Bailey and N. B. Kurland, 'A Review of Telework Research: Findings, New Directions, and Lessons for the Study of Modern Work', *Journal of Organizational Behavior* 23 (2002), 383–400; D. W. McCloskey and M. Igbaria, 'Does "Out of Sight" Mean "Out of Mind"? An Empirical Investigation of the Career Advancement Prospects of Telecommuters', *Information Resources Management Journal* 16 (April–June 2003), 19–34; Sensis, Sensis® Insights Report: Teleworking (Melbourne: Sensis, June 2005).

36 Smith, 'Teleworkers So Near and Yet So Far'.

37 J. Lipnack and J. Stamps, *Virtual Teams: People Working across Boundaries with Technology* (New York: John Wiley & Sons, 2001); L. L. Martins, L. L. Gilson and M. T. Maynard, 'Virtual Teams: What Do We Know and Where Do We Go from Here?', *Journal of Management* 30, no. 6 (2004), 805–35; G. Hertel, S. Geister and U. Konradt, 'Managing Virtual Teams: A Review of Current Empirical Research', *Human Resource Management Review* 15, no. 1 (2005), 69–95.

38 D. Hughes, 'Top of the Corporate Heap', *The Age* (Melbourne), 4 April 2005, 15; C. Kelly et al., *Deriving Value from Corporate Values* (Aspen Institute and Booz Allen Hamilton Inc., February 2005).

39 Middle East Company News, 'Accountability, Teamwork, and Continuous Improvement Define Core Operating Values at DED', Middle East Company News news release (Dubai, 4 January 2005).

40   B. M. Meglino and E. C. Ravlin, 'Individual Values in Organizations: Concepts, Controversies, and Research', *Journal of Management* 24, no. 3 (1998), 351–89; B. R. Agle and C. B. Caldwell, 'Understanding Research on Values in Business', *Business and Society* 38, no. 3 (September 1999), 326–87; S. Hitlin and J. A. Pilavin, 'Values: Reviving a Dormant Concept', *Annual Review of Sociology* 30 (2004), 359–93.

41   K. Kernaghan, 'Integrating Values into Public Service: The Values Statement as Centrepiece', *Public Administration Review* 63, no. 6 (November/December 2003), 711–19. Some of the popular books that emphasise the importance of values include: J. C. Collins and J. I. Porras, *Built to Last: Successful Habits of Visionary Companies* (London: Century, 1995); C. A. O'Reilly III and J. Pfeffer, *Hidden Value* (Cambridge, MA: Harvard Business School Press, 2000); J. M. Kouzes and B. Z. Posner, *The Leadership Challenge*, 3rd edn (San Francisco: Jossey-Bass, 2002).

42   The role of values as a control system is discussed in: T. M. Begley and D. P. Boyd, 'Articulating Corporate Values through Human Resource Policies', *Business Horizons* 43, no. 4 (July 2000), 8–12; M. G. Murphy and K. M. Davey, 'Ambiguity, Ambivalence and Indifference in Organisational Values', *Human Resource Management Journal* 12 (2002), 17–32.

43   'Believe It', *BC Business*, July 2004, 130; 'Multi-Year Study Finds 21% Increase in Americans Who Say Corporate Support of Social Issues Is Important in Building Trust', *Business Wire*, 9 December 2004; J. Milne, 'Do the Right Thing', *MIS UK*, 1 December 2005, 20.

44   M. van Marrewijk, 'Concepts and Definitions of CSR and Corporate Sustainability: Between Agency and Communion', *Journal of Business Ethics* 44 (May 2003), 95–105.

45   S. Zadek, *The Civil Corporation: The New Economy of Corporate Citizenship* (London: Earthscan, 2001), chapter 9; The Warehouse, *This Way Forward: Society and Environment Report 2005* (2005); S. Zambon and A. Del Bello, 'Towards a Stakeholder Responsible Approach: The Constructive Role of Reporting', *Corporate Governance* 5, no. 2 (2005), 130–42.

46   'Wal-Mart to Cut Ties with Bangladesh Factories Using Child Labour', *CBC News* (Toronto), 30 November 2005; P. Foster, 'Heaven Can Wait', *National Post*, 2 July 2005, FP17.

47   M. N. Zald, 'More Fragmentation? Unfinished Business in Linking the Social Sciences and the Humanities', *Administrative Science Quarterly* 41 (1996), 251–61. Concerns about the 'trade deficit' in OB are raised in C. Heath and S. B. Sitkin, 'Big-B Versus Big-O: What Is Organizational About Organizational Behavior?', *Journal of Organizational Behavior* 22 (2001), 43–58.

48   N. Nicholson, 'Evolutionary Psychology: Toward a New View of Human Nature and Organizational Society', *Human Relations* 50 (September 1997), 1053–78; B. D. Pierce and R. White, 'The Evolution of Social Structure: Why Biology Matters', *Academy of Management Review* 24 (October 1999), 843–53; Lawrence and Nohria, *Driven: How Human Nature Shapes Our Choices*.

49   A. Strauss and J. Corbin, *Grounded Theory in Practice* (London: Sage Publications, 1997). For an overview of the importance of qualitative methods in organisational behaviour, see R. P. Gephart Jr, 'Qualitative Research and the Academy of Management Journal', *Academy of Management Journal* 47 (2004), 454–62.

50   C. M. Christensen and M. E. Raynor, 'Why Hard-Nosed Executives Should Care About Management Theory', *Harvard Business Review* (September 2003), 66–74. For an excellent critique of the 'one best way' approach in early management scholarship, see P. F. Drucker, 'Management's New Paradigms', *Forbes* (5 October 1998), 152–77.

51   H. L. Tosi and J. W. Slocum Jr, 'Contingency Theory: Some Suggested Directions', *Journal of Management* 10 (1984), 9–26.

52   D. M. Rousseau and R. J. House, 'Meso Organizational Behavior: Avoiding Three Fundamental Biases', in *Trends in Organizational Behavior*, ed. C. L. Cooper and D. M. Rousseau (Chichester, UK: John Wiley & Sons, 1994), 13–30.

53   F. E. Kast and J. E. Rosenweig, 'General Systems Theory: Applications for Organization and Management', *Academy of Management Journal* (1972), 447–65; P. M. Senge, *The Fifth Discipline: The Art and Practice of the Learning Organization* (New York: Doubleday Currency, 1990); A. De Geus, *The Living Company* (Boston: Harvard Business School Press, 1997); R. T. Pascale, M. Millemann and L. Gioja, *Surfing on the Edge of Chaos* (London: Texere, 2000).

54   V. P. Rindova and S. Kotha, 'Continuous "Morphing": Competing through Dynamic Capabilities, Form, and Function', *Academy of Management Journal* 44 (2001), 1263–80; J. McCann, 'Organizational Effectiveness: Changing Concepts for Changing Environments', *Human Resource Planning* 27, no. 1 (2004), 42–50.

55   R. Martin, 'The Virtue Matrix: Calculating the Return on Corporate Responsibility', *Harvard Business Review* 80 (March 2002), 68–85.

56   M. L. Tushman, M. B. Nadler and D. A. Nadler, *Competing by Design: The Power of Organizational Architecture* (New York: Oxford University Press, 1997).

57   G. Huber, 'Organizational Learning: The Contributing Processes and Literature', *Organizational Science* 2 (1991), 88–115; E. C. Nevis, A. J. DiBella and J. M. Gould, 'Understanding Organizations as Learning Systems', *Sloan Management Review* 36 (1995), 73–85; G. Miles et al., 'Some Conceptual and Research Barriers to the Utilization of Knowledge', *California Management Review* 40 (Spring 1998), 281–8.

58   T. A. Stewart, *Intellectual Capital: The New Wealth of Organizations* (New York: Currency/Doubleday, 1997); H. Saint-Onge and D. Wallace, *Leveraging Communities of Practice for Strategic Advantage* (Boston: Butterworth-Heinemann, 2003), pp. 9–10; J.-A. Johannessen, B. Olsen and J. Olaisen, 'Intellectual Capital as a Holistic Management Philosophy: A Theoretical Perspective', *International Journal of Information Management* 25, no. 2 (2005), 151–71.

59   N. Bontis, 'Assessing Knowledge Assets: A Review of the Models Used to Measure Intellectual Capital', *International Journal of Management Reviews* 3 (2001), 41–60; P. N. Bukh, H. T. Larsen and J. Mouritsen, 'Constructing Intellectual Capital Statements', *Scandinavian Journal of Management* 17 (March 2001), 87–108.

60   There is no complete agreement on the meaning of organisational learning (or learning organisation), and the relationship between organisational learning and knowledge management is still somewhat ambiguous. For example, see: S. C. Goh, 'The Learning Organization: An Empirical Test of a Normative Perspective', *International Journal of Organization Theory & Behavior* 4, no. 3/4 (August 2001), 329–55; B. R. McElyea, 'Knowledge Management, Intellectual Capital, and Learning Organizations: A Triad of Future Management Integration', *Futurics* 26 (2002), 59–65.

61   C. W. Wick and L. S. Leon, 'From Ideas to Actions: Creating a Learning Organization', *Human Resource Management* 34 (Summer 1995), 299–311; L. Falkenberg et al., 'Knowledge Acquisition Processes for Technology Decisions', in *Proceedings of the Academy of Management 2002 Annual Conference* (2002), J1–J6; S. Lloyd, 'Smarter Spending Habits', *Business Review Weekly*, 10 November 2005, 130.

62   W. Cohen and D. Levinthal, 'Absorptive Capacity: A New Perspective on Learning and Innovation', *Administrative Science Quarterly* 35 (1990), 128–52; J. L. Johnson, R. S. Sohi and R. Grewal, 'The Role of Relational Knowledge Stores in Interfirm Partnering', *Journal of Marketing* 68 (July 2004), 21–36; M. Rogers, 'Absorptive Capacity

and Economic Growth: How Do Countries Catch Up?', *Cambridge Journal of Economics* 28, no. 4 (July 2004), 577–96.

63 G. S. Richards and S. C. Goh, 'Implementing Organizational Learning: Toward a Systematic Approach', *The Journal of Public Sector Management* (Autumn 1995), 25–31; C. O'Dell and C. J. Grayson, 'If Only We Knew What We Know: Identification and Transfer of Internal Best Practices', *California Management Review* 40 (Spring 1998), 154–74; R. Ruggles, 'The State of the Notion: Knowledge Management in Practice', *California Management Review* 40 (Spring 1998), 80–9.

64 R. Garud and A. Kumaraswamy, 'Vicious and Virtuous Circles in the Management of Knowledge: The Case of Infosys Technologies', *MIS Quarterly* 29, no. 1 (March 2005), 9–33.

65 E. C. Wenger and W. M. Snyder, 'Communities of Practice: The Organizational Frontier', Harvard Business Review 78 (January–February 2002), 139–45; Saint-Onge and Wallace, *Leveraging Communities of Practice for Strategic Advantage*; M. Thompson, 'Structural and Epistemic Parameters in Communities of Practice', *Organization Science* 16, no. 2 (March–April 2005), 151–64.

66 Saint-Onge and Wallace, *Leveraging Communities of Practice for Strategic Advantage*, chapter 5.

67 D. Cline, 'On a Roll', *Augusta Chronicle*, 2 February 2003, D1.

68 B. P. Sunoo, 'The Sydney Challenge', *Workforce*, September 2000, 70–73; N. Bita and J. Lehmann, 'Five-Ring Circuit for Olympic Organisers', *Australian*, 12 September 2005, 27; E. Semertzaki, 'A Brief but Intense Job', *Information Outlook*, May 2005, 29–35.

69 H. Beazley, J. Boenisch and D. Harden, 'Knowledge Continuity: The New Management Function', *Journal of Organizational Excellence* 22 (2003), 65–81.

70 M. E. McGill and J. W. Slocum Jr, 'Unlearn the Organization', *Organizational Dynamics* 22, no. 2 (1993), 67–79; D. Lei, J. W. Slocum and R. A. Pitts, 'Designing Organizations for Competitive Advantage: The Power of Unlearning and Learning', *Organizational Dynamics* 27 (Winter 1999), 24–38.

INSERT YOUR CD NOW
TO VIEW THE FOOTAGE
THAT CORRESPONDS
TO THESE CASES

VIDEO CASE STUDIES

NEW BELGIUM BREWERY

This video program outlines the various ways in which New Belgium Brewery in Fort Collins, Colorado, tries to operate an environmentally sustainable business. The company accomplishes impressive environmental standards through new technology, alternative forms of energy and waste minimisation. The program reveals these environmentally sustainable strategies and describes how employees buy into this model of doing business.

The owners of the company, Jeff Leabish and Kim Jordan, decided early on what their values and goals were. The overall goal is to make a profit, but for Jeff and Kim there's more to it. Having fun and allowing their employees to have fun with what they do is also important. They were able to visualise the far-reaching effects that this would have on the expansion of their business. By giving the employees a say in the overall company direction, the employees developed a vested interest in seeing the company progress further.

QUESTIONS

1. Discuss the various organisational behaviour topics that are introduced in this video.

2. Discuss how New Belgium Brewery's founders have used aspects of organisational behaviour to gain employee support for the various strategies that have made the company successful.

PART 2

Individual behaviour and processes

CHAPTER 2
Individual behaviour, values and personality

CHAPTER 3
Perception and learning in organisations

CHAPTER 4
Workplace emotions and attitudes

CHAPTER 5
Motivation in the workforce

CHAPTER 6
Applied performance practices

CHAPTER 7
Work-related stress and stress management

VIDEO CASE STUDIES
- Employee loyalty
- Pike Place Fish Market
- Stress in Japan
- The Container Store

CHAPTER 2

Individual behaviour, values and personality

LEARNING OBJECTIVES

After reading this chapter, you should be able to:

- diagram the MARS model

- describe three types of ways to match individual competencies to job requirements

- identify five types of individual behaviour in organisations

- define values and explain why values congruence is important

- define five main values that vary across cultures

- list three ethical principles

- explain how moral intensity, ethical sensitivity and the situation influence ethical behaviour

- identify the 'Big Five' personality dimensions

- summarise the personality concepts behind the Myers–Briggs Type Indicator

- explain how personality relates to Holland's model of vocational choice.

ASB Bank is making employee engagement a cornerstone of its business strategy to become a world-class organisation.

A recent survey of Optus employees revealed trouble ahead. Employee engagement scores at the Australian telecommunications company had tumbled close to the 'serious' zone. 'Our most recent results show that current engagement is lower than we'd like to see,' admits an Optus spokesperson. The report estimated that 60 per cent of 'Optus people are not engaged and are not contributing in full to the achievement of the organisation's goals'. Staff comments suggest that the decline in employee engagement was due to uninspiring management, unclear roles and responsibilities, and lack of support due to outdated procedures and systems.

Employee engagement is receiving a lot of attention at Optus and other organisations these days because it refers to how much employees identify with and are emotionally committed to their work, are cognitively focused on that work, and possess the ability and resources to do so. This collection of beliefs and attitudes ultimately influences the company's productivity, customer satisfaction, profitability and employee retention. For instance, British retailer Marks & Spencer claims that a 1 per cent improvement in the engagement levels of its workforce produces a 2.9 per cent increase in sales per square foot. Australian research estimates that a 5 per cent improvement in employee engagement at a 200-person firm will, on average, reduce employee turnover costs by $240 000 and increase profits by $300 000.

ASB Bank scored well above average in its first employee engagement survey a few years ago, but that wasn't good enough for the New Zealand financial institution. 'We were absolutely shattered,' recalls an ASB Bank executive, who was expecting the firm to be in the top quartile. To boost its employee engagement levels, the Commonwealth Bank of Australia subsidiary produced videos showing how managers with the most engaged subordinates perform their jobs. Managers also meet with staff each month, and the bank's chief executive personally teaches new employees about the company's customer service vision. Today, ASB Bank's employee engagement scores are in the top 10 per cent globally and the company receives some of the highest ratings in New Zealand for customer service

Gallup, the consultancy that measured employee engagement at ASB Bank, estimates that 29 per cent of employees in the United States are highly engaged, compared with 18 per cent in Australia, 17 per cent in New Zealand, 12 per cent in China and Thailand, and only 9 per cent in Singapore and Japan. Approximately two-thirds of employees in Australia, China, Japan and New Zealand and 82 per cent in Singapore and Thailand are 'not engaged'. A third group, the 'actively disengaged', range from 24 per cent in Japan to 6 per cent in Thailand. Gallup warns that actively disengaged employees tend to be disruptive, not just dissatisfied. Surveys by other consultancies reveal similar employee engagement scores across countries in this region.[1]

employee engagement
The extent to which employees identify with and are emotionally committed to their work, are cognitively focused on that work, and possess the ability and resources to be so.

THE GROUNDSWELL OF INTEREST IN employee engagement makes a great deal of sense when we realise that this concept includes most of the drivers of individual behaviour and results. Consider the survey results at Optus. The Australian telecommunications company has low employee engagement scores because employees say they lack motivation (management fails to inspire them), recent changes have increased confusion regarding roles and responsibilities, and some staff complain about bureaucratic rules and poor resources which block them from performing their job more effectively. These conditions are captured within the definition of employee engagement, and they represent three of the four factors that influence employee behaviour and results.

This chapter begins by presenting the MARS model, which outlines the four drivers of individual behaviour and results. Next, the chapter briefly looks at the five main types of individual behaviour in the workplace. The latter half of the chapter focuses on values and personality, two deeply held characteristics of people that influence their attitudes, motivation, and behaviour in the workplace. The section on values describes Schwartz's model of personal values, issues relating to values congruence, the dynamics of cross-cultural values, and key features of ethical values in the workplace. The section on personality introduces the five-factor model of personality, the Myers–Briggs Type Indicator, and other personality characteristics that are often discussed in organisational behaviour research.

MARS MODEL OF INDIVIDUAL BEHAVIOUR AND RESULTS

LEARNING OBJECTIVE

Diagram the MARS model.

Why do individuals behave the way they do and perform well or poorly in the workplace? This question has been the Holy Grail of much research in organisational behaviour, and it is the focus of the next six chapters in this book. The journey begins with the presentation of a basic model of individual behaviour and results (called the MARS model) and an outline of the main types of behaviour in organisational settings. Then the main individual difference topics underlying the MARS model are examined, beginning with two of the most stable influences: values and personality.

The MARS model, illustrated in Exhibit 2.1, is a useful starting point from which to understand the drivers of individual behaviour and the results of that behaviour. The model highlights the four factors that directly influence an employee's voluntary behaviour and resulting performance—motivation, ability, role perceptions and situational factors. These four factors are represented by the acronym 'MARS' in the model's name.[2] The MARS model shows that these four factors have a combined effect on individual performance. If any factor weakens,

EXHIBIT 2.1

MARS model of individual behaviour and results

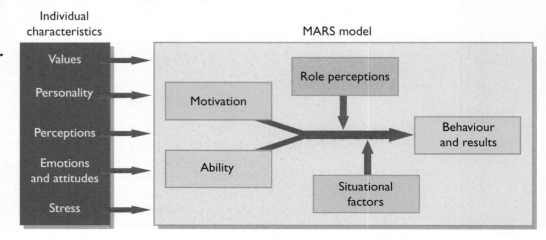

employee performance will decrease. For example, enthusiastic salespeople (motivation) who understand their job duties (role perceptions) and have sufficient resources (situational factors) will not perform their jobs as well if they lack sufficient knowledge and sales skill (ability). Look back at the opening story and you will see that employee engagement captures all four MARS drivers of individual behaviour and results. It is not surprising that employee engagement has become such a popular concept among practitioners!

Exhibit 2.1 also shows that the four factors in the MARS model are influenced by several other individual variables that will be discussed over the next few chapters. Personality and values are the most stable characteristics,[3] so they will be looked at later in this chapter. Emotions, attitudes and stress are much more fluid characteristics, and individual perceptions and learning usually lie somewhere in between. Each of these factors relates to the MARS model in various ways. For example, personal values affect an employee's motivation through emotions and tend to shape role perceptions through the perceptual process. Learning influences ability, role perceptions and motivation, as will be seen in Chapter 3. Before examining these individual characteristics, the four elements of the MARS model are briefly introduced, followed by an overview of the different types of individual behaviour in the workplace.

EMPLOYEE MOTIVATION

Motivation represents the forces within a person that affect his or her direction, intensity and persistence of voluntary behaviour.[4] *Direction* refers to the fact that motivation is goal-oriented, not random. People are motivated to arrive at work on time, finish a project a few hours early, or aim for many other targets. *Intensity* is the amount of effort allocated to the goal. For example, two employees might be motivated to finish their project a few hours early (direction), but only one of them puts forth enough effort (intensity) to achieve this goal. Finally, motivation involves varying levels of *persistence*, that is, continuing the effort for a certain amount of time. Employees sustain their effort until they reach their goal or give up beforehand. Chapter 5 looks more closely at the conceptual foundations of employee motivation, and Chapter 6 considers some applied motivation practices.

motivation The forces within a person that affect the direction, intensity and persistence of voluntary behaviour.

ABILITY

Employee abilities also make a difference in behaviour and task performance. **Ability** includes both the natural aptitudes and the learned capabilities required to successfully complete a task. *Aptitudes* are the natural talents that help employees learn specific tasks more quickly and perform them better. For example, some people have a more natural ability than others to manipulate small objects with their fingers (called 'finger dexterity'). There are many different physical and mental aptitudes, and our ability to acquire skills is affected by these aptitudes. *Learned capabilities* are the skills and knowledge that you have actually acquired. This includes the physical and mental skills you possess as well as the knowledge you acquire and store for later use.

ability Includes both the natural aptitudes and learned capabilities required to complete a task successfully.

Employee competencies

Skills, knowledge, aptitudes, values, drives and other underlying personal characteristics that lead to superior performance are typically bunched together into the concept of **competencies**. Competencies are relevant to an entire job group rather than just to specific jobs. For instance, American Express Australia & New Zealand recently determined that to thrive in an environment of rapid change and globalisation it would require leaders who have strong competencies in commercial excellence, in driving innovation and change, in customer and client focus, and in demonstrating personal excellence.[5] Most large organisations spend a lot of money identifying key competencies, but some competencies are described too broadly to use as a guide to hiring and training people. Also, companies wrongly assume that everyone should have the same set of competencies, whereas the truth seems to be that people with another combination of competencies may be equally effective.[6]

competencies The abilities, values, personality traits and other characteristics of people that lead to superior performance.

Fly-fishing competencies in Chiang Mai

Fly-fishing is barely known in Chiang Mai, Thailand, but lure manufacturers have flocked there for some of the world's best fish-fly making. 'Chiang Mai is to fly tying what Silicon Valley is to computers,' says an executive at Targus Fly & Feather, a Mesa, Arizona, company with large fly-making operations in Thailand. Local residents have a high level of finger dexterity, thanks to centuries of making local handicrafts, and this aptitude is well-suited to fish-fly tying. Even so, Kwanruen Thanomrungruang (shown in photo) and other employees require two months of training and don't become fully proficient at fly tying for up to two years.[7]

AP Photo/Apichart Weerawong

LEARNING OBJECTIVE

Describe three types of ways to match individual competencies to job requirements.

Person–job matching

There are three approaches to matching individual competencies with job requirements. One strategy is to select applicants whose existing competencies best fit the required tasks. This includes comparing each applicant's competencies with the requirements of the job or the work unit. A second approach is to provide training so that employees develop the required skills and knowledge.

The third way to match people with job requirements is to redesign the job so that employees are only given tasks that are within their capabilities. AT&T's customer service operations in Dallas took this approach when it was realised that many employees were overwhelmed by the increasing variety of products (cable, Internet, HDTV, home theatre, etc.). 'Our employees just said "Help! This is way too complex. We're trained on three things and we need help",' recalls an executive at the American telecommunications giant. AT&T's solution was to redesign jobs so that employees could begin with one area of product knowledge, such as video cable, then progress to a second knowledge area when the first product was mastered.[8]

ROLE PERCEPTIONS

At 1:15 am on a summer evening, nearly 1000 passengers travelling on the *Spirit of Tasmania* had an unexpected wake-up call. A fire had started on board the ship as it sailed across Bass Strait for Devonport. The crew sprang into action, waking passengers in each compartment and moving them to the muster stations until the fire was contained. Afterwards, passengers commented on how the crew worked like a 'well-oiled machine'. The Tasmania Fire Service also noted that the quick action by captain and crew prevented the fire from spreading and endangering passengers.[9]

Employees on the *Spirit of Tasmania* acted like a well-oiled machine not just because they had learnt the appropriate skills. They had also developed accurate *role perceptions*. Employees have accurate role perceptions when they understand the specific tasks assigned to them, the relative importance of those tasks, and the preferred behaviours to accomplish those tasks. The most basic way to improve these role perceptions is for staff to receive clear job descriptions and ongoing coaching. For instance, the opening vignette to this chapter described how ASB Bank clarified perceptions about the importance of customer service, and managers watched video programs of colleagues to discover the best way to engage employees. In contrast, some Optus employees said they were confused about roles and responsibilities due to recent changes at the telecommunications company. In other words, employee engagement and job performance are undermined by inaccurate or ambiguous role perceptions.

SITUATIONAL FACTORS

With high levels of motivation and ability, along with clear role perceptions, people will perform well only if the situation also supports their task goals. Situational factors include conditions beyond the employee's immediate control that constrain or facilitate his or her behaviour and performance.[10] Some situational characteristics—such as consumer preferences and economic conditions—originate from the external environment, and consequently are beyond the employee's and organisation's control. However, some situational factors—such as time, people, budgets and physical work facilities—are controlled by others in the organisation. Corporate leaders need to arrange these conditions carefully so employees can achieve their performance potential.

Motivation, ability, role perceptions and situational factors affect all conscious workplace behaviours and their performance outcomes. The next section outlines the five categories of behaviour in organisational settings.

TYPES OF INDIVIDUAL BEHAVIOUR IN ORGANISATIONS

People engage in many different types of behaviour in organisational settings. Exhibit 2.2 highlights the five types of behaviour discussed most often in the organisational behaviour literature: task performance, organisational citizenship, counterproductive work behaviours, joining and staying with the organisation, and work attendance.

LEARNING OBJECTIVE
Identify five types of individual behaviour in organisations.

TASK PERFORMANCE

Task performance refers to goal-directed behaviours under the individual's control that support organisational objectives. Task performance behaviours transform raw materials into goods and services or support and maintain the technical activities.[11] For example, foreign exchange traders

Types of work-related behaviour

EXHIBIT 2.2

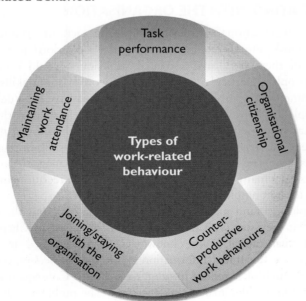

at National Australia Bank make decisions and take actions to exchange currencies. Employees in most jobs have more than one performance dimension. Foreign exchange traders must be able to identify profitable trades, work cooperatively with clients and co-workers in a stressful environment, assist in training new staff, and work on special telecommunications equipment without error. Some of these performance dimensions are more important than others, but only by considering all of them can an employee's contribution to the organisation be fully evaluated.

EXHIBITING ORGANISATIONAL CITIZENSHIP

organisational citizenship
Refers to behaviours that extend beyond the employee's normal job duties.

One of the defining characteristics of engaged employees is that they perform beyond task performance standards or expectations. 'When employees become engaged, they develop a stronger conscientiousness about what they can do,' explains Bill Erikson, vice-chairman of consulting firm Kenexa. 'They will go the extra step, or maybe even the extra mile, to support the interest of the organisation.' In short, engaged employees practise **organisational citizenship**. They help others without selfish intent, are actively involved in organisational activities, avoid unnecessary conflicts, perform tasks beyond normal role requirements, and gracefully tolerate impositions. Several factors described throughout this book explain why some employees are good organisational citizens and others are not. Later in the chapter, for example, we learn that people with a conscientiousness personality trait have higher organisational citizenship.[12]

COUNTERPRODUCTIVE WORK BEHAVIOURS

counterproductive work behaviours (CWBs)
Voluntary behaviours that are likely to either directly or indirectly harm the organisation.

Although organisations benefit from task performance and organisational citizenship, it also needs to be recognised that employees sometimes succumb to **counterproductive work behaviours (CWBs)**—voluntary behaviours that have the potential to directly or indirectly harm the organisation. Organisational behaviour experts have organised CWBs into five categories: abuse of others (e.g. insults and nasty comments), threats (threatening harm), work avoidance (e.g. tardiness), work sabotage (doing work incorrectly), and overt acts (theft). CWBs are not minor concerns. One recent study found that units of an Australian fast-food restaurant chain with higher CWBs had significantly worse performance, whereas organisational citizenship had a relatively minor benefit. Through this book, several ways to minimise counterproductive work behaviours will be identified, including better organisational justice (Chapter 5) and less workplace stress (Chapter 7), as well as looking at the propensity of people with a political personality trait known as Machiavellianism to engage in CWBs (Chapter 12).[13]

JOINING AND STAYING WITH THE ORGANISATION

Task performance, organisational citizenship and the lack of counterproductive work behaviours are obviously important, but if qualified people don't join and stay with the organisation none of these performance-related behaviours would occur. Attracting and retaining talented people is particularly important as worries about skills shortages become front-page news. Some mining projects in Western Australia have been delayed due to a lack of skilled tradespeople. In Whyalla, South Australia, OneSteel has more than three dozen job vacancies in electrical instrumentation alone, and retirement plans for many existing staff will add further pressure to the steelmaker's labour woes. 'There is a skill shortage, there's no doubt about that,' admits OneSteel Whyalla's human resources manager Alan Tidsell.[14] Reality Check 2.1 describes how many companies are addressing this recruitment challenge by paying more attention to their employer brand image.

A reputable employer brand may attract qualified applicants, but the war for talent also includes ensuring that they stay with the company. As discussed in Chapter 1, much of an organisation's intellectual capital is the knowledge carried around in employees' heads. Organisations may try to document information about work processes, corporate values and customer needs, but much of it resides in employees' heads. Consequently, retaining valued employees is a critical knowledge management strategy. The problem is that many employees

COMPANY 'BRAND' ATTRACTS TALENT

MLC has done business in Hong Kong for well over a decade, but the Australian-owned life insurance and financial planning firm is not yet a household name, to either consumers or potential employees. So, MLC has pulled out all the stops to attract the best talent in brand-conscious Hong Kong and is developing its employer brand. The firm recently moved out of older offices to a swanky high-tech centre which is 'a physical manifestation of our employer branding', says Victor Birman, MLC (Hong Kong) general manager for people and culture. The company is also crafting a catchy subtitle to its name that will succinctly state what it's like to work at MLC. 'Ultimately, an employer brand should define what companies promise employees joining them, and what is expected in return,' Birman explains.

Employer branding refers to a public image of what the company stands for (its values) as well as what it offers to employees and expects in return. It is also a powerful way to differentiate a company from others in the minds of potential applicants. Applicants might believe that one organisation has a strong team environment, whereas another is an aggressive competitor that generously rewards its star performers. Each brand attracts a different type of applicant and with varying degrees of success. 'A powerful brand attracts people who are aligned with it,' says Neil Porteous, HR director of Vodafone New Zealand.

Creating an employer brand goes to the core of how the company treats employees. 'Branding has got to be a lot more than brochures and window dressing,' warns Tom Simon, Motorola's senior director of global human resource strategy. 'You can't just go out with some recruiting advertisements. What you do have to do is be ready to tackle management and performance systems and standards—then get all these in sync with one another.'

Aviva Insurance (Thai) Co. Ltd pays a lot of attention to its employer brand. The Bangkok-based subsidiary of the British insurance giant has established several employment practices that appeal to employees and achieve the company's objectives. Aviva also monitors how well its image is coming across by consulting its employees. 'We conduct regular employee focus surveys with all our employees through an international survey provider which … allows us to compare our results with other international companies operating in Thailand,' explains Matthew Grose, an Aviva HR executive in Bangkok. 'It is through listening to our employees that we know whether we're doing a good job in building a strong employer brand.'

Aviva Insurance (Thai) Co. Ltd

Aviva Insurance is creating an employer brand that helps it to attract top-quality talent in Thailand.

Sources: N. Suebsukcharoen, 'Employer "Brands" Matter', *Bangkok Post*, 29 November 2004, B9; E. Silverman, 'Making Your Mark', *Human Resource Executive*, 4 November 2004; T. Metcalfe, 'A Good Image Will Attract the Right Staff', *South China Morning Post* (Hong Kong), 18 June 2005, 4; J. Watkins, 'The Search for Understanding', *New Zealand Management*, July 2005, 34.

don't plan on staying with their current employer for very long. One large-scale survey revealed that nearly two-thirds of Indonesian employees planned to move to a different employer even though the position, area of work and remuneration were the same. A survey of thirteen mining operations across Australia reported an average turnover rate of 24 per cent, with some mining sites experiencing annual employee turnover approaching 60 per cent.[15]

Why do people quit their jobs? Traditionally, organisational behaviour experts have identified low job satisfaction as the main cause of turnover. **Job satisfaction** is a person's evaluation of his or her job and work context (see Chapter 4). Employees become dissatisfied with their employment relationship, which motivates them to search for and join another organisation with better conditions. While job dissatisfaction builds over time and eventually affects turnover, the most recent opinion is that specific 'shock events' need to be considered.[16] These shock events, such as the boss's unfair decision or a conflict episode with a co-worker, create strong emotions that trigger employees to think about and search for alternative employment.

MAINTAINING WORK ATTENDANCE

Along with attracting and retaining employees, organisations need everyone to show up for work at scheduled times. One estimate is that unscheduled absences (i.e. excluding planned holidays) cost Australian business $7 billion annually in lost productivity. According to another study, Australian federal government employees take an average of almost twelve days of unscheduled absences annually, about one-third more than employees in the private sector.[17]

Why are employees absent from work? One factor involves conditions largely beyond the employees' control, such as a major storm, a car breakdown, or sick children with no one else to care for them. Motivation is another factor. Employees who experience job dissatisfaction or work-related stress are more likely to be absent from work or late for work, because taking time off is a way of temporarily withdrawing from stressful or dissatisfying conditions. Absenteeism is also higher in organisations with generous sick leave, because this benefit limits the negative financial impact of taking time away from work. Yet another factor is team norms. One study of Queensland government employees discovered that absenteeism rates changed over time, and that these changing absence levels may be due to changing norms about how much unscheduled time off team members should take.[18]

The MARS model and the five types of individual behaviour and results provide a foundation for the ideas presented over the next few chapters. The remainder of this chapter will look at two of the most stable individual differences: values and personality.

VALUES IN THE WORKPLACE

Westpac has become one of Australia's most popular financial institutions among investors, customers and other stakeholders. According to chief executive David Morgan, the transformation came about by helping employees to understand their personal and shared values. 'Values are the glue you need to mesh the social and economic system in a seamless way,' says Morgan. 'They are deeply rooted in our organisation, they have a real life in the day-to-day experiences of our people. We've always had those values, but one thing we have done in recent years is to make those values more explicit.'[19]

Several best-selling management books conclude that Westpac and other successful companies have a deeply entrenched and long-lasting set of core values.[20] To emulate this success, executives have been keen to identify, communicate and align a set of core values in their own firms. **Values** are stable, evaluative beliefs that guide our preferences for outcomes or courses of action in a variety of situations.[21] They are perceptions about what is good or bad, right or wrong. Values tell us what we 'ought' to do. They serve as a moral compass that directs our motivation and, potentially, our decisions and actions. Values partly define who we are as individuals and as members of groups with similar values.

People arrange values into a hierarchy of preferences, called a *value system*. Some individuals value new challenges more than they value conformity. Others value generosity more than frugality. Each person's unique value system is developed and reinforced through socialisation from parents, religious institutions, friends, personal experiences, and the society in which he or she lives. As such, a person's hierarchy of values is stable and long lasting. For example, one study found that the value systems of a sample of adolescents were remarkably unchanged twenty years later.[22]

Notice that our description of values has focused on individuals, whereas Westpac chief executive David Morgan describes values as though they belong to the organisation. In reality, values exist only within individuals; in other words, they are *personal values*. However, groups of people might hold the same or similar values, so these shared values tend to be ascribed to the team, department, organisation, profession or entire society. The values shared by people throughout an organisation (*organisational values*) will be more fully discussed in Chapter 16 because they are a key part of corporate culture. The values shared across a society (*cultural values*) will receive attention later in this chapter.

Before discussing workplace values in more detail, a distinction needs to be made between espoused and enacted values.[23] *Espoused values* represent the values that people say they use and, in many cases, think they use. Corporate leaders might say that they value environmentalism, creativity and politeness, whether or not they really do value these things in practice. Values are socially desirable, so people create a positive public image by claiming to believe in values that others expect them to embrace. Also, stated corporate values are usually considered espoused values, because, although leaders might abide by them, it is not known whether lower-level employees share this commitment. *Enacted values*, on the other hand, represent the values people actually rely on to guide their decisions and actions. These values-in-use are apparent by watching people in action. Just as we judge an individual's personality by behavioural tendencies, so too we judge enacted values by behavioural tendencies.

TYPES OF VALUES

Values come in many forms, and experts on this topic have devoted considerable attention to organising them into coherent groups. The model in Exhibit 2.3, developed and tested by

EXHIBIT 2.3

Schwartz's values circumplex

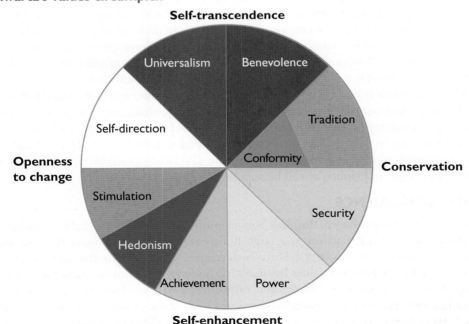

Sources: S. H. Schwartz, 'Universals in the Content and Structure of Values: Theoretical Advances and Empirical Tests in 20 Countries', *Advances in Experimental Social Psychology*, 25 (1992), pp. 1–65; S. H. Schwartz and G. Sagie, 'Value Consensus and Importance: A Cross-national Study', *Journal of Cross-Cultural Psychology*, 31 (July 2000), pp. 465–97.

social psychologist Shalom Schwartz, has become the most widely studied and generally accepted model today.[24] Schwartz reduced dozens of personal values into ten broader domains of values and further organised these domains around two bipolar dimensions.

Along the left side of the horizontal dimension in Schwartz's model is *openness to change*, which represents the extent to which a person is motivated to pursue innovative ways. Openness to change includes the value domains of self-direction (independent thought and action) and stimulation (excitement and challenge). *Conservation*, the opposite end of Schwartz's horizontal dimension, is the extent to which a person is motivated to preserve the status quo. Conservation includes the value clusters of conformity (adherence to social norms and expectations), security (safety and stability) and tradition (moderation and preservation of the status quo).

The vertical dimension in Schwartz's model ranges from self-enhancement to self-transcendence. *Self-enhancement*—how much a person is motivated by self-interest—includes the values of achievement (pursuit of personal success) and power (dominance over others). The opposite of self-enhancement is *self-transcendence*, which refers to the motivation to promote the welfare of others and nature. Self-transcendence includes the values of benevolence (concern for others in one's life) and universalism (concern for the welfare of all people and nature).

VALUES AND INDIVIDUAL BEHAVIOUR

Personal values guide our decisions and actions, but this connection isn't as direct as it sounds. Habitual behaviour tends to be consistent with our values, but our everyday conscious decisions and actions apply our values much less consistently. The main reason for the 'disconnect' between personal values and individual behaviour is that values are abstract concepts that sound good in theory but are less easily followed in practice. A lot of people say that benevolence is an important value to them, yet they don't think about being benevolent in a lot of situations. Benevolence becomes a 'truism' that gets lost in translation in everyday life.

Benevolence and other values do influence decisions and behaviour if three conditions are met.[25] First, a specific value affects our behaviour when something makes us mindful (consciously aware) of that value. Co-workers tend to treat each other with much more respect and consideration immediately after a senior executive has given a speech on the virtues of benevolence in the workplace. The speech makes employees temporarily mindful of this value, so they think about it in their behaviour towards others. Second, even if a particular value is important and people are mindful of it, they still need to have logical reasons in their head for applying that value. In other words, people tend to apply their values only when they can think of specific reasons for doing so. For example, you will be more motivated to switch your holiday time with a co-worker who needs that time off if you are mindful of your value of benevolence and you can think of reasons why it's good to be benevolent.

The third condition that improves the linkage between values and behaviour is the situation. Work environments shape behaviour, at least in the short term, so they necessarily encourage or discourage values-consistent behaviour. The fact is that people's jobs sometimes require them to act in ways that are inconsistent with their personal values. This incongruence between personal values and work requirements can also have a powerful effect on employee attitudes and other behaviours, as will be seen next.

VALUES CONGRUENCE

A few years ago, Copenhagen Business School professor Peter Pruzan held a seminar on workplace values with executives at a large European-based multinational manufacturing company. Working in teams, the executives developed a list of their five most important personal values. The personal values list included honesty, love, beauty, peace of mind and happiness (most of which fall under the categories of universalism and benevolence in Exhibit 2.3). In the afternoon, the teams developed a list of the enacted (not espoused) values of their company. The company values list included success, efficiency, power, competitiveness

Creating congruent values at Coles Myer

Coles Myer staff indicated through employee surveys that they wanted a coherent set of values to help bind the company together. Chief executive John Fletcher and his executive team felt that these values should come from the employees themselves so that personal and organisational values would be highly congruent. To accomplish this, more than 2300 employees across all levels at Australia's largest retailer participated in 203 focus groups around the country. Several dozen employees later met together for two days to condense 153 pages of focus group feedback into four values: integrity, respect and recognition, a passion for excellence, and working together. Next, thousands of Coles Myer managers attended one-day workshops where they developed a better understanding of the four values and what behaviours are associated with those values. The company also revised its performance appraisal system so 20 per cent of managers' bonuses are tied to how well they perform against those values.[27]

Amen Deushian/Newspix

and productivity (most of which are represented by achievement and power in Exhibit 2.3). In other words, the organisation's values were almost completely opposite to the executives' personal values![26]

Executives at the European firm discovered that they needed to dramatically increase **values congruence** within their organisation. Values congruence refers to the similarity of value systems between two entities. In the example of the European manufacturer, the organisation's value system was incongruent with the value systems of its managers (called *person–organisation values congruence*). Research indicates that this form of incongruence is common. Three out of four New Zealand managers surveyed in one study said that their company's values conflict to some extent with their own ethical values. Another study reported that Indian managers saw significant differences between their personal values and organisational practices.[28]

Person–organisation values incongruence has a number of undesirable consequences, including high stress and turnover as well as low organisational citizenship, loyalty and job satisfaction. Values are guideposts, so incongruence also reduces the chance that employees will make decisions compatible with the organisation's values.[29] Does this mean that the most successful organisations perfectly align employee values with the organisation's values? Not at all! While a comfortable degree of values congruence is necessary for the reasons just noted, organisations also benefit from some level of values incongruence. Employees with diverse values offer different perspectives, which often leads to better decision making (see Chapter 8). Moreover, too much congruence can create a 'corporate cult' that potentially undermines creativity, organisational flexibility and business ethics (see Chapter 16).[30]

values congruence A situation wherein two or more entities have similar value systems

Other types of values congruence

A second type of values congruence refers to how closely the values apparent in our actions (enacted values) are consistent with what we say we believe in (espoused values). This *espoused–enacted values congruence* is especially important for people in leadership positions, because any obvious gap between espoused and enacted values undermines their perceived integrity, a critical feature of effective leaders (see Chapter 14).[31] For instance, Westpac regularly surveys its employees to find out the degree to which its managers are acting consistently with the financial institution's espoused values. Even for non-management staff, espoused–enacted values congruence affects how much co-workers can trust each other, which has implications for team dynamics.

A third type of values congruence refers to the compatibility of an organisation's dominant values with the prevailing values of the community or society in which it conducts business.[32] For example, an organisation originating from one country that tries to impose its value system on stakeholders located in another country may experience high employee turnover and have difficult relations with the communities in which the company operates. Management of SC Johnson was aware of this need for alignment for its Australian business. The American healthcare products company has strong paternalistic values in its home country. 'It's a family company with family values,' says Andrew Miedler, SC Johnson's human resource director in Australia. But many Australians would rather keep their work lives separate from their personal lives, so SC Johnson tweaked its values somewhat. 'You can't sell that family company idea in Australia, so we position it as family values with work/life balance,' Miedler explains. Rather than hearing that they are part of the SC Johnson family, the company's Australia employees learn about work/life balance and the company's social responsibility.[33] The next section looks more closely at cross-cultural values.

VALUES ACROSS CULTURES

LEARNING OBJECTIVE

Define five main values that vary across cultures.

Anyone who has worked for some time in another country will know that values differ across cultures. Some cultures value group decisions, whereas others think that the leader should take charge. Meetings in Germany usually start on time, whereas they might be half an hour late in Brazil without much concern. The Asia–Pacific is a region of contrasting cultures, so people in this region need to be particularly sensitive to the fact that cultural differences exist and, although often subtle, can influence decisions and behaviour.

INDIVIDUALISM AND COLLECTIVISM

individualism The extent to which people value independence and personal uniqueness.

collectivism The extent to which people value duty to groups to which they belong as well as group harmony.

Let's start by looking at the two most commonly mentioned cross-cultural values, individualism and collectivism. **Individualism** is the extent to which we value independence and personal uniqueness. Highly individualist people value personal freedom, self-sufficiency and control over their own lives, and have an appreciation of the unique qualities that distinguish them from others. This value relates most closely to the self-direction dimension shown earlier in Exhibit 2.3. **Collectivism** is the extent to which we value our duty to groups to which we belong, and to group harmony. Highly collectivist people define themselves by their group membership and value harmonious relationships within those groups.[34] Collectivism is located within the conservation range of values (security, tradition, conformity) in Exhibit 2.3.

You might think from these definitions that high individualism is the same as low collectivism, and vice versa. Until recently, many scholars thought so, too. However, research indicates that the two concepts are actually unrelated.[35] Some people and cultures might have both high individualism and high collectivism, for example. Someone who highly values duty to one's group does not necessarily give a low priority to personal freedom and self-sufficiency.

How individualistic and collectivistic are people in various countries? Exhibit 2.4 provides the best available answer because it is based on dozens of previous studies combined into a

Individualism and collectivism in selected countries

EXHIBIT 2.4

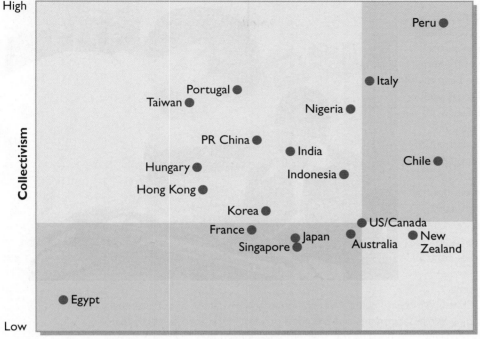

Note: The US/Canada data refers only to people with European heritage in those countries.

Source: Based on information in D. Oyserman, H. M. Coon and M. Kemmelmeier, 'Rethinking Individualism and Collectivism: Evaluation of Theoretical Assumptions and Meta-Analyses', *Psychological Bulletin*, 128 (2002), pp. 3–72. The countries shown here represent only a sample of those in Oyserman's meta-analysis.

massive single analysis. These findings indicate that Australians, Americans, Canadians, and New Zealanders with European heritage are more individualistic than people in many other countries. Only people in some South American countries (such as Chile and Peru) score higher on individualism. In contrast, people from Taiwan, Hong Kong, Korea and China are among those with much lower individualism. Exhibit 2.4 also shows that Australians, New Zealanders, Americans and Canadians with European heritage have relatively low collectivism, whereas people in Italy, Taiwan, Peru, Nigeria and most other countries have higher collectivism.

One notable observation in Exhibit 2.4 is that people in Japan have lower levels of collectivism than people in most other cultures. This is a stark contrast to statements in many cross-cultural books that Japan is one of the most collectivist countries on the planet! The misconception arose because a major study more than twenty years ago that identified Japan as collectivist measured collectivism in a way that bears little resemblance to how the concept is usually defined.[36] Subsequent studies have reported that Japan is relatively low on the collectivist scale (as Exhibit 2.4 reveals), but these persistent results have been slow to replace the old views on the matter.

POWER DISTANCE

Stephen Roberts was born in Australia, but returning to Sydney after nearly a decade as a manager in Asia required a cultural adjustment. 'Managing in Asia was a relatively easy process because no one pushed back,' says Roberts, chief executive of Citigroup Australia/New Zealand. 'I remember arriving in Australia and I was asked to present to an executive committee of our equities team, and it felt like a medical examination. I walked out battered and bruised.'[37]

Stephen Roberts experienced the difference between Australia and every Asian country on the value called **power distance**. Power distance refers to the extent to which people accept an unequal distribution of power in a society.[38] People in Asian countries tend to have high power

power distance The extent to which people accept unequal distribution of power in a society.

Anticipating cross-cultural differences at Lenovo

A few years ago, several Chinese-born managers living in Silicon Valley were recruited to work in Beijing for Lenovo Group, China's giant computer manufacturer. Many of them quit a year later because, after living in the United States for several years, they had difficulty with China's high power distance culture. Every morning, Lenovo employees had to sing the company song. Their whereabouts in and out of the office had to be accounted for throughout the day. Those late for meetings had to stand behind their chair for a minute in humiliation to discourage future tardiness. 'It's very militaristic,' recalls one former Lenovo employee recruited from the United States. 'You just have to do what you're told.' Now, as Lenovo takes control of IBM's personal computer business, cross-cultural differences will probably become

Cancan Chu/Getty Images

apparent for IBM staff in the United States. 'We regard cultural integration as the key factor of our eventual success,' says Lenovo CEO Yang Yuanqing. While Yang points out the good product fit, he acknowledges that there will be 'big cultural conflicts and challenges' in bringing together employees from two diverse cultures.[39]

distance scores (with Malaysia and Philippines among the highest). They accept and value unequal power, value obedience to authority, and are comfortable receiving commands from their superiors without consultation or debate. High power distance individuals also prefer to resolve differences or contradict their boss indirectly through formal procedures rather than directly.

In contrast, people in Australia, New Zealand, Austria, Denmark and other countries with low power distance expect relatively equal power sharing. They view the relationship with their boss as one of interdependence, not dependence; that is, they believe that their boss is also dependent on them, so they expect power sharing and consultation before decisions affecting them are made. As Stephen Roberts discovered soon after returning to Sydney, employees with low power distance are very comfortable approaching and contradicting their boss.

OTHER CROSS-CULTURAL VALUES

uncertainty avoidance The degree to which people tolerate ambiguity or feel threatened by ambiguity and uncertainty.

Cross-cultural researchers have investigated many other values, but the only other two that will be mentioned here are uncertainty avoidance and achievement-nurturing orientation. **Uncertainty avoidance** is the degree to which people tolerate ambiguity (low uncertainty avoidance) or feel threatened by ambiguity and uncertainty (high uncertainty avoidance). Employees with high uncertainty avoidance value structured situations where rules of conduct and decision making are clearly documented. They usually prefer direct rather than indirect or ambiguous communications. Uncertainty avoidance scores tend to be high among people living in Greece, Portugal, Japan and South Korea. Studies report low uncertainty avoidance scores in Singapore and Jamaica, and moderately low scores in Malaysia, Hong Kong and China. Australians, New Zealanders and Americans have similar scores around the middle of the range.

Achievement–nurturing orientation reflects a competitive versus cooperative view of relations with other people.[40] People with a high achievement orientation value assertiveness, competitiveness and materialism. They appreciate people who are tough and favour the acquisition of money and material goods. In contrast, people in nurturing-oriented cultures emphasise relationships and the well-being of others. They focus on human interaction and caring rather than competition and personal success. People in the Netherlands, Sweden and Denmark score very low on achievement orientation (i.e. they have a high nurturing orientation), and those in Thailand have moderately low achievement orientation. In contrast, high achievement orientation scores have been reported in Japan and Hungary. Achievement orientation scores hover around the middle of the range in most Asian countries (other than Japan and Thailand) as well as in New Zealand and Australia.

Before leaving this topic, two concerns need to be raised about the cross-cultural values information provided here.[41] First, the statements about how high or low people in various countries score on power distance, uncertainty avoidance and achievement–nurturing orientation are based on a survey of IBM employees worldwide more than a quarter of a century ago. Over 100 000 IBM staff in dozens of countries completed the survey, but it is possible that these employees do not represent the general population. There is also evidence that values have changed quite a bit in some countries since then. A second concern is the assumption that everyone in a society has similar cultural values. This may be true in a few countries, but multiculturalism—where several micro cultures coexist in the same country—is becoming a common trend. On this point, one study reported significantly different values among Javanese, Batik and Chinese Indonesians. Attributing specific values to an entire society is engaging in a form of stereotyping that limits our ability to understand the more complex reality of that society.

> **achievement–nurturing orientation** A competitive versus cooperative view of relations with other people.

ETHICAL VALUES AND BEHAVIOUR

When pollsters recently asked employers in western Canada to list the most important characteristics they look for when hiring job applicants, the top factor wasn't performance standards, customer service or common sense. Although these characteristics were important, the most important factor in almost every job group was honesty/ethics.[42] Ethics refers to the study of moral principles or values that determine whether actions are right or wrong and outcomes are good or bad. People rely on their ethical values to determine 'the right thing to do'.

New Zealand, Singapore and Australia are recognised around the world for their high ethical standards—they rank among the nine lowest of 155 countries on the global corruption perceptions index, for example—yet these countries and others in this region have their share of business scandals.[43] For instance, in 2005 a United Nations report accused the Australian Wheat Board (AWB) of transferring more than $300 million to former Iraqi president Saddam Hussein through an intricate system of kickbacks; executives at corrugated cardboard box companies in Australia and New Zealand have been removed from their posts due to possible price fixing; several Hong Kong–listed companies have suffered heavy losses through embezzlement by their own executives; and in Japan one of the wealthiest business people in the world retired after allegedly falsifying ownership and financial statements.[44]

THREE ETHICAL PRINCIPLES

To better understand the ethical dilemmas facing organisations, three distinct types of ethical principles need to be considered: utilitarianism, individual rights and distributive justice.[45] Although you might prefer one principle more than the others based on your personal values, all three should be actively considered when putting important ethical issues to the test.

LEARNING OBJECTIVE

List three ethical principles.

- *Utilitarianism.* This principle advises us to seek the greatest good for the greatest number of people. In other words, we should choose the option providing the highest degree of satisfaction to those affected. This is sometimes known as a consequential principle because it focuses on the consequences of our actions, not on how we achieve those consequences. One problem with utilitarianism is that it is almost impossible to evaluate the benefits or costs of many decisions, particularly when stakeholders have wide-ranging needs and values. Another problem is that most of us are uncomfortable engaging in behaviours that seem, well, unethical, to attain results that are ethical.

- *Individual rights*. This principle reflects the belief that all people have entitlements that let them act in a certain way. Some of the most widely cited rights are freedom of movement, physical security, freedom of speech, fair trial and freedom from torture. The individual rights principle includes more than legal rights; it also includes human rights that everyone is granted as a moral norm of society. For example, access to education and knowledge isn't a legal requirement everywhere, but most of us believe that it is a human right. One problem with individual rights is that certain individual rights may conflict with other rights. The shareholders' right to be informed about corporate activities may ultimately conflict with an executive's right to privacy, for example.
- *Distributive justice*. This principle suggests that people who are similar in relevant ways should receive similar benefits and burdens; those who are dissimilar should receive different benefits and burdens in proportion to their dissimilarity. For example, we expect that two employees who contribute equally in their work should receive similar rewards, whereas those who make a lesser contribution should receive less. A variation of the distributive justice principle says that inequalities are acceptable where they benefit the least well off in society. Thus, employees in risky jobs should be paid more if this benefits others who are less well off. One problem with the distributive justice principle is that it is difficult to agree on who is 'similar' and what factors are 'relevant'. Most of us agree that race and gender should not be relevant when distributing pay cheques. But should rewards be determined purely by an employee's performance, or should effort, seniority and other factors also be taken into account?

MORAL INTENSITY, ETHICAL SENSITIVITY AND SITUATIONAL INFLUENCES

LEARNING OBJECTIVE

Explain how moral intensity, ethical sensitivity and the situation influence ethical behaviour.

moral intensity The degree to which an issue demands the application of ethical principles.

ethical sensitivity A personal characteristic that enables people to recognise the presence of an ethical issue and to determine its relative importance.

Along with ethical principles and their underlying values, three other factors that influence ethical conduct in the workplace need to be considered: the moral intensity of the issue, the individual's ethical sensitivity, and situational factors.

Moral intensity is the degree to which an issue demands the application of ethical principles. Decisions with high moral intensity are more important, so the decision maker needs to more carefully apply ethical principles to resolve it. Stealing from your employer is usually considered high on moral intensity, whereas borrowing a company pen for personal use is much lower on the scale. Several factors influence the moral intensity of an issue, such as the extent to which the issue clearly produces good or bad consequences, whether others in the society think it is good or evil, whether the issue quickly affects people, whether the decision maker feels close to the issue, and how much control the person has over the issue.[46]

Even if an issue has high moral intensity, some employees might not recognise its ethical importance because they have low ethical sensitivity. **Ethical sensitivity** is a personal characteristic that enables people to recognise the presence of an ethical issue and to determine its relative importance.[47] Ethically sensitive people are not necessarily more ethical. Rather, they are more likely to recognise whether an issue requires ethical consideration; that is, they can more accurately estimate the moral intensity of the issue. Ethically sensitive people tend to have higher empathy. They also have more information about the specific situation. For example, accountants would be more ethically sensitive regarding the appropriateness of specific accounting procedures than would someone who has not received training in this profession.

The third important factor explaining why good people do bad things is the situation in which the unethical conduct occurs. A few recent surveys have reported that employees regularly experience corporate pressure that leads to selling beyond the customers' needs, lying to the client, or making unrealistic promises. Other surveys have found that most employees believe that they experience so much pressure it compromises their ethical conduct. For instance, nearly two-thirds of the managers in one academic study stated that pressure from top management causes people further down in the hierarchy to compromise their beliefs, whereas 90 per cent of top management disagreed with this statement.[48] The point here is not to justify unethical conduct. Rather, we need to recognise the situational factors that influence wrongdoing so that organisations can correct these problems in the future.

SUPPORTING ETHICAL BEHAVIOUR

Most corporate leaders would agree that ethics are important, yet evidence suggests that few firms in the Asia–Pacific region are systematically developing or monitoring ethical values in their employees. One of the most basic steps in this direction is to develop a code of ethical conduct.[49] Most large and medium-size organisations in the United States have developed and communicate ethical codes of conduct, whereas only about one-third of large Australian companies have done so. Critics point out that ethics codes alone do little to reduce unethical conduct. After all, Enron had a well-developed code of ethical conduct, but that document didn't prevent senior executives from engaging in wholesale accounting fraud, resulting in the energy company's bankruptcy. Still, ethics codes lay the foundation for other strategies to support ethical behaviour.

Many firms with ethics codes bolster their effectiveness through training. For instance, Sun Microsystems puts each of its 35 000 employees worldwide through a basic online ethics training program, while its top 1200 executives participate in a two-day ethics boot

Unethical conduct on ethics tests

The RBC Financial Group has been at the forefront of ethics testing and training for more than twenty years. As part of the Canadian financial institution's strategy to ensure ethical conduct, every employee must complete an online ethics test every two years. The electronic role-play presents a series of scenarios that require ethical judgment, and the results are reviewed by senior management to ensure that employees understand RBC's code of conduct. However, some employees and managers think the exercise is a waste of time. 'People were annoyed that they had to do them,' says a former RBC employee. 'A lot of the account managers thought it was stupid.' Their solution: they asked co-workers who perform well on the test to complete the online test in their place. 'I would just knock these things out,' says the former RBC employee, referring to the number of ethics tests he completed for other RBC staff.[51]

Royal Bank of Canada

camp. Food manufacturer H. J. Heinz Co. is one of many companies that rely on an ethics hotline that employees can use to raise ethical issues or concerns about ethical conduct. At Heinz, the hotline operates around the clock and in 150 languages for its global workforce. 'They know how to use the hotline in China,' comments Jack W. Radke, Heinz's director of ethics. Radke adds that the hotline 'has provided an early warning signal of problems we were not aware of'.[50]

These programs seem to have some influence on ethical conduct, but the most powerful foundation is a culture that supports ethical values and behaviour. 'If you don't have a culture of ethical decision making to begin with, all the controls and compliance regulations you care to deploy won't necessarily prevent ethical misconduct,' warns Devin Brougham, director of Vodafone, the British communications giant. This culture is supported by the ethical conduct and vigilance of corporate leaders. By acting with the highest standards of moral conduct, leaders not only gain support and trust from followers but they role-model the ethical standards that they expect their employees to follow.[52]

PERSONALITY IN ORGANISATIONS

personality The relatively stable pattern of behaviours and consistent internal states that explain a person's behavioural tendencies.

Ethical, cultural and personal values are relatively stable characteristics, so they are an important influence on individual behaviour. Another individual characteristic that has long-term stability is personality. In fact, there is considerable evidence that values and personality traits are interrelated and reinforce each other.[53] **Personality** refers to the relatively stable pattern of behaviours and consistent internal states that explain a person's behavioural tendencies. Personality has both internal and external elements. External traits are the observable behaviours that we rely on to identify someone's personality. For example, we can see that a person is extroverted by the way he or she interacts with other people. The internal states represent the thoughts, values and genetic characteristics that we infer from the observable behaviours. Experts continue to debate the extent to which personality is genetically coded through evolution or shaped from childhood and other early life experiences.[54]

Personality is said to explain behavioural tendencies, because individuals' actions are not perfectly consistent with their personality profile in every situation. Personality traits are less evident in situations where social norms, reward systems and other conditions constrain people's behaviour.[55] For example, talkative people remain relatively quiet in a library where 'no talking' rules are explicit and strictly enforced.

PERSONALITY AND ORGANISATIONAL BEHAVIOUR

A few years ago, 'Patrick' decided to complete a test to find out more about what type of person he is. 'The results were very accurate,' says the partner of a two-person Australian accounting practice. 'There was a series of questionnaires thorough enough to assess what type of personality I was, what type of vocation or occupation I was suited to, and my strengths and weaknesses.' Patrick took the test to demonstrate to his small and medium-sized business clients that this type of assessment can help them in hiring their staff.[56]

Personality is gaining a lot of attention these days from business leaders in both small and large organisations. While aptitude tests have been used for decades, personality tests have had a rocky experience in the selection process. At one time, scholars often explained employee behaviour in terms of personality traits and companies regularly administered personality tests to job applicants. This changed in the 1960s when researchers reported that the relationship between personality and job performance was very weak.[57] They cited problems with measuring personality traits and explained that the connection between personality and performance exists only under very narrowly defined conditions. Companies stopped using personality tests because of concerns that the tests might unfairly discriminate against visible minorities and other identifiable groups.

Over the past decade, personality has regained some of its credibility in organisational settings.[58] Recent studies have reported that specific personality traits predict specific work-related behaviours, stress reactions and emotions fairly well under specific conditions. Experts have reintroduced the idea that effective leaders have identifiable traits and that personality explains some of a person's positive attitudes and life happiness. Personality traits also seem to help people find the jobs that best suit their needs.[59] Personality is a remote concept, so it isn't the best predictor for most jobs, but it is increasingly clear that some personality traits are relevant. Some of the most relevant personality traits for job performance and well-being are found in the Big Five personality dimensions.

THE 'BIG FIVE' PERSONALITY DIMENSIONS

Since the days of Plato, scholars have been trying to develop lists of personality traits. About 100 years ago, a few personality experts tried to catalogue and condense the many personality traits that had been described over the years. They found thousands of words in Roget's Thesaurus and Webster's Dictionary that represented personality traits. They aggregated these words into 171 clusters, then further shrank them down to five abstract personality dimensions. Using more sophisticated techniques, recent investigations identified the same five dimensions—known as the **Big Five personality dimensions**.[60] These five dimensions, represented by the handy acronym CANOE, are outlined in Exhibit 2.5 and described below:

- *Conscientiousness.* Conscientiousness refers to people who are careful, dependable and self-disciplined. Some scholars argue that this dimension also includes the will to achieve. People with low conscientiousness tend to be careless, less thorough, more disorganised and irresponsible.
- *Agreeableness.* This includes the traits of being courteous, good-natured, empathic and caring. Some scholars prefer the label of 'friendly compliance' for this dimension, with its opposite being 'hostile noncompliance'. People with low agreeableness tend to be unco-operative, short-tempered and irritable.
- *Neuroticism.* Neuroticism characterises people with high levels of anxiety, hostility, depression and self-consciousness. In contrast, people with low neuroticism (high emotional stability) are poised, secure and calm.

Big Five personality dimensions The five abstract dimensions representing most personality traits: conscientiousness, emotional stability, openness to experience, agreeableness and extroversion.

LEARNING OBJECTIVE

Identify the 'Big Five' personality dimensions.

The 'Big Five' personality dimensions

EXHIBIT 2.5

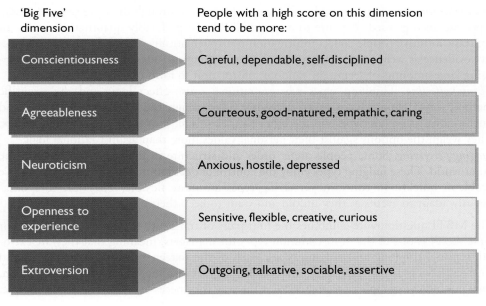

'Big Five' dimension	People with a high score on this dimension tend to be more:
Conscientiousness	Careful, dependable, self-disciplined
Agreeableness	Courteous, good-natured, empathic, caring
Neuroticism	Anxious, hostile, depressed
Openness to experience	Sensitive, flexible, creative, curious
Extroversion	Outgoing, talkative, sociable, assertive

extroversion A 'Big Five' personality dimension that characterises people who are outgoing, talkative, sociable and assertive.

introversion A 'Big Five' personality dimension that characterises people who are quiet, shy and cautious.

- *Openness to experience.* This dimension is the most complex and has the least agreement among scholars. It generally refers to the extent to which people are sensitive, flexible, creative and curious. Those who score low on this dimension tend to be more resistant to change, less open to new ideas, and more fixed in their ways.
- *Extroversion.* **Extroversion** characterises people who are outgoing, talkative, sociable and assertive. The opposite is **introversion**, which refers to those who are quiet, shy and cautious. Introverts do not necessarily lack social skills. Rather, they are more inclined to direct their interests to ideas than to social events. Introverts feel quite comfortable being alone, whereas extroverts do not.

These five personality dimensions affect work-related behaviour and job performance to varying degrees.[61] People with high emotional stability tend to work better than others in high-stressor situations. Those with high agreeableness tend to handle customer relations and conflict-based situations more effectively. However, conscientiousness has taken centre stage as the most valuable personality trait for predicting job performance in almost every job group. Conscientious employees set higher personal goals for themselves, are more motivated and have higher performance expectations than do employees with low levels of conscientiousness. High-conscientiousness employees tend to have high levels of organisational citizenship and work better in workplaces that give employees more freedom than in traditional 'command and control' workplaces. Employees with high conscientiousness as well as agreeableness and emotional stability also tend to provide better customer service.

MYERS–BRIGGS TYPE INDICATOR

Myers–Briggs Type Indicator (MBTI) inventory designed to identify individuals' basic preferences for perceiving and processing information.

More than half a century ago the mother and daughter team of Katherine Briggs and Isabel Briggs-Myers developed the **Myers–Briggs Type Indicator (MBTI)**, a personality inventory designed to identify individuals' basic preferences for perceiving and processing information. The MBTI builds on the personality theory proposed in the 1920s by Swiss psychiatrist Carl Jung that identifies the way people prefer to perceive their environment as well as obtain and process information. Jung suggested that everyone is either extroverted or introverted in orientation and has particular preferences for perceiving (sensing or intuition) and judging or deciding on action (thinking or feeling). The MBTI is designed to measure these as well as a fourth dimension relating to how people orient themselves to the outer world (judging versus perceiving).[62] Extroversion and introversion were discussed earlier, so let's examine the other dimensions:

LEARNING OBJECTIVE

Summarise the personality concepts behind the Myers–Briggs Type Indicator.

- *Sensing/intuition.* Some people like collecting information through their five senses. Sensing types use an organised structure to acquire factual and preferably quantitative details. In contrast, intuitive people collect information nonsystematically. They rely more on subjective evidence as well as their intuition and sheer inspiration. Sensers are capable of synthesising large amounts of seemingly random information to form quick conclusions.
- *Thinking/feeling.* Thinking types rely on rational cause–effect logic and the scientific method (see Chapter 1) to make decisions. They weigh the evidence objectively and unemotionally. Feeling types, on the other hand, consider how their choices affect others. They weigh the options against their personal values more than against rational logic.
- *Judging/perceiving.* Some people prefer order and structure in their relationship with the outer world. These judging types enjoy the control of decision making and want to resolve problems quickly. In contrast, perceiving types are more flexible. They like to spontaneously adapt to events as they unfold and want to keep their options open.

The MBTI questionnaire combines the four pairs of traits into sixteen distinct types. For example, ESTJ is one of the most common types for managers, meaning that they are extroverted, sensing, thinking and judging types. Each of the sixteen types has its strengths and weaknesses. ENTJs are considered natural leaders, ISFJs have a high sense of duty, and so on. These types indicate people's preferences, not the way they necessarily behave all of the time.

Effectiveness of the MBTI

Is the MBTI useful in organisations? Many business leaders think so. The MBTI is one of the most widely used personality tests in work settings and is equally popular for career counselling and executive coaching.[63] Still, evidence regarding the effectiveness of the MBTI and Jung's psychological types is mixed.[64] The MBTI does a reasonably good job of measuring Jung's psychological types. It predicts preferences for information processing in decision making and preferences for particular occupations. However, other evidence is less supportive regarding the MBTI's ability to predict job performance. Overall, the MBTI seems to improve self-awareness for career development and mutual understanding, but it probably should not be used in selecting job applicants.

OTHER PERSONALITY TRAITS

The Big Five personality dimensions and the MBTI don't capture every personality trait. A few others will be discussed in later chapters where they fit specific topics, such as positive and negative emotional traits (Chapter 4), workaholism (Chapter 7) and Machiavellianism (Chapter 12). Two other personality traits that you should know are locus of control and self-monitoring.

Locus of control

Locus of control refers to a generalised belief about the amount of control people have over their own lives. Individuals who feel that they are very much in charge of their own destiny have an internal locus of control; those who think that events in their life are due mainly to fate/luck or powerful others have an external locus of control. Locus of control is a generalised belief, so people with an external locus can feel in control in familiar situations (such as opening a door or serving a customer). However, their underlying locus of control would be apparent in new situations in which control over events is uncertain. Compared with an external locus of control, people with a moderately strong internal locus of control tend to perform better in most employment situations, are more successful in their careers, earn more money, and are better suited for leadership positions. Internals are also more satisfied with their jobs, cope better in stressful situations, and are more motivated by performance-based reward systems.[65]

locus of control A personality trait referring to the extent to which people believe events are within their control.

Self-monitoring

Self-monitoring refers to an individual's level of sensitivity to the expressive behaviour of others and the ability to adapt appropriately to these situational cues. High self-monitors can adjust their behaviour quite easily, whereas low self-monitors are more likely to reveal their emotions, so predicting their behaviour from one situation to the next is relatively easy.[66] The self-monitoring personality trait has been identified as a significant factor in many organisational activities. Employees who are high self-monitors tend to be better at social networking, interpersonal conversations, and leading people. They are also more likely than low self-monitors to be promoted within the organisation and to receive better jobs elsewhere.[67]

self-monitoring A personality trait referring to an individual's level of sensitivity and ability to adapt to situational cues.

PERSONALITY AND VOCATIONAL CHOICE

Self-monitoring, locus of control, conscientiousness and the many other personality traits help us to understand individual behaviour in organisations. One fairly successful application of personality is in the area of vocational choice. Vocational choice is not just about matching your skills with job requirements. It is a complex alignment of personality, values and competencies with the requirements of work and characteristics of the work environment. You might be very talented at a particular job, but your personality and values must also be aligned with what the job offers.

LEARNING OBJECTIVE

Explain how personality relates to Holland's model of vocational choice.

John Holland, a career development scholar, was an early proponent of this notion that career success depends on the degree of congruence between the person and his or her work environment.[68] Holland argued that people can be classified into different types relating to their personality and that they seek out and are more satisfied in work environments that are congruent with their particular profile. Thus, *congruence* refers to the extent to which someone has the same or a similar personality type as the environment in which he or she is working. Some research has found that high congruence leads to better performance, greater satisfaction, and a longer time in that career, but other studies are less supportive of the model.[69]

Holland's six types

Holland's theory classifies individual personalities and work environments into six categories: realistic, investigative, artistic, social, enterprising, and conventional. Exhibit 2.6 defines these types of people and work environments and suggests sample occupations representing those environments. Few people fall squarely into only one of Holland's classifications. Instead, Holland refers to a person's degree of *differentiation*, that is, the extent to which the individual fits into one or several types. A highly differentiated person is aligned with a single category, whereas most people fit into two or more categories.

Since most people fit into more than one personality type, Holland developed a model shaped like a hexagon with each personality type around the points of the model. Consistency refers to the extent to which a person is aligned with similar types, which are next to each other in the hexagon; dissimilar types are opposite. For instance, the enterprising and social types are next to each other in Holland's model, so individuals with both enterprising and social personalities have high consistency.

EXHIBIT 2.6

Holland's six types of personality and work environment

Holland type	Personality traits	Work environment characteristics	Sample occupations
Realistic	Practical, shy, materialistic, stable	Work with hands, machines or tools; focus on tangible results	Assembly worker, dry cleaner, mechanical engineer
Investigative	Analytic, introverted, reserved, curious, precise, independent	Work involves discovering, collecting, and analysing; solving problems	Biologist, dentist, systems analyst
Artistic	Creative, impulsive, idealistic, intuitive, emotional	Work involves creation of new products or ideas, typically in an unstructured setting	Journalist, architect, advertising executive
Social	Sociable, outgoing, conscientious, need for affiliation	Work involves serving or helping others; working in teams	Social worker, nurse, teacher, counsellor
Enterprising	Confident, assertive, energetic, need for power	Work involves leading others; achieving goals through others in a results-oriented setting	Salesperson, stockbroker, politician
Conventional	Dependable, disciplined, orderly, practical, efficient	Work involves systematic manipulation of data or information	Accountant, banker, administrator

Sources: Based on information in D. H. Montross, Z. B. Leibowitz and C. J. Shinkman, *Real People, Real Jobs* (Palo Alto, CA: Davies-Black, 1995); J. H. Greenhaus, *Career Management* (Chicago, Ill.: Dryden, 1987).

Practical implications of Holland's theory

Holland's vocational fit model is the basis of much career counselling today. Still, some aspects of the model don't seem to work. Holland's personality types represent only some of the Big Five personality dimensions, even though other dimensions should be relevant to vocational fit.[70] Also, research has found that some 'opposing' categories in Holland's hexagon are not really opposite to each other. There are also doubts about whether Holland's model can be generalised to other cultures. Aside from these concerns, Holland's model seems to explain individual attitudes and behaviour to some extent, and it is the dominant model of career testing today.[71]

Personality and values lay some of the foundation for our understanding of individual behaviour in organisations. However, people are, of course, also influenced by the environments in which they live and work. These environments are perceived and learned, the two topics presented in the next chapter.

CHAPTER SUMMARY

Individual behaviour is influenced by motivation, ability, role perceptions and situational factors (MARS). Motivation consists of internal forces that affect the direction, intensity and persistence of a person's voluntary choice of behaviour. Ability includes both the natural aptitudes and the learned capabilities required to successfully complete a task. Role perceptions are a person's beliefs about what behaviours are appropriate or necessary in a particular situation. Situational factors are environmental conditions that constrain or facilitate employee behaviour and performance. Collectively, these four factors are included in the concept of employee engagement.

The five main types of workplace behaviour are task performance, organisational citizenship, counterproductive work behaviours, joining and staying with the organisation, and work attendance.

Values are stable, evaluative beliefs that guide our preferences for outcomes or courses of action in a variety of situations. They influence our decisions and our interpretation of what is ethical. People arrange values into a hierarchy of preferences, called a value system. Espoused values—what we say and think we use as values—are different from enacted values, which are values evident from our actions. Shalom Schwartz grouped the dozens of individual values described by scholars over the years into ten broader domains, which are further reduced to four quadrants of a circle.

Values are abstract concepts that are not easily followed in practice. A personal value influences our decisions and actions when (1) something makes us mindful of that value, (2) we can think of specific reasons for applying the value in that situation, and (3) the work environment supports behaviours consistent with the value. Values congruence refers to the similarity of value systems between two entities. Person–organisation values incongruence has a number of undesirable consequences, but some incongruence is also desirable. Espoused–enacted values incongruence is contrary to effective leadership and undermines trust.

Five values that differ across cultures are individualism, collectivism, power distance, uncertainty avoidance, and achievement–nurturing orientation. Three values that guide ethical conduct are utilitarianism, individual rights and distributive justice. Three factors that influence ethical conduct are the extent to which an issue demands ethical principles (moral intensity), the person's ethical sensitivity to the presence and importance of an ethical dilemma, and situational factors that cause people to deviate from their moral values. Companies improve ethical conduct through a code of ethics, ethics training, ethics hot lines, and the conduct of corporate leaders.

Personality refers to the relatively stable pattern of behaviours and consistent internal states that explain a person's behavioural tendencies. Personality is shaped by both heredity and environmental factors. Most personality traits are represented within the Big Five personality dimensions (CANOE): conscientiousness, agreeableness, neuroticism, openness to experience, and extroversion. Conscientiousness is a relatively strong predictor of job performance.

The Myers–Briggs Type Indicator measures how people prefer to focus their attention, collect information, process and evaluate information, and orient themselves to the outer world. Another popular personality trait in organisational behaviour is locus of control, which is a generalised belief about the amount of control people have over their own lives. Another trait, called self-monitoring, refers to an individual's level of sensitivity and ability to adapt to situational cues. Holland's model of vocational choice defines six personalities and their corresponding work environments.

KEY TERMS

ability p. 37
achievement–nurturing orientation p. 49
Big Five personality dimensions p. 53
collectivism p. 46
competencies p. 37
counterproductive work behaviours
  (CWBs) p. 40
employee engagement p. 36
ethical sensitivity p. 50

ethics p. 49
extroversion p. 54
individualism p. 46
introversion p. 54
job satisfaction p. 42
locus of control p. 55
moral intensity p. 50
motivation p. 37
Myers–Briggs Type Indicator (MBTI) p. 54

organisational citizenship p. 40
personality p. 52
power distance p. 47
self-monitoring p. 55
uncertainty avoidance p. 48
values p. 42
values congruence p. 45

DISCUSSION QUESTIONS

1. An insurance company has high levels of absenteeism among the office staff. The head of office administration argues that employees are misusing the company's sick leave benefits. However, some of the mostly female staff members have explained that family responsibilities interfere with work. Using the MARS model, as well as your knowledge of absenteeism behaviour, discuss some of the possible reasons for absenteeism here and how it might be reduced.

2. Most large organisations spend a lot of money identifying the key competencies for superior work performance. What are the potential benefits and pitfalls associated with identifying competencies? Are there alternatives to selecting employees by identifying their competencies?

3. Executives at an Australian state government agency devoted several days to a values identification seminar in which they developed a list of six core values which they believed would make the agency more effective. All employees attended sessions in which they learned about these values. In spite of this effort and ongoing communication regarding the six values, the executive team concluded two years later that employees often made decisions and engaged in behaviours that were inconsistent with these values. Provide three possible explanations for why employees have not enacted the values espoused by top management at this agency.

4. This chapter discussed the concept of values congruence in the context of an employee's personal values and the organisation's

values. But values congruence also relates to the juxtaposition of other pairs of value systems. Explain how values congruence is relevant with respect to organisational versus professional values.

5. People in a particular South American country have high power distance and high collectivism. What does this mean, and what are the implications of this characteristic for a senior executive of a company visiting employees working for the company in that country?

6. In country A, drivers ignore the lines on the road. Three or four rows of cars will be moving quickly along a street or highway where the lines indicate that there should be just two rows of vehicles. Some of the drivers also honk their horns whenever they approach other vehicles. In country B, drivers stay within the indicated lines and use their horns only when there is the risk of an accident. Are drivers in one country more ethical than those in the other country? Why or why not?

7. 'All decisions are ethical decisions.' Comment on this statement, particularly by referring to the concepts of moral intensity and ethical sensitivity.

8. Look over the four pairs of psychological types in the Myers–Briggs Type Indicator and identify the personality type (i.e. the four letters) that would be best for a student in this course. Would this type be appropriate for students in other fields of study (e.g. biology, fine arts)?

PUSHING PAPER CAN BE FUN

A large American city government was putting on a number of seminars for managers of various departments throughout the city. At one of these sessions, the topic discussed was motivation—how public servants could be motivated to do a good job. The plight of a police captain became the central focus of the discussion:

I've got a real problem with my officers. They come on the force as young, inexperienced rookies, and we send them out on the street, either in cars or on a beat. They seem to like the contact they have with the public, the action involved in crime prevention, and the apprehension of criminals. They also like helping people out at fires, accidents and other emergencies.

The problem occurs when they get back to the station. They hate to do the paperwork, and because they dislike it the job is frequently put off or done inadequately. This lack of attention hurts us later on when we get to court. We need clear, factual reports. They must be highly detailed and unambiguous. As soon as one part of a report is shown to be inadequate or incorrect, the rest of the report is suspect. Poor reporting probably causes us to lose more cases than any other factor.

I just don't know how to motivate them to do a better job. We're in a budget crunch and I have absolutely no financial rewards at my disposal. In fact, we'll probably have to lay some people off in the near future. It's hard for me to make the job interesting and challenging because it isn't—it's boring, routine paperwork, and there isn't much you can do about it.

Finally, I can't say to them that their promotions will hinge on the excellence of their paperwork. First of all, they know it's not true. If their performance is adequate, most are more likely to get promoted just by staying on the force a certain number of years than for some specific outstanding act. Second, they were trained to do the job they do out in the streets, not to fill out forms. All through their career it is the arrests and interventions that get noticed.

Some people have suggested a number of things, like using conviction records as a performance criterion. However, we know that's not fair—too many other things are involved. Bad paperwork increases the chance that you lose in court, but good paperwork doesn't necessarily mean you'll win. We tried setting up team competitions based on the excellence of the reports, but the officers caught on to that pretty quickly. No one was getting any type of reward for winning the competition, and they couldn't see any point in busting a gut when there was no payoff.

I just don't know what to do.

Source: T. R. Mitchell and J. R. Larson, Jr., *People in Organizations*, 3rd edn (New York: McGraw-Hill, 1987), p. 184. Used with permission.

QUESTIONS

1. What performance problems is the captain trying to correct?

2. Use the MARS model of individual behaviour and performance to diagnose the possible causes of the unacceptable behaviour.

3. Has the captain considered all possible solutions to the problem? If not, what else might be done?

SKILL BUILDER 2.2

TEAM EXERCISE

COMPARING CULTURAL VALUES

PURPOSE

This exercise is designed to help you determine the extent to which students hold similar assumptions about the values that dominate in other countries.

INSTRUCTIONS

The names in the left column represent labels that a major consulting project identified with business people in a particular country, based on its national culture and values. These names appear in alphabetical order. In the right column are the names of countries, also in alphabetical order, corresponding to the labels in the left column.

Step 1: Working alone, students will connect the labels with the countries by relying on their perceptions of the countries. Each label is associated with only one country, so each label will be connected to only one country, and vice versa. Draw a line to connect the pairs, or put the label number beside the country name.

Step 2: The instructor will form teams of four or five people. Members of each team will compare their results and try to reach consensus on a common set of connecting pairs.

Step 3: Teams or the instructor will post the results, so that everyone can see the extent to which students hold common opinions about business people in other cultures. Class discussion can then focus on the reasons why the results are so similar or different, as well as the implications of the results for working in a global work environment.

VALUES LABELS AND COUNTRY NAMES

Country label (alphabetical)	Country name (alphabetical)
Affable humanists	Australia
Ancient modernisers	Brazil
Commercial catalysts	Canada
Conceptual strategists	China
Efficient manufacturers	France
Ethical statesmen	Germany
Informal egalitarians	India
Modernising traditionalists	Netherlands
Optimistic entrepreneurs	New Zealand
Quality perfectionists	Singapore
Rugged individualists	Taiwan
Serving merchants	United Kingdom
Tolerant traders	United States

Source: Based on R. Rosen, P. Digh, M. Singer and C. Phillips, *Global Literacies* (New York: Simon & Schuster, 2000).

ETHICS DILEMMA VIGNETTES

2.3 SKILL BUILDER

TEAM EXERCISE

PURPOSE

This exercise is designed to make you aware of the ethical dilemmas people face in various business situations, as well as the competing principles and values that operate in these situations.

INSTRUCTIONS

The instructor will form teams of four or five students. Team members will read each case below and discuss the extent to which the company's action in each case was ethical. Teams should be prepared to justify their evaluation using ethics principles and the perceived moral intensity of each incident.

CASE ONE

An employee at a major food retailer wrote a weblog (blog), and in one of his writings he complained that his boss wouldn't let him go home when he felt sick and that his district manager refused to promote him because of his dreadlocks. His blog named the employer, but the employee didn't use his real name. Although all blogs are on the Internet, the employee claims that his was low profile and that it didn't show up when doing a Google search of his name or the company. Still, the employer somehow discovered the blog, figured out the employee's real name, and fired him for 'speaking ill-will of the company in a public domain'.

CASE TWO

Computer printer manufacturers usually sell printers at a low margin over cost and generate much more income from subsequent sales of the high-margin ink cartridges required for each printer. One global printer manufacturer now designs its printers so they work only with ink cartridges made in the same region. Ink cartridges purchased in the United States will not work for the same printer model sold in Europe, for example. This 'region coding' of ink cartridges does not improve performance. Rather, the action prevents consumers and grey marketers from buying the product at a lower price in another region. The company says that this action allows it to maintain stable prices within a region rather than continually changing prices due to currency fluctuations.

CASE THREE

For the past few years the design department of a small (40-employee) company has been using a particular software program, but the three employees who use the software have been complaining for more than a year that the software is out of date and is slowing down their performance. The department agreed to switch to a competing software program costing several thousand dollars. However, the next version won't be released for six months and buying the current version will not allow much discount towards the next version. The company has put in advance orders for the next version. Meanwhile, one employee was able to get a copy of the current version of the software from a friend in the industry. The company has allowed the three employees to use this current version of the software even though they did not pay for it.

SKILL BUILDER | 2.4   IDENTIFYING YOUR SELF-MONITORING PERSONALITY

SELF-ASSESSMENT

PURPOSE
This self-assessment is designed to help you to estimate your level of self-monitoring personality.

INSTRUCTIONS
The statements in this scale refer to personal characteristics that might or might not be characteristic of you. Mark the box indicating the extent to which the statement is true or false about you. This exercise is completed alone so that students can assess themselves honestly without being concerned about social comparison. However, class discussion will focus on the relevance of self-monitoring personality in organisations.

SELF-MONITORING SCALE

Indicate the degree to which you think the following statements are true or false.	Very false	Somewhat false	Slightly more false than true	Slightly more true than false	Somewhat true	Very true
1. In social situations, I have the ability to alter my behaviour if I feel that something else is called for.	❑	❑	❑	❑	❑	❑
2. I am often able to read people's true emotions correctly through their eyes.	❑	❑	❑	❑	❑	❑
3. I have the ability to control the way I come across to people, depending on the impression I wish to give them.	❑	❑	❑	❑	❑	❑
4. In conversations, I am sensitive to even the slightest change in the facial expression of the person I'm conversing with.	❑	❑	❑	❑	❑	❑
5. My powers of intuition are quite good when it comes to understanding others' emotions and motives.	❑	❑	❑	❑	❑	❑
6. I can usually tell when others consider a joke to be in bad taste, even though they may laugh convincingly.	❑	❑	❑	❑	❑	❑
7. When I feel that the image I am portraying isn't working, I can readily change it to something that does.	❑	❑	❑	❑	❑	❑
8. I can usually tell when I've said something inappropriate by reading the listener's eyes.	❑	❑	❑	❑	❑	❑
9. I have trouble changing my behaviour to suit different people and different situations.	❑	❑	❑	❑	❑	❑
10. I have found that I can adjust my behaviour to meet the requirements of any situation I find myself in.	❑	❑	❑	❑	❑	❑
11. If someone is lying to me, I usually know it at once from that person's manner of expression.	❑	❑	❑	❑	❑	❑
12. Even when it might be to my advantage, I have difficulty putting up a good front.	❑	❑	❑	❑	❑	❑
13. Once I know what the situation calls for, it's easy for me to regulate my actions accordingly.	❑	❑	❑	❑	❑	❑

Source: R. D. Lennox and R. N. Wolfe, 'Revision of the Self-Monitoring Scale', *Journal of Personality and Social Psychology*, 46 (June 1984), pp. 1348–64. The response categories in this scale have been altered slightly due to limitations with the original scale responses.

IDENTIFYING YOUR DOMINANT VALUES

2.5 SKILL BUILDER

SELF-ASSESSMENT

FULL EXERCISE ON
STUDENT CD

PURPOSE

This self-assessment is designed to help you to identify your dominant values in Schwartz's values model.

INSTRUCTIONS

This instrument consists of numerous words and phrases, and you are asked to indicate whether each word or phrase is highly opposed or highly similar to your personal values, or some point in between these two extremes. When you have finished answering all items, the results will indicate your values on Schwartz's ten value groups described in this chapter.

INDIVIDUALISM–COLLECTIVISM SCALE

2.6 SKILL BUILDER

SELF-ASSESSMENT

FULL EXERCISE ON
STUDENT CD

PURPOSE

This self-assessment is designed to help you to identify your level of individualism and collectivism.

INSTRUCTIONS

This scale consists of several statements, and you are asked to indicate how well each statement describes you. Read each statement and select the response that best indicates how the statement describes you. You need to be honest with yourself to receive a reasonable estimate of your level of individualism and collectivism.

IDENTIFYING YOUR LOCUS OF CONTROL

2.7 SKILL BUILDER

SELF-ASSESSMENT

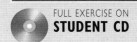
FULL EXERCISE ON
STUDENT CD

PURPOSE

This self-assessment is designed to help you to estimate the extent to which you have an internal or external locus of control personality.

INSTRUCTIONS

This instrument asks you to indicate the degree to which you agree or disagree with each of the statements provided. You need to be honest with yourself in order to obtain a reasonable estimate of your locus of control. The results show your relative position in the internal–external locus continuum and the general meaning of this score.

MATCHING HOLLAND'S CAREER TYPES

2.8 SKILL BUILDER

SELF-ASSESSMENT

FULL EXERCISE ON
STUDENT CD

PURPOSE

This self-assessment is designed to help you to understand Holland's career types.

INSTRUCTIONS

Holland's theory identifies six different types of work environments and occupations in which people work. Few jobs fit purely in one category, but all have a dominant type. Your task is to choose the Holland type that you believe best fits each of the occupations presented in the instrument. While completing this self-assessment, you can open your book to the exhibit describing Holland's six types.

NOTES

1   ISR, 'Hong Kong Ranks Ninth among Ten Countries on Employee Engagement: Major Global Study', ISRInsight news release (Hong Kong: 22 November 2004); J. Robinson, 'ASB Bank: Good Isn't Good Enough', *Gallup Management Journal*, 12 August 2004; E. Beauchesne, 'Just 17% of Canadians "Fully Engaged" by Their Work', *Vancouver Sun*, 19 November 2005, H7; P. Kershaw, 'Happy Days', *Sydney Morning Herald*, 23 August 2005, 6; V. Ratanjee, 'Wake-up Call for Thailand, Inc.', *Gallup Management Journal*, 12 May 2005; M. Sainsbury, 'Optus Morph-Ed into Malcontents', *Australian*, 26 April 2005, 25; M. Sainsbury, 'Optus Contracts Worth $140m Seen at Risk', *Australian*, 25 April 2005, 27.

2   Thanks to senior officers in the Singapore Armed Forces for discovering the handy 'MARS' acronym. Thanks also to Chris Perryer at the University of Western Australia for pointing out that the full model should be called the 'MARS BAR' because the outcomes are 'behaviour and results'! The MARS model is a variation of earlier models and writing by several sources, including: E. E. Lawler III and L. W. Porter, 'Antecedent Attitudes of Effective Managerial Performance', *Organizational Behavior and Human Performance* 2, no. 2 (1967), 122–42; K. F. Kane, 'Special Issue: Situational Constraints and Work Performance', *Human Resource Management Review* 3 (Summer 1993), 83–175.

3   T. A. Judge and R. Illies, 'Relationship of Personality to Performance Motivation: A Meta-Analytic Review', *Journal of Applied Psychology* 87, no. 4 (2002), 797–807; S. Roccas et al., 'The Big Five Personality Factors and Personal Values', *Personality and Social Psychology* 28 (June 2002), 789–801.

4   C. C. Pinder, *Work Motivation in Organizational Behavior* (Upper Saddle River, NJ: Prentice Hall, 1998); G. P. Latham and C. C. Pinder, 'Work Motivation Theory and Research at the Dawn of the Twenty-First Century', *Annual Review of Psychology* 56 (2005), 485–516.

5   K. Brown, 'Putting Leadership Rubber to the Manager Road', *Human Resources Magazine (Australia)*, 15 June 2005.

6   R. Jacobs, 'Using Human Resource Functions to Enhance Emotional Intelligence', in *The Emotionally Intelligent Workplace*, ed. C. Cherniss and D. Goleman (San Francisco: Jossey-Bass, 2001), 159–81.

7   D. D. Gray, 'Thai Town Lures Makers of Fishing Hooks', *Seattle Times*, 14 April 2003.

8   S. Brady, 'Deep in the Heart of AT&T Dallas', *Cable World*, 7 October 2002, 37.

9   D. Rose and C. Waterhouse, '*Spirit* Fire Puts Crew to the Test', *Sunday Tasmanian*, 25 February 2001, 4.

10 Kane, 'Special Issue: Situational Constraints and Work Performance'; S. B. Bacharach and P. Bamberger, 'Beyond Situational Constraints: Job Resources Inadequacy and Individual Performance at Work', *Human Resource Management Review* 5, no. 2 (1995), 79–102; G. Johns, 'Commentary: In Praise of Context', *Journal of Organizational Behavior* 22 (2001), 31–42.

11 J. P. Campbell, 'The Definition and Measurement of Performance in the New Age', in *The Changing Nature of Performance: Implications for Staffing, Motivation, and Development*, ed. D. R. Ilgen and E. D. Pulakos (San Francisco: Jossey-Bass, 1999), 399–429; R. D. Hackett, 'Understanding and Predicting Work Performance in the Canadian Military', *Canadian Journal of Behavioural Science* 34, no. 2 (2002), 131–40.

12 D. W. Organ, 'Organizational Citizenship Behavior: It's Construct Clean-up Time', *Human Performance* 10 (1997), 85–97; J. A. LePine, A. Erez and D. E. Johnson, 'The Nature and Dimensionality of Organizational Citizenship Behavior: A Critical Review and Meta-Analysis', *Journal of Applied Psychology* 87 (February 2002), 52–65; B. Erickson, 'Nature Times Nurture: How Organizations Can Optimize Their People's Contributions', *Journal of Organizational Excellence* 24, no. 1 (Winter 2004), 21–30; M. A. Vey and J. P. Campbell, 'In-Role or Extra-Role Organizational Citizenship Behavior: Which Are We Measuring?', *Human Performance* 17, no. 1 (2004), 119–35.

13 M. Rotundo and P. Sackett, 'The Relative Importance of Task, Citizenship, and Counterproductive Performance to Global Ratings of Job Performance: A Policy-Capturing Approach', *Journal of Applied Psychology* 87 (February 2002), 66–80; P. D. Dunlop and K. Lee, 'Workplace Deviance, Organizational Citizenship Behaviour, and Business Unit Performance: The Bad Apples Do Spoil the Whole Barrel', *Journal of Organizational Behavior* 25 (2004), 67–80.

14 B. Cheesman and H. Trinca, 'Wanted: Warm Bodies', *Australian Financial Review*, 5 July 2005, 60; S. Venning, '40 Jobs Vacant', *Whyalla News (Australia)*, 15 November 2005.

15 'Watson Wyatt Announces Findings of Indonesian Employee Attitude Survey', Watson Wyatt news release (Jakarta: 30 November 2004); 'Research Highlights Mine Industry Worker Turnover', *ABC News Online*, 14 November 2005.

16 T. R. Mitchell, B. C. Holtom and T. W. Lee, 'How to Keep Your Best Employees: Developing an Effective Retention Policy', *Academy of Management Executive* 15 (November 2001), 96–108.

17 D. Spedding, M. Garrett and M. Lewis, *Absence Management in the Australian Public Sector* (Canberra: Auditor-General of Australia, 2002); CCH Australia, *Managing Absenteeism and Sick Leave* (CCH Australia, July 2004).

18 D. A. Harrison and J. J. Martocchio, 'Time for Absenteeism: A 20-Year Review of Origins, Offshoots, and Outcomes', *Journal of Management* 24 (Spring 1998), 305–50; C. M. Mason and M. A. Griffin, 'Group Absenteeism and Positive Affective Tone: A Longitudinal Study', *Journal of Organizational Behavior* 24, no. 6 (2003), 667–87; A. Vaananen et al., 'Job Characteristics, Physical and Psychological Symptoms, and Social Support as Antecedents of Sickness Absence among Men and Women in the Private Industrial Sector', *Social Science & Medicine* 57, no. 5 (2003), 807–24.

19 'Banking on Leadership: Westpac's David Morgan', www.ceoforum.com.au, December 2004; S. Hughes, 'Top of the Corporate Heap', *The Age* (Melbourne), 4 April 2005, 15.

20 Some of the more popular books that encourage executives to develop values statements include: J. C. Collins and J. I. Porras, *Built to Last: Successful Habits of Visionary Companies* (London: Century, 1995); C. A. O'Reilly III and J. Pfeffer, *Hidden Value* (Cambridge, MA: Harvard Business School Press, 2000); J. M. Kouzes and B. Z. Posner, *The Leadership Challenge*, 3rd edn (San Francisco: Jossey-Bass, 2002).

21 B. M. Meglino and E. C. Ravlin, 'Individual Values in Organizations: Concepts, Controversies, and Research', *Journal of Management* 24, no. 3 (1998), 351–89; B. R. Agle and C. B. Caldwell, 'Understanding Research on Values in Business', *Business and Society* 38, no. 3 (September 1999), 326–87; S. Hitlin and J. A. Pilavin, 'Values: Reviving a Dormant Concept', *Annual Review of Sociology* 30 (2004), 359–93.

22 D. Lubinski, D. B. Schmidt and C. P. Benbow, 'A 20-Year Stability Analysis of the Study of Values for Intellectually Gifted Individuals from Adolescence to Adulthood', *Journal of Applied Psychology* 81 (1996), 443–51.

23   B. Kabanoff and J. Daly, 'Espoused Values in Organisations', *Australian Journal of Management* 27, Special issue (2002), 89–104.

24   S. H. Schwartz, 'Universals in the Content and Structure of Values: Theoretical Advances and Empirical Tests in 20 Countries', *Advances in Experimental Social Psychology* 25 (1992), 1–65; S. H. Schwartz, 'Are There Universal Aspects in the Structure and Contents of Human Values?', *Journal of Social Issues* 50 (1994), 19–45; M. Schwartz, 'The Nature of the Relationship between Corporate Codes of Ethics and Behaviour', *Journal of Business Ethics* 32, no. 3 (2001), 247; D. Spini, 'Measurement Equivalence of 10 Value Types from the Schwartz Value Survey across 21 Countries', *Journal of Cross-Cultural Psychology* 34, no. 1 (January 2003), 3–23; S. H. Schwartz and K. Boehnke, 'Evaluating the Structure of Human Values with Confirmatory Factor Analysis', *Journal of Research in Personality* 38, no. 3 (2004), 230–55.

25   G. R. Maio and J. M. Olson, 'Values as Truisms: Evidence and Implications', *Journal of Personality and Social Psychology* 74, no. 2 (1998), 294–311; G. R. Maio et al., 'Addressing Discrepancies between Values and Behavior: The Motivating Effect of Reasons', *Journal of Experimental Social Psychology* 37, no. 2 (2001), 104–17; B. Verplanken and R. W. Holland, 'Motivated Decision Making: Effects of Activation and Self-Centrality of Values on Choices and Behavior', *Journal of Personality and Social Psychology* 82, no. 3 (2002), 434–47; A. Bardi and S. H. Schwartz, 'Values and Behavior: Strength and Structure of Relations', *Personality and Social Psychology Bulletin* 29, no. 10 (October 2003), 1207–20; M. M. Bernard and G. R. Maio, 'Effects of Introspection about Reasons for Values: Extending Research on Values-as-Truisms', *Social Cognition* 21, no. 1 (2003), 1–25.

26   P. Pruzan, 'The Question of Organizational Consciousness: Can Organizations Have Values, Virtues and Visions?', *Journal of Business Ethics* 29 (February 2001), 271–84.

27   Coles Myer Ltd, *Corporate Social Responsibility Report 2005* (Tooronga, Victoria: Coles Myer, July 2005); F. Smith et al., '25 True Leaders', *Australian Financial Review*, 12 August 2005, 62.

28   K. F. Alam, 'Business Ethics in New Zealand Organizations: Views from the Middle and Lower Level Managers', *Journal of Business Ethics* 22 (November 1999), 145–53; S. R. Chatterjee and C. A. L. Pearson, 'Indian Managers in Transition: Orientations, Work Goals, Values and Ethics', *Management International Review* (January 2000), 81–95.

29   A. L. Kristof, 'Person–Organization Fit: An Integrative Review of Its Conceptualizations, Measurement, and Implications', *Personnel Psychology* 49, no. 1 (Spring 1996), 1–49; M. L. Verquer, T. A. Beehr and S. H. Wagner, 'A Meta-Analysis of Relations between Person–Organization Fit and Work Attitudes', *Journal of Vocational Behavior* 63 (2003), 473–89; J. W. Westerman and L. A. Cyr, 'An Integrative Analysis of Person–Organization Fit Theories', *International Journal of Selection and Assessment* 12, no. 3 (September 2004), 252–61.

30   K. M. Eisenhardt, J. L. Kahwajy and L. J. Bourgeois III, 'Conflict and Strategic Choice: How Top Management Teams Disagree', *California Management Review* 39 (Winter 1997), 42–62; D. Arnott, *Corporate Cults* (New York: AMACOM, 1999).

31   T. Simons, 'Behavioral Integrity: The Perceived Alignment between Managers' Words and Deeds as a Research Focus', *Organization Science* 13, no. 1 (Jan–Feb 2002), 18–35.

32   T. A. Joiner, 'The Influence of National Culture and Organizational Culture Alignment on Job Stress and Performance: Evidence from Greece', *Journal of Managerial Psychology* 16 (2001), 229–42; Z. Aycan, R. N. Kanungo and J. B. P. Sinha, 'Organizational Culture and Human Resource Management Practices: The Model of Culture Fit', *Journal of Cross-Cultural Psychology* 30 (July 1999), 501–26.

33   C. Fox, 'Firms Go Warm and Fuzzy to Lure Staff', *Australian Financial Review*, 15 May 2001, 58.

34   D. Oyserman, H. M. Coon and M. Kemmelmeier, 'Rethinking Individualism and Collectivism: Evaluation of Theoretical Assumptions and Meta-Analyses', *Psychological Bulletin* 128 (2002), 3–72; C. P. Earley and C. B. Gibson, 'Taking Stock in Our Progress on Individualism–Collectivism: 100 Years of Solidarity and Community', *Journal of Management* 24 (May 1998), 265–304; F. S. Niles, 'Individualism–Collectivism Revisited', *Cross-Cultural Research* 32 (November 1998), 315–41.

35   Oyserman, Coon, and Kemmelmeier, 'Rethinking Individualism and Collectivism: Evaluation of Theoretical Assumptions and Meta-Analyses'. The relationship between individualism and collectivism is still being debated. Some researchers suggest that there are different types of individualism and collectivism, and some of these types may be opposites. Others say that the lack of association is due to the way we measure these concepts. See: E. G. T. Green, J.-C. Deschamps and D. Paez, 'Variation of Individualism and Collectivism within and between 20 Countries', *Journal of Cross-Cultural Psychology* 36, no. 3 (May 2005), 321–39; S. Oishi et al., 'The Measurement of Values Across Cultures: A Pairwise Comparison Approach', *Journal of Research in Personality* 39, no. 2 (2005), 299–305.

36   M. H. Bond, 'Reclaiming the Individual from Hofstede's Ecological Analysis—a 20-Year Odyssey', *Psychological Bulletin* 128 (2002), 73–7; M. Voronov and J. A. Singer, 'The Myth of Individualism–Collectivism: A Critical Review', *Journal of Social Psychology* 142 (August 2002), 461–80.

37   H. Trinca, 'It's About Soul but Don't Get Too Soft', *Australian Financial Review*, 12 August 2005, 56.

38   G. Hofstede, *Culture's Consequences: Comparing Values, Behaviors, Institutions, and Organizations across Nations*, 2nd edn (Thousand Oaks, CA: Sage, 2001).

39   J. Chao, 'Culture Clash Looms as Lenovo Gobbles IBM Unit', *Palm Beach Post*, 19 December 2004, 3F; D. Roberts and L. Lee, 'East Meets West, Big Time', *Business Week*, 9 May 2005, 74.

40   G. Hofstede, *Cultures and Organizations: Software of the Mind* (New York: McGraw-Hill, 1991). Hofstede used the terms 'masculinity' and 'femininity' for achievement and nurturing orientation respectively. This text has adopted the latter terms to minimise the sexist perspective of the concepts.

41   J. S. Osland et al., 'Beyond Sophisticated Stereotyping: Cultural Sensemaking in Context', *Academy of Management Executive* 14 (February 2000), 65–79; S. S. Sarwono and R. W. Armstrong, 'Microcultural Differences and Perceived Ethical Problems: An International Business Perspective', *Journal of Business Ethics* 30 (March 2001), 41–56; Voronov and Singer, 'The Myth of Individualism–Collectivism: A Critical Review'; N. Jacob, 'Cross-Cultural Investigations: Emerging Concepts', *Journal of Organizational Change Management* 18, no. 5 (2005), 514–28.

42   Business Council of British Columbia, *2004 Biennial Skills and Attributes Survey Report* (Vancouver: Business Council of British Columbia, October 2004).

43   Transparency International, *Transparency International Corruption Perceptions Index 2005* (Berlin, Germany: Transparency International, October 2005).

44   T. Anzai, 'Rise, Fall of Tsutsumi Mirrors Era in Japan', *Nikkei Weekly*, 7 March 2005; J. Moir, 'Dishing the Dirt on China's Corporate Criminals', *South China Morning Post* (Hong Kong), 20 August 2005, 1; I. Porter and G. Costa, 'Internal Spook Fingers Box Man', *The Age* (Melbourne), 1 April 2005, 12; M. Wilkinson and D. Snow, 'Going Against the Grain', *Sydney Morning Herald*, 5 November 2005, 28.

45   P. L. Schumann, 'A Moral Principles Framework for Human Resource Management Ethics', *Human Resource Management Review* 11

(Spring–Summer 2001), 93–111; J. Boss, *Analyzing Moral Issues*, 3rd edn (New York: McGraw-Hill, 2005), chapter 1; M. G. Velasquez, *Business Ethics: Concepts and Cases*, 6th edn (Upper Saddle River, NJ: Prentice Hall, 2006), chapter 2.

46   T. J. Jones, 'Ethical Decision Making by Individuals in Organizations: An Issue Contingent Model', *Academy of Management Review* 16 (1991), 366–95; B. H. Frey, 'The Impact of Moral Intensity on Decision Making in a Business Context', *Journal of Business Ethics* 26 (August 2000), 181–95; D. R. May and K. P. Pauli, 'The Role of Moral Intensity in Ethical Decision Making', *Business and Society* 41 (March 2002), 84–117.

47   J. R. Sparks and S. D. Hunt, 'Marketing Researcher Ethical Sensitivity: Conceptualization, Measurement, and Exploratory Investigation', *Journal of Marketing* 62 (April 1998), 92–109.

48   Alam, 'Business Ethics in New Zealand Organizations: Views from the Middle and Lower Level Managers'; K. Blotnicky, 'Is Business in Moral Decay?', *Chronicle-Herald* (Halifax), 11 June 2000; B. Stoneman and K. K. Holliday, 'Pressure Cooker', *Banking Strategies*, January–February 2001, 13.

49   B. Farrell, D. M. Cobbin and H. M. Farrell, 'Codes of Ethics: Their Evolution, Development and Other Controversies', *Journal of Management Development* 21, no. 2 (2002), 152–63; G. Wood and M. Rimmer, 'Codes of Ethics: What Are They Really and What Should They Be?', *International Journal of Value-Based Management* 16, no. 2 (2003), 181.

50   P. J. Gnazzo and G. R. Wratney, 'Are You Serious About Ethics?', *Across the Board* 40 (July/August 2003), 46ff; T. F. Lindeman, 'A Matter of Choice', *Pittsburgh Post-Gazette*, 30 March 2004; B. Schultz, 'Ethics under Investigation', *Network World*, 26 April 2004; K. Tyler, 'Do the Right Thing', *HRMagazine* 50, no. 2 (February 2005), 99–103.

51   L. Bogomolny, 'Good Housekeeping', *Canadian Business*, 1 March 2004, 87–8.

52   E. Aronson, 'Integrating Leadership Styles and Ethical Perspectives', *Canadian Journal of Administrative Sciences* 18 (December 2001), 266–76; D. R. May et al., 'Developing the Moral Component of Authentic Leadership', *Organizational Dynamics* 32 (2003), 247–60. The Vodafone director quotation is from: R. Van Lee, L. Fabish and N. McGaw, 'The Value of Corporate Values', *Strategy+Business* (Summer 2005), 1–13.

53   Roccas et al., 'The Big Five Personality Factors and Personal Values'.

54   H. C. Triandis and E. M. Suh, 'Cultural Influences on Personality', *Annual Review of Psychology* 53 (2002), 133–60.

55   B. Reynolds and K. Karraker, 'A Big Five Model of Disposition and Situation Interaction: Why a "Helpful" Person May Not Always Behave Helpfully', *New Ideas in Psychology* 21 (April 2003), 1–13; W. Mischel, 'Toward an Integrative Science of the Person', *Annual Review of Psychology* 55 (2004), 1–22.

56   T. Power, 'Psyched Out', *Intheblack*, December 2004, 32–35.

57   R. M. Guion and R. F. Gottier, 'Validity of Personnel Measures in Personnel Selection', *Personnel Psychology* 18 (1965), 135–64; N. Schmitt et al., 'Meta-Analyses of Validity Studies Published between 1964 and 1982 and the Investigation of Study Characteristics', *Personnel Psychology* 37 (1984), 407–22.

58   P. G. Irving, 'On the Use of Personality Measures in Personnel Selection', *Canadian Psychology* 34 (April 1993), 208–14.

59   K. M. DeNeve and H. Cooper, 'The Happy Personality: A Meta-Analysis of 137 Personality Traits and Subjective Well-Being', *Psychological Bulletin* 124 (September 1998), 197–229; T. A. Judge et al., 'Personality and Leadership: A Qualitative and Quantitative Review', *Journal of Applied Psychology* 87, no. 4 (2002), 765–80; R. Ilies,

M. W. Gerhardt and H. Le, 'Individual Differences in Leadership Emergence: Integrating Meta-Analytic Findings and Behavioral Genetics Estimates', *International Journal of Selection and Assessment* 12, no. 3 (September 2004), 207–19.

60   This historical review and the trait descriptions in this section are discussed in: J. M. Digman, 'Personality Structure: Emergence of the Five-Factor Model', *Annual Review of Psychology* 41 (1990), 417–40; M. K. Mount and M. R. Barrick, 'The Big Five Personality Dimensions: Implications for Research and Practice in Human Resources Management', *Research in Personnel and Human Resources Management* 13 (1995), 153–200; R. J. Schneider and L. M. Hough, 'Personality and Industrial/Organizational Psychology', *International Review of Industrial and Organizational Psychology* 10 (1995), 75–129.

61   T. A. Judge and R. Ilies, 'Relationship of Personality to Performance Motivation: A Meta-Analytic Review', *Journal of Applied Psychology* 87, no. 4 (2002), 797–807; A. Witt, L. A. Burke and M. R. Barrick, 'The Interactive Effects of Conscientiousness and Agreeableness on Job Performance', *Journal of Applied Psychology* 87 (February 2002), 164–69.

62   C. G. Jung, *Psychological Types*, trans. H. G. Baynes (Princeton, NJ: Princeton University Press, 1971); I. B. Myers, *The Myers–Briggs Type Indicator* (Palo Alto, CA: Consulting Psychologists Press, 1987).

63   M. Gladwell, 'Personality Plus', *New Yorker*, 20 September 2004, 42–8; R. B. Kennedy and D. A. Kennedy, 'Using the Myers–Briggs Type Indicator in Career Counseling', *Journal of Employment Counseling* 41, no. 1 (March 2004), 38–44.

64   W. L. Johnson et al., 'A Higher Order Analysis of the Factor Structure of the Myers–Briggs Type Indicator', *Measurement and Evaluation in Counseling and Development* 34 (July 2001), 96–108; R. M. Capraro and M. M. Capraro, 'Myers–Briggs Type Indicator Score Reliability across Studies: A Meta-Analytic Reliability Generalization Study', *Educational and Psychological Measurement* 62 (August 2002), 590–602; J. Michael, 'Using the Myers–Briggs Type Indicator as a Tool for Leadership Development? Apply with Caution', *Journal of Leadership & Organizational Studies* 10 (Summer 2003), 68–81.

65   P. E. Spector, 'Behavior in Organizations as a Function of Employee's Locus of Control', *Psychological Bulletin* 91 (1982), 482–97; J. M. Howell and B. J. Avolio, 'Transformational Leadership, Transactional Leadership, Locus of Control, and Support for Innovation: Key Predictors of Consolidated-Business-Unit Performance', *Journal of Applied Psychology* 78 (1993), 891–902; P. E. Spector et al., 'Do National Levels of Individualism and Internal Locus of Control Relate to Well-Being: An Ecological Level International Study', *Journal of Organizational Behavior* 22 (2001), 815–32.

66   M. Snyder, *Public Appearances/Private Realities: The Psychology of Self-Monitoring* (New York: W. H. Freeman, 1987).

67   R. J. Ellis and S. E. Cronshaw, 'Self-Monitoring and Leader Emergence: A Test of Moderator Effects', *Small Group Research* 23 (1992), 113–29; M. Kilduff and D. V. Day, 'Do Chameleons Get Ahead? The Effects of Self-Monitoring on Managerial Careers', *Academy of Management Journal* 37 (1994), 1047–60; M. A. Warech et al., 'Self-Monitoring and 360-Degree Ratings', *Leadership Quarterly* 9 (Winter 1998), 449–73; A. Mehra, M. Kilduff and D. J. Brass, 'The Social Networks of High and Low Self-Monitors: Implications for Workplace Performance', *Administrative Science Quarterly* 46 (March 2001), 121–46.

68   J. L. Holland, *Making Vocational Choices: A Theory of Careers* (Englewood Cliffs, NJ: Prentice Hall, 1973).

69   G. D. Gottfredson and J. L. Holland, 'A Longitudinal Test of the Influence of Congruence: Job Satisfaction, Competency Utilization, and Counterproductive Behavior', *Journal of Counseling Psychology* 37

(1990), 389–98; A. Furnham, 'Vocational Preference and P–O Fit: Reflections on Holland's Theory of Vocational Choice', *Applied Psychology: An International Review* 50 (2001), 5–29.

70 Furnham, 'Vocational Preference and P–O Fit: Reflections on Holland's Theory of Vocational Choice'; R. P. Tett and D. D. Burnett, 'A Personality Trait-Based Interactionist Model of Job Performance', *Journal of Applied Psychology* 88, no. 3 (2003), 500–17; W. Yang,

G. S. Stokes and C. H. Hui, 'Cross-Cultural Validation of Holland's Interest Structure in Chinese Population', *Journal of Vocational Behavior* 67 (2005), 379–96.

71 G. D. Gottfredson, 'John L. Holland's Contributions to Vocational Psychology: A Review and Evaluation', *Journal of Vocational Behavior* 55, no. 1 (1999), 15–40.

CHAPTER 3

Perception and learning in organisations

LEARNING OBJECTIVES

After reading this chapter, you should be able to:

- outline the perceptual process

- explain how we perceive ourselves and others through social identity

- outline the reasons why stereotyping occurs and describe ways to minimise its adverse effects

- describe the attribution process and two attribution errors

- summarise the self-fulfilling prophecy process

- explain how empathy and the Johari Window can help improve our perceptions

- define learning and explain how it affects individual behaviour

- describe the A-B-C model of behaviour modification and the four contingencies of reinforcement

- describe the three features of social learning theory

- summarise the four components of Kolb's experiential learning model.

Vodafone executive Grahame Maher keeps his perceptions in focus by discarding the executive suite and working close to employees every day.

Don't try looking for Grahame Maher in his office; he doesn't have one. Instead, the Australian executive recently appointed as head of Vodafone Sweden uses temporary workspace near employees in various departments. Every few months he packs up his mobile phone, laptop computer, personal organiser and a few files and moves to another department to sharpen his perceptions about the organisation. 'I haven't had an office for years,' said Maher in an interview during his previous job as chief executive of Vodafone Australia. '[Working among employees] is where I learn most about the business.'

Maher doesn't retreat to the executive suite during the bad times, either. His first task as chief executive at Vodafone Australia a few years ago was to cut the company's workforce in half, yet he remained close to his employees. 'In the technology area, where we changed from 800 people to 150 people, I went and sat in the middle of that area so we could talk about it any time and talk about the difficult issues,' says Maher.

Few executives follow Maher's lead by permanently working near front-line staff, but an increasing number improve their perceptions of the business by spending a few days each year working in front-line jobs. Ikea executives work on the shop floor or tend the cash registers during the Swedish retailer's Anti-bureaucracy Week. David Neeleman, the founder of New York–based discount airline JetBlue, works in the trenches each month with his baggage handlers and ticket takers. British department store Debenhams goes one step further; everyone at head office adopts a store for a year and works on the floor of that store once or twice each month.

Aurore Fonte also sharpens her perceptions by working in front-line jobs. 'It reminds us what our people do and how hard the work is,' explains the co-founder of Assetlink Services, the Sydney-based provider of cleaning, security and other services to commercial properties. Fonte experienced the value of sampling front-line work while clearing tables at a food court in Queensland. 'It became apparent that cleaners had to walk [for] seven minutes to wash out a bucket,' she recalls. 'Going back and forth meant a quarter of an hour out of the job each time.' Soon after, Fonte suggested to the shopping complex owner that Assetlink staff could provide better service if a tap and sink were located closer to the food court area.[1]

perception The process of selecting, organising and interpreting information in order to make sense of the world around us.

WORKING IN FRONT-LINE JOBS and keeping in close contact with staff and customers are increasingly recognised as powerful ways for executives to improve their perceptions of their work environment and to learn about the consequences of their actions. **Perception** is the process of receiving information about and making sense of the world around us. It entails deciding which information to notice, how to categorise this information, and how to interpret it within the framework of our existing knowledge. This chapter begins by describing the perceptual process, that is, the dynamics of selecting, organising and interpreting external stimuli. Social identity theory, which has become a leading perceptual theory in organisational behaviour, is then introduced, followed by a description of stereotyping, including ways of minimising stereotype biases in the workplace. Next, attribution, self-fulfilling prophecy and other perceptual issues are looked at, followed by an overview of empathy and the Johari Window as general strategies to minimise perceptual problems.

The opening vignette also refers to the topic of learning, because executives working on the front lines learn about what employees and customers experience every day. Indeed, it is difficult to discuss perceptions without also referring to the knowledge and skills learned from those perceptions, which is why perceptions and learning are combined in this chapter. The concept of learning is introduced in the latter part of the chapter, along with the related concepts of tacit and explicit knowledge. Three perspectives of learning are then looked at: behaviour modification, social learning theory, and experiential learning.

THE PERCEPTUAL PROCESS

LEARNING OBJECTIVE

Outline the perceptual process.

The Greek philosopher Plato wrote long ago that we see reality only as shadows reflected on the rough wall of a cave.[2] In other words, reality is filtered through an imperfect perceptual process. This imperfect process, which is illustrated in Exhibit 3.1, begins when environmental stimuli are received through our senses. Most stimuli are screened out; the rest are organised and interpreted. The resulting perceptions influence our emotions, attitudes and behaviour towards those objects, people and events.[3]

EXHIBIT 3.1

Model of the perceptual process

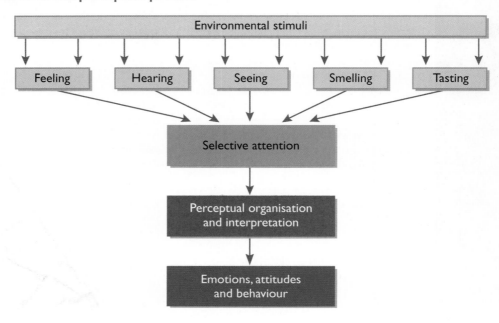

SELECTIVE ATTENTION

Our five senses are constantly bombarded with stimuli. Some things are noticed, but most are screened out. A nurse working in post-operative care might ignore the smell of recently disinfected instruments or the sound of co-workers talking nearby. Yet a small flashing red light on the nurses station console is immediately noticed because it signals that a patient's vital signs are failing. This process of attending to some information received by our senses and ignoring other information is called **selective attention**. Selective attention is influenced by two sets of factors: (1) characteristics of the person or object being perceived, and (2) characteristics of the individual doing the perceiving.[4]

selective attention The process of filtering information received by our senses.

Characteristics of the object

Some things stand out more than others because of their size, intensity, motion, repetition and novelty. The red light on the nurses station console receives attention because it is bright (intensity), flashing (motion) and a rare event (novelty). As for people, two employees having a heated debate would be noticed if the workers in that situation didn't normally raise their voices (novelty and intensity). Notice that selective attention is also influenced by the context in which the target is perceived. You might be aware that a client has a German accent if the meeting takes place in Darwin, but not if the conversation takes place in Germany, particularly if you had been living in Germany for some time. On the contrary, it would be your accent that would be noticed!

Characteristics of the perceiver

Characteristics of the perceiver play an important role in selection attention, much of it without our awareness.[5] When information is received through the senses, our brain quickly and unconsciously assesses whether it is relevant or irrelevant to us. Emotional markers (worry,

Detective theories increase selective attention biases

Good detective work involves more than forming a good theory about the crime. It also involves *not* forming a theory too early in the investigation. 'It is wrong to lock yourself in to a presumption of a motive,' warned ACT detective and acting superintendent Brett McCann during a recent murder investigation in Canberra. 'We are still delving into the deceased's lifestyle to try and come up with motives and we keep a very, very open mind on those.' Detectives eventually need to develop a theory to make sense of disparate pieces of information, but those who form theories too early are more likely to perceptually ignore evidence that seems irrelevant or contrary to the theory. '[They] focus on a suspect, select and filter the evidence that will build a case for conviction, while ignoring or suppressing evidence that points away from guilt,' explains Keith Findley, an American expert in wrongful convictions.[7]

NSW Police

happiness, anger) are attached to the relevant information based on this rapid evaluation, and these emotionally tagged bits of stimuli compete for our conscious attention.

Although largely unconscious, selective attention is also consciously influenced through our anticipation of future events.[6] If you expect a co-worker to send you some important information by email today, that email is likely to get noticed from the daily bombardment of messages. Unfortunately, expectations also delay our awareness of unexpected information. If we form a theory too early regarding a particular customer trend, we might not notice information indicating a different trend. In other words, our expectations and cognitive attention towards one issue tend to reduce our sensitivity to information about other issues. The solution here is to keep an open mind and take in as much information as possible without forming theories too early.

PERCEPTUAL ORGANISATION AND INTERPRETATION

categorical thinking The mostly unconscious process of organising people and objects into preconceived categories that are stored in our long-term memory.

People make sense of information even before they become aware of it. This sense-making partly includes **categorical thinking**—the mostly unconscious process of organising people and objects into preconceived categories that are stored in our long-term memory.[8] Categorical thinking relies on a variety of automatic perceptual grouping principles. Things are often grouped together based on their similarity or proximity to others. If you notice that a group of similar-looking people includes several professors, for instance, you are likely to assume that the others in that group are also professors. Another form of perceptual grouping is based on the need for cognitive closure, such as filling in missing information about what happened at a meeting that you didn't attend (e.g. who was there, where it was held). A third form of grouping occurs when we think we see trends in otherwise ambiguous information. Several research studies have found that people have a natural tendency to see patterns in what are actually random events, such as presumed winning streaks among sports stars or a run of luck in gambling.[9]

Making sense also involves interpreting incoming information, and this happens just as quickly as the brain selects and organises that information. The brain attaches emotional markers to incoming stimuli, which are essentially quick judgments about whether those stimuli are good for us or bad for us. To give you an idea about how quickly and systematically this unconscious perceptual process occurs, consider the following study:[10] Eight observers were shown video clips of university instructors teaching an undergraduate class, and then rated the instructors on several personal characteristics (optimistic, likeable, anxious, active, etc.). The observers did not know the instructors and completed their ratings independently, yet they agreed with each other on many characteristics. Equally important, these ratings matched the ratings completed by students who actually attended the class.

These results may be interesting, but the extraordinary discovery is that the observers formed their perceptions based on as little as *six seconds* of video—three segments of two seconds each selected randomly across the one-hour class! Furthermore, the video didn't have any sound. In spite of these very thin slices of information, the observers developed similar perceptions of the instructor, and those perceptions were comparable to the perceptions formed by students attending the entire class. Other studies have reported parallel results using two fifteen-second video segments of high school teachers, courtroom judges and physicians. Collectively, these 'thin slices' studies reveal that selective attention as well as perceptual organisation and interpretation operate very quickly and to a large extent without our awareness.

Mental models

mental models The broad world views or 'theories-in-use' that people rely on to guide their perceptions and behaviours.

To achieve our goals with some degree of predictability and sanity, we need road maps of the environments in which we live. These road maps, called **mental models**, are internal representations of the external world.[11] They consist of broad world views or templates of the mind that provide enough stability and predictability to guide our preferences and behaviours. For example, most of us have a mental model about attending a class lecture or seminar. We have a set of assumptions and expectations about how people arrive, arrange themselves in the room, ask and answer questions, and so forth. We can create a mental image of what a class would look like in progress.

We rely on mental models to make sense of our environment through perceptual grouping; mental models fill in the missing pieces, including the causal connection between events. Yet mental models may also blind us to seeing the world in different ways. For example, accounting professionals tend to see corporate problems in terms of accounting solutions, whereas marketing professionals see the same problems from a marketing perspective. Mental models also block our recognition of new opportunities. How do we change mental models? It's a tough challenge. After all, we developed models from several years of experience and reinforcement. The most important way to minimise the perceptual problems with mental models is to constantly question them. We need to ask ourselves about the assumptions we make. Working with people from diverse backgrounds is another way to break out of existing mental models. Colleagues from different cultures and areas of expertise tend to have different mental models, so working with them makes your assumptions more obvious.

SOCIAL IDENTITY THEORY

The perceptual process is an interesting combination of our self-perceptions and the perceptions of others. Increasingly, experts around the world (many of them in Australia) are discovering that how we perceive the world depends on how we define ourselves. This connection between self-perception and the perception of others is explained through **social identity theory**.[12] According to social identity theory, people maintain a *social identity* by defining themselves in terms of the groups to which they belong and have an emotional attachment. For instance, someone might have a social identity as a New Zealander, a graduate of the University of Otago and an employee at Fonterra (see Exhibit 3.2). Everyone engages in this social categorisation process because it helps to make sense of where we fit within the social world.

Along with a social identity, people have a *personal identity*—characteristics that make them unique and distinct from people in any particular group. For instance, an unusual achievement that distinguishes you from other people typically becomes a personal identity characteristic. Personal identity refers to something about you as an individual without reference to a larger group. Social identity, on the other hand, defines you in terms of characteristics

social identity theory
A model that explains self-perception and social perception in terms of the person's unique characteristics (personal identity) and membership in various social groups (social identity).

LEARNING OBJECTIVE
Explain how we perceive ourselves and others through social identity.

EXHIBIT 3.2

Self-perception and social perception through social identity

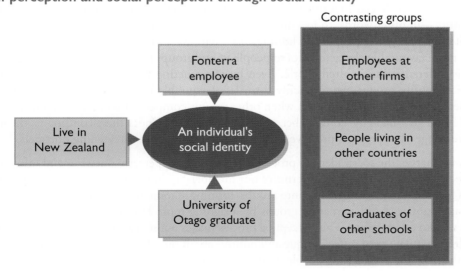

of the group. By perceiving yourself as a Fonterra employee, you are assigning characteristics to yourself that you believe are also characteristics of Fonterra employees in general.

Social identity is a complex combination of many memberships arranged in a hierarchy of importance. One factor determining this importance is how obvious our membership is in the group. We tend to define ourselves by our gender, race, age and other observable characteristics because other people easily identify our membership in those groups. It is difficult to ignore your gender in a class where most other students are the opposite gender, for example. In that context, gender tends to become a stronger defining feature of your social identity than it does in social settings where there are many people of the same gender.

Along with our demographic characteristics, group status is typically an important influence on our social identity. Most of us want to have a positive self-image, so we identify with groups that have higher status or respect. Medical doctors usually define themselves in terms of their profession because of its high status, whereas people in low-status jobs tend to define themselves in terms of non-job groups. Some people define themselves in terms of where they work because their employer has a favourable reputation in the community; other people never mention where they work because their firm has a poor reputation in the community.[13]

PERCEIVING OTHERS THROUGH SOCIAL IDENTITY

Social identity theory explains more than just how we develop self-perceptions. It also explains the dynamics of *social perception*—how we perceive others.[14] This social perception is influenced by three activities in the process of forming and maintaining our social identity: categorisation, homogenisation and differentiation.

- *Categorisation*. Social identity is a comparative process, and that comparison begins with the categorisation of people into distinct groups. By viewing someone (including yourself) as an Australian, for example, you remove that person's individuality and, instead, see him or her as prototypical representative of the group called Australians. This categorisation then allows you to distinguish Australians from people who live in New Zealand, Hong Kong and other countries in the region.
- *Homogenisation*. To simplify the comparison process, we tend to think that people within each group are very similar to each other. For instance, we think Australians collectively have similar attitudes and characteristics, whereas, say, Malaysians collectively have their own set of characteristics. Of course, every individual is unique, but we tend to lose sight of this fact when thinking about our social identity and how we compare with people in other social groups.
- *Differentiation*. Social identity fulfils our inherent need to have a distinct and positive identity—in other words, to feel unique and good about ourselves. To achieve this, we do more than categorise people and homogenise them; we also differentiate groups by assigning more favourable characteristics to people in our groups than to people in other groups. This differentiation is often subtle. Even by constructing favourable images of our own social identity groups, we implicitly form less favourable images of people belonging to other social categories. However, when other groups compete or conflict with our groups, the 'good guy–bad guy' contrast becomes much stronger. Under these conditions, the negative image of opponents preserves our self-image against the threatening outsiders.[15]

To summarise, the social identity process explains how we perceive ourselves and other people. We partly identify ourselves in terms of our membership in social groups. This comparison process includes categorising people into groups, forming a homogeneous image of people within those groups, and differentiating groups by assigning more favourable features to our own groups than to other groups. This perceptual process makes our social world easier to understand and fulfils an innate need to feel unique and positive about ourselves. The social identity process is also the basis for stereotyping people in organisational settings, which is discussed next.

STEREOTYPING IN ORGANISATIONAL SETTINGS

Stereotyping is an extension of social identity theory and a product of our natural process of organising information.[16] The first step in stereotyping occurs when we develop social categories and assign traits that are difficult to observe. For instance, students might form a stereotype that professors are both intelligent and absentminded. Personal experiences shape stereotypes to some extent, but stereotypes are mainly provided to us through cultural upbringing and media images (e.g. movie characters).

The second step in stereotyping involves assigning people to one or more social categories based on easily observable information about them, such as their gender, appearance or physical location. Observable features allow us to assign people to a social group quickly and without much investigation. The third step consists of assigning the stereotyped group's cluster of traits to people identified as members of that group. For example, we tend to think that professors are absentminded because people often include this trait in their stereotype of professors.

WHY STEREOTYPING OCCURS

Stereotyping occurs for three reasons.[17] First, stereotyping relies on categorical thinking which, as discussed earlier, is a natural process to simplify our understanding of the world. We depend on categorical thinking and stereotyping because it is impossible to recall all of the unique characteristics of every person we meet. Second, we have an innate need to understand and anticipate how others will behave. We don't have much information when first meeting someone, so we rely heavily on stereotypes to fill in the missing pieces. As you might expect, people with a stronger need for this cognitive closure have a higher tendency to stereotype others.

The third reason why stereotyping occurs is that it enhances our self-perception and social identity. Recall from social identity theory that we tend to emphasise the positive aspects of the groups to which we belong, which implicitly or explicitly generates less favourable views of people in contrasting groups. This explains why we are particularly motivated to use negative stereotypes towards people who hurt our self-esteem.[18]

PROBLEMS WITH STEREOTYPING

Stereotypes tend to have some inaccuracies, some overestimation or underestimation of real differences, and some degree of accuracy.[19] Still, they cause numerous problems in the workplace that need to be minimised. One concern is that stereotypes do not accurately describe every person in that social category. For instance, the widespread 'bean-counter' stereotype of accountants collectively views people in this profession as 'single-mindedly preoccupied with precision and form, methodical and conservative, and a boring joyless character'.[20] Although this may be true of some accountants, it is certainly not characteristic of all—or even most—people in this profession.

One unfortunate consequence of these negative stereotypes is that they discourage some social groups from entering various professions. As Reality Check 3.1 (overleaf) describes, the 'geek' or 'nerd' stereotype of engineers and computer scientists is partly responsible for the low percentage of women in these occupations. Notice how the individual's social identity also plays an important role in deciding whether to enter these professions.

Another problem with stereotyping is that it lays the foundation for discriminatory behaviour. Most people experience *unintentional (systemic) discrimination*, whereby decision makers rely on stereotypes to establish notions of the 'ideal' person in specific roles. A person who doesn't fit the ideal is likely to receive a less favourable evaluation. For instance, various anecdotes and reports indicate that systemic factors, including work flexibility and effects of the old boys network, prevent female lawyers and accountants in Australia from

stereotyping The process of assigning traits to people based on their membership in a social category.

LEARNING OBJECTIVE

Outline the reasons why stereotyping occurs and describe ways to minimise its adverse effects.

University of Western Australia

STEREOTYPING AND SOCIAL IDENTITY DISCOURAGE WOMEN FROM ENTERING ENGINEERING

Women represent 54 and 58 per cent of university graduates in Australia and New Zealand respectively but only around 15 per cent of university-level engineering and 20 per cent of computer science students. Women are also underrepresented in engineering programs in most (but not all) Asian countries. One reason for this disparity seems to be that the stereotypes of people in engineering and computer science don't fit the social identities that most women want for themselves.

'If you ask a woman to characterise a typical IT professional, she is likely to describe a young man with excess facial hair, sitting behind a computer all day munching pizza and guzzling Coke,' quips Ann Swain, chief executive of the Association of Technology Staffing Companies in the United Kingdom. This concern is supported by an Australian report which concluded that 'the image of the [IT] industry is a major problem and is putting girls off'.

Even if women are not put off by social identity problems, family and friends offer them stereotypic advice. 'It's really not difficult to get girls at high school interested in engineering,' suggests Chris Cook, Dean of Engineering at the University of Wollongong. 'What happens, though, is when they talk to their uncles and aunties and parents ... [they] say it's for men ... I think we still suffer from an overall image which is outdated.'

Kirsty Last, a third-year mechanical engineering student at the University of Wollongong, says that this stereotyping exists in subtle ways. 'People still gasp when I tell them I'm doing engineering,' says Last. She adds that the male stereotype of engineering 'is definitely wrong because women have proven they can do the job just as well as a bloke, and also women can bring many [other] skills to the field'.

To address social identity and stereotyping problems, a few engineering and computer science schools have established summer camps, where high school students gain a more accurate picture of engineering and computer science through hands-on activities. In the United States some of these camps are designed exclusively for high school girls and are led by female faculty or industry professionals. Female engineers or engineering professors also give talks at high schools so girls develop a more balanced view of the field. 'Having school students see females in engineering careers helps to change the perception that engineering is for males only,' says Edith Cowan University Education lecturer Lesley Newhouse-Maiden.

Engineering summer camps, such as this one at the University of Western Australia, help both female and male high school students to cast aside their inaccurate stereotypes of the engineering profession.

Sources: J. Sinclair, 'Breaking Down the Barriers', *The Age* (Melbourne), 30 January 2002, 14; J. E. Godfrey, 'The Culture of Engineering Education and Its Interaction with Gender: A Case Study of a New Zealand University' (PhD thesis, Curtin University of Technology, 2003); L. Mulhall, 'Women Stay on in Tough Environment', *Courier-Mail* (Brisbane), 29 November 2003, E23; L. P. Newhouse-Maiden, 'Hearing Their Voices: Building a Career Development Model for Women in Engineering' (PhD thesis, Curtin University of Technology, 2003); E. Cervini, 'Women Engineer a Gender Imbalance', *Australian Financial Review*, 7 March 2005, 29; C. Trenwith, 'Engineering a Gender Balance', *Illawarra Mercury*, 13 September 2005, 22.

having equal opportunities in those professions. 'A lot of women work harder, try harder and put more hours in than men,' says a female accountant at a mid-size Australian accounting firm. 'But as time goes on, they get disillusioned when they see people getting promoted ahead of them.'[21]

A more overt form of discrimination is **prejudice**, which refers to unfounded negative emotions and attitudes towards people belonging to a particular stereotyped group.[22] Overt prejudice is less apparent today than a few decades ago, but it still exists. The Australian army has taken a hammering recently for several examples of overt racism. In one incident, soldiers dressed as Ku Klux Klan members to taunt non-white soldiers in the unit. Separately, a soldier was reprimanded for posting a website featuring racist jokes and links to the Ku Klux Klan websites in the United States. In a third incident, a soldier with Greek heritage was found hanging with racist words scrawled across his face and arms in felt pen. Although the military concluded that the event was suicide, it could not explain how the soldier's absence wasn't reported for three days. In the most recent incident, a group of Australian soldiers posed for photographs completely naked except for a traditional Arab headdress.[23]

MINIMISING STEREOTYPING BIAS

If stereotyping is such a problem, shouldn't we try to avoid the process altogether? Unfortunately, it's not that simple. Most scholars agree that categorical thinking (including stereotyping) is an automatic and unconscious process. Intensive training can minimise stereotype activation to some extent, but for the most part the process is hardwired in our brain cells.[24] Also remember that stereotyping helps us in several valuable (although fallible) ways, described earlier: to minimise mental effort, to fill in missing information, and to support our social identity. The good news is that, while it is very difficult to prevent the *activation* of stereotypes, we can minimise the *application* of stereotypic information. In other words, we can avoid using our stereotypes in our decisions and actions towards other people. Three strategies for minimising the application of stereotyping are diversity awareness training, meaningful interaction, and decision-making accountability.

Diversity awareness training

Diversity awareness training tries to minimise discrimination by dispelling myths about people from various cultural and demographic groups and by identifying the organisational benefits of diversity and the problems with stereotyping. Some sessions rely on role-playing and other exercises to help employees discover the subtle yet pervasive effects of stereotyping in their decision making and behaviour.[25] Diversity training does not correct deep-rooted prejudice; it probably doesn't even change stereotypes in tolerant people. What diversity training can potentially do, however, is to increase our sensitivity to equality and motivate us to block inaccurate perceptions arising from ingrained stereotypes.

Meaningful interaction

The more meaningful our interactions are with someone, the less we rely on stereotypes to understand that person.[26] This statement, which describes the **contact hypothesis**, sounds simple enough, but in reality it works only under specific conditions. Participants must have close and frequent interaction while working towards a shared goal in a situation where they need to rely on each other (i.e. cooperate rather than compete with each other). Everyone should have equal status in that context and should be engaged in a meaningful task. An hour-long social gathering between executives and front-line employees does not satisfy these conditions. On the other hand, having executives work in front-line jobs, as described at the beginning of the chapter, does seem to represent meaningful interaction. By working in front-line jobs, these executives have equal status with other staff, cooperate towards a common goal, and have close and frequent interaction with front-line employees.

prejudice The unfounded negative emotions towards people belonging to a particular stereotyped group.

contact hypothesis A theory stating that the more we interact with someone, the less we rely on stereotypes to understand that person.

Decision-making accountability

A third way to minimise the biasing effects of stereotyping is to hold employees accountable for their decisions.[27] This accountability encourages more active information processing and, consequently, motivates decision makers to suppress stereotypic perceptions in favour of more precise and logical information. In contrast, less concern about accountability allows decision makers to engage in more passive information processing, which includes more reliance on discriminatory stereotypes.

Overall, social identity theory and stereotyping are central activities in the perceptual process, most of which occurs automatically and unconsciously. Without our awareness, our brain identifies and organises the incoming information around preconceived categories and assigns emotional markers representing an initial reaction to whether the information is good, bad or irrelevant. It may be difficult to prevent this categorisation and activation of stereotypes, but the application of the stereotypes can be consciously controlled in decision making and behaviour. Now let's look at another perceptual activity, called attribution.

ATTRIBUTION THEORY

attribution process The perceptual process of deciding whether an observed behaviour or event is caused largely by internal or external factors.

LEARNING OBJECTIVE

Describe the attribution process and two attribution errors.

The **attribution process** is the process of deciding whether an observed behaviour or event is caused largely by the person (internal factors) or the environment (external factors).[28] Internal factors include the individual's ability or motivation, such as believing that an employee performs the job poorly because he or she lacks the necessary competencies or motivation. External factors include lack of resources, other people, or just luck. An external attribution would occur if we believe that the employee performs the job poorly because he or she doesn't receive sufficient resources to do the task.

People rely on the three attribution rules shown in Exhibit 3.3 to determine whether someone's behaviour has a mainly internal or external attribution. Internal attributions are made when the observed individual has behaved this way in the past (high consistency), behaves like

EXHIBIT 3.3   **Rules of attribution**

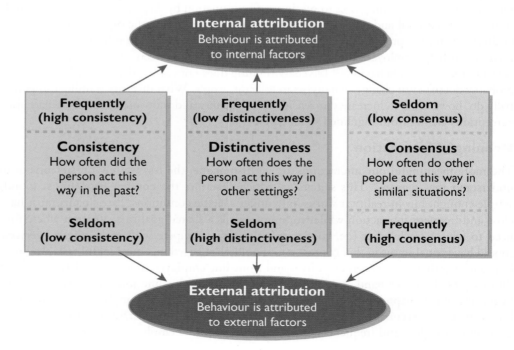

this towards other people or in different situations (low distinctiveness), and other people do not behave this way in similar situations (low consensus). On the other hand, an external attribution is made when there is low consistency, high distinctiveness and high consensus.

Here is an example that will help to clarify the three attribution rules. Suppose that an employee is making poor-quality products one day on a particular machine. We would probably conclude that there is something wrong with the machine (an external attribution) if the employee has made good-quality products on this machine in the past (low consistency), the employee makes good-quality products on other machines (high distinctiveness), and other employees have recently had quality problems on this machine (high consensus). We would make an internal attribution, on the other hand, if the employee usually makes poor-quality products on this machine (high consistency), other employees produce good-quality products on this machine (low consensus), and the employee also makes poor-quality products on other machines (low distinctiveness).[29]

Attributions are an essential part of our perceptual world because they link together the various pieces of that world in cause–effect relationships. As a result, our decisions and actions are influenced by our prior attributions.[30] Students who make internal attributions about their poor performance are more likely to drop out of their programs. Our satisfaction with work accomplishments is influenced to a large degree by whether we take credit for those accomplishments or attribute the success to external causes. Whether employees support or resist organisational change initiatives depends on whether they believe that management introduced those changes due to external pressures or their personal motives.

ATTRIBUTION ERRORS

People are far from perfect when making attributions. One bias, called **fundamental attribution error**, refers to our tendency to see the person rather than the situation as the main cause of that person's behaviour.[31] If an employee is late for work, observers are more likely to conclude that the person is lazy than to assume that external factors have caused the behaviour. One reason why fundamental attribution error occurs is that observers can't easily see the external factors that constrain the person's behaviour. They can't see the traffic jam that caused the person to be late, for instance. Another reason is that we tend to believe in the power of the person; we assume that individuals can overcome situational constraints more than they actually can.

While fairly common in Australia and New Zealand, fundamental attribution error is less common in Asian cultures.[32] The reason for this East–West difference is that Asians are taught from an early age to pay attention to the context in interpersonal relations and to see everything connected in a holistic way. Westerners, on the other hand, learn about the importance and independence of the individual; the person and situation are separate from each other, not seamlessly connected.

Another attribution error, known as **self-serving bias**, is the tendency to attribute our favourable outcomes to internal factors and our failures to external factors. Simply put, we take credit for our successes and blame others or the situation for our mistakes. One recent example is a study that monitored a small government organisation in New Zealand as it introduced a performance management system. The study found that 90 per cent of the employees who received lower-than-expected performance ratings blamed this on their supervisor, the organisation, the appraisal system, or other external causes. Only a handful blamed themselves for the unexpected results. Self-serving bias seems to occur across cultures, although women are somewhat less likely to take credit for their successes under some conditions.[33]

Self-serving bias protects our self-esteem, but it can have the opposite effect for people in leadership positions. We expect leaders to take ownership of their failures, so we have less respect for executives who blame the situation rather than take personal responsibility. Still, self-serving bias is consistently found in annual reports; executives refer to their personal qualities as reasons for the company's gains and to external factors as reasons for the company's losses.[34]

fundamental attribution error The tendency to attribute the behaviour of other people more to internal factors than to external factors.

self-serving bias A perceptual error whereby people tend to attribute their favourable outcomes to internal factors and their failures to external factors.

SELF-FULFILLING PROPHECY

self-fulfilling prophecy
Occurs when our expectations about another person cause that person to act in a way that is consistent with those expectations.

LEARNING OBJECTIVE
Summarise the self-fulfilling prophecy process.

Another important perception—and perceptual error—in organisations is **self-fulfilling prophecy**. Self-fulfilling prophecy occurs when our expectations about another person cause that person to act in a way that is consistent with those expectations. In other words, our perceptions can influence reality. Exhibit 3.4 illustrates the four steps in the self-fulfilling prophecy process, using the example of a supervisor and subordinate:[35]

1. *Expectations formed.* The supervisor forms expectations about the employee's future behaviour and performance. These expectations are sometimes inaccurate, because first impressions are usually formed from limited information.
2. *Behaviour towards the employee.* The supervisor's expectations influence his or her treatment of employees. Specifically, high-expectancy employees (those expected to do well) receive more emotional support through nonverbal cues (e.g. more smiling and eye contact), more frequent and valuable feedback and reinforcement, more challenging goals, better training, and more opportunities to demonstrate their performance.
3. *Effects on the employee.* The supervisor's behaviours have two effects on the employee. First, through better training and more practice opportunities, a high-expectancy employee learns more skills and acquires more knowledge than a low-expectancy employee. Second, the employee becomes more self-confident, which results in higher motivation and a greater willingness to set more challenging goals.[36]
4. *Employee behaviour and performance.* With higher motivation and better skills, high-expectancy employees are more likely to demonstrate desired behaviours and good performance. The supervisor notices this, which supports his or her original perception.

There are plenty of examples of self-fulfilling prophecies in work and school settings.[37] Research has found that women score lower on maths tests when people around them convey a negative stereotype of women regarding their perceived ability to do maths. Women perform better on these tests when they are not exposed to this negative self-fulfilling prophecy. Another study reported that the performance of Israeli Defence Force trainees was influenced by their instructor's expectations regarding the trainee's potential in the program. Self-fulfilling prophecy was at work here because the instructor's expectations were based on a list provided by researchers showing which recruits had high and low potential, even though the researchers had actually listed the trainees randomly.

EXHIBIT 3.4   **The self-fulfilling prophecy cycle**

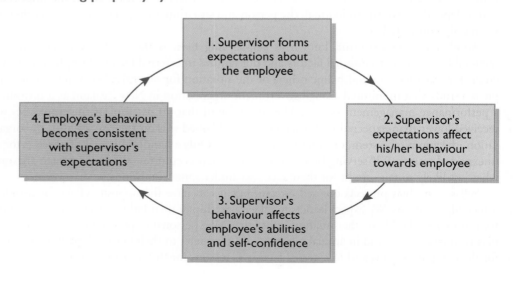

Positive self-fulfilling prophecies strengthen Cocoplans

After only a dozen years in business, Cocoplans is recognised throughout the Philippines as a top-performing pre-needs (superannuation and education) insurance company with excellent customer service. This success is partly due to the way Cocoplans executives perceive their sales staff. 'At Cocoplans, we treat sales people as our internal customers, while plan holders are our external customers,' explains Cocoplans president Caesar T. Michelena. Michelena believes that by treating employees as customers, Cocoplans managers have positive expectations of those employees, which then results in higher performance results. 'It's a self-fulfilling prophecy. If you believe that [employees] will not last, your behaviour towards them will show it ... You get what you expect.' [38]

Courtesy of Cocoplans

CONTINGENCIES OF SELF-FULFILLING PROPHECY

Self-fulfilling prophecies are more powerful under some conditions than others.[39] Manager expectations have a stronger effect on employee behaviour at the beginning of the relationship (i.e. when an employee is first hired) than after the manager and employee have known each other for some time. Self-fulfilling prophecy is also more powerful when several people have an expectation of an individual than when just one person has the expectation. In other words, we might be able to ignore one person's doubts about our potential, but not the collective doubts of several people.

A third factor is the individual's past achievements. Both positive and negative self-fulfilling prophecies have a stronger effect on people with a history of low achievement than on those with a history of high achievement. High achievers are less affected by negative expectations because they can draw on the strength of their successful past experiences. Low achievers don't have these past successes to support their self-esteem, so they give up more easily when they sense their boss's low expectations. Fortunately, the opposite is also true: low achievers respond more favourably than high achievers to positive self-fulfilling prophecy. Low achievers don't receive this positive encouragement very often, so it probably has a strong effect on their motivation to excel.[40]

The main lesson from the self-fulfilling prophecy literature is that leaders need to develop and maintain a positive, yet realistic, expectation towards all employees.[41] This recommendation is consistent with the emerging philosophy of *positive organisational behaviour*, which suggests that focusing on the positive rather than the negative aspects of life will improve organisational success and individual well-being. Perceiving and communicating hope is so important that it is one of the key competencies of physicians and surgeons. Unfortunately, training programs that make leaders aware of the power of positive expectations don't seem to have much effect. Generating positive expectations and hope depends on a corporate culture of support and learning. Hiring supervisors who are inherently optimistic about their staff is another way of increasing the incidence of positive self-fulfilling prophecies.

OTHER PERCEPTUAL ERRORS

Self-fulfilling prophecy, attribution and stereotyping are processes that both assist and interfere with the perceptual process. Four other well-known perceptual biases in organisational settings are primacy effect, recency effect, halo effect, and projection bias.

PRIMACY EFFECT

primacy effect A perceptual error in which we quickly form an opinion of people based on the first information we receive about them.

First impressions are lasting impressions. This well-known saying isn't a cliché; it's a well-researched observation known as the primacy effect. The **primacy effect** refers to our tendency to quickly form an opinion of people based on the first information we receive about them.[42] This rapid perceptual organisation and interpretation occurs because we need to make sense of the world around us. The problem is that first impressions—particularly negative first impressions—are difficult to change. After categorising someone, we tend to select subsequent information that supports our first impression and screen out information that opposes that impression. Negative impressions tend to 'stick' more than positive impressions because negative characteristics are more easily attributed to the person, whereas positive characteristics are often attributed to the situation.

RECENCY EFFECT

recency effect A perceptual error in which the most recent information dominates our perception of others.

The **recency effect** occurs when the most recent information dominates our perceptions.[43] This effect is most common when making an evaluation involving complex information, particularly among people with limited experience. For instance, auditors must digest large volumes of information in their judgments about financial documents, and the most recent information received prior to the decision tends to get weighted more heavily than information received at the beginning of the audit. Similarly, when supervisors evaluate the performance of employees over the previous year, the most recent performance information dominates the evaluation because it is the most easily recalled. Some employees are well aware of the recency effect and use it to their advantage by getting their best work on the manager's desk just before the performance appraisal is conducted.

HALO EFFECT

halo effect A perceptual error whereby our general impression of a person, usually based on one prominent characteristic, colours our perception of other characteristics of that person.

The **halo effect** occurs when our general impression of a person, usually based on one prominent characteristic, colours our perception of other characteristics of that person.[44] If a supervisor who values punctuality notices that an employee is late for work, the supervisor might form a negative image of the employee and evaluate that person's other traits unfavourably as well. Generally, one trait important to the perceiver forms a general impression, and this impression becomes the basis for judgments about other traits. The halo effect is most likely to occur when concrete information about the perceived target is missing or we are not sufficiently motivated to search for it. Instead, we use our general impression of the person to fill in the missing information.

PROJECTION BIAS

projection bias A perceptual error in which we believe that other people have the same beliefs and behaviours that we do.

Projection bias occurs when we believe that other people have the same beliefs and behaviours that we do.[45] If you are eager for a promotion, you might think that others in your position are similarly motivated. If you are thinking of quitting your job, you start to believe that other people are also thinking of quitting. Projection bias is also a defence mechanism to protect our self-esteem. If we break a work rule, projection bias justifies this infraction by claiming that 'everyone does it'. We feel more comfortable with the thought that our negative traits exist in others, so we believe that others also have these traits.

IMPROVING PERCEPTIONS

We can't bypass the perceptual process, but we should make every attempt to minimise perceptual biases and distortions. Earlier, the discussion focused on how diversity awareness, meaningful interaction and accountability practices could minimise the adverse effects of biased stereotypes. Two other broad perceptual improvement practices are developing empathy and improving self-awareness.

LEARNING OBJECTIVE

Explain how empathy and the Johari Window can help improve our perceptions.

IMPROVING PERCEPTIONS THROUGH EMPATHY

Empathy refers to a person's understanding of and sensitivity to the feelings, thoughts and situation of others. Empathy has both a cognitive (thinking) component and an emotional component.[46] The cognitive component, which is sometimes called perspective taking, represents a cognitive awareness of another person's situational and individual circumstances. The emotional component of empathy refers to experiencing the feelings of the other person. You have empathy when actively visualising the other person's situation (perspective taking) and feeling that person's emotions in that situation. Empathising with others improves our sensitivity to the external causes of another person's performance and behaviour, thereby reducing fundamental attribution error. A supervisor who imagines what it's like to be a single mother, for example, would become more sensitive to the external causes of lateness and other events by these employees.

empathy A person's ability to understand and be sensitive to the feelings, thoughts and situation of others.

Our empathy towards others improves through feedback, such as from a supervisor, a co-worker or a coach. Executive coaches also provide empathy-related feedback by attending meetings and later debriefing the executives regarding how well they demonstrated empathy towards others in the meeting.[47] Another way to improve empathy is to literally walk in the other person's shoes. The chapter opened with a description of how several executives are following this practice by working in front-line jobs from time to time. The more you personally experience the environment in which other people live and work, the better you will understand and be sensitive to their needs and expectations.

KNOW YOURSELF: APPLYING THE JOHARI WINDOW

Knowing yourself—becoming more aware of your values, beliefs and prejudices—is a powerful way to improve your perceptions.[48] Let's say that you have had an unpleasant experience with lawyers and developed negative emotions towards people in this profession. Being sensitive to these emotions should enable you to regulate your behaviour more effectively when working with legal professionals. Moreover, if co-workers are aware of your antipathy to lawyers, they are more likely to understand your actions and help you to be objective in the future.

The **Johari Window** is a popular model for understanding how co-workers can increase their mutual understanding.[49] Developed by Joseph Luft and Harry Ingram (hence the name Johari), this model divides information about you into four 'windows'—open, blind, hidden and unknown—based on whether your own values, beliefs and experiences are known to you and to others (see Exhibit 3.5, overleaf). The *open area* includes information about you that is known to both you and others. For example, both you and your co-workers may be aware that you don't like to be near people who smoke cigarettes. The *blind area* refers to information that is known to others but not to you. For example, your colleagues might notice that you are self-conscious and awkward when meeting the company chief executive, but you are unaware of this fact. Information known to you but unknown to others is found in the *hidden area*. We all have personal secrets about our likes, dislikes and personal experiences. Finally, the *unknown area* includes your values, beliefs and experiences that aren't known to you or others.

Johari Window The model of personal and interpersonal understanding that encourages disclosure and feedback to increase the open area and reduce the blind, hidden and unknown areas of oneself.

The main objective of the Johari Window is to increase the size of the open area so that both you and your colleagues are aware of your perceptual limitations. This is partly accomplished by reducing the hidden area through *disclosure*—informing others of your beliefs, feelings and

EXHIBIT 3.5   **Johari Window**

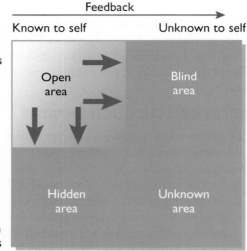

Source: Based on J. Luft, *Group Processes*
(Palo Alto, CA: Mayfield, 1984).

experiences that may influence the work relationship.[50] The open area also increases through *feedback* from others about your behaviours. This information helps you to reduce your blind area, because co-workers often see things in you that you do not see. Finally, the combination of disclosure and feedback occasionally produces revelations about information in the unknown area.

The Johari Window applies to some diversity awareness and meaningful contact activities that were described earlier. By learning about cultural differences and communicating more with people from different backgrounds, we gain a better understanding of their behaviour. Engaging in open dialogue with co-workers also applies the Johari Window. As we communicate with others, we naturally tend to disclose more information about ourselves and eventually feel comfortable providing candid feedback to them.

The perceptual process represents the filter through which information passes from the external environment to our brain. As such, it is really the beginning of the learning process, which is discussed next.

LEARNING IN ORGANISATIONS

LEARNING OBJECTIVE

Define learning and explain how it affects individual behaviour.

learning A relatively permanent change in behaviour that occurs as a result of a person's interaction with the environment.

What do employees at Wipro Technologies appreciate most about working at the Indian software giant? Financial rewards and challenging work are certainly on the list, but one of the top benefits is learning. 'Wipro provides great learning opportunities,' says CEO Vivek Paul. 'The core of how employees think about us and value us revolves around training. It simply isn't something we can back off from.'[51]

Learning is a relatively permanent change in behaviour (or behaviour tendency) that occurs as a result of a person's interaction with the environment. Learning occurs when the learner behaves differently. For example, it can be seen that you have 'learned' computer skills when you operate the keyboard and windows more quickly than before. Learning occurs when interaction with the environment leads to behaviour change. This means that we learn through our senses, such as through study, observation and experience.

Learning influences individual behaviour and performance through three elements of the MARS model (see Chapter 2). First, people acquire skills and knowledge through learning opportunities, which gives them the competencies to perform tasks more effectively. Second, learning clarifies role perceptions. Employees develop a better understanding of their tasks and the relative importance of work activities. Third, learning occurs through feedback, which motivates employees when they see that they are accomplishing the task.

LEARNING EXPLICIT AND TACIT KNOWLEDGE

When employees learn, they acquire both explicit and tacit knowledge. Explicit knowledge is organised and can be communicated from one person to another. The information you receive in a lecture is mainly explicit knowledge, because the instructor packages it and consciously transfers it to you. Explicit knowledge can be written down and given to others.

However, explicit knowledge is really only the tip of the knowledge iceberg. Most of what we know is **tacit knowledge**.[52] You have probably said to someone: 'I can't tell you how to do this, but I can show you.' Tacit knowledge is not documented; rather, it is action-oriented and known below the level of consciousness. Some writers suggest that tacit knowledge also includes the organisation's culture and a team's implicit norms. People know these values and rules exist, but they are difficult to describe and document. Tacit knowledge is acquired through observation and direct experience. For example, airline pilots learn to operate commercial jets more by watching experts and practising on flight simulators than through lectures. They acquire tacit knowledge by directly experiencing the complex interaction of behaviour with the machine's response.

The rest of this chapter introduces three perspectives of learning tacit and explicit knowledge: reinforcement, social learning and direct experience. Each perspective offers a different angle for understanding the dynamics of learning.

tacit knowledge Knowledge embedded in our actions and ways of thinking, and transmitted only through observation and experience.

BEHAVIOUR MODIFICATION: LEARNING THROUGH REINFORCEMENT

One of the oldest perspectives on learning, called **behaviour modification** (also known as *operant conditioning* and *reinforcement theory*), takes the rather extreme view that learning is completely dependent on the environment. Behaviour modification does not question the notion that thinking is part of the learning process, but it views human thoughts as unimportant intermediate stages between behaviour and the environment. The environment teaches us to alter our behaviours so that we maximise positive consequences and minimise adverse consequences.[53]

A-B-CS OF BEHAVIOUR MODIFICATION

The central objective of behaviour modification is to change behaviour (B) by managing its antecedents (A) and its consequences (C). This process is nicely illustrated in the A-B-C model of behaviour modification, shown in Exhibit 3.6.[54]

Antecedents are events preceding the behaviour, informing employees that certain behaviours will have particular consequences. An antecedent may be a sound from your computer signalling that an email has arrived or a request from your supervisor to complete a specific task by

behaviour modification A theory that explains learning in terms of the antecedents and consequences of behaviour.

LEARNING OBJECTIVE

Describe the A-B-C model of behaviour modification and the four contingencies of reinforcement.

A-B-Cs of behaviour modification

EXHIBIT 3.6

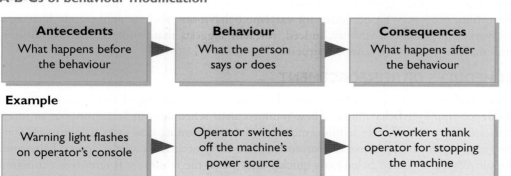

Antecedents What happens before the behaviour	**Behaviour** What the person says or does	**Consequences** What happens after the behaviour

Example

Warning light flashes on operator's console	Operator switches off the machine's power source	Co-workers thank operator for stopping the machine

Sources: Adapted from T. K. Connellan, *How to Improve Human Performance* (New York: Harper & Row, 1978), p. 50; F. Luthans and R. Kreitner, *Organizational Behavior Modification and Beyond* (Glenview, IL: Scott, Foresman, 1985), pp. 85–8.

tomorrow. These antecedents let employees know that a particular action will produce specific consequences. Notice that antecedents do not cause behaviours. The computer sound doesn't cause us to open our email. Rather, the sound is a cue telling us that certain consequences are likely to occur if we engage in certain behaviours.

Although antecedents are important, behaviour modification mainly focuses on the *consequences* of behaviour. Consequences are events following a particular behaviour that influence its future occurrence. Generally speaking, people tend to repeat behaviours that are followed by pleasant consequences and are less likely to repeat behaviours that are followed by unpleasant consequences or no consequences at all.

CONTINGENCIES OF REINFORCEMENT

Behaviour modification identifies four types of consequences that strengthen, maintain or weaken behaviour. These consequences, collectively known as the *contingencies of reinforcement*, include positive reinforcement, punishment, negative reinforcement and extinction.[55]

positive reinforcement Occurs when the introduction of a consequence increases or maintains the frequency or future probability of a behaviour.

punishment Occurs when a consequence decreases the frequency or future probability of a behaviour.

negative reinforcement Occurs when the removal or avoidance of a consequence increases or maintains the frequency or future probability of a behaviour.

extinction Occurs when the target behaviour decreases because no consequence follows it.

- *Positive reinforcement.* **Positive reinforcement** occurs when the *introduction* of a consequence *increases or maintains* the frequency or future probability of a specific behaviour. Receiving a bonus after successfully completing an important project is considered positive reinforcement because it typically increases the probability that you will use those behaviours in the future.
- *Punishment.* **Punishment** occurs when a consequence decreases the frequency or future probability of a behaviour. This consequence typically involves introducing something that employees try to avoid. For instance, most of us would consider a demotion or being ostracised by our co-workers as forms of punishment.[56]
- *Negative reinforcement.* **Negative reinforcement** occurs when the removal or avoidance of a consequence increases or maintains the frequency or future probability of a specific behaviour. Supervisors apply negative reinforcement when they *stop* criticising employees whose substandard performance has improved. When the criticism is withheld, employees are likely to repeat the behaviour that improved their performance. Note that negative reinforcement is not punishment. It actually reinforces behaviour by removing punishment.
- *Extinction.* **Extinction** occurs when the target behaviour decreases because no consequence follows it. In this respect, extinction is a do-nothing strategy. Generally, behaviour that is no longer reinforced tends to disappear; it becomes extinct. For instance, research suggests that when managers stop congratulating employees for their good performance, that performance tends to decline.[57]

Which contingency of reinforcement should we use in the learning process? In most situations, positive reinforcement should follow desired behaviours and extinction (do nothing) should follow undesirable behaviours. This approach is preferred because punishment and negative reinforcement generate negative emotions and attitudes towards the punisher (e.g. supervisor) and the organisation. However, some form of punishment (dismissal, suspension, demotion, etc.) may be necessary for extreme behaviours, such as deliberately hurting a co-worker or stealing inventory. Indeed, research suggests that, under certain conditions, punishment maintains a sense of fairness.[58]

SCHEDULES OF REINFORCEMENT

Along with the types of reinforcement, the frequency and timing of those reinforcers also influence employee behaviours.[59] These reinforcement schedules can be continuous or intermittent. The most effective reinforcement schedule for learning new tasks is *continuous reinforcement*—providing positive reinforcement after every occurrence of the desired behaviour. Employees learn desired behaviours quickly and, when the reinforcer is removed, extinction also occurs very quickly.

The other schedules of reinforcement are intermittent and are distinguished by whether they are based on a period of time (interval) or the number of behavioural events (ratio), and whether that interval or ratio is fixed or variable. Most people get paid with a *fixed interval schedule* because they receive their reinforcement (pay cheque) after a fixed period of time. A *variable interval schedule* is common for promotions. Employees are promoted after a variable amount of time. If you are given the rest of the day off after completing a fixed amount of work (e.g. serving a specific number of customers), you would have experienced a *fixed ratio schedule*—reinforcement after a fixed number of behaviours or accomplishments.

Finally, companies often use a *variable ratio schedule* in which employee behaviour is reinforced after a variable number of times. Salespeople experience variable ratio reinforcement because they make a successful sale (the reinforcer) after a varying number of client calls. They might make four unsuccessful calls before receiving an order on the fifth one, then make ten more calls before receiving the next order, and so on. The variable ratio schedule is a low-cost way to reinforce behaviour, because employees are rewarded infrequently. It is also highly resistant to extinction. Suppose your boss walks into your office at varying times of the day. The chances are that you would work consistently better throughout the day than if your boss visited at exactly 11 am every day. If your boss didn't walk into your office at all on a particular day, you would still expect a visit right up to the end of the day if previous visits had been random.

BEHAVIOUR MODIFICATION IN PRACTICE

Everyone practises behaviour modification in one form or another. We thank people for a job well done, we are silent when displeased, and we sometimes try to punish those who go against our wishes. Behaviour modification also occurs in various formal programs to reduce absenteeism, encourage safe work behaviours, and improve task performance. For example, the Sydney Olympics relied on a variable ratio schedule to reinforce good attendance and a low quit rate among volunteers. Volunteers received a 'passport' which was stamped each time they showed up for work. Each stamped page was later put into a lottery for prizes donated by sponsors, including six ski trips to the IOC headquarters in Switzerland, three Holden cars, and several mountain bikes. Volunteers with more stamped pages had a higher chance of winning a prize.[60]

Another frequent application of behaviour modification is in improving workplace safety. Reality Check 3.2 (overleaf) describes how workplace safety programs have shifted their focus from reinforcing low accident rates to reinforcing safety behaviours. The latter is more consistent with behaviour modification theory, because it focuses on behaviours within the employee's control.

While behaviour modification can be effective, it has several limitations.[61] One problem is 'reward inflation', in which the reinforcer is eventually considered an entitlement. For this reason, most behaviour modification programs must run infrequently and for short durations. A second problem is that some people revolt against the lottery-style variable ratio schedule because they consider gambling unethical. Third, behaviour modification's radical 'behaviourist' philosophy (that human thinking processes are unimportant) has lost favour because it is now evident that people can learn through mental processes, such as observing others and thinking logically about possible consequences.[62] Thus, without throwing away the principles of behaviour modification, most learning experts today also embrace the concepts of social learning theory.

SOCIAL LEARNING THEORY: LEARNING BY OBSERVING

Social learning theory states that much learning occurs by observing others and then modelling the behaviours that lead to favourable outcomes and avoiding behaviours that lead to punishing consequences.[63] Three related features of social learning theory are behaviour modelling, learning behaviour consequences, and self-reinforcement.

LEARNING OBJECTIVE

Describe the three features of social learning theory.

social learning theory A theory stating that much learning occurs by observing others and then modelling the behaviours that lead to favourable outcomes and avoiding behaviours that lead to punishing consequences.

REALITY CHECK 3.2

Employees at ExxonMobil's Fawley refinery in the UK receive various types of reinforcement for safe work behaviours and outcomes.

REINFORCING LAGGING AND LEADING INDICATORS OF WORKPLACE SAFETY

For many years, companies have had workplace safety programs that reward employees for accident-free milestones. For example, employees at Dragon Cement in the United States earn gift certificates for every three months that there is no lost-time injury at the facility. The certificates start at $25 per person and grow by $5 each quarter. The problem with rewarding accident-free milestones and similar 'lagging indicators' is that they really teach employees to avoid reporting accidents. In some cases, employees with broken arms or other injuries requiring rehabilitation have shown up for work because they didn't want to be held responsible for losing everyone's cherished safety bonus.

To some extent, ExxonMobil reinforces lagging indicators. In Malaysia, for instance, the company distributes awards to worksites and contractors with zero lost-time injuries. However, the company mainly reinforces 'leading indicators'—work behaviours that prevent accidents. ExxonMobil's Fawley refinery in the United Kingdom (shown in the photo) introduced a 'Behave Safely Challenge' program in which supervisors rewarded employees and contractors on the spot when they exhibited good safety behaviour or intervened to improve the safe behaviour of co-workers. The company also introduced a system in which co-workers observe each other's safety behaviours.

Lionore Australia also relies on employees to reinforce the safe work behaviour of co-workers on the job. But the mining company discovered that the success of this peer reinforcement system depended on how tactfully employees communicated their observations to the people around them. With this in mind, Lionore Australia launched a training program in which actors re-enacted real workplace incidents involving effective and ineffective communication about safety violations. The humorous yet realistic role-plays provided behaviour modelling for employees so they learnt how to approach colleagues whose behaviour was unsafe.

Sources: 'All Safety Is a Stage', *SafetyWA*, August 2004, pp. 1, 8; ExxonMobil, *UK and Ireland Corporate Citizenship* (ExxonMobil, August 2004); W. Atkinson, 'Safety Incentive Programs: What Works?', *Occupational Hazards*, 11 August 2004; 'Dragon's Concrete Division Passes 6-year Mark Without a Lost-time Injury', Dragon Products Company news release, 6 December 2004; 'ExxonMobil Recognises Employees, Contractors for Outstanding Performances', *Bernama Daily Malaysian News*, 27 June 2005.

BEHAVIOUR MODELLING

People learn by observing the behaviours of a role model on the critical task, remembering the important elements of the observed behaviours, and then practising those behaviours.[64] Behaviour modelling works best when the model is respected and the model's actions are followed by favourable consequences. For instance, recently hired university graduates learn better by watching a previously hired university graduate who successfully performs the task.

Behaviour modelling is a valuable form of learning for two reasons. First, tacit knowledge and skills are mainly acquired from others through observation. The adage that a picture is worth a thousand words applies here. It is difficult to document or verbally explain every detail on how a master baker kneads dough. Instead, this information is more effectively learned by observing the baker's actions and the consequences of those actions. Second, employees have a stronger belief that they can perform the work after seeing someone else perform the task. This effect is particularly strong when observers identify with the model, such as someone who is similar with respect to age, experience and gender. For instance, students are more confident about taking a challenging course when they are mentored by students similar to them who have just completed that course.

LEARNING BEHAVIOUR CONSEQUENCES

A second element of social learning theory says that we learn the consequences of behaviour through logic and observation, not just through direct experience. People logically anticipate desirable consequences after completing a task well and undesirable consequences (punishment or extinction) after performing the job poorly. It just makes sense to expect these outcomes, until we learn otherwise. We also learn behavioural consequences by observing the experiences of other people. This process, known as *vicarious learning*, occurs all the time in organisational settings. You might notice how co-workers mock another employee who dresses formally at work. By observing this incident, you learn about the group's preference for wearing casual attire. You might see how another worker serves customers better by keeping a list of their names, which teaches you to do the same. In each case, you have learned vicariously, not through your own experience.[65]

SELF-REINFORCEMENT

Self-reinforcement, the third element of social learning theory, occurs whenever an employee has control over a reinforcer but doesn't 'take' it until completing a self-set goal.[66] For example, you might be thinking about having a snack after you finish reading the rest of this chapter. You could take a break right now, but you don't use this privilege until you have achieved your goal of reading the chapter. Raiding the refrigerator is a form of self-induced positive reinforcement. Self-reinforcement can take many forms, such as taking a short walk, watching a movie, or simply congratulating yourself for completing the task. Self-reinforcement has become increasingly important because employees are given more control over their working lives and are less dependent on supervisors to dole out positive reinforcement and punishment.

self-reinforcement Occurs whenever someone has control over a reinforcer but delays it until a self-set goal has been completed.

LEARNING THROUGH EXPERIENCE

Mandy Chooi is about to attend a meeting with a lower-level manager who has botched a new assignment. She is also supposed to make a strategy presentation to her boss in three hours, but the telephone won't stop ringing and she is deluged with emails. It's a stressful situation. Fortunately, the challenges facing the Motorola human resources executive from Beijing on this particular day are not real. Chooi is sitting in a simulation to develop and test her leadership skills. 'It was hard. A lot harder than I had expected,' she says. 'It's surprising how realistic and demanding it is.'[67]

Many organisations are shifting their learning strategy away from the classroom and towards a more experiential approach. Classrooms transfer explicit knowledge that has been documented, but most tacit knowledge and skills are acquired through experience as well as

LEARNING OBJECTIVE

Summarise the four components of Kolb's experiential learning model.

EXHIBIT 3.7

Kolb's experiential learning model

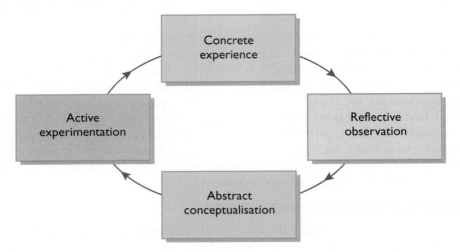

observation. Experiential learning has been conceptualised in many ways, but one of the most enduring perspectives is Kolb's experiential learning model, shown in Exhibit 3.7. This model illustrates experiential learning as a cyclical four-stage process.[68]

Concrete experience involves sensory and emotional engagement in some activity. It is followed by *reflective observation*, which involves listening, watching, recording and elaborating on the experience. The next stage in the learning cycle is *abstract conceptualisation*. This is the stage in which we develop concepts and integrate our observations into logically sound theories. The fourth stage, *active experimentation*, occurs when we test our previous experience, reflection and conceptualisation in a particular context. People tend to prefer some stages more than others and operate better in some stages than in others due to their unique competencies and personality. Still, experiential learning requires all four stages in proper balance.

EXPERIENTIAL LEARNING IN PRACTICE

learning orientation The extent to which an organisation or individual supports knowledge management, particularly opportunities to acquire knowledge through experience and experimentation.

Learning through experience works best in organisations with a strong **learning orientation**, that is, organisations that value learning opportunities and, in particular, the generation of new knowledge while employees perform their jobs. If an employee initially fails to perform a task, the experience might still be a valuable learning opportunity. In other words, organisations encourage employees to appreciate the process of individual and team learning, not just the performance results.

Organisations achieve a learning orientation culture by rewarding experimentation and recognising mistakes as a natural part of the learning process. They encourage employees to take reasonable risks to ultimately discover new and better ways of doing things. Without a learning orientation, mistakes are hidden and problems are more likely to escalate or re-emerge later. It's not surprising, then, that one of the most frequently mentioned lessons from the best performing manufacturers is to expect mistakes. '[Mistakes] are a source of learning and will improve operations in the long run,' explains an executive at Lockheed Martin. '[They] foster the concept that no question is dumb, no idea too wild, and no task or activity is irrelevant.'[70]

Action learning

action learning A variety of experiential learning activities in which employees, usually in teams, are involved in a 'real, complex and stressful problem' with immediate relevance to the company.

One application of workplace experiential learning that has received considerable interest, particularly in Europe, is **action learning**. Action learning occurs when employees, usually in teams, investigate and apply solutions to a situation that is both real and complex, with immediate relevance to the company.[71] In other words, the task becomes the source of learning. Kolb's experiential learning model presented earlier is usually identified as the main template for action learning. Action learning requires concrete experience with a real organisational problem or opportunity, followed by 'learning meetings' in which participants reflect on their observations about that problem or opportunity. They then develop and test a strategy to solve the problem or realise the opportunity. The process also encourages plenty of reflection so the experience becomes a learning process.

Action learning is considered one of the best ways to develop leadership competencies because it combines conceptual knowledge with real-world issues and reflective learning. At the same time, action learning projects often add value to the organisation. 'Action learning has become the primary vehicle for generating creative ideas and building business success at Heineken,' says the chairman of the executive board at the European brewery. MTR Corporation, which operates Hong Kong's commuter train system, recently introduced action learning projects as part of its executive development program. One action learning team discovered a cost savings measure that would fund executive development at MTR for several years.[72]

This chapter has introduced two fundamental activities in human behaviour in the workplace: perceptions and learning. These activities involve receiving information from the environment, organising it, and acting on it as a learning process. Knowledge about perceptions and learning in the workplace lays the foundation for the next chapter, which looks at workplace emotions and attitudes.

Emergency response teams learn through simulations

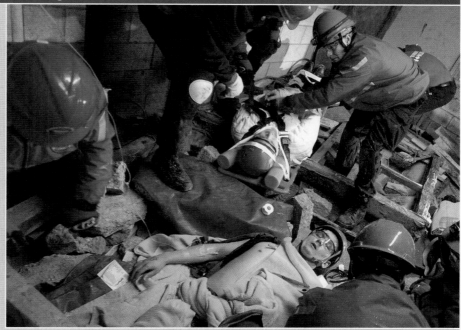

Physicians Jonathan Sherbino and Ivy Chong (far right) prepare to amputate the leg of Wesley Bagshaw who is pinned by a fallen beam in this collapsed building. 'If we don't do this, you're going to die,' says Sherbino in response to Bagshaw's anguished protests. Fortunately for Bagshaw, the bone saw cuts through a pig's leg rather than his own. The entire incident was a mock disaster to help train the Heavy Urban Search and Rescue (HUSAR) team in Toronto, Canada. For four hours, HUSAR crews located the victims with dogs and search equipment at this Toronto Fire Services special operations training centre site, secured the structure, treated Bagshaw and fifteen other 'victims', and extricated them to a mock hospital at a nearby community college. In all, over 300 HUSAR and Greater Toronto medical professionals were involved. 'People from the hospitals love these exercises because they get to try out all the ideas they have and no one is [adversely] affected,' explains one of the event's organisers. 'It was definitely a lot more realistic than anything we've done in the past.'[69]

Michael Stuparyk/Toronto Star

CHAPTER SUMMARY

Perception involves selecting, organising and interpreting information to make sense of the world around us. Selective attention is influenced by the characteristics of the person or object being perceived (i.e. their size, intensity, motion, repetition and novelty), and the characteristics of the person doing the perceiving. Perceptual organisation engages categorical thinking—the mostly unconscious process of organising people and objects into preconceived categories that are stored in our long-term memory. To a large extent, our perceptual interpretation of incoming information also occurs before we are consciously aware of it. Mental models—broad world views or templates of the mind—also help us to make sense of incoming stimuli.

The social identity process explains how we perceive ourselves and other people. We partly identify ourselves in terms of our membership in social groups. This comparison process includes categorising people into groups, forming a homogeneous image of people within those groups, and differentiating groups by assigning more favourable features to our own groups than to other groups.

Stereotyping is a derivative of social identity theory, in which people assign traits to others based on their membership in a social category. Stereotyping economises mental effort, fills in missing information, and enhances our self-perception and social identity. However, it also lays the foundation for prejudice and systemic discrimination. It is very difficult to prevent the activation of stereotyping, but we can minimise the application of stereotypic information in our decisions and actions. Three strategies to minimise the influence of stereotypes are diversity awareness training, meaningful interaction, and decision-making accountability.

The attribution process involves deciding whether the behaviour or event is largely due to the situation (external attributions) or to personal characteristics (internal attributions). Attributions are decided by perceptions of the consistency, distinctiveness and consensus of the behaviour. This process helps us to link together the various pieces of our world in cause–effect relationships, but it is also subject to attribution errors, including fundamental attribution error and self-serving bias.

Self-fulfilling prophecy occurs when our expectations about another person cause that person to act in a way that is consistent with those expectations. Essentially, our expectations affect our behaviour towards the target person, which then affects the employee's opportunities and attitudes, which then influence his or her behaviour. Self-fulfilling prophecies tend to be stronger at the beginning of the relationship (such as when an employee first joins the department), when several people hold the same expectations, and when the employee has a history of low achievement.

Four other perceptual errors commonly noted in organisations are primacy effect, recency effect, halo effect and projection bias. These and other perceptual problems can be minimised through empathy and becoming more aware of our values, beliefs and prejudices (Johari Window).

Learning is a relatively permanent change in behaviour (or behaviour tendency) that occurs as a result of a person's interaction with the environment. Learning influences individual behaviour and performance through ability, role perceptions and motivation. Some learning results in explicit knowledge, which can be verbally transferred between people. But much of what we learn is tacit knowledge, which is embedded in our actions without conscious awareness.

The behaviour modification perspective of learning states that behaviour change occurs by altering the behaviour's antecedents and consequences. Antecedents are environmental stimuli that provoke (not necessarily cause) behaviour. Consequences are events following behaviour that influence its future occurrence. Consequences include positive reinforcement, punishment, negative reinforcement and extinction. The schedules of reinforcement also influence behaviour.

Social learning theory states that much learning occurs by observing others and then modelling those behaviours that seem to lead to favourable outcomes and avoiding behaviours that lead to punishing consequences. It also recognises that people often engage in self-reinforcement. Behaviour modelling is effective because it transfers tacit knowledge and enhances the observer's confidence in performing the task.

Many companies now use experiential learning because employees do not acquire tacit knowledge through formal classroom instruction. Kolb's experiential learning model is a cyclical four-stage process that includes concrete experience, reflective observation, abstract conceptualisation and active experimentation. Action learning is experiential learning in which employees investigate and act on significant organisational issues.

KEY TERMS

action learning p. 91
attribution process p. 78
behaviour modification p. 85
categorical thinking p. 72
contact hypothesis p. 77
empathy p. 83
extinction p. 86
fundamental attribution error p. 79
halo effect p. 82
Johari Window p. 83

learning p. 84
learning orientation p. 91
mental models p. 72
negative reinforcement p. 86
perception p. 70
positive reinforcement p. 86
prejudice p. 77
primacy effect p. 82
projection bias p. 82
punishment p. 86

recency effect p. 82
selective attention p. 71
self-fulfilling prophecy p. 80
self-reinforcement p. 89
self-serving bias p. 79
social identity theory p. 73
social learning theory p. 87
stereotyping p. 75
tacit knowledge p. 85

DISCUSSION QUESTIONS

1. You are part of a task force to increase worker responsiveness to emergencies on the production floor. Identify four factors to be considered when installing a device that will get every employee's attention in an emergency.

2. What mental models do you have about attending a college or university lecture? Are these mental models helpful? Could any of these mental models hold you back from achieving the full benefit of the lecture?

3. Contrast 'personal' and 'social' identity. Do you define yourself in terms of the university or college you attend? Why or why not? What implications does your response have for the future of your university or college?

4. During a diversity management session, a manager suggests that stereotypes are a necessary part of working with others. 'I have to make assumptions about what's in the other person's head, and stereotypes help me do that,' she explains. 'It's better to rely on stereotypes than to enter a working relationship with someone from another culture without any idea of what they believe in!' Discuss the merits of and problems with the manager's statement.

5. Several studies have reported that self-serving bias occurs in corporate annual reports. What does this mean and how would it be apparent in these reports? Provide hypothetical examples of self-serving bias in these documents.

6. Describe how a manager or coach could use the process of self-fulfilling prophecy to enhance an individual's performance.

7. Describe a situation in which you used behaviour modification to influence someone's behaviour. What specifically did you do? What was the result?

8. Why are organisations moving towards the use of experiential approaches to learning? What conditions are required for success?

| SKILL BUILDER | 3.1 | FROM LIPPERT-JOHANSON INC. TO FENWAY |

CASE STUDY

By Lisa V. Williams, Jeewon Cho and Alicia Boisnier, SUNY at Buffalo

PART ONE

Catherine O'Neill was very excited to finally be graduating from Flagship University at the end of the semester. She had always been interested in accounting, following from her father's lifelong occupation, and she very much enjoyed the challenging major. She was involved in many highly regarded student clubs in the business school and worked diligently to earn good grades. Now her commitment to the profession would pay off, she hoped, as she turned her attention to her job search. In late autumn she had on-campus interviews with several firms, but her interview with the prestigious Lippert-Johanson Incorporated (LJI) stood out in her mind as the most attractive opportunity. That's why Catherine was thrilled to learn she had made it to the next level of interviews, to be held at the firm's main office later that month.

When Catherine entered the elegant lobby of LJI's New York City offices, she was immediately impressed by all there was to take in. Catherine had always been one to pay attention to detail, and her acute observations of her environment had been an asset. She was able to see how social and environmental cues told her what was expected of her, and she always set out to meet and exceed those expectations. On a tour of the office, she had already begun to size up her prospective workplace. She appreciated the quiet, focused work atmosphere. She liked how everyone was dressed: most wore suits and their conservative apparel supported the professional attitudes that seemed to be omnipresent. People spoke to her in a formal but friendly manner, and seemed enthusiastic. Some of them even took the time to greet her as she was guided to the conference room for her individual interviews. 'I like the way this place feels and I would love to come to work here every day,' Catherine thought.

Before she knew it, Catherine was sitting in a nicely appointed office with one of the eight managers in the firm. Sandra Jacobs was the picture of a professional woman, and Catherine naturally took her cue from her about how to conduct herself in the interview. The time seemed to go very quickly, although the interview lasted an hour. As soon as Catherine left the office, she could not wait to phone her father about the interview. 'I loved it there and I just know I'm a good fit!' she told her proud father. 'Like them, I believe it is important to have the highest ethical standards and quality of work. Ms Jacobs really emphasised the mission of the firm, as well as its policies. She did say that all the candidates have an excellent skill set and are well qualified for the job, so mostly they are going to base their hiring decision on how well they think each of us will fit into the firm. Reputation is everything to an accounting firm. I learned that from you, Dad!'

After six weeks of apprehensive waiting, Catherine's efforts were rewarded when LJI and another firm contacted her with job offers. Catherine knew she would accept the offer from LJI. She saw the firm as very ethical, with the highest standards for work quality, and an excellent reputation. Catherine was grateful to have been selected from such a competitive hiring process. 'There couldn't be a better choice for me. I'm so proud to become a member of this company!'

Catherine's first few days at LJI were a whirlwind of a newcomer's experiences. She had meetings with her supervisor to discuss the firm mission statement, her role in the firm and what was expected of her. She was also told to spend some time looking at the employee handbook that covers many important policies of the firm, such as dress code, sick time, grievances, the chain of command and job descriptions, and professional ethics. Everyone relied on the handbook to provide clear guidance about what is expected of each employee. Also, Catherine was informed that she would soon begin participating in continuing professional education, which would allow her to update her skills and knowledge in her field. 'This is great,' thought Catherine. 'I'm so glad to know that the firm doesn't just talk about its high standards, it actually follows through with action.'

What Catherine enjoyed most about her new job were her warm and welcoming colleagues who invited her to their group lunches from her first day. They talked about work and home; they seemed close, both professionally and personally. She could see that everyone had a similar attitude towards work: they cared about their work and the firm, they took responsibility for their own tasks, but they also helped one another out. Catherine also got involved in LJI activities outside of work, such as their baseball and soccer teams, happy hours, picnics and parties, and she enjoyed the chance to mingle with her co-workers. In what seemed like no time at all, Catherine started to really see herself as a fully integrated member of LJI.

Before the tax season started, Catherine attended some meetings of the AICPA and other professional accounting societies. There, she met many accountants from other firms who all seemed very impressed when she told them where she worked. Catherine's pride in being a member of LJI grew as she realised how highly regarded the firm is among others in the accounting industry.

PART TWO

For the next seven years, Catherine's career in New York flourished. Her reputation as one of the top tax accountants in her company was well established, and was recognised by colleagues outside the firm as well. However, Catherine entered a new chapter of her life when she married Ted

Lewis, an oncology intern, who could not turn down an offer of residency at a top cancer centre in upstate New York. Wanting to support Ted's once-in-a-lifetime career opportunity, Catherine decided it was time to follow the path of many of her colleagues and leave public accounting for a position that would be more conducive to starting a family. Still, her heart was in the profession, so she took a position as a controller of a small recycling company located a few miles from home. She knew that with this position she could have children and still maintain her career.

Fenway Waste Management is small—about thirty-five employees. There are twenty-five people who work in the warehouse, three administrative assistants, two supervisors, and five people in management. Catherine is finding that she has to adjust to her new position and surroundings. Often she finds herself doing work that formally belongs to someone else; because it is a smaller company managers seem to 'wear many hats'. This is quite different from what she had experienced at LJI. In addition, the warehousemen often have to work with greasy materials, and sometimes track the grease into the offices. Catherine half-laughed and half-worried when she saw a piece of paper pinned to the wall that said 'Clean Up After Yourself!' She supposed that the nature of the business was why the offices are functional, but furnished with old pieces. She couldn't imagine having a business meeting in the office! Also, for most of the employees the casual dress matches the casual attitudes. But Catherine continues to wear a dressed-down version of her formal LJI attire, even though her new co-workers consider her overdressed.

With all the changes that Catherine has experienced, she has maintained one familiar piece of her past. Although it is not required for her new position, Catherine still attends AICPA meetings and makes a point of continuing to update her knowledge of current tax laws. At this year's conference, she told a former colleague, 'Being here, I feel so much more like myself. I am so much more connected to these people and this environment than to those at my new job. It's too bad I don't feel this way at Fenway. I guess I'm just more comfortable with professionals who are similar to me.'

QUESTIONS

PART 1

1. Discuss the social identity issues present in this case.

2. What indicated Catherine's positive evaluation of the groups described in Part 1? How did her evaluations foster her social identity?

3. What theory helps us understand how Catherine learned about appropriate behaviours at Lippert-Johanson Incorporated?

PART 2

1. Compare and contrast Lippert-Johanson Incorporated and Fenway Waste Management.

2. What was Catherine's reaction after joining Fenway and why was her level of social identification different from that of LJI?

3. Is there evidence that Catherine experienced the categorisation–homogenisation–differentiation process? What details support your conclusion?

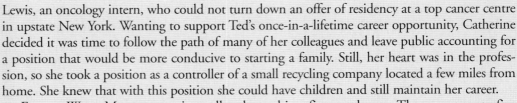

SKILL BUILDER | 3.2   THE LEARNING EXERCISE

CLASS EXERCISE

PURPOSE

This exercise is designed to help you understand how the contingencies of reinforcement in behaviour modification affect learning.

MATERIALS

Any objects normally available in a classroom will be acceptable for this activity.

INSTRUCTIONS

The instructor will ask for three volunteers, who are then briefed outside the classroom. The instructor will spend a few minutes briefing the remaining students in the class about their duties. Then, one of the three volunteers will enter the room to participate in the exercise. When this stage is completed, the second volunteer enters the room and participates in the exercise. When this stage is completed, the third volunteer enters the class and participates in the exercise.

For students to gain the full benefit of this exercise, no other information will be provided here. However, your instructor will have the necessary details to conduct this entertaining activity.

WHO AM I?

3.3 | SKILL BUILDER

TEAM EXERCISE

PURPOSE

This exercise is designed to help you understand the elements and implications of social identity theory.

INSTRUCTIONS

Step 1: Working alone (no discussion with other students), use the space provided below or a piece of paper to write down twelve words or phrases that answer the question 'Who am I?' Write your words or phrases as they come to mind; don't worry about their logical order here. Be sure to fill in all twelve spaces.

Phrases that describe you	Circle S or P
1. I am _____	S P
2. I am _____	S P
3. I am _____	S P
4. I am _____	S P
5. I am _____	S P
6. I am _____	S P
7. I am _____	S P
8. I am _____	S P
9. I am _____	S P
10. I am _____	S P
11. I am _____	S P
12. I am _____	S P

Step 2: Circle the 'S' beside the items that define you in terms of your social identity, such as your demographics and formal or informal membership of a social group or institution (school, company, religious group). Circle the 'P' beside the items that define you in terms of your personal identity; that is, your unique personality, values or experiences that are not connected to any particular social group. Next, underline one or more items that you believe will still be a strong characteristic of you ten years from now.

Sources: M. H. Kuhn and T. S. McPartland, 'An Empirical Investigation of Self-Attitudes', *American Sociological Review*, 19 (February 1954), 68–76; C. Lay and M. Verkuyten, 'Ethnic Identity and Its Relation to Personal Self-Esteem: A Comparison of Canadian-Born and Foreign-Born Chinese Adolescents', *Journal of Social Psychology*, 139 (1999), 288–99; S. L. Grace and K. L. Cramer, 'The Elusive Nature of Self-Measurement: The Self-Construal Scale versus the Twenty Statements Test', *Journal of Social Psychology*, 143 (2003), 649–68.

Step 3: Form small groups. If you have a team project for this course, your project team would work well for this exercise. Compare your list with the lists that others in your group wrote about themselves. Discuss the following questions in your group and prepare notes for class discussion and possible presentation of these questions:

1. Among members of this team, what was the typical percentage of items representing the person's social identity versus personal identity? Did some team members have many more or fewer social identity items compared with other team members? Why do you think these large or small differences in emphasis on social or personal identity occurred?
2. What characteristics did people in your group underline as being the most stable (i.e. remaining the same in ten years from now)? Were these underlined items mostly social or personal identity features? How similar or different were the underlined items among team members?
3. What do these lists say about the dynamics of your group as a team (whether or not your group for this activity is actually involved in a class project for this course)?

SKILL BUILDER | 3.4   ANALYSING CORPORATE ANNUAL REPORTS

WEB EXERCISE

PURPOSE

This exercise is designed to help you diagnose evidence of stereotyping and corporate role models that minimise stereotyping in corporate annual reports.

MATERIALS

Students need to complete their research for this activity prior to class, including selecting a publicly traded company and downloading the past four or more years of its fully illustrated annual reports.

INSTRUCTIONS

The instructor may have students work alone or in groups for this activity. Students will select a company that is publicly traded and that makes its annual reports available on the company website. Ideally, annual reports for at least the past four years should be available, and these reports should be presented in the final illustrated format (typically PDF replicas of the original hard-copy report).

Students will closely examine images in the selected company's recent annual reports in terms of how women, visible minorities and older employees and clients are presented. Specifically, students should be prepared to discuss and provide details in class regarding:

- The percentage of images showing (i.e. visual representation of) women, visible minorities and older workers and clients. Students should also be sensitive to the size and placement of these images on the page and throughout the annual report.
- The roles in which women, visible minorities and older workers and clients are depicted. For example, are women shown more in traditional or non-traditional occupations and non-work roles in these annual reports?
- If several years of annual reports are available, pick one that is a decade or more old and compare its visual representation of and role depiction of women, visible minorities and older employees and clients.

If possible, pick one of the most blatantly stereotypic illustrations you can find in these annual reports to show in class, either as a hard-copy printout or as a computer projection.

ASSESSING YOUR PERSONAL NEED FOR STRUCTURE

PURPOSE

This self-assessment is designed to help you to estimate your personal need for perceptual structure.

INSTRUCTIONS

Read each of the statements below and decide how much you agree with each according to your attitudes, beliefs and experiences. Then use the scoring key in Appendix B of this book to calculate your results. It is important for you to realise that there are no 'right' or 'wrong' answers to these questions. This self-assessment is completed alone so that students rate themselves honestly without concerns of social comparison. However, class discussion will focus on the meaning of the need for structure in terms of how we engage differently in the perceptual process at work and in other settings.

PERSONAL NEED FOR STRUCTURE SCALE

To what extent do you agree or disagree with each of these statements about yourself?	Strongly agree	Moderately agree	Slightly agree	Slightly disagree	Moderately disagree	Strongly disagree
1. It upsets me to go into a situation without knowing what I can expect from it.	❑	❑	❑	❑	❑	❑
2. I'm not bothered by things that interrupt my daily routine.	❑	❑	❑	❑	❑	❑
3. I enjoy being spontaneous.	❑	❑	❑	❑	❑	❑
4. I find that a well-ordered life with regular hours makes my life tedious.	❑	❑	❑	❑	❑	❑
5. I find that a consistent routine enables me to enjoy life more.	❑	❑	❑	❑	❑	❑
6. I enjoy having a clear and structured mode of life.	❑	❑	❑	❑	❑	❑
7. I like to have a place for every thing and everything in its place.	❑	❑	❑	❑	❑	❑
8. I don't like situations that are uncertain.	❑	❑	❑	❑	❑	❑
9. I hate to change my plans at the last minute.	❑	❑	❑	❑	❑	❑
10. I hate to be with people who are unpredictable.	❑	❑	❑	❑	❑	❑
11. I enjoy the exhilaration of being in unpredictable situations.	❑	❑	❑	❑	❑	❑
12. I become uncomfortable when the rules in a situation are not clear.	❑	❑	❑	❑	❑	❑

Source: M.M. Thompson, M.E. Naccarato and K. E. Parker, 'Assessing Cognitive Need: The Development of the Personal Need for Structure and the Personal Fear of Invalidity Scales', paper presented at the annual meeting of the Canadian Psychological Association, Halifax, Nova Scotia (1989).

| **SKILL BUILDER** | **3.6** | ASSESSING YOUR PERSPECTIVE-TAKING (COGNITIVE EMPATHY) |

SELF-ASSESSMENT

FULL EXERCISE ON
STUDENT CD

Empathy is an important perceptual ability in social relations, but the degree to which people empathise varies considerably. This self-assessment provides an estimate of one form of empathy, known as cognitive empathy or perspective-taking. This means that it measures the level of cognitive awareness of another person's situational and individual circumstances. To complete this scale, indicate the degree to which each of the statements presented does or does not describe you very well. You need to be honest with yourself in order to obtain a reasonable estimate of your level of perspective-taking. The results show your relative position along the perspective-taking continuum and the general meaning of this score.

| **SKILL BUILDER** | **3.7** | ASSESSING YOUR EMOTIONAL EMPATHY |

SELF-ASSESSMENT

FULL EXERCISE ON
STUDENT CD

Empathy is an important perceptual ability in social relations, but the degree to which people empathise varies considerably. This self-assessment provides an estimate of one form of empathy, known as emotional empathy. This refers to the extent to which you are able to experience the emotions or feelings of the other person. To complete this scale, indicate the degree to which each of the statements presented does or does not describe you very well. You need to be honest with yourself in order to obtain a reasonable estimate of your level of emotional empathy. The results show your relative position along the emotional empathy continuum and the general meaning of this score.

NOTES

1   N. Hooper, 'Call Me Irresistible', *Australian Financial Review*, 5 December 2003, 38; A. Ferguson, 'Free Radical', *Business Review Weekly*, 12 August 2004, 32; P. Vincent, 'Working—and Loving It', *Sydney Morning Herald*, 21 July 2004, 2; K. Capell, 'Ikea: How the Swedish Retailer Became a Global Cult Brand', *BusinessWeek*, 14 November 2005, 96; L. Morrell, 'Taking the Floor', *Retail Week*, 18 November 2005.

2   Plato, *The Republic*, trans. D. Lee (Harmondsworth, England: Penguin, 1955).

3   R. H. Fazio, D. R. Roskos-Ewoldsen and M. C. Powell, 'Attitudes, Perception, and Attention', in *The Heart's Eye: Emotional Influences in Perception and Attention*, ed. P. M. Niedenthal and S. Kitayama (San Diego, CA: Academic Press, 1994), 197–216.

4   The effect of the target in selective attention is known as 'bottom-up selection'; the effect of the perceiver's psychodynamics on this process is known as 'top-down selection'. C. E. Connor, H. E. Egeth and S. Yantis, 'Visual Attention: Bottom-up versus Top-Down', *Current Biology* 14, no. 19 (2004), R850–2.

5   A. Mack et al., 'Perceptual Organization and Attention', *Cognitive Psychology* 24, no. 4 (1992), 475–501; A. R. Damasio, *Descartes' Error: Emotion, Reason, and the Human Brain* (New York: Putnam Sons, 1994).

6   C. N. Macrae et al., 'Tales of the Unexpected: Executive Function and Person Perception', *Journal of Personality and Social Psychology* 76 (1999), 200–13; C. Frith, 'A Framework for Studying the Neural Basis of Attention', *Neuropsychologia* 39, no. 12 (2001), 1367–71; N. Lavie, 'Distracted and Confused? Selective Attention under Load', *Trends in Cognitive Sciences* 9, no. 2 (2005), 75–82.

7   D. J. Hall, 'The Justice System Isn't Always Just', *Capital Times & Wisconsin State Journal*, 27 November 2005, D1; D. Mclennan, 'Murdered Man "Just Getting Life on Track"', *Canberra Times*, 6 May 2005, 1.

8   C. N. Macrae and G. V. Bodenhausen, 'Social Cognition: Thinking Categorically About Others', *Annual Review of Psychology* 51 (2000), 93–120. For literature on the automaticity of the perceptual organisation and interpretation process, see: J. A. Bargh, 'The Cognitive Monster: The Case against the Controllability of Automatic Stereotype Effects', in *Dual Process Theories in Social Psychology*, ed. S. Chaiken and Y. Trope (New York: Guilford, 1999), 361–82; J. A. Bargh and M. J. Ferguson, 'Beyond Behaviorism: On the Automaticity of Higher Mental Processes', *Psychological Bulletin* 126, no. 6 (2000), 925–45; M. Gladwell, *Blink: The Power of Thinking Without Thinking* (New York: Little, Brown, 2005).

9   E. M. Altmann and B. D. Burns, 'Streak Biases in Decision Making: Data and a Memory Model', *Cognitive Systems Research* 6, no. 1 (2005), 5–16. For discussion of cognitive closure and perception, see: A. W. Kruglanski and D. M. Webster, 'Motivated Closing of the Mind: "Seizing" and "Freezing"', *Psychological Review* 103, no. 2 (1996), 263–83.

10   N. Ambady and R. Rosenthal, 'Half a Minute: Predicting Teacher Evaluations from Thin Slices of Nonverbal Behavior and Physical Attractiveness', *Journal of Personality and Social Psychology* 64, no. 3 (March 1993), 431–41. For other research on thin slices, see: N. Ambady and R. Rosenthal, 'Thin Slices of Expressive Behavior as Predictors of Interpersonal Consequences: A Meta-Analysis', *Psychological Bulletin* 111, no. 2 (1992), 256–74; N. Ambady et al.,

'Surgeons' Tone of Voice: A Clue to Malpractice History', *Surgery* 132, no. 1 (July 2002), 5–9.

11 P. M. Senge, *The Fifth Discipline: The Art and Practice of the Learning Organization* (New York: Doubleday Currency, 1990), chapter 10; P. N. Johnson-Laird, 'Mental Models and Deduction', *Trends in Cognitive Sciences* 5, no. 10 (2001), 434–42; A. B. Markman and D. Gentner, 'Thinking', *Annual Review of Psychology* 52 (2001), 223–47; T. J. Chermack, 'Mental Models in Decision Making and Implications for Human Resource Development', *Advances in Developing Human Resources* 5, no. 4 (2003), 408–22.

12 H. Tajfel, *Social Identity and Intergroup Relations* (Cambridge: Cambridge University Press, 1982); B. E. Ashforth and F. Mael, 'Social Identity Theory and the Organization', *Academy of Management Review* 14 (1989), 20–39; M. A. Hogg and D. J. Terry, 'Social Identity and Self-Categorization Processes in Organizational Contexts', *Academy of Management Review* 25 (January 2000), 121–40; S. A. Haslam, R. A. Eggins and K. J. Reynolds, 'The Aspire Model: Actualizing Social and Personal Identity Resources to Enhance Organizational Outcomes', *Journal of Occupational and Organizational Psychology* 76 (2003), 83–113. Although this topic is labelled 'social identity theory', it also incorporates an extension of social identity theory, called self-categorisation theory.

13 J. E. Dutton, J. M. Dukerich and C. V. Harquail, 'Organizational Images and Member Identification', *Administrative Science Quarterly* 39 (June 1994), 239–63; B. Simon and C. Hastedt, 'Self-Aspects as Social Categories: The Role of Personal Importance and Valence', *European Journal of Social Psychology* 29 (1999), 479–87.

14 M. A. Hogg et al., 'The Social Identity Perspective: Intergroup Relations, Self-Conception, and Small Groups', *Small Group Research* 35, no. 3 (June 2004), 246–76; J. Jetten, R. Spears and T. Postmes, 'Intergroup Distinctiveness and Differentiation: A Meta-Analytic Integration', *Journal of Personality and Social Psychology* 86, no. 6 (2004), 862–79.

15 J. W. Jackson and E. R. Smith, 'Conceptualizing Social Identity: A New Framework and Evidence for the Impact of Different Dimensions', *Personality & Social Psychology Bulletin* 25 (January 1999), 120–35.

16 L. Falkenberg, 'Improving the Accuracy of Stereotypes within the Workplace', *Journal of Management* 16 (1990), 107–18; S. T. Fiske, 'Stereotyping, Prejudice, and Discrimination', in *Handbook of Social Psychology*, ed. D. T. Gilbert, S. T. Fiske and G. Lindzey, 4th edn (New York: McGraw-Hill, 1998), 357–411; Macrae and Bodenhausen, 'Social Cognition: Thinking Categorically About Others'.

17 C. N. Macrae, A. B. Milne and G. V. Bodenhausen, 'Stereotypes as Energy-Saving Devices: A Peek inside the Cognitive Toolbox', *Journal of Personality and Social Psychology* 66 (1994), 37–47; J. W. Sherman et al., 'Stereotype Efficiency Reconsidered: Encoding Flexibility under Cognitive Load', *Journal of Personality and Social Psychology* 75 (1998), 589–606; Macrae and Bodenhausen, 'Social Cognition: Thinking Categorically About Others'.

18 L. Sinclair and Z. Kunda, 'Motivated Stereotyping of Women: She's Fine If She Praised Me but Incompetent If She Criticized Me', *Personality and Social Psychology Bulletin* 26 (November 2000), 1329–42; J. C. Turner and S. A. Haslam, 'Social Identity, Organizations, and Leadership', in *Groups at Work: Theory and Research*, ed. M. E. Turner (Mahwah, NJ: Lawrence Erlbaum Associates, 2001), 25–65.

19 Y. Lee, L. J. Jussim and C. R. McCauley, *Stereotype Accuracy: Toward Appreciating Group Differences* (Washington, DC: American Psychological Association, 1996); S. Madon et al., 'The Accuracy and Power of Sex, Social Class, and Ethnic Stereotypes: A Naturalistic Study in Person Perception', *Personality & Social Psychology Bulletin* 24

(December 1998), 1304–18; F. T. McAndrew, 'A Multicultural Study of Stereotyping in English-Speaking Countries', *Journal of Social Psychology* (August 2000), 487–502.

20 A. L. Friedman and S. R. Lyne, 'The Beancounter Stereotype: Towards a General Model of Stereotype Generation', *Critical Perspectives on Accounting* 12, no. 4 (2001), 423–51.

21 D. Farrant, 'And the Verdict Is … Sexist as Charged', *The Age* (Melbourne), 16 December 2000; M. Priest, 'High Court Pressure for Female Judge', *Australian Financial Review*, 10 November 2004, 1; F. Buffini, 'Boys' Club Still Alive and Well', *Australian Financial Review*, 22 October 2005, 22; E. Kazi, 'Clock Drives Women to Early Highs', *Australian Financial Review*, 21 October 2005, 25.

22 S. O. Gaines and E. S. Reed, 'Prejudice: From Allport to Dubois', *American Psychologist* 50 (February 1995): 96–103; Fiske, 'Stereotyping, Prejudice, and Discrimination'; M. Billig, 'Henri Tajfel's "Cognitive Aspects of Prejudice" and the Psychology of Bigotry', *British Journal of Social Psychology* 41 (2002), 171–88; M. Hewstone, M. Rubin and H. Willis, 'Intergroup Bias', *Annual Review of Psychology* 53 (2002), 575–604.

23 I. Gerard, 'Rotten to the Corps', *Australian*, 19 November 2004, 11; 'Army Chief's Warning KKK Photo May Lead to Officers' Dismissals', *Townsville Bulletin*, 25 June 2005, 7; L. McIlveen, 'Families Fear Cover-up of Racism in the Ranks', *Courier-Mail* (Brisbane), 16 June 2005, 13; L. McIlveen, 'Army Officers' Nude Shame', *Daily Telegraph* (Sydney), 1 December 2005, 9; M. Weatherup, 'Racist Website Probe Ongoing', *Townsville Bulletin*, 10 February 2005, 7.

24 J. A. Bargh and T. L. Chartrand, 'The Unbearable Automaticity of Being', *American Psychologist* 54, no. 7 (July 1999), 462–79; S. T. Fiske, 'What We Know Now About Bias and Intergroup Conflict, the Problem of the Century', *Current Directions in Psychological Science* 11, no. 4 (August 2002), 123–8. For recent evidence that shows that intensive training can minimise stereotype activation, see: K. Kawakami et al., 'Just Say No (to Stereotyping): Effects of Training in the Negation of Stereotypic Associations on Stereotype Activation', *Journal of Personality and Social Psychology* 78, no. 5 (2000), 871–88; E. A. Plant, B. M. Peruche and D. A. Butz, 'Eliminating Automatic Racial Bias: Making Race Non-Diagnostic for Responses to Criminal Suspects', *Journal of Experimental Social Psychology* 41, no. 2 (2005), 141–56.

25 M. Bendick, M. L. Egan and S. M. Lofhjelm, 'Workforce Diversity Training: From Anti-Discrimination Compliance to Organizational Development HR', *Human Resource Planning* 24 (2001), 10–25; L. Roberson, C. T. Kulik and M. B. Pepper, 'Using Needs Assessment to Resolve Controversies in Diversity Training Design', *Group & Organization Management* 28, no. 1 (March 2003), 148–74; D. E. Hogan and M. Mallott, 'Changing Racial Prejudice through Diversity Education', *Journal of College Student Development* 46, no. 2 (March/April 2005), 115–25.

26 T. F. Pettigrew, 'Intergroup Contact Theory', *Annual Review of Psychology* 49 (1998), 65–85; S. Brickson, 'The Impact of Identity Orientation on Individual and Organizational Outcomes in Demographically Diverse Settings', *Academy of Management Review* 25 (January 2000), 82–101; J. Dixon and K. Durrheim, 'Contact and the Ecology of Racial Division: Some Varieties of Informal Segregation', *British Journal of Social Psychology* 42 (March 2003), 1–23.

27 B. F. Reskin, 'The Proximate Causes of Employment Discrimination', *Contemporary Sociology* 29 (March 2000), 319–28.

28 H. H. Kelley, *Attribution in Social Interaction* (Morristown, NJ: General Learning Press, 1971).

29 J. M. Feldman, 'Beyond Attribution Theory: Cognitive Processes in Performance Appraisal', *Journal of Applied Psychology* 66 (1981), 127–48.

30   J. M. Crant and T. S. Bateman, 'Assignment of Credit and Blame for Performance Outcomes', *Academy of Management Journal* 36 (1993), 7–27; B. Weiner, 'Intrapersonal and Interpersonal Theories of Motivation from an Attributional Perspective', *Educational Psychology Review* 12 (2000), 1–14; N. Bacon and P. Blyton, 'Worker Responses to Teamworking: Exploring Employee Attributions of Managerial Motives', *International Journal of Human Resource Management* 16, no. 2 (February 2005), 238–55.

31   Fundamental attribution error is part of a larger phenomenon known as correspondence bias. See: D. T. Gilbert and P. S. Malone, 'The Correspondence Bias', *Psychological Bulletin* 117, no. 1 (1995), 21–38.

32   I. Choi, R. E. Nisbett and A. Norenzayan, 'Causal Attribution across Cultures: Variation and Universality', *Psychological Bulletin* 125, no. 1 (1999), 47–63; D. S. Krull et al., 'The Fundamental Fundamental Attribution Error: Correspondence Bias in Individualist and Collectivist Cultures', *Personality and Social Psychology Bulletin* 25, no. 10 (October 1999), 1208–19; R. E. Nisbett, *The Geography of Thought: How Asians and Westerners Think Differently—and Why* (New York: Free Press, 2003), chapter 5.

33   P. Rosenthal and D. Guest, 'Gender Difference in Managers' Causal Explanations for Their Work Performance: A Study in Two Organizations', *Journal of Occupational & Organizational Psychology* 69 (1996), 145–51. The New Zealand performance ratings study is reported in: P. J. Taylor and J. L. Pierce, 'Effects of Introducing a Performance Management System on Employees' Subsequent Attitudes and Effort', *Public Personnel Management* 28 (Fall 1999), 423–52.

34   F. Lee and L. Z. Tiedens, 'Who's Being Served? "Self-Serving" Attributions in Social Hierarchies', *Organizational Behavior and Human Decision Processes* 84, no. 2 (2001), 254–87; E. W. K. Tsang, 'Self-Serving Attributions in Corporate Annual Reports: A Replicated Study', *Journal of Management Studies* 39, no. 1 (January 2002), 51–65.

35   Similar models are presented in D. Eden, 'Self-Fulfilling Prophecy as a Management Tool: Harnessing Pygmalion', *Academy of Management Review* 9 (1984), 64–73; R. H. G. Field and D. A. Van Seters, 'Management by Expectations (MBE): The Power of Positive Prophecy', *Journal of General Management* 14 (Winter 1988): 19–33; D. O. Trouilloud et al., 'The Influence of Teacher Expectations on Student Achievement in Physical Education Classes: Pygmalion Revisited', *European Journal of Social Psychology* 32 (2002), 591–607.

36   D. Eden, 'Interpersonal Expectations in Organizations', in *Interpersonal Expectations: Theory, Research, and Applications* (Cambridge, UK: Cambridge University Press, 1993), 154–78.

37   D. Eden, 'Pygmalion Goes to Boot Camp: Expectancy, Leadership, and Trainee Performance', *Journal of Applied Psychology* 67 (1982), 194–9; R. P. Brown and E. C. Pinel, 'Stigma on My Mind: Individual Differences in the Experience of Stereotype Threat', *Journal of Experimental Social Psychology* 39, no. 6 (2003), 626–33.

38   A. R. Remo, 'Nurture the Good to Create an Asset', *Philippine Daily Inquirer*, 6 December 2004.

39   S. Madon et al., 'Self-Fulfilling Prophecies: The Synergistic Accumulative Effect of Parents' Beliefs on Children's Drinking Behavior', *Psychological Science* 15, no. 12 (2005), 837–45; A. E. Smith, L. Jussim and J. Eccles, 'Do Self-Fulfilling Prophecies Accumulate, Dissipate, or Remain Stable over Time?', *Journal of Personality and Social Psychology* 77, no. 3 (1999), 548–65.

40   S. Madon, L. Jussim and J. Eccles, 'In Search of the Powerful Self-Fulfilling Prophecy', *Journal of Personality and Social Psychology* 72, no. 4 (April 1997), 791–809.

41   D. Eden et al., 'Implanting Pygmalion Leadership Style through Workshop Training: Seven Field Experiments', *Leadership Quarterly* 11 (2000), 171–210; S. S. White and E. A. Locke, 'Problems with the

Pygmalion Effect and Some Proposed Solutions', *Leadership Quarterly* 11 (Autumn 2000), 389–415; H. A. Wilkinson, 'Hope, False Hope, and Self-Fulfilling Prophecy', *Surgical Neurology* 63, no. 1 (2005), 84–86. For literature on positive organisational behaviour, see: K. Cameron, J. E. Dutton and R. E. Quinn, *Positive Organizational Scholarship: Foundations of a New Discipline* (San Francisco: Berrett Koehler, 2003).

42   C. L. Kleinke, *First Impressions: The Psychology of Encountering Others* (Englewood Cliffs, NJ: Prentice Hall, 1975); E. A. Lind, L. Kray and L. Thompson, 'Primacy Effects in Justice Judgments: Testing Predictions from Fairness Heuristic Theory', *Organizational Behavior and Human Decision Processes* 85 (July 2001), 189–210; O. Ybarra, 'When First Impressions Don't Last: The Role of Isolation and Adaptation Processes in the Revision of Evaluative Impressions', *Social Cognition* 19 (October 2001), 491–520.

43   D. D. Steiner and J. S. Rain, 'Immediate and Delayed Primacy and Recency Effects in Performance Evaluation', *Journal of Applied Psychology* 74 (1989), 136–42; K. T. Trotman, 'Order Effects and Recency: Where Do We Go from Here?', *Accounting & Finance* 40 (2000), 169–82; W. Green, 'Impact of the Timing of an Inherited Explanation on Auditors' Analytical Procedures Judgements', *Accounting and Finance* 44 (2004), 369–92.

44   W. H. Cooper, 'Ubiquitous Halo', *Psychological Bulletin* 90 (1981), 218–44; K. R. Murphy, R. A. Jako and R. L. Anhalt, 'Nature and Consequences of Halo Error: A Critical Analysis', *Journal of Applied Psychology* 78 (1993), 218–25; T. H. Feeley, 'Comment on Halo Effects in Rating and Evaluation Research', *Human Communication Research* 28, no. 4 (October 2002), 578–86.

45   G. G. Sherwood, 'Self-Serving Biases in Person Perception: A Re-Examination of Projection as a Mechanism of Defense', *Psychological Bulletin* 90 (1981), 445–59; R. L. Gross and S. E. Brodt, 'How Assumptions of Consensus Undermine Decision Making', *Sloan Management Review* (January 2001), 86–94.

46   C. Duan and C. E. Hill, 'The Current State of Empathy Research', *Journal of Counseling Psychology* 43 (1996), 261–74; W. G. Stephen and K. A. Finlay, 'The Role of Empathy in Improving Intergroup Relations', *Journal of Social Issues* 55 (Winter 1999), 729–43; S. K. Parker and C. M. Axtell, 'Seeing Another Viewpoint: Antecedents and Outcomes of Employee Perspective Taking', *Academy of Management Journal* 44 (December 2001), 1085–100; G. J. Vreeke and I. L. van der Mark, 'Empathy, an Integrative Model', *New Ideas in Psychology* 21, no. 3 (2003), 177–207.

47   D. Goleman, R. Boyatzis and A. McKee, *The New Leaders* (London: Little, Brown, 2002).

48   T. W. Costello and S. S. Zalkind, *Psychology in Administration: A Research Orientation* (Englewood Cliffs, NJ: Prentice Hall, 1963), pp. 45–6; J. M. Kouzes and B. Z. Posner, *The Leadership Challenge*, 3rd edn (San Francisco: Jossey-Bass, 2002), chapter 3.

49   J. Luft, *Group Processes* (Palo Alto, Calif: Mayfield Publishing, 1984). For a variation of this model, see: J. Hall, 'Communication Revisited', *California Management Review* 15 (Spring 1973), 56–67.

50   L. C. Miller and D. A. Kenny, 'Reciprocity of Self-Disclosure at the Individual and Dyadic Levels: A Social Relations Analysis', *Journal of Personality and Social Psychology* 50 (1986), 713–19.

51   'Wipro: Leadership in the Midst of Rapid Growth', *Knowledge@Wharton*, February 2005.

52   I. Nonaka and H. Takeuchi, *The Knowledge-Creating Company* (New York: Oxford University Press, 1995); E. N. Brockmann and W. P. Anthony, 'Tacit Knowledge and Strategic Decision Making', *Group & Organization Management* 27 (December 2002), 436–55; P. Duguid, '"The Art of Knowing": Social and Tacit Dimensions

of Knowledge and the Limits of the Community of Practice', *The Information Society* 21 (2005), 109–18.

53 B. F. Skinner, *About Behaviorism* (New York: Alfred A. Knopf, 1974); J. Komaki, T. Coombs and S. Schepman, 'Motivational Implications of Reinforcement Theory', in *Motivation and Leadership at Work*, ed. R. M. Steers, L. W. Porter and G. A. Bigley (New York: McGraw-Hill, 1996), 34–52; R. G. Miltenberger, *Behavior Modification: Principles and Procedures* (Pacific Grove, CA: Brooks/Cole, 1997).

54 T. K. Connellan, *How to Improve Human Performance* (New York: Harper & Row, 1978), pp. 48–57; F. Luthans and R. Kreitner, *Organizational Behavior Modification and Beyond* (Glenview, Ill.: Scott, Foresman, 1985), pp. 85–8.

55 Miltenberger, *Behavior Modification: Principles and Procedures*, chapters 4–6.

56 Punishment can also include removing a pleasant consequence, such as when employees must switch from business to economy class flying when their sales fall below the threshold for top-tier sales 'stars'.

57 T. R. Hinkin and C. A. Schriesheim, '"If You Don't Hear from Me You Know You Are Doing Fine"', *Cornell Hotel & Restaurant Administration Quarterly* 45, no. 4 (November 2004), 362–72.

58 L. K. Trevino, 'The Social Effects of Punishment in Organizations: A Justice Perspective', *Academy of Management Review* 17 (1992), 647–76; L. E. Atwater et al., 'Recipient and Observer Reactions to Discipline: Are Managers Experiencing Wishful Thinking?', *Journal of Organizational Behavior* 22, no. 3 (May 2001), 249–70.

59 G. P. Latham and V. L. Huber, 'Schedules of Reinforcement: Lessons from the Past and Issues for the Future', *Journal of Organizational Behavior Management* 13 (1992), 125–49; B. A. Williams, 'Challenges to Timing-Based Theories of Operant Behavior', *Behavioural Processes* 62 (April 2003), 115–23.

60 S. Nixon, 'The Secret to Success Is a Contented Volunteer', *Sydney Morning Herald*, 15 September 2000, p. 15.

61 T. C. Mawhinney, 'Philosophical and Ethical Aspects of Organizational Behavior Management: Some Evaluative Feedback', *Journal of Organizational Behavior Management* 6 (Spring 1984), 5–13; G. A. Merwin, J. A. Thomason and E. E. Sandford, 'A Methodological and Content Review of Organizational Behavior Management in the Private Sector: 1978–1986', *Journal of Organizational Behavior Management* 10 (1989), 39–57; 'New Warnings on the Fine Points of Safety Incentives', *Pay for Performance Report*, September 2002.

62 Bargh and Ferguson, 'Beyond Behaviorism: On the Automaticity of Higher Mental Processes'. Some writers argue that behaviourists long ago accepted the relevance of cognitive processes in behaviour modification. See: I. Kirsch et al., 'The Role of Cognition in Classical and Operant Conditioning', *Journal of Clinical Psychology* 60, no. 4 (April 2004), 369–92.

63 A. Bandura, *Social Foundations of Thought and Action: A Social Cognitive Theory* (Englewood Cliffs, NJ: Prentice Hall, 1986).

64 A. Pescuric and W. C. Byham, 'The New Look of Behavior Modeling', *Training & Development* 50 (July 1996), 24–30.

65 M. E. Schnake, 'Vicarious Punishment in a Work Setting', *Journal of Applied Psychology* 71 (1986), 343–5; Trevino, 'The Social Effects of Punishment in Organizations: A Justice Perspective'; J. B. DeConinck, 'The Effect of Punishment on Sales Managers' Outcome Expectancies and Responses to Unethical Sales Force Behavior', *American Business Review* 21, no. 2 (June 2003), 135–40.

66 A. Bandura, 'Self-Reinforcement: Theoretical and Methodological Considerations', *Behaviorism* 4 (1976), 135–55; C. A. Frayne and J. M. Geringer, 'Self-Management Training for Improving Job Performance: A Field Experiment Involving Salespeople', *Journal of Applied Psychology* 85, no. 3 (June 2000), 361–72; J. B. Vancouver and D. V. Day, 'Industrial and Organisation Research on Self-Regulation: From Constructs to Applications', *Applied Psychology* 54, no. 2 (April 2005), 155–85.

67 D. Woodruff, 'Putting Talent to the Test', *Wall Street Journal Europe*, 14 November 2000, 25. The simulation events described here were experienced by the author of this article, but it is reasonable to assume that Mandy Chooi, who also completed the simulation, experienced similar scenarios.

68 D. A. Kolb, *Experiential Learning* (Englewood Cliffs, NJ: Prentice Hall, 1984); S. Gherardi, D. Nicolini and F. Odella, 'Toward a Social Understanding of How People Learn in Organizations', *Management Learning* 29 (September 1998), 273–97; D. A. Kolb, R. E. Boyatzis and C. Mainemelis, 'Experiential Learning Theory: Previous Research and New Directions', in *Perspectives on Thinking, Learning, and Cognitive Styles*, ed. R. J. Sternberg and L. F. Zhang (Mahwah, NJ: Lawrence Erlbaum, 2001), 227–48.

69 I. Teotonio, 'Rescuers Pull "Victims" from Rubble', *Toronto Star*, 8 April 2005, B01, B03.

70 J. Jusko, 'Always Lessons to Learn', *Industry Week* (15 February 1999), 23; R. Farson and R. Keyes, 'The Failure-Tolerant Leader', *Harvard Business Review* 80 (August 2002), 64–71.

71 R. W. Revans, *The Origin and Growth of Action Learning* (London: Chartwell Bratt, 1982), pp. 626–7; M. J. Marquardt, *Optimizing the Power of Action Learning: Solving Problems and Building Leaders in Real Time* (Palo Alto, CA: Davies-Black, 2004).

72 J. A. Conger and K. Xin, 'Executive Education in the 21st Century', *Journal of Management Education* (February 2000), 73–101; R. M. Fulmer, P. Gibbs and M. Goldsmith, 'Developing Leaders: How Winning Companies Keep on Winning', *Sloan Management Review* (October 2000), 49–59; 'Strategies Needed to Nurture Top Talent', *South China Morning Post* (Hong Kong), 7 August 2004, 4; M. J. Marquardt, 'Harnessing the Power of Action Learning', *T+D*, June 2004, 26–32.

CHAPTER 4

Workplace emotions and attitudes

LEARNING OBJECTIVES

After reading this chapter, you should be able to:

- define emotions and identify the two dimensions around which emotions are organised

- explain how cognitions and emotions influence attitudes and behaviour

- identify the conditions that require emotional labour and the problems associated with it

- describe the four dimensions of emotional intelligence

- summarise the effects of job dissatisfaction in terms of the exit-voice-loyalty-neglect model

- discuss the relationships between job satisfaction and performance as well as job satisfaction and customer satisfaction

- compare the effects of affective and continuance commitment on employee behaviour

- describe five strategies to increase organisational commitment

- contrast transactional and relational psychological contracts.

Along with creating a fun-oriented workplace, Warner Village Theme Parks on Australia's Gold Coast hires staff for their fun-oriented style, which results in happier customers.

Employees seem to enjoy themselves as much as the visitors at Warner Village Theme Parks on Queensland's Gold Coast. The human resources staff of Warner Village Theme Parks say this mutual glee is no accident. 'We hire people who have the potential to have a guest service attitude, and then we train them with skills,' explains Learning and Development Co-ordinator Tony Butler. Shaun McKeogh (Culture and People Development Manager), another Warner Village Theme Parks training specialist, adds that staff members do not follow a prepared script when interacting with guests. Instead, corporate leaders believe that when employees feel happy, so will the guests. 'The guests expect [the park] to be a fun place filled with fun-loving people, [so] we give permission for people to laugh and have fun.'

Fun at work? Sounds like an oxymoron, even at a theme park. But corporate leaders in many industries are realising that generating positive emotions in the workplace pays off in lower employee turnover and better customer service. For example, work seems to be a never-ending party at Auckland radio station MORE FM, where a disco ball hangs from the boardroom ceiling. ANZ's building for call centre and consumer finance staff in Melbourne includes a garden and barbeque area, as well as a play area with air hockey, pinball and snooker. The Malaysian operations of Scope International, a division of British bank Standard Chartered, won an award for bringing fun into the workplace, such as colour coordination days, in which employees wear the same colour of clothing on a particular day.

Cadbury Schweppes Australia turned up the fun meter while also helping the community. The company launched Project Giggles, a surprise campaign to raise funds for The Humour Foundation and boost morale at a time of significant change. The national charity promotes the health benefits of humour, including the work of Clown Doctors who visit hospitals throughout Australia. The philosophy and humour and laughter fits neatly with Cadbury Schweppes' desire to ensure people enjoying working for them, so the uplifting nature of the cause presented a unique opportunity to unite staff in a fun and exciting way. The campaign was launched at key sites with a staff party, featuring balloons, treats, and senior executives dressed in Clown Doctor outfits to encourage everyone to get involved. Fundraising teams, called smile committees, raised funds through 'Cadbury Idol' talent competitions, apple-bobbing competitions, raffle prizes to win a day off work, factory tours and other innovative methods. Not only did employees have fun raising more money than anyone expected (which was matched by Cadbury Schweppes) but they also developed good feelings from Project Giggles' ultimate community value.

These fun and games may seem silly, but some corporate leaders are deadly serious about their value. 'If you want to deliver a good service, you need to create an environment where that can flourish,' says Nigel Malcolm, founder and managing director of Australian fleet management company Fleetcare. 'Don't make it a drag. Have some fun!' '

WORKPLACE EMOTIONS AND ATTITUDES are receiving a lot more attention these days at Cadbury Schweppes, at Warner Village and in many other organisations. This is because emotions and attitudes can make a huge difference to individual behaviour and well-being, as well as to the organisation's performance and customer satisfaction. Over the past decade the field of organisational behaviour has experienced a sea change in thinking about workplace emotions, so this chapter begins by introducing the concept and explaining why researchers are so eager to discover how emotions influence attitudes and behaviour.

Next, the dynamics of emotional labour are considered, including the conditions requiring emotional labour. This is followed by the popular topic of emotional intelligence, in which the components of emotional intelligence and ways of improving this ability are examined. The specific work attitudes of job satisfaction and organisational commitment are then discussed, including their association with various employee behaviours and work performance. Organisational commitment is strongly influenced by the psychological contract, so the final section of the chapter looks briefly at this topic.

EMOTIONS IN THE WORKPLACE

LEARNING OBJECTIVE

Define emotions and identify the two dimensions around which emotions are organised.

Emotions have a profound effect on almost everything we do in the workplace. This is a strong statement, and one that you would rarely find a decade ago in organisational behaviour research or textbooks. For most of its history, the field of organisational behaviour assumed that a person's thoughts and actions were governed primarily by conscious reasoning (called *cognitions*). Yet groundbreaking neuroscience discoveries have revealed that our perceptions, attitudes, decisions and behaviour are influenced by both cognition and emotion, and that the latter often has the greater influence. By ignoring emotionality, many theories have overlooked a large piece of the puzzle about human behaviour in the workplace. Today, organisational behaviour researchers and their colleagues in marketing, economics and many other social sciences are catching up by making emotions a key part of their research and theories.[2]

emotions The feelings experienced towards an object, person or event that create a state of readiness.

So, what are emotions? **Emotions** are physiological, behavioural and psychological episodes experienced towards an object, person or event that create a state of readiness.[3] There are four key elements of this definition. First, emotions are brief events or 'episodes'. Your irritation with a customer, for instance, would typically subside within a few minutes. Second, emotions are directed towards someone or something. We experience joy, fear, anger and other emotional episodes in relation to tasks, customers, public speeches we present, a software program we are using, and so on. This contrasts with *moods*, which are less intense emotional states that are not directed towards anything in particular.[4]

Third, emotions are experiences. They represent changes in a person's physiological condition, such as blood pressure, heart rate and perspiration, as well as changes in behaviour, such as facial expression, voice tone and eye movement. These emotional reactions are involuntary and often occur without our awareness. When aware of these responses, we also develop feelings (worry, fear, boredom) that further mark the emotional experience. The experience of emotion also relates to the fourth element, namely, that emotions put people in a state of readiness. When we get worried, for example, our heart rate and blood pressure increase to make our body better prepared to engage in fight or flight. Emotions are also communications to our conscious selves. Some emotions (e.g. anger, surprise, fear) are particularly strong 'triggers' that interrupt our train of thought, demand our attention, and generate the motivation to take action. They make us aware of events that may affect our survival and well-being.[5]

TYPES OF EMOTIONS

Emotions come in many forms, and experts have generally organised them around two or three dimensions. The most widely recognised arrangement is the Circumplex Model of

Circumplex Model of Emotions

EXHIBIT 4.1

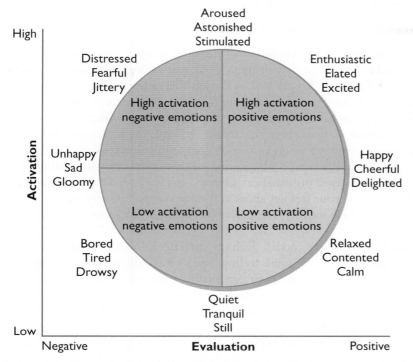

Sources: Adapted from J. Larson, E. Diener and R. E. Lucas, 'Emotion: Models, Measures, and Differences', in R. G. Lord, R. J. Klimoski and R. Kanfer, eds, *Emotions in the Workplace* (San Francisco: Jossey-Bass, 2002), pp. 64–113; J. A. Russell, 'Core Affect and the Psychological Construction of Emotion', *Psychological Review* 110, no. 1 (2003), 145–72.

Emotions shown in Exhibit 4.1, which organises emotions on the basis of their pleasantness and activation (the extent that the emotion produces alertness and motivation to act).[6] Fear, for example, is an unpleasant experience (i.e. we try to avoid conditions that generate fear) and has high activation (i.e. it motivates us to act). Emotions on the opposite side of the circle have the opposite effect. As seen in Exhibit 4.1, calm is the opposite to fear; it is a pleasant experience that produces very little activation in us.

EMOTIONS, ATTITUDES AND BEHAVIOUR

Emotions influence our thoughts and behaviour, but to explain this effect we first need to know about attitudes. **Attitudes** represent the cluster of beliefs, assessed feelings and behavioural intentions towards a person, an object or an event (called an *attitude object*).[7] Attitudes are *judgments*, whereas emotions are *experiences*. In other words, attitudes involve conscious logical reasoning, whereas emotions operate as events, often without our awareness. We also experience most emotions briefly, whereas our attitude towards someone or something is more stable over time.

The three components of attitudes—beliefs, feelings and behavioural intentions—can be illustrated by using people's attitude towards mergers:

- *Beliefs*. These are your established perceptions about the attitude object—what you believe to be true. For example, you might believe that mergers reduce job security for employees in the merged firms. Or you might believe that mergers increase the company's competitiveness in this era of globalisation. These beliefs are perceived facts that you acquire from past experience and other forms of learning.

- *Feelings*. Feelings represent your positive or negative evaluations of the attitude object. Some people think mergers are good; others think they are bad. Your like or dislike of mergers represents your assessed feelings towards the attitude object.

- *Behavioural intentions*. These represent your motivation to engage in a particular behaviour with respect to the attitude object. You might plan to quit rather than stay with the com-

attitudes The cluster of beliefs, assessed feelings and behavioural intentions towards an object.

LEARNING OBJECTIVE

Explain how cognitions and emotions influence attitudes and behaviour.

pany during the merger. Alternatively, you might intend to email the company CEO to say that this merger was a good decision.

Traditional cognitive model of attitudes

Until recently, attitude experts assumed that the three attitude components were connected to each other and to behaviour only through the cognitive (logical reasoning) process, shown on the left side of Exhibit 4.2. Let's look at the left side of the model more closely. First, our beliefs about mergers are formed from various learning experiences, such as reading about the effects of mergers in other organisations or personally experiencing them in the past.

Next, beliefs about mergers shape our feelings towards them. Suppose that you are quite certain that mergers improve an organisation's competitiveness (positive outcome with high probability) and sometimes reduce job security (negative outcome with medium probability) for employees in the merged organisation. Overall, you might have a somewhat positive attitude towards mergers if your feelings about corporate competitiveness are stronger than your feelings about reduced job security. The probability of those outcomes also weights their effect on your feelings.

In the third step of the model, feelings directly influence behavioural intentions.[8] However, two people with the same feelings might have different behavioural intentions based on their past experience and their personality. Some employees with negative feelings towards mergers may intend to quit, whereas others might want to complain about the decision. People choose the behavioural intention that they think will work best or make them feel most comfortable.

In the final step, behavioural intentions are better than feelings or beliefs at predicting a person's behaviour, because they are specific to that behaviour. Even so, behavioural intentions might not predict behaviour very well because intentions represent only the motivation to act, whereas behaviour is also caused by the other three factors in the MARS model—ability, role perceptions and situational factors. You might plan to send an email to management complaining about the announced merger but never get around to it because of a heavy workload and family obligations.

EXHIBIT 4.2   **Model of emotions, attitudes and behaviour**

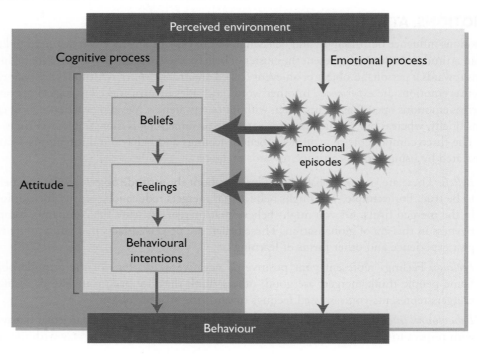

How emotions influence attitudes and behaviour

The cognitive model has dominated attitude research for decades, yet we now know that it only partially describes what really happens.[9] According to neuroscience research, incoming information from our senses is routed to the emotional centre as well as the cognitive (logical reasoning) centre of our brain.[10] The logical reasoning process, depicted on the left side of Exhibit 4.2, has already been described. The right side of Exhibit 4.2 offers a simple depiction of how emotions influence our attitudes and behaviour.

The emotional side of attitude formation begins with the dynamics of the perceptual process, particularly perceptual interpretation, described in Chapter 3. When receiving incoming sensory information, we automatically form emotions regarding that information before consciously thinking about it.[11] More specifically, the emotional centre quickly and imprecisely evaluates whether the incoming sensory information supports or threatens our innate drives, then attaches emotional markers to the information. These are not calculated feelings; they are automatic and unconscious emotional responses based on very thin slices of sensory information.

Returning to the previous example, you might experience excitement, worry, nervousness or happiness upon learning that your company intends to merge with a competitor. The large dots on the right side of Exhibit 4.2 illustrate these multiple emotional episodes triggered by the merger announcement, subsequent thinking about the merger, discussion with co-workers about the merger, and so on. These emotions are transmitted to the logical reasoning process, where they swirl around and ultimately shape our conscious feelings towards the attitude object.[12] Thus, while consciously evaluating the merger—that is, logically figuring out whether it is a good or a bad thing—your emotions have already formed an opinion which then sways your thoughts. If you experience excitement, delight, comfort and other positive emotions whenever you think about or discuss the merger, these positive emotional episodes will lean your logical reasoning towards positive feelings regarding the merger.[13]

Emotions operate automatically and unconsciously most of the time, but research tells us that the logical reasoning process actually 'listens in' on the person's emotions and uses this information when translating beliefs into feelings.[14] When thinking about whether the announced merger is good or bad, we try to understand our emotional reactions to the event, then use this emotional awareness as factual information in our logical evaluation. In some cases, the perceived emotions change the value of some beliefs or the probability that they are true. If you sense that you are worried and nervous about the merger, your logical analysis might pay more attention to your belief about job insecurity and put less weight on your belief that mergers increase the organisation's competitiveness.

You can see how emotions affect workplace attitudes. When performing our jobs or interacting with co-workers, we experience a variety of emotions that shape our longer-term feelings towards the company, our boss, the job itself, and so on. The more we experience positive emotions, the more we form positive attitudes towards the targets of those emotions. Furthermore, we pay attention to our positive emotions to the extent that they offset negative workplace experiences.

The opening paragraphs of this chapter described how several companies inject fun into work so employees experience plenty of positive emotional episodes each day. Warner Village and Scope International and many other firms specifically teach employees four principles developed at Pike Place Fish Market in Seattle, Washington. These Fish! principles—play, make their day, be there, and choose your attitude—help staff to be more upbeat at work and contribute to positive emotions in others. The Fish! principles emerged when Pike Place fishmongers turned a money-losing, morale-draining business into a world-famous attraction by deciding to have fun at work.

Positive emotions through Pike Place Fish! principles

Fishmongers at Pike Place Fish Market in Seattle turned the money-losing, morale-draining business into a world-famous attraction by deciding to have fun at work, such as tossing fish around and joking with customers. Out of this turnaround came four Fish! principles: play, make their day, be there, and choose your attitude. To create an exciting workplace, employees need to learn how to play, just as the fishmongers found ways to enjoy themselves at work. 'Make their day' refers to involving clients and co-workers so they, too, have a positive experience. 'Be there' means that in order to have fun employees need to be focused (not mentally in several places) and actively engaged. 'Choose your attitude' says that, although the environment might contribute to malaise, employees have the power to decide how that environment will affect their emotions, attitudes and behaviour.

AP Photo/Elaine Thomson

K. Mellen, 'Fish! Tackles Workplace Morale,' *Daily Hampshire Gazette*, 24 February, 2003; S. Lundin, H. Paul, and J. Christensen, *FISH! A Remarkable Way to Boost Morale and Improve Results* (New York: Hyperion, 2000)

When cognitions and emotions conflict

The influence of both logical reasoning and emotions on attitudes is most apparent when they disagree with each other. Everyone occasionally experiences this mental tug-of-war, sensing that something isn't right even though they can't think of any logical reason to be concerned. This conflicting experience indicates that our logical analysis of the situation (left side of Exhibit 4.2) can't identify reasons to support the automatic emotional reaction (right side of Exhibit 4.2).[15] Should we pay attention to our emotional response or our logical analysis? This question is not easy to answer because, as just discussed, the emotional and rational processes interact with each other so closely. However, some studies indicate that, while executives tend to make quick decisions based on their gut feelings (emotional response), the best decisions tend to occur when executives spend time logically evaluating the situation.[16] Thus, we should pay attention to both the cognitive and the emotional side of the attitude model, and hope they agree with each other most of the time!

One last observation about the attitude model in Exhibit 4.2 relates to the arrow going directly from the emotional episodes to behaviour. This indicates that people have direct behavioural reactions to their emotions. Even low-intensity emotions automatically change your facial expressions. High-intensity emotions can have a more powerful effect, which is apparent when an upset employee bangs a fist on the desk or an overjoyed colleague embraces someone nearby. These actions are not carefully thought out. They are fairly automatic emotional responses that serve as coping mechanisms in that situation.[17]

Cognitive dissonance

cognitive dissonance Occurs when people perceive an inconsistency between their beliefs, feelings and behaviour.

Emotions and attitudes usually lead to behaviour, but the opposite sometimes occurs through the process of **cognitive dissonance**.[18] Cognitive dissonance occurs when we perceive an inconsistency between our beliefs, feelings and behaviour. This inconsistency creates an uncomfortable feeling that motivates us to change one or more of these elements. Behaviour is usually the most difficult element to change, particularly when it is known to everyone, was done voluntarily, and can't be undone. Thus, we usually change our beliefs and feelings to reduce the inconsistency.

Emotions and personality

This coverage of the dynamics of workplace emotions wouldn't be complete without mentioning that emotions are also partly determined by a person's personality, not just workplace experiences.[19] Some people experience positive emotions as a natural trait. These people are generally extroverted—outgoing, talkative, sociable and assertive (see Chapter 2). In contrast, some people have a personality with a tendency to experience more negative emotions. Positive and negative emotional traits affect a person's attendance, turnover and long-term work attitudes. For example, several studies have found that people with a negative emotional trait have lower levels of job satisfaction. Also, employees with a natural tendency to experience negative emotions tend to have higher levels of job burnout.[20] While these positive and negative personality traits have some effect, other research concludes that the actual situation in which people work has a noticeably stronger influence on their attitudes and behaviour.[21]

MANAGING EMOTIONS AT WORK

The Elbow Room Café is packed and noisy on this Saturday morning. A customer at the restaurant in Vancouver, Canada, half shouts across the room for more coffee. A passing waiter scoffs: 'You want more coffee, get it yourself!' The customer's reaction is to laugh. Another diner complains loudly that he and his party are running late and need their food. This time, restaurant manager Patrick Savoie speaks up: 'If you're in a hurry, you should have gone to McDonald's.' The diner and his companions chuckle.

To the uninitiated, the Elbow Room Café is an emotional basket case, full of irate guests and the rudest staff on Canada's West Coast. But it's all a performance. The café is a place where guests can enjoy good food and play out their emotions about dreadful customer service. 'It's almost like coming to a theatre,' says Savoie, who spends much of his time inventing new ways to insult the clientele.[22]

Whether it is the most insulting service at Elbow Room Café in Vancouver or the friendliest service at Warner Village in Queensland, employees are usually expected to manage their emotions in the workplace. **Emotional labour** refers to the effort, planning and control needed to express organisationally desired emotions during interpersonal transactions.[23] When interacting with co-workers, customers, suppliers and others, employees are expected to abide by *display rules*. These rules are norms requiring employees to display certain emotions and to withhold others.

emotional labour The effort, planning and control needed to express organisationally desired emotions during interpersonal transactions.

CONDITIONS REQUIRING EMOTIONAL LABOUR

In just half a dozen years, Boost Juice has grown from a one-woman operation to a juice-bar phenomenon with more than 150 stores across Australia. The company's success can be attributed to founder Janine Allis's business savvy, the company's health-wise products, and the friendly staff who mix up and serve the delicious concoctions. To ensure that Boost Juice staff are friendly, Allis follows an important recipe for staffing: hire people who 'smile at least once every ten minutes'.[24]

Boost Juice, and just about every other organisation, expects employees to engage in some level of emotional labour. Emotional labour is higher in jobs requiring a variety of emotions (e.g. anger as well as joy) and more intense emotions (e.g. showing delight rather than smiling weakly), as well as in jobs where interaction with clients is frequent and for longer durations. Emotional labour also increases when employees must precisely rather than casually abide by the display rules.[25]

LEARNING OBJECTIVE

Identify the conditions that require and the problems associated with emotional labour.

Localising emotional display rules at Four Seasons Hotels

As one of the world's leading operators of luxury hotels, Toronto-based Four Seasons Hotels and Resorts trains employees and audits hotel performance to ensure that guests consistently experience the highest standards of service quality. Yet Four Seasons also adapts its legendary service to the local culture. 'McDonald's is the same all over. We do not want to be that way; we are not a cookie-cutter company,' says Four Seasons executive David Crowl. One of the most obvious forms of localisation is in the way Four Seasons staff are allowed to display emotions that reflect their own culture. 'What changes [from one country to the next] is that people do it with their own style, grace and personality,' explains Antoine Corinthios, president of Four Seasons' operations in Europe, Middle East and Africa. 'In some cultures you add the strong local temperament. For example, an Italian concierge has his own style and flair. In Turkey or Egypt you experience different hospitality.'[27]

Courtesy of Four Seasons Hotels & Resorts

Emotional display norms across cultures

How much we are expected to hide or reveal our true emotions in public depends to some extent on the culture in which we live. Cultural values in some countries—particularly Ethiopia, Korea, Japan and Austria—expect people to display a neutral emotional demeanour. In the workplace and other public settings, employees try to subdue their emotional expression and minimise physical contact with others. Even voice intonation tends to be monotonic. In other countries—notably Kuwait, Egypt, Spain and Russia—cultural values allow or encourage open display of one's true emotions. People are expected to be transparent in revealing their thoughts and feelings, dramatic in their conversational tones, and animated in their use of nonverbal behaviours to get their message across. These cultural variations in emotional display can be quite noticeable. One survey reported that 83 per cent of Japanese believe that it is inappropriate to become emotional in a business context, compared with 40 per cent of Americans, 34 per cent of French, and only 29 per cent of Italians. In other words, Italians are more likely to accept or tolerate people who display their true emotions at work, whereas this would be considered rude or embarrassing in Japan.[26]

EMOTIONAL DISSONANCE

Emotional labour can be challenging for most of us because it is difficult to conceal true emotions and to display the emotions required by the job. The main problem is that joy, sadness, worry and other emotions automatically activate a complex set of facial muscles that are difficult to prevent, and equally difficult to fake. Our true emotions tend to reveal themselves as subtle gestures, usually without our awareness. Meanwhile, pretending to be cheerful or concerned is difficult because several specific facial muscles and body positions must be coordinated. More often than not, observers see when we are faking and sense that we feel a different emotion.[28]

Emotional labour also tends to create a conflict between required and true emotions, called **emotional dissonance**. The larger the conflict between the required emotions and the true emotions, the more employees tend to experience stress, job burnout and psychological separation from self (i.e. *work alienation*).[29] One way to minimise emotional dissonance is by hiring people with a natural tendency to display the emotions required for the job. This is the approach that Boost Juice (mentioned above) and Warner Village (described at the beginning of the chapter) apply. Rather than specify precise role behaviours that employees must 'act out', both firms hire people who naturally tend to display these emotions and then give them the freedom to interact with customers without a formal script.

But even with a good fit between the person's natural disposition and the required emotions for the job, some acting is required to perform the job. The problem is that most of us engage in *surface acting*; we modify our behaviour to be consistent with required emotions but continue to hold different internal feelings. For instance, we force a smile while greeting a customer who we consider rude. The solution is to follow the practice of great actors, namely, engage in *deep acting*. Deep acting involves changing true emotions to match the required emotions. Rather than feeling irritated by a rude customer, you might view your next interaction with that person as an opportunity to test your sales skills. This change in perspective can potentially generate more positive emotions next time you meet that difficult customer, which produces friendlier displays of emotion.[30] However, it also requires considerable emotional intelligence, which is discussed next.

EMOTIONAL INTELLIGENCE

The $400 million Port Melbourne production facility was GM Holden's largest investment in decades, so executives carefully selected the plant's design team, managers and production staff. Still, it wasn't long before the project unravelled due to infighting and interpersonal tensions. Consultants called in to analyse the problems offered the following solution: employees needed to improve their emotional intelligence. With this advice, the thirty plant design team members and over 300 other employees from production through to management completed training modules on effective self-expression, understanding others, controlling emotions, and related topics. Everyone received an emotional intelligence assessment developed at Swinburne University.

To overcome scepticism about its touchy-feely nature, the emotional intelligence and leadership development program was evaluated to see whether employee scores improved and behaviour changed. The results indicated an average 50 per cent increase on emotional intelligence scores, while behaviour had became much more cooperative and diplomatic. 'It has greatly improved communication within the team and with other teams outside the plant,' said GM Holden quality systems engineer Vesselka Vassileva. Some employees also noted that it had improved their interpersonal behaviour outside the workplace. 'I'm not so aggressive or assertive,' said manufacturing engineer Alf Moore. 'I feel better and it's helped me at home.'[31]

GM Holden's new production facility started up more smoothly than might have occurred because the company paid attention to **emotional intelligence (EI)**. EI is the ability to perceive and express emotion, assimilate emotion in thought, understand and reason with emotion, and regulate emotion in oneself and others.[32] In other words, EI represents a set of *competencies* that allow us to perceive, understand and regulate emotions in ourselves and in others. Exhibit 4.3 (overleaf) illustrates the most recent EI model. According to this model, EI can be organised into four dimensions representing the recognition of emotions in ourselves and in others, as well as the regulation of emotions in ourselves and in others. Each dimension consists of a set of emotional competencies that people must possess in order to fulfil that dimension of emotional intelligence.[33]

emotional dissonance The conflict between required and true emotions.

LEARNING OBJECTIVE
Describe the four dimensions of emotional intelligence.

emotional intelligence (EI) The ability to monitor our own and others' feelings and emotions, to discriminate between them and to use this information to guide our thinking and actions.

EXHIBIT 4.3   **Emotional intelligence competencies model**

	Self (personal competence)	**Other** (social competence)
Recognition of emotions	**Self-awareness** • Emotional self-awareness • Accurate self-assessment • Self-confidence	**Social awareness** • Empathy • Organisational awareness • Service
Regulation of emotions	**Self-management** • Emotional self-control • Transparency • Adaptability • Achievement • Initiative • Optimism	**Relationship management** • Inspirational leadership • Influence • Developing others • Change catalyst • Conflict management • Building bonds • Teamwork and collaboration

Sources: D. Goleman, R. Boyatzis and A. McKee, *Primal Leadership* (Boston: Harvard Business School Press, 2002), chapter 3; D. Goleman, 'An EI-Based Theory of Performance', in C. Cherniss and D. Goleman, eds, *The Emotionally Intelligent Workplace* (San Francisco: Jossey-Bass, 2001), p. 28.

- *Self-awareness*. Self-awareness refers to having a deep understanding of one's own emotions as well as strengths, weaknesses, values and motives. Self-aware people are better able to eavesdrop in on their emotional responses to specific situations and to use this awareness as conscious information.[34]
- *Self-management*. This represents how well we control or redirect our internal states, impulses and resources. It includes keeping disruptive impulses in check, displaying honesty and integrity, being flexible in times of change, maintaining the drive to perform well and seize opportunities, and remaining optimistic even after failure. Self-management involves an inner conversation that guides our behaviour.
- *Social awareness*. Social awareness is mainly about *empathy*—having an understanding of and sensitivity to the feelings, thoughts and situation of others (see Chapter 3). This includes understanding another person's situation, experiencing the other person's emotions, and knowing their needs even though unstated. Social awareness extends beyond empathy to include being organisationally aware, such as sensing office politics and understanding social networks.
- *Relationship management*. This dimension of EI refers to managing other people's emotions. It is linked to a wide variety of practices, such as inspiring others, influencing people's beliefs and feelings, developing others' capabilities, managing change, resolving conflict, cultivating relationships, and supporting teamwork and collaboration. These activities also require effective emotional expression, that is, intentionally communicating emotions to others, usually to influence their emotions and behaviour.

These four dimensions of emotional intelligence form a hierarchy.[35] Self-awareness is the lowest level of EI because it does not require the other dimensions; instead it is a prerequisite for the other three dimensions. Self-management and social awareness are necessarily above self-awareness in the EI hierarchy. You can't manage your own emotions (self-management) if you aren't good at knowing your own emotions (self-awareness). Relationship management is the highest level of EI because it requires all three other dimensions. In other words, we require a high degree of emotional intelligence to master relationship management because this set of competencies requires sufficiently high levels of self-awareness, self-management and social awareness.

EI has its roots in the social intelligence literature introduced more than eighty years ago, but scholars in the main have focused since then on cognitive intelligence (IQ). Now, GM Holden and others are realising that EI is an important set of competencies in the performance of most jobs. As described in Chapter 2, people perform better when their aptitudes—including general intelligence—match the job requirements. But most jobs also involve social interaction, so employees also need emotional intelligence in order to work effectively in social settings. The evidence so far indicates that people with high EI are better at interpersonal relations, perform better in jobs requiring emotional labour, and are more successful in many aspects of job interviews. Teams whose members have high emotional intelligence initially perform better than teams with low EI.[36]

Improving emotional intelligence

Emotional intelligence is related to several personality traits, but the GM Holden experience shows that it can also, to some extent, be learned. Australia Post recently introduced a leadership coaching program using emotional intelligence assessment. Commonwealth Bank, Coles Myer, Telstra and ANZ have also incorporated emotional intelligence assessment and training in their leadership and/or customer service training.[37] Consistent with GM Holden's evaluation, one recent study reported that business students scored higher on emotional intelligence after taking an undergraduate interpersonal skills course.[38] These training programs improve EI to a degree, but the most effective approach is through personal coaching, plenty of practice and frequent feedback. Emotional intelligence also increases with age; it is part of the process called maturity. Overall, emotional intelligence offers considerable potential, but there is still a lot to learn about its measurement and its effects on people in the workplace.[39]

Improving emotional intelligence at ANZ Bank

Executives at ANZ Banking Group learned that they were above average on financial and operational activities but needed improvement with values and social competencies. So, with the guidance of McKinsey & Company, the Australian financial institution introduced a training program in which thousands of ANZ managers learned about emotional intelligence and how to apply these competencies to create 'caring, connected relationships between employees at ANZ, as well as the bank's millions of customers', explains an ANZ executive. 'This transformation is an ongoing journey, which realises the importance of engaging employees on both an emotional and an intellectual level.'[40]

Australian and New Zealand Banking Group Ltd

So far, this chapter has laid out the model of emotions and attitudes, but specific workplace attitudes also need to be understood. The next two sections of the chapter look at two of the most widely studied attitudes: job satisfaction and organisational commitment.

JOB SATISFACTION

Job satisfaction, a person's evaluation of his or her job and work context, is probably the most studied attitude in organisational behaviour.[41] It is an *appraisal* of the perceived job characteristics, work environment and emotional experiences at work. Satisfied employees have a favourable evaluation of their job, based on their observations and emotional experiences. Job satisfaction is really a collection of attitudes about different aspects of the job and work context. You might like your co-workers but be less satisfied with the workload, for instance.

How satisfied are we at work? Pollsters are focusing more on employee engagement than job satisfaction these days, but global survey results, including those shown in Exhibit 4.4, reveal a wide disparity of satisfaction across the region. Employees in India are apparently among the most satisfied in the world. Another survey estimates that people in the Philippines also have high levels of job satisfaction. Almost half of the Australians seem to be very satisfied with work, ranking eighth out of thirty-nine countries. In contrast, few employees in China, South Korea and Japan indicated that they are very satisfied.[42]

It is probably fair to conclude that employees in India and Australia are more satisfied than in some other parts of the world, but we also need to be somewhat cautious about these and other job satisfaction surveys. One problem is that surveys often use a single direct question, such as 'How satisfied are you with your job?'. Many dissatisfied employees are reluctant to reveal their feelings in a direct question, because this is tantamount to admitting that they made a poor job choice and are not enjoying life. For instance, one recent survey found that although most employees in Malaysia say they are satisfied with their job and work environment, only

EXHIBIT 4.4

Job satisfaction across cultures

Percentage very satisfied

Denmark	61
India	55
Norway	54
US	50
Ireland	49
Canada	48
Germany	48
Australia	46
Mexico	44
Slovenia	40
UK	38
Argentina	36
Austria	36
Israel	33
Brazil	28
France	24
Japan	16
S. Korea	14
China	11
Czech Rep.	11
Ukraine	10
Hungary	9

Source: Based on Ipsos-Reid survey of 9300 employees in 39 countries in the middle of the Year 2000. See 'Ipsos-Reid Global Poll Finds Major Differences in Employee Satisfaction around the World', Ipsos-Reid News Release, 8 January 2001. A sample of 22 countries across the range is shown here, including all of the top scoring countries.

http://www.galtglobalreview.com/world/satisfied_workers.html

55 per cent would recommend their company to others and less than half would stay if a comparable job were available in another company.[43]

A second problem is that cultural values make it difficult to compare job satisfaction across countries. People in China, South Korea and Japan tend to subdue their emotions in public, so they probably avoid extreme survey ratings such as 'very satisfied'. A third problem is that job satisfaction changes with economic conditions. Employees with the highest job satisfaction in this survey tend to be in countries where the economy was booming at the time of the survey.[44]

JOB SATISFACTION AND WORK BEHAVIOUR

Annette Verschuren, an executive at American retail giant Home Depot, pays a lot of attention to job satisfaction. 'I can tell you within two seconds of entering a store whether morale is good,' says Verschuren. The main reason for her interest is that job satisfaction is a key driver to corporate success. 'With an unhappy workforce you have nothing and you will never be great,' Verschuren warns.[45] Home Depot and a flock of other firms around the world are paying a lot more attention to job satisfaction these days. In some firms, executive bonuses depend partly on employee satisfaction ratings. The reason for this attention is simple: job satisfaction affects many of the individual behaviours introduced in Chapter 2.

A useful template to organise and understand the consequences of job dissatisfaction is the **exit-voice-loyalty-neglect (EVLN) model**. As the name suggests, the EVLN model identifies four ways that employees respond to dissatisfaction:[46]

- *Exit* refers to leaving the organisation, transferring to another work unit, or at least trying to make the exit. Employee turnover is a well-established outcome of job dissatisfaction, particularly for employees with better job opportunities elsewhere. Exit usually follows specific 'shock events', such as when your boss treats you unfairly.[47] These shock events generate strong emotions that energise employees to think about alternative employment.
- *Voice* refers to any attempt to change, rather than escape from, the dissatisfying situation. Voice can be a constructive response, such as recommending ways for management to improve the situation, or it can be more confrontational, such as by filing formal grievances.[48] In the extreme, some employees might engage in counterproductive behaviours to get attention and force changes in the organisation.
- *Loyalty* has been described in different ways, but the most widely held view is that 'loyalists' are employees who respond to dissatisfaction by patiently waiting—some say they 'suffer in silence'—for the problem to work itself out or get resolved by others.[49]
- *Neglect* includes reducing work effort, paying less attention to quality, and increasing absenteeism and lateness. It is generally considered a passive activity that has negative consequences for the organisation.

Which of the four EVLN alternatives do employees use? It depends on the person and the situation. One determining factor is the availability of alternative employment. With poor job prospects, employees are less likely to use the exit option. Those who identify with the organisation are also more likely to use voice rather than exit. People with a high conscientiousness personality are less likely to engage in neglect and more likely to engage in voice. Some experts suggest that employees differ in their EVLN behaviour depending on whether they have high or low collectivism. Finally, past experience influences our choice of action. Employees who were unsuccessful with voice in the past are more likely to engage in exit or neglect when experiencing job dissatisfaction in the future.[50]

JOB SATISFACTION AND PERFORMANCE

One of the oldest beliefs in the business world is that 'a happy worker is a productive worker'. Is this statement true? Organisational behaviour scholars have seesawed on this question for the past century. Long ago, they were reasonably confident that the statement was true. Later,

LEARNING OBJECTIVE

Summarise the effects of job dissatisfaction in terms of the exit-voice-loyalty-neglect model.

exit-voice-loyalty-neglect (EVLN) model The four ways, as indicated in the name, that employees respond to job dissatisfaction.

LEARNING OBJECTIVE

Discuss the relationships between job satisfaction and performance as well as job satisfaction and customer satisfaction.

doubts emerged as studies found a weak or negligible association between job satisfaction and task performance.[51] Now, the evidence suggests that the popular saying may be correct after all. Citing problems with the earlier studies, a groundbreaking analysis recently concluded that there is a *moderate* relationship between job satisfaction and job performance. In other words, happy workers really are more productive workers *to some extent*.[52]

Even with a moderate association between job satisfaction and performance, there are a few underlying reasons why the relationship isn't even stronger.[53] One argument is that general attitudes (such as job satisfaction) don't predict specific behaviours very well. As seen with the EVLN model, job dissatisfaction can lead to a variety of outcomes rather than lower job performance (neglect). Some employees continue to work productively while they complain (voice), look for another job (exit) or patiently wait for the problem to be fixed (loyalty).

A second explanation is that job performance leads to job satisfaction (rather than vice versa), but only when performance is linked to valued rewards. High performers receive more rewards and, consequently, are more satisfied than low-performing employees who receive fewer rewards. The connection between job satisfaction and performance isn't stronger because many organisations do not reward good performance. The third explanation is that job satisfaction might influence employee motivation, but this has little influence on performance in jobs where employees have minimal control over their job output (such as assembly line work). This point explains why the job satisfaction–performance relationship is strongest in complex jobs, where employees have more freedom to perform their work or to slack off.

JOB SATISFACTION AND CUSTOMER SATISFACTION

Along with the job satisfaction–performance relationship, corporate leaders are making strong statements that happy employees produce happy customers. 'The last three minutes of the shopping mile is the thing that counts,' says Coles-Myer chief executive John Fletcher. 'If the person at the register is not happy, they can transmit that to the customer and they can say, "I'm not coming back here again".' Shona Bishop agrees with that view. 'We made a philosophical decision based on the service/profit chain,' says the general manager of sales and service at the Bank of New Zealand. 'Happy staff means happy customers, which means shareholders are also happy.'[54]

Fortunately, research generally agrees that job satisfaction has a positive effect on customer satisfaction.[55] There are two main reasons for this relationship. First, employees are usually in a more positive mood when they feel satisfied with their job and working conditions. Employees in a good mood display friendliness and positive emotions more naturally and frequently, and this creates positive emotions for customers. Second, satisfied employees are less likely to quit their jobs, so they have better knowledge and skills and thus are better able to serve the clients. Lower turnover also means that customers are served by the same employees, so there is more consistent service. There is some evidence that customers build their loyalty to specific employees, not to the organisation, so keeping employee turnover low tends to build customer loyalty.[56]

Before leaving this topic, it's worth mentioning that job satisfaction does more than improve work behaviours and customer satisfaction. Job satisfaction is also an ethical issue that influences the organisation's reputation in the community. People spend a large portion of their time working in organisations, and many societies now expect companies to provide work environments that are safe and enjoyable. Indeed, employees in several countries closely monitor ratings of the best companies to work for, an indication that employee satisfaction is a virtue worth considerable goodwill to employers. This virtue is apparent when an organisation has low job satisfaction. The company tries to hide this fact and, when morale problems become public, corporate leaders are usually quick to improve the situation.

Outback restaurants build on employee–customer satisfaction relationship

Outback Steakhouse, Inc., has become a phenomenal success story in America's competitive restaurant industry. In 1988 Outback's four partners each opened a restaurant in Tampa, Florida, based on popular images of casual lifestyle and tucker in the land Down Under. Today, Outback's 65 000 employees work in 1100 restaurants around the United States and Canada. The Australian theme launched the company's success, but Outback founder and CEO, Chris Sullivan, said that the quality of the staff deserves as much credit. Long before scholars pointed out that satisfied employees provide better customer service, Outback was applying this principle. 'Outback's theory of success is that you hire the right people and take care of them,' explained Sullivan and three colleagues in a recent journal article. The company creates a culture that supports energised employees who stay with the company and provide excellent service. This service makes customers happy, which means that they come back to the restaurant and also refer Outback to friends. The result of such customer satisfaction is higher sales and improved company profits.[57]

Courtesy of Outback Steakhouse

ORGANISATIONAL COMMITMENT

Along with job satisfaction, organisational behaviour researchers have been very interested in an attitude called organisational commitment. **Organisational commitment** refers to the employee's emotional attachment to, identification with and involvement in a particular organisation.[58] This definition refers specifically to *affective commitment* because it is an emotional attachment—our feelings of loyalty—to the organisation.

Another form of commitment, called **continuance commitment**, occurs when employees believe it is in their own personal interest to remain with the organisation. It is a calculative rather than an emotional attachment to the organisation.[59] Employees have high continuance commitment when they do not particularly identify with the organisation where they work but feel bound to remain there because it would be too costly to quit. This reluctance to quit may be due to the risk of losing a large bonus by leaving early or because they are well established in the community where they work.[60]

CONSEQUENCES OF ORGANISATIONAL COMMITMENT

Corporate leaders have good reason to pay close attention to employee loyalty, because it can be a significant competitive advantage. Employees with high levels of affective commitment are less likely to quit their jobs and be absent from work. Organisational commitment also improves customer satisfaction, because long-tenure employees have a better knowledge of work practices, and clients like to do business with the same employees. Employees with high affective commitment also have higher work motivation and organisational citizenship, as well as somewhat higher job performance.[61]

organisational commitment
The employee's emotional attachment to, identification with and involvement in a particular organisation.

continuance commitment
A bond felt by an employee that motivates him or her to stay only because leaving would be costly.

LEARNING OBJECTIVE

Compare the effects of affective and continuance commitment on employee behaviour.

Employees can also have too much affective commitment. One concern is that organisational loyalty reduces turnover, which may limit the organisation's opportunity to hire new employees with different knowledge and fresh perspectives. Another concern is that loyalty results in conformity, which can undermine creativity and ethical conduct. For instance, a former executive at Arthur Andersen claims that one reason for the accounting firm's downfall was that it created a cult-like level of employee loyalty which meant that no one questioned or second-guessed top management's decisions.[62]

Consequences of continuance commitment

Creating too much affective commitment is probably a small problem compared with company practices that increase continuance commitment. Many firms tie employees financially to the organisation through low-cost loans, share options, deferred bonuses and other 'golden handcuffs'. For instance, when AMP went through a turbulent restructuring not long ago, the Australian insurance and investment company paid out $38 million in retention bonuses as a financial incentive for its top 160 executives to remain with the company.[63] Continuance commitment might also be higher in one-company towns because there are few employers to choose from, employees may have difficulty selling their home when leaving to work elsewhere, and people don't want to give up the relaxed lifestyle of these small communities.

All of these financial, employment and personal factors reduce turnover, but they also increase continuance commitment, not affective commitment. Research suggests that employees with high levels of continuance commitment have *lower* performance ratings and are *less* likely to engage in organisational citizenship behaviours! Furthermore, unionised employees with high continuance commitment are more likely to use formal grievances, whereas employees with high affective commitment engage in more constructive problem solving when employee–employer relations sour.[64] Although some level of financial connection may be necessary, employers should not confuse continuance commitment with employee loyalty. Employers still need to win employees' hearts (affective commitment) beyond tying them financially to the organisation (continuance commitment).

BUILDING ORGANISATIONAL COMMITMENT

LEARNING OBJECTIVE

Describe five strategies to increase organisational commitment.

There are almost as many ways to build organisational loyalty as topics in this textbook, but the following list is most prominent in the literature.

- *Justice and support.* Affective commitment is higher in organisations that fulfil their obligations to employees and abide by humanitarian values such as fairness, courtesy, forgiveness and moral integrity. These values relate to the concept of organisational justice, which is discussed in the next chapter. Similarly, organisations that support employee well-being tend to cultivate higher levels of loyalty in return.[65]
- *Shared values.* The definition of affective commitment refers to a person's identification with the organisation, and that identification is highest when employees believe that their values are congruent with the organisation's dominant values. Also, employees experience more comfort and predictability when they agree with the values underlying corporate decisions. This comfort increases their motivation to stay with the organisation.[66]
- *Trust.* **Trust** is a psychological state comprising the intention to accept vulnerability based on positive expectations of the intent or behaviour of another person.[67] Trust means putting faith in the other person or group. It is also a reciprocal activity: to receive trust, you must demonstrate trust. Employees identify with and feel obliged to work for an organisation only when they trust its leaders. This explains why layoffs are one of the greatest blows to employee loyalty; by reducing job security, companies reduce the trust employees have in their employer and the employment relationship.[68]
- *Organisational comprehension.* Affective commitment is a person's identification with the company, so it makes sense that this attitude is strengthened when employees understand

trust A psychological state comprising the intention to accept vulnerability based on positive expectations of the intent or behaviour of another person.

the company, including its past, present and future. Thus, loyalty tends to increase with open and rapid communication to and from corporate leaders, as well as with opportunities to interact with co-workers across the organisation.[69]

- *Employee involvement.* Employee involvement increases affective commitment by strengthening the employee's social identity with the organisation. Employees feel that they are part of the organisation when they take part in decisions that guide the organisation's future. Employee involvement also builds loyalty, because giving this power is a demonstration of the company's trust in its employees.

Look closely at some of the recommendations above and you will see that one of the key influences on organisational commitment is the employment relationship. In particular, affective commitment is sensitive to how well the organisation fulfils the psychological contract.

PSYCHOLOGICAL CONTRACTS

A few years ago employees at Westpac's mortgage processing operation in Adelaide were 'deeply shocked' to learn that they would be outsourced. Westpac was going to hand the entire unit over to an American company that provides technology services. The deal would ensure that the 1200 mortgage processing employees at the centre kept their jobs, but it meant that Westpac would no longer be their employer.[70]

Westpac's mortgage processing employees experienced the shock of having their psychological contract violated. This isn't unusual. According to one university study, 24 per cent of employees are 'chronically' angry at work, mostly because they feel their employer violated basic promises and didn't fulfil the psychological contract.[71] The **psychological contract** refers to the individual's beliefs about the terms and conditions of a reciprocal exchange agreement between that person and another party. This is inherently perceptual, so one person's understanding of the psychological contract may differ from the other party's understanding of it. In employment relationships, psychological contracts consist of beliefs about what the employee is entitled to receive and is obliged to offer the employer in return.[72] For example, Westpac employees believed that the bank would employ them as long as they worked at the Adelaide processing centre. Being handed over to another company clearly violated their expectations.

TYPES OF PSYCHOLOGICAL CONTRACTS

Psychological contracts vary in many ways.[73] One of the most fundamental differences is the extent to which they are transactional or relational. As Exhibit 4.5 indicates, *transactional*

LEARNING OBJECTIVE

Contrast transactional and relational psychological contracts.

psychological contract
The individual's beliefs about the terms and conditions of a reciprocal exchange agreement between that person and another party.

Types of psychological contracts in employment

EXHIBIT 4.5

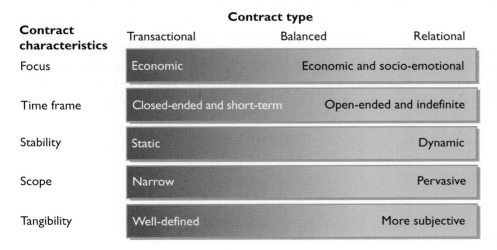

Contract characteristics	Contract type		
	Transactional	Balanced	Relational
Focus	Economic	Economic and socio-emotional	
Time frame	Closed-ended and short-term	Open-ended and indefinite	
Stability	Static		Dynamic
Scope	Narrow		Pervasive
Tangibility	Well-defined		More subjective

Sources: Based on information in D. M. Rousseau and J. M. Parks, 'The Contracts of Individuals and Organisations', *Research in Organisational Behavior* 15 (1993), 1–43; D. M. Rousseau, *Psychological Contracts in Organisations* (Thousand Oaks, CA: Sage, 1995).

contracts are primarily short-term economic exchanges. Responsibilities are well defined around a fairly narrow set of obligations that do not change over the life of the contract. People hired in temporary positions and as consultants tend to have transactional contracts. To some extent, new employees also form transactional contracts until they develop a sense of continuity with the organisation.

Relational contracts, on the other hand, are rather like marriages; they are long-term attachments that encompass a broad array of subjective mutual obligations. Employees with a relational psychological contract are more willing to contribute their time and effort without expecting the organisation to pay back this debt in the short term. Relational contracts are also dynamic, meaning that the parties are more flexible regarding when they expect a payback for their contribution to the relationship. Not surprisingly, organisational citizenship behaviours are more likely to prevail under relational than transactional contracts. Permanent employees are more likely to believe they have a relational contract.

PSYCHOLOGICAL CONTRACTS ACROSS CULTURES AND GENERATIONS

Psychological contracts are influenced by the social contexts in which the contracting process occurs.[74] In other words, they vary across cultures and groups of employees based on their unique cultures and cohort experiences. For instance, employees in Australia and New Zealand expect some involvement in company decisions (i.e. they have low power distance), whereas employees in Taiwan and Mexico are more willing to accept arbitrary orders from their supervisors (i.e. they have high power distance).

Psychological contracts also seem to vary across the generations. A few decades ago, many employees around the Pacific Rim (at least, those in white-collar jobs) could expect secure jobs with steady promotions through the hierarchy. They often devoted their entire lives to the same company, put in regular hours, and rarely thought about changing employers. Some older employees still hold on to these expectations, whereas fewer people under thirty make these conditions part of their psychological contract because they have never experienced that degree of employment stability.

Japan has experienced this shift towards employability much more recently, but perhaps more dramatically due to its extended recession of the 1990s. This shift has produced some rather startling changes in the psychological contract expectations of many young Japanese. As Reality Check 4.1 describes, new employment relationships and economic turbulence have given rise to a large cohort of 'freeters'—young people who hop from one job to the next, usually with a distinctly transactional psychological contract. In a country where loyalty has been the gold standard of employee expectations for decades, the opposing psychological contract expectations of freeters has motivated the Japanese government to introduce various schemes that will change their views on the employment relationship.

Psychological contracts are changing, as is the entire field of organisational behaviour, as new knowledge about emotions in the workplace is embraced. Emotional brain centres, emotional labour, emotional intelligence and other topics in this chapter were unheard of ten or fifteen years ago. Now they are essential reading to improve our grasp of the complex dynamics of employee attitudes and behaviour. You will see several references to emotions-related concepts throughout this book, including in the next chapter on employee motivation.

JAPAN'S FREETERS BRING A NEW PSYCHOLOGICAL CONTRACT TO THE WORKPLACE

Tatsuhiro Nakayama scoffs at the 'live-to-work' philosophy that his parents embraced. 'I don't feel like working and I don't have any problems with it,' says the 26-year-old who lives in Tokyo with financial support from his parents when not earning money in odd jobs. Nakayama is one of more than 2 million 'freeters' in Japan, which is double the number of a decade ago. Freeters are young people, including university graduates, who scrape by with low-paying part-time jobs.

The original explanation for the burgeoning freeter population was that Japan's struggling economy prevented young people from entering meaningful jobs. However, recent surveys indicate that a large portion of freeters don't try to find permanent jobs, don't worry at all about long-term careers, and think that job-hopping is a badge of honour. They prefer a psychological contract with employers that is short-term, transactional and flexible—just the opposite to what their parents expected in an employment relationship.

'Living as a freeter, I get more freedom and I like that,' says Mika Onodera, a 28-year-old bakery employee in Tokyo. Onodera, who shares an apartment with her sister, is on her fifth job in as many years. 'Although I cut back on my spending, I have enough money to go out with friends and live comfortably.'

Worried that a generation of freeters will undermine Japan's already fragile economy, several government departments have developed a counterattack, including funds for more school counsellors and a program to teach elementary school pupils the importance of full-time employment. Another government program provides financial aid to companies who hire freeters so they can 'test-drive' a permanent job.

The government's test-drive program seems to be having some effect. 'You can't tell much about a job just by reading the description in a classified ad,' says Hidenobu Kawai, a 23-year-old freeter who accepted employment through the government program with Yoshida Taro Co., a trading house in Tokyo. 'After I actually started working, I realised the job suited me.'

More than 2 million young Japanese have become 'freeters', casual workers with an equally casual psychological contract that emphasises personal freedom over loyalty.

Sources: 'Officials Worry as Younger Japanese Embrace "Freeting"', *Taipei Times*, 4 June 2003, p. 12; C. Fujioka, 'Idle Young Adults Threaten Japan's Workforce', *Reuters News*, 28 February 2005; 'Ministry Scheme Lets you Test-drive a Job', *Yomiuri Shimbun* (Tokyo), 22 April 2005.

AP Photo/Koji Sasahara

CHAPTER SUMMARY

Emotions are physiological, behavioural and psychological episodes experienced in relation to an object, person or event that create a state of readiness. Emotions are typically organised into a bi-polar circle (circumplex) based on their pleasantness and activation. Emotions differ from attitudes, which represent the cluster of beliefs, feelings and behavioural intentions towards a person, object or event. Beliefs are a person's established perceptions about the attitude object. Feelings are positive or negative evaluations of the attitude object. Behavioural intentions represent a motivation to engage in a particular behaviour with respect to the target.

Attitudes have traditionally been described as a process in which we logically calculate our feelings towards the attitude object based on an analysis of our beliefs. Thus, beliefs predict feelings, which predict behavioural intentions, which predict behaviour. But this traditional perspective overlooks the role of emotions, which have an important influence on attitudes and behaviour. Emotions typically form before we think through situations, so they influence this rational attitude formation process. This dual process is apparent when we internally experience a conflict between what logically seems good or bad and what we emotionally feel is good or bad in a situation. Emotions also affect behaviour directly.

Behaviour sometimes influences our subsequent attitudes through cognitive dissonance. People also have personality traits which affect their emotions and attitudes.

Emotional labour refers to the effort, planning and control needed to express organisationally desired emotions during interpersonal transactions. This is more common in jobs requiring a variety of emotions and more intense emotions, as well as where interaction with clients is frequent and for longer durations. The extent to which we are expected to hide or reveal our true emotions in public depends to some extent on the culture in which we live.

Emotional labour can be challenging for most people because it is difficult to conceal true emotions and to display the emotions required by the job. It also creates emotional dissonance when required emotions and true emotions are incompatible with each other. Deep acting can minimise this dissonance, as can the practice of hiring people with a natural tendency to display desired emotions.

Emotional intelligence is the ability to perceive and express emotion, assimilate emotion in thought, understand and reason with emotion, and regulate emotion in oneself and others. This concept includes four components arranged in a hierarchy: self-awareness, self-management, social awareness, and relationship management. Emotional intelligence can be learned to some extent, particularly through personal coaching.

Job satisfaction represents a person's evaluation of his or her job and work context. Surveys on job satisfaction reveal a broad dispersion of scores throughout Asia, Australia and New Zealand. However, these results may be somewhat inflated by the use of single-item questions and distorted by cultural differences. The exit-voice-loyalty-neglect model outlines four possible consequences of job dissatisfaction. Job satisfaction has a moderate relationship with job performance and with customer satisfaction. Job satisfaction is also a moral obligation in many societies.

Affective organisational commitment (loyalty) refers to the employee's emotional attachment to, identification with and involvement in a particular organisation. This contrasts with continuance commitment, which is a calculative bond with the organisation. Affective commitment improves motivation and organisational citizenship, and leads to higher job performance, whereas continuance commitment is associated with lower performance and organisational citizenship. Companies build loyalty through justice and support, shared values, trust, organisational comprehension and employee involvement.

The psychological contract refers to the individual's beliefs about the terms and conditions of a reciprocal exchange agreement between that person and another party. Transactional psychological contracts are primarily short-term economic exchanges, whereas relational contracts are long-term attachments that encompass a broad array of subjective mutual obligations. Psychological contracts seem to vary across cultures as well as across generations of employees.

KEY TERMS

attitudes p. 107
cognitive dissonance p. 110
continuance commitment p. 119
emotional dissonance p. 113
emotional intelligence (EI) p. 113

emotional labour p. 111
emotions p. 106
exit-voice-loyalty-neglect (EVLN)
  model p. 117
job satisfaction p. 116

organisational commitment p. 107
psychological contract p. 121
trust p. 120

DISCUSSION QUESTIONS

1. After a few months on the job, Susan has experienced several emotional episodes ranging from frustration to joy about the work she has been assigned. Explain how these emotions affect Susan's level of job satisfaction with the work itself.

2. A recent study reported that tertiary education instructors are frequently required to engage in emotional labour. Identify the situations in which emotional labour is required for this job. In your opinion, is emotional labour more troublesome for college instructors or for telephone operators working at an emergency service?

3. 'Emotional intelligence is more important than cognitive intelligence in influencing an individual's success.' Do you agree or disagree with this statement? Support your perspective.

4. Describe a time when you effectively managed someone's emotions. What happened? What was the result?

5. The latest employee satisfaction survey in your organisation indicates that employees are unhappy with some aspects of the organisation. However, management tends to pay attention to the single-item question asking employees to indicate their overall satisfaction with the job. The results of this item indicate that 86 per cent of staff members are very or somewhat satisfied, so management concludes that the other results refer to issues that are probably not important to employees. Explain why management's interpretation of these results may be inaccurate.

6. 'Happy employees create happy customers.' Explain why this statement might be true, and identify conditions in which it might not be true.

7. What factors influence an employee's organisational loyalty?

8. This chapter argues that psychological contracts vary across cultures and generations. Identify some of the psychological contract expectations around which younger and older employees differ in the country in which you live.

FRAN HAYDEN JOINS DAIRY ENGINEERING

4.1 | SKILL BUILDER

CASE STUDY

By Glyn Jones, University of Waikato

Dairy Engineering (NZ) Ltd has its headquarters in Hamilton, New Zealand, with manufacturing plants in South Auckland and Christchurch. The company manufactures equipment for the dairy industry. In its early years it focused on the domestic market but in the last five years has expanded into the export market. The company employs 450 people, which makes it a large company by New Zealand standards.

The case focuses on events in the Accounting Department at head office, which is organised into two sections, Cost Accounting and Management Information Services (MIS). The Accounting Department is structured as shown in the table overleaf.

FRAN, THE NEW GRADUATE

Fran Hayden had recently graduated with a Bachelor of Management Studies (BMS) degree from the University of Waikato where she proved to be a high achiever. Fran was interested in a position with Dairy Engineering for the following reasons:

- the opportunity to gain practical experience
- the high starting salary offered in the industry
- a boyfriend in the city.

Fran sent her curriculum vitae to the company and two weeks later she was invited to an interview with the chief accountant. She was surprised at the end of the interview to be offered the position of assistant cost accountant. Fran said she would like to think it over. Two

Name	Position	Description
Rob Poor	Chief accountant	Rob is the Accounting Department manager. He is 40 years old, a qualified accountant with a chartered accounting (ACA) qualification. He has been with the company for six years. He is an unassuming person regarded as a bit 'soft' by his staff.
Vernon Moore	Chief cost accountant	Vernon is 30 years old, also a graduate with an ACA qualification. He joined the company 18 months ago. He is considered an easy-going type and is well liked by his staff.
Peter Bruton	Management accountant	Peter is 37 years old with a science degree in dairy technology. He is studying part-time for a management degree through Massey University. He is regarded as 'moody' and is not well liked by his staff.

weeks later, when she had still not replied, she received a telephone call from Rob Poor asking if she was going to take the position. Although not totally convinced that it was what she wanted, Fran decided to accept the offer.

THE FIRST DAY AT WORK

Like many of her peers, Fran was glad to be leaving university after four years of study. She was looking forward to having money to spend as well as reducing her student debt. In order to 'look the part' she had gone further into debt to buy new 'corporate clothing'.

On reporting to the Accounting Department, she got her first shock in the 'real world'. No one was expecting her! Even worse, she found that there was no vacancy for her in Cost Accounting. Instead, she had been assigned to MIS.

Fran was taken to MIS by one of her new colleagues, Mike, who introduced her to the others in the MIS section, Tom and Adrian. They seemed to be a friendly bunch, as apparently was her boss, Peter Bruton, who explained that her main duties were to assist with compiling information for the monthly management report known as 'Big Brother'.

After two weeks the time came for compiling 'Big Brother'. Fran found that her part was almost entirely clerical and consisted of photocopying, collating, binding, punching and stamping the pages of the report. She then had to hand-deliver copies of the report to the senior manager at headquarters.

After 'Big Brother' was completed, Fran found she had little to do. She began to wonder why MIS needed four people.

THE BIG OPPORTUNITY

One afternoon, out of the blue, the chief accountant called Fran to his office to tell her about a management workshop to be held in Auckland the following week on performance measurement. Rob talked about the importance of staff development, and said that he would like to see one of his younger staff attending the workshop. He then asked Fran if she would be interested. She jumped at the opportunity. Unfortunately her boss was away on two weeks leave at the time, but Rob said he would talk to him about the workshop when he returned.

Fran enjoyed the workshop, particularly rubbing shoulders with experienced managers, living in a classy hotel and generally acting the management part. Even before leaving Auckland, she wrote a detailed report on the workshop for the chief accountant.

On her return to Hamilton, however, she found that all was far from well.

The evening before going back to work, Fran was telephoned by her colleague Mike with some disturbing news. When Peter had returned to work to find that Fran was in Auckland, he had been furious, complaining that he had not been consulted and that his authority was being undermined. He had said, 'Fran is no longer employed in this section.'

Fran returned to work full of trepidation, only to find that the expected encounter with her boss did not take place because he was in Christchurch. She handed two copies of her report on the workshop to the chief accountant's secretary before taking the opportunity of her boss's absence to seek the advice of her colleagues.

'I'm really worried,' said Fran. 'What do you think I should do?'

'Stop worrying about it,' said Adrian. 'He's just letting off steam. I've seen this all before. He'll get over it.'

'Come on, get serious,' said Fran. 'He is my boss! He can make things very difficult for me.'

'I think you should talk with Rob,' suggested Mike. 'After all, he's the one who suggested you go. It's not like it was your idea. He has to stick up for you.'

The next day Fran managed to get an appointment with the chief accountant. She started by saying that she had found the workshop very useful. She then brought up her fears about Peter's displeasure with her attendance at the workshop, to which the chief accountant responded: 'Well, yes, he was a bit upset, but don't worry, I will sort it out. The report was really good. By the way, I think you should treat it as confidential. Don't show it to anyone or discuss it with anyone. Is that okay? Don't worry about this. I assure you that I will sort it out.'

Fran left the meeting feeling reassured but also a bit puzzled, wondering whether Rob had really read her report already.

On Thursday Peter returned to work, and just before lunch he called Fran into his office, where he proceeded to attack her verbally, saying that she had 'connived' behind his back to attend the workshop and that she had never asked for his permission. He said that he realised she was an intelligent 'girl' but that she was 'sneaky'. He went on: 'You'd better realise which side your bread is buttered on—that for better or worse you are in my section. No other section would want you.'

He then called Mike in and said, 'I don't want Fran wasting more time. She is not to make private calls from work.'

Later, in 'confidence', he told Janet, one of the administration clerks, 'Fran has far too much work to catch up on. Don't go talking to her.'

Naturally Janet did tell Fran!

The following week, Vernon Moore happened to pass Fran in the corridor and stopped to talk with her. Fran had met Vernon only briefly during her first week in the company and was surprised when he asked her why she looked so miserable. She explained what had happened and he said that they had better talk with the chief accountant. He took Fran with him to Rob's office. Fran listened as Vernon outlined the situation to Rob. Fran then made it clear that if Peter continued to treat her this way she would have to ask for a transfer. She also said that there was not enough work in MIS to keep her occupied for more than a day or so each week.

The chief accountant listened and then asked her to give him a written report of what had happened since she had joined the company, including the latest incident with her boss. This, he said, would be brought up at the next senior management meeting. On the weekend Fran wrote the report, which included a request for a transfer out of MIS on the basis of the lack of work and her boss's attitude towards her. On Monday morning she handed her report to the chief accountant's secretary.

Fran expected a reply but by early afternoon had heard nothing. At the end of the day, Peter called all his staff into his office. He was obviously in a good mood and told them that he had put his plan for revising 'Big Brother' to the management meeting and had received an

enthusiastic response. As he spoke, Fran noticed the colour draining out of Mike's face. Later, Mike told her that what Peter was describing was his revision plan, not Peter's. Mike resolved never to give his boss another one of his ideas. 'He just uses other people's brains. But that's the last time he uses mine,' he said.

Fran drove home from work feeling despondent. She wished she had never joined the company. Her job was boring, almost entirely clerical, and certainly did not require a degree. She was also taking the stresses home, resulting in quarrels with her boyfriend and her flatmates.

Fran concluded that she had only two alternatives: a transfer or resignation. But to leave her job after less than five months would hardly impress any future employer. In desperation, she went to talk with Vernon, who she thought would be sympathetic, but there she received more unwelcome news. He told her that, contrary to Fran's expectation, the chief accountant had not confronted Peter at the senior management meeting. In fact, the chief accountant had been eclipsed by Peter's presentation about the revision of 'Big Brother' and had not attempted to raise the issue.

Vernon was frank with her: the only solution was to either transfer or resign. Then, to Fran's surprise, he suggested she apply for a position in his section that would become vacant in three weeks time. One of his assistant accountants was leaving to go overseas at short notice and he did not have a replacement. Vernon cautioned, however, that Fran's only chance was to apply directly to the chief accountant. That would force the issue, he believed. With a formal, written application before him, the chief accountant would have to make a decision. Just as certainly, Peter would resist the request. Later Fran drafted a letter to Rob requesting that she be transferred from MIS to the upcoming position in Cost Accounting.

THE CONFRONTATION

Next morning, Fran took her request to the chief accountant, but after reading it he said: 'You really needn't have done this, you know. I intended dealing with the situation.'

Fran left Rob's office wondering what to believe. From her desk she watched as Peter made his way across to the chief accountant's office. The meeting was brief. Five minutes later he left Rob's office and as he passed by her desk he said, in a loud voice, 'Fran, you are finished in this company.'

Fran saw her colleagues duck their heads down and pretend to be working. No one envied the position she was in. She wondered how, in such a short time, she has ended up in this situation.

QUESTIONS

1. Describe Fran's emotions and attitudes since joining Dairy Engineering. How have they changed, and why?

2. Describe Fran's level of loyalty (affective commitment) and explain why she has this level of loyalty.

3. Discuss Fran's psychological contract with Dairy Engineering.

4. What would you have done in Fran's position? What should she do now?

5. What pressures do you think the main participants might be under in this case?

6. What skills might have enabled Fran to better cope with the situation? Can these skills be taught in business schools?

STEM-AND-PROBE INTERVIEW ACTIVITY

PURPOSE
To help students experience the effects of emotional experiences on behaviour.

INSTRUCTIONS
This simple yet powerful exercise consists of students conducting and receiving a detailed stem-and-probe interview with other students in the class. Each student will have an opportunity to interview and be interviewed. However, to increase the variation and novelty of the experience, the student conducting the first interview should *not* be interviewed by the student who had just been interviewed. Instead, the instructor should form groups of four students (two pairs) at the beginning of the exercise, or have two pairs of students swap after the first round. Each of the two sets of interviews should take ten to fifteen minutes and use a stem-and-probe interview method.

The *stem-and-probe interviewing* method attempts to receive more detail from the interviewee than typically occurs in semi-structured or structured interviews. The main interview question, called the 'stem', is followed by probing questions that encourage the interviewee to provide additional details relating to a particular incident or situation. (The stem question for this exercise is provided below.) There are several 'probes' that the interviewer can use to elicit more detail, and the best probe depends on the circumstances, such as what information has already been provided. Some common probe questions include: 'Tell me more about that', 'What did you do next?', 'Could you explain that further, please?', and 'What else can you remember about that event?'. Notice that all of these probes are open-ended; they are not closed questions such as 'Is there anything else you want to tell me?', in which a simple 'Yes' or 'No' is possible. Stem-and-probe interviewing also improves when the interviewer engages in active listening and isn't afraid of silence—giving the interviewee time to think and motivating the interviewee to fill in the silence with new information.

In both sets of interviews, the 'stem' question is:

'Describe two or three things you did in the past week that made someone else feel better.'

Through this interview process, the interviewer's task is to receive as much information as possible (that the interviewee is willing to divulge) about these two or three things that the interviewee chooses to describe.

Following the two sets of interviews (where each student has interviewed and been interviewed once), the class will discuss the emotional and attitudinal dynamics of the activity.

RANKING JOBS ON THEIR EMOTIONAL LABOUR

PURPOSE
This exercise is designed to help you understand the jobs in which people tend to experience higher or lower degrees of emotional labour.

INSTRUCTIONS
Step 1: Individually rank-order the extent to which the jobs listed below require emotional labour. In other words, assign a '1' to the job you believe requires the most effort, planning and control to express organisationally desired emotions during interpersonal transactions. Assign a '10' to the job you believe requires the least amount of emotional labour. Mark your rankings in column 1.
Step 2: The instructor will form teams of four or five members and each team will rank-order the items based on consensus (not simply averaging the individual rankings). These results are placed in column 2.

Step 3: The instructor will provide expert ranking information. This information should be written in column 3. Students then calculate the differences in columns 4 and 5.

Step 4: The class will compare the results and discuss the features of jobs with high emotional labour.

OCCUPATIONAL EMOTIONAL LABOUR SCORING SHEET					
Occupation	(1) Individual ranking	(2) Team ranking	(3) Expert ranking	(4) Absolute difference of 1 and 3	(5) Absolute difference of 2 and 3
Bartender					
Cashier					
Dental hygienist					
Insurance adjuster					
Lawyer					
Librarian					
Postal clerk					
Registered nurse					
Social worker					
Television announcer					
TOTAL (The lower the score, the better)					
				Your score	Team score

SKILL BUILDER | **4.4**   COLLEGE AND UNIVERSITY COMMITMENT SCALE

SELF-ASSESSMENT

STUDENT CD

PURPOSE

This self-assessment is designed to help you understand the concept of organisational commitment and to assess your commitment to the college or university you are currently attending.

OVERVIEW

The concept of commitment is as relevant to students enrolled in college or university courses as it is to employees working in various organisations. This self-assessment is an adaptation of a popular organisational commitment instrument, and refers to your commitment to the college or university where you are attending this program.

INSTRUCTIONS

Read each of the statements below and circle the response that best fits your personal belief. Then use the scoring key in Appendix B of this book to calculate your results. This self-assessment is completed alone so that students rate themselves honestly without concerns of social comparison. However, class discussion will focus on the meaning of the different types of organisational commitment and how well this scale applies to the commitment of students towards the college or university they are attending.

COLLEGE OR UNIVERSITY COMMITMENT SCALE

Indicate the degree to which you think the following statements are true or false.	Strongly agree	Moderately agree	Slightly agree	Neutral	Slightly disagree	Moderately disagree	Strongly disagree
1. I would be very happy to complete the rest of my education at this institution.	❑	❑	❑	❑	❑	❑	❑
2. One of the difficulties of leaving this institution is that there are few alternatives.	❑	❑	❑	❑	❑	❑	❑
3. I really feel as if this institution's problems are my own.	❑	❑	❑	❑	❑	❑	❑
4. Right now, staying enrolled at this institution is a matter of necessity as much as desire.	❑	❑	❑	❑	❑	❑	❑
5. I do not feel a strong sense of belonging to this institution.	❑	❑	❑	❑	❑	❑	❑
6. It would be very hard for me to leave this institution right now even if I wanted to.	❑	❑	❑	❑	❑	❑	❑
7. I do not feel emotionally attached to this institution.	❑	❑	❑	❑	❑	❑	❑
8. Too much of my life would be disrupted if I decided to move to a different institution now.	❑	❑	❑	❑	❑	❑	❑
9. I do not feel like part of the 'family' at this institution.	❑	❑	❑	❑	❑	❑	❑
10. I feel that I have too few options to consider leaving this institution.	❑	❑	❑	❑	❑	❑	❑
11. This institution has a great deal of personal meaning for me.	❑	❑	❑	❑	❑	❑	❑
12. If I had not already put so much of myself into this institution, I might consider completing my education elsewhere.	❑	❑	❑	❑	❑	❑	❑

Source: Adapted from J. P. Meyer, N. J. Allen and C. A. Smith, 'Commitment to Organizations and Occupations: Extension and Test of a Three-Component Model', *Journal of Applied Psychology*, 78 (1993), pp. 538–51.

SKILL BUILDER | 4.5   DISPOSITIONAL MOOD SCALE

SELF-ASSESSMENT

FULL EXERCISE ON
STUDENT CD

This self-assessment is designed to help you understand mood states or personality traits of emotions and to assess your own mood or emotion personality. The self-assessment consists of several words representing various emotions that you might have experienced. For each word presented, indicate the extent to which you have felt this way generally across all situations *over the past six months*. You need to be honest with yourself in order to receive a reasonable estimate of your mood state or personality trait on these scales. The results provide an estimate of your level on two emotional personality scales. This instrument is widely used in research, but it is only an estimate. You should not assume that the results are accurate without a more complete assessment by a trained professional.

NOTES

1   M. A. Tan, 'Management: Having Fun at Work', *The Edge Malaysia*, 10 February 2003; S. Wisenthal, 'Star System', *Australian Financial Review*, 3 December 2004, 35; C. Bennett, 'Memo Boss: Create Some Fun', *Sunday Times* (Perth), 27 November 2005, 23; B. Flagler, 'The 20 Best Places to Work', *Unlimited*, March 2005; B. Hatch, 'Staring at Walls Can Be Productive Too', *Australian Financial Review*, 20 September 2005, 59; Humour Foundation, 'Project Giggles', (Humour Foundation, 2005), www.humourfoundation.com.au (accessed 14 December 2005); K. O'Meara, 'Project Giggles Builds Community Spirit Inside and Out', *Communication World*, March/April 2005, 36–7.

2   The centrality of emotions in marketing, economics and sociology is discussed in: G. Loewenstein, 'Emotions in Economic Theory and Economic Behavior', *American Economic Review* 90, no. 2 (May 2000), 426–32; D. S. Massey, 'A Brief History of Human Society: The Origin and Role of Emotion in Social Life', *American Sociological Review* 67 (February 2002), 1–29; J. O'Shaughnessy and N. J. O'Shaughnessy, *The Marketing Power of Emotion* (New York: Oxford University Press, 2003).

3   The definition presented here is constructed from information in the following sources: N. M. Ashkanasy, W. J. Zerbe and C. E. J. Hartel, 'Introduction: Managing Emotions in a Changing Workplace', in *Managing Emotions in the Workplace*, ed. N. M. Ashkanasy, W. J. Zerbe and C. E. J. Hartel (Armonk, NY: M. E. Sharpe, 2002), 3–18; H. M. Weiss, 'Conceptual and Empirical Foundations for the Study of Affect at Work', in *Emotions in the Workplace*, ed. R. G. Lord, R. J. Klimoski and R. Kanfer (San Francisco: Jossey-Bass, 2002), 20–63. However, the meaning of emotions is still being debated. See, for example, M. Cabanac, 'What Is Emotion?', *Behavioural Processes* 60 (2002), 69–83.

4   R. Kanfer and R. J. Klimoski, 'Affect and Work: Looking Back to the Future', in *Emotions in the Workplace*, ed. R. G. Lord, R. J. Klimoski and R. Kanfer (San Francisco: Jossey-Bass, 2002), 473–90; J. A. Russell, 'Core Affect and the Psychological Construction of Emotion', *Psychological Review* 110, no. 1 (2003), 145–72.

5   R. B. Zajonc, 'Emotions', in *Handbook of Social Psychology*, ed. D. T. Gilbert, S. T. Fiske and L. Gardner (New York: Oxford University Press, 1998), 591–634.

6   N. A. Remington, L. R. Fabrigar and P. S. Visser, 'Re-examining the Circumplex Model of Affect', *Journal of Personality and Social Psychology* 79, no. 2 (2000), 286–300; R. J. Larson, E. Diener and R. E. Lucas, 'Emotion: Models, Measures, and Differences', in *Emotions in the Workplace*, ed. R. G. Lord, R. J. Klimoski and R. Kanfer (San Francisco: Jossey-Bass, 2002), 64–113.

7   A. H. Eagly and S. Chaiken, *The Psychology of Attitudes* (Orlando, FL: Harcourt Brace Jovanovich, 1993); A. P. Brief, *Attitudes in and around Organizations* (Thousand Oaks, CA: Sage, 1998). There is ongoing debate about whether attitudes represent only feelings or all three components described here. However, those who adopt the single-factor perspective still refer to beliefs as the cognitive *component* of attitudes. For example, see I. Ajzen, 'Nature and Operation of Attitudes', *Annual Review of Psychology* 52 (2001), 27–58.

8   S. D. Farley and M. F. Stasson, 'Relative Influences of Affect and Cognition on Behavior: Are Feelings or Beliefs More Related to Blood Donation Intentions?', *Experimental Psychology* 50, no. 1 (2003), 55–62.

9   C. D. Fisher, 'Mood and Emotions While Working: Missing Pieces of Job Satisfaction?', *Journal of Organizational Behavior* 21 (2000), 185–202; M. Pergini and R. P. Bagozzi, 'The Role of Desires and Anticipated Emotions in Goal-Directed Behaviors: Broadening and Deepening the Theory of Planned Behavior', *British Journal of Social Psychology* 40 (March 2001), 79–98; J. D. Morris et al., 'The Power of Affect: Predicting Intention', *Journal of Advertising Research* 42 (May–June 2002), 7–17. For a review of the predictability of the traditional attitude model, see C. J. Armitage and M. Conner, 'Efficacy of the Theory of Planned Behavior: A Meta-Analytic Review', *British Journal of Social Psychology* 40 (2001), 471–99.

10 This explanation refers to a singular 'cognitive (logical reasoning) centre' and 'emotional centre'. While many scholars do refer to a single location for most emotional transactions, an emerging view is that both the emotional and rational 'centres' are distributed throughout the brain. J. Schulkin, B. L. Thompson and J. B. Rosen, 'Demythologizing the Emotions: Adaptation, Cognition, and Visceral Representations of Emotion in the Nervous System', *Brain and Cognition (Affective Neuroscience)* 52 (June 2003), 15–23.

11 J. A. Bargh and M. J. Ferguson, 'Beyond Behaviorism: On the Automaticity of Higher Mental Processes', *Psychological Bulletin* 126, no. 6 (2000), 925–45; R. H. Fazio, 'On the Automatic Activation of Associated Evaluations: An Overview', *Cognition and Emotion* 15, no. 2 (2001), 115–41; M. Gladwell, *Blink: The Power of Thinking without Thinking* (New York: Little, Brown, 2005).

12 A. R. Damasio, *Descartes' Error: Emotion, Reason, and the Human Brain* (New York: Putnam Sons, 1994); A. Damasio, *The Feeling of What Happens* (New York: Harcourt Brace and Co., 1999); P. Ekman, 'Basic Emotions', in *Handbook of Cognition and Emotion*, ed. T. Dalgleish and M. Power (San Francisco: Jossey-Bass, 1999), 45–60; J. E. LeDoux, 'Emotion Circuits in the Brain', *Annual Review of Neuroscience* 23

(2000), 155–84; R. J. Dolan, 'Emotion, Cognition, and Behavior', *Science* 298, no. 5596 (8 November 2002), 1191–4.

13   H. M. Weiss and R. Cropanzano, 'Affective Events Theory: A Theoretical Discussion of the Structure, Causes, and Consequences of Affective Experiences at Work', *Research in Organizational Behavior* 18 (1996), 1–74.

14   N. Schwarz, 'Emotion, Cognition, and Decision Making', *Cognition and Emotion* 14, no. 4 (2000), 433–40; M. T. Pham, 'The Logic of Feeling', *Journal of Consumer Psychology* 14, no. 4 (2004), 360–9.

15   G. R. Maio, V. M. Esses and D. W. Bell, 'Examining Conflict between Components of Attitudes: Ambivalence and Inconsistency Are Distinct Constructs', *Canadian Journal of Behavioural Science* 32, no. 2 (2000), 71–83.

16   P. C. Nutt, *Why Decisions Fail* (San Francisco, CA: Berrett-Koehler, 2002); S. Finkelstein, *Why Smart Executives Fail* (New York: Viking, 2003); P. C. Nutt, 'Search During Decision Making', *European Journal of Operational Research* 160 (2005), 851–76.

17   Weiss and Cropanzano, 'Affective Events Theory'.

18   L. Festinger, *A Theory of Cognitive Dissonance* (Evanston, Ill.: Row, Peterson, 1957); G. R. Salancik, 'Commitment and the Control of Organizational Behavior and Belief', in *New Directions in Organizational Behavior*, ed. B. M. Staw and G. R. Salancik (Chicago: St. Clair, 1977), 1–54; A. D. Galinsky, J. Stone and J. Cooper, 'The Reinstatement of Dissonance and Psychological Discomfort Following Failed Affirmation', *European Journal of Social Psychology* 30, no. 1 (2000), 123–47.

19   T. A. Judge, E. A. Locke and C. C. Durham, 'The Dispositional Causes of Job Satisfaction: A Core Evaluations Approach', *Research in Organizational Behavior* 19 (1997), 151–88; A. P. Brief and H. M. Weiss, 'Organizational Behavior: Affect in the Workplace', *Annual Review of Psychology* 53 (2002), 279–307.

20   C. M. Brotheridge and A. A. Grandey, 'Emotional Labor and Burnout: Comparing Two Perspectives of "People Work"', *Journal of Vocational Behavior* 60 (2002), 17–39; P. G. Irving, D. F. Coleman and D. R. Bobocel, 'The Moderating Effect of Negative Affectivity in the Procedural Justice–Job Satisfaction Relation', *Canadian Journal of Behavioural Science* 37, no. 1 (January 2005), 20–32.

21   J. Schaubroeck, D. C. Ganster and B. Kemmerer, 'Does Trait Affect Promote Job Attitude Stability?', *Journal of Organizational Behavior* 17 (1996), 191–6; C. Dormann and D. Zapf, 'Job Satisfaction: A Meta-Analysis of Stabilities', *Journal of Organizational Behavior* 22 (2001), 483–504.

22   R. Corelli, 'Dishing out Rudeness', *Maclean's*, 11 January 1999, 44–7; D. Matheson, 'A Vancouver Cafe Where Rudeness Is Welcomed', *Canada AM, CTV Television* (11 January 2000).

23   B. E. Ashforth and R. H. Humphrey, 'Emotional Labor in Service Roles: The Influence of Identity', *Academy of Management Review* 18 (1993), 88–115. For a recent review of the emotional labour concept, see T. M. Glomb and M. J. Tews, 'Emotional Labor: A Conceptualization and Scale Development', *Journal of Vocational Behavior* 64, no. 1 (2004), 1–23.

24   C. Cooper, 'The Wizards of Biz', *Bulletin*, 8 November 2005; E. Ross, 'Help Wanted Urgently', *Business Review Weekly*, 27 January 2005, 40.

25   J. A. Morris and D. C. Feldman, 'The Dimensions, Antecedents, and Consequences of Emotional Labor', *Academy of Management Review* 21 (1996), 986–1010; D. Zapf, 'Emotion Work and Psychological Well-Being: A Review of the Literature and Some Conceptual Considerations', *Human Resource Management Review* 12 (2002), 237–68.

26   E. Forman, '"Diversity Concerns Grow as Companies Head Overseas", Consultant Says', *Sun-Sentinel* (Fort Lauderdale, FL), 26

June 1995. Cultural differences in emotional expression are discussed in: F. Trompenaars, 'Resolving International Conflict: Culture and Business Strategy', *Business Strategy Review* 7, no. 3 (Autumn 1996), 51–68; F. Trompenaars and C. Hampden-Turner, *Riding the Waves of Culture*, 2nd edn (New York: McGraw-Hill, 1998), chapter 6.

27   R. Hallowell, D. Bowen and C.-I. Knoop, 'Four Seasons Goes to Paris', *Academy of Management Executive* 16, no. 4 (November 2002), 7–24.

28   This relates to the automaticity of emotion, which is summarised in: P. Winkielman and K. C. Berridge, 'Unconscious Emotion', *Current Directions in Psychological Science* 13, no. 3 (2004), 120–3; K. N. Ochsner and J. J. Gross, 'The Cognitive Control of Emotions', *TRENDS in Cognitive Sciences* 9, no. 5 (May 2005), 242–9.

29   W. J. Zerbe, 'Emotional Dissonance and Employee Well-Being', in *Managing Emotions in the Workplace*, ed. N. M. Ashkanasy, W. J. Zerbe and C. E. J. Hartel (Armonk, NY: M. E. Sharpe, 2002), 189–214; R. Cropanzano, H. M. Weiss and S. M. Elias, 'The Impact of Display Rules and Emotional Labor on Psychological Well-Being at Work', *Research in Occupational Stress and Well Being* 3 (2003), 45–89.

30   Brotheridge and Grandey, 'Emotional Labor and Burnout: Comparing Two Perspectives of "People Work"'; Zapf, 'Emotion Work and Psychological Well-Being'; J. M. Diefendorff, M. H. Croyle and R. H. Gosserand, 'The Dimensionality and Antecedents of Emotional Labor Strategies', *Journal of Vocational Behavior* 66, no. 2 (2005), 339–57.

31   C. Fox, 'Shifting Gears', *Australian Financial Review*, 13 August 2004, 28; J. Thomson, 'True Team Spirit', *Business Review Weekly*, 18 March 2004, 92.

32   J. D. Mayer, P. Salovey and D. R. Caruso, 'Models of Emotional Intelligence', in *Handbook of Human Intelligence*, ed. R. J. Sternberg, 2nd edn (New York: Cambridge University Press, 2000), 396–420. This definition is also recognised in: C. Cherniss, 'Emotional Intelligence and Organizational Effectiveness', in *The Emotionally Intelligent Workplace*, ed. C. Cherniss and D. Goleman (San Francisco: Jossey-Bass, 2001), 3–12; M. Zeidner, G. Matthews and R. D. Roberts, 'Emotional Intelligence in the Workplace: A Critical Review', *Applied Psychology: An International Review* 53, no. 3 (2004), 371–99.

33   These four dimensions of emotional intelligence are discussed in detail in D. Goleman, R. Boyatzis and A. McKee, *Primal Leadership* (Boston: Harvard Business School Press, 2002), chapter 3. Slight variations of this model are presented in: R. Boyatzis, D. Goleman and K. S. Rhee, 'Clustering Competence in Emotional Intelligence', in *The Handbook of Emotional Intelligence*, ed. R. Bar-On and J. D. A. Parker (San Francisco: Jossey-Bass, 2000), 343–62; D. Goleman, 'An EI-Based Theory of Performance', in *The Emotionally Intelligent Workplace*, ed. C. Cherniss and D. Goleman (San Francisco: Jossey-Bass, 2001), 27–44.

34   H. A. Elfenbein and N. Ambady, 'Predicting Workplace Outcomes from the Ability to Eavesdrop on Feelings', *Journal of Applied Psychology* 87, no. 5 (2002), 963–71.

35   The hierarchical nature of the four EI dimensions is discussed by Goleman, but is more explicit in the Salovey and Mayer model. See D. R. Caruso and P. Salovey, *The Emotionally Intelligent Manager* (San Francisco: Jossey-Bass, 2004).

36   P. J. Jordan et al., 'Workgroup Emotional Intelligence: Scale Development and Relationship to Team Process Effectiveness and Goal Focus', *Human Resource Management Review* 12 (2002), 195–214; H. Nel, W. S. De Villiers and A. S. Engelbrecht, 'The Influence of Emotional Intelligence on Performance in a Call Centre Environment', in *First International Conference on Contemporary Management*, ed. A. Travaglione et al. (Adelaide, Australia, 1–2 September 2003), 81–90; P. N. Lopes et al., 'Emotional Intelligence and Social Interaction', *Personality and Social Psychology Bulletin* 30, no. 8 (August 2004), 1018–34; C. S. Daus and N. M. Ashkanasy, 'The Case for the

Ability-Based Model of Emotional Intelligence in Organizational Behavior', *Journal of Organizational Behavior* 26 (2005), 453–66. Not all studies have found that EI predicts job performance. See: S. Newsome, A. L. Day and V. M. Catano, 'Assessing the Predictive Validity of Emotional Intelligence', *Personality and Individual Differences*, no. 29 (December 2000), 1005–16; A. L. Day and S. A. Carroll, 'Using an Ability-Based Measure of Emotional Intelligence to Predict Individual Performance, Group Performance, and Group Citizenship Behaviours', *Personality and Individual Differences* 36 (2004), 1443–58.

37   S. C. Clark, R. Callister and R. Wallace, 'Undergraduate Management Skills Courses and Students' Emotional Intelligence', *Journal of Management Education* 27, no. 1 (February 2003), 3–23; K. Brown, 'Emotional Intelligence: Is It Ready for the Workplace?', *Human Resources* (Australia), 5 April 2005.

38   R. J. Grossman, 'Emotions at Work', *Health Forum Journal*, no. 43 (Sept–Oct 2000), 18–22; J. Brown, 'School Board, Employment Centers Test Emotional Intelligence', *Technology in Government*, no. 8 (April 2001), 9; Clark, Callister and Wallace, 'Undergraduate Management Skills Courses and Students' Emotional Intelligence'.

39   For recent critiques of emotional intelligence, see: F. J. Landy, 'Some Historical and Scientific Issues Related to Research on Emotional Intelligence', *Journal of Organizational Behavior* 26 (2005), 411–24; E. A. Locke, 'Why Emotional Intelligence Is an Invalid Concept', *Journal of Organizational Behavior* 26 (2005), 425–31.

40   ANZ Banking Group, *The Journey* (Melbourne: ANZ Banking Group, November 2002); L. Cossar, 'IQ? But How Does Your EQ Rate?', *Business Review Weekly* (22 August 2002), 68; C. Nader, 'EQ Begins to Edge out IQ as Desirable Quality in the Boss', *Sunday Age* (Melbourne), 18 May 2003, 10; C. Fox and A. Cornell, 'The ANZ Experience', *Australian Financial Review*, 12 March 2004, 30.

41   E. A. Locke, 'The Nature and Causes of Job Satisfaction', in *Handbook of Industrial and Organizational Psychology*, ed. M. Dunnette (Chicago: Rand McNally, 1976), 1297–350; H. M. Weiss, 'Deconstructing Job Satisfaction: Separating Evaluations, Beliefs and Affective Experiences', *Human Resource Management Review*, no. 12 (2002), 173–94. Some definitions still include emotion as an element of job satisfaction, whereas the definition presented in this book views emotion as a cause of job satisfaction. Also, this definition views job satisfaction as a 'collection of attitudes', not several 'facets' of job satisfaction.

42   Ipsos-Reid, 'Ipsos-Reid Global Poll Finds Major Differences in Employee Satisfaction around the World', news release (Toronto: 8 January 2001). These results are similar to other global satisfaction surveys. See International Survey Research, *Employee Satisfaction in the World's 10 Largest Economies: Globalization or Diversity?* (Chicago: International Survey Research, 2002).

43   W. W. Worldwide, 'Malaysian Workers More Satisfied with Their Jobs Than Their Companies' Leadership and Supervision Practices', Watson Wyatt Worldwide News release (Kuala Lumpur: 30 November 2004).

44   The problems with measuring attitudes and values across cultures is discussed in: G. Law, 'If You're Happy & You Know It, Tick the Box', *Management-Auckland*, no. 45 (March 1998), 34–7; P. E. Spector et al., 'Do National Levels of Individualism and Internal Locus of Control Relate to Well-Being: An Ecological Level International Study', *Journal of Organizational Behavior*, no. 22 (2001), 815–32; L. Saari and T. A. Judge, 'Employee Attitudes and Job Satisfaction', *Human Resource Management* 43, no. 4 (Winter 2004), 395–407.

45   M. Troy, 'Motivating Your Workforce: A Home Depot Case Study', *DSN Retailing Today*, 10 June 2002, 29.

46   M. J. Withey and W. H. Cooper, 'Predicting Exit, Voice, Loyalty, and Neglect', *Administrative Science Quarterly*, no. 34 (1989), 521–39; W. H. Turnley and D. C. Feldman, 'The Impact of Psychological

Contract Violations on Exit, Voice, Loyalty, and Neglect', *Human Relations*, no. 52 (July 1999), 895–922.

47   T. R. Mitchell, B. C. Holtom and T. W. Lee, 'How to Keep Your Best Employees: Developing an Effective Retention Policy', *Academy of Management Executive* 15 (November 2001), 96–108; C. P. Maertz and M. A. Campion, 'Profiles of Quitting: Integrating Process and Content Turnover Theory', *Academy of Management Journal* 47, no. 4 (2004), 566–82.

48   A. A. Luchak, 'What Kind of Voice Do Loyal Employees Use?', *British Journal of Industrial Relations* 41 (March 2003), 115–34.

49   J. D. Hibbard, N. Kumar and L. W. Stern, 'Examining the Impact of Destructive Acts in Marketing Channel Relationships', *Journal of Marketing Research* 38 (February 2001), 45–61; J. Zhou and J. M. George, 'When Job Dissatisfaction Leads to Creativity: Encouraging the Expression of Voice', *Academy of Management Journal* 44 (August 2001), 682–96.

50   M. J. Withey and I. R. Gellatly, 'Situational and Dispositional Determinants of Exit, Voice, Loyalty and Neglect', *Proceedings of the Administrative Sciences Association of Canada, Organizational Behaviour Division* (June 1998); M. J. Withey and I. R. Gellatly, 'Exit, Voice, Loyalty and Neglect: Assessing the Influence of Prior Effectiveness and Personality', *Proceedings of the Administrative Sciences Association of Canada, Organizational Behaviour Division* 20 (1999), 110–19.

51   D. P. Schwab and L. L. Cummings, 'Theories of Performance and Satisfaction: A Review', *Industrial Relations* 9 (1970), 408–30; M. T. Iaffaldano and P. M. Muchinsky, 'Job Satisfaction and Job Performance: A Meta-Analysis', *Psychological Bulletin* 97 (1985), 251–73.

52   T. A. Judge et al., 'The Job Satisfaction–Job Performance Relationship: A Qualitative and Quantitative Review', *Psychological Bulletin* 127 (2001), 376–407; Saari and Judge, 'Employee Attitudes and Job Satisfaction'.

53   Judge et al., 'The Job Satisfaction–Job Performance Relationship: A Qualitative and Quantitative Review'.

54   'Fixed Shifts Key to Customer Service at BNZ Call Centres', *EEO Trust Work & Life Bulletin*, June 2005, 3; F. Smith et al., '25 True Leaders', *Australian Financial Review*, 12 August 2005, 62.

55   J. I. Heskett, W. E. Sasser and L. A. Schlesinger, *The Service Profit Chain* (New York: Free Press, 1997); D. J. Koys, 'The Effects of Employee Satisfaction, Organizational Citizenship Behavior, and Turnover on Organizational Effectiveness: A Unit-Level, Longitudinal Study', *Personnel Psychology* 54 (April 2001), 101–14; W.-C. Tsai and Y.-M. Huang, 'Mechanisms Linking Employee Affective Delivery and Customer Behavioral Intentions', *Journal of Applied Psychology* 87, no. 5 (2002), 1001–8; T. DeCotiis et al., 'How Outback Steakhouse Created a Great Place to Work, Have Fun, and Make Money', *Journal of Organizational Excellence* 23, no. 4 (Autumn 2004), 23–33; G. A. Gelade and S. Young, 'Test of a Service Profit Chain Model in the Retail Banking Sector', *Journal of Occupational & Organizational Psychology* 78 (2005), 1–22. However, some studies have found only a weak relationship between employee attitudes and sales outcomes.

56   P. Guenzi and O. Pelloni, 'The Impact of Interpersonal Relationships on Customer Satisfaction and Loyalty to the Service Provider', *International Journal of Service Industry Management* 15, no. 3–4 (2004), 365–84; S. J. Bell, S. Auh and K. Smalley, 'Customer Relationship Dynamics: Service Quality and Customer Loyalty in the Context of Varying Levels of Customer Expertise and Switching Costs', *Journal of the Academy of Marketing Science* 33, no. 2 (Spring 2005), 169–83.

57   DeCotiis et al., 'How Outback Steakhouse Created a Great Place to Work, Have Fun, and Make Money'.

58 R. T. Mowday, L. W. Porter and R. M. Steers, *Employee Organization Linkages: The Psychology of Commitment, Absenteeism, and Turnover* (New York: Academic Press, 1982).

59 J. P. Meyer, 'Organizational Commitment', *International Review of Industrial and Organizational Psychology* 12 (1997), 175–228. Along with affective and continuance commitment, Meyer identifies 'normative commitment', which refers to employee feelings of obligation to remain with the organisation. This commitment has been excluded so that students focus on the two most common perspectives of commitment.

60 R. D. Hackett, P. Bycio and P. A. Hausdorf, 'Further Assessments of Meyer and Allen's (1991) Three-Component Model of Organizational Commitment', *Journal of Applied Psychology* 79 (1994), 15–23.

61 F. F. Reichheld, *The Loyalty Effect* (Boston: Harvard Business School Press, 1996), chapter 4; J. P. Meyer et al., 'Affective, Continuance, and Normative Commitment to the Organization: A Meta-Analysis of Antecedents, Correlates, and Consequences', *Journal of Vocational Behavior* 61 (2002), 20–52; M. Riketta, 'Attitudinal Organizational Commitment and Job Performance: A Meta-Analysis', *Journal of Organizational Behavior* 23 (2002), 257–66.

62 B. L. Toffler, *Final Accounting: Ambition, Greed, and the Fall of Arthur Andersen* (New York: Broadway Books, 2003).

63 T. Boreham and G. Newman, 'AMP Slaps on the Golden Cuffs', *Australian*, 17 October 2003, 17.

64 J. P. Meyer et al., 'Organizational Commitment and Job Performance: It's the Nature of the Commitment That Counts', *Journal of Applied Psychology* 74 (1989), 152–6; A. A. Luchak and I. R. Gellatly, 'What Kind of Commitment Does a Final-Earnings Pension Plan Elicit?', *Relations Industrielles* 56 (Spring 2001), 394–417; Z. X. Chen and A. M. Francesco, 'The Relationship between the Three Components of Commitment and Employee Performance in China', *Journal of Vocational Behavior* 62, no. 3 (2003), 490–510; D. M. Powell and J. P. Meyer, 'Side-Bet Theory and the Three-Component Model of Organizational Commitment', *Journal of Vocational Behavior* 65, no. 1 (2004), 157–77.

65 E. W. Morrison and S. L. Robinson, 'When Employees Feel Betrayed: A Model of How Psychological Contract Violation Develops', *Academy of Management Review* 22 (1997), 226–56; J. E. Finegan, 'The Impact of Person and Organizational Values on Organizational Commitment', *Journal of Occupational and Organizational Psychology* 73 (June 2000), 149–69.

66 D. M. Cable and T. A. Judge, 'Person–Organization Fit, Job Choice Decisions, and Organizational Entry', *Organizational Behavior and Human Decision Processes* 67, no. 3 (1996), 294–311; T. J. Kalliath, A. C. Bluedorn and M. J. Strube, 'A Test of Value Congruence Effects', *Journal of Organizational Behavior* 20, no. 7 (1999), 1175–98; J. W. Westerman and L. A. Cyr, 'An Integrative Analysis of Person–Organization Fit Theories', *International Journal of Selection and Assessment* 12, no. 3 (September 2004), 252–61.

67 D. M. Rousseau et al., 'Not So Different after All: A Cross-Discipline View of Trust', *Academy of Management Review* 23 (1998), 393–404.

68 S. Ashford, C. Lee and P. Bobko, 'Content, Causes, and Consequences of Job Insecurity: A Theory-Based Measure and Substantive Test', *Academy of Management Journal* 32 (1989), 803–29; C. Hendry and R. Jenkins, 'Psychological Contracts and New Deals', *Human Resource Management Journal* 7 (1997), 38–44.

69 T. S. Heffner and J. R. Rentsch, 'Organizational Commitment and Social Interaction: A Multiple Constituencies Approach', *Journal of Vocational Behavior* 59 (2001), 471–90.

70 A. Keane, 'Westpac Outsource Proposal', *The Advertiser* (Adelaide), 5 May 2001.

71 P. Kruger, 'Betrayed by Work', *Fast Company*, November 1999, 182.

72 S. L. Robinson, M. S. Kraatz and D. M. Rousseau, 'Changing Obligations and the Psychological Contract: A Longitudinal Study', *Academy of Management Journal* 37 (1994), 137–52; Morrison and Robinson, 'When Employees Feel Betrayed: A Model of How Psychological Contract Violation Develops'.

73 D. M. Rousseau, *Psychological Contracts in Organizations* (Thousand Oaks, CA: Sage, 1995); M. Janssens, L. Sels and I. Van den Brande, 'Multiple Types of Psychological Contracts: A Six-Cluster Solution', *Human Relations* 56, no. 11 (2003), 1349–78.

74 P. R. Sparrow, 'Reappraising Psychological Contracting: Lessons for the Field of Human-Resource Development from Cross-Cultural and Occupational Psychology Research', *International Studies of Management & Organization* 28 (March 1998), 30–63; D. C. Thomas, K. Au and E. C. Ravlin, 'Cultural Variation and the Psychological Contract', *Journal of Organizational Behavior* 24 (2003), 451–71.

CHAPTER 5

Motivation in the workplace

LEARNING OBJECTIVES

After reading this chapter, you should be able to:

- state three reasons why motivating employees has become more challenging in recent years

- explain why Maslow's needs hierarchy theory is not as good a model of employee motivation as has been popularly believed

- describe four-drive theory and explain how these drives influence motivation and behaviour

- summarise McClelland's learned needs theory, including the three needs he studied

- discuss the practical implications of motivation theories that studied needs and drives

- diagram the expectancy theory model and discuss its practical implications for motivating employees

- describe the characteristics of effective goal setting and feedback

- summarise the equity theory model, including how people try to reduce feelings of inequity

- identify the factors that influence procedural justice, as well as the consequences of procedural justice.

David Gachuru lives by a motto that motivates employees more than money can buy: 'If an employee's work calls for a thumbs-up, I will appreciate him or her as many times as possible.' Translating this advice into practice is a daily event for the general manager of Panafric Hotel in Nairobi, Kenya. In addition to thanking staff personally and through emails, Gachuru holds bi-monthly meetings where top performing employees are congratulated and receive paid holidays with their family. Employee achievements are also celebrated in the hotel's newsletter, which is distributed to guests as well as employees. The hotel even holds parties for high-achieving employees on their last day of work.

Panafric Hotel and other firms are returning to good old-fashioned praise and recognition to motivate staff. Share options can evaporate and incentive plans might backfire, whereas a few words of appreciation almost always create a warm glow of satisfaction and renewed energy. According to Grant Thornton human resources manager Larn Mulligan, employees at the Brisbane accounting firm actually prefer praise to money. 'Feedback from staff has been that what's important is the act of saying "thank you" rather than seeing a few extra dollars on their payslip,' he says. Grant Thornton staff who receive good feedback from clients or walk the extra mile receive various forms of recognition, including movie tickets, professional massages, and a fun drive at the Holden Performance Driving Centre. 'We're not trying to create a cash culture but a culture of celebrating,' Mulligan explains.

Panafric Hotel in Nairobi, Kenya, motivates its employees through plenty of praise and recognition. 'If an employee's work calls for a thumbs-up, I will appreciate him or her as many times as possible,' says Panafric general manager David Gachuru, shown in this photo (left) presenting an award to employee of the month, Matayo Moyale.

Along with recognition from managers, approximately one-third of large American firms rely on peer recognition as one of the ways to motivate employees. Among them is Yum Brands Inc., the parent company of KFC, Taco Bell and Pizza Hut. Yum discovered the power of peer recognition from its Australian KFC operations, where managers had created a system in which employees reward colleagues with 'Champs' cards, an acronym for KFC's values (cleanliness, hospitality, etc.). Yum executives have since adapted KFC Australia's peer recognition activity in its restaurants around the world.

The Ritz Carlton Hotel in Kuala Lumpur applies a similar peer recognition process using First Class Cards. Nancy Teoh, the hotel's human resources manager, explains that 'congratulatory messages or words of appreciation are written down by any member of the team to another and even . . . from the hotel and corporate senior leaders'. Teoh adds: 'This serves as a motivational aspect of the work environment.'[1]

LEARNING OBJECTIVE

State three reasons why motivating employees has become more challenging in recent years.

FIRST CLASS CARDS AT RITZ CARLTON HOTEL, Champs cards at KFC Australia and various celebrations for good performance at Panafric Hotel are designed to maintain and improve employee motivation. Motivation refers to the forces within a person that affect the direction, intensity and persistence of voluntary behaviour.[2] Motivated employees are willing to exert a particular level of effort (intensity), for a certain amount of time (persistence), towards a particular goal (direction). Motivation is one of the four essential drivers of individual behaviour and performance (see the MARS model in Chapter 2) and consequently is an integral component of employee engagement. An engaged workforce is an important predictor of the organisation's competitiveness, so it is easy to see why employee motivation is continuously on the minds of corporate leaders.

The quest for a motivated and engaged workforce has not been easy, however. Most employers—92 per cent of them, according to one major survey—say that motivating employees has become more challenging. Three factors seem to be responsible for this increasing challenge. First, globalisation, information technology, corporate restructuring and other changes have dramatically altered the employment relationship. These changes potentially undermine the levels of trust and commitment necessary to energise employees beyond minimum standards.[3]

Second, in decades past, companies typically relied on armies of supervisors to closely monitor employee behaviour and performance. Even if commitment and trust were low, employees performed their jobs with the boss watching them closely. But most companies thinned out their supervisory ranks when they flattened the organisational structure to reduce costs. Supervisors now have many more employees, so it is not possible to keep a watchful eye out for laggards. This is just as well, because today's educated workforce resents the old 'command-and-control' approach to performance management. Most people enjoy the feeling of being motivated, but this requires the right conditions, so employers need to search for more contemporary ways to motivate staff.

The third challenge is that a new generation of employees has brought different expectations to the workplace. A few years ago, various writers disparaged Generation-X and Generation-Y employees as slackers, cynics, whiners and malcontents. Now it is known that the problem wasn't their lack of motivational potential; it was that employers didn't know how to motivate them! It seems that many companies still haven't figured this out: according to one report, more than 40 per cent of employees aged 25 to 34 sometimes or frequently feel demotivated, compared with 30 per cent of 35- to 44-year-olds and just 18 per cent of 45- to 54-year-olds.[4]

This chapter begins the process of understanding employee motivation by looking at the core theories of motivation in organisational settings. A description of Maslow's needs hierarchy theory opens the chapter, and the shortfalls of this incredibly popular theory as well as other needs hierarchy models are explained. The text then turns to four-drive theory and McClelland's learned needs theory, both of which offer more promise. Next, the chapter examines a rational decision model of employee motivation, called expectancy theory. The third section of the chapter covers the key elements of goal setting and feedback, including the topics of multisource feedback and executive coaching. The final section of the chapter looks at organisational justice, including the dimensions and dynamics of equity theory and procedural justice.

NEEDS, DRIVES AND EMPLOYEE MOTIVATION

needs Deficiencies that energise or trigger behaviours to satisfy those needs.

Motivation begins with individual needs and their underlying drives. In spite of some confusion in the literature regarding 'needs' and 'drives', **needs** are defined here as deficiencies that energise or trigger behaviours to satisfy those needs. Unfulfilled needs create a tension that makes us want to find ways to reduce or satisfy those needs. The stronger your needs, the more motivated you are to satisfy them. Conversely, a satisfied need does not motivate. **Drives** are instinctive or innate tendencies to seek certain goals or maintain internal stability. Drives are hardwired in the brain—everyone has the same drives—and they probably exist to help the species survive.[5] Needs are typically produced by drives, but they may also be strengthened through learning (reinforcement) and through social forces such as culture and childhood upbringing. Needs and drives will be discussed later in the section, after a description of Maslow's theory and other needs hierarchy theories.

MASLOW'S NEEDS HIERARCHY THEORY

More people have probably heard about **Maslow's needs hierarchy** theory than any other concept in organisational behaviour. Developed by psychologist Abraham Maslow in the 1940s, the model has been applied in almost every human pursuit, from marketing products to rehabilitating prison inmates. This incredible popularity is rather odd, considering that most research has reported little or no support for the theory. According to his later journal entries, even Maslow was amazed that people had accepted his theory wholeheartedly without any critique. Normally, a theory that fails to live up to its predictions is laid to rest. However, Maslow's model is described here because of its significant historic value.

The needs hierarchy model emerged out of Maslow's concern that scholars had splintered needs and drives into dozens of categories, each studied in isolation using non-typical subjects (usually animals or people with severe psychological dysfunctions).[6] He argued that isolating narrowly defined needs and drives was inappropriate, because human behaviour is typically initiated by more than one of these needs or drives, with varying degrees of influence on that behaviour. While most scholars at the time focused on drive deprivation (particularly hunger), Maslow suggested that need gratification is just as important and that higher-level needs (such as status) are influenced by social dynamics and culture, not just instincts. Maslow's call for a more holistic, humanistic and positive approach to human motivation research was a significant shift in thinking which largely remains with us today.

Maslow's needs hierarchy theory takes a holistic approach by condensing the long list of needs into a hierarchy of five basic categories.[7] As Exhibit 5.1 illustrates, physiological needs (need for food, air, water, shelter, etc.) are at the bottom of the hierarchy. Next are safety needs—the need for a secure and stable environment and the absence of pain, threat or illness.

drives Instinctive or innate tendencies to seek certain goals or maintain internal stability.

Maslow's needs hierarchy A motivation theory of needs arranged in a hierarchy, whereby people are motivated to fulfill a higher need as a lower one becomes gratified.

LEARNING OBJECTIVE

Explain why Maslow's needs hierarchy theory is not as good a model of employee motivation that is popularly believed.

Maslow's needs hierarchy

EXHIBIT 5.1

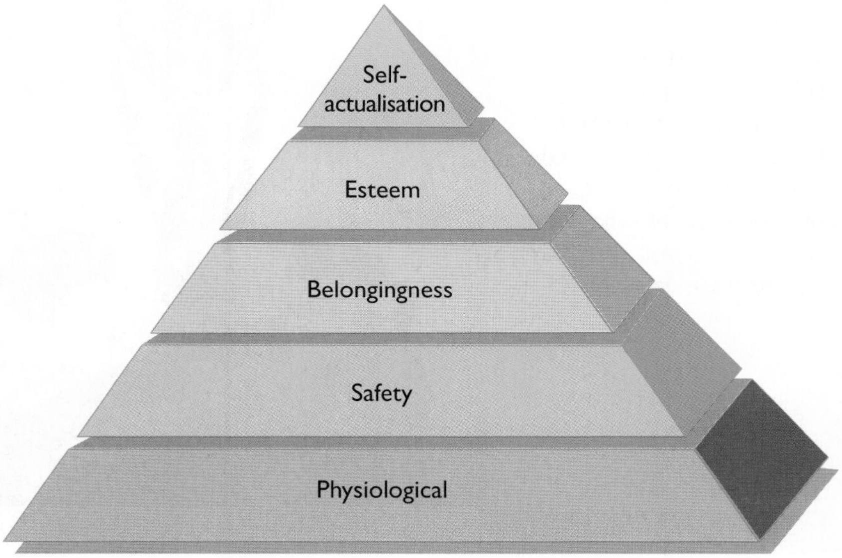

- Self-actualisation
- Esteem
- Belongingness
- Safety
- Physiological

Source: Based on information in: A. H. Maslow, 'A Theory of Human Motivation', *Psychological Review* 50 (1943), 370–96.

self-actualisation The need for self-fulfilment in reaching one's potential.

Belongingness includes the need for love, affection and interaction with other people. Esteem includes self-esteem through personal achievement as well as social esteem through recognition and respect from others. At the top of the hierarchy is **self-actualisation**, which represents the need for self-fulfilment—a sense that the person's potential has been realised. In addition to these five, Maslow described the need to know and the need for aesthetic beauty as two needs that do not fit within the hierarchy.

Maslow says that we are motivated simultaneously by several needs, but the strongest source is the lowest unsatisfied need at the time. As the person satisfies a lower-level need, the next higher need in the hierarchy becomes the primary motivator and remains so even if never satisfied. Physiological needs are initially the most important and people are motivated to satisfy them first. As they become gratified, safety needs emerge as the strongest motivator. As safety needs are satisfied, belongingness needs become most important, and so forth. The exception to this need fulfilment process is self-actualisation; as people experience self-actualisation, they desire more rather than less of this need. Thus, while the bottom four groups are *deficiency needs* because they become activated when unfulfilled, self-actualisation is known as a *growth need* because it continues to develop even when fulfilled.

Evaluating needs hierarchy theory

As mentioned earlier, Maslow's needs hierarchy theory has not received much scientific support.[8] Researchers have found that needs do not cluster neatly around the hierarchy's five categories. Also, gratification of one need level does not necessarily lead to increased motivation to satisfy the next higher need level. Some people can be very hungry and yet strive to fulfil their social needs; others can self-actualise while working in a risky environment. The theory also assumes that need priorities shift over months or years, whereas the importance of a particular need probably changes more quickly with the situation.

Self-actualising to achieve the impossible

Neil Carswell thrives on challenges. This was apparent not long after Carswell joined Branded Products Pty Ltd a few years ago. 'He jumped in with both feet and worked hard,' says John Whitaker, owner of the Dandenong, Victoria, promotional products company. Carswell's strong need for self-actualisation was recently demonstrated when he received a last-minute call from a major Australian telecommunications company for 1125 T-shirts, each with an individual slogan. Branded Products had previously received orders for 500 T-shirts with the same slogan, but this was a different matter. Rather than dismiss the impossible request, Carswell worked through a long weekend, completing the task and delivering the individually branded promotional items on time. Carswell, who was one of the top finalists in a national employee of the year award, says he enjoys 'playing Sherlock Holmes' and solving these unusual and difficult customer requests.[11]

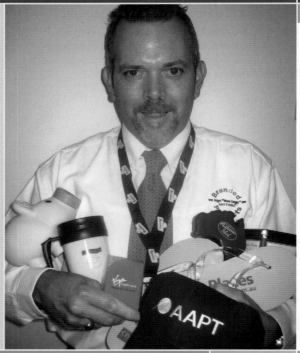

Branded Products Pty Ltd

In spite of the flaws of needs hierarchy theory, Maslow made an important contribution in shifting research away from studies of narrowly defined needs and drives and raising awareness of the importance of social and cultural factors, not just hunger-like instincts. But Maslow's most important contribution is his work on self-actualisation, which he considered far more important than the needs hierarchy model.[9] Throughout his career, Maslow emphasised that people are naturally motivated to reach their potential (once lower needs are fulfilled), and that organisations and societies need to be structured to help people continue and develop this motivation. Maslow called for more 'enlightened management' to provide meaningful work and freedom, rather than tedious work with oppressive bureaucratic controls, so that employees could experience self-actualisation and fulfil their other needs.[10]

What's wrong with needs hierarchy models?

Maslow's theory is not the only attempt to map employee needs onto a hierarchy. The most comprehensive of the alternative models is **ERG theory**, which re-organises Maslow's five groups into three—existence, relatedness and growth.[12] Maslow's theory explained only how people progress up the hierarchy, whereas ERG theory also describes how people regress down the hierarchy when they fail to fulfil their higher needs. ERG theory seems to explain human motivation somewhat better than Maslow's needs hierarchy, but that's mainly because it is easier to cluster human needs around ERG's three categories than Maslow's five categories. Otherwise, the research findings are fairly clear that ERG theory only marginally improves our understanding of human needs.[13]

Why have Maslow's needs hierarchy, ERG theory and other needs hierarchies largely failed to explain the dynamics of employee needs? The most glaring explanation is that people don't fit into a single universal needs hierarchy. We can think of acquaintances who seem addicted to social status even though they haven't fulfilled all of their lower needs, or who consider personal development and growth an ongoing priority over social relations. There is increasing evidence that needs hierarchies are unique, not universal, because a person's needs are strongly influenced by his or her social identity and values.[14] People with a strong social identity tend to emphasise social needs, whereas those with a strong personal identity focus more on their self-actualisation needs.

Values also influence a person's unique needs hierarchy.[15] If your fundamental values lean towards stimulation and self-direction, you probably pay a lot of attention to self-actualisation needs. If power and achievement are at the top of your value system, status needs might be strongest most of the time. This connection between values and needs suggests that a needs hierarchy is unique to each person and can change over time, just as values change over a lifetime. In summary, human beings seem to have a personal and somewhat flexible needs hierarchy, not one that is hardwired in human nature, as needs hierarchy theories assume.

FOUR-DRIVE THEORY

Motivation experts have mostly abandoned needs hierarchy theories, but not the notion that needs and drives are relevant. On the contrary, recent discoveries in neuroscience have prompted experts to reconsider a more coherent and integrated approach to innate drives. Building on recent research on innate drives, emotions and social intelligence, Harvard Business School professors Paul Lawrence and Nitin Nohria have proposed **four-drive theory** to explain human motivation.[16] This model is both holistic (it pulls together the many drives and needs) and humanistic (it considers human thought and social influences rather than just instinct). These were two conditions that Maslow felt were essential for a solid theory of human motivation.

Four fundamental drives

Four-drive theory organises drives into four categories: the drive to acquire, to bond, to learn and to defend. These drives are innate and universal, meaning that they are hardwired in our

ERG theory A motivation theory of three instinctive needs arranged in a hierarchy, in which people progress to the next higher need when a lower one is fulfilled, and regress to a lower need if unable to fulfil a higher one.

four-drive theory A motivation theory based on the innate drives to acquire, bond, learn, and defend that incorporates both emotions and rationality.

LEARNING OBJECTIVE

Describe four-drive theory and explain how these drives influence motivation and behaviour.

brains through evolution and are found in everyone. They are also independent of each other, so one drive is neither dependent on nor inherently inferior or superior to another drive. Four-drive theory also states that these four drives are a complete set; there are no other fundamental drives excluded from the model. Another key feature is that three of the four drives are 'proactive', meaning that we regularly try to fulfil them. Thus, any notion of fulfilling drives is temporary, at best.

- *Drive to acquire*. This is the drive to seek, take, control and retain objects and personal experiences. The drive to acquire extends beyond basic food and water; it includes the need for relative status and recognition in society. Thus, it is the foundation of competition and the basis of our need for esteem. Four-drive theory states that the drive to acquire is insatiable, because the purpose of human motivation is to achieve a higher position than others, not just to fulfil one's physiological needs.
- *Drive to bond*. This is the drive to form social relationships with others and develop mutual caring commitments. It also explains why people form social identities by aligning their self-image with various social groups (see Chapter 3). Research indicates that people invest considerable time and effort in forming and maintaining relationships without any special circumstances or ulterior motives. Indeed, recent evidence indicates that people who lack social contact are more prone to serious health problems.[17] The drive to bond motivates people to cooperate, and consequently is a fundamental ingredient in the success of organisations and the development of societies.
- *Drive to learn*. This is the drive to satisfy our curiosity, to know and understand ourselves and the environment around us. When observing something that is inconsistent with or beyond our current knowledge, we experience a tension that motivates us to close that information gap. In fact, studies in the 1950s revealed that people who are removed from any novel information will crave even boring information (outdated stock reports) to satisfy their drive to learn![18] The drive to learn is related to the higher-order needs of growth and self-actualisation described earlier.
- *Drive to defend*. This is the drive to protect ourselves physically and socially. Probably the first drive to develop, it creates a 'fight-or-flight' response in the face of personal danger. The drive to defend goes beyond protecting our physical self. It includes defending our relationships, our acquisitions and our belief systems. The drive to defend is always reactive—it is triggered by threat. In contrast, the other three drives are always proactive—we actively seek to improve our acquisitions, relationships and knowledge.

How drives influence employee motivation

To understand how these four drives translate into employee motivation, recall from previous chapters that our perceptions of the external world are influenced by our emotions. Every meaningful bit of information we receive is quickly and unconsciously tagged with emotional markers that subsequently shape our logical analysis of the situation. Our motivation to act is a result of rational thinking influenced by these emotional markers.[19]

The four drives fit into this tango of emotionality and rationality because they determine which emotional markers, if any, are attached to the perceived information. For example, suppose your department has just received a new computer program that you are curious to try out (triggered by your drive to learn). However, your boss says that you are not experienced enough to use the new system yet, which makes you somewhat angry (triggered by your drive to defend against the 'inexperience' insult). Both the curiosity about the software program and the anger resulting from the boss's beliefs about your experience demand your attention and energise you to act. The key point here is that the four innate drives determine which emotions are generated in each situation.

Four-drive theory further explains that this process is conscious (humanistic) rather than instinctive, because these drives produce independent and often competing signals that require

Four-drive theory of motivation

EXHIBIT 5.2

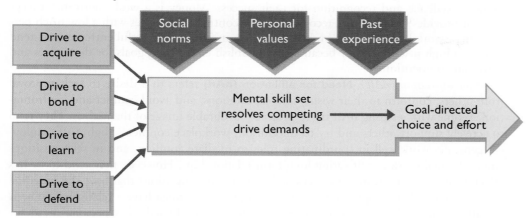

Source: Based on information in
P. R. Lawrence and N. Nohria, *Driven:
How Human Nature Shapes Our Choices*
(San Francisco: Jossey-Bass, 2002).

our attention.[20] As Exhibit 5.2 illustrates, we resolve these dilemmas through a built-in skill set that takes into account social norms, past experience and personal values. The result is goal-directed decision making and effort that fits within the constraints of cultural and moral expectations. In other words, our conscious analysis of competing demands from the four drives generates needs that energise us to act in ways acceptable to society and our own moral compass.

Evaluating four-drive theory

Four-drive theory potentially offers a rich explanation for employee motivation. It avoids the assumption found in needs hierarchy theories that everyone has the same needs hierarchy. Instead, it explains how our needs are based on innate drives, how emotions are generated from those drives in the context of a specific situation, and how personal experience and cultural values influence the intensity, persistence and direction of effort. Four-drive theory also provides a much clearer understanding about the role of emotional intelligence in employee motivation and behaviour. Employees with high emotional intelligence are more sensitive to competing demands from the four drives, are better able to avoid impulsive behaviour from those drives, and can judge the best way to act to fulfil those drive demands in a social context.

Four-drive theory is based on some fairly solid evidence regarding (1) the existence and dynamics of the four innate drives, and (2) the interaction of emotions and cognitions (logical thinking) in employee behaviour. However, the overall model is quite new and requires much more work to clarify the role of skill sets in forming goal-directed choice and effort. The theory also ignores the fact that the needs can be strengthened through learning. Four-drive theory probably accommodates the notion of learned needs, but it does not explain them. Fortunately, other motivational researchers, notably David McClelland, have provided some clarification about learned needs, which are examined next.

THEORY OF LEARNED NEEDS

At the beginning of this chapter, it was explained that needs typically originate from drives. For instance, your need for social interaction with co-workers is usually created out of the innate drive to bond. But needs can also be strengthened through reinforcement, including through childhood learning, parental styles and social norms. Psychologist David McClelland popularised the idea of learned needs years ago through his research on three learned needs: achievement, power and affiliation.

- *Need for achievement (nAch).* People with a strong **need for achievement (nAch)** want to accomplish reasonably challenging goals through their own effort. They prefer working alone rather than in teams and they choose tasks with a moderate degree of risk

**LEARNING
OBJECTIVE**

*Summarise McClelland's learned
needs theory, including the three
needs he studied.*

**need for achievement
(nAch)** A learned need in
which people want to accomplish
reasonably challenging goals
through their own efforts, like
to be successful in competitive
situations, and desire
unambiguous feedback regarding
their success.

(i.e. neither too easy nor impossible to complete). High nAch people also desire unambiguous feedback and recognition for their success. Money is a weak motivator, except when it provides feedback and recognition.[21] In contrast, employees with a low nAch perform their work better when money is used as an incentive. Successful entrepreneurs tend to have a high nAch, possibly because they establish challenging goals for themselves and thrive on competition.[22]

- *Need for affiliation (nAff).* **Need for affiliation (nAff)** refers to a desire to seek approval from others, conform to their wishes and expectations, and avoid conflict and confrontation. People with a strong nAff try to project a favourable image of themselves. They tend to actively support others and try to smooth out workplace conflicts. High nAff employees generally work well in coordinating roles to mediate conflicts, and in sales positions where the main task is cultivating long-term relationships. However, they tend to be less effective at allocating scarce resources and making other decisions that have the potential to generate conflict. People in decision-making positions must have a relatively low need for affiliation so that their choices and actions are not biased by a personal need for approval.[23]

- *Need for power (nPow).* People with a high **need for power (nPow)** want to exercise control over others and are concerned about maintaining their leadership position. They frequently rely on persuasive communication, make more suggestions in meetings, and tend to publicly evaluate situations more frequently. McClelland pointed out that there are two types of nPow. Those who enjoy their power for its own sake, use it to advance personal interests and wear it as a status symbol have *personalised power*. Others mainly have a high need for *socialised power* because they desire power as a means to help others.[24] McClelland argues that to be effective leaders should have a high need for socialised rather than personalised power. They have a high degree of altruism and social responsibility and are concerned about the effect of their actions on others.

Learning needs

McClelland argued that achievement, affiliation and power needs can be strengthened through learning, so he developed training programs for this purpose. In his achievement motivation program, trainees write achievement-oriented stories and practise achievement-oriented behaviours in business games. They also complete a detailed achievement plan for the next two years and form a reference group with other trainees to maintain their new-found achievement motive style.[25] These programs seem to work. Participants attending a need for achievement course in India subsequently started more new businesses, had greater community involvement, invested more in expanding their businesses, and employed twice as many people as non-participants. Research on similar achievement-motive courses for American small-business owners reported dramatic increases in the profitability of the participants' businesses.

PRACTICAL IMPLICATIONS OF NEEDS AND DRIVE-BASED THEORIES

LEARNING OBJECTIVE

Discuss the practical implications of motivation theories that studied needs and drives.

Four-drives theory, learned needs theory and Maslow's research on self-actualisation offer a few practical recommendations. Lawrence and Nohria provide the following advice from four-drive theory: ensure that individual jobs and workplaces provide a balanced opportunity to fulfil the drive to acquire, to bond, to learn and to defend.[26] There are really two key recommendations here. The first one is that everyone in the workplace needs to regularly fulfil all four drives. This is in sharp contrast to the ill-fated needs hierarchy theories, which suggested that employees are motivated mainly by one need at a time. Four-drive theory says that all of us continuously seek fulfilment of our innate drives. Thus, the best workplaces for motivation and morale provide sufficient rewards, learning opportunities, social interaction and so forth for all employees.

Sony suffers from lack of four-drive balance

Companies that help employees fulfil one drive but not the others will face long-term problems. This conclusion from four-drive theory seems to explain the current challenges facing Sony. The Japanese company which led the electronics world a decade ago with its Walkman and Playstation innovations is now struggling to keep up with its competitors. One reason for the current difficulties is that Sony executives allowed a hyper-competitive culture to develop where engineers were encouraged to outdo each other rather than work together. This competitive culture fed employees' drive to acquire, but the lack of balance with the drive to bond led to infighting and information hoarding. For instance, competitive rivalries within Sony delayed the company's launch of a digital music player and online music service to compete with Apple's iPod and iTunes music website.[27]

Charles Gupton/Getty Images

The second recommendation from four-drive theory is that these four drives must be kept in 'balance'; that is, organisations should avoid too much or too little opportunity to fulfil each drive. The reason for this advice is that the four drives counterbalance each other. Companies that help employees fulfil one drive but not the others will face long-term problems. An organisation that energises the drive to acquire without the drive to bond may eventually suffer from organisational politics and dysfunctional conflict. Change and novelty in the workplace will aid the drive to learn, but too much of it will trigger the drive to defend to such an extent that employees become territorial and resistant to change. Creating a workplace that supports the drive to bond can, at extreme levels, undermine the diversity and constructive debate required for effective decision making.

Another recommendation from the needs-/drives-based theories is to offer employees a choice of rewards rather than give everyone the same specific reward. Although people possess the same drives and require their ongoing fulfilment, people differ in their needs at any given time. Due to their unique values system and social learning, some employees have a strong need to achieve whereas others are motivated more by social factors. A narrow application of this recommendation is to let employees choose their own rewards from catalogues. At a broader level, employees need to have career choices and diverse opportunities to discover and experience their potential. One of the enduring recommendations from Maslow's work on self-actualisation is that employees must have sufficient freedom to discover their potential. It cannot be assumed or dictated by management.

EXPECTANCY THEORY OF MOTIVATION

The theories described so far mainly explain what motivates employees. But how do these drives and needs translate into specific effort and behaviour? One of the best theories to answer this question is the expectancy theory of motivation. **Expectancy theory** is based on

LEARNING OBJECTIVE

Diagram the expectancy theory model and discuss its practical implications for motivating employees.

expectancy theory The motivation theory based on the idea that work effort is directed towards behaviours that people believe will lead to desired outcomes.

the idea that work effort is directed towards behaviours that people believe will lead to desired outcomes.[28] Through experience, we develop expectations about whether we can achieve various levels of job performance. We also develop expectations about whether job performance and work behaviours lead to particular outcomes. Finally, we naturally direct our effort towards outcomes that help us fulfil our needs.

Expectancy theory model

The expectancy theory model is presented in Exhibit 5.3. The key variable of interest in expectancy theory is *effort*—the individual's actual exertion of energy. An individual's effort level depends on three factors: effort-to-performance (E-to-P) expectancy, performance-to-outcome (P-to-O) expectancy, and outcome valences (V). Employee motivation is influenced by all three components of the expectancy theory model. If any component weakens, motivation weakens.

E-to-P expectancy

The *effort-to-performance (E-to-P) expectancy* is the individual's perception that his or her effort will result in a particular level of performance. Expectancy is defined as a probability, and therefore ranges from 0.0 to 1.0. In some situations, employees may believe that they can unquestionably accomplish the task (a probability of 1.0). In other situations, they expect that even their highest level of effort will not result in the desired performance level (a probability of 0.0). For instance, unless you are an expert skier, you probably aren't motivated to try some of the black-diamond ski runs at New Zealand's Mt Hutt. The reason is a very low E-to-P expectancy. Even your best effort won't get you down the hill feet first! In most cases, the E-to-P expectancy falls somewhere between the two extremes.

P-to-O expectancy

The *performance-to-outcome (P-to-O) expectancy* is the perceived probability that a specific behaviour or performance level will lead to specific outcomes. This probability is developed from previous learning. For example, students learn from experience that skipping class either ruins their chance of a good grade or has no effect at all. In extreme cases, employees may believe that accomplishing a particular task (performance) will definitely result in a particular outcome (a probability of 1.0), or they may believe that this outcome will have no effect on successful performance (a probability of 0.0). More often, the P-to-O expectancy falls somewhere between the two extremes.

One important issue in P-to-O expectancies is which outcomes we think about. We certainly don't evaluate the P-to-O expectancy for every possible outcome; there are too many of

EXHIBIT 5.3   **Expectancy theory of motivation**

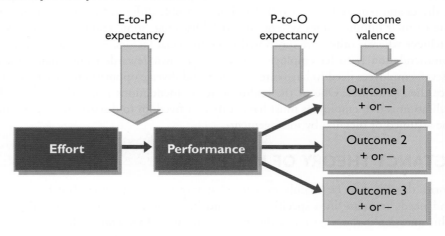

them. Instead, we think only about outcomes of interest to us at the time. On one occasion, your motivation to complete a task may be fuelled mainly by the likelihood of getting off work early to meet friends. At other times, your motivation to complete the same task may be based more on the P-to-O expectancy of a promotion or pay increase. The main point is that your motivation depends on the probability that a behaviour or job performance level will result in outcomes that you think about.

Outcome valences

The third element in expectancy theory is the **valence** of each outcome that you consider. Valence refers to the anticipated satisfaction or dissatisfaction that an individual feels towards an outcome. It ranges from negative to positive. (The actual range doesn't matter; it may be from −1 to +1, or from −100 to +100.) An outcome valence represents a person's anticipated satisfaction with the outcome.[29] Outcomes have a positive valence when they are consistent with our values and satisfy our needs; they have a negative valence when they oppose our values and inhibit need fulfilment. If you have a strong need for social interaction, for example, you would value group activities and other events that help to fulfil that need. Outcomes that move you further away from fulfilling your social need—such as working alone from home—will have a strong negative valence.

valence The anticipated satisfaction or dissatisfaction that an individual feels towards an outcome.

EXPECTANCY THEORY IN PRACTICE

One of the appealing characteristics of expectancy theory is that it provides clear guidelines for increasing employee motivation by altering the person's E-to-P expectancies, P-to-O expectancies, and/or outcome valences.[30] Several practical implications of expectancy theory are listed in Exhibit 5.4 and described below.

Increasing E-to-P expectancies

E-to-P expectancies are influenced by the individual's belief that he or she can successfully complete the task. Some companies increase this can-do attitude by assuring employees that

Practical applications of expectancy theory

EXHIBIT 5.4

Expectancy theory component	Objective	Applications
E→P expectancies	To increase the belief that employees are capable of performing the job successfully	• Select people with the required skills and knowledge. • Provide required training and clarify job requirements. • Provide sufficient time and resources. • Assign simpler or fewer tasks until employees can master them (shaping). • Provide examples of similar employees who have successfully performed the task. • Provide coaching to people who lack self-confidence.
P→O expectancies	To increase the belief that good performance will result in certain (valued) outcomes	• Measure job performance accurately. • Clearly explain the outcomes that will result from successful performance. • Describe how the employee's rewards were based on past performance. • Provide examples of other employees whose good performance has resulted in higher rewards.
Valences of outcomes	To increase expected value of outcomes resulting from desired performance	• Distribute rewards that employees value. • Individualise rewards. • Minimise the presence of countervalent outcomes.

they have the necessary competencies, clear role perceptions and necessary resources to reach the desired levels of performance. Matching employees to jobs based on their abilities and clearly communicating the tasks required for the job are important parts of this process. Similarly, E-to-P expectancies are learned, so behavioural modelling and supportive feedback (positive reinforcement) typically strengthen the individual's belief that he/she is able to perform the task.[31]

Increasing P-to-O expectancies

The most obvious ways to improve P-to-O expectancies are to measure employee performance accurately and distribute more valued rewards to those with higher job performance. Unfortunately, many organisations have difficulty putting this straightforward idea into practice. Some executives are reluctant to withhold rewards for poor performance because they don't want to experience conflict with employees. Others don't measure employee performance very well. For instance, fewer than half of the 6000 employees surveyed in one study said they knew how to increase their base pay or cash bonuses. In other words, most employees and managers have a generally low P-to-O expectancy regarding their pay cheques.[32] Chapter 6 looks at reasons why rewards aren't connected to job performance.

P-to-O expectancies are perceptions, so employees should believe that higher performance will result in higher rewards. Having a performance-based reward system is important, but this fact must be communicated. When rewards are distributed, employees should understand how their rewards have been based on past performance. More generally, companies need to regularly communicate the existence of a performance-based reward system through examples, anecdotes and public ceremonies.

Increasing outcome valences

Performance outcomes influence work effort only when those outcomes are valued by employees. This brings us back to what we learned from the needs-/drives-based theories of motivation, namely that companies should develop more individualised reward systems so that employees who perform well are offered a choice of rewards. Expectancy theory also emphasises the need to discover and neutralise countervalent outcomes. These are performance outcomes that have negative valences, thereby reducing the effectiveness of existing reward systems. For example, peer pressure may cause some employees to perform their jobs at the minimum standard even though formal rewards and the job itself would otherwise motivate them to perform at higher levels.

DOES EXPECTANCY THEORY FIT REALITY?

Expectancy theory remains one of the better theories for predicting work effort and motivation. In particular, it plays a valuable role by detailing a person's thinking process when translating the competing demands of the four drives into specific effort. Expectancy theory has been applied to a wide variety of studies, such as predicting student motivation to participate in teaching evaluations, using a decision support system, leaving the organisation, and engaging in organisational citizenship behaviours.[33] Research also indicates that expectancy theory predicts employee motivation in different cultures.[34]

One limitation is that expectancy theory seems to ignore the central role of emotions in employee effort and behaviour. As discussed earlier in this chapter and in previous chapters, emotions serve an adaptive function that demand our attention and energise us to take action. The valence element of expectancy theory captures some of this emotional process, but only peripherally. Thus, theorists probably need to redesign the expectancy theory model in light of new information about the importance of emotions in motivation and behaviour.

GOAL SETTING AND FEEDBACK

Walk into almost any call centre around the Pacific Rim and you will notice that performance is judged on several metrics, such as average time to answer the call, length of time per call, and abandon rates (customers who hang up before the call is handled by a customer service representative). Some call centres have large electronic boards showing how many customers are waiting, the average time they have been waiting, and the average time before someone talks to them. Employees sometimes receive feedback on their computer, such as the average length of time for each call at their workstation. Meanwhile, supervisors spend much of their time monitoring customer calls—usually several calls per month per employee—and regularly coaching employees based on those observations.

Call centres rely on goal setting and feedback to motivate employees and achieve superior performance.[35] **Goal setting** is the process of motivating employees and clarifying their role perceptions by establishing performance objectives. It potentially improves employee performance in two ways: (1) by stretching the intensity and persistence of effort, and (2) by giving employees clearer role perceptions so that their effort is channelled towards behaviours that will improve work performance.

CHARACTERISTICS OF EFFECTIVE GOALS

Goal setting is more complex than simply telling someone to 'do your best'. Instead, it requires six conditions to maximise task effort and performance: specific goals, relevant goals, challenging goals, goal commitment, participation in goal formation (sometimes), and goal feedback.[37]

- *Specific goals.* Employees put more effort into a task when they work towards specific goals rather than 'do your best' targets.[38] Specific goals have measurable levels of change over a specific and relatively short time frame, such as 'reduce scrap rate by 7 per cent over the next six months'. Specific goals communicate precise performance expectations, so employees can direct their effort more efficiently and reliably.
- *Relevant goals.* Goals must also be relevant to the individual's job and within his or her control. For example, a goal to reduce waste materials would have little value if employees didn't have much control over waste in the production process.

LEARNING OBJECTIVE

Describe the characteristics of effective goal setting and feedback.

goal setting The process of motivating employees and clarifying their role perceptions by establishing performance objectives.

Stretch goals send Speedera staff to the beach

Near the end of a recent financial quarter, Speedera Network's 120 employees in Bangalore, India, and Santa Clara, California, received an enticing challenge from founder and CEO Ajit Gupta: 'If we pull together to achieve our business targets [for the next quarter], then we'll all be on a beach in May.' Employees at the Internet applications company (now merged with Akamai) even voted on the preferred destination (a Hawaiian resort). Speedera would cover employee expenses as well as 50 per cent of a spouse's or family member's expenses for four days. Everyone worked feverishly towards the company's goals, which included a hefty increase in revenue. Their motivation was further fuelled by constant reminders of the Hawaiian trip. 'The offices were transformed to look like tropical islands,' says Gupta. Staff also received postcards and brochures with tempting images of the resort and its attractions. Much to everyone's delight, the company achieved its goals and Speedera staff from both countries had a memorable bonding experience on Hawaiian beaches.[36]

Courtesy of Akamai

- *Challenging goals*. Challenging goals (rather than easy ones) cause people to raise the intensity and persistence of their work effort and to think through information more actively. They also fulfil a person's achievement or growth needs when the goal is achieved. General Electric, Goldman Sachs and many other organisations emphasise *stretch goals*. These goals don't just stretch your abilities and motivation; they are goals that you don't know how to reach, so you need to be creative to achieve them.[39]
- *Goal commitment*. Although goals should be challenging, employees also need to be committed to accomplishing the goals. Thus, managers need to find an optimal level of goal difficulty where the goals are challenging yet employees are still motivated to achieve them.[40] This is the same as the E-to-P expectancy discussed in the section on expectancy theory. The lower the E-to-P expectancy that the goal can be accomplished, the less committed (motivated) the employee is to the goal.
- *Goal participation* (sometimes). Goal setting is usually (but not always) more effective when employees participate in setting the goals.[41] Employees identify more with goals they are involved in setting than goals assigned by a supervisor. In fact, today's workforce increasingly expects to be involved in goal setting and other decisions that affect them. Participation may also improve goal quality, because employees have valuable information and knowledge that may not be known to managers who normally develop these goals alone. Thus, participation ensures that employees buy into the goals and have the competencies and resources necessary to accomplish them.
- *Goal feedback*. Feedback is another necessary condition for effective goal setting.[42] **Feedback** is any information that people receive about the consequences of their behaviour. Feedback lets us know whether we have achieved the goal or are properly directing our effort towards it. Feedback is also an essential ingredient in motivation because our growth needs can't be satisfied unless we receive information on goal accomplishment. Feedback is so central to goal setting that it will be looked at more closely next.

feedback Any information that people receive about the consequences of their behaviour.

CHARACTERISTICS OF EFFECTIVE FEEDBACK

Feedback is a key ingredient in goal setting and employee performance. It communicates what behaviours are appropriate or necessary in a particular situation (i.e. clarifies role perceptions) and improves ability by frequently providing information to correct performance problems. Information that identifies a gap between the actual and the ideal performance is known as *corrective feedback*, because it raises awareness of performance errors and identifies ways to correct those errors.

A third benefit is that, under some conditions, feedback motivates employees. This is particularly true when feedback is positive, such as the peer-to-peer recognition activities described in the chapter's opening vignette. These recognition programs communicate feedback as rewards, so they have the double benefit of informing employees about their performance and fulfilling their needs. Constructive feedback can also be motivating when employees have a strong 'can-do' attitude towards the task and a learning orientation. For these people, less-than-ideal performance feedback triggers the drive to learn (improve their performance), not their drive to defend.[43]

Many of the characteristics of effective goal setting also apply to effective feedback (see Exhibit 5.5). First, feedback should be *specific*. The information provided should be connected to the details of the goal, rather than subjective and general phrases such as 'your sales are going well'. Second, feedback must be *relevant*; it must relate to the individual's behaviour rather than to conditions beyond the individual's control. This ensures that the feedback is not distorted by situational factors. Third, feedback should be *timely*; it should be available as soon as possible after the behaviour or results. Timeliness helps employees see a clear association between their behaviour and its consequences.

Fourth, feedback should be *sufficiently frequent*. How frequent is 'sufficiently'? The answer depends on at least two things. One consideration is the employee's knowledge and

Characteristics of effective feedback

EXHIBIT 5.5

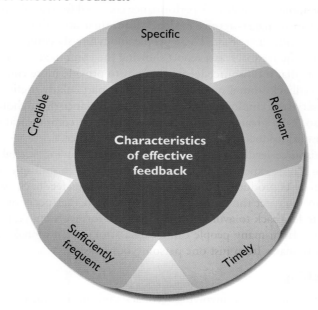

experience with the task. Feedback is a form of reinforcement, so employees working on new tasks should receive more frequent corrective feedback because they require more behaviour guidance and reinforcement (see Chapter 3). Employees who are repeating familiar tasks can receive less frequent feedback. The second factor is how long it takes to complete the task. Feedback is necessarily less frequent in jobs with a long cycle time (e.g. executives and scientists) than in jobs with a short cycle time (e.g. supermarket checkout operator). The final characteristic of effective feedback is that it should be *credible*. Employees are more likely to accept feedback (particularly corrective feedback) from trustworthy and credible sources.

SOURCES OF FEEDBACK

Feedback can originate from non-social or social sources. Non-social sources provide feedback without someone communicating that information. The opening paragraph to this section mentioned that call centres have various forms of non-social feedback, such as electronic displays showing how many callers are waiting and the average time they have been waiting.[44] Some professionals have 'executive dashboards' on their computer screens that display the latest measures of sales, inventory and other indicators of corporate success. The job itself can be a non-social source of feedback. Many employees see the results of their work effort while making a product or providing a service where good and poor performance is fairly obvious.

Social sources of feedback include supervisors, clients, co-workers and anyone else who communicates information about the employee's behaviour or results. Supervisors in some call centres meet with each employee a few times every month to review monitored calls and discuss ways to improve those events. In most other organisations, employees receive formal feedback maybe once or twice a year, but informal feedback occurs more often. Customer surveys have become a popular form of feedback for teams of employees, such as staff at a bank branch.

Multisource (360-degree) feedback

Each year, managers at Microsoft Malaysia receive feedback from a full circle of people, including direct reports, peers, bosses, vendors, customers and partners. A similar review occurs for the software company's managers in many other countries. The Australian federal government also relies on this process, called **multisource** or **360-degree feedback**, to assist the career and

multisource (360-degree) feedback Performance feedback received from a full circle of people around an employee.

leadership development of its senior executive group. As the name implies, multisource feedback is information about an employee's performance collected from a full circle of people. The Australian government managers receive feedback from their boss, four subordinates and two other people familiar with their work. These people anonymously complete the online survey, and managers receive the feedback as a report showing the combined results.[45]

Research suggests that multisource feedback tends to provide more complete and accurate information than feedback from a supervisor alone. It is particularly useful when the supervisor is unable to observe the employee's behaviour or performance throughout the year. Lower-level employees also feel a greater sense of fairness and open communication when they are able to provide upward feedback about their boss's performance.[46]

However, multisource feedback also creates challenges. Having several people review so many other people can be expensive and time-consuming. With multiple opinions, the 360-degree process can also produce ambiguous and conflicting feedback, so employees may require guidance to interpret the results. A third concern is that peers may provide inflated rather than accurate feedback to avoid conflicts over the forthcoming year. A final concern is that critical feedback from many people can create a stronger emotional reaction than if the critical judgment originates from just one person (your boss).[47]

Executive coaching

executive coaching A helping relationship using behavioural methods to assist clients in identifying and achieving goals for their professional performance and personal satisfaction.

Another rapidly growing practice involving feedback and motivation is **executive coaching**, which uses a wide variety of behavioural methods to assist clients to identify and achieve goals for their performance and well-being. Executive coaching is usually conducted by an external consultant and is essentially one-on-one 'just-in-time' personal development using feedback and other techniques. Coaches do not provide answers to the employee's problems. Rather,

P&O Nedlloyd's Australian chief gets coached

Soon after his promotion to general manager of P&O Nedlloyd in Australia, Bob Kemp hired an executive coach to help him discover and repair his vulnerabilities. He was particularly keen to shore up his self-awareness skills because, as the top executive, there was no one above him at the shipping and logistics firm to regularly monitor his interpersonal style as a leader. Over several sessions, the executive coach teased out Kemp's weak spots, such as his listening skills and being approachable. Before long, Kemp's colleagues and wife noticed a positive change. 'Very early in the process, people started telling me I was changing and I started to feel more at ease in the new role,' Kemp recalls. He also noticed that people were 'walking out of my office with a slightly more positive attitude'.[49]

David Geraghty/Newspix

they are 'thought partners' who offer accurate feedback, open dialogue and constructive encouragement to improve the client's performance and personal well-being.

The evidence so far is that executives who work with an executive coach perform better than those who do not. Coaching comes in many forms, so this positive result should be treated cautiously. Still, executive coaching has become a popular form of feedback and development for executives throughout the Pacific Rim. For instance, a few years ago Alison Clark was burning out from overwork, and her business, Tickles Child Care Centre in Te Puke, New Zealand, was suffering from high staff turnover. With the guidance of an executive coach, Clark discovered the leadership issues she needed to address in order to improve the business and her personal life. The ongoing coaching has had a demonstrable effect: Clark has recently earned New Zealand-wide awards for her entrepreneurship and team development.[48]

Choosing feedback sources

With so many sources of feedback—executive coaching, multisource feedback, executive dashboards, customer surveys, equipment gauges, nonverbal communication from your boss, and so on—which one works best under which conditions? The preferred feedback source depends on the purpose of the information. To learn about their progress towards the accomplishment of a goal, employees usually prefer non-social feedback sources, such as computer printouts or feedback directly from the job. This is because information from non-social sources is considered more accurate than information from social sources. Corrective feedback from non-social sources is also less damaging to self-esteem. This is probably just as well, because social sources tend to delay negative information, leave some of it out, and distort the bad news in a positive way.[50] When employees want to improve their self-image, they seek out positive feedback from social sources. It feels better to have co-workers say that you are performing the job well than to discover this from a computer printout.

EVALUATING GOAL SETTING AND FEEDBACK

A recent survey of organisational behaviour researchers recently identified goal setting as one of the top OB theories in terms of validity and usefulness.[51] This high score is not surprising given the impressive research support and wide application of this concept in a variety of settings. In partnership with goal setting, feedback also has an excellent reputation for improving employee motivation and performance.

Nevertheless, both goal setting and feedback have a few limitations.[52] One problem is that combining goals with monetary incentives can motivate employees to set up easy rather than difficult goals. In some cases, employees have negotiated goals with their supervisor that have already been completed! Another limitation is that goal setting potentially focuses employees on a narrow subset of measurable performance indicators while ignoring aspects of job performance that are difficult to measure. The saying 'What gets measured gets done' applies here. A third problem is that setting performance goals is effective in established jobs, but seems to interfere with the learning process in new, complex jobs. Thus, we need to be careful not to apply goal setting where an intense learning process is occurring.

ORGANISATIONAL JUSTICE

Taiwan has legislation guaranteeing gender equality in the workplace, but over half of the 4000 working women recently surveyed in that country say that men get paid more for doing the same work. 'It's unfair,' says Hsieh Hsuen-Hui, a senior trade specialist at an export company in Taipei. 'Monthly salaries that male colleagues receive are about NT$10 000 (A$415) higher than what I get, even though we are doing the same job.' Hsieh's boss believes that men should be paid higher wages since they are more flexible when it comes to overseas business travel. Some employers openly say that they pay men more because they have a greater need

distributive justice The perceived fairness in outcomes we receive relative to our contribution and the outcomes and contributions of others.

procedural justice The fairness of the procedures used to decide the distribution of resources.

LEARNING OBJECTIVE

Summarise the equity theory model, including how people try to reduce feelings of inequity.

equity theory A theory that explains how people develop perceptions of fairness in the distribution and exchange of resources.

for income as the breadwinners. But Hsieh and other women claim that neither reason justifies the significant pay differences. 'We have tried to express our dissatisfaction, but our boss says those are the rules of the game and anyone who doesn't agree can just leave,' says Hsieh.[53]

Most corporate leaders know that treating employees fairly is both morally correct and good for employee motivation, loyalty and well-being. Yet the feelings of injustice that Hsieh Hsuen-Hui describes are regular occurrences in a variety of situations. These incidents can be minimised by applying two forms of organisational justice: distributive justice and procedural justice.[54] **Distributive justice** refers to the perceived fairness in the outcomes we receive relative to our contribution and the outcomes and contributions of others. **Procedural justice**, on the other hand, refers to the fairness of the procedures used to decide the distribution of resources. Hsieh Hsuen-Hui felt distributive injustice because male colleagues were paid significantly more than she was, even though their contribution to the organisation was comparable. Hsieh also experienced procedural injustice because of the way her boss responded to her concerns.

DISTRIBUTIVE JUSTICE AND EQUITY THEORY

The first thing we usually think about and experience in situations of injustice is distributive injustice—the belief (and its emotional response) that the distribution of pay and other outcomes is unfair. What is considered 'fair' varies with each person and situation. We apply an *equality principle* when we believe that everyone in the group should receive the same outcomes. Companies apply this principle when allocating some employee benefits and parking spaces, for example. The *need principle* is applied when we believe that those with the greatest need should receive more outcomes than others with less need. As mentioned above, some Taiwanese employers use the need principle to justify paying men more than women; they say that men need the higher pay because they are the family breadwinners. Hsieh Hsuen-Hui applied the *equity principle* by inferring that people should be paid in proportion to their contribution. The equity principle is the most common distributive justice rule in organisational settings, so let's look at it in more detail.

Elements of equity theory

To explain how the equity principle operates in our heads, organisational behaviour scholars developed **equity theory**, which says that employees determine feelings of equity by comparing their own outcome/input ratio with the outcome/input ratio of some other person.[55] The outcome/input ratio is the value of the outcomes you receive divided by the value of inputs you provide in the exchange relationship. Hsieh Hsuen-Hui probably included her level of responsibility, effort and performance as inputs. Other inputs might include skills, experience, status and amount of time worked. Outcomes are the things employees receive from the organisation in exchange for the inputs. In the case of Hsieh Hsuen-Hui, the main outcome is the pay cheque. Some other outcomes might be promotions, recognition or an office with a window.

Equity theory states that we compare our outcome/input ratio with a comparison other.[56] Hsieh Hsuen-Hui compared herself with her male colleagues in similar positions. However, the comparison other may be another person, a group of people, or even yourself in the past. It may be someone in the same job, another job or another organisation. Chief executives have no direct comparison within the firm, so they tend to compare themselves with their counterparts in other organisations. Some research suggests that employees frequently collect information on several referents to form a 'generalised' comparison other.[57] For the most part, however, the comparison other varies from one person to the next and is not easily identifiable.

Equity evaluation

We form an equity evaluation after determining our own outcome/input ratio and comparing this with the comparison other's ratio. Let's consider the experience of Hsieh Hsuen-Hui

Equity theory model

EXHIBIT 5.6

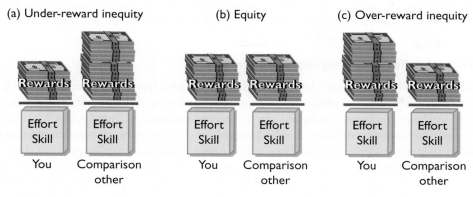

(a) Under-reward inequity   (b) Equity   (c) Over-reward inequity

again. Hsieh feels *under-reward* inequity because her male counterparts receive higher outcomes (pay) for inputs that are, at best, comparable to what she contributes. This condition is illustrated in Exhibit 5.6(a).

In the equity condition, Hsieh would believe that her outcome/input ratio is similar to the ratio of her male colleagues. Specifically, if she believes that she provides the same inputs as the male senior trade specialists, she would feel equity if both the men and the women received the same pay and other outcomes (see Exhibit 5.6(b)). If the male senior trade specialists claim that they make a greater contribution because they have more flexibility, they would have feelings of equity only if they received proportionally more pay than Hsieh and the other female trade specialists. It is also possible that some male trade specialists experience *over-reward* inequity (Exhibit 5.6(c)). They would feel that their jobs have the same value as Hsieh's job, yet they earn more money. However, over-reward inequity isn't as common as under-reward inequity.

Correcting inequity feelings

People experience an emotional tension when they perceive inequities, and, when sufficiently strong, the tension motivates them to reduce the inequities. Research has identified several reactions that people have to inequity. Some actions are reasonable, whereas others are dysfunctional, and some are illegal, such as theft and sabotage. Here are the main ways that people correct inequity feelings when they are under-rewarded compared with a co-worker (a comparison other):[58]

- *Reduce inputs.* Perform at a lower level, give fewer helpful suggestions, or engage in less organisational citizenship behaviour.
- *Increase outcomes.* Ask for a pay increase, or make unauthorised use of company resources.
- *Increase comparison other's inputs.* Subtly ask the better-off co-worker to do a larger share of the work to justify his/her higher pay or other outcomes.
- *Reduce comparison other's outcomes.* Ask the boss to stop giving favourable treatment to the co-worker.
- *Change perceptions.* Believe that the co-worker really is doing more (e.g. working longer hours), or that the higher outcomes (e.g. better office) he/she receives really aren't so much better.
- *Change the comparison other.* Compare yourself to someone else closer to your situation (job duties, pay scale).
- *Leave the field.* Avoid thinking about the inequity by keeping away from the office where the co-worker is located, taking more sick leave, moving to another department, or quitting the job.

Although the categories remain the same, people who feel over-reward inequity would, of course, act differently. For example, over-rewarded employees don't usually correct this tension by working harder. Instead, they might encourage the referent to work at a more leisurely pace or, equally likely, change their perceptions to justify why they are given more favourable outcomes. As the author Pierre Burton once said: 'I was underpaid for the first half of my life. I don't mind being overpaid for the second half.'[59]

Individual differences: equity sensitivity

equity sensitivity A person's outcome/input preferences and reaction to various outcome/input ratios.

Thus far, equity theory has been described as though everyone has the same feelings of inequity in a particular situation. The reality, however, is that people vary in their **equity sensitivity**, that is, their outcome/input preferences and reaction to various outcome/input ratios.[60] At one end of the equity sensitivity continuum are the 'benevolents'—people who are tolerant of situations in which they are under-rewarded. They might prefer equal outcome/input ratios, but they don't mind if others receive more than they do for the same inputs. In the middle are people who fit the standard equity theory model. These 'equity sensitives' want their outcome/input ratio to be equal to the outcome/input ratio of the comparison other. Equity sensitives feel increasing inequity as the ratios become different. At the other end are the 'entitleds'. These people feel more comfortable in situations in which they receive proportionately more than others. They might accept having the same outcome/input ratio as others, but they would prefer receiving more than others performing the same work.[61]

Evaluating equity theory

Equity theory is widely studied and is quite successful at predicting various situations involving feelings of workplace injustice, such as major baseball league salary disputes and remuneration of British CEOs.[62] Feelings of inequity are regular occurrences in every workplace. Some tensions are minor and temporary misunderstandings of the situation; others produce emotions or, worse, major theft and sabotage of company resources. Feelings of inequity are based on the moral principle of distributive justice (see Chapter 2), so companies that act unfairly towards their employees also face the charge of unethical conduct. Reality Check 5.1 describes a popular movement in the United Kingdom where employees (and shareholders) publicly berate 'fat cat' CEOs for being paid much more than they are worth when compared with the pay cheques of their staff. These exhibitions aren't just appealing to the logic of inequity; they are publicly leveraging the moral argument against overpaid chief executives.

In spite of its research support, equity theory has a few limitations. One concern is that the theory isn't sufficiently specific to predict employee motivation and behaviour. It doesn't indicate which inputs or outcomes are most valuable, and it doesn't identify the comparison other against which the outcome/input ratio is evaluated. These vague and very flexible elements may explain why organisational behaviour scholars think that equity theory is highly valid but only moderately useful.[63]

A second problem is that equity theory incorrectly assumes that people are individualistic, rational and selfish. In reality, people are social creatures who define themselves as members of various group memberships (see social identity theory in Chapter 3). They share goals with other members of these groups and commit themselves to the norms of their groups. A third limitation is that recent studies have found that equity theory accounts for only some of our feelings of fairness or justice in the workplace. Scholars now say that procedural justice, which is looked at next, is at least as important as distributive justice.

PROCEDURAL JUSTICE

LEARNING OBJECTIVE

Identify the factors that influence procedural justice, as well as the consequences of procedural justice.

For many years, organisational behaviour scholars believed that distributive justice was more important than procedural justice in explaining employee motivation, attitudes and behaviour. This belief was based on the assumption that people are driven mainly by self-interest, so they try to maximise their personal outcomes. Today, we know that people seek justice for its own sake, not just as a means to improve their pay cheque. Thus, procedural jus-

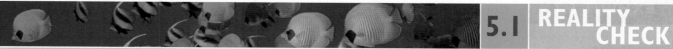

5.1 REALITY CHECK

PROTESTING UNFAIR 'FAT CAT' PAY IN THE UNITED KINGDOM

Cats have become an increasingly common sight at corporate annual general meetings throughout the United Kingdom. More precisely, dozens of people have been dressing up as 'fat cats' in business suits as a way of protesting the generous pay cheques of British executives. Labour unions are behind many of these antics, but institutional investors and private shareholders are also expressing their feelings of unfairness by voting against executive remuneration.

Over half of GlaxoSmithKline's shareholders opposed an A$47.5 million golden parachute that chief executive Jean-Pierre Garnier would be paid if fired from the pharmaceutical giant. A larger percentage of shareholders also opposed or abstained from voting for overly generous pay packages for executives at advertising group WPP and engineering group BAE Systems.

Critics say there is plenty of reason for the theatrics and shareholder unrest against executive pay. Piers Morgan was ousted as editor of the *Daily Mirror* after the British tabloid lost 800 000 readers and, in an embarrassing incident, was revealed to have published fake photos of Iraqi prisoner abuse while under Morgan's watch. In spite of these failings, Morgan was sent out the door with A$4 million—a buyout of the remaining two years of his contract. Sir Phillip Watts didn't suffer too badly, either, with his A$2.4 million farewell handshake from Shell. Under Watts' command, the Anglo–Dutch oil giant admitted overstating its gas and oil reserves by more than 20 per cent.

Employees and commuters were also miffed recently when Network Rail bosses gave themselves healthy bonuses soon after hundreds of staff were laid off. The publicly owned rail company's chief executive and deputy officer each received a bonus of over A$230 000. 'It is hard to understand how Network Rail bosses can sack 650 experienced managers last year to save costs and justify six-figure bonuses for themselves six months later,' complained a spokesperson for the union representing the company's office staff.

British protesters express their anger over unfair executive pay by dressing as 'fat cats' in business suits outside the company's annual general meeting.

© Simon Clark

Sources: K. Walker, 'Rail Fat Cats Scandal', *The Express* (London), 3 June 2004, 10; H. Jones, 'Fat Cats Rewarded for Failure', *The Express* (London), 28 August 2004, 48–49; W. Wallace, 'British Shareholders Battle "American-Style" Exec Pay', *Los Angeles Times*, 2 June 2003, 5; 'Handfuls of Protesters Decrying "Fat Cat" Paycheques', *Canadian Press*, 25 May 2003; 'Heads, They Win', *The Guardian*, 9 May 2003.

tice seems to be as important as (some experts say more important than) distributive justice in explaining employee attitudes, motivation and behaviour.[65]

Structural rules of justice

Procedural justice is influenced by both structural rules and social rules (see Exhibit 5.7, overleaf).[65] Structural rules represent the policies and practices that decision makers should follow. The most frequently identified structural rule in procedural justice research is people's belief that they should have a 'voice' in the decision process.[66] Voice allows employees to convey what they believe are relevant facts and views to the decision maker. Voice also provides a 'value-expressive' function; employees tend to feel better after having an opportunity to speak their mind. Other structural rules are that the decision maker is unbiased, relies on complete and accurate information, applies existing policies consistently, has listened to all sides of the dispute, and allows the decision to be appealed to a higher authority.[67]

EXHIBIT 5.7   Components of organisational justice

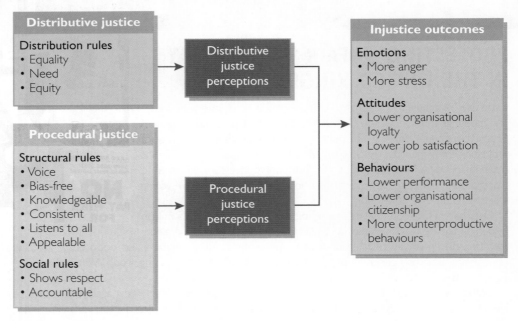

Social rules of justice

Along with structural rules, procedural justice is influenced by social rules, that is, how well the decision maker treats employees during the process. The two key social rules are respect and accountability. Employees feel greater procedural justice when they are treated with respect. For instance, one study found that non-white nurses who experienced racism tended to file grievances only after experiencing disrespectful treatment in their attempt to resolve the racist situation. Another study found that employees with repetitive strain injuries were more likely to file workers' compensation claims after experiencing disrespectful behaviour from management. A third, recent study noted that employees have stronger feelings of injustice when the manager has a reputation for treating people unfairly most of the time.[68]

The other social rule that has attracted attention is accountability. People believe that they are entitled to explanations about decisions, particularly when the results have potentially negative consequences for them. For instance, suppose that a co-worker receives a better office than you do (distributive injustice). The chances are that you will feel less injustice after hearing the decision maker's explanation for that decision.

Consequences of procedural injustice

Procedural justice has a strong influence on a person's emotions and motivation. Employees tend to experience anger towards the source of an injustice, which generates various response behaviours that scholars categorise as either withdrawal or aggression.[69] Notice how these response behaviours are similar to the fight-or-flight responses described earlier in the chapter regarding situations that activate our drive to defend. Withdrawal behaviours might include avoiding those who acted unjustly or being less willing to comply with their future requests. For instance, employees who believe that their boss relies on an unfair decision process may be less likely to 'walk the extra mile' in the future and might complete any assigned work only at a minimal standard.

Aggressive responses to procedural injustice include several counterproductive work behaviours, such as sabotage, theft, conflict and acts of violence.[70] However, most employees who experience injustice respond with milder forms of retaliation, such as showing indignation and denouncing the decision maker's competence. Research suggests that being treated unfairly undermines our self-esteem and social status, particularly when others see that we have been unjustly treated. Consequently, employees retaliate to restore their self-esteem and reinstate their status and power in the relationship with the perpetrator of the injustice. Employees also engage in these counterproductive behaviours to educate the decision maker, thereby minimising the chance of future injustices.[71]

ORGANISATIONAL JUSTICE IN PRACTICE

One of the clearest lessons from equity theory is that people need to continually be treated fairly in the distribution of organisational rewards. Unfortunately, this is perhaps one of life's greatest challenges because most people seem to have unique opinions about the value of inputs and outcomes. Decision makers need to carefully understand these dynamics, along with the distribution rules—equity, equality or need—that the organisation wants to apply. The procedural justice literature points out that justice also depends on whether employees believe that the decision-making process follows a fair set of rules and that they are personally treated fairly in that process.

In spite of the many challenges of creating justice in the workplace, managers can improve their procedural fairness through training programs. In one study, supervisors participated in role-play exercises to develop several procedural justice practices in the disciplinary process, such as maintaining the employee's privacy, giving employees some control over the process, avoiding arbitrariness, and exhibiting a supportive demeanour. Judges subsequently rated supervisors who received the procedural justice training as behaving more fairly than supervisors who did not receive the training. In another study, managers received procedural justice training through lectures, case studies, role-playing and discussion. Three months later, subordinates of the trained managers had significantly higher organisational citizenship behaviours than the subordinates of managers who did not receive the training.[72] Overall, it seems that justice can be improved in the workplace.

CHAPTER SUMMARY

Motivation refers to the forces within a person that affect his or her direction, intensity and persistence of voluntary behaviour in the workplace. Motivation has become more challenging because of an increasingly turbulent work environment, the removal of direct supervision as a motivational instrument, and the lack of understanding about what motivates the new generations of people entering the workforce.

Maslow's needs hierarchy groups needs into a hierarchy of five levels and states that the lowest needs are initially the most important, but the higher needs become more important as the lower ones are satisfied. Although very popular, the theory lacks research support, as does ERG theory, which attempted to overcome some of the limitations in Maslow's needs hierarchy. Both models assume that everyone has the same hierarchy, whereas the emerging evidence suggests that needs hierarchies vary from one person to the next based on their social identity and personal values.

Four-drive theory states that everyone has four innate drives—the drive to acquire, to bond, to learn and to defend. These drives create emotional markers that motivate people. The drives generate competing emotions, however, so people consciously reconcile these competing impulses through a skill set that considers social norms, past experience and personal values. Four-drive theory offers considerable potential for understanding employee motivation, but it still requires clarification and research to understand how people translate competing emotions into motivated behaviour.

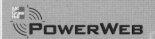

McClelland's learned needs theory argues that needs can be strengthened through learning. The three needs studied in this respect have been the need for achievement, the need for power and the need for affiliation.

The practical implication of needs-/drives-based motivation theories is that corporate leaders need to provide opportunities for everyone in the workplace to regularly fulfil all four drives, that organisations should avoid too much or too little opportunity to fulfil each drive, and that employees should be offered a choice of rewards rather than given the same reward as everyone else.

Expectancy theory states that work effort is determined by the perception that effort will result in a particular level of performance (E-to-P expectancy), the perception that a specific behaviour or performance level will lead to specific outcomes (P-to-O expectancy), and the valences that the person feels for those outcomes. The E-to-P expectancy increases by improving the employee's ability and confidence to perform the job. The P-to-O expectancy increases by measuring performance accurately, distributing higher rewards to better performers, and showing employees that rewards are performance-based. Outcome valences increase by finding out what employees want and using these resources as rewards.

Goal setting is the process of motivating employees and clarifying their role perceptions by establishing performance objectives. Goals are more effective when they are specific, relevant and challenging, have employee commitment, and are accompanied by meaningful feedback. Participative goal setting is important in some situations. Effective feedback is specific, relevant, timely, credible and sufficiently frequent (which depends on the length of the task cycle and the employee's knowledge/experience with the task). Two increasingly popular forms of feedback are multisource (360-degree) assessment and executive coaching. Feedback from non-social sources is also beneficial.

Organisational justice consists of distributive justice (perceived fairness in the outcomes received relative to personal contributions and the outcomes and contributions of others) and procedural justice (fairness of the procedures used to decide the distribution of resources). Equity theory, which considers the most common principle applied in distributive justice, has four elements: outcome/input ratio, comparison other, equity evaluation, and consequences of inequity. The theory also explains what people are motivated to do when they feel inequitably treated. Equity sensitivity is a personal characteristic that explains why people react differently to varying degrees of inequity.

Procedural justice is influenced by both structural rules and social rules. Structural rules represent the policies and practices that decision makers should follow; the most frequently identified is giving employees 'voice' in the decision process. Social rules refer to standards of interpersonal conduct between employees and decision makers; they are best observed by showing respect and providing accountability for decisions. Procedural justice is as important as distributive justice, and it influences organisational commitment, trust and various withdrawal and aggression behaviours.

KEY TERMS

distributive justice p. 154
drives p. 139
equity sensitivity p. 156
equity theory p. 154
ERG theory p. 141
executive coaching p. 152
expectancy theory p. 146

feedback p. 150
four-drive theory p. 141
goal setting p. 149
Maslow's needs hierarchy p. 139
motivation p. 138
multisource (360-degree) feedback p. 151
need for achievement (nAch) p. 143

need for affiliation (nAff) p. 144
need for power (nPow) p. 144
needs p. 138
procedural justice p. 154
self-actualisation p. 140
valence p. 147

DISCUSSION QUESTIONS

1. This chapter begins by suggesting that motivating employees has become more challenging in recent years, partly because younger employees (Generation-X and Generation-Y) have different expectations from baby boomers. How do you think these younger and older generation groups differ in their expectations? Generally speaking, what would motivate a typical Generation-Y employee (under 25 years old) at work more than a typical baby boomer (over 45 years old)?

2. Four-drive theory is conceptually different from Maslow's needs hierarchy (as well as ERG theory) in several ways. Describe these differences. At the same time, needs are typically based on drives, so the four drives should parallel the seven needs that Maslow identified (five in the hierarchy and two additional needs). Map Maslow's needs onto the four drives in four-drive theory.

3. Use all three components of expectancy theory to explain why some employees are motivated to show up for work during a severe storm whereas others make no effort to leave their home.

4. What are the limitations of expectancy theory in predicting an individual's work effort and behaviour?

5. Using your knowledge of the characteristics of effective goals, establish two meaningful goals related to your performance in this class.

6. When do employees prefer feedback from non-social rather than social sources? Explain why non-social sources are preferred under these conditions.

7. Several service representatives are upset that the newly hired representative with no previous experience will be paid $3000 a year above the usual starting salary in the pay range. The department manager explained that the new hire would not accept the entry-level rate, so the company raised the offer by $3000. All five reps currently earn salaries near the top of the scale ($15 000 higher than the new recruit), although they all started at the minimum starting salary a few years earlier. Use equity theory to explain why the five service representatives have inequity feelings in this situation.

8. Organisational injustice can occur in the classroom as well as in the workplace. Identify classroom situations in which you have experienced feelings of injustice. What can instructors do to maintain an environment that fosters both distributive and procedural justice?

BUDDY'S SNACK COMPANY

5.1 | SKILL BUILDER

CASE STUDY

By Russell Casey, Clayton State University, and Gloria Thompson, University of Phoenix

Buddy's Snack Company is a family-owned company in Colorado. Buddy Forest started the business in 1951 by selling homemade potato chips out of the back of his truck. Today Buddy's is a $36 million snack food company struggling to regain market share lost to Frito-Lay and others. In the early 1980s, Buddy passed the business onto his son, Buddy Jr, who is now grooming his son, Mark, to succeed himself as head of the company.

Six months ago, Mark joined Buddy's Snacks as a salesperson and after four months was quickly promoted to sales manager. Mark recently graduated from a local university with an MBA in Marketing, and Buddy Jr was hoping that Mark would be able to implement strategies that could help turn the company around. One of Mark's initial strategies was to introduce a new sales performance management system. As part of this approach, any salesperson who received a below-average performance rating would be required to attend a mandatory coaching session with his/her supervisor. Mark is hoping that these coaching sessions will motivate his employees to increase their sales. This case describes the reaction of three salespeople who have been required to attend a coaching session because of their low performance over the previous quarter.

LYNDA LEWIS

Lynda is a hard worker who takes pride in her work ethic. She has spent a lot of time reading the training material and learning selling techniques, viewing training videos in her own time and accompanying top salespeople on their calls. Lynda has no problem asking for advice and doing whatever needs to be done to learn the business. Everyone agrees that Lynda has a cheery attitude and is a real 'team player', giving the company 150 per cent at all times. It has been a tough quarter for Lynda due to the downturn in the economy, but she is doing her best to make sales for the company. Lynda doesn't feel that failure to make quota during this past quarter is due to lack of effort, but just bad luck in the economy. She is hopeful that things will turn around in the next quarter.

Lynda is upset with Mark for insisting that she attend the coaching session, because this is the first time in three years that her sales quota has not been met. Although Lynda is willing to do whatever it takes to be successful, she is concerned that the coaching sessions will be held on a Saturday. Doesn't Mark realise that Lynda is raising three boys by herself and that weekends are an important time for her family? Because Lynda is a dedicated employee she will somehow manage to rearrange the family's schedule.

Lynda is now very concerned about how her efforts are being perceived by Mark. After all, she exceeded the sales quota in the previous quarter, yet did not receive a 'thank you' or 'good job' for that effort. The entire experience has left Lynda unmotivated and questioning her future with the company.

MICHAEL BENJAMIN

Michael is happy to have his job at Buddy's Snack Company, although he doesn't really like sales work very much. Michael accepted the position because he felt that he wouldn't have to work hard and would have a lot of free time during the day. Michael was sent to coaching mainly because his customer satisfaction reports were low; in fact, they were the lowest in the company. Michael tends to give 'canned' presentations and does not listen closely to the customer's needs. Consequently, Michael makes numerous errors in new sales orders, which delays shipments and loses business and goodwill for Buddy's Snack Company. Michael doesn't really care, since most of his customers do not spend much money and he doesn't think it is worth his while to take extra care.

There has been a recent change in the company commission structure. Instead of selling to the warehouse stores and possibly earning a high commission, Michael is now forced to sell to lower-volume convenience stores. In other words, he will have to sell twice as much product to earn the same amount of money. Michael does not think this change in commission is fair, and he feels that the coaching session will be a waste of time. He feels that the other members of the sales team are getting all of the good leads and that is why they are so successful. Michael doesn't socialise with others in the office and attributes others' success and promotions to 'who they know' in the company rather than the fact that they are hard workers. He feels that no matter how much effort is put into the job, he will never be adequately rewarded.

KYLE SHERBO

For three of the last five years Kyle was the number one salesperson in the division and had hopes of being promoted to sales manager. When Mark joined the company, Kyle worked closely with Buddy Jr to help Mark learn all facets of the business. Kyle thought that this close relationship with Buddy Jr would assure his promotion to the coveted position of sales manager and was devastated to learn that Mark had received the promotion.

During the past quarter there was a noticeable change in Kyle's work habits. It had become commonplace for Kyle to be late for appointments or to miss them entirely, to not return phone calls and to not follow-up on leads. His sales performance declined dramatically, which resulted in a drastic loss of income. Although Kyle had been dedicated and fiercely loyal to Buddy Jr and

the company for many years, he is now looking for other employment. Buddy's Snacks is located in a rural community, which leaves Kyle with limited job opportunities. He was, however, offered a position as a sales manager with a competing company in a larger town, but Kyle's wife refuses to leave the area because of her strong family ties. Kyle is bitter and resentful of his current situation and now faces a mandatory coaching session that will be conducted by Mark.

QUESTIONS

1. Use equity theory to explain how these three employees reacted to this situation.
2. Explain the motivation of these three employees in terms of the expectancy theory of motivation.

NEEDS PRIORITY EXERCISE

5.2 | SKILL BUILDER

TEAM EXERCISE

PURPOSE

This class exercise is designed to help you understand the characteristics and contingencies of employee needs in the workplace.

INSTRUCTIONS

Step 1: The table below lists in alphabetical order fourteen characteristics of the job or work environment. Working alone, use the far-left column to rank-order these characteristics in terms of how important they are to you personally. Write in '1' beside the most important characteristic, '2' for the second most important and so on through to '14' for the least important characteristic on the list.

Step 2: In the second column, rank-order these characteristics in the order that you think human resource managers believe their employees would rank them.

Step 3: Your instructor will provide results of a recent large-scale survey of employees. When these results are presented, identify the reasons for any noticeable differences. Relate the differences to your understanding of the emerging view of employee needs and drives in work settings.

Importance to YOU	What HR managers believe are important to employees	Characteristics of the job or work environment
_____	_____	Autonomy and independence
_____	_____	Benefits (health care, dental, etc.)
_____	_____	Career development opportunities
_____	_____	Communication between employees and senior management
_____	_____	Compensation/pay
_____	_____	Feeling safe in the work environment
_____	_____	Flexibility to balance work–life issues
_____	_____	Job security
_____	_____	Job-specific training
_____	_____	Management recognition of employee job performance
_____	_____	Opportunities to use skills/abilities
_____	_____	Organisation's commitment to professional development
_____	_____	Relationship with immediate supervisor
_____	_____	The work itself

SKILL BUILDER | 5.3 — MEASURING YOUR EQUITY SENSITIVITY

SELF-ASSESSMENT

STUDENT CD

PURPOSE

This self-assessment is designed to help you to estimate your level of equity sensitivity.

INSTRUCTIONS

Read each of the statements below and circle the response that you believe best reflects your position regarding each statement. Then use the scoring key in Appendix B to calculate your results. This exercise is completed alone so that students can assess themselves honestly without concerns of social comparison. However, class discussion will focus on equity theory and the effect of equity sensitivity on perceptions of fairness in the workplace.

EQUITY PREFERENCE QUESTIONNAIRE

To what extent do you agree or disagree that ...	Strongly agree	Agree	Neutral	Disagree	Strongly disagree
1. I prefer to do as little as possible at work while getting as much as I can from my employer.	1	2	3	4	5
2. I am most satisfied at work when I have to do as little as possible.	1	2	3	4	5
3. When I am at my job, I think of ways to get out of work.	1	2	3	4	5
4. If I could get away with it, I would try to work just a little bit slower than the boss expects.	1	2	3	4	5
5. It is really satisfying to me when I can get something for nothing at work.	1	2	3	4	5
6. It is the smart employee who gets as much as he/she can while giving as little as possible in return.	1	2	3	4	5
7. Employees who are more concerned about what they can get from their employer than what they can give to their employer are the wisest.	1	2	3	4	5
8. When I have completed my task for the day, I help out other employees who have yet to complete their tasks.	1	2	3	4	5
9. Even if I receive low wages and poor benefits from my employer, I would still try to do my best at my job.	1	2	3	4	5
10. If I had to work hard all day at my job, I would probably quit.	1	2	3	4	5
11. I feel obligated to do more than I am paid to do at work.	1	2	3	4	5
12. At work, my greatest concern is whether or not I am doing the best job I can.	1	2	3	4	5
13. A job which requires me to be busy during the day is better than a job which allows me a lot of loafing.	1	2	3	4	5
14. At work, I feel uneasy when there is little work for me to do.	1	2	3	4	5
15. I would become very dissatisfied with my job if I had little or no work to do.	1	2	3	4	5
16. All other things being equal, it is better to have a job with a lot of duties and responsibilities than one with few duties and responsibilities.	1	2	3	4	5

Source: Reprinted from K.S. Sauleya and A.G. Bedeian, 'Equity Sensitivity: Construction of a Measure and Examination of Its Psychometric Properties', *Journal of Management*, 26 (September 2000), pp. 885–910. Copyright © 2000, with permission from Elsevier.

MEASURING YOUR GROWTH–NEED STRENGTH

5.4 | **SKILL BUILDER**

SELF ASSESSMENT

FULL EXERCISE ON
STUDENT CD

Abraham Maslow's needs hierarchy theory distinguished between deficiency needs and growth needs. Deficiency needs become activated when unfulfilled, such as the need for food or belongingness. Growth needs, on the other hand, continue to develop even when temporarily fulfilled. Maslow identified self-actualisation as the only category of growth needs. Research has found that Maslow's needs hierarchy theory overall doesn't fit reality, but specific elements such as the concept of growth needs have not been rejected. This self-assessment is designed to estimate your level of growth-need strength. This instrument asks you to consider what it is about a job that is most important to you. Indicate which of the two jobs you personally would prefer if you had to make a choice between them. In answering each question, assume that everything else about the jobs is the same. Pay attention only to the characteristics actually listed.

NOTES

1   W. L. Lee, 'Net Value: That Loving Feeling', *The Edge Financial Daily* (Malaysia), 25 April 2005; L. Molina, 'Novel Staff Incentive Program Pays Off', *Courier-Mail* (Brisbane), 2 September 2005, 35; N. Mwaura, 'Honour Staff for Good Work', *Daily Nation* (Nairobi, Kenya), 27 September 2005; E. White, 'Praise from Peers Goes a Long Way', *Wall Street Journal*, 19 December 2005, B3.

2   C. C. Pinder, *Work Motivation in Organizational Behavior* (Upper Saddle River, NJ: Prentice-Hall, 1998); R. M. Steers, R. T. Mowday and D. L. Shapiro, 'The Future of Work Motivation Theory', *Academy of Management Review* 29 (2004), 379–87.

3   'Towers Perrin Study Finds, Despite Layoffs and Slow Economy, a New, More Complex Power Game Is Emerging between Employers and Employees', Business Wire news release (New York, 30 August 2001); K. V. Rondeau and T. H. Wagar, 'Downsizing and Organizational Restructuring: What Is the Impact on Hospital Performance?', *International Journal of Public Administration* 26 (2003), 1647–68.

4   C. Lachnit, 'The Young and the Dispirited', *Workforce* 81 (August 2002), 18; S. H. Applebaum, M. Serena and B. T. Shapiro, 'Generation X and the Boomers: Organizational Myths and Literary Realities', *Management Research News* 27, no. 11/12 (2004), 1–28. Motivation and needs across generations is also discussed in R. Zemke and B. Filipczak, *Generations at Work: Managing the Clash of Veterans, Boomers, Xers, and Nexters in Your Workplace* (NY: AMACOM, 2000).

5   T. V. Sewards and M. A. Sewards, 'Fear and Power-Dominance Drive Motivation: Neural Representations and Pathways Mediating Sensory and Mnemonic Inputs, and Outputs to Premotor Structures', *Neuroscience and Biobehavioral Reviews* 26 (2002), 553–79; K. C. Berridge, 'Motivation Concepts in Behavioral Neuroscience', *Physiology & Behavior* 81, no. 2 (2004), 179–209.

6   A. H. Maslow, 'A Preface to Motivation Theory', *Psychosomatic Medicine* 5 (1943), 85–92.

7   A. H. Maslow, 'A Theory of Human Motivation', *Psychological Review* 50 (1943), 370–96; A. H. Maslow, *Motivation and Personality* (New York: Harper & Row, 1954).

8   D. T. Hall and K. E. Nougaim, 'An Examination of Maslow's Need Hierarchy in an Organizational Setting', *Organizational Behavior and Human Performance* 3, no. 1 (1968), 12; M. A. Wahba and L. G. Bridwell, 'Maslow Reconsidered: A Review of Research on the Need Hierarchy Theory', *Organizational Behavior and Human Performance* 15 (1976), 212–40; E. L. Betz, 'Two Tests of Maslow's Theory of Need Fulfillment', *Journal of Vocational Behavior* 24, no. 2 (1984), 204–20; P. A. Corning, 'Biological Adaptation in Human Societies: A "Basic Needs" Approach', *Journal of Bioeconomics* 2, no. 1 (2000), 41–86.

9   K. Dye, A. J. Mills and T. G. Weatherbee, 'Maslow: Man Interrupted—Reading Management Theory in Context', February 2005, Wolfville, NS.

10   A. H. Maslow, *Maslow on Management* (New York: John Wiley & Sons, 1998).

11   M. Marshall, 'Making His Own Brand in Business', *Oakleigh Monash/Springvale Dandenong Leader* (Victoria), 21 September 2005, 14.

12   C. P. Alderfer, *Existence, Relatedness, and Growth* (New York: Free Press, 1972).

13   J. Rauschenberger, N. Schmitt and J. E. Hunter, 'A Test of the Need Hierarchy Concept by a Markov Model of Change in Need Strength', *Administrative Science Quarterly* 25, no. 4 (December 1980), 654–70; J. P. Wanous and A. A. Zwany, 'A Cross-Sectional Test of Need Hierarchy Theory', *Organizational Behavior and Human Performance* 18 (1977), 78–97.

14   S. A. Haslam, C. Powell and J. Turner, 'Social Identity, Self-Categorization, and Work Motivation: Rethinking the Contribution of the Group to Positive and Sustainable Organisational Outcomes', *Applied Psychology: An International Review* 49 (July 2000), 319–39; E. A. Locke, 'Motivation, Cognition, and Action: An Analysis of Studies of Task Goals and Knowledge', *Applied Psychology: An International Review* 49 (2000), 408–29.

15   B. A. Agle and C. B. Caldwell, 'Understanding Research on Values in Business', *Business and Society* 38 (September 1999), 326–87; B. Verplanken and R. W. Holland, 'Motivated Decision Making: Effects of Activation and Self-Centrality of Values on Choices and Behavior', *Journal of Personality and Social Psychology* 82, no. 3 (2002), 434–47; S. Hitlin and J. A. Pilavin, 'Values: Reviving a Dormant Concept', *Annual Review of Sociology* 30 (2004), 359–93.

16   P. R. Lawrence and N. Nohria, *Driven: How Human Nature Shapes Our Choices* (San Francisco: Jossey-Bass, 2002).

17 R. E. Baumeister and M. R. Leary, 'The Need to Belong: Desire for Interpersonal Attachments as a Fundamental Human Motivation', *Psychological Bulletin* 117 (1995), 497–529; S. Kirkey, 'Being Shy, Unsociable Is Bad for Your Health, Study Finds', *Ottawa Citizen*, 21 November 2005, A1.

18 W. H. Bexton, W. Heron and T. H. Scott, 'Effects of Decreased Variation in the Sensory Environment', *Canadian Journal of Psychology* 8 (1954), 70–6; G. Loewenstein, 'The Psychology of Curiosity: A Review and Reinterpretation', *Psychological Bulletin* 116, no. 1 (1994), 75–98.

19 A. R. Damasio, *Descartes' Error: Emotion, Reason, and the Human Brain* (New York: Putnam Sons, 1994); J. E. LeDoux, 'Emotion Circuits in the Brain', *Annual Review of Neuroscience* 23 (2000), 155–84; P. Winkielman and K. C. Berridge, 'Unconscious Emotion', *Current Directions in Psychological Science* 13, no. 3 (2004), 120–3.

20 Lawrence and Nohria, *Driven: How Human Nature Shapes Our Choices*, pp. 145–7.

21 D. C. McClelland, *The Achieving Society* (New York: Van Nostrand Reinhold, 1961).

22 S. Shane, E. A. Locke and C. J. Collins, 'Entrepreneurial Motivation', *Human Resource Management Review* 13, no. 2 (2003), 257–79.

23 D. C. McClelland and D. H. Burnham, 'Power Is the Great Motivator', *Harvard Business Review* 73 (January–February 1995), 126–39; J. L. Thomas, M. W. Dickson and P. D. Bliese, 'Values Predicting Leader Performance in the US Army Reserve Officer Training Corps Assessment Center: Evidence for a Personality-Mediated Model', *Leadership Quarterly* 12, no. 2 (2001), 181–96.

24 D. Vredenburgh and Y. Brender, 'The Hierarchical Abuse of Power in Work Organizations', *Journal of Business Ethics* 17 (September 1998), 1337–47.

25 D. Miron and D. C. McClelland, 'The Impact of Achievement Motivation Training on Small Business', *California Management Review* 21 (1979), 13–28.

26 Lawrence and Nohria, *Driven: How Human Nature Shapes Our Choices*, chapter 11.

27 P. Dvorak, 'Out of Tune', *Wall Street Journal*, 29 June 2005, A1.

28 Expectancy theory of motivation in work settings originated in V. H. Vroom, *Work and Motivation* (New York: Wiley, 1964). The version of expectancy theory presented here was developed by Edward Lawler. Lawler's model provides a clearer presentation of the model's three components. P-to-O expectancy is similar to 'instrumentality' in Vroom's original expectancy theory model. The difference is that instrumentality is a correlation whereas P-to-O expectancy is a probability. See: J. P. Campbell et al., *Managerial Behavior, Performance, and Effectiveness* (New York: McGraw-Hill, 1970); E. E. Lawler III, *Motivation in Work Organizations* (Monterey, CA: Brooks-Cole, 1973); D. A. Nadler and E. E. Lawler, 'Motivation: A Diagnostic Approach', in *Perspectives on Behavior in Organizations*, ed. J. R. Hackman, E. E. Lawler III and L. W. Porter, 2nd edn (New York: McGraw-Hill, 1983), 67–78.

29 M. Zeelenberg et al., 'Emotional Reactions to the Outcomes of Decisions: The Role of Counterfactual Thought in the Experience of Regret and Disappointment', *Organizational Behavior and Human Decision Processes* 75, no. 2 (1998), 117–41; B. A. Mellers, 'Choice and the Relative Pleasure of Consequences', *Psychological Bulletin* 126, no. 6 (November 2000), 910–24; R. P. Bagozzi, U. M. Dholakia and S. Basuroy, 'How Effortful Decisions Get Enacted: The Motivating Role of Decision Processes, Desires, and Anticipated Emotions', *Journal of Behavioral Decision Making* 16, no. 4 (October 2003), 273–95.

30 Nadler and Lawler, 'Motivation: A Diagnostic Approach'.

31 T. Janz, 'Manipulating Subjective Expectancy through Feedback: A Laboratory Study of the Expectancy–Performance Relationship', *Journal of Applied Psychology* 67 (1982), 480–5; K. A. Karl, A. M. O'Leary-Kelly and J. J. Martoccio, 'The Impact of Feedback and Self-Efficacy on Performance in Training', *Journal of Organizational Behavior* 14 (1993), 379–94; R. G. Lord, P. J. Hanges and E. G. Godfrey, 'Integrating Neural Networks into Decision-Making and Motivational Theory: Rethinking Vie Theory', *Canadian Psychology* 44, no. 1 (2003), 21–38.

32 P. W. Mulvey et al., *The Knowledge of Pay Study: E-Mails from the Frontline* (Scottsdale, Arizona: WorldatWork, 2002).

33 M. L. Ambrose and C. T. Kulik, 'Old Friends, New Faces: Motivation Research in the 1990s', *Journal of Management* 25 (May 1999), 231–92; C. L. Haworth and P. E. Levy, 'The Importance of Instrumentality Beliefs in the Prediction of Organizational Citizenship Behaviors', *Journal of Vocational Behavior* 59 (August 2001), 64–75; Y. Chen, A. Gupta and L. Hoshower, 'Marketing Students' Perceptions of Teaching Evaluations: An Application of Expectancy Theory', *Marketing Education Review* 14, no. 2 (Summer 2004), 23–36.

34 T. Matsui and I. Terai, 'A Cross-Cultural Study of the Validity of the Expectancy Theory of Motivation', *Journal of Applied Psychology* 60 (1979), 263–5; D. H. B. Welsh, F. Luthans and S. M. Sommer, 'Managing Russian Factory Workers: The Impact of US-Based Behavioral and Participative Techniques', *Academy of Management Journal* 36 (1993), 58–79.

35 K. H. Doerr and T. R. Mitchell, 'Impact of Material Flow Policies and Goals on Job Outcomes', *Journal of Applied Psychology* 81 (1996), 142–52; L. A. Wilk and W. K. Redmon, 'The Effects of Feedback and Goal Setting on the Productivity and Satisfaction of University Admissions Staff', *Journal of Organizational Behavior Management* 18 (1998), 45–68.

36 A. Prayag, 'All Work and More Play', *Business Line (The Hindu)*, 13 July 2005, 4; S. Rajagopalan, 'Bangalore to Hawaii, an All-Paid Holiday', *Hindustan Times*, 7 May 2005; J. A. Singh, 'Hola for Success!', *Business Standard* (India), 4 June 2005.

37 G. P. Latham, 'Goal Setting: A Five-Step Approach to Behavior Change', *Organizational Dynamics* 32, no. 3 (2003), 309–18; E. A. Locke and G. P. Latham, *A Theory of Goal Setting and Task Performance* (Englewood Cliffs, NJ: Prentice Hall, 1990). Some practitioners rely on the acronym 'SMART' goals, referring to goals that are specific, measurable, acceptable, relevant and timely. However, this list overlaps key elements (e.g. specific goals *are* measurable and timely) and overlooks the key elements of challenging and feedback-related.

38 K. Tasa, T. Brown and G. H. Seijts, 'The Effects of Proximal, Outcome and Learning Goals on Information Seeking and Complex Task Performance', *Proceedings of the Annual Conference of the Administrative Sciences Association of Canada, Organizational Behavior Division* 23, no. 5 (2002), 11–20.

39 K. R. Thompson, W. A. Hochwarter and N. J. Mathys, 'Stretch Targets: What Makes Them Effective?', *Academy of Management Executive* 11 (August 1997), 48–60; S. Kerr and S. Landauer, 'Using Stretch Goals to Promote Organizational Effectiveness and Personal Growth: General Electric and Goldman Sachs', *Academy of Management Executive* 18, no. 4 (2004), 134–8.

40 A. Li and A. B. Butler, 'The Effects of Participation in Goal Setting and Goal Rationales on Goal Commitment: An Exploration of Justice Mediators', *Journal of Business and Psychology* 19, no. 1 (Fall 2004), 37–51.

41 Locke and Latham, *A Theory of Goal Setting and Task Performance*, chapters 6 and 7; J. Wegge, 'Participation in Group Goal Setting: Some Novel Findings and a Comprehensive Model as a New Ending

to an Old Story', *Applied Psychology: An International Review* 49 (2000), 498–516.

42   M. London, E. M. Mone and J. C. Scott, 'Performance Management and Assessment: Methods for Improved Rater Accuracy and Employee Goal Setting', *Human Resource Management* 43, no. 4 (Winter 2004), 319–36; G. P. Latham and C. C. Pinder, 'Work Motivation Theory and Research at the Dawn of the Twenty-First Century', *Annual Review of Psychology* 56 (2005), 485–516.

43   S. P. Brown, S. Ganesan and G. Challagalla, 'Self-Efficacy as a Moderator of Information-Seeking Effectiveness', *Journal of Applied Psychology* 86, no. 5 (2001), 1043–51; P. A. Heslin and G. P. Latham, 'The Effect of Upward Feedback on Managerial Behaviour', *Applied Psychology: An International Review* 53, no. 1 (2004), 23–37; D. Van-Dijk and A. N. Kluger, 'Feedback Sign Effect on Motivation: Is It Moderated by Regulatory Focus?', *Applied Psychology: An International Review* 53, no. 1 (2004), 113–35; J. E. Bono and A. E. Colbert, 'Understanding Responses to Multi-Source Feedback: The Role of Core Self-Evaluations', *Personnel Psychology* 58, no. 1 (Spring 2005), 171–203.

44   L. Hollman, 'Seeing the Writing on the Wall', *Call Center* (August 2002), 37.

45   Australian Public Service Commission, '360 Degree Feedback on Senior Executive Leadership Capabilities' (Canberra: Australian Government, 2005), http://www.apsc.gov.au/leadership/feedback.htm (accessed 22 December 2005); K. Singh, 'Hewitt Best Employers in Malaysia 2005 Awards', *Edge Malaysia*, 25 April 2005.

46   W. W. Tornow and M. London, *Maximizing the Value of 360-Degree Feedback: A Process for Successful Individual and Organizational Development* (San Francisco: Jossey-Bass, 1998); L. E. Atwater, D. A Waldman and J. F. Brett, 'Understanding and Optimizing Multisource Feedback', *Human Resource Management Journal* 41 (Summer 2002), 193–208; J. W. Smither, M. London and R. R. Reilly, 'Does Performance Improve Following Multisource Feedback? A Theoretical Model, Meta-Analysis, and Review of Empirical Findings', *Personnel Psychology* 58, no. 1 (2005), 33–66.

47   A. S. DeNisi and A. N. Kluger, 'Feedback Effectiveness: Can 360-Degree Appraisals Be Improved?', *Academy of Management Executive* 14 (February 2000), 129–39; M. A. Peiperl, 'Getting 360 Degree Feedback Right', *Harvard Business Review* 79 (January 2001), 142–7; 'Perils & Payoffs of Multi-Rater Feedback Programs', *Pay for Performance Report* (May 2003), 1; M.-G. Seo, L. F. Barrett and J. M. Bartunek, 'The Role of Affective Experience in Work Motivation', *Academy of Management Review* 29 (2004), 423–49.

48   J. W. Smither et al., 'Can Working with an Executive Coach Improve Multisource Feedback Ratings over Time? A Quasi-Experimental Field Study', *Personnel Psychology* 56 (Spring 2003), 23–44; C. Udy, 'Coaching a Winner', *Bay of Plenty Times* (New Zealand), 23 November 2005, P01.

49   E. Ross, 'Know Yourself', *Business Review Weekly*, 17 March 2005, 86.

50   S. J. Ashford and G. B. Northcraft, 'Conveying More (or Less) Than We Realize: The Role of Impression Management in Feedback Seeking', *Organizational Behavior and Human Decision Processes* 53 (1992), 310–34; M. London, 'Giving Feedback: Source-Centered Antecedents and Consequences of Constructive and Destructive Feedback', *Human Resource Management Review* 5 (1995), 159–88; J. R. Williams et al., 'Increasing Feedback Seeking in Public Contexts: It Takes Two (or More) to Tango', *Journal of Applied Psychology* 84 (December 1999), 969–76.

51   J. B. Miner, 'The Rated Importance, Scientific Validity, and Practical Usefulness of Organizational Behavior Theories: A Quantitative Review', *Academy of Management Learning and Education* 2, no. 3 (2003), 250–68. Also see C. C. Pinder, *Work Motivation in Organizational Behavior* (Upper Saddle River, NJ: Prentice-Hall, 1997), p. 384.

52   P. M. Wright, 'Goal Setting and Monetary Incentives: Motivational Tools That Can Work Too Well', *Compensation and Benefits Review* 26 (May–June 1994), 41–9; E. A. Locke and G. P. Latham, 'Building a Practically Useful Theory of Goal Setting and Task Motivation: A 35-Year Odyssey', *American Psychologist* 57, no. 9 (2002), 705–17.

53   A. Lue, 'Women Seethe over Gender Gap in Salaries', *Taipei Times*, 6 March 2003.

54   J. Greenberg and E. A. Lind, 'The Pursuit of Organizational Justice: From Conceptualization to Implication to Application', in *Industrial and Organizational Psychology: Linking Theory with Practice*, ed. C. L. Cooper and E. A. Locke (London: Blackwell, 2000), 72–108; R. Cropanzano and M. Schminke, 'Using Social Justice to Build Effective Work Groups', in *Groups at Work: Theory and Research*, ed. M. E. Turner (Mahwah, NJ: Lawrence Erlbaum Associates, 2001), 143–71; D. T. Miller, 'Disrespect and the Experience of Injustice', *Annual Review of Psychology* 52 (2001), 527–53.

55   J. S. Adams, 'Toward an Understanding of Inequity', *Journal of Abnormal and Social Psychology* 67 (1963), 422–36; R. T. Mowday, 'Equity Theory Predictions of Behavior in Organizations', in *Motivation and Work Behavior*, ed. L. W. Porter and R. M. Steers, 5th edn (New York: McGraw-Hill, 1991), 111–31; R. Cropanzano and J. Greenberg, 'Progress in Organizational Justice: Tunneling through the Maze', in *International Review of Industrial and Organizational Psychology*, ed. C. L. Cooper and I. T. Robertson (New York: Wiley, 1997), 317–72; L. A. Powell, 'Justice Judgments as Complex Psychocultural Constructions: An Equity-Based Heuristic for Mapping Two- and Three-Dimensional Fairness Representations in Perceptual Space', *Journal of Cross-Cultural Psychology* 36, no. 1 (January 2005), 48–73.

56   C. T. Kulik and M. L. Ambrose, 'Personal and Situational Determinants of Referent Choice', *Academy of Management Review* 17 (1992), 212–37; G. Blau, 'Testing the Effect of Level and Importance of Pay Referents on Pay Level Satisfaction', *Human Relations* 47 (1994), 1251–68.

57   T. P. Summers and A. S. DeNisi, 'In Search of Adams' Other: Re-examination of Referents Used in the Evaluation of Pay', *Human Relations* 43 (1990), 497–511.

58   Y. Cohen-Charash and P. E. Spector, 'The Role of Justice in Organizations: A Meta-Analysis', *Organizational Behavior and Human Decision Processes* 86 (November 2001), 278–321.

59   Canadian Press, 'Pierre Berton, Canadian Cultural Icon, Enjoyed Long and Colourful Career', *Times Colonist* (Victoria, BC), 30 November 2004.

60   K. S. Sauleya and A. G. Bedeian, 'Equity Sensitivity: Construction of a Measure and Examination of Its Psychometric Properties', *Journal of Management* 26 (September 2000), 885–910.

61   The meaning of these three groups has evolved over the years. These definitions are based on W. C. King Jr and E. W. Miles, 'The Measurement of Equity Sensitivity', *Journal of Occupational and Organizational Psychology* 67 (1994), 133–42.

62   M. Ezzamel and R. Watson, 'Pay Comparability across and within UK Boards: An Empirical Analysis of the Cash Pay Awards to CEOs and Other Board Members', *Journal of Management Studies* 39, no. 2 (March 2002), 207–32; J. Fizel, A. C. Krautman and L. Hadley, 'Equity and Arbitration in Major League Baseball', *Managerial and Decision Economics* 23, no. 7 (October–November 2002), 427–35.

63   Miner, 'The Rated Importance, Scientific Validity, and Practical Usefulness of Organizational Behavior Theories: A Quantitative Review'.

64   Cohen-Charash and Spector, 'The Role of Justice in Organizations: A Meta-Analysis'; J. A. Colquitt et al., 'Justice at the Millennium: A Meta-Analytic Review of 25 Years of Organizational Justice Research', *Journal of Applied Psychology* 86 (2001), 425–45.

65   Several types of justice have been identified and there is some debate as to whether they represent forms of procedural justice or are distinct from procedural and distributive justice. The discussion here adopts the former view, which seems to dominate the literature. C. Viswesvaran and D. S. Ones, 'Examining the Construct of Organizational Justice: A Meta-Analytic Evaluation of Relations with Work Attitudes and Behaviors', *Journal of Business Ethics* 38 (July 2002), 193–203.

66   Greenberg and Lind, 'The Pursuit of Organizational Justice: From Conceptualization to Implication to Application'. For a recent study of voice and injustice, see J. B. Olson-Buchanan and W. R. Boswell, 'The Role of Employee Loyalty and Formality in Voicing Discontent', *Journal of Applied Psychology* 87, no. 6 (2002), 1167–74.

67   R. Folger and J. Greenberg, 'Procedural Justice: An Interpretive Analysis of Personnel Systems', *Research in Personnel and Human Resources Management* 3 (1985), 141–83; L. B. Bingham, 'Mediating Employment Disputes: Perceptions of Redress at the United States Postal Service', *Review of Public Personnel Administration* 17 (Spring 1997), 20–30.

68   R. Hagey et al., 'Immigrant Nurses' Experience of Racism', *Journal of Nursing Scholarship* 33 (Fourth Quarter 2001), 389–95; K. Roberts and K. S. Markel, 'Claiming in the Name of Fairness: Organizational Justice and the Decision to File for Workplace Injury Compensation', *Journal of Occupational Health Psychology* 6 (October 2001), 332–47;

D. A. Jones and D. P. Skarlicki, 'The Effects of Overhearing Peers Discuss an Authority's Fairness Reputation on Reactions to Subsequent Treatment', *Journal of Applied Psychology* 90, no. 2 (2005), 363–72.

69   Miller, 'Disrespect and the Experience of Injustice'.

70   S. Fox, P. E. Spector and E. W. Miles, 'Counterproductive Work Behavior (CWB) in Response to Job Stressors and Organizational Justice: Some Mediator and Moderator Tests for Autonomy and Emotions', *Journal of Vocational Behavior* 59 (2001), 291–309; I. M. Jawahar, 'A Model of Organizational Justice and Workplace Aggression', *Journal of Management* 28, no. 6 (2002), 811–34; M. M. LeBlanc and J. Barling, 'Workplace Aggression', *Current Directions in Psychological Science* 13, no. 1 (2004), 9–12.

71   M. L. Ambrose, M. A. Seabright and M. Schminke, 'Sabotage in the Workplace: The Role of Organizational Injustice', *Organizational Behavior and Human Decision Processes* 89, no. 1 (2002), 947–65.

72   N. D. Cole and G. P. Latham, 'Effects of Training in Procedural Justice on Perceptions of Disciplinary Fairness by Unionized Employees and Disciplinary Subject Matter Experts', *Journal of Applied Psychology* 82 (1997), 699–705. D. P. Skarlicki and G. P. Latham, 'Increasing Citizenship Behavior within a Labor Union: A Test of Organizational Justice Theory', *Journal of Applied Psychology* 81 (1996), 161–9.

CHAPTER 6

Applied performance practices

LEARNING OBJECTIVES

After reading this chapter, you should be able to:

- discuss the advantages and disadvantages of the four reward objectives

- identify two team-level and four organisational-level performance-based rewards

- describe five ways to improve reward effectiveness

- discuss the advantages and disadvantages of job specialisation

- diagram the job characteristics model of job design

- identify three strategies to improve employee motivation through job design

- define empowerment and identify strategies to support empowerment

- describe the five elements of self-leadership.

K ambuku is the name of one of the largest tusked elephants in Africa. It is also the symbolic title for a 'people focused, value added' initiative that has transformed Pretoria Portland Cement (PPC) into a performance-oriented company and one of South Africa's best employers. The transformation began at the beginning of the new millennium, when PPC faced the realities of a dismantled cement cartel that had previously protected its income, as well as the entry of LaFarge and other global competitors into South Africa.

'We realised if we were going to compete with the best players in the world here in Southern Africa, our people had to be the best in the world,' says PPC chief executive John Gomersall. The company had a long way to go. At the time, PPC was a top-down, autocratic organisation where managers gave 'oodles of supervision and checking that people do the right things and a very instructive culture', says Gomersall. Morale was low and the company's operational and financial performance had been dismal over the previous five years.

A Kambuku team consisting of engineers and plant managers was set up to 'get every employee to come to work with a sense of purpose, work with excitement and go home with satisfaction'. The team recommended giving departments and teams more autonomy and responsibility for achieving their targets, encouraging employees to acquire more skills so they could perform multiple

The Kambuku process improved employee performance and well-being at Pretoria Portland Cement in South Africa through job design, performance-based rewards, and empowerment.

jobs, and keeping everyone fully informed of developments and their roles in the company. The Kambuku process is supported by formal awards, incentives, and a gainsharing plan in which employees earn bonuses each year for improving productivity. 'We have passed the ownership to the people,' says Gomersall.

This application of job design, rewards and empowerment has made PPC one of the most productive and competitive cement companies in Africa. 'We attribute our ongoing success and strength to the fact that every employee in the company has the opportunity to make a contribution and be recognised for their input to achieving success,' says chief operating officer Orrie Fenn. 'Empowered employees ensure a committed workforce, which eventually translates into sustainable business performance.'

Shonisani Modau, a shift supervisor at PPC's Hercules plant in Pretoria, has not only noticed the transformation; he feels it. 'You know what I like best about this job?' he says. 'It's driving to work in the morning, knowing what PPC wants to achieve and how that affects me and the Hercules plant. I understand how my performance fits in. There's nothing worse than not knowing what your contribution is and how it affects the company. We know what our goals are, and why.'[1]

THE OPENING STORY HIGHLIGHTS the importance of rewards, job design and empowerment in the success of Pretoria Portland Cement. This chapter looks at each of these applied performance practices as well as a fourth practice, self-leadership. The chapter begins with an overview of financial reward practices, including the different types of rewards and how to implement rewards effectively. Next, it looks at the dynamics of job design, including specific job design strategies to motivate employees. The elements of empowerment are then considered, as well as conditions that support empowerment. The final part of the chapter explains how employees manage their own performance through self-leadership.

FINANCIAL REWARD PRACTICES

Financial rewards are probably the oldest—and certainly the most fundamental—applied performance practice in organisational settings. At the most basic level, financial rewards represent a form of exchange; employees provide their labour, skill and knowledge in return for money and benefits from the organisation. From this perspective, money and related rewards align employee goals with organisational goals.

However, financial rewards do much more than pay employees for their contribution to organisational objectives. They are a symbol of success, a reinforcer and motivator, a reflection of one's performance, and a source of reduced anxiety. With so many different purposes, it is little wonder that people rank pay and benefits as two of the most important features in the employment relationship.[2]

The value and meaning of money also vary considerably from one person to the next. One large-scale survey revealed that men in almost all of the forty-three countries studied attach more importance or value to money than do women. This result is consistent with public opinion polls—one of 2000 Australian employees and the other of 4000 'high-performing' American employees—which reported that money is a higher priority for men than for women, particularly as a symbol of power and status.[3] Cultural values also seem to influence the meaning and value of money. People in countries with high power distance (such as China and Japan) tend to have a high respect for money and make it a priority, whereas people in countries with a strong egalitarian culture (such as Australia, New Zealand and Scandinavian countries) are discouraged from openly talking about money or displaying their personal wealth.[4]

Financial rewards come in many forms, and can be organised into the four specific objectives identified in Exhibit 6.1: membership and seniority, job status, competencies, and performance.

LEARNING OBJECTIVE

Discuss the advantages and disadvantages of the four reward objectives.

MEMBERSHIP- AND SENIORITY-BASED REWARDS

Membership- and seniority-based rewards (sometimes called 'pay for pulse') represent the largest part of most pay cheques. Some employee benefits, such as free or discounted meals in the company cafeteria, remain the same for everyone, whereas others increase with seniority. Many Asian companies distribute a '13th month' bonus which every employee expects to receive each year. The Australian Navy pays completion bonuses of up to $15 000 per year so its engineers stay with the organisation.[5] These membership- and seniority-based rewards potentially attract job applicants (particularly those who desire predictable income) and reduce turnover. However, they do not directly motivate job performance; on the contrary, they discourage poor performers from seeking out work better suited to their abilities. Instead, the good performers are lured to better-paying jobs. Some of these rewards are also golden handcuffs, which, as discussed in Chapter 4, can potentially weaken job performance by creating continuance commitment.

JOB STATUS–BASED REWARDS

Almost every organisation rewards employees to some extent based on the status or worth of the jobs they occupy. In Australia, the national awards system has historically established much

EXHIBIT 6.1

Reward objectives, advantages and disadvantages

Reward objective	Sample rewards	Advantages	Disadvantages
Membership/ seniority	• Fixed pay • Most employee benefits • Paid time off	• May attract applicants • Minimises stress of insecurity • Reduces turnover	• Doesn't directly motivate performance • May discourage poor performers from leaving • Golden handcuffs may undermine performance
Job status	• Promotion-based pay increase • Status-based benefits	• Tries to maintain internal equity • Minimises pay discrimination • Motivates employees to compete for promotions	• Encourages hierarchy, which may increase costs and reduce responsiveness • Reinforces status differences • Motivates job competition and exaggerated job worth
Competencies	• Pay increase based on competency • Skill-based pay	• Improves workforce flexibility • Tends to improve quality • Consistent with employability	• Subjective measurement of competencies • Skill-based pay plans can be expensive
Task performance	• Commissions • Merit pay • Gainsharing • Profit-sharing • Stock options	• Motivates task performance • Attracts performance-oriented applicants • Organisational rewards create an ownership culture • Pay variability may avoid layoffs during downturns	• May weaken job content motivation • May distance reward giver from receiver • May discourage creativity • Tends to address symptoms, not underlying causes of behaviour

Sources: Based on information in D. H. Montross, Z. B. Leibowitz and C. J. Shinkman, *Real People, Real Jobs* (Palo Alto, CA: Davies-Black, 1995); J. H. Greenhaus, *Career Management* (Chicago, Ill.: Dryden, 1987).

of this hierarchy of pay across jobs and industries. With the shift to enterprise bargaining and individual contracts, some companies are relying more on **job evaluation** to assess the worth of each job within the organisation. Most job evaluation methods give higher value to jobs that require more skill and effort, have more responsibility, and have more difficult working conditions. As an example, nurses on the Cook Islands received a pay increase after consulting firm PricewaterhouseCoopers determined that nurses were paid less than other jobs requiring similar skill, effort and responsibility.[7] Aside from receiving higher pay, employees with more valued jobs sometimes receive larger offices, company-paid vehicles, and other perks.

Job status–based rewards maintain feelings of equity (that people in higher valued jobs should get higher pay) and motivate employees to compete for promotions. However, at a time when companies are trying to be more cost efficient and responsive to the external environment, job status–based rewards potentially do the opposite by encouraging a bureaucratic hierarchy. These rewards also reinforce a status mentality, whereas Generation-X and Generation-Y employees expect a more egalitarian workplace. Furthermore, status-based pay potentially motivates employees to compete with each other for higher status jobs and to raise the value of their own jobs by exaggerating job duties and hoarding resources.[8]

job evaluation Systematically evaluating the worth of jobs within an organisation by measuring their required skill, effort, responsibility and working conditions.

COMPETENCY-BASED REWARDS

Many firms have shifted from status-based to competency-based rewards. The National Health Service (NHS) in the United Kingdom is a recent example. Every job in the NHS is now described in terms of the required skills and knowledge. Employees receive annual pay increases through a wide pay band (ranging from lowest to highest pay for that job) based on how well they meet the job's competency requirements.[9] Skill-based pay is a variation of competency-based rewards, in which employees are rewarded for the number of skill modules mastered and consequently the number of jobs they can perform.

Japanese firms reward age, seniority and babies

Since World War II, employees in most large Japanese companies have received pay rates and increases determined entirely by their age or seniority, usually topping out at around age forty-five. Not even the value of the specific jobs performed affected how much employees earned. Tough times in the 1990s forced many Japanese firms to introduce performance-based pay systems, in which annual pay increases varied with the employee's contribution. The shift towards pay-for-performance continues today, but labour groups continue to oppose them, and a few companies have not been happy with the results. Concerned that employees were becoming too stressed over their variable pay rates each year, Tokai Rubber Industries Ltd recently re-introduced an age-based bonus pay system. 'Even during that period [when they can't perform as well as expected], we raise salaries according to their age,' says Tokai Rubber president Akira Fujii. Meanwhile, Japanese firms are replacing monthly family allowances (where employees receive higher pay for the number of children they support) with a one-time lump-sum childbirth bonus. For example, employees at Daiwa House Industry Co. in Osaka previously received an extra A\$60 per month for each child. Now the company pays a one-time lump sum of \$11 500 when a child is born.[6]

Jason Dewey/Getty Images

Competency-based rewards improve workforce flexibility by motivating employees to learn a variety of skills and thereby perform a variety of jobs. Product or service quality tends to improve, because employees with multiple skills are more likely to understand the work process and know how to improve it. Competency-based rewards are also consistent with employability, because they reward employees who continuously learn skills that will keep them employed. One potential problem is that measuring competencies can be subjective, particularly when described as personality traits or personal values. Skill-based pay systems measure specific skills, so they are usually more objective. However, they are expensive, because employees spend more time learning new tasks.[10]

PERFORMANCE-BASED REWARDS

Performance-based rewards have existed since Babylonian days in the twentieth century BC, but their popularity has increased dramatically over the past two decades.[11] Here is an overview of some of the most popular individual, team and organisational performance-based rewards.

Individual rewards

Many employees receive individual bonuses or awards for accomplishing a specific task or exceeding annual performance goals. At Pretoria Portland Cement, described at the beginning of this chapter, individual employees receive awards for suggestions that improve productivity. Hong Kong communications company PCCW rewards employees with up to one month's pay if they exceed their performance goals.[12] Real estate agents and other salespeople typically earn commissions, in which their pay increases with sales volume. Piece-rate systems reward employees based on the number of units produced.

Team rewards

Most brokerage firms on Wall Street and many organisations in other industries and countries are shifting their focus from individuals to teams. Consequently, employees are finding that a larger part of their total pay cheque is determined by team performance. Forward Media is a case in point. 'We have seen individual incentive programs fail,' says James Ward, who co-founded the Sydney-based enterprise software consulting firm a decade ago with his wife, Nadia. 'We set a group revenue target for each team, then give people a bonus according to the profit their team achieves.'[13]

Rather than calculating bonuses from team sales or profit, **gainsharing plans** award bonuses based on cost savings and productivity improvements. Employees at Pretoria Portland Cement receive gainsharing bonuses determined by improvements in output at their cement factory relative to labour and other inputs required. The majority of mining companies in North America have a gainsharing bonus system, typically where mining teams share the cost savings of extracting more ore at a lower cost. With considerable caution, American hospitals have introduced gainsharing programs where surgeons and other medical staff are rewarded for cost reductions in surgery and patient care.[14] Gainsharing plans tend to improve team dynamics, knowledge sharing and pay satisfaction. They also create a reasonably strong link between effort and performance, because much of the cost reduction and labour efficiency is within the team's control.

Organisational rewards

Along with individual and team-based rewards, many firms rely on organisational-level rewards to motivate employees. **Employee share ownership plans (ESOPs)** encourage employees to buy shares in the company, usually at a discounted price or with a no-interest loan. Employees are subsequently rewarded through dividends and market appreciation of the shares. Only about 6 per cent of the Australian workforce holds shares through these plans, although it is as high as 30 per cent of employees in the banking and communications sectors. Fosters Group and Lend Lease are among the Australian companies with broad-based ESOPs (available to most or all employees). Beca, the New Zealand–based engineering and related services company is owned entirely by its 1500 employees located in two dozen countries. Dairibord Zimbabwe employees own more than one-fifth of the outstanding shares of the Zimbabwe dairy products company. Most Dairibord workers who bought a few thousand shares a decade ago are now millionaires from the share appreciation and receive a sizeable bonus from the annual dividend.[15]

Share options are a variation of ESOPs, giving employees the right to purchase shares from the company at a future date at a predetermined price up to a fixed expiry date. Silex Systems Limited, a Sydney-based technology company specialising in isotopes, uses share options to motivate its three dozen employees. In 2005, for instance, Silex employees were granted the right to purchase a predetermined number of shares for an exercise price of $0.85 per share. If the company's share price rises above $0.85 at any time between 2007 and 2010, employees can buy the shares at $0.85 each and earn the capital gain. If the share price remains below $0.85 through to 2010, employees would allow the options to expire at no cost to them. The intention of share options is to motivate employees to increase the company's success and thus raise the company's share price, so they reap the value above the exercise price of the share options.[16]

Profit-sharing plans, a third organisational-level reward, calculate bonuses from the previous year's level of corporate profits. Redarc Electronics, the South Australian electronic voltage converter manufacturer, pays all employees the same bonus amount calculated from the company's profits each year. A fourth organisational-level reward strategy, called **balanced scorecard (BSC)**, is a goal-oriented performance measurement system that rewards people (typically executives) for improving performance on a composite of financial, customer and

LEARNING OBJECTIVE

Identify two team-level and four organisational-level performance-based rewards.

gainsharing plan A reward system in which team members earn bonuses for reducing costs and increasing labour efficiency in their work process.

employee share ownership plans (ESOPs) A reward system that encourages employees to buy shares of the company.

share options A reward system that gives employees the right to purchase company shares at a future date at a predetermined price.

profit-sharing plan A reward system that pays bonuses to employees based on the previous year's level of corporate profits.

balanced scorecard (BSC) A reward system that pays bonuses for improved results on a composite of financial, customer, internal process and employee factors.

Western Water's scorecard success

After Western Water senior managers and board members had devoted three months of bi-weekly meetings to develop a focused strategy, the Victorian water utility introduced a balanced scorecard (BSC) to improve staff awareness of, and motivation towards, this strategy. 'The Balanced Scorecard was implemented across all areas of the business to measure and report on performance against our corporate vision, which is to be a leading service provider as judged by our customers,' says chief executive John Wilkinson (shown in photo with staff members Suzanne Evans (left) and Julie Green). Western Water's balanced scorecard model includes measures in five key areas: customer, stakeholder, financial, internal processes, and learning and growth. Each month a team of managers across the utility's six functional units meets to monitor progress towards specific goals in the five areas. For example, Western Water has a goal of achieving 100 per cent recycled water within the next couple of years, so this target is included in the balanced scorecard. Since introducing BSC, Western Water's performance has soared. It has also received CPA Australia's Public Sector Organisation of the Year award and is one of two Australian companies to be inducted into the Balanced Scorecard Hall of Fame.[18]

Western Water

internal processes, as well as employee factors. The better the measurement improvements across these dimensions, the larger the bonus awarded. For instance, KT (formerly Korea Telecom) relied on BSC to transform the former government-owned telephone company into a more competitive business after privatisation. 'It guided our employees with clear direction and balanced perspectives,' says Song Young-han, KT's executive senior vice-president. 'By gathering all the employees around BSC, we were able to concentrate our foundation for the performance-oriented organisation culture.'[17]

Evaluating organisational-level rewards

How effective are organisational-level rewards? ESOPs, share options and balanced scorecards tend to create an 'ownership culture' in which employees feel aligned with the organisation's success. Balanced scorecards have the added benefit of aligning rewards to several specific measures of organisational performance. However, Australian scholars have recently pointed out that BSC is potentially more subjective and requires a particular corporate culture in order for it to be implemented effectively. Profit sharing tends to create less ownership culture, but it has the advantage of automatically adjusting employee compensation with the firm's prosperity, thereby reducing the need for layoffs or negotiated pay reductions during recessions.[19]

The main problem with ESOPs, share options and profit sharing (and to a lesser degree balanced scorecards) is that employees often perceive a weak connection between individual effort and corporate profits or the value of company shares. Even in small firms, the company's share price or profitability is influenced by economic conditions, competition, and other factors beyond the employee's immediate control. This low individual performance-to-outcome expectancy weakens employee motivation. Another concern is that many companies in a few countries (such as the United States) use ESOPs as a replacement for employee superannuation. This is a risky strategy, because the pension funds lack diversification. If the company goes bankrupt, employees lose both their jobs and a large portion of their retirement nest egg.[20]

IMPROVING REWARD EFFECTIVENESS

LEARNING OBJECTIVE

Describe five ways to improve reward effectiveness.

Performance-based rewards have come under attack over the years for discouraging creativity, distancing management from employees, distracting employees from the meaningfulness of the work itself, and being quick fixes that ignore the true causes of poor performance. While these issues have kernels of truth under specific circumstances, they do not necessarily mean that performance-based pay should be abandoned. On the contrary, the top-performing companies around the world are more likely to have performance-based rewards.[21] Reward systems do motivate most employees, but only under the right conditions. Here are some of the more important strategies to improve reward effectiveness.

Link rewards to performance

Behaviour modification theory (Chapter 3) and expectancy theory (Chapter 5) both recommend that employees who perform well should be rewarded more than those who perform poorly. Unfortunately, this simple principle seems to be unusually difficult to apply. In one recent large-scale survey, fewer than half of Malaysian employees said they believe their company rewards high performance or deals appropriately with poor performers. Employees particularly get ruffled by the subjectivity and bias in annual performance appraisals. 'After the last one I was spitting,' recalls an IT employee in New Zealand. 'I was getting graded on projects and activities I hadn't even agreed to take on!'[22]

How can we improve the pay–performance linkage? Inconsistencies and bias can be minimised by introducing gainsharing, ESOPs and other plans that use objective performance measures. Where subjective measures of performance are necessary, companies should rely on multiple sources of information, such as 360-degree feedback. Companies also need to apply rewards soon after the performance occurs, and in a large enough dose (such as a bonus rather than a pay increase) so that employees experience positive emotions when they receive the reward.[23]

Ensure that rewards are relevant

Companies need to align rewards with performance within the employee's control. The more employees see a 'line of sight' between their daily actions and the reward, the more they are motivated to improve performance. BHP-Billiton applies this principle by rewarding bonuses to top executives based on the company's overall performance, whereas front-line mining staff earn bonuses based on the production output, safety performance and other local indicators. Reward systems also need to correct for situational factors. Salespeople in one region may have higher sales because the economy is stronger there than elsewhere, so sales bonuses need to be adjusted for these economic factors.

Use team rewards for interdependent jobs

Team rewards should be used rather than individual rewards when employees work in highly interdependent jobs, because it is difficult to measure individual performance in these situations. Team rewards also encourage cooperation, which is more important when work is highly interdependent. A third benefit of team rewards is that they tend to support employee preferences for team-based work. One concern, however, is that employees (particularly the most productive ones) in Australia, New Zealand and many other low-collectivism cultures prefer rewards based on their individual performance rather than team performance.[24]

Ensure that rewards are valued

It seems obvious that rewards work best when they are valued. Yet companies sometimes make false assumptions about what employees want, with unfortunate consequences. The solution, of course, is to ask employees what they value. Campbell Soup did this a few years ago at its distribution centres in Canada. Executives thought that the employees would ask for more money in a special team reward program. Instead, distribution staff suggested a less expensive but more valued reward: a leather jacket with the Campbell Soup logo on the back.[25]

Watch out for unintended consequences

Performance-based reward systems sometimes have an unexpected—and undesirable—effect on employee behaviours. Consider the pizza company that decided to reward its drivers for on-time delivery. The plan got more hot pizzas to customers on time, but it also increased the accident rates of its drivers because the incentive motivated them to drive recklessly.[26] Reality Check 6.1 describes a few other examples where reward systems had unintended consequences. The solution here is to carefully think through the consequences of rewards and, where possible, test incentives in a pilot project before applying them across the organisation.

REALITY CHECK   6.1

WHEN REWARDS GO WRONG

There is an old saying that 'what gets rewarded gets done'. But what companies reward isn't always what they had intended their employees to do. Here are a few dramatic examples:

Share options are supposed to motivate executives to improve corporate performance. Instead, they seem to motivate some leaders to inflate share values through dodgy accounting practices. Recent research estimates that for every 25 per cent increase in share options awarded to executives, the risk of fraud rises by 68 per cent. The companies with the largest corporate frauds in recent years have, on average, eight times as many options as similar companies that did not experience fraud.

Integrated steel companies often rewarded managers for increased labour efficiency. The lower the labour hours required to produce a ton of steel, the larger the manager's bonus. Unfortunately, the firms usually didn't count the work of outside contractors in the formula, so the reward system motivated managers to hire expensive contractors in the production process. By employing more contractors, the cost of production actually increased, not decreased.

Toyota rewards its dealerships based on customer satisfaction surveys, not just car sales. What Toyota discovered, however, is that this motivates dealers to increase satisfaction scores, not customer satisfaction. One Toyota dealership received high ratings because it offered free detailing to every customer who indicated they were 'very satisfied' on the survey form. The dealership even had a special copy of the survey showing clients which boxes to check off. This increased customer ratings, but not customer satisfaction.

Donnelly Mirrors (now part of Magna International) introduced a gainsharing plan that motivated employees to reduce labour but not material costs. Employees at the car-parts manufacturer knew they worked faster with sharp grinding wheels, so they replaced the expensive diamond wheels more often. This action reduced labour costs, thereby giving employees the gainsharing bonus. However, the labour savings were easily offset by the much higher costs for the grinding wheels.

Sources: F. F. Reichheld, *The Loyalty Effect* (Boston, MA: Harvard University Press, 1996), 236; D. R. Spitzer, 'Power Rewards: Rewards That Really Motivate', *Management Review* (May 1996), 45–50; J. A. Byrne, 'How To Fix Corporate Governance', *Business Week*, 6 May 2002, p. 68; A. Holeck, 'Griffith, Ind., Native Takes Over as Steel Plant Manager', *Northwest Indiana Times*, 25 May 2003; H. Connon, 'Overhyped, Overpaid and Overextended', *The Observer* (London), 20 March 2005, p. 5.

Financial rewards come in many forms and influence employees in complex ways. A recent survey identified money as the top motivator to inspire and retain employees in China.[27] However, no one should assume that pay and benefits are important everywhere, and they certainly are not the only ways to motivate and retain employees. 'At the end of the year [employees] see the benefits by way of their incentive or gainshare bonus, but incentives alone are not enough,' advises John Gomersall, chief executive of Pretoria Portland Cement, the company discussed at the beginning of the chapter. 'Through the process, the lives of all of our employees both at work and at home have been enriched.'[28] In other words, companies motivate employees mainly by designing interesting and challenging jobs, which is discussed next.

JOB DESIGN PRACTICES

How do you build a better job? That question has challenged organisational behaviour experts as well as psychologists, engineers and economists for centuries. Some jobs have very few tasks and usually require very little skill. Other jobs are immensely complex and require years of experience and learning to master them. From one extreme to the other, jobs have different effects on work efficiency and employee motivation. The challenge, at least from the organisation's perspective, is to find the right combination so work is performed efficiently but employees are motivated and engaged.[29] This challenge requires careful **job design**—the process of assigning tasks to a job, including the interdependency of those tasks with other jobs. A job is a set of tasks performed by one person. To understand this issue more fully, let's begin by describing early job design efforts aimed at increasing work efficiency through job specialisation.

job design The process of assigning tasks to a job, including the interdependency of those tasks with other jobs.

JOB DESIGN AND WORK EFFICIENCY

At the Magna Steyr manufacturing plant in Graz, Austria, one of the five lines of production employees assemble Chrysler's European mini-van. On average, assembly workers on this line take three minutes to attach their assigned pieces to the chassis. In North America, where Chrysler owns more than a dozen production plants, employees assembling the same vehicle have an average job cycle time of 64.5 seconds. The difference isn't that Austrian employees are slower. Rather, each of Magna's Austrian employees is assigned more parts to assemble compared with Chrysler's North American employees.[30]

LEARNING OBJECTIVE

Discuss the advantages and disadvantages of job specialisation.

Employees assembling Chrysler vehicles in Austria and North America perform jobs with a high degree of **job specialisation**. Job specialisation occurs when the work required to build a car—or any other product or service—is subdivided into separate jobs assigned to different people. Each resulting job includes a narrow subset of tasks, usually completed in a short 'cycle time'. The cycle time is the time required to complete the task before starting over with a new work unit. For the Magna employees in Austria, the cycle time is about three minutes. For Chrysler assembly workers in North America, the cycle time is about one minute.

job specialisation The result of division of labour in which each job includes a subset of the tasks required to complete the product or service.

The economic benefits of dividing work into specialised jobs have been described and applied for at least two millennia. More than 2300 years ago the Chinese philosopher Mencius and the Greek philosopher Plato noted that division of labour improves work efficiency. In AD 1436, the waterways of Venice became an assembly line loading ten galleons in just six hours. More than 200 years ago, economist Adam Smith described a small factory where ten pin-makers collectively produced as many as 48 000 pins per day because they performed specialised tasks such as straightening, cutting, sharpening, grinding and whitening the pins. In contrast, Smith claimed that if these ten people worked alone making complete pins they would collectively produce no more than 200 pins per day.[31]

One reason why job specialisation potentially increases work efficiency is that employees have fewer tasks to juggle and therefore spend less time changing activities. They also require fewer physical and mental skills to accomplish the work, so less time and resources are needed for training. A third reason is that employees practise their tasks more frequently with shorter work cycles, so jobs are mastered quickly. A fourth reason is that employees with specific aptitudes or skills can be matched more precisely to the jobs for which they are best suited.[32]

Scientific management

scientific management
Involves systematically partitioning work into its smallest elements and standardising tasks to achieve maximum efficiency.

One of the strongest advocates of job specialisation was Frederick Winslow Taylor, an American industrial engineer who introduced the principles of **scientific management** in the early 1900s.[33] Scientific management consists of a toolkit of activities. Some of these interventions—training, goal setting and work incentives—are common today but were rare until Taylor popularised them. However, scientific management is mainly associated with high levels of job specialisation and standardisation of tasks in order to achieve maximum efficiency.

According to Taylor, the most effective companies have detailed procedures and work practices developed by engineers, enforced by supervisors, and executed by employees. Even the supervisor's tasks should be divided: one person manages operational efficiency, another manages inspection, and another is the disciplinarian. Taylor and other industrial engineers demonstrated that scientific management significantly improves work efficiency. No doubt, some of the increased productivity can be credited to the training, goal setting and work incentives, but job specialisation quickly became popular in its own right.

Frederick Taylor and his contemporaries focused on how job specialisation reduces labour 'waste' by improving the mechanical efficiency of work (i.e. matching skills, faster learning, less switch-over time). Yet they didn't seem to notice how this extreme job specialisation has an adverse effect on employee attitudes and motivation. Some jobs—such as assembling Chrysler mini-vans—are so specialised that they quickly become tedious, trivial and socially isolating. Employee turnover and absenteeism tends to be higher in specialised jobs with very short time cycles. Companies sometimes have to pay higher wages to attract job applicants to this dissatisfying, narrowly defined work.[34]

Job specialisation often reduces work quality because employees see only a small part of the process. As one observer of a car assembly line reported: 'Often [employees] did not know how their jobs related to the total picture. Not knowing, there was no incentive to strive for quality—what did quality even mean as it related to a bracket whose function you did not understand?'[35]

Equally important, Taylor's reliance on job specialisation to improve employee performance ignores the motivational potential of jobs. As jobs become specialised, the work tends to become easier to perform but less motivating. As jobs become more complex, work motivation increases but the ability to master the job decreases. Maximum job performance occurs somewhere between these two extremes, where most people can eventually perform the job tasks efficiently, yet the work is interesting.

JOB DESIGN AND WORK MOTIVATION

motivator–hygiene theory
Herzberg's theory stating that employees are primarily motivated by growth and esteem needs, not by lower-level needs.

Industrial engineers may have overlooked the motivational effect of job characteristics, but it is now the central focus of many job design changes. Organisational behaviour scholar Frederick Herzberg is credited with shifting the spotlight when he introduced **motivator-hygiene theory** in the 1950s.[36] Motivator-hygiene theory proposes that employees experience job satisfaction when they fulfil growth and esteem needs (called motivators), and they experience dissatisfaction when they have poor working conditions, job security and other factors categorised as lower order needs (called hygienes). Herzberg argued that only characteristics of the job itself motivate employees, whereas the hygiene factors merely prevent dissatisfaction. It might seem obvious to us today that the job itself is a source of motivation, but it was radical thinking when Herzberg proposed the idea.

job characteristics model
A job design model that relates the motivational properties of jobs to specific personal and organisational consequences of those properties.

Motivator-hygiene theory didn't find much research support, but Herzberg's ideas generated new thinking about the motivational potential of the job itself.[37] Out of subsequent research emerged the **job characteristics model**, shown in Exhibit 6.2. The job characteristics

The job characteristics model

EXHIBIT 6.2

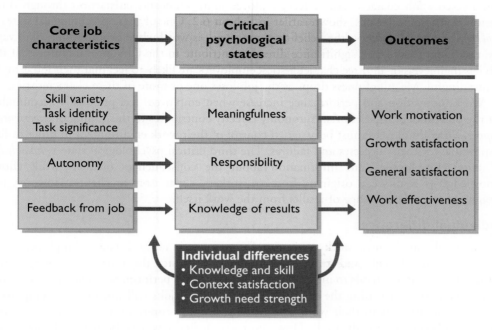

Source: J. R. Hackman and G. Oldham, *Work Redesign* (Reading, MA: Addison-Wesley, 1980), p. 90. Used with permission of Pearson Education.

LEARNING OBJECTIVE

Diagram the job characteristics model of job design.

model identifies five core job dimensions that produce three psychological states. Employees who experience these psychological states tend to have higher levels of internal work motivation (motivation from the work itself), job satisfaction (particularly satisfaction with the work itself), and work effectiveness.[38]

Core job characteristics

The job characteristics model identifies five core job characteristics. Under the right conditions, employees are more motivated and satisfied when jobs have higher levels of these characteristics.

- *Skill variety*. **Skill variety** refers to the use of different skills and talents to complete a range of work activities. For example, sales clerks who normally only serve customers might be assigned the additional duties of stocking inventory and changing storefront displays.
- *Task identity*. **Task identity** is the degree to which a job requires completion of a whole or identifiable piece of work, such as assembling an entire broadband modem rather than just soldering in the circuitry.
- *Task significance*. **Task significance** is the degree to which the job affects the organisation and/or larger society. Recall from the opening story to this chapter that Shonisani Modau said: 'There's nothing worse than not knowing what your contribution is and how it affects the company.' Fortunately, the shift supervisor at Pretoria Portland Cement's Hercules plant in Pretoria has plenty of task significance. 'I understand how my performance fits in,' said Modau.[39]
- *Autonomy*. Jobs with high levels of **autonomy** provide freedom, independence, and discretion in scheduling the work and determining the procedures to be used to complete the work. In autonomous jobs, employees make their own decisions rather than relying on detailed instructions from supervisors or procedure manuals.
- *Job feedback*. Job feedback is the degree to which employees can tell how well they are doing based on direct sensory information from the job itself. Airline pilots can tell how well they land their aircraft and road crews can see how well they have prepared the road bed and laid the bitumen.

skill variety The extent to which employees must use different skills and talents to perform tasks within their job.

task identity The degree to which a job requires completion of a whole or an identifiable piece of work.

task significance The degree to which the job has a substantial impact on the organisation and/or larger society.

autonomy The degree to which a job gives employees the freedom, independence and discretion to schedule their work and determine the procedures used in completing it.

Critical psychological states

The five core job characteristics affect employee motivation and satisfaction through three critical psychological states, shown earlier in Exhibit 6.2. One of these psychological states is *experienced meaningfulness*—the belief that one's work is worthwhile or important. Skill variety, task identity and task significance directly contribute to the job's meaningfulness. If the job has high levels of all three characteristics, employees are likely to feel that their job is highly meaningful. Meaningfulness drops as the job loses one or more of these characteristics.

Work motivation and performance increase when employees feel personally accountable for the outcomes of their efforts. Autonomy directly contributes to this feeling of *experienced responsibility*. Employees must be assigned control of their work environment in order to feel responsible for their successes and failures. The third critical psychological state is *knowledge of results*. Employees want information about the consequences of their work effort. Knowledge of results can originate from co-workers, supervisors or clients. However, job design focuses on knowledge of results from the work itself.

Individual differences

Job design doesn't increase work motivation for everyone in every situation. Employees must have the required skills and knowledge in order to master the more challenging work. Otherwise, job design tends to increase stress and reduce job performance. The original model also suggests that increasing the motivational potential of jobs will not motivate employees who are dissatisfied with their work context (e.g. working conditions, job security) or who have a low score on growth needs. However, research findings have been mixed, suggesting that employees might be motivated by job design no matter how they feel about their job context or how high or low they score on growth need strength.[40]

LEARNING OBJECTIVE

Identify three strategies to improve employee motivation through job design.

job rotation The practice of moving employees from one job to another.

JOB DESIGN PRACTICES THAT MOTIVATE

Three main strategies can increase the motivational potential of jobs: job rotation, job enlargement and job enrichment. This section also identifies several ways to implement job enrichment.

Job rotation

Job rotation is the practice of moving employees from one job to another. At Baxter Corp's dialysis solution plant, for example, employees on the haemodialysis product line rotate several times each day through the three assembly-line positions as well as two non-assembly jobs (forklift operator and warehouse loader).[41] The medical products company and other organisations introduce job rotation for three reasons. First, it minimises health risks from repetitive strain and heavy lifting, because employees use different muscles and physical positions in the various jobs. Second, it supports multiskilling (employees learn several jobs), which increases workforce flexibility in the production process and in finding replacements for those on holidays. A third benefit of job rotation is that it potentially reduces the boredom of highly repetitive jobs. On Baxter's haemodialysis product line, the warehouse and forklift jobs are more intellectually stimulating, so working on these tasks breaks the tedium of the repetitive assembly-line jobs.

Job enlargement

job enlargement Increasing the number of tasks employees perform within their job.

Job enlargement adds tasks to an existing job. This might involve combining two or more complete jobs into one, or just adding one or two more tasks to an existing job. Either way, skill variety increases because there are more tasks to perform. Video journalists represent a clear example of an enlarged job. As Exhibit 6.3 illustrates, a traditional news team consists of a camera operator, a sound and lighting specialist, and the journalist who writes and presents or narrates the story. A video journalist performs all of these tasks.

Job enlargement significantly improves work efficiency and flexibility. However, research suggests that simply giving employees more tasks won't affect motivation, performance or

Job enlargement of video journalists

EXHIBIT 6.3

Traditional news team

Video journalist

Employee 1
Operates camera

Employee 2
Operates sound

Employee 3
Reports story

**Operates camera
Operates sound
Reports story**

job satisfaction. Instead, these benefits result only when skill variety is combined with more autonomy and job knowledge.[42] In other words, employees are motivated when they perform a variety of tasks *and* have the freedom and knowledge to structure their work to achieve the highest satisfaction and performance. These job characteristics are at the heart of job enrichment.

Job enrichment

Job enrichment occurs when employees are given more responsibility for scheduling, coordinating and planning their own work.[43] Generally, people in enriched jobs experience higher job satisfaction and work motivation, along with lower absenteeism and turnover. Productivity is also higher when task identity and job feedback are improved. Product and service quality tends to improve because job enrichment increases the job-holder's felt responsibility for and sense of ownership of the product or service.[44]

One way to increase job enrichment is by combining highly interdependent tasks into one job. This *natural grouping* approach is reflected in the video journalist job. As noted earlier, video journalist is an enlarged job, but it is also an example of job enrichment because it naturally groups tasks together to complete an entire product (i.e. a news clip). By forming natural work units, job-holders have stronger feelings of responsibility for an identifiable body of work. They feel a sense of ownership and therefore tend to increase job quality. Forming natural work units increases task identity and task significance because employees perform a complete product or service and can more readily see how their work affects others.

A second job enrichment strategy, called *establishing client relationships*, involves putting employees in direct contact with their clients rather than using the supervisor as a go-between. By being directly responsible for specific clients, employees have more information and can make decisions affecting those clients.[46] Establishing client relationships also increases task significance, because employees see a line-of-sight connection between their work and the consequences for customers. This was apparent among medical secretaries at a large regional hospital in Sweden after the hospital reduced its workforce by 10 per cent and gave the secretaries expanded job duties. Although these employees experienced more stress from the higher workloads, some of them also felt more motivated and satisfied because they now had direct interaction with patients. 'Before, I never saw a patient; now they have a face,' says one medical secretary. 'I feel satisfied and pleased with myself; you feel someone needs you.'[47]

job enrichment Occurs when employees are given more responsibility for scheduling, coordinating and planning their own work.

Video journalists experience job enrichment

Traditionally, up to four people are required to shoot a video news clip: a reporter, a camera operator, a sound operator and a production editor. Now, thanks to technology and innovative thinking about job design in the newsroom, many documentaries and some nightly news clips are created by one person, called a video journalist (VJ). Thom Cookes, one of Australia's most celebrated VJs, points out that multiskilled VJ work is challenging, particularly in his remote assignments for SBS's *Dateline*. 'Working as a one-person crew, especially in remote locations like the New Guinea highlands, can be a huge task, even if you have all the skills,' says Cookes. 'You are thinking of five things at once and suffer a high level of paranoia—have you got all the shots you need? Is the sound okay? Will you bring back the yarn you want?' A traditional crew of three or four people can keep all of these issues in mind. At the same time, Cookes acknowledges that VJs are far more flexible than traditional crews and can be less intimidating to the people being interviewed. It is also much more interesting work. 'Doing what we do is a big ask of the journalists but it is incredibly rewarding,' says Cookes (shown in photo). 'It is the best job I have ever had in journalism.'[45]

Special Broadcasting Services/Thom Cookes

Forming natural task groups and establishing client relationships are common ways to enrich jobs, but the heart of the job enrichment philosophy is to give employees more autonomy over their work. This basic idea is at the core of one of the most widely mentioned—and often misunderstood—practices, known as empowerment.

EMPOWERMENT PRACTICES

LEARNING OBJECTIVE

Define empowerment and identify strategies to support empowerment.

A large American hotel had a policy that, if guests questioned their bill, front-desk staff were supposed to defend the bill no matter what. If a guest then asked to speak with the manager, the manager would override the charge. The hotel manager believed that this 'good cop, bad cop' approach was useful, but Rick Garlick, a consultant hired by the hotel, suggested that they immediately change the policy. Instead, front-desk staff should have the autonomy to decide alone whether the complaint was justified. 'Empowering employees was one of a number of key improvements in manager–staff relations that ultimately resulted in much higher guest satisfaction,' says Garlick. 'The hotel's guest satisfaction scores went from being near the bottom to being one of the best rated in the chain within a few months.'[48]

empowerment A psychological concept in which people experience more self-determination, meaning, competence and impact regarding their role in the organisation.

Empowerment is a term that has been loosely tossed around in corporate circles and has been the subject of considerable debate among academics. However, the most widely accepted definition is that empowerment is a psychological concept represented by four dimensions: self-determination, meaning, competence, and impact of the individual's role in the organisation. Empowerment consists of all four dimensions. If any dimension weakens, the employee's sense of empowerment will weaken.[49]

- *Self-determination*. Empowered employees feel that they have freedom, independence and discretion over their work activities.
- *Meaning*. Employees who feel empowered care about their work and believe that what they do is important.
- *Competence*. Empowered people are confident about their ability to perform the work well and have a capacity to grow with new challenges.
- *Impact*. Empowered employees view themselves as active participants in the organisation; that is, their decisions and actions have an influence on the company's success.

From this definition, you can see that empowerment is not a personality trait, although personality might influence the extent to which someone feels empowered. People also experience degrees of empowerment, which can vary from one work environment to the next. One company that sets the standard for extreme empowerment is Semco Corporation, SA. Reality Check 6.2 describes how the Brazilian conglomerate has become world famous for giving

6.2 REALITY CHECK

THE EMPOWERMENT OF SEMCO

Most executives like to say that they empower their workforce, but few come close to the work arrangements at Semco Corporation, SA. 'Can an organisation let people do what they want, when they want and how they want?' asks Ricardo Semler, who took over his father's marine pump business in São Paulo, Brazil, twenty years ago. The answer appears to be 'Yes'. Today, Semco pushes the limits of empowerment at its dozen businesses—high-tech mixing equipment, inventory control and environmental resources management, to name a few—with 3000 employees and $160 million revenue.

Organised into small groups of six to ten people, Semco employees choose their objectives every six months, hire their co-workers, work out their budgets, set their own salaries, decide when to come to work, and even elect their own bosses. Semco factory workers have chosen future factory sites that management didn't like, and commissioned an artist to paint the entire plant like a canvas.

The success of Semco's approach to empowerment was recently demonstrated when Carrefour, the French supermarket chain, hired Semco to take inventory at its forty-two Brazilian hypermarkets on June 30th. The assignment required 1000 workers in twenty cities on the same day, a major challenge for any firm. Unfortunately, June 30th also turned out to be the day that Brazil played in the World Cup soccer finals. If Brazil won the game (which it did), employers could count on losing 40 per cent of their employees to street celebrations. Semco managers asked employees to figure out among themselves how to confront this dilemma, which they did. Semco completed the task on time. In fact, a week later Brazil's second largest supermarket chain asked Semco to take inventory because the competitor hired for the job didn't have enough staff show up to count inventory during the World Cup final.

Semco may have radical empowerment, but Semler says that the company is 'only 50 or 60 per cent where we'd like to be'. Semler believes that replacing head office with several satellite offices around São Paulo would give employees even more opportunity for empowerment. 'If you don't know where people are, you can't possibly keep an eye on them,' Semler says. 'All that's left to judge on is performance.'

Ricardo Semler, shown here with staff in hammocks at head office, has taken empowerment to the extreme at Brazilian conglomerate Semco Corporation.

Photo courtesy of Semco

Sources: 'Ricardo Semler Set Them Free', *CIO Insight* (April 2004), p. 30; S. Caulkin, 'Who's in Charge Here?', *The Observer*, 27 April 2003, p. 9; S. Moss, 'Portrait: "Idleness is good"', *The Guardian*, 17 April 2003, p. 8; D. Gardner, 'A Boss Who's Crazy about his Workers', *Sunday Herald* (Scotland), 13 April 2003, p. 6; R. Semler, *The Seven-Day Weekend* (Century, London, 2003).

employees complete freedom, even if the employees' actions overrule managers and the company owner, Ricardo Semler.

The chances are that you have heard corporate leaders say they are 'empowering' the workforce. What these executives really mean is that they are changing the work environment to support empowerment.[50] Numerous individual, job design and organisational or work context factors support empowerment. At the individual level, employees must possess the necessary competencies to be able to perform the work as well as handle the additional decision-making requirements. While other individual factors have been proposed (e.g. locus of control), they do not seem to have any real effect on whether employees feel empowered.[51]

Job characteristics clearly influence the dynamics of empowerment.[52] To generate beliefs about self-determination, employees must work in jobs with a high degree of autonomy and minimal bureaucratic control. To maintain a sense of meaningfulness, jobs must have high levels of task identity and task significance. And to maintain a sense of self-confidence, jobs must provide sufficient feedback.

Several organisational and work context factors also influence empowerment. Employees experience more empowerment in organisations in which information and other resources are easily accessible. Empowerment also requires a learning orientation culture. In other words, empowerment flourishes in organisations that appreciate the value of the employee learning and that accept reasonable mistakes as a natural part of the learning process. Furthermore, empowerment requires corporate leaders who trust employees and are willing to take the risks that empowerment creates. 'Executives must give up control and trust the power of talent,' advises Ricardo Semler, head of Semco Corporation in São Paulo, Brazil.[53]

With the right individuals, job characteristics and organisational environment, empowerment can have a noticeable effect on motivation and performance. For instance, a study of bank employees concluded that empowerment improved customer service and tended to reduce conflict between employees and their supervisors. Other research links empowerment with higher trust in management, which ultimately influences job satisfaction, belief and acceptance of organisational goals and values, and organisational commitment. Empowerment also tends to increase personal initiative, because employees identify with their work and assume more psychological ownership of it.[54]

SELF-LEADERSHIP PRACTICES

LEARNING OBJECTIVE

Describe the five elements of self-leadership.

self-leadership The process of influencing oneself to establish the self-direction and self-motivation needed to perform a task.

John Ilham has come a long way from the preschool boy who arrived in Melbourne from Turkey with little more than the suitcases that his parents brought with them. Today, 'Crazy John' Ilham is one of Australia's most successful entrepreneurs, operating Australia's largest independent mobile-phone operation. What is Ilham's secret to success? 'I have always found one should never look to others for motivation,' he says. 'Self-motivation must be the key to any successful business.'[55]

Most of the concepts introduced in this chapter and Chapter 5 have assumed that corporate leaders do things to motivate employees. Certainly, these theories and practices are valuable, but they overlook the point that John Ilham has made, namely, that successful people ultimately motivate and manage themselves. In other words, they engage in self-leadership.

Self-leadership refers to the process of influencing oneself to establish the self-direction and self-motivation needed to perform a task.[56] This concept includes a toolkit of behavioural activities borrowed from social learning theory and goal setting. It also includes constructive thought processes that have been extensively studied in sports psychology. Overall, self-leadership takes the view that individuals mostly regulate their own actions through these behavioural and cognitive (thought) activities.

Although we are in the early stages of understanding the dynamics of self-leadership, Exhibit 6.4 identifies the five main elements of this process. These elements, which generally

Elements of self-leadership

EXHIBIT 6.4

| Personal goal setting | ▸ | Constructive thought patterns | ▸ | Designing natural rewards | ▸ | Self-monitoring | ▸ | Self-reinforcement |

follow each other in a sequence, are personal goal setting, constructive thought patterns, designing natural rewards, self-monitoring and self reinforcement.[57]

PERSONAL GOAL SETTING

The first step in self-leadership is to set goals for your own work effort. This applies the ideas learned in Chapter 5 on goal setting, such as identifying goals that are specific, relevant and challenging. The main difference is that self-leadership involves setting goals alone, rather than having them assigned by or jointly decided with a supervisor. Research suggests that employees are more focused and perform better when they set their own goals, particularly in combination with other self-leadership practices.[58]

CONSTRUCTIVE THOUGHT PATTERNS

Before beginning a task and while performing it, employees should engage in positive (constructive) thoughts about that work and its accomplishment. In particular, employees are more motivated and better prepared to accomplish a task after they have engaged in positive self-talk and mental imagery.

Positive self-talk

Do you ever talk to yourself? Most of us do, according to a major study of university students.[59] **Self-talk** refers to any situation in which we talk to ourselves about our own thoughts or actions. Some of this internal communication assists the decision-making process, such as

self-talk Talking to ourselves about our own thoughts or actions for the purpose of increasing our self-confidence and navigating through decisions in a future event.

Self-leadership puts accountant in fast forward

At twenty-four, Katarina Vicelik is already a senior tax consultant with PricewaterhouseCoopers in Sydney and is working towards becoming a chartered accountant. Vicelik plans to take a master's degree after completing her accountancy exams, is looking at work opportunities in Europe, and wants to reach managerial level within three years. Vicelik regularly sets goals for herself, and reflects on where her future should be headed. In other words, she has moved well along in her career by practising self-leadership. 'If you want to make the most out of your career, anywhere, you've got to be self-motivated,' she advises. 'That's the only way you're going to get ahead.'[60]

Angela Brkic

weighing the advantages of a particular choice. Self-leadership is mostly interested in evaluative self-talk, in which you evaluate your capabilities and accomplishments.

The problem is that most evaluative self-talk is negative; we criticise ourselves much more than we encourage or congratulate ourselves. Negative self-talk undermines our confidence and our potential to perform a particular task. In contrast, positive self-talk creates a 'can-do' belief and thereby increases motivation by raising our effort-to-performance expectancy. We often hear that professional athletes 'psych' themselves up before an important event. They tell themselves that they can achieve their goal and that they have practised enough to reach that goal. They are motivating themselves through self-talk.

Mental imagery

mental imagery Mentally practising a task and visualising its successful completion.

You've probably heard the phrase 'I'll cross that bridge when I come to it'. Self-leadership takes the opposite view. It suggests that we need to practise a task mentally and imagine successfully performing it beforehand. This process, known as **mental imagery**, has two parts. One part involves mentally practising the task, anticipating obstacles to goal accomplishment, and working out solutions to those obstacles before they occur. By mentally walking through the activities required to accomplish the task, we begin to see problems that may occur. We can then imagine what responses would be best for each contingency.[61]

While one part of mental imagery helps us to anticipate things that could go wrong, the other part involves visualising successful completion of the task. We imagine the experience of completing the task and the positive results that follow. Everyone daydreams and fantasises about being in a successful situation. You might imagine yourself being promoted to your boss's job, receiving a prestigious award or taking time off work. This visualisation increases goal commitment and motivates us to complete the task effectively.

DESIGNING NATURAL REWARDS

Self-leadership recognises that employees actively craft their jobs. To varying degrees, they can alter tasks and work relationships to make the work more motivating.[62] One way to build natural rewards into the job is to alter the way a task is accomplished. People often have enough discretion in their jobs to make slight changes to suit their needs and preferences. For instance, you might try out a new software program to design an idea, rather than sketch the image with pencil. By using the new software, you are adding challenge to a task that may have otherwise been mundane.

SELF-MONITORING

Self-monitoring is the process of keeping track at regular intervals of one's progress towards a goal using naturally occurring feedback. It also includes designing artificial feedback where natural feedback does not occur. Salespeople might arrange to receive monthly reports on sales levels in their territory. Production staff might have gauges or computer feedback systems installed so they can see how many errors are made on the production line. Research suggests that people who have control over the timing of performance feedback perform their tasks better than those with feedback assigned by others.[63]

SELF-REINFORCEMENT

Self-leadership includes the social learning theory concept of self-reinforcement. Self-reinforcement occurs whenever an employee has control over a reinforcer but doesn't 'take' the reinforcer until completing a self-set goal.[64] A common example is taking a break after reaching a predetermined stage of your work. The work break is a self-induced form of positive reinforcement. Self-reinforcement also occurs when you decide to do a more enjoyable task after completing a task that you dislike. For example, after slogging through a difficult report, you might decide to spend some time catching up on industry news by scanning websites.

SELF-LEADERSHIP IN PRACTICE

Self-leadership is shaping up to be a valuable applied performance practice in organisational settings. A respectable body of research shows consistent support for most elements of self-leadership. Self-set goals and self-monitoring increased the frequency of wearing safety equipment among employees in a mining operation. Airline employees who received constructive thought training experienced better mental performance, enthusiasm and job satisfaction than co-workers who did not receive this training. Mental imagery helped supervisors and process engineers in a pulp and paper mill to transfer what they learned in an interpersonal communication skills class back to the job.[65] Studies also indicate that self-set goals and constructive thought processes improved individual performance in swimming, tennis, ice skating, soccer and other sports. Indeed, studies show that almost all Olympic athletes rely on mental rehearsal and positive self-talk to achieve their performance goals.[66]

Self-leadership behaviours are more frequently found in people with specific personality characteristics, notably conscientiousness and extroversion.[67] However, one of the benefits of self-leadership is that it can be learned. Training programs have helped employees to improve their self-leadership skills. Organisations can also encourage self-leadership by providing sufficient autonomy and establishing rewards that reinforce self-leadership behaviours. Employees are also more likely to engage in self-monitoring in companies that emphasise continuous measurement of performance. Overall, self-leadership promises to be an important concept and practice for improving employee motivation and performance.

Self-leadership, job design, empowerment and rewards are valuable approaches to improving employee performance. However, performance is also affected by work-related stress. As discussed in the next chapter, too much stress is causing numerous problems with employee performance and well-being, but there are also ways to combat this epidemic.

CHAPTER SUMMARY

Money and other financial rewards are a fundamental part of the employment relationship, but their value and meaning varies from one person to the next. Organisations reward employees for their membership and seniority, job status, competencies and performance. Membership-based rewards may attract job applicants and seniority-based rewards reduce turnover, but these reward objectives tend to discourage turnover among those with the lowest performance. Rewards based on job status try to maintain internal equity and motivate employees to compete for promotions. However, they tend to encourage bureaucratic hierarchy, support status differences, and motivate employees to compete and hoard resources. Competency-based rewards are becoming increasingly popular because they improve workforce flexibility and are consistent with the emerging idea of employability. However, they tend to be subjectively measured and can result in higher costs as employees spend more time learning new skills.

Awards, bonuses, commissions and other individual performance-based rewards have existed for centuries and are widely used. Many companies are shifting to team-based rewards such as gain-sharing plans and to organisational rewards such as employee stock ownership plans (ESOPs), stock options, profit sharing and balanced scorecards. ESOPs and stock options create an ownership culture, but employees often perceive a weak connection between individual performance and the organisational reward.

Financial rewards have a number of limitations, but reward effectiveness can be improved in several ways. Organisational leaders should ensure that rewards are linked to work performance, rewards are aligned with performance within the employee's control, team rewards are used where jobs are interdependent, rewards are valued by employees, and rewards have no unintended consequences.

Job design refers to the process of assigning tasks to a job, including the interdependency of those tasks with other jobs. Job specialisation subdivides work into separate jobs for different people. This increases work efficiency because employees master the tasks quickly, spend less time changing tasks, require less training, and can be matched more closely with the jobs best suited to their skills. However, job specialisation may reduce work motivation, create mental health problems, lower product or service quality, and increase costs through discontentment, absenteeism and turnover.

Contemporary job design strategies reverse job specialisation through job rotation, job enlargement and job enrichment. The job characteristics model is a template for job redesign that specifies core job dimensions, psychological states and individual differences. Organisations introduce job rotation to reduce job boredom, develop a more flexible workforce, and reduce the incidence of repetitive strain injuries. Two ways to enrich jobs are clustering tasks into natural groups and establishing client relationships.

Empowerment is a psychological concept represented by four dimensions: self-determination, meaning, competence, and impact regarding the individual's role in the organisation. Individual characteristics seem to have a minor influence on empowerment. Job design is a major influence, particularly autonomy, task identity, task significance and job feedback. Empowerment is also supported at the organisational level through a learning orientation culture, sufficient information and resources, and corporate leaders who trust employees.

Self-leadership is the process of influencing oneself to establish the self-direction and self-motivation needed to perform a task. This includes personal goal setting, constructive thought patterns, designing natural rewards, self-monitoring and self-reinforcement. Constructive thought patterns include self-talk and mental imagery. Self-talk refers to any situation in which a person talks to himself or herself about his or her own thoughts or actions. Mental imagery involves mentally practising a task and imagining successfully performing it.

KEY TERMS

autonomy p.181
balanced scorecard (BSC) p. 175
employee share ownership plans (ESOPS) p. 175
empowerment p. 184
gainsharing plan p. 175
job characteristics model p. 180
job design p. 179

job enlargement p. 182
job enrichment p. 183
job evaluation p. 174
job rotation p. 182
job specialisation p. 179
mental imagery p. 188
motivator-hygiene theory p. 180
profit-sharing plan p. 175

scientific management p. 180
self-leadership p. 186
self-talk p. 187
skill variety p. 181
share options p. 175
task identity p. 181
task significance p. 181

DISCUSSION QUESTIONS

1. As a consultant, you have been asked to recommend either a gainsharing plan or a profit-sharing plan for employees who work in the four regional distribution and warehousing facilities of a large retail organisation. Which reward system would you recommend? Explain your answer.

2. You are a member of a team responsible for developing performance measures for your college or university department or faculty unit based on the balanced scorecard approach. Identify one performance measurement for each of the following factors: financial, customer satisfaction, internal processes and employee performance.

3. Mullewa Tyre Pty Ltd redesigned its production facilities around a team-based system. However, the company president believes that employees will not be motivated unless they receive incentives based on their individual performance. Give three explanations for why Mullewa Tyre should introduce team-based rather than individual rewards in this setting.

4. What can organisations do to increase the effectiveness of financial rewards?

5. Most of us have watched pizzas being made while waiting in a pizzeria. What level of job specialisation do you usually notice in these operations? Why does this high or low level of specialisation exist? If some pizzerias have different levels of specialisation than others, identify the contingencies that might explain these differences.

6. Can a manager or supervisor 'empower' an employee? Discuss fully.

7. Describe a time when you practised self-leadership to successfully perform a task. With reference to each step in the self-leadership process, describe what you did to achieve this success.

8. Can self-leadership replace formal leadership in an organisational setting?

THE REGENCY GRAND HOTEL

6.1 | SKILL BUILDER

CASE STUDY

By Lisa Ho, under the supervision of Steven L. McShane

The Regency Grand Hotel is a five-star hotel in Bangkok, Thailand. The hotel was established fifteen years ago by a local consortium of investors and has been operated by a Thai general manager since that time. The hotel is one of Bangkok's most prestigious hotels and its 700 employees have enjoyed the prestige of being associated with the hotel. The hotel provides good welfare benefits, above-market-rate salaries, and job security. In addition, a good year-end bonus amounting to four months' salary was given to employees regardless of the hotel's overall performance during the year.

Recently, the Regency was sold to a large American hotel chain that was very keen to expand its operations into Thailand. When the acquisition was announced, the Thai general manager decided to take early retirement. The American hotel chain kept all of the Regency employees, although a few were transferred to other positions. John Becker, an American with ten years management experience with the hotel chain, was appointed as the new general manager of the Regency Grand Hotel. He was selected because of his previous successes in integrating newly acquired hotels in the United States. In most of the previous acquisitions, Becker had taken over operations with poor profitability and low morale.

Becker is a strong believer in empowerment. He expects employees to go beyond guidelines and standards to consider guest needs on a case-to-case basis. That is, employees must be guest-oriented at all times so as to provide excellent customer service. From his US experience, Becker had found that empowerment increases employee motivation, performance and job satisfaction, all of which contribute to a hotel's profitability and customer service ratings. Soon after becoming general manager in the Regency, Becker introduced the practice of empowerment in order to replicate the successes that he had achieved back home.

At the Regency Grand Hotel the employees had always worked according to management's instructions. Their responsibility was to ensure that the instructions from their managers were carried out diligently and conscientiously. Innovation and creativity had been discouraged under the previous management. Indeed, employees were punished for their mistakes and discouraged from trying out ideas that had not been approved by management. As a result, employees were afraid to be innovative and to take risks.

Becker met with the Regency's managers and department heads to explain that empowerment would be introduced in the hotel. He told them that employees must be empowered with decision-making authority so that they could use their initiative, creativity and judgment to satisfy guests' needs or to handle problems effectively and efficiently. However, he stressed that employees were to refer the more complex issues and decisions to their superiors, who were to coach and assist rather than provide direct orders. Furthermore, Becker stressed that mistakes would be allowed but that he would not tolerate the same mistake being made more than twice. He advised his managers and department heads not to consult him about minor decisions or to bring minor issues or problems to him. However, they were to discuss any important matters with him. He concluded the meeting by asking for feedback. Several managers and department heads told him that they liked the idea and would support it, while others simply nodded their heads. Becker was pleased with the response, and was eager to have his plan implemented.

In the past, the Regency had emphasised administrative control, resulting in many bureaucratic procedures throughout the organisation. For example, the front-counter employees needed to seek approval from their manager before they could upgrade guests to another category of room. The front-counter manager would then have to submit a report to the general manager justifying the upgrade. Soon after his meeting with the managers, Becker reduced the number of bureaucratic rules at the Regency and allocated more decision-making authority to front-line employees. This action upset those who had previously made these kinds of decisions, and several of them left the hotel.

Becker also began spending a large portion of his time observing and interacting with the employees at the front desk, lobby, restaurants and various departments. This direct interaction with Becker helped many employees to understand what he expected of them. However, the employees had difficulty distinguishing between a major and a minor issue or decision. More often than not, supervisors would reverse employee decisions by stating that they were major issues requiring management approval. Employees who displayed initiative and made good decisions in satisfying the needs of the guests rarely received any positive feedback from their supervisors. Eventually, most of these employees lost confidence in their decision-making ability and reverted back to relying on their superiors.

Not long after the implementation of the practice of empowerment, Becker realised that his subordinates were consulting him more frequently than before. Most of them came to him with minor issues and consulted him before making minor decisions. He was spending most of his time attending to their concerns. Soon he began to feel highly frustrated and exhausted, and often would tell his secretary that 'unless the hotel is on fire, don't let anyone disturb me'.

Becker thought that the practice of empowerment would bring benefits to the hotel. Contrary to his expectation, the overall performance of the hotel began to deteriorate. The number of guest complaints had increased from being minimal to there being a significant number of formal written complaints every month. Many other guests voiced their dissatisfaction verbally to hotel employees. The number of mistakes made by employees was also on the increase. Becker was very upset when two of the local newspapers and an overseas newspaper published negative feedback about the hotel in terms of service standards. He was even more distressed when an international travel magazine described the hotel as 'one of Asia's nightmare hotels'.

The stress levels of the employees had been mounting ever since the introduction of the practice of empowerment. Absenteeism due to illness was increasing at an alarming rate. In addition, the employee turnover rate had reached an all-time high. The good working relationships that had existed under the old management had been severely strained. The employees were no longer united and supportive of each other. They were quick to 'point the finger at' or 'backstab' one another when mistakes were made and problems occurred.

QUESTIONS

1. Identify the symptoms indicating that problems exist in this case.

2. Diagnose the problems in this case using organisational behaviour concepts.

3. Recommend solutions that overcome or minimise the problems and symptoms in this case.

Note: This case is based on true events, but the industry and names have been changed.

IS STUDENT WORK ENRICHED?

6.2 | SKILL BUILDER

TEAM EXERCISE

PURPOSE

This exercise is designed to help you to learn how to measure the motivational potential of jobs and to evaluate the extent to which jobs should be further enriched.

INSTRUCTIONS

Being a student is like a job in several ways. You have tasks to perform and someone (such as your instructor) oversees your work. Although few people want to be students for most of their lives (the pay rate is too low!), it may be interesting to determine how enriched your job is as a student.

Step 1: Students are placed into teams (preferably four or five people).

Step 2: Working alone, each student completes both sets of measures in this exercise. Then, using the guidelines below, they individually calculate the score for the five core job characteristics as well as the overall motivating potential score for the job.

Step 3: Members of each team compare their individual results. The group should identify differences of opinion for each core job characteristic. They should also note which core job characteristics have the lowest scores and recommend how these scores could be increased.

Step 4: The entire class will now meet to discuss the results of the exercise. The instructor may ask some teams to present their comparisons and recommendations for a particular core job characteristic.

JOB DIAGNOSTIC SURVEY

Circle the number on the right that best describes student work.	Very little			Moderately			Very much
1. To what extent does student work permit you to decide on your own how to go about doing the work?	1	2	3	4	5	6	7
2. To what extent does student work involve doing a whole or identifiable piece of work, rather than a small portion of the overall work process?	1	2	3	4	5	6	7
3. To what extent does student work require you to do many different things, using a variety of your skills/talents?	1	2	3	4	5	6	7
4. To what extent are the results of your work as a student likely to significantly affect the lives and well-being of other people (e.g. within your institution, your family, society)?	1	2	3	4	5	6	7
5. To what extent does working on student activities provide information about your performance?	1	2	3	4	5	6	7

Circle the number on the right that best describes student work.	Very inaccurate			Uncertain			Very accurate
6. Being a student requires me to use a number of complex and high-level skills.	1	2	3	4	5	6	7
7. Student work is arranged so that I do not have the chance to do an entire piece of work from beginning to end.	1	2	3	4	5	6	7
8. Doing the work required of students provides many chances for me to figure out how well I am doing.	1	2	3	4	5	6	7
9. The work students must do is quite simple and repetitive.	1	2	3	4	5	6	7
10. The work of a student is one where a lot of other people can be affected by how well the work gets done.	1	2	3	4	5	6	7
11. Student work denies me any chance to use my personal initiative or judgment in carrying out the work.	1	2	3	4	5	6	7
12. Student work provides me with the chance to completely finish the pieces of work I begin.	1	2	3	4	5	6	7
13. Doing student work by itself provides very few clues about whether or not I am performing well.	1	2	3	4	5	6	7
14. As a student, I have considerable opportunity for independence and freedom in how I do the work.	1	2	3	4	5	6	7
15. The work I perform as a student is not very significant or important in the broader scheme of things.	1	2	3	4	5	6	7

Adapted from the Job Diagnostic Survey, developed by J. R. Hackman and G. R. Oldham. The authors have released any copyright ownership of this scale (see J. R. Hackman and G. Oldham, *Work Redesign*, Reading, MA, Addison-Wesley, 1980, p. 275).

CALCULATING THE MOTIVATING POTENTIAL SCORE

Scoring core job characteristics: Use the following set of calculations to estimate the motivating potential score for the job of being a student. Use your answers from the Job Diagnostic Survey that you completed above.

Skill variety (SV) $\dfrac{\text{Question } 3 + 6 + 9}{3} = \underline{}$

Task identity (TI) $\dfrac{\text{Question } 2 + 7 + 12}{3} = \underline{}$

Task significance (TS) $\dfrac{\text{Question } 4 + 10 + 15}{3} = \underline{}$

Autonomy $\dfrac{\text{Question } 1 + 11 + 14}{3} = \underline{}$

Job feedback $\dfrac{\text{Question } 5 + 8 + 13}{3} = \underline{}$

Calculating motivating potential score (MPS): Use the following formula and the results above to calculate the motivating potential score. Notice that skill variety, task identity and task significance are averaged before being multiplied by the score for autonomy and job feedback.

$$\left(\frac{SV + TI + TS}{3}\right) \times \text{Autonomy} \times \text{Job feedback}$$

$$\left(\frac{\underline{} + \underline{} + \underline{}}{3}\right) \times \underline{} \times \underline{} = \underline{}$$

WHAT IS YOUR ATTITUDE TOWARDS MONEY?

6.3 SKILL BUILDER

SELF-ASSESSMENT

FULL EXERCISE ON
STUDENT CD

PURPOSE

This exercise is designed to help you to understand the types of attitudes towards money and to assess your attitude towards money.

INSTRUCTIONS

Read each of the statements below and circle the response that you believe best reflects your position regarding each statement. Then use the scoring key in Appendix B to calculate your results. This exercise is completed alone so that students can assess themselves honestly without concerns of social comparison. However, class discussion will focus on the meaning of money, including the dimensions measured here and other aspects of money that may have an influence on behaviour in the workplace.

MONEY ATTITUDE SCALE

To what extent do you agree or disagree that ...	Strongly agree	Agree	Neutral	Disagree	Strongly disagree
1. I sometimes purchase things because I know they will impress other people.	5	4	3	2	1
2. I regularly put money aside for the future.	5	4	3	2	1
3. I tend to get worried about decisions involving money.	5	4	3	2	1
4. I believe that financial wealth is one of the most important signs of a person's success.	5	4	3	2	1
5. I keep a close watch on how much money I have.	5	4	3	2	1
6. I feel nervous when I don't have enough money.	5	4	3	2	1
7. I tend to show more respect to people who are wealthier than I am.	5	4	3	2	1
8. I follow a careful financial budget.	5	4	3	2	1
9. I worry about being financially secure.	5	4	3	2	1
10. I sometimes boast about my financial wealth or how much money I make.	5	4	3	2	1
11. I keep track of my investments and financial wealth.	5	4	3	2	1
12. I usually say 'I can't afford it', even when I can afford something.	5	4	3	2	1

Sources: Adapted from J. A. Roberts and C. J. Sepulveda, 'Demographics and Money Attitudes: A Test of Yamauchi and Templer's (1982) Money Attitude Scale in Mexico', *Personality and Individual Differences* 27 (July 1999), pp. 19–35; K. Yamauchi and D. Templer, 'The Development of a Money Attitudes Scale', *Journal of Personality Assessment* 46 (1982), pp. 522–8.

SKILL BUILDER | 6.4 — ASSESSING YOUR SELF-LEADERSHIP

SELF-ASSESSMENT

FULL EXERCISE ON
STUDENT CD

PURPOSE

This exercise is designed to help you understand self-leadership concepts and to assess your self-leadership tendencies.

INSTRUCTIONS

Indicate the extent to which each statement in this instrument describes you very well or not at all. Complete each item honestly to get the best estimate of your score on each self-leadership dimension.

SKILL BUILDER | 6.5 — STUDENT EMPOWERMENT SCALE

SELF-ASSESSMENT

FULL EXERCISE ON
STUDENT CD

PURPOSE

This exercise is designed to help you understand the dimensions of empowerment and to assess your level of empowerment as a student.

INSTRUCTIONS

Empowerment is a concept that applies to people in a variety of situations. This instrument is specifically adapted to your position as a student at this college or university. Indicate the extent to which you agree or disagree with each statement in this instrument, then request the results, which provide an overall score as well as scores on each of the four dimensions of empowerment. Complete each item honestly to get the best estimate of your level of empowerment.

NOTES

1   D. Furlonger, 'Best Company to Work For', *Financial Mail* (South Africa), 30 September 2005, 20; A. Hogg, 'John Gomersall: CEO, PPC' (South Africa, 26 October 2005), http://www.moneyweb.co.za/specials/corp_gov/509689.htm (accessed 4 January 2006); Pretoria Portland Cement, 'PPC Wins Best Company to Work for 2005', Meropa Communications news release (Sandton, South Africa, 29 September 2005). Information was also collected from the 2003, 2004 and 2005 annual reports of Pretoria Portland Cement.

2   H. Das, 'The Four Faces of Pay: An Investigation into How Canadian Managers View Pay', *International Journal of Commerce & Management* 12 (2002), 18–40. For recent ratings of the importance of pay and benefits, see P. Babcock, 'Find What Workers Want', *HRMagazine*, April 2005, 50–6.

3   R. Lynn, *The Secret of the Miracle Economy* (London: SAE, 1991), cited in A. Furnham and R. Okamura, 'Your Money or Your Life: Behavioral and Emotional Predictors of Money Pathology', *Human Relations* 52 (September 1999), 1157–77. The opinion polls are summarised in: J. O'Rourke, 'Show Boys the Money and Tell Girls You Care', *Sun-Herald* (Sydney), 10 December 2000, 43; M. Steen, 'Study Looks at What Good Employees Want from a Company', *San Jose Mercury* (19 December 2000).

4   A. Furnham, B. D. Kirkcaldy and R. Lynn, 'National Attitudes to Competitiveness, Money, and Work among Young People: First, Second, and Third World Differences', *Human Relations* 47 (January 1994), 119–32; V. K. G. Lim, 'Money Matters: An Empirical Investigation of Money, Face and Confucian Work Ethic', *Personality and Individual Differences* 35 (2003), 953–70; T. L.-P. Tang, A. Furnham and G. M.-T. Davis, 'A Cross-Cultural Comparison of the Money Ethic, the Protestant Work Ethic, and Job Satisfaction: Taiwan, the USA, and the UK', *International Journal of Organization Theory and Behavior* 6, no. 2 (Summer 2003), 175–94.

5   Commonwealth of Australia. Defence Public Affairs, 'Boost for Navy's Warfare Sailors', AAP MediaNet news release (14 December 2005).

6   'Seniority Pay System Seeing Revival', *Kyodo News* (Tokyo), 29 March 2004; 'More Firms Offering Childbirth Allowances', *Daily Yomiuri* (Tokyo), 29 September 2005, 4.

7   'Cook Islands Nurses Set to Receive Pay Rise', *Pacific News Agency Service* (Rarotonga), 19 October 2005.

8   E. E. Lawler III, *Rewarding Excellence: Pay Strategies for the New Economy* (San Francisco: Jossey-Bass, 2000), 30–5, 109–19; R. McNabb and K. Whitfield, 'Job Evaluation and High Performance Work Practices: Compatible or Conflictual?', *Journal of Management Studies* 38 (March 2001), 293–312.

9   'Changing Times in the NHS', *Personnel Today*, 7 December 2004, 9.

10 E. E. Lawler III, 'From Job-Based to Competency-Based Organizations', *Journal of Organizational Behavior* 15 (1994), 3–15; R. L. Heneman, G. E. Ledford Jr and M. T. Gresham, 'The Changing Nature of Work and Its Effects on Compensation Design and Delivery', in *Compensation in Organizations: Current Research and Practice*, ed. S. Rynes and B. Gerhart (San Francisco: Jossey-Bass, 2000), 195–240; B. Murray and B. Gerhart, 'Skill-Based Pay and Skill Seeking', *Human Resource Management Review* 10 (August 2000), 271–87; R. J. Long, 'Paying for Knowledge: Does It Pay?', *Canadian HR Reporter*, 28 March 2005, 12–13; J. D. Shaw et al., 'Success and Survival of Skill-Based Pay Plans', *Journal of Management* 31, no. 1 (February 2005), 28–49.

11 E. B. Peach and D. A. Wren, 'Pay for Performance from Antiquity to the 1950s', *Journal of Organizational Behavior Management* (1992), 5–26.

12 C. Petrie, 'PCCW Puts the Focus on Rewarding Staff', *South China Morning Post* (Hong Kong), 17 July 2004, 4.

13 K. Walters, 'Dream Team', *Business Review Weekly*, 13 October 2005, 92.

14 J. M. Welch, 'Gainsharing Returns: Hospitals and Physicians Join to Reduce Costs', *Journal of Health Care Compliance* 7, no. 3 (May/June 2005), 39–42. For evaluations of gainsharing programs, see: L. R. Gomez-Mejia, T. M. Welbourne and R. M. Wiseman, 'The Role of Risk Sharing and Risk Taking under Gainsharing', *Academy of Management Review* 25 (July 2000), 492–507; K. M. Bartol and A. Srivastava, 'Encouraging Knowledge Sharing: The Role of Organizational Reward System', *Journal of Leadership & Organizational Studies* 9 (Summer 2002), 64–76.

15 C. Rukuni, 'Employee Share Schemes Change Workers' Fortunes', *LiquidAfrica*, 9 October 2004; 'Beca Co-Founder Receives an Entrepreneurship Award', *Scoop* (Auckland), 13 October 2005; 'Winners of the "ESOP of the Year" for 2005–2006 Announced' (Sydney: Australian Employee Ownership Association, December 2005), www.aeoa.org.au (accessed 15 January 2006); 'Trends and Statistics on ESO in Australia' (Canberra: Commonwealth of Australia, 2006), www.workplace.gov.au (accessed 15 January 2006).

16 The source of share options at Silex Systems Limited is Silex Systems Limited, *Silex Annual Report 2005* (Sydney: Silex Systems Limited, October 2006).

17 'KT Seeks New Growth Engines', *Korea Herald*, 2 March 2004.

18 E. Charles, 'Final Score', *Australian CPA*, July 2003, 30; Western Water, 'Western Water Honoured with Hall of Fame Award', Western Water news release (Gisborne, 30 November 2004).

19 J. Chelius and R. S. Smith, 'Profit Sharing and Employment Stability', *Industrial and Labor Relations Review* 43 (1990), 256s–73s; S. H. Wagner, C. P. Parkers and N. D. Christiansen, 'Employees That Think and Act Like Owners: Effects of Ownership Beliefs and Behaviors on Organizational Effectiveness', *Personnel Psychology* 56, no. 4 (Winter 2003), 847–71; G. Ledford, M. Lucy and P. Leblanc, 'The Effects of Stock Ownership on Employee Attitudes and Behavior: Evidence from the Rewards at Work Studies', *Perspectives* (Sibson), January 2004; P. Andon, J. Baxter and H. Mahama, 'The Balanced Scorecard: Slogans, Seduction, and State of Play', *Australian Accounting Review* 15, no. 1 (March 2005), 29–38.

20 A. J. Maggs, 'Enron, ESOPs, and Fiduciary Duty', *Benefits Law Journal* 16, no. 3 (Autumn 2003), 42–52; C. Brodzinski, 'Esop's Fables Can Make Coverage Risky', *National Underwriter. P & C*, 13 June 2005, 16–17. The popularity of ESOPs and profit sharing in fast-growth Canadian firms is described in J. Myers, 'Dream Teams', *Profit*, June 2003, 24.

21 J. Pfeffer, *The Human Equation* (Boston: Harvard Business School Press, 1998); B. N. Pfau and I. T. Kay, *The Human Capital Edge* (New York: McGraw-Hill, 2002). The problems with performance-based pay are discussed in: W. C. Hammer, 'How to Ruin Motivation with Pay', *Compensation Review* 7, no. 3 (1975), 17–27; A. Kohn, *Punished by Rewards* (Boston: Houghton Mifflin, 1993); M. O'Donnell and J. O'Brian, 'Performance-Based Pay in the Australian Public Service', *Review of Public Personnel Administration* 20 (Spring 2000), 20–34; M. Beer and M. D. Cannon, 'Promise and Peril of Implementing Pay-for-Performance', *Human Resource Management* 43, no. 1 (Spring 2004), 3–48.

22 W. Wyatt, 'Workmalaysia', (Kuala Lumpur: Watson Wyatt, 2004), http://www.watsonwyatt.com/asia-pacific/research/workasia/workmy_keyfindings.asp (accessed 2 December 2005); S. Allen, 'Finding Value in Employee Reviews', *Dominion Post* (Wellington), 22 July 2005, 4.

23 S. Kerr, 'Organization Rewards: Practical, Cost-Neutral Alternatives That You May Know but Don't Practice', *Organizational Dynamics* 28 (Summer 1999), 61–70.

24 J. S. DeMatteo, L. T. Eby and E. Sundstrom, 'Team-Based Rewards: Current Empirical Evidence and Directions for Future Research', *Research in Organizational Behavior* 20 (1998), 141–83; S. Rynes, B. Gerhart and L. Parks, 'Personnel Psychology: Performance Evaluation and Pay for Performance', *Annual Review of Psychology* 56 (2005), 571–600.

25 'Dream Teams', *Human Resources Professional* (November 1994), 17–19.

26 D. R. Spitzer, 'Power Rewards: Rewards That Really Motivate', *Management Review* (May 1996), 45–50. For a classic discussion on the unintended consequences of pay, see S. Kerr, 'On the Folly of Rewarding A, While Hoping for B', *Academy of Management Journal* 18 (1975), 769–83.

27 'Cash Is King in the Work Force', *Shanghai Daily*, 26 September 2005.

28 Pretoria Portland Cement, *Annual Report, 2003* (Sandton, South Africa: Pretoria Portland Cement, December 2003).

29 J. R. Edwards, J. A. Scully and M. D. Brtek, 'The Nature and Outcomes of Work: A Replication and Extension of Interdisciplinary Work-Design Research', *Journal of Applied Psychology* 85, no. 6 (2000), 860–8; F. P. Morgeson and M. A. Campion, 'Minimizing Tradeoffs When Redesigning Work: Evidence from a Longitudinal Quasi-Experiment', *Personnel Psychology* 55, no. 3 (Autumn 2002), 589–612.

30 P. Siekman, 'This Is Not a BMW Plant', *Fortune*, 18 April 2005, 208.

31 Accel-Team, 'Scientific Management: Lessons from Ancient History through the Industrial Revolution', www.accel-team.com; A. Smith, *The Wealth of Nations* (London: Dent, 1910).

32 H. Fayol, *General and Industrial Management*, trans. C. Storrs (London: Pitman, 1949); E. E. Lawler III, *Motivation in Work Organizations* (Monterey, CA: Brooks/Cole, 1973), chapter 7; M. A. Campion, 'Ability Requirement Implications of Job Design: An Interdisciplinary Perspective', *Personnel Psychology* 42 (1989), 1–24.

33 F. W. Taylor, *The Principles of Scientific Management* (New York: Harper & Row, 1911); R. Kanigel, *The One Best Way: Frederick Winslow Taylor and the Enigma of Efficiency* (NY: Viking, 1997).

34 C. R. Walker and R. H. Guest, *The Man on the Assembly Line* (Cambridge, MA: Harvard University Press, 1952); W. F. Dowling, 'Job Redesign on the Assembly Line: Farewell to Blue-Collar Blues?', *Organizational Dynamics* (Autumn 1973), 51–67; E. E. Lawler III, *High-Involvement Management* (San Francisco: Jossey-Bass, 1986).

35 M. Keller, *Rude Awakening* (New York: Harper Perennial, 1989), p. 128.

36 F. Herzberg, B. Mausner and B. B. Snyderman, *The Motivation to Work* (New York: Wiley, 1959).

37 S. K. Parker, T. D. Wall and J. L. Cordery, 'Future Work Design Research and Practice: Towards an Elaborated Model of Work Design', *Journal of Occupational and Organizational Psychology* 74 (November 2001), 413–40. For a decisive critique of motivator-hygiene theory, see N. King, 'Clarification and Evaluation of the Two Factor Theory of Job Satisfaction', *Psychological Bulletin* 74 (1970), 18–31.

38 J. R. Hackman and G. Oldham, *Work Redesign* (Reading, MA: Addison-Wesley, 1980).

39 Furlonger, 'Best Company to Work For'.

40 J. E. Champoux, 'A Multivariate Test of the Job Characteristics Theory of Work Motivation', *Journal of Organizational Behavior* 12, no. 5 (September 1991), 431–46; R. B. Tiegs, L. E. Tetrick and Y. Fried, 'Growth Need Strength and Context Satisfactions as Moderators of the Relations of the Job Characteristics Model', *Journal of Management* 18, no. 3 (September 1992), 575–93.

41 M. Ouellette, 'Rotate Workers to Reduce Repetitive Strain Injuries', *Plant*, 22 September 2003, 17.

42 M. A. Campion and C. L. McClelland, 'Follow-up and Extension of the Interdisciplinary Costs and Benefits of Enlarged Jobs', *Journal of Applied Psychology* 78 (1993), 339–51; N. G. Dodd and D. C. Ganster, 'The Interactive Effects of Variety, Autonomy, and Feedback on Attitudes and Performance', *Journal of Organizational Behavior* 17 (1996), 329–47.

43 J. R. Hackman et al., 'A New Strategy for Job Enrichment', *California Management Review* 17, no. 4 (1975), 57–71; R. W. Griffin, *Task Design: An Integrative Approach* (Glenview, IL: Scott Foresman, 1982).

44 P. E. Spector and S. M. Jex, 'Relations of Job Characteristics from Multiple Data Sources with Employee Affect, Absence, Turnover Intentions, and Health', *Journal of Applied Psychology* 76 (1991), 46–53; P. Osterman, 'How Common Is Workplace Transformation and Who Adopts It?', *Industrial and Labor Relations Review* 47 (1994), 173–88; R. Saavedra and S. K. Kwun, 'Affective States in Job Characteristics Theory', *Journal of Organizational Behavior* 21 (2000), 131–46.

45 G. Barker, 'One for the Road', *Sydney Morning Herald*, 27 September 2004, 6; S. Quinn, 'Tools of War', *The Age* (Melbourne), 2 June 2005, 8.

46 Hackman and Oldham, *Work Redesign*, pp. 137–8.

47 A. Hertting et al., 'Personnel Reductions and Structural Changes in Health Care: Work–Life Experiences of Medical Secretaries', *Journal of Psychosomatic Research* 54 (February 2003), 161–70.

48 K. Tyler, 'The Boss Makes the Weather', *HRMagazine*, May 2004, 93–6.

49 This definition is based mostly on G. M. Spreitzer and R. E. Quinn, '*A Company of Leaders: Five Disiplines for Unleashing the Power in Your Workforce*' (San Francisco: Jossey-Bass, 2001). However, most elements of the definition appear in other discussions of empowerment. See, for example: R. Forrester, 'Empowerment: Rejuvenating a Potent Idea', *Academy of Management Executive* 14 (August 2000), 67–80; W. A. Randolph, 'Re-Thinking Empowerment: Why Is It So Hard to Achieve?', *Organizational Dynamics* 29 (November 2000), 94–107; S. T. Menon, 'Employee Empowerment: An Integrative Psychological Approach', *Applied Psychology: An International Review* 50 (2001), 153–80.

50 The positive relationship between these structural empowerment conditions and psychological empowerment is reported in H. K. S. Laschinger et al., 'A Longitudinal Analysis of the Impact of Workplace Empowerment on Work Satisfaction', *Journal of Organizational Behavior* 25, no. 4 (June 2004), 527–45.

51 C. S. Koberg et al., 'Antecedents and Outcomes of Empowerment', *Group and Organization Management* 24 (1999), 71–91; Y. Melhem, 'The Antecedents of Customer-Contact Employees' Empowerment', *Employee Relations* 26, no. 1/2 (2004), 72–93.

52 B. J. Niehoff et al., 'The Influence of Empowerment and Job Enrichment on Employee Loyalty in a Downsizing Environment', *Group and Organization Management* 26 (March 2001), 93–113; J. Yoon, 'The Role of Structure and Motivation for Workplace Empowerment: The Case of Korean Employees', *Social Psychology Quarterly* 64 (June 2001), 195–206; T. D. Wall, J. L. Cordery and C. W. Clegg, 'Empowerment, Performance, and Operational Uncertainty: A Theoretical Integration', *Applied Psychology: An International Review* 51 (2002), 146–69.

53 R. Semler, *The Seven-Day Weekend* (London: Century, 2003), p. 61. The organisational factors affecting empowerment are discussed in: G. M. Spreitzer, 'Social Structural Characteristics of Psychological Empowerment', *Academy of Management Journal* 39 (April 1996), 483–504; J. Godard, 'High Performance and the Transformation of

Work? The Implications of Alternative Work Practices for the Experience and Outcomes of Work', *Industrial & Labor Relations Review* 54 (July 2001), 776–805; P. A. Miller, P. Goddard and H. K. Spence Laschinger, 'Evaluating Physical Therapists' Perception of Empowerment Using Kanter's Theory of Structural Power in Organizations', *Physical Therapy* 81 (December 2001), 1880–8.

54 J.-C. Chebat and P. Kollias, 'The Impact of Empowerment on Customer Contact Employees' Role in Service Organizations', *Journal of Service Research* 3 (August 2000), 66–81; H. K. S. Laschinger, J. Finegan and J. Shamian, 'The Impact of Workplace Empowerment, Organizational Trust on Staff Nurses' Work Satisfaction and Organizational Commitment', *Health Care Management Review* 26 (Summer 2001), 7–23.

55 S. Dow, 'Secret of Success', *Sun Herald (Sunday Life)* (Sydney), 22 May 2005, 14.

56 C. P. Neck and C. C. Manz, 'Thought Self-Leadership: The Impact of Mental Strategies Training on Employee Cognition, Behavior, and Affect', *Journal of Organizational Behavior* 17 (1996), 445–67.

57 C. C. Manz, 'Self-Leadership: Toward an Expanded Theory of Self-Influence Processes in Organizations', *Academy of Management Review* 11 (1986), 585–600; C. C. Manz and C. Neck, *Mastering Self-Leadership*, 3rd edn (Upper Saddle River, NJ: Prentice Hall, 2004).

58 O. J. Strickland and M. Galimba, 'Managing Time: The Effects of Personal Goal Setting on Resource Allocation Strategy and Task Performance', *Journal of Psychology* 135 (July 2001), 357–67.

59 R. M. Duncan and J. A. Cheyne, 'Incidence and Functions of Self-Reported Private Speech in Young Adults: A Self-Verbalization Questionnaire', *Canadian Journal of Behavioral Science* 31 (April 1999), 133–6.

60 J. Woods, 'Upwardly Mobile', *Sydney Morning Herald*, 13 April 2005, 9.

61 J. E. Driscoll, C. Copper and A. Moran, 'Does Mental Practice Enhance Performance?', *Journal of Applied Psychology* 79 (1994), 481–92; C. P. Neck, G. L. Stewart and C. C. Manz, 'Thought Self-Leadership as a Framework for Enhancing the Performance of Performance Appraisers', *Journal of Applied Behavioral Science* 31 (September 1995), 278–302. Some research separates mental imagery from mental practice, whereas most studies combine both into the one concept.

62 A. Wrzesniewski and J. E. Dutton, 'Crafting a Job: Revisioning Employees as Active Crafters of Their Work', *Academy of Management Review* 26 (April 2001), 179–201.

63 M. I. Bopp, S. J. Glynn and R. A. Henning, *Self-Management of Performance Feedback During Computer-Based Work by Individuals and Two-Person Work Teams*, paper presented at the APA-NIOSH conference (March 1999).

64 A. W. Logue, *Self-Control: Waiting Until Tomorrow for What You Want Today* (Englewood Cliffs, NJ: Prentice Hall, 1995).

65 Neck and Manz, 'Thought Self-Leadership: The Impact of Mental Strategies Training on Employee Cognition, Behavior, and Affect'; A. M. Saks and B. E. Ashforth, 'Proactive Socialization and Behavioral Self-Management', *Journal of Vocational Behavior* 48 (1996), 301–23; L. Morin and G. Latham, 'The Effect of Mental Practice and Goal Setting as a Transfer of Training Intervention on Supervisors' Self-Efficacy and Communication Skills: An Exploratory Study', *Applied Psychology: An International Review* 49 (July 2000), 566–78; J. S. Hickman and E. S. Geller, 'A Safety Self-Management Intervention for Mining Operations', *Journal of Safety Research* 34 (2003), 299–308.

66 S. Ming and G. L. Martin, 'Single-Subject Evaluation of a Self-Talk Package for Improving Figure Skating Performance', *Sport Psychologist* 10 (1996), 227–38; D. Landin and E. P. Hebert, 'The Influence of Self-Talk on the Performance of Skilled Female Tennis Players', *Journal of Applied Sport Psychology* 11 (September 1999), 263–82; K. E. Thiese and S. Huddleston, 'The Use of Psychological Skills by Female Collegiate Swimmers', *Journal of Sport Behavior* (December 1999), 602–10; J. Bauman, 'The Gold Medal Mind', *Psychology Today* 33 (May 2000), 62–9; A. Papaioannou et al., 'Combined Effect of Goal Setting and Self-Talk in Performance of a Soccer-Shooting Task', *Perceptual and Motor Skills* 98, no. 1 (February 2004), 89–99.

67 J. Houghton et al., 'The Relationship between Self-Leadership and Personality: A Comparison of Hierarchical Factor Structures', *Journal of Managerial Psychology* 19, no. 4 (2004), 427–41. For a discussion of constructive thought patterns in the context of organisations, see J. Godwin, C. P. Neck and J. Houghton, 'The Impact of Thought Self-Leadership on Individual Goal Performance: A Cognitive Perspective', *Journal of Management Development* 18 (1999), 153–69.

CHAPTER 7

Work-related stress and stress management

LEARNING OBJECTIVES

After reading this chapter, you should be able to:

- define stress and describe the stress experience

- outline the stress process from stressors to consequences

- identify the different types of stressors in the workplace

- explain why a stressor might produce different stress levels in two people

- discuss the physiological, psychological and behavioural effects of stress

- identify five ways to manage workplace stress.

John Pakos, shown in this busy waiting room at Woodcroft Medical Centre near Adelaide, and many other physicians across Australia are experiencing work overload due to a chronic shortage of doctors.

One of the more distressing tasks that Carol Oates performs is turning away prospective patients. 'It's dreadful to have to say "sorry we can't see you"', says the practice manager at Channel Medical Centre in Kingston, a fast-growing suburb of Hobart, Tasmania. Channel's three full-time and three part-time GPs already see up to fifty patients each day on eleven-hour shifts, and the clinic has been unable to find enough doctors to ease the workload. 'It is full-on work. The days are long,' says Oates. 'There are days when doctors work through without a break, sometimes not even a cup of tea, starting at about 8 and finishing at 7.30.'

The doctor shortage is also taking its toll at the Woodcroft Medical Centre near Adelaide, where seven doctors (3.5 full-time equivalent) are trying to cope with the needs of 10 000 registered patients. The phones start ringing at 8.15 am and rarely stop until the clinic closes. 'The first hour every day is just crazy, as patients scramble to get an appointment,' says Woodcroft's principal GP, John Pakos, who closed his books to new patients three years ago. 'We have been struggling. A lot of other surgeries around us have closed.'

While doctors in Kingston, Woodcroft and other suburban communities have their share of work overload, the shortage of medical talent and its effect on practitioners is even more acute in country Australia. 'Many of the rural doctors are overworked and under a lot of stress,' warns Tony Van Der Spek, who runs a practice in Bendigo, Victoria, where the doctor-to-patient ratio is 1:2000.

Robert McKimm was one of three obstetricians in Sale, Victoria, two decades ago, but he was the only remaining obstetrician in the 1990s. Fortunately, a second specialist recently moved into the area to ease the workload. 'If you lose a certain number of your colleagues, you get more and more responsibility thrown on your shoulders, to the point where it's no longer a viable lifestyle,' says McKimm.

Christine Jeffries-Stokes has had an equally challenging time. For two years the Kalgoorlie doctor was the only paediatrician between Perth and Alice Springs, robbing her of any personal time off. 'I have been doing this for ten years now and I have repeatedly told the Health Department that I cannot keep going on like this—my health and my family are suffering,' she wrote in a letter to the Western Australia government. A second specialist now works in the area and a third doctor from Perth is completing paediatric training in Kalgoorlie. 'Hopefully it's just going to make my life normal,' said Jeffries-Stokes on hearing about the most recent appointment.[1]

WORKING LONGER HOURS and receiving less time off is a serious concern among doctors in Australia. But they are not alone in the rising tide of work-related stress. The Royal New Zealand College of General Practitioners warns that many doctors in that country plan to leave the profession, mainly because they are ready to retire but many also because they have had enough of the high workloads. 'They use words like "stressed", "burnt out", "frustrated" and "exhausted",' says College president Jonathan Fox. Research by Medibank Private Health reported that 53 per cent of Australian employees across all occupations feel under pressure a significant amount of the time. More than 20 per cent said they feel exhausted on the job. Another Australian survey reported that 79 per cent of workers lose sleep thinking about work or are obsessed about their jobs in their spare time.[2]

Of course, stress isn't just an affliction in Australia and New Zealand. A survey of 4700 people across Asia reported that one-third were feeling more stress than in the recent past, down from 41 per cent two years earlier when the economy was less robust. People in Taiwan report the highest stress; those in Thailand report the lowest stress. The Japanese government, which tracks work-related stress every five years, has found that the percentage of Japanese employees who feel 'strong worry, anxiety or stress at work or in daily working life' has increased from 51 per cent in 1982 to almost two-thirds of the population today. According to a Gallup poll, 80 per cent of Americans feel too much stress on the job; nearly half indicate that they need help coping with it. Approximately one in every four employees in the United Kingdom feels 'very or extremely stressed', and this condition has become the top cause of absenteeism there.[3]

This chapter looks at the dynamics of work-related stress and how to manage it. It begins by describing the stress experience. Next, the causes and consequences of stress are examined, along with the factors that cause some people to experience stress when others do not. The final section of the chapter looks at ways to manage work-related stress from an organisational perspective and an individual perspective.

WHAT IS STRESS?

stress An individual's adaptive response to a situation that is perceived as challenging or threatening to the person's well-being.

Stress is an adaptive response to a situation that is perceived as challenging or threatening to the person's well-being.[4] The stress response is a complex emotion that produces physiological changes to prepare us for 'fight or flight', to defend against the threat or flee from it. Specifically, our heart rate increases, muscles tighten, breathing speeds up and perspiration increases. Our body also moves more blood to the brain, releases adrenaline and other hormones, fuels the system by releasing more glucose and fatty acids, activates systems that sharpen our senses, and conserves resources by shutting down our immune system.

We often hear about stress as a negative consequence of modern living. People are stressed from overwork, job insecurity, information overload and the increasing pace of life. These events produce *distress*—the degree of physiological, psychological and behavioural deviation from healthy functioning. There is also a positive side to stress, called *eustress*, which refers to the healthy, positive, constructive outcome of stressful events and the stress response. Eustress is the stress experience in moderation, enough to activate and motivate people so that they can achieve goals, change their environments and succeed in life's challenges. In other words, we need some stress to survive.[5] However, most research focuses on *distress*, because it is a significant concern in organisational settings. Employees frequently experience enough stress to hurt their job performance and increase their risk of mental and physical health problems. Consequently, the discussion will focus more on distress than on eustress.

LEARNING OBJECTIVE

Define stress and describe the stress experience.

GENERAL ADAPTATION SYNDROME

general adaptation syndrome A model of the stress experience, consisting of three stages: alarm reaction, resistance and exhaustion.

The stress experience was first documented fifty years ago by stress research pioneer Hans Selye.[6] Selye determined that people have a fairly consistent physiological response to stressful situations. This response, called the **general adaptation syndrome**, provides an automatic

Selye's general adaptation syndrome

EXHIBIT 7.1

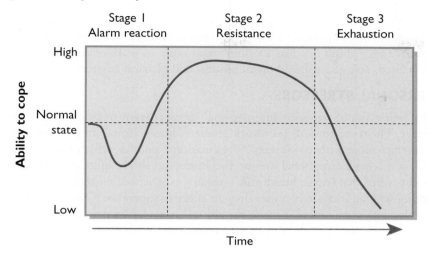

Source: Adapted from H. Selye, *The Stress of Life* (New York: McGraw-Hill, 1956).

defence system to help us cope with environmental demands. Exhibit 7.1 illustrates the three stages of the general adaptation syndrome: alarm, resistance and exhaustion. The line in this exhibit shows the individual's energy and ability to cope with the stressful situation.

Alarm reaction

The alarm reaction stage occurs when a threat or challenge activates the physiological stress responses noted earlier, such as increased respiration rate, blood pressure, heartbeat and muscle tension. The individual's energy level and coping effectiveness decrease in response to the initial shock. In extreme situations, this shock can result in incapacity or death because the body is unable to generate enough energy quickly enough. Most of the time, the alarm reaction alerts the person to the environmental condition and prepares the body for the resistance stage.

Resistance

The person's ability to cope with the environmental demand rises above the normal state during the resistance stage because the body activates various biochemical, psychological and behavioural mechanisms. For example, the body has a higher than normal level of adrenaline and glucose during this stage, which gives it more energy to overcome or remove the source of the stress. At the same time, the body shuts down the immune system to focus energy on the source of the stress. This explains why people are more likely to catch a cold or other illness when they experience prolonged stress.

Exhaustion

People have a limited resistance capacity, and if the source of stress persists they will eventually move into the exhaustion stage. In most work situations, the general adaptation syndrome process ends long before total exhaustion. Employees resolve tense situations before the destructive consequences of stress become manifest, or they withdraw from the stressful situation, rebuild their survival capabilities, and return later to the stressful environment with renewed energy. However, people who frequently experience the general adaptation syndrome have increased risk of long-term physiological and psychological damage.[7]

The general adaptation syndrome describes the stress experience, but this is only part of the picture. To effectively manage work-related stress, its causes and consequences must be understood, as well as individual differences in the stress experience.

stressors The causes of stress, including any environmental conditions that place a physical or emotional demand on the person.

LEARNING OBJECTIVE

Outline the stress process from stressors to consequences.

LEARNING OBJECTIVE

Identify the different types of stressors in the workplace.

STRESSORS: THE CAUSES OF STRESS

Stressors, the causes of stress, include any environmental conditions that place a physical or emotional demand on the person.[8] There are numerous stressors in organisational settings and other life activities. Exhibit 7.2 lists the four main types of work-related stressors: interpersonal, role-related, task control, and organisational and physical environment stressors.

INTERPERSONAL STRESSORS

Among the four types of stressors, interpersonal stressors seem to be the most pervasive in the workplace. The trend towards teamwork generates interpersonal stressors because employees must interact more with co-workers. Organisational politics, which will be discussed in Chapter 12, is another interpersonal stressor. Bad bosses can also be quite stressful. For instance, one study discovered that female health-care assistants experienced much higher blood pressure when working with an ineffective rather than an effective supervisor. Over a sustained period, the higher blood pressure would increase the risk of stroke by 38 per cent![9] Two other interpersonal stressors are workplace violence and harassment, which are discussed next.

Workplace violence

Workplace violence immediately brings to mind the United States, where approximately 600 employees are murdered on the job each year and 2 million others experience lesser forms of physical violence. While these figures are troubling, violence is also a serious stressor in several industries in the Pacific Rim region. One recent study estimated that 17 per cent of juvenile justice employees and 12 per cent of health-care workers in Australia experienced physical assault within the previous year. Another survey reported that more than half of Queensland nurses had experienced some form of workplace violence within the previous three months.[10]

EXHIBIT 7.2	**Causes and consequences of stress**

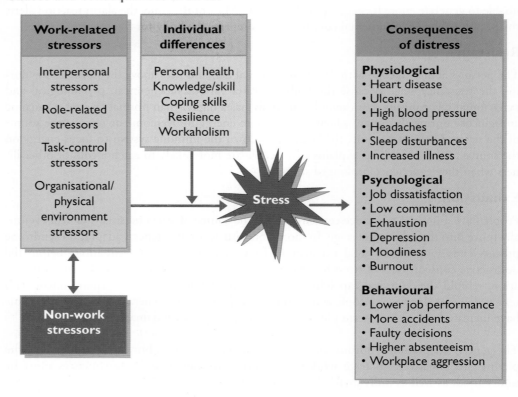

Victims of workplace violence experience severe stress symptoms. Those who observe the violence also tend to experience stress. After a serious workplace incident, counsellors assist many employees, not just the direct victims. Even employees who have not directly experienced or observed violence may show signs of stress if they work in jobs that expose them to a high incidence of violence.

Psychological and sexual harassment

For almost seven years Devander Naidu took more abuse from his boss than most of us would experience in a lifetime. The assistant security and fire control manager received ongoing verbal abuse, racial taunts (Naidu is Indo-Fijian), threats of physical violence, swearing, insults to his wife, and lewd behaviour from News Ltd's senior manager responsible for security and fire. The manager also forced Naidu to perform construction work at his (the manager's) home during work hours. Naidu complained about these incidents to his manager at Group 4 Securitas, the security firm that actually employed him, but the Group 4 manager did little to help, fearing loss of the News Ltd contract. Over time, Naidu developed severe depression and post-traumatic stress disorder as a result of the psychological abuse. The senior manager was sacked after News Ltd's internal investigation found sufficient evidence of his behaviour problems. (Naidu's situation became known only when News Ltd investigated claims by female staff that the senior manager had sexually harassed them.) Naidu later sued News Ltd and Group 4 for their failure to stop the senior manager's harassment, and won compensation.[11]

The New South Wales Supreme Court concluded that Naidu experienced extreme and prolonged **psychological harassment**. Psychological harassment includes repeated and hostile or unwanted conduct, verbal comments, actions or gestures that affect an employee's dignity or psychological or physical integrity and that result in a harmful work environment for the employee. This covers a broad landscape of behaviours, from threats and bullying to subtle yet persistent forms of incivility.[12] Psychological harassment has become such a problem that some European governments explicitly prohibit it in the workplace. When the province of Quebec, Canada, recently passed the first workplace anti-harassment legislation in North America, more than 2500 complaints were received in the first year alone![13]

Psychological harassment also permeates throughout many Australian workplaces. A New South Wales Law Society survey reported that more than half of the 1800 lawyers polled have been bullied or intimidated. Three separate studies estimate that between 15 and 26 per cent of government employees in Tasmania, Victoria and South Australia experience harassment each year from their managers, fellow employees or clients. Research by WorkSafe Victoria estimates that 15 per cent of employees in that state had been subjected to some form of bullying in the previous year. In Western Australia, WorkSafe reported 311 claims of workplace bullying in 2004, up from just eleven claims three years earlier.[14]

Sexual harassment is a variation of harassment in which a person's employment or job performance is conditional on unwanted sexual relations (called *quid pro quo*), and/or the person experiences sexual conduct from others (such as posting pornographic material) that unreasonably interferes with work performance or creates an intimidating, hostile or offensive working environment (called *hostile work environment*). One study points out that men tend to have a narrower interpretation than do women about what constitutes a hostile work environment, so they sometimes engage in this form of sexual harassment without being aware of their transgressions.[15] Another issue is that sexual harassment sometimes escalates into psychological harassment after the alleged victim complains of the sexual wrongdoing.

Psychological and sexual harassment are stressful experiences that undermine employee well-being and performance. Past behaviour is the best predictor of future behaviour, so companies should carefully screen applicants in terms of past incidents. Multi-source feedback is another valuable tool to let employees know that co-workers and direct reports find their behaviour intimidating or sexually inappropriate. Along with these practices, companies need

psychological harassment
Repeated and hostile or unwanted conduct, verbal comments, actions or gestures that affect an employee's dignity or psychological or physical integrity and that result in a harmful work environment for the employee.

sexual harassment
Unwelcome conduct of a sexual nature that detrimentally affects the work environment or leads to adverse job-related consequences for its victims.

to develop a grievance, mediation or other conflict resolution process that employees trust when they become victims of workplace harassment.

ROLE-RELATED STRESSORS

role conflict Incongruity or incompatibility of expectations associated with the person's role.

Role-related stressors include conditions where employees have difficulty understanding, reconciling or performing the various roles in their lives. Three types of role-related stressors are role conflict, role ambiguity and work overload. **Role conflict** refers to the degree of incongruity or incompatibility of expectations associated with the person's role. Some people experience stress when they have two roles that conflict with each other. For example, various studies have recently reported this inter-role conflict among human service workers and health-care providers, where workloads and bureaucratic procedures interfered with their ability to serve clients or patients.[16] Role conflict also occurs when an employee's personal values are incompatible with the organisational values, a topic that was detailed in Chapter 2.

role ambiguity A lack of clarity and predictability of the outcomes of one's behaviour.

Role ambiguity refers to the lack of clarity and predictability of the outcomes of one's behaviour. Role ambiguity produces unclear role perceptions, which has a direct effect on job performance. It is also a source of stress in a variety of situations, such as joining an organisation or working in a new joint venture, because people are uncertain about task and social expectations.[17]

Work overload

A half-century ago, social scientists predicted that technology would allow employees to enjoy a fifteen-hour work-week at full pay by 2030. So far, it hasn't turned out that way. As the opening story to this chapter revealed, doctors in many parts of Australia are experiencing stress due to *work overload*—working more hours and more intensely during those hours than they can reasonably cope with. Doctors in small communities throughout New Zealand and in parts of Asia also experience this stressor. Work overload extends beyond the medical community. Two-thirds of managers in Singapore work more than fifty hours each week, as do 23 per cent of Australian employees in all occupations. Korea, Hong Kong, Turkey, India and Singapore top the list of countries where the hours of work are much higher than the hours of leisure. The Philippines, Thailand, Brazil, Argentina and Canada have the highest ratio of leisure hours exceeding work hours.[18]

Why do employees work such long hours? One explanation is the combined effects of technology and globalisation. 'Everyone in this industry is working harder now because of email, wireless access and globalisation,' says Christopher Lochhead, chief marketing officer of Mercury Interactive, a California-based consultancy with offices in thirty-five countries. 'You can't even get a rest on the weekend,' he says. A second cause, according to a recent Australian study, is that many people are caught up in consumerism; they want to buy more goods and services, which requires more income through longer working hours. A third reason, called the 'ideal worker norm', is that professionals expect themselves and others to work longer hours. For many, toiling away far beyond the normal work-week is a badge of honour, a symbol of their superhuman capacity to perform better than others. The ideal worker norm is particularly strong in Japan, Korea, China and other Asian cultures. As Reality Check 7.1 describes, the effect of this long-hours cultural value is *karoshi*—death from overwork.[19]

TASK-CONTROL STRESSORS

As a private driver for an executive in Jakarta, Eddy knows that traffic jams are a way of life in Indonesia's largest city. 'Jakarta is traffic congestion,' he complains. 'All of the streets in the city are crowded with vehicles. It is impossible to avoid this distressing fact every day.' Eddy's boss complains when traffic jams make him late for appointments, which makes matters even more stressful. 'Even watching soccer on TV or talking to my wife doesn't get rid of my stress. It's driving me mad.'[20] Eddy and many other people experience stress due to a lack of task

7.1

KAROSHI: DEATH BY OVERWORK CONTINUES TO INVADE ASIA

Yoichi Kawamoto typically worked eight hours each day, then did an extra six hours of unpaid overtime. The 52-year-old manager at a machinery firm in the southern Japanese city of Kobe also felt obliged to work on Saturdays and holidays. One day, Kawamoto penned a short note, saying: 'Overtime work with no pay, or not enough. Being forced to stay late.' The note was written in English, presumably to hide the message from his colleagues. Kawamoto died a few days later. 'His death, from a massive heart attack, was almost spontaneous,' Kawamoto's wife recalls. 'Those long working hours killed him.'

Yoichi Kawamoto was a victim of *karoshi*—death from overwork. The Japanese government recorded 157 cases of *karoshi* in the most recent year, but this number includes only situations where family members claimed and received compensation. Experts say that the *karoshi* death toll in Japan is probably closer to 10 000, and that up to one million white-collar employees are at risk. According to the Japanese government, employees who work more than eighty hours of overtime per month have a significantly higher risk of *karoshi*. Currently, more than 20 per cent of male Japanese employees exceed that level of overtime. In spite of the increasing number of *karoshi* cases, the Japanese government recently announced plans to abolish the limits on overtime for some white-collar workers.

Japanese workers are not the only ones dropping dead from long hours of work. Both South Korea (which is among the countries with the world's highest average work hours) and Taiwan are paying close attention to workplace casualties that appear to result from working too many continuous hours. China is another country where several young Chinese executives, professionals, academics and factory workers have apparently died from overwork. Chinese media are now using the term *guolaosi*, meaning 'overwork death'.

Several investigations suggest that *guolaosi* is a concern in China even though the government does not officially discuss it. A study of journalists in China's major news outlets revealed that the average age of death was forty-six years. Another investigation reported that academics at Zhongguancun, Beijing's Silicon Valley, died at an average age of fifty-three years, down from a decade earlier when the average age at death was fifty-eight years. A third study of mortality among academics also found that the average age of death was the early fifties. These startling statistics were recently made more human when two young faculty members at China's top engineering school died suddenly. Both apparently suffered from exhaustion and stress from overwork.

Larry Dale Gordon/Getty Images

Employees in Japan, China and other countries are literally dropping dead from overwork.

Sources: M. Schreiber, 'Die (Working) Hard, with a Vengeance', *Japan Times*, 6 April 2003; C. B. Meek, 'The Dark Side of Japanese Management in the 1990s: Karoshi and Ijime in the Japanese Workplace', *Journal of Managerial Psychology* 19, no. 3 (2004), 312–31; N. You, 'Work for Life, Rather than Live to Work', *China Daily*, 26 March 2005; J. Ryall, 'Limits on Overtime to Go, Despite Work-Stress Complaints', *South China Morning Post*, 30 April 2005, 11; J. Shi, 'Beijing's High Flyers Dying to Get Ahead', *South China Morning Post*, 8 October 2005, 8.

control. Along with driving through congested traffic, low task control occurs where the employee's work is paced by a machine, the job involves monitoring equipment, or the work schedule is controlled by someone else. Computers, mobile phones and other technology also increase stress by limiting a person's control of time and privacy.[21]

The degree to which low task control is a stressor increases with the burden of responsibility that an employee must carry. Assembly-line workers have low task control, but their stress can also be fairly low if their level of responsibility is also low. In contrast, sports coaches are under immense pressure to win games (high responsibility), yet have little control over what happens on the playing field (low task control). Similarly, Eddy (the Jakarta driver) is under pressure to get his employer to a particular destination on time (high responsibility), yet he has little control over traffic congestion (low task control).

ORGANISATIONAL AND PHYSICAL ENVIRONMENT STRESSORS

Organisational and physical environment stressors come in many forms. Downsizing is stressful for those who lose their jobs, but even those who keep their jobs (called 'layoff survivors') experience stress because of the reduced job security, the chaos of change, the additional workload, and the guilt of having a job as others lose theirs. For example, one study reported that long-term sick leave doubled among surviving government employees in Finland after a major downsizing.[22] Physical work environment stressors include excessive noise and poor lighting. People working in dangerous work environments also tend to experience high stress levels.

WORK–NON-WORK STRESSORS

The stress model shown earlier in Exhibit 7.2 has a two-way arrow, indicating that stressors from work spill over into non-work and vice versa.[24] There are three types of work–non-work stressors: time-based, strain-based and role-based conflict.

Time-based conflict

Time-based conflict refers to the challenge of balancing the time demanded by work with family and other non-work activities. Time-based conflict relates back to the work overload stressor described earlier. The problem of longer working hours (as well as working more intensely during those hours) is compounded by the fact that employees have little time or energy left for themselves and their family. Inflexible work schedules, business travel and

Medical staff endure the stress of SARS

In just six months, severe acute respiratory syndrome (SARS) infected 8000 people worldwide and took the lives of more than 800 of them. Medical staff at Hong Kong's Prince of Wales hospital (shown here) were on the front-line of that epidemic and experienced highly stressful circumstances, because no one knew how the virus spread or what medical interventions would work. Prince of Wales nurse Joanna Pong recalls one incident in which an elderly SARS patient suffering from dementia lowered her mask and coughed hard at Pong. 'It was a scary feeling,' says Pong, who fortunately did not catch the disease. Employees were also exhausted by overwork and the challenges of wearing uncomfortable body suits, goggles, gloves and tight-fitting masks throughout their shift. 'Working with a mask on all day is incredibly exhausting,' says Prince of Wales nurse Josephine Chung Yuen-man. 'Some of my colleagues have lost a lot of weight due to all the stress.'[23]

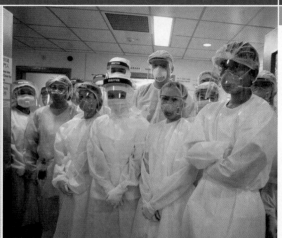

AP Photo/Vincent Yu

rotating shift schedules also take a heavy toll, because they reduce the ability to effectively juggle work and non-work.[25] Time-based conflict is usually more acute for women than for men, because housework and childcare continue to fall more on their shoulders as a 'second shift' in most dual-career families.

Strain-based conflict

Strain-based conflict occurs when stress from one domain spills over to the other. Relationship problems, financial difficulties and the loss of a loved one usually top the list of non-work stressors. New responsibilities, such as marriage, the birth of a child, and a mortgage, are also stressful to most people. Stress at work also spills over to an employee's personal life and often becomes the foundation of stressful relations with family and friends. In support of this, one study found that fathers who experience stress at work engage in dysfunctional parenting behaviours, which then lead to their children having behaviour problems at school.[26]

Role behaviour conflict

A third stressor, called role behaviour conflict, occurs when people are expected to act at work quite differently from when in non-work roles. For instance, people who act logically and impersonally at work have difficulty switching to a more compassionate behavioural style in their personal lives. Thus, stress occurs in this adjustment from one role to the other.[27]

Stress and occupations

Several studies have attempted to identify which jobs have more stressors than others.[28] These lists are not in complete agreement, but Exhibit 7.3 identifies a representative sample of jobs and their relative level of stressors. This information needs to be viewed with some caution, however. One problem with rating occupations in terms of their stress levels is that a particular occupation may have considerably different tasks and job environments across organisations and societies. A nurse's job may be less stressful in a small-town medical clinic, for instance, than in the emergency room of a large city hospital.

Another important point to remember when looking at Exhibit 7.3 is that a major stressor to one person may be less significant to another. Thus, not everyone in so-called high-stress occupations actually experiences more stress than people in other occupations. High-stress jobs have more stressors, but people don't experience more stress if they are carefully selected and trained for this type of work. The next section discusses individual differences in stress.

Stressors in occupations

EXHIBIT 7.3

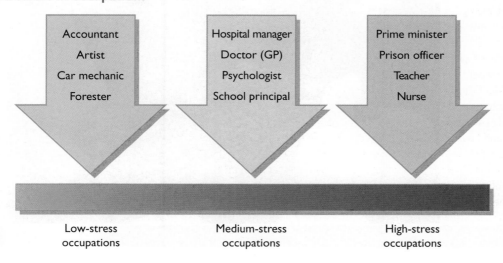

Accountant	Hospital manager	Prime minister
Artist	Doctor (GP)	Prison officer
Car mechanic	Psychologist	Teacher
Forester	School principal	Nurse

Low-stress occupations | Medium-stress occupations | High-stress occupations

**LEARNING
OBJECTIVE**

*Explain why a stressor might
produce different stress levels in
two people.*

INDIVIDUAL DIFFERENCES IN STRESS

People have different stress experiences when exposed to the same stressor due to unique personal characteristics. One reason is that they have different threshold levels of resistance to the stressor. Younger employees generally experience fewer and less severe stress symptoms than older employees because they have a larger store of energy to cope with high stress levels. Exercise and healthy lifestyles (including work-free holidays), discussed later in the chapter, are ways to manage stress, because these activities rebuild this store of energy. A second reason for different stress outcomes is that people use different coping strategies, some of which are more effective than others. Research suggests that employees who try to ignore or deny the existence of a stressor suffer more in the long run than those who try to find ways to weaken the stressor and seek social support.[29]

The third reason why some people experience less stress than others in the same situation is that they have different beliefs about the threat and their ability to withstand it. This explanation has two parts. The first part refers to the notion that people with more knowledge and skill usually feel more confident about successfully managing or overcoming the threat. Someone who flies a plane for the first time tends to experience much more stress than an experienced pilot, for instance. The second part refers to the idea that people who are optimistic, confident and often experience positive emotions tend to feel less stress.[30] This characteristic extends beyond the person's knowledge and skill; it refers to an important emerging concept, known as resilience.

RESILIENCE AND STRESS

resilience The capability of
individuals to cope successfully in
the face of significant change,
adversity or risk.

Resilience is the capability of individuals to cope successfully in the face of significant change, adversity or risk. Everyone has some resiliency; it occurs every time we pull through stressful experiences. Although the word literally means to 'leap back', resilience in this context mainly refers to withstanding adversity rather than recovering from it. While everyone needs to recuperate to some extent following a stressful experience, people with high resilience are better able to maintain an equilibrium, and, consequently, have lost little ground in the first place. In fact, some writers believe that resilience moves people to a higher plateau after the adversity.[32]

Stress-free at Finster Honey Farms

Working around honeybees is a heart-thumping experience for most people. But Hakija Pehlic (shown here) doesn't worry when he pushes his nose through a layer of European honeybees to better determine the type of honey produced on a honeycomb frame. Pehlic, a beekeeper at Finster Honey Farms in Schuyler, New York, doesn't experience much stress in this situation because he is trained to know when it's safe to smell the honey and how to avoid getting stung. Most of the time, says Pehlic, honeybees are gentle insects that won't bother you. Maybe so, but you probably shouldn't try this at home.[31]

Heather Ainsworth, *Observer-Dispatch* (Utica, NY)

Experts have looked at the characteristics of resilience from different perspectives. One perspective is that resilient people have personality traits that generate more optimism, confidence and positive emotions. These traits include high extroversion, low neuroticism, internal locus of control, high tolerance of change and high self-esteem.[33]

A second perspective is that resilience involves specific competencies and behaviours to respond and adapt more effectively to stressors. Research indicates that resilient people have higher emotional intelligence and good problem-solving skills. They also apply productive coping strategies, such as analysing the sources of stress and finding ways to neutralise these problems. In contrast, people with low resilience tend to avoid the stressors or deny the existence of them.[34]

The third perspective is that resilience is an inner force that motivates us to move forward. This emerging view is connected to the concept of self-actualisation that psychologist Abraham Maslow popularised and made his life's work a half-century ago (see Chapter 5). It is also connected to recent organisational behaviour writing on *workplace spirituality*, which investigates a person's inner strength and how it nurtures and is nurtured by the workplace. Resilience as an inner force has some empirical support. Research has found that resilience is stronger when people have a sense of purpose and are in touch with their personal values.[35]

WORKAHOLISM AND STRESS

While resilience helps people to withstand stress, another personal characteristic—workaholism—attracts more stressors and weakens the capacity to cope with them. The classic **workaholic** (also called *work addict*) is highly involved in work, feels compelled or driven to work because of inner pressures, and has a low enjoyment of work. He or she is compulsive and preoccupied with work, often to the exclusion and detriment of personal health, intimate relationships and family. Work addicts are typically hard-driving, competitive individuals who tend to be impatient, lose their temper, and interrupt others during conversations.[36] These latter characteristics are collectively known as **Type A behaviour pattern.**

How many people are workaholics? The evidence is still scant and much of it comes from questionable popular-press sources. A survey of 1000 Australians found that 35 per cent consider themselves to be workaholics. Using a similar question, Statistics Canada reported that 30 per cent of adults in that country consider themselves classic workaholics. Self-reports in the United States range from 27 to 30 per cent. Using a more robust and detailed workaholism measure, other studies estimate that 18 per cent of Australian women psychologists and 16 per cent of MBA alumni from a Canadian university are work addicts.[37]

The studies of Australian women psychologists and Canadian MBA alumni also report on two other forms of workaholism. *Enthusiastic addicts* have high work involvement, a strong drive to succeed and high work enjoyment. Approximately 18 per cent of the psychologists and 19 per cent of the MBA alumni fell into this category. People who belong to the third type of workaholism, called *work enthusiasts*, have high work involvement and work enjoyment, but a low drive to succeed. Approximately 11 per cent of the psychologists and 14 per cent of the MBA alumni were of this type.

Workaholism is relevant to our discussion of stress because classic work addicts are more prone to job stress and burnout. They also have significantly higher scores on depression, anxiety and anger than do non-workaholics, as well as lower job and career satisfaction. Furthermore, work addicts of both sexes report more health complaints.[38]

CONSEQUENCES OF DISTRESS

The previous sections on workplace stressors and individual differences in stress have made some reference to the various outcomes of the stress experience. These stress consequences are typically grouped in terms of physiological, psychological and behavioural consequences.

workaholic A person who is highly involved in work, feels compelled to work and has a low enjoyment of work.

Type A behaviour pattern A behaviour pattern associated with people having premature coronary heart disease; type As tend to be impatient, lose their temper, talk rapidly and interrupt others.

LEARNING OBJECTIVE
Discuss the physiological, psychological and behavioural effects of stress.

PHYSIOLOGICAL CONSEQUENCES

Stress takes its toll on the human body.[39] The stress response shuts down the immune system, which makes the body more vulnerable to virus and bacterial infection. Many people experience tension headaches due to stress. Others get muscle pain and related back problems. These physiological ailments are attributed to muscle contractions that occur when people are exposed to stressors.

Cardiovascular disease is one of the most disturbing effects of stress in modern society. Strokes and heart attacks were rare a century ago but are now one of the leading causes of death among adults in Australia and other countries. The good news is that deaths due to heart disease and strokes have decreased markedly over the past decade (at least in Australia), largely due to better diet and lifestyle. Still, various investigations, including a recent global study, have found that stress is a significant cause of heart attacks. Equally disturbing is a study of over 60 000 people in Norway which found that those with high scores on an anxiety test were 25 per cent more likely to have premalignant tumours seven years later.[40]

PSYCHOLOGICAL CONSEQUENCES

Stress produces various psychological consequences, including job dissatisfaction, moodiness, depression and lower organisational commitment.[41] Emotional fatigue is another psychological consequence of stress and is related to job burnout.

Job burnout

job burnout The process of emotional exhaustion, cynicism and reduced efficacy (lower feelings of personal accomplishment) resulting from prolonged exposure to stress.

Job burnout refers to the process of emotional exhaustion, cynicism and reduced feelings of personal accomplishment resulting from prolonged exposure to stress.[42] It is a complex process that includes the dynamics of stress, coping strategies and stress consequences. Burnout is caused by excessive demands made on people who serve or frequently interact with others. In other words, burnout is mainly due to interpersonal and role-related stressors, and is most common in the helping occupations (e.g. nurses, teachers, police officers).

Exhibit 7.4 diagrams the relationship between the three components of job burnout. *Emotional exhaustion*, the first stage, is characterised by a lack of energy, tiredness, and a feeling that one's emotional resources are depleted. Emotional exhaustion is sometimes called 'compassion fatigue' because the employee no longer feels able to give as much support and care to clients.

EXHIBIT 7.4   **The job burnout process**

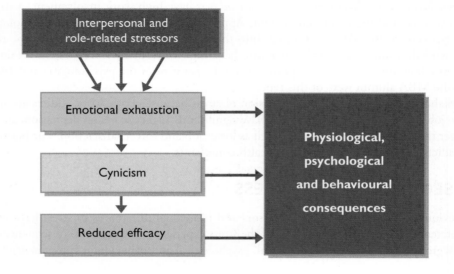

Cynicism (also called *depersonalisation*) follows emotional exhaustion. It is identified by an indifferent attitude towards work and the treatment of others as objects rather than people. At this stage, employees become emotionally detached from clients and cynical about the organisation. This detachment is to the point of callousness, far beyond the normal level in the helping occupations. Cynicism is also apparent when employees strictly follow the rules and regulations rather than try to understand the client's needs and search for a mutually acceptable solution.

Reduced professional efficacy (also called *reduced personal accomplishment*), the final component of job burnout, refers to feelings of diminished confidence in the ability to perform the job well. In these situations, employees develop a sense of learned helplessness as they no longer believe that their efforts make a difference.

BEHAVIOURAL CONSEQUENCES

Moderate levels of stress focus our attention and concentrate resources where they are most needed. But when stress becomes distress, job performance falls, memory becomes impaired, workplace accidents are more frequent, and decisions are less effective.[43] You have probably experienced this in an exam or an emergency work situation. You forget important information, make mistakes and otherwise 'draw a blank' under intense pressure.

Overstressed employees also tend to have higher levels of absenteeism. One reason is that stress makes people susceptible to viruses and bacterial infections. The other reason is that absenteeism is a coping mechanism. At a basic level, human beings react to stress through 'fight or flight'. Absenteeism is a form of flight—temporarily withdrawing from the stressful situation so that there is an opportunity to re-energise. Companies may try to minimise absenteeism, but it sometimes helps employees avoid the exhaustion stage of the stress experience.[44]

Workplace aggression

Workplace aggression is more than the serious interpersonal stressor described earlier. It is also an increasingly worrisome behavioural consequence of stress. Aggression represents the fight (instead of flight) reaction to stress. In its mildest form, employees engage in verbal harassment. They 'fly off the handle' and are less likely to empathise with co-workers. Like most forms of workplace behaviour, co-worker aggression is caused by both the person and the situation. While certain individuals are more likely to be aggressive, their behaviour is also usually to some extent a consequence of extreme stress.[45] In particular, employees are more likely to engage in aggressive behaviour if they believe they have been treated unfairly, experience other forms of frustration beyond their personal control, and work in physical environments that are stressful (e.g. hot, noisy).

MANAGING WORK-RELATED STRESS

Not long ago, Koh Ching Hong would dutifully arrive at work around 7.30 in the morning and stay until 10 at night. The managing director of Fuji Xerox in Singapore would continue working at home for a few more hours, sending off email messages listing tasks to be completed by employees 'first thing in the morning'. Eventually, Koh realised that the relentless pace was defeating a higher purpose. 'It came to a point that the people whom I worked so hard to provide for, my family, weren't getting to see me,' said the father of three children. Today, Koh is out of the office by 6.30 pm and shoos his staff out at the same time. Fuji Xerox also gives staff the opportunity to work from home as well as flexibility regarding when they want to begin and end their work day.[46]

Koh Ching Hong was fortunate. He was able to change his work habits and improve conditions for his 500 employees before matters got worse. Unfortunately, many people deny the existence of their stress until it is too late. This avoidance strategy creates a vicious cycle,

LEARNING OBJECTIVE

Identify five ways to manage workplace stress.

EXHIBIT 7.5   Stress management strategies

because the failure to cope with stress becomes another stressor on top of the one that created the stress in the first place. The solution is for both employers and employees to discover the toolkit of effective stress management strategies identified in Exhibit 7.5, and to determine which ones are best for the situation.[47]

REMOVE THE STRESSOR

From the categories in Exhibit 7.5, some writers argue that the only way companies can effectively manage stress is by removing the stressors that cause unnecessary strain and job burnout. Other stress management strategies may keep employees 'stress-fit', but they don't solve the fundamental causes of stress.

Removing the stressor usually begins by identifying areas of high stress and determining its main causes. Ericsson Canada conducts this diagnosis through an annual survey which includes a stress index. Executives at the telecommunications company use the index to identify departments where stress problems may be developing. 'We look at those scores and if there appears to be a problem in a particular group, we put in action plans to try and remedy and improve the work situation that may be causing the stress,' explains Ericsson Canada vice-president Peter Buddo.[48]

An important, but very difficult, approach to stress reduction is changing the corporate culture to support a work–life balance rather than dysfunctional workaholism. Another strategy is to give employees more control over their work and work environment. Role-related stressors can be minimised by selecting and assigning employees to positions that match their competencies. Noise and safety risks are stressful, so improving these conditions would also go a long way towards minimising stress in the workplace. Workplace harassment can be minimised by carefully selecting employees and having clear guidelines of behaviour and feedback to those who violate those standards.[49]

Employees can also take an active role in removing stressors. If stress is caused by ambiguous role expectations, for example, employees might seek out more information from others to clarify these expectations. If a particular piece of work is too challenging, they might break it into smaller sets of tasks so that the overall project is less threatening or wearing. To some extent, employees can also minimise workplace harassment by learning to identify early warning signs of aggression in customers and co-workers and by developing interpersonal skills that dissipate aggression.

Work–life balance initiatives

In a variety of ways, companies can help employees experience a better balance between their work and their personal lives. Five of the most common work–life balance initiatives are flexible work time, job sharing, teleworking, personal leave and childcare support.

- *Flexible work time.* Some firms are flexible on the hours, days and amount of time that employees work. For instance, at various times over the past decade Veronica Harley has adjusted her work hours at Deloitte New Zealand from four days to as little as eighteen hours per week. At one point she took three years off work to raise her family. 'Every time I want to adjust my hours they have been able to accommodate me,' says Harley. 'And people don't write me off because I'm part-time. I got promoted to senior manager when I was working 18 hours a week.'[51]
- *Job sharing.* Job sharing splits a career position between two people so they experience less time-based stress between work and family. They typically work different parts of the week, with some overlapping work time in the weekly schedule to coordinate activities. Although traditionally aimed at non-management positions, job sharing is also starting to occur in executive jobs.[52]
- *Teleworking.* Chapter 1 described how an increasing number of employees are teleworking. This eliminates the stress of commuting to work and makes it easier to fulfil family obligations, such as temporarily leaving the home office to pick the kids up from school. Research suggests that teleworkers experience a healthier work–life balance.[53] However, teleworking may increase stress for those who crave social interaction and who lack the space and privacy necessary to work at home.

Sara Lee makes work more flexible

When Tanya Crampton took maternity leave to have her first child, her employer, Sara Lee Bakery in Lisarow, New South Wales, was very supportive of her need for a different work arrangement. 'Sara Lee have been really good to me with my hours and their flexibility,' says Crampton, who had worked full-time in marketing for six years prior to her maternity leave. After nine months, the marketing professional returned to work for eight hours per week. Now, with three young children, she works ten to fifteen hours per week, mostly from home (as shown in the photo). 'I still go in to work at least once a week for a meeting, but they are worked around my schedule which is great,' says Crampton, who might move back to the office two days per week when two of her children are at school next year.[50]

Troy Snook/Newspix

- *Personal leave.* Employees in most countries are granted paid maternity leave; many are also eligible for paternity and other personal time off. Australia, New Zealand and the United States stand out as the only high-income countries without legislated paid maternity leave, although one-third of large and medium-sized firms in Australia do offer paid maternity leave. Victoria University in Melbourne, for example, offers fourteen weeks on full pay and thirty-eight weeks at 60 per cent pay.[54]
- *Childcare support.* Governments in Australia, Canada and other countries are grappling with childcare support policies for working parents. Meanwhile, a small percentage of employers in this region offer childcare support, either subsidising the cost or offering on-site facilities. Westpac is a role model in this respect, with six on-site childcare centres for its employees located around Australia.[55] Childcare support reduces stress, because employees are less rushed to drop off children and less worried during the day about how well they are doing.

Given the high levels of work–life conflict discussed earlier, you would think that organisations would be encouraging their employees to apply these initiatives. The reality, according to some critics, is that, although these practices are available, employees either feel guilty about using them or are discouraged from using them. To ensure that employees actually develop a work–life balance, the top 500 managers at accounting firm RSM McGladrey Inc. receive annual 360-degree reviews in which peers, subordinates and managers rate how well the executive respects and encourages 'balance of work and personal life priorities' among employees.[56]

WITHDRAW FROM THE STRESSOR

Removing the stressor may be the ideal solution, but it is often not feasible. An alternative strategy is to permanently or temporarily remove employees from the stressor. Permanent withdrawal occurs when employees are transferred to jobs that better fit their competencies and values.

Temporary withdrawal strategies

Temporarily withdrawing from stressors is the most frequent way that employees manage stress. SAS Institute employees in Cary, North Carolina, enjoy live piano recitals at lunch. Consulting firms Segal Co. in New York and Vielife in London have nap rooms where staff can recover with a few winks of sleep. Admiral Insurance doesn't have sleep facilities yet, but

Singing the stress away

When employees at Liggett-Stashower Inc. need a short break from the daily stresses of work, they retreat to one of three theme rooms specially designed for creativity and respite. Staff at the Cleveland advertising firm can enter the bowling room and knock down a few pins. Or they might try out the Zen room, which serves as a quiet, relaxing place to think. The third room is a karaoke room where frustrated employees can belt out tunes. 'The higher the stress level, the more singing there is going on,' says Kristen Flynn, a Liggett art director.[58]

Courtesy of Liggett-Stashower Inc.

the Welsh insurance company offers other ways for employees to take temporary breaks from work. 'We have an Indian head-masseur who visits monthly, we have a number of chill-out rooms with sofas, TVs and games consoles for all staff to use, and we are currently trialling a "relaxation chair", which reclines and massages the user while playing chilled-out music through headphones,' says an Admiral Insurance spokesperson.[57]

Personal days off and holidays represent somewhat longer temporary withdrawals from stressful conditions. Oxygen Business Solutions in Auckland offers employees two 'wellness' days per year 'so people can call in and say they're too well to come to work today', says Oxygen chief executive Mike Smith. Sabbaticals represent an extended version of holidays, whereby employees take up to several months of paid leave after several years of service. Australia is one of the few countries with legislation that provides long-service leave (essentially a sabbatical). Generally, Australians receive two or three months of paid leave after ten or fifteen years of service. IBM, Colliers International and a few other firms in Australia and New Zealand offer unpaid sabbaticals. 'Sabbaticals result in happier, healthier employees,' says Colliers managing director Mark Synnott, who has taken four sabbaticals during his career. 'People recharge their batteries and come back clear-headed and motivated.'[59]

CHANGE STRESS PERCEPTIONS

As mentioned, employees often experience different levels of stress in the same situation because they have different levels of self-confidence and optimism. Consequently, corporate leaders need to look at ways that employees can strengthen their confidence and self-esteem so that job challenges are not perceived as threatening. Self-leadership practices seem to help here. For example, positive self-talk can boost self-confidence. A study of newly hired accountants reported that personal goal setting and self-reinforcement can also reduce the stress that people experience when they enter new work settings.[60] Humour can also improve optimism and create positive emotions by taking some psychological weight off the situation.

CONTROL THE CONSEQUENCES OF STRESS

Coping with workplace stress also involves controlling its consequences. For this reason, many companies have fitness centres where employees can keep in shape. Research indicates that physical exercise reduces the physiological consequences of stress by helping employees moderate their breathing, heart rate, muscle tension and stomach acidity.[61] Another way to control the physiological consequences of stress is through relaxation and meditation. For instance, employees at pharmaceutical company AstraZeneca practise a form of meditation called Qi Gong during department meetings and coffee breaks. Research has found that Qi Gong and other forms of meditation reduce anxiety, blood pressure and muscle tension, and moderate breathing and heart rate.[62]

Along with fitness and relaxation/meditation, many firms have shifted to the broader approach of wellness programs. These programs educate and support employees in better nutrition and fitness, regular sleep and other good health habits. For example, CSBP, the fertiliser division of Westfarmers in Kwinana, Western Australia, offers employees audiometric testing, immunisations, subsidies for health club membership, on-site Pilates classes and beach fitness sessions.[63]

Many large employers offer **employee assistance programs (EAPs)**—counselling services that help employees overcome personal or organisational stressors and adopt more effective coping mechanisms. Most EAPs are 'broad-brush' programs that assist employees on any work or personal problems. Family problems often represent the largest percentage of EAP referrals, although this varies with industry and location. For instance, major banks provide post-trauma stress counselling for employees after a robbery. EAPs can be one of the most effective stress management interventions; the counselling helps employees to understand the stressors and to acquire and practise stress management skills.[64]

employee assistance programs (EAPs)
Counselling services that help employees overcome personal or organisational stressors and adopt more effective coping mechanisms.

RECEIVE SOCIAL SUPPORT

Social support from co-workers, supervisors, family members, friends and others is generally regarded as one of the more effective stress management practices. However, this benefit occurs when the stressed individual reaches out for support, not when the support is imposed by others. Social support refers to the person's interpersonal transactions with others and involves providing either emotional or informational support to buffer the stress experience. Seeking social support is called a 'tend and befriend' response to stress, and research suggests that women often follow this route rather than the 'fight-or-flight' alternative that was mentioned earlier in the chapter.[65]

Social support reduces stress in at least three ways.[66] First, employees improve their perception that they are valued and worthy. This, in turn, increases resilience because they have higher self-esteem and confidence to cope with the stressor. Second, social support provides information to help employees interpret, comprehend and possibly remove the stressor. For instance, co-workers might reduce a new employee's stress by describing ways to handle difficult customers. Finally, emotional support from others can directly help to buffer the stress experience. This last point reflects the idea that 'misery loves company'. People seek out and benefit from the emotional support of others when they face threatening situations.[67]

Social support is an important way to cope with stress that everyone can practise by maintaining friendships. This includes helping others when they are dealing with the stressors of life. Organisations can facilitate social support by providing opportunities for social interaction among employees as well as their families. People in leadership roles also need to practise a supportive leadership style when employees work under stressful conditions and need this social support. Mentoring relationships with more senior employees may also help junior employees cope with organisational stressors.

CHAPTER SUMMARY

Stress is an adaptive response to a situation that is perceived as challenging or threatening to the person's well-being. Distress represents high stress levels that have negative consequences, whereas eustress represents the moderately low stress levels needed to activate people. The stress experience, called the general adaptation syndrome, involves moving through three stages: alarm, resistance and exhaustion. The stress model shows that stress is caused by stressors, but the effect of these stressors on stress is moderated by individual characteristics.

Stressors are the causes of stress and include any environmental conditions that place a physical or emotional demand on the person. Stressors are found in the physical work environment, the employee's various life roles, interpersonal relations, and organisational activities and conditions. Conflicts between work and non-work obligations are a frequent source of employee stress.

Two people exposed to the same stressor may experience different stress levels because they have different threshold levels of resistance to the stressor, use different coping strategies, or have different beliefs about the threat and their ability to withstand it. People experience less stress when they have high resilience—the capability of individuals to cope successfully in the face of significant change, adversity or risk. Classic workaholics (work addicts)—those who are highly involved in work, feel compelled or driven to work because of inner pressures, and have a low enjoyment of work—tend to experience more stress.

Intense or prolonged stress can cause physiological symptoms, such as cardiovascular disease, headaches and muscle pain. Psychologically, stress reduces job satisfaction and organisational commitment, and increases moodiness, depression and job burnout. Job burnout refers to the process of emotional exhaustion, cynicism and reduced efficacy resulting from prolonged exposure to stress. It is mainly due to interpersonal and role-related stressors and is most common in the helping occupations. Behavioural symptoms of stress include lower job performance, poorer decisions, more workplace accidents, higher absenteeism and more workplace aggression.

Many interventions are available to manage work-related stress. Some directly remove unnecessary stressors or remove employees from the stressful environment. Others help employees alter their interpretation of the environment so that it is not viewed as a serious stressor. Wellness programs encourage employees to build better physical defences against stress experiences. Social support provides emotional, informational and material resource support to buffer the stress experience.

E-STUDENT

PowerWeb

International articles related to organisational behaviour are available at the Online Learning Centre at www.mhhe.com/au/mcshane2e.

MaxMARK

There are approximately thirty interactive questions on work-related stress and stress management waiting online at www.mhhe.com/au/mcshane2e. The questions are written with additional feedback for incorrect answers, and text excerpts with page references for follow-up study.

KEY TERMS

employee assistance programs (EAPs)
  p. 217
general adaptation syndrome p. 202
job burnout p. 212
psychological harassment p. 205

resilience p. 210
role ambiguity p. 206
role conflict p. 206
sexual harassment p. 205
stress p. 202

stressors p. 204
Type A behaviour pattern p. 211
workaholic p. 211

DISCUSSION QUESTIONS

1. Several websites—including www.unitedmedia.com/comics/dilbert/ and www.cartoonbank.com—use humour to describe problems that people experience at work. Scan through these and other websites and see what types of work-related stressors are described.

2. Is being a full-time college or university student a stressful role? Why or why not? Contrast your response with other students' perspectives.

3. Two recent university graduates join the same major newspaper as journalists. Both work long hours and have tight deadlines to complete their stories. They are under constant pressure to scout out new leads and be the first to report new controversies. One journalist is increasingly fatigued and despondent and has taken several days of sick leave. The other is getting the work done and seems to enjoy the challenges. Use your knowledge of stress to explain why these two journalists are reacting differently to their jobs.

4. Resilience is an individual characteristic that plays an important role in moderating the effect of stressors. Suppose that you

have been put in charge of a task force in a large government department to ensure that employees are highly resilient. What would you and your task force do to accomplish this objective?

5. If you were asked to identify people who are classic workaholics (work addicts), what would you look for?

6. A friend says that he is burned out by his job. What questions might you ask this friend in order to determine whether he is really experiencing job burnout?

7. What should organisations do to reduce employee stress? What is the responsibility of an employee to manage stress effectively? How might fitness programs help employees working in stressful situations?

8. A senior official of a labour union stated: 'All stress management does is help people cope with poor management. [Employers] should really be into stress reduction.' Discuss the accuracy of this statement.

SKILL BUILDER 7.1

CASE STUDY

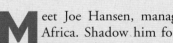

A TYPICAL DAY FOR JOE HANSEN, MANAGING DIRECTOR

By Hazel Bothma, University of Cape Town, South Africa

Meet Joe Hansen, managing director of Magical Connections, Cape Town, South Africa. Shadow him for a day and see the challenges and stressors he faces in his daily work.

Buzzzz. Joe turns over and switches off the alarm. It's 6 am and he toys with the idea of going for a run. However, last night, like many before that, he stayed up late working, so he decides to postpone the run and catch another thirty minutes sleep. Fate intervenes within five minutes as he hears his eighteen-month-old daughter start to cry. Joe looks over at his wife, and decides to let her sleep. She had to take care of their daughter last night, as he had to work until 11 pm. Dragging himself out of bed, he fetches his wailing daughter and goes to the kitchen to prepare her bottle. While in the kitchen he balances his daughter on his lap, turns on his laptop and grimaces as his machine shows him forty-two new emails. He thinks back to a time before email and mobile phones became popular, and, although he would be the first to admit that he couldn't do without these new technologies, he realises that in many ways the boundaries between work and home life have become blurred. Joe knows that, like many of his colleagues in the IT sector, he finds it hard to separate the two. His daughter is now feeding quietly in her cot and this gives Joe the opportunity to start responding to the emails and deleting much of the junk mail he receives. At 6.45 he jumps in the shower, still feeling tired and preparing himself for a day of work. As he combs his hair he notices the first touch of grey—only thirty-eight, he thinks wryly to himself, and starting to go grey. He wonders if his late hours and pressure from work is the culprit. It is now 7.15 and Joe needs to get to the office. No time for breakfast. Instead he gulps down his second cup of strong coffee, promising himself that from tomorrow he will make time to eat before work.

THE MORNING COMMUTE

As Joe sets off in his car to work, the early morning traffic is beginning to grow. He thinks that at least he is not on his way to the airport for one of his frequent business trips; these trips leave him exhausted and with mountains of work to complete on his return. Hardly ten minutes into the drive, his mobile phone rings. It is Justin, one of his team managers, requesting a meeting with him today to discuss why some of the teams are not reaching their targets. Joe thinks back to his first job at one of the major banks. Teamwork was nonexistent then, and as he was at the bottom of the managerial rung he was hardly ever consulted or asked to make decisions. The situation is very different now, especially in the information technology sector. Joe's company, Magical Connections, has very few managers, with most of the twenty-two staff working in teams. This is a far cry from his days in the bank when he was one of 500 employees, faceless in a hierarchical company. Many of the people that Joe worked with in the banking industry are still there. For Joe it remains a constant challenge to keep competent staff, as many leave after about two years for other IT companies, or even leave the country to seek work elsewhere. Despite this, Joe does not miss the way work used to be organised in the bank, and he likes the way his company is structured. The division of labour within Magical Connections helps its progress; the tasks are divided logically, and there isn't the frustration of a huge bureaucracy.

THE OFFICE DAY BEGINS

As Joe walks into the office, he is met by Alan who is pacing up and down the reception area. The company is anxiously waiting for new parts from Taiwan to arrive. Alan explains that the parts have landed at the port in Durban, but Customs is holding them up, as some document seems to be missing. The companies that have been promised the various parts have been ringing Alan to find out where they are. Alan looks near breaking point as he explains heatedly to Joe the pressure of having to deal with irate customers who want everything now. Joe is empathetic as he too constantly faces pressure from all sides. After briefly brainstorming solutions to this crisis with Alan, Joe eagerly helps himself to his third cup of coffee, hoping that the caffeine will perk him up, and although it is only 10 o'clock he finds a cigarette in his desk drawer and goes outside to smoke. He is well aware of the health risks (not to mention the wrath he would face if his wife found out), but as always the day seems packed with obstacles and Joe uses this five minutes to be on his own.

At 11 o'clock Joe sits down with one of the teams to discuss targets. Justin, one of the team members, starts the meeting by accusing Sharon of not performing adequately and thereby jeopardising the team's target. Justin rants that he is tired of having to work even harder to make up for Sharon's poor performance. As Joe listens, he is aware that Justin's antagonistic nature is not helping the meeting, and that a lack of good interpersonal skills hinders the effective working of the team. Added to this, he is going to have to ascertain what is causing Sharon to fail to meet her targets. Joe makes a mental note to try and organise some training on interpersonal skills for all the teams. It is imperative that the teams at Magical Connections are effective, as this translates into remaining competitive at both a national and a global level, which is a cornerstone to the company's survival.

Dan, Joe's old school friend, phones him at 1 pm to see if he would like to join him for lunch. Joe laughs down the phone and reminds Dan that he has not had a lunch break in the past two years. He thinks longingly of a quiet lunch, good food and stimulating company, but knows that he has too much to do. Justin is still angry about the poor team performance, and Joe needs to deal with this issue as soon as possible. Dan good-naturedly tells him that as MD he should be delegating more and enjoying some time off. He has a point, thinks Joe. Empowerment is still a relatively new concept in South Africa, but Joe knows that if he delegated more of his work to younger staff, and allowed them to make more decisions, it would free him up to think about long-term strategies for his company. But today is not the day for a lunch-break, so a hamburger and chips from the canteen will have to do.

At 2.30 pm Fiona walks into his office and tells Joe of her intention to leave the company. Joe's heart sinks at the thought, as she is one of the brightest staff members. The company will now have to try and attract a suitable person, and of course retain them. The recruitment and selection of a new person will be time-consuming and Joe makes a mental note to start the process.

At 4 pm Joe is lying on a table in his office having a massage. All employees are entitled to a thirty-minute massage once a week. This practice, requested by the staff, began a month ago. With gentle music and the smell of aromatherapy oils lingering in the air, Joe feels the release of tension as his knotted muscles are worked under the masseur's able hands. What a great idea this has turned out to be.

STARTING THE SECOND SHIFT

With a bulging briefcase, Joe manages to leave the office at 6 pm, aware that his wife, who has been looking after their daughter all day, will be exhausted and desperate for him to come home and help. He has about six new computer journals he needs to read, and a page of websites someone gave him that he needs to explore. The constant pressure to keep abreast of the flood of information within this industry is an overwhelming feature of Joe's life. Added to this, Joe realises that next week he needs to undertake a vendor computer-training course, which will keep him out of the office. There is a constant need for re-training in order to stay abreast of latest developments.

As Joe starts his twenty-minute drive home he puts on a new CD and starts humming to his favourite track. The humming soon changes to a full-throated bellow as he sings the chorus out aloud and makes drumming noises on the steering wheel. However, a phone call on a work-related issue interrupts this pleasant interlude. As he ends the call, Joe thinks to himself that this weekend he is going to take his wife and daughter away for a break—perhaps to the mountains, where they can relax as a family, and he can spend some time talking to his wife. He grins to himself—no mobile phone and no laptop. With that comforting thought, he thinks about the challenges he faces tomorrow and in the future. Magical Connections needs to remain a company that is fast, flexible, responsive, resilient and creative, and Joe looks forward to helping that happen. Despite the challenges of his job, Joe loves his work and finds it stimulating and rewarding.

QUESTIONS

1. Identify the stressors facing Joe.

2. How do you think Joe could go about managing his stress more effectively?

3. Would it be fair to argue that employees within the IT sector experience higher levels of stress than, say, employees within the banking or manufacturing sectors?

STAGE FRIGHT!

PURPOSE
This exercise is designed to help you to diagnose a common stressful situation and determine how stress management practices apply to the situation.

BACKGROUND
Stage fright—including the fear of public speaking—is one of the most stressful experiences many people have in everyday life. According to some estimates, nearly three-quarters of us frequently get stage fright, even when speaking or acting in front of a small audience. Stage fright is an excellent topic for this team activity on stress management because the psychological and physiological symptoms of stage fright are really symptoms of stress. In other words, stage fright is the stress experience in a specific context involving a public audience. Based on the personal experiences of team members, your team is asked to identify the symptoms of stage fright and to determine specific stress management activities that will effectively combat it.

INSTRUCTIONS
Step 1: Students are organised into teams, typically four to six students per team. Ideally, each team should have one or more people who acknowledge that they have experienced stage fright.

Step 2: Each team's first task is to identify the symptoms of stage fright. The best way to organise these symptoms is to look at the three categories of stress outcomes described in the chapter: physiological, psychological and behavioural. The specific stage fright symptoms may be different from the stress outcomes described in the chapter, but the three broad categories would be relevant. Teams should be prepared to identify several symptoms and to present one or two specific examples based on the experiences of team members. (Remember that individual students are not required to describe their experiences to the entire class.)

Step 3: Each team's second task is to identify specific strategies people could apply or have applied to minimise stage fright. The five categories of stress management presented in the chapter will provide a useful template with which to organise the specific stage fright management activities. Each team should document several strategies and be able to present one or two specific examples to illustrate some of the strategies.

Step 4: The class will congregate to hear each team's analysis of the symptoms and solutions to stage fright. This information will then be compared with the stress experience and the stress management practices respectively.

CONNOR–DAVIDSON RESILIENCE SCALE (CD-RISC)

PURPOSE
This self-assessment is designed to help you to estimate your personal level of resilience.

INSTRUCTIONS
Check the box indicating the extent to which each statement is true for you *over the past month*. Then use the scoring key in Appendix B of this book to calculate your results. It is important for you to realise that there are no 'right' or 'wrong' answers to these questions. This self-assessment is completed alone so that you can complete the instrument honestly without concerns of social comparison. However, class discussion will focus on the meaning of resilience and how it relates to workplace stress.

CONNOR–DAVIDSON RESILIENCE SCALE (CD-RISC)

To what extent are these statements true about you over the past month?	Not at all true	Rarely true	Sometimes true	Often true	True nearly all of the time
1. I am able to adapt to change.	❑	❑	❑	❑	❑
2. I have close and secure relationships.	❑	❑	❑	❑	❑
3. I take pride in my achievements.	❑	❑	❑	❑	❑
4. I work to attain my goals.	❑	❑	❑	❑	❑
5. I feel in control of my life.	❑	❑	❑	❑	❑
6. I have a strong sense of purpose.	❑	❑	❑	❑	❑
7. I see the humorous side of things.	❑	❑	❑	❑	❑
8. Things happen for a reason.	❑	❑	❑	❑	❑
9. I have to act on a hunch.	❑	❑	❑	❑	❑
10. I can handle unpleasant feelings.	❑	❑	❑	❑	❑
11. Sometimes fate or God can help.	❑	❑	❑	❑	❑
12. I can deal with whatever comes my way.	❑	❑	❑	❑	❑
13. Past success gives me confidence for new challenges.	❑	❑	❑	❑	❑
14. Coping with stress strengthens me.	❑	❑	❑	❑	❑
15. I like challenges.	❑	❑	❑	❑	❑
16. I can make unpopular or difficult decisions.	❑	❑	❑	❑	❑
17. I think of myself as a strong person.	❑	❑	❑	❑	❑
18. When things look hopeless, I don't give up.	❑	❑	❑	❑	❑
19. I give my best effort, no matter what.	❑	❑	❑	❑	❑
20. I can achieve my goals.	❑	❑	❑	❑	❑
21. I am not easily discouraged by failure.	❑	❑	❑	❑	❑
22. I tend to bounce back after a hardship or illness.	❑	❑	❑	❑	❑
23. I know where to turn to for help.	❑	❑	❑	❑	❑
24. Under pressure, I focus and think clearly.	❑	❑	❑	❑	❑
25. I prefer to take the lead in problem solving.	❑	❑	❑	❑	❑

Source: K. M. Connor and J. R. T. Davidson, 'Development of a New Resilience Scale: The Connor–Davidson Resilience Scale (CD-RISC)', *Depression and Anxiety* 18, no. 2 (2003), 76–82.

SKILL BUILDER | 7.4   WORK ADDICTION RISK TEST

SELF-ASSESSMENT

FULL EXERCISE ON
STUDENT CD

This self-assessment is designed to help you to identify the extent to which you are a workaholic. The instrument presents several statements, and asks you to indicate the extent to which each statement is true of your work habits. You need to be honest with yourself in order to obtain a reasonable estimate of your level of workaholism.

PERCEIVED STRESS SCALE

7.5 | SKILL BUILDER

SELF-ASSESSMENT

FULL EXERCISE ON
STUDENT CD

This self-assessment is designed to help you to estimate your perceived general level of stress. The items in this scale ask you about your feelings and thoughts during the last month. In each case, indicate how often you felt or thought a certain way. You need to be honest with yourself in order to obtain a reasonable estimate of your general level of stress.

STRESS COPING PREFERENCE SCALE

7.6 | SKILL BUILDER

SELF-ASSESSMENT

FULL EXERCISE ON
STUDENT CD

This self-assessment is designed to help you to identify the type of coping strategy you prefer to use in stressful situations. The scale lists a variety of things you might do when faced with a stressful situation. You are asked how often you tend to react in these ways. You need to be honest with yourself in order to obtain a reasonable estimate of your preferred coping strategy.

NOTES

1   K. Holland and S.-J. Tasker, 'For Children's Sake', *Kalgoorlie Miner*, 1 October 2004, 1; 'Doctors in Daily Battle to Cope', *The Advertiser* (South Australia), 28 October 2005, 4; A. Cresswell, 'Bush Obstetrics "Facing Collapse"', *The Australian*, 14 February 2005, 1; M. Naidoo, 'GP Shortage Hits Kingston', *Hobart Mercury*, 17 November 2005, 11; T. Sadleir, 'New Baby Doctor for City', *Kalgoorlie Miner*, 19 November 2005, 10; B. Roberts, 'Push for Rural Doctors', *Herald Sun* (Melbourne), 1 February 2006, 28.

2   S. Kidson, 'Nelson GPs Fear for the Future', *Nelson Mail* (New Zealand), 12 December 2005, 1; S. Moran, 'Balance Your Life, Unplug the Phone', *Australian Financial Review*, 8 January 2005, 6; D. Passmore, 'We're All Sick of Work', *Sunday Mail* (Brisbane), 27 November 2005, 45.

3   T. Haratani, 'Job Stress Trends in Japan', in *Job Stress Trends in East Asia (Proceedings of the First East-Asia Job Stress Meeting)*, ed. A. Tsutsumi (Waseda University, Tokyo, 8 January 2000), 4–10; 'New Survey: Americans Stressed More Than Ever', *PR Newswire*, 26 June 2003; 'India's Call Centers Suffer High Quit Rate', *CNET Asia*, 8 August 2003; S. James, 'Work Stress Taking Larger Financial Toll', *Reuters*, 9 August 2003; 'Hong Kong People Still Most Stressed in Asia— Survey', *Reuters News*, 2 November 2004; Mind, *Stress and Mental Health in the Workplace* (London: Mind, May 2005).

4   J. C. Quick et al., *Preventive Stress Management in Organizations* (Washington, DC: American Psychological Association, 1997), 3–4; R. S. DeFrank and J. M. Ivancevich, 'Stress on the Job: An Executive Update', *Academy of Management Executive* 12 (August 1998), 55–66.

5   Quick et al., *Preventive Stress Management in Organizations*, 5–6; B. L. Simmons and D. L. Nelson, 'Eustress at Work: The Relationship between Hope and Health in Hospital Nurses', *Health Care Management Review* 26, no. 4 (October 2001), 7ff.

6   H. Selye, *Stress without Distress* (Philadelphia: J. B. Lippincott, 1974).

7   S. E. Taylor, R. L. Repetti and T. Seeman, 'Health Psychology: What Is an Unhealthy Environment and How Does It Get under the Skin?', *Annual Review of Psychology* 48 (1997), 411–47.

8   K. Danna and R. W. Griffin, 'Health and Well-Being in the Workplace: A Review and Synthesis of the Literature', *Journal of Management* (Spring 1999), 357–84.

9   N. Wager, G. Fieldman and T. Hussey, 'The Effect on Ambulatory Blood Pressure of Working under Favourably and Unfavourably

Perceived Supervisors', *Occupational and Environmental Medicine* 60, no. 7 (1 July 2003), 468–74. For further details on the stressful effects of bad bosses, see E. K. Kelloway et al., 'Poor Leadership', in *Handbook of Workplace Stress*, ed. J. Barling, E. K. Kelloway and M. Frone (Thousand Oaks, CA: Sage, 2005), 89–112.

10 'Violence, Stress up for Nurses', *AAP News*, 13 July 2005; C. Mayhew and D. Chappell, 'Violence in the Workplace', *Medical Journal of Australia* 183, no. 7 (2005), 346–7.

11 New South Wales Supreme Court, *Naidu v. Group 4 Securitas Pty Ltd & Anor*, NSWSC, 24 June 2005.

12 This is a slight variation of the definition in the Quebec anti-harassment legislation. See www.cnt.gouv.qc.ca. For related definitions and discussion of workplace incivility, see H. Cowiea et al., 'Measuring Workplace Bullying', *Aggression and Violent Behavior* 7 (2002), 33–51; C. M. Pearson and C. L. Porath, 'On the Nature, Consequences and Remedies of Workplace Incivility: No Time for "Nice"? Think Again', *Academy of Management Executive* 19, no. 1 (February 2005), 7–18.

13 T. Goldenberg, 'Thousands of Workers Intimidated on Job: Study', *Montreal Gazette*, 11 June 2005, A9.

14 'Bullies Stronger', *Herald-Sun* (Melbourne), 23 September 2005, 18; J. Chapman, 'Half Public Servants See Work Bullying', *The Advertiser* (South Australia), 10 November 2005, 25; J. Strutt, 'More Report Workplace Bullying', *West Australian*, 9 September 2005, 34; S. Toomey, 'Bullying Alive and Kicking', *The Australian*, 16 July 2005, 9; M. Paine, 'Survey Shame for PS Office Bullies', *Hobart Mercury*, 18 January 2006, 1; F. Tomazin, 'Bullying Rife in Public Service', *The Age* (Melbourne), 16 January 2006, 1.

15 V. Schultz, 'Reconceptualizing Sexual Harassment', *Yale Law Journal* 107 (April 1998), 1683–805; M. Rotundo, D.-H. Nguyen and P. R. Sackett, 'A Meta-Analytic Review of Gender Differences in Perceptions of Sexual Harassment', *Journal of Applied Psychology* 86 (October 2001), 914–22.

16 E. K. Kelloway and J. Barling, 'Job Characteristics, Role Stress and Mental Health', *Journal of Occupational Psychology* 64 (1991), 291–304; M. Siegall and L. L. Cummings, 'Stress and Organizational Role Conflict', *Genetic, Social, and General Psychology Monographs* 12 (1995), 65–95; J. Lait and J. E. Wallace, 'Stress at Work: A Study of Organizational–Professional Conflict and Unmet Expectations', *Relations Industrielles* 57, no. 3 (Summer 2002), 463–87; E. Grunfeld et al.,

'Job Stress and Job Satisfaction of Cancer Care Workers', *Psycho-Oncology* 14, no. 1 (May 2005), 61–9.

17   A. M. Saks and B. E. Ashforth, 'Proactive Socialization and Behavioral Self-Management', *Journal of Vocational Behavior* 48 (1996), 301–23; A. Nygaard and R. Dahlstrom, 'Role Stress and Effectiveness in Horizontal Alliances', *Journal of Marketing* 66 (April 2002), 61–82.

18   'Work Hard? Play Hard? It's Not the Countries You Might Think', *PR Newswire Europe*, 9 November 2004; S.-A. Chia and E. Toh, 'Give Employees a Break', *Straits Times* (Singapore), 23 July 2005. Past predictions of future work hours are described in B. K. Hunnicutt, *Kellogg's Six-Hour Day* (Philadelphia: Temple University Press, 1996).

19   R. Drago, D. Black and M. Wooden, *The Persistence of Long Work Hours*, Melbourne Institute Working Paper Series (Melbourne: Melbourne Institute of Applied Economic and Social Research, University of Melbourne, August 2005).

20   L. Wahyudi S., 'Traffic Congestion Makes Me Crazy', *Jakarta Post*, 18 March 2003. Traffic congestion is linked to stress in G. W. Evans, R. E. Wener and D. Phillips, 'The Morning Rush Hour: Predictability and Commuter Stress', *Environment and Behaviour* 34 (July 2002), 521–30.

21   F. Kittell et al., 'Job Conditions and Fibrinogen in 14,226 Belgian Workers: The Belstress Study', *European Heart Journal* 23 (2002), 1841–8; S. K. Parker, 'Longitudinal Effects of Lean Production on Employee Outcomes and the Mediating Role of Work Characteristics', *Journal of Applied Psychology* 88, no. 4 (2003), 620–34.

22   R. J. Burke and C. L. Cooper, *The Organization in Crisis: Downsizing, Restructuring, and Privatization* (Oxford, UK: Blackwell, 2000); M. Kivimaki et al., 'Factors Underlying the Effect of Organizational Downsizing on Health of Employees: Longitudinal Cohort Study', *British Medical Journal* 320 (8 April 2000), 971–5; M. Sverke, J. Hellgren and K. Näswall, 'No Security: A Meta-Analysis and Review of Job Insecurity and Its Consequences', *Journal of Occupational Health Psychology* 7 (July 2002), 242–64; R. J. Burke, 'Correlates of Nursing Staff Survivor Responses to Hospital Restructuring and Downsizing', *Health Care Manager* 24, no. 2 (2005), 141–9.

23   K. Bradsher, 'SARS Takes High Toll on Nurses', *International Herald Tribune*, 10 May 2003, 1; N. Law, 'Behind the Mask: Josephine Chung Yuen-Man', *South China Morning Post* (Hong Kong), 1 May 2003, 5; H. Luk, 'Hong Kong's SARS-Stressed Nurses Describe Pressure, Isolation', *Associated Press* (22 May 2003), 4; J. G. W. S. Wong et al., 'Psychological Responses to the SARS Outbreak in Healthcare Students in Hong Kong', *Medical Teacher* 26, no. 7 (2004), 657–63.

24   L. T. Eby et al., 'Work and Family Research in IO/OB: Content Analysis and Review of the Literature (1980–2002)', *Journal of Vocational Behavior* 66, no. 1 (2005), 124–97.

25   C. Higgins and L. Duxbury, *The 2001 National Work–Life Conflict Study: Report One, Final Report* (Ottawa: Health Canada, March 2002); M. Shields, 'Shift Work and Health', *Health Reports (Statistics Canada)* 13 (Spring 2002), 11–34.

26   W. Stewart and J. Barling, 'Fathers' Work Experiences Effect on Children's Behaviors Via Job-Related Affect and Parenting Behaviors', *Journal of Organizational Behavior* 17 (1996), 221–32; E. K. Kelloway, B. H. Gottlieb and L. Barham, 'The Source, Nature, and Direction of Work and Family Conflict: A Longitudinal Investigation', *Journal of Occupational Health Psychology* 4 (October 1999), 337–46.

27   A. S. Wharton and R. J. Erickson, 'Managing Emotions on the Job and at Home: Understanding the Consequences of Multiple Emotional Roles', *Academy of Management Review* (1993), 457–86.

28   B. Keil, 'The 10 Most Stressful Jobs in NYC', *New York Post*, 6 April 1999, 50; A. Smith et al., *The Scale of Occupational Stress: A Further Analysis of the Impact of Demographic Factors and Type of Job* (Sudbury, Suffolk: United Kingdom, Health & Safety Executive, 2000).

29   S. J. Havlovic and J. P. Keenen, 'Coping with Work Stress: The Influence of Individual Differences; Handbook on Job Stress [Special Issue]', *Journal of Social Behavior and Personality* 6 (1991), 199–212.

30   S. C. Segerstrom et al., 'Optimism Is Associated with Mood, Coping, and Immune Change in Response to Stress', *Journal of Personality & Social Psychology* 74 (June 1998), 1646–55; S. M. Jex et al., 'The Impact of Self-Efficacy on Stressor–Strain Relations: Coping Style as an Explanatory Mechanism', *Journal of Applied Psychology* 86 (2001), 401–9.

31   J. L. Hernandez, 'What's the Buzz in Schuyler? Just Ask Beekeeper Finster', *Observer-Dispatch* (Utica, NY), 23 June 2003.

32   S. S. Luthar, D. Cicchetti and B. Becker, 'The Construct of Resilience: A Critical Evaluation and Guidelines for Future Work', *Child Development* 71, no. 3 (May–June 2000), 543–62; F. Luthans, 'The Need for and Meaning of Positive Organizational Behavior', *Journal of Organizational Behavior* 23 (2002), 695–706; G. A. Bonanno, 'Loss, Trauma, and Human Resilience: Have We Underestimated the Human Capacity to Thrive after Extremely Aversive Events?', *American Psychologist* 59, no. 1 (2004), 20–8.

33   K. M. Connor and J. R. T. Davidson, 'Development of a New Resilience Scale: The Connor–Davidson Resilience Scale (CD-RISC)', *Depression and Anxiety* 18, no. 2 (2003), 76–82; M. M. Tugade, B. L. Fredrickson and L. Feldman Barrett, 'Psychological Resilience and Positive Emotional Granularity: Examining the Benefits of Positive Emotions on Coping and Health', *Journal of Personality* 72, no. 6 (2004), 1161–90; L. Campbell-Sills, S. L. Cohan and M. B. Stein, 'Relationship of Resilience to Personality, Coping, and Psychiatric Symptoms in Young Adults', *Behaviour Research and Therapy*, in press (2006).

34   M. Beasley, T. Thompson and J. Davidson, 'Resilience in Response to Life Stress: The Effects of Coping Style and Cognitive Hardiness', *Personality and Individual Differences* 34, no. 1 (2003), 77–95; I. Tsaousis and I. Nikolaou, 'Exploring the Relationship of Emotional Intelligence with Physical and Psychological Health Functioning', *Stress and Health* 21, no. 2 (2005), 77–86.

35   Y. Kim and L. Seidlitz, 'Spirituality Moderates the Effect of Stress on Emotional and Physical Adjustment', *Personality and Individual Differences* 32, no. 8 (June 2002), 1377–90; G. E. Richardson, 'The Metatheory of Resilience and Resiliency', *Journal of Clinical Psychology* 58, no. 3 (2002), 307–21.

36   J. T. Spence and A. S. Robbins, 'Workaholism: Definition, Measurement and Preliminary Results', *Journal of Personality Assessment* 58 (1992), 160–78; R. J. Burke, 'Workaholism in Organizations: Psychological and Physical Well-Being Consequences', *Stress Medicine* 16, no. 1 (2000), 11–16; I. Harpaz and R. Snir, 'Workaholism: Its Definition and Nature', *Human Relations* 56 (2003), 291–319; R. J. Burke, A. M. Richardson and M. Martinussen, 'Workaholism among Norwegian Senior Managers: New Research Directions', *International Journal of Management* 21, no. 4 (December 2004), 415–26.

37   R. J. Burke, 'Workaholism and Extra-Work Satisfactions', *International Journal of Organizational Analysis* 7 (1999), 352–64; A. Kemeny, 'Driven to Excel: A Portrait of Canada's Workaholics', *Canadian Social Trends* (Spring 2002), 2–7; R. J. Burke, F. Oberklaid and Z. Burgess, 'Workaholism among Australian Women Psychologists: Antecedents and Consequences', *International Journal of Management* 21, no. 3 (September 2004), 263–77; Moran, 'Balance Your Life, Unplug the Phone'.

38   R. J. Burke and G. MacDermid, 'Are Workaholics Job Satisfied and Successful in Their Careers?', *Career Development International* 4 (1999), 277–82; R. J. Burke and S. Matthiesen, 'Short Communication: Workaholism among Norwegian Journalists: Antecedents and Consequences', *Stress and Health* 20, no. 5 (2004), 301–8.

39   D. Ganster, M. Fox and D. Dwyer, 'Explaining Employees' Health Care Costs: A Prospective Examination of Stressful Job Demands, Personal Control, and Physiological Reactivity', *Journal of Applied Psychology* 86 (May 2001), 954–64.

40 M. Kivimaki et al., 'Work Stress and Risk of Cardiovascular Mortality: Prospective Cohort Study of Industrial Employees', *British Medical Journal* 325 (19 October 2002), 857–60; 'Banishing the Blues Could Cut the Chances of Cancer', *The Scotsman* (23 June 2003); A. Rosengren et al., 'Association of Psychosocial Risk Factors with Risk of Acute Myocardial Infarction in 11 119 Cases and 13 648 Controls from 52 Countries (the Interheart Study): Case-Control Study', *The Lancet* 364, no. 9438 (11 September 2004), 953–62; S. Yusuf et al., 'Effect of Potentially Modifiable Risk Factors Associated with Myocardial Infarction in 52 Countries (the Interheart Study): Case-Control Study', *The Lancet* 364, no. 9438 (11 September 2004), 937–52.

41 R. C. Kessler, 'The Effects of Stressful Life Events on Depression', *Annual Review of Psychology* 48 (1997), 191–214; M. Jamal and V. V. Baba, 'Job Stress and Burnout among Canadian Managers and Nurses: An Empirical Examination', *Canadian Journal of Public Health* 91, no. 6 (November–December 2000), 454–8.

42 C. Maslach, W. B. Schaufeli and M. P. Leiter, 'Job Burnout', *Annual Review of Psychology* 52 (2001), 397–422; J. R. B. Halbesleben and M. R. Buckley, 'Burnout in Organizational Life', *Journal of Management* 30, no. 6 (2004), 859–79.

43 M. Jamal, 'Job Stress and Job Performance Controversy: An Empirical Assessment', *Organizational Behavior and Human Performance* 33 (1984), 1–21; G. Keinan, 'Decision Making under Stress: Scanning of Alternatives under Controllable and Uncontrollable Threats', *Journal of Personality and Social Psychology* 52 (1987), 638–44. The positive effects of moderate stress are reported in: L. Van Dyne, K. A. Jehn and A. Cummings, 'Differential Effects of Strain on Two Forms of Work Performance: Individual Employee Sales and Creativity', *Journal of Organizational Behavior* 23, no. 1 (2002), 57–74; E. Chajut and D. Algom, 'Selective Attention Improves under Stress: Implications for Theories of Social Cognition', *Journal of Personality and Social Psychology* 85, no. 2 (2003), 231–48.

44 R. D. Hackett and P. Bycio, 'An Evaluation of Employee Absenteeism as a Coping Mechanism among Hospital Nurses', *Journal of Occupational & Organizational Psychology* 69 (December 1996), 327–38; A. Vaananen et al., 'Job Characteristics, Physical and Psychological Symptoms, and Social Support as Antecedents of Sickness Absence among Men and Women in the Private Industrial Sector', *Social Science & Medicine* 57, no. 5 (September 2003), 807–24; L. Tourigny, V. V. Baba and T. R. Lituchy, 'Job Burnout among Airline Employees in Japan: A Study of the Buffering Effects of Absence and Supervisory Support', *International Journal of Cross Cultural Management* 5, no. 1 (April 2005), 67–85.

45 L. Greenburg and J. Barling, 'Predicting Employee Aggression against Co-workers, Subordinates and Supervisors: The Roles of Person Behaviors and Perceived Workplace Factors', *Journal of Organizational Behavior* 20 (1999), 897–913; H. Steensma, 'Violence in the Workplace: The Explanatory Strength of Social (in)Justice Theories', in *The Justice Motive in Everyday Life*, ed. M. Ross and D. T. Miller (New York: Cambridge University Press, 2002), 149–67; J. D. Leck, 'Violence in the Canadian Workplace', *Journal of the American Academy of Business* 7, no. 2 (September 2005), 308–15.

46 Chia and Toh, 'Give Employees a Break'.

47 Siegall and Cummings, 'Stress and Organizational Role Conflict'.

48 'Employee Wellness', *Canadian HR Reporter* (23 February 2004), 9–12.

49 J. L. Howard, 'Workplace Violence in Organizations: An Exploratory Study of Organizational Prevention Techniques', *Employee Responsibilities and Rights Journal* 13 (June 2001), 57–75.

50 A. McCumstie, 'Sara Lee Makes Life Easier', *Central Coast Express Advocate*, 1 June 2004, 21.

51 N. Mandow, 'Nine-to-Five R.I.P.', *IDG Unlimited*, August 2005.

52 C. R. Cunningham and S. S. Murray, 'Two Executives, One Career', *Harvard Business Review* 83, no. 2 (February 2005), 125–31.

53 S. R. Madsen, 'The Effects of Home-Based Teleworking on Work–Family Conflict', *Human Resource Development Quarterly* 14, no. 1 (2003), 35–58.

54 K. Hansen, 'Mum's the Word', *Intheblack*, June 2005, 32–6.

55 S. McLean, 'Happy Employees a Work in Progress', *Courier-Mail* (Brisbane), 2 April 2005, L06.

56 M. Blair-Loy and A. S. Wharton, 'Employees' Use of Work–Family Policies and the Workplace Social Context', *Social Forces* 80 (March 2002), 813–45; M. Jackson, 'Managers Measured by Charges' Work–Life Accountability Programs Let Firms Calculate Progress', *Boston Globe*, 2 February 2003, G1.

57 'Office Stress? Just Sleep on It', *Western Mail* (Cardiff, Wales), 2 November 2004, 12; K. Redford, 'Is It Time to Get Bossy?', *Employee Benefits* (UK), 7 December 2005, S25; J. Saranow, 'Anybody Want to Take a Nap?', *Wall Street Journal*, 24 January 2005, R5.

58 S. Moreland, 'Strike up Creativity', *Crain's Cleveland Business*, 14 April 2003, 3.

59 V. Bland, 'Sabbaticals Ideal Refresher', *New Zealand Herald*, 31 August 2005; R. Schwarz, 'Keeping the Workers Happy', *Dominion Post* (Auckland), 4 April 2005, 10. On the value of sabbaticals, see A. E. Carr and T. L.-P. Tang, 'Sabbaticals and Employee Motivation: Benefits, Concerns, and Implications', *Journal of Education for Business* 80, no. 3 (January–February 2005), 160–4.

60 M. Waung, 'The Effects of Self-Regulatory Coping Orientation on Newcomer Adjustment and Job Survival', *Personnel Psychology* 48 (1995), 633–50; Saks and Ashforth, 'Proactive Socialization and Behavioral Self-Management'.

61 W. M. Ensel and N. Lin, 'Physical Fitness and the Stress Process', *Journal of Community Psychology* 32, no. 1 (January 2004), 81–101.

62 S. Armour, 'Rising Job Stress Could Affect Bottom Line', *USA Today*, 29 July 2003; V. A. Barnes, F. A. Treiber and M. H. Johnson, 'Impact of Transcendental Meditation on Ambulatory Blood Pressure in African-American Adolescents', *American Journal of Hypertension* 17, no. 4 (2004), 366–9; M. S. Lee et al., 'Effects of Qi-Training on Anxiety and Plasma Concentrations of Cortisol, Acth, and Aldosterone: A Randomized Placebo-Controlled Pilot Study', *Stress and Health* 20, no. 5 (2004), 243–8; P. Manikonda et al., 'Influence of Non-Pharmacological Treatment (Contemplative Meditation and Breathing Technique) on Stress Induced Hypertension: a Randomized Controlled Study', *American Journal of Hypertension* 18, no. 5, Supplement 1 (2005), A89–A90.

63 Danna and Griffin, 'Health and Well-Being in the Workplace: A Review and Synthesis of the Literature'; S. Peacock, 'Healthy Workers Give Business a Booster Shot', *West Australian*, 19 June 2004, 74.

64 T. Rotarius, A. Liberman and J. S. Liberman, 'Employee Assistance Programs: A Prevention and Treatment Prescription for Problems in Health Care Organizations', *Health Care Manager* 19 (September 2000), 24–31; J. J. L. van der Klink et al., 'The Benefits of Interventions for Work-Related Stress', *American Journal of Public Health* 91 (February 2001), 270–6.

65 S. E. Taylor et al., 'Biobehavioral Responses to Stress in Females: Tend-and-Befriend, Not Fight-or-Flight', *Psychological Review* 107, no. 3 (July 2000), 411–29; R. Eisler and D. S. Levine, 'Nurture, Nature, and Caring: We Are Not Prisoners of Our Genes', *Brain and Mind* 3 (2002), 9–52; J. T. Deelstra et al., 'Receiving Instrumental Support at Work: When Help Is Not Welcome', *Journal of Applied Psychology* 88, no. 2 (2003), 324–31.

66 J. S. House, *Work Stress and Social Support* (Reading, Mass: Addison-Wesley, 1981).

67 S. Schachter, *The Psychology of Affiliation* (Stanford, CA: Stanford University Press, 1959).

INSERT YOUR CD NOW
TO VIEW THE FOOTAGE
THAT CORRESPONDS
TO THESE CASES

EMPLOYEE LOYALTY

Not so long ago, companies offered secure employment. In return, workers showed their loyalty by remaining with one company for most of their careers. Not any more! This video program illustrates how dramatically times have changed. Joel Baglole received an internship at the Toronto Star and later was offered a full-time job. Baglole happily accepted the position, but quit six weeks later when the prestigious Wall Street Journal offered him a job. Baglole explains why he has no obligation to be loyal to the Toronto Star, whereas Toronto Star publisher John Honderich believes that loyalty is important and should be expected. This program also examines ways that the Toronto Star and other companies try to increase employee loyalty.

QUESTIONS

1. Which, if any, of the five strategies to build organisational commitment would be effective in this situation involving Joel Baglole?

2. Explain how Joel Baglole's psychological contract is influenced by organisational loyalty in this situation.

PIKE PLACE FISH MARKET

Fifteen years ago, Pike Place Fish Market in Seattle had unhappy employees and was in financial trouble. Rather than close up shop, owner John Yokoyama sought help from consultant Jim Bergquist to improve his leadership skills and energise the workforce. Rather than rule as a tyrant, Yokoyama learned how to actively involve employees in the business. Soon, staff felt more empowered and gained more enjoyment from their work. They also began to actively have fun at work, including setting goals as a game, throwing fish to each other as sport, and pretending they were 'world famous'. Today, thanks to these and other strategies described in this video case, Pike Place is world famous. The little shop has become a tourist attraction and customers from California to New York call in orders.

QUESTIONS

1. Based on the model of emotions and attitudes in Chapter 4, explain how the changes at Pike Place Fish Market improved job satisfaction and reduced turnover. How did these attitude changes affect customer satisfaction?

2. Goal setting is discussed as an important activity at Pike Place. Evaluate the effectiveness of this goal setting process in the context of the characteristics of effective goals described in Chapter 5 of this textbook.

3. How is coaching applied at Pike Place, and how does this coaching influence employee performance?

VIDEO CASE STUDIES

INSERT YOUR CD NOW
TO VIEW THE FOOTAGE
THAT CORRESPONDS
TO THESE CASES

STRESS IN JAPAN

Stress from overwork has become an epidemic in Japan. Japanese have been educated to obey their seniors when they are told what to do. Not being able to say no to situations that result in work overload is part of Japanese workplace culture. This video program consists of two segments that illustrate the degree to which some Japanese employees are overworked, as well as the consequences of their overwork. The first segment follows a typical day of a Japanese manager, from his two-hour morning commute to his late-night working hours. The program also shows how he is under constant pressure to improve efficiency, and how he carries a heavy burden from the responsibility of having to do better. The second segment describes how *karoshi*—death from overwork—took the life of 23-year-old Yoshika. It reconstructs Yoshiko's work life as a graphic artist up to the time when she died suddenly on the job due to a brain hemorrhage.

QUESTIONS

1. Identify the various sources of stress (i.e. stressors) that the Japanese manager in the first segment is likely to experience each day. Does he do anything to try to manage his stress?

2. What conditions led up to the karoshi death of Yoshika? Are these conditions commonly found in the country in which you live?

THE CONTAINER STORE

Walk into any of The Container Store locations and you'll immediately notice two things: great products and very happy and motivated employees. Indeed, *Fortune* magazine places the retailer as either the number 1 or number 2 among the best companies to work for in America. In this video case study, co-founders Garrett Boone and Kip Tindell tell us what makes The Container Store such a success story in employee satisfaction, motivation and performance. The Container Store helps its employees to feel emotionally secure by creating an environment with the proper values, stressing integrity, honesty and open communication. In achieving this, they have also created a family-like atmosphere that meets the social needs to feel loved, accepted and a part of the group.

The program reveals the company's cultural values and business practices that attract so many job applicants and make The Container Store a role model in superior customer service.

QUESTIONS

1. Using the MARS model of individual behaviour and performance, explain how specific practices at The Container Store increase employee performance and customer satisfaction.

2. What applied performance practices are applied at The Container Store? Are they used effectively here? Why or why not?

3. Discuss the importance of values at The Container Store. What values are important at this retailer and how do they influence employee behaviour?

PART 3

Team processes

CHAPTER 8
Decision making and creativity

CHAPTER 9
Foundations of team dynamics

CHAPTER 10
Developing high-performance teams

CHAPTER 11
Communicating in teams and organisations

CHAPTER 12
Power and influence in the workplace

CHAPTER 13
Conflict and negotiation in the workplace

CHAPTER 14
Leadership in organisational settings

VIDEO CASE STUDIES
• Bully Broads
• Celebrity CEO charisma

CHAPTER 8

Decision making and creativity

LEARNING OBJECTIVES

After reading this chapter, you should be able to:

- explain why people have difficulty identifying problems and opportunities

- contrast the rational choice paradigm with how people actually evaluate and choose alternatives

- describe three ways that emotions influence the selection of alternatives

- outline how intuition operates

- describe four causes of escalation of commitment

- describe four benefits of employee involvement in decision making

- identify four contingencies that affect the optimal level of employee involvement

- outline the four steps in the creative process

- describe the characteristics of employees and the workplace that support creativity.

Rising Sun Pictures and other computer graphics firms in Australia and New Zealand emphasise creative decision making and employee involvement.

What does fire look like when it emanates from a magic goblet? That question occupied the minds of employees at Rising Sun Pictures when the Adelaide-based visual special effects (VFX) firm was given the challenge of animating the magic goblet in the Harry Potter film *Goblet of Fire*. 'The goblet had to feel alive, like it had a personality,' explains James Whitlam, Rising Sun's head of production. 'It was important that it felt unpredictable as well as mesmerising and beautiful.'

Australia and New Zealand have become creative hotspots for Hollywood special effects and other postproduction work. Along with the work on *Goblet of Fire*, Rising Sun provided some of the animated sequences in *Sky Captain and the World of Tomorrow*, *Batman Begins* and *Charlotte's Web*. Weta Digital in Wellington, New Zealand, is credited with much of the animation in *King Kong*, the Lord of the Rings trilogy and *I, Robot*.

Hollywood studios have outsourced the toughest VFX jobs to Australia and New Zealand firms because the employees in these firms are able to meet the impossible expectations and deadlines. They do this by pushing the limits of technology and imagination. 'Directors all want the same thing,' says Toby Grime, a designer at Sydney-based VFX company Animal Logic. 'They say, "I want a never-been-seen-before effect".' Animal Logic has delivered those breakthrough digital effects in The Matrix trilogy, *Moulin Rouge* and *House of the Flying Daggers*.

Chris Godfrey, who co-founded Animal Logic in the early 1990s, believes that the company's work environment and Australia's freewheeling culture contribute to the creative output. 'We're pretty laid-back, don't take ourselves too seriously and we like to have fun in everything we do, which I believe is reflected in our work,' says Godfrey. 'Our culture and approach allow us to be a lot more accessible, creative and innovative.'

Employees in these Australian and New Zealand VFX firms also have an inventive thinking style and the persistence to turn creative ideas into reality. 'What's exciting is having to keep having new ideas and trying to push the boundaries,' says Jeremy Howdin, an Animal Logic 3-D supervisor whose team was recently nominated for an Emmy visual effects award for the television series *Farscape*.

Justen Marshall, one of Howdin's co-workers, agrees. 'Half the pleasure of this job is achieving the impossible,' he says. Eventually, Marshall believes, VFX technology will dominate the film industry. 'The ultimate goal is to make a film that is completely computer-generated and completely realistic. It will free our minds to be as creative as we want.'[1]

Paramount Pictures/Brooklyn Films

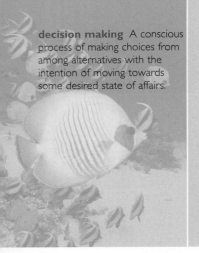

decision making A conscious process of making choices from among alternatives with the intention of moving towards some desired state of affairs.

Employees at Animal Logic, Weta Digital and Rising Sun Pictures are in the creativity business, but every organisation depends on creativity to some extent in almost all its decisions. Decision making is a conscious process of making choices from among alternatives with the intention of moving towards some desired state of affairs.[2] This chapter begins by outlining the rational choice paradigm of decision making. This perspective is then examined more critically by recognising how people identify problems and opportunities, choose between alternatives, and evaluate the success of their decisions differently from the rational model. Bounded rationality, escalation of commitment, and intuition are three of the more prominent topics in this section. Next, the role of employee involvement in decision making is explored, including the benefits of involvement and the factors that determine the optimal level of involvement. The final section of the chapter examines the factors that support creativity in decision making, including the characteristics of creative people, work environments that support creativity, and creativity activities.

RATIONAL CHOICE PARADIGM OF DECISION MAKING

rational choice paradigm A deeply held view that people should and can make decisions based on pure logic and with all information.

How do people make decisions in organisations? For most of written history, philosophers, economists and scholars in Western societies have stated or assumed that people should—and typically do—make decisions based on pure logic or rationality. This rational choice paradigm began 2500 years ago when Plato and his contemporaries in ancient Greece raised logical debate and reasoning to a fine art. A few centuries later, Greek and Roman Stoics insisted that one should always 'follow where reason leads' rather than fall victim to passion and emotions. About 500 years ago, several European philosophers emphasised that the ability to make logical decisions is one of the most important accomplishments of human beings. In the mid-1800s, while working at the Royal Mint in Australia, William Stanley Jevons began to develop the first mathematical rational choice model, which later scholars refined for economics, operations research and other decision sciences.[3]

Exhibit 8.1 illustrates the rational choice process.[4] The first step is to identify the problem or recognise an opportunity. A problem is a deviation between the current and the desired situation—the gap between 'what is' and 'what ought to be'. This deviation is a symptom of

EXHIBIT 8.1   Rational choice decision-making process

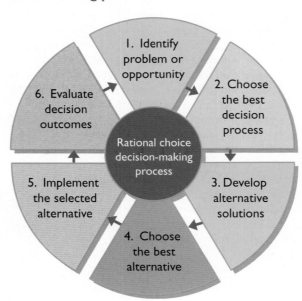

1. Identify problem or opportunity
2. Choose the best decision process
3. Develop alternative solutions
4. Choose the best alternative
5. Implement the selected alternative
6. Evaluate decision outcomes

Rational choice decision-making process

more fundamental root causes that need to be corrected.[5] An opportunity is a deviation between current expectations and a potentially better situation that was not previously expected. In other words, decision makers realise that some decisions may produce results beyond current goals or expectations.

The second step involves deciding how to process the decision.[6] One issue is whether the decision maker has enough information or needs to involve others in the process. Later in the chapter we'll examine whether and how much others should be involved in the decision. Another issue is whether the decision is programmed or non-programmed. *Programmed decisions* follow standard operating procedures; they have been resolved in the past, so the optimal solution has already been identified and documented. In contrast, *non-programmed decisions* require all steps in the decision model because the problems are new, complex or ill-defined. The third step is to develop a list of possible solutions. This usually begins by searching for ready-made solutions, such as practices that have worked well on similar problems. If an acceptable solution cannot be found, decision makers need to design a custom-made solution or modify an existing one.

The fourth step is to choose from among the alternatives. The rational choice paradigm assumes that people naturally select the alternative with the highest *subjective expected utility*.[7] Subjective expected utility refers to how much the selected alternative benefits or satisfies the decision maker. Figuring out the alternative with the highest utility (total value or happiness) involves identifying all the outcomes that would occur if the alternative is selected and estimating the amount of satisfaction the person would feel from each of those outcomes. This is incredibly complex, but rational choice assumes that everyone does this calculation without any problem. The fifth step is to implement the selected alternative. This is followed by the sixth step, evaluating whether the gap has narrowed between 'what is' and 'what ought to be'. Ideally, this information should come from systematic benchmarks, so that relevant feedback is objective and easily observed.

PROBLEMS WITH THE RATIONAL CHOICE PARADIGM

The rational choice paradigm seems so logical, yet it is rarely practised in reality. One reason is that the model assumes that people are efficient and logical information processing machines. But as the next few pages will reveal, people have difficulty recognising problems; they cannot (or will not) simultaneously process the huge volume of information needed to identify the best solution; and they have difficulty recognising when their choices have failed. The second reason why the rational model doesn't fit reality is that it focuses on logical thinking and completely ignores the fact that emotions also influence—perhaps even dominate— the decision-making process. As this chapter will reveal, emotions both support and interfere with our quest to make better decisions.[8] With these points in mind, let's look again at each step of decision making, but with more detail about what really happens.

IDENTIFYING PROBLEMS AND OPPORTUNITIES

When Albert Einstein was asked how he would save the world in one hour, he replied that the first fifty-five minutes should be spent defining the problem and the last five minutes solving it.[9] Einstein's point is that problem identification is not just the first step in decision making; it is arguably the most important step. But problems and opportunities do not appear on our desks as well-labelled objects. Instead, decision makers translate information into evidence that something is wrong or that an opportunity is available.

To some extent, this discovery process occurs through conscious evaluation of the facts and persuasive arguments by other people. But what is becoming increasingly apparent is that a fair amount of problem recognition actually occurs during the mostly unconscious processes of perceptual selective attention and attitude formation (described in Chapter 3 and 4 respectively).[10] Specifically, we evaluate information as soon as we perceive it by attaching emotional

LEARNING OBJECTIVE

Explain why people have difficulty identifying problems and opportunities.

markers (anger, caution, delight, etc.) to that information. These automatic emotional responses, together with logical analysis and the emotions triggered by that analysis, determine whether we perceive something as a problem, an opportunity or irrelevant.

Let's say that a worried-looking colleague tells you that the company's salesperson in Queensland has just quit. Your initial reaction (emotions generated upon hearing the news that the salesperson has quit) might be worry and frustration. Meanwhile, the rational part of your brain works through this information, recalling from memory the related knowledge that the Queensland salesperson's performance was mediocre and that an excellent salesperson at another company wants to join your firm in that state. What initially felt like a problem was really an opportunity, based on your rational analysis of the situation. The initial emotions of worry or frustration might have been wrong in this situation, but sometimes your emotions provide a good indicator of problems or opportunities.

PROBLEMS WITH PROBLEM IDENTIFICATION

Several problems occur during the problem identification stage.[11] One concern is that employees, clients and other stakeholders with vested interests try to influence the decision maker's perceptions of problems or opportunities. This persuasion 'frames' the person's view of the situation, which short-circuits a full assessment of the problem or opportunity. A second biasing effect is that under some conditions people block out negative information as a coping mechanism. Their brain refuses to see information that threatens their self-esteem. A third perceptual challenge is that mental models blind people from seeing opportunities that deviate from the status quo. If an idea doesn't fit the existing mental model of how things should work, the idea is dismissed as unworkable or undesirable. Reality Check 8.1 describes how narrow mental models are the source of several famous missed or near-missed opportunities.

A fourth barrier to effective problem identification is that decision makers often exhibit faulty diagnostic skills.[12] One diagnostic flaw is that leaders are expected to be decisive, and this decisive image motivates them to zero in on a problem without sufficiently analysing the facts. Another diagnostic skill flaw is the tendency to define problems in terms of their solutions. Someone who says 'The problem is that we need more control over our suppliers' has fallen into this trap. Notice that this statement focuses on a solution (controlling suppliers), whereas proper diagnosis would determine the cause of the symptoms before jumping to solutions.

This focus on solutions occurs because it gives decision makers a sense of comforting clarity in ambiguous situations. People want to make sense of their immediate environment, so alternatives are unconsciously evaluated (tagged with emotions) as soon as they are identified, not just consciously evaluated later through logical analysis.[13] Solutions that worked well in the past are typically viewed favourably, even though they were applied under different circumstances, because these known solutions increase closure and predictability. Some executives are known for cutting the workforce whenever they face problems; others introduce a new customer service program as their favourite solution to a variety of problems. The point here is that decision makers tend to look at problems from the perspective of the ready-made solutions that worked for them in the past.

IDENTIFYING PROBLEMS AND OPPORTUNITIES MORE EFFECTIVELY

Recognising problems and opportunities will always be a challenge, but the process can be improved through awareness of these perceptual and diagnostic limitations. By keeping in mind that mental models restrict a person's perspective of the world, decision makers are more motivated to consider other perspectives of reality. A second method of minimising perceptual and diagnostic weaknesses is to discuss the situation with colleagues. Decision makers discover blind spots in problem identification by hearing how others perceive certain information and diagnose problems. Opportunities also become apparent when outsiders explore this information from their different mental models. Third, leaders require willpower to resist appearing decisive when

FAMOUS MISSED OPPORTUNITIES

Mental models create road maps that guide our decisions. Unfortunately, these maps also potentially block our ability to see emerging problems and opportunities. Here are a few famous examples.

Graphical user interfaces, mice, windows, pull-down menus, laser printing, distributed computing and Ethernet technologies weren't invented by Apple, Microsoft or IBM. These essential elements of contemporary personal computing originated in the 1970s from researchers at Xerox PARC. Unfortunately, Xerox executives were so focused on their photocopier business that they didn't bother to patent most of these inventions. Xerox has successfully applied some of its laser technology, but the lost value of Xerox PARC's other computing discoveries is much larger than the entire photocopier industry today.

CP/Everett Collection

Nia Vardalos wrote a comedy screenplay based on incidents involving her Greek-Canadian family. None of Hollywood's literary agents were interested. 'They all said it's not good; it's not funny,' said Vardalos, who honed her writing and acting skills at the Second City comedy group. Undeterred, Vardalos turned the script into a successful one-woman show in Los Angeles. None of Hollywood's talent agents accepted her invitation to see the show, but when actors Rita Wilson and Tom Hanks watched her skits, they immediately supported her in making a movie. Even with Hanks on board, Hollywood studios rejected the script, but HBO agreed to provide a paltry US$2.5 million 'as a favour' to Hanks. With a budget of only US$5 million, *My Big Fat Greek Wedding* became one of the highest grossing independent films of all time. The screenplay that no one in Hollywood wanted was also nominated for an Oscar.

When the World Wide Web burst onto the cyberspace scene in the early 1990s, Bill Gates wondered what all the fuss was about. Even as late as 1996, the Microsoft founder lampooned investors for their love-in with companies that made Internet products. However, Gates eventually realised the error in his mental model of computing. Making up for lost time, Microsoft bought Hotmail and other Web-savvy companies, and added Internet support to its Windows operating system.

The best television commercial in history (as rated by *Advertising Age*) almost didn't see the light of day. The Apple Macintosh 'Why 1984 won't be like 1984' clip features a female athlete hurling a sledgehammer at a giant TV screen of an Orwellian Big Brother, liberating thousands of subjugated followers. Apple initially rejected the ad agency's (Chiat-Day) now-memorable phrase in an Apple II newspaper ad, but agreed to use the theme to launch the Macintosh computer during the 1984 Superbowl. The Macintosh team and sales force were ecstatic with rough cuts of the ad, but every outside director on Apple's board despised it. One remarked that it was the worst commercial of all time; another insisted that Apple immediately change its ad agency. Based on the board's reaction, Apple CEO John Sculley asked Chiat-Day to cancel the Superbowl ad space. Fortunately, the agency claimed it could only sell off some of the time, so Apple had to show the commercial. The single sixty-second ad shown during the Superbowl had such a huge effect that it was featured on evening news over the next several days. A month later, Apple's board members applauded the Macintosh team for a successful launch and apologised for their misjudgment of the commercial.

Nia Vardalos's comedy screenplay about her Greek-Canadian family was rejected by Hollywood literary agents and studios, yet it eventually became the top-grossing independent film in history and was nominated for an Oscar.

Sources: T. Abate, 'Meet Bill Gates, Stand-Up Comic', *San Francisco Examiner*, 13 March 1996, p. D1; O. Port, 'Xerox Won't Duplicate Past Errors', *Business Week*, 29 September 1997, p. 98; B. Campbell and M. Conron, 'Xerox Ready to Hit Another Home Run', *Ottawa Citizen*, 28 June 1999; P. Nason, 'A Big Fat Hollywood Success Story', *United Press International*, 12 December 2002; M. McCarthy, 'Top 20 in 20 Years: Apple Computer—1984', *Adweek Online*, www.adweek.com/adweek/creative/top20_20years/index.jsp (accessed 16 January 2003); A. Hertzfeld, '1984', www.folklore.org (accessed 31 July 2005).

a more thoughtful examination of the situation should occur. Finally, successful decision makers experience 'divine discontent'. They are never satisfied with the status quo, and this aversion to complacency creates a mind-set that actively searches for problems and opportunities.[14]

EVALUATING AND CHOOSING ALTERNATIVES

LEARNING OBJECTIVE

Contrast the rational choice paradigm with how people actually evaluate and choose alternatives.

bounded rationality
Processing limited and imperfect information and satisficing rather than maximising when choosing between alternatives.

According to the rational choice paradigm of decision making, people rely on logic to evaluate alternatives and choose between them. This paradigm assumes that decision makers have well-articulated and agreed-on organisational goals, that they efficiently and simultaneously process facts about all alternatives and the consequences of those alternatives, and that they choose the alternative with the highest payoff.

Nobel Prize–winning organisational scholar Herbert Simon questioned these assumptions half a century ago. He argued that people engage in **bounded rationality** because they process limited and imperfect information and rarely select the best choice.[15] Simon and other organisational behaviour experts demonstrated that how people evaluate and choose between alternatives differs from the rational choice paradigm in several ways, as illustrated in Exhibit 8.2. These differences are so significant that even economists have shifted from rational choice to bounded rationality assumptions in their theories. Let's look at these differences in terms of goals, information processing and maximisation.

PROBLEMS WITH GOALS

We need clear goals in order to choose the best solution. Goals identify 'what ought to be' and therefore provide a standard against which each alternative is evaluated. The reality, however, is that organisational goals are often ambiguous or in conflict with each other. One survey found that 25 per cent of managers and employees felt that decisions were delayed because of difficulty agreeing on what they wanted the decision to achieve.[16]

EXHIBIT 8.2

Rational choice assumptions versus organisational behaviour findings about choosing alternatives

Rational choice paradigm assumptions	Observations from organisational behaviour
Goals are clear, compatible and agreed upon	Goals are ambiguous, in conflict and lack full support
Decision makers can calculate all alternatives and their outcomes	Decision makers have limited information processing abilities
Decision makers evaluate all alternatives simultaneously	Decision makers evaluate alternatives sequentially
Decision makers use absolute standards to evaluate alternatives	Decision makers evaluate alternatives against an implicit favourite
Decision makers use factual information to choose alternatives	Decision makers process perceptually distorted information
Decision makers choose the alternative with the highest pay-off	Decision makers choose the alternative that is good enough (satisficing)

PROBLEMS WITH INFORMATION PROCESSING

People do not make perfectly rational decisions because they don't process information very well. One problem is that decision makers can't possibly think through all of the alternatives and the outcomes of those alternatives. Consequently, they look at only a few alternatives and only some of the main outcomes of those alternatives.[17] For example, there may be dozens of computer brands to choose from and dozens of features to consider, yet people typically evaluate only a few brands and a few features.

A related problem is that decision makers typically look at alternatives sequentially rather than all at the same time. As a new alternative comes along, it is immediately compared with an **implicit favourite**. An implicit favourite is an alternative that the decision maker prefers and is used as a comparison against which other choices are judged. The implicit favourite is formed very early and usually unconsciously in the decision-making process, which means that it is not necessarily the best choice to compare against the others.[18]

Although the implicit favourite comparison process works well some of the time, it more often undermines effective decision making because people unconsciously distort information in order to favour their implicit favourite over the alternative choices. Specifically, they tend to forget the limitations of the implicit favourite and the advantages of the alternative. Decision makers also overweight factors where the implicit favourite is better and underweight areas where the alternative is superior.[19] This effect was observed in a study of auditing students who had to decide whether the company described in a case had significant financial problems. Those who decided that the company did have significant problems distorted the available information to make those problems appear worse. Students who felt that the financial problems were not significant enough to report in a formal audit minimised any reference to the negative information in their case reports.[20]

> **implicit favourite** The decision maker's preferred alternative against which all other choices are judged.

PROBLEMS WITH MAXIMISATION

Decision makers tend to select the alternative that is acceptable or 'good enough', rather than the one with the highest payoff (i.e. the highest subjective expected utility). In other words, they engage in **satisficing** rather than maximising. Satisficing occurs because it isn't possible to identify every alternative, and information about available alternatives is imperfect or ambiguous. Satisficing also occurs because, as mentioned earlier, decision makers tend to evaluate alternatives sequentially, rather than all at the same time. They evaluate each alternative against the implicit favourite and eventually select an option that scores above a subjective minimum point considered to be good enough to satisfy their needs or preferences.[21]

> **satisficing** Selecting a solution that is satisfactory or 'good enough', rather than optimal or 'the best'.

EVALUATING OPPORTUNITIES

Opportunities are just as important as problems, but the process of discovering an opportunity is quite different from the process of problem solving. According to a recent study of decision failures, decision makers do not evaluate several alternatives when they find an opportunity; after all, the opportunity *is* the solution, so why look for others! An opportunity is usually experienced as an exciting and rare revelation, so decision makers tend to have an emotional attachment to it. Unfortunately, this emotional preference motivates decision makers to apply the opportunity and short-circuit any detailed evaluation of it.[22]

EMOTIONS AND MAKING CHOICES

Herbert Simon and many other experts have presented plenty of evidence that people do not evaluate alternatives nearly as well as is assumed by the rational choice paradigm. However, these experts neglected to mention another glaring weakness with rational choice—it completely ignores the effect of emotions in human decision making. Just as both the rational and emotional brain centres alert us to problems, they also influence our choice of alternatives.

LEARNING OBJECTIVE

Describe three ways that emotions influence the selection of alternatives.

Emotions affect the evaluation of alternatives in three ways. First, the emotional marker process described earlier in the chapter—as well as in Chapters 3, 4 and 5—determines our preferences for each alternative. Our brain very quickly attaches specific emotions to information about each alternative, and our preferred alternative is strongly influenced by those initial emotional markers. Of course, logical analysis also influences which alternative we choose, but it requires strong logical evidence to change our initial preferences (initial emotional markers). But even logical analysis depends on emotions to sway our decision. Specifically, neuroscientific evidence says that information produced from logical analysis is also tagged with emotional markers which then motivate us to choose or avoid a particular alternative. Ultimately, emotions, not rational logic, energise us to make the preferred choice. (People with damaged emotional brain centres have difficulty making choices.)

Second, a considerable body of literature, much of it in Australia, indicates that moods and specific emotions influence the *process* of evaluating alternatives. For instance, we pay more attention to details when in a negative mood, possibly because a negative mood signals that there is something wrong that requires attention. When in a positive mood, on the other hand, we pay less attention to details and rely on a more programmed decision routine. Regarding specific emotions, decision makers rely on stereotypes and other shortcuts to speed up the choice process when they experience anger. Anger also makes them more optimistic about the success of risky alternatives, whereas the emotion of fear tends to make them less optimistic.[23]

The third way that emotions influence the evaluation of alternatives is through a process called 'emotions as information'. Marketing experts have found that we listen in on our emotions to provide guidance when making choices.[24] Most emotional experiences remain below the radar screen of awareness, but sufficiently intense emotions are picked up consciously and figured into our decision. Suppose that you are in the process of choosing one of several advertising firms to work with your company. You would logically consider several factors, such as previous experience, the agency's resources, and so on. But you would probably also pay attention to your gut feeling about each agency. If you sense positive feelings about a particular advertising firm, those conscious assessments of your emotions tend to get weighted into the decision. Some people pay a lot of attention to these gut feelings, and personality tests such as the Myers–Briggs Type Indicator (see Chapter 2) identify those who listen in on their emotions more than others.[25] But all of us use our emotions as information to some degree. This phenomenon ties directly into our next topic, intuition.

INTUITION AND MAKING CHOICES

LEARNING OBJECTIVE

Outline how intuition operates.

intuition The ability to know when a problem or opportunity exists and to select the best course of action without conscious reasoning.

Linda, a trainee nurse in the neonatal intensive care unit of a hospital, was responsible for Melissa, a premature baby with no problems other than needing support to grow out of her sensitive condition. One day, Melissa was a little sleepier than normal and was a bit lethargic during feeding. A spot on her heel where a blood sample had been taken was bleeding slightly, but that might have been due to a sloppy sample prick. Melissa's temperature had also dropped slightly over several checks, but was still within the normal range. None of these conditions would seem unusual to most people, including trainee Linda. But when Darlene, an experienced nurse, happened to walk by, she immediately sensed that Melissa 'just looked funny', as she put it. After reviewing the baby's charts and asking Linda a few questions, Darlene rushed to call a physician with the details. The physician immediately prescribed antibiotics to correct what a blood test later confirmed was sepsis.[26]

The gut instinct that helped Darlene save this baby's life is known as **intuition**—the ability to know when a problem or opportunity exists and to select the best course of action without conscious reasoning.[27] Intuition is both an emotional experience and a rapid unconscious analytic process. As mentioned in the previous section, the gut feelings we experience are emotional signals that have enough intensity to make us consciously aware of them. These signals warn us of impending danger, such as a sick baby, or motivate us to take advantage of an opportunity. Some intuition also directs us to preferred choices relative to other alternatives in that situation.

All gut feelings are emotional signals, but not all emotional signals are intuition. The key distinction is that intuition involves rapidly comparing what we see or otherwise sense with deeply held patterns learned through experience.[28] These templates represent tacit knowledge that has been implicitly acquired over time. When a template fits or doesn't fit the current situation, emotions are produced that motivate us to act. Intuition also relies on mental models, internal representations of the external world that allow us to anticipate future events from current observations. Darlene's years of experience produced mental templates of unhealthy babies that matched what she saw on that fateful day. Studies have also found that chess masters receive emotional signals when they sense an opportunity through quick observation of a chessboard. They can't immediately explain why they see a favourable move on the chessboard—they just feel it.

As mentioned, some emotional signals (gut feelings) are not intuition because they are not based on well-grounded templates or mental models. Instead, they occur when we compare the current situation with our templates and mental models of distant circumstances, which may or may not be relevant. Thus, whether the emotions we experience in a situation represent intuition or not depends largely on our level of experience in that situation.

So far, intuition has been described as an emotional experience (gut feeling) and a process of pattern matching in which we compare the current situation with well-established templates and mental models. Intuition also relies on *action scripts*—pre-programmed routines for responding to pattern matches or mismatches.[29] Action scripts are programmed decision routines; they provide instant road maps to follow without consciously evaluating the alternatives. These action scripts are generic, so we need to consciously adapt them to the specific situation, but they speed up the decision–action process.

MAKING CHOICES MORE EFFECTIVELY

It is very difficult to get around the human limitations of making choices, but a few strategies may help. One important discovery is that decisions tend to have a higher failure rate when leaders are decisive rather than contemplative about the available options. Of course, problems also arise when decisions take too long, but research indicates that a lack of logical analysis is a greater concern. By systematically evaluating alternatives, decision makers minimise the implicit favourite and satisficing problems that occur when relying on general subjective judgments. Intuition still figures in this analysis, but so does careful consideration of relevant information.[30]

Another issue is how to minimise the adverse effects of emotions on the decision process. The first recommendation here is that we need to be constantly aware that decisions are influenced by both rational and emotional processes. With this awareness, some decision makers deliberately revisit important issues so they look at the information in different moods and have allowed their initial emotions to subside. Others practise **scenario planning**, in which they anticipate emergencies long before they occur, so that alternative courses of action are evaluated without the pressure and emotions that occur during real emergencies.[31]

scenario planning A systematic process of thinking about alternative futures and what the organisation should do to anticipate and react to those environments.

EVALUATING DECISION OUTCOMES

Contrary to the rational choice paradigm, decision makers aren't completely honest with themselves when evaluating the effectiveness of their decisions. One concern is that after making a choice decision makers tend to support their choice by forgetting or downplaying the negative features of the selected alternative and emphasising its positive features. This perceptual distortion, known as **post-decisional justification**, results from the need for decision makers

post-decisional justification Justifying choices by unconsciously inflating the quality of the selected option and deflating the quality of the discarded options.

to maintain their self-esteem.[32] Post-decisional justification gives people an excessively optimistic evaluation of their decisions, but only until they receive very clear and undeniable information to the contrary. Unfortunately, it also inflates the decision maker's initial evaluation of the decision, so reality often comes as a painful shock when objective feedback is finally received.

ESCALATION OF COMMITMENT

escalation of commitment
The tendency to repeat an apparently bad decision or to allocate more resources to a failing course of action.

A second problem when evaluating decision outcomes is **escalation of commitment**—the tendency to repeat an apparently bad decision or to allocate more resources to a failing course of action.[33] There are plenty of escalation examples, including an ill-fated baggage-handling system at Denver International Airport, a subway extension project in Tokyo, BHP-Billiton's hot briquetted iron (HBI) plant in Western Australia, the Pacificat ferries in British Columbia, Canada, and development of the Concorde supersonic airliner. (In some fields of science, escalation of commitment is called the 'Concorde fallacy'.) One of the most dramatic examples is Scotland's new parliament building. The project began in 1997 with an estimated cost of A$110 million and completion by 2001. Instead, due to several escalation influences and other decision debacles, the building opened in 2004 at a cost exceeding A$1 billion.[34]

Escalation of commitment at BHP-Billiton's HBI plant

In 1994 BHP announced that it would build the world's largest hot briquetted iron (HBI) plant near Port Hedland, Western Australia. The HBI plant would cost $1.4 billion, produce two million tonnes of the small iron bricks per year, and be at full production within four years. A dozen years later the company closed the plant after pouring almost $3 billion into it. BHP could have cut these losses by half if it had cancelled the project in 1997 when experts first warned of the cost overruns, but executives continued to throw more money into the project. In 1998 BHP's chief operating officer acknowledged that the HBI project 'did get out of control, absolutely out of control', but assured investors that the final cost would fall somewhere between $2.2 and $2.4 billion. In 2001, when costs had reached $2.6 billion, management of the then-merged BHP-Billiton continued to support the project, saying the 'decision is very straightforward—it is about managing the value of an existing investment'. Production at the plant was stopped in 2004 after an accident cost the life of one employee and seriously injured two others. The plant was finally closed the following year.[35]

Megan Powell/WAN

Causes of escalating commitment

Why are people led deeper and deeper into failing projects? There are several reasons, including self-justification, prospect theory effect, perceptual blinders, and closing costs.

- *Self-justification.* Individuals are motivated to maintain their course of action when they have a high need to justify their decision. This self-justification is particularly evident when decision makers are personally identified with the project and have staked their reputations to some extent on the project's success.[36] This is probably the main reason why BHP executives initially ignored or denied cost overruns at the BHP-Billiton hot briquetted iron plant in Western Australia (see photo).
- *Prospect theory effect.* You might think that people would dislike losing $50 just as much as they would like receiving $50, but that isn't true for most people. People actually dislike losing a particular amount more than they like gaining the same amount. People also take fewer risks to receive gains and take more risks to avoid losses. This effect, called **prospect theory**, is a second explanation for escalation of commitment. Stopping a project is a certain loss, which is more painful to most people than the uncertainty of success associated with continuing to fund the project. Given the choice, decision makers choose the less painful option.[37] The prospect theory effect might have been an influence in the escalation of commitment at BHP-Billiton's hot briquetted iron project. In spite of the numerous setbacks, senior executives restated their confidence on at least three occasions spanning five years that the project would get back on track.
- *Perceptual blinders.* Escalation of commitment sometimes occurs because decision makers do not see the problems soon enough. They unconsciously screen out or explain away negative information to protect their self-esteem. Serious problems initially look like random errors along the trend line to success. Even when they see that something is wrong, the information is sufficiently ambiguous for it to be misinterpreted or justified.
- *Closing costs.* Even when a project's success is in doubt, decision makers will persist because the costs of ending the project are high or unknown. Terminating a major project may involve large financial penalties, a bad public image or personal political costs. Closing costs definitely played a role in the escalation of BHP's plant in Western Australia. There were concerns that terminating the project would cost up to $1 billion in forfeited contracts and obligations.

These four conditions make escalation of commitment look irrational. Usually it is, but there are exceptions. Recent studies suggest that throwing more money into a failing project is sometimes a logical attempt to further understand an ambiguous situation. This strategy is essentially a variation of testing unknown waters. By adding more resources, the decision maker gains new information about the effectiveness of these funds, which provides more feedback about the project's future success. This strategy is particularly common where the project has high closing costs.[38]

EVALUATING DECISION OUTCOMES MORE EFFECTIVELY

One of the most effective ways to minimise escalation of commitment and post-decisional justification is to separate decision choosers from decision evaluators. This minimises the self-justification effect because the person responsible for evaluating the decision is not connected to the original decision. A second strategy is to publicly establish a preset level at which the decision is abandoned or re-evaluated. This is similar to a stop-loss order in the share market, whereby the share is sold if it falls below a certain price. The problem with this solution is that conditions are often so complex that it is difficult to identify an appropriate point at which to abandon a project.[39]

A third strategy is to find a source of systematic and clear feedback.[40] For example, BHP-Billiton executives might have minimised the escalation problem at the hot briquetted iron plant if they had received less ambiguous and conflicting information about the true costs of the project during the first few years. Finally, projects might have less risk of escalation if

LEARNING OBJECTIVE

Describe four causes of escalation of commitment.

prospect theory An effect in which losing a particular amount is more disliked than gaining the same amount.

several people are involved. Co-workers continuously monitor each other and might notice problems sooner than someone working alone on a project. Employee involvement offers these and other benefits to the decision-making process, as discussed next.

EMPLOYEE INVOLVEMENT IN DECISION MAKING

employee involvement The degree to which employees influence how their work is organised and carried out.

In this world of rapid change and increasing complexity, leaders rarely have enough information to make the best decision alone. Whether this information is about reducing costs or improving the customer experience, employee involvement can potentially solve problems or realise opportunities more effectively. **Employee involvement** (also called *participative management*) refers to the degree to which employees influence how their work is organised and carried out.[41] At the lowest level, participation involves asking employees for information. They do not make recommendations and might not even know what the problem is about. At a moderate level of involvement, employees are told about the problem and provide recommendations to the decision maker. At the highest level of involvement, the entire decision-making process is handed over to employees. They identify the problem, choose the best alternative and implement their choice.

Every organisation has some form and various levels of employee involvement. Employees at one of Alinta Limited's Australian power stations showed senior management how they could save tens of thousands of dollars by making parts in their workshop rather than outsourcing the work. RAC Western Australia employees were actively involved in decisions about designing and outfitting the company's new building in Perth. 'Staff had workshops every month to focus on a different element of the building, and that interaction made the transition much easier and gives a real sense of ownership,' says the building's interior designer, Gary Giles. And at hard disk manufacturer Komag Malaysia, seven-person self-directed work teams make decisions in their own work areas to achieve corporate objectives.[42]

High involvement keeps Thai Carbon Black in the black

Thai Carbon Black, which makes the black colouring agent in tyres, inks and many other products, views all of its employees as problem solvers. 'The "can do" attitude of every employee is important,' says Subburaman Srinivasan, president of the Thai–Indian joint venture. Each year, employees submit over 600 productivity improvement suggestions, placing their ideas in one of the little red boxes located around the site. Participatory management meetings are held every month, where employees are encouraged to come up with new ideas on ways to improve day-to-day operations. For instance, the company cut its transport costs by more than 10 per cent after employees developed a special shipping bag which allowed packers to stuff more product into the same volume. Thanks in part to this emphasis on employee

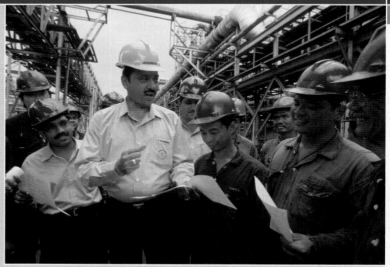

Yvan Cohen/OnAsia.com

involvement, Thai Carbon Black is one of the few companies outside Japan to receive the Deming Prize for total quality management. It has also received the Thailand Quality Class award, *Forbes* magazine's recognition as one of the best-managed companies, and Hewitt Associates' ranking as one of the best employers in Asia and Thailand.[43]

BENEFITS OF EMPLOYEE INVOLVEMENT

For the past half-century organisational behaviour scholars have advised that employee involvement potentially improves decision-making quality and commitment.[44] Involving employees can lead to improved decision quality because problems are recognised more quickly and they are defined more accurately. Employees are, in many respects, the sensors of the organisation's environment. When the organisation's activities misalign with customer expectations, employees are usually the first to know. Employee involvement ensures that everyone in the organisation is quickly alerted to these problems.[45]

Employee involvement can also potentially improve the number and quality of solutions generated. In a well-managed meeting, team members create synergy by pooling their knowledge to form new alternatives. In other words, several people working together have the potential to generate more and better solutions than the same people working alone. A third benefit is that employee involvement often improves the likelihood of choosing the best alternative. This occurs because the decision is reviewed by people with diverse perspectives and a broad representation of values.[46]

Along with improving decision quality, employee involvement tends to strengthen employee commitment to the decision. Rather than viewing themselves as agents of someone else's decision, staff members feel personally responsible for the success of the decision. It also has positive effects on employee motivation, satisfaction and turnover. A recent Australian study reported that employee involvement also increases skill variety, feelings of autonomy, and task identity, all of which increase job enrichment and potentially employee motivation. Participation is also a critical practice in organisational change, because employees are more motivated to implement the decisions and less likely to resist changes resulting from the decisions. As a respected organisational behaviour expert concluded: 'The new organisational realities are that top-down decision making is not sufficiently responsive to the dynamic organisational environment. Employees must be actively involved in decisions—or completely take over many decisions.'[47]

CONTINGENCIES OF EMPLOYEE INVOLVEMENT

If employee involvement is so wonderful, why don't leaders leave all decisions to employees? The answer is that the optimal level of employee involvement depends on the situation. The employee involvement model, shown in Exhibit 8.3, lists four contingencies: decision structure, source of decision knowledge, decision commitment, and risk of conflict in the decision process.

LEARNING OBJECTIVE

Describe four benefits of employee involvement in decision making.

LEARNING OBJECTIVE

Identify four contingencies that affect the optimal level of employee involvement.

EXHIBIT 8.3

Model of employee involvement in decision making

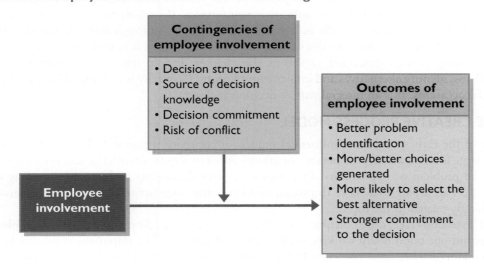

Contingencies of employee involvement
- Decision structure
- Source of decision knowledge
- Decision commitment
- Risk of conflict

Employee involvement

Outcomes of employee involvement
- Better problem identification
- More/better choices generated
- More likely to select the best alternative
- Stronger commitment to the decision

- *Decision structure.* As mentioned earlier, some decisions are programmed, whereas others are non-programmed. Programmed decisions are less likely to need employee involvement, because the solutions are already worked out from past experience. In other words, the benefits of employee involvement increase with the novelty and complexity of the problem or opportunity.
- *Source of decision knowledge.* Subordinates should be involved in some level of decision making when the leader lacks sufficient knowledge and subordinates have additional information that will improve the decision quality. In many cases, employees are closer to customers and production activities, so they often know where the company can save money, improve product or service quality and realise opportunities. This is particularly true for complex decisions where employees are more likely to possess the relevant information.[48]
- *Decision commitment.* Participation tends to improve employee commitment to the decision. If employees are unlikely to accept a decision made without their involvement, some level of participation is usually necessary.
- *Risk of conflict.* Two types of conflict undermine the benefits of employee involvement. First, if employee goals and norms conflict with the organisation's goals, only a low level of employee involvement is advisable. Second, the degree of involvement depends on whether employees will reach agreement on the preferred solution. If conflict is likely, then high involvement (i.e. where employees make the decision alone) would be difficult to achieve.

Employee involvement is an important component of the decision-making process. To make the best decisions, there needs to be involvement by people who have the most valuable information and who will increase commitment to implement the decision. Another important component of decision making is creativity, which is discussed next.

CREATIVITY

LEARNING OBJECTIVE

Outline the four steps in the creative process.

creativity The development of original ideas that make a socially recognised contribution.

Parcel delivery might seem like a routine business, but that's not the way the folks at Yamato Transport Company see it. The Japanese company invented door-to-door next-day parcel delivery in Japan and its name is now synonymous with the service. Yamato was also the first to offer 'cool takkyubin' (delivering chilled or frozen items to any address) and to deliver customers' ski equipment to resorts and homes. To keep better track of shipments, customers receive the mobile telephone numbers of Yamato's delivery personnel, not just the distribution centres. One local branch office is testing the use of lockers at train stations around Japan for pickup and delivery locations, notifying customers by email of the delivery times.[49]

Yamato Transport is successful in Japan's fiercely competitive delivery service industry because it relies on creativity for innovative new services. **Creativity** is the development of original ideas that make a socially recognised contribution.[50] Although there are unique conditions for creativity (which are discussed in the next few pages), it is really part of the decision-making process described earlier in the chapter. People rely on creativity to find problems, identify alternatives and implement solutions. Creativity is not something saved for special occasions. It is an integral part of decision making.

THE CREATIVE PROCESS MODEL

One of the earliest and most influential models of creativity is shown in Exhibit 8.4.[51] The first stage is preparation—the person's or group's effort to acquire knowledge and skills regarding the problem or opportunity. Preparation involves developing a clear understanding of what you are trying to achieve through a novel solution, then actively studying information seemingly related to the topic.

The second stage, called incubation, is the stage of reflective thought. We put the problem aside, but our mind is still working on it in the background.[52] The important condition here is to maintain a low-level awareness by frequently revisiting the problem. Incubation does not

The creative process model

EXHIBIT 8.4

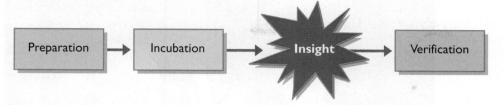

mean that you forget about the problem or issue. Incubation assists **divergent thinking**—reframing the problem in a unique way and generating different approaches to the issue. This contrasts with convergent thinking—calculating the conventionally accepted 'right answer' to a logical problem. Divergent thinking breaks us away from existing mental models so we can apply concepts or processes from completely different areas of life. Consider the following classic example. Years ago the experimental bulbs in Thomas Edison's lab kept falling off their fixtures, until a technician wondered whether the threaded caps that screwed down tightly on kerosene bottles would work on light bulbs. They did, and the design remains to this day.[53]

Insight, the third stage of creativity, refers to the experience of suddenly becoming aware of a unique idea.[54] Insight is often visually depicted as a light bulb, but a better image would be a brief flash of light or perhaps a flickering candle, because these bits of inspiration are fleeting and can be quickly lost if not documented. For this reason, many creative people keep a journal or notebook nearby at all times, so that they can jot down these flickering ideas before they disappear. Also, these ideas don't keep a particular schedule; they might come to you at any time of day or night. Insights are merely rough ideas. Their usefulness still requires verification through conscious evaluation and experimentation. Thus, although verification is labelled the final stage of creativity, it is really the beginning of a long process of experimentation and further creativity.

CREATIVE PEOPLE AND WORK ENVIRONMENTS

Rising Sun Pictures, Weta Digital and Animal Logic have an impressive portfolio of digital animation accomplishments which appear seamlessly throughout many of today's blockbuster films. As described in the opening story to this chapter, these Australian and New Zealand companies have achieved this success by finding creative people and putting them in an environment that encourages creative ideas. In other words, creativity is a function of both the person and the situation.

Characteristics of creative people

Everyone is creative, but some people seem to be more creative than others. Four of the main features of creative people are intelligence, persistence, subject-matter knowledge and experience, and an inventive thinking style. First, creative people have the above-average intelligence needed to synthesise information, analyse ideas, and apply the ideas.[55] Like the fictional sleuth Sherlock Holmes, creative people recognise the significance of small bits of information and are able to connect them in ways that no one else could imagine. Then, they have the capacity to evaluate the potential usefulness of their ideas.

Persistence is the second feature of creative people. The fact is that innovations derive more from trial and error than from intelligence and experience. Persistence drives creative people to continue developing and testing after others have given up. In other words, people who develop more creative products and services are those who develop more ideas that don't work. Thomas Edison emphasised this point in his famous statement that genius is 1 per cent inspiration and 99 per cent perspiration. Edison and his staff discovered hundreds of ways *not* to build a light bulb before they got it right! This persistence is based on a high need for achievement and a moderate or high degree of self-confidence.[56]

divergent thinking Reframing a problem in a unique way and generating different approaches to the issue.

LEARNING OBJECTIVE

Describe the characteristics of employees and the workplace that support creativity.

Persistence becomes the cure for peptic ulcers

AFP/Getty Images

Australians Barry Marshall (left) and Robin Warren (right) faced plenty of doubters when they first proposed that peptic ulcers are caused by specific bacteria. The prevailing belief was that these ulcers were caused by weak stomach linings, gastric acid and unhealthy diets. Few believed that bacteria could survive, let alone thrive, in the highly acidic stomach environment. Marshall and Warren's initial research supported the bacteria theory, but their paper almost didn't get published because none of the reviewers believed the findings! The paper was eventually published after a British researcher replicated the results in his lab. Bacteria experts soon embraced the theory, but most stomach ulcer experts remained sceptical. To further convince the doubters, Marshall ingested the bacteria into his healthy stomach and developed symptoms within a few days. 'It took ten years and there was a lot of opposition,' recalls one expert. '[But Marshall] had this enormous self-belief that what he'd found was right.' Marshall and Warren were recently awarded the Nobel Prize in medicine for their discovery. Fittingly, the Nobel committee acknowledged their 'tenacity and a prepared mind challenging prevailing dogmas'.[57]

A third feature of creative people is that they possess sufficient knowledge of the subject and experience in it.[58] Creativity experts explain that discovering new ideas requires knowledge of the fundamentals. For example, 1960s rock group The Beatles produced most of their songs only after they had played together for several years. They developed extensive experience singing and adapting the music of other people before their creative talents soared.

Although knowledge and experience may be important in one sense, they can also undermine creativity because people develop mental models that lead to 'mindless behaviour', whereby they stop questioning their assumptions.[59] This explains why some corporate leaders like to hire people from other industries and areas of expertise. For instance, Ballard Power Systems founder Geoffrey Ballard hired a chemist to develop a better battery. When the chemist protested that he didn't know anything about batteries, Ballard replied: 'That's fine. I don't want someone who knows batteries. They know what won't work.'[60] Ballard explained that he wanted to hire people who would question and investigate what experts had stopped questioning.

The fourth characteristic of creative people is that they have an inventive thinking style. Creative types are divergent thinkers and risk takers. They are not bothered about making mistakes or working with ambiguous information. They take a broad view of problems, don't like to abide by rules or status, and are unconcerned about social approval of their actions.[61]

Organisational conditions supporting creativity

Hiring creative people is only part of the creativity equation. Corporate leaders also need to maintain a work environment that supports the creative process for everyone.[62] However, as Australian writers have recently warned, it is overly simplistic to identify one best environment in which creativity flourishes. Instead, we need to recognise that creativity emerges through different combinations of processes, mechanisms and structures.[63] With this caveat in mind, here are some of the conditions that seem to encourage creative thinking.

One of the most important conditions is that the organisation has a learning orientation; that is, leaders recognise that employees will make reasonable mistakes as part of the creative process. Motivation from the job itself is another important condition for creativity.[64] Employees tend to be more creative when they believe that their work has a substantial impact on the organisation and/or larger society (i.e. task significance) and when they have the freedom to pursue novel ideas without bureaucratic delays (i.e. autonomy). Creativity is about changing things, and change is possible only when employees have the authority to experiment. More generally, jobs encourage creativity when they are challenging and aligned with the employee's competencies.

Along with supporting a learning orientation and intrinsically motivating jobs, companies foster creativity through open communication and sufficient resources. They provide a reasonable level of job security, which explains why creativity suffers during times of downsizing and corporate restructuring.[65] To some degree, creativity also improves with support from leaders and co-workers. One recent study reported that effective product champions provide enthusiastic support for new ideas. Other studies suggest that co-worker support can improve creativity in some situations, whereas competition among co-workers improves creativity in other situations.[66] Similarly, it isn't clear how much pressure should be exerted on employees to produce creative ideas. Extreme time pressures are well-known creativity inhibitors, but a lack of pressure doesn't seem to produce the highest creativity either.

ACTIVITIES THAT ENCOURAGE CREATIVITY

Along with hiring creative people and giving them a supportive work environment, organisations have introduced numerous activities that attempt to crank up the creative potential. One set of activities encourages employees to redefine the problem. This occurs when old projects that have been set aside are revisited. After a few months of neglect, these projects might be seen in new ways.[67] Another strategy involves asking people unfamiliar with the issue (preferably with different expertise) to explore the problem with you. You would state the objectives and give some facts, then let the other person ask questions to further understand the situation. By verbalising the problem, listening to questions and hearing what others think, you are more likely to gain new perspectives on the issue.[68]

A second set of creativity activities, known as *associative play*, ranges from art classes to impromptu storytelling. Employees at mobile phone company Vodacom and financial institution ABSA have used Lego blocks to build models that mapped out where they wanted their company to go in the future. These South African companies also engaged employees in impromptu storytelling, in which participants randomly contributed to the development of characters and storyline. OMD, the British media giant, gets the creative juices flowing by sending employees to two-day retreats in the countryside where they play grapefruit croquet, chant like medieval monks, and pretend to be dog collars. 'Being creative is a bit like an emotion—we need to be stimulated,' explains Harriet Frost, one of OMD's specialists in building creativity. 'The same is true for our imagination and its ability to come up with new ideas. You can't just sit in a room and devise hundreds of ideas.'[69]

Another associative play activity, called *morphological analysis*, involves listing different dimensions of a system and the elements of each dimension, then looking at each combination. This encourages people to carefully examine combinations that initially seem nonsensical. Tyson Foods, the world's largest poultry producer, applied this activity to identify new ways to serve chicken for lunch. The marketing and research team assigned to this task focused on three categories: occasion, packaging and taste. Next, the team worked through numerous combinations of items in the three categories. This created unusual ideas, such as cheese chicken pasta (taste) in pizza boxes (packaging) for concessions at baseball games (occasion). Later, the team looked more closely at the feasibility of these combinations and sent them to customer focus groups for further testing.[70]

A third set of activities that encourages creativity in organisations is known as *cross-pollination*.[71] Cross-pollination occurs when people from different areas of the organisation exchange ideas. IDEO, the California-based product design company, does this by encouraging employees to consider how features of one product they've worked on might be relevant to another. Cross-pollination also occurs through formal events where employees from different parts of the organisation share their knowledge through presentations.

Cross-pollination highlights the fact that creativity rarely occurs alone. Some creative people may be individualistic, but most creative ideas are generated through teams and informal social interaction. This probably explains why Jonathon Ive, the award-winning designer of Apple Computer products, always refers to his team's creativity rather than his own. 'The only time you'll hear [Jonathan Ive] use the word "I" is when he's naming some of the products he helped make famous: iMac, iBook, iPod,' says one writer.[73] The next chapter introduces the main concepts in team effectiveness. Then, Chapter 10 discusses high-performance teams, including ways to improve team decision making and creativity.

Radically creative

Radical Entertainment, a division of Vivendi Universal Games, pulls out all the stops to support employee creativity. 'Hit games are made by people who have the freedom and support to put unconventional ideas in motion,' explains Ian Wilkinson, founder and CEO of the electronic games developer. 'So, we give our employees the autonomy to drive real change, whatever their role in the company. No other game developer offers this level of creative freedom.' To drive home this creative focus, Wilkinson (third from right in the photo) lunches with a group of employees, listening to their suggestions and reinforcing company values, including 'Take risks, always learn'. Radical also encourages employees to cross-pollinate ideas through a monthly 'game fair' day, in which teams show off their products and make presentations to other employees. The result of this creative environment is a series of game hits, including *The Incredible Hulk* and *The Simpsons: Hit and Run*.[72]

Ron Sangha Photograph Ltd. Used by permission of Radical Entertainment Inc.

CHAPTER SUMMARY

Decision making is a conscious process of making choices among one or more alternatives with the intention of moving towards some desired state of affairs. The rational choice paradigm of decision making includes identifying problems and opportunities, choosing the best decision style, developing alternative solutions, choosing the best solution, implementing the selected alternative, and evaluating the decision outcomes.

Persuasion by stakeholders, perceptual biases and poor diagnostic skills affect our ability to identify problems and opportunities. We can minimise these challenges by being aware of the human limitations and discussing the situation with colleagues.

Evaluating and choosing alternatives is often challenging, because organisational goals are ambiguous or in conflict, human information processing is incomplete and subjective, and people tend to satisfice rather than maximise. Decision makers also short-circuit the evaluation process when faced with an opportunity rather than a problem. Emotions shape our preferences for alternatives and the process we follow to evaluate alternatives. We also listen in to our emotions for guidance when making decisions. This latter activity relates to intuition—the ability to know when a problem or opportunity exists and to select the best course of action without conscious reasoning. Intuition is both an emotional experience and a rapid unconscious analytic process that involves both pattern matching and action scripts.

People generally make better choices by systematically evaluating alternatives. Scenario planning can help to make future decisions without the pressure and emotions that occur during real emergencies.

Post-decisional justification and escalation of commitment make it difficult to evaluate decision outcomes accurately. Escalation is mainly caused by self-justification, the prospect theory effect, perceptual blinders, and closing costs. These problems are minimised by separating decision choosers from decision evaluators, establishing a preset level at which the decision is abandoned or re-evaluated, relying on systematic and clear feedback about the project's success, and involving several people in the decision making.

Employee involvement (or participation) refers to the degree to which employees influence how their work is organised and carried out. The level of participation may range from an employee providing specific information to management without knowing the problem or issue, to complete involvement in all phases of the decision process. Employee involvement may lead to higher decision quality and commitment, but several contingencies need to be considered, including the decision structure, the source of decision knowledge, the decision commitment, and the risk of conflict.

Creativity is the development of original ideas that make a socially recognised contribution. The four creativity stages are preparation, incubation, insight and verification. Incubation assists divergent thinking, which involves reframing the problem in a unique way and generating different approaches to the issue.

Four of the main features of creative people are intelligence, subject-matter knowledge and experience, persistence, and an inventive thinking style. Creativity is also strengthened for everyone when the work environment supports a learning orientation, the job has high intrinsic motivation, the organisation provides a reasonable level of job security, and project leaders provide appropriate goals, time pressure and resources. Three types of activities that encourage creativity are redefining the problem, associative play and cross-pollination.

KEY TERMS

bounded rationality p. 238
creativity p. 246
decision making p. 234
divergent thinking p. 247
employee involvement p. 244

escalation of commitment p. 242
implicit favourite p. 239
intuition p. 240
post-decisional justification p. 241
prospect theory p. 243

rational choice paradigm p. 234
satisficing p. 239
scenario planning p. 241

DISCUSSION QUESTIONS

1. A management consultant is hired by a manufacturing firm to determine the best site for its next production facility. The consultant has had several meetings with the company's senior executives regarding the factors to consider when making the recommendation. Discuss the decision-making problems that might prevent the consultant from choosing the best site location.

2. You have been asked to personally recommend a new travel agency to handle all airfare, accommodation and related travel needs for your organisation of 500 staff. One of your colleagues, who is responsible for the company's economic planning, suggests that the best travel agent could be selected mathematically by inputting the relevant factors for each agency and the weight (importance) of each factor. What decision-making approach is your colleague recommending? Is this recommendation a good idea in this situation? Why or why not?

3. Intuition is both an emotional experience and an unconscious analytic process. One problem, however, is that not all emotions signalling that there is a problem or opportunity represent intuition. Explain how we would know if our 'gut feelings' are intuition or not, and if they are not intuition, suggest what might be causing them.

4. A developer received financial backing for a new business financial centre along a derelict section of the waterfront, a few miles from the current downtown area of a large European city. The idea was to build several high-rise structures, attract large tenants to the sites, and have the city extend transportation systems out to the new centre. Over the next decade the developer believed that others would build in the area, thereby attracting the regional or national offices of many financial institutions. Interest from potential tenants was much lower than initially predicted and the city did not build transportation systems as quickly as expected. Still, the builder proceeded with the original plans. Only after financial support was curtailed did the developer reconsider the project. Using your knowledge of escalation of commitment, discuss three possible reasons why the developer was motivated to continue with the project.

5. Ancient Book Company has a problem with new book projects. Even when others are aware that a book is far behind schedule and may engender little public interest, sponsoring editors are reluctant to terminate contracts with authors that they have signed. The result is that editors invest more time with these projects than on more fruitful projects. As a form of escalation of commitment, describe two methods that Ancient Book Company can use to minimise this problem.

6. Employee involvement applies just as well to the classroom as to the office or factory floor. Explain how student involvement in classroom decisions typically made by the instructor alone might improve decision quality. What potential problems might occur in this process?

7. Think of a time when you experienced the creative process. Maybe you woke up with a brilliant (but usually sketchy and incomplete) idea, or you solved a baffling problem while doing something else. Describe this incident to your class and explain how the experience followed the creative process.

8. Two characteristics of creative people are that they have relevant experience and are persistent in their quest. Does this mean that people with the most experience and the highest need for achievement are the most creative? Explain your answer.

SKILL BUILDER 8.1   EMPLOYEE INVOLVEMENT CASES

CASE STUDY

CASE 1: THE SUGAR SUBSTITUTE RESEARCH DECISION

You are the head of research and development (R&D) for a major beer company. While working on a new beer product, one of the scientists in your unit seems to have tentatively identified a new chemical compound that has few calories but tastes closer to sugar than current sugar substitutes. The company has no foreseeable need for this product, but it could be patented and licensed to manufacturers in the food industry.

The sugar substitute discovery is in its preliminary stages and requires considerable time and resources before it would be commercially viable. This means that it would necessarily take some resources away from other projects in the lab. The sugar substitute project is beyond your technical expertise, but some of the R&D lab researchers are familiar with that field of chemistry. As with most forms of research, it is difficult to determine the amount of research required to further identify and perfect the sugar substitute. You do not know how much demand is expected for this product. Your department has a decision process for funding projects that are behind schedule. However, there are no rules or precedents about funding projects that would be licensed but not used by the organisation.

The company's R&D budget is limited and other scientists in your work group have recently complained that they require more resources and financial support to get their projects completed. Some of these other R&D projects hold promise for future beer sales. You believe that most researchers in the R&D unit are committed to ensuring that the company's goals are achieved.

CASE 2: COAST GUARD CUTTER DECISION PROBLEM

You are the captain of a 72-metre Coast Guard cutter, with a crew of sixteen, including officers. Your mission is general at-sea search and rescue. At 2 am this morning, while en route to your home port after a routine 28-day patrol, you received word from the nearest Coast Guard station that a small plane had crashed 100 kilometres offshore. You obtained all the available information concerning the location of the crash, informed your crew of the mission, and set a new course at maximum speed for the scene to begin a search for survivors and wreckage.

You have now been searching for twenty hours. Your search operation has been increasingly impaired by rough seas, and there is evidence of a severe storm building. The atmospherics associated with the deteriorating weather have made communications with the Coast Guard station impossible. A decision must be made shortly about whether to abandon the search and place your vessel on a course that would ride out the storm (thereby protecting the vessel and the crew, but relegating any possible survivors to almost certain death from exposure) or to continue a potentially futile search and the risks it would entail.

Before losing communications, you received an update weather advisory concerning the severity and duration of the storm. Although the crew members are extremely conscientious about their responsibility, you believe that they would be divided on the decision about whether to leave or to stay.

Source: The New Leadership: Managing Participation in Organizations, V.H. Vroom and A.G. Jago, 1987. Copyright © 1987 V.H. Vroom and A.G Jago. Reprinted by permission of the authors.

QUESTIONS *(for both cases)*

1. To what extent should your subordinates be involved in this decision? Select one of the following levels of involvement:

   • No involvement. You make the decision alone without any participation from subordinates.

   • Low involvement. You ask one or more subordinates for information relating to the problem, but you don't ask for their recommendations and might not mention the problem to them.

   • Medium involvement. You describe the problem to one or more subordinates (alone or in a meeting) and ask for any relevant information as well as their recommendations on the issue. However, you make the final decision, which might or might not reflect their advice.

   • High involvement. You describe the problem to subordinates. They discuss the matter, identify a solution without your involvement (unless they invite your ideas), and implement that solution. You have agreed to support their decision.

2. What factors led you to choose this level of employee involvement rather than the others?

3. What problems might occur if less or more involvement occurred in this case (where possible)?

SKILL BUILDER | 8.2

CLASS EXERCISE

FOR WHAT IT'S WORTH

PURPOSE
This exercise is designed to help you understand issues related to making perfectly rational decisions.

MATERIALS
The instructor will either bring to class or show as a computer image three products. Students will need their student number (or a driver's licence or other piece of numeric identity).

INSTRUCTIONS
Step 1: The instructor will show the three products (or image of the products) to the class and describe the features of each product so students are sufficiently informed of their features and functions. The instructor will *not* provide any information about the price paid for the products or their market value.

Step 2: Working alone, each student will write down at the top of the calculation sheet below the last two digits of his/her student number (or driver's licence or other identification if a student number is not available). Each student will also write down in the left column the name of each product shown by the instructor. Then, each student will circle 'Yes' or 'No' for each product, indicating whether he/she would be willing to pay the dollar equivalent of the two-digit number for each product if looking to purchase such a product.

Step 3: In the right-hand column of the calculation sheet, each student (still working alone) will write down the maximum dollar value they would be willing to pay for each product if they were looking to purchase such a product.

Step 4: After completing their calculations alone, students will be organised into four or five groups as specified by the instructor. Group size is unimportant, but the instructor's criterion for organising teams is very important and must be followed. Each team will calculate the average price that students within that group were willing to pay for each product. The team will also calculate the percentage of people within the group who indicated 'Yes' (were willing to purchase at the stated price) for each product.

Step 5: Each team will report its three average maximum willingness-to-pay prices as well as the percentage of students in the team who indicated 'Yes' for each product. The instructor will outline a concept relevant to rational decision making and how that concept relates to this exercise.

FOR WHAT IT'S WORTH CALCULATION SHEET

Two-digit number: ___ ___

Product name	Willing to pay two-digit number price for this product? (Circle your answer)		Maximum willingness to pay for this product
	NO	YES	$ ___ ___ ___:00
	NO	YES	$ ___ ___ ___:00
	NO	YES	$ ___ ___ ___:00

Source: Based on information in D. Ariely, G. Loewenstein and D. Prelec, "'Coherent Arbitrariness': Stable Demand Curves Without Stable Preferences', *Quarterly Journal of Economics*, February 2003, pp. 73–105.

WHERE IN THE WORLD ARE WE?

PURPOSE

This exercise is designed to help you understand the potential advantages of involving others in decisions rather than making decisions alone.

MATERIALS

Students require an unmarked copy of the map of Asia with grid marks (overleaf). Students are not allowed to look at any other maps or use any other materials. The instructor will provide a list of communities located somewhere on the map. The instructor will also provide copies of the answer sheet after students have individually and in teams estimated the locations of communities.

INSTRUCTIONS

Step 1: Write down in the table below the list of communities identified by your instructor. Then, working alone, estimate the location in the map of these communities, all of which are in Asia. For example, mark a small '1' on the map on the spot where you believe the first community is located. Mark a small '2' where you think the second community is located, and so on. Be sure to number each location clearly and with numbers small enough to fit within one grid space.

Step 2: The instructor will organise students into approximately equal teams (typically five or six people per team). Working with your team members, reach a consensus on the location of each community listed. The instructor might provide teams with a separate copy of the map, or each member can identify the team's numbers using a different coloured pen on their individual maps. The team's decision for each location should occur by consensus, not by voting or averaging.

Step 3: The instructor will provide or display an answer sheet, showing the correct locations of the communities. Using this answer sheet, students will count the minimum number of grid squares between the location they individually marked and the true location of each community. Write the number of grid squares in the second column of the table, then add up the total. Next, count the minimum number of grid squares between the location the team marked and the true location of each community. Write the number of grid squares in the third column, then add up the total.

Step 4: The instructor will ask for information about the totals and the class will discuss the implication of these results for employee involvement and decision making.

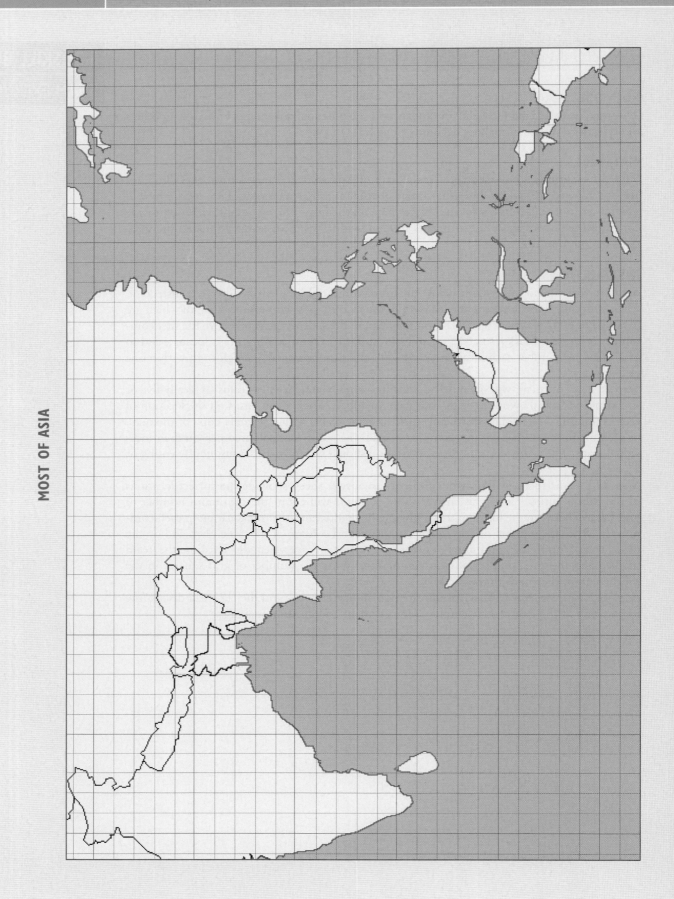

MOST OF ASIA

LIST OF SELECTED COMMUNITIES IN ASIA

Number	Community	Individual distance in grid units from the true location	Team distance in grid units from the true location
1			
2			
3			
4			
5			
6			
7			
8			
		Total	Total

© 2002 Steven L. McShane

WINTER SURVIVAL EXERCISE

8.4 | **SKILL BUILDER**

TEAM EXERCISE

PURPOSE
This exercise is designed to help you understand the potential advantages of involving others in decisions rather than making decisions alone.

INSTRUCTIONS
Step 1: Read the 'Situation' below. Then, working alone, rank-order the twelve items shown in the table below according to their importance to your survival. In the 'Individual ranking' column, indicate the most important item with '1', going through to '12' for the least important. Keep in mind the reasons why each item is or is not important.

Step 2: The instructor will divide the class into small teams (four to six people). Each team will rank-order the items in the second column. Team rankings should be based on consensus, not simply averaging the individual rankings.

Step 3: When the teams have completed their rankings, the instructor will provide the expert's ranking, which can be entered in the third column.

Step 4: Each student will compute the absolute difference (i.e. ignore minus signs) between the individual ranking and the expert's ranking, record this information in column four, and sum the absolute values at the bottom of column four.

Step 5: In column five, record the absolute difference between the team's ranking and the expert's ranking, and sum these absolute scores at the bottom. A class discussion will follow regarding the implications of these results for employee involvement and decision making.

SITUATION
You have just crash-landed somewhere in the woods of southern Manitoba or possibly northern Minnesota. It is 11.32 am in mid-January. The small plane in which you were travelling crashed on a small lake. The pilot and co-pilot were killed. Shortly after the crash, the plane

sank completely into the lake with the pilot's and co-pilot's bodies inside. Everyone else on the flight escaped serious injury and was able to get to dry land before the plane went down and without getting wet.

The crash came suddenly before the pilot had time to radio for help or inform anyone of your position. Since the pilot was trying to avoid a storm, you know that the plane was considerably off course. The pilot announced shortly before the crash that you were 70 kilometres north-west of a small town that is the nearest known habitation.

You are in a wilderness area made up of thick woods broken by many lakes and rivers. The snow depth varies from above the ankles in windswept areas to more than knee-deep where it has drifted. The last weather report indicated that the temperature would reach −10 degrees Celsius in the daytime and −25 degrees at night. There is plenty of dead wood in the area around the lake. You and the other surviving passengers are dressed in winter clothing appropriate for city wear—suits, pantsuits, street shoes and overcoats. While escaping from the plane, your group salvaged the twelve items listed in the chart below. You may assume that the number of persons in the group is the same as the number in your group, and that you have agreed to stay together.

WINTER SURVIVAL TALLY SHEET

Items	Step 1 Your individual ranking	Step 2 Your team's ranking	Step 3 Survival expert's ranking	Step 4 Difference between steps 1 and 3	Step 5 Difference between steps 2 and 3
Ball of steel wool					
Newspapers					
Compass					
Hand axe					
Cigarette lighter					
45-calibre pistol					
Section air map					
Canvas					
Shirt and pants					
Can of shortening (animal fat)					
Whiskey					
Chocolate bars					
			Total		
		The lower the score, the better		**Your score**	**Your team score**

Source: Adapted from 'Winter Survival', in D. Johnson and F. Johnson, *Joining Together*, 3rd edn (Englewood Cliffs, NJ: Prentice Hall, 1984).

CREATIVITY BRAINBUSTERS

PURPOSE

This exercise is designed to help students understand the dynamics of creativity and team problem solving.

INSTRUCTIONS

This exercise may be completed alone or in teams of three or four people. If teams are formed, students who already know the solutions to one or more of these problems should identify themselves and serve as silent observers. When finished (or, more likely, time is up), the instructor will review the solutions and discuss the implications of the exercise. In particular, be prepared to discuss what you needed to solve these puzzles and what may have prevented you from solving them more quickly (or at all).

1. DOUBLE-CIRCLE PROBLEM

Draw two circles, one inside the other, with a single line and with neither circle touching the other (as shown at right). In other words, you must draw both of these circles without lifting your pen (or other writing instrument).

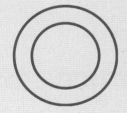

2. NINE-DOT PROBLEM

At right are nine dots. Without lifting your pencil, draw no more than four straight lines that pass through all nine dots.

3. NINE-DOT PROBLEM REVISITED

Referring to the nine-dot diagram above, describe how, without lifting your pencil, you could pass a pencil line through all dots with three or fewer straight lines.

4. WORD SEARCH

In the following line of letters, cross out five letters so that the remaining letters, without altering their sequence, spell a familiar English word.

C F R I V E E L A T E T I T E V R S E

5. BURNING ROPES

You have two pieces of rope of unequal length and a box of matches. In spite of their different lengths, each piece of rope takes one hour to burn; however, parts of each rope burn at unequal speeds. For example, the first half of one piece might burn in ten minutes. Use these materials to accurately determine when forty-five minutes has elapsed.

MEASURING YOUR CREATIVE PERSONALITY

STUDENT CD

PURPOSE

This self-assessment is designed to help you to measure the extent to which you have a creative personality.

INSTRUCTIONS

Listed below is an adjective checklist with thirty words that may or may not describe you. Put a mark in the box beside the words that you think accurately describe you. DO NOT mark the boxes for words that do not describe you. When finished, you can score the test using the scoring key in Appendix B. This exercise is completed alone so students can assess themselves without concerns of social comparison. However, class discussion will focus on how this scale might be applied in organisations, and the limitations of measuring creativity in work settings.

ADJECTIVE CHECKLIST

Affected	❑	Honest	❑	Reflective	❑
Capable	❑	Humorous	❑	Resourceful	❑
Cautious	❑	Individualistic	❑	Self-confident	❑
Clever	❑	Informal	❑	Sexy	❑
Commonplace	❑	Insightful	❑	Sincere	❑
Confident	❑	Intelligent	❑	Snobbish	❑
Conservative	❑	Inventive	❑	Submissive	❑
Conventional	❑	Mannerly	❑	Suspicious	❑
Dissatisfied	❑	Narrow interests	❑	Unconventional	❑
Egotistical	❑	Original	❑	Wide interests	❑

Source: Adapted from and based on information in H. G. Gough and A. B. Heilbrun Jr, *The Adjective Check List Manual* (Palo Alto, CA: Consulting Psychologists Press, 1965).

SKILL BUILDER 8.7   TESTING YOUR CREATIVE BENCH STRENGTH

SELF-ASSESSMENT

FULL EXERCISE ON
STUDENT CD

This self-assessment takes the form of a self-scoring quiz. It consists of twelve questions that require divergent thinking to identify the correct answers. For each question, type in your answer in the space provided. When finished, look at the correct answer for each question, along with the explanation for that answer.

SKILL BUILDER 8.8   DECISION-MAKING STYLE INVENTORY

SELF-ASSESSMENT

FULL EXERCISE ON
STUDENT CD

People have different styles of decision making that are reflected in how they identify problems or opportunities and make choices. This self-assessment estimates your decision-making style through a series of statements describing how individuals go about making important decisions. Indicate whether you agree or disagree with each statement. Answer each item as truthfully as possible so that you get an accurate estimate of your decision-making style. This exercise is completed alone so students can assess themselves honestly without concerns of social comparison. However, class discussion will focus on the decision-making style that people prefer in organisational settings.

NOTES

1   D. Teutsch, 'Designing the Perfect Human', *Sun Herald* (Sydney), 3 October 2004, 69; 'Animated Discussion', *In the Black*, December 2005, 26; 'Stars of Post-Production', *Variety*, 22–28 August 2005, A6; L. Chant, 'Wizard at Work', *Sunday Mail* (Adelaide), 20 November 2005, 1; A. Shea, 'Film', *Qantas Australia Way*, March 2005, 71–2.

2   F. A. Shull Jr, A. L. Delbecq and L. L. Cummings, *Organizational Decision Making* (New York: McGraw-Hill, 1970), 31.

3   M. V. White, 'Jevons in Australia: A Reassessment', *The Economic Record* 58 (1982), 32–45; R. E. Nisbett, *The Geography of Thought: How Asians and Westerners Think Differently—and Why* (New York: Free Press, 2003); D. Baltzly, 'Stoicism' (Stanford Encyclopedia of Philosophy, 2004), http://plato.stanford.edu/entries/stoicism/ (accessed 8 March 2005); R. Hanna, 'Kant's Theory of Judgment' (Stanford Encyclopedia of Philosophy, 2004),

http://plato.stanford.edu/entries/kant-judgment/ (accessed 12 March 2005).

4   This model is adapted from several sources, including: H. A. Simon, *The New Science of Management Decision* (New York: Harper & Row, 1960); H. Mintzberg, D. Raisinghani and A. Théorét, 'The Structure of "Unstructured" Decision Processes', *Administrative Science Quarterly* 21 (1976), 246–75; W. C. Wedley and R. H. G. Field, 'A Predecision Support System', *Academy of Management Review* 9 (1984), 696–703.

5   P. F. Drucker, *The Practice of Management* (New York: Harper & Brothers, 1954), 353–7; B. M. Bass, *Organizational Decision Making* (Homewood, Ill.: Irwin, 1983), chapter 3.

6   L. R. Beach and T. R. Mitchell, 'A Contingency Model for the Selection of Decision Strategies', *Academy of Management Review* 3 (1978), 439–49; I. L. Janis, *Crucial Decisions* (New York: The Free Press, 1989), 35–7; W. Zhongtuo, 'Meta-Decision Making: Concepts and Paradigm', *Systematic Practice and Action Research* 13, no. 1 (February 2000), 111–15.

7   J. G. March and H. A. Simon, *Organizations* (New York: John Wiley & Sons, 1958).

8   N. Schwarz, 'Social Judgment and Attitudes: Warmer, More Social, and Less Conscious', *European Journal of Social Psychology* 30 (2000), 149–76; N. M. Ashkanasy and C. E. J. Hartel, 'Managing Emotions in Decision-Making', in *Managing Emotions in the Workplace*, ed. N. M. Ashkanasy, W. J. Zerbe and C. E. J. Hartel (Armonk, NY: M. E. Sharpe, 2002); S. Maitlis and H. Ozcelik, 'Toxic Decision Processes: A Study of Emotion and Organizational Decision Making', *Organization Science* 15, no. 4 (July–August 2004), 375–93.

9   A. Howard, 'Opinion', *Computing*, 8 July 1999, 18.

10 A. R. Damasio, *Descartes' Error: Emotion, Reason, and the Human Brain* (New York: Putnam Sons, 1994); P. Winkielman and K. C. Berridge, 'Unconscious Emotion', *Current Directions in Psychological Science* 13, no. 3 (2004), 120–3; A. Bechara and A. R. Damasio, 'The Somatic Marker Hypothesis: A Neural Theory of Economic Decision', *Games and Economic Behavior* 52, no. 2 (2005), 336–72.

11 T. K. Das and B. S. Teng, 'Cognitive Biases and Strategic Decision Processes: An Integrative Perspective', *Journal of Management Studies* 36, no. 6 (November 1999), 757–78; P. Bijttebier, H. Vertommen and G. V. Steene, 'Assessment of Cognitive Coping Styles: A Closer Look at Situation-Response Inventories', *Clinical Psychology Review* 21, no. 1 (2001), 85–104; P. C. Nutt, 'Expanding the Search for Alternatives During Strategic Decision-Making', *Academy of Management Executive* 18, no. 4 (November 2004), 13–28.

12 P. C. Nutt, *Why Decisions Fail* (San Francisco, CA: Berrett-Koehler, 2002); S. Finkelstein, *Why Smart Executives Fail* (New York: Viking, 2003).

13 E. Witte, 'Field Research on Complex Decision-Making Processes—the Phase Theorem', *International Studies of Management and Organization* (1972), 156–82; J. A. Bargh and T. L. Chartrand, 'The Unbearable Automaticity of Being', *American Psychologist* 54, no. 7 (July 1999), 462–79.

14 R. Rothenberg, 'Ram Charan: The Thought Leader Interview', *strategy + business* (Fall 2004).

15 H. A. Simon, *Administrative Behavior*, 2nd edn (New York: The Free Press, 1957); H. A. Simon, 'Rational Decision Making in Business Organizations', *American Economic Review* 69, no. 4 (September 1979), 493–513.

16 D. Sandahl and C. Hewes, 'Decision Making at Digital Speed', *Pharmaceutical Executive* 21 (August 2001), 62.

17 Simon, *Administrative Behavior*, xxv, 80–4.

18 P. O. Soelberg, 'Unprogrammed Decision Making', *Industrial Management Review* 8 (1967), 19–29; J. E. Russo, V. H. Medvec and M. G. Meloy, 'The Distortion of Information During Decisions', *Organizational Behavior & Human Decision Processes* 66 (1996), 102–10.

19 A. L. Brownstein, 'Biased Predecision Processing', *Psychological Bulletin* 129, no. 4 (2003), 545–68.

20 F. Phillips, 'The Distortion of Criteria after Decision-Making', *Organizational Behavior and Human Decision Processes* 88 (2002), 769–84.

21 H. A. Simon, 'Rational Choice and the Structure of Environments', *Psychological Review* 63 (1956), 129–38; H. Schwartz, 'Herbert Simon and Behavioral Economics', *Journal of Socio-Economics* 31 (2002), 181–9.

22 P. C. Nutt, 'Search during Decision Making', *European Journal of Operational Research* 160 (2005), 851–76.

23 J. P. Forgas, 'Affective Intelligence: Towards Understanding the Role of Affect in Social Thinking and Behavior', in *Emotional Intelligence in Everyday Life*, ed. J. V. Ciarrochi, J. P. Forgas and J. D. Mayer (New York: Psychology Press, 2001), 46–65; J. P. Forgas and J. M. George, 'Affective Influences on Judgments and Behavior in Organizations: An Information Processing Perspective', *Organizational Behavior and Human Decision Processes* 86 (September 2001), 3–34; G. Loewenstein and J. S. Lerner, 'The Role of Affect in Decision Making', in *Handbook of Affective Sciences*, ed. R. J. Davidson, K. R. Scherer and H. H. Goldsmith (New York: Oxford University Press, 2003), 619–42; J. S. Lerner, D. A. Small and G. Loewenstein, 'Heart Strings and Purse Strings: Carryover Effects of Emotions on Economic Decisions', *Psychological Science* 15, no. 5 (2004), 337–41.

24 M. T. Pham, 'The Logic of Feeling', *Journal of Consumer Psychology* 14 (September 2004), 360–9; N. Schwarz, 'Metacognitive Experiences in Consumer Judgment and Decision Making', *Journal of Consumer Psychology* 14 (September 2004), 332–49.

25 L. Sjöberg, 'Intuitive vs. Analytical Decision Making: Which Is Preferred?', *Scandinavian Journal of Management* 19 (2003), 17–29.

26 G. Klein, *Intuition at Work* (New York: Currency/Doubleday, 2003), 3–7.

27 W. H. Agor, 'The Logic of Intuition', *Organizational Dynamics* (Winter 1986), 5–18; H. A. Simon, 'Making Management Decisions: The Role of Intuition and Emotion', *Academy of Management Executive* (February 1987), 57–64; O. Behling and N. L. Eckel, 'Making Sense out of Intuition', *Academy of Management Executive* 5 (February 1991), 46–54.

28 M. D. Lieberman, 'Intuition: A Social Cognitive Neuroscience Approach', *Psychological Bulletin* 126 (2000), 109–37; Klein, *Intuition at Work*; E. Dane and M. G. Pratt, 'Intuition: Its Boundaries and Role in Organizational Decision-Making', in *Academy of Management Best Papers Proceedings* (New Orleans, 2004), A1–6.

29 Klein, *Intuition at Work*, 12–13, 16–17.

30 Y. Ganzach, A. H. Kluger and N. Klayman, 'Making Decisions from an Interview: Expert Measurement and Mechanical Combination', *Personnel Psychology* 53 (Spring 2000), 1–20; A. M. Hayashi, 'When to Trust Your Gut', *Harvard Business Review* 79 (February 2001), 59–65. Evidence of high failure rates from quick decisions is reported in Nutt, *Why Decisions Fail*, and Nutt, 'Search During Decision Making'.

31 P. Goodwin and G. Wright, 'Enhancing Strategy Evaluation in Scenario Planning: A Role for Decision Analysis', *Journal of Management Studies* 38 (January 2001), 1–16; R. Bradfield et al., 'The Origins and Evolution of Scenario Techniques in Long Range Business Planning', *Futures* 37, no. 8 (2005), 795–812.

32 R. N. Taylor, *Behavioral Decision Making* (Glenview, Ill.: Scott, Foresman, 1984), 163–6.

33 G. Whyte, 'Escalating Commitment to a Course of Action: A Reinterpretation', *Academy of Management Review* 11 (1986), 311–21; J. Brockner, 'The Escalation of Commitment to a Failing Course of Action: Toward Theoretical Progress', *Academy of Management Review* 17, no. 1 (January 1992), 39–61.

34 J. Lorinc, 'Power Failure', *Canadian Business*, November 1992, 50–8; P. Ayton and H. Arkes, 'Call It Quits', *New Scientist* (20 June 1998); M. Fackler, 'Tokyo's Newest Subway Line a Saga of Hubris, Humiliation', *Associated Press Newswires* (20 July 1999); P. Gallagher, 'New Bid to Rein in Rising Costs of Scots Parliament', *Aberdeen Press and Journal* (Scotland), 11 June 2003, 1; I. Swanson, 'Holyrood Firms Face Grilling over Costs', *Evening News* (Edinburgh), 6 June 2003, 2.

35 M. Dixon and I. Howarth, 'Pilbarra Plant to Give BHP World Lead', *Australian Financial Review*, 15 August 1994, 23; P. Armstrong, 'HBI Cost Systems Ran "out of Control"', *West Australian* (Perth), 27 June 1998, 67; M. Weir, 'HBI Wins a Lifeline—for Now', *West Australian* (Perth), 15 December 2000; J. Phaceas, 'BHP Eyes New Roles for Jinxed Boodarie', *West Australian* (Perth), 12 November 2004, 48; 'Dropped Like a Hot Briquette', *Australian Mining*, September 2005, 6.

36 F. D. Schoorman and P. J. Holahan, 'Psychological Antecedents of Escalation Behavior: Effects of Choice, Responsibility, and Decision Consequences', *Journal of Applied Psychology* 81 (1996), 786–93.

37 G. Whyte, 'Escalating Commitment in Individual and Group Decision Making: A Prospect Theory Approach', *Organizational Behavior and Human Decision Processes* 54 (1993), 430–55; D. J. Sharp and S. B. Salter, 'Project Escalation and Sunk Costs: A Test of the International Generalizability of Agency and Prospect Theories', *Journal of International Business Studies* 28, no. 1 (1997), 101–21.

38 J. D. Bragger et al., 'When Success Breeds Failure: History, Hysteresis, and Delayed Exit Decisions', *Journal of Applied Psychology* 88, no. 1 (2003), 6–14. A second logical reason for escalation, called the martingale strategy, is described in J. A. Aloysius, 'Rational Escalation of Costs by Playing a Sequence of Unfavorable Gambles: The Martingale', *Journal of Economic Behavior & Organization* 51 (2003), 111–29.

39 I. Simonson and B. M. Staw, 'De-Escalation Strategies: A Comparison of Techniques for Reducing Commitment to Losing Courses of Action', *Journal of Applied Psychology* 77 (1992), 419–26; W. Boulding, R. Morgan and R. Staelin, 'Pulling the Plug to Stop the New Product Drain', *Journal of Marketing Research*, no. 34 (1997), 164–76; B. M. Staw, K. W. Koput and S. G. Barsade, 'Escalation at the Credit Window: A Longitudinal Study of Bank Executives' Recognition and Write-Off of Problem Loans', *Journal of Applied Psychology*, no. 82 (1997), 130–42; M. Keil and D. Robey, 'Turning around Troubled Software Projects: An Exploratory Study of the De-escalation of Commitment to Failing Courses of Action', *Journal of Management Information Systems* 15 (Spring 1999), 63–87.

40 D. Ghosh, 'De-Escalation Strategies: Some Experimental Evidence', *Behavioral Research in Accounting*, no. 9 (1997), 88–112.

41 M. Fenton-O'Creevy, 'Employee Involvement and the Middle Manager: Saboteur or Scapegoat?', *Human Resource Management Journal*, no. 11 (2001), 24–40. Also see V. H. Vroom and A. G. Jago, *The New Leadership: Managing Participation in Organizations* (Englewood Cliffs, NJ: Prentice Hall, 1988).

42 M. Jacobs, 'RAC's New Home Builds Brand', *WA Business News* (Perth), 29 September 2005; A. Limited, *Annual Report, 2004* (Perth: Alinta Limited, February 2005); M. A. Tan, 'Hewitt Best Employers in Malaysia 2005 Awards', *The Edge Malaysia*, 25 April 2005.

43 S. W. Crispin, 'Workers' Paradise', *Far Eastern Economic Review*, 17 April 2003, 40–1; 'Thai Carbon Black: Worker-Driven Focus Key to Firm's Success', *The Nation* (Thailand), 3 June 2004.

44 Some of the early OB writing on employee involvement includes: C. Argyris, *Personality and Organization* (New York: Harper & Row, 1957); D. McGregor, *The Human Side of Enterprise* (New York: McGraw-Hill, 1960); R. Likert, *New Patterns of Management* (New York: McGraw-Hill, 1961).

45 A. G. Robinson and D. M. Schroeder, *Ideas Are Free* (San Francisco: Berrett-Koehler, 2004).

46 A. Kleingeld, H. Van Tuijl and J. A. Algera, 'Participation in the Design of Performance Management Systems: A Quasi-Experimental Field Study', *Journal of Organizational Behavior* 25, no. 7 (2004), 831–51.

47 K. T. Dirks, L. L. Cummings and J. L. Pierce, 'Psychological Ownership in Organizations: Conditions under Which Individuals Promote and Resist Change', *Research in Organizational Change and Development*, no. 9 (1996), 1–23; J. P. Walsh and S.-F. Tseng, 'The Effects of Job Characteristics on Active Effort at Work', *Work & Occupations*, no. 25 (February 1998), 74–96; B. Scott-Ladd and V. Marshall, 'Participation in Decision Making: A Matter of Context?', *Leadership & Organization Development Journal* 25, no. 8 (2004), 646–62. The quotation is from E. E. Lawler III, *Rewarding Excellence: Pay Strategies for the New Economy* (San Francisco: Jossey-Bass, 2000), 23–4.

48 G. P. Latham, D. C. Winters and E. A. Locke, 'Cognitive and Motivational Effects of Participation: A Mediator Study', *Journal of Organizational Behavior*, no. 15 (1994), 49–63; J. A. Wagner III et al., 'Cognitive and Motivational Frameworks in US Research on Participation: A Meta-Analysis of Primary Effects', *Journal of Organizational Behavior*, no. 18 (1997), 49–65.

49 Y. Utsunomiya, 'Yamato Continues to Deliver New Ideas', *Japan Times*, 8 July 2003; 'Yamato Transport Co., Ltd—SWOT Analysis', *Datamonitor Company Profiles*, 7 July 2004.

50 J. Zhou and C. E. Shalley, 'Research on Employee Creativity: A Critical Review and Directions for Future Research', *Research in Personnel and Human Resources Management* 22 (2003), 165–217; M. A. Runco, 'Creativity', *Annual Review of Psychology* 55 (2004), 657–87.

51 B. Kabanoff and J. R. Rossiter, 'Recent Developments in Applied Creativity', *International Review of Industrial and Organizational Psychology*, no. 9 (1994), 283–324.

52 R. S. Nickerson, 'Enhancing Creativity', in *Handbook of Creativity*, ed. R. J. Sternberg (New York: Cambridge University Press, 1999), 392–430.

53 R. I. Sutton, *Weird Ideas That Work* (New York: Free Press, 2002), 26.

54 For a thorough discussion of insight, see R. J. Sternberg and J. E. Davidson, *The Nature of Insight* (Cambridge, MA: MIT Press, 1995).

55 R. J. Sternberg and L. A. O' Hara, 'Creativity and Intelligence', in *Handbook of Creativity*, ed. R. J. Sternberg (New York: Cambridge University Press, 1999), 251–72; S. Taggar, 'Individual Creativity and Group Ability to Utilize Individual Creative Resources: A Multilevel Model', *Academy of Management Journal* 45 (April 2002), 315–30.

56 G. J. Feist, 'The Influence of Personality on Artistic and Scientific Creativity', in *Handbook of Creativity*, ed. R. J. Sternberg (New York: Cambridge University Press, 1999), 273–96; Sutton, *Weird Ideas That Work*, 8–9, chapter 10.

57 V. Laurie, 'Gut Instinct', *The Australian Magazine*, 10 December 2005, 1; J. Robotham, 'Of Guts and Glory', *Sydney Morning Herald*, 5 October 2005, 16; M. Irving, 'Nobel Deeds, Words of Praise', *West Australian* (Perth), 14 January 2006, 4. Some facts are also found in Robin Warren's 2005 Nobel lecture. See J. Robin Warren, 'Nobel Lecture: The Ease and Difficulty of a New Discovery', RealVideo presentation at: http://nobelprize.org/medicine/laureates/2005/warren-lecture.html

58 R. W. Weisberg, 'Creativity and Knowledge: A Challenge to Theories', in *Handbook of Creativity*, ed. R. J. Sternberg (New York: Cambridge University Press, 1999), 226–50.

59 Sutton, *Weird Ideas That Work*, 121, 153–4; C. Andriopoulos, 'Six Paradoxes in Managing Creativity: An Embracing Act', *Long Range Planning* 36 (2003), 375–88.

60 T. Koppell, *Powering the Future* (New York: Wiley, 1999), 15.

61 D. K. Simonton, 'Creativity: Cognitive, Personal, Developmental, and Social Aspects', *American Psychologist* 55 (January 2000), 151–8.

62 M. D. Mumford, 'Managing Creative People: Strategies and Tactics for Innovation', *Human Resource Management Review* 10 (Autumn 2000), 313–51; T. M. Amabile et al., 'Leader Behaviors and the Work Environment for Creativity: Perceived Leader Support', *The Leadership Quarterly* 15, no. 1 (2004), 5–32; C. E. Shalley, J. Zhou and G. R. Oldham, 'The Effects of Personal and Contextual Characteristics on Creativity: Where Should We Go from Here?', *Journal of Management* 30, no. 6 (2004), 933–58.

63 R. Westwood and D. R. Low, 'The Multicultural Muse: Culture, Creativity and Innovation', *International Journal of Cross Cultural Management* 3, no. 2 (2003), 235–59.

64 T. M. Amabile, 'Motivating Creativity in Organizations: On Doing What You Love and Loving What You Do', *California Management Review* 40 (Fall 1997), 39–58; A. Cummings and G. R. Oldham, 'Enhancing Creativity: Managing Work Contexts for the High Potential Employee', *California Management Review*, no. 40 (Fall 1997), 22–38.

65 T. M. Amabile, 'Changes in the Work Environment for Creativity During Downsizing', *Academy of Management Journal* 42 (December 1999), 630–40.

66 J. M. Howell and K. Boies, 'Champions of Technological Innovation: The Influence of Contextual Knowledge, Role Orientation, Idea Generation, and Idea Promotion on Champion Emergence', *The Leadership Quarterly* 15, no. 1 (2004), 123–43; Shalley, Zhou and Oldham, 'The Effects of Personal and Contextual Characteristics on Creativity'.

67 A. Hiam, 'Obstacles to Creativity—and How You Can Remove Them', *Futurist* 32 (October 1998), 30–4.

68 M. A. West, *Developing Creativity in Organizations* (Leicester, UK: BPS Books, 1997), 33–5.

69 S. Hemsley, 'Seeking the Source of Innovation', *Media Week*, 16 August 2005, 22; S. Planting, 'When You Need to Get Serious, Get Playful', *Financial Mail* (South Africa), 4 February 2005, 14.

70 J. Neff, 'At Eureka Ranch, Execs Doff Wing Tips, Fire up Ideas', *Advertising Age*, 9 March 1998, 28–9.

71 A. Hargadon and R. I. Sutton, 'Building an Innovation Factory', *Harvard Business Review* 78 (May–June 2000), 157–66; T. Kelley, *The Art of Innovation* (New York: Currency Doubleday, 2001), 158–62.

72 P. Withers, 'Few Rules Rule', *B. C. Business*, January 2002, 24; G. Huston, I. Wilkinson and D. Kellogg, 'Dare to Be Great', *B.C. Business*, May 2004, 28–9; P. Withers and L. Kloet, 'The Best Companies to Work for in B.C.', *B.C. Business*, December 2004, 37–53.

73 K. S. Brown, 'The Apple of Jonathan Ive's Eye', *Investor's Business Daily*, 19 September 2003.

CHAPTER 9

Foundations of team dynamics

LEARNING OBJECTIVES

After reading this chapter, you should be able to:

- define teams
- distinguish teams from informal groups
- outline the model of team effectiveness
- identify six organisational and team environmental elements that influence team effectiveness
- explain the influence on team effectiveness of the team's task, composition and size
- describe the five stages of team development
- identify three factors that shape team norms
- list six factors that influence team cohesiveness
- discuss the limitations of teams
- explain how companies minimise social loafing.

GM Holden relies on teamwork to design and manufacture new products, as well as concept cars such as the Efijy shown here.

G M Holden's global reputation for design is soaring, thanks to the innovation and productivity of its forward-thinking design teams. The Australian car-maker's capabilities came to the fore in the late 1990s when eight designers from the Commodore VT project secretly worked on a souped-up coupe version, the Monaro. 'It had to stay quiet,' said Michael Simcoe, who led the clandestine Monaro 'skunkworks' group. 'It wasn't an official Holden project and management hadn't asked us to produce a coupe. It was all after-hours work; people stayed on at the office instead of going straight home at night and they even came in on weekends to make it happen.'

The project was so secret that the lounge-room wall at one team member's home was used to complete the first full-size line drawings. Holden executives were told about the Monaro project just five months before the Sydney Auto Show. With formal approval, the team scrambled to build the demonstrator model, which quickly grabbed world attention and resulted in more than 45 000 global sales over the Monaro's four-year life span.

'[The Monaro] freed up the minds of people at Holden,' says Simcoe, who is now head of new car design at General Motors headquarters in Detroit. 'The effect has been that the public perceives Holden as a leader, and has been good for the company's credibility here and overseas.'

Indeed, Holden encouraged design teams to debut stunning new vehicles at every Australian car show in the following years. Some designs subsequently went into production, such as the S3X, a four-wheel drive SUV engineered jointly with GM Daewoo's design crew. Others, such as the funky retro Efijy, were purely concept cars that allowed design teams to push the limits of their creative spirit.

The Monaro skunkworks project also catapulted GM Holden into the parent company's global design arena. Holden design and engineering teams are now responsible for developing one of GM's latest global vehicle platforms. The company has also installed 'groundbreaking' computer technology, allowing Holden designers and engineers to work on virtual teams with other GM specialists around the world. For example, Holden's VE Commodore team members participate in virtual teams with counterparts in Detroit to maintain global compatibility of parts and engineering standards. Similarly, a virtual team of Holden and Daewoo employees created the S3X four-wheel drive SUV. 'The production version of [the S3X] will represent a true collaboration between various parts of General Motors operations in the Asia–Pacific region,' Holden managing director Denny Mooney recently proclaimed.[1]

GM HOLDEN DOESN'T RELY on the creativity of individuals working alone to design next-generation vehicles; it requires teamwork to complete the daunting work of combining style, engineering and efficient product design. Organisations ultimately consist of individuals, but corporate leaders are discovering that people working alone usually lack sufficient knowledge or capacity to achieve organisational objectives. SANS Fibres, the South African manufacturer of synthetic fibre and polyester polymers, relies on the team approach to eliminate waste, maximise manufacturing flow, minimise inventories, and meet customer requirements. Cadbury Schweppes counts on dedicated teams for innovation in Australia and New Zealand. 'We operate cross-functional category teams,' explains Mark Smith, managing director of the confectionery company. 'Our R&D teams are directly linked to our commercial teams, and participate in all aspects of our growth agenda.' And teamwork is so important at FedEx Singapore that the US-based courier company recently launched a television commercial on the island-state highlighting how teams solve the most difficult problems to get packages delivered on time.[2]

This chapter looks at the complex conditions that make teams more or less effective in organisational settings. The chapter begins by explaining why people join informal groups and why organisations rely on teams. Most of the chapter examines each part of this model, including team and organisational environment, team design, and the team processes of development, norms, roles and cohesiveness.

TEAMS AND GROUPS

teams Groups of two or more people who interact with and influence each other, are mutually accountable for achieving common objectives, and perceive themselves as a social entity within an organisation.

LEARNING OBJECTIVE

Define teams.

Teams are groups of two or more people who interact with and influence each other, are mutually accountable for achieving common goals associated with organisational objectives, and perceive themselves as a social entity within an organisation.[3] All teams exist to fulfil some purpose, such as assembling a product, providing a service, designing a new manufacturing facility, or making an important decision. Team members are held together by their interdependence and need for collaboration to achieve common goals. All teams require some form of communication so members can coordinate and share common objectives. Team members also influence each other, although some members are more influential than others regarding the team's goals and activities.

Exhibit 9.1 briefly describes various types of (usually) formal work teams in organisations. Notice that some teams are permanent, while others are temporary. Some are involved in making products or providing services, while others exist to make decisions or share knowledge. Each of these types of teams has been created deliberately to serve an organisational purpose. Some teams, such as the secret Monaro 'skunkworks' group, are not initially sanctioned by management, yet are called 'teams' because members clearly work towards an organisation objective.

groups People with a unifying relationship.

LEARNING OBJECTIVE

Distinguish teams from informal groups.

All teams are **groups** because they consist of people with a unifying relationship. But not all groups are teams; some groups are just people assembled together without any necessary interdependence or organisationally focused objective. Along with formal work teams, organisations consist of *informal groups*. Informal groups are not initiated by the organisation and usually do not perform organisational goals (thus they are 'informal'). Instead, they exist primarily for the benefit of their members. The groups you meet with for lunch and chat with in the hallway are informal groups. In each case, you associate with these groups for your own benefit.

WHY RELY ON TEAMS?

GM Holden, Cadbury Schweppes, Fedex Singapore and many other organisations have put a lot of energy into transforming their organisations into team-based structures. In fact, one major survey of human resource professionals concluded: 'Teams are now an integral part of

Several types of formal teams in organisations

EXHIBIT 9.1

Team type	Description
Departmental teams	Employees have similar or complementary skills located in the same unit of a functional structure; there is usually minimal task interdependence because each person works with employees in other departments.
Production/ service/ leadership teams	Typically multiskilled (employees have diverse competencies), team members collectively produce a common product/service or make ongoing decisions; production/service teams typically have an assembly line type of interdependence, whereas leadership teams tend to have tight interactive (reciprocal) interdependence.
Self-directed work teams	These are similar to production/service teams except that (1) they produce an entire product or subassembly that has low interdependence with other work units, and (2) they have very high autonomy (no supervisors) and usually control inputs, flow and outputs.
Advisory teams	These entities provide recommendations to decision makers (e.g. committees, advisory councils, work councils and review panels); they may be temporary but are often permanent, some with frequent rotation of members.
Task force (project) teams	The assignment of these usually multiskilled, temporary entities is to solve a problem, realise an opportunity, or develop a product or service.
Skunkworks	Skunkworks are multiskilled entities that are usually located away from the organisation and are relatively free of its hierarchy; these teams are often initiated by an entrepreneurial team leader (innovation champion) who borrows people and resources (bootlegging) to create a product or develop a service.
Virtual teams	These are formal teams whose members operate across space, time and organisational boundaries and are linked through information technologies to achieve organisational tasks; they may be a temporary task force or a permanent service team.
Communities of practice	These may be formally designed, but are usually informal groups bound together by shared expertise and passion for a particular activity or interest; they are often similar to virtual teams in that many rely on information technologies as the main source of interaction, but their purpose is to share information, not make a product or provide a service.

workplace management.' Why all the fuss about teams? The answer to this question has a long history, dating back to research on British coal mining in the 1940s and the Japanese economic miracle of the 1970s.[4] These early studies revealed that, under the right conditions, teams make better decisions, develop products and services, and create a more energised workforce compared with employees working alone. 'I always remind people that team achievements, not individual ones, count most in a company like Nokia,' says Bruce Lam, who oversees Nokia's mobile phone operations in Hong Kong and Macau.[5]

As a form of employee involvement, teams are generally more successful than individuals working alone at identifying problems, developing alternatives and choosing from those alternatives. For instance, GM Holden's design teams consist of experts from various disciplines who collectively produce more innovative and cutting-edge vehicles than an individual working alone. Similarly, team members can quickly share information and coordinate tasks, whereas these processes are slower and prone to more errors in traditional departments led by supervisors. Teams typically provide superior customer service because they provide more breadth of knowledge and expertise to customers than individual 'stars' can offer.

Wall Street discovers the benefits of teamwork

A few years ago, Paul Tramontano was typical of most Wall Street advisors in single-handedly providing advice to hundreds of clients. Not any more. The Smith Barney financial consultant realised that clients needed a wider variety of services than any one person could deliver, so he and two other partners formed an eleven-person team, including technical specialists, to complement his own focus on financial, estate planning and advisory business. 'That's why I think the team approach is the model for what this industry will look like,' says Tramontano. In fact, teams have become the rage throughout the investment industry. Nearly 40 per cent of Smith Barney advisors are now assigned to teams. Merrill Lynch has organised over half of its financial advisors into 3000 teams. When Mark Mobius, who oversees emerging-market investments at Templeton Asset in Singapore, was asked whether individual fund managers are the real 'brands' for a mutual fund, Mobius quickly replied: 'The funds are actually run by teams of people and do not depend on one person.'[6]

Paul Thomas/Getty Images

In many situations, individuals are potentially more energised or engaged when working in teams. People have a drive to bond and are motivated to fulfil the goals of groups to which they belong. For instance, one study reported that employees had a stronger sense of belongingness when they worked in teams rather than alone.[7] Another consideration is that people potentially have higher motivation to complete complex tasks in a team because the effort-to-performance expectancy would be much lower if performing the entire task alone.

WHY PEOPLE BELONG TO INFORMAL GROUPS

Employees are not required to join informal groups, yet they exist throughout organisations. One reason is that human beings are social animals. Experts suggest that our drive to bond is hardwired evolutionary development, which includes the drive to belong to informal groups.[8] This is evident from the fact that people invest considerable time and effort forming and maintaining social relationships without any special circumstances or ulterior motives. A second explanation is provided by social identity theory, which states that individuals define themselves by their group affiliations. Thus, we join informal groups—particularly groups viewed favourably by others and that are similar to our existing values—because they shape and reinforce our self-image.[9]

A third reason that people join informal groups is that they accomplish tasks that cannot be achieved by individuals working alone. For example, employees will sometimes form a group to oppose organisational changes, because the group collectively has more power than individuals complaining alone. A fourth explanation for informal groups is that in stressful situations we are comforted by the mere presence of other people and are therefore motivated to be near them. When in danger, people congregate near each other even though it serves no apparent purpose. Similarly, employees tend to mingle more often when hearing rumours that the company might be sold.[10]

A MODEL OF TEAM EFFECTIVENESS

You might have noticed that the earlier discussion hedged the glorification of teams by saying that they are 'potentially' better than individuals 'under the right conditions'. The reason for this cautious writing is that many organisations have introduced team structures that later became spectacular failures. Why are some teams effective while others fail? This question has challenged organisational researchers for some time and, as you might expect, numerous models of team effectiveness have been proposed over the years.[11]

Let's begin by clarifying the meaning of **team effectiveness**. Team effectiveness refers to how the team affects the organisation, individual team members, and the team's existence.[12] First, most teams exist to serve some purpose relating to the organisation or other system in which the group operates. Some informal groups also have task-oriented (although not organisationally mandated) goals, such as sharing information in an informal community of practice.

Second, team effectiveness relies on the satisfaction and well-being of its members. People join groups to fulfil their personal needs, so effectiveness is partly measured by this need fulfilment. Finally, team effectiveness includes the team's viability—its ability to survive. It must be able to maintain the commitment of its members, particularly during the turbulence of the team's development. Without this commitment, people leave and the team will fall apart. It must also secure sufficient resources and find a benevolent environment in which to operate.

Exhibit 9.2 presents the model of team effectiveness that will be examined closely in the rest of this chapter. The discussion begins by looking at elements of the team's and the organisation's environment that influence team design, processes and outcomes.

LEARNING OBJECTIVE
Outline the model of team effectiveness.

team effectiveness The extent to which a team achieves its objectives, achieves the needs and objectives of its members and sustains itself over time.

Model of team effectiveness

EXHIBIT 9.2

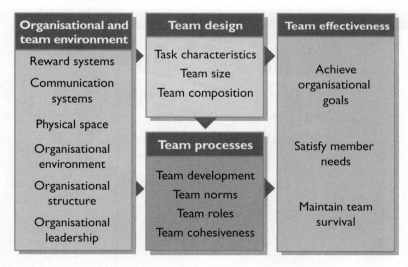

ORGANISATIONAL AND TEAM ENVIRONMENT

Our discussion of team effectiveness logically begins with the contextual factors that influence the team's design, processes and outcomes.[13] There are many elements in the organisational and team environment that influence team effectiveness. Six of the most important elements are reward systems, communication systems, physical space, organisational environment, organisational structure and organisational leadership.

LEARNING OBJECTIVE
Identify six organisational and team environmental elements that influence team effectiveness.

- *Reward systems.* Team members tend to work together more effectively when they are at least partly rewarded for team performance.[14] This doesn't mean that everyone on the team should receive the same amount of pay based on the team's performance. On the contrary, research indicates that employees in Australia, New Zealand and other Western cultures work better in teams when their rewards are based on a combination of individual and team performance.

- *Communication systems.* A poorly designed communication system can starve a team of valuable information and feedback, or it may swamp it with information overload. As will be seen in the next chapter, communication systems are particularly important when team members are geographically dispersed. This critical factor explains why, as the opening story to this chapter mentioned, GM Holden invested heavily in information technology for its Australian designers when working with team members located in other countries.

- *Physical space.* The layout of an office or manufacturing facility does more than improve communication among team members. It also shapes employee perceptions about being together as a team and influences the team's ability to accomplish tasks. For instance, Medibank executives say that teamwork improved dramatically when the Melbourne-based health insurer moved employees from several headquarters buildings and 150 offices into a single headquarters building and just fourteen offices.[15] Toyota also relies on physical space to create a team environment. The Japanese car-maker puts everyone involved in product design in a large room (called an *obeya*) so they have a sense of being a team and can communicate more quickly and effectively.

- *Organisational environment.* Team success depends on the company's external environment. If the organisation cannot secure resources, for instance, the team cannot fulfil its performance targets. Similarly, high demand for the team's output creates feelings of success, which motivates team members to stay with the team. A competitive environment can motivate employees to work together more closely.

Toyota's *obeya* improves team dynamics

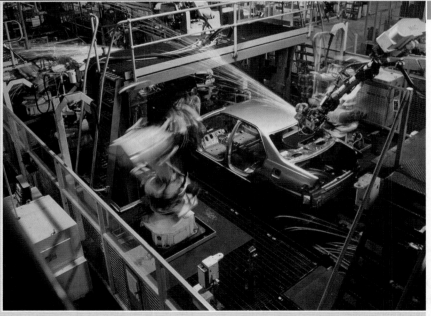

As with most car-makers, Toyota relies on engineers, design stylists, suppliers, assembly workers and marketing people to help design new vehicles. But rather than have these people meet every week to identify and assess new product features, Toyota moves these three dozen people out of their departments and into one big room as a team. About the size of a basketball court, the *obeya* (Japanese for 'big room') arrangement has cut Toyota's product development time and costs by 25 and 50 per cent respectively. 'The reason *obeya* works so well is that it's all about immediate face-to-face human contact,' explains Atsushi Niimi, president of Toyota Motor Manufacturing North America. Max Gillard, who oversees Toyota's *obeya* in Melbourne, Australia, adds that everyone in the *obeya* can hear conversations between a few people, which encourages others to join the discussion. 'There is a hubbub,' says Gillard. 'You can go there and feel the excitement of the place. It is not like an office environment where people sit quietly tapping away at their computers.'[16]

Toyota Motor Corporation Australia Ltd

- *Organisational structure*. Many teams fail because the organisational structure does not support them. Teams work better when there are few layers of management and teams are given autonomy and responsibility for their work. This structure encourages interaction with team members rather than with supervisors. Teams also flourish when employees are organised around work processes rather than specialised skills. This structure increases interaction among team members.[17]
- *Organisational leadership*. Teams require ongoing support from senior executives to align rewards, organisational structure, communication systems and other elements of team context. They also require team leaders or facilitators who provide coaching and support. Team leaders are also enablers, meaning that they ensure that teams have the authority to solve their own problems and resources to accomplish their tasks.[18] Leaders also maintain a value system that supports team performance more than individual success.

TEAM DESIGN FEATURES

There are several elements to consider when designing an effective team. Three of the main design elements are task characteristics, team size and team composition. As seen earlier in the team effectiveness model (Exhibit 9.2), these design features influence team effectiveness directly as well as indirectly through team processes, described later.

LEARNING OBJECTIVE

Explain the influence on team effectiveness of the team's task, composition and size.

TASK CHARACTERISTICS

More than a decade ago, Varian Australia introduced continuous improvement process (CIP) teams to assist productivity improvement. A recent evaluation found that while CIP teams reduced the product development cycle by up to 50 per cent, most fell apart after a few years. One of the main problems, the company discovered, was that many CIP teams ran out of ways to improve productivity. Others gave up because they were assigned projects beyond their capability.[19]

This incident at Varian Australia reveals that whether teams flourish or fail is partly determined by their assigned tasks or goals. However, organisational behaviour experts are still figuring out the best types of work for teams.[20] As Varian Australia learnt, tasks must be within the team's skill set. Some research also says that teams are more effective when their tasks are well-structured, because the clear structure makes it easier to coordinate work among several people. At the same time, other studies indicate that teams flourish more on complex tasks because the complexity motivates them to work together as a team. The difficulty here is that, while task structure and task complexity aren't opposites, it can be difficult to find complex work that is well structured.

Task interdependence

One task characteristic that is definitely important for teams is **task interdependence**—the extent to which team members must share common inputs to their individual tasks, need to interact in the process of executing their work, or receive outcomes (such as rewards) that are partly determined by the performance of others.[21] The higher the level of task interdependence, the greater the need for teams rather than individuals working alone.

task interdependence The degree to which a task requires employees to share common inputs or outcomes, or requires them to interact in the process of executing their work.

Teams are well suited to highly interdependent tasks, because people coordinate better when working together than when working separately. Employees tend to be motivated and more satisfied working on teams when their tasks are highly interdependent. However, this motivation and satisfaction occurs only when team members have the same job goals, such as serving the same clients or collectively assembling the same product. In contrast, frustration is more likely to occur when each team member has unique goals (such as serving different clients) but must depend on other team members (high task interdependence) to achieve those unique goals.[22] The solution here is to ensure that task interdependence is highest when team members share the same goals and is minimised when employees are working towards different goals.

| **EXHIBIT 9.3** | **Levels of task interdependence** |

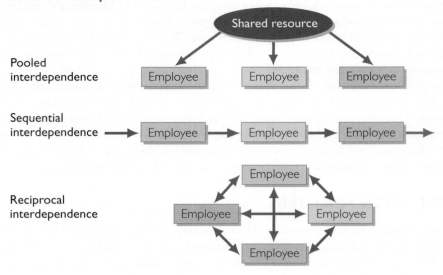

Exhibit 9.3 illustrates three levels of task interdependence.[23] Pooled interdependence is the lowest level of interdependence (other than independence), in which individuals operate independently except for reliance on a common resource or authority. Employees share a common payroll, cafeteria and other organisational resources. In most cases, they will work well alone rather than in teams if pooled interdependence is the highest relationship among them.

Sequential interdependence occurs where the output of one person becomes the direct input for another person or unit. This interdependent linkage is found in most assembly lines. Although employees in the production line process usually work alone, they are sufficiently interdependent that Toyota and other companies create teams around these processes. Reciprocal interdependence represents the highest level of interdependence, in which work output is exchanged back and forth among individuals. Employees with reciprocal interdependence should almost always be organised into teams to facilitate coordination in their interwoven relationship.

TEAM SIZE

Jim Hassell is a strong believer in teamwork, but the managing director of Sun Microsystems in Australia and New Zealand also recognises that putting together the best team requires careful consideration of the optimal size. '[A] big challenge in building a team is getting the number of people in the team right. You need to have a balance between having enough people to do all the things that need to be done, while keeping the team small enough so that it is cohesive and can make decisions effectively and speedily.'[24]

Team size is an important concern for Jim Hassell and other executives. Some writers claim that a team should consist of no more than ten people, but the optimal team size really depends on several factors, such as the number of people required to complete the work and the amount of coordination needed to work together. As Hassell described, the general rule is that teams should be large enough to provide the necessary competencies and perspectives to perform the work, yet small enough to maintain efficient coordination and the meaningful involvement of each member.[25]

Larger teams are typically less effective because members consume more time and effort coordinating their roles and resolving differences. For instance, some of the continuous improvement process teams at Varian Australia (described earlier) suffered because they had more than a dozen members, making it difficult to reach agreement on ideas. In these larger teams, individuals have less opportunity to participate and consequently are less likely to feel that they are contributing to the team's success. Larger work units tend to break into informal subgroups around common interests and work activities, leading members to form stronger commitments to their subgroup than to the larger team.

TEAM COMPOSITION

When Hewlett-Packard Co. (H-P) hires new talent, it doesn't just look for technical skills and knowledge. The high-tech computer manufacturer looks for job applicants who fit into a team environment. 'It's important for candidates to prove to us that they can work well with others,' explains business-development manager Bill Avey. 'We're looking for people who value the different perspectives that each individual brings to a team.' Avey describes how H-P recruiters will ask applicants to recall a time they worked in a group to solve a problem. 'Successful candidates tend to show how they got differences out in the open and reached a resolution as a team,' says Avey.[26]

Hewlett-Packard has a strong team orientation, so it carefully selects people with the necessary motivation and competencies for teamwork. Teams require members who are motivated to remain team members. In particular, they must be motivated to work together rather than alone, abide by the team's rules of conduct, and buy in to the team's goals. Employees with a strong collectivist orientation—those who value group goals more than their own personal goals—tend to perform better in work teams.[27] Effective team members also possess valuable skills and knowledge for the team's objectives, and are able to work well with others. Notably, research suggests that high-performing team members demonstrate more cooperative behaviour towards others and generally have more emotional intelligence.[28]

Team diversity

Another important dimension of team composition is the diversity of team members.[29] **Homogeneous teams** include members with common technical expertise, demographics (age, sex), ethnicity, experiences or values, whereas **heterogeneous teams** have members with diverse personal characteristics and backgrounds. Some forms of diversity are apparent on the surface, such as differences in sex and race. Deep-level diversity, on the other hand, refers to differences in the personalities, values, attitudes and other psychological characteristics of team members. Surface-level diversity is apparent as soon as the team forms, whereas deep-level diversity emerges over time as team members discover each other's values and beliefs.[30]

Should teams be homogeneous or heterogeneous? Both have advantages and disadvantages, and their relative effectiveness depends on the situation.[32] Heterogeneous teams experience more conflict and take longer to develop. They are susceptible to 'faultlines'—hypothetical dividing lines that may split a team into subgroups along gender, ethnic, professional or other dimensions. Teams with strong faultlines—such as where team members fall into two or more distinct demographic groups—have a higher risk of dysfunctional conflict and other behaviours that undermine team effectiveness. Under these circumstances, leaders need to restructure the work to minimise interaction among these subgroups.[33] In contrast, members of homogeneous teams experience higher satisfaction, less conflict and better interpersonal relations. Consequently, homogeneous teams tend to be more effective on tasks requiring a high degree of cooperation and coordination, such as emergency response teams.

Although heterogeneous teams have their difficulties, they are generally more effective than homogeneous teams in executive groups and in other situations involving complex problems requiring innovative solutions. One reason is that people from different backgrounds see a problem or an opportunity from different perspectives. A second reason is that they usually have a broader knowledge base. For example, GM Holden design teams (described in the opening story) are necessarily composed of a diverse group of people who have deep knowledge in several fields, ranging from engine design to upholstery materials. Without these heterogeneous characteristics, the teams would be much less effective in their assigned tasks.

homogeneous teams
Teams that include members with common technical expertise, demographics (age, gender), ethnicity, experiences or values.

heterogeneous teams
Teams that include members with diverse personal characteristics and backgrounds.

Team diversity in Shell's Gourami Business Challenge

Shell discovered long ago that it isn't easy to measure team competencies in a job interview. Instead, the global energy company launched the Shell Gourami Business Challenge, a five-day event in which four dozen engineering and business university students are split into several teams (exploration, refining, finance, marketing, etc.) and must develop and present a five-year business strategy for Shell in the fictitious nation of Gourami. Introduced in Europe a decade ago, the first Asian version of the Gourami game was recently held at Langkawi, Malaysia, and included students from Australia, China, Egypt, Korea, Malaysia, the Philippines and Singapore. Participants first attended a cultural sensitivity briefing, but the effects of team diversity were still apparent when the game began. One Filipino student felt some initial tension because the Australians were 'more straightforward and tell you right

Shell International Ltd

away if you're doing something right or wrong'. A Singaporean participant explained how she actively pushed her team one day, then took more of a back seat the following day. 'I didn't want to appear too bossy. It's about group effort.' An Australian participant said the Gourami game made him realise how diversity affects the team's development and performance. 'I learnt how cultural aspects can affect the way a team works together, and how to handle working with an international group.'[31]

A third reason why heterogeneous teams are generally more effective than homogeneous teams is that the diversity provides representation to the team's constituents, such as other departments or clients from similarly diverse backgrounds. When a team represents various professions or departments, those constituents are more likely to accept and support the team's decisions and actions.

TEAM PROCESSES

Two sets of elements in the team effectiveness model have been looked at so far: (1) organisational and team environment, and (2) team design. The next few pages will discuss the third set of team effectiveness elements, collectively known as team processes. These processes—team development, norms, roles and cohesiveness—are influenced by both team design and organisational and team environment factors.

TEAM DEVELOPMENT

A few years ago the National Transportation Safety Board (NTSB) in the United States studied the circumstances under which aeroplane cockpit crews were most likely to have accidents

LEARNING OBJECTIVE

Describe the five stages of team development.

and related problems. What they discovered was startling: 73 per cent of all incidents took place on the crew's first day, and 44 per cent occurred on the crew's very first flight together. This isn't an isolated example. NASA studied the fatigue of pilots after they returned from multiple-day trips. Fatigued pilots made more errors in the NASA flight simulator, as one would expect. But the NASA researchers didn't expect the discovery that fatigued crews who had worked together made fewer errors than did rested crews who had not yet flown together.[34]

The NTSB and NASA studies reveal that team members must resolve several issues and pass through several stages of development before emerging as an effective work unit. They must get to know each other, understand their respective roles, discover appropriate and inappropriate behaviours, and learn how to coordinate their work or social activities. The longer that team members work together, the better they develop common mental models, mutual understanding, and effective performance routines to complete the work.

The five-stage model of team development, shown in Exhibit 9.4, provides a general outline of how teams evolve by forming, storming, norming, performing and eventually adjourning.[35] The model shows teams progressing from one stage to the next in an orderly fashion, but the dashed lines illustrate that they might also fall back to an earlier stage of development as new members join or other conditions disrupt the team's maturity.

1. *Forming*. The first stage of team development is a period of testing and orientation in which members learn about each other and evaluate the benefits and costs of continued membership. People tend to be polite during this stage and will defer to the existing authority of a formal or informal leader who must provide an initial set of rules and

Stages of team development

EXHIBIT 9.4

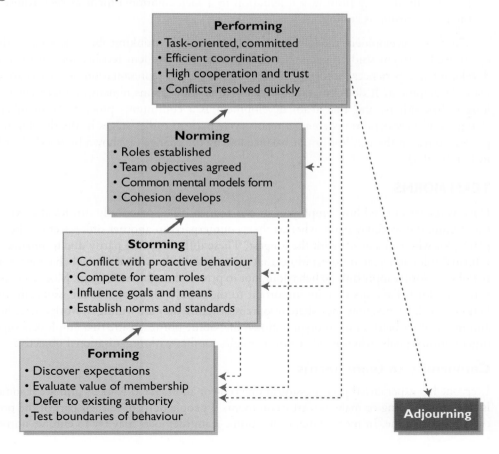

Performing
- Task-oriented, committed
- Efficient coordination
- High cooperation and trust
- Conflicts resolved quickly

Norming
- Roles established
- Team objectives agreed
- Common mental models form
- Cohesion develops

Storming
- Conflict with proactive behaviour
- Compete for team roles
- Influence goals and means
- Establish norms and standards

Forming
- Discover expectations
- Evaluate value of membership
- Defer to existing authority
- Test boundaries of behaviour

Adjourning

structures for interaction. Members try to find out what is expected of them and how they will fit into the team.

2. *Storming*. The storming stage is marked by interpersonal conflict as members become more proactive and compete for various team roles. Coalitions may form to influence the team's goals and means of goal attainment. Members try to establish norms of appropriate behaviour and performance standards. This is a tenuous stage in the team's development, particularly when the leader is autocratic and lacks the necessary conflict-management skills.

3. *Norming*. During the norming stage, the team develops its first real sense of cohesion as roles are established and a consensus forms around group objectives. Members have developed relatively similar mental models, so they have common expectations and assumptions about how the team's goals should be accomplished. They have developed a common team-based mental model that allows them to interact more efficiently so they can move into the next stage, performing.[36]

4. *Performing*. The team becomes more task-oriented in the performing stage. Team members have learnt to coordinate and resolve conflicts more efficiently. Further coordination improvements must occasionally be addressed, but the greater emphasis is on task accomplishment. In high-performance teams, members are highly cooperative, have a high level of trust in each other, are committed to group objectives and identify with the team. There is a climate of mutual support in which team members feel comfortable about taking risks, making errors or asking for help.[37]

5. *Adjourning*. Most work teams and informal groups eventually end. Task forces disband when their project is completed. Informal work groups may reach this stage when several members leave the organisation or are reassigned elsewhere. Some teams adjourn as a result of layoffs or plant shutdowns. Whatever the cause of team adjournment, members shift their attention away from task orientation to a socioemotional focus as they realise that their relationship is ending.

The team development model is a useful framework for thinking about how teams develop. Indeed, a recent study suggests that it fits nicely with student recollections of their team development experiences.[38] Still, the model is not a perfect representation of the dynamics of team development. It does not explicitly show that some teams remain in a particular stage longer than others, and that team development is a continuous process. As membership changes and new conditions emerge, teams cycle back to earlier stages in the developmental process to regain the equilibrium or balance lost by the change (as shown by the dashed lines in Exhibit 9.4).

TEAM NORMS

norms The informal rules and expectations that groups establish to regulate the behaviour of their members.

Have you ever noticed how employees in one branch office practically run for the exit door the minute the workday ends, whereas their counterparts in another office seem to be competing for who can stay at work the longest? These differences are partly due to **norms**—the informal rules and shared expectations that groups establish to regulate the behaviour of their members. Norms apply only to behaviour, not to private thoughts or feelings. Moreover, norms exist only for behaviours that are important to the team.[40] Norms guide the way team members deal with clients, how they share resources, whether they are willing to work longer hours, and many other behaviours in organisational life. Some norms ensure that employees support organisational goals, whereas other norms might conflict with organisational objectives.

LEARNING OBJECTIVE

Identify three factors that shape team norms.

Conformity to team norms

Everyone has experienced peer pressure at one time or another. Co-workers grimace if someone is late for a meeting or make sarcastic comments if people don't have their part of the project completed on time. In more extreme situations, team members may try to enforce norms by

Sky-high team development

Courtesy of United States Navy

Reaching the 'performing' stage of team development isn't just a goal for the Blue Angels; it's an absolute necessity to ensure that the US Navy's aerial demonstration team completes its manoeuvres with near-perfect timing. Although highly experienced before joining the squad, the pilots put in long hours of practice to reach the pinnacle of team development. The F/A-18A Hornets initially fly with a large space between them, but the team gradually tightens up the formation over the ten-week training program until the fighter jets are at times only 50 centimetres apart. Lt Cdr John Saccomando, who flies the No. 2 position, explains that the training improves trust and common mental models about each manoeuvre. 'I know exactly what [the lead] jet is going to do, and when,' he says. 'It takes a while to build that confidence.' Team development is also sped up through candid debriefings after every practice. 'We close the door, and there's no rank,' says Saccomando, who is expected to offer frank feedback to commanding officer and flight leader Cdr Stephen R. Foley. Foley points out that the safety and success of the Blue Angels depend on how well the team development process works. 'The team concept is what makes [everything] here click,' Foley emphasises.[39]

temporarily ostracising deviant co-workers or threatening to terminate their membership. This heavy-handed peer pressure isn't as rare as you might think. One survey revealed that 20 per cent of Australian employees have been pressured by their colleagues to slack off at work. Half the time, the peer pressure occurred because colleagues didn't want to look like poor performers against their more productive co-workers.[41]

Norms are also directly reinforced through praise from high-status members, more access to valued resources, or other rewards available to the team. But team members often conform to prevailing norms without direct reinforcement or punishment because they identify with the group and want to align their behaviour with the team's values. The more tightly the person's social identity is connected to the group, the more the individual is motivated to avoid negative sanctions from that group.[42] This effect is particularly strong in new members because they are uncertain of their status and want to demonstrate their membership of the team. Reality Check 9.1 (overleaf) provides an extreme example of the consequences of team norms and conformity in organisational settings.

REALITY CHECK 9.1

ELITE NEW ZEALAND PRISON TEAM'S 'CULTURE OF OBEDIENCE'

Members of a special emergency response team congregated at dawn for a covert mission. The sixteen hand-picked and specially trained members based at Paparua Prison, New Zealand, were supposed to reduce prison violence, prevent drugs from entering prisons and improve prisoner compliance. But the mission on this day was different. The response team was hunting for an escapee, a rooster belonging to a member of the response team that had escaped to a neighbouring farm.

This is just one of the bizarre incidents involving the Canterbury Emergency Response Unit (CERU), dubbed the 'Goon Squad' by its adversaries. The team worked independently of the prison officers and had its own distinctive black uniforms. Unfortunately, at least two government reports and a court case concluded that CERU had developed a distinctive set of norms, some of which violated Corrections Department policies.

Officials heard claims that the team falsified time sheets, juggled the work roster for personal gain, used department vehicles for personal use, used unnecessary intimidation on inmates, consumed alcohol on duty, acted inappropriately in public, and hunted wayward roosters on company time. CERU also conducted missions in the outside community even though its mandate was restricted to the prison. 'Our focus moved to a policeman's role, which we should not have been doing,' admits one former member.

None of the members complained during the unit's existence because of 'a culture of obedience'. For example, when one member refused to go to a party, others in the unit allegedly went to his home, restrained him, hit him over the head with an axe handle, handcuffed him, and dragged him along to the party.

'The most chilling thing about the team was an apparent fear of authority among members, leading to a culture of obedience and silence,' says an executive member of the Howard League for Penal Reform. 'In effect, they became a law unto themselves.'

Sources: Y. Martin, 'Goon Squad', *The Press* (Christchurch), 9 June 2001, 2; Y. Martin, 'The Goon Squad—The Fallout Continues', *The Press (Christchurch)*, 16 August 2003, 15; Y. Martin, 'Prison Riot Teams Back in Favour', *The Press* (Christchurch), 2 October 2004, 9; Y. Martin, 'Squad Suited up for Trouble', *The Press* (Christchurch), 19 January 2005, 17.

How team norms develop

Norms develop as soon as teams form, because people need to anticipate or predict how others will act. Even subtle events during the team's formation, such as how team members initially greet each other and where they sit in the first meetings, can initiate norms that are later difficult to change. At first, most norms are fuzzy, such as 'team members should communicate frequently with each other'. Over time, norms tend to become more specific, such as 'check and reply to your email daily'.[43]

Norms form as team members discover behaviours that help them function more effectively (such as the need to respond quickly to email). In particular, a critical event in the team's history can trigger the formation of a norm or sharpen a previously vague one. As an example, if a co-worker slipped on metal scraps and seriously injured herself, team members might develop a strong norm to keep the work area clean. Along with the effect of initial experiences and critical events, a third influence on team norms is the past experiences and values that members bring to the team. If most people who join a new team value work/life balance, norms are likely to develop that discourage long hours and work overload.[44]

Preventing and changing dysfunctional team norms

Team norms often become deeply anchored, so the best way to avoid norms that undermine organisational success or employee well-being is to establish desirable norms when the team is first formed. As was just mentioned, norms form from the values that people bring to the team, so one strategy is to select people with the appropriate values. If organisational leaders want their teams to have strong safety norms, they should hire people who already value safety.

Another strategy is to clearly state desirable norms as soon as the team is created. For instance, when Four Seasons Hotels and Resorts opens a new hotel, it forms a 35-person task force of respected staff from other Four Seasons hotels to get the new hotel up and running. Their mandate also includes helping to 'Four Seasonise' the new staff by watching for behaviours and decisions that are inconsistent with the Four Seasons way of doing things. 'The task force helps establish norms [in the new hotel],' explains a Four Seasons manager who has served on these task forces.[45]

Of course, most teams are not just starting up, so how can norms change in older teams? One way is for the leader to explicitly discuss the counterproductive norm with team members, using persuasive communication tactics. For example, the surgical team of one hospital had developed a norm of arriving late for operations. Patients and other hospital staff often waited thirty minutes or more for the team to arrive. The hospital CEO eventually spoke to the surgical team members about their lateness and, through moral suasion, convinced them to arrive for operating room procedures no more than five minutes late.[46]

Team-based reward systems can sometimes weaken counterproductive norms. Unfortunately, the pressure to conform to the counterproductive norm is sometimes stronger than the financial incentive. This problem is demonstrated in the classic story of a pyjama factory where employees were paid under a piece-rate system. Some individuals in the group were able to process up to 100 units per hour and thereby earn more money, but they all chose to abide by the group norm of 50 units per hour. Only after the team was disbanded did the strong performers working alone increase their performance to 100 units per hour.[47]

Finally, a dysfunctional norm may be so deeply ingrained that the best strategy is to disband the group and replace it with people who have more favourable norms. Organisational leaders should seize the opportunity to introduce performance-oriented norms when the new team is formed, and select members who will bring desirable norms to the group. For instance, the Canterbury Emergency Response Unit (CERU) described in Reality Check 9.1 was disbanded when the extent of its wayward norms became apparent. More recently, the New Zealand government announced plans to launch a new emergency team, but advised former CERU members in writing that selecting them for the new team 'would not be appropriate at this time'.[48]

TEAM ROLES

All work teams and informal groups have various roles necessary to coordinate the team's task and maintain the team's functioning. A **role** is a set of behaviours that people are expected to perform because they hold certain positions in a team and organisation.[49] Some roles help the team achieve its goals; other roles maintain relationships so the team survives and team members fulfil their needs. Some team roles are formally assigned to specific people. For example, team leaders are usually expected to initiate discussion, ensure that all members have an opportunity to present their views, and help the team reach agreement on the issues discussed. But team members often take on various roles informally based on their personality, values and expertise. These role preferences are usually worked out during the storming stage of team development. However, in a dynamic environment, team members often need to assume various roles temporarily as the need arises.[50]

role A set of behaviours that people are expected to perform because they hold certain positions in a team and organisation.

EXHIBIT 9.5

Belbin's team roles

Role label	Role description
Plant	Creative, imaginative, unorthodox. Solves difficult problems.
Coordinator	Mature, confident, a good chairperson. Clarifies goals, promotes decision making, delegates well.
Monitor evaluator	Sober, strategic and discerning. Sees all options. Judges accurately.
Implementer	Disciplined, reliable, conservative and efficient. Turns ideas into practical actions.
Completer finisher	Painstaking, conscientious, anxious. Searches out errors and omissions. Delivers on time.
Resource investigator	Extrovert, enthusiastic, communicative. Explores opportunities. Develops contacts.
Shaper	Challenging, dynamic, thrives on pressure. The drive and courage to overcome obstacles.
Teamworker	Cooperative, mild, perceptive and diplomatic. Listens, builds, averts friction.
Specialist	Single-minded, self-starting, dedicated. Provides knowledge and skills in rare supply.

Source: R. M. Belbin, *Team Roles at Work* (Oxford, UK: Butterworth-Heinemann, 1993). Reprinted with permission of Belbin Associates (www.belbin.com).

Various team role theories have been proposed over the years, but Meredith Belbin's team role theory is the most popular.[51] The model identifies nine team roles (see Exhibit 9.5) that are related to specific personality characteristics. People have a natural preference for one role or another, although they can adjust to a secondary role. Belbin's model emphasises that all nine roles must be engaged for optimal team performance. Moreover, certain team roles should dominate at various stages of the team's project or activities. For example, shapers and coordinators are key figures when the team is identifying its needs, whereas completers and implementers are most important during the follow-through stage of the team's project.

How accurate is Belbin's team roles model? The evidence is mixed.[52] Research indicates that teams do require a balance of roles, and that people do tend to prefer one type of role. However, Belbin's nine roles typically boil down to six or seven roles in empirical studies. For example, the implementer and completer roles are the same or too similar to distinguish from each other. Scholars have also criticised how Belbin's roles are measured, which creates difficulty in determining the accuracy of the model. Overall, teams do have a variety of roles that must be fulfilled for team effectiveness, but researchers are still trying to figure out what these roles are and how to measure them.

TEAM COHESIVENESS

Team cohesiveness The degree of attraction people feel towards the team and their motivation to remain members.

Team cohesiveness—the degree of attraction people feel towards the team and their motivation to remain members—is considered an important factor in a team's success.[53] Employees feel cohesiveness when they believe that the team will help them achieve their personal goals, fulfil their need for affiliation or status, or provide social support during times of crisis or trouble. Cohesiveness is an emotional experience, not just a calculation of whether to stay or leave the team. It exists when team members make the team part of their social identity. Cohesiveness is the glue or *esprit de corps* that holds the group together and ensures that its members fulfil their obligations.

LEARNING OBJECTIVE

List six factors that influence team cohesiveness.

Influences on team cohesiveness

Several factors influence team cohesiveness: member similarity, team size, member interaction, difficult entry, team success, and external competition or challenges. For the most part, these factors reflect the individual's social identity with the group and beliefs about how team membership will fulfil personal needs.[54] Several of these factors are related to our earlier discussion about why people join informal groups and how teams develop. Specifically, teams become more cohesive as they reach higher stages of development and are more attractive to potential members.

- *Member similarity.* As discussed earlier in the chapter, highly diverse teams potentially create faultlines that can lead to factious subgroups and higher turnover among team members. Other research has found that people with similar values have a higher attraction to each other. Collectively, these findings suggest that homogeneous teams are more cohesive than heterogeneous teams. However, not all forms of diversity reduce cohesion. For example, teams consisting of people from different job groups seem to gel together just as well as teams of people from the same job.[55]

- *Team size.* Smaller teams tend to be more cohesive than larger teams because it is easier for a few people to agree on goals and coordinate work activities. The smallest teams aren't always the most cohesive, however. Small teams are less cohesive when they lack enough members to perform the required tasks. Thus, team cohesiveness is potentially greatest when teams are as small as possible, yet large enough to accomplish the required tasks.

- *Member interaction.* Teams tend to be more cohesive when team members interact with each other fairly regularly. This occurs when team members perform highly interdependent tasks and work in the same physical area.

- *Somewhat difficult entry.* Teams tend to be more cohesive when entry to the team is restricted. The more elite the team, the more prestige it confers on its members and the more they tend to value their membership in the unit. Existing team members are also more willing to welcome and support new members after they have 'passed the test', possibly because they have shared the same entry experience. This raises the issue of how difficult the initiation for entry into the team should be. Research suggests that severe initiations can potentially lead to humiliation and psychological distance from the group, even for those who successfully endure the initiation.[56]

- *Team success.* Cohesion is both emotional and instrumental, with the latter referring to the notion that people feel more cohesion in teams that fulfil their goals. Consequently, cohesion increases with the team's level of success.[57] Furthermore, individuals are more likely to attach their social identity to successful teams than to those with a string of failures. Team leaders can increase cohesiveness by regularly communicating and celebrating the team's successes. Note that this can create a spiral effect. Successful teams are more cohesive and, under certain conditions, increased cohesiveness increases the team's success.

- *External competition and challenges.* Team cohesiveness tends to increase when members face external competition or a valued objective that is challenging. This might include a threat from an external competitor or friendly competition from other teams. These conditions tend to increase cohesiveness because employees value the team's ability to overcome the threat or competition if they can't solve the problem individually. They also value their membership as a form of social support. Organisations need to be careful about the degree of external threat, however. Evidence suggests that teams are less effective when external threats are severe. Although cohesiveness tends to increase, external threats are stressful and cause teams to make less effective decisions under these conditions.[58]

Team cohesion among Australian submariners

Crew members of Australia's Collins-class submarines work in an environment that creates powerful team cohesiveness. Applicants must pass a rigorous selection process, and successful submariners eventually receive their 'dolphins', the gold badge of distinction. 'Submariners, like aviators, simply work in a more dangerous environment,' explained a former commander of the Royal Australian Navy's submarine squadron. 'The result is greater professionalism and a strong esprit de corps.' Team cohesiveness became even more apparent after crew members of the HMAS *Dechaineux* survived a serious flood while the submarine was at maximum depth. Fortunately, the crew's quick actions and the vessel's capabilities averted tragedy. 'Everyone was really proud of the way the boat behaved and the way we all got through it—there was a lot of pride,' said Lieutenant Commander Geoff Wadley, who was the officer in charge when the incident took place off the coast of Western Australia. 'It really brought the crew together.'[59]

Australian Government Department of Defence

Consequences of team cohesiveness

Every team must have some minimal level of cohesiveness to maintain its existence. People who belong to high-cohesion teams are motivated to maintain their membership and to help the team perform effectively. Compared with low-cohesion teams, high-cohesion team members spend more time together, share information more frequently, and are more satisfied with each other. They provide each other with better social support in stressful situations.[60]

Members of high-cohesion teams are generally more sensitive to each other's needs and develop better interpersonal relationships, thereby reducing dysfunctional conflict. When conflict does arise, members tend to resolve these differences swiftly and effectively. With better cooperation and more conformity to norms, high-cohesion teams usually perform better than low-cohesion teams. However, the relationship is a little more complex. Exhibit 9.6 illustrates how the effect of cohesiveness on team performance depends on the extent to which team norms are consistent with organisational goals. Cohesive teams will probably have lower task performance when norms conflict with organisational objectives, because cohesiveness motivates employees to perform at a level more consistent with group norms.[61]

Effect of team cohesiveness on task performance

EXHIBIT 9.6

	Low ← Team cohesiveness → High	
Team norms support company goals	Moderately high task performance	High task performance
Team norms conflict with company goals	Moderately low task performance	Low task performance

Low   High

Team cohesiveness

THE TROUBLE WITH TEAMS

As explained near the start of this chapter, organisational leaders are placing a lot more emphasis on teams these days. While this chapter has outlined the benefits of teams, the reality is that teams aren't always needed.[62] Sometimes a quick and decisive action by one person is more appropriate. Some tasks are also performed just as easily by one person as by a group. 'The now-fashionable team in which everybody works with everybody on everything from the beginning is rapidly becoming a disappointment,' warned the late management guru Peter Drucker.[63]

A second problem is that teams take time to develop and maintain. Scholars refer to these hidden costs as **process losses**—resources (including time and energy) expended towards team development and maintenance rather than the task.[64] It is much more efficient for an individual to work out an issue alone than to resolve differences of opinion with other people. The process loss problem becomes apparent when adding new people to the team. The group has to recycle through the team development process to bring everyone up to speed. The software industry even has a name for this. 'Brooks's law' says that adding more people to a late software project only makes it later. Researchers point out that the cost of process losses may be offset by the benefits of teams. Unfortunately, few companies conduct a cost–benefit analysis of their team activities.[65]

A third problem is that teams require the right environment in order to flourish. Many companies forget this point by putting people in teams without changing anything else. As noted earlier, teams require appropriate rewards, communication systems, team leadership, and other conditions. Without these, the shift to a team structure could be a waste of time. At the same time, critics suggest that changing these environmental conditions to improve teamwork could result in higher costs than benefits for the overall organisation.[66]

LEARNING OBJECTIVE

Discuss the limitations of teams.

process losses Resources (including time and energy) expended towards team development and maintenance rather than the task.

social loafing A situation in which people exert less effort (and usually perform at a lower level) when working in groups than when working alone.

LEARNING OBJECTIVE

Explain how companies minimise social loafing.

SOCIAL LOAFING

Perhaps the best-known limitation of teams is the risk of productivity loss due to **social loafing**. Social loafing occurs when people exert less effort (and usually perform at a lower level) when working in groups than when working alone.[67] A few scholars question whether social loafing is common, but students can certainly report many instances of this problem in their team projects!

Social loafing is most likely to occur in large teams where individual output is difficult to identify. This particularly includes situations in which team members work alone towards a common output pool (i.e. they have low task interdependence). Under these conditions, employees aren't as worried that their performance will be noticed. Social loafing is less likely to occur when the task is interesting, because individuals have a higher intrinsic motivation to perform their duties. It is less common when the group's objective is important, possibly because individuals experience more pressure from other team members to perform well. Finally, social loafing occurs less frequently among members with a strong collectivist value, because they value group membership and believe in working towards group objectives.[68]

How to minimise social loafing

By understanding the causes of social loafing, ways to minimise the problem can be identified. Some of the strategies listed below reduce social loafing by making each member's performance more visible. Others increase each member's motivation to perform his or her tasks within the group.[69]

- *Form smaller teams.* Splitting the team into several smaller groups reduces social loafing because each person's performance becomes more noticeable and important for team performance. A smaller group also potentially increases cohesiveness, so would-be shirkers feel a greater obligation to perform fully for their team.
- *Specialise tasks.* Each person's contribution is easier to see when each team member performs a different work activity. For example, rather than pooling their effort for all incoming customer inquiries, each customer service representative might be assigned a particular type of client.
- *Measure individual performance.* Social loafing is minimised when each member's contribution is measured. Of course, individual performance is difficult to measure in some team activities, such as problem-solving projects in which the team's performance depends on one person discovering the best answer.
- *Increase job enrichment.* Social loafing is minimised when team members are assigned more motivating jobs, such as those requiring more skill variety or having direct contact with clients. More generally, social loafing is less common among employees with high job satisfaction.
- *Select motivated employees.* Social loafing can be minimised by carefully selecting job applicants who are motivated by the task and have a collectivist value orientation. Those with a collectivist value are motivated to work harder for the team because they value their membership in the group.

This chapter has laid the foundation for an understanding of team dynamics. To build an effective team requires time, the right combination of team members, and the right environment. These ingredients of environment and team processes will be applied in the next chapter, which looks at high-performance teams, including self-directed teams and virtual teams.

CHAPTER SUMMARY

Teams are groups of two or more people who interact and influence each other, are mutually accountable for achieving common objectives, and perceive themselves as a social entity within an organisation. All teams are groups, because they consist of people with a unifying relationship, but not all groups are teams, because some groups do not have purposive interaction.

Groups can be categorised in terms of their permanence (teams versus informal groups) and formality in the organisation. Informal groups exist primarily for the benefit of their members rather than for the organisation. Teams have become popular because they tend to make better decisions, support the knowledge management process, and provide superior customer service. In many situations, employees are potentially more energised and engaged working in teams rather than alone.

Team effectiveness includes the group's ability to survive, to achieve its system-based objectives, and to fulfil the needs of its members. The model of team effectiveness considers the team and organisational environment, the team design and team processes. The team or organisational environment influences team effectiveness directly, as well as through team design and team processes. Six elements in the organisational and team environment that influence team effectiveness are reward systems, communication systems, physical space, organisational environment, organisational structure and organisational leadership.

Three team design elements are task characteristics, team size and team composition. Teams tend to be more effective when they work on well-structured or complex tasks. The need for teamwork increases with task interdependence. Teams should be large enough to perform the work, yet small enough for efficient coordination and meaningful involvement. Effective teams are composed of people with the competencies and motivation to perform tasks in a team environment. Heterogeneous teams operate best on complex projects and problems requiring innovative solutions.

Teams develop through the stages of forming, storming, norming, performing and eventually adjourning. Teams develop norms to regulate and guide member behaviour. These norms may be influenced by initial experiences, critical events, and the values and experiences that team members bring to the group. Team members also have roles—a set of behaviours they are expected to perform because they hold certain positions in a team and organisation.

Cohesiveness is the degree of attraction people feel towards the team and their motivation to remain members. Cohesiveness increases with member similarity, smaller team size, higher degree of interaction, somewhat difficult entry, team success and external challenges. Teams need some level of cohesiveness to survive, but high-cohesive units have higher task performance only when their norms do not conflict with organisational objectives.

Teams are not always beneficial or necessary. Moreover, they have hidden costs, known as process losses, and require particular environments in order to flourish. Teams often fail because they are not set up in a supportive environment. Social loafing is another potential problem with teams. This is the tendency for individuals to perform at a lower level when working in groups than when alone. Social loafing can be minimised by making each member's performance more visible and increasing each member's motivation to perform his or her tasks within the group.

KEY TERMS

groups p. 266
heterogeneous teams p. 273
homogeneous teams p. 273
norms p. 276

process losses p. 283
role p. 279
social loafing p. 284
task interdependence p. 271

team cohesiveness p. 280
team effectiveness p. 269
teams p. 266

DISCUSSION QUESTIONS

1. Informal groups exist in almost every form of social organisation. What types of informal groups exist in your classroom? Why are students motivated to belong to these informal groups?

2. You have been asked to lead a complex software project over the next year that requires the full-time involvement of approximately 100 people with diverse skills and backgrounds. Using your knowledge of team size, how can you develop an effective team under these conditions?

3. You have been put in charge of a cross-functional task force that will develop enhanced Internet banking services for retail customers. The team includes representatives from marketing, information services, customer service and accounting, all of whom will move to the same location at headquarters for three months. Describe the behaviours you might observe during each stage of the team's development.

4. You have just been transferred from the Christchurch office to the Wellington office of your company, a New Zealand–wide sales organisation of electrical products for developers and contractors. In Christchurch, team members regularly called customers after a sale to ask whether the products had arrived on time and whether they were satisfied. But when you moved to the Wellington office, no one seemed to make these follow-up calls. A recently hired co-worker explained that other co-workers discouraged her from making those calls. Later, another co-worker suggested that your follow-up calls were making everyone else look lazy. Give three possible reasons why the norms in the Christchurch office might be different from those in the Wellington office, even though the customers, products, sales commissions and other characteristics of the workplace are almost identical.

5. An employee at a financial services firm recently made the following comment about his team, using a sporting metaphor: 'Our team has a great bunch of people. But just like a baseball team, some people need to hit the home run, whereas others have to play catcher. Some need to be coaches and others have to be experts at fixing the equipment every day. The problem with our team is that we don't have people in some of these other jobs. As a result, our team isn't performing as well as it should.' What team dynamics topic is this person mainly referring to, and what is he saying about his team in the context of that topic?

6. You have been assigned to a class project with five other students, none of whom you have met before. To what extent would team cohesiveness improve your team's performance on this project? What actions would you recommend to build team cohesiveness among team members in this situation?

7. Collins-class submarine crews were described in this chapter as a highly cohesive team. From the description provided, what factors contribute to this cohesion?

8. The late management guru Peter Drucker said: 'The now-fashionable team in which everybody works with everybody on everything from the beginning is rapidly becoming a disappointment.' Discuss three problems associated with teams.

SKILL BUILDER | 9.1

CASE STUDY

TREETOP FOREST PRODUCTS

Treetop Forest Products Ltd is a sawmill operation in Oregon, USA, that is owned by a major forest products company but operates independently of headquarters. It was built thirty years ago and was completely updated with new machinery five years ago. Treetop receives raw logs from the area for cutting and planing into building-grade timber, mostly 2-by-4 and 2-by-6 pieces of standard lengths. Higher-grade logs leave Treetop's sawmill department in finished form and are sent directly to the packaging department. The remaining 40 per cent of sawmill output consists of cuts from lower-grade logs, requiring further work by the planing department.

Treetop has one general manager, sixteen supervisors and support staff, and 180 unionised employees. The unionised employees are paid an hourly rate specified in the collective agreement, whereas management and support staff are paid a monthly salary. The mill is divided into six operating departments: boom, sawmill, planer, packaging, shipping and maintenance. The sawmill, boom and packaging departments operate a morning shift starting at 6 am and an afternoon shift starting at 2 pm. Employees in these departments rotate shifts every two weeks. The planer and shipping departments operate only morning shifts. Maintenance employees work the night shift (starting at 10 pm).

Each department, except for packaging, has a supervisor on every work shift. The planer supervisor is responsible for the packaging department on the morning shift, and the sawmill supervisor is responsible for the packaging department on the afternoon shift. However, the packaging operation is housed in a separate building from the other departments, so supervisors seldom visit the packaging department. This is particularly true for the afternoon shift, because the sawmill supervisor is the furthest distance from the packaging building.

PACKAGING QUALITY

Ninety per cent of Treetop's product is sold on the international market through Westboard Co., a large marketing agency. Westboard represents all forest products mills owned by Treetop's parent company as well as several other clients in the region. The market for building-grade timber is very price competitive, because there are numerous mills selling a relatively undifferentiated product. However, some differentiation does occur in product packaging and presentation. Buyers will look closely at the packaging when deciding whether to buy from Treetop or another mill.

To encourage its clients to package their products better, Westboard sponsors a monthly package quality award. The marketing agency samples and rates its clients' packages daily, and the sawmill with the highest score at the end of the month is awarded a plaque. Package quality is a combination of how the timber is piled (e.g. defects turned in), where the bands and dunnage are placed, how neatly the stencil and seal are applied, the stencil's accuracy, and how neatly and tightly the plastic wrap is attached.

Treetop Forest Products has won Westboard's packaging quality award several times over the past five years, and received high ratings in the months that it didn't win. However, the mill's ratings have started to decline over the past year or two, and several clients have complained about the appearance of the finished product. A few large customers switched to competitors' timber, saying that the decision was based on the substandard appearance of Treetop's packaging when it arrived in their timber yard.

BOTTLENECK IN PACKAGING

The planing and sawmilling departments have significantly increased productivity over the past couple of years. The sawmill operation recently set a new productivity record on a single day. The planer operation has increased productivity to the point where last year it reduced operations to just one (rather than two) shifts per day. These productivity improvements are due to better operator training, fewer machine breakdowns and better selection of raw logs. (Sawmill cuts from high-quality logs usually do not require planing work.)

Productivity levels in the boom, shipping and maintenance departments have remained constant. However, the packaging department has recorded decreasing productivity over the past couple of years, with the result that a large backlog of finished product is typically stockpiled outside the packaging building. The morning shift of the packaging department is unable to keep up with the combined production of the sawmill and planer departments, so the unpackaged output is left for the afternoon shift. Unfortunately, the afternoon shift packages even less product than the morning shift, so the backlog continues to build. The backlog adds to Treetop's inventory costs and increases the risk of damaged stock.

Treetop has added Saturday overtime shifts as well as extra hours before and after the regular shifts for the packaging department employees to process this backlog. Last month the packaging department employed 10 per cent of the workforce but accounted for 85 per cent of the overtime. This is frustrating for Treetop's management, because time and motion studies recently confirmed that the packaging department is capable of processing all of the daily

sawmill and planer production without overtime. Moreover, with employees earning one and a half or two times their regular pay on overtime, Treetop's cost competitiveness suffers.

Employees and supervisors at Treetop are aware that people in the packaging department tend to extend lunch by ten minutes and coffee breaks by five minutes, and typically leave work a few minutes before the end of the shift. This abuse has worsened recently, particularly on the afternoon shift. Employees who are temporarily assigned to the packaging department also seem to participate in this time loss pattern after a few days. Although they are punctual and productive in other departments, these temporary employees soon adopt the packaging crew's informal schedule when assigned to that department.

QUESTIONS

1. Based on your knowledge of team dynamics, explain why the packaging department is less productive than are other teams at Treetop.

2. How should Treetop change the non-productive norms that exist in the packaging group?

3. What structural and other changes would you recommend that may improve this situation in the long term?

SKILL BUILDER | 9.2　　TEAM TOWER POWER

TEAM EXERCISE

PURPOSE

This exercise is designed to help you understand team roles, team development and other issues in the development and maintenance of effective teams.

MATERIALS

The instructor will provide enough Lego pieces or similar materials for each team to complete the assigned task. All teams should have an identical (or very similar) amount of pieces and the same type of pieces. The instructor will need a measuring tape and stopwatch. Students may use writing materials during the design stage (Stage 2). The instructor will distribute a 'Team Objectives Sheet' and 'Tower Specifications Effectiveness Sheet' to all teams.

INSTRUCTIONS

Step 1: The instructor will divide the class into teams. Depending on class size and space available, teams may have between four and seven members, but all should be of approximately equal size.

Step 2: Each team is given twenty minutes to design a tower that uses only the materials provided, is freestanding, and provides an optimal return on investment. Team members may wish to draw their tower on paper or a flip chart to assist in the design. Teams are free to practise building their tower during this stage. Preferably, teams are assigned to separate rooms so the design can be created privately. During this stage, each team will complete the Team Objectives Sheet distributed by the instructor. This sheet requires the Tower Specifications Effectiveness Sheet, also distributed by the instructor.

Step 3: Each team will show the instructor that it has completed its Team Objectives Sheet. Then, with all teams in the same room, the instructor will announce the start of the construction phase. The time taken for construction will be closely monitored and the instructor will occasionally call out the time elapsed (particularly if there is no clock in the room).

Step 4: Each team will advise the instructor as soon as it has completed its tower. The team will write down the time elapsed that the instructor has determined. It may be asked to assist the instructor by counting the number of blocks used and the height of the tower. This information is also written on the Team Objectives Sheet. The team then calculates its profit.

Step 5: After presenting the results, the class will discuss the team dynamics elements that contribute to team effectiveness. Team members will discuss their strategy, division of labour (team roles), expertise within the team, and other elements of team dynamics.

Source: Several published and online sources describe variations of this exercise, but it has no known origin.

TEAM ROLES PREFERENCES SCALE

9.3 SKILL BUILDER

SELF-ASSESSMENT

STUDENT CD

PURPOSE
This self-assessment is designed to help you to identify your preferred roles in meetings and similar team activities.

INSTRUCTIONS
Read each of the statements below and circle the response that you believe best reflects your position regarding each statement. Then use the scoring key in Appendix B to calculate your results for each team role. This exercise is completed alone so students can assess themselves honestly without concerns of social comparison. However, class discussion will focus on the roles that people assume in team settings. This scale assesses only a few team roles.

TEAM ROLES PREFERENCES SCALE

Circle the number that best reflects your position regarding each of these statements.	Does not describe me at all	Does not describe me very well	Describes me somewhat	Describes me well	Describes me very well
1. I usually take responsibility for getting the team to agree on what the meeting should accomplish.	1	2	3	4	5
2. I tend to summarise to other team members what the team has accomplished so far.	1	2	3	4	5
3. I'm usually the person who helps other team members overcome their disagreements.	1	2	3	4	5
4. I try to ensure that everyone gets heard on issues.	1	2	3	4	5
5. I'm usually the person who helps the team determine how to organise the discussion.	1	2	3	4	5
6. I praise other team members for their ideas more than do others in the meetings.	1	2	3	4	5
7. People tend to rely on me to keep track of what has been said in meetings.	1	2	3	4	5
8. The team typically counts on me to prevent debates from getting out of hand.	1	2	3	4	5
9. I tend to say things that make the group feel optimistic about its accomplishments.	1	2	3	4	5
10. Team members usually count on me to give everyone a chance to speak.	1	2	3	4	5
11. In most meetings, I am less likely than others to 'put down' the ideas of team-mates.	1	2	3	4	5
12. I actively help team-mates to resolve their differences in meetings.	1	2	3	4	5
13. I actively encourage quiet team members to describe their ideas on each issue.	1	2	3	4	5
14. People tend to rely on me to clarify the purpose of the meeting.	1	2	3	4	5
15. I like to be the person who takes notes or minutes of the meeting.	1	2	3	4	5

NOTES

1   A. Doak, 'New-Age Style, Old-Fashioned Grunt, but How Will It Look with Fluffy Dice?', *The Age* (Melbourne), 16 October 1998, 4; W. Webster, 'How a Star Was Born', *Daily Telegraph* (Sydney), 17 October 1998, 11; R. Edgar, 'Designers Front up to World Stage', *The Age* (Melbourne), 11 February 2004, 6; 'Holden Heaven', *Bay of Plenty Times* (Tauranga, NZ), 21 October 2005, M04–5; 'How Holden Sees Seven-Seater', *Gold Coast Bulletin*, 16 November 2005, 12; M. Taylor, 'Hard Road for Holden', *Bulletin*, 12 April 2005.

2   P. Haw, 'Learning from Lean Principles', *Business Day* (South Africa), 7 July 2003, 7; '"Stepping Stones" Highlights Fedex Teamwork', *BusinessWorld*, 23 September 2005, S3/9; S. Lloyd, 'Smarter Spending Habits', *Business Review Weekly*, 10 November 2005, 130.

3   This definition and very similar variations are found in: M. E. Shaw, *Group Dynamics*, 3rd edn (New York: McGraw-Hill, 1981), 8; S. A. Mohrman, S. G. Cohen and A. M. Mohrman Jr., *Designing Team-Based Organizations: New Forms for Knowledge Work* (San Francisco: Jossey-Bass, 1995), 39–40; M. A. West, 'Preface: Introducing Work Group Psychology', in *Handbook of Work Group Psychology*, ed. M. A. West (Chichester, UK: Wiley, 1996), xxvi; S. G. Cohen and D. E. Bailey, 'What Makes Teams Work: Group Effectiveness Research from the Shop Floor to the Executive Suite', *Journal of Management* 23 (May 1997), 239–90; E. Sundstrom, 'The Challenges of Supporting Work Team Effectiveness', in *Supporting Work Team Effectiveness*, ed. E. Sundstrom and Associates (San Francisco, CA: Jossey-Bass, 1999), 6–9.

4   M. Moldaschl and W. Weber, 'The "Three Waves" of Industrial Group Work: Historical Reflections on Current Research on Group Work', *Human Relations* 51 (March 1998), 347–88. The survey quotation is found in 'What Makes Teams Work?', *HRfocus* (April 2002), 17. Several popular books in the 1980s encouraged team work, based on the Japanese economic miracle. These books included: W. Ouchi, *Theory Z: How American Management Can Meet the Japanese Challenge* (Reading, Mass.: Addison-Wesley, 1981); R. T. Pascale and A. G. Athos, *Art of Japanese Management* (New York: Simon and Schuster, 1982).

5   C. R. Emery and L. D. Fredenhall, 'The Effect of Teams on Firm Profitability and Customer Satisfaction', *Journal of Service Research* 4 (February 2002), 217–29; G. S. Van der Vegt and O. Janssen, 'Joint Impact of Interdependence and Group Diversity on Innovation', *Journal of Management* 29 (2003), 729–51. Bruce Lam's quotation is found in J. Cremer, 'Nokia Sets the Tone for Teamwork', *South China Morning Post*, 18 December 2004, 4.

6   S. Konig, 'The Challenge of Teams', *On Wall Street*, August 2003; D. Jamieson, '8 Most Common Myths About Teams', *On Wall Street*, May 2005; H. J. Stock, 'A "Cheat Sheet" to Cross Sell', *Bank Investment Consultant*, April 2005, 28; L. Wei, 'Brokers Increasingly Use Teamwork', *Wall Street Journal*, 23 February 2005.

7   J. Godard, 'High Performance and the Transformation of Work? The Implications of Alternative Work Practices for the Experience and Outcomes of Work', *Industrial & Labor Relations Review* 54 (July 2001), 776–805.

8   B. D. Pierce and R. White, 'The Evolution of Social Structure: Why Biology Matters', *Academy of Management Review* 24 (October 1999), 843–53; P. R. Lawrence and N. Nohria, *Driven: How Human Nature Shapes Our Choices* (San Francisco: Jossey-Bass, 2002); J. R. Spoor and J. R. Kelly, 'The Evolutionary Significance of Affect in Groups: Communication and Group Bonding', *Group Processes & Intergroup Relations* 7, no. 4 (2004), 398–412.

9   M. A. Hogg et al., 'The Social Identity Perspective: Intergroup Relations, Self-Conception, and Small Groups', *Small Group Research* 35, no. 3 (June 2004), 246–76; N. Michinov, E. Michinov and M. C. Toczek-Capelle, 'Social Identity, Group Processes, and Performance in Synchronous Computer-Mediated Communication', *Group Dynamics: Theory, Research, and Practice* 8, no. 1 (2004), 27–39; M. Van Vugt and C. M. Hart, 'Social Identity as Social Glue: The Origins of Group Loyalty', *Journal of Personality and Social Psychology* 86, no. 4 (2004), 585–98.

10 S. Schacter, *The Psychology of Affiliation* (Stanford, CA: Stanford University Press, 1959), 12–19; R. Eisler and D. S. Levine, 'Nurture, Nature, and Caring: We Are Not Prisoners of Our Genes', *Brain and Mind* 3 (2002), 9–52; A. C. DeVries, E. R. Glasper and C. E. Detillion, 'Social Modulation of Stress Responses', *Physiology & Behavior* 79, no. 3 (August 2003), 399–407.

11 M. A. West, C. S. Borrill and K. L. Unsworth, 'Team Effectiveness in Organizations', International Review of Industrial and Organizational Psychology 13 (1998), 1–48; R. Forrester and A. B. Drexler, 'A Model for Team-Based Organization Performance', *Academy of Management Executive* 13 (August 1999), 36–49; J. E. McGrath, H. Arrow and J. L. Berdahl, 'The Study of Groups: Past, Present, and Future', Personality & Social Psychology Review 4, no. 1 (2000), 95–105; M. A. Marks, J. E. Mathieu and S. J. Zaccaro, 'A Temporally Based Framework and Taxonomy of Team Processes', *Academy of Management Review* 26, no. 3 (July 2001), 356–76.

12 G. P. Shea and R. A. Guzzo, 'Group Effectiveness: What Really Matters?', *Sloan Management Review* 27 (1987), 33–46; J. R. Hackman et al., 'Team Effectiveness in Theory and in Practice', in *Industrial and Organizational Psychology: Linking Theory with Practice*, ed. C. L. Cooper and E. A. Locke (Oxford, UK: Blackwell, 2000), 109–29.

13 J. N. Choi, 'External Activities and Team Effectiveness: Review and Theoretical Development', *Small Group Research* 33 (April 2002), 181–208; T. L. Doolen, M. E. Hacker and E. M. Van Aken, 'The Impact of Organizational Context on Work Team Effectiveness: A Study of Production Team', *IEEE Transactions on Engineering Management* 50, no. 3 (August 2003), 285–96.

14 J. S. DeMatteo, L. T. Eby and E. Sundstrom, 'Team-Based Rewards: Current Empirical Evidence and Directions for Future Research', *Research in Organizational Behavior* 20 (1998), 141–83; E. E. Lawler III, *Rewarding Excellence: Pay Strategies for the New Economy* (San Francisco: Jossey-Bass, 2000), 207–14; G. Hertel, S. Geister and U. Konradt, 'Managing Virtual Teams: A Review of Current Empirical Research', *Human Resource Management Review* 15 (2005), 69–95.

15 S. Dabkowski, 'Healthy Diagnosis Deems Medibank Might Be Fit to Float', *The Age* (Melbourne), 3 October 2005, 1.

16 A. Niimi, 'The Slow and Steady Climb toward True North', Toyota Motor Manufacturing North America news release (7 August 2003); B. Andrews, 'Room with Many Views', *Business Review Weekly*, 15 January 2004, 68.

17 R. Wageman, 'Case Study: Critical Success Factors for Creating Superb Self-Managing Teams at Xerox', *Compensation and Benefits Review* 29 (September–October 1997), 31–41; G. Gard, K. Lindström and M. Dallner, 'Towards a Learning Organization: The Introduction of a Client-Centered Team-Based Organization in Administrative Surveying Work', *Applied Ergonomics* 34 (2003), 97–105.

18 S. D. Dionne et al., 'Transformational Leadership and Team Performance', *Journal of Organizational Change Management* 17, no. 2 (2004), 177–93.

19 A. S. Sohal, M. Terziovski and A. Zutshi, 'Team-Based Strategy at Varian Australia: A Case Study', *Technovation* 23 (2003), 349–57.

20 M. A. Campion, E. M. Papper and G. J. Medsker, 'Relations between Work Team Characteristics and Effectiveness: A Replication and Extension', *Personnel Psychology* 49 (1996), 429–52; D. C. Man and S. S. K. Lam, 'The Effects of Job Complexity and Autonomy on Cohesiveness in Collectivistic and Individualistic Work Groups: A Cross-Cultural Analysis', *Journal of Organizational Behavior* 24 (2003), 979–1001.

21 R. Wageman, 'The Meaning of Interdependence', in *Groups at Work: Theory and Research*, ed. M. E. Turner (Mahwah, NJ: Lawrence Erlbaum Associates, 2001), 197–217.

22 R. Wageman, 'Interdependence and Group Effectiveness', *Administrative Science Quarterly* 40 (1995), 145–80; G. S. Van der Vegt, J. M. Emans and E. Van de Vliert, 'Patterns of Interdependence in Work Teams: A Two-Level Investigation of the Relations with Job and Team Satisfaction', *Personnel Psychology* 54 (Spring 2001), 51–69; S. M. Gully et al., 'A Meta-Analysis of Team-Efficacy, Potency, and Performance: Interdependence and Level of Analysis as Moderators of Observed Relationships', *Journal of Applied Psychology* 87, no. 5 (October 2002), 819–32.

23 J. D. Thompson, *Organizations in Action* (New York: McGraw-Hill, 1967), 54–6. One concern with Thompson's typology is that it isn't clear how much more interdependence is created by each of these three forms. See: G. Van der Vegt and E. Van de Vliert, 'Intragroup Interdependence and Effectiveness: Review and Proposed Directions for Theory and Practice', *Journal of Managerial Psychology* 17, no. 1/2 (2002), 50–67.

24 J. O'Toole and D. Tessmann-Keys, 'The Power of Many: Building a High-Performance Management Team', *ceoforum.com.au*, March 2003.

25 G. Stasser, 'Pooling of Unshared Information during Group Discussion', in *Group Process and Productivity*, ed. S. Worchel, W. Wood and J. A. Simpson (Newbury Park, California: Sage, 1992), J. R. Katzenbach and D. K. Smith, *The Wisdom of Teams: Creating the High-Performance Organization* (Boston: Harvard University Press, 1993), 45–7.

26 S. E. Nedleman, 'Recruiters Reveal Their Top Interview Questions', *Financial News Online*, 16 February 2005.

27 P. C. Earley, 'East Meets West Meets Mideast: Further Explorations of Collectivistic and Individualistic Work Groups', *Academy of Management Journal* 36 (1993), 319–48; L. T. Eby and G. H. Dobbins, 'Collectivist Orientation in Teams: An Individual and Group-Level Analysis', *Journal of Organizational Behavior* 18 (1997), 275–95; S. B. Alavi and J. McCormick, 'Theoretical and Measurement Issues for Studies of Collective Orientation in Team Contexts', *Small Group Research* 35, no. 2 (April 2004), 111–27.

28 M. R. Barrick et al., 'Relating Member Ability and Personality to Work-Team Processes and Team Effectiveness', *Journal of Applied Psychology* 83 (1998), 377–91; S. Sonnentag, 'Excellent Performance: The Role of Communication and Cooperation Processes', *Applied Psychology: An International Review* 49 (2000), 483–97.

29 S. E. Jackson and A. Joshi, 'Diversity in Social Context: A Multi-Attribute, Multilevel Analysis of Team Diversity and Sales Performance', *Journal of Organizational Behavior* 25 (2004), 675–702; D. van Knippenberg, C. K. W. De Dreu and A. C. Homan, 'Work Group Diversity and Group Performance: An Integrative Model and Research Agenda', *Journal of Applied Psychology* 89, no. 6 (2004), 1008–22.

30 D. A. Harrison et al., 'Time, Teams, and Task Performance: Changing Effects of Surface- and Deep-Level Diversity on Group Functioning', *Academy of Management Journal* 45 (October 2002), 1029–45.

31 S. Ganesan, 'Reality-Style Recruitment', *Malaysia Star*, 9 October 2005; Z. Nazeer, 'You're Hired!' *The New Paper* (Singapore), 31 October 2005; J. Ng, 'Shell Uses "the Apprentice" Contest to Recruit Staff', *Straits Times* (Singapore), 3 October 2005.

32 K. Y. Williams, C.A. O'Reilly, 'Demography and Diversity in Organizations: A Review of 40 Years of Research', in *Research in Organizational Behavior*, ed. B. M. Staw and L. L. Cummings (Greenwich, CT: JAI, 1998), 77–140; C. M. Riordan, 'Relational Demography within Groups: Past Developments, Contradictions, and New Directions', in *Research in Personnel and Human Resources Management*, ed. G. R. Ferris (Greenwich, CT: JAI, 2000), 131–73.

33 D. C. Lau and J. K. Murnighan, 'Interactions within Groups and Subgroups: The Effects of Demographic Faultlines', *Academy of Management Journal* 48, no. 4 (August 2005), 645–59.

34 The NTSB and NASA studies are summarised in J. R. Hackman, 'New Rules for Team Building', *Optimize* (July 2002), 50–62.

35 B. W. Tuckman and M. A. C. Jensen, 'Stages of Small-Group Development Revisited', *Group and Organization Studies* 2 (1977), 419–42.

36 J. E. Mathieu and G. F. Goodwin, 'The Influence of Shared Mental Models on Team Process and Performance', *Journal of Applied Psychology* 85 (April 2000), 273–84.

37 A. Edmondson, 'Psychological Safety and Learning Behavior in Work Teams', *Administrative Science Quarterly* 44 (1999), 350–83.

38 D. L. Miller, 'The Stages of Group Development: A Retrospective Study of Dynamic Team Processes', *Canadian Journal of Administrative Sciences* 20, no. 2 (2003), 121–34. For other models of team development, see: J. G. Gersick, 'Time and Transition in Work Teams: Toward a New Model of Group Development', *Academy of Management Journal* 31 (March 1988), 9–41; J. E. Jones and W. L. Bearley, 'Facilitating Team Development: A View from the Field', *Group Facilitation* 3 (Spring 2001), 56–65; H. Arrow et al., 'Time, Change, and Development: The Temporal Perspective on Groups', *Small Group Research* 35, no. 1 (February 2004), 73–105.

39 W. B. Scott, 'Blue Angels', *Aviation Week & Space Technology*, 21 March 2005, 50–7.

40 D. C. Feldman, 'The Development and Enforcement of Group Norms', *Academy of Management Review* 9 (1984), 47–53; E. Fehr and U. Fischbacher, 'Social Norms and Human Cooperation', *Trends in Cognitive Sciences* 8, no. 4 (2004), 185–90.

41 'Employees Terrorized by Peer Pressure in the Workplace', *Morgan & Banks news release*, September 2000. For further discussion on sanctions applied to people who outperform others in the group, see J. J. Exline and M. Lobel, 'The Perils of Outperformance: Sensitivity about Being the Target of a Threatening Upward Comparison', *Psychological Bulletin* 125, no. 3 (1999), 307–37.

42 N. Ellemers and F. Rink, 'Identity in Work Groups: The Beneficial and Detrimental Consequences of Multiple Identities and Group Norms for Collaboration and Group Performance', *Advances in Group Processes* 22 (2005), 1–41.

43 C. R. Graham, 'A Model of Norm Development for Computer-Mediated Teamwork', *Small Group Research* 34, no. 3 (June 2003), 322–52.

44 J. J. Dose and R. J. Klimoski, 'The Diversity of Diversity: Work Values Effects on Formative Team Processes', *Human Resource Management Review* 9, no. 1 (Spring 1999), 83–108.

45 R. Hallowell, D. Bowen and C.-I. Knoop, 'Four Seasons Goes to Paris', *Academy of Management Executive* 16, no. 4 (November 2002), 7–24.

46 L. Y. Chan and B. E. Lynn, 'Operating in Turbulent Times: How Ontario's Hospitals Are Meeting the Current Funding Crisis', *Health Care Management Review* 23, no. 3 (1998), 7–18.

47 L. Coch and J. R. P. French, Jr., 'Overcoming Resistance to Change', *Human Relations* 1 (1948), 512–32.

48 Y. Martin, 'Prison Riot Teams Back in Favour', *The Press* (Christchurch, NZ), 2 October 2004, 9.

49 A. P. Hare, 'Types of Roles in Small Groups: A Bit of History and a Current Perspective', *Small Group Research* 25 (1994), 443–8.

50 S. H. N. Leung, J. W. K. Chan and W. B. Lee, 'The Dynamic Team Role Behavior: The Approaches of Investigation', *Team Performance Management* 9 (2003), 84–90.

51 R. M. Belbin, *Team Roles at Work* (Oxford, UK: Butterworth-Heinemann, 1993).

52 W. G. Broucek and G. Randell, 'An Assessment of the Construct Validity of the Belbin Self-Perception Inventory and Observer's Assessment from the Perspective of the Five-Factor Model', *Journal of Occupational and Organizational Psychology* 69 (December 1996), 389; S. G. Fisher, T. A. Hunter and W. D. K. Macrosson, 'The Structure of Belbin's Team Roles', *Journal of Occupational and Organizational Psychology* 71 (September 1998), 283–8; J. S. Prichard and N. A. Stanton, 'Testing Belbin's Team Role Theory of Effective Groups', *Journal of Management Development* 18 (1999), 652–65; G. Fisher, T. A. Hunter and W. D. K. Macrosson, 'Belbin's Team Role Theory: For Non-Managers Also?', *Journal of Managerial Psychology* 17 (2002), 14–20.

53 C. R. Evans and K. L. Dion, 'Group Cohesion and Performance: A Meta-Analysis', *Small Group Research* 22 (1991), 175–86; B. Mullen and C. Copper, 'The Relation between Group Cohesiveness and Performance: An Integration', *Psychological Bulletin* 115 (1994), 210–27; A. V. Carron et al., 'Cohesion and Performance in Sport: A Meta-Analysis', *Journal of Sport and Exercise Psychology* 24 (2002), 168–88; D. J. Beal et al., 'Cohesion and Performance in Groups: A Meta-Analytic Clarification of Construct Relations', *Journal of Applied Psychology* 88, no. 6 (2003), 989–1004.

54 N. Ellemers, R. Spears and B. Doosie, 'Self and Social Identity', *Annual Review of Psychology* 53 (2002), 161–86; K. M. Sheldon and B. A. Bettencourt, 'Psychological Need-Satisfaction and Subjective Well-Being within Social Groups', *British Journal of Social Psychology* 41 (2002), 25–38.

55 K. A. Jehn, G. B. Northcraft and M. A. Neale, 'Why Differences Make a Difference: A Field Study of Diversity, Conflict, and Performance in Workgroups', *Administrative Science Quarterly* 44, no. 4 (1999), 741–63; van Knippenberg, De Dreu and Homan, 'Work Group Diversity and Group Performance: An Integrative Model and Research Agenda'. For evidence that diversity/similarity does not always influence cohesion, see S. S. Webber and L. M. Donahue, 'Impact of Highly and Less Job-Related Diversity on Work Group Cohesion and Performance: A Meta-Analysis', *Journal of Management* 27, no. 2 (2001), 141–62.

56 E. Aronson and J. Mills, 'The Effects of Severity of Initiation on Liking for a Group', *Journal of Abnormal and Social Psychology* 59 (1959), 177–81; J. E. Hautaluoma and R. S. Enge, 'Early Socialization into a Work Group: Severity of Initiations Revisited', *Journal of Social Behavior & Personality* 6 (1991), 725–48.

57 Mullen and Copper, 'The Relation between Group Cohesiveness and Performance: An Integration'.

58 M. Rempel and R. J. Fisher, 'Perceived Threat, Cohesion, and Group Problem Solving in Intergroup Conflict', *International Journal of Conflict Management* 8 (1997), 216–34; M. E. Turner and T. Horvitz, 'The Dilemma of Threat: Group Effectiveness and Ineffectiveness under Adversity', in *Groups at Work: Theory and Research*, ed. M. E. Turner (Mahwah, NJ: Lawrence Erlbaum Associates, 2001), 445–70.

59 T. Macknay, 'Subculture', *Scoop*, Spring 2000; C. Stewart, '20 Seconds to Disaster', *The Australian Magazine*, 23 July 2005, 1.

60 W. Piper et al., 'Cohesion as a Basic Bond in Groups', *Human Relations* 36 (1983), 93–108; C. A. O'Reilly, D. E. Caldwell and W. P. Barnett, 'Work Group Demography, Social Integration, and Turnover', *Administrative Science Quarterly* 34 (1989), 21–37.

61 C. Langfred, 'Is Group Cohesiveness a Double-Edged Sword? An Investigation of the Effects of Cohesiveness on Performance', *Small Group Research* 29 (1998): 124–43; K. L. Gammage, A. V. Carron and P. A. Estabrooks, 'Team Cohesion and Individual Productivity: The Influence of the Norm for Productivity and the Identifiability of Individual Effort', *Small Group Research* 32 (February 2001), 3–18.

62 'The Trouble with Teams', *Economist* (14 January 1995), 6; H. Robbins and M. Finley, *Why Teams Don't Work* (Princeton, NJ: Peterson's/Pacesetters, 1995), chapter 20; E. A. Locke et al., 'The Importance of the Individual in an Age of Groupism', in *Groups at Work: Theory and Research*, ed. M. E. Turner (Mahwah, NJ: Lawrence Erbaum Associates, 2001), 501–28; N. J. Allen and T. D. Hecht, 'The "Romance of Teams": Toward an Understanding of Its Psychological Underpinnings and Implications', *Journal of Occupational and Organizational Psychology* 77 (2004), 439–61.

63 P. Panchak, 'The Future Manufacturing', *Industry Week* 247 (21 September 1998), 96–105.

64 I. D. Steiner, *Group Process and Productivity* (New York: Academic Press, 1972); N. L. Kerr and S. R. Tindale, 'Group Performance and Decision Making', *Annual Review of Psychology* 55 (2004), 623–55.

65 D. Dunphy and B. Bryant, 'Teams: Panaceas or Prescriptions for Improved Performance?', *Human Relations* 49 (1996), 677–99. For a discussion of Brooks's Law, see F. P. Brooks, ed., *The Mythical Man-Month: Essays on Software Engineering*, 2nd edn (Reading, Mass.: Addison-Wesley, 1995).

66 R. Cross, 'Looking before You Leap: Assessing the Jump to Teams in Knowledge-Based Work', *Business Horizons* (September 2000); Q. R. Skrabec Jr., 'The Myth of Teams', *Industrial Management* (September–October 2002), 25–7.

67 S. J. Karau and K. D. Williams, 'Social Loafing: A Meta-Analytic Review and Theoretical Integration', *Journal of Personality and Social Psychology* 65 (1993), 681–706; R. C. Liden et al., 'Social Loafing: A Field Investigation', *Journal of Management* 30 (2004), 285–304.

68 M. Erez and A. Somech, 'Is Group Productivity Loss the Rule or the Exception? Effects of Culture and Group-Based Motivation', *Academy of Management Journal* 39 (1996), 1513–37; Kerr and Tindale, 'Group Performance and Decision Making'.

69 E. Kidwell and N. Bennett, 'Employee Propensity to Withhold Effort: A Conceptual Model to Intersect Three Avenues of Research', *Academy of Management Review* 19 (1993), 429–56; J. M. George, 'Asymmetrical Effects of Rewards and Punishments: The Case of Social Loafing', *Journal of Occupational and Organizational Psychology* 68 (1995), 327–38; T. A. Judge and T. D. Chandler, 'Individual-Level Determinants of Employee Shirking', *Relations Industrielles* 51 (1996), 468–86.

CHAPTER 10

Developing high-performance teams

LEARNING OBJECTIVES

After reading this chapter, you should be able to:

- identify the characteristics of self-directed work teams (SDWTs)

- describe the four conditions in sociotechnical systems theory that support SDWTs

- summarise three challenges to SDWTs

- explain why virtual teams have become more common in organisations

- describe the role of communication systems, task structure, team size and team composition in virtual team effectiveness

- summarise the three levels of trust in teams

- identify five problems facing teams when making decisions

- describe the five structures for team decision making

- discuss the potential benefits and limitations of brainstorming

- outline the four types of team building.

Started more than sixty years ago as the original business of Hewlett-Packard founders William Hewlett and David Packard, Agilent Technologies is on the cutting edge of major trends in digital electronics and optical and wireless communications. It is also on the cutting edge of a globally distributed organisational structure where most employees work in virtual teams. The company closed its forty-eight US sales offices in 2003 and instructed its employees on how to work from home. In Australia, more than half of Agilent's 170 employees report to a manager located in another country. Its employees work with human resources staff in Malaysia, IT and finance staff in Singapore, and accounts payable/receivable staff in India.

Agilent has provided a variety of technologies to assist its distributed teams. It was an early adopter of web-based meeting tools, which offer virtual whiteboards, brainstorming rooms, breakout space for sub-group discussions, and video or voice conferencing. Yet, although its employees are in the high-tech business (most work in Melbourne at the company's global research and development centre for network testing equipment), Agilent Australia country manager Grant Marshall acknowledges that virtual teams can be challenging.

Employees at Agilent Technologies Australia are learning to work more effectively in global virtual teams.

'I think the initial reaction was one of frustration,' says Marshall. 'When you have everyone in the same place, you can get people in a room to talk through issues—at least things seem to be easier! When the team is virtual, you have to be much more structured in how you communicate with your team.' Marshall explains that virtual team members lack the nonverbal cues that exist in face-to-face meetings, so team dynamics require more sensitivity to the limited interpersonal information available. The company also provides cross-cultural training to increase employees' sensitivity to different interpretations of their words and actions.

Team development is another challenge that Agilent employees are working to overcome in a virtual team environment. Marshall strengthens the bonding process with his virtual team by scheduling a 'coffee pot chat' meeting once each month. 'All the virtual team [members] call in via a conference line,' Marshall explains. 'There is no specific pre-planned business agenda—the objective is to discuss general activities of what we have been doing.' The casual meeting lasts fifteen minutes to half an hour and includes such topics as 'personal accomplishments, sporting activities, films, holidays etc.—the type of discussion that you might have around the coffee station'.[1]

AGILENT TECHNOLOGIES IS forging new directions in building high-performance virtual teams. Years earlier, as a division of Hewlett-Packard (it was spun off in 1999), the company excelled in developing high-performance face-to-face teams. This chapter extends the discussion of teams by focusing on high-performance teams, including self-directed work teams, virtual teams, effective decision making in teams, and team-building strategies. It begins by introducing the features of self-directed work teams, as well as the elements of sociotechnical systems theory, on which these high-performance teams are based. Next, it looks at the increasing popularity of virtual teams and summarises current research on how to ensure that these virtual teams are effective. It also looks at the important topic of trust in virtual teams and other groups. The chapter then focuses on effective decision making in teams, including challenges and strategies to minimise problems with effective team decision making. The last section of the chapter looks at various team-building strategies.

SELF-DIRECTED WORK TEAMS

LEARNING OBJECTIVE

Identify the characteristics of self-directed work teams (SDWTs).

self-directed work teams (SDWTs) Cross-functional work groups organised around work processes, that complete an entire piece of work requiring several interdependent tasks, and that have substantial autonomy over the execution of those tasks.

Griffith University Library in Queensland has taken the leap towards becoming a high-performance organisation. Employees in the library's technical services section are organised into two teams—one for monographs and the other for serials. Each team has complete responsibility for ordering, receiving, cataloguing and other tasks in the work process. Team members participate in all decisions within the work process, including hiring new staff. Employees in the section also receive rewards and recognition tied to the achievement of the team's performance targets. 'The self-managed team model, in which all team members are aware of targets and work together to achieve them, has proven to be very successful,' says Glenda Smith, a team leader at Griffith University Library.[2]

Griffith University Library and many other organisations have adopted a form of work structure that relies on **self-directed work teams (SDWTs)**. There is limited information on how popular SDWTs are in Australia, New Zealand or Asia, but surveys estimate that somewhere between one-third and two-thirds of the medium and large organisations in the United States use these high-performance teams for part of their operations.[3]

SDWTs complete an entire piece of work requiring several interdependent tasks and have substantial autonomy over the execution of these tasks. These teams vary somewhat from one

EXHIBIT 10.1   **Features of self-directed work teams**

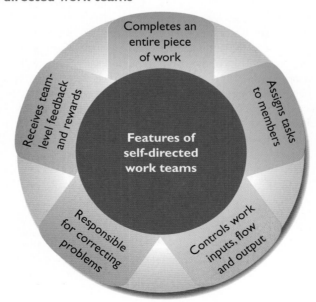

firm to the next, but they generally have the features listed in Exhibit 10.1.[4] First, SDWTs complete an entire piece of work, whether it's a product, a service, or part of a larger product or service. For instance, each library team at Griffith University is responsible for the entire process from ordering to maintaining either monographs or serial publications. Second, the team—not the supervisors—assigns tasks that individual team members perform. In other words, the team plans, organises and controls work activities with little or no direct involvement of a higher-status supervisor.

Third, SDWTs control most work inputs, flows and outputs. This occurs at Griffith University Library, where team members work directly with suppliers (publishers) on the input side and with students and other customers on the output side. Fourth, SDWTs are responsible for correcting work-flow problems as they occur. In other words, the teams maintain their own quality and logistical control. Fifth, SDWTs receive team-level feedback and rewards. This recognises and reinforces the fact that the team—not individuals—is responsible for the work, although team members may also receive individual feedback and rewards.

You may have noticed from this description that members of SDWTs have enriched and enlarged jobs. The team's work includes all the tasks required to make an entire product or provide the service. The team is also mostly responsible for scheduling, coordinating and planning these tasks.[5] Self-directed work teams were initially designed around production processes. However, they are also found in administrative and service activities, banking services, city government administration, and customer assistance teams in courier services. These service tasks are well suited to self-directed work teams when employees have interdependent tasks and decisions require the knowledge and experience of several people.[6]

SOCIOTECHNICAL SYSTEMS THEORY AND SDWTS

How do companies create successful self-directed work teams? To answer this question, we need to look at **sociotechnical systems (STS) theory**, which is the main source of current SDWT practices. STS theory was introduced during the 1940s at Britain's Tavistock Institute, where researchers had been studying the effects of technology on coal mining in the United Kingdom.[7]

The Tavistock researchers observed that the new coal-mining technology (called the 'long wall' method) led to lower, not higher, job performance. They analysed the causes of this problem and established the idea that organisations need 'joint optimisation' between the social and technical systems of the work unit. In other words, they need to introduce technology in a way that creates the best structure for semi-autonomous work teams. Moreover, the Tavistock group concluded that teams should be sufficiently autonomous so that they can control the main 'variances' in the system. This means that the team must control the factors with the greatest impact on quality, quantity and the cost of the product or service. From this overview of STS, four main conditions for high-performance SDWTs can be identified.[8]

> **sociotechnical systems (STS) theory** A theory stating that effective work sites have joint optimisation of their social and technological systems, and that teams should have sufficient autonomy to control key variances in the work process.

SDWTs are a primary work unit

STS theory suggests that self-directed teams work best when they are a primary work unit; in other words, when they are responsible for making an entire product, providing a service, or otherwise completing an entire work process. By making an entire product or service, the team is sufficiently independent that it can make adjustments without interfering with, or having interference from, other work units. At the same time, the primary work unit ensures that employees perform interdependent subtasks within their team so they have a sense of cohesiveness by working towards a common goal.[9]

LEARNING OBJECTIVE

Describe the four conditions in sociotechnical systems theory that support SDWTs.

SDWTs have sufficient autonomy

STS theory says that an SDWT must have sufficient autonomy to manage the work process. The team should be able to organise and coordinate work among its members to respond more quickly and effectively to its environment. This autonomy also motivates team members

REALITY CHECK 10.1

Don Golding

These Celestica team members completely redesigned the cell's work process, reflecting their company's movement towards self-directed work teams.

CELESTICA'S LEAN SELF-DIRECTED WORK TEAMS

From the day it was spun off from IBM ten years ago, Celestica Inc. has been under intense pressure to reduce costs. The global manufacturer of circuit boards and other electronic equipment for Dell, IBM, Hewlett-Packard and many others has moved some work to low-wage countries, but it has also remained competitive by relying on high-performance teams and lean manufacturing practices.

A few years ago, Celestica began the process of transforming its traditional assembly lines into team-based units. Using sociotechnical systems principles, teams mapped out work processes and identified key factors that they could control to improve efficiency and quality. Now, Celestica is pushing development of self-directed teams further through lean manufacturing initiatives. 'It's about moving away from complex IT types of systems so everyone can be involved in making improvements,' explains Rob Hemmant, Celestica's global lean architect.

Shown in this photo with Hemmant (third from right) are employees from one of Celestica's North American teams responsible for repairing rejected parts from other cells (team units) for reintroduction into the manufacturing process. The team participated in a four-day *kaizen* blitz, during which they completely reorganised their physical space and work flow to remove wasteful activities and resources.

'We implemented a U-shaped cell from incoming repair material to outgoing products,' says rework team member Muhammad Khan (fourth from left). Khan adds that the blitz cut space, time and distance, resulting in an impressive 86 per cent reduction in lead times. These *kaizen* blitzes are so successful that Celestica runs an average of three of them every week at various sites around the world.

Along with improving efficiency, *kaizen* blitzes and their underlying lean manufacturing principles push teams to become more autonomous and self-sufficient. For instance, the team shown in this photo previously had to get approval from an engineering group before repairing certain circuit boards; now, team members decide among themselves whether the boards should be repaired.

'People are starting to get involved and you can see the culture is starting to change,' points out cell engineer Chris Barlosky (second from left at back in the photo). 'The [*kaizen*] events are designed to empower operators so they can run the cell on their own. There's more ownership for the tools, machines and processes and they're eager to see improvements.'

Sources: R. Dyck and N. Halpern, 'Team-Based Organisations Redesign at Celestica', *Journal for Quality & Participation* 22 (September–October 1999), 36–40; B. Jorgensen, 'Look before You Leap', *Electronic Business* 30, no. 12 (2004), 35–36; D. McCutcheon, 'Chipping Away: Celestica's Toronto Plant Cuts Waste Blitz by Blitz', *Advanced Manufacturing* 6, no. 6 (November/December 2004), 23.

through feelings of empowerment. These features are apparent in Reality Check 10.1, where Celestica, the global electronic equipment manufacturer, is evolving towards a self-directed team structure based on a lean manufacturing philosophy and practices.

SDWTs control key variances

STS theory says that high-performance SDWTs have control over 'key variances'. These variances represent the disturbances or interruptions in the work process that affect the quality or performance of the product or service. For instance, the mixture of ingredients would be a key variance for employees in food processing because the mixture is within the team's control and it influences the quality of the final product. In contrast, applying STS offers little advantage when the primary causes of good or poor performance are mainly due to technology, supplies or other factors beyond the team's control.

SDWTs operate under joint optimisation

Perhaps the most crucial feature of STS theory is **joint optimisation**—the notion that the work process needs to balance the social and technical subsystems.[10] In particular, the technological system should be implemented in a way that encourages or facilitates team dynamics, job enrichment and meaningful feedback. This idea of joint optimisation was quite radical in the 1940s, a time when many thought that technology dictated how employees should be organised. In many cases, the technology resulted in people working alone with little opportunity to directly coordinate their work or share knowledge and ideas. Sociotechnical systems theory, on the other hand, says that companies can and must introduce technology so that it supports a semi-autonomous, team-based structure.

joint optimisation A key requirement in sociotechnical systems theory that a balance must be struck between social and technical systems to maximise an operation's effectiveness.

APPLYING STS THEORY AND SELF-DIRECTED WORK TEAMS

Although self-directed work teams receive less fanfare here than in the United States and Europe, such teams have been successfully implemented at ALCOA Australia, Davao Light & Power Co. in the Philippines, Work and Income New Zealand, the Western Australian State Revenue Department, and Aztec Software in Mumbai, India, among many others.[11] Numerous studies have found that, with a few important caveats to consider, self-directed work teams make a difference.

A decade ago, Canon Inc. introduced self-directed teams at all twenty-nine of its Japanese plants. The camera and copier company claims that a team of half a dozen people can now produce as much as thirty people in the old assembly-line system. One study found that car dealership service garages that organise employees into self-directed teams were significantly more profitable than service garages where employees work without a team structure. Another study reported that both short- and long-term measures of customer satisfaction increased after street-cleaning employees in a German city were organised into SDWTs.[12]

STS theory provides some guidance for designing self-directed work teams, but it doesn't provide enough detail regarding the optimal alignment of the social and technical systems. Volvo's Uddevalla manufacturing plant in Sweden is a case in point.[13] Opened in 1988 as a model of sociotechnical design, the Uddevalla plant replaced the traditional assembly line with fixed workstations at which teams of approximately twenty employees assembled and installed components in an unfinished car chassis. The work structure created a strong team orientation, but productivity was among the lowest in the car industry. (Producing a car at Uddevalla took fifty hours versus twenty-five hours at a traditional Volvo plant and thirteen hours at a Toyota plant.)

The Uddevalla plant was shut down in 1993 and re-opened two years later. The plant still makes use of highly skilled teams, but they are organised around a more traditional assembly-line process (similar to Toyota's production system). Some writers argue that organisational politics and poor market demand closed the Uddevalla experiment prematurely. However,

Federal Signal recently had a very similar experience in its truck assembly plant in the United States. It seems that both Volvo and Federal Signal failed to identify the best alignment of the social and technical subsystems.

CHALLENGES TO SELF-DIRECTED WORK TEAMS

Along with determining the best combination of social and technical subsystems, corporate leaders need to recognise and overcome at least three potential barriers to self-directed work teams: cross-cultural issues, management resistance, and employee and labour union resistance.

Cross-cultural issues

SDWTs are difficult to implement in high power distance cultures.[14] Employees in these cultures are more comfortable when supervisors give them directions, whereas low power distance employees value their involvement in decisions. One study reported that employees in Mexico (which has a high power distance culture) expect managers to make decisions affecting their work, whereas SDWTs emphasise self-initiative and individual responsibility within teams. Some writers also suggest that SDWTs are more difficult to implement in cultures with low collectivism because employees are less comfortable collaborating and working interdependently with co-workers.[15]

Management resistance

Poet Robert Frost once wrote, 'The brain is a wonderful organ; it starts working the moment you get up in the morning and does not stop until you get into the office.' Frost's humour highlights the fact that many organisations expect employees to park their brains at the door. Consistent with this view, studies report that supervisors and higher-level managers are often the main source of resistance to the transition to self-directed work teams. Their main worry is losing power when employees gain power through empowered teams. Some are concerned that their jobs will lose value, whereas others believe that they will not have any jobs at all.[16]

Self-directed teams operate best when supervisors shift from 'hands-on' controllers to 'hands off' facilitators, but many supervisors have difficulty changing their style. This was one of the biggest stumbling blocks to self-directed work teams at a TRW car-parts plant. Many supervisors kept slipping back into their command-and-control supervisory style. As one TRW employee explains: 'One of the toughest things for some of them was to shift from being a boss to a coach, moving from saying "I know what's good for you" to "How can I help you?"' Research suggests that supervisors are less likely to resist self-directed work teams when they have personally worked in a high-involvement workplace and receive considerable training in their new facilitation role.[17]

Employee and labour union resistance

Employees sometimes oppose SDWTs because they require new skills or appear to require more work. Many feel uncomfortable as they explore their new roles, and they may be worried that they lack the skills to adapt to the new work requirements. For instance, professional surveyors at a Swedish company reported increased stress when their company introduced customer-focused self-directed teams.[19]

Labour unions supported the early experiments in sociotechnical change in Europe and India, but some unions in other parts of the world have reservations about SDWTs.[20] One concern is that teams improve productivity at the price of higher stress levels among employees, which is sometimes true. Another worry is that SDWTs require more flexibility by reversing work rules and removing job categories that unions have negotiated over the years. Labour union leaders are therefore concerned that regaining these hard-fought union member rights will be a difficult battle.

Learning to lead self-directed teams

When Standard Motor Products (SMP) introduced self-directed work teams at its Kansas plant, supervisors had a tough challenge replacing their command-and-control management style with something closer to a mentor or facilitator. 'It wasn't easy for managers who were raised in the top-down authority model,' recalls Darrel Ray, the nationally recognised consultant who worked with the car-parts company during the transition. 'It is far easier to be a tyrant than it is to be a psychologist or a teacher,' explains distribution manager Don Wakefield. Steve Domann was one of the managers who had difficulty adjusting. 'I thought about quitting when the changes were announced,' says Domann, who now oversees plant work teams as a team developer. 'Some of the old management team couldn't conform to the team, but I'm glad I did.'[18]

In spite of these challenges, self-directed work teams offer enormous potential for organisations when they are implemented under the right conditions, as specified by sociotechnical systems theory. Meanwhile, information technologies and knowledge work have enabled virtual teams to gain popularity. The next section examines this new breed of team, including strategies to create high-performance virtual teams.

VIRTUAL TEAMS

As discussed in the opening vignette to this chapter, Agilent Technologies Australia increasingly relies on virtual teams. Virtual teams are teams whose members operate across space, time and organisational boundaries and are linked through information technologies to achieve organisational tasks.21 Virtual teams are similar to face-to-face teams in the sense that they consist of two or more people who interact and influence each other, are mutually accountable for achieving common goals associated with organisational objectives, and perceive themselves as a social entity within an organisation. However, virtual teams differ from traditional teams in two ways: (1) they are not usually co-located (work in the same physical area), and (2) due to their lack of co-location, members of virtual teams depend primarily on information technologies rather than face-to-face interaction to communicate and coordinate their work effort.

Virtual teams are one of the most significant developments in organisations over the past decade. One reason for their popularity is that Internet, intranets, instant messaging, virtual whiteboards and other products have made it easier than in the past to communicate with and coordinate people at a distance.[22] The shift from production-based to knowledge-based work has also made virtual teamwork feasible. Information technologies allow people to exchange knowledge work, such as software code, product development plans, and ideas for strategic decisions. In contrast, relying on virtual teams for production work, in which people develop physical objects, is less feasible.

Information technologies and knowledge-based work make virtual teams possible, but two other factors—globalisation and knowledge management—make them increasingly necessary. As described in Chapter 1, companies are opening businesses overseas, forming tight alliances with companies located elsewhere, and serving customers who want global support. These global conditions require a correspondingly global response in the form of virtual teams that

LEARNING OBJECTIVE

Explain why virtual teams have become more common in organisations.

coordinate these operations. As one IBM manager stated: 'IBM is a global company working in 170 countries in the world. Just that alone would dictate that we do work with people we've never met face to face and may never meet.'[23]

Invensys PLC, the British-based process and control engineering company, relies on information technologies to make the best use of its far-reaching talent, often organising employees into virtual teams at a moment's notice. 'Our development projects operate in a virtual mode and [gather] people from multiple sites based on project needs,' explains Joe Ayers, a manager at Invensys's process simulation unit in California. 'It is common for projects to utilise developers from three different time zones in a "follow the sun" development mode.'[24]

Along with aiding global coordination, virtual teams support knowledge management by allowing and encouraging employees to share and use knowledge in distributed operations. This is one of the main drivers behind the popularity of virtual teams at Agilent Technologies. The company's global research and development centre for router testing technologies is in Melbourne, but it relies on the expertise of employees in many other countries. Similarly, as was mentioned in Chapter 9, Holden GM's design team in Australia shares expertise with engineers at General Motor's design units in Detroit, South Korea (GM Daewoo) and other parts of the world.

DESIGNING HIGH-PERFORMANCE VIRTUAL TEAMS

LEARNING OBJECTIVE

Describe the role of communication systems, task structure, team size and team composition in virtual team effectiveness.

As with all teams, high-performance virtual teams are affected by the elements of the team effectiveness model discussed in Chapter 9. Exhibit 10.2 outlines the key design issues for virtual teams, which are discussed next.

Virtual team environment

Reward systems, communication systems, the organisational environment, the organisational structure and leadership influence the effectiveness of all teams, including virtual teams. Communication systems are particularly important because, unlike conventional teams, virtual teams cannot rely on face-to-face meetings whenever they wish. As will be seen in the next chapter, face-to-face communication transfers the highest volume and complexity of information and offers the timeliest feedback. In contrast, email, telephone and other information technologies fall far behind in their ability to exchange information. 'Having a four- to five-hour discussion is hard to do by phone, especially where you need to read body language,' says

EXHIBIT 10.2

Designing high-performance virtual teams

Team design element	Special virtual team requirements
Team environment	• Virtual teams need several communication channels available to offset lack of face-to-face communication.
Team tasks	• Virtual teams operate better with structured tasks rather than complex and ambiguous tasks.
Team size and composition	• Virtual teams usually require smaller team size than conventional teams. • Virtual team members must have skills in communicating through information technology and be able to process multiple threads of conversation. • Virtual team members are more likely than conventional team members to require cross-cultural awareness and knowledge.
Team processes	• Virtual team development and cohesiveness require some face-to-face interaction, particularly when the team forms.

an executive at accounting giant PricewaterhouseCoopers. Even videoconferencing, which seems similar to face-to-face meetings, actually communicates much less than we realise.[25]

To become a high-performance virtual team, the organisation needs to provide a variety of communication media so that virtual team members have the freedom to creatively combine these media to match the task demands.[26] For instance, virtual team members might rely on email to coordinate routine tasks but quickly switch to videoconferences and electronic whiteboards when emergencies arise. The lack of face-to-face communication isn't all bad news for virtual teams. Working through email or intranet systems can minimise status differences related to language skills. Team members whose first language is not English may be overwhelmed into silence in face-to-face meetings but have time to craft persuasive messages in cyberspace.

Virtual team tasks

Experts suggest that virtual teams operate best with structured tasks requiring only moderate levels of task interdependence.[27] Consider the task structure of client service engineers at BakBone Software. Each day, BakBone engineers in San Diego pick up customer support problems passed on from colleagues in Maryland and England. At the end of the workday, they pass some of these projects on to BakBone co-workers in Tokyo. The assignments sent on to Tokyo must be stated clearly, because overseas co-workers can't ask questions in the middle of San Diego's night.

BakBone's virtual team works well with these structured tasks, whereas the lack of co-location makes it difficult for them to consult and communicate on complex and ambiguous tasks. 'You don't have the time for open-ended conversation [in a virtual team],' admits BakBone engineer Roger Rodriguez. 'You can't informally brainstorm with someone.'[28] Generally, complex and ambiguous tasks should be assigned to co-located teams. Similarly, virtual teams should work on tasks requiring moderate levels of interdependence among team members. High levels of interdependence require more intense communication, so they are better assigned to co-located teams.

Virtual team size and composition

The problems of team size that were discussed in the previous chapter are amplified in virtual teams due to the limits of information technologies. In other words, virtual teams need to be smaller than comparable co-located teams in order to develop as quickly and coordinate as effectively. The team composition issues covered in Chapter 9 apply to virtual teams, with the added requirement that virtual team members need additional communication skills. They need to be sensitive to emotional reactions to emails and listen to more subtle nonverbal signals in teleconferences. 'On a call, I use subtle listening,' explains Procter & Gamble executive Karim Ladak, whose virtual team members live in six cities around the world. 'I listen for a quiver or a pause. And even then I know that I can very quickly miss something.'[29]

Virtual teams often span across cultures, so team members must also be aware of cross-cultural issues. For example, one study reported that virtual teams of American and Belgian college students were easily confused by differing conventions in the use of commas versus decimal points in numbers (e.g. $2.953 million versus $2,953 million). They also experienced cultural differences in socialising. The American students were willing to engage in social communication after they completed the assignment, whereas the Belgian students were more interested in developing a relationship with their partners before beginning work on the project.[30]

Team processes

Team development and cohesiveness are particular concerns for virtual teams because they lack the face-to-face interaction that supports these processes. For example, one recent university study found that face-to-face teams communicate better than virtual teams during the early stages of a project; it was only after gaining experience that virtual teams shared information as openly as face-to face teams. Other studies have reported that employees who work at a distance (such as through telework) from other team members tend to feel less connected with their team.[31]

There is no 'virtual' solution to this dilemma. Some companies try to ensure that virtual team members have good skills for communicating across distances. Another solution, ironically, is to have virtual team members meet face-to-face once in a while. For instance, when staff from Shell Canada and IBM Canada formed a virtual team to build an electronic customer-access system for Shell, they began with an 'all hands' face-to-face gathering to assist the team development process. The two firms also made a rule that the dispersed team members should have face-to-face contact at least once every six weeks throughout the project. Without this, 'after about five or six weeks we found some of that communication would start to break down,' says Sharon Hartung, the IBM co-manager for the project.[32]

TEAM TRUST

Any relationship—including the relationships among virtual team members—depends on a certain degree of trust between the parties.[34] Trust is a psychological state comprising the intention to accept vulnerability based on positive expectations of the intent or behaviour of another person. A high level of trust occurs when others affect you in situations where you are at risk, but you believe they will not harm you.

Trust has been discussed as both beliefs and conscious feelings about the relationship and the other party. In other words, a person both logically evaluates the situation as trustworthy and feels that it is trustworthy.[35] Trust can also be understood in terms of the foundation of that trust. From this perspective, people trust others based on three platforms: calculus, knowledge and identification (see Exhibit 10.3).

- *Calculus-based trust.* This minimal level of trust refers to an expected consistency of behaviour based on deterrence. Each party believes that the other will deliver on its promises because punishments will be administered if they fail.[36] For example, most employees have at least calculus-based trust because co-workers could get fired if they attempted to undermine another employee's work effort.

LEARNING OBJECTIVE

Summarise the three levels of trust in teams.

Keeping PwC's virtual teams in touch

PricewaterhouseCoopers (PwC) employs 190 training professionals in seventy offices across the United States. These professionals, along with many more consultants and academics who provide employee development services, routinely form virtual teams for new projects. The global accounting firm supports these virtual teams with the latest information technology, but even the techno-savvy professionals in PwC's training group know that it takes more than technology to bond people together. When Scott Patterson, PwC's e-learning manager in Atlanta, establishes a new project team, he relies on the old-fashioned way to build team spirit. 'I always try to do the kickoff meeting face-to-face,' says Patterson. 'We also try to bring the group back together for major milestones in a project.' Patterson explains that bringing virtual team members together once in a while is the best way to 'build enthusiasm and to get clear about everyone's roles and responsibilities'.[33]

PricewaterhouseCoopers

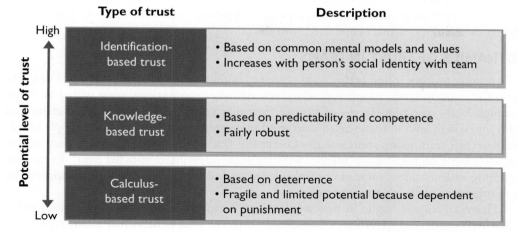

Three platforms of trust in teams

EXHIBIT 10.3

- *Knowledge-based trust.* Knowledge-based trust is grounded on the other party's predictability. The more we understand others and can predict what they will do in the future, the more we trust them, up to a moderate level. For instance, employees are more willing to trust leaders who 'walk the talk' because their actions are aligned with their words. Even if we don't agree with the leader, this consistency generates some level of trust. Knowledge-based trust also relates to confidence in the other person's ability or competence. People trust others based on their known or perceived expertise, such as when they trust a doctor.[37]
- *Identification-based trust.* This third type of trust is based on mutual understanding and an emotional bond between the parties. Identification occurs when one party thinks like, feels like and responds like the other party. High-performance teams exhibit this level of trust because they share the same values and mental models. Identification-based trust is connected to the concept of social identity; the more you define yourself in terms of membership of the team, the more trust you have in that team.[38]

These three foundations of trust are arranged in a hierarchy. Calculus-based trust offers the lowest potential trust because it is easily broken by a violation of expectations. Generally, calculus-based trust alone cannot sustain a team's relationship, because it relies on deterrence. Relationships don't become very strong when based only on the threat of punishment if one party fails to deliver its promises. Knowledge-based trust offers a higher potential level of trust and is more stable because it develops over time. Suppose that another member of your virtual team had submitted documentation to you on schedule in the past, but it arrived late this time. Knowledge-based trust might be dented by this incident, but it will not be broken. Through knowledge-based trust, you 'know' that the late delivery is probably an exception, because it deviates from the co-worker's past actions.

Identification-based trust is potentially the strongest and most robust of all three. The individual's self-image (social identity) is based partly on membership in the team and he/she believes their values highly overlap, so any transgressions by other team members are quickly forgiven. People are more reluctant to acknowledge a violation of this high-level trust because it strikes at the heart of their self-image.

INDIVIDUAL DIFFERENCES IN TRUST

Along with these three platforms of trust, the level of trust depends on a person's general *propensity to trust.*[39] Some people are inherently more willing than others to trust in a given situation. When joining a new work team, you might initially have very high trust in your new team-mates, whereas another new team member might feel only a moderate level of trust.

This difference is due to each individual's personality, values and socialisation experiences. Our willingness to trust others also varies with the emotions experienced at the moment. In particular, we trust people more when experiencing pleasant emotions than when angry, even when those emotions aren't connected with the other person.

DYNAMICS OF TRUST IN TEAMS

A common misconception is that team members build trust from a low level when they first join the team. In truth, people typically join a virtual or conventional team with a moderate or high level—not a low level—of trust in their new co-workers. The main explanation for this initial high level of trust (called *swift trust*) in organisational settings is that people usually believe their team-mates are reasonably competent (knowledge-based trust) and they tend to develop some degree of social identity with the team (identification-based trust). Even when working with strangers, most of us display some level of trust, if only because it supports our self-impression of being a nice person.[40]

However, trust is fragile in new relationships because it is based on assumptions rather than well-established experience. Consequently, recent studies of virtual teams report that trust tends to decrease rather than increase over time. In other words, new team members experience trust violations, which pushes their trust to a lower level. Employees who join the team with identification-based trust tend to drop back to knowledge-based or perhaps calculus-based trust. Declining trust is particularly challenging in virtual teams, because research identifies communication among team members as an important condition for sustaining trust. Equally important, employees become less forgiving and less cooperative towards others as their level of trust decreases, which undermines team and organisational effectiveness.[41]

TEAM DECISION MAKING

Self-directed work teams, virtual teams and practically all other groups are involved to some degree in making decisions. Under certain conditions, teams are more effective than individuals at identifying problems, choosing alternatives and evaluating their decisions. To leverage these benefits, however, the constraints on effective team decision making need to be understood. These constraints will be looked at, followed by specific team structures that try to overcome such constraints.

CONSTRAINTS ON TEAM DECISION MAKING

Anyone who has spent a reasonable amount of time in the workplace can list several ways in which teams stumble in decision making. Five of the most common problems are time constraints, evaluation apprehension, pressure to conform, groupthink and group polarisation.

Time constraints

There's a saying that 'committees keep minutes and waste hours'. This reflects the fact that teams take longer than individuals to make decisions.[42] Unlike individuals, teams require extra time to organise, coordinate and socialise. The larger the group, the more time required to make a decision. Team members need time to learn about each other and build rapport. They need to manage an imperfect communication process so that there is sufficient understanding of each other's ideas. They also need to coordinate roles and rules of order within the decision process.

Another time-related constraint found in most team structures is that only one person can speak at a time.[43] This problem, known as **production blocking**, undermines idea generation in several ways. First, team members need to listen in on the conversation to find an opportune time to speak up, and this monitoring makes it difficult for them to concentrate on their own ideas. Second, ideas are fleeting, so the longer a member waits to speak up, the more likely

these flickering ideas will die out. Third, team members might remember their fleeting thoughts by concentrating on them, but this causes them to pay less attention to the conversation. By ignoring what others are saying, team members miss other potentially good ideas as well as the opportunity to convey their ideas to others in the group.

Evaluation apprehension

Individuals are reluctant to mention ideas that seem silly because they believe (often correctly) that other team members are silently evaluating them.[44] This **evaluation apprehension** is based on the individual's desire to create a favourable self-presentation and need to protect self-esteem. It is most common in meetings attended by people with different levels of status or expertise, or when members formally evaluate each other's performance throughout the year (as in 360-degree feedback). Creative ideas often sound bizarre or illogical when presented, so evaluation apprehension tends to discourage employees from mentioning them in front of co-workers.

evaluation apprehension When individuals are reluctant to mention ideas that seem silly because they believe (often correctly) that other team members are silently evaluating them.

Pressure to conform

Recall from the previous chapter that cohesiveness leads individual members to conform to the team's norms. This control keeps the group organised around common goals, but it may also cause team members to suppress their dissenting opinions, particularly when a strong team norm is related to the issue. When someone does state a point of view that violates the majority opinion, other members might punish the violator or try to persuade him or her that the opinion is incorrect. Conformity can also be subtle. To some extent, we depend on the opinions that others hold to validate our own views. If co-workers don't agree with us, then we begin to question our own opinions even without overt peer pressure.

Groupthink

One team decision-making problem that most people have heard about is **groupthink**—the tendency of highly cohesive groups to value consensus at the price of decision quality.[45] Groupthink goes beyond the problem of conformity by focusing on how decisions go awry when team members try to maintain harmony. This desire for harmony exists as a group norm and is most apparent when team members have a strong social identity with the group. Along with a desire for harmony, groupthink supposedly occurs when the team is isolated from outsiders, the team leader is opinionated (rather than impartial), the team is under stress due to an external threat, the team has experienced recent failures or other decision-making problems, and the team lacks clear guidance from corporate policies or procedures.

groupthink The tendency of highly cohesive groups to value consensus at the price of decision quality.

The concept of groupthink gets mixed reviews from researchers because some of the above-mentioned groupthink characteristics actually improve rather than undermine the team decision-making process, in some situations.[46] Other aspects of the concept do create problems in team decision making. For example, groupthink characteristics cause teams to be highly confident in their decisions. One recent study reported that highly confident teams are less attentive in decision making than moderately confident teams. This is consistent with previous evidence that overconfident executive groups make sloppy decisions because they are complacent and have a false sense of invulnerability.[47]

Group polarisation

Group polarisation refers to the tendency of teams to make more extreme decisions than individuals working alone.[48] Suppose that a group of people meets to decide on the future of a new product. Individual team members might come to the meeting with various degrees of support or opposition to the product's future. Yet, by the end of the meeting, chances are that the team will agree on a more extreme solution than the average person had when the meeting began.

group polarisation The tendency of teams to make more extreme decisions than individuals working alone.

EXHIBIT 10.4   **The group polarisation process**

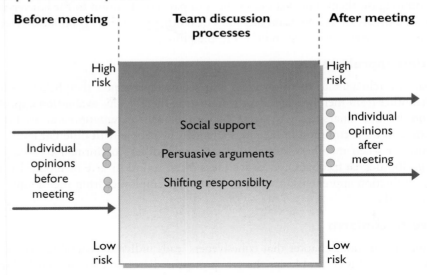

There are three reasons why group polarisation occurs (see Exhibit 10.4). First, team members become comfortable with more extreme positions when they realise that co-workers also generally support the same position. Second, persuasive arguments favouring the dominant position convince doubtful members and help form a consensus around the extreme option. Finally, individuals feel less personally responsible for the decision consequences because the decision is made by the team. Social support, persuasion and shifting responsibility explain why teams make *extreme* decisions, but they also make *riskier* decisions because of the natural tendency to take higher risks when facing certain losses. This tendency is due to the prospect theory effect described in Chapter 8—people try to avoid losses because they are more painful than the equivalent gain.[49]

TEAM STRUCTURES TO IMPROVE CREATIVITY AND DECISION MAKING

LEARNING OBJECTIVE

Describe the five structures for team decision making.

The constraints on team decision making are potentially serious, but several solutions also emerge from these bad-news studies. Team members need to be confident in their decision making, but not so confident that they collectively feel invulnerable. This calls for team norms that encourage critical thinking as well as team membership that maintains sufficient diversity. Team leaders and other powerful members can sway the rest of the group, so checks and balances need to be in place to avoid the adverse effects of this power. Another practice is to maintain an optimal team size. The group should be large enough that members possess the collective knowledge to resolve the problem, yet small enough that the team doesn't consume too much time or restrict individual input.

Team structures also help to minimise the problems described over the previous few pages. Five team structures potentially improve creativity and decision making in team settings: constructive conflict, brainstorming, electronic brainstorming, the Delphi method and the nominal group technique.

Constructive conflict

constructive conflict Occurs when team members debate their different perceptions about an issue in a way that keeps the conflict focused on the task rather than people.

Constructive conflict occurs when team members debate their different perceptions about an issue in a way that keeps the conflict focused on the task rather than people. This conflict is called 'constructive' because participants pay attention to facts and logic and avoid statements that generate emotional conflict. The main advantage of this debate is that it presents different points of view, and thus encourages everyone to re-examine their assumptions and logic.

NASA encourages constructive conflict

The ill-fated flight of the space shuttle *Columbia* was a wake-up call for how NASA's mission management team makes decisions. The *Columbia* accident investigation team concluded that concerns raised by engineers were either deflected or watered-down because the mission management team appeared to be 'immersed in a culture of invincibility' and hierarchical authority discouraged constructive debate. If top decision makers had more fully considered the extent of damage during takeoff, they might have been able to save *Columbia's* seven crew members. To foster more open communications and constructive debate, the mission management team's assigned-seating rectangular table has been replaced by a C-shaped arrangement where people sit wherever they want (shown in photo). None of the twenty-four members stands out above the others in the new set-up. Around the walls of the room are pearls of wisdom reminding everyone of the pitfalls of team decision making. 'People in groups tend to agree on courses of action which, as individuals, they know are stupid,' warns one poster.[51]

Johnson Space Center/NASA

One problem with constructive conflict is that it is difficult to apply; healthy debate can slide into personal attacks. Also, the effect of constructive conflict on team decision making is inconsistent. Some research indicates that debate—even criticism—can be good for team decision making, whereas others say that all forms of conflict can be detrimental to teams. Until this issue gets sorted out, constructive conflict should be used cautiously.[50]

Brainstorming

In the 1950s, advertising executive Alex Osborn wanted to find a better way for teams to generate creative ideas.[52] Osborn's solution, called **brainstorming**, requires team members to abide by four rules. Osborn believed that these rules encourage divergent thinking while minimising evaluation apprehension and other team dynamics problems.

- *Speak freely.* Brainstorming welcomes wild and wacky ideas because these become the seeds of divergent thinking in the creative process. Crazy suggestions are sometimes crazy only because they break out of the mould set by existing mental models.
- *Don't criticise.* Team members are more likely to contribute wild and wacky ideas if no one tries to mock or criticise them. Thus, a distinctive rule in brainstorming is that no one is allowed to criticise any ideas that are presented.
- *Provide as many ideas as possible.* Brainstorming is based on the idea that quantity breeds quality. In other words, teams generate better ideas when they generate many ideas. This relates to the belief that divergent thinking occurs after traditional ideas have been exhausted. Therefore, the group should think of as many possible solutions as they can and go well beyond the traditional solutions to a problem.
- *Build on the ideas of others.* Team members are encouraged to 'piggyback' or 'hitchhike', that is, combine and improve on the ideas already presented. Building on existing ideas encourages the synergy of employee involvement that was mentioned in Chapter 8.

Brainstorming is a well-known team structure for encouraging creative ideas. Yet for several years researchers concluded that this practice was ineffective. Lab studies found that brainstorming groups generated fewer ideas, largely because production blocking and evaluation apprehension still interfered with team dynamics.[53] However, these conclusions contrast with

brainstorming A freewheeling, face-to-face meeting where team members aren't allowed to criticise, but are encouraged to speak freely, generate as many ideas as possible, and build on the ideas of others.

LEARNING OBJECTIVE

Discuss the potential benefits and limitations of brainstorming.

more recent real-world evidence that highly creative firms such as IDEO, the California product design firm, thrive on brainstorming.

There are a few explanations for why the lab studies differ from real-world evidence.[54] First, the lab studies measured the number of ideas generated, whereas brainstorming seems to provide more creative ideas, which is the main reason that companies use brainstorming. Evaluation apprehension may be a problem for students brainstorming in lab experiments, but it is less of a problem in high-performing teams that trust each other and embrace a learning orientation culture. The lab studies also overlooked the fact that brainstorming participants interact and participate directly, thereby increasing decision acceptance and team cohesiveness.

Brainstorming sessions also provide valuable nonverbal communication that spreads enthusiasm, which, in turn, provides a more creative climate. Clients are sometimes involved in brainstorming sessions, so these positive emotions may produce higher customer satisfaction than if people are working alone on the product. Overall, while brainstorming might not always be the best team structure, it seems to be more valuable than some of the earlier research studies indicated.

Electronic brainstorming

electronic brainstorming
Using special computer software, participants share ideas while minimising the team dynamics problems inherent in traditional brainstorming sessions.

Electronic brainstorming tries to minimise many of the problems described earlier with face-to-face brainstorming by having people generate and share ideas through computers. A facilitator begins the process by posting a question. Participants then enter their answers or ideas on their computer terminal. Soon after, everyone's ideas are posted anonymously and randomly on the computer screens or at the front of the room. Participants eventually vote electronically on the ideas presented. Face-to-face discussion usually follows the electronic brainstorming process.

Research indicates that electronic brainstorming generates more ideas than traditional brainstorming and more creative ideas than traditional interacting teams. Participants also tend to be more satisfied, motivated and confident in the decision-making exercise than in other team structures.[55] One reason for these favourable outcomes is that electronic brainstorming significantly reduces production blocking. Participants are able to document their ideas as soon as they pop into their heads, rather than wait their turn to communicate.[56] The process also supports creative synergy because participants can easily develop new ideas from those generated by other people. Electronic brainstorming also minimises the problem of evaluation apprehension, because ideas are posted anonymously.

Despite these numerous advantages, electronic brainstorming is not widely used by corporate leaders. One possible reason is that it might be too structured and technology-bound for some executives. Furthermore, some decision makers may feel threatened by the honesty of statements generated through this process and by their limited ability to control the discussion. A third explanation is that electronic brainstorming may work for certain types of decisions, but not for others. For example, electronic brainstorming may be less effective than face-to-face meetings where effective decision making is less important than social bonding and emotional interaction.[57] Overall, electronic brainstorming can significantly improve decision making under the right conditions, but more research is required to identify those conditions.

Delphi method

Delphi method A structured team decision-making process of systematically pooling the collective knowledge of experts on a particular subject to make decisions, predict the future or identify opposing views.

The **Delphi method** was developed by the RAND think tank in the 1950s and has regained attention over the past decade. Delphi systematically pools the collective knowledge of experts on a particular subject to make decisions, predict the future, identify opposing views (called dissensus) or identify multiple causes of events.[58] One recent example is a Delphi analysis of the causes of increasing obesity among Australians. Fifty experts identified a range of causes, then in a second round rank-ordered the importance of each cause, along with an explanation of their rankings. The results revealed a dissensus of opinion about why Australians are gaining weight.[59]

There are a few variations, but most Delphi groups have the following features. They do not meet face to face; in fact, participants are often located in different parts of the world and may not know each other's identity. As with electronic brainstorming, Delphi participants do not know who 'owns' the ideas submitted. Typically, Delphi group members submit possible solutions or comments regarding an issue to the central convener, although computer technology is turning this stage into an automatic compilation process. The compiled results are returned to the panel for a second round of comments. This process may be repeated a few more times until consensus or dissensus emerges.

Nominal group technique

Nominal group technique is a variation of traditional brainstorming that tries to combine individual efficiencies with team dynamics.[60] The method is called nominal because participants form a group in name only during two stages of decision making. This process, shown in Exhibit 10.5, first involves the individual, then the group, and finally the individual again. After the problem is described, team members silently and independently write down as many solutions as they can. During the group stage, participants describe their solutions to the other team members, usually in a round-robin format. As with brainstorming, there is no criticism or debate, although members are encouraged to ask for clarification of the ideas presented. In the final stage, participants silently and independently rank-order or vote on each proposed solution.

Nominal group technique tends to generate a higher number of ideas and better quality ideas compared with traditional interacting and possibly brainstorming groups.[61] Due to its high degree of structure, nominal group technique usually maintains a high task orientation and a relatively low potential for conflict within the team. However, team cohesiveness is generally lower in nominal decisions because the structure minimises social interaction. Production blocking and evaluation apprehension still occur to some extent.

nominal group technique A structured team decision-making process whereby team members independently write down ideas, describe and clarify them to the group, and then independently rank or vote on them.

TEAM BUILDING

HellermannTyton's sixty senior marketing executives recently gathered in what appeared to be the middle of a South American jungle. In reality, the executives at the global maker of wire and cable products were participating in a team-building exercise located in a private wildlife reserve in Naples, Florida, complete with giraffes, leopards, chimpanzees and alligators. 'You would never think we were still in Naples, but we were,' says Terry Tuttle, HellermannTyton's vice-president of marketing. The safari-themed program tested the managers' teamwork, communication and leadership skills in a realistic setting. One activity even put participants up close with a live alligator. 'Although many were sceptical at first, you could see the teams

Nominal group technique

EXHIBIT 10.5

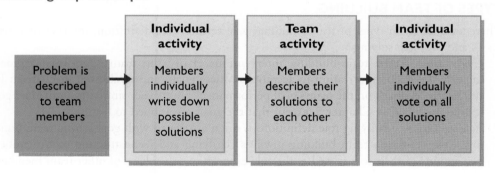

Volunteering builds better teams

Many companies are turning to charity work and community volunteering as ways to build better teams in the workplace. Deakin University holds an annual team-building day in which employees work together to contribute to charities. Recently, more than 100 building and grounds employees from Deakin helped to improve facilities at a donation-run children's camp. Give India's annual Dream Run marathon in Mumbai was oversubscribed as dozens of companies wanted to participate. 'There's participation from across the board, so it's a great bonding event,' says an executive at Prudential ICICI Asset Management. The Hong Kong operation of German electronics company Siemens is improving team dynamics by encouraging employees

Siemens Ltd

to work with social services organisation St James' Settlement. '[Charity work] is a great opportunity for people to get to know each other in an environment where they're all doing exactly the same task so there's no hierarchy,' says Kathryn Wightman-Beaven, at the accounting firm where 40 per cent of the 4500 staff volunteer on an annual basis. 'It really does help people to understand each other and build teams.'[64]

form and build with each exercise,' says Tuttle. 'By the end, everyone was pumped up. We established camaraderie as a group that is essential to getting business goals accomplished throughout the year.'[62]

The executives at HellermannTyton rejuvenated team dynamics through **team building**— any formal activity intended to improve the development and functioning of a work team.[63] Some team-building activities also reshape team norms and strengthen cohesiveness. Team building is sometimes applied to newly established teams because team members are at the earliest stages of team development. However, it is more common among existing teams, such as at HellermannTyton, where employees need to re-establish camaraderie or where the team has regressed to earlier stages of team development. Team building is therefore most appropriate when the team experiences high membership turnover or members have lost focus on their respective roles and team objectives.

team building Any formal activity intended to improve the development and functioning of a team.

TYPES OF TEAM BUILDING

There are four main types of team building: goal setting, role definition, interpersonal processes and problem solving.[65]

LEARNING OBJECTIVE

Outline the four types of team building.

- *Goal setting.* Some team-building interventions clarify the team's performance goals, increase the team's motivation to accomplish these goals, and establish a mechanism for systematic feedback on the team's goal performance. This is very similar to individual goal setting described in Chapter 5, except that the goals are applied to teams.
- *Role definition.* Clarifying role definitions is often associated with goal-setting team building. Role definition team building involves clarifying and reconstructing each member's perceptions of their role as well as the role expectations they have of other team members.

Various interventions may be applied, ranging from open discussion to structured analysis of the work process. Role definition encompasses the emerging concept of *team mental models*. Recall from Chapter 3 that mental models are internal representations of the external world. Research studies indicate that team processes and performance depend on how well team-mates share common mental models about how they should work together.[66] Team-building activities help team members to clarify and form a more unified perspective of their team mental models.

- *Interpersonal processes*. This category of team building covers a broad territory. Conflict management fits under this heading, both as a symptom to identify the team's underlying weaknesses and as an ongoing interpersonal process that team members learn to continuously manage constructively. Early team-building interventions relied on direct confrontation sessions to give the sources of conflict an airing. This can work with professional facilitation, but experts warn that open dialogue is not always the most effective way to solve team conflicts.[67] Another interpersonal process is building (or rebuilding) trust among team members. Popular interventions such as wilderness team activities, paintball wars and obstacle course challenges are typically offered to build trust. 'If two colleagues hold the rope for you while you're climbing 10 metres up, that is truly team-building,' explains Jan Antwerpes, a partner in a German communications consulting firm. 'It also shows your colleagues that you care for them.'[68]

- *Problem solving*. This type of team building focuses on decision making, including the issues mentioned earlier in the chapter and the decision-making process described in Chapter 8. To improve their problem-solving skills, some teams participate in simulation games that require team decisions in hypothetical situations.

IS TEAM BUILDING EFFECTIVE?

Are team-building interventions effective? Is the money well spent? So far, the answer is an equivocal 'maybe'. Studies suggest that some team-building activities are successful, but just as many fail to build high-performance teams.[69] One problem is that corporate leaders assume that team-building activities are general solutions to general team problems. No one bothers to diagnose the team's specific needs (e.g. problem solving, interpersonal processes) because the team-building intervention is assumed to be a broad-brush solution. A better approach is to begin with a sound diagnosis of the team's health, then select team-building interventions that address weaknesses.[70]

Another problem is that corporate leaders tend to view team building as a one-shot medical inoculation that every team should receive when it is formed. In truth, team building is an ongoing process, not a three-day jumpstart. Some experts suggest, for example, that wilderness experiences often fail because they rarely include follow-up consultation to ensure that team learning is transferred back to the workplace.[71]

Finally, it must be remembered that team building occurs on the job, not just on an obstacle course or in a national park. Organisations should encourage team members to reflect on their work experiences and to experiment with just-in-time learning for team development. This dialogue requires open communication, so employees can clarify expectations, coordinate work activities, and build common mental models of working together. The next chapter looks at the dynamics of communicating in teams and organisations.

CHAPTER SUMMARY

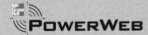
Self-directed work teams (SDWTs) complete an entire piece of work requiring several interdependent tasks and have substantial autonomy over the execution of these tasks. Sociotechnical systems (STS) theory identifies four main conditions for high-performance SDWTs. SDWTs must be a primary work unit, have sufficient autonomy, have control over key variances, and operate under joint optimisation.

STS theory has been widely supported since its origins in the 1950s. However, it is not very helpful at identifying the optimal alignment of the social and technical system. SDWTs also face cross-cultural issues, management resistance, and labour union and employee resistance.

Virtual teams are teams whose members operate across space, time and organisational boundaries and are linked through information technologies to achieve organisational tasks. Unlike conventional teams, virtual team members are not co-located, so they are more dependent on information technologies rather than face-to-face interaction. Virtual teams are gaining in popularity because information technology and knowledge-based work make it easier to collaborate from a distance. Virtual teams are becoming increasingly necessary because they represent a natural part of the knowledge management process. Moreover, as companies globalise, they must rely more on virtual teams than co-located teams to coordinate operations at distant sites.

Several elements in the team effectiveness model stand out as important issues for virtual teams. High-performance virtual teams require a variety of communication media, and virtual team members need to creatively combine these media to match the task demands. Virtual teams operate better with structured rather than complex and ambiguous tasks. They usually cannot maintain as large a team as is possible in conventional teams. Members of virtual teams require special skills in communication systems and should be aware of cross-cultural issues. Virtual team members should also meet face to face on occasion, particularly when the team forms, to assist team development and cohesiveness.

Trust is important in team dynamics, particularly in virtual teams. Trust is a psychological state comprising the intention to accept vulnerability based on positive expectations of the intent or behaviour of another person. The minimum level of trust is calculus-based trust, which is based on deterrence. Teams cannot survive with this level of trust. Knowledge-based trust is a higher level of trust and is grounded on the other party's predictability. The highest level of trust, called identification-based trust, is based on mutual understanding and an emotional bond between the parties. Most employees join a team with a fairly high level of trust, which tends to decline over time.

Team decisions are impeded by time constraints, evaluation apprehension, conformity to peer pressure, groupthink and group polarisation. Production blocking—where only one person typically speaks at a time—is a form of time constraint on teams. Evaluation apprehension occurs when employees believe that others are silently evaluating them, so they avoid stating seemingly silly ideas. Conformity keeps team members aligned with team goals, but it also tends to suppress dissenting opinions. Groupthink is the tendency of highly cohesive groups to value consensus at the price of decision quality. Group polarisation refers to the tendency of teams to make more extreme decisions than individuals working alone.

To minimise decision-making problems, teams should be moderately (not highly) confident, ensure that the team leader does not dominate, maintain an optimal team size, and ensure that team norms support critical thinking. Five team structures that potentially improve team decision making are constructive conflict, brainstorming, electronic brainstorming, the Delphi method and the nominal group technique. Constructive conflict occurs when team members debate their different perceptions about an issue in a way that keeps the conflict focused on the task rather than people. Brainstorming requires team members to speak freely, avoid criticism, provide as many ideas as possible, and build on the ideas of others. Electronic brainstorming uses computer software to share ideas while minimising team dynamics problems. The Delphi method systematically pools the collective knowledge of experts on a particular subject without face-to-face meetings. In the nominal group technique, participants write down ideas alone, describe these ideas in a group, then silently vote on these ideas.

Team building is any formal activity intended to improve the development and functioning of a work team. Four team-building strategies are goal setting, role definition, interpersonal processes and problem solving. Some team-building events succeed, but companies often fail to consider the contingencies of team building.

KEY TERMS

brainstorming p. 309
constructive conflict p. 308
Delphi method p. 310
electronic brainstorming p. 310
evaluation apprehension p. 307

group polarisation p. 307
groupthink p. 307
joint optimisation p. 299
nominal group technique p. 311
production blocking p. 306

self-directed work teams (SDWTs) p. 296
sociotechnical systems (STS) theory p. 297
team building p. 312
trust p. 304
virtual teams p. 301

DISCUSSION QUESTIONS

1. How do self-directed work teams differ from conventional teams?

2. Advanced Telecom Pty Ltd has successfully introduced self-directed work teams at its operations throughout Australia and New Zealand. The company now wants to introduce SDWTs at its plants in Thailand and Mexico. What potential cross-cultural challenges might Advanced Telecom experience as it introduces SDWTs in these high power distance countries?

3. A chicken processing company wants to build a processing plant designed around sociotechnical systems principles. In a traditional chicken processing plant, employees work in separate departments—cleaning and cutting, cooking, packaging, and warehousing. The cooking and packaging processes are controlled by separate workstations in the traditional plant. How would the company change this operation according to sociotechnical systems design?

4. What can organisations do to reduce management resistance to self-directed work teams?

5. Suppose the instructor for this course assigned you to a project team consisting of three other students who are currently taking similar courses in Ireland, India and Brazil. All students speak English and have similar expertise in the topic. Use your knowledge of virtual teams to discuss the problems that your team might face, compared with a team of local students who can meet face to face.

6. What can virtual teams do to sustain trust among team members?

7. Some firms in this region have turned to volunteering as a form of team building, whereby a group of employees spends a day working together on a community project, often outside their expertise. In what ways might volunteering be an effective team-building activity?

8. Bangalore Technologies wants to use brainstorming with its employees and customers to identify new uses for its technology. Advise Bangalore's CEO about the potential benefits of brainstorming, as well as its potential limitations.

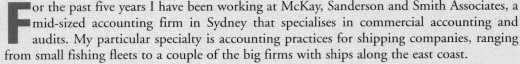

SKILL BUILDER | 10.1   THE SHIPPING INDUSTRY ACCOUNTING TEAM

CASE STUDY

For the past five years I have been working at McKay, Sanderson and Smith Associates, a mid-sized accounting firm in Sydney that specialises in commercial accounting and audits. My particular specialty is accounting practices for shipping companies, ranging from small fishing fleets to a couple of the big firms with ships along the east coast.

About eighteen months ago, McKay, Sanderson and Smith Associates became part of a large merger involving two other accounting firms. These firms have offices in Melbourne, Brisbane and Perth. Although the other two accounting firms were much larger than McKay, all three firms agreed to avoid centralising the business around one office in Sydney. Instead, the new firm—called Goldberg, Choo and McKay Associates—would rely on teams across the country to 'leverage the synergies of our collective knowledge' (an often-cited statement from the managing partner soon after the merger).

The merger affected me personally a year ago when my boss (a senior partner and vice-president of the merged firm) announced that I would be working closely with three people from the other two firms to become the firm's new shipping industry accounting team. The other 'team members' were Elias in Melbourne, Susan in Brisbane and Brad in Perth. I had met Elias briefly at a meeting in Melbourne during the merger, but had never met Susan or Brad, although I knew that they were shipping accounting professionals at the other firms.

Initially, the shipping 'team' activities involved emailing each other about new contracts and prospective clients. Later, we were asked to submit joint monthly reports on accounting statements and issues. Normally, I submitted my own monthly reports, which summarised activities involving my own clients. Coordinating the monthly report with three other people took much more time, particularly since different accounting documentation procedures across the three firms were still being resolved. It took numerous emails and a few telephone calls to work out a reasonable monthly report style.

During this aggravating process, it became apparent—to me at least—that this 'team's' business was costing me more time than it was worth. Moreover, Brad in Perth didn't have a clue about how to communicate with the rest of us. He rarely replied to emails. Instead, he often used the telephone voice-mail system, which resulted in lots of telephone tag. Brad arrives at work at 9.30 am in Perth (and is often late!), which is early afternoon in Brisbane. My typical work hours are from 7.30 am to 3.30 pm, allowing me to chauffeur my kids after school to sports and music lessons. So Brad and I have a window of less than three hours in which to share information.

The biggest nuisance with the shipping specialist accounting team started two weeks ago when the firm asked the four of us to develop a new strategy for attracting more shipping firm business. This new strategic plan is a messy business. Somehow we have to share our thoughts on various approaches, agree on a new plan, and write a unified submission to the managing partner. Already the project is taking most of my time, just writing and responding to emails and talking in conference calls (which none of us did much of before the team was formed).

Susan and Brad have already had two or three 'misunderstandings' via email about their different perspectives on delicate matters in the strategic plan. The worst of these disagreements required a conference call with all of us to resolve. Except for the most basic matters, it seems that we can't understand each other, let alone agree on key issues. Thank goodness Brad lives on the other side of the country, because I would go crazy if I had to have him working with me in the Sydney office. While Elias and I seem to agree on most points, the overall team can't form a common vision or strategy. I don't know how Elias, Susan or Brad feel, but I would be quite happy to work somewhere that did not require any of these long-distance team headaches.

QUESTIONS

1. What type of team was formed here? Was it necessary, in your opinion?

2. Use the team effectiveness model in Chapter 9 and related information in this chapter to identify the strengths and weaknesses of this team's environment, design and processes.

3. Assuming that these four people must continue to work as a team, recommend ways to improve the team's effectiveness.

EGG DROP EXERCISE

10.2 | SKILL BUILDER

TEAM EXERCISE

PURPOSE
This exercise is designed to help you understand the dynamics of high-performance teams.

MATERIALS
The instructor will provide various raw materials with which to complete this task. The instructor will also distribute a cost sheet to each team, and will post the rules for managers and workers. Rule violations will attract penalties that increase the cost of production.

TEAM TASK
The team's task is to design and build a protective device that will allow a raw egg (provided by the instructor) to be dropped from a great height without breaking. The team wins if its egg does not break using the lowest-priced device.

The origin of this exercise, which is widely available in many forms, is not known.

INSTRUCTIONS

Step 1: The instructor will divide the class into teams, with approximately six people in each team. Team members will divide into groups of 'managers' and 'workers'. The team can have as many people as the group thinks are needed for managers and workers as long as all team members are assigned to one of these roles. Note from the cost sheet that managers and workers represent a cost to your project's budget.

Step 2: Within the time allotted by the instructor, each team's managers will design the device to protect the egg. Workers and managers will then purchase supplies from the store, and workers will then build the egg-protection device. Team members should read the rules carefully to avoid penalty costs.

SKILL BUILDER | 10.3   THE TEAM PLAYER INVENTORY

SELF-ASSESSMENT

By Theresa Kline, University of Calgary

STUDENT CD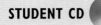

PURPOSE

This exercise is designed to help you estimate the extent to which you are positively predisposed to work in teams.

INSTRUCTIONS

Read each of the statements below and circle the response that you believe best indicates the extent to which you agree or disagree with that statement. Then use the scoring key in Appendix B to calculate your results for each scale. This exercise is completed alone so students assess themselves honestly without concerns of social comparison. However, class discussion will focus on the characteristics of individuals who are more or less compatible with working in self-directed work teams.

THE TEAM PLAYER INVENTORY

To what extent do you agree or disagree that ...?	Completely disagree	Disagree somewhat	Neither agree nor disagree	Agree somewhat	Completely agree
1. I enjoy working on team projects.	❏	❏	❏	❏	❏
2. Team project work easily allows others not to 'pull their weight'.	❏	❏	❏	❏	❏
3. Work that is done as a team is better than the work done individually.	❏	❏	❏	❏	❏
4. I do my best work alone rather than in a team.	❏	❏	❏	❏	❏
5. Team work is overrated in terms of the actual results produced.	❏	❏	❏	❏	❏
6. Working in a team gets me to think more creatively.	❏	❏	❏	❏	❏
7. Teams are used too often when individual work would be more effective.	❏	❏	❏	❏	❏
8. My own work is enhanced when I am in a team situation.	❏	❏	❏	❏	❏
9. My experiences working in team situations have been primarily negative.	❏	❏	❏	❏	❏
10. More solutions or ideas are generated when working in a team situation than when working alone.	❏	❏	❏	❏	❏

Source: T. J. B. Kline, 'The Team Player Inventory: Reliability and Validity of a Measure of Predisposition towards Organizational Team Working Environments', *Journal for Specialists in Group Work,* 24 (1999), pp. 102–12. Reprinted by permission of Sage Publications, Inc.

PROPENSITY TO TRUST SCALE

FULL EXERCISE ON
STUDENT CD

Trust is a psychological state comprising the intention to accept vulnerability based on positive expectations of the intent or behaviour of another person. While trust varies from one situation to the next, some people have a higher or lower propensity to trust. In other words, some people are highly trusting of others, even when first meeting them, whereas others have difficulty trusting anyone, even over a long time. This self-assessment provides an estimate of your propensity to trust. Indicate your preferred response to each statement, being honest with yourself for each item. This self-assessment is completed alone, although class discussion will focus on the meaning of propensity to trust, why it varies from one person to the next, and how it affects teamwork.

NOTES

1   'Leading a Virtual Team: Agilent's Grant Marshall', *ceoforum.com.au*, March 2005; 'Supporting Australian Innovation', *Electronics News*, 11 January 2005; M. Conlin, 'The Easiest Commute of All', *Business Week*, 12 December 2005, 78.

2   G. Smith, 'Quantitative Measures of Performance in Serials: A Team-based Approach', *Serials Review* 26 (October–December 2000), pp. 30–6.

3   S. G. Cohen, G. E. Ledford Jr and G. M. Spreitzer, 'A Predictive Model of Self-Managing Work Team Effectiveness', *Human Relations* 49 (1996), 643–76; E. E. Lawler, *Organizing for High Performance* (San Francisco: Jossey-Bass, 2001).

4   S. A. Mohrman, S. G. Cohen and A. M. Mohrman Jr, *Designing Team-Based Organizations: New Forms for Knowledge Work* (San Francisco: Jossey-Bass, 1995); B. L. Kirkman and D. L. Shapiro, 'The Impact of Cultural Values on Employee Resistance to Teams: Toward a Model of Globalized Self-Managing Work Team Effectiveness', *Academy of Management Review* 22 (July 1997), 730–57; D. E. Yeatts and C. Hyten, *High-Performing Self-Managed Work Teams: A Comparison of Theory and Practice* (Thousand Oaks, CA: Sage, 1998).

5   P. S. Goodman, R. Devadas and T. L. G. Hughson, 'Groups and Productivity: Analyzing the Effectiveness of Self-Managing Teams', in *Productivity in Organizations*, eds J. P. Campbell, R. J. Campbell, and Associates (San Francisco: Jossey-Bass, 1988), 295–327.

6   D. Tjosvold, *Teamwork for Customers* (San Francisco: Jossey-Bass, 1993); J. Childs, 'Five Years and Counting: The Path to Self-Directed Work Teams', *Hospital Materiel Management Quarterly* 18 (May 1997), 34–43; A. de Jong and K. de Ruyter, 'Adaptive Versus Proactive Behavior in Service Recovery: The Role of Self-Managing Teams', *Decision Sciences* 35, no. 3 (2004), 457–91.

7   E. L. Trist et al., *Organizational Choice* (London: Tavistock, 1963); N. Adler and P. Docherty, 'Bringing Business into Sociotechnical Theory and Practice', *Human Relations* 51, no. 3 (1998), 319–45; R. J. Torraco, 'Work Design Theory: A Review and Critique with Implications for Human Resource Development', *Human Resource Development Quarterly* 16, no. 1 (Spring 2005), 85–109.

8   The main components of sociotechnical systems are discussed in: M. Moldaschl and W. G. Weber, 'The "Three Waves" of Industrial Group Work: Historical Reflections on Current Research on Group Work', *Human Relations* 51 (March 1998), 259–87; W. Niepce and E. Molleman, 'Work Design Issues in Lean Production from Sociotechnical System Perspective: Neo-Taylorism or the Next Step in Sociotechnical Design?', *Human Relations* 51, no. 3 (March 1998), 259–87.

9   E. Ulich and W. G. Weber, 'Dimensions, Criteria, and Evaluation of Work Group Autonomy', in *Handbook of Work Group Psychology*, ed. M. A. West (Chichester, UK: John Wiley and Sons, 1996), 247–82.

10 K. P. Carson and G. L. Stewart, 'Job Analysis and the Sociotechnical Approach to Quality: A Critical Examination', *Journal of Quality Management* 1 (1996), 49–65; C. C. Manz and G. L. Stewart, 'Attaining Flexible Stability by Integrating Total Quality Management and Socio-Technical Systems Theory', *Organization Science* 8 (1997), 59–70.

11 P. McDonald and A. Sharma, 'Toward Work Teams within a New Zealand Public Service Organization', in *Annual Conference of the Center for the Study of Work Teams* (Fort Worth, Texas, 1994); C. Q. Francisco, 'Making a Company Grow', *BusinessWorld* (Manila, Philippines), 16 January 2004, 27; 'Aztec Software Ranked 11th in Top 25 Great Places to Work in India', *Hindustan Times* (Mumbai, India), 4 February 2006.

12 C. R. Emery and L. D. Fredendall, 'The Effect of Teams on Firm Profitability and Customer Satisfaction', *Journal of Service Research* 4 (February 2002), 217–29; I. M. Kunii, 'He Put the Flash Back in Canon', *Business Week,* 16 September 2002, 40; A. Krause and H. Dunckel, 'Work Design and Customer Satisfaction: Effects of the Implementation of Semi-Autonomous Group Work on Customer Satisfaction Considering Employee Satisfaction and Group Performance' (translated abstract), *Zeitschrift fur Arbeits-und Organisationspsychologie* 47, no. 4 (2003), 182–93.

13 J. P. Womack, D. T. Jones and D. Roos, *The Machine That Changed the World* (New York: Macmillan, 1990); P. S. Adler and R. E. Cole, 'Designed for Learning: A Tale of Two Auto Plants', *Sloan Management Review* 34 (Spring 1993), 85–94; C. Berggren, 'Volvo Uddevalla: A Dead Horse or a Car Dealer's Dream?', in *Actes du GERPISA* (May 1993), 129–43; J. Å. Granath, 'Torslanda to Uddevalla Via Kalmar: A Journey in Production Practice in Volvo', paper presented at Seminário Internacional Reestruturação Produtiva, Flexibilidade do Trabalho e Novas Competências Profissionais COPPE/UFRJ, Rio de Janeiro, Brazil, 24–25 August 1998; Emery and Fredendall, 'The Effect of Teams on Firm Profitability and Customer Satisfaction'; J. Boudreau et al., 'On the Interface between Operations and Human Resources Management', *Manufacturing & Service Operations Management* 5, no. 3 (Summer 2003), 179–202.

14 C. E. Nicholls, H. W. Lane and M. B. Brechu, 'Taking Self-Managed Teams to Mexico', *Academy of Management Executive* 13 (August 1999), 15–25; B. L. Kirkman and D. L. Shapiro, 'The Impact of Cultural Values on Job Satisfaction and Organizational Commitment in Self-Managing Work Teams: The Mediating Role of Employee Resistance', *Academy of Management Journal* 44 (June 2001), 557–69.

15 C. Pavett and T. Morris, 'Management Styles within a Multinational Corporation: A Five Country Comparative Study', *Human Relations* 48 (1995), 1171–91; Kirkman and Shapiro, 'The Impact of Cultural Values on Employee Resistance to Teams: Toward a Model of Globalized Self-Managing Work Team Effectiveness'; C. Robert and T. M. Probst, 'Empowerment and Continuous Improvement in the United States, Mexico, Poland, and India', *Journal of Applied Psychology* 85 (October 2000), 643–58.

16 C. C. Manz, D. E. Keating and A. Donnellon, 'Preparing for an Organizational Change to Employee Self-Management: The Managerial Transition', *Organizational Dynamics* 19 (Autumn 1990), 15–26; J. D. Orsburn and L. Moran, *The New Self-Directed Work Teams: Mastering the Challenge* (New York: McGraw-Hill, 2000), chapter 11. The Robert Frost quotation is found at: www.quoteland.com.

17 M. Fenton-O'Creevy, 'Employee Involvement and the Middle Manager: Saboteur or Scapegoat?', *Human Resource Management Journal* 11 (2001), 24–40; R. Wageman, 'How Leaders Foster Self-Managing Team Effectiveness', *Organization Science* 12, no. 5 (September–October 2001), 559–77; C. Douglas and W. L. Gardner, 'Transition to Self-Directed Work Teams: Implications of Transition Time and Self-Monitoring for Managers' Use of Influence Tactics', *Journal of Organizational Behavior* 25 (2004), 47–65. The TRW quotation is found in: J. Jusko, 'Always Lessons to Learn', *Industry Week*, 15 February 1999, 23–30.

18 D. Stafford, 'Sharing the Driver's Seat', *Kansas City Star*, 11 June 2002, D1.

19 G. Garda, K. Lindstrom and M. Dallnera, 'Towards a Learning Organization: The Introduction of a Client-Centered Team-Based Organization in Administrative Surveying Work', *Applied Ergonomics* 34 (2003), 97–105.

20 R. Hodson, 'Dignity in the Workplace under Participative Management: Alienation and Freedom Revisited', *American Sociological Review* 61 (1996), 719–38; R. Yonatan and H. Lam, 'Union Responses to Quality Improvement Initiatives: Factors Shaping Support and Resistance', *Journal of Labor Research* 20 (Winter 1999), 111–31.

21 J. Lipnack and J. Stamps, *Virtual Teams: People Working across Boundaries with Technology* (New York: John Wiley and Sons, 2001); B. S. Bell and W. J. Kozlowski, 'A Typology of Virtual Teams: Implications for Effective Leadership', *Group & Organization Management* 27 (March 2002), 14–49; G. Hertel, S. Geister and U. Konradt, 'Managing Virtual Teams: A Review of Current Empirical Research', *Human Resource Management Review* 15 (2005), 69–95.

22 G. Gilder, *Telecosm: How Infinite Bandwidth Will Revolutionize Our World* (New York: Free Press, 2001); L. L. Martins, L. L. Gilson and M. T. Maynard, 'Virtual Teams: What Do We Know and Where Do We Go From Here?', *Journal of Management* 30, no. 6 (2004), 805–35. The Novartis quotation is from S. Murray, 'Pros and Cons of Technology: The Corporate Agenda: Managing Virtual Teams', *Financial Times* (London), 27 May 2002, 6.

23 J. S. Lureya and M. S. Raisinghani, 'An Empirical Study of Best Practices in Virtual Teams', *Information & Management* 38 (2001), 523–44; Y. L. Doz, J. F. P. Santos and P. J. Williamson, 'The Metanational Advantage', *Optimize* (May 2002), 45ff; K. Marron, 'Close Encounters of the Faceless Kind', *Globe & Mail*, 9 February 2005, C1.

24 D. Robb, 'Global Workgroups', *Computerworld*, 15 August 2005, 37–8.

25 Martins, Gilson and Maynard, 'Virtual Teams'. The quotation is found in S. Gasper, 'Virtual Teams, Real Benefits', *Network World*, 24 September 2001, 45.

26 D. Robey, H. M. Khoo and C. Powers, 'Situated Learning in Cross-Functional Virtual Teams', *Technical Communication* (February 2000), 51–66.

27 Lureya and Raisinghani, 'An Empirical Study of Best Practices in Virtual Teams'.

28 S. Alexander, 'Virtual Teams Going Global', *InfoWorld*, 13 November 2000, 55–6.

29 S. Prashad, 'Building Trust Tricky for "Virtual" Teams', *Toronto Star*, 23 October 2003, K06.

30 S. Van Ryssen and S. H. Godar, 'Going International without Going International: Multinational Virtual Teams', *Journal of International Management* 6 (2000), 49–60.

31 B. J. Alge, C. Wiethoff and H. J. Klein, 'When Does the Medium Matter? Knowledge-Building Experiences and Opportunities in Decision-Making Teams', *Organizational Behavior and Human Decision Processes* 91, no. 1 (2003), 26–37; D. Robey, K. S. Schwaig and L. Jin, 'Intertwining Material and Virtual Work', *Information & Organization* 13 (2003), 111–29; U. Bernard, R. Gfrörer and B. Staffelbach, 'Der Einfluss Von Telearbeit Auf Das Team: Empirisch Analysiert Am Beispiel Eines Versicherungsunternehmens' (translated abstract), *Zeitschrift für Personalforschung* 19, no. 2 (2005), 120–38.

32 G. Buckler, 'Staking One for the Team', *Computing Canada*, 22 October 2004, 16.

33 J. Gordon, 'Do Your Virtual Teams Deliver Only Virtual Performance?', *Training*, June 2005, 20–4.

34 S. L. Robinson, 'Trust and Breach of the Psychological Contract', *Administrative Science Quarterly* 41 (1996), 574–99; D. M. Rousseau et al., 'Not So Different after All: A Cross-Discipline View of Trust', *Academy of Management Review* 23 (1998), 393–404; D. L. Duarte and N. T. Snyder, *Mastering Virtual Teams: Strategies, Tools, and Techniques That Succeed*, 2nd edn (San Francisco, CA: Jossey-Bass, 2000), 139–55; A. C. Costa, 'Work Team Trust and Effectiveness', *Personnel Review* 32, no. 5 (2003), 605–24; S. Kiffin-Petersen, 'Trust: A Neglected Variable in Team Effectiveness Research', *Journal of the Australian and New Zealand Academy of Management* 10, no. 1 (2004), 38–53.

35 D. J. McAllister, 'Affect- and Cognition-Based Trust as Foundations for Interpersonal Cooperation in Organizations', *Academy of Management Journal* 38, no. 1 (February 1995), 24–59; M. Williams, 'In Whom We Trust: Group Membership as an Affective Context for Trust Development', *Academy of Management Review* 26, no. 3 (July 2001), 377–96.

36 O. E. Williamson, 'Calculativeness, Trust, and Economic Organization', *Journal of Law and Economics* 36, no. 1 (1993), 453–86.

37 E. M. Whitener et al., 'Managers as Initiators of Trust: An Exchange Relationship Framework for Understanding Managerial Trustworthy Behavior', *Academy of Management Review* 23 (July 1998), 513–30; J M. Kouzes and B. Z. Posner, *The Leadership Challenge*, 3rd edn (San Francisco: Jossey-Bass, 2002), chapter 2; T. Simons, 'Behavioral Integrity: The Perceived Alignment between Managers' Words and Deeds as a Research Focus', *Organization Science* 13, no. 1 (January–February 2002), 18–35.

38 M. A. Hogg et al., 'The Social Identity Perspective: Intergroup Relations, Self-Conception, and Small Groups', *Small Group Research* 35, no. 3 (June 2004), 246–76.

39 J. R. Dunn and M. E. Schweitzer, 'Feeling and Believing: The Influence of Emotion on Trust', *Journal of Personality and Social Psychology* 88, no. 5 (May 2005), 736–48; H. Gill et al., 'Antecedents of Trust: Establishing a Boundary Condition for the Relation between Propensity to Trust and Intention to Trust', *Journal of Business and Psychology* 19, no. 3 (Spring 2005), 287–302.

40 T. K. Das and B. Teng, 'Between Trust and Control: Developing Confidence in Partner Cooperation in Alliances', *Academy of*

Management Review 23 (1998), 491–512; S. L. Jarvenpaa and D. E. Leidner, 'Communication and Trust in Global Virtual Teams', *Organization Science* 10 (1999), 791–815; J. K. Murnighan, J. M. Oesch and M. Pillutla, 'Player Types and Self-Impression Management in Dictatorship Games: Two Experiments', *Games and Economic Behavior* 37, no. 2 (2001), 388–414; M. M. Pillutla, D. Malhotra and J. Keith Murnighan, 'Attributions of Trust and the Calculus of Reciprocity', *Journal of Experimental Social Psychology* 39, no. 5 (2003), 448–55.

41 K. T. Dirks and D. L. Ferrin, 'The Role of Trust in Organizations', *Organization Science* 12, no. 4 (July–August 2004), 450–67.

42 V. H. Vroom and A. G. Jago, *The New Leadership* (Englewood Cliffs, NJ: Prentice-Hall, 1988), 28–9.

43 M. Diehl and W. Stroebe, 'Productivity Loss in Idea-Generating Groups: Tracking Down the Blocking Effects', *Journal of Personality and Social Psychology* 61 (1991), 392–403; R. B. Gallupe et al., 'Blocking Electronic Brainstorms', *Journal of Applied Psychology* 79 (1994), 77–86; B. A. Nijstad, W. Stroebe and H. F. M. Lodewijkx, 'Production Blocking and Idea Generation: Does Blocking Interfere with Cognitive Processes?', *Journal of Experimental Social Psychology* 39, no. 6 (November 2003), 531–48.

44 B. E. Irmer, P. Bordia and D. Abusah, 'Evaluation Apprehension and Perceived Benefits in Interpersonal and Database Knowledge Sharing', *Academy of Management Proceedings* (2002), B1–6.

45 I. L. Janis, *Groupthink: Psychological Studies of Policy Decisions and Fiascos*, 2nd edn (Boston: Houghton Mifflin, 1982); J. K. Esser, 'Alive and Well after 25 Years: A Review of Groupthink Research', *Organizational Behavior and Human Decision Processes* 73, no. 2–3 (1998), 116–41.

46 J. N. Choi and M. U. Kim, 'The Organizational Application of Groupthink and Its Limitations in Organizations', *Journal of Applied Psychology* 84, no. 2 (April 1999), 297–306; N. L. Kerr and S. R. Tindale, 'Group Performance and Decision Making', *Annual Review of Psychology* 55 (2004), 623–55.

47 D. Miller, *The Icarus Paradox: How Exceptional Companies Bring About Their Own Downfall* (New York: HarperBusiness, 1990); S. Finkelstein, *Why Smart Executives Fail* (New York: Viking, 2003); K. Tasa and G. Whyte, 'Collective Efficacy and Vigilant Problem Solving in Group Decision Making: A Non-Linear Model', *Organizational Behavior and Human Decision Processes* 96, no. 2 (March 2005), 119–29.

48 D. Isenberg, 'Group Polarization: A Critical Review and Meta-Analysis', *Journal of Personality and Social Psychology* 50 (1986), 1141–51; C. McGarty et al., 'Group Polarization as Conformity to the Prototypical Group Member', *British Journal of Social Psychology* 31 (1992), 1–20; C. R. Sunstein, 'Deliberative Trouble? Why Groups Go to Extremes', *Yale Law Journal* 110, no. 1 (October 2000), 71–119.

49 D. Friedman, 'Monty Hall's Three Doors: Construction and Deconstruction of a Choice Anomaly', *American Economic Review* 88 (September 1998), 933–46; D. Kahneman, 'Maps of Bounded Rationality: Psychology for Behavioral Economics', *American Economic Review* 93, no. 5 (December 2003), 1449–75.

50 K. M. Eisenhardt, J. L. Kahwajy and L. J. Bourgeois III, 'Conflict and Strategic Choice: How Top Management Teams Disagree', *California Management Review* 39 (1997), 42–62; R. Sutton, *Weird Ideas That Work* (New York: Free Press, 2002); C. J. Nemeth et al., 'The Liberating Role of Conflict in Group Creativity: A Study in Two Countries', *European Journal of Social Psychology* 34, no. 4 (2004), 365–74. For discussion on how all conflict is potentially detrimental to teams, see: C. K. W. De Dreu and L. R. Weingart, 'Task Versus Relationship Conflict, Team Performance, and Team Member Satisfaction: A Meta-Analysis', *Journal of Applied Psychology* 88

(August 2003), 587–604; P. Hinds and D. E. Bailey, 'Out of Sight, Out of Sync: Understanding Conflict in Distributed Teams', *Organization Science* 14, no. 6 (2003), 615–32.

51 K. Darce, 'Ground Control: NASA Attempts a Cultural Shift', *Seattle Times*, 24 April 2005, A3; R. Shelton, 'NASA Attempts to Change Mindset in Wake of *Columbia* Tragedy', *Macon Telegraph* (Macon, GA), 7 July 2005.

52 A. F. Osborn, *Applied Imagination* (New York: Scribner, 1957).

53 B. Mullen, C. Johnson and E. Salas, 'Productivity Loss in Brainstorming Groups: A Meta-Analytic Integration', *Basic and Applied Psychology* 12 (1991), 2–23. For recent evidence that group brainstorming is beneficial, see: V. R. Brown and P. B. Paulus, 'Making Group Brainstorming More Effective: Recommendations from an Associative Memory Perspective', *Current Directions in Psychological Science* 11, no. 6 (2002), 208–12; K. Leggett Dugosh and P. B. Paulus, 'Cognitive and Social Comparison Processes in Brainstorming', *Journal of Experimental Social Psychology* 41, no. 3 (2005), 313–20.

54 R. I. Sutton and A. Hargadon, 'Brainstorming Groups in Context: Effectiveness in a Product Design Firm', *Administrative Science Quarterly* 41 (1996), 685–718; T. Kelley, *The Art of Innovation* (New York: Currency Doubleday, 2001), chapter 4.

55 R. B. Gallupe, L. M. Bastianutti and W. H. Cooper, 'Unblocking Brainstorms', *Journal of Applied Psychology* 76 (1991), 137–42; W. H. Cooper et al., 'Some Liberating Effects of Anonymous Electronic Brainstorming', *Small Group Research* 29, no. 2 (April 1998), 147–78; A. R. Dennis, B. H. Wixom and R. J. Vandenberg, 'Understanding Fit and Appropriation Effects in Group Support Systems Via Meta-Analysis', *MIS Quarterly* 25, no. 2 (June 2001), 167–93; D. S. Kerr and U. S. Murthy, 'Divergent and Convergent Idea Generation in Teams: A Comparison of Computer-Mediated and Face-to-Face Communication', *Group Decision and Negotiation* 13, no. 4 (July 2004), 381–99.

56 P. Bordia, 'Face-to-Face Versus Computer-Mediated Communication: A Synthesis of the Experimental Literature', *Journal of Business Communication* 34 (1997), 99–120; P. B. Paulus and H.-C. Yang, 'Idea Generation in Groups: A Basis for Creativity in Organizations', *Organizational Behavior and Human Decision Processes* 82, no. 1 (2000), 76–87.

57 B. Kabanoff and J. R. Rossiter, 'Recent Developments in Applied Creativity', *International Review of Industrial and Organizational Psychology* 9 (1994), 283–324; A. Pinsoneault et al., 'Electronic Brainstorming: The Illusion of Productivity', *Information Systems Research* 10 (1999), 110–33.

58 H. A. Linstone and M. Turoff, *The Delphi Method: Techniques and Applications* (Reading, MA: Addison-Wesley, 1975); P. M. Mullen, 'Delphi: Myths and Reality', *Journal of Health Organization and Management* 17, no. 1 (2003), 37–51.

59 C. Banwell et al., 'Reflections on Expert Consensus: A Case Study of the Social Trends Contributing to Obesity', *European Journal of Public Health* 15, no. 6 (December 2005), 564–8.

60 A. L. Delbecq, A. H. Van de Ven and D. H. Gustafson, *Group Techniques for Program Planning: A Guide to Nominal Group and Delphi Processes* (Middleton, Wis.: Green Briar Press, 1986).

61 S. Frankel, 'NGT + MDS: An Adaptation of the Nominal Group Technique for Ill-Structured Problems', *Journal of Applied Behavioral Science* 23 (1987), 543–51; H. Barki and A. Pinsonneault, 'Small Group Brainstorming and Idea Quality: Is Electronic Brainstorming the Most Effective Approach?', *Small Group Research* 32, no. 2 (April 2001), 158–205.

62 A. Graham, 'Teambuilding Reveals Its Serious Side', *Corporate Meetings & Incentives*, May 2005, S6–11.

63   W. G. Dyer, *Team Building: Current Issues and New Alternatives*, 3rd edn (Reading, MA: Addison-Wesley, 1995); C. A. Beatty and B. A. Barker, *Building Smart Teams: Roadmap to High Performance* (Thousand Oaks, CA: Sage Publications, 2004).

64   'Cottage Event a Labour of Love for Deakin Workers', *Geelong Advertiser* (Victoria, Australia), 17 February 2004, 20; 'Charity Work Proves Successful Tool for Team', *South China Morning Post* (Hong Kong), 23 November 2004, 8; S. Williams, 'Thanks, but No Thanks', *Australian Financial Review*, 20 August 2005, 32; V. Doctor, 'Corporates Are Game for a Dream Run', *Economic Times* (India), 12 January 2006.

65   M. Beer, *Organizational Change and Development: A Systems View* (Santa Monica, CA: Goodyear, 1980), 143–6; E. Sundstrom, K. P. De Meuse and D. Futrell, 'Work Teams: Applications and Effectiveness', *American Psychologist* 45 (1990), 120–33.

66   J. Langan-Fox and J. Anglim, 'Mental Models, Team Mental Models, and Performance: Process, Development, and Future Directions', *Human Factors and Ergonomics in Manufacturing* 14, no. 4 (2004), 331–52; J. E. Mathieu et al., 'Scaling the Quality of Team-mates' Mental Models: Equifinality and Normative Comparisons', *Journal of Organizational Behavior* 26 (2005), 37–56.

67   R. Beckhard, 'The Confrontation Meeting', *Harvard Business Review* 45, no. 4 (1967), 159–65; H. D. Glover, 'Organizational Change and Development: The Consequences of Misuse', *Leadership & Organization Development Journal* 13, no. 1 (1992), 9–16. For recent discussion about problems with confrontation in teams, see M. A. Von Glinow, D. L. Shapiro and J. M. Brett, 'Can We *Talk*, and Should We? Managing Emotional Conflict in Multinational Teams', *Academy of Management Review* 29, no. 4 (2004), 578–92.

68   'German Businesswoman Demands End to Fun at Work', *Reuters*, 9 July 2003.

69   R. W. Woodman and J. J. Sherwood, 'The Role of Team Development in Organizational Effectiveness: A Critical Review', *Psychological Bulletin* 88 (1980), 166–86.

70   L. Mealiea and R. Baltazar, 'A Strategic Guide for Building Effective Teams', *Personnel Management* 34, no. 2 (Summer 2005), 141–60.

71   G. E. Huszczo, 'Training for Team Building', *Training and Development Journal* 44 (February 1990), 37–43; P. McGraw, 'Back from the Mountain: Outdoor Management Development Programs and How to Ensure the Transfer of Skills to the Workplace', *Asia Pacific Journal of Human Resources* 31 (Spring 1993), 52–61.

CHAPTER 11

Communicating in teams and organisations

How can corporate leaders conduct a casual conversation with a few thousand employees? Telecom New Zealand chief executive Theresa Gattung handles the task through her personal weblog, called Theresa Online. Gattung writes occasional musings in her blog (as these weblogs or online journals are called) on issues ranging from corporate developments to long-term product strategies. The site even includes an option for employees to submit their questions to Gattung. Molli Hoos, who oversees internal communications at Telecom, says Gattung's blog brings 'her closer to employees and gives them an opportunity to communicate directly with her. People like the opportunity to ask her questions directly. In a company as large as ours there isn't an opportunity for her to get out and meet all staff members.'

Corporate blogs have gained so much popularity as a form of internal communication that Sun Microsystems, IBM, Google and a few other firms provide resources for employees to create their own personal blogs. IBM has several outward-facing blogs for customers, but its inward-facing (i.e. restricted to IBM employees) BlogCentral hosts more than 3000 personal blogs created by employees who want to share their thoughts and experiences with co-workers.

Telecom New Zealand chief executive Theresa Gattung adds a personal touch to corporate communication through her personal weblog, Theresa Online.

'We have seen a lot of different uses of blogs within the firewall,' says Jason Goldman, Blogger product manager at Google. 'People keeping track of meeting notes, sharing diagnostics information, sharing snippets of code, as well as more personal uses, like letting co-workers know what they're thinking about and what they're up to.'

Corporate and employee blogs also create complications. When Microsoft Australia employee Cameron O'Reilly wrote in his personal blog that Microsoft has 'great products but average marketing', the company warned him that the content was inappropriate and unprofessional. O'Reilly quit after a heated debate with his supervisor about the blog. One of India's most popular bloggers also experienced problems after she posted unflattering remarks about her co-workers. 'My co-workers found the blog and some rather blunt things I had said about them,' said the blogger, known as eM. 'I realised that I couldn't just write about everything.'

In spite of these risks, Sun Microsystems not only encourages its employees to blog but allows anyone to view most of the blogs. 'Why hide your voice?' asks Andy Lark, the New Zealand–born vice-president of marketing at Sun. 'Our employees are smart and will ultimately do the right thing. And some of them write really well. Blogs improve communication, inside and out.'

LEARNING OBJECTIVE

Explain the importance of communication and diagram the communication process.

IT'S ALMOST A CLICHÉ TO say that information technologies have transformed communication in organisations. Yet we may still be at the beginning of this revolution. Wire cablegrams and telephones introduced a century ago are giving way to email, instant messaging, weblogs and podcasting. Each of these inventions creates fascinating changes in how people interact with each other in the workplace. Communication refers to the process by which information is transmitted and *understood* between two or more people. The word 'understood' is emphasised because transmitting the sender's intended meaning is the essence of good communication.

Telecom New Zealand, Sun Microsystems and other large organisations require innovative strategies to keep communication pathways open. In fact, a recent survey of thousands of employees in a dozen Australian companies reported that only 42 per cent were satisfied with the company's internal communication. The highest communication satisfaction score among these twelve firms was only 52 per cent.[2] Smaller businesses may have fewer structural bottlenecks, but they, too, can suffer from subtle communication problems.

Effective communication is vital to all organisations because it coordinates employees, fulfils employee needs, supports knowledge management and improves decision making.[3] First, the ability to exchange information is an essential part of the coordination process, allowing employees to develop common mental models that synchronise their work. Second, communication is the glue that holds people together. It helps people satisfy their drive to bond and, as part of the dynamics of social support, eases work-related stress.

Communication is also a key driver in knowledge management. It brings knowledge into the organisation and distributes it to employees who require that information. As such, it minimises the 'silos of knowledge' problem that undermines an organisation's potential. Fourth, communication influences the quality of decision making. Individuals rarely have enough information alone to make decisions on the complex matters facing businesses today. Instead, problem solvers require information from co-workers, subordinates and anyone else with relevant knowledge.

This chapter begins by presenting a model of the communication process and discussing the various communication channels, including computer-mediated communication. Next, the factors to consider when choosing a communication medium are presented, followed by barriers to effective communication. The chapter then presents some options for communicating in organisational hierarchies and describes the pervasive organisational grapevine. The latter part of the chapter examines cross-cultural and gender differences in communication and outlines strategies to improve interpersonal communication.

A MODEL OF COMMUNICATION

The communication model presented in Exhibit 11.1 provides a useful 'conduit' metaphor for thinking about the communication process.[4] According to this model, communication flows through channels between the sender and the receiver. The sender forms a message and encodes it into words, gestures, voice intonations and other symbols or signs. Next, the encoded message is transmitted to the intended receiver through one or more communication channels (media). The receiver senses the incoming message and decodes it into something meaningful. Ideally, the decoded meaning is what the sender had intended.

In most situations, the sender looks for evidence that the other person has received and understood the transmitted message. This feedback may be a formal acknowledgment, such as 'Yes, I know what you mean', or indirect evidence from the receiver's subsequent actions. Notice that feedback repeats the communication process. Intended feedback is encoded, transmitted, received and decoded from the receiver to the sender of the original message.

This model recognises that communication is not a free-flowing conduit. Rather, the transmission of meaning from one person to another is hampered by noise—the psychological,

EXHIBIT 11.1

The communication process model

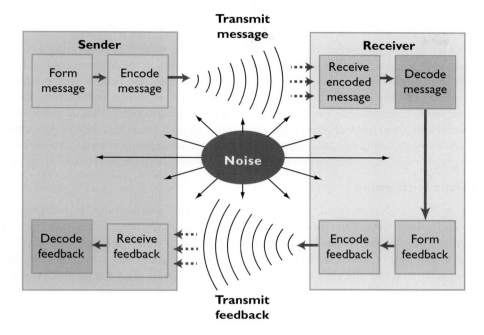

social and structural barriers that distort and obscure the sender's intended message. If any part of the communication process is distorted or broken, the sender and the receiver will not have a common understanding of the message.

COMMUNICATION CHANNELS

A critical part of the communication model is the channel or medium through which information is transmitted. There are two main types of channels: verbal and nonverbal. Verbal communication includes any oral or written means of transmitting meaning through words. Nonverbal communication, which is discussed later, is any part of communication that does not use words.

VERBAL COMMUNICATION

Different forms of verbal communication should be used in different situations. Face-to-face interaction is usually better than written methods for transmitting emotions and persuading the receiver. This is because nonverbal cues accompany oral communications, such as voice intonations and the use of silence. Furthermore, face-to-face interaction provides the sender with immediate feedback from the receiver and the opportunity to adjust the emotional tone of the message accordingly. Written communication is more appropriate for recording and presenting technical details. This is because ideas are easier to follow when written down than when communicated aurally. Traditionally, written communication has been slow to develop and transmit, but electronic mail, weblogs and other computer-mediated communication channels have significantly improved written communication efficiency.

Computer-mediated communication

Electronic mail (email) is revolutionising the way people communicate in organisational settings. It has also become the medium of choice in most workplaces, because messages can be quickly formed, edited and stored. Information can be appended and transmitted to many people with a simple click of a mouse. Email is asynchronous (messages are sent and received at different times), so there is no need to coordinate a communication session. This technology also allows fairly random access of information; you can select any message in any order, skip to different parts of a message, and search for any word in any message on your computer.

Email tends to be the preferred medium for coordinating work (e.g. confirming a co-worker's production schedule) and for sending well-defined information for decision making. It often increases the volume of communication and significantly alters the flow of that information within groups and throughout the organisation.[5] Specifically, it reduces some face-to-face and telephone communication but increases communication with people further up the hierarchy. Some social and organisational status differences still exist with email, but they are less apparent than in face-to-face communication. Email also reduces many selective attention biases, because it hides people's age, race, weight and other features that are observable in face-to-face meetings.

Problems with email

LEARNING OBJECTIVE

Describe problems with communicating through electronic mail.

flaming The act of sending an emotionally charged electronic mail message to others.

In spite of the wonders of email, anyone who has used this communication medium knows that it has its limitations. One problem is that email is an ineffective medium for communicating emotions. People rely on facial expressions and other nonverbal cues to interpret the emotional meaning of words, and email lacks this parallel communication medium. Email aficionados try to clarify the emotional tone of their messages by inserting graphic faces called emoticons, or 'smileys'.[6]

A second problem with email is that it seems to reduce our politeness and respect for others. This is mostly evident through the increased frequency of **flaming**—the act of sending an emotionally charged message to others. There are two explanations for this lack of diplomacy. First, people can quickly write and post email messages before their emotions subside, whereas cooler thoughts have usually prevailed before traditional memos or letters are sent. Second, email is an impersonal medium, allowing employees to write things that they would never say verbally in face-to-face conversation. Fortunately, research has found that politeness and respect increase as team members get to know each other and when companies establish explicit norms and rules of communication.[7]

A third problem is that email is an inefficient medium for communicating in ambiguous, complex and novel situations. The communicating parties lack mutual mental models, so they need to transmit a large number of emails to share enough information. Two-way face-to-face communication is a much more effective medium under these circumstances, but many employees are reluctant to break out of the email dialogue. AMP, the Australian financial services firm, experimented with a 'no email day' so employees would discover other forms of internal communication.[8] Reality Check 11.1 describes how Liverpool City Council and other British organisations also believe that some things are better discussed in person than in cyberspace.

A fourth difficulty with email is that it contributes to information overload, which will be discussed in more detail later in the chapter. Many email users are overwhelmed by hundreds of messages each week, many of which are either unnecessary or irrelevant to the receiver. This occurs because emails can be easily created and copied to thousands of people through group mailbox systems. Email overload may eventually decrease as people become more familiar with it, but this trend may take a while.

Other computer-mediated communication

Intranets, extranets, Blackberry wireless emailing, instant messaging, blogging, podcasting and other forms of computer-mediated communication are fuelling the hyperfast world of corporate information sharing. The opening story to this chapter described how blogs enable executives to communicate more personally with employees. Sun Microsystems and a few other firms support employee blogs because they empower staff to share information both internally and externally, and let co-workers know more about each other. Blogs also allow

11.1 REALITY CHECK

BRITISH ORGANISATIONS BAN EMAIL TO REDISCOVER THE ART OF CONVERSATION

For the past 800 years, citizens in the port city of Liverpool, England, have relied on face-to-face communication to conduct trade and resolve their differences. But leaders at Liverpool City Council are concerned that email is becoming a threat to the noble practice of dialogue among its employees. 'We'd seen a doubling in internal emails and found a lot of emails were unnecessary,' says David Henshaw, chief executive of Liverpool City Council. 'A lot of the stuff could be dealt with over the phone, or by getting up and walking to the person next to you.'

To battle email overload, Henshaw has asked his employees to avoid using this medium of communication on Wednesdays. So far, Henshaw's own email flow has dropped from 250 per day to just 25 on that day. Not everyone is convinced that the ban will last for long. 'In business the pressure is on,' says Leicestershire Chamber of Commerce chief executive Martin Traynor. 'If people email you in the morning, by lunch they're asking why you haven't emailed back.'

Perhaps so, but Liverpool City Council is not alone in its quest for more old-fashioned face-to-face conversation. Nestlé Rowntree executives asked staff to hit the email 'send' button less often on Fridays to 'reduce needless information flow across the organisation'. Camelot, the British lottery operator, also discouraged emails on the last day of the workweek. 'We needed to make staff more aware of other forms of communication,' explained a Camelot spokesperson.

Phones 4U CEO John Caudwell became so fed-up with the time wasted with email that he has banned his 2500 employees from emailing each other at all. Email is allowed only sparingly at the British mobile phone company, when communicating with customers who insist on using it. 'The quality and efficiency of communication have increased in one fell swoop,' says Caudwell. 'Things are getting done and people aren't tied to their personal computers.'

> Liverpool City Council has banned email one day a week so employees rediscover the benefits of face-to-face communication.

Sources: R. Steiner and M. Chittenden, 'Office Workers Told to Take an E-mail Holiday', *Sunday Times* (London), 4 March 2001, p. 8; O. Burkeman, 'Post Modern', *The Guardian* (London), 20 June 2001; 'Does E-Mail Really Help Us Get the Message?', *Leicester Mercury*, 31 August 2002; D. J. Horgan, 'You've Got Conversation', *CIO Magazine*, 15 October 2002; M. Greenwood, 'I Have Banned Emails … They are the Cancer of Modern Business', *The Mirror* (London), 19 September 2003, p. 11.

firms to archive discussions, something that is less easily done in instant messaging. Podcasting may become another electronic communication medium that gains favour in organisations. Although primarily aimed at the public, podcasts—radio-like programs formatted for digital music players and computer music software—are starting to appear as messages from executives to employees and customers alike.[9]

Instant messaging (IM) is another emerging form of electronic communication that has gained popularity in some organisations. IM is more efficient than email because messages are brief (usually just a sentence or two with acronyms and sound-alike letters for words) and appear on the receiver's screen as soon as they are sent. IM also creates real-time communities of practice as employees form clustered conversations around specific fields of expertise. Another advantage is that employees soon develop the capability of carrying on several IM conversations at the same time. 'No matter how good you are on the phone, the best you can do is carry on two conversations at once,' says one New York City broker. 'With IM, I can have six going at once . . . That allows me to get my job done and serve clients better.'[10]

NONVERBAL COMMUNICATION

Nonverbal communication includes facial gestures, voice intonation, physical distance, and even silence. This communication channel is necessary where noise or physical distance prevents effective verbal exchanges and the need for immediate feedback precludes written communication. But even in quiet face-to-face meetings, most information is communicated nonverbally. Rather like a parallel conversation, nonverbal cues signal subtle information to both parties, such as reinforcing their interest in the verbal conversation or demonstrating their relative status in the relationship.[11]

Nonverbal communication differs from verbal communication in a couple of ways. First, it is less rule-bound than verbal communication. We receive a lot of formal training on how to understand spoken words, but very little on understanding the nonverbal signals that accompany those words. Consequently, nonverbal cues are generally more ambiguous and susceptible to misinterpretation. At the same time, many facial expressions (such as smiling) are hardwired and universal, thereby providing the only reliable means of communicating across cultures. This point is powerfully illustrated in Reality Check 11.2. To overcome language and physical noise barriers, the quick-thinking leader of a coalition forces unit during the Iraq war relied on nonverbal communication to communicate the unit's friendly intentions, thereby narrowly avoiding a potentially deadly incident.

The other difference between verbal and nonverbal communication is that the former is typically conscious, whereas most nonverbal communication is automatic and unconscious. We normally plan the words we say or write, but we rarely plan every blink, smile or other gesture during a conversation. Indeed, as Reality Check 11.2 demonstrated, many of these facial expressions communicate the same meaning across cultures because they are hardwired, unconscious or preconscious responses to human emotions.[12] For example, pleasant emotions cause the brain centre to widen the mouth, whereas negative emotions produce constricted facial expressions (squinting eyes, pursed lips, etc.).

Emotional contagion

One of the most fascinating effects of emotions on nonverbal communication is the phenomenon called **emotional contagion**, which is the automatic process of 'catching' or sharing another person's emotions by mimicking that person's facial expressions and other nonverbal behaviour. Consider what happens when you see a co-worker accidentally bang his or her head against a filing cabinet. The chances are that you wince and put your hand on your own head as if *you* had hit the cabinet. Similarly, while listening to someone describe a positive event, you tend to smile and exhibit other emotional displays of happiness. While some of our nonverbal communication is planned, emotional contagion represents unconscious behaviour—we automatically mimic and synchronise our nonverbal behaviours with other people.[13]

Emotional contagion serves three purposes. First, mimicry provides continuous feedback, communicating that we understand and empathise with the sender. To consider the significance of this, imagine employees remaining expressionless after watching a co-worker bang his or her head! The lack of parallel behaviour conveys a lack of understanding or caring. Second, mimicking the nonverbal behaviours of other people seems to be a way of receiving emotional meaning from those people. If a co-worker is angry with a client, your tendency to frown and show anger while listening helps you share that emotion more fully. In other words, we receive meaning by expressing the sender's emotions as well as by listening to the sender's words.

The third function of emotional contagion is to fulfil the drive to bond that was described in Chapter 5. Social solidarity is built out of each member's awareness of a collective sentiment. Through nonverbal expressions of emotional contagion, people see that others feel the same emotions that they feel. This strengthens team cohesiveness by providing evidence of member similarity.[14]

LEARNING OBJECTIVE

Identify two ways in which nonverbal communication differs from verbal communication.

emotional contagion The automatic and unconscious tendency to mimic and synchronise one's own nonverbal behaviours with those of other people.

NONVERBAL GESTURES HELP CROWD CONTROL DURING IRAQ WAR

The southern Iraqi city of Najaf is home to one of Islam's holiest sites, the Ali Mosque. The site is believed to be the final resting place of Ali, son-in-law of the prophet Mohammed. It is also home to Grand Ayatollah Ali Hussein Sistani, one of the most revered Shiites in the Muslim world and a potential supporter of US efforts to introduce a more moderate government in Iraq.

One week before Saddam Hussein's regime was overthrown, Sistani sent word that he wanted to meet with senior officers of the American forces. Fearing assassination, he also asked for soldiers to secure his compound, located along the Golden Road near the mosque. But when 130 soldiers from the 101st Airborne's 2nd Battalion, 327th Infantry and their gun trucks turned onto the Golden Road to provide security, hundreds of Iraqis in the area started to get angry. Clerics tried to explain to the crowd why the Americans were approaching, but they were drowned out. The crowd assumed that the Americans would try to enter and possibly attack the sacred mosque.

The chanting got louder as the quickly growing crowd approached the soldiers. Anticipating a potentially deadly situation, Lieutenant Colonel Christopher Hughes, the battalion's commander, picked up a loudspeaker and called out the unit's nickname: 'No Slack Soldiers!' Then he commanded, 'All No Slack Soldiers, take a knee.' According to journalists witnessing the incident, every soldier immediately knelt down on one knee. Hughes then called out, 'All No Slack Soldiers, point your weapons at the ground.' Again, the soldiers complied.

With the crowd still chanting in anger, Hughes spoke through the loudspeaker a third time. 'All No Slack Soldiers, smile,' he commanded. 'Smile, guys, everybody smile.' And in this intensely difficult situation, the kneeling troops showed the friendliest smile they could muster towards the crowd.

Eyewitnesses say that these nonverbal gestures started to work. Some people in the crowd smiled back at the Americans and stopped chanting. But insurgents in the crowd (apparently Hussein supporters planted to misinform the crowd) continued to yell. So Hughes spoke one more time: 'All vehicles, all No Slack Soldiers, calmly stand up and withdraw from this situation. We'll go so the people understand we are not trying to hurt him [the Grand Ayatollah]. C'mon, Bravo, back off. Smile and wave and back off.' And with that, the soldiers walked backwards for 100 metres, then turned around and returned to their compound.

Sources: W. Allison, 'March to Mosque Provokes Worst Fears', *St Petersburg Times* (Florida), 4 April 2003, p. 1A; 'All Things Considered', *National Public Radio (NPR)*, 4 April 2003; R. Chilcote, 'Iraqis Mistakenly Believe Soldiers Have Their Sights on a Sacred Landmark', *CNN*, 4 April 2003.

CHOOSING THE BEST COMMUNICATION CHANNELS

Employees perform better if they can quickly determine the best communication channels for the situation and are flexible enough to use different methods as the occasion requires. But which communication channels are the most appropriate? This question was partly answered in the evaluation of the different communication channels. However, two additional contingencies worth noting are media richness and symbolic meaning.

MEDIA RICHNESS

Aristocrat Leisure's financial status was a shambles when Simon Kelly stepped into the chief financial officer role a few years ago. His previous job in the food industry, where profit margins are razor thin, gave Kelly a solid grounding in cutting costs and reducing working capital.

Kelly also felt that inventory costs could be reduced at the Sydney-based gaming technology company, but the lists of numbers in the monthly inventory cost reports were too austere. Instead, by asking Aristocrat's financial staff to prepare a narrative analysis along with the numbers, Kelly and his staff identified several problems with surplus and obsolete stock held at twelve warehouses around the world.[15]

By requesting more detailed inventory reports, Simon Kelly was matching the communication medium's richness with the requirements of the situation. **Media richness** refers to the medium's *data-carrying capacity*—the volume and variety of information that can be transmitted during a specific time.[16] Exhibit 11.2 illustrates various communication channels arranged in a hierarchy of richness, with face-to-face interaction at the top and lean data-only reports at the bottom.

The media richness hierarchy is determined by three factors. First, rich media simultaneously use multiple communication media. For instance, face-to-face communication scores high on media richness because it includes both verbal and nonverbal information exchange, whereas inventory reports rely only on verbal (written) information. Second, rich media allow immediate feedback from receiver to sender, whereas feedback in lean media is delayed or nonexistent. Third, rich media allow the sender to customise the message to the receiver. Face-to-face conversations are developed specifically for one or a few people, whereas financial reports have low media richness because one size fits all; everyone gets the same information.

Exhibit 11.2 also shows that rich media are better than lean media when the communication situation is non-routine and ambiguous. In non-routine situations (such as an unexpected and unusual emergency), the sender and receiver have little common experience, so they need to transmit a large volume of information with immediate feedback. Lean media work well in routine situations because the sender and receiver have common expectations through shared mental models. Ambiguous situations also require rich media because the parties must share large amounts of information with immediate feedback in order to resolve multiple and conflicting interpretations of their observations and experiences.[17]

media richness The data-carrying capacity of a communication medium, including the volume and variety of information it can transmit.

LEARNING OBJECTIVE

Identify two conditions requiring a channel with high media richness.

EXHIBIT 11.2

Media richness hierarchy

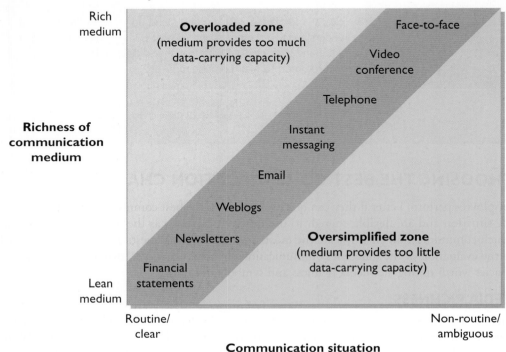

Sources: Based on R. Lengel and R. Daft, 'The Selection of Communication Media as an Executive Skill', *Academy of Management Executive* 2, no. 3 (August 1988), p. 226; R. L. Daft and R. H. Lengel, 'Information Richness: A New Approach to Managerial Behavior and Organization Design', *Research in Organizational Behavior*, 1984, p. 199.

What happens when we choose the wrong level of media richness for the situation? When the situation is routine or clear, using a rich medium—such as holding a special meeting—would seem like a waste of time. On the other hand, if a unique and ambiguous issue is handled through email or another lean medium, then issues take longer to resolve and misunderstandings are more likely to occur.

Evaluating media richness theory

Research studying traditional channels (face-to-face, written memos, etc.) generally supports the media richness proposition—that rich media are better than lean media when the situation is non-routine and/or ambiguous. But the evidence is mixed when emerging information technologies are considered. One reason for this inconsistency is that the communicator's previous experience with email, IM and other means of communication that do not exist naturally need to be taken into account. People who have plenty of experience with a particular communication medium can 'push' the amount of media richness normally possible through that information channel. Experienced Blackberry users, for instance, can whip through messages in a flash, whereas new users struggle to type email notes and organise incoming messages. Experience is less relevant with verbal conversation, report writing and other traditional methods because they are learned early in life and, indeed, may be hardwired in our evolutionary development.[18]

A second factor to consider is the communicator's previous experience with the receiver. The more two or more people share common mental models, the less information exchange is required to communicate new meanings. People who know each other have similar 'codebooks', so the sender can communicate with fewer words or other symbols and doesn't need to check as closely that the message has been understood. Without this common codebook, the sender needs to add in more redundancy (such as saying the same thing in two different ways) and requires more efficient feedback to ensure that the receiver has understood the message.

SYMBOLIC MEANING OF THE MEDIUM

'The medium is the message.'[19] This famous phrase by communications guru Marshall McLuhan means that the channel of communication has social consequences as much as (or perhaps more than) the content that passes through that medium. McLuhan was referring mainly to the influence of television and other 'new media' on society, but this concept applies equally well to how the symbolic meaning of a communication medium influences our interpretation of the message and the relationship between sender and receiver.

The medium-as-message principle was apparent when KPMG gave layoff notices to hundreds of its British employees via email. The public swiftly criticised the consulting firm, not because of the content of the message but because of the medium through which it had been transmitted. Ironically, KPMG had delivered the bad news by email because most employees had specifically asked for this method. Yet even the KPMG executives who sent the layoff notices were hesitant. 'I was horrified about telling staff via email as I knew it would make us look callous,' admitted one executive.[20] The point here is that we need to be sensitive to the symbolic meaning of the communication medium to ensure that it amplifies rather than misinterprets the meaning found in the message content.

COMMUNICATION BARRIERS (NOISE)

In spite of the best intentions of sender and receiver to communicate, several barriers inhibit the effective exchange of information. As author George Bernard Shaw wrote, 'The greatest problem with communication is the illusion that it has been accomplished.' Four pervasive communication barriers (called 'noise' in Exhibit 11.1) are *perceptions*, *filtering*, *language* and *information overload*. Later, cross-cultural and gender communication barriers will also be investigated.

LEARNING OBJECTIVE

Identify four common communication barriers.

PERCEPTIONS

The perceptual process determines what messages we select or screen out, as well as how the selected information is organised and interpreted. This can be a significant source of noise in the communication process if the sender and receiver have different perceptual frames and mental models. For instance, corporate leaders are watched closely by employees, and the most inane words or gestures are interpreted with great meaning even though they often occur without intention.

FILTERING

Some messages are filtered or stopped altogether on their way up or down the organisational hierarchy. Filtering may involve deleting or delaying negative information or using less harsh words so that events sound more favourable.[21] Employees and supervisors usually filter communication to create a good impression of themselves to superiors. Filtering is most common where the organisation rewards employees who communicate mainly positive information and punishes those who convey bad news. John Stewart admits that reducing filtering isn't easy. 'We have been trying hard to get people to be more open,' says the chief executive of National Australia Bank. 'To do that, you have to make sure your senior people are listening to staff when they bring problems to them, and not killing the messenger ... You have to do it, otherwise people will stop telling you and then nothing gets fixed.'[22]

LANGUAGE BARRIERS

Language problems can be a huge source of communication noise. Recall from Exhibit 11.1 that the sender encodes the message and the receiver decodes it. To make this process work, both parties need to have the same 'codebook'; that is, they need to have a mutual understanding of what the words or other symbols being sent mean. Even when both people speak the same language, they might interpret words and phrases differently. If someone says 'Would you like to check the figures again?', he or she may be politely *telling* you to double-check the figures, or might be merely *asking* if you want to do this.

This language ambiguity isn't always dysfunctional noise.[23] Corporate leaders sometimes rely on metaphors and other vague language to describe ill-defined or complex ideas. Ambiguity is also used to avoid conveying or creating undesirable emotions. For example, one recent study reported that people rely on more ambiguous language when communicating with people who have different values and beliefs. In these situations, ambiguity minimises the risk of conflict.

Along with ambiguity, people who generally speak the same language might not understand specific jargon within that language. **Jargon** consists of technical language and acronyms as well as recognised words with specialised meaning in specific organisations or social groups. Some jargon can improve communication efficiency when both sender and receiver understand this specialised language. But technical experts (including organisational behaviour teachers!) sometimes use jargon without realising that listeners don't have the codebook to translate those particular words. In fact, one recent survey found that people react negatively to unnecessary jargon, which is probably contrary to the sender's intention to look 'cool' by using the latest buzzwords.[24]

jargon Technical language and acronyms as well as recognised words with specialised meanings in specific organisations or groups.

INFORMATION OVERLOAD

John Teres estimates that about 300 email messages stream into his computer every day. The national executive officer for the Australian Society of Association Executives spends half an hour every morning identifying the urgent ones, then devotes up to one third of his workday replying to the others. Even with this regimented process, Tores falls behind to the point that his inbox is filled with more than 3000 messages. 'The scary thing is, I've got 500 in there that I haven't read,' says Teres. 'It's grown and grown and grown.'[25]

Dynamics of information overload

EXHIBIT 11.3

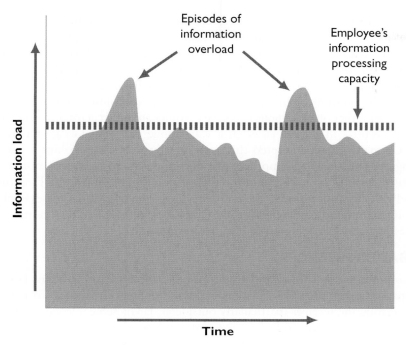

John Teres probably receives plenty of communication beyond email messages. Add in voice mail, mobile phone text messages, website scanning, PDF file downloads, hard-copy documents and other sources of incoming information and you have a perfect recipe for **information overload**.[26] Information overload occurs when the volume of information received exceeds the person's capacity to get through it. Employees have a certain *information processing capacity*—the amount of information that they are able to process in a fixed unit of time. At the same time, jobs have a varying *information load*—the amount of information to be processed per unit of time.[27] As Exhibit 11.3 illustrates, information overload occurs whenever the job's information load exceeds the individual's information processing capacity.

Information overload creates noise in the communication system, because information gets overlooked or misinterpreted when people can't process it fast enough. It has also become a common cause of workplace stress. These problems can be minimised by increasing our information processing capacity, reducing the job's information load, or through a combination of both. Information processing capacity increases when we learn to read faster, scan through documents more efficiently, and remove distractions that slow information processing speed. Time management also increases information processing capacity. When information overload is temporary, information processing capacity can increase by working longer hours.

Three strategies help us to reduce information load: buffering, omitting and summarising.[28] Consider Microsoft chairman Bill Gates. Gates receives approximately 300 emails daily from Microsoft addresses that are outside a core group of people; these emails are buffered; that is, they are routed to an assistant who reads each and sends Gates only the thirty or so messages considered essential reading. Gates also applies the omitting strategy by using software rules to redirect emails from distribution lists, non-essential sources and junk mail (spam). These emails are dumped into preassigned folders to be read later, if ever. Gates probably also relies on the summarising strategy by reading executive summaries rather than entire reports on some issues.

Perceptions, filtering, language barriers and information overload are not the only sources of noise in the communication process, but they are probably the most common. Noise also occurs when we communicate across cultures or genders, both of which are discussed next.

information overload A condition in which the volume of information received exceeds the person's capacity to process it.

CROSS-CULTURAL AND GENDER COMMUNICATION

In a world of increasing globalisation and cultural diversity, organisations face new opportunities as well as communication challenges.[29] Language is the most obvious cross-cultural communications challenge. Words are easily misunderstood in verbal communication, either because the receiver has a limited vocabulary or because the sender's accent distorts the usual sound of some words. The issue is further complicated in global organisations where employees from non-English countries often rely on English as the common business language. The problem discussed earlier of ambiguous language becomes amplified across cultures. For example, a French executive might call an event a 'catastrophe' as a casual exaggeration, whereas someone in Germany usually interprets this word literally as an earth-shaking event.[30]

Mastering the same language improves one dimension of cross-cultural communication, but problems may still occur when interpreting voice intonation. Middle Easterners tend to speak loudly to show sincerity and interest in the discussion, whereas Japanese people tend to speak softly to communicate politeness or humility. These different cultural norms regarding voice loudness may cause one person to misinterpret the other.

NONVERBAL DIFFERENCES

Nonverbal communication is more important in some cultures than in others. For example, people in Japan interpret more of a message's meaning from nonverbal cues. To avoid offending or embarrassing the receiver (particularly outsiders), Japanese people will often say what the other person wants to hear (called *tatemae*) but send more subtle nonverbal cues indicating the sender's true feelings (called *honne*). A Japanese colleague might politely reject your business proposal by saying 'I will think about that' while sending non-verbal signals that he or she is not really interested. 'In Japan, they have seven ways to say no; they never want to offend,' advises Rick Davidson, global CIO at Manpower, Inc. 'Sometimes they nod their head, and you think you have an agreement, but they're just saying, "I hear you".'[31]

Many unconscious or involuntary nonverbal cues (such as smiling) have the same meaning around the world, but deliberate gestures often have different interpretations. For example,

Thumbs-up for cross-cultural (mis)communication

Patricia Oliveira made several cultural adjustments when she moved from Brazil to Australia. One of the more humorous incidents occurred in the Melbourne office where she works. A co-worker would stick his thumbs up when asked about something, signalling that everything was okay. But the gesture had a totally different meaning to Oliveiri and other people from Brazil. 'He asked me why I was laughing and I had to explain that in Brazil that sign means something not very nice,' recalls Oliveiri. 'After that, everyone started doing it to the boss. It was really funny.'[33]

Mark M. Lawrence/CORBIS

most of us shake our head from side to side to say 'No', but a variation of head shaking means 'I understand' to many people in India. Filipinos raise their eyebrows to give an affirmative answer, yet Arabs interpret this expression (along with clicking one's tongue) as a negative response. Most Westerners are taught to maintain eye contact with the speaker to show interest and respect, yet Australian Aborigines, among others, learn at an early age to show respect by looking down when an older or more senior person is talking to them.[32]

Even the common handshake communicates different meanings across cultures. Westerners tend to appreciate a firm handshake as a sign of strength and warmth in a friendship or business relationship. In contrast, many Asians and Middle Easterners favour a loose grip and regard a firm clench as aggressive. Germans prefer one good handshake stroke, whereas anything less than five or six strokes may symbolise a lack of trust in Spain. If this isn't confusing enough, people from some cultures view any touching in public—including handshakes—as a sign of rudeness.

Silence and conversational overlaps

Communication includes silence, but its use and meaning vary from one culture to another.[34] A recent study estimated that silence and pauses represented 30 per cent of conversation time between Japanese doctors and patients, compared with only 8 per cent of the time between American doctors and patients. Why is there more silence in Japanese conversations? In Japan, silence symbolises respect and indicates that the listener is thoughtfully contemplating what has just been said.[35] Empathy is also important in Japan, and this shared understanding is demonstrated without using words. In contrast, most people in Australia, India and many other cultures view silence as a *lack* of communication and often interpret long breaks as a sign of disagreement.

Conversational overlaps also send different messages in different cultures. Japanese people usually stop talking when they are interrupted, whereas talking over the other person's speech is more common in Brazil and some other countries. The difference in communication behaviour is, again, due to interpretations. Talking while someone is speaking to you is considered quite rude in Japan, whereas Brazilians are more likely to interpret this as the person's interest and involvement in the conversation.

GENDER DIFFERENCES IN COMMUNICATION

After reading popular-press books on how men and women communicate, you might come to the conclusion that they are completely different life forms.[36] In reality, men and women have similar communication practices, but there are subtle distinctions that can occasionally lead to misunderstanding and conflict. One distinction is that men are more likely than women to view conversations as negotiations of relative status and power. They assert their power by directly giving advice to others (e.g. 'You should do the following') and using combative language. There is also evidence that men dominate the talk time in conversations with women, as well as interrupt more and adjust their speaking style less than do women.[37]

Men also engage in more 'report talk', in which the primary function of the conversation is impersonal and efficient information exchange. Women also do report talk, particularly when conversing with men, but conversations among women have a higher incidence of relationship building through 'rapport talk'. Rather than asserting status, women use indirect requests such as 'Have you considered . . . ?' Similarly, women apologise more often and seek advice from others more quickly than do men. Finally, research fairly consistently indicates that women are more sensitive than men to nonverbal cues in face-to-face meetings.[38]

Both men and women usually understand each other, but these subtle differences are occasional irritants. For instance, female scientists have complained that adversarial interaction among male scientists makes it difficult for women to participate in meaningful dialogue.[39] Another irritant occurs when women seek empathy but receive male dominance in response. Specifically, women sometimes discuss their personal experiences and problems to develop

LEARNING OBJECTIVE

Discuss the degree to which men and women communicate differently.

closeness with the receiver. But when men hear problems, they quickly suggest solutions because this asserts their control over the situation. As well as frustrating a woman's need for common understanding, the advice actually says: 'You and I are different; you have the problem and I have the answer.' Meanwhile, men become frustrated because they can't understand why women don't appreciate their advice.

IMPROVING INTERPERSONAL COMMUNICATION

Effective interpersonal communication depends on the sender's ability to get the message across and the receiver's performance as an active listener. This section outlines these two essential features of effective interpersonal communication.

GETTING YOUR MESSAGE ACROSS

This chapter began with the statement that effective communication occurs when the other person receives and understands the message. To accomplish this difficult task, the sender must learn to empathise with the receiver, repeat the message, choose an appropriate time for the conversation, and be descriptive rather than evaluative.

- *Empathise*. Recall from Chapters 3 and 4 that empathy is a person's ability to understand and be sensitive to the feelings, thoughts and situation of others. In conversations this involves putting yourself in the receiver's shoes when encoding the message. For instance, be sensitive to words that may be ambiguous or trigger the wrong emotional response.
- *Repeat the message*. Rephrase the key points a couple of times. The saying 'Tell them what you're going to tell them; tell them; then tell them what you've told them' reflects this need for redundancy.
- *Use timing effectively*. Your message competes with other messages and noise, so find a time when the receiver is less likely to be distracted by these other matters.
- *Be descriptive*. Focus on the problem, not the person, if you have negative information to convey. People stop listening when the information attacks their self-esteem. Also, suggest things the listener can do to improve, rather than point to him or her as a problem.

ACTIVE LISTENING

'Nature gave people two ears but only one tongue, which is a gentle hint that they should listen more than they talk.'[40] To follow this sage advice, we need to recognise that listening is a process of actively sensing the sender's signals, evaluating them accurately, and responding appropriately. These three components of listening—sensing, evaluating and responding—reflect the listener's side of the communication model described at the beginning of the chapter. Listeners receive the sender's signals, decode them as intended, and provide appropriate and timely feedback to the sender (see Exhibit 11.4). Active listeners constantly cycle through sensing, evaluating and responding during the conversation and engage in various activities to improve these processes.[41]

Sensing

Sensing is the process of receiving signals from the sender and paying attention to them. These signals include the words spoken, the nature of the sounds (speed of speech, tone of voice, etc.) and nonverbal cues. Active listeners improve sensing by postponing evaluation, avoiding interruptions and maintaining interest.

- *Postpone evaluation*. Many listeners become victims of first impressions. They quickly form an opinion of the speaker's message and subsequently screen out important information. Active listeners, on the other hand, try to stay as open-minded as possible by delaying evaluation of the message until the speaker has finished.

Active listening process and strategies

EXHIBIT 11.4

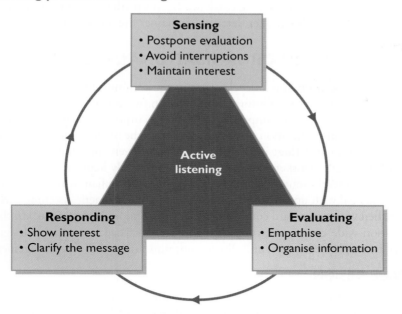

- *Avoid interruptions.* Interrupting the speaker's conversation has two negative effects on the sensing process. First, it disrupts the speaker's idea, so the listener does not receive the entire message. Second, interruptions tend to second-guess what the speaker is trying to say, which contributes to the problem of evaluating the speaker's ideas too early.
- *Maintain interest.* As with any behaviour, active listening requires motivation. Too often we close our minds soon after a conversation begins because the subject is boring. Instead, active listeners maintain interest by taking the view—probably an accurate one—that there is always something of value in a conversation; it's just a matter of actively looking for it.

Evaluating

This component of listening includes understanding the message meaning, evaluating the message, and remembering the message. To improve their evaluation of the conversation, active listeners empathise with the speaker and organise information received during the conversation.

- *Empathise.* Active listeners try to understand and be sensitive to the speaker's feelings, thoughts and situation. Empathy is a critical skill in active listening because the verbal and nonverbal cues from the conversation are accurately interpreted from the other person's point of view.
- *Organise information.* Listeners process information three times faster than the average rate of speech (450 words per minute versus 125 words per minute), so they are easily distracted. Active listeners use this spare time to organise the information into key points. In fact, it's a good idea to imagine that you must summarise what people have said after they have finished speaking.

Responding

Responding, the third component of listening, is feedback to the sender, which motivates and directs the speaker's communication. Active listeners do this by showing interest and clarifying the message.

- *Show interest.* Active listeners show interest by maintaining sufficient eye contact and sending back channel signals such as 'Oh, really!' and 'I see' during appropriate breaks in the conversation.

- *Clarify the message.* Active listeners provide feedback by rephrasing the speaker's ideas at appropriate breaks ('So you're saying that . . . ?'). This further demonstrates interest in the conversation and helps the speaker determine whether the message has been understood.

COMMUNICATING IN ORGANISATIONAL HIERARCHIES

LEARNING OBJECTIVE

Summarise four communication strategies in organisational hierarchies.

So far, the focus has been on 'micro-level' issues in the communication process, namely, the dynamics of sending and receiving information between two people in various situations. But in this era when knowledge is a competitive advantage, corporate leaders also need to maintain an open flow of communication up, down and across the organisation. At least two recent Australian polls indicate that there is a lot of room for improvement. One survey reported that 69 per cent of blue-collar workers say that they are completely kept out of the loop by their bosses. A survey of several thousand employees in a dozen Australian firms found that only 40 per cent were satisfied with upward communication and management 'listening', while 38 per cent were satisfied with downward communication from senior management.[42] In this section, four organisation-wide communication strategies are discussed: workspace design; e-zines, blogs and wikis; employee surveys; and direct communication with top management.

WORKSPACE DESIGN

The ability and motivation to communicate is, to some extent, influenced by the physical space in which employees work. The location and design of hallways, offices, cubicles and communal areas (cafeterias, lifts) shape who employees speak to as well as the frequency of

National@Docklands building encourages chance encounters

Communication was a top priority when National Australia Bank designed National@Docklands, the financial institution's new campus-like headquarters in Melbourne. Each of the site's two buildings has a hollow core cross-hatched with walkways, gantries and stairways that draw employees into the open environment. Workstations are located in open offices, while the building provides numerous study areas, cafés and other 'bump spaces' to encourage communication during chance interactions. 'In the traditional building, closed rooms or separate lifts keep people apart; even traditional open-plan offices don't always encourage community,' said an NAB executive. 'But great things can start from one idea, from a chance conversation. Docklands will encourage people to meet, to bump into one another; it will increase the chance for that flow of ideas.'[44]

John Gollins/Bligh Voller Nield Architects

that communication. Pixar Animation Studios designed its building in a way that encourages ongoing informal communication within team clusters. At the same time, the company's campus near San Francisco, California, is designed such that employees share knowledge through happenstance interactions with people on other teams. Pixar executives call this the 'bathroom effect', because team members must leave their isolated pods to fetch their mail, have lunch or visit the rest room. 'It promotes that chance encounter,' says Pixar creative director John Lasseter. 'You run into people constantly. It worked from the minute we arrived. We just blossomed here.'[43]

Another increasingly popular workspace strategy is to replace traditional offices with open space arrangements, where all employees (including management) work in the same open area. Anecdotal evidence suggests that people do communicate more often with fewer walls between them. However, research also suggests that open office design potentially increases employee stress due to the loss of privacy and personal space. According to an analysis of 13 000 employee surveys in forty major organisations, the most important function of workspace is to provide a place to concentrate on work without distraction. The second most important function is to support informal communication with co-workers.[45] In other words, workspace needs to balance privacy with opportunities for social interaction.

E-ZINES, BLOGS AND WIKIS

For decades employees have received official company news through hard-copy newsletters and magazines. Many firms still use these communication devices, but most have supplemented or replaced them completely with web-based information sources. Web-based or PDF-only format newsletters, called *e-zines*, are inexpensive and allow companies to post new information quickly. However, information from e-zines tends to be brief, because many employees have difficulty reading long articles on a computer screen.[46]

The opening story to this chapter described how *blogs* are entering the corporate world as another communication vehicle. Blogs written by senior executives offer direct communication to employees and, if written casually, have a personal touch that makes the information more credible than formal magazines. Executive blogs also allow employees to submit their comments, which isn't possible in e-zines or newsletters. In addition to executive blogs, Matsushita and a few other firms are also turning to employee blogs, in which people in a work unit post updates of events in their area.

Wikis (Hawaiian for 'fast') are a collaborative variation of blogs in which anyone in a group can write, edit or remove material from the website. Wikipedia, the popular online encyclopedia, is a massive example of a wiki. The Melbourne Wireless Group, a nonprofit group setting up a metro-wide wireless network, uses a wiki to keep its technical documents up to date. Wikis are also slowly finding their way into traditional organisations. Employees at Aperture Technologies Inc. use wikis to write documentation, brainstorm ideas and coordinate marketing projects. 'Wikis allow this collaboration much better than anything else, so we get things done faster,' says Aperture founder Nicholas Pisarro Jr.[47]

EMPLOYEE SURVEYS

Most of the 'best companies to work for' conduct regular employee opinion surveys in order to monitor worker morale, particularly as part of broader measures of corporate performance. For example, Bell Canada surveys its 60 000 employees each year using eighty-four questions on several themes, including career mobility, job challenge, information sharing and trust in the company's leadership. Canada's largest telephone company also has quarterly 'pulse surveys' that measure attitudes about specific policies, such as early retirement. These employee surveys have resulted in numerous corporate changes, such as switching from company-driven to flexible benefits.[48]

DIRECT COMMUNICATION WITH TOP MANAGEMENT

management by walking around (MBWA) A communication practice in which executives get out of their offices and learn from others in the organisation through face-to-face dialogue.

'The best fertiliser in any field is that of the farmer's footsteps!' This old Chinese saying means that farms are most successful when the farmers spend time in the fields directly observing the crop's development. In an organisational context, this means that to fully understand the issues, senior executives need to get out of the executive suite and meet directly with employees at all levels and on their turf. Nearly forty years ago people at Hewlett-Packard coined a phrase for this communication strategy: **management by walking around (MBWA)**.[49] MBWA became an operational mandate at Guild Insurance & Financial Services in order to boost employee engagement and clarify the company's strategic plan. Executives at the Hawthorn, Victoria, liability and indemnity insurance company spend a good deal of their time 'walking the floor', that is, talking face-to-face with employees around the country. Today, 85 per cent of Guild Insurance employees say that the company does an excellent job of keeping employees informed.[50]

Along with MBWA, executives are getting more direct communication with employees through 'town hall meetings', where large groups of employees hear about a merger or other special news directly from the key decision makers. Others attend employee round-table forums to hear opinions from a small representation of staff about various issues. All of these direct communication strategies potentially minimise filtering, because executives listen directly to employees. They also help executives acquire a deeper understanding of internal organisational problems. A third benefit of direct communication is that employees might have more empathy for decisions made further up the corporate hierarchy.

Kowloon Shangri-La's 'state of the hotel' meetings

Communicating with employees can be a challenge when the organisation is a large hotel that operates around the clock. But these conditions haven't prevented senior management at Kowloon Shangri-La from holding 'state of the hotel' meetings with all 700 staff twice each year. Two sessions are held, one in the morning and the other in the afternoon, so that all employees at the Hong Kong hotel can attend without leaving the hotel short-staffed. General manager Mark Heywood conducts no-holds-barred sessions in which employees are updated on the hotel's financial performance, upcoming events and renovations. 'It's a chance to communicate about the good, the bad and the ugly,' says Heywood. 'We don't just share good news and positive things.' He also outlines his vision for the hotel and reinforces its 'one team—one way' culture.[51]

Shangri-La International Hotel Management Ltd

COMMUNICATING THROUGH THE GRAPEVINE

No matter how much corporate leaders try to communicate through e-zines, blogs, wikis, surveys, MBWA and other means, employees will still rely on the oldest communication channel: the corporate **grapevine**. The grapevine is an unstructured and informal network founded on social relationships rather than organisational charts or job descriptions. What do employees think about the grapevine? Surveys of employees in two US firms (one in Florida and the other in California) provide the answer. Both surveys found that almost all employees use the grapevine but very few of them prefer this source of information. The Californian survey also reported that only one-third of employees believe that grapevine information is credible. In other words, employees turn to the grapevine when they have few other options.[52]

GRAPEVINE CHARACTERISTICS

Research conducted several decades ago reported that the grapevine transmits information very rapidly in all directions throughout the organisation. The typical pattern is a cluster chain, whereby a few people actively transmit rumours to many others. The grapevine works through informal social networks, so it is more active where employees have similar backgrounds and are able to communicate easily. Many rumours seem to have at least a kernel of truth, possibly because they are transmitted through media-rich communication channels (e.g. face-to-face) and employees are motivated to communicate effectively. Nevertheless, the grapevine distorts information by deleting fine details and exaggerating key points of the story.[53]

Some of these characteristics might still be true today, but other features of the grapevine would have changed due to the dramatic effects of information technologies in the workplace. Email, instant messages and even blogs have replaced the traditional chats at the water cooler as sources of gossip. Social networks have expanded as employees communicate with each other around the globe, not just with the occupant of the next cubicle. Public blogs and web forums have extended gossip to anyone, not just employees connected to social networks.

GRAPEVINE BENEFITS AND LIMITATIONS

Should the grapevine be encouraged, tolerated or quashed? This question is difficult to answer because the grapevine has both benefits and limitations.[54] One benefit, as mentioned earlier, is that employees rely on the grapevine when information is not available through formal channels. It is also the main conduit through which organisational stories and other symbols of the organisation's culture are communicated. A third benefit of the grapevine is that this social interaction relieves anxiety. This explains why rumour mills are most active during times of uncertainty.[55] Finally, the grapevine is associated with the drive to bond. Being a recipient of gossip is a sign of inclusion, according to evolutionary psychologists. Trying to quash the grapevine is, in some respects, an attempt to undermine the natural human drive for social interaction.[56]

While the grapevine offers these benefits, it is not the preferred communication medium. Grapevine information is sometimes so distorted that it escalates rather than reduces employee anxiety. Furthermore, employees develop more negative attitudes towards the organisation when management is slower than the grapevine in communicating information. What should corporate leaders do with the grapevine? The best advice seems to be to listen to the grapevine as a signal of employee anxiety, then correct the cause of this anxiety. Some companies also listen to the grapevine and step in to correct blatant errors and fabrications. Most importantly, corporate leaders need to view the grapevine as a competitor, and eventually win the challenge to inform employees before they receive the news through the grapevine.

grapevine An unstructured and informal communication network founded on social relationships rather than organisational charts or job descriptions.

CHAPTER SUMMARY

Communication refers to the process by which information is transmitted and *understood* between two or more people. Communication supports work coordination, employee well-being, knowledge management and decision making. The communication process involves forming, encoding and transmitting the intended message to a receiver, who then decodes the message and provides feedback to the sender. Effective communication occurs when the sender's thoughts are transmitted to and understood by the intended receiver.

Electronic mail (email) is an increasingly popular way to communicate, and it has changed communication patterns in organisational settings. However, email is an ineffective channel for communicating emotions, tends to reduce politeness and respect, is an inefficient medium for communicating in ambiguous, complex and novel situations, and contributes to information overload. Instant messaging, blogs and podcasts are also gaining in popularity in organisations.

Nonverbal communication includes facial gestures, voice intonation, physical distance and even silence. Unlike verbal communication, nonverbal communication is less rule-bound and is mostly automatic and unconscious. Emotional contagion refers to the automatic and unconscious tendency to mimic and synchronise our nonverbal behaviours with other people. The most appropriate communication medium depends on its data-carrying capacity (media richness) and its symbolic meaning to the receiver. Non-routine and ambiguous situations require rich media.

Several barriers create noise in the communication process. People misinterpret messages because of perceptual biases. Some information is filtered out as it gets passed up the hierarchy. Jargon and ambiguous language are barriers when the sender and receiver have different interpretations of the words and symbols used. People also screen out or misinterpret messages due to information overload.

Globalisation and workforce diversity have brought new communication challenges. Words are easily misunderstood in verbal communication, either because the receiver has a limited vocabulary or because the sender's accent distorts the usual sound of some words. Voice intonation, silence and nonverbal cues have different meanings and importance in different cultures. There are also some communication differences between men and women; for example, men have a tendency to exert status and engage in report talk in conversations, whereas women use more rapport talk and are more sensitive than are men to nonverbal cues.

To get a message across, the sender must learn to empathise with the receiver, repeat the message, choose an appropriate time for the conversation, and be descriptive rather than evaluative. Listening includes sensing, evaluating and responding. Active listeners support these processes by postponing evaluation, avoiding interruptions, maintaining interest, empathising, organising information, showing interest and clarifying the message.

Some companies try to encourage informal communication through workspace design, although open offices run the risk of increasing stress and reducing the ability to concentrate on work. Many larger organisations also rely on e-zines to communicate corporate news. Employee surveys are widely used to measure employee attitudes or involve employees in corporate decisions. Some executives also meet directly with employees, through 'management by walking around' or other arrangements, to facilitate communication across the organisation.

In any organisation, employees rely on the grapevine, particularly during times of uncertainty. The grapevine is an unstructured and informal network founded on social relationships rather than organisational charts or job descriptions. Although early research identified several unique features of the grapevine, some of these features may be changing as the Internet plays an increasing role in grapevine communication.

KEY TERMS

communication p. 326
emotional contagion p. 331
flaming p. 328

grapevine p. 343
information overload p. 335
jargon p. 334

management by walking around
  (MBWA) p. 342
media richness p. 332

DISCUSSION QUESTIONS

1. A company in a country that is just entering the information age intends to introduce electronic mail for office staff at its three buildings located throughout the city. Describe two benefits as well as two potential problems that employees might experience with this medium.

2. Corporate and employee blogs might become increasingly popular over the next few years. What are the advantages and disadvantages of this communication medium?

3. Marshall McLuhan coined the popular phrase 'The medium is the message'. What does this phrase mean, and why should we be aware of it when communicating in organisations?

4. Why is emotional contagion important in organisations and what effect does the increasing reliance on email have on this phenomenon?

5. Under what conditions, if any, do you think it is appropriate to use email to notify an employee that he or she has been laid off or sacked? Why is email usually considered an inappropriate channel to convey this information?

6. Explain why men and women are sometimes frustrated with each other's communication behaviours.

7. In your opinion, has the introduction of email and other information technologies increased or decreased the amount of information flowing through the corporate grapevine? Explain your answer.

8. Wikis are collaborative websites where anyone in the group can post, edit or delete any information. Where might this communication technology be most useful in organisations?

BRIDGING THE TWO WORLDS: THE ORGANISATIONAL DILEMMA

11.1 | SKILL BUILDER

CASE STUDY

By William Todorovic, Purdue University

I had been hired by Aluminium Elements Corp. (AEC) and it was my first day of work. I was twenty-six years old, and I was now the manager of AEC's customer service group which looked after customers, logistics and some of the raw material purchasing. My superior, George, was the vice-president of the company. AEC manufactured most of its products, a majority of which were destined for the construction industry, from aluminium.

As I walked around the shop floor, the employees appeared to be concentrating on their jobs, barely noticing me. Management held daily meetings, in which various production issues were discussed. No one from the shop floor was invited to the meeting, unless there was a specific problem. Later I also learned that management had separate washrooms and separate lunchrooms, as well as other perks which floor employees did not have. Most of the floor employees felt that management, although polite on the surface, did not really feel it had anything to learn from the floor employees.

John, who worked on the aluminium slitter, a crucial operation required before any other operations could commence, had a number of unpleasant encounters with George. As a result, George usually sent written memos to the floor in order to avoid a direct confrontation with John. Because the directions in the memos were complex, the memos were often more than two pages in length.

One morning, as I was walking around, I noticed that John was very upset. Feeling that perhaps there was something I could do, I approached John and asked him if I could help. He indicated that everything was just fine. From the look of the situation, and John's body language, I felt that he was willing to talk but he knew that this was not the way things were done at AEC. Tony, who worked at the machine next to John's, then cursed and said that the office guys only cared about schedules, not about the people down on the floor. I told him that I had only been working here for a week, and thought that I could address some of their issues. Tony gave me a strange look, shook his head and went back to his machine. I could hear him still swearing as I left. Later I realised that most of the office staff were offended by Tony's language.

On the way back to my office, Lesley, a recently hired engineer from Russia, approached me and pointed out that the employees were not accustomed to management talking to them. Management only issued orders and made demands. As we discussed the different perceptions between office and floor staff, we were interrupted by a very loud lunch bell, which startled me. I was happy to join Lesley for lunch, but she asked me why I was not eating in the managers' lunch room. I replied that if I was going to understand how AEC worked, I had to get to know all the people better. In addition, I realised that this was not how things were done, and wondered about the nature of this apparent division between the management and the floor. In the lunchroom, the other workers were amazed to see me there, commenting that I was new and had not learned the ropes yet.

After lunch I asked George, my supervisor, about his recent confrontation with John. George was surprised that John had been upset, and exclaimed, 'I just wanted John to know that he had done a great job, and as a result we would be able to ship on time one large order to the West Coast. If fact, I thought I was complimenting him.'

Earlier, Lesley had indicated that certain behaviour was expected from management, and therefore from me. I did not think that this behaviour worked, and besides it was not what I believed or how I cared to behave. For the next couple of months I simply walked around the floor and took every opportunity to talk to the shop-floor employees. Often when the employees related specific information about their workplaces, I felt that it went over my head. Frequently I had to write down the information and revisit it later. I made a point of listening to them, identifying where they were coming from, and trying to understand them. I needed to keep my mind open to new ideas. Because the shop employees expected me to make requests and demands, I made a point of not doing any of that. Soon, the employees became friendly, and started to accept me as one of their own, or at least as a different type of management person.

During my third month of work the employees showed me how to improve the scheduling of jobs, especially those on the aluminium slitter. In fact, the greatest contribution was made by John who demonstrated better ways to combine the most common slitting sizes and how to reduce waste by retaining some of the 'common-sized' material for new orders. Seeing the opportunity, I programmed a spreadsheet to calculate and track inventory. This, in addition to better planning and forecasting, allowed us to reduce our new-order turnarounds from four or five weeks to in by 10 am and out by 5 pm on the same day.

By the time I had been employed for four months, members from other departments were coming to me and asking me to relay messages to the shop employees. When I asked why they were delegating this task to me, they stated that I spoke the same language as the shop employees. Increasingly, I became the messenger for the office to shop floor communication.

One morning George called me into his office and complimented me on the levels of customer service, and the improvements that had been achieved. As we talked, I mentioned that we could not have done it without John's help. 'He really knows his stuff, and he is good,' I said. I suggested that we consider him for some type of promotion. I hoped that this would be a positive gesture that would improve the communication between the office and the shop floor.

George turned and pulled a flyer out of his desk. 'There is a management skills seminar on in a couple of weeks. Do you think we should send John to it?'

'That is a great idea,' I exclaimed. 'Perhaps it would be good if he were to receive the news from you directly, George.' George agreed, and after discussing some other issues, we parted company.

That afternoon, John came into my office, upset and ready to quit. 'After all my effort and work, you guys are sending me for training seminars. So, am I not good enough for you?'

QUESTIONS

1. What barriers to effective communication existed in Aluminium Elements Corp? How did the author deal with these? What would you do differently?

2. Identify and discuss why John was upset at the end of the case. What do you recommend the writer should do at this time?

ANALYSING THE BLOGOSPHERE

PURPOSE

This exercise is designed to help you understand the dynamics of corporate blogs as a way to communicate in organisations.

INSTRUCTIONS

The activity is usually completed in between classes. The instructor will divide the class into teams (although the exercise can also be done by individuals). Each team will identify a corporate blog (written by a company or government executive and aimed at customers, employees or the wider community). The team will analyse the content of the selected blog and answer the following questions (preferably with brief samples where applicable).

1. Who is the main intended audience of the blog?
2. To what extent do you think this blog attracts the attention of its intended audience? Explain.
3. What are the main topics in recent postings about this organisation? Are they mostly good or bad news? Why?

ACTIVE LISTENING EXERCISE

Mary Gander, Winona State University

PURPOSE

This exercise is designed to help you understand the dynamics of active listening in conversations and to help develop active listening skills.

INSTRUCTIONS

For each of the four vignettes presented below, student teams (or students working individually) will compose three statements that demonstrate active listening. Specifically, one statement will indicate that you show empathy for the situation; the second will ask for clarification and detail in a non-judgmental way; the third will provide non-evaluative feedback to the speaker. Here are details about each of the three types of responses:

- *Showing empathy. Acknowledge feelings.* Sometimes it sounds like the speaker wants you to agree with him/her but in reality the person mainly wants you to understand how he or she feels. 'Acknowledging feelings' involves taking in the speaker's statements but looking at the 'whole message', including body language, tone of voice and level of arousal, and trying to determine what emotion the speaker is conveying. Then you let the speaker know that you realise he or she is feeling that emotion by acknowledging it in a sentence.

- *Asking for clarification and detail while withholding your judgment and own opinions.* This conveys that you are making a good effort to understand and not just trying to push your opinions onto the speaker. To formulate a relevant question in asking for more clarification, you will have to listen carefully to what is said. Frame your question in a way that indicates that you are trying to understand in more detail; often asking for a specific example is useful. This also helps the speaker evaluate his or her own opinions and perspective.

- *Providing non-evaluative feedback. Feeding back the message you heard.* This will allow the speaker to determine whether he/she has really got the message across to you and will help prevent troublesome miscommunication. It will also help the speaker become more aware of how he/she is coming across to another person (self-evaluation). Think about what the speaker is conveying and paraphrase it in your own words, and say it back to the speaker (without judging the correctness or merit of what was said), asking him/her if that is the intended meaning.

After teams (or individual students) have prepared the three statements for each vignette, the instructor will ask them to present their statements and explain how these statements satisfy the active listening criteria.

VIGNETTE 1

A colleague stops by your desk and says, 'I am tired of the lack of leadership around here. The boss is so wishy-washy, he can't get tough with some of the slackers around here. They just keep milking the company, living off the rest of us. Why doesn't management do something about these guys? And *you* are always so supportive of the boss; he's not as good as you make him out to be.'

VIGNETTE 2

Your co-worker stops by your cubicle, her voice and body language showing stress, frustration and even some fear. You know she has been working hard and has a strong need to get her work done on time and done well. You are trying to concentrate on some work and have had a number of interruptions already. She abruptly interrupts you and says, 'This project is turning out to be a mess. Why can't the other three people on my team quit fighting each other?'

VIGNETTE 3

One of your subordinates is working on an important project. He is an engineer who has good technical skills and knowledge and was selected for the project team because of that. He stops by your office and appears to be quite agitated. His voice is loud and strained and his face has a look of bewilderment. He says, 'I'm supposed to be working with four other people from four other departments on this new project, but they never listen to my ideas and seem to hardly know I'm at the meeting!'

VIGNETTE 4

Your subordinate comes into your office in a state of agitation, and asks if she can talk to you. She is polite and sits down. She seems calm and does not have an angry look on her face. However, she says, 'It seems like you consistently make up lousy schedules. You are unfair and unrealistic in the kinds of assignments you give certain people, me included. Everyone else is so intimidated that they don't complain, but I think you need to know that this isn't right and it's got to change.'

CROSS-CULTURAL COMMUNICATION GAME

PURPOSE

This exercise is designed to develop and test your knowledge of cross-cultural differences in communication and etiquette.

MATERIALS

The instructor will provide one set of question/answer cards for each pair of teams.

INSTRUCTIONS

Step 1: The class is divided into an even number of teams. Ideally, each team would have three students. (Two- or four-student teams are possible if matched with an equal-sized team.) Each team is then paired with another team and the paired teams (Team 'A' and Team 'B') are assigned a private space away from other matched teams.

Step 2: The instructor will hand each pair of teams a stack of cards with the multiple-choice questions face down. These cards have questions and answers about cross-cultural differences in communication and etiquette. No books or other aids are allowed.

Step 3: The exercise begins with a member of Team A picking up one card from the top of the pile and asking the question on that card to both people on Team B. The information given to Team B includes the question and all alternatives listed on the card. Team B has thirty seconds after the question and alternatives have been read to give an answer. Team B earns one point if the correct answer is given. If Team B's answer is incorrect, however, Team A earns that point. Correct answers to each question are indicated on the card and, of course, should not be revealed until the question is correctly answered or time is up. Whether or not Team B answers correctly, it picks up the next card on the pile and asks the question to members of Team A. In other words, cards are read alternatively to each team. This procedure is repeated until all of the cards have been read or time has elapsed. The team receiving the most points wins.

Important note: The textbook provides very little information pertaining to the questions in this exercise. Rather, you must rely on past learning, logic and luck to win.

© 2001 Steven L. McShane

ACTIVE LISTENING SKILLS INVENTORY

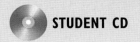 **STUDENT CD**

PURPOSE

This self-assessment is designed to help you estimate your strengths and weaknesses on various dimensions of active listening.

INSTRUCTIONS

Think back to face-to-face conversations you have had with a co-worker or client in the office, in the hallway, on the factory floor or in another setting. Indicate the extent to which each item below describes your behaviour during those conversations. Answer each item as truthfully as possible so that you get an accurate estimate of where your active listening skills need improvement. Then use the scoring key in Appendix B to calculate your results for each scale. This exercise is completed alone so that students can assess themselves honestly without concerns of social comparison. However, class discussion will focus on the important elements of active listening.

ACTIVE LISTENING SKILLS INVENTORY

Circle the best response to the right that indicates the extent to which each statement describes you when listening to others.	Not at all	A little	Somewhat	Very much	Score
1. I keep an open mind about the speaker's point of view until he/she has finished talking.	❑	❑	❑	❑	_____
2. While listening, I mentally sort out the speaker's ideas in a way that makes sense to me.	❑	❑	❑	❑	_____
3. I stop the speaker and give my opinion when I disagree with something he/she has said.	❑	❑	❑	❑	_____
4. People can often tell when I'm not concentrating on what they are saying.	❑	❑	❑	❑	_____
5. I don't evaluate what a person is saying until he/she has finished talking.	❑	❑	❑	❑	_____
6. When someone takes a long time to present a simple idea, I let my mind wander to other things.	❑	❑	❑	❑	_____
7. I jump into conversations to present my views rather than wait and risk forgetting what I wanted to say.	❑	❑	❑	❑	_____
8. I nod my head and make other gestures to show I'm interested in the conversation.	❑	❑	❑	❑	_____
9. I can usually keep focused on what people are saying to me even when the person doesn't sound interesting.	❑	❑	❑	❑	_____
10. Rather than organising the speaker's ideas, I usually expect the person to summarise them for me.	❑	❑	❑	❑	_____
11. I always say things like 'I see' or 'uh-huh' so people will know that I'm really listening to them.	❑	❑	❑	❑	_____
12. While listening, I concentrate on what is being said and regularly organise the information.	❑	❑	❑	❑	_____
13. While the speaker is talking, I quickly determine whether I like or dislike his/her ideas.	❑	❑	❑	❑	_____
14. I pay close attention to what people are saying even when they are explaining something I already know.	❑	❑	❑	❑	_____
15. I don't give my opinion until I'm sure the other person has finished talking.	❑	❑	❑	❑	_____

NOTES

1   C. Keall, 'Workplace Blogging', *IDG Unlimited*, 23 August 2004; J. C. Perez, Google Sees Benefits in Corporate Blogging', *Network World*, 29 November 2004, 28; M. Delio, 'The Enterprise Blogosphere', *InfoWorld*, 28 March 2005, 42–7; R. Schwarz, 'Blogs Go Corporate', *Dominion Post* (Auckland), 10 October 2005, 10; T. Tharakan, 'Bloggers Beware! Big Brother Is Watching', *Press Trust of India*, 9 November 2005; Y. Y. Yeo, 'Blogs Go Corporate', *Straits Times* (Singapore), 2 October 2005.

2   R. Gray, 'Finding the Right Direction', *Communication World*, November–December 2004, 26–32.

3   I. Nonaka and H. Takeuchi, *The Knowledge-Creating Company* (New York: Oxford University Press, 1995); R. T. Barker and M. R. Camarata, 'The Role of Communication in Creating and Maintaining a

Learning Organization: Preconditions, Indicators, and Disciplines', *Journal of Business Communication* 35 (October 1998), 443–67; D. Te'eni, 'A Cognitive-Affective Model of Organizational Communication for Designing IT', *MIS Quarterly* 25 (June 2001), 251–312.

4   C. E. Shannon and W. Weaver, *The Mathematical Theory of Communication* (Urbana, Ill.: University of Illinois Press, 1949); K. J. Krone, F. M. Jablin and L. L. Putnam, 'Communication Theory and Organizational Communication: Multiple Perspectives', in *Handbook of Organizational Communication: An Interdisciplinary Perspective*, ed. F. M. Jablin et al. (Newbury Park, California: Sage, 1987), 18–40.

5   W. Lucas, 'Effects of E-Mail on the Organization', *European Management Journal* 16, no. 1 (February 1998), 18–30; D. A. Owens,

M. A. Neale and R. I. Sutton, 'Technologies of Status Management Status Dynamics in E-Mail Communications', *Research on Managing Groups and Teams* 3 (2000), 205–30; N. Ducheneaut and L. A. Watts, 'In Search of Coherence: A Review of E-Mail Research', *Human–Computer Interaction* 20, no. 1-2 (2005), 11–48.

6   J. B. Walther, 'Language and Communication Technology: Introduction to the Special Issue', *Journal of Language and Social Psychology* 23, no. 4 (December 2004), 384–96; J. B. Walther, T. Loh and L. Granka, 'Let Me Count the Ways: The Interchange of Verbal and Nonverbal Cues in Computer-Mediated and Face-to-Face Affinity', *Journal of Language and Social Psychology* 24, no. 1 (March 2005), 36–65.

7   G. Hertel, S. Geister and U. Konradt, 'Managing Virtual Teams: A Review of Current Empirical Research', *Human Resource Management Review* 15 (2005), 69–95; H. Lee, 'Behavioral Strategies for Dealing with Flaming in an Online Forum', *The Sociological Quarterly* 46, no. 2 (2005), 385–403.

8   H. Zampetakis, 'Business Out to Show Email Who's the Boss', *The Age* (Melbourne), 19 August 2003, 3.

9   K. Restivo, 'Coming to an iPod Near You', *National Post*, 16 July 2005, FP4.

10 D. Robb, 'Ready or Not … Instant Messaging Has Arrived as a Financial Planning Tool', *Journal of Financial Planning* (July 2001), 12–14; J. Black, 'Why Offices Are Now Open Secrets', *Business Week* (17 September 2003); A. F. Cameron and J. Webster, 'Unintended Consequences of Emerging Communication Technologies: Instant Messaging in the Workplace', *Computers in Human Behavior* 21, no. 1 (2005), 85–103.

11 L. Z. Tiedens and A. R. Fragale, 'Power Moves: Complementarity in Dominant and Submissive Nonverbal Behavior', *Journal of Personality and Social Psychology* 84, no. 3 (2003), 558–68.

12 P. Ekman and E. Rosenberg, *What the Face Reveals: Basic and Applied Studies of Spontaneous Expression Using the Facial Action Coding System* (Oxford, England: Oxford University Press, 1997); P. Winkielman and K. C. Berridge, 'Unconscious Emotion', *Current Directions in Psychological Science* 13, no. 3 (2004), 120–3.

13 E. Hatfield, J. T. Cacioppo and R. L. Rapson, *Emotional Contagion* (Cambridge, UK: Cambridge University Press, 1993); S. G. Barsade, 'The Ripple Effect: Emotional Contagion and Its Influence on Group Behavior', *Administrative Science Quarterly* 47 (December 2002), 644–75; M. Sonnby-Borgstrom, P. Jonsson and O. Svensson, 'Emotional Empathy as Related to Mimicry Reactions at Different Levels of Information Processing', *Journal of Nonverbal Behavior* 27 (Spring 2003), 3–23.

14 J. R. Kelly and S. G. Barsade, 'Mood and Emotions in Small Groups and Work Teams', *Organizational Behavior and Human Decision Processes* 86 (September 2001), 99–130.

15 B. Andrews, 'Winning Hand', *Business Review Weekly*, 14 April 2005, 72.

16 R. L. Daft and R. H. Lengel, 'Information Richness: A New Approach to Managerial Behavior and Organization Design', *Research in Organizational Behavior* 6 (1984), 191–233; R. H. Lengel and R. L. Daft, 'The Selection of Communication Media as an Executive Skill', *Academy of Management Executive* 2 (1988), 225–32.

17 R. E. Rice, 'Task Analyzability, Use of New Media, and Effectiveness: A Multi-Site Exploration of Media Richness', *Organization Science* 3 (1992), 475–500.

18 J. R. Carlson and R. W. Zmud, 'Channel Expansion Theory and the Experiential Nature of Media Richness Perceptions', *Academy of Management Journal* 42 (April 1999), 153–70; N. Kock, 'Media Richness or Media Naturalness? The Evolution of Our Biological Communication Apparatus and Its Influence on Our Behavior toward E-Communication Tools', *IEEE Transactions on Professional Communication* 48, no. 2 (June 2005), 117–30.

19 M. McLuhan, *Understanding Media: The Extensions of Man* (New York: McGraw-Hill, 1964).

20 K. Griffiths, 'KPMG Sacks 670 Employees by E-Mail', *The Independent* (London), 5 November 2002, 19; P. Nelson, 'Work Practices', *Personnel Today*, 12 November 2002, 2.

21 D. Goleman, R. Boyatzis and A. McKee, *Primal Leaders* (Boston: Harvard Business School Press, 2002), pp. 92–5.

22 J. Kavanaugh, 'National Emergency', *Business Review Weekly*, 3 November 2005, 32.

23 L. L. Putnam, N. Phillips and P. Chapman, 'Metaphors of Communication and Organization', in *Handbook of Organization Studies*, ed. S. R. Clegg, C. Hardy and W. R. Nord (London: Sage, 1996), 373–408; G. Morgan, *Images of Organization*, 2nd edn (Thousand Oaks, CA: Sage, 1997); M. Rubini and H. Sigall, 'Taking the Edge Off of Disagreement: Linguistic Abstractness and Self-Presentation to a Heterogeneous Audience', *European Journal of Social Psychology* 32 (2002), 343–51.

24 K. M. Jackson, 'Buzzword Backlash Looks to Purge Jibba-Jabba from Corporate-Speak', *Boston Globe*, 17 April 2005, G1.

25 D. Stonehouse, 'Email', *Sun Herald* (Sydney), 26 June 2005, 26.

26 T. Koski, 'Reflections on Information Glut and Other Issues in Knowledge Productivity', *Futures* 33 (August 2001), 483–95; D. D. Dawley and W. P. Anthony, 'User Perceptions of E-Mail at Work', *Journal of Business and Technical Communication* 17, no. 2 (April 2003), 170–200; 'Email Brings Costs and Fatigue', *Western News* (University of Western Ontario) (London, Ontario), 9 July 2004.

27 A. G. Schick, L. A. Gordon and S. Haka, 'Information Overload: A Temporal Approach', *Accounting, Organizations & Society* 15 (1990), 199–220; A. Edmunds and A. Morris, 'The Problem of Information Overload in Business Organisations: A Review of the Literature', *International Journal of Information Management* 20 (2000), 17–28.

28 D. Kirkpatrick, 'Gates and Ozzie: How to Escape E-Mail Hell', *Fortune*, 27 June 2005, 169–71.

29 D. C. Thomas and K. Inkson, *Cultural Intelligence: People Skills for Global Business* (San Francisco: Berrett-Koehler, 2004), chapter 6; D. Welch, L. Welch and R. Piekkari, 'Speaking in Tongues', *International Studies of Management & Organization* 35, no. 1 (Spring 2005), 10–27.

30 D. Woodruff, 'Crossing Culture Divide Early Clears Merger Paths', *Asian Wall Street Journal*, 28 May 2001, 9.

31 M. Brandel, 'Global CIO', *Computerworld*, 21 November 2005, 39–41. *Tatemae* and *honne* are discussed in: H. Yamada, *American and Japanese Business Discourse: A Comparison of Interaction Styles* (Norwood, NJ: Ablex, 1992), p. 34; R. M. March, *Reading the Japanese Mind* (Tokyo: Kodansha International, 1996), chapter 1.

32 P. Harris and R. Moran, *Managing Cultural Differences* (Houston: Gulf, 1987); H. Blagg, 'A Just Measure of Shame?', *British Journal of Criminology* 37 (Autumn 1997), 481–501; R. E. Axtell, *Gestures: The Do's and Taboos of Body Language around the World*, revised edn (New York: Wiley, 1998).

33 M. Griffin, 'The Office, Australian Style', *Sunday Age* (22 June 2003), 6.

34 S. Ohtaki, T. Ohtaki and M. D. Fetters, 'Doctor–Patient Communication: A Comparison of the USA and Japan', *Family Practice* 20 (June 2003), 276–82; M. Fujio, 'Silence During Intercultural Communication: A Case Study', *Corporate Communications* 9, no. 4 (2004), 331–9.

35 D. C. Barnlund, *Communication Styles of Japanese and Americans: Images and Realities* (Belmont, Calif.: Wadsworth, 1988); Yamada, *American and Japanese Business Discourse: A Comparison of Interaction Styles*, chapter 2; H. Yamada, *Different Games, Different Rules* (New York: Oxford University Press, 1997), pp. 76–9.

36   This stereotypic notion is prevalent throughout J. Gray, *Men Are from Mars, Women Are from Venus* (New York: Harper Collins, 1992). For a critique of this view, see J. T. Wood, 'A Critical Response to John Gray's Mars and Venus Portrayals of Men and Women', *Southern Communication Journal* 67 (Winter 2002), 201–10.

37   D. Tannen, *You Just Don't Understand: Men and Women in Conversation* (New York: Ballentine Books, 1990); D. Tannen, *Talking from 9 to 5* (New York: Avon, 1994); M. Crawford, *Talking Difference: On Gender and Language* (Thousand Oaks, CA: Sage, 1995), pp. 41–4; L. L. Namy, L. C. Nygaard and D. Sauerteig, 'Gender Differences in Vocal Accommodation: The Role of Perception', *Journal of Language and Social Psychology* 21, no. 4 (December 2002), 422–32.

38   A. Mulac et al., '"Uh-Huh. What's That All About?" Differing Interpretations of Conversational Backchannels and Questions as Sources of Miscommunication across Gender Boundaries', *Communication Research* 25 (December 1998), 641–68; N. M. Sussman and D. H. Tyson, 'Sex and Power: Gender Differences in Computer-Mediated Interactions', *Computers in Human Behavior* 16 (2000), 381–94; D. R. Caruso and P. Salovey, *The Emotionally Intelligent Manager* (San Francisco: Jossey-Bass, 2004), p. 23.

39   P. Tripp-Knowles, 'A Review of the Literature on Barriers Encountered by Women in Science Academia', *Resources for Feminist Research* 24 (Spring/Summer 1995), 28–34.

40   Cited in K. Davis and J. W. Newstrom, *Human Behavior at Work: Organizational Behavior*, 7th edn (New York: McGraw-Hill, 1985), p. 438.

41   The three components of listening discussed here are based on several recent studies in the field of marketing, including: S. B. Castleberry, C. D. Shepherd and R. Ridnour, 'Effective Interpersonal Listening in the Personal Selling Environment: Conceptualization, Measurement, and Nomological Validity', *Journal of Marketing Theory and Practice* 7 (Winter 1999), 30–8; L. B. Comer and T. Drollinger, 'Active Empathetic Listening and Selling Success: A Conceptual Framework', *Journal of Personal Selling & Sales Management* 19 (Winter 1999), 15–29; K. de Ruyter and M. G. M. Wetzels, 'The Impact of Perceived Listening Behavior in Voice-to-Voice Service Encounters', *Journal of Service Research* 2 (February 2000), 276–84.

42   Gray, 'Finding the Right Direction'; Talent2, 'Tight-lipped Bosses Play the "Keep the Workers in the Dark" Game!', Talent2 news release (Melbourne: 11 August 2005).

43   S. P. Means, 'Playing at Pixar', *Salt Lake Tribune* (Utah), 30 May 2003, D1; G. Whipp, 'Swimming against the Tide', *Daily News of Los Angeles*, 30 May 2003, U6.

44   C. Fox and A. Cornell, 'Too Little, Too Late', *Australian Financial Review*, 12 March 2004, 30; S. Drake and G. Brawn, 'National@Docklands', *Architecture Australia* 94, no. 1 (January–February 2005), 62–71.

45   G. Evans and D. Johnson, 'Stress and Open-Office Noise', *Journal of Applied Psychology* 85 (2000), 779–83; F. Russo, 'My Kingdom for a Door', *Time Magazine*, 23 October 2000, B1.

46   B. Sosnin, 'Digital Newsletters "E-Volutionize" Employee Communications', *HRMagazine*, May 2001, 99–107.

47   R. D. Hof, 'Something Wiki Comes This Way', *BusinessWeek*, 7 June 2004, 128; K. Swisher, 'Boomtown: "Wiki" May Alter How Employees Work Together', *Wall Street Journal*, 29 July 2004, B1; Delio, 'The Enterprise Blogosphere'.

48   S. Greengard, 'Employee Surveys: Ask the Right Questions, Probe the Answers for Insight', *Workforce Management*, December 2004, 76.

49   The original term is 'management by *wandering* around', but this has been replaced with 'walking' over the years. See: W. Ouchi, *Theory Z* (New York: Avon Books, 1981), pp. 176–7; T. Peters and R. Waterman, *In Search of Excellence* (New York: Harper and Row, 1982), p. 122.

50   L. Huxley, 'Aligning People and Strategy at Guild IFS', *Strategic HR Review* 3, no. 6 (September–October 2004), 16–19.

51   R. Rodwell, 'Regular Staff Meetings Help Build Morale', *South China Morning Post* (Hong Kong), 27 August 2005, 4.

52   R. Rousos, 'Trust in Leaders Lacking at Utility', *The Ledger* (Lakeland, Fl.), 29 July 2003, B1; B. Whitworth and B. Riccomini, 'Management Communication: Unlocking Higher Employee Performance', *Communication World*, March–April 2005, 18–21.

53   K. Davis, 'Management Communication and the Grapevine', *Harvard Business Review* 31 (September–October 1953), 43–9; W. L. Davis and J. R. O'Connor, 'Serial Transmission of Information: A Study of the Grapevine', *Journal of Applied Communication Research* 5 (1977), 61–72.

54   H. Mintzberg, *The Structuring of Organizations* (Englewood Cliffs, NJ: Prentice Hall, 1979), pp. 46–53; D. Krackhardt and J. R. Hanson, 'Informal Networks: The Company Behind the Chart', *Harvard Business Review* 71 (July–August 1993), 104–11.

55   C. J. Walker and C. A. Beckerle, 'The Effect of State Anxiety on Rumour Transmission', *Journal of Social Behaviour & Personality* 2 (August 1987), 353–60; R. L. Rosnow, 'Inside Rumor: A Personal Journey', *American Psychologist* 46 (May 1991), 484–96; M. Noon and R. Delbridge, 'News from Behind My Hand: Gossip in Organizations', *Organization Studies* 14 (1993), 23–36.

56   N. Nicholson, 'Evolutionary Psychology: Toward a New View of Human Nature and Organizational Society', *Human Relations* 50 (September 1997), 1053–78.

CHAPTER 12

Power and influence in the workplace

LEARNING OBJECTIVES

After reading this chapter, you should be able to:

- define the meaning of power and counterpower

- describe the five bases of power in organisations

- explain how information relates to power in organisations

- discuss the four contingencies of power

- summarise the eight types of influence tactics

- discuss three contingencies to consider when deciding which influence tactic to use

- distinguish influence from organisational politics

- describe the organisational conditions and personal characteristics that support organisational politics

- identify ways to minimise organisational politics.

National Australia Bank rogue trader Luke Duffy and his colleagues created losses of $350 million, thanks in part to Duffy's power and influence tactics.

For three long days, junior trader Dennis Gentilin received the cold shoulder from his boss, Luke Duffy. Duffy, who ran National Australia Bank's (NAB) foreign currency options desk in Melbourne, had discovered that Gentilin had complained to Duffy's boss, Gary Dillon, that Duffy was altering transaction records to 'smooth' his group's profits. Smoothing (which includes carrying forward trading losses) was apparently common at one time, but traders had recently been warned to stop the practice.

On the fourth day, Duffy called Gentilin into a private meeting and, according to Gentilin, launched into a tirade: 'I felt like … killing someone the other day,' he'd said pointedly to Gentilin. 'If you want to stay in the team, I demand loyalty and don't want you going to Dillon about what's happening in the team.'

Duffy was apparently accustomed to getting his way. According to Gentilin, Duffy, Dillon and a few other senior traders were 'untouchables'' who were given free rein at NAB because of their expertise. 'They just created this power base where they were laws unto themselves,' claimed Gentilin.

Anyone who interfered with Duffy's plans was apparently mocked into submission. For example, Duffy taunted a co-worker in London who he thought was too sceptical and conservative, calling him 'the London stench boy'. This, Duffy said later in court, was because he was 'always making a stink about things, whether they were going on, both good and bad, and you could smell the stink coming from London'.

Soon after his private meeting with Duffy, Gentilin was transferred to NAB's London office, still working in the foreign exchange group. Duffy's unit in Melbourne continued to fudge the numbers so that upper management wouldn't notice any problems with the trading results. But when the group bet the wrong way against a rising Australian dollar, the cover-ups escalated, including the creation of fictitious trades to offset the losses. The idea was that they could recover the losses and receive their cherished bonuses by year end.

Fatefully, Gentilin got wind of the problems from London, so he asked Vanessa McCallum, a junior NAB trader in Melbourne, to have other people look into Duffy's transactions. McCallum later acknowledged that she was terrified about asking for the audit. 'My greatest fear was, if nothing is wrong I'm going to have to leave the desk because you had to be loyal to Luke [Duffy],' explained McCallum, who no longer works at the bank.

What senior NAB executives discovered shook the Australian bank to its core. Duffy and other senior traders had become a rogue team that amassed $350 million in losses in one year. Their unrestrained power and influence kept everyone (except Gentilin and McCallum) in line, resulting in countless transaction record irregularities and over 800 breaches of the bank's trading limits. Duffy and a few other traders were jailed for securities violations. Several NAB executives, including the chief executive and the chairman, lost their jobs.[1]

The National Australia Bank saga illustrates how power and influence can have profound consequences for employee behaviour and the organisation's success. Although NAB's story has an unhappy ending, power and influence can equally lead to ethical conduct and improve corporate performance. The reality is that no one escapes from organisational power and influence. They exist in every business and, according to some writers, in every decision and action.

This chapter unfolds as follows: First, power is defined and a basic model depicting the dynamics of power in organisational settings is presented. The chapter then discusses the five bases of power, as well as information as a power base. Next, the contingencies necessary to translate those sources into meaningful power are described. The latter part of the chapter examines the various types of influence in organisational settings as well as the contingencies of effective influence strategies. The final section of the chapter looks at situations in which influence becomes organisational politics, and discusses ways of minimising dysfunctional politics.

THE MEANING OF POWER

power The capacity of a person, team or organisation to influence others.

LEARNING OBJECTIVE

Define the meaning of power and counterpower.

counterpower The capacity of a person, team or organisation to keep a more powerful person or group in the exchange relationship.

Power is the capacity of a person, team or organisation to influence others.[2] Power is not the act of changing others' attitudes or behaviour; it is only the potential to do so. People frequently have power they do not use; they might not even know they have power.

The most basic prerequisite of power is that one person or group believes it is dependent on another person or group for something of value.[3] This relationship is shown in Exhibit 12.1, where Person A has power over Person B by controlling something that Person B needs in order to achieve his or her goals. You might have power over others by controlling a desired job assignment, useful information, important resources, or even the privilege of being associated with you! In the opening story, Luke Duffy wielded power because he controlled the job security and workplace resources of the NAB foreign exchange staff. To make matters more complex, power is ultimately a perception, so people might gain power simply by convincing others that they have something of value. Thus, power exists when others believe that someone controls resources that they want.[4]

Although power requires dependence, it is really more accurate to say that the parties are interdependent. One party may be more dependent than the other, but the relationship exists only when each party has something of value to the other. Exhibit 12.1 shows a thinner dashed line to illustrate the weaker party's (Person B's) power over the dominant participant (Person A). This **counterpower**, as it is known, is strong enough to maintain Person A's participation in the exchange relationship. For example, executives have power over subordinates by controlling their job security and promotional opportunities. At the same time, employees have counterpower by controlling the ability to work productively and thereby creating a positive impression of the supervisor to his or her boss. Counterpower usually motivates executives to apply their power judiciously so that the relationship is not broken.

EXHIBIT 12.1

Dependence in the power relationship

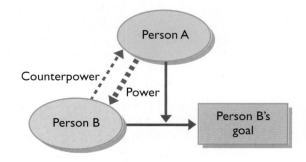

A model of power within organisations

EXHIBIT 12.2

Sources of power

Legitimate
Reward
Coercive
Expert
Referent

→ **Power over others**

Contingencies of power

Substitutability
Centrality
Discretion
Visibility

A MODEL OF POWER IN ORGANISATIONS

Power involves more than just dependence. As seen in Exhibit 12.2, the model of power includes both power sources and contingencies. It indicates that power is derived from five sources: legitimate, reward, coercive, expert and referent. The model also indicates that these sources yield power only under certain conditions. The four contingencies of power include the employee's or department's substitutability, centrality, discretion and visibility. Finally, as will be discussed later, the type of power applied affects the type of influence the power-holder has over the other person or work unit.

SOURCES OF POWER IN ORGANISATIONS

More than forty years ago, social scientists John French and Bertrand Raven listed five sources of power within organisations: legitimate, reward, coercive, expert and referent. Many researchers have studied these five power bases and searched for others. For the most part, French and Raven's list remains intact.[5] The first three power bases are derived from the power-holder's position; that is, the person receives these power bases because of the specific authority or roles he or she is assigned in the organisation. The latter two sources of power originate from the power-holder's own characteristics. In other words, people bring these power bases to the organisation.

LEARNING OBJECTIVE

Describe the five bases of power in organisations.

LEGITIMATE POWER

Legitimate power is an agreement between organisational members that people in certain roles can request certain behaviours of others. This perceived right comes from formal job descriptions as well as informal rules of conduct. Executives have considerable legitimate power, but all employees also have this power based on company rules and government laws.[6] For example, an organisation might give employees the right to request customer files if this information is required for their job.

Legitimate power depends on more than job descriptions. It also depends on mutual agreement from those expected to abide by this authority. Your boss's power to make you work overtime partly depends on your agreement to this power. Stories and movies about mutinies, such as *The Caine Mutiny* and *Crimson Tide*, illustrate this point. More frequently, employees question their boss's right to make them stay late or perform unsafe tasks and other activities.

legitimate power The capacity to influence others through formal authority.

Legitimate power meets a mutiny

Crimson Tide is a riveting novel and film about the limits of legitimate power. When radical Russian nationalists threaten to start World War III, the nuclear submarine USS *Alabama* is told to prepare for retaliation with its own nuclear arsenal. The signal to launch does come in, but the message is not completed before the sub goes into silent mode. *Alabama's* commander, Captain Frank Ramsey (Gene Hackman, at right in photo), is ready to have his crew push the button, whereas Lieutenant Commander Ron Hunter (Denzel Washington, at left in photo) opposes this decision. What ensues is a mutiny that divides the loyalties of *Alabama's* crew. The story illustrates how Captain Ramsey's decision and its consequences tested the limits of his legitimate power over his crew.

Thus, legitimate power is the person's authority to make discretionary decisions as long as followers accept this discretion.[7]

People in high power distance cultures (i.e. those who accept an unequal distribution of power) are more likely to comply with legitimate power than are people in low power distance cultures. Legitimate power is also stronger in some organisations than in others. A 3M scientist might continue to work on a project after being told by superiors to stop working on it because the 3M culture supports an entrepreneurial spirit, which includes ignoring your boss's authority from time to time. More generally, employees are becoming less tolerant of legitimate power. They increasingly expect to be involved in decisions rather than be told what to do.[8] Thus, the command style of leadership that often guided employee behaviour in the past must be replaced by other forms, particularly expert and referent power, which are described later.

REWARD POWER

Reward power is derived form the person's ability to control the allocation of rewards valued by others and to remove negative sanctions (i.e. negative reinforcement). Managers have formal authority that gives them power over the distribution of organisational rewards such as pay, promotions, time off, holiday schedules and work assignments. Employees also have reward power over their bosses through the use of 360-degree feedback systems. Employee feedback affects supervisors' promotions and other rewards, so they tend to behave differently towards employees after 360-degree feedback is introduced.

COERCIVE POWER

Coercive power is the ability to apply punishment. In the opening story to this chapter, Luke Duffy demonstrated his coercive power by allegedly reprimanding employees and threatening them into submission. Employees also have coercive power, ranging from sarcasm to ostracism, which they can use to ensure that co-workers conform to team norms. Many firms rely on the coercive power of team members to control co-worker behaviour.

For instance, when asked how AirAsia maintained attendance and productivity when the Kuala Lumpur–based discount airline removed the time clocks, chief executive Tony Fernandes replied: 'Simple. Peer pressure sees to that. The fellow employees, who are putting their shoulders to the wheel, will see to that.' Coca-Cola Amatil also relies on co-workers to guide employee behaviour through coercive power. 'Peer pressure helps people to conform,' explains the company's managing director for New Zealand and Fiji. 'We find individuals will take up issues of behaviour with others.'[9]

EXPERT POWER

For the most part, legitimate power, reward power and coercive power originate from the position. In contrast, expert power originates from within the person. It is an individual's or work unit's capacity to influence others by possessing knowledge or skills that the others value. Luke Duffy and the other 'untouchables' mentioned in the opening story had expert power over more senior executives at National Australia Bank, apparently to the point that they performed much of their work with minimal checks and balances. Employees are also gaining expert power as our society moves from an industrial to a knowledge-based economy.[10] The reason is that employee knowledge becomes the means of production and is ultimately outside the control of those who own the company. And without this control over production, owners are more dependent on employees to achieve their corporate objectives.

REFERENT POWER

People have **referent power** when others identify with them, like them or otherwise respect them. As with expert power, referent power comes from within the person. It is largely a function of the person's interpersonal skills and usually develops slowly. Referent power is often associated with charismatic leadership. *Charisma* can be defined as a form of interpersonal attraction whereby followers develop a respect for and trust in the charismatic individual.[11]

referent power The capacity to influence others based on an identification with and respect for the power-holder.

INFORMATION AND POWER

Information is power.[12] This statement is increasingly relevant in a knowledge-based economy. Information power exists in two forms. First, people gain information power when they control the flow of information to others. These information gatekeepers can alter perceptions of the situation, and can restrict information as a resource that others need in order to accomplish their work. For example, supervisors tend to have more information power in a centralised hierarchy where information flows through them to employees. But when information systems (such as intranets and corporate blogs) bypass supervisors, the supervisors' information power declines.[13]

Second, information power is higher for those who can help firms cope with environmental uncertainties. Organisations value this ability to cope because it allows them to more easily secure resources, introduce more efficient work processes, and estimate demand for their outputs. In other words, coping increases the organisation's adaptability to its environment. Individuals and work units gain power by offering one or more of the following ways to cope with uncertainty, with the first being the most powerful:[14]

- *Prevention.* The most effective strategy is to prevent environmental changes from occurring. For example, financial experts acquire power by preventing the organisation from experiencing a cash shortage or defaulting on loans.
- *Forecasting.* The next best strategy is to predict environmental changes or variations. In this respect, marketing specialists gain power by predicting changes in consumer preferences.
- *Absorption.* People and work units also gain power by absorbing or neutralising the impact of environmental shifts as they occur. An example is the ability of maintenance crews to come to the rescue when machines break down and the production process stops.

LEARNING OBJECTIVE

Explain how information relates to power in organisations.

Trendspotters have information power

People who can forecast the future are worth their weight in gold. The reason is this: information about the future helps companies to cope with environmental uncertainties. Corporate leaders can ramp up production to cash in on growing demand, and can take corrective action to minimise damage from falling demand. 'It's good to have advance-warning radar about what's happening among consumers,' says London-based trendspotter Zoe Lazarus. Lazarus and Richard Welch in New York (both shown here) jointly lead a trend analysis unit for Lowe Worldwide, one of several ad agencies that have recently introduced trend analysis teams that peer into the future. Along with scanning offbeat magazines (*Sleazenation*, *Relax*), Lazarus and Welch anticipate social changes by listening to more than 500 bartenders, photographers, disc jockeys, architects, journalists, designers and other 'influencers' in fifty-two cities across several countries. '[We're] looking for leading-edge trends that will eventually filter into the mainstream in one to two years' time, changing patterns in leisure behaviour, holiday destinations, music choices, as well as fashion trends,' Lazarus explains.[15]

Courtesy of Lowe Worldwide

CONTINGENCIES OF POWER

LEARNING OBJECTIVE

Discuss the four contingencies of power.

If you have expert power by virtue of your ability to forecast and possibly even prevent dramatic changes in the organisation's environment, does this expertise mean that you are influential? Not necessarily. As seen earlier in Exhibit 12.2, power bases generate power only under certain conditions. The four conditions—called the contingencies of power—are substitutability, centrality, discretion and visibility.[16] These are not sources of power; rather, they determine the extent to which people can leverage their power bases. You may have lots of expert power, but you won't be able to influence others with this power base if the contingency factors are not in place.

SUBSTITUTABILITY

substitutability The extent to which people who are dependent on a resource have alternatives.

Substitutability refers to the availability of alternatives. Power is strongest when someone has a monopoly over a valued resource. Conversely, power decreases as the number of alternative sources of the critical resource increases. If you were the only person in your organisation to have expertise in an important issue, you would be more powerful than if several people in the company possessed this valued knowledge. Substitutability refers not only to other sources that offer the resource but also to substitutions of the resource itself. For instance, labour unions are weakened when companies introduce technologies that replace the need for unionised staff. At one time, a strike by telephone employees would have shut down operations, but computerised systems and other technological innovations now ensure that telephone operations continue during labour strikes and reduce the need for telephone operators during normal operations. Technology is a substitute for employees and consequently reduces union power.

How do people and work units increase their power through non-substitutability? There are several ways, although not all of them are ethical. Some of them are described here for your information—not necessarily for you to practise.

- *Controlling tasks*. Governments pass laws that give certain professions an exclusive right to perform particular tasks. As an example, most countries require publicly traded corporations to have their financial statements audited by a specific accounting group (certified public accountants, chartered accountants, etc.). The simmering conflict between medical doctors and nurse practitioners in some countries is also based around the exclusive right of doctors to perform specific medical procedures that nurse practitioners want within their mandate.

- *Controlling knowledge.* Professions control access to the knowledge of their work domain, such as through restricted enrolment in educational programs. Knowledge is also restricted on the job. Several years ago, maintenance workers in a French tobacco processing plant had become very powerful because they controlled the knowledge required to repair the tobacco machines.[17] The maintenance manuals had mysteriously disappeared and the machines had been redesigned enough that only the maintenance staff knew how to fix them if they broke down (which they often did). Knowing the power of non-substitutability, maintenance staff carefully avoided documenting the repair procedures and didn't talk to production employees about their trade knowledge.

- *Controlling labour.* Aside from their knowledge resource, people gain power by controlling the availability of their labour. Labour unions attempt to organise as many people as possible within a particular trade or industry so that employers have no other source of labour supply. Unions have an easier time increasing wages when their members produce almost all of a particular product or service in the industry. The union's power during a strike is significantly weakened when the employer can continue production by using outside contractors or other non-union facilities.

- *Differentiation.* Differentiation occurs when an individual or work unit claims to have a unique resource—such as raw materials or knowledge— that others would want. By definition, the uniqueness of this resource means that no one else has it. The tactic here isn't so much the non-substitutability of the resource but making others believe that the resource is unique. Some people claim that consultants use this tactic. They take skills and knowledge that many consulting firms can provide and wrap them into a package (with the latest buzz words, of course) so that it looks like a service that no one else can offer.

CENTRALITY

Centrality refers to the degree and nature of interdependence between the power-holder and others.[18] Airline pilots have high centrality because their actions affect many people and because their actions quickly affect other people. Think about your own centrality for a moment. If you decided not to show up for work or school tomorrow, how many people would be affected, and how much time would pass before they were affected? If you have high centrality, most people in the organisation would be adversely affected by your absence, and they would be affected quickly.

centrality The degree and nature of interdependence between the power-holder and others.

DISCRETION

The freedom to exercise judgment—to make decisions without referring to a specific rule or receiving permission from someone else—is another important contingency of power in organisations. Consider the plight of first-line supervisors. It may seem that they have legitimate and reward power over employees, but this power is often curtailed by specific rules. This lack of discretion makes supervisors largely powerless even though they may have access to some of the power bases described earlier in the chapter. 'Middle managers are very much "piggy-in-the-middle",' complained a middle manager at Britain's National Health System. 'They have little power, only what senior managers are allowed to give them.'[20]

VISIBILITY

Several years ago as a junior copywriter at advertising agency Chiat/Day, Mimi Cook submitted an idea for a potential client to her boss, who then presented it to co-founder Jay Chiat. Chiat was thrilled with the concept, but Cook's boss 'never mentioned the idea came from

Gate Gourmet dispute reveals its centrality to British Airways

Gate Gourmet's dispute with its union couldn't have come at a worse time for its major customer, British Airways (BA). When the caterer's staff went on strike (or were sacked, as they claimed) in early August, the impact on BA's operations was both immediate and devastating. BA was forced to cancel flights out of Heathrow Airport because it had no food for its long-haul flights and because its own baggage handlers walked off in support of Gate Gourmet staff (many of whom were spouses). August is Europe's busiest holiday time, so BA's closure left 110 000 passengers stranded over the two days of chaos. The effect of Gate Gourmet's dispute extended far beyond

Stephen Chernin/Getty Images

London. BA passengers were stranded in several other cities around the world because BA did not have planes in place to fly them to their destination. 'This unprecedented move is a result of the crippling operational impact of unofficial industrial action,' said BA chief executive Rod Eddington about the decision to cancel flights. The dispute was also poor timing for Eddington. The Australian executive's retirement was scheduled for the following month.[19]

me', recalls Cook. Cook confronted her boss, who claimed that the oversight was unintentional. But when a similar incident occurred a few months later, Cook left the agency for another firm.[21]

Mimi Cook, who has since progressed to associate creative director at another ad agency, knows that power does not flow to unknown people in the organisation. Those who control valued resources or knowledge will yield power only when others are aware of these power bases—in other words, when they are visible. One way to increase visibility is to take people-oriented jobs and work on projects that require frequent interaction with senior executives. 'You can take visibility in steps,' advises a pharmaceutical executive. 'You can start by making yourself visible in a small group, such as a staff meeting. Then when you're comfortable with that, seek out larger arenas.'[22]

Employees also gain visibility by being, quite literally, visible. Some people strategically move into offices or cubicles where co-workers pass most often (such as closest to the lift or office lunch room). People often use public symbols as subtle (and not-so-subtle) cues to make their power sources known to others. Many professionals display their educational diplomas and awards on office walls to remind visitors of their expertise. Medical professionals wear white coats with a stethoscope around their neck to symbolise their legitimate and expert power in hospital settings. Until they moved to an open-office design, executives at Melbourne-based financial services firm Axa Australia measured their legitimate power by the size of their office. 'The size of the office could be measured by the number of ceiling tiles and people used to count them to check how big it was,' recalls an Axa executive.[23]

mentoring The process of learning the ropes of organisational life from a senior person within the company.

Another way to increase visibility is through **mentoring**—the process of learning the ropes of organisational life from a senior person within the company. Mentors give protégés more visible and meaningful work opportunities and open doors for them to meet more senior people in the organisation. Mentors also teach these newcomers influence tactics supported by the organisation's senior decision makers.[24]

NETWORKING AND POWER

'It's not what you know but who you know that counts!' This often-heard statement reflects the reality that employees get ahead not just by developing their competencies but by **networking**—cultivating social relationships with others to accomplish one's goals. Networking increases a person's power in three ways. First, networks represent a critical component of *social capital*, the knowledge and other resources available to people or social units (teams, organisations) due to a durable network that connects them to others. Networks consist of people who trust each other, which increases the flow of knowledge among those within the network. The more you network, the more likely you are to receive valuable information that increases your expert power in the organisation.[25]

Second, people tend to identify more with partners within their own networks, which increases referent power among people within each network. This network-based referent power may lead to more favourable decisions by others in the network. Finally, effective networkers are better known by others in the organisation, so their talents are more readily recognised. This power increases when networkers place themselves in strategic positions in the network, thereby gaining centrality.[26] For example, these people might be regarded as the main sources for distributing information in the network or who keep the network connected through informal gatherings.

Networking is a natural part of the informal organisation, yet it can create a formidable barrier to those who are not actively connected to it.[27] Women are often excluded from powerful networks because they do not participate in golf games and other male-dominated social events. That's what Deloitte and Touche executives discovered when they investigated why so many junior female employees left the accounting and consulting firm before reaching partnership level. The firm now relies on mentoring, formal women's network groups, and measurement of career progress to ensure that female staff members have the same career development opportunities as their male colleagues.[28]

networking Cultivating social relationships with others to accomplish one's goals.

INFLUENCING OTHERS

Thus far, the focus has been on the sources and contingencies of power. But power is only the capacity to influence others. It represents the potential to change someone's attitudes and behaviour. **Influence**, on the other hand, refers to any behaviour that attempts to alter someone's attitudes or behaviour.[29] Influence is power in motion. It applies one or more power bases to get people to alter their beliefs, feelings and activities. Consequently, the focus in the remainder of the chapter is on how people use power to influence others.

Influence tactics are woven throughout the social fabric of all organisations. This is because influence is an essential process through which people coordinate their efforts and act in concert to achieve organisational objectives. Indeed, influence is central to the definition of leadership. Influence operates down, across and up the corporate hierarchy. Executives ensure that subordinates complete required tasks. Employees influence co-workers to help them with their job assignments. Subordinates engage in upward influence tactics so that corporate leaders make decisions compatible with subordinates' needs and expectations.

influence Any behaviour that attempts to alter another person's attitudes or behaviour.

TYPES OF INFLUENCE TACTICS

Organisational behaviour researchers have devoted considerable attention to the various types of influence tactics found in organisational settings. A groundbreaking study twenty-five years ago identified several influence strategies, but recent evidence suggests that some of them overlap.[30] The original list also seems to have a Western bias that ignores influence tactics used in Asian and other cultures.[31] With these caveats in mind, this discussion will focus on the following influence tactics identified in the current literature (see Exhibit 12.3, overleaf): silent authority,

LEARNING OBJECTIVE

Summarise the eight types of influence tactics.

assertiveness, information control, coalition formation, upward appeal, ingratiation and impression management, persuasion, and exchange. The first five are known as hard influence tactics because they force behaviour change through position power (legitimate, reward and coercion). The latter three—ingratiation and impression management, persuasion and exchange—are called soft tactics because they rely more on personal sources of power (referent, expert) and appeal to the target person's attitudes and needs.

Silent authority

The silent application of authority occurs where someone complies with a request because of the requester's legitimate power as well as the target person's role expectations. This condition is often referred to as deference to authority.[32] Deference occurs when you comply with your boss's request to complete a particular task. If the task is within your job scope and your boss has the right to make the request, this influence strategy operates without negotiation, threats, persuasion or other tactics.

Silent authority is often overlooked as an influence strategy, but it is the most common form of influence in high power distance cultures. Employees comply with supervisor requests without question because they respect the supervisor's higher authority in the organisation. Silent authority also occurs when leaders influence subordinates through role-modelling. One study reported that Japanese managers typically influence subordinates by engaging in the behaviours that they want the employees to mimic.[33]

Assertiveness

In contrast to silent authority, assertiveness might be called 'vocal authority' because it involves actively applying legitimate and coercive power to influence others. Assertiveness includes persistently reminding the target of his or her obligations, frequently checking the target's work, confronting the target, and using threats of sanctions to force compliance. Assertiveness typically applies or threatens to apply punishment if the target does not comply. Explicit or implicit threats range from job loss to losing face by letting down the team. Extreme forms of assertiveness include blackmailing colleagues, such as by threatening to reveal the other person's previously unknown failures unless he or she complies with a request. Associates claim that Luke Duffy influenced his staff at National Australia Bank largely through assertiveness, including threatening to sack them if they didn't keep quiet and follow his wishes.

Information control

Luke Duffy also used information control as an influence tactic. Specifically, the rogue NAB trader hid hundreds of illegal transactions from his boss and other executives in order to avoid their involvement in the unit's trading problems. Information control involves explicitly manipulating others' access to information for the purpose of changing their attitudes and/or behaviour. With limited access to potentially valuable information, others are at a disadvantage. While the NAB incident is more extreme than most, hiding information isn't unusual in organisations. Almost half of the employees in one major survey believe that people keep their colleagues in the dark about work issues if it helps their own cause. Employees also influence executive decisions by screening out (filtering) information flowing up the hierarchy. Indeed, one recent study found that CEOs also influence their board of directors by selectively feeding information to board members.[34]

Coalition formation

coalition A group that attempts to influence people outside the group by pooling the resources and power of its members.

When people lack sufficient power alone to influence others in the organisation, they might form a **coalition** of people who support the proposed change. A coalition is influential in three ways.[35] First, it pools the power and resources of many people, so the coalition potentially has more influence than any number of people operating alone. Second, the coalition's mere

Types of influence tactics in organisations

EXHIBIT 12.3

Influence tactic	Description
Silent authority	Influencing behaviour through legitimate power without explicitly referring to that power base
Assertiveness	Actively applying legitimate and coercive power by applying pressure or threats
Information control	Explicitly manipulating other people's access to information for the purpose of changing their attitudes and/or behaviour
Coalition formation	Forming a group that attempts to influence others by pooling the resources and power of its members
Upward appeal	Gaining support from one or more people with higher authority or expertise
Ingratiation/impression management	Attempting to increase liking by, or perceived similarity to, some targeted person
Persuasion	Using logical arguments, factual evidence and emotional appeals to convince people of the value of a request
Exchange	Promising benefits or resources in exchange for the target person's compliance

existence can be a source of power by symbolising the legitimacy of the issue. In other words, a coalition creates a sense that the issue deserves attention because it has broad support. Third, coalitions tap into the power of the social identity process introduced in Chapter 3. A coalition is essentially an informal group that advocates a new set of norms and behaviours. If the coalition has a broad-based membership (i.e. its members come from various parts of the organisation), other employees are more likely to identify with the group and consequently accept the ideas it is proposing.

Upward appeal

Have you ever had a disagreement with a colleague in which one of you eventually says, 'I'm sure the boss (or teacher) will agree with me on this. Let's find out!' This tactic—called **upward appeal**—is a form of coalition in which one or more members is someone with higher authority or expertise. Upward appeal ranges from a formal alliance to the perception of informal support from someone with higher authority or expertise. Upward appeal also includes relying on the authority of the firm as an entity without approaching anyone further up the hierarchy. For instance, one study reported that Japanese managers remind employees of their obligation to support the organisation's objectives.[36] By reminding the target that your request is consistent with the organisation's overarching goals, you are implying support from senior executives without formally involving anyone with higher authority in the situation.

upward appeal A type of coalition in which one or more members is someone with higher authority or expertise.

Ingratiation and impression management

Upward appeals, assertiveness, information control, coalitions and upward appeals are forceful ways to influence other people. At the opposite extreme is a 'soft' influence tactic called ingratiation. **Ingratiation** includes any attempt to increase liking by, or perceived similarity to, some targeted person.[37] Flattering your boss in front of others, helping co-workers with their work,

ingratiation Any attempt to increase the extent to which a target person likes us or perceives that he or she is similar to us.

exhibiting similar attitudes (e.g. agreeing with your boss's proposal to change company policies) and seeking the other person's counsel (e.g. asking for his or her 'expert' advice) are all examples of ingratiation. Collectively, ingratiation behaviours are better than most other forms of influence at predicting career success (performance appraisal feedback, salaries and promotions).[38]

Ingratiation is potentially influential because it increases the perceived similarity of the source of ingratiation to the target person, which causes the target person to form more favourable opinions of the ingratiator. However, people who are obvious in their ingratiation risk losing any influence because their behaviours are considered insincere and self-serving. The terms 'apple polishing' and 'brown-nosing' are applied to those who ingratiate to excess or in ways that suggest selfish motives for the ingratiation. Not surprisingly, research indicates that people who engage in high levels of ingratiation are less (not more) influential and less likely to get promoted.[39]

Ingratiation is part of a larger influence tactic known as impression management. **Impression management** is the practice of actively shaping our public images.[40] These public images might be crafted as being important, vulnerable, threatening or pleasant. For the most part, employees routinely engage in pleasant impression management behaviours to satisfy the basic norms of social behaviour, such as the way they dress and how they behave towards colleagues and customers. Impression management is a common strategy for people trying to get ahead in the workplace. For instance, almost all job applicants in a recent study relied on one or more types of impression management.

An extreme form of impression management occurs when people pad their résumé. One study found that 21 per cent of Australian job applicants had misrepresented their qualifications. Recent examples include two doctors in Queensland, a television chief executive in New Zealand, and a teenager who obtained employment on Great Keppel Island by claiming to be qualified as a registered nurse.[41] As with ingratiation, employees who use too much impression management tend to be less influential because their behaviours are viewed as insincere.[42]

impression management
The practice of actively shaping our public image.

Persuasion

persuasion Using logical arguments, facts and emotional appeals to encourage people to accept a request or message.

Persuasion is one of the most effective influence strategies for career success. The ability to present facts, logical arguments and emotional appeals to change another person's attitudes and behaviour is not just an acceptable way to influence others; in many societies it is a noble art and a quality of effective leaders. The literature on influence strategies has typically described persuasion as the use of reason through factual evidence and logical arguments. However, recent studies have begun to adopt a 'dual process' perspective in which persuasion is influenced by both the individual's emotional reaction and a rational interpretation of incoming information.[43] Thus, persuasion is an attempt to convince people by using emotional appeals as well as factual evidence and logical arguments.

The effectiveness of persuasion as an influence tactic depends on the characteristics of the persuader, the message content, the communication medium and the audience being persuaded.[45] What makes one person more persuasive than another? One factor is the person's perceived expertise. Persuasion attempts are more successful when listeners believe that the speaker is knowledgeable about the topic. People are also more persuasive when they demonstrate credibility, such as when the persuader does not seem to profit from the persuasion attempt and states a few points against the position.[46]

Message content is more important than the messenger when the issue is important to the audience. Persuasive message content acknowledges several points of view so the audience does not feel cornered by the speaker. The message should also be limited to a few strong arguments, which are repeated a few times but not too frequently. The message content should use emotional appeals (such as graphically showing the unfortunate consequences of a bad decision), but only in combination with logical arguments so the audience doesn't feel manipulated. Also, emotional appeals should always be accompanied by specific recommendations to

Steve Jobs' persuasiveness creates a reality distortion field

Wearing his trademark black turtleneck and faded blue jeans, Apple Computer co-founder and CEO Steve Jobs is famous for stirring up crowds with evangelical fervour as he draws them into his 'reality distortion field'. A reality distortion field occurs when people are caught in Steve Jobs' visionary headlights. Apple Computer manager Bud Tribble borrowed the phrase from the television series *Star Trek* to describe Jobs' overwhelming persuasiveness. 'In his presence, reality is malleable,' Tribble explained to newly hired Andy Hertzfeld in 1981. 'He [Jobs] can convince anyone of practically anything. It wears off when he's not around, but it makes it hard to have realistic schedules.' As one journalist wrote: 'Drift too close to Jobs in the grip of one of his manias and you can get sucked in, like a wayward asteroid straying into Jupiter's gravitational zone.'[44]

AFP/Getty Images

overcome the threat. Finally, message content is more persuasive when the audience is warned about opposing arguments. This **inoculation effect** causes listeners to generate counterarguments to the anticipated future persuasion attempts, which makes them less effective.[47]

Two other considerations when persuading people are the medium of communication and the characteristics of the audience. Generally, persuasion works best in face-to-face conversations and through other media-rich communication channels. The personal nature of face-to-face communication increases the persuader's credibility, and the richness of this channel provides faster feedback that the influence strategy is working. With respect to audience characteristics, it is more difficult to persuade people who have high self-esteem and intelligence, as well as those whose targeted attitudes are strongly connected to their self-identity.[48]

Exchange

Exchange activities involve the promise of benefits or resources in exchange for the target person's compliance with your request. This tactic also includes reminding the target of past benefits or favours, with the expectation that the target will now make up for that debt. The norm of reciprocity is a central and explicit theme in exchange strategies. According to the norm of reciprocity, individuals are expected to help those who have helped them.[49] Negotiation, which is discussed more fully in Chapter 13, is also an integral part of exchange influence activities. For instance, you might negotiate with your boss for a day off in return for working a less desirable shift at a future date. Networking is another form of exchange as an influence strategy. Active networkers build up 'exchange credits' by helping colleagues in the short-term for reciprocal benefits in the long-term.

Networking as an influence strategy is a deeply ingrained practice in several cultures. The Chinese term *guanxi* refers to special relationships and active interpersonal connectedness. It is based on traditional Confucian values of helping others without expecting future repayment. However, some writers suggest that the original interpretation and practice of *guanxi* has shifted to include implicit long-term reciprocity, which can slip into cronyism. As a result, some Asian governments are discouraging *guanxi*-based decisions, preferring more

inoculation effect A persuasive communication strategy of warning listeners that others will try to influence them in the future and that they should be wary about the opponent's arguments.

arms-length transactions in business and government decisions.[50] *Blat* is a Russian word that also refers to special relationships or connections. Unlike *guanxi*, however, blat was originally associated with survival during times of scarcity and continues to have a connotation of self-interest and possible illegality.[51]

CONSEQUENCES AND CONTINGENCIES OF INFLUENCE TACTICS

Now that the main strategies used to influence people have been covered, you are probably asking: Which influence tactics are best? The best way to answer this question is to identify the three ways in which people react when others try to influence them: resistance, compliance or commitment.[52] *Resistance* occurs when people or work units oppose the behaviour desired by the influencer, and consequently argue about it, refuse to engage in the behaviour, or delay engaging in it. *Compliance* occurs when people are motivated to implement the influencer's request at a minimal level of effort and for purely instrumental reasons. Without external sources to prompt the desired behaviour, it would not occur. *Commitment* is the strongest form of influence, whereby people identify with the influencer's request and are highly motivated to implement it even when extrinsic sources of motivation are no longer present.

Research has found that people generally react more favourably to 'soft' tactics such as friendly persuasion and subtle ingratiation than to 'hard' tactics such as upward appeal and assertiveness (see Exhibit 12.4). Soft tactics rely on personal power bases (expert and referent power), which tend to build commitment to the influencer's request. For example, co-workers tend to 'buy in' to people's ideas when they apply moderate levels of ingratiation and impression management tactics or use persuasion based on expertise. In contrast, hard influence tactics rely on position power (legitimate, reward and coercion), so they tend to produce compliance or, worse, resistance. Hard tactics also tend to undermine trust, which can hurt future relationships. For example, the potential influence of coalitions is sometimes limited when the group's forcefulness is threatening to those being influenced.[53]

EXHIBIT 12.4

Consequences of hard and soft influence tactics

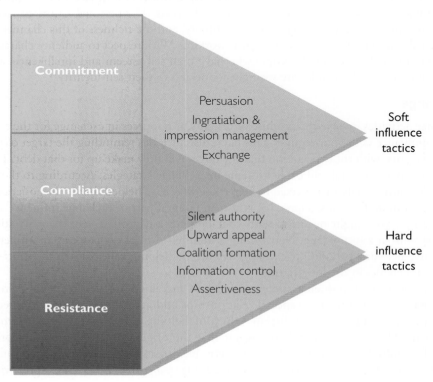

Upward, downward or lateral influence

Aside from the general preference for soft rather than hard tactics, the most appropriate influence strategy depends on a few contingencies. One consideration is whether the person being influenced is higher, lower or at the same level in the organisation. Employees have some legitimate power over their boss, but they may face adverse career consequences by being too assertive with this power. Similarly, it may be more acceptable for supervisors to control information access than for employees to control what information they distribute to co-workers and people at higher levels in the organisation.

LEARNING OBJECTIVE

Discuss three contingencies to consider when deciding which influence tactic to use.

Influencer's power base

A second contingency is the influencer's power base. Those with expertise tend to be more successful using persuasion, whereas those with a strong legitimate power base are usually more successful applying silent authority.[54]

Personal and cultural values

Studies indicate that personal values guide our preference for some influence methods more than others.[55] The general trend in Australia, New Zealand and elsewhere is towards softer influence tactics, because younger employees tend to have more egalitarian values compared with employees near retirement. As such, silent authority and assertiveness are tolerated less than they were a few decades ago. Acceptance of influence tactics also varies across cultures. Research indicates that American managers and subordinates alike often rely on ingratiation because it minimises conflict and supports a trusting relationship. In contrast, managers in Hong Kong and other high power distance cultures rely less on ingratiation, possibly because this tactic disrupts the more distant roles that managers and employees expect in these cultures. Instead, as noted earlier, influence through exchange tends to be more common and accepted in Asian cultures because of the importance of interpersonal relationships (*guanxi*).

Gender differences in influence tactics

Men and women seem to differ in their use of influence tactics. Some writers say that men are more likely than women to rely on direct impression management tactics. Specifically, men tend to advertise their achievements and take personal credit for the successes of those reporting to them, whereas women are more reluctant to focus the spotlight on themselves, preferring instead to share the credit with others. At the same time, women are more likely to apologise—personally take the blame—even for problems not caused by them. Men are more likely to assign blame and less likely to assume it.[56]

Some research also suggests that women generally have difficulty exerting some forms of influence in organisations, and this has limited their promotional opportunities. In particular, women are viewed as less (not more) influential when they try to directly influence others by exerting their authority or expertise. In job interviews, for example, direct and assertive female job applicants were less likely to be hired than were male applicants using the same influence tactics. Similarly, women who directly disagreed in conversations were less influential than women who agreed with the speaker.[57] These findings suggest that women may face problems applying 'hard' influence tactics such as assertiveness. Instead, until stereotypes change, women need to rely on softer and more indirect influence strategies, such as ingratiation.

INFLUENCE TACTICS AND ORGANISATIONAL POLITICS

You might have noticed that organisational politics has not been mentioned yet, even though some of the practices or examples described over the past few pages are usually considered political tactics. The phrase was carefully avoided because, for the most part, 'organisational

LEARNING OBJECTIVE

Distinguish influence from organisational politics.

politics' is in the eye of the beholder. One person might perceive a co-worker's attempt to influence their boss as normal behaviour, whereas another person might perceive the tactic as brazen organisational politics. This is why experts mainly discuss influence tactics as behaviours and organisational politics as perceptions. The influence tactics described earlier are behaviours that might be considered organisational politics, or they might be considered acceptable behaviour. It all depends on the observer's perception of the situation.[58]

When are influence tactics perceived as **organisational politics**? Increasingly, organisational behaviour researchers say that influence tactics are organisational politics when they seem to benefit the perpetrators at the expense of others and usually the entire organisation or work unit. Organisational politics have a number of negative effects. Those who believe that their organisation is steeped in organisational politics have lower job satisfaction, organisational commitment and organisational citizenship, as well as high levels of work-related stress. Employees affected by organisational politics also engage in more 'neglect' behaviours, such as reducing their work effort, paying less attention to quality, and increasing their absenteeism and lateness.[59]

Some incidents involving organisational politics have devastating effects on the organisation. The opening story to this chapter is one such example. Luke Duffy's political acts of hiding transactions and threatening or criticising those who attempted to report the wrongdoing ultimately resulted in huge losses for the bank. Reality Check 12.1 described an even more extreme example, whereby WorldCom executives used their assertiveness, information control and other influence practices to protect their financial interests. These actions eventually led to the largest accounting fraud and bankruptcy in American history.

CONDITIONS SUPPORTING ORGANISATIONAL POLITICS

Organisational politics flourish under the right conditions.[60] One of those conditions is scarce resources. When budgets are slashed, people rely on political tactics to safeguard their resources and maintain the status quo. Office politics also flourish when resource allocation decisions are ambiguous, complex or lack formal rules. This occurs because decision makers are given more discretion over resource allocation, so potential recipients of those resources use political tactics to influence the factors that should be considered in the decision. Organisational change encourages political behaviours for this reason. Change creates uncertainty and ambiguity as the company moves from an old set of rules and practices to a new set. During these times, employees apply political strategies to protect their valued resources, position and self-image.[61]

Organisational politics also become commonplace when they are tolerated and transparently supported by the organisation.[62] Companies sometimes promote people who are the best politicians, not necessarily the best talent to run the company. If left unchecked, organisational politics can paralyse an organisation as people focus more on protecting themselves than fulfilling their roles. Political activity becomes self-reinforcing unless the conditions supporting political behaviour are altered.

Personal characteristics

Several personal characteristics affect a person's motivation to engage in organisational politics.[63] Some people have a strong need for personal as opposed to socialised power. They seek power for its own sake and use political tactics to acquire more power. People with an internal locus of control are more likely than those with an external locus of control to engage in political behaviours. This does not mean that internals are naturally political; rather, they are more likely to use influence tactics when political conditions are present because, unlike externals, they feel very much in charge of their own destiny.

Some individuals have strong **Machiavellian values**. Machiavellianism is named after Niccolò Machiavelli, the sixteenth-century Italian philosopher who wrote *The Prince*, a famous treatise

organisational politics
Behaviours that others perceive as self-serving tactics for personal gain at the expense of other people and possibly the organisation.

LEARNING OBJECTIVE

Describe the organisational conditions and personal characteristics that support organisational politics.

Machiavellian values The belief that deceit is a natural and acceptable way to influence others.

POLITICS AT WORLDCOM LEAD TO RECORD-BREAKING ACCOUNTING FRAUD

Bernie Ebbers built WorldCom, Inc. (now MCI, Inc.) into one of the world's largest telecommunications firms. Yet he and chief financial officer (CFO) Scott Sullivan have become better known for creating a massive corporate accounting fraud that led to the largest bankruptcy in US history. Two investigative reports and subsequent court cases concluded that WorldCom executives were responsible for fraudulent or unsupported accounting entries amounting to billions of dollars. How did this mammoth accounting scandal occur without anyone raising the alarm? Evidence suggests that Ebbers and Sullivan held considerable power and influence that prevented accounting staff from complaining, or even knowing, about the fraud.

Ebbers' inner circle had tight control over the flow of all financial information. The geographically dispersed accounting groups were discouraged from sharing information. Ebbers' group also restricted the distribution of company-level financial reports and prevented sensitive reports from being prepared at all. Accountants didn't have access to the computer files where some of the largest fraudulent entries were made. As a result, employees had to rely on Ebbers' executive team to justify the accounting entries that were requested.

Another reason why employees complied with questionable accounting practices was that CFO Scott Sullivan wielded immense personal power. He was considered a 'whiz kid' with impeccable integrity, and had won the prestigious 'CFO Excellence Award'. Thus, when Sullivan's office asked staff to make questionable entries, some accountants assumed that Sullivan had found an innovative—and legal—accounting loophole. If Sullivan's expert power didn't work, other executives took a more coercive approach. Employees cited incidents where they had been publicly berated for questioning headquarters' decisions and intimidated if they asked for more information. When one employee at a branch refused to alter an accounting entry, WorldCom's controller threatened to fly in from WorldCom's Mississippi headquarters to make the change himself. The employee changed the entry.

Ebbers had similar influence over WorldCom's board of directors. Sources indicate that his personal charisma and intolerance of dissension produced a passive board that rubber-stamped most of his recommendations. As one report concluded: 'The Board of Directors appears to have embraced suggestions by Mr Ebbers without question or dissent, even under circumstances where its members now readily acknowledge they had significant misgivings regarding his recommended course of action.'

Martin H. Simon/Corbis

Former WorldCom CEO Bernard Ebbers (left) and chief financial officer Scott Sullivan (right) who, along with other executives, perpetrated one of the largest cases of accounting fraud in history by using influence tactics for personal gain.

Sources: United States Bankruptcy Court, Southern District of New York. In Re: WorldCom, Inc., et al., Debtors. Chapter 11 Case No. 02-15533 (AJG), Jointly Administered Second Interim Report of Dick Thornburgh, Bankruptcy Court Examiner, 9 June 2003; Report of Investigation by the Special Investigative Committee of the Board of Directors of WorldCom, Inc. Dennis R. Beresford, Nicholas Deb Katzenbach, C. B. Rogers, Jr, Counsel, Wilmer, Cutler & Pickering, Accounting Advisors, PricewaterhouseCoopers Llp, 31 March 2003. Also see: T. Catan et al., 'Before the Fall', *Financial Times* (London), 19 December 2002, 17; J. O'Donnell and A. Backover, 'Ebbers' High-Risk Act Came Crashing Down on Him', *USA Today*, 12 December 2002, B1; C. Stern, 'Ebbers Dominated Board, Report Says', *Washington Post*, 5 November 2002, E1; D. S. Hilzenrath, 'How a Distinguished Roster of Board Members Failed to Detect Company's Problems', *Washington Post*, 16 June 2003, E1; S. Pulliam and A. Latour, 'Lost Connection', *Wall Street Journal*, 12 January 2005, A1; S. Rosenbush, 'Five Lessons of the WorldCom Debacle', *Business Week Online*, 16 March 2005.

about political behaviour. People with high Machiavellian values are comfortable with getting more than they deserve, and they believe that deceit is a natural and acceptable way to achieve this goal. They seldom trust co-workers and tend to use cruder influence tactics, such as bypassing one's boss or being assertive, to get their own way.[64] The opening vignette to this chapter suggests that National Australia Bank's rogue trader displayed Machiavellian characteristics, including rough assertiveness and controlling information.

Minimising organisational politics and its consequences

LEARNING OBJECTIVE

Identify ways to minimise organisational politics.

The conditions that fuel organisational politics also give us some clues about how to control dysfunctional political activities.[65] One strategy to keep organisational politics in check is to introduce clear rules and regulations to specify the use of scarce resources. Corporate leaders also need to actively support the all-channels communication structure described earlier in the chapter so that political employees do not misuse power through information control. As mentioned, organisational politics can become a problem during times of organisational change. Effective organisational change practices—particularly training and involvement— can minimise uncertainty and consequently politics during the change process.

Organisational political behaviour is either supported or punished, depending on team norms and the organisation's culture. Thus, leaders need to actively manage group norms to curtail self-serving influence activities. They also need to support organisational values that oppose political tactics, such as altruism and customer-focus. One of the most important strategies is for leaders to become role models of organisational citizenship rather than symbols of successful organisational politicians.

Along with minimising organisational politics, companies can limit the adverse effects of political perceptions by giving employees more control over their work and keeping them informed of organisational events. Research has found that employees who are kept informed of what is going on in the organisation and who are involved in organisational decisions are less likely to experience stress, job dissatisfaction and absenteeism as a result of organisational politics.

CHAPTER SUMMARY

Power is the capacity to influence others. It exists when one party perceives that he or she is dependent on the other for something of value. However, the dependent person must also have counterpower—some power over the dominant party—to maintain the relationship.

There are five power bases. Legitimate power is an agreement between organisational members that people in certain roles can request certain behaviours of others. Reward power is derived from the ability to control the allocation of rewards valued by others and to remove negative sanctions. Coercive power is the ability to apply punishment. Expert power is the capacity to influence others by possessing knowledge or skills that they value. People have referent power when others identify with them, like them, or otherwise respect them.

Information plays an important role in organisational power. Employees gain power by controlling the flow of information that others need and by being able to cope with uncertainties related to important organisational goals.

Four contingencies determine whether these power bases translate into real power. Individuals and work units are more powerful when they are non-substitutable, that is, there is a lack of alternatives. Employees, work units and organisations reduce substitutability by controlling tasks, knowledge and labour, and by differentiating themselves from competitors. A second contingency is centrality. People have more power when they have high centrality, that is, when the number of people affected is large and people are quickly affected by their actions. Discretion, the third contingency of power, refers to the freedom to exercise judgment. Power increases when people have freedom to use their power. The fourth contingency, visibility, refers to the idea that power increases to the extent that a person's or work unit's competencies are known to others.

Networking involves cultivating social relationships with others to accomplish one's goals. This activity increases an individual's expert and referent power as well as visibility and possibly centrality. However, networking can limit opportunities for people outside the network, as many women in senior management positions have discovered.

Influence refers to any behaviour that attempts to alter someone's attitudes or behaviour. The most widely studied influence tactics are silent authority, assertiveness, information control, coalition formation, upward appeal, ingratiation and impression management, persuasion and exchange. 'Soft' influence tactics such as friendly persuasion and subtle ingratiation are more acceptable than 'hard' tactics such as upward appeal and assertiveness. However, the most appropriate influence tactic also depends on the influencer's power base, whether the person being influenced is higher, lower or at the same level in the organisation, and personal and cultural values regarding influence behaviour.

Organisational politics are influence tactics that others perceive to be self-serving behaviours at the expense of others and sometimes contrary to the interests of the entire organisation or work unit. Organisational political behaviour is more prevalent when scarce resources are allocated using complex and ambiguous decisions, and when the organisation tolerates or rewards political behaviour. Individuals with a high need for personal power, an internal locus of control and strong Machiavellian values have a high propensity to use political tactics.

Organisational politics can be minimised by providing clear rules for resource allocation, establishing a free flow of information, using education and involvement during organisational change, supporting team norms and a corporate culture that discourage dysfunctional politics, and having leaders who role-model organisational citizenship rather than political savvy.

KEY TERMS

centrality p. 361
coalition p. 364
counterpower p. 356
impression management p. 366
influence p. 363
ingratiation p. 365

inoculation effect p. 367
legitimate power p. 357
Machiavellian values p. 370
mentoring p. 362
networking p. 363
organisational politics p. 370

persuasion p. 366
power p. 356
referent power p. 359
substitutability p. 360
upward appeal p. 365

DISCUSSION QUESTIONS

1. What role does counterpower play in the power relationship? Give an example of your own encounter with counterpower at school or work.

2. Several years ago the major league baseball players association in the United States went on strike in September, just before the World Series started. The players' contracts expired in the spring, but the players held off the strike until September when they would lose only one-sixth of their salaries. In contrast, a September strike would hurt the owners financially because they earn a large portion of their revenue during the playoffs. As one player explained: 'If we strike next spring, there's nothing stopping [the club owners] from letting us go until next June or July because they don't have that much at stake.' Use your knowledge of the sources and contingencies of power to explain why the baseball players association had more power in negotiations by walking out in September rather than in March.

3. You have just been hired as a brand manager of toothpaste for a large consumer products company. Your job mainly involves encouraging the advertising and production groups to promote and manufacture your product more effectively. These departments are not under your direct authority, although company procedures indicate that they must complete certain tasks requested by brand managers. Describe the sources of power you can use to ensure that the advertising and production departments will help you make and sell toothpaste more effectively.

4. How does networking increase a person's power? What networking strategies could you initiate now to potentially enhance your future career success?

5. Discuss the eight influence tactics described in this chapter in terms of how they are used by students to influence college instructors. Which influence tactic is applied most often? Which is applied least often, in your opinion? To what extent is each influence tactic considered acceptable behaviour or organisational politics?

6. How do cultural differences affect the following influence factors: (a) silent authority, and (b) upward appeal?

7. A few years ago the CEO of Apple Computer invited Steve Jobs (who was not associated with the company at the time) to serve as a special adviser and raise morale among Apple employees and customers. While doing this, Jobs spent more time advising the CEO on how to cut costs, redraw the organisation chart and hire new people. Before long, most of the top people at Apple were Jobs's colleagues, who began to systematically evaluate and weed out teams of Apple employees. While publicly supporting Apple's CEO, Jobs privately criticised him, and, in a show of non-confidence, sold 1.5 million shares of Apple stock he had received. This action caught the attention of Apple's board of directors, who soon after decided to replace the CEO with Jobs. The CEO claimed that Jobs was a conniving back-stabber who used political tactics to get his way. Others suggest that Apple would be out of business today if Jobs hadn't taken over the company. In your opinion, were Steve Jobs's actions examples of organisational politics? Justify your answer.

8. This book frequently emphasises that successful companies engage in knowledge management. How do political tactics interfere with knowledge management objectives?

SKILL BUILDER | 12.1   NIRVANA ART GALLERY

CASE STUDY

By Christine Ho, University of Adelaide

It was an irony not lost on many of the employees of Nirvana Art Gallery. This gallery was far from being a place of harmony and joy. In fact, some of the employees preferred to refer to management using the acronym 'NAG' in a derogatory manner.

Nirvana was regarded as one of the leading museums of art in Australia. Its collection of Australian art was one of the oldest and best known in the country. The museum also housed an enviable Aboriginal collection and an international collection of considerable breadth and depth.

Rod was the assistant curator for the Curatorial unit. Despite his job title, his time was divided between the Curatorial and Research units because there was not enough work in the former to keep him occupied from week to week. It was agreed between the managers of the two units that he would work on Monday to Wednesday at Curatorial and then the remaining days at Research. While Rod would have preferred to work solely for Curatorial because that was where his interests lay, he was in no position to argue with either manager. He hoped that when he finished his PhD in art history he would be employed full-time in Curatorial where he could fully utilise his specialised knowledge and achieve his aspiration to be a curator.

Rod did not particularly enjoy coming to work on Thursdays. The research he was asked to do was okay, although it was not particularly stimulating. However, he convinced himself that it was useful to understand the functions of the different units in the gallery and not restrict himself to purely curatorial issues. The Research unit was quite small and the staff were very serious. Because they worked in close proximity to each other, he tried to be friendly towards them while they worked.

When he kept getting frowns and annoyed looks from his colleagues, it became obvious that they did not like being interrupted. Further, they assumed that he did not have enough work to do, so they kept giving him more tasks. He found himself falling behind and having to ask for permission to stay late to finish his work. Because the gallery housed expensive artworks, security was tight. All staff were expected to leave by 5 pm and not return until the following morning after 8 am. Management was very strict about granting permission to stay late, because Security had to be notified so that alarm systems could be adjusted and monitored accordingly. But because the Research manager, Nelly, often stayed late, she was happy to grant Rod permission as well.

One Friday morning, Rod met with Nelly to give her the report he had written on business plans.

'Thanks, Rod. It looks good,' said Nelly, as she flipped through the document. 'You're still working on that draft document on the current spending and budget allocation for this year, aren't you? Andrew can help you with that.'

Rod hesitated. 'Oh, I think I have all the necessary information, and I'm sure Andrew is busy anyway. If I stay late tonight, I might be able to give it to you before I leave work.'

'What's wrong?' asked Nelly.

'It's nothing. I just always get the impression that I'm disturbing everyone in Research. They seem busy all the time and don't seem to have time for anything but work. I'm more of a sociable person, and like to talk with others while I work.'

Nelly gave him a look which Rod didn't know how to decipher. I hope she doesn't think I'm complaining about my job or my colleagues, Rod thought to himself as he walked out of her office. He liked the fact that no one was breathing down his neck all the time. And the last thing he needed was to create any animosity between himself and the rest of Research. It was bad enough that they never invited him when they went out for lunch together. But he wished they would at least say 'hi' to him from time to time.

The following Thursday, when Nelly came into the Research area to talk to one of the researchers, she came by Rod's desk to say that she had read both of the reports he had finished last week, thanked him for his hard work, and asked how his work was going. He appreciated the attention. Over the following weeks, when he was in Research Nelly would often come by and talk to him. This sometimes included complimenting him on his appearance: how his shirt colour emphasised his eyes, or his new stylish haircut made him look more handsome. At least someone is talking to me, thought Rod. He felt that her comments were a little inappropriate, but he accepted them graciously and with a smile, making sure that he kept his comments professional. He also tried to minimise how often he had to stay late at work so as not to give the wrong impression, but this was difficult given his workload.

It wasn't long before the other researchers noticed the attention Nelly was giving to Rod. He became aware of the surreptitious looks he received whenever she spoke to him, but thought he was being paranoid. A couple of times when he had walked into the research area some of the researchers who had been talking in low voices stopped when they saw him.

What's going on? wondered Rod. It was not like he was not pulling his weight. He got the projects done on time even though he worked only two days in Research, and Nelly said he was doing a good job. Rod went home that weekend pleased that for once he did not have to work late.

He arrived at work on Monday in good spirits. He had studied all weekend and had nearly completed his final draft of his PhD thesis. He always enjoyed working in the Curatorial unit. He found his work preparing upcoming exhibitions interesting. Further, he quite liked the Curatorial team. His manager, Sarah, was approachable, and despite being the most junior member his colleagues regularly asked for his input during the weekly Monday meetings. The team was friendly and he found he had a lot in common with many of them, and sometimes he would go to lunch with them. Working in Curatorial also meant that he was not in Research. Here he did not have to put up with Nelly's comments, which were beginning to make him feel quite uncomfortable, and he did not have to put up with the whispers or the silent stares he got from his Research colleagues. Rod was about to start working on a catalogue for an Aboriginal art exhibition the gallery was hosting next month, when Nelly walked in.

'Rod, you're looking sexy today. Andrew is away sick. Can you come and work in Research today?' she asked.

'Um, I can't, Nelly. We're really busy in Curatorial at the moment. We've got this exhibition coming up and we're behind. Claire is on maternity leave and two others in Curatorial are sick with that flu that's going around at the moment. Sorry, but I can't.'

Nelly frowned and left without a backward glance. I'll be at Research soon enough on Thursday anyway, thought Rod.

Later that day, Rod received an email from Nelly.

> *Rod,*
>
> *There has been a change in your work arrangement, to start this week. The assistant director and I have decided that instead of working in Curatorial for three days and Research for two days, you will now work in Curatorial on Monday and Tuesday, and then on Wednesday switch over to Research for the rest of the week.*
>
> *Nelly*

Rod began to feel panicky. The whole point of this job was to gain curatorial experience, which was why he had changed his PhD status to part-time. He went to see Sarah to see if she could get his work assignment changed back. Unfortunately, Sarah only confirmed the arrangement.

'There's nothing I can do about this, Rod. I wish I could, but Nelly helped me get this job. You're a valuable member of Curatorial and we both know that everyone on the team is flat out with the others away sick or on leave. But Nelly has more authority than me and is good friends with the assistant director.'

When Rod arrived in Research on Wednesday, Nelly told him that the desk arrangements were to be changed around. His desk was now visible from her office. Other things began to change in Research as well. Nelly rarely spoke to him except to pass on job assignments. And because he was there an extra day each week, he was able to complete his tasks without having to stay after hours. Rod was pleased about that. However, as the weeks passed, there were not enough tasks to keep him occupied and he'd be told to 'find something to do'. He felt as if he was wasting his time, especially since Curatorial continued to be short-staffed and Research was now brimming with staff. Rod hated that sometimes he had to pretend to be busy.

To make matters worse, Nelly had started to greet his arrival at work with remarks like 'So *now* you've decided to turn up to work' or 'Getting our beauty sleep, were we?' His fellow researchers began to chime in with similar snide remarks, such as 'While you've been having your latte, we've been at work since 8 am.'

It was getting unbearable in Research for Rod. His colleagues were talking to him now, but he would have preferred it if they were not.

At lunch with some of the Curatorial staff one day, he told them about the email.

'You'll just have to do the time with Research and hope that you get back on the good side of Nelly,' one of them said. 'She may eventually change things back so that you can work more in Curatorial. She's a NAG who likes to use her power over others. It's happened before.'

Note: This case is based on actual events.

QUESTIONS

1. What sources of power and contingencies of power seem to help Nelly get her way?

2. Describe the influence tactics applied by Nelly, by Rod's co-workers in the Research department, and by Rod. Which influence tactics, in your opinion, would be considered organisational politics in this situation?

3. If you were Rod, what would you do in the situation?

BUDGET DELIBERATIONS

12.2 SKILL BUILDER

TEAM EXERCISE

By Sharon Card

PURPOSE

This exercise is designed to help you understand some of the power dynamics and influence tactics that occur across hierarchical levels in organisations.

MATERIALS

This activity works best where one small room leads to a larger room, which leads to a larger area.

INSTRUCTIONS

These instructions are based on a class size of about thirty students. The instructor may adjust the size of the first two groups slightly for larger classes. The instructor will organise students as follows. A few (3 or 4) students are assigned the position of executives. They are preferably located in a secluded office or corner of a large classroom. Another six to eight students are assigned positions as middle managers. These people will ideally be located in an adjoining room or space, allowing privacy for the executives. The remaining students represent the non-management employees in the organisation. They are located in an open area outside the executive and management rooms.

RULES

Members of the executive group are free to enter the space of either the middle management group or the non-management group and to communicate whatever they wish, whenever they wish. Members of the middle management group may enter the space of the non-management group whenever they wish, but must request permission to enter the executive group's space. The executive group can refuse the middle management group's request. Members of the non-management group are not allowed to disturb the top group in any way unless specifically invited by members of the executive group. The non-management group does have the right to request permission to communicate with the middle management group. The middle management group can refuse the lower group's request.

TASK

Your organisation is in the process of preparing a budget. The challenge is to balance needs with the financial resources. Of course, the needs are greater than the resources. The instructor will distribute a budget sheet showing a list of budget requests and their costs. Each group has control over a portion of the budget and must decide how to spend the money over which they have control. Non-management has discretion over a relatively small portion and the executive group has discretion over the greatest portion. The exercise is finished when the organisation has negotiated a satisfactory budget, or until the instructor calls 'time's up'. The class will then debrief with the following questions and others the instructor might ask.

QUESTIONS

1. What can we learn from this exercise about power in organisational hierarchies?
2. How is this exercise similar to relations in real organisations?
3. How did students in each group feel about the amount of power they held?
4. How did they exercise their power in relations with the other groups?

SKILL BUILDER | 12.3   UPWARD INFLUENCE SCALE

SELF-ASSESSMENT

PURPOSE

This exercise is designed to help you understand several ways of influencing people up the organisational hierarchy, as well as help you estimate your preferred upward influence tactics.

INSTRUCTIONS

Read each of the statements below and circle the response that you believe best indicates how often you engaged in that behaviour over the past six months. Then use the scoring key in Appendix B to calculate your results. This exercise is completed alone so that students can assess themselves honestly without concerns of social comparison. However, class discussion will focus on the types of influence in organisations and the conditions under which particular influence tactics are most and least appropriate.

UPWARD INFLUENCE SCALE

How often in the past 6 months have you engaged in the behaviours?	Never	Seldom	Occasionally	Frequently	Almost always
1. I obtain the support of my co-workers in persuading my manager to act on my request.	1	2	3	4	5
2. I offer an exchange in which I will do something that my manager wants if he or she will do what I want.	1	2	3	4	5
3. I act in a very humble and polite manner while making my request.	1	2	3	4	5
4. I appeal to higher management to put pressure on my manager.	1	2	3	4	5
5. I remind my manager of how I have helped him or her in the past and imply that now I expect compliance with my request.	1	2	3	4	5
6. I go out of my way to make my manager feel good about me, before asking him or her to do what I want.	1	2	3	4	5
7. I use logical arguments in order to convince my manager.	1	2	3	4	5

continued ▶

UPWARD INFLUENCE SCALE *continued*

How often in the past 6 months have you engaged in the behaviours?	Never	Seldom	Occasionally	Frequently	Almost always
8. I have a face-to-face confrontation with my manager in which I forcefully state what I want.	1	2	3	4	5
9. I act in a friendly manner towards my manager before making my request.	1	2	3	4	5
10. I present facts, figures and other information to my manager in support of my position.	1	2	3	4	5
11. I obtain the support and cooperation of my subordinates to back up my request.	1	2	3	4	5
12. I obtain the informal support of higher management to back me.	1	2	3	4	5
13. I offer to make a personal sacrifice such as giving up my free time if my manager will do what I want.	1	2	3	4	5
14. I very carefully explain to my manager the reasons for my request.	1	2	3	4	5
15. I verbally express my anger to my manager in order to get what I want.	1	2	3	4	5
16. I use a forceful manner; I try such things as demands, the setting of deadlines, and the expression of strong emotion.	1	2	3	4	5
17. I rely on the chain of command—on people higher up in the organisation who have power over my supervisor.	1	2	3	4	5
18. I mobilise other people in the organisation to help me in influencing my supervisor.	1	2	3	4	5

Source: C. Schriesheim and T. Hinkin, 'Influence Tactics Used by Subordinates: A Theoretical and Empirical Analysis and Refinement of the Kipnis, Schmidt, and Wilkinson subscales', *Journal of Applied Psychology*, 75 (1990), pp. 246–57.

GUANXI ORIENTATION SCALE

12.4 SKILL BUILDER

SELF-ASSESSMENT

FULL EXERCISE ON
STUDENT CD

Guanxi, which is translated as 'interpersonal connections', is an important element of doing business in China and some other Asian countries with strong Confucian cultural values. *Guanxi* is based on traditional Confucian values of helping others without expecting future repayment. This instrument estimates your *guanxi* orientation, that is, the extent to which you accept and apply *guanxi* values. This self-assessment is completed alone so that students rate themselves honestly without concerns of social comparison. However, class discussion will focus on the meaning of *guanxi* and its relevance for organisational power and influence.

MACHIAVELLIANISM SCALE

12.5 SKILL BUILDER

SELF-ASSESSMENT

FULL EXERCISE ON
STUDENT CD

Machiavellianism is named after Niccolo Machiavelli, the sixteenth-century Italian philosopher who wrote *The Prince*, a famous treatise about political behaviour. Out of Machiavelli's work emerged this instrument that estimates the degree to which you have a Machiavellian personality. Indicate the extent to which you agree or disagree that each statement in this instrument describes you. Complete each item honestly to get the best estimate of your level of Machiavellianism.

SKILL BUILDER | 12.6   PERCEPTIONS OF POLITICS SCALE (POPS)

SELF-ASSESSMENT

FULL EXERCISE ON **STUDENT CD**

Organisations have been called 'political arenas'—environments in which political tactics are common because decisions are ambiguous and resources are scarce. This instrument estimates the degree to which you believe that the college or university where you attend classes has a politicised culture. The scale consists of several statements that might or might not describe the institution you attend. The statements refer to the administration of the institution, not the classroom. Indicate the extent to which you agree or disagree with each statement.

NOTES

1   R. Gluyas, 'Fear and Loathing in NAB's Forex Fiasco', *Australian*, 6 August 2005, 35; E. Johnston, '"Anything Goes," Ex-Trader Says', *Australian Financial Review*, 2 August 2005, 3; E. Johnston, 'Expletives and Stench in Hothouse of NAB Dealers', *Australian Financial Review*, 6 August 2005, 3.

2   For a discussion of the definition of power, see: H. Mintzberg, *Power in and around Organizations* (Englewood Cliffs, NJ: Prentice Hall, 1983), chapter 1; J. Pfeffer, *Managing with Power* (Boston: Harvard Business University Press, 1992), pp. 17, 30; J. Pfeffer, *New Directions in Organizational Theory* (New York: Oxford University Press, 1997), chapter 6; J. M. Whitmeyer, 'Power through Appointment', *Social Science Research* 29 (2000), 535–55.

3   R. A. Dahl, 'The Concept of Power', *Behavioral Science* 2 (1957), 201–18; R. M. Emerson, 'Power–Dependence Relations', *American Sociological Review* 27 (1962), 31–41; A. M. Pettigrew, *The Politics of Organizational Decision-Making* (London: Tavistock, 1973).

4   K. M. Bartol and D. C. Martin, 'When Politics Pays: Factors Influencing Managerial Compensation Decisions', *Personnel Psychology* 43 (1990), 599–614; D. J. Brass and M. E. Burkhardt, 'Potential Power and Power Use: An Investigation of Structure and Behavior', *Academy of Management Journal* 36 (1993), 441–70.

5   J. R. P. French and B. Raven, 'The Bases of Social Power', in *Studies in Social Power*, ed. D. Cartwright (Ann Arbor, Michigan: University of Michigan Press, 1959), 150–67; P. Podsakoff and C. Schreisheim, 'Field Studies of French and Raven's Bases of Power: Critique, Analysis, and Suggestions for Future Research', *Psychological Bulletin* 97 (1985), 387–411; S. Finkelstein, 'Power in Top Management Teams: Dimensions. Measurement, and Validation', *Academy of Management Journal* 35 (1992), 505–38; P. P. Carson and K. D. Carson, 'Social Power Bases: A Meta-Analytic Examination of Interrelationships and Outcomes', *Journal of Applied Social Psychology* 23 (1993), 1150–69.

6   B. H. Raven, 'The Bases of Power: Origins and Recent Developments', *Journal of Social Issues* 49 (1993), 227–51; G. A. Yukl, *Leadership in Organizations*, 3rd edn (Englewood Cliffs, NJ: Prentice Hall, 1994), p. 13.

7   C. Barnard, *The Function of the Executive* (Cambridge, MA: Harvard University Press, 1938); C. Hardy and S. R. Clegg, 'Some Dare Call It Power', in *Handbook of Organization Studies*, ed. S. R. Clegg, C. Hardy and W. R. Nord (London: Sage, 1996), 622–41.

8   L. A. Conger, *Winning 'Em Over: A New Model for Managing in the Age of Persuasion* (New York: Simon & Schuster, 1998), Appendix A.

9   V. Bland, 'Writing on the Walls', *New Zealand Herald*, 28 February 2004, C11; L. S. Sya, 'Flying to Greater Heights', *New Sunday Times* (Kuala Lumpur), 31 July 2005, 14.

10 P. F. Drucker, 'The New Workforce', *The Economist*, 3 November 2001, 8–12.

11 J. D. Kudisch and M. L. Poteet, 'Expert Power, Referent Power, and Charisma: Toward the Resolution of a Theoretical Debate', *Journal of Business & Psychology* 10 (Winter 1995), 177–95; H. L. Tosi et al., 'CEO Charisma, Compensation, and Firm Performance', *Leadership Quarterly* 15, no. 3 (2004), 405–20.

12 G. Yukl and C. M. Falbe, 'Importance of Different Power Sources in Downward and Lateral Relations', *Journal of Applied Psychology* 76 (1991), 416–23; B. H. Raven, 'Kurt Lewin Address: Influence, Power, Religion, and the Mechanisms of Social Control', *Journal of Social Issues* 55 (Spring 1999), 161–86.

13 P. L. Dawes, D. Y. Lee and G. R. Dowling, 'Information Control and Influence in Emergent Buying Centers', *Journal of Marketing* 62, no. 3 (July 1998), 55–68; D. J. Brass et al., 'Taking Stock of Networks and Organizations: A Multilevel Perspective', *Academy of Management Journal* 47, no. 6 (December 2004), 795–817.

14 C. R. Hinings et al., 'Structural Conditions of Intraorganizational Power', *Administrative Science Quarterly* 19 (1974), 22–44. Also see C. S. Saunders, 'The Strategic Contingency Theory of Power: Multiple Perspectives', *The Journal of Management Studies* 27 (1990), 1–21.

15 S. Elliott, 'Hunting for the Next Cool in Advertising', *New York Times*, 1 December 2003, C19; S. Delaney, 'Predicting the Birth of the Cool', *The Independent* (London), 5 September 2005, 15; A. McMains, 'Trend-Spotting Division Adds to Lowe's Evolution', *Adweek*, 11 April 2005, 11.

16 D. J. Hickson et al., 'A Strategic Contingencies' Theory of Intraorganizational Power', *Administrative Science Quarterly* 16 (1971), 216–27; Hinings et al., 'Structural Conditions of Intraorganizational Power'; R. M. Kanter, 'Power Failure in Management Circuits', *Harvard Business Review* (July–August 1979), 65–75.

17 M. Crozier, *The Bureaucratic Phenomenon* (London: Tavistock, 1964).

18 Hickson et al., 'A Strategic Contingencies' Theory of Intraorganizational Power'; J. D. Hackman, 'Power and Centrality in the Allocation of Resources in Colleges and Universities', *Administrative Science Quarterly* 30 (1985), 61–77; Brass and Burkhardt, 'Potential Power and Power Use: An Investigation of Structure and Behavior'.

19 A. Jameson and E. Judge, 'Mournful Swansong for the BA Boss', *The Times* (London), 13 August 2005, 8; S. Lekic, 'Tens of Thousands Stranded as British Airways Cancels Flights over Labor Dispute', *Associated Press*, 13 August 2005; M. Milner and M. Honigsbaum, 'Chaos as BA Flights Grounded', *The Guardian* (London), 12 August 2005, 1.

20 Kanter, 'Power Failure in Management Circuits'; B. E. Ashforth, 'The Experience of Powerlessness in Organizations', *Organizational Behavior and Human Decision Processes* 43 (1989), 207–42; L. Holden, 'European Managers: HRM and an Evolving Role', *European Business Review* 12 (2000).

21 J. Voight, 'When Credit Is Not Due', *Adweek*, 1 March 2004, 24.

22 R. Madell, 'Ground Floor', *Pharmaceutical Executive (Women in Pharma Supplement)*, June 2000, 24–31.

23 N. Lindsay, 'Office Fit-out Doctors Turn the Tables', *Australian Financial Review*, 7 January 2000, 31.

24 B. R. Ragins, 'Diversified Mentoring Relationships in Organizations: A Power Perspective', *Academy of Management Review* 22 (1997), 482–521; M. C. Higgins and K. E. Kram, 'Reconceptualizing Mentoring at Work: A Developmental Network Perspective', *Academy of Management Review* 26 (April 2001), 264–88.

25 D. Krackhardt and J. R. Hanson, 'Informal Networks: The Company Behind the Chart', *Harvard Business Review* 71 (July–August 1993), 104–11; P. S. Adler and S.-W. Kwon, 'Social Capital: Prospects for a New Concept', *Academy of Management Review* 27, no. 1 (2002), 17–40.

26 A. Mehra, M. Kilduff and D. J. Brass, 'The Social Networks of High and Low Self-Monitors: Implications for Workplace Performance', *Administrative Science Quarterly* 46 (March 2001), 121–46.

27 B. R. Ragins and E. Sundstrom, 'Gender and Power in Organizations: A Longitudinal Perspective', *Psychological Bulletin* 105 (1989), 51–88; M. Linehan, 'Barriers to Women's Participation in International Management', *European Business Review* 13 (2001).

28 D. M. McCracken, 'Winning the Talent War for Women: Sometimes It Takes a Revolution', *Harvard Business Review* (November–December 2000), 159–67; D. L. Nelson and R. J. Burke, 'Women Executives: Health, Stress, and Success', *Academy of Management Executive* 14 (May 2000), 107–21.

29 K. Atuahene-Gima and H. Li, 'Marketing's Influence Tactics in New Product Development: A Study of High Technology Firms in China', *Journal of Product Innovation Management* 17 (2000), 451–70; A. Somech and A. Drach-Zahavy, 'Relative Power and Influence Strategy: The Effects of Agent/Target Organizational Power on Superiors' Choices of Influence Strategies', *Journal of Organizational Behavior* 23 (2002), 167–79.

30 D. Kipnis, S. M. Schmidt and I. Wilkinson, 'Intraorganizational Influence Tactics: Explorations in Getting One's Way', *Journal of Applied Psychology* 65 (1980), 440–52. Also see: C. Schriesheim and T. Hinkin, 'Influence Tactics Used by Subordinates: A Theoretical and Empirical Analysis and Refinement of the Kipnis, Schmidt, and Wilkinson Subscales', *Journal of Applied Psychology* 75 (1990), 246–57; W. A. Hochwarter et al., 'A Re-examination of Schriesheim and Hinkin's (1990) Measure of Upward Influence', *Educational and Psychological Measurement* 60 (October 2000), 755–71.

31 Some of the more thorough lists of influence tactics are presented in: A. Rao and K. Hashimoto, 'Universal and Culturally Specific Aspects of Managerial Influence: A Study of Japanese Managers', *Leadership Quarterly* 8 (1997), 295–312; L. A. McFarland, A. M. Ryan and S. D. Kriska, 'Field Study Investigation of Applicant Use of Influence Tactics in a Selection Interview', *Journal of Psychology* 136 (July 2002), 383–98.

32 R. B. Cialdini and N. J. Goldstein, 'Social Influence: Compliance and Conformity', *Annual Review of Psychology* 55 (2004), 591–621.

33 Rao and Hashimoto, 'Universal and Culturally Specific Aspects of Managerial Influence'. Silent authority as an influence tactic in non-Western cultures is also discussed in S. F. Pasa, 'Leadership Influence in a High Power Distance and Collectivist Culture', *Leadership & Organization Development Journal* 21 (2000), 414–26.

34 'Be Part of the Team If You Want to Catch the Eye', *Birmingham Post* (UK), 31 August 2000, 14; S. Maitlis, 'Taking It from the Top: How CEOs Influence (and Fail to Influence) Their Boards', *Organization Studies* 25, no. 8 (2004), 1275–311.

35 A. T. Cobb, 'Toward the Study of Organizational Coalitions: Participant Concerns and Activities in a Simulated Organizational Setting', *Human Relations* 44 (1991), 1057–79; E. A. Mannix, 'Organizations as Resource Dilemmas: The Effects of Power Balance on Coalition Formation in Small Groups', *Organizational Behavior and Human Decision Processes* 55 (1993), 1–22; D. J. Terry, M. A. Hogg and K. M. White, 'The Theory of Planned Behavior: Self-Identity, Social Identity and Group Norms', *British Journal of Social Psychology* 38 (September 1999), 225–44.

36 Rao and Hashimoto, 'Universal and Culturally Specific Aspects of Managerial Influence'.

37 D. Strutton and L. E. Pelton, 'Effects of Ingratiation on Lateral Relationship Quality within Sales Team Settings', *Journal of Business Research* 43 (1998), 1–12; R. Vonk, 'Self-Serving Interpretations of Flattery: Why Ingratiation Works', *Journal of Personality and Social Psychology* 82 (2002), 515–26.

38 C. A. Higgins, T. A. Judge and G. R. Ferris, 'Influence Tactics and Work Outcomes: A Meta-Analysis', *Journal of Organizational Behavior* 24 (2003), 90–106.

39 D. Strutton, L. E. Pelton and J. F. Tanner, Jr, 'Shall We Gather in the Garden: The Effect of Ingratiatory Behaviors on Buyer Trust in Salespeople', *Industrial Marketing Management* 25 (1996), 151–62; J. O'Neil, 'An Investigation of the Sources of Influence of Corporate Public Relations Practitioners', *Public Relations Review* 29 (June 2003), 159–69.

40 A. Rao and S. M. Schmidt, 'Upward Impression Management: Goals, Influence Strategies, and Consequences', *Human Relations* 48 (1995), 147–67.

41 A. Mascarenhas, 'Two out of 10 Lie in Their Job Résumés', *Sydney Morning Herald*, 26 November 2004, 2; J. Lill, 'Unqualified Teen Took Job as Nurse', *Courier-Mail* (Brisbane), 16 September 2005, 8.

42 A. P. J. Ellis et al., 'The Use of Impression Management Tactics in Structured Interviews: A Function of Question Type?', *Journal of Applied Psychology* 87 (December 2002), 1200–8; M. C. Bolino and W. H. Tunley, 'More Than One Way to Make an Impression: Exploring Profiles of Impression Management', *Journal of Management* 29 (2003), 141–60.

43 J. Dillard and E. Peck, 'Persuasion and the Structure of Affect: Dual Systems and Discrete Emotions as Complementary Models', *Human Communication Research* 27 (2000), 38–68; S. Fox and Y. Amichai-Hamburger, 'The Power of Emotional Appeals in Promoting Organizational Change Programs', *Academy of Management Executive* 15 (November 2001), 84–94; E. H. H. J. Das, J. B. F. de Wit and W. Stroebe, 'Fear Appeals Motivate Acceptance of Action Recommendations: Evidence for a Positive Bias in the Processing of Persuasive Messages', *Personality and Social Psychology Bulletin* 29 (May 2003), 650–64; R. Buck et al., 'Emotion and Reason in Persuasion: Applying the Ari Model and the Casc Scale', *Journal of Business Research* 57, no. 6 (2004), 647–56.

44 S. Gilmor, 'Ahead of the Curve', *Infoworld* (13 January 2003), 58; M. Hiltzik, 'Apple CEO's Visions Don't Guarantee Sustained Gains', *Los Angeles Times* (14 April 2003), C1. The origin of 'reality distortion field' is described at www.folklore.org.

45 A. P. Brief, *Attitudes in and around Organizations* (Thousand Oaks, CA: Sage, 1998), pp. 69–84; D. J. O'Keefe, *Persuasion: Theory and Research* (Thousand Oaks, CA: Sage Publications, 2002).

46 Conger, *Winning 'Em Over: A New Model for Managing in the Age of Persuasion*; J. J. Jiang, G. Klein and R. G. Vedder, 'Persuasive Expert Systems: The Influence of Confidence and Discrepancy', *Computers in Human Behavior* 16 (March 2000), 99–109.

47 These and other features of message content in persuasion are detailed in: R. Petty and J. Cacioppo, *Attitudes and Persuasion: Classic and Contemporary Approaches* (Dubuque, Iowa: W. C. Brown, 1981); D. G. Linz and S. Penrod, 'Increasing Attorney Persuasiveness in the Courtroom', *Law and Psychology Review* 8 (1984), 1–47; M. Pfau, E. A. Szabo and J. Anderson, 'The Role and Impact of Affect in the Process of Resistance to Persuasion', *Human Communication Research* 27 (April 2001), 216–52; O'Keefe, *Persuasion: Theory and Research*, chapter 9.

48 N. Rhodes and W. Wood, 'Self-Esteem and Intelligence Affect Influenceability: The Mediating Role of Message Reception', *Psychological Bulletin* 111, no. 1 (1992), 156–71.

49 A. W. Gouldner, 'The Norm of Reciprocity: A Preliminary Statement', *American Sociological Review* 25 (1960), 161–78.

50 Y. Fan, 'Questioning *Guanxi*: Definition, Classification, and Implications', *International Business Review* 11 (2002), 543–61; D. Tan and R. S. Snell, 'The Third Eye: Exploring *Guanxi* and Relational Morality in the Workplace', *Journal of Business Ethics* 41 (December 2002), 361–84; W. R. Vanhonacker, 'When Good *Guanxi* Turns Bad', *Harvard Business Review* 82, no. 4 (April 2004), 18–19.

51 A. Ledeneva, *Russia's Economy of Favors: Blat, Networking and Informal Exchange* (New York: Cambridge University Press, 1998); S. Michailova and V. Worm, 'Personal Networking in Russia and China: *Blat* and *Guanxi*', *European Management Journal* 21 (2003), 509–19.

52 C. M. Falbe and G. Yukl, 'Consequences for Managers of Using Single Influence Tactics and Combinations of Tactics', *Academy of Management Journal* 35 (1992), 638–52.

53 Falbe and Yukl, 'Consequences for Managers of Using Single Influence Tactics and Combinations of Tactics'; Atuahene-Gima and Li, 'Marketing's Influence Tactics in New Product Development'.

54 R. C. Ringer and R. W. Boss, 'Hospital Professionals' Use of Upward Influence Tactics', *Journal of Managerial Issues* 12 (2000), 92–108.

55 G. Blickle, 'Do Work Values Predict the Use of Intraorganizational Influence Strategies?', *Journal of Applied Social Psychology* 30, no. 1 (January 2000), 196–205; P. P. Fu et al., 'The Impact of Societal Cultural Values and Individual Social Beliefs on the Perceived Effectiveness of Managerial Influence Strategies: A Meso Approach', *Journal of International Business Studies* 35, no. 4 (July 2004), 284–305.

56 D. Tannen, *Talking from 9 to 5* (New York: Avon, 1994), chapter 2; M. Crawford, *Talking Difference: On Gender and Language* (Thousand Oaks, CA: Sage, 1995), pp. 41–4.

57 S. Mann, 'Politics and Power in Organizations: Why Women Lose Out', *Leadership & Organization Development Journal* 16 (1995), 9–15; E. H. Buttner and M. McEnally, 'The Interactive Effect of Influence Tactic, Applicant Gender, and Type of Job on Hiring Recommendations', *Sex Roles* 34 (1996), 581–91; L. L. Carli, 'Gender, Interpersonal Power, and Social Influence', *Journal of Social Issues* 55 (Spring 1999), 81–99.

58 This definition of organisational politics has become the dominant perspective over the past fifteen years. See: G. R. Ferris and K. M. Kacmar, 'Perceptions of Organizational Politics', *Journal of Management* 18 (1992), 93–116; R. Cropanzano et al., 'The Relationship of Organizational Politics and Support to Work Behaviors, Attitudes, and Stress', *Journal of Organizational Behavior* 18 (1997), 159–80; E. Vigoda and A. Cohen, 'Influence Tactics and Perceptions of Organizational Politics: A Longitudinal Study', *Journal of Business Research* 55 (2002), 311–24. However, organisational politics were previously viewed as influence tactics outside the formal role that could be either selfish or altruistic. This older definition is less common today, possibly because it is incongruent with popular views of politics and because it overlaps too much with the concept of influence. For the older perspective of organisational politics, see J. Pfeffer, *Power in Organizations* (Boston: Pitman, 1981), and Mintzberg, *Power in and around Organizations*.

59 K. M. Kacmar and R. A. Baron, 'Organizational Politics: The State of the Field, Links to Related Processes, and an Agenda for Future Research', in *Research in Personnel and Human Resources Management*, ed. G. R. Ferris (Greenwich, CT: JAI Press, 1999), 1–39; L. A. Witt, T. F. Hilton and W. A. Hochwarter, 'Addressing Politics in Matrix Teams', *Group & Organization Management* 26 (June 2001), 230–47; E. Vigoda, 'Stress-Related Aftermaths to Workplace Politics: The Relationships among Politics, Job Distress, and Aggressive Behavior in Organizations', *Journal of Organizational Behavior* 23 (2002), 571–91.

60 C. Hardy, *Strategies for Retrenchment and Turnaround: The Politics of Survival* (Berlin: Walter de Gruyter, 1990), chapter 14; M. C. Andrews and K. M. Kacmar, 'Discriminating among Organizational Politics, Justice, and Support', *Journal of Organizational Behavior* 22 (2001), 347–66.

61 S. Blazejewski and W. Dorow, 'Managing Organizational Politics for Radical Change: The Case of Beiersdorf-Lechia S.A., Poznan', *Journal of World Business* 38 (August 2003), 204–23.

62 H. Mintzberg, 'The Organization as Political Arena', *Journal of Management Studies* 22 (1985), 133–54; G. R. Ferris, G. S. Russ and P. M. Fandt, 'Politics in Organizations', in *Impression Management in the Organization*, ed. R. A. Giacalone and P. Rosenfeld (Hillsdale, NJ: Erlbaum, 1989), 143–70.

63 L. W. Porter, R. W. Allen and H. L. Angle, 'The Politics of Upward Influence in Organizations', *Research in Organizational Behavior* 3 (1981), 120–2; R. J. House, 'Power and Personality in Complex Organizations', *Research in Organizational Behavior* 10 (1988), 305–57.

64 R. Christie and F. Geis, *Studies in Machiavellianism* (New York: Academic Press, 1970); S. M. Farmer et al., 'Putting Upward Influence Strategies in Context', *Journal of Organizational Behavior* 18 (1997), 17–42; K. S. Sauleya and A. G. Bedeian, 'Equity Sensitivity: Construction of a Measure and Examination of Its Psychometric Properties', *Journal of Management* 26 (September 2000), 885–910.

65 G. R. Ferris et al., 'Perceptions of Organizational Politics: Prediction, Stress-Related Implications, and Outcomes', *Human Relations* 49 (1996), 233–63.

CHAPTER 13

Conflict and negotiation in the workplace

LEARNING OBJECTIVES

After reading this chapter, you should be able to:

- outline the conflict process

- discuss the advantages and disadvantages of conflict in organisations

- distinguish constructive from socioemotional conflict

- identify six sources of organisational conflict

- outline the five interpersonal styles of conflict management

- summarise six structural approaches to managing conflict

- outline four situational influences on negotiations

- compare and contrast the three types of third-party dispute resolution.

In 2002 British conglomerate Virgin Group wanted an Australian partner to inject funds into its fledgling airline, Virgin Blue, while satisfying Australian share ownership regulations. A partner was found in Patrick Corp, the feisty transportation and stevedoring firm best known for dramatically increasing Australia's seaport productivity a few years earlier by breaking the waterfront union's control. But rather than remaining a cooperative partner, Patrick successfully launched a hostile bid in early 2005 for majority ownership of Virgin Blue. Chris Corrigan, Patrick's chief executive, claims he took control away from Virgin Group because the airline could be better managed to improve its profitability.

Publicly, Virgin Group founder Richard Branson was philosophical about giving up control of Virgin Blue, even meeting Corrigan over drinks soon after the transfer of power (as shown in the photo). But sources say that Branson actually went 'ballistic' when Corrigan announced the takeover. 'We'd like our baby back,' Branson said candidly a few months later. 'It was snatched in a way we didn't appreciate at the time.'

With 25 per cent ownership of the airline, Branson and his Virgin Group board members also clashed with Corrigan and his Patrick-dominated board over the airline's direction. 'We have had some strong debates on the board,' admits Branson. Branson alleges that since the Patrick takeover Virgin Blue has 'lost its heart' and needs to be liberated from 'wheelers and dealers'. Also, while Corrigan was focused on cutting costs, Virgin Group wanted Virgin Blue to launch a frequent

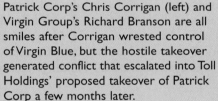

Patrick Corp's Chris Corrigan (left) and Virgin Group's Richard Branson are all smiles after Corrigan wrested control of Virgin Blue, but the hostile takeover generated conflict that escalated into Toll Holdings' proposed takeover of Patrick Corp a few months later.

flyer program, a loyal credit card, improved on-time performance, and other strategies to capture the business market. The two factions also disagreed over hedging against fuel costs.

Given this situation, Branson must have been delighted to receive a call from Paul Little, chief executive of rival Australian transportation company Toll Holdings. Little told Branson that he was about to launch a takeover of Patrick Corp and, if successful, pledged to help Branson regain control of Virgin Blue. (Toll was mainly interested in Patrick's seaport and container assets.) The two had discussed this possibility when Patrick was taking control of Virgin Blue, but Toll had needed more time to launch its assault. Toll Holdings executives had also approached Patrick executives within the past year about a merger of equals, but their proposal had been rejected.

Toll Holdings' bid to acquire Patrick is more complicated and conflict-ridden than a typical battle between two transportation industry rivals. Both firms are also partners in Australia's national rail freight service Pacific National (PN). Toll's takeover announcement immediately put PN into turmoil. Toll and Patrick representatives on PN's board fought about most resolutions; they couldn't even agree on the minutes of the previous meeting! PN executives took such a battering from the conflict that PN's chief executive and at least two others quit in frustration over the internal squabbling, the strong words and the personal threats.

In one interview, Chris Corrigan summed up relations inside PN during Toll's takeover bid by proposing the following tongue-in-cheek recruitment ad for a new PN chief executive: 'Great opportunity to come into a dysfunctional organisation. Work for two shareholders who are at each other's throats. Expect to receive the occasional barrage of emails and the odd derogatory, blasphemous phone message.'[1]

conflict The process in which one party perceives that its interests are being opposed or negatively affected by another party.

THE DISPUTE BETWEEN PATRICK CORP, Toll Holdings and Virgin Group may be an unusually high-stakes display of discord between business partners, but it illustrates several dimensions of conflict that will be discussed in this chapter. Conflict is a process in which one party perceives that its interests are being opposed or negatively affected by another party.[2] This chapter looks at the dynamics of conflict in organisational settings. It begins by describing the conflict process and discussing the consequences and sources of conflict in organisational settings. Five conflict management styles are then described, followed by a discussion of the structural approaches to conflict management. The last two sections of the chapter introduce two procedures for resolving conflict: negotiation and third-party conflict resolution.

THE CONFLICT PROCESS

LEARNING OBJECTIVE

Outline the conflict process.

When someone describes an incident involving conflict, they usually refer to the observable part of conflict—the angry words, shouting matches and actions that symbolise opposition. But this manifest conflict is only a small part of the conflict process. As Exhibit 13.1 illustrates, the conflict process begins with the sources of conflict.[3] Incompatible goals, different values and other conditions lead one or both parties to perceive that conflict exists. These sources of conflict will be looked at closely later in the chapter, because understanding and changing them is the key to effective conflict management.

CONFLICT PERCEPTIONS AND EMOTIONS

At some point the sources of conflict lead one or both parties to perceive that conflict exists. They become aware that one party's statements and actions are incompatible with their own goals. These perceptions usually interact with emotions experienced about the conflict. The Patrick–Toll–Virgin dispute is riddled with such emotions. Richard Branson, the typically smiling founder of Virgin Group, was said to have gone 'ballistic' when told of Patrick's surprise takeover of Virgin Blue. The resignation of Pacific National's chief executive was apparently triggered by angry emails and voice messages from a Toll Holdings executive who accused PN's neutral CEO of supporting Patrick Corp.

MANIFEST CONFLICT

Conflict perceptions and emotions usually manifest themselves in the decisions and overt behaviours of one party towards the other. These conflict episodes can range from subtle nonverbal behaviours to warlike aggression. When people experience high levels of conflict emotions,

EXHIBIT 13.1

The conflict process

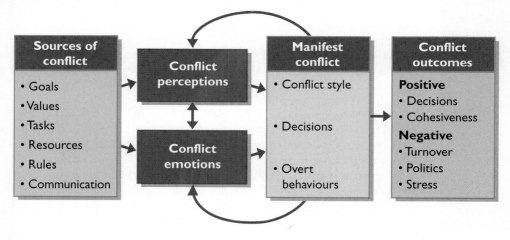

they often have difficulty finding the words and expressions that communicate effectively without further irritating the relationship.[4] Conflict is also manifested by the style each side uses to resolve the conflict. Some people tend to avoid the conflict, whereas others try to defeat those with opposing views. Conflict management styles will be described later in the chapter. At this point, you should know that these styles influence the other party's perceptions and actions regarding the conflict, which then either diffuses or further escalates the conflict.

CONFLICT ESCALATION CYCLE

The conflict process in Exhibit 13.1 shows arrows looping back from manifest conflict to conflict perceptions and emotions. These loops represent the fact that the conflict process is really a series of episodes that potentially link in an escalation cycle or spiral.[5] It doesn't take much to start this conflict cycle—just an inappropriate comment, a misunderstanding, or an action that lacks diplomacy. These behaviours communicate to the other party in a way that creates a perception of conflict. If the first party did not intend to demonstrate conflict, the second party's response may create that perception.

If the conflict remains focused on perceptions, both parties can often resolve the conflict through logical analysis. However, the communication process has enough ambiguity that a wrong look or word may trigger strong emotions and set the stage for further conflict escalation. These distorted beliefs and emotions reduce each side's motivation to communicate, making it more difficult for them to discover common ground and ultimately resolve the conflict. The parties then rely more on stereotypes and emotions to reinforce their perceptions of the other party. Some structural conditions increase the likelihood of conflict escalation. Employees who are more confrontational and less diplomatic also tend to escalate conflict.[6]

CONFLICT OUTCOMES

The battle for control at Patrick Corp, Toll Holdings and Virgin Group illustrates some of the dysfunctional consequences of conflict: verbal barbs from both parties, management actions that have questionable benefits for stakeholders, resignation of key executives, and public statements that may damage the underlying value of each party's assets. Even at lower levels in the organisation, employees are distracted from their work by internal feuds and engage in dysfunctional behaviours such as withholding valuable knowledge and other resources. Ongoing conflict also increases stress and turnover, while reducing organisational commitment and job satisfaction. At the intergroup level, conflict with people outside the team may cause team members to become more insular, increasing their cohesiveness while distancing themselves from outsiders who are critical of the team's past decisions.[7]

Given these problems, it's not surprising that people normally associate **conflict management** with reducing or removing conflict. However, conflict management refers to interventions that alter the level and form of conflict in ways that maximise its benefits and minimise its dysfunctional consequences. This sometimes means increasing the level of constructive conflict (also known as *task-related conflict*).[8] Recall from Chapter 10 that constructive conflict occurs when team members debate their different perceptions about an issue in a way that keeps the conflict focused on the task rather than people. This form of conflict tests the logic of arguments and encourages participants to re-examine their basic assumptions about the problem and its possible solution. For example, Tharman Shanmugaratnam, Singapore's Minister of Education and deputy chairman of the Monetary Authority of Singapore, encourages debate among his staff to challenge old mind-sets. 'We argue ferociously internally,' says Shanmugaratnam. 'There's no discernible hierarchy in many of these debates.'[9]

The challenge is to engage in constructive conflict without having it escalate into **socioemotional conflict** (also known as *relationship conflict*). When socioemotional conflict dominates, differences are viewed as personal attacks rather than attempts to resolve an issue. The parties become defensive and competitive towards each other, which motivates them to

LEARNING OBJECTIVE

Discuss the advantages and disadvantages of conflict in organisations.

LEARNING OBJECTIVE

Distinguish constructive from socioemotional conflict.

conflict management
Interventions that alter the level and form of conflict in ways that maximise its benefits and minimise its dysfunctional consequences.

socioemotional conflict
Any situation where people view their differences as personal attacks rather than attempts to resolve an issue.

Constructive conflict improves Kiwi board decisions

Jim Syme knows a thing or two about using constructive conflict to improve decision making in corporate board meetings. Recently voted QBE Insurance chairperson of the year, the New Zealand executive chairs several boards, including Kiwi Income Property Trust, Waste Management New Zealand, Abano (formerly Eldercare) and Software of Excellence. Syme is considered a 'gentleman' with high integrity in his boardroom behaviour, but he is quick to point out that being polite and respectful doesn't mean shying away from constructive conflict. 'The relationships need to be strong enough to support rigorous and constructive debate by all directors and to ensure there is a strong and effective relationship between the board and the chief executive,' says Syme. He explains that actively debating an issue encourages directors on the board to think carefully through the logic of the situation. 'It is critical that an important issue in front of us is well debated so that we get the right decision,' Syme advises.[10]

Kiwi Income Property Trust

reduce communication and information sharing. Once again, the model nicely reflects events in the Patrick–Toll–Virgin dispute. In fact, relations between Paul Little at Toll Holdings and Chris Corrigan at Patrick Corp had deteriorated to the point where 'it's probably gone a bit too far', Little acknowledged. As for reduced communication, Little quipped: 'There's been no phone calls to ask about the weather in that area of the country.'[11]

Minimising socioemotional conflict

The solution here seems obvious: encourage constructive conflict for better decision making and minimise socioemotional conflict in order to avoid dysfunctional emotions and behaviours. This sounds good in theory, but recent evidence suggests that separating these two types of conflict isn't easy. Most of us experience some degree of socioemotional conflict during or after any constructive debate.[12] In other words, it is difficult to suppress defensive emotions when trying to resolve conflicts calmly and rationally. Fortunately, conflict management experts have identified three strategies that might reduce the level of socioemotional conflict during constructive conflict episodes.[13]

- *Emotional intelligence.* Socioemotional conflict is less likely to occur, or is less likely to escalate, when team members have high levels of emotional intelligence. Emotionally intelligent employees are better able to regulate their emotions during debate, which reduces the risk of escalating perceptions of interpersonal hostility. People with high emotional intelligence are also more likely to view a co-worker's emotional reaction as valuable information about that person's needs and expectations, rather than as a personal attack.
- *Cohesive team.* Socioemotional conflict is suppressed when the conflict occurs within a highly cohesive team. The longer people work together, get to know each other, and develop mutual trust with each other, the more latitude they give to each other to show emotions without being personally offended. Strong cohesion also allows people to know about and anticipate the behaviours and emotions of their team-mates. Another benefit is that cohesion produces a stronger social identity with the group, so team members are

motivated to avoid escalating socioemotional conflict during otherwise emotionally turbulent discussions.

- *Supportive team norms.* Various team norms can hold socioemotional conflict at bay during constructive debate. When team norms encourage openness, for instance, team members learn to appreciate honest dialogue without personally reacting to any emotional display during the disagreements. Other norms might discourage team members from displaying negative emotions towards co-workers. Team norms also encourage tactics that diffuse socioemotional conflict when it first appears. For instance, research has found that teams with low socioemotional conflict use humour to maintain positive group emotions, which offsets negative feelings that team members might develop towards some co-workers during debate.

SOURCES OF CONFLICT IN ORGANISATIONS

Manifest conflict is just the tip of the proverbial iceberg. What we really need to understand are the sources of this conflict, which lie under the surface. The six main conditions that cause conflict in organisational settings are shown in Exhibit 13.2 and described over the next few pages.

LEARNING OBJECTIVE

Identify six sources of organisational conflict.

INCOMPATIBLE GOALS

A common source of conflict is goal incompatibility.[14] Goal incompatibility occurs when one person's or unit's goals seem to interfere with another person's or unit's goals. This source of conflict is apparent in the Patrick–Toll–Virgin conflict. Chris Corrigan's takeover of and subsequent strategic plans for Virgin Blue (namely to reduce costs and increase profitability) created conflict because they were incompatible with Richard Branson's plans for the airline (namely to expand services for business passengers and maintain an employee-focused culture).

Goal incompatibility also exists between Paul Little at Toll Holdings and Chris Corrigan at Patrick Corp. Little wants to form an integrated freight handling group that would be able to transport materials and products between manufacturing operations in Asia and warehouses in Australia. Corrigan doesn't see that goal as a viable option, claims Little, who concludes that Corrigan is 'devoid of vision'.[15] This goal incompatibility led to the takeover proposal because

Sources of conflict in organisations

EXHIBIT 13.2

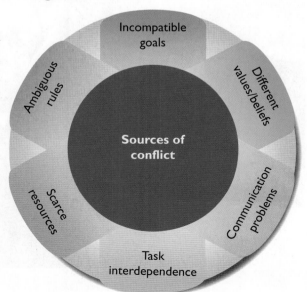

Toll Holdings needs some of Patrick's waterfront and container businesses in order to achieve regional dominance in transportation and logistics. Meanwhile, Toll's takeover proposal threatens Corrigan's goals for Patrick Corp.

DIFFERENTIATION

Not long ago a British automotive company proposed a friendly buyout of an Italian firm. Executives at both companies were excited about the opportunities for sharing distribution channels and manufacturing technologies. But the grand vision of a merged company turned into a nightmare as executives began meeting to discuss the details. Their backgrounds and experiences were so different that they were endlessly confused and constantly apologising to the other side for oversights and misunderstandings. At one meeting—the last, as it turned out—the president of the Italian firm stood up and, smiling sadly, said, 'I believe we all know what is the problem here . . . it seems your forward is our reverse; your down, our up; your right, our wrong. Let us finish now, before war is declared.'[16]

These automotive executives discovered that conflict is often caused by different values and beliefs due to unique backgrounds, experiences or training. Mergers and joint ventures often produce conflict because they bring together people with divergent corporate cultures. Employees and executives fight over the 'right way' to do things because of their unique experiences in the separate companies. This differentiation is another contributing factor in the conflicts described in the opening story. Virgin Group's Richard Branson complained that Patrick Corp had a 'wheeler and dealer' culture that was diametrically opposed to Virgin Blue's employee-friendly and customer-focused culture. Paul Little also says that relations between Toll Holdings and Patrick Corp have been strained because of their divergent approaches to doing business.

Conflict also occurs when people from one culture are guided by deeply held values that are at odds with the values applied by people from another culture. This form of differentiation conflict was illustrated in a recent study of two Australian organisations, which found

Cultural differences spark conflict between Godrej and P&G

Corporate and national culture differences can create serious conflicts in international joint ventures. That's what executives at Procter & Gamble (P&G) in the United States and at Godrej Soaps (now Godrej Industries) in India recently discovered. The family-owned Godrej group had a centralised structure in which top-management decisions were unchallenged. But soon after the partnership began, junior P&G executives thought nothing of openly challenging senior management's decisions. Similarly, top managers at Godrej Soaps could meet the chairman only by appointment, whereas junior P&G managers would walk into senior executives' offices without notice, and call the executives by their first names. After three years of these tensions, the two companies ended their joint venture in mutual frustration.[20]

AAP/AP

that the type, frequency and duration of conflict among employees with diverse cultural backgrounds was sometimes triggered by cultural assumptions about space and privacy. One employee at an Australian childcare agency said: 'I am Latin American and we are very open and very informal about things. I'm sitting in my office and people come along and they will talk to me and I don't have any problems.' In contrast, she noted that the European librarian in her office was uncomfortable with spontaneous socialising. The study also reported that some employees decorated their work area with cultural artefacts, whereas employees from other cultures felt this personalisation was inappropriate.[17] In each case, cultural differences make it difficult for each party to understand or accept the other party's preferences and actions.

Yet another source of differentiation is cross-generational.[18] Younger and older employees have different needs, different expectations and somewhat different values, which sometimes produces conflicting preferences and actions. Generational gaps have always existed, but this source of conflict is more common today because employees across age groups work together more than ever before. Virtual teams further amplify these cross-cultural and cross-generational conflicts, because virtual teams have more difficulty than face-to-face (co-located) teams when it comes to establishing common mental models, norms and temporal rhythms.[19]

TASK INTERDEPENDENCE

Conflict tends to increase with the level of task interdependence. Task interdependence exists when team members (a) must share common inputs to their individual tasks, (b) need to interact in the process of executing their work, or (c) receive outcomes (such as rewards) that are partly determined by the performance of others. The higher the level of task interdependence, the greater the risk of conflict, because there is a greater chance that each side will disrupt or interfere with the other side's goals.[21]

Other than complete independence, employees tend to have the lowest risk of conflict when working with others in a pooled interdependence relationship. Pooled interdependence occurs where individuals operate independently except for reliance on a common resource or authority (see Chapter 9). The potential for conflict is higher in sequential interdependence work relationships, such as an assembly line. The highest risk of conflict tends to occur in reciprocal interdependence situations. With reciprocal interdependence, employees are highly dependent on each other, and consequently have a higher probability of interfering with each other's work and personal goals.

SCARCE RESOURCES

Resource scarcity generates conflict because each person or unit that requires the same resource necessarily undermines others who also need that resource to fulfil their goals. Consider the feud between Arthur Andersen's partners, described in Reality Check 13.1 (overleaf). These consultants share the same resource—client fees—and the more one consultant receives, the less others receive. This conflict wouldn't exist if clients were plentiful and revenues flowed freely, but of course that is rarely the case. Consequently, each group's goals interfere with the goals of other groups because there isn't enough of the resource for everyone.

AMBIGUOUS RULES

Ambiguous rules breed conflict (as does the complete lack of rules). This occurs because uncertainty increases the risk that one party intends to interfere with the other party's goals. Ambiguity also encourages political tactics, and in some cases employees enter a free-for-all battle to win decisions in their favour. The fee feud at Arthur Andersen (described in Reality Check 13.1) was partly caused by the limited resource (clients and their fees) but also by a lack of rules regarding how to divide up this resource. In particular, the now defunct accounting and consulting firm lacked clear guidelines to determine who should be the engagement partner, so partners battled over this ambiguous decision.

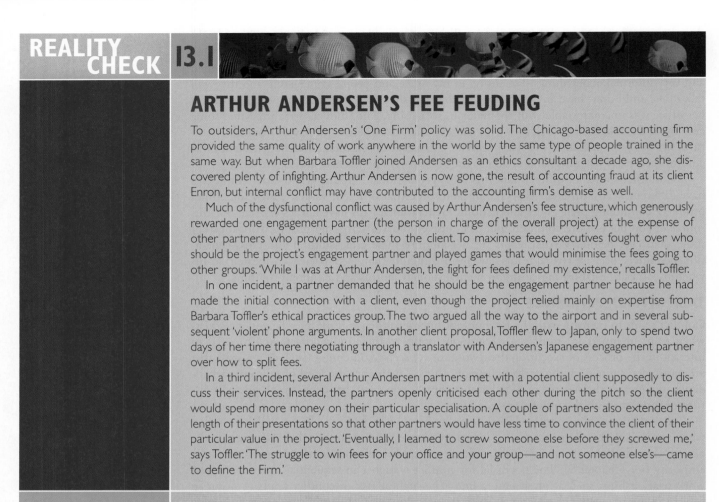

REALITY CHECK 13.1

ARTHUR ANDERSEN'S FEE FEUDING

To outsiders, Arthur Andersen's 'One Firm' policy was solid. The Chicago-based accounting firm provided the same quality of work anywhere in the world by the same type of people trained in the same way. But when Barbara Toffler joined Andersen as an ethics consultant a decade ago, she discovered plenty of infighting. Arthur Andersen is now gone, the result of accounting fraud at its client Enron, but internal conflict may have contributed to the accounting firm's demise as well.

Much of the dysfunctional conflict was caused by Arthur Andersen's fee structure, which generously rewarded one engagement partner (the person in charge of the overall project) at the expense of other partners who provided services to the client. To maximise fees, executives fought over who should be the project's engagement partner and played games that would minimise the fees going to other groups. 'While I was at Arthur Andersen, the fight for fees defined my existence,' recalls Toffler.

In one incident, a partner demanded that he should be the engagement partner because he had made the initial connection with a client, even though the project relied mainly on expertise from Barbara Toffler's ethical practices group. The two argued all the way to the airport and in several subsequent 'violent' phone arguments. In another client proposal, Toffler flew to Japan, only to spend two days of her time there negotiating through a translator with Andersen's Japanese engagement partner over how to split fees.

In a third incident, several Arthur Andersen partners met with a potential client supposedly to discuss their services. Instead, the partners openly criticised each other during the pitch so the client would spend more money on their particular specialisation. A couple of partners also extended the length of their presentations so that other partners would have less time to convince the client of their particular value in the project. 'Eventually, I learned to screw someone else before they screwed me,' says Toffler. 'The struggle to win fees for your office and your group—and not someone else's—came to define the Firm.'

Source: Adapted from B. L. Toffler, *Final Accounting: Ambition, Greed, and the Fall of Arthur Andersen* (New York: Broadway Books, 2003).

COMMUNICATION PROBLEMS

Conflict often occurs as a result of a lack of opportunity, ability or motivation to communicate effectively. Let's look at each of these causes. First, when two parties lack the opportunity to communicate, they tend to use stereotypes to explain past behaviours and anticipate future actions. Unfortunately, stereotypes are sufficiently subjective that emotions can negatively distort the meaning of an opponent's actions, thereby escalating perceptions of conflict. Furthermore, without direct interaction the two sides have less psychological empathy for each other. Second, some people lack the necessary skills to communicate in a diplomatic, non-confrontational manner. When one party communicates its disagreement in an arrogant way, opponents are more likely to heighten their perception of the conflict. Arrogant behaviour also sends a message that one side intends to be competitive rather than cooperative. This may lead the other party to reciprocate with a similar conflict management style.[22] Consequently, as explained earlier, ineffective communication often leads to an escalation in the conflict cycle.

Ineffective communication can also lead to a third problem: less motivation to communicate in the future. Socioemotional conflict is uncomfortable, so people avoid interacting with others in a conflictive relationship. Unfortunately, less communication can further escalate the conflict because there is less opportunity to empathise with the opponent's situation, and the feuding parties are more likely to rely on distorted stereotypes to perceive each other. In fact, conflict tends to further distort these stereotypes through the social identity process (see Chapter 3). People begin to see competitors less favourably so that their self-image remains strong during these threats.[23]

Lack of motivation to communicate also explains (along with different values and beliefs, described earlier) why conflict is more common in cross-cultural relationships. People tend to feel uncomfortable or awkward interacting with co-workers from different cultures, so they are less motivated to engage in dialogue with them. With limited communication, people rely more on stereotypes to fill in missing information. They also tend to misunderstand each other's verbal and nonverbal signals, further escalating the conflict.[24]

INTERPERSONAL CONFLICT MANAGEMENT STYLES

The six structural conditions described above set the stage for conflict. The conflict process identified in Exhibit 13.1 illustrated that these sources of conflict lead to perceptions and emotions. Some people enter a conflict with a **win–win orientation**. This is the perception that the parties will find a mutually beneficial solution to their disagreement. They believe that the resources at stake are expandable rather than fixed if the parties work together to find a creative solution. Other people enter a conflict with a **win–lose orientation**. They adopt the belief that the parties are drawing from a fixed pie, so the more one party receives, the less the other party will receive.

Conflict tends to escalate when the parties develop a win–lose orientation, because they rely on power and politics to gain advantage. A win–lose orientation may occasionally be appropriate when the conflict really is over a fixed resource, but few organisational conflicts are due to perfectly opposing interests with fixed resources. Some degree of win-win orientation is usually advantageous—that is, believing that each side's goals are not perfectly opposing. One possibility is that each party needs different parts of the resource. Another possibility is that various parts of the shared resource have different levels of value to each side.

Consider the example of a supplier and a customer resolving a disagreement over the price of a product. Initially, this seems like a clear win–lose situation—the supplier wants to receive more money for the product, whereas the customer wants to pay less money for it. Yet further discussion may reveal that the customer would be willing to pay more if the product could be provided earlier than originally arranged. The vendor may actually value that earlier delivery because it saves inventory costs. By looking at the bigger picture, both parties can often discover common ground.[25]

Adopting a win–win or win–lose orientation influences our conflict management style, that is, how we act towards the other person. The five conflict resolution styles described below can be placed in a two-dimensional grid reflecting the person's degree of concern for his or her own interests and concern for the other party's interests (see Exhibit 13.3, overleaf). Problem solving is the only style that represents a purely win–win orientation. The other four styles represent variations of the win–lose approach.

- *Problem solving.* Problem solving tries to find a mutually beneficial solution for both parties. Information sharing is an important feature of this style because both parties collaborate to identify common ground and potential solutions that satisfy both (or all) of them.
- *Avoiding.* Avoiding tries to smooth over conflicts or avoid conflict situations altogether. It represents a low concern for both self and the other party; in other words, avoiders try to suppress thinking about the conflict. For example, some employees will rearrange their work area or tasks to minimise interaction with certain co-workers.[26]
- *Forcing.* Forcing tries to win the conflict at the other's expense. This style, which has the strongest win–lose orientation, relies on some of the 'hard' influence tactics described in Chapter 12, particularly assertiveness, to get one's own way.

win–win orientation The belief that the parties will find a mutually beneficial solution to their disagreement.

win–lose orientation The belief that conflicting parties are drawing from a fixed pie, so the more one party receives, the less the other party will receive.

LEARNING OBJECTIVE

Outline the five interpersonal styles of conflict management.

Source: C. K. W. de Dreu, A. Evers,
B. Beersma, E. S. Kluwer and A. Nauta,
'A Theory-based Measure of Conflict
Management Strategies in the
Workplace', *Journal of Organizational
Behavior*, 22 (2001), pp. 645–68.
For earlier variations of this model, see
T. L. Ruble and K. Thomas, 'Support for
a Two-Dimensional Model of Conflict
Behavior', *Organizational Behavior and
Human Performance*, 16 (1976), p. 145.

EXHIBIT 13.3   **Interpersonal conflict management styles**

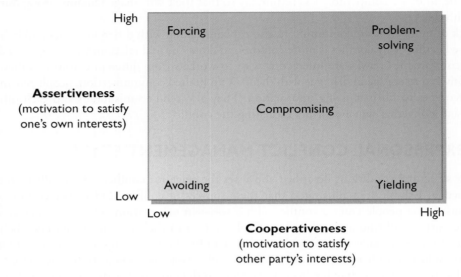

- *Yielding*. Yielding involves giving in completely to the other side's wishes, or at least cooperating with little or no attention to your own interests. This style involves making unilateral concessions and unconditional promises, as well as offering help with no expectation of reciprocal help.
- *Compromising*. Compromising involves looking for a position in which your losses are offset by equally valued gains. It involves matching the other party's concessions, making conditional promises or threats, and actively searching for a middle ground between the interests of the two parties.[27]

CHOOSING THE BEST CONFLICT MANAGEMENT STYLE

Most of us have a preferred conflict management style, but the best style varies with the situation.[28] The forcing style of conflict resolution may be necessary in situations where you know you are correct and the dispute requires a quick solution, such as when the other party is engaging in unethical conduct. This style may also be necessary if the other party would take advantage of more cooperative strategies. However, satisfying your own interests without considering the other party's interests creates considerable risk. Reality Check 13.2 describes how Telstra chief executive Sol Trujillo applied his trademark forcing style, which may have unleashed more resistance from government officials and regulators rather than increasing their compliance to reduce regulatory control over Australia's largest telecommunications company.

The problem-solving style is the preferred approach to resolving conflict in many situations because it is the only one that actively tries to optimise the value for both parties. However, this style works well only when the parties do not have perfectly opposing interests and when they have enough trust and openness to share information. You might think that avoiding is an ineffective conflict management strategy, but it is actually the best approach where conflict has become socioemotional or where negotiating has a higher cost than the benefits of conflict resolution.[29] At the same time, conflict avoidance should not be a long-term solution where the conflict persists, because it increases the other party's frustration.

The yielding style may be appropriate when the other party has substantially more power or the issue is not as important to you as to the other party. On the other hand, yielding behaviours may give the other side unrealistically high expectations, thereby motivating them to seek more from you in the future. In the long run, yielding may produce more conflict

TELSTRA'S NEW EXECUTIVE TEAM TRIES A FORCING CONFLICT HANDLING STYLE

James Davies/Fairfax Photos

Sol Trujillo, the new Telstra chief executive, had barely stepped off the plane from the United States when he boldly warned the Australian government that Telstra was shackled with regulations and policies 'that belonged to the last century' and were unfair to customers. He also met with fund managers, encouraging them to join him in fighting government regulations.

Trujillo quickly filled most of Telstra's top jobs with his American associates, who also applied a tough-talking style. 'Our struggle is against a repressive, intrusive, draconian, punitive system of regulation,' said Phil Burgess, one of Trujillo's most outspoken American imports, hired as Telstra's communication and policy advisor. Less than a month into his new job, Burgess frankly warned government bureaucrats in Canberra that Trujillo's executive team might freeze investment if it didn't get its way. He also boldly stated that he wouldn't recommend Telstra shares to his mother.

The Australian government, which held half of Telstra's shares when Trujillo came on board, was both surprised and offended. Telstra's previous chief executive had maintained a cosy relationship with government officials, even sending an advance copy of any speech that might seem somewhat assertive. Now, Telstra's incoming executive team was publicly browbeating its largest shareholder and quickly sinking Telstra's shares at a time when the government was eager to sell them. '[Trujillo] feels if he pokes us in the eye he'll get what he wants,' suggested one government insider. 'His ways have baffled ministers. We're Australian—we're not used to bolshie tactics from companies.'

Pundits claim that Telstra's board hired Trujillo precisely because of his forceful reputation with government regulators. One former US telecommunications commissioner recalled that, while leading American telecommunications firm US West, Trujillo 'took an attitude of our way or the highway'. Colorado lobbyist Chuck Malick was more blunt. 'I'm really glad [Trujillo is] in Australia and not in the US,' he said. 'Somebody like Sol, he either gets 100 per cent or he is not happy.'

But Trujillo's forcing conflict handling style might not have been the best approach in this situation. Calling Trujillo's executive team a 'disgrace', Prime Minister John Howard ordered Telstra's chairman to rein in the new executive team. Some writers suggest that Trujillo's behaviour has given government officials ammunition to further increase, rather than reduce, the level of government regulation, because they see Trujillo as a preview of what Telstra will be like when the company is free from government ownership.

Trujillo's style also stirred up the Australian Competition and Consumer Commission (ACCC), which applies the regulations that Trujillo is criticising. 'This is so simple: don't engage in anti-competitive conduct,' says ACCC chief Graeme Samuel. 'Telstra seems to think that it ought to be separate from the law, that it's above the law ... And if Telstra, the dominant player in the industry, can't operate in a competitive market, then management needs to take a long hard look at itself.'

Meanwhile, Trujillo isn't sure what all the fuss is about. 'I believe in collaboration, not fighting,' he said. 'What I am trying to do is expand some of the conversation.'

> The forcing style used by Telstra chief executive Sol Trujillo and his imported American executives might not have been the best approach in handling conflict with government leaders.

Sources: L. Bell, 'Trujillo Wages War on Regulation, Mendoza on Trujillo', *Australian Broadcasting Corporation*, 7 September 2005; M. Charles, 'How the Amigos Were Gunned Down', *Herald-Sun* (Sydney), 20 August 2005, 91; D. Crowe, 'The Government's Worst Nightmare', *Australian Financial Review*, 6 August 2005, 19; G. Elliott and M. Sainsbury, 'Telstra Boss Has Form on Stoushes', *Australian*, 10 September 2005, 1; M. Grattan, 'Trujillo's Bad Connection', *The Age* (Melbourne), 17 August 2005, 19; M. Grattan and J. Koutsoukis, 'Mexican Stand-Off', *The Age* (Melbourne), 2 September 2005, 11; A. Kohler, 'Canberra Prepares for Hurricane Sol', *Sydney Morning Herald*, 17 August 2005, 25; J. McCullough, 'Bushies Warm to Sol's Message', *Courier-Mail* (Brisbane), 4 August 2005, 2.

rather than resolve it. The compromising style may be best when there is little hope for mutual gain through problem solving, where both parties have equal power, and where both are under time pressure to settle their differences. However, compromise is rarely a final solution and may cause the parties to overlook options for mutual gain.

CULTURAL AND GENDER DIFFERENCES IN CONFLICT MANAGEMENT STYLES

Cultural differences are more than just a source of conflict. Cultural background also affects the preferred conflict management style.[30] Research from Australia and other countries suggests that people from collectivist cultures—where group goals are valued more than individual goals—are motivated to maintain harmonious relations, and, consequently, are more likely than those from low collectivist cultures to manage disagreements through avoidance or problem solving.

Some writers suggest that men and women also tend to rely on different conflict management styles.[31] Generally speaking, women pay more attention than do men to the relationship between the parties. Consequently, they tend to adopt a problem-solving style in business settings and are more willing to compromise to protect the relationship. Men tend to be more competitive and take a short-term orientation to the relationship. Of course, we must be cautious about these observations because gender has a weak influence on conflict management style.

STRUCTURAL APPROACHES TO CONFLICT MANAGEMENT

Conflict management styles refer to how we approach the other party in a conflict situation. But conflict management also involves altering the underlying structural causes of potential conflict. The main structural approaches are identified in Exhibit 13.4. Although this section discusses ways to reduce conflict, it should be kept in mind that conflict management sometimes calls for increasing conflict. This occurs mainly by reversing the strategies described over the next few pages.[32]

EMPHASISING SUPERORDINATE GOALS

Superordinate goals are common objectives held by conflicting parties that are more important than the departmental or individual goals on which the conflict is based. By increasing com-

LEARNING OBJECTIVE

Summarise six structural approaches to managing conflict.

superordinate goals
A common objective held by conflicting parties that is more important than their conflicting departmental or individual goals.

EXHIBIT 13.4

Structural approaches to conflict management

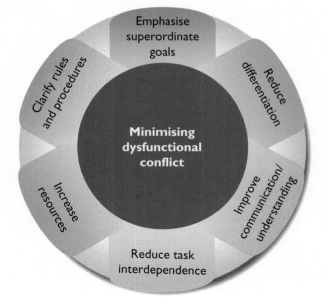

mitment to corporate-wide goals, employees place less emphasis on competing individual or departmental-level goals and therefore feel less conflict with co-workers regarding them. Superordinate goals also potentially reduce the problem of differentiation because they establish a common frame of reference. For example, one study revealed that marketing managers in Hong Kong, China, Japan and the United States were more likely to develop a collaborative conflict management style when executives aligned departmental goals with corporate objectives.[33]

REDUCING DIFFERENTIATION

Another way to minimise dysfunctional conflict is to reduce the differences that produce the conflict in the first place. The more employees think they have common backgrounds or experiences with co-workers, the more motivated they are to coordinate their activities and resolve conflict through constructive discussion with those co-workers.[34] One way to increase this commonality is by creating common experiences. The Manila Diamond Hotel in the Philippines accomplishes this by rotating staff across different departments. 'In Manila Diamond, there is no turf mentality,' explains the hotel's marketing manager. 'We all work together. We even share each other's jobs whenever necessary.' Multinational peacekeeping forces reduce differentiation among troops from the representative nations by providing opportunities for them to socialise and engage in common activities, including eating together.[35]

IMPROVING COMMUNICATION AND UNDERSTANDING

Brisbane City Council law enforcers receive a regular barrage of verbal abuse and occasionally physical attacks when fining people who violate parking, sprinkler and animal regulations. To help them in these potentially volatile situations, Brisbane's inspectors are completing a course at the police academy on tactical communication skills. Along with making a threat assessment, they are learning to stay calm and use communication skills that diffuse rather than escalate the conflict. 'I think it is very hard for someone to stay angry at you when you are just staying nice and calm,' says council law officer Jodie Greer, who recently completed the program.[37]

Toyota drums out differences

Employees at Toyota Motor Sales USA are drumming their way to a common bond and cooperation. Over the past three years more than 3000 Toyota employees have visited the car-maker's training centre (University of Toyota) in Torrance, California, to participate in drum circles. Typically in groups of fifteen to fifty from one department, employees would begin banging on one of the 150 percussion instruments available in the drum room. Few have played a percussion instrument before, so the first attempt is rarely worth recording. 'At first, it sounds pretty terrible, with everyone competing to be the loudest,' admits Ron Johnson, Toyota's resident drum guru and a training centre manager in Torrance. But most groups soon find a common beat without any guidance or conductor. Johnson recalls his first drum circle experience: 'I'll never forget the spirit that came alive inside me. In a matter of moments, perfect strangers came together in synchronistic rhythm to share a common vision.' By the end of the hour-long event, most groups have formed a special bond that apparently increases their cooperation and sense of unity when they return to their jobs.[36]

Edward Carreon/Newshouse News Service

Brisbane City Council law enforcers are discovering that communication plays a vital role in managing conflict. In this situation, verbal and nonverbal communication signals the law enforcers' passive response to the initial aggression, which in most cases diffuses the conflict. The program also teaches the law enforcers to provide logical explanations that deflect the hostilities and open up more attentive dialogue. People are more likely to listen to reason when their hostile behaviour does not evoke hostility in return.

Communication is also important in other organisational circumstances where two warring factions need to understand each other better. This recommendation relates back to the contact hypothesis described in Chapter 3. Specifically, the more meaningful an interaction we have with someone, the less we rely on stereotypes to understand that person.[38] This positive effect is more pronounced when people work closely and frequently together on a meaningful task which requires that they rely on each other (i.e. cooperate rather than compete with each other). Another important ingredient is that the parties have equal status in that context.

There are two important caveats regarding the communication–understanding strategy. First, this strategy should be applied only *after* differentiation between the two sides has been reduced. If perceived differentiation remains high, attempts to manage conflict through dialogue might have the opposite effect, because defence mechanisms are more likely to kick into action. Specifically, when forced to interact with people who we believe are quite different and in conflict with us, we tend to select information that reinforces that view rather than try to understand them better.[39] Thus, communication and understanding interventions are effective only when differentiation is sufficiently low.

Second, resolving differences through direct communication with the opposing party is a distinctly Western strategy that is not as comfortably applied in most parts of Asia and in other collectivist cultures.[40] As noted earlier, people in high collectivist cultures prefer an avoidance conflict management style because it is the most consistent with harmony and face saving. Direct communication is a high-risk strategy because it easily threatens the need to save face and maintain harmony.

Talking circles

Where avoidance is ineffective in the long run, some collectivist groups engage in structured forms of dialogue that enable communication with less risk of upsetting harmony. One such practice in several indigenous cultures around the world is the talking circle.[41] A talking circle is an ancient group process used to educate, make decisions and repair group harmony due to conflict. Participants sit in a circle and often begin with a song, a prayer, shaking hands with the nearest person, or some other communal activity. They then share their experiences, information and stories relating to the issue.

A talking stick or other natural object (rock, feather) is held by the person speaking, which minimises interruptions and dysfunctional verbal reactions by others. Talking circles are not aimed at solving problems through negotiated discussion. In fact, talking circle norms usually discourage participants from responding to someone else's statements. Rather, the emphasis is on healing relationships and restoring harmony, typically through the circle's communal experience and improved understanding of each person's views. Talking circles are rare in business organisations, but they have been applied in meetings between Aboriginal peoples and government in Australia.

REDUCING TASK INTERDEPENDENCE

Conflict increases with the level of interdependence, so minimising dysfunctional conflict might involve reducing the level of interdependence between the parties. If cost-effective, this might occur by dividing the shared resource so that each party has exclusive use of part of it. Sequentially or reciprocally interdependent jobs might be combined so that they form a pooled interdependence. For example, rather than having one employee serve customers and another operate the cash register, each employee could handle both customer activities alone. Buffers also help to reduce task interdependence between people. Buffers include resources, such as adding more inventory between people who perform sequential tasks. Organisations also use human buffers—people who serve as intermediaries between interdependent people or work units who do not get along through direct interaction.

INCREASING RESOURCES

An obvious way to reduce conflict due to resource scarcity is to increase the amount of resources available. Corporate decision makers might quickly dismiss this solution because of the costs involved. However, they need to carefully compare these costs with the costs of dysfunctional conflict arising out of resource scarcity.

CLARIFYING RULES AND PROCEDURES

Conflicts that arise from ambiguous rules can be minimised by establishing rules and procedures. Armstrong World Industries, Inc. applied this strategy when consultants and information systems employees clashed while working together on development of a client–server network. Information systems employees at the flooring and building materials company thought they should be in charge, whereas consultants believed they had the senior role. Also, the consultants wanted to work long hours and take Friday off to fly home, whereas Armstrong employees wanted to work regular hours. The company reduced these conflicts by having both parties agree on specific responsibilities and roles. The agreement also assigned two senior executives at the companies to establish rules if future disagreements arose.[42]

Rules establish changes to the terms of interdependence, such as an employee's hours of work or a supplier's fulfilment of an order. In most cases, the parties affected by these rules are involved in the process of deciding the terms of interdependence. By redefining the terms of interdependence, the strategy of clarifying rules is part of the larger process of negotiation.

RESOLVING CONFLICT THROUGH NEGOTIATION

Think back through yesterday's events. Maybe you had to work out an agreement with other students about what tasks to complete for a team project. The chances are that you shared transportation with someone, so you had to clarify the timing of the ride. Then perhaps there was the question of who made dinner. Each of these daily events created potential conflict, and they were resolved through negotiation. **Negotiation** occurs whenever two or more conflicting parties attempt to resolve their divergent goals by redefining the terms of their interdependence. In other words, people negotiate when they think that discussion can produce a more satisfactory arrangement (at least for them) in their exchange of goods or services.

negotiation Occurs whenever two or more conflicting parties attempt to resolve their divergent goals by redefining the terms of their interdependence.

As you can see, negotiation is not an obscure practice reserved for labour and management bosses when hammering out a workplace agreement. Everyone negotiates, every day. Most of the time you don't even realise that you are in negotiations. Negotiation is particularly evident in the workplace because employees work interdependently with each other. They negotiate with their supervisors over next month's work assignments, with customers over the sale and delivery schedules of their product, and with co-workers over when to have lunch. And yes, they occasionally negotiate with each other in labour disputes and workplace agreements.

Some writers suggest that negotiations are more successful when the parties adopt a problem-solving style, whereas others caution that this conflict management style is sometimes costly.[43] We know that any win–lose style (forcing, yielding, etc.) is unlikely to produce the optimal solution, because the parties have not shared information necessary to discover a mutually satisfactory solution. On the other hand, we must be careful about adopting an openly problem-solving style until mutual trust has been established.

The concern with the problem-solving style is that information is power, so information sharing gives the other party more power to leverage a better deal if the opportunity occurs. Skilled negotiators often adopt a cautious problem-solving style at the outset by sharing information slowly and determining whether the other side will reciprocate. In this respect, they try to establish trust with the other party.[44] They switch to one of the win–lose styles only when it becomes apparent that a win–win solution is not possible or the other party is unwilling to share information with a cooperative orientation.

BARGAINING ZONE MODEL OF NEGOTIATIONS

The negotiation process moves each party along a continuum, with an area of potential overlap called the *bargaining zone*.[45] Exhibit 13.5 displays one possible bargaining zone situation. This linear diagram illustrates a purely win–lose situation; one side's gain will be the other's loss. However, the bargaining zone model can also be applied to situations in which both sides potentially gain from the negotiations. As this model illustrates, the parties typically establish three main negotiating points. The *initial offer point* is the team's opening offer to the other party. This may be its best expectation or a pie-in-the-sky starting point. The *target point* is the team's realistic goal or expectation for a final agreement. The *resistance point* is the point beyond which the team will make no further concessions.

The parties begin negotiations by describing their initial offer point for each item on the agenda. In most cases, the participants know that this is only a starting point that will change as both sides offer concessions. In win–lose situations, neither the target nor the resistance point is revealed to the other party. However, people try to discover the other side's resistance point because this knowledge helps them determine how much they can gain without breaking off negotiations. When the parties have a win–win orientation, on the other hand, the objective is to find a creative solution that keeps everyone close to their initial offer points. They hope to find an arrangement by which each side loses relatively little value on some issues and gains significantly more on other issues.

SITUATIONAL INFLUENCES ON NEGOTIATIONS

The effectiveness of negotiating depends on both the situation and the behaviours of the negotiators. Four of the most important situational factors are location, physical setting, time and audience.

LEARNING OBJECTIVE

Outline four situational influences on negotiations.

EXHIBIT 13.5   Bargaining zone model of negotiations

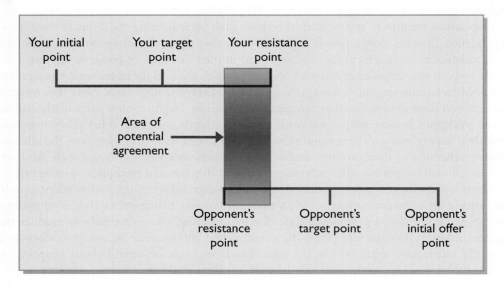

Your initial point   Your target point   Your resistance point

Area of potential agreement

Opponent's resistance point   Opponent's target point   Opponent's initial offer point

Location

It is easier to negotiate on your own turf because you are familiar with the negotiating environment and are able to maintain comfortable routines.[46] Also, there is no need to cope with travel-related stress or depend on others for resources during the negotiation. Of course, you can't walk out of negotiations as easily when on your own turf, but this is usually a minor issue. Considering these strategic benefits of home turf, many negotiators agree to neutral territory. Telephones, videoconferences and other forms of information technology potentially avoid territorial issues, but skilled negotiators usually prefer the media richness of face-to-face meetings. Frank Lowy, co-founder of Australian retail property giant Westfield Group, says that telephones are 'too cold' for negotiating. 'From a voice I don't get all the cues I need. I go by touch and feel and I need to see the other person.'[47]

Physical setting

The physical distance between the parties and the formality of the setting can influence the parties' orientation towards each other and the disputed issues. So can the seating arrangements. People who sit face to face are more likely to develop a win–lose orientation towards the conflict situation. In contrast, some negotiation groups deliberately intersperse participants around the table to convey a win–win orientation. Others arrange the seating so that both parties face a white board, reflecting the notion that both parties face the same problem or issue.

Time passage and deadlines

The more time people invest in negotiations, the stronger is their commitment to reaching an agreement. This increases the motivation to resolve the conflict, but it also fuels the escalation of commitment problems described in Chapter 8. For example, the more time put into negotiations, the stronger the tendency to make unwarranted concessions so that the negotiations do not fail.

Time deadlines may be useful to the extent that they motivate the parties to complete negotiations. However, time pressures are usually a liability in negotiations.[48] One problem is that time pressure inhibits a problem-solving conflict management style, because the parties have less time to exchange information or present flexible offers. Negotiators under time pressure also process information less effectively, so they have less creative ability to discover a win–win solution to the conflict. There is also anecdotal evidence that negotiators make excessive concessions and soften their demands more rapidly as the deadline approaches.

Audience characteristics

Most negotiators have audiences—anyone with a vested interest in the negotiation outcomes, such as executives, other team members or the general public. Negotiators tend to act in one way when their audience observes the negotiation or has detailed information about the process and in another way when the audience sees only the end results.[49] When the audience has direct surveillance over the proceedings, negotiators tend to be more competitive, less willing to make concessions, and more likely to engage in political tactics against the other party. This 'hardline' behaviour shows the audience that the negotiator is working for their interests. With their audience watching, negotiators also have more interest in saving face.

NEGOTIATOR BEHAVIOURS

Negotiator behaviours play an important role in resolving conflict. Four of the most important behaviours are setting goals, gathering information, communicating effectively and making concessions.

- *Preparation and goal setting.* Research has consistently reported that people have more favourable negotiation results when they prepare for the negotiation and set goals.[50] In particular, negotiators should carefully think through their initial offer, their target points and their resistance points. They need to consider alternative strategies in case the negotiation fails. Negotiators also need to check their underlying assumptions, as well as their goals and values. Equally important is the need to research what the other party wants from the negotiation.

- *Gathering information.* 'Seek to understand before you seek to be understood.' This popular philosophy from management guru Stephen Covey applies to effective negotiations. It means that we should spend time listening closely to the other party and asking for details.[51] One way to improve the information-gathering process is to have a team of people participate in negotiations. Asian companies tend to have large negotiation teams for this purpose.[52] With more information about the opponent's interests and needs, negotiators are better able to discover low-cost concessions or proposals that will satisfy the other side.

- *Communicating effectively.* Effective negotiators communicate in a way that maintains effective relationships between the parties. Specifically, they minimise socioemotional conflict by focusing on issues rather than people. Effective negotiators also avoid irritating statements such as 'I think you'll agree that this is a generous offer'. Third, effective negotiators are masters of persuasion. They structure the content of their message so it is accepted by others, not merely understood.[53]

- *Making concessions.* Concessions are important because (1) they enable the parties to move towards the area of potential agreement, (2) they symbolise each party's motivation to bargain in good faith, and (3) they tell the other party of the relative importance of the negotiating items.[54] How many concessions should you make? This varies with the other party's expectations and the level of trust between you. For instance, many Chinese negotiators are wary of people who change their position during the early stages of negotiations. Similarly, some writers warn that Russian negotiators tend to view concessions as a sign of weakness rather than a sign of trust.[55] Generally, the best strategy is to be moderately tough and give just enough concessions to communicate sincerity and motivation to resolve the conflict.[56] Being too tough can undermine relations between the parties; giving too many concessions implies weakness and encourages the other party to use power and resistance.

THIRD-PARTY CONFLICT RESOLUTION

third-party conflict resolution Any attempt by a relatively neutral person to help the parties resolve their differences.

LEARNING OBJECTIVE

Compare and contrast the three types of third-party dispute resolution.

Most of this chapter has focused on people directly involved in a conflict, yet many disputes in organisational settings are resolved with the assistance of a third party. **Third-party conflict resolution** is any attempt by a relatively neutral person to help the parties resolve their differences. There are generally three types of third-party dispute resolution activities: arbitration, inquisition and mediation. These activities can be classified by their level of control over the decision (see Exhibit 13.6).[57]

- *Arbitration.* Arbitrators have high control over the final decision but low control over the process. Executives engage in this strategy by following previously agreed rules of due process, listening to arguments from the disputing employees, and making a binding decision. Arbitration is applied as the final stage of grievances by unionised employees, but it is also becoming more common in non-union conflicts.

- *Inquisition.* Inquisitors control all discussion about the conflict. Like arbitrators, they have high decision control because they choose the form of conflict resolution. However, inquisitors also have high process control because they choose which information to examine and how to examine it, and they generally decide how the conflict resolution process will be handled.

- *Mediation.* Mediators have high control over the intervention process. In fact, their main purpose is to manage the process and context of interaction between the disputing parties. However, the parties make the final decision about how to resolve their differences. Thus, mediators have little or no control over the conflict resolution decision.

Types of third-party intervention

EXHIBIT 13.6

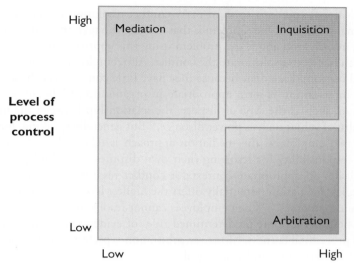

CHOOSING THE BEST THIRD-PARTY INTERVENTION STRATEGY

Team leaders, executives and co-workers regularly intervene in disputes between employees and departments. Sometimes they adopt a mediator role; at other times they serve as arbitrators. However, research suggests that people in positions of authority (e.g. managers) usually adopt an inquisitional approach whereby they dominate the intervention process as well as making a binding decision.[58] Managers like the inquisition approach because it is consistent

More listening, less inquisition to resolve workplace conflict

Research suggests that managers prefer an inquisitional approach to resolving conflicts among employees; they decide the conflict solution as well as the process to determine that solution. But this command-and-control approach is often the least effective strategy, partly because employees don't have any voice or control when managers get involved. Steve Lancken, a professional mediator in Sydney, believes that managers need to step back and allow the disputants to give their points of view. 'It's more about listening than talking, understanding what someone's got to say before reacting,' Lancken explains. 'When people don't feel as if they have been heard, their level of anger and anxiety increases. So the first tip to dealing with conflict is to listen and to demonstrate that you have heard what the other person has to say.'[60]

with the decision-oriented nature of managerial jobs, gives them control over the conflict process and outcome, and tends to resolve disputes efficiently.

However, the inquisitional approach to third-party conflict resolution is usually the least effective in organisational settings.[59] One problem is that leaders who take an inquisitional role tend to collect limited information about the problem using this approach, so their imposed decision may produce an ineffective solution to the conflict. Also, employees often view inquisitional procedures and outcomes as unfair because they have little control over the approach.

Which third-party intervention is most appropriate in organisations? The answer partly depends on the situation, such as the type of dispute, the relationship between the manager and employees, and cultural values such as power distance.[61] But generally speaking, for everyday disputes between two employees, the mediation approach is usually best, because this gives employees more responsibility for resolving their own disputes. The third-party representative merely establishes an appropriate context for conflict resolution. Although not as efficient as other strategies, mediation potentially offers the highest level of employee satisfaction with the process and outcomes.[62] When employees cannot resolve their differences, arbitration seems to work best, because the predetermined rules of evidence and other processes create a higher sense of procedural fairness. Moreover, arbitration is preferred where the organisation's goals should take priority over individual goals.

CHAPTER SUMMARY

Conflict is the process in which one party perceives that its interests are being opposed or negatively affected by another party. The conflict process begins with the sources of conflict. These sources lead one or both sides to perceive a conflict and to experience conflict emotions. This, in turn, produces manifest conflict, such as behaviours towards the other side. The conflict process often escalates through a series of episodes.

Conflict management maximises the benefits and minimises the dysfunctional consequences of conflict. Constructive conflict, a possible benefit of conflict, occurs when team members debate their different perceptions about an issue in a way that keeps the conflict focused on the task rather than people. Socioemotional conflict, a negative outcome, occurs when differences are viewed as personal attacks rather than attempts to resolve an issue. Socioemotional conflict tends to emerge in most constructive conflict episodes, but it is less likely to dominate when the parties are emotionally intelligent, have a cohesive team, and have supportive team norms. The main problems with conflict are that it may lead to job stress, dissatisfaction and turnover.

Conflict tends to increase when people have incompatible goals, differentiation (different values and beliefs), interdependent tasks, scarce resources, ambiguous rules and problems communicating with each other. Conflict is more common in a multicultural workforce because of greater differentiation and communication problems among employees.

People with a win–win orientation believe that the parties will find a mutually beneficial solution to their disagreement. Those with a win–lose orientation adopt the belief that the parties are drawing from a fixed pie. The win–lose orientation tends to escalate conflict. Among the five interpersonal conflict management styles, only problem solving represents a purely win–win orientation. The four other styles—avoiding, forcing, yielding and compromising—adopt some variation of a win–lose orientation. Women and people with high collectivism tend to use a problem-solving or avoidance style more than men and people with high individualism.

Structural approaches to conflict management include emphasising superordinate goals, reducing differentiation, improving communication and understanding, reducing task interdependence, increasing resources, and clarifying rules and procedures. These elements can also be altered to stimulate conflict.

Negotiation occurs whenever two or more conflicting parties attempt to resolve their divergent goals by redefining the terms of their interdependence. Negotiations are influenced by several situational factors, including location, physical setting, time passage and deadlines, and audience. Important negotiator behaviours include preparation and goal setting, gathering information, communicating effectively and making concessions.

Third-party conflict resolution is any attempt by a relatively neutral person to help the parties resolve their differences. The three main forms of third-party dispute resolution are mediation, arbitration and inquisition. Managers tend to use an inquisition approach, although mediation and arbitration are more appropriate, depending on the situation.

KEY TERMS

conflict p. 386
conflict management p. 387
constructive conflict p. 387

negotiation p. 399
socioemotional conflict p. 387
superordinate goals p. 396

third-party conflict resolution p. 402
win–lose orientation p. 393
win–win orientation p. 393

DISCUSSION QUESTIONS

1. Distinguish constructive conflict from socioemotional conflict and explain how to apply the former without having the latter become a problem.

2. The chief executive of Creative Toys Pty Ltd read about cooperation in Japanese companies and vowed to bring this same philosophy to his company. The goal was to avoid all conflict, so that employees would work cooperatively and be happier at Creative Toys. Discuss the merits and limitations of the proposed conflict avoidance policy.

3. Conflict between managers emerged soon after a French company acquired a Swedish firm. The Swedes perceived the French management as hierarchical and arrogant, whereas the French thought the Swedes were naive, cautious and lacking an achievement orientation. Describe ways to reduce dysfunctional conflict in this situation.

4. This chapter describes three levels of task interdependence that exist in interpersonal and intergroup relationships. Identify examples of these three levels in your work or university activities. How do these three levels affect the potential for conflict for you?

5. Jane has just been appointed purchasing manager of Wollongong Technologies. The previous purchasing manager, who recently retired, was known for his 'winner-take-all' approach to suppliers. He continually fought for more discounts

and was sceptical about any special deals proposed by suppliers. A few suppliers refused to do business with Wollongong Technologies, but senior management was confident that the former purchasing manager's approach minimised the company's costs. Jane wants to try a more problem-solving approach to working with suppliers. Will her approach work? How should she adopt a more problem-solving approach in future negotiations with suppliers?

6. You are a special assistant to the commander-in-chief of a peacekeeping mission to a war-torn part of the world. The unit consists of a few thousand peacekeeping troops from Australia, France, India and four other countries. The troops will work together for approximately one year. What strategies would you recommend to improve mutual understanding and to minimise conflict among these troops?

7. Suppose that you head one of five divisions in a multinational organisation and are about to begin this year's budget deliberations at headquarters. What are the characteristics of your audience in these negotiations and what effect might they have on your negotiation behaviour?

8. Managers tend to use an inquisitional approach to resolving disputes between employees and departments. Describe the inquisitional approach and discuss its appropriateness in organisational settings.

SKILL BUILDER | 13.1   CONFLICT IN CLOSE QUARTERS

CASE STUDY

A team of psychologists at Moscow's Institute for Biomedical Problems (IBMP) wanted to learn more about the dynamics of long-term isolation in space. This knowledge would be applied to the International Space Station, a joint project of several countries that would send people into space for more than six months. It would eventually include a trip to Mars taking up to three years.

The IBMP psychologists set up a replica of the Mir space station in Moscow. They then arranged for three international researchers from Japan, Canada and Austria to spend 110 days isolated in a chamber the size of a train carriage. This chamber joined a smaller chamber where four Russian cosmonauts had already completed half of their 240 days of isolation. This was the first time an international crew had been involved in the studies. None of the participants spoke English as their first language, yet they communicated throughout their stay in English at varying levels of proficiency.

Judith Lapierre, a French-Canadian, was the only female in the experiment. As well as having a PhD in public health and social medicine, Lapierre had studied space sociology at the International Space University in France, and had conducted isolation research in the

Antarctic. This was her fourth trip to Russia, where she had learned the language. The mission was supposed to have a second female participant from the Japanese space program, but she had not been selected by IBMP.

The Japanese and Austrian participants viewed the participation of a woman as a favourable factor, says Lapierre. For example, to make the surroundings more comfortable, they rearranged the furniture, hung posters on the wall, and put a tablecloth on the kitchen table. 'We adapted our environment, whereas the Russians just viewed it as something to be endured,' she explains. 'We decorated for Christmas, because I'm the kind of person who likes to host people.'

NEW YEAR'S EVE TURMOIL

Ironically, it was at one of those social events, the New Year's Eve party, that events took a turn for the worse. After drinking vodka (allowed by the Russian space agency), two of the Russian cosmonauts got into a fistfight that left blood splattered on the chamber walls. At one point a colleague hid the knives in the station's kitchen because of fears that the two Russians might have stabbed each other. The two cosmonauts, who generally did not get along, had to be restrained by other men. Soon after that brawl, the Russian commander grabbed Lapierre, dragged her out of view of the television monitoring cameras, and kissed her aggressively—twice. Lapierre fought him off, but the message didn't register. He tried to kiss her again the next morning.

The next day the international crew complained to IBMP about the behaviour of the Russian cosmonauts. The Russian institute apparently took no action against any of the aggressors. Instead, the institute's psychologists replied that the incidents were part of the experiment. They wanted crew members to solve their personal problems with mature discussion, without asking for outside help. 'You have to understand that Mir is an autonomous object, far away from anything,' Vadim Gushin, the IBMP psychologist in charge of the project, explained after the experiment had ended in March. 'If the crew can't solve problems among themselves, they can't work together.'

Following IBMP's response, the international crew wrote a scathing letter to the Russian institute and the space agencies involved in the experiment. 'We had never expected such events to take place in a highly controlled scientific experiment where individuals go through a multi-step selection process,' they wrote. 'If we had known . . . we would not have joined it as subjects.' The letter also complained about IBMP's response to their concerns.

Informed of the New Year's Eve incident, the Japanese space program convened an emergency meeting on 2 January to address the incidents. Soon after, the Japanese team member quit, apparently shocked by IBMP's inaction. He was replaced with a Russian researcher on the international team. Ten days after the fight—a little over a month after the international team began the mission—the doors between the Russians' chamber and the international crew's chamber were barred at the request of the international research team. Lapierre later emphasised that this action was taken because of concerns about violence, not the incident involving her.

A STOLEN KISS OR SEXUAL HARASSMENT

By the end of the experiment in March, news of the fistfight between the cosmonauts and the commander's attempts to kiss Lapierre had reached the public. Russian scientists attempted to play down the kissing incident by saying that it was one fleeting kiss, a clash of cultures, and a female participant who was too emotional.

'In the West, some kinds of kissing are regarded as sexual harassment. In our culture it's nothing,' said Russian scientist Vadim Gushin in one interview. In another interview he explained: 'The problem of sexual harassment is given a lot of attention in North America but less in Europe. In Russia it is even less of an issue, not because we are more or less moral than the rest of the world; we just have different priorities.'

Judith Lapierre says the kissing incident was tolerable compared with this reaction from the Russian scientists who conducted the experiment. 'They don't get it at all,' she complained. 'They don't think anything is wrong. I'm more frustrated than ever. The worst thing is that they don't realise it was wrong.'

Norbert Kraft, the Austrian scientist on the international team, also disagreed with the Russian interpretation of events. 'They're trying to protect themselves,' he says. 'They're trying to put the fault on others. But this is not a cultural issue. If a woman doesn't want to be kissed, it is not acceptable.'

QUESTIONS

1. Identify the different conflict episodes that exist in this case? Who was in conflict with whom?

2. What are the sources of conflict for these conflict incidents?

3. What conflict management style(s) did Lapierre, the international team and Gushin use to resolve these conflicts? What style(s) would have worked best in these situations?

4. What conflict management interventions were applied here? Did they work? What alternative strategies would work best in this situation and in the future?

The facts of this case were pieced together by Steven L. McShane from the following sources: G. Sinclair Jr, 'If You Scream in Space, Does Anyone Hear?', *Winnipeg Free Press*, 5 May 2000, p. A4; S. Martin, 'Reining in the Space Cowboys', *Globe & Mail*, 19 April 2000, p. R1; M. Gray, 'A Space Dream Sours', *Maclean's*, 17 April 2000, p. 26; E. Niiler, 'In Search of the Perfect Astronaut', *Boston Globe*, 4 April 2000, p. E4; J. Tracy, '110-Day Isolation Ends in Sullen ... Isolation', *Moscow Times*, 30 March 2000, p. 1; M. Warren, 'A Mir Kiss?', *Daily Telegraph* (London), 30 March 2000, p. 22; G. York, 'Canadian's Harassment Complaint Scorned', *Globe & Mail*, 25 March 2000, p. A2; S. Nolen, 'Lust in Space', *Globe & Mail*, 24 March 2000, p. A3.

SKILL BUILDER | 13.2   UGLI ORANGE ROLE-PLAY

TEAM EXERCISE

PURPOSE
This exercise is designed to help you understand the dynamics of interpersonal and intergroup conflict as well as the effectiveness of negotiation strategies under specific conditions.

MATERIALS
The instructor will distribute roles for Dr Roland, Dr Jones and a few observers. Ideally, each negotiation should occur in a private area away from other negotiations.

INSTRUCTIONS
Step 1: The instructor will divide the class into an even number of teams of three people each, with one participant left over for each team formed (e.g. six observers if there are six teams). One-half of the teams will take the role of Dr Roland and the other half will be Dr Jones. The instructor will distribute the roles after the teams have been formed.

Step 2: Members within each team are given ten minutes (or other time limit stated by the instructor) to learn their roles and decide their negotiating strategy.

Step 3: After reading their roles and discussing their strategy, each Dr Jones team is matched with a Dr Roland team to conduct negotiations. Observers will receive observation forms from the instructor, and two observers will be assigned to watch the paired teams during pre-negotiations and subsequent negotiations.

Step 4: As soon as Roland and Jones reach agreement or at the end of the time allotted for the negotiation (whichever comes first), the Roland and Jones teams report to the instructor for further instruction.

Step 5: At the end of the exercise, the class will congregate to discuss the negotiations. Observers, negotiators and instructors will then discuss their observations and experiences and the implications for conflict management and negotiation.

This exercise was developed by Robert J. House, Wharton Business School, University of Pennsylvania. A similar incident is also attributed to earlier writing by R. R. Blake and J. S. Mouton.

THE DUTCH TEST FOR CONFLICT HANDLING

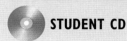 **STUDENT CD**

PURPOSE
This self-assessment is designed to help you to identify your preferred conflict management style.

INSTRUCTIONS
Read each of the statements below and circle the response that you believe best reflects your position regarding each statement. Then use the scoring key in Appendix B to calculate your results for each conflict management style. This exercise is completed alone so students can assess themselves honestly without concerns of social comparison. However, class discussion will focus on the different conflict management styles and the situations in which each is most appropriate.

DUTCH TEST FOR CONFLICT HANDLING

When I have a conflict at work, I do the following:	Not at all				Very much
1. I give in to the wishes of the other party.	1	2	3	4	5
2. I try to realise a middle-of-the-road solution.	1	2	3	4	5
3. I push my own point of view.	1	2	3	4	5
4. I examine issues until I find a solution that really satisfies me and the other party.	1	2	3	4	5
5. I avoid confrontation about our differences.	1	2	3	4	5
6. I concur with the other party.	1	2	3	4	5
7. I emphasise that we have to find a compromise solution.	1	2	3	4	5
8. I search for gains.	1	2	3	4	5
9. I stand for my own and other's goals and interests.	1	2	3	4	5
10. I avoid differences of opinion as much as possible.	1	2	3	4	5
11. I try to accommodate the other party.	1	2	3	4	5
12. I insist we both give in a little.	1	2	3	4	5
13. I fight for a good outcome for myself.	1	2	3	4	5
14. I examine ideas from both sides to find a mutually optimal solution.	1	2	3	4	5
15. I try to make differences seem less severe.	1	2	3	4	5
16. I adapt to the parties' goals and interests.	1	2	3	4	5
17. I strive whenever possible towards a fifty-fifty compromise.	1	2	3	4	5
18. I do everything to win.	1	2	3	4	5
19. I work out a solution that serves my own and other's interests as well as possible.	1	2	3	4	5
20. I try to avoid a confrontation with the other.	1	2	3	4	5

Source: C. K. W. de Dreu, A. Evers, B. Beersma, E. S. Kluwer and A. Nauta, 'A Theory-based Measure of Conflict Management Strategies in the Workplace', *Journal of Organizational Behavior*, vol. 22. Copyright © 2001 John Wiley & Sons Limited. Reproduced with permission.

NOTES

1   'Corrigan Speaks out over Toll Holdings' Takeover Bid', *Australian Broadcasting Corporation*, 18 September 2005; A. Clark, 'Branson in Battle for Virgin Blue', *The Guardian* (London), 5 October 2005, 23; T. Harcourt, 'Toll, Patrick Clash in Rail Boardroom', *Australian Financial Review*, 25 October 2005, 14; A. Hughes, 'PN Chief Resigns over "Threats"', *Australian Financial Review*, 15 October 2005, 15; P. Williams, 'Corrigan Promises Toll Boss the Fight of His Life', *Australian Financial Review*, 21 October 2005, 1; L. Wood, 'Juggernauts: How the Two Titans of Transport Collided Head On', *The Age* (Melbourne), 22 October 2005, 15.

2   J. A. Wall and R. R. Callister, 'Conflict and Its Management', *Journal of Management*, 21 (1995), 515–58; M. A. Rahim, 'Toward a Theory of Managing Organizational Conflict', *International Journal of Conflict Management* 13, no. 3 (2002), 206–35.

3   L. Pondy, 'Organizational Conflict: Concepts and Models', *Administrative Science Quarterly* 2 (1967), 296–320; K. W. Thomas, 'Conflict and Negotiation Processes in Organizations', in *Handbook of Industrial and Organizational Psychology*, ed. M. D. Dunnette and L. M. Hough, 2nd edn (Palo Alto, CA: Consulting Psychologists Press, 1992), 651–718.

4   M. A. Von Glinow, D. L. Shapiro and J. M. Brett, 'Can We Talk, and Should We? Managing Emotional Conflict in Multicultural Teams', *Academy of Management Review* 29, no. 4 (2004), 578–92.

5   G. E. Martin and T. J. Bergman, 'The Dynamics of Behavioral Response to Conflict in the Workplace', *Journal of Occupational & Organizational Psychology* 69 (December 1996), 377–87; J. M. Brett, D. L. Shapiro and A. L. Lytle, 'Breaking the Bonds of Reciprocity in Negotiations', *Academy of Management Journal* 41 (August 1998), 410–24.

6   H. Witteman, 'Analyzing Interpersonal Conflict: Nature of Awareness, Type of Initiating Event, Situational Perceptions, and Management Styles', *Western Journal of Communications* 56 (1992), 248–80; Wall and Callister, 'Conflict and Its Management'.

7   M. Rempel and R. J. Fisher, 'Perceived Threat, Cohesion, and Group Problem Solving in Intergroup Conflict', *International Journal of Conflict Management* 8 (1997), 216–34.

8   D. Tjosvold, *The Conflict-Positive Organization* (Reading, MA: Addison-Wesley, 1991); K. M. Eisenhardt, J. L. Kahwajy and L. J. Bourgeois III, 'Conflict and Strategic Choice: How Top Management Teams Disagree', *California Management Review* 39 (Winter 1997), 42–62; L. H. Pelled, K. M. Eisenhardt and K. R. Xin, 'Exploring the Black Box: An Analysis of Work Group Diversity, Conflict, and Performance', *Administrative Science Quarterly* 44 (March 1999), 1–28; S. Schulz-Hardt, M. Jochims and D. Frey, 'Productive Conflict in Group Decision Making: Genuine and Contrived Dissent as Strategies to Counteract Biased Information Seeking', *Organizational Behavior and Human Decision Processes* 88 (2002), 563–86.

9   'Power to the First Movers', *Sunday Times* (Singapore), 9 April 2000, 9.

10 Trans-Tasman Business Circle, 'Waste Management New Zealand—a Formula for Success', www.transtasmanbusiness.com.au/syme_akl.html (accessed 5 October 2005); R. Birchfield, 'The Management Interview: Jim Syme', *New Zealand Management* (May 2004), 32.

11 Wood, 'Juggernauts: How the Two Titans of Transport Collided Head On'.

12 C. K. W. De Dreu and L. R. Weingart, 'Task Versus Relationship Conflict, Team Performance, and Team Member Satisfaction: A Meta-Analysis', *Journal of Applied Psychology* 88 (August 2003), 587–604.

13 J. Yang and K. W. Mossholder, 'Decoupling Task and Relationship Conflict: The Role of Intergroup Emotional Processing', *Journal of Organizational Behavior* 25 (2004), 589–605.

14 R. E. Walton and J. M. Dutton, 'The Management of Conflict: A Model and Review', *Administrative Science Quarterly* 14 (1969), 73–84.

15 Wood, 'Juggernauts: How the Two Titans of Transport Collided Head On'.

16 D. M. Brock, D. Barry and D. C. Thomas, '"Your Forward Is Our Reverse, Your Right, Our Wrong": Rethinking Multinational Planning Processes in Light of National Culture', *International Business Review* 9 (2000), 687–701.

17 O. B. Ayoko and C. E. J. Härtel, 'The Role of Space as Both a Conflict Trigger and a Conflict Control Mechanism in Culturally Heterogeneous Workgroups', *Applied Psychology: An International Journal* 52, no. 3 (2003), 383–412.

18 R. Zemke and B. Filipczak, *Generations at Work: Managing the Clash of Veterans, Boomers, Xers, and Nexters in Your Workplace* (New York: Amacom, 1999); P. Harris, 'Boomers vs. Echo Boomer: The Work War', *T+D* (May 2005), 44–9.

19 P. Hinds and D. E. Bailey, 'Out of Sight, out of Sync: Understanding Conflict in Distributed Teams', *Organization Science* 14, no. 6 (2003), 615–32; P. Hinds and M. Mortensen, 'Understanding Conflict in Geographically Distributed Teams: The Moderating Effects of Shared Identity, Shared Context, and Spontaneous Communication', *Organization Science* 16, no. 3 (May–June 2005), 290–307.

20 P. Sangameshwaran and A. Sharma, 'Lessons from Corporate Divorce', *Business Standard* (India), 12 June 2001, 1.

21 P. C. Earley and G. B. Northcraft, 'Goal Setting, Resource Interdependence, and Conflict Management', in *Managing Conflict: An Interdisciplinary Approach*, ed. M. A. Rahim (New York: Praeger, 1989), 161–70; K. Jelin, 'A Multimethod Examination of the Benefits and Detriments of Intragroup Conflict', *Administrative Science Quarterly* 40 (1995), 245–82.

22 K. A. Jehn and C. Bendersky, 'Intragroup Conflict in Organizations: A Contingency Perspective on the Conflict–Outcome Relationship', *Research in Organizational Behavior* 25 (2003), 187–242.

23 J. Jetten, R. Spears and T. Postmes, 'Intergroup Distinctiveness and Differentiation: A Meta-Analytic Integration', *Journal of Personality and Social Psychology* 86, no. 6 (2004), 862–79.

24 Von Glinow, Shapiro and Brett, 'Can We Talk, and Should We?'.

25 J. M. Brett, *Negotiating Globally: How to Negotiate Deals, Resolve Disputes, and Make Decisions across Cultural Boundaries* (San Francisco: Jossey-Bass, 2001); R. J. Lewicki et al., *Negotiation*, 4th edn (Burr Ridge, Ill.: McGraw-Hill/Irwin, 2003), chapter 4.

26 Jelin, 'A Multimethod Examination of the Benefits and Detriments of Intragroup Conflict'.

27 C. K. W. De Dreu et al., 'A Theory-Based Measure of Conflict Management Strategies in the Workplace', *Journal of Organizational Behavior* 22 (2001), 645–68.

28 D. W. Johnson et al., 'Effects of Cooperative, Competitive, and Individualistic Goal Structures on Achievement: A Meta-Analysis', *Psychological Bulletin* 89 (1981), 47–62; D. Tjosvold, *Working Together to Get Things Done* (Lexington, Mass.: Lexington, 1986); C. K. W. De Dreu, E. Giebels and E. Van de Vliert, 'Social Motives and Trust in Integrative Negotiation: The Disruptive Effects of Punitive Capability', *Journal of Applied Psychology* 83, no. 3 (June 1998), 408–22.

29 C. K. W. De Dreu and A. E. M. Van Vianen, 'Managing Relationship Conflict and the Effectiveness of Organizational Teams', *Journal of Organizational Behavior* 22 (2001), 309–28; Lewicki et al., *Negotiation*, pp. 35–6.

30 S. Ting-Toomey, J. G. Oetzel and K. Yee-Jung, 'Self-Construal Types and Conflict Management Styles', *Communication Reports* 14 (Summer 2001), 87–104; C. H. Tinsley, 'How Negotiators Get to Yes: Predicting the Constellation of Strategies Used across Cultures to Negotiate Conflict', *Journal of Applied Psychology* 86, no. 4 (2001), 583–93; F. P. Brew and D. R. Cairns, 'Styles of Managing Interpersonal Workplace Conflict in Relation to Status and Face Concern: A Study with Anglos and Chinese', *International Journal of Conflict Management* 15, no. 1 (2004), 27–57; C. L. Wang et al., 'Conflict Handling Styles in International Joint Ventures: A Cross-Cultural and Cross-National Comparison', *Management International Review* 45, no. 1 (2005), 3–21.

31 N. Brewer, P. Mitchell and N. Weber, 'Gender Role, Organizational Status, and Conflict Management Styles', *International Journal of Conflict Management* 13 (2002), 78–95; N. B. Florea et al., 'Negotiating from Mars to Venus: Gender in Simulated International Negotiations', *Simulation & Gaming* 34 (June 2003), 226–48.

32 E. Van de Vliert, 'Escalative Intervention in Small Group Conflicts', *Journal of Applied Behavioral Science* 21 (Winter 1985), 19–36.

33 M. Sherif, 'Superordinate Goals in the Reduction of Intergroup Conflict', *American Journal of Sociology* 68 (1958), 349–58; K. M. Eisenhardt, J. L. Kahwajy and L. J. Bourgeois III, 'How Management Teams Can Have a Good Fight', *Harvard Business Review* (July–August 1997), 77–85; X. M. Song, J. Xile and B. Dyer, 'Antecedents and Consequences of Marketing Managers' Conflict-Handling Behaviors', *Journal of Marketing* 64 (January 2000), 50–66.

34 H. C. Triandis, 'The Future of Workforce Diversity in International Organisations: A Commentary', *Applied Psychology: An International Journal* 52, no. 3 (2003), 486–95.

35 E. Elron, B. Shamir and E. Ben Ari, 'Why Don't They Fight Each Other? Cultural Diversity and Operational Unity in Multinational Forces', *Armed Forces & Society* 26 (October 1999), 73–97; 'Teamwork Polishes This Diamond', *Philippine Daily Inquirer*, 4 October 2000, 10.

36 K. R. Lewis, '(Drum) Beatings Build Corporate Spirit', *Star Tribune* (Minneapolis, Minn.), 3 June 2003, 3E; 'Oh What a Feeling!', *Music Trades*, May 2004, 94–5; D. Cole, 'Joining the Tom-Tom Club', *US News & World Report*, 22 March 2004, D12.

37 A. Pavey, 'Charming! Parking Inspectors Learn How to Be Nice', *Sunday Mail* (Brisbane), 19 June 2005, 15.

38 T. F. Pettigrew, 'Intergroup Contact Theory', *Annual Review of Psychology* 49 (1998), 65–85; S. Brickson, 'The Impact of Identity Orientation on Individual and Organizational Outcomes in Demographically Diverse Settings', *Academy of Management Review* 25 (January 2000), 82–101; J. Dixon and K. Durrheim, 'Contact and the Ecology of Racial Division: Some Varieties of Informal Segregation', *British Journal of Social Psychology* 42 (March 2003), 1–23.

39 Triandis, 'The Future of Workforce Diversity in International Organisations'.

40 Von Glinow, Shapiro and Brett, 'Can We Talk, and Should We?'.

41 P. O. Walker, 'Decolonizing Conflict Resolution: Addressing the Ontological Violence of Westernization', *American Indian Quarterly* 28, no. 3/4 (July 2004), 527–49; Native Dispute Resolution Network, 'Glossary of Terms', (Tucson, Arizona, 2005), http://nativenetwork.ecr.gov (accessed 15 September 2005).

42 E. Horwitt, 'Knowledge, Knowledge, Who's Got the Knowledge?', *Computerworld*, 8 April 1996, 80, 81, 84.

43 For a critical view of the problem-solving style in negotiation, see J. M. Brett, 'Managing Organizational Conflict', *Professional Psychology: Research and Practice* 15 (1984), 664–78.

44 R. E. Fells, 'Developing Trust in Negotiation', *Employee Relations* 15 (1993), 33–45; R. E. Fells, 'Overcoming the Dilemmas in Walton and Mckersie's Mixed Bargaining Strategy', *Industrial Relations (Laval)* 53 (March 1998), 300–25.

45 R. Stagner and H. Rosen, *Psychology of Union—Management Relations* (Belmont, CA: Wadsworth, 1965), pp. 95–6, 108–10; R. E. Walton and R. B. McKersie, *A Behavioral Theory of Labor Negotiations: An Analysis of a Social Interaction System* (New York: McGraw-Hill, 1965), pp. 41–6; L. Thompson, *The Mind and Heart of the Negotiator* (Upper Saddle River, NJ: Prentice-Hall, 1998), chapter 2.

46 J. W. Salacuse and J. Z. Rubin, 'Your Place or Mine? Site Location and Negotiation', *Negotiation Journal* 6 (January 1990), 5–10; J. Mayfield et al., 'How Location Impacts International Business Negotiations', *Review of Business* 19 (December 1998), 21–4.

47 J. Margo, 'The Persuaders', *Boss Magazine*, 29 December 2000, 38. For a full discussion of the advantages and disadvantages of face-to-face and alternative negotiations situations, see M. H. Bazerman et al., 'Negotiation', *Annual Review of Psychology* 51 (2000), 279–314.

48 A. F. Stuhlmacher, T. L. Gillespie and M. V. Champagne, 'The Impact of Time Pressure in Negotiation: A Meta-Analysis', *International Journal of Conflict Management* 9, no. 2 (April 1998), 97–116; C. K. W. De Dreu, 'Time Pressure and Closing of the Mind in Negotiation', *Organizational Behavior and Human Decision Processes* 91 (July 2003), 280–95. However, one recent study reported that speeding up these concessions leads to better negotiated outcomes. See D. A. Moore, 'Myopic Prediction, Self-Destructive Secrecy, and the Unexpected Benefits of Revealing Final Deadlines in Negotiation', *Organizational Behavior and Human Decision Processes* 94, no. 2 (2004), 125–39.

49 Lewicki et al., *Negotiation*, pp. 298–322.

50 S. Doctoroff, 'Re-engineering Negotiations', *Sloan Management Review* 39 (March 1998), 63–71; D. C. Zetik and A. F. Stuhlmacher, 'Goal Setting and Negotiation Performance: A Meta-Analysis', *Group Processes & Intergroup Relations* 5 (January 2002), 35–52.

51 L. L. Thompson, 'Information Exchange in Negotiation', *Journal of Experimental Social Psychology* 27 (1991), 161–79.

52 L. Thompson, E. Peterson and S. E. Brodt, 'Team Negotiation: An Examination of Integrative and Distributive Bargaining', *Journal of Personality and Social Psychology* 70 (1996), 66–78; Y. Paik and R. L. Tung, 'Negotiating with East Asians: How to Attain "Win–Win" Outcomes', *Management International Review* 39 (1999), 103–22.

53 D. J. O'Keefe, *Persuasion: Theory and Research* (Thousand Oaks, CA: Sage Publications, 2002).

54 Lewicki et al., *Negotiation*, pp. 90–6; S. Kwon and L. R. Weingart, 'Unilateral Concessions from the Other Party: Concession Behavior, Attributions, and Negotiation Judgments', *Journal of Applied Psychology* 89, no. 2 (2004), 263–78.

55 J. J. Zhao, 'The Chinese Approach to International Business Negotiation', *Journal of Business Communication* (July 2000), 209–37; N. Crundwell, 'US–Russian Negotiating Strategies', *BISNIS Bulletin*, October 2003, 5–6.

56 J. Z. Rubin and B. R. Brown, *The Social Psychology of Bargaining and Negotiation* (New York: Academic Press, 1976), chapter 9.

57 L. L. Putnam, 'Beyond Third Party Role: Disputes and Managerial Intervention', *Employee Responsibilities and Rights Journal* 7 (1994), 23–36; A. R. Elangovan, 'The Manager as the Third Party: Deciding How to Intervene in Employee Disputes', in *Negotiation: Readings, Exercises, and Cases*, eds R. J. Lewicki, J. A. Litterer and D. Saunders, 3rd edn (New York: McGraw-Hill, 1999), 458–69. For a somewhat different taxonomy of managerial conflict intervention, see P. G. Irving and J. P. Meyer, 'A Multidimensional Scaling Analysis of Managerial Third-Party Conflict Intervention Strategies', *Canadian Journal of Behavioural Science* 29, no. 1 (January 1997), 7–18.

58 B. H. Sheppard, 'Managers as Inquisitors: Lessons from the Law', in *Bargaining inside Organizations*, ed. M. H. Bazerman and R. J. Lewicki (Beverly Hills, CA: Sage, 1983); N. H. Kim, D. W. Sohn and J. A. Wall, 'Korean Leaders' (and Subordinates') Conflict Management', *International Journal of Conflict Management* 10, no. 2 (April 1999), 130–53.

59 R. Karambayya and J. M. Brett, 'Managers Handling Disputes: Third Party Roles and Perceptions of Fairness', *Academy of Management Journal* 32 (1989), 687–704; R. Cropanzano et al., 'Disputant Reactions to Managerial Conflict Resolution Tactics', *Group & Organization Management* 24 (June 1999), 124–53.

60 'Give Peace a Chance in the Workplace', *Daily Telegraph* (Sydney), 11 August 2004, 56; J. Woods, 'My Career and Where I'm Taking It', *Sydney Morning Herald*, 23 March 2005, 24.

61 A. R. Elangovan, 'Managerial Intervention in Organizational Disputes: Testing a Prescriptive Model of Strategy Selection', *International Journal of Conflict Management* 4 (1998), 301–35; P. S. Nugent, 'Managing Conflict: Third-Party Interventions for Managers', *Academy of Management Executive* 16, no. 1 (February 2002), 139–54.

62 J. P. Meyer, J. M. Gemmell and P. G. Irving, 'Evaluating the Management of Interpersonal Conflict in Organizations: A Factor-Analytic Study of Outcome Criteria', *Canadian Journal of Administrative Sciences* 14 (1997), 1–13.

CHAPTER 14

Leadership in organisational settings

LEARNING OBJECTIVES

After reading this chapter, you should be able to:

- define leadership

- list seven competencies of effective leaders

- describe the people-oriented and task-oriented leadership styles

- outline the path–goal theory of leadership

- contrast transactional with transformational leadership

- describe the four elements of transformational leadership

- explain how perceptions of followers influence leadership

- discuss the influence of culture on perceptions of effective leaders

- discuss the similarities and differences in the leadership styles of women and men.

Infosis

Infosys has grown into one of India's largest and most successful information technology companies, and chief executive Nandan Nilekani wants to maintain that momentum by focusing his attention on leadership development. 'Given our pace of growth, transferring the values and beliefs, the DNA of the organisation, to the next generations of leaders is one of my most important functions,' says Nilekani, who is actively involved in the company's leadership development workshops and mentoring activities.

Building a strong cadre of leaders required Nilekani and his executive team to carefully think about the meaning of effective leadership. 'We believe our future leaders need to learn how to set direction, to create a shared vision, encourage execution excellence, embrace inclusive meritocracy,' he says. Nilekani particularly emphasises the importance of values and vision. 'In essence, leadership is about dreaming the impossible and helping followers achieve the same. Moreover, the dream has to be built on sound and context-invariant values to sustain the enthusiasm and energy of people over a long time.'

'In essence, leadership is about dreaming the impossible and helping followers achieve the same,' says Nandan Nilekani, chief executive of Infosys, one of India's largest and most successful information technology companies.

Nandan Nilekani's prototype of an effective leader sounds remarkably similar to the characteristics of Australia's 'best bosses', reported by Hewitt Associates in its annual surveys of Australia's best-managed companies. What the top executives of the best companies have in common is that 'they all understand from a long-term perspective that you've got to have excited, passionate employees if the organisation is to prosper,' says Hewitt Associate's Australian managing director John Williams.

Effective leaders aren't necessarily charismatic heroes. 'We've tried to look at whether successful companies have charismatic leadership,' says Williams. 'We are pretty confident that is not the case. The CEOs are passionate and committed and respected, but definitely not charismatic.' Coles Myer chief executive John Fletcher echoes this point. 'The key about leadership is, it isn't about you,' Fletcher advises. 'The best leaders are often listeners who are watching their people do it rather than doing it themselves.' Microsoft Australia chief executive Steve Vamos makes a similar observation. 'It's not about having all the answers. The role of the leader is to create environments where others can do great work—and then to get out of the way.'

leadership Influencing, motivating and enabling others to contribute towards the effectiveness and success of the organisations of which they are members.

LEARNING OBJECTIVE

Define leadership.

THE WORLD IS CHANGING, and so is our concept of leadership. Gone is yesteryear's image of the command-and-control boss. Also gone is the more recent view that leaders charismatic heroes. Instead, as Nandan Nilekani, John Fletcher, Steve Vamos and consultants at Hewitt Associates stated in the opening vignette, leadership is about values, vision, enabling and coaching. A few years ago, fifty-four leadership experts from thirty-eight countries reached a consensus that leadership is about influencing, motivating and enabling others to contribute towards the effectiveness and success of the organisations of which they are members.[2] Leaders apply various forms of influence—from subtle persuasion to direct application of power—to ensure that followers have the motivation and role clarity to achieve specified goals. Leaders also arrange the work environment—such as allocating resources and altering communication patterns—so that employees can achieve corporate objectives more easily.

Leadership isn't restricted to the executive suite. Anyone in the organisation may be a leader in various ways and at various times.[3] This view is known as shared leadership or the leaderful organisation. Effective self-directed work teams, for example, consist of members who share leadership responsibilities or otherwise allocate this role to a responsible coordinator. For example, W. L. Gore & Associates is organised around self-directed work teams and consequently has few formal leaders. Yet, when asked in the company's annual survey 'Are you a leader?', more than 50 per cent of Gore employees answered 'Yes'.[4]

PERSPECTIVES OF LEADERSHIP

Leadership has been contemplated since the days of Greek philosophers and it is one of the most popular research topics among organisational behaviour scholars. This has resulted in an enormous volume of leadership literature, most of which can be organised into the five perspectives shown in Exhibit 14.1.[5] Although some of these perspectives are currently more popular than others, each helps us to understand this complex issue more fully.

Some research examines leadership competencies, whereas other research looks at leadership behaviours. More recent studies have looked at leadership from a contingency approach by considering the appropriate leader behaviours in different settings. Currently, the most popular perspective is that leaders transform organisations through their vision, communication

EXHIBIT 14.1   **Perspectives of leadership**

and ability to build commitment. Finally, an emerging perspective suggests that leadership is mainly a perceptual bias. We distort reality and attribute events to leaders because we feel more comfortable believing that a competent individual is at the organisation's helm. This chapter explores each of these five perspectives of leadership. In the final section, cross-cultural and gender issues in organisational leadership are considered.

COMPETENCY (TRAIT) PERSPECTIVE OF LEADERSHIP

LEARNING OBJECTIVE

List seven competencies of effective leaders.

Margaret Leung Ko May-yee is a confident leader with high integrity, who balances the drive to succeed with the emotional intelligence of working effectively in teams. 'You should not overlook mistakes—even your own,' advises the Hong Kong-based global co-head of HSBC's commercial banking division. 'You must be fair, however, because you are engaged in team work, otherwise the outcome would be failure.' Leung says the reason she feels comfortable in the traditionally Anglo-male company (which has become more culturally diverse in recent years) is due to her upbringing as the only girl with three brothers. 'If I thought something was wrong, or could be done better, I would speak out,' says Leung of her confidence in business meetings. Leung also has a sharp intellect and a deep knowledge of the business from a quarter of a century working at HSBC and being mentored by its current and past chief executives.[6]

Self-confidence, integrity, a drive to succeed, emotional intelligence, intelligence and knowledge of the business: these characteristics of Margaret Leung Ko May-yee reflect the notion that people require specific competencies in order to fulfil leadership roles. Since the beginning of recorded civilisation, people have been interested in the traits that distinguish great leaders from the rest of us. A major review in the late 1940s concluded that no consistent list of traits could be distilled from the hundreds of studies conducted up to that time. A subsequent review suggested that a few traits are consistently associated with effective leaders, but most are unrelated to effective leadership.[7] These conclusions caused many scholars to give up their search for the personal characteristics that distinguish effective leaders.

Over the past decade, leadership researchers and consultants have returned to the notion that leadership requires specific personal characteristics. One recent study established that inherited personality characteristics significantly influence *leadership emergence*—the perception that someone is a leader—in a leaderless situation.[8] More striking, however, is the resurgence in interest in discovering leadership *competencies* that enable companies to select future leaders and to provide leadership development programs.[9] Competencies encompass a broad range of personal characteristics, including knowledge, skills, abilities and values. The recent leadership literature identifies seven competencies that are characteristic of effective leaders (see Exhibit 14.2, overleaf):[10]

- *Emotional intelligence*. Research in Australia and elsewhere points to emotional intelligence as an important attribute of effective leaders.[11] People with emotional intelligence have the ability to perceive and express emotion, assimilate emotion in thought, understand and reason with emotion, and regulate emotion in themselves and others (see Chapter 4). Effective leaders are able to empathise, build rapport and network with others. The contingency leadership perspective described later in the chapter assumes that effective leaders have sufficient emotional intelligence to adjust their behaviour to match the situation.

- *Integrity*. This refers to the leader's truthfulness and tendency to translate words into deeds. The characteristic is sometimes called *authentic leadership* because the individual acts with sincerity. He or she has a high moral capacity to judge dilemmas based on sound values and to act accordingly. Several large-scale studies have reported that integrity or honesty is the most important characteristic of effective leaders. Employees want honest leaders whom they can trust.[12] The problem is that most employees don't trust their leaders and don't think they have integrity. Half of the Australian employees polled said that revelations about business wrongdoing had undermined their trust in employers. Another recent

EXHIBIT 14.2   Seven competencies of effective leaders

Leadership trait	Description
Emotional intelligence	The leader's ability to monitor his or her own and others' emotions, discriminate between them, and use the information to guide his or her thoughts and actions.
Integrity	The leader's truthfulness and tendency to translate words into deeds.
Drive	The leader's inner motivation to pursue goals.
Leadership motivation	The leader's need for socialised power to accomplish team or organisational goals.
Self-confidence	The leader's belief in his/her own leadership skills and ability to achieve objectives.
Intelligence	The leader's above-average cognitive ability, needed to process enormous amounts of information.
Knowledge of the business	The leader's understanding of the company's environment, in order to make more intuitive decisions.

Sources: Most elements of this list were derived from S. A. Kirkpatrick and E. A. Locke, 'Leadership: Do Traits Matter?', *Academy of Management Executive*, 5 (May 1991), pp. 48–60. Several of the ideas are also discussed in: H. B. Gregersen, A. J. Morrison and J. S. Black, 'Developing Leaders for the Global Frontier', *Sloan Management Review*, 40 (Fall 1998), pp. 21–32; R. J. House and R. N. Aditya, 'The Social Scientific Study of Leadership: Quo Vadis?', *Journal of Management*, 23 (1997), pp. 409–73.

survey reported that less than one-third of the 115 000 Asian workers polled are satisfied with their level of trust in management.[13]

- *Drive.* Leaders have a high need for achievement (see Chapter 5). They have a strong desire to compete in the marketplace and to take their company into uncharted waters. This drive represents the inner motivation that leaders possess to pursue their goals and to encourage others to work towards theirs. Drive inspires an inquisitiveness and a need to learn.
- *Leadership motivation.* Leaders have a strong need for power because they want to influence others (see Chapter 5). However, they tend to have a need for 'socialised power', because their motivation is constrained by a strong sense of altruism and social responsibility. In other words, effective leaders try to gain power so that they can influence others to accomplish goals that benefit the team or organisation.[14]
- *Self-confidence.* Margaret Leung Ko May-yee and other leaders demonstrate confidence in their leadership skills and their ability to achieve objectives. Effective leaders are typically extroverted—outgoing, sociable, talkative and assertive—but they also manage to remain humble.
- *Intelligence.* Leaders have above-average cognitive ability, but they aren't necessarily geniuses. Rather, they have superior ability to analyse a variety of complex alternatives and opportunities.
- *Knowledge of the business.* Effective leaders know the business environment in which they operate. This knowledge helps them to intuitively recognise opportunities and understand the organisation's capacity to capture those opportunities.

COMPETENCY (TRAIT) PERSPECTIVE LIMITATIONS AND PRACTICAL IMPLICATIONS

Although the competency perspective is gaining popularity (again), it assumes that all leaders have the same personal characteristics and that all of these qualities are equally important in all situations. This is probably a false assumption; leadership is far too complex to have a

Gail Kelly's leadership competencies help St George Bank's success

St George Bank has experienced phenomenal success over the past few years, and many point to Gail Kelly as part of the reason for this success. 'Her enthusiasms are clearly evident and that flows through to her staff and into business growth,' says one investment analyst. 'She seems to be highly energetic and seems to be a motivating force,' says another. Kelly is applauded for her interpersonal skills and integrity, but also for her persistent drive to get results. 'Her focus on execution is just enormous,' says a member of Kelly's executive team. 'There is no room not to deliver.'[15]

St George Bank Limited

universal list of traits that apply to every condition. Some competencies might not be important all the time. Another limitation is that alternative combinations of competencies may be equally successful. In other words, people with two different sets of competencies might be equally good leaders.[16]

As will be seen later in the chapter, several leadership researchers have also warned that some personal characteristics might influence only our perception that someone is a leader, not whether the individual really makes a difference to the organisation's success. People who exhibit self-confidence, extroversion and other traits are called leaders because they fit our stereotype of an effective leader. Or we might see a successful person, call that person a leader, and then attribute unobservable traits that we consider essential for great leaders.

Aside from these limitations, the competency perspective recognises that some people possess personal characteristics that offer them a higher potential to be great leaders. The most obvious implication of this is that organisations are turning to competency-based methods to hire people with strong leadership potential. The competency perspective of leadership does not imply that leadership is something you are either born with or must live without. On the contrary, competencies indicate leadership potential, not leadership performance. People with these characteristics become effective leaders only after they have developed and mastered the necessary leadership behaviours. People with somewhat lower leadership competencies may become very effective leaders because they have leveraged their potential more fully.

BEHAVIOURAL PERSPECTIVE OF LEADERSHIP

In the 1940s and 1950s leadership experts at several universities launched an intensive research investigation to answer the question 'What behaviours make leaders effective?'. Questionnaires were administered to employees, asking them to rate their supervisors on a large number of behaviours. These studies distilled two clusters of leadership behaviours from thousands of leadership behaviour items.[17]

LEARNING OBJECTIVE

Describe the people-oriented and task-oriented leadership styles.

One cluster represented people-oriented behaviours. This included showing trust in and respect for subordinates, demonstrating a genuine concern for their needs, and having a desire to look out for their welfare. Leaders with a strong people-oriented style listen to employee suggestions, do personal favours for employees, support their interests when required, and treat employees as equals.

The other cluster represented a task-oriented leadership style and included behaviours that define and structure work roles. Task-oriented leaders assign employees to specific tasks, clarify their work duties and procedures, ensure that they follow company rules, and push them to reach their performance capacity. They establish stretch goals and challenge employees to push beyond those high standards.

CHOOSING TASK- VERSUS PEOPLE-ORIENTED LEADERSHIP

Should leaders be task-oriented or people-oriented? This is a difficult question to answer because each style has its advantages and disadvantages. Recent evidence suggests that both styles are positively associated with leader effectiveness, but differences are often apparent only in very high or very low levels of each style. Generally, absenteeism, grievances, turnover and job dissatisfaction are higher among employees who work with supervisors who have very low levels of people-oriented leadership. Job performance is lower among employees who work for supervisors with low levels of task-oriented leadership.[18] Research suggests that university students value task-oriented instructors because they want clear objectives and well-prepared lectures that abide by the unit's objectives.[19]

One problem with the behavioural leadership perspective is that the two categories are broad generalisations that mask specific behaviours within each category. For instance, task-oriented leadership includes planning work activities, clarifying roles and monitoring operations and performance. Each of these clusters of activities is fairly distinct and likely to have a different effect on employee well-being and performance. A second concern is that the behavioural approach assumes that high levels of both styles are best in all situations. In reality, the best leadership style depends on the situation.[20] On a positive note, the behavioural perspective lays the foundation for two of the main leadership styles—people-oriented and task-oriented—found in many contemporary leadership theories. These contemporary theories adopt a contingency perspective, which is described next.

CONTINGENCY PERSPECTIVE OF LEADERSHIP

The contingency perspective of leadership is based on the idea that the most appropriate leadership style depends on the situation. Most (although not all) contingency leadership theories assume that effective leaders must be both insightful and flexible.[21] They must be able to adapt their behaviours and styles to the immediate situation. This isn't easy to do, however. Leaders typically have a preferred style. It takes considerable effort for leaders to learn when and how to alter their styles to match the situation. As noted earlier, leaders must have high emotional intelligence so they can diagnose the circumstances and match their behaviours accordingly.

LEARNING OBJECTIVE

Outline the path–goal theory of leadership.

path–goal leadership theory
A contingency theory of leadership based on the expectancy theory of motivation that relates several leadership styles to specific employee and situational contingencies.

PATH–GOAL THEORY OF LEADERSHIP

Several contingency theories have been proposed over the years, but **path–goal leadership theory** has withstood scientific critique better than the others. The theory has its roots in the expectancy theory of motivation (see Chapter 5).[22] Early research incorporated expectancy theory into the study of how leader behaviours influence employee perceptions of expectancies (paths) between employee effort and performance (goals). Out of this early work was born path–goal theory as a contingency leadership model.

Using the language of expectancy theory (Chapter 5), path–goal theory states that effective leaders strengthen the performance-to-outcome expectancy and valences of those outcomes, thereby ensuring that employees who perform their jobs well have a higher degree of need fulfilment than employees who perform poorly. Effective leaders also strengthen the effort-to-performance expectancy by providing the information, support and other resources necessary to help employees complete their tasks.[23] In other words, path–goal theory advocates **servant leadership**.[24] Servant leaders do not view leadership as a position of power; rather, they are coaches, stewards and facilitators. Leadership is an obligation to understand employee needs and to facilitate their work performance. Servant leaders ask 'How can I help you?' rather than expecting employees to serve them. As Microsoft Australia chief executive Steve Vamos stated at the beginning of the chapter: 'The role of the leader is to create environments where others can do great work—and then to get out of the way.'

servant leadership The belief that leaders serve followers by understanding their needs and facilitating their work performance.

PATH–GOAL LEADERSHIP STYLES

Exhibit 14.3 presents the path–goal theory of leadership. This model specifically highlights four leadership styles and several contingency factors leading to three indicators of leader effectiveness. The four leadership styles are:[25]

- *Directive.* These are clarifying behaviours that provide a psychological structure for subordinates. The leader clarifies performance goals, the means to reach those goals, and the standards against which performance will be judged. It also includes judicious use of rewards and disciplinary actions. Directive leadership is the same as the task-oriented leadership described earlier and echoes the discussion in Chapter 2 on the importance of clear role perceptions in employee performance. One study reported that the Australian managers interviewed dislike using the directive style because it sets them apart as 'the boss' and is generally tedious.[26]

- *Supportive.* These behaviours provide psychological support for subordinates. The leader is friendly and approachable, makes the work more pleasant, treats employees with equal respect, and shows concern for the status, needs and well-being of employees. Supportive leadership is the same as the people-oriented leadership described earlier and reflects the benefits of social support to help employees cope with stressful situations.

Path–goal leadership theory

EXHIBIT 14.3

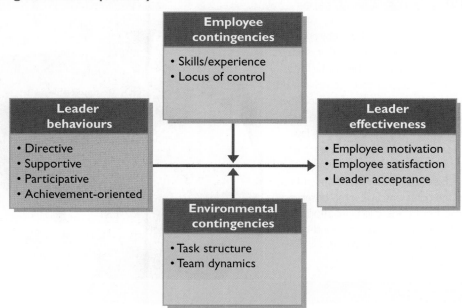

- *Participative*. These behaviours encourage and facilitate subordinates' involvement in decisions beyond their normal work activities. The leader consults with employees, asks for their suggestions, and takes these ideas into serious consideration before making a decision. Participative leadership relates to involving employees in decisions (see Chapter 8).
- *Achievement-oriented*. These behaviours encourage employees to reach their peak performance. The leader sets challenging goals, expects employees to perform at their highest level, continuously seeks improvement in employee performance, and shows a high degree of confidence that employees will assume responsibility and accomplish challenging goals. Achievement-oriented leadership applies goal-setting theory (Chapter 5) as well as positive expectations in self-fulfilling prophecy (Chapter 3).

The path–goal model contends that effective leaders are capable of selecting the most appropriate behavioural style (or styles) for each situation. Leaders might simultaneously use two or more styles. For example, they might be both supportive and participative in a specific situation.

CONTINGENCIES OF PATH–GOAL THEORY

As a contingency theory, path–goal theory states that each of these four leadership styles will be effective in some situations but not in others. The path–goal leadership model specifies two sets of situational variables that moderate the relationship between a leader's style and effectiveness: (1) employee characteristics, and (2) characteristics of the employee's work environment. Several contingencies have already been studied within the path–goal framework, and the model is open for more variables in the future.[28] However, only four contingencies are reviewed here (see Exhibit 14.4).

Skill and experience

A combination of directive and supportive leadership is best for employees who are (or perceive themselves to be) inexperienced and unskilled.[29] Directive leadership gives subordinates information about how to accomplish the task, whereas supportive leadership helps them cope with the uncertainties of unfamiliar work situations. Directive leadership is detrimental when employees are skilled and experienced, because it introduces too much supervisory control.

Chrysler CEO cuts costs with directive/achievement leadership styles

Chrysler Group is under intense pressure to cut costs and thereby avoid the troubles that General Motors is facing. This mandate makes Chrysler's recently appointed chief executive, Tom LaSorda, ideal for the job. LaSorda (shown here with Chrysler employees in Mexico) sets tough goals and looks for ways to improve efficiency by clocking how much time employees lose moving from one station to the next. 'With every second you've lost productivity,' explains LaSorda. 'That's kind of how my mind works.' A few years ago LaSorda applied his combination of directive and achievement-oriented leadership, as well as self-taught knowledge of lean manufacturing practices, to turn a money-losing Eastern European motor vehicle plant into one of the most efficient operations on the continent. Still, some observers believe that LaSorda also needs to move from transactional to more transformational leadership. 'Tom LaSorda, who's more of a nuts-and-bolts type of guy, needs to take it to the next level and set Chrysler up for the next decade,' suggests motor vehicle consultant Michael Robinet.[27]

D. Lopez-Mills/Associated Press

EXHIBIT 14.4

Selected contingencies of path–goal theory

	Directive	Supportive	Participative	Achievement-oriented
Employee contingencies				
Skill and experience	Low	Low	High	High
Locus of control	External	External	Internal	Internal
Environmental contingencies				
Task structure	Non-routine	Routine	Non-routine	?
Team dynamics	Negative norms	Low cohesion	Positive norms	?

Locus of control

Recall from Chapter 2 that people with an internal locus of control believe that they have control over their work environment. Consequently, these employees prefer participative and achievement-oriented leadership styles and may become frustrated with a directive style. In contrast, people with an external locus of control believe that their performance is due more to luck and fate, so they tend to be more satisfied with directive and supportive leadership.

Task structure

Leaders should adopt the directive style when the task is non-routine, because this style minimises the role ambiguity that tends to occur in these complex work situations (particularly for inexperienced employees).[30] The directive style is ineffective when employees have routine and simple tasks because the manager's guidance serves no purpose and may be viewed as unnecessarily close control. Employees in highly routine and simple jobs may require supportive leadership to help them cope with the tedious nature of the work and lack of control over the pace of work. Participative leadership is preferred for employees performing non-routine tasks, because the lack of rules and procedures gives them more discretion to achieve challenging goals. The participative style is ineffective for employees in routine tasks because they lack discretion over their work.

Team dynamics

Cohesive teams with performance-oriented norms act as a substitute for most leader interventions. High team cohesiveness substitutes for supportive leadership, whereas performance-oriented team norms substitute for directive and possibly achievement-oriented leadership. Thus, when team cohesiveness is low, leaders should use the supportive style. Leaders should apply a directive style to counteract team norms that oppose the team's formal objectives. For example, the team leader may need to use legitimate power if team members have developed a norm to 'take it easy' rather than get a project completed on time.

PRACTICAL IMPLICATIONS AND LIMITATIONS OF PATH–GOAL THEORY

Path–goal theory has received more research support than other contingency leadership models, but the evidence is far from complete. A few contingencies (i.e. task structure) do not have a clear-cut association with any leadership style. Other contingencies and leadership styles in the path–goal leadership model haven't received research investigation at all, as indicated by the question marks in Exhibit 14.4.[31] The path–goal model was expanded a few years ago to include more leadership styles and contingencies, but these additions have received limited investigation.

Another concern is that as path–goal theory expands, the model may become too complex for practical use. Although the expanded model provides a closer representation of the complexity of leadership, it may become too cumbersome for training people in leadership styles. Few people would be able to remember all the contingencies and the appropriate leadership styles for those contingencies. In spite of these limitations, path–goal theory remains a relatively robust contingency leadership theory.

OTHER CONTINGENCY THEORIES

As was noted at the beginning of the chapter, numerous leadership theories have developed over the years. Most of them are found in the contingency perspective of leadership. Some overlap with the path–goal model in terms of leadership styles, but most use simpler and more abstract contingencies. Two will be briefly mentioned here because of their popularity and their historical significance.

SITUATIONAL LEADERSHIP THEORY

situational leadership theory Developed by Hersey and Blanchard, the model suggests that effective leaders vary their style with the 'readiness' of followers.

One of the most popular contingency theories among practitioners is the **situational leadership theory (SLT)**, also called the life-cycle theory of leadership, developed by Paul Hersey and Ken Blanchard.[32] SLT suggests that effective leaders vary their style with the 'readiness' of followers. (An earlier version of the model called this 'maturity'.) 'Readiness' refers to the employee's or work team's ability and willingness to accomplish a specific task. 'Ability' refers to the extent to which the follower has the skills and knowledge to perform the task without the leader's guidance. 'Willingness' refers to the follower's self-motivation and commitment to perform the assigned task. The model compresses these distinct concepts into a single situational condition.

The situational leadership model also identifies four leadership styles—telling, selling, participating and delegating—that Hersey and Blanchard distinguish in terms of the amount of directive and supportive behaviour provided. For example, 'telling' has high task behaviour and low supportive behaviour. The situational leadership model has four quadrants, with each quadrant showing the leadership style that is most appropriate under different circumstances.

In spite of its popularity, several studies and at least three reviews have concluded that the situational leadership model lacks empirical support.[33] Only one part of the model apparently works: namely that leaders should use 'telling' (i.e. a directive style) when employees lack motivation and ability. (Recall that this is also documented in path–goal theory.) The model's elegant simplicity is attractive and entertaining, but most parts don't represent reality very well.

FIEDLER'S CONTINGENCY MODEL

Fiedler's contingency model Developed by Fred Fiedler, the model suggests that leader effectiveness depends on whether the person's natural leadership style is appropriately matched to the situation.

Fiedler's contingency model, developed by Fred Fiedler and his associates, is the earliest contingency theory of leadership.[34] According to this model, leader effectiveness depends on whether the person's natural leadership style is appropriately matched to the situation. The theory examines two leadership styles that essentially correspond to the previously described people-oriented and task-oriented styles. Unfortunately, Fiedler's model relies on a questionnaire that does not measure either leadership style very well.

Fiedler's model suggests that the best leadership style depends on the level of *situational control*: that is, the degree of power and influence that the leader possesses in a particular situation. Situational control is affected by three factors, in the following order of importance: leader–member relations, task structure and position power.[35] 'Leader–member relations' is the degree to which employees trust and respect the leader and are willing to follow his or her guidance. 'Task structure' refers to the clarity or ambiguity of operating procedures. 'Position power' is the extent to which the leader possesses legitimate, reward and coercive power over subordinates. These three contingencies form the eight possible combinations of *situation favourableness* from the leader's viewpoint. Good leader–member relations, high task structure and strong position power create the most favourable situation for the leader, because he or she has the most power and influence under these conditions.

Fiedler has gained considerable respect for pioneering the first contingency theory of leadership. However, his theory has fared less well. As mentioned, the leadership-style scale used by Fiedler has been widely criticised. There is also no scientific justification for placing the three situational control factors in a hierarchy. Moreover, it seems that leader–member relations are actually an indicator of leader effectiveness (as in path–goal theory) rather than a situational factor. Finally, the theory considers only two leadership styles whereas other models present a more complex and realistic array of behaviour options. These concerns explain why the theory has limited empirical support.[36]

Changing the situation to match the leader's natural style

Fiedler's contingency model may have become a historical footnote, but it does make an important and lasting contribution by suggesting that leadership style is related to the individual's personality and, consequently, is relatively stable over time. Leaders might be able to alter their style temporarily, but they tend to use a preferred style in the long term. More recent scholars have also proposed that leadership styles are more 'hard-wired' than most contingency leadership theories assume.[37]

If leadership style is influenced by a person's personality, organisations should engineer the situation to fit the leader's dominant style, rather than expect leaders to change their style with the situation. A directive leader might be assigned inexperienced employees who need direction rather than seasoned people who work less effectively under a directive style. Alternatively, companies might transfer supervisors to workplaces where their dominant style fits best. For instance, directive leaders might be parachuted into work teams with counterproductive norms, whereas leaders who prefer a supportive style should be sent to departments in which employees face work pressures and other stressors.

LEADERSHIP SUBSTITUTES

We have looked at theories that recommend using different leadership styles in various situations. But one theory, called **leadership substitutes**, identifies conditions that either limit the leader's ability to influence subordinates or make that particular leadership style unnecessary. The literature identifies several conditions that might substitute for task-oriented or people-oriented leadership. For example, performance-based reward systems keep employees directed towards organisational goals, so they might replace or reduce the need for task-oriented leadership. Task-oriented leadership is also less important when employees are skilled and experienced. Notice how these propositions are similar to path–goal leadership theory, namely that directive leadership is unnecessary—and may be detrimental—when employees are skilled or experienced.[38]

Some research suggests that effective leaders help team members learn to lead themselves through leadership substitutes; in other words, co-workers substitute for leadership in high-involvement team structures.[39] Co-workers instruct new employees, thereby providing directive leadership. They also provide social support, which reduces stress among fellow employees. Teams with norms that support organisational goals may substitute for achievement-oriented leadership, because employees encourage (or pressure) co-workers to stretch their performance levels.[40]

Self-leadership—the process of influencing oneself to establish the self-direction and self-motivation needed to perform a task (see Chapter 6)—is another possible leadership substitute.[41] Employees with high self-leadership set their own goals, reinforce their own behaviour, maintain positive thought processes and monitor their own performance, thereby managing both personal motivation and abilities. As employees become more proficient in self-leadership, they presumably require less supervision to keep them focused and energised towards organisational objectives.

leadership substitutes
A theory that identifies contingencies that either limit the leader's ability to influence subordinates or make that particular leadership style unnecessary.

The leadership substitutes model has intuitive appeal, but the evidence so far is mixed. Some studies show that a few substitutes do replace the need for task- or people-oriented leadership, but others do not. The messiness of statistically testing for leadership substitutes may account for some problems, but a few writers contend that the limited support is evidence that leadership plays a critical role regardless of the situation.[42] At this point it can be concluded that a few conditions (such as self-directed work teams, self-leadership and reward systems) might reduce the importance of task- or people-oriented leadership, but they probably won't completely replace leaders in these roles.

TRANSFORMATIONAL PERSPECTIVE OF LEADERSHIP

transformational leadership
A leadership perspective that explains how leaders change teams or organisations by creating, communicating and modelling a vision for the organisation or work unit, and inspiring employees to strive for that vision.

In the opening vignette to this chapter, Infosys chief executive Nandan Nilekani stated that effective leaders create a shared vision and encourage excellent execution towards that vision. Leadership, he explains, is essentially 'about dreaming the impossible and helping followers achieve the same'. Nandan Nilekani is referring to **transformational leadership**. Transformational leaders are agents of change. They create, communicate and model a shared vision for the team or organisation, and inspire followers to strive for that vision.[43]

TRANSFORMATIONAL VERSUS TRANSACTIONAL LEADERSHIP

transactional leadership
Leadership that helps organisations achieve their current objectives more efficiently, such as linking job performance to valued rewards and ensuring that employees have the resources needed to get the job done.

Transformational leadership differs from **transactional leadership**.[44] Transactional leadership is 'managing'—helping organisations achieve their current objectives more efficiently, such as by linking job performance to valued rewards and ensuring that employees have the resources needed to get the job done. The contingency and behavioural theories described earlier adopt the transactional perspective because they focus on leader behaviours that improve employee performance and satisfaction. In contrast, transformational leadership is about 'leading'— changing the organisation's strategies and culture so that they have a better fit with the surrounding environment.[45] Transformational leaders are change agents who energise and direct employees to a new set of corporate values and behaviours.

LEARNING OBJECTIVE

Contrast transactional with transformational leadership.

Organisations require both transactional and transformational leadership.[46] Transactional leadership improves organisational efficiency, whereas transformational leadership steers companies onto a better course of action. Transformational leadership is particularly important in organisations that require significant alignment with the external environment. Unfortunately, too many leaders get trapped in the daily managerial activities that represent transactional leadership.[47] They lose touch with the transformational aspect of effective leadership. Without transformational leaders, organisations stagnate and eventually become seriously misaligned with their environments.

TRANSFORMATIONAL VERSUS CHARISMATIC LEADERSHIP

One topic that has generated some confusion and controversy is the distinction between transformational and charismatic leadership.[48] Many researchers either use the words interchangeably, as if they have the same meaning, or view charismatic leadership as an essential ingredient of transformational leadership. Others take this view further by suggesting that charismatic leadership is the highest degree of transformational leadership.

However, the emerging view, which this book adopts, comes from a third group of experts who contend that charisma is distinct from transformational leadership. These academics point out that charisma is a personal trait that provides referent power over followers, whereas transformational leadership is a set of behaviours that people use to lead the change process.[49] Charismatic leaders might be transformational leaders; indeed, their personal power through charisma is a tool to change the behaviour of followers. However, some research points out that charismatic or 'heroic' leaders easily build allegiance in followers but do not necessarily change the organisation. Other research suggests that charismatic leaders produce dependent followers, whereas transformational leaders have the opposite effect: they support follower empowerment, which tends to reduce dependence on the leader.[50]

The distinction between charismatic and transformational leadership is illustrated in recent leadership dynamics at Procter & Gamble. The American household goods company lost market share and innovativeness under the previous charismatic leader. Yet, as Reality Check 14.1 describes, it has experienced a dramatic turnaround under Alan G. Lafley, who is

14.1 REALITY CHECK

PROCTER & GAMBLE TRADES CHARISMA FOR TRANSFORMATIONAL SUBSTANCE

AP/World Wide Photos

A few days after becoming CEO of Procter & Gamble (P&G), Alan George Lafley made an impression by walking unannounced into a dinner party of executives who had moved to other companies. This act was highly symbolic, because the household goods giant famously promoted from within and treated people who left the company before retirement as outcasts. P&G was in trouble—it lacked new products and its existing offerings were under siege from competitors—so Lafley's visit to P&G alumni (the first such visit by a P&G CEO) quickly signalled that the company would embrace ideas and people from outside the organisation.

In addition to greeting former employees, Lafley incessantly communicates the mantra that 'the consumer is boss' and that the company's future depends on creativity. Far from the heroic charismatic style of P&G's previous CEO, who failed to turn the company around and was ousted in just eighteen months, Lafley is distinctly 'unassuming' with 'a humble demeanour that belies his status'. One industry observer is more blunt: 'If there were fifteen people sitting around the conference table, it wouldn't be obvious that he was the CEO.'

Yet Lafley has transformed P&G where others could not. His calm self-assurance, consistent vision and symbolic and strategic actions towards a more customer-friendly and innovative organisation have provided the direction and clarity that the company lacked. Importantly, Lafley also walks the talk: his behaviour is closely aligned with the message that he conveys. He restructured the company, pruned costs, made significant acquisitions (Gillette and Clairol), and rekindled a spirit of innovation through special creativity teams. Lafley is also out in the field for ten to fifteen days each year, meeting with customers and closely observing what they like and don't like about the company's and competitors' products.

To instil the creative spirit at the top, Lafley took P&G's entire forty-person leadership council to a one-day innovation workshop in San Francisco led by design firm IDEO. IDEO also built an innovation centre (called 'the Gym') where P&G staff learn brainstorming, prototyping, observation and other ways to become more innovative. Lafley revamped the executive offices into an open-space plan that improves information sharing. He has also hired an army of creative people from other organisations and paired them with long-service P&G staff. The result: P&G has become the industry's hotspot for innovation, its market share and profitability have experienced sustained growth, and its stock price has soared.

A. G. Lafley has turned around beleaguered Procter & Gamble through transformational leadership behaviours without being charismatic or heroic.

Sources: K. Brooker and J. Schlosser, 'The Un-CEO', *Fortune,* 16 September 2002, 88–93; B. Nussbaum, 'The Power of Design', *BusinessWeek,* 17 May 2004, 86; N. Buckley, 'The Calm Reinventor', *Financial Times* (London), 29 January 2005, 11; S. Ellison, 'Women's Touch Guides P&G Chief's Firm Hand in Company Turnaround', *Wall Street Journal Europe,* 1 June 2005, A1; S. Hill Jr, 'P&G's Turnaround Proves Listening to Customer Pays', *Manufacturing Business Technology,* July 2005, 64; J. Tylee, 'Procter's Creative Gamble', *Campaign,* 18 March 2005, 24–6.

not known for being charismatic. Instead, Lafley applies the classic elements of transformational leadership that are described next.

ELEMENTS OF TRANSFORMATIONAL LEADERSHIP

There are several descriptions of transformational leadership, but most include the four elements illustrated in Exhibit 14.5. These elements include creating a strategic vision, communicating the vision, modelling the vision and building commitment towards the vision.

Creating a strategic vision

Transformational leaders shape a strategic vision of a realistic and attractive future that bonds employees together and focuses their energy towards a superordinate organisational goal. A shared strategic vision represents the substance of transformational leadership. It reflects a future for the company or work unit that is ultimately accepted and valued by organisational members. Strategic vision creates a 'higher purpose' or superordinate goal that energises and unifies employees.[51] A strategic vision might originate with the leader, but it is just as likely to emerge from employees, clients, suppliers or other constituents. A shared strategic vision plays an important role in organisational effectiveness.[52] Visions offer the motivational benefits of goal setting, but are compelling future states that bond employees and motivate them to strive for those objectives. Visions are typically described in a way that distinguishes them from the current situation, yet makes the goal both appealing and achievable.

Communicating the vision

If vision is the substance of transformational leadership, then communicating that vision is the process. Transformational leaders communicate meaning and elevate the importance of the visionary goal to employees. They frame messages around a grand purpose with emotional appeal that captivates employees and other corporate stakeholders. Framing helps transformational leaders establish a common mental model so that the group or organisation will act collectively towards the desirable goal.[53]

Transformational leaders bring their visions to life through symbols, metaphors, stories and other vehicles that transcend plain language. Metaphors borrow images of other experiences, thereby creating richer meaning of the vision that has not yet been experienced. As

---

EXHIBIT 14.5   **Elements of transformational leadership**

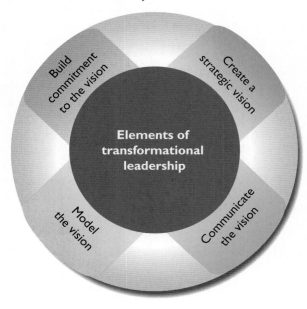

Haier Group CEO takes symbolism to the extreme

In the 1980s, so the story goes, Zhang Ruimin, the newly appointed chief executive of Haier Group, was so incensed by the poor quality of the products built at the company's factory in the Chinese port city of Qingdao that he picked up a sledgehammer and smashed several washing machines. Zhang had just taken over the state-owned appliance manufacturer and saw the need for radical change. Today, the legendary sledgehammer is displayed in a glass case on Haier's shop floor in Qindao, which has been transformed into a model of modern efficiency. Thousands of employees dressed in clean uniforms work in pristine workshops, while a fully automated logistics centre and advanced research and development program help to produce

superior quality appliances. Haier Group has become China's first truly multinational company with plants around the world. By relying on Japanese quality control and American-style management practices, Zhang's dream of making Haier a global brand is becoming a reality.[57]

an example, when George Cohen faced the difficult challenge of opening McDonald's restaurants in Moscow, he frequently reminded his team members that they were establishing 'hamburger diplomacy'.[54]

Modelling the vision

Transformational leaders not only talk about a vision; they enact it. They 'walk the talk' by stepping outside the executive suite and doing things that symbolise the vision.[55] They are also reliable and persistent in their actions, thereby legitimising the vision and providing further evidence that they can be trusted. Leaders walk the talk through significant events, but they also alter mundane activities—meeting agendas, office locations, executive schedules—to make them consistent with the vision and its underlying values. Modelling the vision is important because employees and other stakeholders are executive watchers who look for behaviours that symbolise values and expectations. The greater the consistency between the leader's words and actions, the more employees will believe and follow the leader. Walking the talk also builds employee trust, because trust is partly determined by the consistency of the person's actions.

Unfortunately, it seems that many leaders in this region fail to walk the talk. A recent survey of Taiwanese employees estimated that only 28 per cent believe that senior management behaves in accordance with the company's core values. A global survey reported that only 53 per cent of employees in Australia and 63 per cent in Singapore believe that leaders in their company make decisions that are consistent with company values. These scores are comparable to results in France, Netherlands, Germany and the United Kingdom, but well below Canada, where 76 per cent gave a favourable evaluation of their leaders. 'There are lots of people who talk a good story, but very few deliver one,' warns Peter Farrell, the Australian founder and chief executive of ResMed, which leads the world in technology that corrects sleep disorders. 'You've got to mean what you say, say what you mean, and be consistent.'[56]

Building commitment towards the vision

Transforming a vision into reality requires employee commitment. Transformational leaders build this commitment in several ways. Their words, symbols and stories build a contagious enthusiasm that energises people to adopt the vision as their own. Leaders demonstrate a 'can do' attitude by enacting their vision and staying on course. Their persistence and consistency reflect an image of honesty, trust and integrity. Finally, leaders build commitment by involving employees in the process of shaping the organisation's vision.

EVALUATING THE TRANSFORMATIONAL LEADERSHIP PERSPECTIVE

Transformational leaders do make a difference. Subordinates are more satisfied and have higher affective organisational commitment under transformational leaders. They also perform their jobs better, engage in more organisational citizenship behaviours, and make better or more creative decisions. One study of bank branches also reported that organisational commitment and financial performance seemed to increase where the branch manager had completed a transformational leadership training program.[58]

Transformational leadership is currently the most popular leadership perspective, but it faces a number of challenges. One problem is that some writers engage in circular logic by defining transformational leadership in terms of the leader's success.[59] They suggest that leaders are transformational when they successfully bring about change, rather than whether they engage in certain behaviours that are called transformational. Another concern is that the transformational leadership model seems to be universal rather than contingency-oriented. Only very recently have writers begun to explore the idea that transformational leadership is more appropriate in some situations than others.[60] For instance, transformational leadership is probably more appropriate when organisations need to adapt than when environmental conditions are stable. Preliminary evidence suggests that the transformational leadership perspective is relevant across cultures. However, specific elements of transformational leadership, such as the way visions are formed and communicated, may be more appropriate in Western societies than in other cultures.

IMPLICIT LEADERSHIP PERSPECTIVE

implicit leadership theory
A theory stating that people rely on preconceived traits to evaluate others as leaders, and that they tend to inflate the influence of leadership on organisational events.

The competency, behaviour, contingency and transformational leadership perspectives make the basic assumption that leaders 'make a difference'. Certainly, there is evidence that senior executives do influence organisational performance. However, leaders might have less influence than most of us would like to believe. Some leadership experts suggest that people inflate the importance of leadership in explaining organisational events. These processes, which include stereotyping, attribution errors and the need for situational control, are collectively called **implicit leadership theory**.[61]

LEARNING OBJECTIVE

Explain how perceptions of followers influence leadership.

STEREOTYPING LEADERSHIP

Implicit leadership theory states that everyone has preconceived notions about the features and behaviours of an effective leader. These perceptions are stereotypes or prototypes of idealised leadership that develop through socialisation within the family and society.[62] Mental images of an ideal leader shape our expectations and acceptance of people as leaders which, in turn, affect their ability to influence us as followers. We rely on leadership stereotypes partly because a leader's success might not be known for months or possibly years. Consequently, employees depend on immediate information to decide whether the leader is effective. If the leader fits the mould, employees are more confident that the leader is effective.[63]

ATTRIBUTING LEADERSHIP

Implicit leadership is also influenced by attribution errors. Research has found that (at least in Western cultures) people tend to attribute organisational events to the leader, even when those events are largely caused by factors beyond the leader's control. This attribution is partly caused by fundamental attribution error (see Chapter 3) in which leaders are given credit or blame for the company's success or failure because employees do not readily see the external forces that also influence these events. Leaders reinforce this belief by taking credit for organisational successes.[64]

NEED FOR SITUATIONAL CONTROL

A third perceptual distortion of leadership suggests that people want to believe that leaders make a difference. There are two basic reasons for this belief.[65] First, leadership is a useful way for us to simplify life events. It is easier to explain organisational successes and failures in terms of the leader's ability than by analysing a complex array of other forces. For example, there are usually many reasons why a company fails to change quickly enough in the marketplace, yet we tend to simplify this explanation down to the notion that the company CEO or some other corporate leader was ineffective.

Second, there is a strong tendency in Australia, New Zealand and other Western cultures to believe that life events are generated more from people than from uncontrollable natural forces.[66] This illusion of control is satisfied by believing that events result from the rational actions of leaders. In short, employees feel better believing that leaders make a difference, so they actively look for evidence that this is so.

The implicit leadership perspective questions the importance of leadership, but it also provides valuable advice on how to improve leadership acceptance. This approach highlights the fact that leadership is a perception of followers as much as the actual behaviours and characteristics of people calling themselves leaders. Potential leaders must be sensitive to this fact, understand what followers expect, and act accordingly. Individuals who do not make an effort to fit leadership prototypes will have more difficulty bringing about necessary organisational change.

CROSS-CULTURAL AND GENDER ISSUES IN LEADERSHIP

Along with the five perspectives of leadership presented throughout this chapter, it needs to be kept in mind that societal cultural values and practices affect what leaders do. Culture shapes the leader's values and norms, which influence his or her decisions and actions. These cultural values also shape the expectations that followers have of their leaders. This is apparent in Reality Check 14.2 (overleaf), which looks into the 'ubuntu' values that shape the preferred leadership behaviours and style in Africa.

LEARNING OBJECTIVE

Discuss the influence of culture on perceptions of effective leaders.

An executive who acts inconsistently with cultural expectations is more likely to be perceived as an ineffective leader. Moreover, leaders who deviate from those values may experience various forms of influence to get them to conform to the leadership norms and expectations of that society. In other words, implicit leadership theory described in the previous section explains differences in leadership practices across cultures.

Over the past few years, 150 researchers from dozens of countries have worked together on Project GLOBE (Global Leadership and Organisational Behaviour Effectiveness) to identify the effects of cultural values on leadership.[67] The project organised countries into ten regional clusters, of which Australia and New Zealand are grouped into the 'Anglo' cluster with the United States, Great Britain and Canada. The results of this massive investigation are just beginning to appear, but preliminary work suggests that some features of leadership are universal and some differ across cultures.

Specifically, the GLOBE Project reports that 'charismatic visionary' is a universally recognised concept, and that middle managers around the world believe that it is a characteristic of effective leaders. 'Charismatic visionary' represents a cluster of concepts, including visionary, inspirational, performance-orientation, integrity and decisiveness.[68] In contrast, participative leadership is perceived as characteristic of effective leadership in low power distance cultures

REALITY CHECK 14.2

LEADING THROUGH *UBUNTU* VALUES

Woven into the fabric of African society is the concept of *ubuntu*. *Ubuntu* represents a collection of values, including harmony, compassion, respect, human dignity and collective unity. It is 'that profound African sense that each of us is human through the humanity of other human beings,' explains former South African president Nelson Mandela. *Ubuntu* is often described through the Zulu maxim *umuntu ngumuntu ngabantu*. Archbishop Desmond Tutu offers this translation: 'We believe that a person is a person through other persons; that my humanity is caught up, bound up and inextricably in yours.'

The *ubuntu* value system provides a framework for how people should lead others in Africa, whether in politics or in organisations. First, *ubuntu* is about connectedness, so leaders must be comfortable with the highly participative process of making decisions through consensus. Everyone must have a chance to speak without imposed tight time restrictions. The process itself will determine the time required. This consensus process does not call for leadership abdication; rather, it requires leaders to coach, facilitate and possibly mediate as the group moves towards mutual agreement.

Along with building consensus, *ubuntu* values a collective respect for everyone in the system. It places the good of the community above self-interest—to help others as an inherent part of your own well-being. For leaders, this condition requires the ability to give support to followers, to mediate differences, and to serve followers rather than have followers serve them. The heroic leader who steps in front—and typically looks down from a higher plateau—is not consistent with *ubuntu*. Instead, leaders are respected for their wisdom and ability, so *ubuntu* selects leaders for their age and experience.

Ubuntu is 'that profound African sense that each of us is human through the humanity of other human beings', explains Nelson Mandela.

EPA Photos/EPA/Kim Ludbrook/Corbis

Sources: L. van der Colff, 'Leadership Lessons from the African Tree', *Management Decision* 41 (2003), pp. 257–61; L. van der Colff, 'Ubuntu, Isivivane and Uhluhlasa: The Meaning of Leadership and Management in South Africa', *Equity-Skills News & Views*, 1 (December 2002/January 2003); L. D. Krause and R. Powell, 'Preparing School Leaders in Post-apartheid South Africa: A Survey of Leadership Preferences of Principals in Western Cape', *Journal of Leadership Studies* 8 (January 2002), pp. 63ff; M. P. Mangaliso, 'Building Competitive Advantage from Ubuntu: Management Lessons from South Africa', *Academy of Management Executive* 15 (August 2001), pp. 23–43; speech by President Nelson Mandela at his 80th birthday party, Kruger National Park, 16 July 1998.

but less so in high power distance cultures. For instance, one study reported that Mexican employees expect managers to make decisions affecting their work. Mexico is a high power distance culture, so followers expect leaders to apply their authority rather than delegate their power most of the time.[69] In summary, there are similarities and differences in the concept and preferred practice of leadership across cultures.

GENDER DIFFERENCES IN LEADERSHIP

LEARNING OBJECTIVE

Discuss similarities and differences in the leadership styles of women and men.

Do women lead differently from men? Several writers think so. They suggest that women have an interactive style that includes more people-oriented and participative leadership.[70] They also believe that women are more relationship-oriented, cooperative, nurturing and emotional in their leadership roles. They further assert that these qualities make women particularly well suited to leadership roles at a time when companies are adopting a stronger emphasis on teams and employee involvement. These arguments are consistent with sex role stereotypes, namely that men tend to be more task-oriented whereas women are more people-oriented.

Are these stereotypes true? Do women adopt more people-oriented and participative leadership styles? The answer is 'no' and 'yes' respectively. Leadership studies outside university laboratories (i.e. in real work settings) have generally found that male and female leaders do not differ in their levels of task-oriented or people-oriented leadership. The main explanation is that real-world jobs require similar behaviour from male and female job incumbents.[71]

However, women do adopt a participative leadership style more readily than their male counterparts. One possible reason is that, compared with boys, girls are often raised to be more egalitarian and less status-oriented, which is consistent with being participative. There is also some evidence that women have somewhat better interpersonal skills than men, and this translates into their relatively greater use of the participative leadership style. A third explanation is that subordinates expect female leaders to be more participative, based on their own sex stereotypes, so female leaders comply with follower expectations to some extent.

Several recent surveys report that women are rated higher than men on the emerging leadership qualities of coaching, teamwork and empowering employees.[72] Yet research also suggests that women are evaluated negatively when they try to apply the full range of leadership styles, particularly the more directive and autocratic approaches. Thus, ironically, women may be well suited to contemporary leadership roles, yet they often continue to face limitations of leadership through the gender stereotypes and prototypes of leaders held by followers.[73] Overall, both male and female leaders must be sensitive to the fact that followers have expectations about how leaders should act, and negative evaluations may go to leaders who deviate from those expectations.

CHAPTER SUMMARY

Leadership is a complex concept that is defined as the ability to influence, motivate and enable others to contribute towards the effectiveness and success of the organisations of which they are members. Leaders use influence to motivate followers, and arrange the work environment so that they do the job more effectively. Leaders exist throughout the organisation, not just in the executive suite.

The competency perspective tries to identify the characteristics of effective leaders. Recent writing suggests that leaders have emotional intelligence, integrity, drive, leadership motivation, self-confidence, above-average intelligence, and knowledge of the business. The behavioural perspective of leadership identified two clusters of leader behaviour, people-oriented and task-oriented. People-oriented behaviours include showing mutual trust and respect for subordinates, demonstrating a genuine concern for their needs, and having a desire to look out for their welfare. Task-oriented behaviours include assigning employees to specific tasks, clarifying their work duties and procedures, ensuring that they follow company rules, and pushing them to reach their performance capacity.

The contingency perspective of leadership takes the view that effective leaders diagnose the situation and adapt their style to fit that situation. The path–goal model is the prominent contingency theory that identifies four leadership styles—directive, supportive, participative and achievement-oriented—and several contingencies relating to the characteristics of the employee and of the situation.

Two other contingency leadership theories include the situational leadership theory and Fiedler's contingency theory. Research support is quite weak for both theories. However, a lasting element of Fiedler's theory is the idea that leaders have natural styles, and consequently companies need to change the leader's environment to suit his or her style. Leadership substitutes theory identifies contingencies that either limit the leader's ability to influence subordinates or make that particular leadership style unnecessary.

Transformational leaders create a strategic vision, communicate that vision through framing and the use of metaphors, model the vision by 'walking the talk' and acting consistently, and build commitment towards the vision. This contrasts with transactional leadership, which involves linking job performance to valued rewards and ensuring that employees have the resources needed to get the job done. The contingency and behavioural perspectives adopt the transactional view of leadership.

According to the implicit leadership perspective, people inflate the importance of leadership through attribution, stereotyping and a fundamental need for human control. Implicit leadership theory is evident across cultures, because cultural values shape the behaviours that followers expect of their leaders.

Cultural values also influence the leader's personal values which, in turn, influence his or her leadership practices. The GLOBE Project data reveal that there are similarities and differences in the concept and preferred practice of leadership across cultures. Women generally do not differ from men in the degree of people-oriented or task-oriented leadership. However, female leaders more often adopt a participative style. Research also suggests that people evaluate female leaders based on gender stereotypes, which may result in higher or lower ratings.

KEY TERMS

Fiedler's contingency model p. 422
implicit leadership theory p. 428
leadership p. 414

leadership substitutes p. 423
path–goal leadership theory p. 418
servant leadership p. 419

situational leadership theory p. 422
transactional leadership p. 424
transformational leadership p. 424

DISCUSSION QUESTIONS

1. Why is it important for top executives to value and support leadership demonstrated at all levels of the organisation?

2. Find two newspaper ads for management or executive positions. What leadership competencies are mentioned in these ads? If you were on the selection panel, what methods would you use to identify these competencies in job applicants?

3. Consider your favourite teacher. What people-oriented and task-oriented leadership behaviours did he or she use effectively? In general, do you think students prefer an instructor who is more people-oriented or one who is more task-oriented? Explain your preference.

4. Your employees are skilled and experienced customer service representatives who perform non-routine tasks, such as solving unique customer problems or special needs with the company's equipment. Use path–goal theory to identify the most appropriate leadership style(s) you should use in this situation. Fully explain your answer and discuss why other styles are inappropriate.

5. Transformational leadership is currently the most popular perspective of leadership. However, it is far from perfect. Discuss the limitations of transformational leadership.

6. This chapter emphasised that charismatic leadership is not the same as transformational leadership. Still, charisma is often mentioned in the discussions about leadership. In your opinion, how does charisma relate to leadership?

7. Identify a current political leader (e.g. prime minister, premier, or mayor of your city) and his or her recent accomplishments. Now, using the implicit leadership perspective, think of ways that these accomplishments may be overstated. In other words, explain why they may be due to factors other than the leader.

8. You hear two people debating the merits of women as leaders. One person claims that women make better leaders than men because women are more sensitive to their employees' needs and involve them in organisational decisions. The other person counters that, although these leadership styles may be increasingly important, most women have trouble gaining acceptance as leaders when they face tough situations in which a more autocratic style is required. Discuss the accuracy of the comments made.

JOSH MARTIN

14.1 SKILL BUILDER

CASE STUDY

By Joseph C. Santora, Essex County College and TSTDCG, Inc., and James C. Sarros, Monash University

Josh Martin, a 41-year-old administrator at the Centre Street Settlement House, a non-profit social service agency with seventy employees and more than $6 million in assets, sat pensively at his desk located outside the executive suite. He thought to himself, 'No, it can't be. I can't have been working here for twenty years. Where did the time go?'

Martin has spent his entire adult life working at the Centre Street Settlement House. He began his career there immediately after graduating from university with a degree in economics, and very slowly climbed the narrow administrative ladder from his initial position as the director of a government-funded project to his current position as the deputy agency administrator. In addition, for the past five years he has been serving as the president of the agency's for-profit construction company. He reports directly to Tom Saunders, the autocratic executive director of the agency.

Martin, a competent administrator, often gets things done through his participative leadership style. In the last few years, Martin's job responsibilities have increased exponentially. He fills many informational, decisional and interpersonal managerial roles for the agency. Six months ago he was given the added responsibility of processing invoices for agency vendors and consultants, authority he shares in common with Saunders and the agency's accountant.

Martin is rewarded handsomely for his role in the non-profit agency. Last year he earned $90 000, plus a liberal fringe benefits package that included an agency car, a pension plan, a

medical health plan (including dental), a month's holiday leave, fifteen paid public holidays, and unlimited sick time. Although he has received an annual cost-of-living allowance, Martin has no written contractual agreement and essentially serves at the pleasure of Saunders.

Martin pays a high personal price for his attractive compensation package. He is on-call twenty-four hours a day, complete with a beeper. Each Sunday morning Martin attends a mandatory agency strategy meeting required of all agency managers.

Over the years Martin has tolerated Saunders' erratic mood swings and his inattentiveness to agency details, but tension between the two men has reached a high point in recent months. For example, two months ago Martin called in sick because he was suffering from a severe bout of the flu. Martin's absence forced Saunders to cancel an important meeting in order to supervise an agency fiscal audit. Saunders responded to Martin's absence in an irrational fashion by focusing on a small piece of tile missing from the cafeteria floor. He screamed at two employees who were eating lunch in the cafeteria.

'You see,' he said, 'Martin doesn't give a damn about anything in this agency. I always have to make sure things get done around here. Just look at the floor! There's a piece of tile missing!' Mary Thompson and Elizabeth Duncan, two veteran employees, seemed shocked by Saunders' reaction to the missing piece of tile. As Saunders stormed out of the cafeteria throwing his hands in the air, Mary turned to Elizabeth and whispered, 'Saunders is really going off the deep end. Without Josh nothing would get done around here. I don't see how Saunders can blame Josh for every little problem. I wonder how long Josh can take this unfair treatment.' Elizabeth nodded her head in agreement.

A month after this incident, Martin recommended pay increases for two employees who had received excellent performance appraisals by their supervisors. Martin believed that a 2 per cent raise, admittedly only a symbolic raise, would provide motivation, would increase morale, and would not seriously jeopardise the agency's budget. When Martin proposed the raises to Saunders at the Thursday weekly fiscal meeting, Saunders vehemently rejected his proposal, ranting: 'Everybody wants a raise around here. It's about time people started doing more work and stopped whining about money. Let's move on to the next agenda item.'

As Saunders closed the weekly staff meeting, he said, 'I'm the leader of this agency. I have to manage everything for this agency to run effectively.' Phil Jones, the director of field operations, turned to Paul Lindstrom, the fiscal officer, and whispered, 'Sure, Saunders is the director of this agency, but he couldn't manage his way out of a paper bag. Without Josh, this place would be in total chaos. Josh listens to us and tries to implement some of our ideas to make life simpler around here.'

Martin has often contemplated resigning from the agency to seek other public sector employment. However, he believes that such opportunities are rare since he is a middle-aged, white male. Besides, Saunders knows just about every agency CEO in the public sector. Martin believes that Saunders would find out that he had applied for a job as soon as his resumé reached an agency personnel department. Moreover, Martin feels that his long tenure with the agency may be detrimental; most prospective employers would be suspicious of his motives for leaving the settlement house after some two decades of service. Martin mused, 'Perhaps I stayed too long at the dance.' Finally, given the present economic conditions, many public sector agencies would be reluctant to match his salary and benefits package—at least not in his first few years of service.

Martin is uncertain of his options at this point. On a personal note, although his wife is gainfully employed and possesses good technical skills and experience in the printing industry, Martin still needs to maintain his present standard of living to support his family, including his two university-student daughters, a $100 000 mortgage on his home, and other financial obligations. He has significant non-profit and for-profit experience and excellent managerial and leadership skills. Yet he wonders if there is any way out of his current situation.

QUESTIONS

1. Describe the two different leadership styles used by Josh Martin and Tom Saunders. Do the two different styles tell you anything about leadership traits? Do you think there is any resolution to the organisational problems resulting from the conflicting leadership styles?

2. What are the characteristics/elements of an effective leader? Do you think Saunders is an effective leader? Why or why not? Is Martin an effective leader? Why or why not?

3. Does Josh Martin have any way out of his current situation? What would you do if you were he?

LEADERSHIP DIAGNOSTIC ANALYSIS

14.2 SKILL BUILDER

TEAM EXERCISE

PURPOSE

To help students learn about the different path–goal leadership styles and when to apply each style.

INSTRUCTIONS

Step 1: Students individually write down two incidents in which someone had been an effective manager or leader of them. The leader and situation might be from work, a sports team, a student work group, or any other setting where leadership might emerge. For example, students might describe how their supervisor in a summer job pushed them to reach higher performance goals than they would have otherwise achieved. Rather than general statements, each incident should state the actual behaviours that the leader used (e.g. 'My boss sat down with me and we agreed on specific targets and deadlines, then he said several times over the next few weeks that I was capable of reaching those goals'). Each incident requires only two or three sentences.

Step 2: After everyone has written their two incidents, the instructor will form small groups (typically four or five students). Each team will answer the following questions for each incident presented in that team:

- Which path–goal theory leadership style(s)—directive, supportive, participative or achievement-oriented—did the leader apply in this incident?
- Ask the person who wrote the incident about the conditions that made this leadership style (or these styles, if more than one was used) appropriate in this situation. The team should list these contingency factors clearly and, where possible, connect them to the contingencies described in path–goal theory. (*Note*: the team might identify path–goal leadership contingencies that are not described in this book. These, too, should be noted and discussed.)

Step 3: After the teams have diagnosed the incidents, each team will describe to the entire class the most interesting incidents as well as its diagnosis of that incident. Other teams will critique the diagnosis. Any leadership contingencies not mentioned in the textbook should also be presented and discussed.

LEADERSHIP DIMENSIONS INSTRUMENT

14.3 SKILL BUILDER

SELF-ASSESSMENT

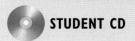 **STUDENT CD**

PURPOSE

This assessment is designed to help you to understand two important dimensions of leadership and to identify which of these dimensions is more prominent in your supervisor, team leader, coach or other person to whom you are accountable.

INSTRUCTIONS

Read each of the statements below and circle the response that you believe best describes your supervisor. You may substitute 'supervisor' with anyone else to whom you are accountable, such as a team leader, a CEO, a course instructor or a sports coach. Then use the scoring key in Appendix B to calculate the results for each leadership dimension. After completing the assessment, be prepared to discuss in class the distinctions between the leadership dimensions.

LEADERSHIP DIMENSIONS INSTRUMENT

My supervisor ...	Strongly agree	Agree	Neutral	Disagree	Strongly disagree
1. Focuses attention on irregularities, mistakes, exceptions and deviations from what is expected of me.	5	4	3	2	1
2. Engages in words and deeds that enhance his/her image of competence.	5	4	3	2	1
3. Monitors performance for errors needing correction.	5	4	3	2	1
4. Serves as a role model for me.	5	4	3	2	1
5. Points out what I will receive if I do what is required.	5	4	3	2	1
6. Instils pride in being associated with him/her.	5	4	3	2	1
7. Keeps careful track of mistakes.	5	4	3	2	1
8. Can be trusted to help me overcome any obstacle.	5	4	3	2	1
9. Tells me what to do to be rewarded for my efforts.	5	4	3	2	1
10. Makes me aware of strongly held values, ideals and aspirations which are shared in common.	5	4	3	2	1
11. Is alert for failure to meet standards.	5	4	3	2	1
12. Mobilises a collective sense of mission.	5	4	3	2	1
13. Works out agreements with me on what I will receive if I do what needs to be done.	5	4	3	2	1
14. Articulates a vision of future opportunities.	5	4	3	2	1
15. Talks about special rewards for good work.	5	4	3	2	1
16. Talks optimistically about the future.	5	4	3	2	1

Source: Items and dimensions are adapted from D. N. Den Hartog, J. J. Van Muijen and P. L. Koopman, 'Transactional Versus Transformational Leadership: An Analysis of the MLQ', *Journal of Occupational & Organizational Psychology* 70 (March 1997), pp. 19–34. Den Hartog et al. label transactional leadership as 'rational–objective leadership' and label transformational leadership as 'inspirational leadership'. Many of their items may have originated from B. M. Bass and B. J. Avolio, *Manual for the Multifactor Leadership Questionnaire* (Palo Alto, CA: Consulting Psychologists Press, 1989).

NOTES

1   C. Fox, 'Choose Me', *Australian Financial Review*, 9 July 2004, 18; N. Nilekani, 'How Do I Develop Next Generation Leaders', *Economic Times* (India), 25 November 2005; F. Smith et al., '25 True Leaders', *Australian Financial Review*, 12 August 2005, 62; D. Tarrant, 'The Leading Edge', *Bulletin*, 15 November 2005.

2   R. House, M. Javidan and P. Dorfman, 'Project Globe: An Introduction', *Applied Psychology: An International Review* 50 (2001), 489–505; R. House et al., 'Understanding Cultures and Implicit Leadership Theories across the Globe: An Introduction to Project Globe', *Journal of World Business* 37 (2002), 3–10.

3   R. G. Isaac, W. J. Zerbe and D. C. Pitt, 'Leadership and Motivation: The Effective Application of Expectancy Theory', *Journal of Managerial Issues* 13 (Summer 2001), 212–26; C. L. Pearce and J. A. Conger, eds, *Shared Leadership: Reframing the Hows and Whys of Leadership* (Thousand Oaks, CA: Sage, 2003); J. S. Nielson, *The Myth of Leadership* (Palo Alto, CA: Davies-Black, 2004).

4   J. Raelin, 'Preparing for Leaderful Practice', *T&D*, March 2004, 64.

5   Many of these perspectives are summarised in R. N. Kanungo, 'Leadership in Organizations: Looking Ahead to the 21st Century', *Canadian Psychology* 39 (Spring 1998), 71–82; G. A. Yukl, *Leadership in Organizations*, 6th edn (Upper Saddle River, NJ: Pearson Education, 2006).

6   M. Chan, 'Leung Sitting Pretty in HSBC Executive Suite', *South China Morning Post* (Hong Kong), 22 August 2005, 20.

7   R. M. Stogdill, *Handbook of Leadership* (New York: The Free Press, 1974), chapter 5.

8   R. Ilies, M. W. Gerhardt and H. Le, 'Individual Differences in Leadership Emergence: Integrating Meta-Analytic Findings and Behavioral Genetics Estimates', *International Journal of Selection and Assessment* 12, no. 3 (September 2004), 207–19.

9   J. Intagliata, D. Ulrich and N. Smallwood, 'Leveraging Leadership Competencies to Produce Leadership Brand: Creating Distinctiveness by Focusing on Strategy and Results', *Human Resources Planning* 23,

no. 4 (2000), 12–23; J. A. Conger and D. A. Ready, 'Rethinking Leadership Competencies', *Leader to Leader* (Spring 2004), 41–7; S. J. Zaccaro, C. Kemp and P. Bader, 'Leader Traits and Attributes', in *The Nature of Leadership*, ed. J. Antonakis, A. T. Cianciolo and R. J. Sternberg (Thousand Oaks, CA: Sage, 2004), 101–24.

10 This list is based on: S. A. Kirkpatrick and E. A. Locke, 'Leadership: Do Traits Matter?', *Academy of Management Executive* 5 (May 1991), 48–60; R. M. Aditya, R. J. House and S. Kerr, 'Theory and Practice of Leadership: Into the New Millennium', in *Industrial and Organizational Psychology: Linking Theory with Practice*, ed. C. L. Cooper and E. A. Locke (Oxford, UK: Blackwell, 2000), 130–65; D. Goleman, R. Boyatzis and A. McKee, *Primal Leaders* (Boston: Harvard Business School Press, 2002); T. A. Judge et al., 'Personality and Leadership: A Qualitative and Quantitative Review', *Journal of Applied Psychology* 87, no. 4 (August 2002), 765–80; T A. Judge, A. E. Colbert and R. Ilies, 'Intelligence and Leadership: A Quantitative Review and Test of Theoretical Propositions', *Journal of Applied Psychology* 89, no. 3 (June 2004), 542–52.

11 J. George, 'Emotions and Leadership: The Role of Emotional Intelligence', *Human Relations* 53 (August 2000), 1027–55; Goleman, Boyatzis and McKee, *Primal Leaders*; R. G. Lord and R. J. Hall, 'Identity, Deep Structure and the Development of Leadership Skill', *Leadership Quarterly* 16, no. 4 (August 2005), 591–615; C. Skinner and P. Spurgeon, 'Valuing Empathy and Emotional Intelligence in Health Leadership: A Study of Empathy, Leadership Behaviour and Outcome Effectiveness', *Health Services Management Research* 18, no. 1 (February 2005), 1–12.

12 D. R. May et al., 'The Moral Component of Authentic Leadership', *Organizational Dynamics* 32 (August 2003), 247–60. The large-scale studies are reported in: C. Savoye, 'Workers Say Honesty Is Best Company Policy', *Christian Science Monitor*, 15 June 2000; J. M. Kouzes and B. Z. Posner, *The Leadership Challenge*, 3rd edn (San Francisco: Jossey-Bass, 2002), chapter 2; J. Schettler, 'Leadership in Corporate America', *Training & Development*, September 2002, 66–73.

13 'Workers Lack Faith in Employers', *The Age* (Melbourne), 23 September 2003; Watson Wyatt Worldwide, 'Asia–Pacific Workers Satisfied with Jobs Despite Some Misgivings with Management and Pay', Watson Wyatt Worldwide news release (Singapore, 16 November 2004).

14 R. J. House and R. N. Aditya, 'The Social Scientific Study of Leadership: Quo Vadis?', *Journal of Management* 23 (1997), 409–73.

15 A. Cornell and J. Moullakas, 'Just How Great Is Gail Kelly?', *Australian Financial Review*, 7 May 2005, 20; C. Wright, 'Best in Show: Rating Our Top Dogs', *Australian Financial Review*, 13 July 2005, 27.

16 R. Jacobs, 'Using Human Resource Functions to Enhance Emotional Intelligence', in *The Emotionally Intelligent Workplace*, ed. C. Cherniss and D. Goleman (San Francisco: Jossey-Bass, 2001), 161–3; Conger and Ready, 'Rethinking Leadership Competencies'.

17 P. G. Northouse, *Leadership: Theory and Practice*, 3rd edn (Thousand Oaks, CA: Sage, 2004), chapter 4; Yukl, *Leadership in Organizations*, chapter 3.

18 A. K. Korman, 'Consideration, Initiating Structure, and Organizational Criteria—a Review', *Personnel Psychology* 19 (1966), 349–62; E. A. Fleishman, 'Twenty Years of Consideration and Structure', in *Current Developments in the Study of Leadership*, ed. E. A. Fleishman and J. C. Hunt (Carbondale, Ill.: Southern Illinois University Press, 1973), 1–40; T. A. Judge, R. F. Piccolo and R. Ilies, 'The Forgotten Ones? The Validity of Consideration and Initiating Structure in Leadership Research', *Journal of Applied Psychology* 89, no. 1 (2004), 36–51; Yukl, *Leadership in Organizations*, pp. 62–75.

19 V. V. Baba, 'Serendipity in Leadership: Initiating Structure and Consideration in the Classroom', *Human Relations* 42 (1989), 509–25.

20 S. Kerr et al., 'Towards a Contingency Theory of Leadership Based upon the Consideration and Initiating Structure Literature', *Organizational Behavior and Human Performance* 12 (1974), 62–82; L. L. Larson, J. G. Hunt and R. N. Osbom, 'The Great Hi–Hi Leader Behavior Myth: A Lesson from Occam's Razor', *Academy of Management Journal* 19 (1976), 628–41.

21 R. Tannenbaum and W. H. Schmidt, 'How to Choose a Leadership Pattern', *Harvard Business Review* (May–June 1973), 162–80.

22 For a thorough study of how expectancy theory of motivation relates to leadership, see R. G. Isaac, W. J. Zerbe and D. C. Pitt, 'Leadership and Motivation: The Effective Application of Expectancy Theory', *Journal of Managerial Issues* 13 (Summer 2001), 212–26.

23 R. J. House, 'A Path–Goal Theory of Leader Effectiveness', *Administrative Science Quarterly* 16 (1971), 321–38; M. G. Evans, 'Extensions of a Path–Goal Theory of Motivation', *Journal of Applied Psychology* 59 (1974), 172–8; R. J. House and T. R. Mitchell, 'Path–Goal Theory of Leadership', *Journal of Contemporary Business* (Autumn 1974), 81–97; M. G. Evans, 'Path–Goal Theory of Leadership', in *Leadership*, ed. L. L. Neider and C. A. Schriesheim (Greenwich, CT: Information Age Publishing, 2002), 115–38.

24 Various thoughts on servant leadership are presented in L. C. Spears and M. Lawrence, eds, *Focus on Leadership: Servant-Leadership* (New York: John Wiley & Sons, 2002).

25 R. J. House, 'Path–Goal Theory of Leadership: Lessons, Legacy, and a Reformulated Theory', *Leadership Quarterly* 7 (1996), 323–52.

26 G. Avery and J. Ryan, 'Applying Situational Leadership in Australia', *Journal of Management Development* 21, no. 3/4 (2002), 242–62.

27 D.-A. Durbin, 'New Chrysler Boss LaSorda Gears up to Improve Efficiency', *St Louis Post-Dispatch*, 21 August 2005, E1.

28 J. Indvik, 'Path–Goal Theory of Leadership: A Meta-Analysis', *Academy of Management Proceedings* (1986), 189–92; J. C. Wofford and L. Z. Liska, 'Path–Goal Theories of Leadership: A Meta-Analysis', *Journal of Management* 19 (1993), 857–76.

29 J. D. Houghton and S. K. Yoho, 'Toward a Contingency Model of Leadership and Psychological Empowerment: When Should Self-Leadership Be Encouraged?', *Journal of Leadership & Organizational Studies* 11, no. 4 (2005), 65–83.

30 R. T. Keller, 'A Test of the Path–Goal Theory of Leadership with Need for Clarity as a Moderator in Research and Development Organizations', *Journal of Applied Psychology* 74 (1989), 208–12.

31 C. A. Schriesheim and L. L. Neider, 'Path–Goal Leadership Theory: The Long and Winding Road', *Leadership Quarterly* 7 (1996), 317–21.

32 P. Hersey and K. H. Blanchard, *Management of Organizational Behavior: Utilizing Human Resources*, 5th edn (Englewood Cliffs, NJ: Prentice Hall, 1988).

33 R. P. Vecchio, 'Situational Leadership Theory: An Examination of a Prescriptive Theory', *Journal of Applied Psychology* 72 (1987), 444–51; W. Blank, J. R. Weitzel and S. G. Green, 'A Test of the Situational Leadership Theory', *Personnel Psychology* 43 (1990), 579–97; C. L. Graeff, 'Evolution of Situational Leadership Theory: A Critical Review', *Leadership Quarterly* 8 (1997), 153–70.

34 F. E. Fiedler, *A Theory of Leadership Effectiveness* (New York: McGraw-Hill, 1967); F. E. Fiedler and M. M. Chemers, *Leadership and Effective Management* (Glenview, Ill.: Scott, Foresman, 1974).

35 F. E. Fiedler, 'Engineer the Job to Fit the Manager', *Harvard Business Review* 43, no. 5 (1965), 115–22.

36 For a summary of criticisms, see Yukl, *Leadership in Organizations*, pp. 217–18.

37   N. Nicholson, *Executive Instinct* (New York: Crown, 2000).

38   This observation has also been made by C. A. Schriesheim, 'Substitutes-for-Leadership Theory: Development and Basic Concepts', *Leadership Quarterly* 8 (1997), 103–8.

39   D. F. Elloy and A. Randolph, 'The Effect of Superleader Behavior on Autonomous Work Groups in a Government Operated Railway Service', *Public Personnel Management* 26 (Summer 1997), 257–72; C. C. Manz and H. Sims Jr, *The New SuperLeadership: Leading Others to Lead Themselves* (San Francisco: Berrett-Koehler, 2001).

40   M. L. Loughry, 'Co-workers Are Watching: Performance Implications of Peer Monitoring', *Academy of Management Proceedings* (2002), O1–O6.

41   C. C. Manz and C. Neck, *Mastering Self-Leadership*, 3rd edn (Upper Saddle River, NJ: Prentice Hall, 2004).

42   P. M. Podsakoff and S. B. MacKenzie, 'Kerr and Jermier's Substitutes for Leadership Model: Background, Empirical Assessment, and Suggestions for Future Research', *Leadership Quarterly* 8 (1997), 117–32; S. D. Dionne et al., 'Neutralizing Substitutes for Leadership Theory: Leadership Effects and Common-Source Bias', *Journal of Applied Psychology* 87, no. 3 (June 2002), 454–64; J. R. Villa et al., 'Problems with Detecting Moderators in Leadership Research Using Moderated Multiple Regression', *Leadership Quarterly* 14, no. 1 (February 2003), 3–23; S. D. Dionne et al., 'Substitutes for Leadership, or Not', *The Leadership Quarterly* 16, no. 1 (2005), 169–93.

43   J. M. Burns, *Leadership* (New York: Harper & Row, 1978); B. M. Bass, *Transformational Leadership: Industrial, Military, and Educational Impact* (Hillsdale, NJ: Erlbaum, 1998); S. B. Proctor-Thomson and K. W. Parry, 'What the Best Leaders Look Like', in *Leadership in the Antipodes: Findings, Implications and a Leader Profile*, ed. K. W. Parry (Wellington, NZ: Institute of Policy Studies and Centre for the Study of Leadership, 2001), 166–91; B. J. Avolio and F. J. Yammarino, eds, *Transformational and Charismatic Leadership: The Road Ahead* (Greenwich, CT: JAI Press, 2002).

44   V. L. Goodwin, J. C. Wofford and J. L. Whittington, 'A Theoretical and Empirical Extension to the Transformational Leadership Construct', *Journal of Organizational Behaviour*, 22 (November 2001), pp. 759–74.

45   A. Zaleznik, 'Managers and Leaders: Are They Different?', *Harvard Business Review* 55, no. 5 (1977), 67–78; W. Bennis and B. Nanus, *Leaders: The Strategies for Taking Charge* (New York: Harper & Row, 1985); R. H. G. Field, 'Leadership Defined: Web Images Reveal the Differences between Leadership and Management', in *Annual Conference of the Administrative Sciences Association of Canada, Organizational Behavior Division*, ed. P. Mudrack (Winnipeg, Manitoba, 25–28 May 2002), 93.

46   Both transformational and transactional leadership improve work unit performance. See B. M. Bass et al., 'Predicting Unit Performance by Assessing Transformational and Transactional Leadership', *Journal of Applied Psychology* 88 (April 2003), 207–18.

47   For a discussion on the tendency to slide from transformational to transactional leadership, see W. Bennis, *An Invented Life: Reflections on Leadership and Change* (Reading, MA: Addison-Wesley, 1993).

48   R. J. House, 'A 1976 Theory of Charismatic Leadership', in *Leadership: The Cutting Edge*, ed. J. G. Hunt and L. L. Larson (Carbondale, Ill.: Southern Illinois University Press, 1977), 189–207; J. A. Conger, 'Charismatic and Transformational Leadership in Organizations: An Insider's Perspective on These Developing Streams of Research', *Leadership Quarterly* 10 (Summer 1999), 145–79.

49   J. E. Barbuto, Jr, 'Taking the Charisma out of Transformational Leadership', *Journal of Social Behavior & Personality* 12 (September 1997), 689–97; Y. A. Nur, 'Charisma and Managerial Leadership: The Gift That Never Was', *Business Horizons* 41 (July 1998), 19–26; M. D. Mumford and J. R. Van Doorn, 'The Leadership of Pragmatism—Reconsidering Franklin in the Age of Charisma', *Leadership Quarterly* 12, no. 3 (Fall 2001), 279–309.

50   R. E. De Vries, R. A. Roe and T. C. B. Taillieu, 'On Charisma and Need for Leadership', *European Journal of Work and Organizational Psychology* 8 (1999), 109–33; R. Khurana, *Searching for a Corporate Savior: The Irrational Quest for Charismatic CEOs* (Princeton, NJ: Princeton University Press, 2002).

51   Bennis and Nanus, *Leaders*, pp. 27–33, 89; I. M. Levin, 'Vision Revisited', *Journal of Applied Behavioral Science* 36 (March 2000), 91–107; J. R. Sparks and J. A. Schenk, 'Explaining the Effects of Transformational Leadership: An Investigation of the Effects of Higher-Order Motives in Multilevel Marketing Organizations', *Journal of Organizational Behavior* 22 (2001), 849–69; D. Christenson and D. H. T. Walker, 'Understanding the Role of "Vision" in Project Success', *Project Management Journal* 35, no. 3 (September 2004), 39–52; R. E. Quinn, *Building the Bridge as You Walk on It: A Guide for Leading Change* (San Francisco: Jossey-Bass, 2004), chapter 11.

52   J. R. Baum, E. A. Locke and S. A. Kirkpatrick, 'A Longitudinal Study of the Relation of Vision and Vision Communication to Venture Growth in Entrepreneurial Firms', *Journal of Applied Psychology* 83 (1998), 43–54; S. L. Hoe and S. L. McShane, 'Leadership Antecedents of Informal Knowledge Acquisition and Dissemination', *International Journal of Organisational Behaviour* 5 (2002), 282–91.

53   J. A. Conger, 'Inspiring Others: The Language of Leadership', *Academy of Management Executive* 5 (February 1991), 31–45; G. T. Fairhurst and R. A. Sarr, *The Art of Framing: Managing the Language of Leadership* (San Francisco, CA: Jossey-Bass, 1996); A. E. Rafferty and M. A. Griffin, 'Dimensions of Transformational Leadership: Conceptual and Empirical Extensions', *Leadership Quarterly* 15, no. 3 (2004), 329–54.

54   L. Black, 'Hamburger Diplomacy', *Report on Business Magazine*, August 1988, 30–6.

55   D. E. Berlew, 'Leadership and Organizational Excitement', *California Management Review* 17, no. 2 (Winter 1974), 21–30; Bennis and Nanus, *Leaders*, pp. 43–55; T. Simons, 'Behavioral Integrity: The Perceived Alignment between Managers' Words and Deeds as a Research Focus', *Organization Science* 13, no. 1 (January–February 2002), 18–35.

56   M. Webb, 'Executive Profile: Peter C. Farrell', *San Diego Business Journal*, 24 March 2003, 32; P. Benesh, 'He Likes Them Breathing Easy', *Investor's Business Daily*, 13 September 2005, A04. The two surveys are reported in: ISR, 'Driving an Innovative Culture: Insights from Global Research and Implications for Businesses in Hong Kong' (ISR, 2004), www.isrsurveys.com.au/pdf/insight/IHRM%20Show-18Nov04.pdf (accessed 22 December 2005); Watson Wyatt Worldwide, 'Worktaiwan: Key Findings' (Singapore: Watson Wyatt Worldwide, 2004), www.watsonwyatt.com/asia-pacific/research/workasia/worktw_keyfindings.asp (accessed 2 December 2005).

57   'Emerging Market Corporates', *The Banker*, 1 July 2003; G. Chellam, 'Haier Story a Smash-Hit', *New Zealand Herald*, 20 September 2003; D. J. Lynch, 'CEO Pushes China's Haier as Global Brand', *USA Today*, 3 January 2003, 1B.

58   J. Barling, T. Weber and E. K. Kelloway, Effects of Transformational Leadership Training on Attitudinal and Financial Outcomes: A Field Experiment', *Journal of Applied Psychology* 81 (1996), 827–32.

59   A. Bryman, 'Leadership in Organizations', in *Handbook of Organization Studies*, eds S. R. Clegg, C. Hardy and W. R. Nord (Thousand Oaks, CA: Sage, 1996), 276–92.

60 B. S. Pawar and K. K. Eastman, 'The Nature and Implications of Contextual Influences on Transformational Leadership: A Conceptual Examination', *Academy of Management Review* 22 (1997), 80–109; C. P. Egri and S. Herman, 'Leadership in the North American Environmental Sector: Values, Leadership Styles, and Contexts of Environmental Leaders and Their Organizations', *Academy of Management Journal* 43, no. 4 (2000), 571–604.

61 J. R. Meindl, 'On Leadership: An Alternative to the Conventional Wisdom', *Research in Organizational Behavior* 12 (1990), 159–203; L. R. Offermann, J. J. K. Kennedy and P. W. Wirtz, 'Implicit Leadership Theories: Content, Structure, and Generalizability', *Leadership Quarterly* 5, no. 1 (1994), 43–58; R. J. Hall and R. G. Lord, 'Multi-Level Information Processing Explanations of Followers' Leadership Perceptions', *Leadership Quarterly* 6 (1995), 265–87; O. Epitropaki and R. Martin, 'Implicit Leadership Theories in Applied Settings: Factor Structure, Generalizability, and Stability over Time', *Journal of Applied Psychology* 89, no. 2 (2004), 293–310.

62 L. M. A. Chong and D. C. Thomas, 'Leadership Perceptions in Cross-Cultural Context: Pakeha and Pacific Islanders in New Zealand', *Leadership Quarterly* 8 (1997), 275–93; R. G. Lord et al., 'Contextual Constraints on Prototype Generation and Their Multilevel Consequences for Leadership Perceptions', *The Leadership Quarterly* 12, no. 3 (2001), 311–38; T. Keller, 'Parental Images as a Guide to Leadership Sensemaking: An Attachment Perspective on Implicit Leadership Theories', *Leadership Quarterly* 14 (2003), 141–60.

63 S. F. Cronshaw and R. G. Lord, 'Effects of Categorization, Attribution, and Encoding Processes on Leadership Perceptions', *Journal of Applied Psychology* 72 (1987), 97–106; J. L. Nye and D. R. Forsyth, 'The Effects of Prototype-Based Biases on Leadership Appraisals: A Test of Leadership Categorization Theory', *Small Group Research* 22 (1991), 360–79.

64 R. Weber et al., 'The Illusion of Leadership: Misattribution of Cause in Coordination Games', *Organization Science* 12, no. 5 (2001), 582–98; N. Ensari and S. E. Murphy, 'Cross-Cultural Variations in Leadership Perceptions and Attribution of Charisma to the Leader', *Organizational Behavior and Human Decision Processes* 92 (2003), 52–66; M. L. A. Hayward, V. P. Rindova and T. G. Pollock, 'Believing One's Own Press: The Causes and Consequences of CEO Celebrity', *Strategic Management Journal* 25, no. 7 (July 2004), 637–53.

65 Meindl, 'On Leadership: An Alternative to the Conventional Wisdom', p. 163.

66 J. Pfeffer, 'The Ambiguity of Leadership', *Academy of Management Review* 2 (1977), 102–12.

67 Six of the Project GLOBE clusters are described in a special issue of the *Journal of World Business* 37 (2000). For an overview of Project GLOBE, see: House, Javidan and Dorfman, 'Project Globe: An Introduction'; House et al., 'Understanding Cultures and Implicit Leadership Theories across the Globe: An Introduction to Project Globe'.

68 J. C. Jesiuno, 'Latin Europe Cluster: From South to North', *Journal of World Business* 37 (2002), 88. Another GLOBE study of Iranian managers also reported that charismatic visionary stands out as a primary leadership dimension. See: A. Dastmalchian, M. Javidan and K. Alam, 'Effective Leadership and Culture in Iran: An Empirical Study', *Applied Psychology: An International Review* 50 (2001), 532–58.

69 D. N. Den Hartog et al., 'Culture Specific and Cross-Cultural Generalizable Implicit Leadership Theories: Are Attributes of Charismatic/Transformational Leadership Universally Endorsed?', *Leadership Quarterly* 10 (1999), 219–56; F. C. Brodbeck et al., 'Cultural Variation of Leadership Prototypes across 22 European Countries', *Journal of Occupational and Organizational Psychology* 73 (2000), 1–29; E. Szabo et al., 'The Europe Cluster: Where Employees Have a Voice', *Journal of World Business* 37 (2002), 55–68. The Mexican study is reported in C. E. Nicholls, H. W. Lane and M. B. Brechu, 'Taking Self-Managed Teams to Mexico', *Academy of Management Executive* 13 (August 1999), 15–25.

70 J. B. Rosener, 'Ways Women Lead', *Harvard Business Review* 68 (November–December 1990), 119–25; S. H. Appelbaum and B. T. Shapiro, 'Why Can't Men Lead Like Women?', *Leadership and Organization Development Journal* 14 (1993), 28–34; N. Wood, 'Venus Rules', *Incentive* 172 (February 1998), 22–7.

71 G. N. Powell, 'One More Time: Do Female and Male Managers Differ?', *Academy of Management Executive* 4 (1990), 68–75; M. L. van Engen and T. M. Willemsen, 'Sex and Leadership Styles: A Meta-Analysis of Research Published in the 1990s', *Psychological Reports* 94, no. 1 (February 2004), 3–18.

72 R. Sharpe, 'As Leaders, Women Rule', *Business Week*, 20 November 2000, 74; M. Sappenfield, 'Women, It Seems, Are Better Bosses', *Christian Science Monitor*, 16 January 2001; A. H. Eagly and L. L. Carli, 'The Female Leadership Advantage: An Evaluation of the Evidence', *The Leadership Quarterly* 14, no. 6 (December 2003), 807–34; A. H. Eagly, M. C. Johannesen-Schmidt and M. L. van Engen, 'Transformational, Transactional, and Laissez-Faire Leadership Styles: A Meta-Analysis Comparing Women and Men', *Psychological Bulletin* 129 (July 2003), 569–91.

73 A. H. Eagly, S. J. Karau and M. G. Makhijani, 'Gender and the Effectiveness of Leaders: A Meta-Analysis', *Psychological Bulletin* 117 (1995), 125–45; J. G. Oakley, 'Gender-Based Barriers to Senior Management Positions: Understanding the Scarcity of Female CEOs', *Journal of Business Ethics* 27 (2000), 821–34; N. Z. Stelter, 'Gender Differences in Leadership: Current Social Issues and Future Organizational Implications', *Journal of Leadership Studies* 8 (2002), 88–99; M. E. Heilman et al., 'Penalties for Success: Reactions to Women Who Succeed at Male Gender-Typed Tasks', *Journal of Applied Psychology* 89, no. 3 (2004), 416–27; A. H. Eagly, 'Achieving Relational Authenticity in Leadership: Does Gender Matter?', *The Leadership Quarterly* 16, no. 3 (June 2005), 459–74.

VIDEO CASE STUDIES

BULLY BROADS

Women executives in Silicon Valley who seem to be over-aggressive are sent to (or voluntarily join) a reform program called the Bully Broads Program. The program provides executive coaching as well as group activities to curb the impulse to influence others through too much assertiveness. But while the program has value in changing behaviour, its founder and participants also believe that there is a double standard operating: aggressive male executives aren't sent to similar programs, and there is still an expectation that women should act in a more gentle way than men.

QUESTIONS

1. Use your knowledge of power and influence in the workplace to explain why aggressive women are told to be less aggressive whereas this behaviour is seen as acceptable in men.

2. Are there workplaces where the organisational political climate makes it more conducive to aggressive female leaders?

VIDEO CASE STUDIES

INSERT YOUR CD NOW TO VIEW THE FOOTAGE THAT CORRESPONDS TO THESE CASES

CELEBRITY CEO CHARISMA

Does the cult of CEO charisma really make a difference to company profits? This video program takes a brief look at chief executives who acted like super-heroes but failed to deliver, as well as a few low-key executives who really made a difference. The program hears from Harvard business school professor Rakesh Khurana, author of *Searching for a Corporate Savior*, a book warning that charismatic leaders are not necessarily effective leaders.

1. Why do company boards tend to hire charismatic CEOs?

2. What can corporate boards do to minimise the charisma effect when filling chief executive officer and other senior executive positions?

QUESTIONS

PART 4

Organisational processes

CHAPTER 15
Organisational structure

CHAPTER 16
Organisational culture

CHAPTER 17
Organisational change

VIDEO CASE STUDIES
- Childcare help
- Home sweet home, work sweet work

CHAPTER 15

Organisational structure

LEARNING OBJECTIVES

After reading this chapter, you should be able to:

- describe three types of coordination in organisational structures

- explain why firms can have flatter structures than previously believed

- discuss the dynamics of centralisation and formalisation as organisations get larger and older

- contrast functional structures with divisional structures

- explain why geographic divisional structures are becoming less common than other divisional structures

- outline the features and advantages of the matrix structure

- describe the features of team-based organisational structures

- discuss the merits of the network structure

- summarise the contingencies of organisational design

- explain how organisational strategy relates to organisational structure.

Globalisation is playing havoc with the organisational structures of advertising agencies. Some multinational firms, such as Samsung, have centralised marketing decisions, requiring ad firms to also concentrate their expertise globally. Yet other companies, such as Coca-Cola and Procter & Gamble, have positioned their advertising decisions at the regional level, so agencies serving these clients need to offer both regional and global expertise. Meanwhile, believing that global advertising firms are too bureaucratic, several client companies are turning to boutique agencies for local expertise.

Australian advertising executive Chris Clarke may have found an organisational structure that satisfies this mishmash of client needs. Clarke launched Nitro, a virtual agency in which each local office has account service staff, but a global creative 'swat' team is parachuted in as required. Nitro began in Shanghai and within three years had expanded to New York, London, Taipei, Hong Kong, Sydney and Melbourne. Its global billings have already reached A$400 million.

Boutique advertising firm Nitro relies on an organisational structure that keeps it nimble and responsive to customer needs.

Nitro's balance of regional decentralisation and global centralisation gives clients direct access to the agency's top creative teams, who move from hub to hub and sometimes work in clients' offices. Clarke also intends to keep Nitro boutique-size by limiting the number of clients. 'We want to remain small, as a certain size gives us the ability to be fast and nimble,' he says. Wei Wei Chen, Nitro's head of operations for Greater China, says that the company's unique structure minimises the bureaucracy of most global agencies. 'The speed at which we can move gives us a competitive edge. We believe in erasing the line between departments and between us and the client.'

Nitro isn't alone in designing an organisational structure aligned with the need for global and regional balance. Lowe Worldwide recently introduced a 'lighthouse structure' which reorganised its offices in ninety-one countries around a dozen 'lighthouses', or centres of creativity, in key markets. 'The Lighthouse structure eliminates the bureaucratic system of regional management and pools resources, talent and processes,' explains one executive at the London-based ad agency. Another adds: '[The Lighthouse structure] means access to top-flight talent around the world—talent that has access to local markets and the creativity and flexibility to execute.'[1]

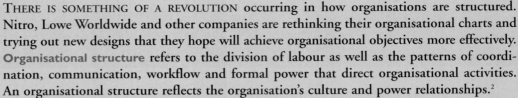

THERE IS SOMETHING OF A REVOLUTION occurring in how organisations are structured. Nitro, Lowe Worldwide and other companies are rethinking their organisational charts and trying out new designs that they hope will achieve organisational objectives more effectively. **Organisational structure** refers to the division of labour as well as the patterns of coordination, communication, workflow and formal power that direct organisational activities. An organisational structure reflects the organisation's culture and power relationships.[2]

Organisational structures are frequently used as tools for change because they establish new communication patterns and align employee behaviour with the corporate vision.[3] For example, to steer Charles Schwab & Co. out of its financial trouble, founder Charles Schwab held a two-day marathon session in which the company's top executives were asked to redraw the organisation chart in a way that would make the company simpler, more decentralised and refocused on the customer. Every executive in the room, including those whose jobs would be erased from the new structure, were asked for their input.[4]

This chapter begins by considering the two fundamental processes in organisational structure: division of labour and coordination. This is followed by a detailed investigation of the four main elements of organisational structure: span of control, centralisation, formalisation and departmentalisation. The latter part of the chapter examines the contingencies of organisational design, including the external environment, organisational size, technology and strategy.

DIVISION OF LABOUR AND COORDINATION

All organisational structures include two fundamental requirements: the division of labour into distinct tasks and the coordination of that labour so that employees are able to accomplish common goals.[5] Organisations are groups of people who work interdependently towards some purpose. To efficiently accomplish their goals, these groups typically divide the work into manageable chunks, particularly when there are many different tasks to perform. They also introduce various coordinating mechanisms to ensure that everyone is working effectively towards the same objectives.

DIVISION OF LABOUR

Division of labour refers to the subdivision of work into separate jobs assigned to different people. Subdivided work leads to job specialisation, because each job now includes a narrow subset of the tasks necessary to complete the product or service. Launching a space shuttle at NASA, for example, requires tens of thousands of specific tasks that are divided among thousands of people. Tasks are also divided vertically, such as having supervisors coordinate work while employees perform the work.

Work is divided into specialised jobs because it potentially increases work efficiency.[6] Job incumbents can master their tasks quickly because work cycles are very short. Less time is wasted changing from one task to another. Training costs are reduced because employees require fewer physical and mental skills to accomplish the assigned work. Finally, job specialisation makes it easier to match people with specific aptitudes or skills to the jobs for which they are best suited.

COORDINATING WORK ACTIVITIES

LEARNING OBJECTIVE

Describe three types of coordination in organisational structures.

As soon as people divide work among themselves, coordinating mechanisms are needed to ensure that everyone works in concert. Every organisation—from the two-person corner convenience store to the largest corporate entity—uses one or more of the following coordinating mechanisms:[7] informal communication, formal hierarchy and standardisation (see Exhibit 15.1).

Coordinating mechanisms in organisations

EXHIBIT 15.1

Form of coordination	Description	Sub-types
Informal communication	Sharing information on mutual tasks; forming common mental models to synchronise work activities	• Direct communication • Liaison roles • Integrator roles
Formal hierarchy	Assigning legitimate power to individuals, who then use this power to direct work processes and allocate resources	• Direct supervision • Corporate structure
Standardisation	Creating routine patterns of behaviour or output	• Standardised skills • Standardised processes • Standardised output

Source: Based on information in J. Galbraith, *Designing Complex Organisations* (Reading, MA: Addison-Wesley, 1973), pp. 8–19; H. Mintzberg, *The Structuring of Organisations* (Englewood Cliffs, NJ: Prentice Hall, 1979), chapter 1; D. A. Nadler and M. L. Tushman, *Competing by Design: The Power of Organisational Architecture* (New York: Oxford University Press, 1997), chapter 6.

Coordination through informal communication

Informal communication is a coordinating mechanism in all organisations. This includes sharing information on mutual tasks as well as forming common mental models so that employees synchronise work activities using the same mental road map.[8] Informal communication is vital in non-routine and ambiguous situations, because employees can exchange a large volume of information through face-to-face communication and other media-rich channels.

Coordination through informal communication is easiest in small firms such as Nitro, although information technologies have further leveraged this coordinating mechanism in large organisations. Companies employing thousands of people, such as Brisbane-based Flight Centre travel agency, also support informal communication by keeping each workplace small. Toyota and other car-makers further support this coordinating mechanism by occasionally moving dozens of employees responsible for developing a new product into one large room.[9]

Larger organisations also encourage coordination through informal communication by creating *integrator roles*. These people are responsible for coordinating a work process by encouraging employees in each work unit to share information and informally coordinate work activities. Integrators do not have authority over the people involved in that process, so they must rely on persuasion and commitment. Brand managers at Procter & Gamble co-ordinate work among marketing, production and design groups.[10]

Coordination through formal hierarchy

Informal communication is the most flexible form of coordination, but it can be time consuming. Consequently, as organisations grow, they develop a second coordinating mechanism: formal hierarchy. Hierarchy assigns legitimate power to individuals, who then use this power to direct work processes and allocate resources. In other words, work is coordinated through direct supervision. Any organisation with a formal structure coordinates work to some extent through the formal hierarchy. For instance, senior production coordinators at Animal Logic, the Sydney-based computer graphics company, are responsible for ensuring that employees on their team remain on schedule and that their respective tasks are compatible with tasks completed by other team members.

The formal hierarchy also coordinates work among executives through the division of organisational activities. If the organisation is divided into geographic areas, the structure gives the regional group leaders legitimate power over executives responsible for production, customer service and other activities in those areas. If the organisation is divided into product groups, the heads of those groups have the right to coordinate work across regions.

The formal hierarchy has traditionally been applauded as the optimal coordinating mechanism for large organisations. A century ago, administrative scholars argued that organisations are most effective where managers exercise their authority and employees receive orders from only one supervisor. Coordination should occur through the chain of command: that is, up the hierarchy and across to the other work unit.[11]

Coordination through formal hierarchy may have been popular with classic organisational theorists, but it can be an inefficient coordinating mechanism. Without relying on other coordinating mechanisms, managers are able to supervise only a limited number of employees. As the business grows, the number of supervisors and layers of management must also increase, resulting in a costly bureaucracy. Also, communicating through the chain of command is rarely as fast or accurate as direct communication between employees. A third concern is that today's workforce is less tolerant of rigid structures. For instance, Pretoria Portland Cement is one of South Africa's best places to work, partly because it minimises formal hierarchy as a coordinating mechanism.

Coordination through standardisation

Standardisation, the third means of coordination, involves creating routine patterns of behaviour or output. This coordinating mechanism takes three distinct forms:

- *Standardised processes.* Quality and consistency of a product or service can often be improved by standardising work activities through job descriptions and procedures.[12] This coordinating mechanism is feasible when the work is routine (such as mass production) or simple (such as making pizzas), but is less effective in non-routine and complex work such as product design.
- *Standardised outputs.* This form of standardisation involves ensuring that individuals and work units have clearly defined goals and output measures (e.g. customer satisfaction,

Medical team coordinates through expertise

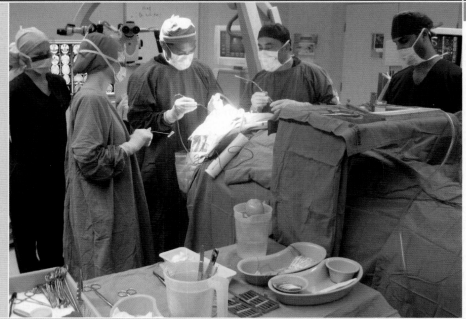

Led by Dr Charlie Teo, Director of the Centre for Minimally Invasive Surgery at Prince of Wales Private Hospital in Sydney, this surgery team is divided into specialised jobs so that each person has the required competencies for each position. To some extent, surgical work is coordinated through informal communication. However, much of the work activity can occur without discussion because team members also coordinate through standardisation of skills. Through extensive training, each medical professional has learned precise role behaviours so that his or her task activities are coordinated with others on the surgical team.

Charlie Teo

production efficiency). For instance, to coordinate the work of salespeople, companies assign sales targets rather than specific behaviours.

- *Standardised skills.* When work activities are too complex to standardise through processes or goals, companies often coordinate work effort by extensively training employees or hiring people who have learned precise role behaviours from educational programs. This form of coordination is used in hospital operating rooms. Surgeons, nurses and other operating room professionals coordinate their work more through training than through goals or company rules.

Division of labour and coordination of work represent the two fundamental ingredients of all organisations. How the work is divided, who makes the decisions, which coordinating mechanisms are emphasised and other issues are related to the four elements of organisational structure.

ELEMENTS OF ORGANISATIONAL STRUCTURE

Every company is configured in terms of four basic elements of organisational structure. This section introduces three of them: span of control, centralisation and formalisation. The fourth element—departmentalisation—is presented in the next section.

SPAN OF CONTROL

Span of control refers to the number of people directly reporting to the next level in the hierarchy. Almost 100 years ago French engineer and administrative theorist Henri Fayol strongly recommended the formal hierarchy as the primary coordinating mechanism. Consequently, he prescribed a relatively narrow span of control, typically no more than twenty employees per supervisor and six supervisors per manager. These prescriptions were based on the assumption that managers simply cannot monitor and control any more subordinates closely enough. Today we know better. The best performing manufacturing plants currently have an average of thirty-eight production employees per supervisor.[13]

What's the secret here? Did Fayol and others miscalculate the optimal span of control? The answer is that Fayol and many other scholars sympathetic to hierarchical control believed that employees should 'do' the work, whereas supervisors and other management personnel should monitor employee behaviour and make most of the decisions. In contrast, the best performing manufacturing operations today rely on self-directed work teams, so direct supervision (formal hierarchy) is just a back-up coordinating mechanism. The underlying principle here is that the optimal span of control depends on the presence of other coordinating mechanisms. Self-directed work teams supplement direct supervision with informal communication and specialised knowledge.[14]

Along with the presence of other coordinating mechanisms, the best span of control depends on the nature of the task. A wider span of control is possible when employees perform routine tasks, whereas a narrower span of control is required when employees perform novel or complex tasks. Routine tasks have few exceptions, so there is less need for direction or advice from supervisors, whereas novel or complex tasks tend to require more supervisory decisions or coaching. This principle is illustrated in a survey of American property/casualty insurers. The average span of control in commercial policy processing departments is around fifteen employees per supervisor, whereas the span of control is 6.1 in claims service and 5.5 in commercial underwriting. Staff members in the latter two departments perform more technical work, so they have more novel and complex tasks. Commercial policy processing, on the other hand, is production-like work where tasks are routine and have few exceptions.[15]

A third influence on span of control is the degree of interdependence among employees within the department or team. One recent study of airline flight departure crews reported that supervisors responsible for highly interdependent teams need to provide more feedback

span of control The number of people directly reporting to the next level in the organisational hierarchy.

LEARNING OBJECTIVE

Explain why firms can have flatter structures than previously believed.

and coaching than where employees have less interdependence. When tasks are highly interdependent, employees lack unique performance indicators for their own work, so supervisory feedback must be introduced. This increased coaching and feedback means that supervisors need a narrower span of control when managing highly interdependent teams.[16]

Tall and flat structures

BASF's European Seal Sands plant recently organised employees into self-directed work teams and dramatically restructured the work process. These actions did much more than increase efficiency and lower costs at the bulk chemical plant. They also chopped out several layers of hierarchy. 'Seven levels of management have been cut basically to two,' says a BASF executive.[17]

BASF's European Seal Sands plant joins a long list of companies that are moving towards flatter organisational structures. This trend towards delayering—moving from a tall to a flat structure—is partly in response to the recommendations of management gurus. Nearly twenty years ago, for example, management guru Tom Peters challenged corporate leaders to cut the number of layers to three within a facility and to five within the entire organisation.[18] The main reasons why BASF and other companies are moving towards flatter organisational structures is that it potentially cuts overhead costs and puts decision makers closer to front-line staff and information about customer needs. With fewer managers, employees might also experience more empowerment due to their greater autonomy in regard to their work roles.

However, some organisational experts warn that corporate leaders may be cutting out too much hierarchy. They argue that the much-maligned 'middle managers' serve a valuable function by controlling work activities and managing corporate growth. Moreover, companies will always need hierarchy because someone has to make the quick decisions and represent a source of appeal over conflicts.[19] The conclusion here is that there is an optimal level of delayering in most organisations. Flatter structures offer several benefits, but cutting out too much management can offset these benefits.

One last point before leaving this topic: the size of an organisation's hierarchy depends on both the average span of control and the number of people employed by the organisation. Exhibit 15.2 illustrates this principle. A tall structure has many hierarchical levels, each with a

EXHIBIT 15.2　Span of control and tall/flat structures

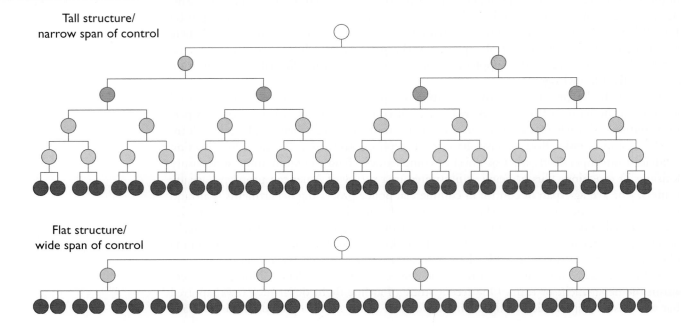

Tall structure/
narrow span of control

Flat structure/
wide span of control

relatively narrow span of control, whereas a flat structure has few levels, each with a wide span of control Larger organisations that depend on hierarchy for coordination necessarily develop taller structures. For instance, Microsoft is considered a high-involvement organisation, yet it has at least seven levels of corporate hierarchy to coordinate its tens of thousands of employees.[20]

CENTRALISATION AND DECENTRALISATION

Centralisation and decentralisation represent a second element of organisational design. **Centralisation** means that formal decision-making authority is held by a small group of people, typically those at the top of the organisational hierarchy. Most organisations begin with centralised structures, as the founder makes most of the decisions and tries to direct the business towards his or her vision. But as organisations grow they diversify and their environments become more complex. Senior executives are not able to process all the decisions that significantly influence the business. Consequently, larger organisations tend to *decentralise*, that is, they disperse decision authority and power throughout the organisation.

Soon after becoming chief executive of Barrick Gold Corp., Greg Wilkins recognised that large firms can't remain centralised forever. 'Barrick had always been run on this command-and-control model, a centrist approach that saw all the decision making made in Toronto,' Wilkins said. 'That worked while the company was small and operating only in North America. But all of a sudden we are in four continents and seven countries and it becomes pretty clear that you just can't do it any more.' The company has since decentralised its operations around three regions of the world.[21]

The optimal level of centralisation or decentralisation depends on several contingencies that will be examined later in the chapter. However, it is appropriate to mention here that different degrees of decentralisation can occur simultaneously in different parts of the organisation. Nestlé has decentralised marketing decisions to remain responsive to local markets. At the same time, the Swiss-based food company has centralised production, logistics and supply-chain management activities to improve cost efficiencies and avoid having too much complexity

centralisation The degree to which formal decision authority is held by a small group of people, typically those at the top of the organisational hierarchy.

LEARNING OBJECTIVE

Discuss the dynamics of centralisation and formalisation as organisations get larger and older.

Malaysian government decentralises for better service

The Malaysian government recently concluded that the centralised organisational structure in most government agencies, in which the department head makes most of the decisions, is the main culprit causing long queues, slow service and frustrated clients. To improve this situation, the government advised department heads to delegate more decision-making authority to lower level staff. 'Department heads who are responsible for decision making should empower their subordinates and allow them to make decisions in their absence so that the public will not be inconvenienced,' says the Malaysian government's Chief Secretary, Tan Sri Samsudin Osman. The government also encourages departments to set up 'centres for decision making' as part of the decentralisation process. Along with improving customer service, the government believes that decentralisation will reduce the incidence of corruption. 'If there is no proper delegation of authority and there are no centres for decision-making, then there are a lot of opportunities to do negative things,' explains a senior government official.[23]

Munshi Ahmed/OnAsia.com

across the organisation. 'If you are too decentralised, you can become too complicated—you get too much complexity in your production system,' explains Nestlé CEO Peter Brabeck.[22] Firms also tend to rapidly centralise during times of turbulence and organisational crisis. When the problems are over, the company should decentralise decisions again, although this reversal tends to occur slowly because leaders are reluctant to give up decision-making power.

FORMALISATION

Have you ever wondered why McDonald's hamburgers in Sydney look and taste the same as the McDonald's hamburgers in Singapore? The reason is that the fast-food company has engineered out all variation through formalisation. **Formalisation** is the degree to which organisations standardise behaviour through rules, procedures, formal training and related mechanisms.[24] In other words, formalisation represents the establishment of standardisation as a coordinating mechanism.

McDonald's Restaurants has a formalised structure because it relies heavily on standardisation of work processes as a coordinating mechanism. Employees have precisely defined roles, right down to how much mustard should be dispensed, how many pickles should be applied, and how long each hamburger should be cooked. In contrast, Nitro, described in the opening story to this chapter, has relatively little formalisation because job descriptions and output expectations are broadly defined to accommodate varying tasks and responsibilities.

Older companies tend to become more formalised because work activities become routinised, making them easier to document into standardised practices. Larger companies formalise as a coordinating mechanism, because direct supervision and informal communication among employees do not operate as easily. External influences, such as government safety legislation and strict accounting rules, also encourage formalisation.

Problems with formalisation

Formalisation may increase efficiency and compliance, but it can also create problems. Rules and procedures reduce organisational flexibility, so employees follow prescribed behaviours even when the situation clearly calls for a customised response. Thus, high levels of formalisation undermine a learning orientation required for knowledge management and creativity. Some work rules become so convoluted that organisational efficiency would decline if they were actually followed as prescribed. Labour unions sometimes invoke work-to-rule strikes, in which their members closely follow the formalised rules and procedures established by an organisation. This tactic is effective because the company's productivity actually falls when employees follow the rules that are supposed to guide their behaviour.

Formalised structures are fine for employees who value a stable workplace, but many employees today feel disempowered—they lack a feeling of self-determination, meaning, competence and the impact of their organisational role—when working in highly formalised organisations. Finally, rules and procedures have been known to take on a life of their own in some organisations. They become the focus of attention rather than the organisation's ultimate objectives of producing a product or service and serving its dominant stakeholders.

MECHANISTIC VERSUS ORGANIC STRUCTURES

Span of control, centralisation and formalisation have been discussed together because they usually cluster into two forms: mechanistic and organic structures.[25] A **mechanistic structure** is characterised by a narrow span of control and a high degree of formalisation and centralisation. Mechanistic structures have many rules and procedures, limited decision making at lower levels, tall hierarchies of people in specialised roles, and vertical rather than horizontal communication flows. Tasks are rigidly defined, and are altered only when sanctioned by higher authorities.

Companies with an **organic structure** have the opposite characteristics. Nitro, the boutique advertising firm described at the beginning of the chapter, is a clear example of an organic structure because it has a wide span of control, decentralised decision making and little formalisation. Tasks are fluid, adjusting to new situations and organisational needs. The organic structure values knowledge and takes the view that information may be located anywhere in the organisation rather than only among senior executives. Thus, communication flows in all directions with little concern for the formal hierarchy.

Mechanistic structures operate best in stable environments because they rely on efficiency and routine behaviours. However, as emphasised throughout this book, most organisations operate in a world of dramatic change. Information technology, globalisation, a changing workforce and other factors have strengthened the need for more organic structures that are flexible and responsive to these changes. Organic structures are also more compatible with knowledge and quality management, because they emphasise information sharing rather than hierarchy and status.[26]

FORMS OF DEPARTMENTALISATION

Span of control, centralisation, and formalisation are important elements of organisational structure, but most people think about organisational charts when the discussion of organisational structure arises. The organisational chart represents the fourth element in the structuring of organisations, called departmentalisation. Departmentalisation specifies how employees and their activities are grouped together. It is a fundamental strategy for coordinating organisational activities because it influences organisational behaviour in the following ways.[27]

- Departmentalisation establishes the chain of command, that is, the system of common supervision among positions and units within the organisation. It frames the membership of formal work teams and typically determines which positions and units must share resources. Thus, departmentalisation establishes interdependencies among employees and subunits.
- Departmentalisation focuses people around common mental models or ways of thinking, such as serving clients, developing products or supporting a particular skill set. This focus is typically anchored around the common budgets and measures of performance assigned to employees within each departmental unit.
- Departmentalisation encourages coordination through informal communication among people and subunits. With common supervision and resources, members within each configuration typically work near each other, so they can use frequent and informal interaction to get the work done.

There are almost as many organisational charts as there are businesses, but five pure types of departmentalisation can be identified: simple, functional, divisional, matrix and team-based. In addition, this section describes the network structure, which extends beyond internal departments.

Simple structure

Most companies begin with a *simple structure*.[28] They employ only a few people and typically offer only one distinct product or service. There is minimal hierarchy, usually just employees reporting to the owners. Employees are grouped into broadly defined roles because there are insufficient economies of scale to assign them to specialised roles. The simple structure is highly flexible and minimises the walls that form between employees in other structures. However, the simple structure usually depends on the owner's direct supervision to coordinate work activities, so it is very difficult to operate as the company grows and becomes more complex.

FUNCTIONAL STRUCTURE

Organisations that grow large enough use functional structures at some level of the hierarchy or at some time in their history. A **functional structure** organises employees around specific

LEARNING OBJECTIVE

Contrast functional structures with divisional structures.

functional structure An organisational structure that organises employees around specific knowledge or other resources.

Boost Juice outgrows its simple structure

When Janine Allis opened her first Boost Juice store in Adelaide, she didn't employ many staff to fill in the organisational chart. 'I've had to do everything from painting the floor to doing the dishes, to typing up the million email addresses to put in the databases,' she recalls. The simple organisational structure consisted of Allis, a few employees, and her husband who assisted with marketing and franchising. Boost Juice grew to five stores within the first year, then mushroomed through franchising over the next five years to almost 200 stores employing 1600 people. Along the way, the company hired people for marketing, information technology, franchising, human resources, training and other functions. As these departments developed, Boost Juice's simple structure morphed into a functional structure. And as Allis and her corporate board eye franchise opportunities in New Zealand, Dubai, Chile, Hong Kong and other countries, Boost Juice may soon need to revise its organisational structure again.[29]

Boost Juice Pty Ltd

knowledge or other resources. Employees with marketing expertise are grouped into a marketing unit, those with production skills are located in manufacturing, engineers are found in product development, and so on. Organisations with functional structures are typically centralised to coordinate their activities effectively. Standardisation of work processes is the most common form of coordination used in a functional structure.

Evaluating the functional structure

The functional structure encourages specialisation and increases employees' identification with their profession. It permits greater specialisation so that the organisation has expertise in each area. Direct supervision is easier, because managers have a background in that functional area and employees approach them with common problems and issues. Finally, the functional structure creates common pools of talent that typically serve everyone in the organisation. This provides more economies of scale than if functional specialists are spread over different parts of the organisation.[30]

The functional structure also has limitations.[31] Grouping employees around their skills tends to focus attention on those skills and related professional needs rather than on the company's products/services or client needs. Unless people are transferred from one function to the next, they might not develop a broader understanding of the business. Compared with other structures, the functional structure usually produces higher dysfunctional conflict and poorer coordination in serving clients or developing products. These problems occur because employees need to work with co-workers in other departments to complete organisational tasks, yet they have different subgoals and mental models of ideal work. Together, these problems require substantial formal controls and coordination when people are organised around functions.

DIVISIONAL STRUCTURE

The **divisional structure** groups employees around geographic areas, outputs (products/services) or clients. This type of structure creates mini-businesses that may operate as subsidiaries rather than departments (sometimes called *strategic business units*); they are far more autonomous than functional departments. Exhibit 15.3 illustrates the three pure forms of divisional structure. The *geographic structure* organises employees around distinct regions of the country or globe. Exhibit 15.3(a) illustrates a geographic divisionalised structure recently adopted by Barrick Gold Corp. The *product/service structure* organises work around distinct outputs. Exhibit 15.3(b) illustrates this type of structure at Philips. The Dutch electronics company divides its workforce mainly into five product divisions, ranging from consumer electronics to semiconductors. The *client structure* represents the third form of divisional structure, in which employees are organised around specific customer groups. Exhibit 15.3(c) illustrates the customer-focused structure similar to one adopted by the US Internal Revenue Service.[32]

Which form of divisionalisation should large organisations adopt? The answer depends mainly on the primary source of environmental diversity or uncertainty.[33] Suppose that an organisation has one type of product sold to people across the country. If customer needs vary across regions, or if state governments impose different regulations on the product, then a geographic structure would be best in order to be more vigilant of this diversity. On the other hand, if the

divisional structure An organisational structure that groups employees around geographic areas, clients or outputs.

EXHIBIT 15.3

Three types of divisional structure

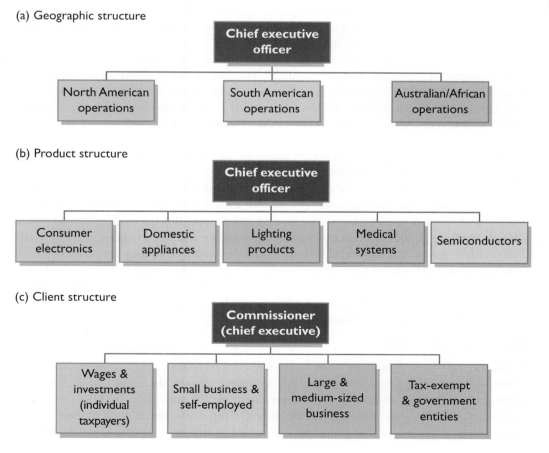

(a) Geographic structure

- Chief executive officer
  - North American operations
  - South American operations
  - Australian/African operations

(b) Product structure

- Chief executive officer
  - Consumer electronics
  - Domestic appliances
  - Lighting products
  - Medical systems
  - Semiconductors

(c) Client structure

- Commissioner (chief executive)
  - Wages & investments (individual taxpayers)
  - Small business & self-employed
  - Large & medium-sized business
  - Tax-exempt & government entities

company sells several types of products across the country and customer preferences and government regulations are similar everywhere, a product structure would probably work best.

Coca-Cola, Nestlé and many other food and beverage companies are organised mainly around geographic regions because consumer tastes and preferred marketing strategies vary considerably around the world. Even though McDonald's makes the same Big Mac around the planet, it has more fish products in Hong Kong and more vegetarian products in India, in line with traditional diets in those countries. Philips, on the other hand, is organised around products because consumer preferences are similar within each group. Hospitals from Geneva (Switzerland) to Santiago (Chile) purchase similar medical equipment from Philips, whereas the business of manufacturing and selling medical equipment is quite different from Philips' semiconductor business.

Many divisionalised companies are moving away from geographical structures.[34] One reason for this is that clients can purchase online and communicate with businesses from almost anywhere in the world, so local representation is less critical. Reduced geographic variation is another reason for the shift away from geographical structures; freer trade has reduced government intervention for many products, and consumer preferences for many products and services are becoming more similar, or converging, around the world. The third reason is that large companies increasingly have global business customers who demand one global point of purchase, not one in every country or region.

Evaluating the divisionalised structure

The divisional form is a building block structure, because it accommodates growth relatively easily. Related products or clients can be added to existing divisions with little need for additional learning. Different products, services or clients can be accommodated by sprouting a new division. Organisations typically reorganise around divisional structures as they expand into distinct products, services and domains of operation, because coordinating functional units becomes too unwieldy with increasing diversity.[35]

These advantages are offset by a number of limitations. First, the divisionalised structure tends to duplicate resources, such as production equipment and engineering or information technology expertise. Also, unless the division is quite large, resources are not used as efficiently as in functional structures where resources are pooled across the entire organisation. The divisionalised structure also creates silos of knowledge. Expertise is spread throughout the various business units, which reduces the ability and perhaps motivation of these people to share their knowledge with counterparts in other divisions. In contrast, a functional structure groups experts together, which supports knowledge sharing.

Finally, as explained above, the preferred divisionalised structure depends on the company's primary source of environmental diversity or uncertainty. This principle seems to be applied easily enough at Coca-Cola, McDonald's and Philips. But the decision is really quite difficult, because global organisations experience diversity and uncertainties in many ways. The decision also affects political dynamics in the organisation. If corporate leaders switch from a geographic to a product structure, people who led the geographical fiefdoms suddenly find themselves lower on the hierarchy than the product chiefs. Consequently, global organisations revise their structures back and forth, with each transition usually resulting in one or more executives leaving the company.

MATRIX STRUCTURE

Ralph Szygenda faced a dilemma when he became General Motors' first corporate chief information officer.[36] His group had to serve the company's regional divisions, and each region's information technology needs differed to some extent. At the same time, GM has five diverse IT services, such as product development and supply-chain management. Each of these services requires deep expertise, so staff providing one service would have quite different knowledge

LEARNING OBJECTIVE

Explain why geographic divisional structures are becoming less common than other divisional structures.

LEARNING OBJECTIVE

Outline the features and advantages of the matrix structure.

from staff providing one of the other IT services. The dilemma was whether to organise GM's hundreds of IT employees around a geographic or a process structure.

Szygenda's solution was to do both by adopting a **matrix structure**. A matrix structure overlays two organisational forms in order to leverage the benefits that each has to offer. GM's IT group is organised around both geography and processes, as Exhibit 15.4 illustrates. The processes dimension is led by five process information officers (PIOs), each of whom is responsible for specific IT processes around the world. These PIOs report only to Szygenda. The geographic dimension is led by five regional chief information officers (CIOs) who are responsible for IT functions in each of GM's five regions around the world. These CIOs report to Szygenda as well as to the heads of their respective geographic business division. For example, the North American CIO reports to Szygenda and to the president of GM North America. Because they work closely with GM's regional executives and understand their priorities, the regional CIOs control the region's IT budget. This means that GM's PIOs compete with each other for financial resources towards IT projects in their specialisation.

The matrix structure that organises hundreds of IT professionals at General Motors is just one of many possible matrix structure combinations. Most global firms with a matrix structure have geography on one dimension, but the other dimension might be products/services (such as GM's IT processes) or client groups. Instead of combining two divisional forms, some project-based firms overlap a functional structure with project teams. Electronic games companies sometimes use this structure. Employees are assigned to a cross-functional team responsible for a specific game project, yet they also belong to a permanent functional unit (design, audio, programming, etc.) from which they are redistributed when their work is completed on a particular project.[37]

matrix structure A type of departmentalisation that overlays two organisational forms in order to leverage the benefits of both.

Simplified matrix structure of GM's IT division

EXHIBIT 15.4

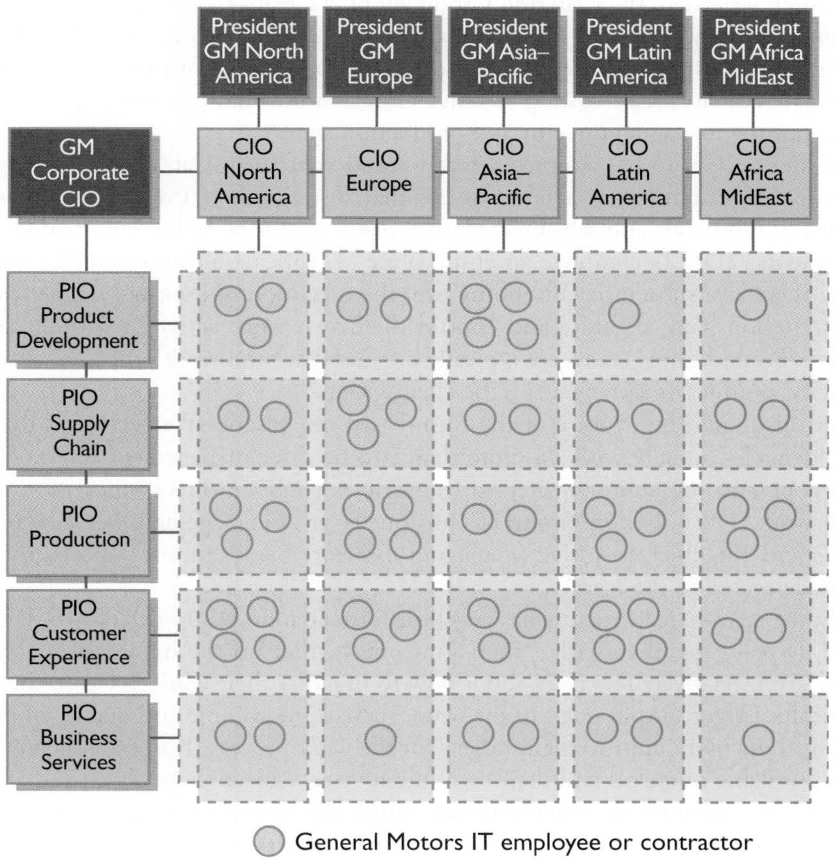

General Motors IT employee or contractor

Evaluating the matrix structure

The matrix structure usually optimises the use of resources and expertise, making it ideal for project-based organisations with fluctuating workloads. When properly managed, it improves communication efficiency, project flexibility and innovation compared with purely functional or divisional designs. It focuses employees on serving clients or creating products, yet keeps expertise organised around their specialisation so knowledge sharing improves and resources are used more efficiently. The matrix structure is also a logical choice when, as in the case of GM's IT group, two different dimensions are equally important. Structures determine executive power and what is important; the matrix structure works when two different dimensions deserve equal attention.

In spite of these advantages, the matrix structure has several well-known problems.[38] One concern is that it increases goal conflict and ambiguity. Employees working at the matrix level have two bosses and, consequently, two sets of priorities which aren't always aligned with each other. Project leaders might squabble over specific employees who are assigned to other projects. They might also disagree with employee decisions, but the employee's functional leader has more say than the project leader as to the individual's technical competence.

Another challenge is that the existence of two bosses can dilute accountability. In a functional or divisionalised structure, one manager is responsible for everything, even the most unexpected issues. But in a matrix structure, the unusual problems don't get resolved because neither manager takes ownership of them.[39] As a result of conflict and ambiguity in matrix structures, some employees experience more stress, and some managers are less satisfied with their work arrangements.

TEAM-BASED STRUCTURE

LEARNING OBJECTIVE

Describe the features of team-based organisational structures.

team-based structure A type of departmentalisation with a flat hierarchy and relatively little formalisation, consisting of self-directed work teams responsible for various work processes.

About a dozen years ago, the Criterion Group adopted a team-based organisation to improve quality and efficiency. The New Zealand manufacturer of ready-to-assemble furniture organises its 150 production employees into self-directed work teams with their own performance indicators and activity-based costing systems. Criterion now has just one layer of eight managers between the managing director and production staff.[40]

The Criterion Group has adopted a **team-based structure** in its production operations. The team-based structure has a few features that distinguish it from other organisational forms. First, it is built around self-directed work teams (SDWTs) rather than traditional teams or departments. SDWTs complete an entire piece of work requiring several interdependent tasks, and they have substantial autonomy over the execution of their tasks. The teams operating at Criterion plan, organise and control their own work activities without traditional supervision. Second, these teams are typically organised around work processes, such as making a specific product or serving a specific client group.

A third distinguishing feature of the team-based organisational structure is that it has a very flat hierarchy, usually with no more than two or three management levels. This flatter structure is possible because self-directed teams do not rely on direct supervision to coordinate their work. The Criterion Group has just one layer of management between production employees and the chief executive (managing director) because most supervisory activities have been delegated to the team.

Finally, the team-based structure has very little formalisation. Almost all day-to-day decisions are made by team members rather than someone further up the organisational hierarchy. Teams are given relatively few rules about how to organise their work. Instead, the executive team typically assigns output goals to the team, such as the volume and quality of product or service, or productivity improvement targets for the work process. Teams are then encouraged to use the available resources and their own initiative to achieve those objectives.

Team-based structures are usually found within the manufacturing operations of larger divisionalised structures. For example, American car-parts giant TRW Automotive has a team-based structure in many of its 200 plants, but these plants are linked together within the company's divisionalised structure. However, a small number of firms apply the team-based structure from top to bottom. Boutique ad agency Nitro is one such example, because employees work in teams without any departmentalisation. Perhaps the most famous example of this extreme level of team-based structure is W. L. Gore & Associates, which is described in Reality Check 15.1.

15.1 REALITY CHECK

THE EXTREME TEAM STRUCTURE OF W. L. GORE & ASSOCIATES

Diane Davidson admits that her first few months at W. L. Gore & Associates Inc. were a bit frustrating. 'When I arrived at Gore, I didn't know who did what,' recalls the apparel industry sales executive hired to market Gore-Tex fabrics to brand-name designers. 'I wondered how anything got done here. It was driving me crazy.' Davidson kept asking her 'starting sponsor' who her boss was, but the sponsor firmly replied 'Stop using the B-word'. Gore must have managers, she thought, but they probably downplay their status. But there really aren't any bosses, not in the traditional sense. 'Your team is your boss, because you don't want to let them down,' Davidson eventually learned. 'Everyone's your boss, and no one's your boss.'

From its beginnings in 1958, the Delaware-based manufacturer of fabrics (Gore-Tex), electronics and industrial and medical products has organised most of its employees (or 'associates', as they are known) around self-directed teams. The company has an incredibly flat hierarchy with a high degree of decentralised authority. Associates make day-to-day decisions within their expertise without approval from anyone higher up. Bigger issues, such as hiring and compensating staff, are decided by teams. 'We make our own decisions and everything is discussed as well,' explains Phyllis Tait, a medical business support leader at Gore's UK business unit.

The company has a divisional structure, organised around products and clients, with divisions such as Fabrics, Medical, Electronics and Industrial. But most of Gore's 7000 associates work at forty-five self-sufficient manufacturing and sales offices around the world. Each facility is deliberately limited to about 200 people so staff can coordinate effectively through informal communication. Within the units, new projects are started through individual initiative and support from others. 'There is no positional power,' explains a Gore team leader. 'You are only a leader if teams decide to respect and follow you.'

As Diane Davidson discovered, Gore operates without job titles, job descriptions or a formal chain of command. This ambiguous structure was established so that associates could be creative and responsive and coordinate directly with people in other areas of the organisation. 'You go to whomever you need to get things done,' says Gore sales veteran Tom Erickson. 'If I want to talk to a person on the manufacturing line about a particular job, I just go out and talk to him. That's one thing that sets us apart. There's no fear of any person going over another's head.'

W. L. Gore & Associates has an extreme team-based organisational structure that eliminates the traditional hierarchy. 'There's no fear of any person going over another's head,' says Gore sales veteran Tom Erickson, shown here (left) with a co-worker, John Cusick, in Gore's testing room.

© Bill Cramer

Sources: 'The Firm That Lets Staff Breathe', *Sunday Times* (London), 24 March 2002; A. Brown, 'Satisfaction All in a Day's Work for Top 3', *Evening News* (Edinburgh, Scotland), 23 March 2002, 13; M. Weinreb, 'Power to the People', *Sales & Marketing Management*, April 2003, 30–5; L. D. Maloney, 'Smiles in the Workplace', *Test & Measurement World*, March 2004, 5; A. Deutschman, 'The Fabric of Creativity', *Fast Company*, December 2004, 54–9.

Evaluating the team-based structure

The team-based organisation represents an increasingly popular structure because it is usually more responsive and flexible than the traditional functional or divisionalised structures.[41] It tends to reduce costs because teams have less reliance on formal hierarchy (direct supervision). A cross-functional team structure improves communication and cooperation across traditional boundaries. With greater autonomy, this structure also allows quicker and more informed decision making.[42] For this reason, some hospitals have shifted from functional departments to cross-functional teams. Teams composed of nurses, radiologists, anaesthetists, a pharmacology representative, possibly social workers, a rehabilitation therapist and other specialists communicate and coordinate more efficiently, thereby reducing delays and errors.[43]

Against these benefits, the team-based structure can be costly to maintain due to the need for ongoing interpersonal skills training. Teamwork potentially takes more time to coordinate than formal hierarchy during the early stages of team development. Employees may experience more stress due to increased ambiguity in their roles. Team leaders also experience more stress due to increased conflict, loss of functional power, and unclear career progression ladders.[44]

NETWORK STRUCTURE

LEARNING OBJECTIVE

Discuss the merits of the network structure.

network structure An alliance of several organisations for the purpose of creating a product or serving a client.

BMW isn't eager to let you know this, but some of its vehicles, designed and constructed with Germanic precision, are not designed or constructed by BMW or in Germany. The BMW X3, for example, was not only assembled by car-parts giant Magna International in Austria, but much of the vehicle's engineering was designed by Magna specialists. BMW is the hub organisation that owns and markets the brand and coordinates Magna and other organisations involved in BMW's network of supplies.[45]

BMW is moving towards a **network structure** as it creates an alliance of several organisations for the purpose of creating a product or serving a client.[46] Exhibit 15.5 illustrates a hypothetical example of the network structure, which typically consists of several satellite organisations beehived around a 'hub' or 'core' firm. The core firm 'orchestrates' the network

EXHIBIT 15.5   **A network structure**

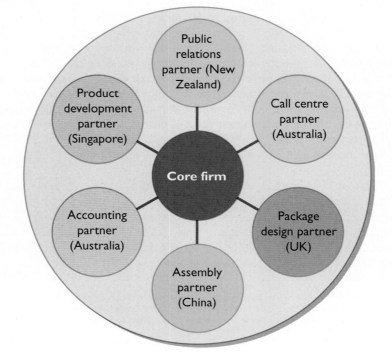

process and provides one or two other core competencies, such as marketing or product development. In the BMW example, BMW is the hub that provides marketing and distribution, whereas a variety of firms perform most other functions. The core firm might be the main contact with customers, but most of the product or service delivery and support activities are farmed out to satellite organisations located anywhere in the world. Extranets (web-based networks with partners) and other technologies ensure that information flows easily and openly between the core firm and its array of satellites.[47]

One of the main forces pushing towards a network structure is the recognition that an organisation has only a few *core competencies*. A core competency is a knowledge base that resides throughout the organisation and provides a strategic advantage. As companies discover their core competencies, they concentrate on those competencies and outsource most other activities to organisations whose core competency is performing those tasks.

Companies are also more likely to form network structures when technology is changing quickly and production processes are complex or varied.[48] Many firms cannot keep up with the hyperfast changes in information technology, so they have outsourced their entire information systems departments to IBM, EDS and other firms that specialise in information systems services. Similarly, many high-technology firms form networks with Celestica and other electronics equipment manufacturers because they have expertise in diverse production processes.

Virtual corporations

The network structure generally performs a patterned set of tasks for all clients. In contrast, some network structures—known as **virtual corporations**—represent several independent companies that form unique partnership teams to provide customised products or services, usually to specific clients, for a limited time.[49] Host Universal is a good example of this. The British advertising firm has no employees or clients. Instead, it serves a specific project by forming a unique team of partners, who then disband when the project is finished. 'At Host we have no clients or employees, which enables us to pull the most effective teams together from our network without foisting redundant skills, fees and hierarchy onto clients,' explains one of Host's founding partners.[50]

Virtual corporations exist temporarily and reshape themselves quickly to fit immediate needs. When an opportunity emerges, a unique combination of partners in the alliance forms a virtual corporation that works on the assignment until it is completed. Virtual corporations are self-organising, which means that they arrange their own communication patterns and roles to fit the situation. The relationship between the partners is mutually determined rather than imposed by a core firm.

Evaluating the network structure

For several years, organisational behaviour theorists have argued that organisational leaders must develop a metaphor of organisations as plasma-like organisms rather than rigid machines.[51] Network structures come close to the organism metaphor because they offer the flexibility to realign their structure with changing environmental requirements. If customers demand a new product or service, the core firm forms new alliances with other firms offering the appropriate resources. For example, by working with Magna International, BMW was probably able to develop and launch the X3 vehicle much sooner than if it had performed the necessary tasks on its own. When BMW needs a different type of manufacturing, it isn't saddled with non-essential facilities and resources. Network structures also offer efficiencies because the core firm becomes globally competitive as it shops worldwide for subcontractors with the best people and the best technology at the best price. Indeed, the pressures of global competition have made network structures more vital, and computer-based information technology has made them possible.[52]

A potential disadvantage of network structures is that they expose the core firm to market forces. Other companies may bid up the price for subcontractors, whereas the short-term cost

virtual corporations
Network structures representing several independent companies that form unique partnership teams to provide customised products or services, usually to specific clients, for a limited time.

would be lower if the company hired its own employees to provide this function. Another problem is that, although information technology makes worldwide communication much easier, it will never replace the degree of control that organisations have when manufacturing, marketing and other functions are in-house. The core firm can use arm's-length incentives and contract provisions to maintain the subcontractor's quality, but these actions are relatively crude compared with those used to maintain the performance of in-house employees.

CONTINGENCIES OF ORGANISATIONAL DESIGN

LEARNING OBJECTIVE

Summarise the contingencies of organisational design.

Most organisational behaviour theories and concepts have contingencies—ideas that work well in one situation might not work as well in another situation. The contingency approach is certainly relevant when choosing the most appropriate organisational structure.[53] In this section, four contingencies of organisational design are introduced: external environment, size, technology and strategy.

EXTERNAL ENVIRONMENT

The best structure for an organisation depends on its external environment. The external environment includes anything outside the organisation, including most stakeholders (e.g. clients, suppliers, government), resources (e.g. raw materials, human resources, information, finances) and competitors. Four characteristics of external environments influence the type of organisational structure best suited to a particular situation: dynamism, complexity, diversity and hostility.[54]

- *Dynamic vs stable environments.* Dynamic environments have a high rate of change, leading to novel situations and a lack of identifiable patterns. Organic structures, including the team-based structure at Nitro, are better suited to this type of environment so that the organisation can adapt more quickly to changes.[55] In contrast, stable environments are characterised by regular cycles of activity and steady changes in supply and demand for inputs and outputs. Events are more predictable, enabling the firm to apply rules and procedures. Mechanistic structures are more efficient when the environment is predictable, so they tend to work better than organic structures under these conditions.

- *Complex versus simple environments.* Complex environments have many elements, whereas simple environments have few things to monitor. As an example, a major university library operates in a more complex environment than a small-town or suburban public library. The university library's clients require several types of services—book borrowing, online full-text databases, research centres, course reserve collections, and so on. A public library has fewer of these demands placed on it. The more complex the environment, the more decentralised the organisation should become. Decentralisation is a logical response to complexity, because decisions are pushed down to people and subunits with the necessary information to make informed choices.

- *Diverse versus integrated environments.* Organisations located in diverse environments have a greater variety of products or services, clients and regions. In contrast, an integrated environment has only one client, product and geographic area. The more diversified the environment, the more the firm needs to use a divisionalised form aligned with that diversity. If it sells a single product around the world, for example, a geographic divisionalised structure would align best with the firm's geographic diversity.

- *Hostile versus munificent environments.* Firms located in a hostile environment face resource scarcity and more competition in the marketplace. Hostile environments are typically dynamic ones because they reduce the predictability of access to resources and demand for outputs. Organic structures tend to be best in hostile environments. However, when the environment is extremely hostile—such as when raw materials are in short supply—organisations tend to temporarily centralise so that decisions can be made more quickly and

7-Eleven's centralised–decentralised structure

7-Eleven tries to leverage the buying power and efficiencies of its 25 000 stores in nineteen countries by centralising decisions about information technology and supplier purchasing. At the same time, the convenience store chain's customers from Australia to Japan to North America have diverse preferences. This diversity exists even within countries. For example, weather and special events can be dramatically different from one city to the next, which means that product demand will also vary. To thrive in this diverse and complex environment, 7-Eleven's business in the United States has what it calls a 'centrally decentralised' structure in which store managers make local inventory decisions using a centralised inventory management system. Along with ongoing product training and guidance from regional consultants, store managers have the best information about their customers and can respond quickly to local market needs. 'We could never predict a busload of football players on a Friday night, but the store manager can,' explains 7-Eleven president and CEO Jim Keyes, shown in this photo with a 7-Eleven employee.[56]

Courtesy of 7-Eleven Inc.

executives feel more comfortable being in control.[57] Ironically, centralisation may result in lower-quality decisions during organisational crises, because top management has less information, particularly when the environment is complex.

ORGANISATIONAL SIZE

Larger organisations should have different structures from smaller organisations.[58] As the number of employees increases, job specialisation increases due to a greater division of labour. This greater division of labour requires more elaborate coordinating mechanisms. Thus, larger firms make greater use of standardisation (particularly work processes and outcomes) to coordinate work activities. These coordinating mechanisms create an administrative hierarchy and greater formalisation. Historically, larger organisations have made less use of informal communication as a coordinating mechanism. However, emerging information technologies and increased emphasis on empowerment have caused informal communication to regain its importance in large firms.[59]

Larger organisations also tend to be more decentralised. Executives have neither the time nor the expertise to process all the decisions that significantly influence the business as it grows. Therefore, decision-making authority is pushed down to lower levels, where incumbents are able to cope with the narrower range of issues under their control.

TECHNOLOGY

Technology is another factor to consider when designing the best organisational structure for the situation.[60] Technology refers to the mechanisms or processes by which an organisation turns out its product or service. One technological contingency is its *variability*, the number of exceptions to standard procedures that tend to occur. In work processes with low variability, jobs are routine and follow standard operating procedures. Another contingency is *analysability*, the predictability or difficulty of the required work. The less analysable the work, the more it requires experts with sufficient discretion to address the work challenges.

Assembly-line technology has low variability and high analysability; the jobs are routine and highly predictable. This type of technology works best with a structure consisting of high formalisation and centralisation. When employees perform tasks with high variety and low analysability, they apply their skills to unique situations with little opportunity for repetition.

Research project teams operate under these conditions. Situations such as this call for an organic structure, one with low formalisation, highly decentralised decision-making authority, and coordination mainly through informal communication among team members.

High variety and high analysability tasks have many exceptions to routines, but these exceptions can usually be resolved through standard procedures. Maintenance groups and engineering design teams experience these conditions. Work units that fall into this category should use an organic structure, but it is possible to have somewhat greater formalisation and centralisation due to the analysability of problems. Skilled tradespeople tend to work in situations with low variety and low analysability. Their tasks involve few exceptions, but the problems that arise are difficult to resolve. This situation allows more centralisation and formalisation than in a purely organic structure, but coordination must include informal communication among the skilled employees so that unique problems can be resolved.

ORGANISATIONAL STRATEGY

organisational strategy
The way an organisation positions itself in its setting in relation to its stakeholders, given the organisation's resources, capabilities and mission.

LEARNING OBJECTIVE

Explain how organisational strategy relates to organisational structure.

Organisational strategy refers to the way the organisation positions itself in its setting in relation to its stakeholders, given the organisation's resources, capabilities and mission.[61] In other words, strategy represents the decisions and actions applied to achieve the organisation's goals. Although size, technology and the environment influence the optimal organisational structure, these contingencies do not necessarily determine structure. Instead, corporate leaders formulate and implement strategies that shape the characteristics of these contingencies as well as the organisation's resulting structure.

This concept is summed up with the simple phrase: structure follows strategy.[62] Organisational leaders decide how large to grow and which technologies to use. They take steps to define and manipulate their environments, rather than let the organisation's fate be entirely determined by external influences. Furthermore, organisational structures don't evolve as a natural response to these contingencies. Instead, they result from organisational decisions. Thus, organisational strategy influences both the contingencies of structure and the structure itself.

The 'structure follows strategy' thesis has become the dominant perspective of business policy and strategic management. An important aspect of this view is that organisations can choose the environments in which they want to operate. Some businesses adopt a *differentiation strategy* by bringing unique products to the market or by attracting clients who want customised goods and services. They try to distinguish their outputs from those provided by other firms through marketing, providing special services, and innovation. Others adopt a *cost leadership strategy*, in which they maximise productivity and are thereby able to offer popular products or services at a competitive price.[63]

The type of organisational strategy selected leads to the best organisational structure to adopt.[64] Organisations with a cost leadership strategy should adopt a mechanistic, functional structure with high levels of job specialisation and standardised work processes. This is similar to the routine technology category described earlier, because they maximise production and service efficiency. A differentiation strategy, on the other hand, requires more customised relations with clients. A matrix or team-based structure with less centralisation and formalisation is most appropriate here, so that technical specialists are able to coordinate their work activities more closely with the client's needs. Overall, it is now apparent that organisational structure is influenced by size, technology and the environment, but the organisation's strategy may reshape these elements and loosen their connection to organisational structure.

CHAPTER SUMMARY

Organisational structure refers to the division of labour as well as the patterns of coordination, communication, workflow and formal power that direct organisational activities. All organisational structures divide labour into distinct tasks and coordinate that labour to accomplish common goals. The primary means of coordination are informal communication, formal hierarchy and standardisation.

The four basic elements of organisational structure include span of control, centralisation, formalisation and departmentalisation. At one time, scholars suggested that firms should have a tall hierarchy with a narrow span of control. However, the span of control can be much wider when other coordinating mechanisms are present. The span of control should be narrower in situations where employees perform novel or complex tasks and where their work is highly interdependent with their co-workers' work.

Centralisation occurs when formal decision authority is held by a small group of people, typically senior executives. Many companies decentralise as they become larger and more complex, because senior executives lack the necessary time and expertise to process all the decisions that significantly influence the business. Formalisation is the degree to which organisations standardise behaviour through rules, procedures, formal training and related mechanisms. Companies become more formalised as they get older and larger.

Span of control, centralisation and formalisation cluster into mechanistic and organic structures. A mechanistic structure is characterised by a narrow span of control and a high degree of formalisation and centralisation. Companies with an organic structure have the opposite characteristics.

Departmentalisation specifies how employees and their activities are grouped together. It establishes the chain of command, focuses people around common mental models, and encourages coordination through informal communication among people and subunits. A functional structure organises employees around specific knowledge or other resources. This fosters greater specialisation and improves direct supervision, but increases conflict in serving clients or developing products. It also focuses employee attention on functional skills rather than on the company's product or service or its clients' needs.

A divisional structure groups employees around geographic areas, clients or outputs. This structure accommodates growth and focuses employee attention on products or customers rather than tasks. However, this structure creates silos of knowledge and duplication of resources. The matrix structure combines two types of structure to leverage the benefits of both types. However, this approach requires more coordination than functional or pure divisional structures, may dilute accountability, and increases conflict.

Team-based structures are very flat, have low formalisation and organise self-directed teams around work processes rather than functional specialties. A network structure is an alliance of several organisations for the purpose of creating a product or serving a client. Virtual corporations are network structures that can quickly reorganise themselves to suit the client's requirements.

The best organisational structure depends on the firm's external environment, size, technology and strategy. The optimal structure depends on whether the environment is dynamic or stable, complex or simple, diverse or integrated, and hostile or munificent. As organisations increase in size, they become more decentralised and more formalised, with greater job specialisation and elaborate coordinating mechanisms. The work unit's technology—including variety of work and analysability of problems—influences whether to adopt an organic or a mechanistic structure. These contingencies influence but do not necessarily determine structure. Instead, corporate leaders formulate and implement strategies that shape the characteristics of these contingencies as well as the organisation's resulting structure.

KEY TERMS

centralisation p. 451
divisional structure p. 455
formalisation p. 452
functional structure p. 453
matrix structure p. 457

mechanistic structure p. 452
network structure p. 460
organic structure p. 452
organisational strategy p. 464
organisational structure p. 446

span of control p. 449
team-based structure p. 458
virtual corporations p. 461

DISCUSSION QUESTIONS

1. Boutique advertising agency Nitro has an organic, team-based structure. What coordinating mechanism dominates in this type of organisational structure? Describe the extent and form in which the other two forms of coordination might be apparent at Nitro.

2. Think about the business school or other organisational unit whose classes you are currently attending. What is the dominant coordinating mechanism used to guide or control the instructor? Why is this coordinating mechanism used in this situation?

3. Administrative theorists concluded many decades ago that the most effective organisations have a narrow span of control. Yet today's top-performing manufacturing firms have a wide span of control. Why is this possible? Under what circumstances, if any, should manufacturing firms have a narrow span of control?

4. If one could identify 'trends' in organisational structure, one of them would be decentralisation. Why is decentralisation becoming more common in contemporary organisations? What should companies consider when determining the degree of decentralisation?

5. Diversified Technologies Ltd (DTL) makes four types of products, each type to be sold to different types of clients. For example, one product is sold exclusively to motor vehicle repair shops, whereas another is used mainly in hospitals. Customer expectations and needs are surprisingly similar throughout the world. However, the company has separate marketing, product design and manufacturing facilities in Asia, North America, Europe and South America, because until recently each jurisdiction had unique regulations governing the production and sales of these products. However, several governments have begun the process of deregulating the products that DTL designs and manufactures, and trade agreements have opened several markets to foreign-made products. Which form of departmentalisation might be best for DTL if deregulation and trade agreements occur?

6. Why are many organisations moving away from the geographic divisional structure?

7. From an employee's perspective, what are the advantages and disadvantages of working in a matrix structure?

8. Suppose that you have been hired as a consultant to diagnose the environmental characteristics of your college or university. How would you describe the institution's external environment? Is the institution's existing structure appropriate for this environment?

SKILL BUILDER | 15.1   FTCA: REGIONAL AND HEADQUARTERS RELATIONS

CASE STUDY

By Swee C. Goh, University of Ottawa

The FTCA is a government organisation that provides services to the public but also serves an enforcement role. It employs over 20 000 people, who are located at headquarters and in a large number of regional offices across the country. Most staff members are involved with direct counter-type services for both individuals and businesses. This includes collections, inquiries, payments and audits. The agency also has large centres in various parts of the country to process forms and payments submitted by individuals and businesses.

FTCA is a typical federal government department; many employees are unionised and have experienced numerous changes over the years. Because of the increasing complexity of regulations and the need to be more cost effective in the delivery of services, FTCA has evolved into an organisation that uses technology to a great extent. The agency's leaders increasingly emphasise the need for easier and faster service and turnaround in dealing with clients. They also expect staff to depend more on electronic means of communication for interaction with the public.

As the population has grown over the years, the regional offices of this government organisation have expanded. Each regional office is headed by an Assistant Deputy Minister (ADM) who has a budget and an increasing number of staff for the various functional activities related to the region, such as a manager for information systems. Every region also has offices located in the major cities. The directors of these city centre offices report directly to the regional ADM. The regional ADMs report directly to the Deputy Minister (DM) who is the overall head of the department.

FTCA'S DUAL REPORTING STRUCTURE

FTCA has a strong emphasis on centralised control, particularly in the functional units. This emphasis occurs because of legislative requirements as well as the fact that the agency has extensive direct interaction with the public. For example, one functional unit at headquarters (HQ) is responsible for collections and enforcement. If a regional manager has the same functional activity, FTCA executives believe that that person should be accountable to the HQ functional ADM. However, as mentioned earlier, the regional manager also reports directly to the regional ADM and the budget for the department comes from the regional budget allocations and not from the HQ functional group.

This arrangement produces a dual reporting relationship for regional functional managers. Regional managers complain that this situation is very awkward. Who is the real boss under the circumstances: the regional ADM or the functional HQ ADM for these managers? Also, who should be responsible for evaluating the work performance of these dual-reporting regional managers? And if a regional manager makes a serious error, which of the two supervisors of that manager is ultimately accountable?

The potential for confusion about responsibility and accountability has made the roles and reporting relationships of the senior managers very vague. The occurrences of conflict between regional managers and HQ managers have also increased.

INVESTIGATING FTCA'S GROWING PROBLEM

In order to deal with this growing problem, a consultant was brought in to do an independent evaluation of the current organisation structure of FTCA. The consultant asked for an organisation chart of FTCA, which is shown overleaf. The consultant became aware of the concerns described above by conducting interviews with various staff members throughout the agency. Other information such as budgets and financial allocations, some earlier organisational studies and the mandate of the department were also provided to the consultant.

The discussions with staff members were very interesting. Some viewed this issue as a people problem and not a structural one. They suggested that if regional and HQ managers learned how to cooperate and work with each other this would not be an issue at all. That is, they should take a shared responsibility approach and try to work together. But the view of the HQ functional groups was very different. They argued that FTCA is a functional organisation so these functional unit leaders should have authority and power over regional managers performing the same function. In effect, these regional managers should report to the functional unit ADMs or at least be accountable to HQ policies and objectives.

To compound the problem, the regional managers saw this problem completely differently again. They argued that the functional HQ managers should have a policy development function. On an annual basis they should develop broad objectives and targets in consultation with regional managers. Once approved, it is the responsibility of the regional managers to carry them out in light of the environment and the constraints they face. The functional unit ADMs oppose the regional managers' position, pointing out that if the regional managers do not achieve their objectives, the functional ADMs suffer the consequences.

After hearing these views, the consultant formed the opinion that this was an intractable and complex problem that could be related to both people and structure. The consultant also noted

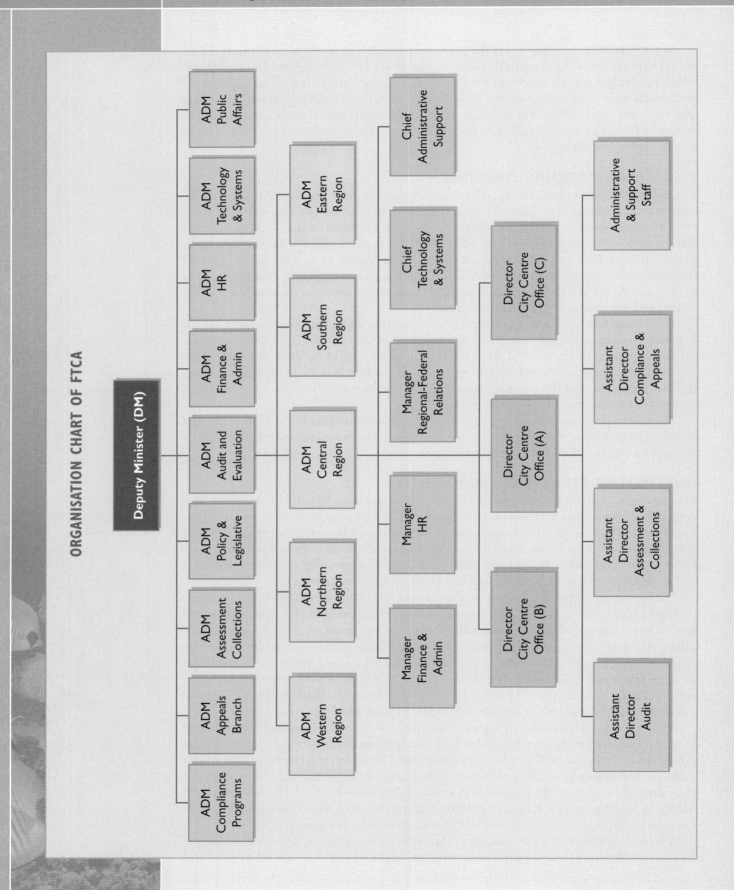

ORGANISATION CHART OF FTCA

Deputy Minister (DM)

ADM Compliance Programs

ADM Appeals Branch

ADM Assessment Collections

ADM Policy & Legislative

ADM Audit and Evaluation

ADM Finance & Admin

ADM HR

ADM Technology & Systems

ADM Public Affairs

ADM Western Region

ADM Northern Region

ADM Central Region

ADM Southern Region

ADM Eastern Region

Manager Finance & Admin

Manager HR

Manager Regional-Federal Relations

Chief Technology & Systems

Chief Administrative Support

Director City Centre Office (B)

Director City Centre Office (A)

Director City Centre Office (C)

Assistant Director Audit

Assistant Director Assessment & Collections

Assistant Director Compliance & Appeals

Administrative & Support Staff

that the regional budgets were huge, sometimes larger than the budgets for functional groups at HQ. Regional ADMs also met infrequently—only once a month—with the deputy minister and functional ADMs at HQ. Most of the time the regions seem to operate fairly autonomously, whereas the deputy minister seems to have ongoing involvement with the functional ADMs.

An HQ staff member observed that over time the regional offices seem to be getting bigger and bigger, and the result has been that they have become fairly autonomous, with functional staff that mirror the staff functions at HQ. The implication is that the regional staff will soon view the functional units at headquarters as a distant group which only sets policy that the regions can interpret or ignore as they please.

A functional ADM with several years of seniority at FTCA warned that the functional units must have some control audit and other functional activities in the region. The ADM explained that without clear roles, reporting relationships and accountabilities between the region and HQ, FTCA will not be able to provide citizens with transparent and fair treatment in the services under their mandate.

The regional ADMs, however, saw their responsibilities as facilitating horizontal coordination within the region to ensure that actions and decisions are consistent and reflect the legislative responsibility of the department.

After a month of study and discussions with staff at FTCA, the consultant realised that this was not going to be an easy problem to resolve. There were also rumblings as the project progressed that some regional ADMs did not like the idea of restructuring FTCA to deal with this issue. They seem to have considerable clout and power in the organisation as a group and would resist any change to the status quo.

As the consultant sat down to write the report, a number of critical questions became apparent. Some of these include: Is FTCA a purely functional organisation? Can the accountability issues be resolved through an acceptable organisational process and people training without the need for restructuring? What about power, politics and conflict in this situation? Finally, will resistance to change become a problem as well?

Source: Adapted from C. Harvey and K. Morouney, *Journal of Management Education* 22 (June 1998), pp. 425–9. Used with permission of the authors.

QUESTIONS

1. Describe the current organisation structure of FTCA. What is it? What are the strengths and weaknesses of such a structure?

2. Can FTCA operate effectively as a purely functional structure?

3. What roles do power and politics play in the current situation?

4. What kind of conflict is FTCA experiencing between HQ and regional managers?

5. Suggest a practical and workable solution to the problem at FTCA. If a restructuring is part of your solution, describe what the structure would look like and justify from your knowledge of organisation theory and design why it would work (i.e. improve the working relationship between headquarters and regional staff).

ORGANISATIONAL STRUCTURE AND DESIGN: THE CLUB ED EXERCISE

15.2 SKILL BUILDER

TEAM EXERCISE

By Cheryl Harvey and Kim Morouney, Wilfred Laurier University

PURPOSE

This exercise is designed to help you understand the issues to consider when designing organisations at various stages of growth.

MATERIALS

Each student team should have enough overhead transparencies or flip chart sheets to display several organisational charts.

INSTRUCTIONS

Each team discusses the scenario presented. The first scenario is presented below. The instructor will facilitate discussion and notify teams when to begin the next step. The exercise and debriefing require approximately ninety minutes, although fewer scenarios can reduce the time somewhat.

Step 1: Students are placed in teams (typically four or five people).

Step 2: After reading Scenario 1, each team will design an organisational chart (departmentalisation) that is most appropriate for this situation. Students should be able to describe the type of structure drawn and explain why it is appropriate. The structure should be drawn on an overhead transparency or flip chart for others to see during later class discussion. The instructor will set a fixed time (e.g. 15 minutes) to complete this task.

> SCENARIO 1: Determined never to endure another cold, rainy Melbourne winter, you decide to establish a new resort business on a South Pacific island accessible to air travellers. The resort is under construction and is scheduled to open one year from now. You decide it is time to draw up an organisational chart for this new venture, called Club Ed.

Step 3: At the end of the time allowed, the instructor will present Scenario 2 and each team will be asked to draw another organisational chart to suit that situation. Again, students should be able to describe the type of structure drawn and explain why it is appropriate.

Step 4: At the end of the time allowed, the instructor will present Scenario 3 and each team will be asked to draw another organisational chart to suit that situation.

Step 5: Depending on the time available, the instructor might present a fourth scenario. The class will gather to present their designs for each scenario. During each presentation, teams should describe the type of structure drawn and explain why it is appropriate.

SKILL BUILDER | 15.3   IDENTIFYING YOUR PREFERRED ORGANISATIONAL STRUCTURE

SELF-ASSESSMENT

STUDENT CD

PURPOSE

This exercise is designed to help you understand how an organisation's structure influences the personal needs and values of people working in that structure.

INSTRUCTIONS

Personal values influence how comfortable you are working in different organisational structures. You might prefer an organisation with clearly defined rules or no rules at all. You might prefer a firm where almost any employee can make important decisions, or where important decisions are screened by senior executives. Read the statements below and indicate the extent to which you would like to work in an organisation with that characteristic. When finished, use the scoring key in Appendix B to calculate your results. This self-assessment is completed alone so that students can complete the assessment honestly without concerns of social comparison. However, class discussion will focus on the elements of organisational design and their relationship to personal needs and values.

ORGANISATIONAL STRUCTURE PREFERENCE SCALE

I would like to work in an organisation where ...	Not at all	A little	Somewhat	Very much	Score
1. A person's career ladder has several steps towards higher status and responsibility.	❏	❏	❏	❏	_____
2. Employees perform their work with few rules to limit their discretion.	❏	❏	❏	❏	_____
3. Responsibility is pushed down to employees who perform the work.	❏	❏	❏	❏	_____
4. Supervisors have few employees, so they work closely with each person.	❏	❏	❏	❏	_____
5. Senior executives make most decisions to ensure that the company is consistent in its actions.	❏	❏	❏	❏	_____
6. Jobs are clearly defined so there is no confusion over who is responsible for various tasks.	❏	❏	❏	❏	_____
7. Employees have their say on issues, but senior executives make most of the decisions.	❏	❏	❏	❏	_____
8. Job descriptions are broadly stated or nonexistent.	❏	❏	❏	❏	_____
9. Everyone's work is tightly synchronised around top management's operating plans.	❏	❏	❏	❏	_____
10. Most work is performed in teams without close supervision.	❏	❏	❏	❏	_____
11. Work gets done through informal discussion with co-workers rather than through formal rules.	❏	❏	❏	❏	_____
12. Supervisors have so many employees that they can't watch anyone very closely.	❏	❏	❏	❏	_____
13. Everyone has clearly understood goals, expectations and job duties.	❏	❏	❏	❏	_____
14. Senior executives assign overall goals, but leave daily decisions to front-line teams.	❏	❏	❏	❏	_____
15. Even in a large company, the CEO is only three or four levels above the lowest position.	❏	❏	❏	❏	_____

NOTES

1   L. Sinclair, 'Morris Vows to Aid and Abet Nitro', *Australian*, 30 September 2004, 21; 'Nimble Nitro Steals a March on the Big Networks', *Marketing Week*, 9 June 2005, 13; P. Chatterjee, '"India Vital Part of Our Jigsaw"', *Business Line (The Hindu)* (India), 17 November 2005, 1; S. Elliott, 'Watch Out, Giant Agencies. Boutique Shops Like Nitro Are Winning Some Big Clients', *New York Times*, 4 April 2005, 6; E. Hall, 'Nitro Takes "Substantial" Chunk of UK's Soul', *Advertising Age*, 18 April 2005, 22; A. Hargrave-Silk, 'Chen Named Chairman for Nitro Greater China', *Media*, 6 May 2005; N. Shatrujeet, 'The Light at Lowe', *Economic Times* (India), 29 June 2005. Also see www.nitro-group.com.

2   S. Ranson, R. Hinings and R. Greenwood, 'The Structuring of Organizational Structure', *Administrative Science Quarterly* 25 (1980), 1–14.

3   J.-E. Johanson, 'Intraorganizational Influence', *Management Communication Quarterly* 13 (February 2000), 393–435.

4   B. Morris, 'Charles Schwab's Big Challenge', *Fortune*, 30 May 2005, 88.

5   H. Mintzberg, *The Structuring of Organizations* (Englewood Cliffs, NJ: Prentice Hall, 1979), 2–3.

6   E. E. Lawler III, *Motivation in Work Organizations* (Monterey, CA: Brooks/Cole, 1973); M. A. Campion, 'Ability Requirement Implications of Job Design: An Interdisciplinary Perspective', *Personnel Psychology* 42 (1989), 1–24.

7   Mintzberg, *The Structuring of Organizations*, 2–8; D. A. Nadler and M. L. Tushman, *Competing by Design: The Power of Organizational Architecture* (NY: Oxford University Press, 1997), chapter 6.

8   C. Downs, P. Clampitt and A. L. Pfeiffer, 'Communication and Organizational Outcomes', in *Handbook of Organizational Communication*, ed. G. Goldhaber and G. Barnett (Norwood, NJ: Ablex, 1988), 171–211; I. Nonaka and H. Takeuchi, *The Knowledge-Creating Company* (New York: Oxford University Press, 1995).

9   A. L. Patti, J. P. Gilbert and S. Hartman, 'Physical Co-Location and the Success of New Product Development Projects', *Engineering Management Journal* 9 (September 1997), 31–7; M. Hoque, M. Akter and Y. Monden, 'Concurrent Engineering: A Compromise Approach to Develop a Feasible and Customer-Pleasing Product', *International Journal of Production Research* 43, no. 8 (15 April 2005), 1607–24.

10 For a discussion of the role of brand manager at Procter & Gamble, see C. Peale, 'Branded for Success', *Cincinnati Enquirer* (20 May 2001), A1. Details about how to design integrator roles in organisational structures are presented in J. R. Galbraith, *Designing Organizations* (San Francisco: Jossey-Bass, 2002), 66–72.

11 Fayol's work is summarised in J. B. Miner, *Theories of Organizational Structure and Process* (Chicago: Dryden, 1982), 358–66.

12 Y.-M. Hsieh and A. Tien-Hsieh, 'Enhancement of Service Quality with Job Standardisation', *Service Industries Journal* 21 (July 2001), 147–66.

13 D. Drickhamer, 'Lessons from the Leading Edge', *Industry Week*, 21 February 2000, 23–6.

14 D. D. Van Fleet and A. G. Bedeian, 'A History of the Span of Management', *Academy of Management Review* 2 (1977), 356–72; Mintzberg, *The Structuring of Organizations*, chapter 8.

15 J. Greenwald, 'Ward Compares the Best with the Rest', *Business Insurance*, 26 August 2002, 16.

16 J. H. Gittell, 'Supervisory Span, Relational Coordination and Flight Departure Performance: A Reassessment of Postbureaucracy Theory', *Organization Science* 12, no. 4 (July–August 2001), 468–83.

17 'BASF Culling Saves (GBP) 4m', *Personnel Today* (19 February 2002), 3.

18 T. Peters, *Thriving on Chaos* (New York: Knopf, 1987), 359.

19 Q. N. Huy, 'In Praise of Middle Managers', *Harvard Business Review* 79 (September 2001), 72–9; H. J. Leavitt, *Top Down: Why Hierarchies Are Here to Stay and How to Manage Them More Effectively* (Cambridge: Harvard Business School Press, 2005).

20 The number of layers at Microsoft is inferred from F. Jebb, 'Don't Call Me Sir', *Management Today* (August 1998), 44–7.

21 W. Stueck, 'Revamped Barrick Keeps Eyes on the Hunt for the Golden Prize', *Globe & Mail*, 17 September 2005, B4.

22 P. Brabeck, 'The Business Case against Revolution: An Interview with Nestlé's Peter Brabeck', *Harvard Business Review* 79 (February 2001), 112; H. A. Richardson et al., 'Does Decentralization Make a Difference for the Organization? An Examination of the Boundary Conditions Circumscribing Decentralized Decision-Making and Organizational Financial Performance', *Journal of Management* 28, no. 2 (2002), 217–44; G. Masado, 'To Centralize or Decentralize?', *Optimize*, May 2005, 58.

23 'Set up Decision-Making Centres to Speed up Approvals-Cuepacs', *Bernama Daily Malaysian News*, 30 June 2005; S. Singh and M. Kaur, 'Who Can I Speak To? Sorry, Officer Not In', *New Straits Times* (Kuala Lumpur), 28 December 2005.

24 Mintzberg, *The Structuring of Organizations*, chapter 5.

25 T. Burns and G. Stalker, *The Management of Innovation* (London: Tavistock, 1961).

26 J. Tata, S. Prasad and R. Thom, 'The Influence of Organizational Structure on the Effectiveness of TQM Programs', *Journal of Managerial Issues* 11, no. 4 (Winter 1999), 440–53; A. Lam, 'Tacit Knowledge, Organizational Learning and Societal Institutions: An Integrated Framework', *Organization Studies* 21 (May 2000), 487–513.

27 Mintzberg, *The Structuring of Organizations*, 106.

28 Mintzberg, *The Structuring of Organizations*, chapter 17.

29 J. Hall, 'Liquid Assets', *Voyeur Magazine* (VirginBlue), January 2004; R. O'Neill, 'Small Tricks, Big Business', *The Age* (Melbourne), 14 December 2004, 1; C. Cooper, 'The Wizards of Biz', *The Bulletin*, 8 November 2005. Some information also originates from Boost Juice's website: www.boostjuice.com.

30 Galbraith, *Designing Organizations*, 23–5.

31 E. E. Lawler III, *Rewarding Excellence: Pay Strategies for the New Economy* (San Francisco: Jossey-Bass, 2000), 31–4.

32 These structures were identified from corporate websites and annual reports. The companies include a mixture of other structures, so the charts shown are adapted for learning purposes.

33 M. Goold and A. Campbell, 'Do You Have a Well-Designed Organization?', *Harvard Business Review* 80 (March 2002), 117–24.

34 J. R. Galbraith, 'Structuring Global Organizations', in *Tomorrow's Organization*, ed. S. A. Mohrman et al. (San Francisco: Jossey-Bass, 1998), 103–29; C. Homburg, J. P. Workman Jr and O. Jensen, 'Fundamental Changes in Marketing Organization: The Movement toward a Customer-focused Organizational Structure', *Academy of Marketing Science Journal* 28 (Fall 2000), 459–78; T. H. Davenport, J. G. Harris and A. K. Kohli, 'How Do They Know Their Customers So Well?', *Sloan Management Review* 42 (Winter 2001), 63–73; J. R. Galbraith, 'Organizing to Deliver Solutions', *Organizational Dynamics* 31 (2002), 194–207.

35 D. Robey, *Designing Organizations*, 3rd edn (Homewood, Ill.: Irwin, 1991), 191–7.

36 J. Teresko, 'Transforming GM', *Industry Week*, December/January 2002, 34–8; E. Prewitt, 'GM's Matrix Reloads', *CIO Magazine*, 1 September 2003.

37 R. C. Ford and W. A. Randolph, 'Cross-Functional Structures: A Review and Integration of Matrix Organization and Project Management', *Journal of Management* 18 (1992), 267–94. For a discussion of matrix structures in an electronic games company, see R. Muzyka and G. Zeschuk, 'Managing Multiple Projects', *Game Developer*, March 2003, 34–42.

38 G. Calabrese, 'Communication and Co-Operation in Product Development: A Case Study of a European Car Producer', *R & D Management* 27 (July 1997), 239–52; T. Sy and L. S. D'Annunzio, 'Challenges and Strategies of Matrix Organizations: Top-Level and Mid-Level Managers' Perspectives', *Human Resource Planning* 28, no. 1 (2005), 39–48.

39 Nadler and Tushman, *Competing by Design*, chapter 6; M. Goold and A. Campbell, 'Structured Networks: Towards the Well-Designed Matrix', *Long Range Planning* 36, no. 5 (October 2003), 427–39.

40 C. Campbell-Hunt et al., *World Famous in New Zealand* (Auckland: University of Auckland Press, 2001), 89.

41 J. R. Galbraith, E. E. Lawler III and Associates, *Organizing for the Future: The New Logic for Managing Complex Organizations* (San Francisco, CA: Jossey-Bass, 1993); R. Bettis and M. Hitt, 'The New Competitive Landscape', *Strategic Management Journal* 16 (1995), 7–19.

42 P. C. Ensign, 'Interdependence, Coordination, and Structure in Complex Organizations: Implications for Organization Design', *Mid-Atlantic Journal of Business* 34 (March 1998), 5–22.

43 M. M. Fanning, 'A Circular Organization Chart Promotes a Hospital-Wide Focus on Teams', *Hospital & Health Services Administration* 42 (June 1997), 243–54; L. Y. Chan and B. E. Lynn, 'Operating in Turbulent Times: How Ontario's Hospitals Are Meeting the Current Funding Crisis', *Health Care Management Review* 23 (June 1998), 7–18.

44 R. Cross, 'Looking Before You Leap: Assessing the Jump to Teams in Knowledge-Based Work', *Business Horizons* (September 2000);

M. Fenton-O'Creevy, 'Employee Involvement and the Middle Manager: Saboteur or Scapegoat?', *Human Resource Management Journal* 11 (2001), 24–40; G. Garda, K. Lindstrom and M. Dallnera, 'Towards a Learning Organization: The Introduction of a Client-Centered Team-Based Organization in Administrative Surveying Work', *Applied Ergonomics* 34 (2003), 97–105; C. Douglas and W. L. Gardner, 'Transition to Self-Directed Work Teams: Implications of Transition Time and Self-Monitoring for Managers' Use of Influence Tactics', *Journal of Organizational Behavior* 25 (2004), 47–65.

45 P. Siekman, 'This Is Not a BMW Plant', *Fortune*, 18 April 2005, 208.

46 R. F. Miles and C. C. Snow, 'The New Network Firm: A Spherical Structure Built on a Human Investment Philosophy', *Organizational Dynamics* 23, no. 4 (1995), 5–18; C. Baldwin and K. Clark, 'Managing in an Age of Modularity', *Harvard Business Review* 75 (September–October 1997), 84–93.

47 J. Hagel III and M. Singer, 'Unbundling the Corporation', *Harvard Business Review* 77 (March–April 1999), 133–41; R. Hacki and J. Lighton, 'The Future of the Networked Company', *McKinsey Quarterly* 3 (2001), 26–39.

48 M. A. Schilling and H. K. Steensma, 'The Use of Modular Organizational Forms: An Industry-Level Analysis', *Academy of Management Journal* 44 (December 2001), 1149–68.

49 W. H. Davidow and T. W. Malone, *The Virtual Corporation* (New York: Harper Business, 1992); L. Fried, *Managing Information Technology in Turbulent Times* (New York: John Wiley and Sons, 1995).

50 C. Taylor, 'Agency Teams Balancing in an Ever-Changing Media World', *Media Week* (1 June 2001), 20.

51 G. Morgan, *Images of Organization*, 2nd edn (Newbury Park: Sage, 1996); G. Morgan, *Imagin-I-Zation: New Mindsets for Seeing, Organizing and Managing* (Thousand Oaks, CA: Sage, 1997).

52 H. Chesbrough and D. J. Teece, 'When Is Virtual Virtuous? Organizing for Innovation', *Harvard Business Review* (January–February 1996), 65–73; P. M. J. Christie and R. Levary, 'Virtual Corporations: Recipe for Success', *Industrial Management* 40 (July 1998), 7–11.

53 L. Donaldson, *The Contingency Theory of Organizations* (Thousand Oaks, CA: Sage, 2001); J. Birkenshaw, R. Nobel and J. Ridderstrâle, 'Knowledge as a Contingency Variable: Do the Characteristics of Knowledge Predict Organizational Structure?', *Organization Science* 13, no. 3 (May–June 2002), 274–89.

54 P. R. Lawrence and J. W. Lorsch, *Organization and Environment* (Homewood, Ill.: Irwin, 1967); Mintzberg, *The Structuring of Organizations*, chapter 15.

55 Burns and Stalker, *The Management of Innovation*; Lawrence and Lorsch, *Organization and Environment*.

56 J. G. Kelley, 'Slurpees and Sausages: 7-Eleven Holds School', *Richmond (Va.) Times-Dispatch*, 12 March 2004, C1; S. Marling, 'The 24-Hour Supply Chain', *InformationWeek*, 26 January 2004, 43.

57 Mintzberg, *The Structuring of Organizations*, 282.

58 D. S. Pugh and C. R. Hinings, *Organizational Structure: Extensions and Replications* (Farnborough, England: Lexington Books, 1976); Mintzberg, *The Structuring of Organizations*, chapter 13.

59 G. Hertel, S. Geister and U. Konradt, 'Managing Virtual Teams: A Review of Current Empirical Research', *Human Resource Management Review* 15 (2005), 69–95.

60 C. Perrow, 'A Framework for the Comparative Analysis of Organizations', *American Sociological Review* 32 (1967), 194–208; D. Gerwin, 'The Comparative Analysis of Structure and Technology: A Critical Appraisal', *Academy of Management Review* 4, no. 1 (1979), 41–51; C. C. Miller et al., 'Understanding Technology–Structure Relationships: Theory Development and Meta-Analytic Theory Testing', *Academy of Management Journal* 34, no. 2 (1991), 370–99.

61 R. H. Kilmann, *Beyond the Quick Fix* (San Francisco: Jossey-Bass, 1984), 38.

62 A. D. Chandler, *Strategy and Structure* (Cambridge, Mass.: MIT Press, 1962).

63 A. M. Porter, *Competitive Strategy* (New York: The Free Press, 1980).

64 D. Miller, 'Configurations of Strategy and Structure', *Strategic Management Journal* 7 (1986), 233–49.

CHAPTER 16

Organisational culture

LEARNING OBJECTIVES

After reading this chapter, you should be able to:

- describe the elements of organisational culture

- discuss the importance of organisational subcultures

- list four categories of artefacts through which corporate culture is deciphered

- identify three functions of organisational culture

- discuss the conditions under which cultural strength improves corporate performance.

- compare and contrast four strategies for merging organisational cultures

- identify five strategies to strengthen an organisation's culture

- describe the stages of organisational socialisation

- explain how realistic job previews assist the socialisation process.

In 2001 Carter Holt Harvey decided to spin-off its information technology (IT) group into a consulting business called Oxygen Business Solutions. The New Zealand forest products company was not in the IT business and Carter executives felt that its 200 IT employees would become more efficient and customer-focused if they competed in the open market. Today, Oxygen has excelled in customer service and competitiveness, recently becoming the largest dedicated SAP (a popular enterprise software) solutions company in the region. Oxygen has more than sixty clients throughout Australia and New Zealand and employs more than 350 people out of Melbourne, Sydney, Wellington and its head office in Auckland.

Chief executive Mike Smith thinks that the company's carefully crafted culture is a key ingredient in this success, because cultural values, beliefs and assumptions guide employee behaviour and shape the company's public image. 'We've recognised that our people and the way they deliver to customers is an extension of our culture and brand,' he explains.

Auckland-based Oxygen Business Solutions has become a successful IT services provider on both sides of the Tasman by developing a strong organisational culture aligned with its environment and its employee values.

Oxygen employees began to transform the company's culture by identifying the values by which they would want to work. 'We ran focus groups with staff, did an e-survey and got feedback on the values they thought would be important if they owned the business,' says Smith. 'The staff came up with seven new values: real, grow, support, fun, zest, imagine and shine.'

Next, groups of Oxygen employees participated in offsite seminars where they were asked to identify their personal values, then compare those values with the ideal culture identified in the earlier focus groups and surveys. 'That [event] was an eye-opener for people,' Smith recalls. 'It is too easy to get caught up in day-to-day things and not see what is important in your own life.'

This process of articulating ideal values and comparing them against personal values has reshaped Oxygen's culture and contributed to the IT services firm's success, but Oxygen's managers know that corporate culture change takes time. 'We are making our values overt, but over time they will become subconscious and inherent in the organisation,' explains Oxygen's general manager of people. 'I see this as a journey. It is not something where we put a big tick in a column and say it is done.'

organisational culture
The basic pattern of shared assumptions, values and beliefs considered to be the correct way of thinking about and acting on problems and opportunities facing the organisation.

Oxygen Business Solution's phenomenal success is a testament to the power of organisational culture. **Organisational culture** is the basic pattern of shared assumptions, values and beliefs considered to be the correct way of thinking about and acting on problems and opportunities facing the organisation. It defines what is important and unimportant in the company. You might think of it as the organisation's DNA—invisible to the naked eye, yet a powerful template that shapes what happens in the workplace.[2]

This chapter begins by examining the elements of organisational culture and how culture is deciphered through artefacts. This is followed by a discussion about the relationship between organisational culture and corporate performance, including the effects of cultural strength, fit and adaptability. The discussion then turns to the issue of mergers and corporate culture, followed by specific strategies for maintaining a strong organisational culture. The last section of the chapter zooms in on employee socialisation, which is identified as one of the more important ways to strengthen organisational culture.

ELEMENTS OF ORGANISATIONAL CULTURE

LEARNING OBJECTIVE

Describe the elements of organisational culture.

As Exhibit 16.1 illustrates, the assumptions, values and beliefs that represent organisational culture operate beneath the surface of behaviour. *Assumptions* are the shared mental models that people rely on to guide their perceptions and behaviours. They represent the deepest part of organisational culture because they are unconscious and taken for granted. At Oxygen, for example, growth and shining customer orientation aren't just valued; they are assumed to be the best way to ensure the company's success. *Beliefs* represent the individual's perceptions of reality. *Values* are more stable, evaluative beliefs that guide our preferences for outcomes or courses of action in a variety of situations.[3] They help us define what is right or wrong, or good or bad, in the world.

CONTENT OF ORGANISATIONAL CULTURE

Organisations differ in their cultural content, that is, in the relative ordering of beliefs, values and assumptions. Consider the following companies and their apparent dominant cultures:

- *ICICI Bank.* India's second largest bank exudes a performance-oriented culture. Its organisational practices place a premium on training, career development, goal setting and pay-for-performance, all with the intent of maximising employee performance and customer

EXHIBIT 16.1   **Elements of organisational culture**

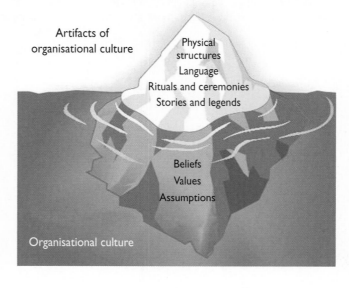

Artifacts of organisational culture

Physical structures
Language
Rituals and ceremonies
Stories and legends

Beliefs
Values
Assumptions

Organisational culture

Colliers International's egalitarian culture

Colliers International is Australia's leading commercial property service agency with twenty-two offices in Australia and 248 offices worldwide. Yet, in spite of its size, complex management hierarchy is not part of the corporate culture. The company embraces innovative open-plan office environments for all staff, to create a dynamic learning environment. The corner-office hierarchy is not part of the culture. Instead, the senior directors of the company occupy the same office space as other staff. The pay structure is also designed to reward performance, not hierarchical status.[7]

Colliers International Property Consultants

service. 'We believe in defining clear performance for employees and empowering them to achieve their goals,' says ICICI Bank executive director Kalpana Morparia. 'This has helped to create a culture of high performance across the organisation.'[4]

- *Wal-Mart, Inc.* Stroll through Wal-Mart's headquarters in Bentonville, Arkansas, and you will find a workplace that almost screams out frugality and efficiency. The world's largest retailer has a Spartan waiting room for suppliers, rather like a government office waiting area. Visitors pay for their own soft drinks and coffee. In each of the building's inexpensive cubicles, employees sit at inexpensive desks finding ways to squeeze more efficiencies and lower costs out of suppliers as well as their own work processes.[5]

- *Technology One.* Employees who join this Brisbane-based enterprise software systems developer soon learn that 'The TechOne Way' values entrepreneurship and innovation. 'Our success comes from our shared values, our entrepreneurial spirit and our innovation,' says the company's mission statement. 'We call this the TechOne Way. The way in which each of us embraces these ideals is of critical importance.'[6]

Performance-oriented. Efficiency-oriented. Entrepreneurial. How many corporate cultural values are there? No one knows for certain. There are dozens of individual and cross-cultural values, so there are probably as many organisational values. Some writers and consultants have attempted to classify organisational cultures into a few categories with catchy labels such as 'mercenaries' and 'communes'. Although these typologies might reflect the values of a few organisations, they oversimplify the diversity of cultural values in organisations. Worse, the oversimplification tends to distort rather than clarify attempts to diagnose corporate culture.

ORGANISATIONAL SUBCULTURES

A discussion about organisational culture is actually referring to the *dominant culture*, that is, the themes shared most widely by the organisation's members. However, organisations are also comprised of *subcultures* located throughout its various divisions, geographic regions and occupational groups.[8] Some subcultures enhance the dominant culture by espousing parallel assumptions, values and beliefs; others are called *countercultures* because they directly oppose the organisation's core values.

Subcultures, particularly countercultures, have the potential to create conflict and dissension among employees, but they also serve two important functions.[9] First, they maintain the organisation's standards of performance and ethical behaviour. Employees who hold countercultural values are an important source of surveillance and critique of the dominant order. They encourage constructive conflict and more creative thinking about how the organisation should interact with its environment. By preventing employees from blindly following one set of values, subcultures help the organisation to abide by society's ethical values.

The second function of subcultures is that they are the spawning grounds for emerging values that keep the firm aligned with the needs of customers, suppliers, society and other stakeholders. Companies eventually need to replace their dominant values with ones that are more appropriate for the changing environment. If subcultures are suppressed, the organisation may take longer to discover and adopt values aligned with the emerging environment.

DECIPHERING ORGANISATIONAL CULTURE THROUGH ARTEFACTS

artefacts The observable symbols and signs of an organisation's culture.

An organisation's cultural assumptions, values and beliefs can't be seen directly. Instead, as Exhibit 16.1 illustrated, organisational culture is deciphered indirectly through **artefacts**. Artefacts are the observable symbols and signs of an organisation's culture, such as the way visitors are greeted, the physical layout, and how employees are rewarded.[10] Understanding a company's culture requires more than surveying employees. It requires a painstaking assessment of many artefacts, because they are subtle and often ambiguous.[11]

Thus, discovering an organisation's culture is very much like an anthropological investigation of a new society. It involves observing workplace behaviour, listening for unique language in everyday conversations, studying written documents, and interviewing staff about corporate stories. The four broad categories of artefacts are organisational stories and legends, rituals and ceremonies, language, and physical structures and symbols.

ORGANISATIONAL STORIES AND LEGENDS

In 1847 William Arnott sailed to Australia to join his convict father and to make his fortune on the Bathurst goldfields. Arnott wasn't much good at finding gold, but his skills as a journeyman pastrycook in Scotland served him well after he set up a bakery shop in Newcastle. Through innovative products and quality control, Arnott had expanded into Sydney by the 1880s and had introduced one of Australia's most enduring products, the Milk Arrowroot biscuit. Other innovations followed, including Iced Vovos, Salada crackers and Sao biscuits.[12]

Arnott's was purchased a few years ago by US-based Campbell Soup Company, but this story still reflects the company's strong culture of quality and innovation. Stories and legends about past corporate incidents serve as powerful social prescriptions of the way things should (or should not) be done. They provide human realism to corporate expectations, individual performance standards, and assumptions about the way things should work around the organisation. Stories are important artefacts because they personalise the culture and generate emotions that help people to remember lessons within these stories. Stories have the greatest effect at communicating corporate culture when they describe real people, are assumed to be true, and are remembered by employees throughout the organisation. Stories are also prescriptive; they advise people what to do or not to do.[13]

RITUALS AND CEREMONIES

rituals The programmed routines of daily organisational life that dramatise the organisation's culture.

Rituals are the programmed routines of daily organisational life that dramatise the organisation's culture. They include how visitors are greeted, how often senior executives visit subordinates, how people communicate with each other, how much time employees take for lunch, and so on. For instance, BMW's fast-paced culture is quite literally apparent in the way employees walk

Mayo Clinic's cultural expedition

The Mayo Clinic has a well-established culture at its original clinic in Rochester, Minnesota, but maintaining that culture in its expanding operations in Florida and Arizona has been challenging. 'We were struggling with growing pains [and] we didn't want to lose the culture, [so] we were looking at how to keep the heritage alive,' explains Matt McElrath, Mayo Clinic human resources director in Arizona. The Mayo Clinic retained anthropologist Linda Catlin to decipher Mayo's culture and identify ways to reinforce it at the two newer sites. Catlin shadowed employees and posed as a patient to observe what happens in waiting rooms. 'She did countless interviews, joined physicians on patient visits and even spent time in the operating room,' says McElrath. At the end of her six-week cultural expedition, Catlin submitted a report outlining Mayo's culture and how its satellite operations varied from that culture. The Clinic adopted all of Catlin's eleven recommendations, such as requiring all new physicians at the three sites to attend an orientation in Rochester where they learn about Mayo's history and values.[15]

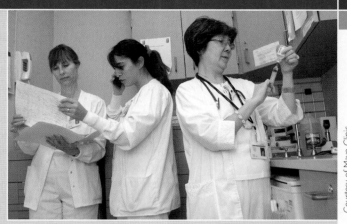

Courtesy of Mayo Clinic

around the German car-maker's offices. 'When you move through the corridors and hallways of other companies' buildings, people kind of crawl, they walk slowly,' says BMW board of management chairman Helmut Panke on a visit to the company's Singapore offices. 'But BMW people tend to move faster—whether it's here in Singapore, Seoul or Munich.'[14]

Ceremonies are more formal artefacts than rituals. Ceremonies are planned activities conducted specifically for the benefit of an audience, such as publicly rewarding (or punishing) employees, or celebrating the launch of a new product or newly won contract.

ceremonies Planned and usually dramatic displays of organisational culture, conducted specifically for the benefit of an audience.

ORGANISATIONAL LANGUAGE

The language of the workplace speaks volumes about the company's culture. How employees address co-workers, describe customers, express anger and greet stakeholders are all verbal symbols of cultural values. The importance of language in culture was apparent when San Francisco–based discount broker Charles Schwab & Co. acquired highbrow New York–based private bank US Trust. In meetings immediately following the acquisition, US Trust executives insisted on using the term 'clients' rather than 'customers', the term that Schwab executives used freely. This language reflects the long-term and deep relationship that US Trust staff have with their clients, compared with the more impersonal connection between Schwab's staff and their customers.[16]

Language also highlights values held by organisational subcultures. For instance, consultants working at Whirlpool kept hearing employees talk about the appliance company's 'PowerPoint culture'. This phrase, which names Microsoft's presentation software, is a critique of Whirlpool's hierarchical culture in which communication is one-way (from executives to employees).[17]

PHYSICAL STRUCTURES AND SYMBOLS

Winston Churchill once said, 'We shape our buildings; thereafter, they shape us.'[18] The former British prime minister was reminding us that buildings both reflect and influence an organisation's culture. The size, shape, location and age of a building might suggest the company's emphasis on teamwork, environmental friendliness, flexibility or any other set of values.

Even if the building doesn't make much of a statement, there is a treasure trove of physical artefacts inside. Desks, chairs, office space and wall hangings (or lack of them) are just a few of the items that might convey cultural meaning. Stroll through the head office of Flight Centre in Brisbane and you realise that this is a frugal, egalitarian culture. The global travel agency has no individual offices and no secretarial staff, and chief executive Graham Turner shares a small, narrow, unadorned and rather gloomy room with six others.[19] Each of these artefacts alone might not say much, but put enough of them together and the company's cultural values become easy to decipher.

Buildings and their décor have such a strong influence on organisational culture that some leaders are designing offices to reflect what they want the company's culture to become, rather than its current culture. National Australia Bank's (NAB) National@Docklands, a low-rise campus-like building in Melbourne's docklands area, is a case in point. The building's open design and colourful décor are symbolic of a more open, egalitarian and creative culture, compared with the closed hierarchical culture that NAB executives are trying to shed. The docklands building project was initiated when executives realised that MLC, a financial services firm that NAB had acquired a few years earlier, was able to change its culture after moving into its funky headquarters in Sydney. 'There's no doubt that MLC has moved its culture over the last few years to a more open and transparent style which is a good example for the rest of the group to follow,' admitted a NAB executive.[20]

ORGANISATIONAL CULTURE AND PERFORMANCE

Does organisational culture affect corporate performance? Mike Smith and other executives at Oxygen Business Solutions think so. As the opening story to this chapter described, the Auckland-based IT consulting firm spent a lot of time and money identifying a dominant culture that would best fit its competitive environment and the values of its staff. Several writers also claim that companies with strong cultures are more likely to be successful.[21]

A strong organisational culture exists when most employees across all subunits hold the dominant values. The company's values are also institutionalised through well-established artefacts, thereby making it difficult for those values to change. Furthermore, strong cultures tend to be long lasting; some can be traced back to the beliefs and values established by the company's founder. In contrast, companies have weak cultures when the dominant values are short-lived and held mainly by a few people at the top of the organisation.

A strong corporate culture is potentially good for business, because it serves three important functions:

LEARNING OBJECTIVE

Identify three functions of organisational culture.

- *Control system.* Organisational culture is a deeply embedded form of social control that influences employee decisions and behaviour.[22] Culture is pervasive and operates unconsciously. You might think of it as an automatic pilot, directing employees in ways that are consistent with organisational expectations.
- *Social glue.* Organisational culture is the 'social glue' that bonds people together and makes them feel part of the organisational experience.[23] Employees are motivated to internalise the organisation's dominant culture because it fulfils their need for social identity. This social glue is increasingly important as a way to attract new staff and retain top performers.
- *Sense-making.* Organisational culture assists the sense-making process.[24] It helps employees understand what goes on and why things happen in the company. Corporate culture also makes it easier for them to understand what is expected of them and to interact with other employees who know the culture and believe in it.

LEARNING OBJECTIVE

Discuss the conditions under which cultural strength improves corporate performance.

ORGANISATIONAL CULTURE STRENGTH AND FIT

Although strong cultures do seem to offer the three benefits listed here, this does not necessarily mean that companies with strong cultures have higher performance. On the contrary,

Organisational culture and performance

EXHIBIT 16.2

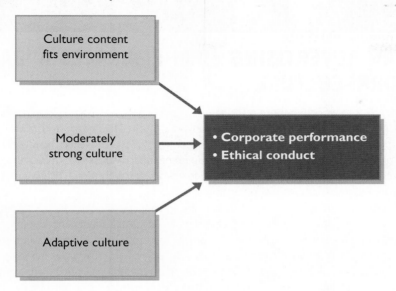

studies have found only a modestly positive relationship between culture strength and success.[25] One reason for the weak relationship is that a strong culture increases organisational performance only when the cultural content is appropriate for the organisation's environment (see Exhibit 16.2). This alignment is apparent at Oxygen Business Solutions, described in the chapter's opening story. Oxygen adopted a more customer-focused and responsive culture in order to survive in the highly competitive IT services industry. When a firm's strong culture is misaligned with its environment, it is unable to serve its customers and other dominant stakeholders effectively. As Reality Check 16.1 (overleaf) describes, Judith Mair developed a strong 'back to work' culture at her German advertising and web design firm because she believed that the typical 'cool' cultures at other firms contributed to their downfall.

A second reason why companies with strong cultures aren't necessarily more effective is that strong cultures lock decision makers into mental models that blind them to new opportunities and unique problems. Thus, strong cultures might cause decision makers to overlook or incorrectly define subtle misalignments between the organisation's activities and the changing environment. Several bankrupt steel manufacturers in the United States apparently suffered from this problem. 'It was 100 years of integrated culture,' recalls Mittal Steel vice-president John Mang, III who worked at one of the now-bankrupt firms for three decades. 'People in the organisation are inbreds, including myself. You grew up in the culture; you didn't see anything else ... It is a culture from within so you have these rose-coloured glasses that everything's fine.'[26]

A third consideration is that very strong cultures tend to suppress dissenting subcultural values. As noted earlier, subcultures encourage constructive conflict, which improves creative thinking and offers some level of ethical vigilance over the dominant culture. In the long run, the subculture's nascent values could become important dominant values as the environment changes. Strong cultures suppress subcultures, thereby undermining these benefits.

ADAPTIVE CULTURES

So far, the discussion has highlighted that strong cultures are more effective when the cultural values are aligned with the organisation's environment. Also, no corporate culture should be so strong that it blinds employees to alternative viewpoints or completely suppresses dissenting subcultures. One last point to add to this discussion is that organisations are more likely

GERMAN ADVERTISING FIRM EMBRACES A 'BACK TO WORK' CULTURE

It's time to get back to work! No more office games or pool tables. No more flexible hours. No more casual dress. No Christmas party this year … or any year. In a rebellion against new economy work practices, a small advertising and web design firm in Cologne, Germany, is returning to a no-nonsense, disciplined corporate culture. 'The office is not an amusement park,' advises Judith Mair, the thirty-year-old entrepreneur who started Mair & Company a few years ago with three colleagues. 'Work is just work, and that's exactly what it needs to become again.'

Mair & Company's business-like culture is apparent as soon as you enter its offices. Mair and her co-workers wear company uniforms: smart blue suits when visiting clients and blue-grey tracksuits at the office. Everyone addresses each other formally by their family name. Smiling is not required; it's not even encouraged. Non-work topics are discussed only during official five-minute breaks. The offices are spartan: no pictures on the white walls and no personal items that would distract employees from their duties. New Age gibberish from America, such as 'team spirit', 'workflow' and 'brainstorming', is strictly verboten.

The corporate culture also advocates strict working hours from 9 am to 5.30 pm and minimal socialising afterwards. Weekend work is forbidden and no one is allowed to take work home. 'It's dangerous if work and free time are being mixed up,' Mair warns, suggesting that employees experience more stress when their company tries to take over their life beyond normal working hours.

These cultural artefacts are not dictums from the CEO. Mair & Company shifted away from the typical dot-com culture after seeing many other German Internet companies flounder. Employees also found it stressful to act like a 'cool' young firm by dressing in the latest fashions and having company drinks in hip bars. 'Yeah, it's strict, but it's okay,' says co-worker Vanessa Plotkin, who helped to develop the disciplined culture. 'It works.'

Many Germans also think Mair & Company's culture 'works' in today's tough economy. Mair's recently published book about her company's culture, called *Schluss mit Lustig* (meaning 'End the Fun'), has been snapped up by German business leaders looking for ways to survive in Germany's current economic slump.

Sources: R. Boyes, 'Germans Told: Work Is Not Fun', *The Times* (London), 6 December 2002, 20; T. Paterson, 'German Woman Boss Puts Back Clock to Outlaw Fun', *Telegraph* (London), 8 December 2002; K. James, 'Germany Concern Looks at Making the Workplace Stricter and Less Friendly'. *Marketplace: Minnesota Public Radio*, 9 January 2003; K. Gehmlich, 'Work Is Just Work', *Globe & Mail*, 11 July 2003, C7; B. Bloch, 'Controls Freaks Work Wonders on Shop Floor', *Daily Telegraph* (London), 6 October 2005, 6.

adaptive culture An organisational culture in which employees focus on the changing needs of customers and other stakeholders, and support initiatives to keep pace with those changes.

to succeed when they have an adaptive culture.[27] An **adaptive culture** exists when employees focus on the changing needs of customers and other stakeholders, and support initiatives to keep pace with these changes.

Organisational culture experts are starting to piece together the elements of adaptive cultures.[28] First and foremost, adaptive cultures have an external focus. Employees hold a common mental model that change is both necessary and inevitable in order to keep pace with a changing external environment. Second, employees in adaptive cultures pay as much attention to organisational processes as they do to organisational goals. They engage in continuous improvement of internal processes (production, customer service, etc.) to serve external stakeholders.

Third, employees in adaptive cultures have a strong sense of ownership. They assume responsibility for the organisation's performance. In other words, they believe in 'it's our job' rather than 'it's not my job'. Fourth, adaptive cultures are proactive and quick. Employees seek out opportunities; they don't wait for them to arrive. They act swiftly to learn through discovery rather than engage in 'paralysis by analysis'.

ORGANISATIONAL CULTURE AND BUSINESS ETHICS

An organisation's culture influences more than just the bottom line; it can also potentially influence the organisation's ethical conduct. This makes sense because, as discussed in Chapter 2, good behaviour is driven by ethical values. An organisation can guide the conduct of its employees by embedding ethical values in its dominant culture.

Organisational culture is also a potential source of ethical problems when it applies excessive control over employees. All organisations require some values congruence. As explained in Chapter 2, this congruence ensures that employees make decisions that are compatible with organisational objectives. Congruence also improves employee satisfaction, loyalty and tenure (i.e. low turnover). But a few organisations imprint their cultural values so strongly on employees that they risk becoming corporate cults. They take over employees' lives and rob people of their individualism.

This cult-like phenomenon was apparently one of the factors that led to the downfall of Arthur Andersen. The accounting firm's uniting principle, called 'One Firm', emphasised consistent service throughout the world by developing Andersen employees in the same way. Andersen carefully selected university graduates with compatible values, then subjected these 'green beans' to a powerful indoctrination process to further imprint Andersen's culture. This production of Andersen think-alikes, called 'Androids', improved service consistency, but it also undermined the ethics of individualism.[29] Thus, an organisation's culture should be consistent with society's ethical values and the culture should not be so strong that it undermines individual freedom.

Citibank's culture pushes ethical boundaries

Citibank Japan director Koichiro Kitade thrived in Citigroup's intensely bottom-line corporate culture. Each year his group exceeded the ever-increasing targets set by Citigroup's top executives in New York. Over six years, Citibank Japan increased its clientele tenfold and delivered profits that outscored all other private banks in the company's huge network. Unfortunately, the Japanese government's financial watchdog recently concluded that Citibank's culture also encouraged Kitade to push aside ethical and financial compliance rules. Japan's regulator accused Citibank of constructing 'a law-evading sales system', citing infractions ranging from grossly overcharging clients to helping them to falsify profit and manipulate stock. With eighty-three infractions, Citigroup was told to close some of its Japanese operations. 'It's our fault, because all we talk about is delivering the numbers. We've done this forever,' admits Citigroup chief executive Charles Prince. The photo shows Prince (right) with a colleague bowing at a Tokyo news conference in apology for the violations. Prince fired several top executives in Tokyo and New York and is now on a mission to change Citibank's culture. He has a major challenge ahead of him. The Dow Jones news service reports that Citigroup has an 'established reputation for pushing the limits of acceptable banking behaviour'.[30]

Yuriko Nakao/Reuters

MERGING ORGANISATIONAL CULTURES

Corporate culture was on the minds of BHP executives a few years ago as they contemplated a merger with the huge South African resources company Billiton plc. 'Obviously one of the questions when you get into a merger is: Is one culture going to dominate or do you create a new one?' said a BHP executive at the time. 'Lots of mergers have failed to realise what they purported to because they failed to look at the people or culture side of the business.' To ensure that the BHP–Billiton merger wasn't another casualty, the two firms set up a committee to address the cultural issues and plan the integration of the two firms. The committee began by taking a 'cultural swab' from both companies. What they found was two businesses in cultural transition, so it was possible to form a composite culture that took the best of both firms.[31]

The BHP–Billiton merger went more smoothly and successfully than most because its leaders paid attention to the risk of organisational culture differences. Unfortunately, it is an exception. Various studies report that between 60 and 75 per cent of all mergers fail to return a positive investment. Often, corporate leaders are so focused on the financial or marketing logistics of a merger that they forget to conduct due-diligence audits on their respective corporate cultures.[32]

The corporate world is littered with mergers that have failed or have had a difficult gestation because of clashing organisational cultures. IBM's acquisition of PricewaterhouseCooper's (PwC) consulting business has recently turned into a well-publicised culture clash in Australia and elsewhere. IBMers tend to be cost conscious and flexible, whereas PwC staff are accustomed to flying business class and having a large, personal office (IBMers tend to hot-desk). PwC staff are also much more conservative than their IBM counterparts. At one event in Melbourne, a senior IBM executive was dressed as American tennis star Andre Agassi. 'The IBMers went mad that time, nuts, standing and cheering. They loved it,' recalls one onlooker. 'The PwC folk were stunned. Silent.' Less than two years after IBM had acquired PwC's consulting business, up to one-quarter of PwC's partners had apparently quit.[33]

Charles Schwab & Co.'s acquisition of US Trust is another example of a corporate culture clash. Reality Check 16.2 describes how the diametrically opposing cultures of the discount brokerage firm and the 'old money' firm undermined job performance, increased dysfunctional conflict, and resulted in lost talent.

BICULTURAL AUDIT

bicultural audit Diagnoses cultural relations between companies prior to a merger and determines the extent to which cultural clashes are likely to occur.

Organisational leaders can minimise these cultural collisions and fulfil their duty of due diligence by conducting a bicultural audit. A **bicultural audit** diagnoses cultural relations between the companies and determines the extent to which cultural clashes are likely to occur. The bicultural audit process begins by identifying cultural differences between the merging companies. Next, the bicultural audit data are analysed to determine which differences between the two firms will result in conflict and which cultural values provide common ground on which to build a cultural foundation in the merged organisation. The final stage involves identifying strategies and preparing action plans to bridge the two organisations' cultures.

STRATEGIES TO MERGE DIFFERENT ORGANISATIONAL CULTURES

LEARNING OBJECTIVE

Compare and contrast four strategies for merging organisational cultures.

In some cases, the bicultural audit results in a decision to end merger talks because the two cultures are too different to merge effectively. However, even with substantially different cultures, two companies may form a workable union if they apply the appropriate merger strategy. The four main strategies for merging different corporate cultures are assimilation, deculturation, integration and separation (see Exhibit 16.3, overleaf).[34]

SCHWAB SUFFERS THE PERILS OF CLASHING CULTURES

During the peak of the dot-com boom, the then-CEO of Charles Schwab & Co., David Pottruck, was convinced that as investors got wealthier they would migrate from the San Francisco-based discount broker to full-service firms that offered more personalised service. So Schwab paid top dollar to acquire US Trust, a highbrow New York-based private bank that only served those clients who had at least $10 million to invest. Schwab customers who got wealthy would be shunted over to US Trust for more personalised service.

The strategy backfired, partly because Schwab's customers still wanted cheap trades as they got wealthier, and partly because Schwab ignored the acquisition's cultural dynamics. Schwab's culture values rapid change, cost-cutting frugality, process efficiency, and egalitarianism. Schwab employees see themselves as nimble nonconformists who empower millions of people through low-cost Internet-based stock trading. In contrast, US Trust was an exclusive club that was slow to adopt technology and preferred to admit new clients through referrals from existing clients. Clients were pampered by 'wealth advisers' who earned huge bonuses and worked in an environment that reeked of luxury.

While negotiating the takeover, US Trust executives expressed concern about these cultural differences, so Schwab agreed to leave the firm as a separate entity. This separation strategy didn't last very long. Schwab cut US Trust's lucrative bonuses and tied annual rewards to Schwab's financial performance. US Trust executives were pushed to cut costs and set more aggressive goals. Schwab even tried to acculturate several hundred US Trust employees with a board game that used a giant mat showing hills, streams and a mountain with founder Charles Schwab's face carved into the side. US Trust staff complained that the game was demeaning, particularly wearing smocks as they played the role of investors.

In meetings immediately following the acquisition, US Trust executives winced when Schwab frequently used the term *customers*. They reminded Schwab's staff that US Trust has *clients*, which implies much more of a long-term relationship. US Trust advisers also resisted Schwab's referrals of newly minted millionaires in blue jeans. 'We were flabbergasted,' said one Schwab board member of the cultural clash. 'Some of the US Trust officers simply refused to accept our referrals.'

When the depth of cultural intransigence became apparent, Pottruck replaced US Trust's CEO with Schwab executive Alan Weber. Weber later insisted that 'there is no culture clash', because Schwab 'never tried to change the nature of the organisation'. Meanwhile, sources say that more than 300 US Trust wealth advisers have defected to competitors since the acquisition, taking many valued clients with them. Pottruck lost his job as Schwab CEO, in part because the US Trust acquisition stumbled. The acquisition is now worth less than half of its original purchase price.

'Here are two first-class companies, but structural and cultural problems keep the combination from the kind of success they expected,' explained a financial adviser in Florida.

Sources: F. Vogelstein and E. Florian, 'Can Schwab Get Its Mojo Back?', *Fortune*, 17 September 2001, 93; B. Morris, 'When Bad Things Happen to Good Companies', *Fortune*, 8 December 2003, 78; S. Craig and K. Brown, 'Schwab Ousts Pottruck as CEO', *Wall Street Journal*, 21 July 2004, A1; R. Frank, 'US Trust Feels Effects of Switch', *Wall Street Journal*, 21 July 2004, A8; R. Frank and S. Craig, 'White-Shoe Shuffle', *Wall Street Journal*, 15 September 2004, A1; C. Harrington, 'Made in Heaven? Watching the Watchovia-Tanager Union', *Accounting Today*, 20 December 2004, 18; J. Kador, 'Cultures in Conflict', *Registered Rep.*, October 2004, 43.

EXHIBIT 16.3	**Strategies for merging different organisational cultures**

Merger strategy	Description	When it works best
Assimilation	The acquired company embraces the acquiring firm's culture.	When the acquired firm has a weak culture.
Deculturation	The acquiring firm imposes its culture on an unwilling acquired firm.	It rarely works; it may be necessary only when acquired firm's culture doesn't work but employees don't realise it.
Integration	The two or more cultures are combined into a new composite culture.	When existing cultures can be improved.
Separation	The merging companies remain distinct entities with minimal exchange of culture or organisational practices.	When firms operate successfully in different businesses requiring different cultures.

Source: Based on ideas in A. R. Malekazedeh and A. Nahavandi, 'Making Mergers Work by Managing Cultures', *Journal of Business Strategy*, May/June 1990, pp. 55–7; K. W. Smith, 'A Brand-New Culture for the Merged Firm', *Mergers and Acquisitions*, 35 (June 2000), pp. 45–50.

Assimilation

Assimilation occurs when employees at the acquired company willingly embrace the cultural values of the acquiring organisation. Typically, this strategy works best when the acquired company has a weak dysfunctional culture whereas the acquiring company's culture is strong and aligned with the external environment. Assimilation seldom produces a cultural clash because the acquired firm's culture is weak and employees are looking for better cultural alternatives.

Deculturation

Assimilation is rare. Employees usually resist organisational change, particularly when they are asked to throw away organisational values that were similar to their personal values. Under these conditions, some acquiring companies apply a *deculturation* strategy by imposing their culture and business practices on the acquired organisation. The acquiring firm strips away artefacts and reward systems that support the old culture. People who cannot adopt the acquiring company's culture are often terminated. Deculturation may be necessary when the acquired firm's culture doesn't work but employees aren't convinced of this. However, the strategy is difficult to apply effectively because the acquired firm's employees resist the cultural intrusions from the buying firm, thereby delaying or undermining the merger process.

Integration

A third strategy is to combine the two or more cultures into a new composite culture that preserves the best features of the previous cultures. Integration is slow and potentially risky, because there are many forces preserving the existing cultures. Still, this strategy should be considered when the companies have relatively weak cultures, or when their cultures include several overlapping values. Integration also works best when people realise that their existing cultures are ineffective, and they are therefore motivated to adopt a new set of dominant values.

Separation

A separation strategy occurs where the merging companies agree to remain distinct entities with minimal exchange of culture or organisational practices. This strategy is most appropriate when the two merging companies are in unrelated industries or operate in different countries, because the most appropriate cultural values tend to differ by industry and national culture. Discount brokerage firm Charles Schwab & Co. tried to apply a separation strategy when it first acquired US Trust. However, as described in Reality Check 16.2, this separation strategy didn't last long. In fact, this is one of many examples where executives in the acquiring firm have had difficulty keeping their hands off the acquired firm. According to one survey, only 15 per cent of acquiring firms leave the acquired organisation as a stand-alone unit.[35]

CHANGING AND STRENGTHENING ORGANISATIONAL CULTURE

Changing the culture is often necessary in order to improve the organisation's long-term success, but this transformation can be tremendously difficult. Oxygen Business Solutions in New Zealand and BHP-Billiton in Australia are rare exceptions. Transforming the organisation's culture requires the change management toolkit that will be discussed in the next chapter. Corporate leaders need to make employees aware of the urgency for change. They then need to 'unfreeze' the existing culture by removing artefacts that represent that culture and 'refreeze' the new culture by introducing artefacts that communicate and reinforce the new values.

STRENGTHENING ORGANISATIONAL CULTURE

Artefacts communicate and reinforce the new corporate culture, but ways to strengthen that culture further also need to be considered. Five approaches that are commonly cited in the literature are the actions of founders and leaders, introducing culturally consistent rewards, maintaining a stable workforce, managing the cultural network, and selecting and socialising new employees (see Exhibit 16.4).

LEARNING OBJECTIVE

Identify five strategies to strengthen an organisation's culture.

Actions of founders and leaders

Founders establish an organisation's culture through their vision and concerted actions.[36] You can see this at retail giant Harvey Norman, where company chairman and co-founder Gerry Harvey has established a culture that is aggressive, demanding and frugal, yet pays attention to the development of its franchisees. Subsequent leaders can break the organisation away

Strategies for strengthening organisational culture

EXHIBIT 16.4

from the founder's values. This shift was apparent at Haier Group, the Chinese white goods manufacturer that chief executive Zhang Ruimin transformed from a state-owned bureaucracy to a global competitor in twenty years. Chen Biting achieved a similar cultural shift at Shenhua Group, China's largest coal producer.[37] In both cases, these leaders were visionaries who applied the transformational leadership concepts described in Chapter 14. Transformational leaders alter and strengthen organisational culture by communicating and enacting their vision of the future.

Introducing culturally consistent rewards

Reward systems strengthen corporate culture when they are consistent with cultural values.[38] For example, Husky Injection Molding Systems has an unusual stock incentive program that supports its environmentalist culture. Employees at the plastics equipment manufacturer earn one-twentieth of a company share for each seedling they plant, one share for each month of car pooling, and so on. The idea is to align rewards to the cultural values the company wants to reinforce.

Maintaining a stable workforce

An organisation's culture is embedded in the minds of its employees. Organisational stories are rarely written down; rituals and ceremonies do not usually exist in procedure manuals; organisational metaphors are not found in corporate directories. Thus, organisations depend on a stable workforce to communicate and reinforce the dominant beliefs and values. The organisation's culture can literally disintegrate during periods of high turnover and precipitous downsizing because the corporate memory leaves with these employees.[39] Conversely, corporate leaders who want to change the corporate culture have accelerated the turnover of senior executives and older employees who held the cultural values in place.

Managing the cultural network

Organisational culture is learned, so an effective network of cultural transmission is necessary to strengthen the company's underlying assumptions, values and beliefs. According to Max De Pree, former CEO of furniture manufacturer Herman Miller Inc., every organisation needs 'tribal storytellers' to keep the organisation's history and culture alive.[40] The cultural network exists through the organisational grapevine. It is also supported through frequent opportunities for interaction so employees and organisational leaders can share stories and re-enact rituals. Company magazines and other media can further strengthen organisational culture by communicating cultural values and beliefs more efficiently.

Selecting and socialising employees

Organisational culture is strengthened by hiring people who already embrace the cultural values. A good person–organisation fit reinforces the culture; it also improves job satisfaction and organisational loyalty because new hires with values compatible to the corporate culture adjust more quickly to the organisation.[41] Job applicants also pay attention to corporate culture during the hiring process. They look at corporate culture artefacts to determine whether the company's values are compatible with their own.

organisational socialisation
The process by which individuals learn the values, expected behaviours and social knowledge necessary to assume their roles in the organisation.

Along with selecting people with compatible values, companies maintain strong cultures through the process of organisational socialisation. **Organisational socialisation** refers to the process by which individuals learn the values, expected behaviours, and social knowledge necessary to assume their roles in the organisation.[42] By communicating the company's dominant values, job candidates and new hires tend to internalise these values more quickly and deeply. Socialisation is an important process for absorbing corporate culture as well as helping newcomers to adjust to co-workers, work procedures, and other corporate realities. Thus, the final section of this chapter looks more closely at the organisational socialisation process.

Socialising newcomers into Flight Centre's culture

Flight Centre is a runaway success story of the Australian travel industry. Part of this success comes from the company's unique culture, which it carefully maintains through the selection and socialisation of new staff. 'Through our induction, the first thing that people learn when they come into our organisation is what our culture and what our philosophies are and what that means to them,' says chief executive and co-founder Graham Turner. 'We have a very comprehensive system to make sure that we employ the right people.' Louise Mullane describes how Flight Centre made sure that she was comfortable with the travel agency's culture. 'I had a couple of interviews and then spent a day at the 277 store to see how I fitted in,' says Mullane, who now works at the Flight Centre store in Newmarket, an Auckland, New Zealand, suburb. 'I got a real feel for the job, the people and what was expected of me.'[43]

APN New Zealand Herald

ORGANISATIONAL SOCIALISATION

Nadia Ramos had plenty of job opportunities after graduating from business school, but Canadian financial institution Bank of Nova Scotia (ScotiaBank) won the contest hands down. Ramos was impressed by the opportunity for overseas field assignments and the panel interview with senior managers in commercial banking. But it was the little things that really won Ramos over to ScotiaBank. Rather than seeing only the company boardroom and company recruiters, Ramos toured the offices where she would actually work and met with fellow international banking associates who immediately welcomed her to the team and offered advice for apartment hunting in Toronto. ScotiaBank also assigned a buddy to help Ramos adjust to the workplace over the first two years. 'We have to make sure, once they are in the door, that they start having a great experience as an employee—and that we haven't over-promised,' says a ScotiaBank executive.[44]

ScotiaBank successfully brings employees into the organisation by going beyond selecting applicants with the right competencies. It relies on several organisational socialisation practices to help newcomers learn about and adjust to the company's culture, physical layout, procedures and so on. Research indicates that when employees are effectively socialised into the organisation, they tend to perform better and have higher job satisfaction.[45]

Organisational socialisation is a process of both learning and adjustment. It is a learning process because newcomers try to make sense of the company's physical workplace, social dynamics and strategic/cultural environment. They learn about the organisation's performance expectations, power dynamics, corporate culture, company history and jargon. Organisational socialisation is also a process of adjustment, because individuals need to adapt to their new work environment. They develop new work roles that reconfigure their social identity, adopt new team norms, and practise new behaviours. Research reports that the adjustment process is fairly rapid for many people, usually within a few months. However, newcomers with diverse work experience seem to adjust better than those with limited previous experience, possibly because they have a larger toolkit of knowledge and skills to make the adjustment possible.[46]

Newcomers absorb the organisation's dominant culture to varying degrees. Some people deeply internalise the company's culture; a few others rebel against these attempts to change their mental models and values. Ideally, newcomers adopt a level of 'creative individualism' in which they accept the essential elements of the organisation's culture and team norms, yet maintain a healthy individualism that challenges the dysfunctional elements of organisational life.

STAGES OF SOCIALISATION

LEARNING OBJECTIVE

Describe the stages of organisational socialisation.

Socialisation is a continuous process, beginning long before the first day of employment and continuing throughout one's career within the company. However, it is most intense when people move across organisational boundaries, such as when they first join a company or get transferred to an international assignment. Each of these transitions is a process that can be divided into three stages. Our focus here is on the socialisation of new employees, so the three stages are called pre-employment socialisation, encounter, and role management (see Exhibit 16.5). These stages parallel the individual's transition from outsider, to newcomer, and then to insider.[47]

Stage 1: Pre-employment socialisation

Think back to the months and weeks before you began working in a new job (or attending a new university). You actively searched for information about the company, formed expectations about working there, and felt some anticipation about fitting into that environment. The pre-employment socialisation stage encompasses all of the learning and adjustment that occurs prior to the first day of work in a new position. In fact, a large part of the socialisation adjustment process occurs prior to the first day of work.[48]

The main problem with pre-employment socialisation is that individuals are outsiders, so they must rely on friends, employment interviews, recruiting literature and other indirect information to form expectations about what it is like to work in the organisation. Furthermore, the information exchange between applicants and employers is usually less than perfectly honest.[49] Job applicants might distort their résumés, while employers hide their blemishes by presenting overly positive images of organisational life. Job applicants avoid asking sensitive questions—about things such as pay increases and fast promotions—in order to maintain a good image.

To make matters worse, job applicants tend to engage in post-decisional justification during pre-employment socialisation. Before the first day of work, they tend to increase the importance of favourable elements of the job and justify or completely forget about some negative elements. At the same time, they reduce the perceived quality of job offers that they turned down. Employers often distort their expectations of new hires in the same way.

EXHIBIT 16.5

Stages of organisational socialisation

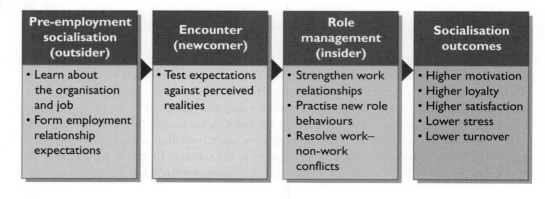

Pre-employment socialisation (outsider)	Encounter (newcomer)	Role management (insider)	Socialisation outcomes
• Learn about the organisation and job • Form employment relationship expectations	• Test expectations against perceived realities	• Strengthen work relationships • Practise new role behaviours • Resolve work–non-work conflicts	• Higher motivation • Higher loyalty • Higher satisfaction • Lower stress • Lower turnover

Reality shock in India's call centres

Rajit Gangadharan thought his dream had come true when offered a job at a call centre in Bangalore, India. The recent business school graduate looked forward to the fun office environment, decent salary, free entertainment passes, and working with customers half a world away. But it didn't take long for Gangadharan to discover the downside of the job, including long night shifts, irregular eating times, and few opportunities to meet his old friends. 'Social life is nil in such a job,' complains Gangadharan, who no longer works in a call centre. A survey by NFO WorldGroup reports that Gangadharan is typical of call centre employees in India. They are well educated and highly qualified, yet their high job expectations result in reality shock and turnover rates of 30 to 50 per cent.[53]

Gideon Mendel/CORBIS

The result is that both parties develop higher expectations of each other than will be fulfilled during the encounter stage.

Stage 2: Encounter

The first day on the job typically marks the beginning of the encounter stage of organisational socialisation. This is the stage in which newcomers test their prior expectations with the perceived realities. Many jobs fail the test. Consider Duncan McNee, the secondary English and PE teacher from Brisbane, Australia, who accepted a teaching post in the United Kingdom. McNee expected a challenging new adventure teaching in another country. Instead, he was soon shocked by the severity of student behaviour problems. 'Even in the worst schools where I taught in Australia the kids still had some respect,' says McNee. 'But over here there seems to be a complete lack of it. I've had chairs being thrown around, textbooks thrown out of windows and fights.'[50]

Duncan McNee experienced **reality shock** because the behaviour of students was much worse than he had imagined. Reality shock occurs when newcomers perceive discrepancies between their pre-employment expectations and the on-the-job reality.[51] The larger the gap, the stronger the reality shock. Reality shock doesn't necessarily occur on the first day; it might develop over several weeks or even months as newcomers develop a better understanding of their new work environment. Along with experiencing unmet expectations, reality shock occurs when newcomers are overwhelmed by the experience of sudden entry into a new work environment. They experience the stress of information overload and have difficulty adjusting quickly to their new role.

It might have been difficult for McNee and other Australians to imagine the discipline problems that exist in UK schools, but reality shock is common in many organisations. For example, Australian human resource executives indicate that the most common reason that recently hired employees give for quitting is that their expectations have not been met. This is supported by another survey reporting that 73 per cent of Australian Generation-X employees say that the reality of a new job rarely matches the promise.[52]

Stage 3: Role management

During the role-management stage in the socialisation process, employees settle in as they make the transition from newcomers to insiders. They strengthen relationships with co-workers and supervisors, practise new role behaviours, and adopt attitudes and values consistent with their

reality shock Occurs when newcomers perceive discrepancies between pre-employment expectations and on-the-job reality.

new position and organisation. Role management also involves resolving the conflicts between work and nonwork activities. In particular, employees must redistribute their time and energy between work and family, reschedule recreational activities, and deal with changing perceptions and values in the context of other life roles. They must address any discrepancies between their existing values and those emphasised by the organisational culture. New social identities are formed that are more compatible with the work environment.

IMPROVING THE SOCIALISATION PROCESS

LEARNING OBJECTIVE

Explain how realistic job previews assist the socialisation process.

realistic job preview (RJP)
Giving job applicants a balance of positive and negative information about the job and work context.

Executives at Dun & Bradstreet Australasia knew that they had a problem a few years ago when up to 40 per cent of their Generation-Y recruits quit within a couple of years of being hired. According to several Gen-Y staff, the business information and credit risk services company misrepresented the job ('over-glamorised the position big time', said one employee) in its advertisements, interviews and induction sessions. To correct the problem, Dun & Bradstreet changed its recruitment message by 'talking down' the job. It also changed internal processes to align more with Gen-Y expectations, such as introducing a mentoring program, increasing base salaries, and expanding its involvement in charities.[54]

Dun & Bradstreet Australasia executives improved the socialisation process by offering a more **realistic job preview (RJP)**—a balance of positive and negative information about the job and work context.[55] Companies often exaggerate the positive features of the job and neglect to mention the undesirable elements in the hope that the best applicants will get hooked into joining the organisation. In contrast, an RJP helps job applicants to decide for themselves whether their skills, needs and values are compatible with the job and the organisation.

For example, applicants for jobs in the West Australian police service watch an RJP consisting of a video showing various police tasks, followed by a discussion of police work with current West Australian police officers and civilian staff. Applicants' partners and family members are also invited to attend so they gain a better understanding of the work and how it will affect them. The police service hopes that the RJP will correct the unrealistic view of police work depicted in television soap operas and police dramas. 'The aim of the realistic job preview is to ensure all applicants have a true and realistic understanding of the role of police in the community and the many and varied tasks (both good and bad) that they can expect to encounter during their service,' explains the Western Australia police service website.[56]

Although RJPs scare away some applicants, they tend to reduce turnover and increase job performance.[57] This occurs because RJPs help applicants develop more accurate pre-employment expectations that, in turn, minimise reality shock. RJPs represent a type of vaccination by preparing employees for the more challenging and troublesome aspects of work life. There is also some evidence that RJPs increase organisational loyalty. A possible explanation for this is that companies providing candid information are easier to trust. They also show respect for the psychological contract and concern for employee welfare.[58]

Socialisation agents

Nadia Ramos received plenty of support to help her adjust to a career at ScotiaBank. As mentioned at the beginning of this section on organisational socialisation, Ramos's future co-workers welcomed her to the team and offered advice on finding an apartment. ScotiaBank also assigned an experienced employee (a buddy) to offer Ramos special assistance and guidance. Clearly, ScotiaBank leaders seem to be aware that a lot of organisational socialisation occurs informally through socialisation agents, which includes co-workers, bosses, and even friends who work for the company.

Supervisors usually provide technical information, performance feedback and information about job duties. They also improve the socialisation process by giving newcomers reasonably challenging first assignments, buffering them from excessive demands, and helping them form social ties with co-workers.[59] Co-workers are particularly important socialisation agents because they are easily accessible, can answer questions when problems arise, and serve as role models for appropriate behaviour. New employees tend to receive this information and support when co-workers integrate them into the work team.

Co-workers also aid the socialisation process by being flexible and tolerant in their inter-actions with the new hires. Newcomers who quickly form social relations with co-workers tend to have a less traumatic socialisation experience and are less likely to quit their jobs within the first year of employment.[60] The challenge is for organisations to ensure that co-workers offer the necessary support (such as through buddy systems whereby newcomers are assigned to co-workers for sources of information and social support).

CHAPTER SUMMARY

Organisational culture is the basic pattern of shared assumptions, values and beliefs that govern behaviour within a particular organisation. Assumptions are the shared mental models or theories-in-use that people rely on to guide their perceptions and behaviours. Beliefs represent the individual's perceptions of reality. Values are more stable, long-lasting beliefs about what is important. They help us define what is right or wrong, or good or bad, in the world. Culture content refers to the relative ordering of beliefs, values and assumptions.

Organisations have subcultures as well as the dominant culture. Subcultures maintain the organisation's standards of performance and ethical behaviour. They are also the source of emerging values that replace aging core values.

Artefacts are the observable symbols and signs of an organisation's culture. Four broad categories of artefacts include organisational stories and legends, rituals and ceremonies, language, physical structures and symbols. Understanding an organisation's culture requires assessment of many artefacts, because they are subtle and often ambiguous.

Organisational culture has three main functions. It is a deeply embedded form of social control. It is also the 'social glue' that bonds people together and makes them feel part of the organisational experience. Third, corporate culture helps employees make sense of the workplace.

Companies with strong cultures generally perform better than those with weak cultures, but only when the cultural content is appropriate for the organisation's environment. Also, the culture should not be so strong that it drives out dissenting values, which may form emerging values for the future. Organisations should have adaptive cultures so that employees focus on the need for change and support initiatives and leadership that keeps pace with these changes.

Organisational culture relates to business ethics in two ways. First, corporate cultures can support the ethical values of society, thereby reinforcing ethical conduct. Second, some cultures are so strong that they rob a person's individualism and discourage constructive conflict.

Mergers should include a bicultural audit to diagnose the compatibility of the organisational cultures. The four main strategies for merging different corporate cultures are integration, deculturation, assimilation and separation.

Organisational culture may be strengthened through the actions of founders and leaders, introducing culturally consistent rewards, maintaining a stable workforce, managing the cultural network, and selecting and socialising employees.

Organisational socialisation is the process by which individuals learn the values, expected behaviours and social knowledge necessary to assume their roles in the organisation. It is a process of both learning about the work context and adjusting to new work roles, team norms and behaviours. Employees typically pass through three socialisation stages: pre-employment, encounter, and role management. To improve the socialisation process, organisations should introduce realistic job previews (RJPs) and recognise the value of socialisation agents in the process.

KEY TERMS

adaptive culture p. 482
artefacts p. 478
bicultural audit p. 482

ceremonies p. 478
organisational culture p. 476
organisational socialisation p. 488

realistic job preview (RJP) p. 492
reality shock p. 491
rituals p. 478

DISCUSSION QUESTIONS

1. Superb Consultants has submitted a proposal to analyse the cultural values of your organisation. The proposal states that Superb has developed a revolutionary new survey to tap the company's true culture. The survey takes just ten minutes to complete and the consultants say that results can be based on a small sample of employees. Discuss the merits and limitations of this proposal.

2. Some people suggest that the most effective organisations have the strongest cultures. What do we mean by the 'strength' of organisational culture, and what possible problems are there with a strong organisational culture?

3. The CEO of a manufacturing firm wants everyone to support the organisation's dominant culture of lean efficiency and hard work. The CEO has introduced a new reward system to reinforce this culture, and personally interviews all professional and managerial applicants to ensure that they bring similar values to the organisation. Some employees who criticised these values had their careers sidelined until they left. Two mid-level managers were sacked for supporting contrary values, such as work–life balance. Based on your knowledge of organisational subcultures, what potential problems is the CEO creating?

4. Identify at least two artefacts you have observed in your department or faculty from each of these four broad categories:
(a) organisational stories and legends

(b) rituals and ceremonies

(c) language

(d) physical structures and symbols.

5. 'Organisations are more likely to succeed when they have an adaptive culture.' What can an organisation do to foster an adaptive culture?

6. Acme Pty Ltd is planning to acquire Beta Pty Ltd, which operates in a different industry. Acme's culture is entrepreneurial and fast-paced, whereas Beta employees value slow, deliberate decision making by consensus. Which merger strategy would you recommend to minimise culture shock when Acme acquires Beta? Explain your answer.

7. Suppose you are asked by senior officers of a city government to identify ways to reinforce a new culture of teamwork and collaboration. The senior executive group clearly supports these values, but it wants everyone in the organisation to embrace them. Identify four types of activities that would strengthen these cultural values.

8. ScotiaBank, Flight Centre and other organisations rely on current employees to socialise new recruits. What are the advantages of relying on this type of socialisation agent? What problems can you foresee (or you have personally experienced) with co-worker socialisation practices?

SKILL BUILDER | 16.1

HILLTON'S TRANSFORMATION

CASE STUDY

Twenty years ago, Hillton was a town of 30 000 residents that served as an outer suburb of a large metropolitan area. The local council treated employees like family and gave them a great deal of autonomy in their work. Everyone in the organisation (including the two labour unions representing employees) implicitly agreed that the leaders and supervisors of the organisation should rise through the ranks based on their experience. Few people were ever hired from the outside into middle or senior management positions. The rule of employment at Hillton was to learn the job skills, maintain a reasonably good work record, and wait your turn for promotion.

Hillton has grown rapidly since the mid-1980s. As the population grew, so did the municipality's workforce to keep pace with the increasing demand for municipal services. This meant that employees were promoted fairly quickly and were almost guaranteed employment. In fact, until recently Hillton had never laid off an employee. The organisation's culture could be described as one of entitlement and comfort. Neither the elected councillors nor Hillton's chief executive officer bothered the departmental managers about their work. There were few cost controls, because the rapid growth placed more emphasis on keeping up with the population expansion. The public became somewhat more critical of the poor services, including road construction at inconvenient times and the apparent lack of respect some employees showed for rate-payers.

During these expansion years, Hillton directed more of its budget into 'outside' (also called 'hard') municipal services. These included road building, utility construction and maintenance, fire and police protection, recreational facilities and land use control. This emphasis occurred because an expanding population demanded more of these services and most of the council's senior managers came from the outside services group. For example, Hillton's chief executive officer for many years was a road development engineer. The 'inside' workers (rates, community services, etc.) tended to have less seniority and their departments were given less priority.

As commuter and road systems developed, Hillton attracted more upwardly mobile professionals into the community. Some infrastructure demands continued, but now these suburban dwellers wanted more of the 'soft' services, such as libraries, social activities and community services. They also began complaining about the way the municipality was being run. The population had more than tripled by the early 1990s, and it was increasingly apparent that the organisation needed more corporate planning, information systems, organisation development and cost control systems. In various ways, residents voiced their concerns that the municipality was not providing the quality of management that they would expect from a city of Hillton's size.

In 1996 a new mayor and council replaced most of the previous incumbents, mainly on the platform of improving the municipality's management structure. The new council gave the chief executive officer, along with two other senior managers, an early retirement buyout package. Rather than promoting from the lower ranks, council decided to fill all three positions with qualified candidates from large municipal corporations elsewhere in the state. In the following year, several long-term managers left and at least half of those positions were filled by people from outside the organisation.

In less than two years, Hillton had eight senior or departmental managers who had been hired from other municipalities, and these people played a key role in changing the organisation's value system. The eight managers were called the 'professionals' by employees, usually with negative connotations. The managers worked closely with each other to change the way middle and lower-level managers operated. They brought in a new computer system and emphasised cost controls where managers had previously had complete autonomy. Promotions were increasingly based more on merit than seniority.

The new managers frequently announced in meetings and newsletters that municipal employees must provide superlative customer service, and that Hillton would become one of the most customer-friendly places for citizens and those who did business with the municipality. To this end, these managers were quick to support the public's increasing demand for more 'soft' services such as expanded library services and recreational activities. And when population growth recently flattened out, the chief executive officer and other professionals gained council support to lay off a few of the outside workers due to the lack of demand for 'hard' services.

One of the most significant changes was that the 'outside' departments no longer held dominant positions in city management. Most of the 'professional' managers had worked exclusively in administrative and related inside jobs. Two had Master of Business Administration degrees. This led to some tension between the professional managers and the older outside managers.

Even before the layoffs, the managers of outside departments resisted the changes more than others. These managers complained that their employees with the highest seniority had been turned down for promotions. They argued for more generous budgets and warned that infrastructure problems would cause an increase in liability claims. Informally, these outside managers were supported by the labour union representing the outside workers. The union leaders tried to bargain for more job guarantees, whereas the union representing the inside

workers focused more on improving wages and benefits. Leaders of the outside union made several statements in the local media that the city had 'lost its heart' and that the public would suffer from the actions of the new professionals.

QUESTIONS

1. Contrast Hillton's earlier corporate culture with the emerging set of cultural values.

2. Considering the difficulty of changing organisational culture, why does Hillton's management seem to have been successful in this transformation?

3. Identify two other strategies that the city might consider to reinforce the new set of corporate values.

SKILL BUILDER | 16.2   DIAGNOSING CORPORATE CULTURE PROCLAMATIONS

WEB EXERCISE

PURPOSE

To understand the importance and contents in which corporate culture is identified and discussed in organisations.

INSTRUCTIONS

This exercise is a take-home activity, although it can be completed in classes with computers and Internet connections. The instructor will divide the class into small teams (typically four or five people per team). Each team is assigned a specific industry, such as energy, biotechnology or computer hardware.

The team's task is to search the websites of several companies in the selected industry for company statements about their corporate culture. Use the company website search engine (if it exists) to find documents with key phrases such as 'corporate culture' or 'company values'.

In the next class, or at the end of the time allotted in the current class, students will report on their observations by answering the following three discussion questions.

QUESTIONS

1. What values seem to dominate the corporate culture of the companies you searched? Are these values similar or diverse across companies in the industry?

2. What was the broader content of the web pages in which the companies described or mentioned their corporate culture?

3. Do companies in this industry refer to their corporate culture on their websites more or less than companies in other industries searched by teams in the class?

SKILL BUILDER | 16.3   TRUTH IN ADVERTISING

TEAM EXERCISE

PURPOSE

This team activity is designed to help you diagnose the degree to which recruitment advertisements and brochures provide realistic previews of the job and/or organisation.

MATERIALS

The instructor will bring to class either recruiting brochures or newspaper advertisements.

INSTRUCTIONS

The instructor will place students into teams and give them copies of recruiting brochures and/or advertisements. The instructor might assign one lengthy brochure or, alternatively, several newspaper advertisements. All teams should receive the same materials so that everyone is familiar with the items and results can be compared. Teams will evaluate the recruiting material and answer the following questions for each item.

QUESTIONS

1. What information in the text of this brochure/advertisement identifies conditions or activities in the organisation or job that some applicants may not like?

2. If there are photographs or images of people at work, do they show only positive conditions, or do some show conditions or events that some applicants may not like?

3. After reading this item, would you say that it provides a realistic preview of the job and/or organisation?

CORPORATE CULTURE PREFERENCE SCALE

16.4 SKILL BUILDER

SELF-ASSESSMENT

FULL EXERCISE ON
STUDENT CD

PURPOSE
This self-assessment is designed to help you identify a corporate culture that fits most closely with your personal values and assumptions.

INSTRUCTIONS
Read each pair of statements in the Corporate Culture Preference Scale and circle the statement that describes the organisation you would prefer to work in. Then use the scoring key in Appendix B to calculate your results for each subscale. The scale does not attempt to measure your preference for every corporate culture, just a few of the more common varieties. Also, keep in mind that none of these corporate cultures is inherently good or bad. The focus here is on how well you fit within each of them. This exercise is completed alone so students can assess themselves honestly without concerns of social comparison. However, class discussion will focus on the importance of matching job applicants to the organisation's dominant values.

CORPORATE CULTURE PREFERENCE SCALE

I would prefer to work in an organisation:

1a	Where employees work well together in teams.	**OR**	**1b**	That produces highly respected products or services.
2a	Where top management maintains a sense of order in the workplace.	**OR**	**2b**	Where the organisation listens to customers and responds quickly to their needs.
3a	Where employees are treated fairly.	**OR**	**3b**	Where employees continuously search for ways to work more efficiently.
4a	Where employees adapt quickly to new work requirements.	**OR**	**4b**	Where corporate leaders work hard to keep employees happy.
5a	Where senior executives receive special benefits not available to other employees.	**OR**	**5b**	Where employees are proud when the organisation achieves its performance goals.
6a	Where employees who perform the best get paid the most.	**OR**	**6b**	Where senior executives are respected.
7a	Where everyone gets their job done like clockwork.	**OR**	**7b**	That is on top of new innovations in the industry.
8a	Where employees receive assistance to overcome any personal problems.	**OR**	**8b**	Where employees abide by company rules.
9a	That is always experimenting with new ideas in the marketplace.	**OR**	**9b**	That expects everyone to put in 110 per cent for peak performance.
10a	That quickly benefits from market opportunities.	**OR**	**10b**	Where employees are always kept informed of what's happening in the organisation.
11a	That can quickly respond to competitive threats.	**OR**	**11b**	Where most decisions are made by the top executives.
12a	Where management keeps everything under control.	**OR**	**12b**	Where employees care for each other.

NOTES

1   'Oxygen Is a Breath of Fresh Air', *New Zealand Herald*, 11 August 2004, E32; 'Oxygen Gives the Kiss of Life (Outsourcing: A Special Advertising Report)', *Australian*, 21 January 2005, 23; P. Broekhuyse, 'Eyes on Asia for Oxygen Culture Vulture Dickinson', *Australian*, 3 May 2005, 36; K. McLaughlin, 'Sales Looms for Carter's High-Flyer', *National Business Review* (NZ), 20 May 2005.

2   A. Williams, P. Dobson and M. Walters, *Changing Culture: New Organizational Approaches* (London: Institute of Personnel Management, 1989); E. H. Schein, 'What Is Culture?', in *Reframing Organizational Culture*, eds P. J. Frost et al. (Beverly Hills, CA: Sage, 1991), 243–53.

3   B. M. Meglino and E. C. Ravlin, 'Individual Values in Organizations: Concepts, Controversies, and Research', *Journal of Management* 24, no. 3 (1998), 351–89; B. R. Agle and C. B. Caldwell, 'Understanding Research on Values in Business', *Business and Society* 38, no. 3 (September 1999), 326–87; S. Hitlin and J. A. Pilavin, 'Values: Reviving a Dormant Concept', *Annual Review of Sociology* 30 (2004), 359–93.

4   'New-Age Banks Bet on Variable Pay Plan', *Business Line* (India), 22 September 2003; 'Golden Handshake, the ICICI Bank Way', *Financial Express* (India), 6 July 2003.

5   A. D'Innocenzio, 'Wal-Mart's Town Becomes New Address for Corporate America', *Associated Press*, 19 September 2003; J. Useem, 'One Nation under Wal-Mart', *Fortune*, 3 March 2003, 65–78.

6   Technology One, 'The TechOne Way' (Brisbane: Technology One, n.d.), pdf file from Technology One website (accessed 11 November 2005).

7   C. Houston, '$10bn Man Is Still the First among Equals', *The Age* (Melbourne), 17 September 2005, 2.

8   J. S. Ott, *The Organizational Culture Perspective* (Pacific Grove, CA: Brooks/Cole, 1989), pp. 45–7; S. Sackmann, 'Culture and Subcultures: An Analysis of Organizational Knowledge', *Administrative Science Quarterly* 37 (1992), 140–61.

9   A. Sinclair, 'Approaches to Organizational Culture and Ethics', *Journal of Business Ethics* 12 (1993); A. Boisnier and J. Chatman, 'The Role of Subcultures in Agile Organizations', in *Leading and Managing People in Dynamic Organizations*, eds R. Petersen and E. Mannix (Mahwah, NJ: Lawrence Erlbaum Associates, 2003), 87–112.

10 Ott, *The Organizational Culture Perspective*, chapter 2; J. S. Pederson and J. S. Sorensen, *Organizational Cultures in Theory and Practice* (Aldershot, England: Gower, 1989), pp. 27–9; M. O. Jones, *Studying Organizational Symbolism: What, How, Why?* (Thousand Oaks, CA: Sage, 1996).

11 E. H. Schein, 'Organizational Culture', *American Psychologist* (February 1990), 109–19; A. Furnham and B. Gunter, 'Corporate Culture: Definition, Diagnosis, and Change', *International Review of Industrial and Organizational Psychology* 8 (1993), 233–61; E. H. Schein, *The Corporate Culture Survival Guide* (San Francisco: Jossey-Bass, 1999), chapter 4.

12 This history is found in G. Tippet, 'One People One Destiny One Biscuit', *The Age* (Melbourne), 4 May 2001.

13 A. L. Wilkins, 'Organizational Stories as Symbols Which Control the Organization', in *Organizational Symbolism*, eds L. R. Pondy et al. (Greenwich, CT: JAI Press, 1984), 81–92; R. Zemke, 'Storytelling: Back to a Basic', *Training* 27 (March 1990), 44–50; J. C. Meyer, 'Tell Me a Story: Eliciting Organizational Values from Narratives', *Communication Quarterly* 43 (1995), 210–24; W. Swap et al., 'Using Mentoring and Storytelling to Transfer Knowledge in the Workplace', *Journal of Management Information Systems* 18 (Summer 2001), 95–114.

14 'The Ultimate Chairman', *Business Times Singapore*, 3 September 2005.

15 M. Doehrman, 'Anthropologists—Deep in the Corporate Bush', *Daily Record* (Kansas City, MO), 19 July 2005, 1.

16 R. Frank and S. Craig, 'White-Shoe Shuffle', *Wall Street Journal*, 15 September 2004, A1.

17 R. E. Quinn and N. T. Snyder, 'Advance Change Theory: Culture Change at Whirlpool Corporation', in *The Leader's Change Handbook*, eds J. A. Conger, G. M. Spreitzer and E. E. Lawler III (San Francisco: Jossey-Bass, 1999), 162–93.

18 Churchill apparently made this statement on 28 October 1943 in the British House of Commons, when London, damaged by bombings in World War II, was about to be rebuilt.

19 S. K. Witcher, 'Flight Centre Founder Prides Company on Being Deliberately Unconventional', *Wall Street Journal*, 11 December 2000, C15; E. Johnston, 'Elf Boys', *Boss Magazine*, 8 June 2001, 26.

20 J. Hewett, 'Office Politics', *Australian Financial Review*, 27 September 2003, 29.

21 T. E. Deal and A. A. Kennedy, *Corporate Cultures* (Reading, Mass.: Addison-Wesley, 1982); J. B. Barney, 'Organizational Culture: Can It Be a Source of Sustained Competitive Advantage?', *Academy of Management Review* 11 (1986), 656–65; C. Siehl and J. Martin, 'Organizational Culture: A Key to Financial Performance?', in *Organizational Climate and Culture*, ed. B. Schneider (San Francisco, CA: Jossey-Bass, 1990), 241–81.

22 C. A. O'Reilly and J. A. Chatman, 'Culture as Social Control: Corporations, Cults, and Commitment', *Research in Organizational Behavior* 18 (1996), 157–200; J. C. Helms Mills and A. J. Mills, 'Rules, Sensemaking, Formative Contexts, and Discourse in the Gendering of Organizational Culture', in *International Handbook of Organizational Climate and Culture*, eds N. Ashkanasy, C. Wilderom and M. Peterson (Thousand Oaks, CA: Sage, 2000), 55–70; J. A. Chatman and S. E. Cha, 'Leading by Leveraging Culture', *California Management Review* 45 (Summer 2003), 20–34.

23 B. Ashforth and F. Mael, 'Social Identity Theory and the Organization', *Academy of Management Review* 14 (1989), 20–39.

24 M. R. Louis, 'Surprise and Sensemaking: What Newcomers Experience in Entering Unfamiliar Organizational Settings', *Administrative Science Quarterly* 25 (1980), 226–51; S. G. Harris, 'Organizational Culture and Individual Sensemaking: A Schema-Based Perspective', *Organization Science* 5 (1994), 309–21.

25 D. R. Denison, *Corporate Culture and Organizational Effectiveness* (New York: Wiley, 1990); G. G. Gordon and N. DiTomasco, 'Predicting Corporate Performance from Organizational Culture', *Journal of Management Studies* 29 (1992), 783–98; J. P. Kotter and J. L. Heskett, *Corporate Culture and Performance* (New York: Free Press, 1992).

26 A. Holeck, 'Griffith, Ind., Native Takes over as Steel Plant Manager', *The Times* (Munster, Indiana), 24 May 2003.

27 Kotter and Heskett, *Corporate Culture and Performance*; J. P. Kotter, 'Cultures and Coalitions', *Executive Excellence* 15 (March 1998), 14–15.

28 The features of adaptive cultures are described in W. F. Joyce, *Megachange: How Today's Leading Companies Have Transformed Their Workforces* (NY: Free Press, 1999).

29 D. Griesing, '"Boot Camp" Failed to Teach All They Could Be', *Chicago Tribune*, 21 April 2002, C1; B. L. Toffler, *Final Accounting: Ambition, Greed, and the Fall of Arthur Andersen* (New York: Broadway Books, 2003).

30 'Japanese Officials Order Citibank to Halt Some Operations', *Dow Jones Business News*, 17 September 2004; 'Citigroup CEO Prince Holds Press Conference in Japan', *Business Wire* (Tokyo), 25 October 2004; A. Morse, 'Citigroup Extends Apology to Japan', *Wall Street Journal*, 26 October 2004, A3; M. Pacelle, M. Fackler and A. Morse, 'Mission Control', *Wall Street Journal*, 22 December 2004, A1.

31 C. Fox, 'Mergers and Desires II', *Business Review Weekly*, 11 May 2001.

32 Schein, *The Corporate Culture Survival Guide*, chapter 8; M. L. Marks, 'Mixed Signals', *Across the Board* (May 2000), 21–6; J. P. Daly, R. W. Pouder and B. Kabanoff, 'The Effects of Initial Differences in Firms' Espoused Values on Their Postmerger Performance', *Journal of Applied Behavioral Science* 40, no. 3 (September 2004), 323–43. The merger failure rates are cited in: G. Costa, 'More to Mergers Than Just Doing the Deal', *Sydney Morning Herald*, 8 January 2004; J. Kirby, 'The Trouble with Mergers', *Canadian Business*, 16–29 February 2004, 64.

33 E. Connors, 'Not Drowning, Dancing', *Australian Financial Review*, 12 November 2004, 22.

34 A. R. Malekazedeh and A. Nahavandi, 'Making Mergers Work by Managing Cultures', *Journal of Business Strategy* (May–June 1990), 55–7; K. W. Smith, 'A Brand-New Culture for the Merged Firm', *Mergers and Acquisitions* 35 (June 2000), 45–50.

35 Hewitt Associates, 'Mergers and Acquisitions May Be Driven by Business Strategy—but Often Stumble over People and Culture Issues', PR Newswire news release (Lincolnshire, IL, 3 August 1998).

36 E. H. Schein, 'The Role of the Founder in Creating Organizational Culture', *Organizational Dynamics* 12, no. 1 (Summer 1983), 13–28; R. House, M. Javidan and P. Dorfman, 'Project Globe: An Introduction', *Applied Psychology: An International Review* 50 (2001), 489–505; R. House et al., 'Understanding Cultures and Implicit Leadership Theories across the Globe: An Introduction to Project Globe', *Journal of World Business* 37 (2002), 3–10.

37 K. K. Spors, 'Against the Grain', *Wall Street Journal*, 27 September 2004, R6; 'Chen Lights a Fire under Shenhua Energy', *South China Morning Post* (Hong Kong), 7 November 2005, 14.

38 J. Kerr and J. W. Slocum Jr, 'Managing Corporate Culture through Reward Systems', *Academy of Management Executive* 1 (May 1987), 99–107; K. R. Thompson and F. Luthans, 'Organizational Culture: A Behavioral Perspective', in *Organizational Climate and Culture*, ed. B. Schneider (San Francisco: Jossey-Bass, 1990), 319–44.

39 K. McNeil and J. D. Thompson, 'The Regeneration of Social Organizations', *American Sociological Review* 36 (1971), 624–37; W. G. Ouchi and A. M. Jaeger, 'Type Z Organization: Stability in the Midst of Mobility', *Academy of Management Review* 3 (1978), 305–14.

40 M. De Pree, *Leadership Is an Art* (East Lansing, MI: Michigan State University Press, 1987).

41 D. M. Cable and T. A. Judge, 'Person–Organization Fit, Job Choice Decisions, and Organizational Entry', *Organizational Behavior and Human Decision Processes* 67, no. 3 (1996), 294; A. E. M. Van Vianen, 'Person–Organization Fit: The Match between Newcomers' and Recruiters' Preferences for Organizational Cultures', *Personnel Psychology* 53 (Spring 2000), 113–49; K. J. Lauver and A. Kristof-Brown, 'Distinguishing between Employees' Perceptions of Person–Job and Person–Organization Fit', *Journal of Vocational Behavior* 59, no. 3 (December 2001), 454–70; J. W. Westerman and L. A. Cyr, 'An Integrative Analysis of Person–Organization Fit Theories', *International Journal of Selection and Assessment* 12, no. 3 (September 2004), 252–61.

42 J. Van Maanen, 'Breaking In: Socialization to Work', in *Handbook of Work, Organization, and Society*, ed. R. Dubin (Chicago: Rand McNally, 1976).

43 Johnston, 'Elf Boys'; S. Hart, 'Beat the New Job Blues', *New Zealand Herald*, 24 January 2005, D01.

44 V. Galt, 'Kid-Glove Approach Woos New Grads', *Globe & Mail*, 9 March 2005, C1.

45 C. L. Adkins, 'Previous Work Experience and Organizational Socialization: A Longitudinal Examination', *Academy of Management Journal* 38 (1995), 839–62; J. D. Kammeyer-Mueller and C. R. Wanberg,

'Unwrapping the Organizational Entry Process: Disentangling Multiple Antecedents and Their Pathways to Adjustment', *Journal of Applied Psychology* 88, no. 5 (2003), 779–94.

46 J. M. Beyer and D. R. Hannah, 'Building on the Past: Enacting Established Personal Identities in a New Work Setting', *Organization Science* 13 (November/December 2002), 636–52; H. D. C. Thomas and N. Anderson, 'Newcomer Adjustment: The Relationship between Organizational Socialization Tactics, Information Acquisition and Attitudes', *Journal of Occupational and Organizational Psychology* 75 (December 2002), 423–37.

47 L. W. Porter, E. E. Lawler III and J. R. Hackman, *Behavior in Organizations* (New York: McGraw-Hill, 1975), pp. 163–7; Van Maanen, 'Breaking In: Socialization to Work'; D. C. Feldman, 'The Multiple Socialization of Organization Members', *Academy of Management Review* 6 (1981), 309–18.

48 B. E. Ashforth and A. M. Saks, 'Socialization Tactics: Longitudinal Effects on Newcomer Adjustment', *Academy of Management Journal* 39 (1996), 149–78; Kammeyer-Mueller and Wanberg, 'Unwrapping the Organizational Entry Process'.

49 Porter, Lawler III, and Hackman, *Behavior in Organizations*, chapter 5.

50 E. Fitzmaurice, 'A Hard Lesson', *Sun Herald* (Sydney), 11 March 2001, 50.

51 Louis, 'Surprise and Sensemaking: What Newcomers Experience in Entering Unfamiliar Organizational Settings'.

52 P. Yelland, 'Computer Savvy, Fickle and Wanted', *Sydney Morning Herald*, 30 January 2001, 4. Also see S. L. Robinson and D. M. Rousseau, 'Violating the Psychological Contract: Not the Exception but the Norm', *Journal of Organizational Behavior* 15 (1994), 245–59.

53 S. Barancik, 'Different World, Same Old Stress', *St Petersburg Times* (Florida), 3 September 2003; A. Daga, 'Dial C for Crisis at India's Call Centres', *The Age* (Melbourne), 12 July 2003.

54 L. Gettler, 'Gen X Marks Time, and Hard Graft Is Y's Affront', *The Age* (Melbourne), 26 October 2005, 14; L. Hoffman, 'Gen Y Here and Now', *Australian*, 20 August 2005, 9.

55 J. A. Breaugh, *Recruitment: Science and Practice* (Boston: PWS-Kent, 1992); J. P. Wanous, *Organizational Entry* (Reading, Mass.: Addison-Wesley, 1992).

56 D. Benda, 'Laying Down the Law', *West Australian* (Perth), 19 September 2000, 2; Western Australia Police Service, 'Step Forward: Realistic Job Preview', (Perth, 2005), www.stepforward.wa.gov.au/realistic-job-preview.php (accessed 11 November 2005).

57 J. M. Phillips, 'Effects of Realistic Job Previews on Multiple Organizational Outcomes: A Meta-Analysis', *Academy of Management Journal* 41 (December 1998), 673–90.

58 Y. Ganzach et al., 'Social Exchange and Organizational Commitment: Decision-Making Training for Job Choice as an Alternative to the Realistic Job Preview', *Personnel Psychology* 55 (Autumn 2002), 613–37.

59 C. Ostroff and S. W. J. Koslowski, 'Organizational Socialization as a Learning Process: The Role of Information Acquisition', *Personnel Psychology* 45 (1992), 849–74; E. W. Morrison, 'Newcomer Information Seeking: Exploring Types, Modes, Sources, and Outcomes', *Academy of Management Journal* 36 (1993), 557–89; U. Anakwe and J. H. Greenhaus, 'Effective Socialization of Employees: Socialization Content Perspective', *Journal of Managerial Issues* 11, no. 3 (Fall 1999), 315–29.

60 S. L. McShane, 'Effect of Socialization Agents on the Organizational Adjustment of New Employees' (Big Sky, Montana: Annual Conference of the Western Academy of Management, March 1988).

CHAPTER 17

Organisational change

LEARNING OBJECTIVES

After reading this chapter, you should be able to:

- describe the elements of Lewin's force field analysis model

- outline six reasons why people resist organisational change

- discuss six strategies to minimise resistance to change

- outline the conditions for effectively diffusing change from a pilot project

- describe the action research approach to organisational change

- outline the 'Four-D' model of appreciative inquiry and explain how this approach differs from action research

- explain how parallel learning structures assist the change process

- discuss four ethical issues in organisational change.

Medibank Private is Australia's largest, and only national, health fund with nearly three million members. In the three years to 2005 the government-owned health fund achieved the most dramatic financial turnaround in its thirty-year history, while recording increases in levels of customer satisfaction and staff morale. This followed a dramatic financial loss in 2002 when the health fund also suffered from low employee morale and high turnover. George Savvides, previously Australian chief executive of a global medical supplies company, was hired as the managing director in April 2002 to turn the fund around. Savvides acted quickly. Looking at all profit restoration opportunities, including overhead reduction, he cut or reassigned one-third of the executive team. This action reduced costs by removing a layer of management and built a change-oriented executive team that agreed to 'deliver the corporate surgery' and rebuild the organisation. It also symbolised to employees that Savvides was serious about improving the organisation and turning it around. 'The first thing we had to do was to clear the decks and that meant getting our own house in order,' says Savvides in reference to the management

Employee involvement through quality action teams helped transform Medibank Private into a profitable medical insurer.

changes. 'You cannot start the journey of change without looking at what we did internally first.'

During his first six months, Savvides also met twice with staff around the country in forty group sessions to find out what needed changing and to outline his vision of how that change can occur. Later, he reorganised employees from 150 offices into just fourteen offices, and moved most of the central operations from four buildings around Melbourne into one building at Melbourne's Docklands. 'We've moved into a great new building and a lot of things have changed. We've got better communication and teamwork,' Savvides explains. 'In fixing the company, we had to make certain everyone knew that every employee was equally valuable. That builds teamwork and equity.'

The greatest momentum for change, however, came through a continuous improvement process that involved nearly three dozen quality action teams (QATs). Each QAT, which included employees from all levels of the organisation, investigated ways to improve a specific area of the business, then delivered its verdict and recommendations directly to Medibank Private's board of directors. 'The board took a direct feed from frontline quality action teams,' recalls Derek Linsell, the change agent that Savvides hired to help guide the turnaround.

The QAT recommendations saved millions of dollars by identifying better ways to serve customers and complete work processes. Within one year, Medibank Private was able to seek out a small net profit. Two years later, the health fund had the lowest cost structure in the industry and was highly profitable even with lower premium increases than the industry average.[1]

MEDIBANK PRIVATE WAS TRANSFORMED from a health fund running at a loss into a financially healthy and employee-friendly organisation because it applied many of the practices we will describe in this chapter on managing change. George Savvides ensured that employees had developed an urgency for change, he demonstrated his commitment to this change through redeployment of executives and re-organising the business. Then he relied on employee involvement and empowerment to determine the best way to change and build employee commitment to the change process.

This chapter begins by introducing Lewin's model of change and its component parts. This includes sources of resistance to change, ways to minimise this resistance, and stabilizing desired behaviours. Next, this chapter examines three approaches to organisational change– action research, appreciative inquiry, and parallel learning structures. The last section of this chapter considers both cross-cultural and ethical issues in organisational change.

LEWIN'S FORCE FIELD ANALYSIS MODEL

force field analysis Kurt Lewin's model of system-wide change that helps change agents diagnose the forces that drive and restrain proposed organisational change.

LEARNING OBJECTIVE

Describe the elements of Lewin's force field analysis model.

Social psychologist Kurt Lewin developed the force field analysis model to help explain how the change process works (see Exhibit 17.1).[2] Although developed more than fifty years ago, Lewin's **force field analysis** model remains the prominent way of viewing this process.

One side of the force field model represents the driving forces that push organisations towards a new state of affairs. Chapter 1 described some of the driving forces in the external environment, including globalisation, virtual work and a changing workforce. Along with these external forces, corporate leaders create driving forces within the organisation so the organisation anticipates the external forces. These internally originating forces are difficult to apply because they lack external justifications, so effective transformational leadership as well as structural change mechanisms are necessary to legitimate and support internal driving forces.

The other side of Lewin's model represents the *restraining forces* that maintain the status quo. These restraining forces are commonly called 'resistance to change' because they appear as employee behaviours that block the change process. Stability occurs when the driving and restraining forces are roughly in equilibrium; that is, they are of approximately equal strength in opposite directions.

EXHIBIT 17.1

Lewin's force field analysis model

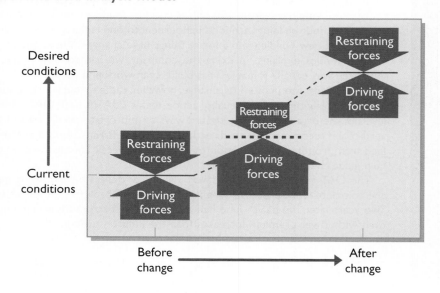

Lewin's force field model emphasises that effective change occurs by **unfreezing** the current situation, moving to a desired condition, and then **refreezing** the system so that it remains in this desired state. Unfreezing involves producing disequilibrium between the driving and restraining forces. As we will describe later, this may occur by increasing the driving forces, reducing the restraining forces, or having a combination of both. Refreezing occurs when the organisation's systems and structures are aligned with the desired behaviours. They must support and reinforce the new role patterns and prevent the organisation from slipping back into the old way of doing things. Over the next few pages, we use Lewin's model to understand why change is blocked and how the process can evolve more smoothly.

unfreezing The first part of the change process whereby the change agent produces disequilibrium between the driving and restraining forces.

refreezing The latter part of the change process in which systems and conditions are introduced that reinforce and maintain the desired behaviours.

RESTRAINING FORCES

In his two tumultuous years as CEO, Jacques Nasser heaped a lot of change on employees at Ford Motor Company in Detroit. Nasser, who began his career at Ford Australia, tried to shift the US car-maker from engineering prowess to 'cyber-savviness', from quality to efficiency, and from an old-boys' club to a performance-focused competitor. In one year he rammed through a performance review system that took General Electric nearly a decade to implement. The changes were too much for many Ford employees. Some engineers grumbled that quality had declined; employees stung by the performance system launched age-discrimination lawsuits. 'When you induce change, you get a reaction,' explains a senior Ford executive. 'I have letters from employees congratulating us. I have letters from employees doing the opposite.' In the latter group was the Ford family, who eventually replaced Nasser with William Clay Ford as CEO.[3]

Resistance to change isn't unique to the Ford Motor Company. According to various surveys, more than 40 per cent of executives identify employee resistance as the most important barrier to corporate restructuring or improved performance. This is consistent with a recent survey in which 800 Australian employees admitted that they don't follow through with organisational changes because they 'like to keep things the way they are' or the changes seem to be too complicated or time wasting. Almost half of the Australian employees also complained that 'the new initiatives get announced with great fanfare and then you never hear about them again'.[4]

FBI meets its own resistance

In 1993, following the first terrorist attacks on the World Trade Centre, the US Federal Bureau of Investigation (FBI) promised to refocus from a reactive law-enforcement agency (solving crimes) to a proactive domestic intelligence agency (preventing terrorism). Yet, two government reports recently concluded that resistance from FBI staff has hampered this change process. One report even stated that both the FBI and the CIA 'seem to be working harder and harder just to maintain a status quo that is increasingly irrelevant to the new challenges'. The reports claim that FBI employees and managers are unable or unwilling to change because solving crimes (rather than intelligence gathering) is burned into their mind-set, routines, career paths and decentralised structure. Most FBI field managers were trained in law enforcement, so they continue to give preferential treatment and resources to enforcement rather than terrorist-prevention initiatives. An information access barrier called 'the wall' further isolates FBI intelligence officers from the mainstream criminal investigation staff. Historical turf wars with the CIA have also undermined FBI respect for the bureau's intelligence gathering initiative. 'One of the most difficult things one has to do is to bring an entity through the development of a change of business practices,' FBI director Robert Mueller recently admitted.[5]

AP/Wide World Photos

LEARNING OBJECTIVE

Outline six reasons why people resist organisational change.

Employee resistance takes many forms, including passive noncompliance, complaints, absenteeism, turnover and collective action (e.g. strikes, walkouts). In extreme cases of resistance, the chief change agent eventually leaves or is pushed out. This resistance is a symptom of deeper problems in the change process, so rather than directly correcting incidences of passive noncompliance, change agents need to understand why employees are not changing their behaviour in the desired ways.[6] In some situations, employees may be worried about the *consequences* of change, such as that the new conditions will take away their power and status. In other situations, employees show resistance because of concerns about the *process* of change itself, such as the effort required to break old habits and learn new skills. The main reasons why people resist change are shown in Exhibit 17.2 and are described below:[7]

Direct costs. People tend to block actions that result in higher direct costs or lower benefits than the existing situation. Ford employees who received low performance ratings resisted change because it threatened their job security and career development.

- *Saving face.* Some people resist change as a political strategy to 'prove' that the decision is wrong or that the person encouraging change is incompetent. This occurred when senior executives in a manufacturing firm bought a computer other than the system recommended by the information systems department. Soon after the system was in place, several information systems employees let minor implementation problems escalate to demonstrate that senior management had made a poor decision.
- *Fear of the unknown.* People resist change out of worry that they cannot adjust to the new work requirements. This fear of the unknown increases the *risk* of personal loss. For example, one company owner wanted sales staff to telephone rather than personally visit prospective customers. With no experience in telephone sales, they complained about the changes. Some even avoided the training program that taught them how to make telephone sales.[8]
- *Breaking routines.* Chapter 1 described how organisations need to unlearn, not just learn. This means that employees need to abandon the behavioural routines that are no longer appropriate. Unfortunately, people are creatures of habit. They like to stay within their comfort zones by continuing routine role patterns that make life predictable. Consequently, many people resist organisational changes that force employees out of their comfort zones and require the investment of time and energy learning new role patterns.
- *Incongruent organisational systems.* Rewards, selection, training and other control systems ensure that employees maintain desired role patterns. Yet the organisational systems that maintain stability also discourage employees from adopting new ways. The implication, of course, is that organisational systems must be altered to fit the desired change. Unfortunately,

EXHIBIT 17.2　　**Forces resisting organisational change**

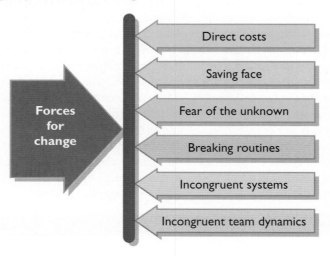

control systems can be difficult to change, particularly when they have supported role patterns that worked well in the past.[9]

- *Incongruent team dynamics.* Teams develop and enforce conformity to a set of norms that guide behaviour. However, conformity to existing team norms may discourage employees from accepting organisational change. Team norms that conflict with the desired changes need to be altered.

UNFREEZING, CHANGING AND REFREEZING

According to Lewin's force field analysis model, effective change occurs by unfreezing the current situation, moving to a desired condition, and then refreezing the system so that it remains in this desired state. Unfreezing occurs when the driving forces are stronger than the restraining forces. This happens by making the driving forces stronger, weakening or removing the restraining forces, or a combination of both.

With respect to the first option, driving forces must increase enough to motivate change. Change rarely occurs by increasing driving forces alone, however, because the restraining forces often adjust to counterbalance the driving forces. It is rather like the coils of a mattress. The harder corporate leaders push for change, the stronger the restraining forces push back. This antagonism threatens the change effort by producing tension and conflict within the organisation. The preferred option is to both increase the driving forces and reduce or remove the restraining forces. Increasing the driving forces creates an urgency for change, whereas reducing the restraining forces minimises resistance to change.

CREATING AN URGENCY FOR CHANGE

It is almost a cliché to say that organisations today operate in more dynamic, fast-paced environments than they did a few decades ago. These environmental pressures represent the driving forces that push employees out of their comfort zones. They energise people to face the risks that change creates. 'One principle I applied across all three organisations [where I have been chief executive] was to be absolutely honest about the current state of the business and [to have] a preparedness to state the truth about failings,' says Medibank chief executive George Savvides, who applied this principle when reorganising his management team and when meeting with Medibank employees around Australia.[10]

In many organisations, however, corporate leaders buffer employees from the external environment to such an extent that external driving forces are hardly felt by anyone below the top executive level. Simon Kelly discovered this problem when he joined Aristocrat Leisure as chief financial officer. Kelly was hired to help turn around the Sydney-based gaming technology firm, which had suffered significant losses as well as top management problems. What surprised Kelly was that Aristocrat's employees seemed blissfully unaware of the company's woes. 'They managed to divorce themselves very well from the turmoil that was going on at the executive and board levels and in the media,' Kelly recalls. Only when Kelly and the incoming chief executive communicated the company's predicament did staff become more receptive to new attitudes and practices regarding reducing costs. The point here is that the change process must begin by informing employees about the company's performance, competitive threats, changing consumer trends, impending government regulations, and other driving forces.[11]

Customer-driven change

Shell Europe has a well-known brand name, excellent assets and highly qualified staff, but a few years ago these three ingredients weren't achieving Shell's financial goals or meeting its customer needs. To make matters worse, many Shell executives believed that Shell Europe's performance was quite satisfactory. So, to create an urgency for change, the European executives were loaded onto buses and taken out to talk with customers and with employees who work with customers every day. 'We called these "bus rides". The idea was to encourage people to think back from the customer's perspective rather than from the head office,' explains Shell Europe's vice-president of retailing. 'The bus rides were difficult for a lot of people who, in their work history, had hardly ever had to talk to a customer and find out what was good and not so good about Shell from the customer's standpoint.'[12]

Shell Europe is one of many organisations that have fuelled the urgency for change by putting employees in direct contact with customers. Dissatisfied customers represent a compelling driving force for change because of the adverse consequences for the organisation's survival and success. Customers also provide a human element that further energises employees to change current behaviour patterns.[13]

Urging change without external forces

Exposing employees to external forces can strengthen the urgency for change, but leaders often need to begin the change process before problems come knocking at the company's door. 'You want to create a burning platform for change even when there isn't a need for one,' says Steve Bennett, CEO of financial software company Intuit.[14] Creating an urgency for change when the organisation is riding high requires a lot of persuasive influence that helps employees visualise future competitive threats and environmental shifts.

For instance, Apple Computer's iPod dominates the digital music market, but Steve Jobs wants the company to be its own toughest competitor. Just when sales of the iPod Mini were soaring, Jobs challenged a gathering of 100 top executives and engineers to develop a better product to replace it. 'Playing it safe is the most dangerous thing we can do,' Jobs warned. Nine months later the company launched the iPod Nano, which replaced the still-popular iPod Mini before competitors could offer a better alternative.[15]

LEARNING OBJECTIVE

Discuss six strategies to minimise resistance to change.

REDUCING THE RESTRAINING FORCES

Effective change requires more than making employees aware of the driving forces. It also involves reducing or removing the restraining forces. Exhibit 17.3 summarises six ways to

---

Coles Myer chief maintains the momentum for change

Coles Myer chief executive John Fletcher has led the challenging task of transforming Australia's largest retailer into a more nimble and customer-focused organisation. The change process is starting to show positive results, including a more engaged workforce and better customer service. But Fletcher points out that, as the company becomes more successful, his role as a change agent becomes even more difficult. 'The thing now is to maintain momentum; it's critical in change programs when things start to look good,' Fletcher advises. 'Change programs are easier when things are bad. When things improve, people relax and think, we're there.'[16]

Coles Myer Ltd

Methods for minimising resistance to change

EXHIBIT 17.3

Strategy	Example	When used	Problems
Communication	Customer complaint letters shown to employees.	When employees don't feel an urgency for change, or don't know how the change will affect them.	Time-consuming and potentially costly.
Learning	Employees learn how to work in teams as company adopts a team-based structure.	When employees need to break old routines and adopt new role patterns.	Time-consuming and potentially costly.
Employee involvement	Company forms task force to recommend new customer service practices.	When the change effort needs more employee commitment, some employees need to save face, and/or employee ideas would improve decisions about the change strategy. Very time-consuming.	Might also lead to conflict and poor decisions if employees' interests are incompatible with organisational needs.
Stress management	Employees attend sessions to discuss their worries about the change.	When communication, training and involvement do not sufficiently ease employee worries.	Time-consuming and potentially expensive. Some methods may not reduce stress for all employees.
Negotiation	Employees agree to replace strict job categories with multiskilling in return for increased job security.	When employees will clearly lose something of value from the change and would not otherwise support the new conditions. Also necessary when the company must change quickly.	May be expensive, particularly if other employees want to negotiate their support. Also tends to produce compliance but not commitment to the change.
Coercion	Company CEO tells managers to 'get on board' the change or leave.	When other strategies are ineffective and the company needs to change quickly.	Can lead to more subtle forms of resistance, as well as long-term antagonism towards the change agent.

Sources: Adapted from J. P. Kotter and L. A. Schlesinger, 'Choosing Strategies for Change', *Harvard Business Review* 57 (1979), pp. 106–14; P. R. Lawrence, 'How to Deal with Resistance to Change', *Harvard Business Review* (May–June 1954), pp. 49–57.

overcome employee resistance. Communication, learning, employee involvement and stress management try to reduce the restraining forces and, if feasible, should be attempted first.[17] However, negotiation and coercion are necessary for people who will clearly lose something from the change and when the speed of change is critical.

Communication

Honest and frequent communication is the highest priority and first strategy required for any organisational change.[18] Communication improves the change process in at least two ways. First, it is the conduit through which employees typically learn about the driving forces for change. Whether through meetings with senior management or by directly meeting with disgruntled customers, employees become energised to change. Second, communication can potentially reduce fear of the unknown. The more corporate leaders communicate their images of the future, the more easily employees can visualise their own role in that future. This effort may also begin the process of adjusting team norms to be more consistent with the new reality.

Learning

Learning is an important process in most change initiatives because employees require new knowledge and skills to fit the organisation's evolving requirements. When a company introduces a new sales database, for instance, representatives need to learn how to adapt their previous behaviour patterns to benefit from the new system. Action learning, which was described in Chapter 3, is another potentially powerful learning process for organisational change because it develops management skills while discovering ways to improve the organisation.[19] Coaching is yet another form of learning that provides more personalised feedback and direction during the learning process. Coaching and other forms of learning are time consuming, but they help employees break routines by learning new role patterns.

Employee involvement

Except in times of extreme urgency or where employee interests are incompatible with the organisation's needs, employee involvement is almost an essential part of the change process. Rather than viewing themselves as agents of someone else's decision, employees feel personally responsible for the success of the change effort.[20] Involvement also minimises problems of saving face and fear of the unknown. Furthermore, the complexity of today's work environment demands that more people provide ideas regarding the best direction of the change effort. These benefits of employee involvement played a vital role in the transformation of Medibank Private, as mentioned at the beginning of the chapter. Reality Check 17.1 describes how employee involvement also helped the dramatic transformation of Nissan Motor Company. Soon after Carlos Ghosn became CEO of the Japanese car-maker, he formed a dozen cross-functional management teams and gave them three months to identify ways to save the company from possible bankruptcy.

future search System-wide group sessions, usually lasting a few days, in which participants identify trends and identify ways to adapt to those changes.

Minimising resistance to change through employee involvement is also possible in large organisations through **future search** events. These conferences, which were first developed by Australian change expert Fred Emery and his British colleague Eric Trist in 1960 to assist the merger of two British aerospace firms, are large group sessions, usually lasting a few days, in which participants identify the environmental trends and establish strategic solutions for those conditions. Experts on various topics are sometimes brought in to speak during lunch or dinner. Future search conferences 'put the entire system in the room', meaning that they try to involve as many employees and other stakeholders as possible associated with the organisational system. These multi-day events ask participants to identify trends or issues and establish strategic solutions for those conditions.[21]

The city of Greater Bendigo recently held a three-day future search conference in which various community groups (sport and recreation, the environment, arts, youth, planning and business) met with city councillors to reflect on the Victorian city's development and peer into its future. The city of Cairns held a similar session soon afterwards. A few years ago, the state of Tasmania held an unprecedented future search conference, called Tasmania Together, involving 14 000 individuals and organisations in sixty formal community discussions. Several private sector organisations—including Ikea, Microsoft, the US Forest Service, Whole Foods Market and Richmond Savings Credit Union—have held future search conferences to engage employees and other stakeholders in a future vision for those organisations.

Future search meetings potentially minimise resistance to change and assist the quality of the change process, but they also have limitations.[22] One problem is that involving so many

17.1   **REALITY CHECK**

CARLOS GHOSN RELIES ON HIGH INVOLVEMENT TO TRANSFORM NISSAN

Nissan Motor Company was on the brink of bankruptcy when French car-maker Renault purchased a controlling interest and installed Carlos Ghosn as the effective head of the Japanese car-maker. Along with Nissan's known problems of high debt and plummeting market share, Ghosn (pronounced 'gone') saw that Nissan managers had no apparent sense of urgency for change. 'Even though the evidence is against them, they sit down and they watch the problem a little bit longer,' says Ghosn.

Ghosn's challenge was to act quickly, yet minimise the inevitable resistance that arises when an outsider tries to change traditional Japanese business practices. 'I was non-Nissan, non-Japanese,' he says. 'I knew that if I tried to dictate changes from above, the effort would backfire, undermining morale and productivity. But if I was too passive, the company would simply continue its downward spiral.'

To resolve this dilemma, Ghosn formed nine cross-functional teams of ten middle managers each, and gave them the mandate to identify innovative proposals for a specific area (marketing, manufacturing, etc.) within three months. Each team could form sub-teams with additional people to analyse issues in more detail. In all, over 500 middle managers and other employees were involved in the so-called 'Nissan Revival Plan'.

After a slow start—Nissan managers weren't accustomed to such authority or working with colleagues across functions or cultures—ideas began to flow, as Ghosn stuck to his deadline, reminded team members of the car-maker's desperate situation, and encouraged teams to break traditions. Three months later the nine teams submitted a bold plan to close three assembly plants, eliminate thousands of jobs, cut the number of suppliers by half, reduce purchasing costs by 20 per cent, return to profitability, cut the company's debt by half, and introduce twenty-two new models within the next two years.

Although risky, Ghosn accepted all of the proposals. Moreover, when revealing the plan publicly on the eve of the annual Tokyo Motor Show, Ghosn added his own commitment to the plan: 'If you ask people to go through a difficult period of time, they have to trust that you're sharing it with them,' Ghosn explains. 'So I said that if we did not fulfil our commitments, I would resign.'

Ghosn's strategy for organisational change and the Nissan Revival Plan worked. Within twelve months the car-maker had increased sales and market share, and posted its first profit in seven years. The company has introduced innovative models and expanded operations. Ghosn has received high praise throughout Japan and abroad, and has since become head of Renault.

Carlos Ghosn launched a turnaround at Nissan Motor Company that saved the Japanese car-maker and relied on change management practices rarely seen in Japan.

Sources: C. Lebner, 'Nissan Motor Co.', *Fast Company*, July 2002, 80; C. Dawson, 'On Your Marks', *Business Week*, 17 March 2003, 52; D. Magee, *Turn Around: How Carlos Ghosn Rescued Nissan* (New York: HarperCollins, 2003); C. Ghosn and P. Riès, *Shift: Inside Nissan's Historic Revival* (New York: Currency Doubleday, 2005).

© Eriko Sugita/Reuters/Corbis

people invariably limits the opportunity to contribute and increases the risk that a few people will dominate the process. Another concern is that these events generate high expectations about an ideal future state that is difficult to satisfy in practice. Furthermore, some executives forget that future search conferences and other forms of employee involvement require follow-up action. If employees do not see meaningful decisions and actions resulting from these meetings, they begin to question the credibility of the process and are more cynical of similar subsequent change management activities.[23]

Stress management

Organisational change is a stressful experience for many people because it threatens self-esteem and creates uncertainty about the future. Communication, learning and employee involvement can reduce some of these stressors. However, research indicates that companies also need to introduce stress management practices to help employees cope with the changes.[24] In particular, stress management minimises resistance by removing some of the direct costs and fear of the unknown of the change process. Stress also saps energy, so minimising stress potentially increases employee motivation to support the change process.

Negotiation

As long as people resist change, organisational change strategies will require some influence tactics. Negotiation is a form of influence that involves the promise of benefits or resources in exchange for the target person's compliance with the influencer's request. This strategy potentially activates those who would otherwise lose out from the change. However, it merely gains compliance, rather than commitment to the change effort, so it might not be effective in the long term.

Coercion

If all else fails, leaders rely on coercion to change organisations. Coercion can include persistently reminding people of their obligations, frequently monitoring behaviour to ensure compliance, confronting people who do not change, and using threats of sanctions to force compliance. Replacing people who will not support the change is an extreme step, but it is neither rare nor, in some cases, inappropriate. For example, the opening vignette to this chapter noted that George Savvides sacked or reassigned one-third of his senior management group within the first 100 days of his tenure as the new chief executive of Medibank Private. Savvides explains that leaders need to have in place an executive team who buy into the company's vision before employees can be expected to support the change effort towards that vision.

Replacing staff is a radical form of organisational 'unlearning' (see Chapter 1) because replacing executives removes knowledge of the organisation's past routines. This potentially opens up opportunities for new practices to take hold.[25] At the same time, coercion is a risky strategy because survivors (employees who are not fired) may have less trust in corporate leaders and engage in more political tactics to protect their own job security.

REFREEZING THE DESIRED CONDITIONS

Unfreezing and changing behaviour patterns won't result in lasting change. People are creatures of habit, so they easily slip back into past patterns. Therefore, leaders need to refreeze the new behaviours by realigning organisational systems and team dynamics with the desired changes.[27] One of the most popular refreezing strategies is to realign the reward system around desired behaviour and outcomes.[28] Feedback, information systems, organisational structures and the physical layout of buildings are among the other tools that can be used to refreeze desired behaviours.

Change the principal, change the school

A few years ago, test results at Sun Valley Middle School were so low that the San Fernando Valley, California, school was put on a US federal government watch list for closer scrutiny. The Los Angeles unified school district tried to help the principal and staff to improve, but to no avail. When a state audit reported that the school suffered from poor management, unsanitary conditions and uneven classroom instruction, the school district applied a more radical change strategy: it replaced Sun Valley's principal and four assistant principals with new leaders. Sun Valley's new principal, Jeff Davis (shown with students in this photo), introduced extra English language instruction, reorganised class locations, and launched team teaching to foster a more collegial atmosphere among staff. Sun Valley still has a long way to go, but student test scores in maths and English have tripled over the past three years. 'That school is absolutely headed in the right direction,' says Sue Shannon, superintendent of schools in the eastern San Fernando Valley.[26]

© 2004 Brian Vander Brug, Los Angeles Times

STRATEGIC VISIONS, CHANGE AGENTS AND DIFFUSING CHANGE

Kurt Lewin's force field analysis model is a useful template to explain the dynamics of organisational change. But it overlooks three other ingredients in effective change processes: strategic visions, change agents and diffusing change. Every successful change requires a well-articulated and appealing vision of the desired future state.[29] This was apparent at Medibank Private, where chief executive George Savvides quickly developed and communicated the view that the medical insurance company must engage in continuous improvement to become much more cost efficient. The leader's vision provides a sense of direction and establishes the critical success factors against which the real changes are evaluated. It also minimises employee fear of the unknown and provides a better understanding about what behaviours employees must learn for the future state.

CHANGE AGENTS

Every organisational change, whether large or small, requires one or more change agents. A **change agent** is anyone who possesses enough knowledge and power to guide and facilitate the change effort. Change agents come in different forms, and more than one person is often required to serve these different roles. Transformational leaders such as George Savvides are the primary agents of change because they form a vision of the desired future state, communicate that vision in ways that are meaningful to others, behave in ways that are consistent with the vision, and build commitment to the vision.[30] Transformational leaders are the architects who shape the overall direction for the change effort and motivate employees to achieve that objective.

change agent Anyone who possesses enough knowledge and power to guide and facilitate the organisational change effort.

Organisational change also requires transactional leaders who implement the change by aligning the behaviour of individual employees on a day-to-day basis with the organisation's new goals.[31] If a company wants to provide better customer service, then supervisors and other transactional leaders need to arrange rewards, resources, feedback and other conditions that support better customer service behaviours in employees. Consultants from either inside or outside the organisation represent a third change agent role. For instance, Derek Linsell was hired as Medibank Private's 'Innovation and Continuous Improvement Advocate', essentially an internal consultant to help guide the change process and maintain the momentum. Consultants typically bring unique expertise to the change process through a toolkit of change processes, some of which are introduced later in the chapter. Finally, just as employees are encouraged to become leaders any time and anywhere, they also assist the change process as role models for others to follow in the change process.

DIFFUSION OF CHANGE

LEARNING OBJECTIVE

Outline the conditions for effectively diffusing change from a pilot project.

Change agents often test the transformation process with a pilot project, and then diffuse what has been learned from this experience to other parts of the organisation. Unlike centralised, system-wide changes, pilot projects are more flexible and less risky.[32] The pilot project approach also makes it easier to select organisational groups that are most ready for change, which increases the pilot project's success.

But how do we ensure that the change process started in the pilot project is adopted by other segments of the organisation? The MARS model introduced in Chapter 2 offers a useful template to organise the answer to this question. First, employees are more likely to adopt the practices of a pilot project when they are motivated to do so.[33] This occurs when they see that the pilot project is successful and people in the pilot project receive recognition and rewards for changing their previous work practices. Diffusion also requires supervisor support and reinforcement of the desired behaviours. More generally, change agents need to minimise the sources of resistance to change that were discussed earlier in the chapter.

Second, employees must have the ability—the required skills and knowledge—to adopt the practices introduced in the pilot project. According to innovation diffusion studies, people adopt ideas more readily when they have an opportunity to interact and learn from others who have already applied the new practices.[34] Thus, pilot projects get diffused when employees in the original pilot are dispersed to other work units as role models and knowledge sources.

Third, pilot projects get diffused when employees have clear role perceptions; that is, they understand how the practices in a pilot project apply to them even though in a completely different functional area. For instance, accounting department employees won't easily recognise how they can adopt quality improvement practices developed by employees in the production department. The challenge here is for change agents to provide guidance that is neither too specific, because it might not seem relevant to other areas of the organisation, nor too abstract, because this makes the instructions too vague. Finally, employees require supportive situational factors, including the resources and time necessary to adopt the practices demonstrated in the pilot project.

THREE APPROACHES TO ORGANISATIONAL CHANGE

So far, the chapter has looked at the dynamics of change that occur every day in organisations. However, organisational change agents and consultants also apply various approaches to organisational change. This section introduces three of the leading approaches to organisational change: action research, appreciative inquiry and parallel learning structures.

ACTION RESEARCH APPROACH

LEARNING OBJECTIVE

Describe the action research approach to organisational change.

action research A data-based, problem-oriented process that diagnoses the need for change, introduces the intervention, and then evaluates and stabilises the desired changes.

Along with introducing the force field model, Kurt Lewin recommended an **action research** approach to the change process. Action research takes the view that meaningful change is a combination of action-orientation (changing attitudes and behaviour) and research orientation (testing theory).[35] On the one hand, the change process needs to be action-oriented because the ultimate goal is to bring about change. An action orientation involves diagnosing current problems and applying interventions that resolve those problems. On the other hand, the change process is a research study because change agents apply a conceptual framework (such as team dynamics or organisational culture) to a real situation. As with any good research, the change process involves collecting data to diagnose problems more effectively and to systematically evaluate how well the theory works in practice. In other words, action research embraces the notion of organisational learning and knowledge management (see Chapter 1).[36]

Within this dual framework of action and research, the action research approach adopts an open systems view. It recognises that organisations have many interdependent parts, so change agents need to anticipate both the intended and the unintended consequences of their interventions. Action research is also a highly participative process, because open systems change requires both the knowledge and the commitment of members within that system. Indeed, employees are essentially co-researchers as well as participants in the intervention. Overall, action research is a data-based, problem-oriented process that diagnoses the need for change, introduces the intervention, and then evaluates and stabilises the desired changes (see Exhibit 17.4).[37]

1. *Form client–consultant relationship.* Action research usually assumes that the change agent originates outside the system (such as a consultant), so the process begins by forming the client–consultant relationship. Consultants need to determine the client's readiness for change, including whether people are motivated to participate in the process, are open to meaningful change, and possess the abilities to complete the process.

2. *Diagnose the need for change.* Action research is a problem-oriented activity that carefully diagnoses the problem through systematic analysis of the situation. Organisational diagnosis identifies the appropriate direction for the change effort by gathering and analysing data about an ongoing system, such as through interviews and surveys of employees and other stakeholders. Organisational diagnosis also includes employee involvement in agreeing on the appropriate change method, the schedule for these actions, and the expected standards of successful change.

3. *Introduce intervention.* This stage in the action research model applies one or more actions to correct the problem. It may include any of the prescriptions mentioned in this textbook, such as building more effective teams, managing conflict, building a better organisational structure, or changing the corporate culture. An important issue is how quickly the changes should occur.[38] Some experts recommend *incremental change*, in which the organisation fine-tunes the system and takes small steps towards a desired state. Others claim that *quantum change* is often required, in which the system is overhauled decisively and quickly. Quantum change is usually traumatic to employees and offers little opportunity for correction. But incremental change is also risky when the organisation is seriously misaligned with its environment, thereby threatening its survival.

The action research process

EXHIBIT 17.4

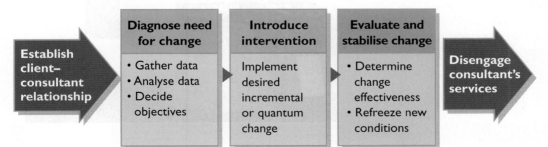

4. *Evaluate and stabilise change.* Action research recommends evaluating the effectiveness of the intervention against the standards established in the diagnostic stage. Unfortunately, even when these standards are clearly stated, the effectiveness of an intervention might not be apparent for several years, or might be difficult to separate from other factors. If the activity has the desired effect, the change agent and participants need to stabilise the new conditions. This refers to the refreezing process described earlier. Rewards, information systems, team norms and other conditions are redesigned so that they support the new values and behaviours.

The action research approach has dominated organisational change thinking ever since it was introduced in the 1940s. However, some experts complain that the problem-oriented nature of action research—in which something is wrong that must be fixed—focuses on the negative dynamics of the group or system rather than its positive opportunities and potential. This concern with action research has led to the development of a more positive approach to organisational change, called 'appreciative inquiry'.[39]

APPRECIATIVE INQUIRY APPROACH

appreciative inquiry An organisational change strategy that directs the group's attention away from its own problems and focuses participants on the group's potential and positive elements.

Appreciative inquiry tries to break out of the problem-solving mentality of traditional change management practices by reframing relationships around the positive and the possible. It searches for organisational (or team) strengths and capabilities, then adapts or applies that knowledge for further success and well-being. Appreciative inquiry is therefore deeply grounded in the emerging philosophy of *positive organisational behaviour*, which suggests that focusing on the positive rather than the negative aspects of life will improve organisational success and individual well-being.[40]

Canadian Tire's appreciative journey

Canadian Tire CEO Wayne Sales (pictured) and his executive team wanted to hear from employees and store-owners about what makes the Canadian hardware and car-parts retailer so successful. They then planned to rebuild its core values around those positive experiences. Appreciative inquiry played an important role in this re-visioning process. Internal consultants conducted interviews with 377 staff across the organisation, asking them to describe occasions on which they felt the retailer was working at its best and what they valued most about the company. Some people described the excitement of the holiday season when products flew out the door. Others recalled the teamwork of employees volunteering to work late to clean up a store after a major delivery. These incidents were organised around six team values, which the executive team discussed and affirmed. The company then held a one-day conference in which middle and senior management developed a common understanding of these values. Next, store managers discussed the six team values with their staff and participated in an exercise in which employees visualised a good news story about the company's success.[42]

Toronto Star

The Four-D model of appreciative inquiry

EXHIBIT 17.5

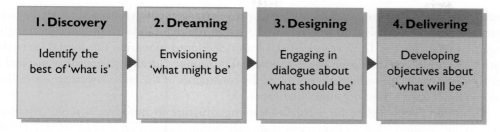

1. Discovery	**2. Dreaming**	**3. Designing**	**4. Delivering**
Identify the best of 'what is'	Envisioning 'what might be'	Engaging in dialogue about 'what should be'	Developing objectives about 'what will be'

Source: Based on F. J. Barrett and D. L. Cooperrider, 'Generative Metaphor Intervention: A New Approach for Working with Systems Divided by Conflict and Caught in Defensive Perception', *Journal of Applied Behavioral Science*, 26 (1990), p. 229; D. Whitney and C. Schau, 'Appreciative Inquiry: An Innovative Process For Organization Change', *Employment Relations Today*, 25 (Spring 1998), pp. 11–21; J. M. Watkins and B. J. Mohr, *Appreciative Inquiry: Change at the Speed of Imagination* (San Francisco: Jossey-Bass, 2001), pp. 25, 42–5.

Appreciative inquiry typically directs its inquiry towards successful events and successful organisations or work units. This external focus becomes a form of behavioural modelling, but it also increases open dialogue by redirecting the group's attention away from its own problems. Appreciative inquiry is especially useful when participants are aware of their 'problems' or already suffer from enough negativity in their relationships. The positive orientation of appreciative inquiry enables groups to overcome these negative tensions and build a more hopeful perspective of their future by focusing on what is possible. [41]

The Four-D model of appreciative inquiry (named after its four stages) shown in Exhibit 17.5 begins with *discovery*—identifying the positive elements of the observed events or organisation. [43] This might involve documenting positive customer experiences elsewhere in the organisation. Or it might include interviewing members of another organisation to discover its fundamental strengths. As participants discuss their findings, they shift into the *dreaming* stage by envisioning what might be possible in an ideal organisation. By directing their attention to a theoretically ideal organisation or situation, participants feel safer revealing their hopes and aspirations than if they were discussing their own organisation or predicament.

As participants make their private thoughts public to the group, the process shifts into the third stage, called *designing*. Designing involves the process of dialogue, in which participants listen with selfless receptivity to each other's models and assumptions and eventually form a collective model for thinking within the team. In effect, they create a common image of what should be. As this model takes shape, group members shift the focus back to their own situation. In the final stage of appreciative inquiry, called *delivering*, participants establish specific objectives and direction for their own organisation based on their model of what will be.

Appreciative inquiry was developed twenty years ago, but it really only gained popularity a few years ago, partly due to success stories at AVON Mexico, American Express, Green Mountain Coffee Roasters and Hunter Douglas, among others. Although less common in this part of the world, it has been applied in India by Wipro Technologies in the high-technology service firm's team development process, as well as by executives at ANZ Information Technology. 'Every organisation has some success factors that have to be explored and built upon and we tried to do it at ANZ,' say Shabbir Merchant, the consultant responsible for the appreciative inquiry intervention. [44]

Although appreciative inquiry shows promise as an approach to organisational change, experts warn that it requires a particular mind-set among participants where they are willing to let go of the problem-oriented approach, and where leaders are willing to accept appreciative inquiry's less structured process. [45] Another concern is that research has not yet examined the contingencies of this approach. [46] Specifically, we don't yet know under what conditions appreciate inquiry is the best approach to organisational change, and under what conditions it is less effective. Overall, appreciative inquiry has much to offer the organisational change process, but we are just beginning to understand its potential and limitations.

LEARNING OBJECTIVE

Outline the 'Four-D' model of appreciative inquiry and explain how this approach differs from action research.

parallel learning structures
Highly participative groups constructed alongside (i.e. parallel to) the formal organisation with the purpose of increasing the organisation's learning and producing meaningful organisational change.

LEARNING OBJECTIVE

Explain how parallel learning structures assist the change process.

PARALLEL LEARNING STRUCTURE APPROACH

Parallel learning structures are highly participative arrangements, composed of people from most levels of the organisation who follow the action research model to produce meaningful organisational change. They are social structures developed alongside the formal hierarchy with the purpose of increasing the organisation's learning.[47] Ideally, participants in parallel learning structures are sufficiently free from the constraints of the larger organisation so they can more effectively solve organisational issues.

Royal Dutch/Shell relied on a parallel learning structure to introduce a more customer-focused organisation.[48] Rather than try to change the entire organisation at once, executives held week-long 'retail boot camps' with six country teams of front-line people (e.g. service station managers, truck drivers, marketing professionals). Participants learned about competitive trends in their regions and were taught powerful marketing tools to identify new opportunities. The teams then returned home to study their market and develop proposals for improvement.

Four months later, boot camp teams returned for a second workshop where each proposal was critiqued by Royal/Dutch Shell executives. Each team had sixty days to put its ideas into action, then return for a third workshop to analyse what worked and what didn't. This parallel learning process did much more than introduce new marketing ideas. It created enthusiasm in participants that spread contagiously to their co-workers, including managers above them, when they returned to their home countries.

CROSS-CULTURAL AND ETHICAL ISSUES IN ORGANISATIONAL CHANGE

One significant concern with some organisational change interventions is that they originate in the United States and other Western countries and may conflict with cultural values in some other countries.[49] A few experts point out that this Western perspective of change is linear, such as in Lewin's force field model shown earlier. It also assumes that the change process is punctuated by tension and overt conflict. Indeed, some organisational change practices encourage the open display of conflict.

But change as a linear and conflict-ridden process is incompatible with cultures that view change as a natural cyclical process with harmony and equilibrium as the objectives.[50] For instance, people in many Asian countries try to minimise conflict in order to respect others and save face.[51] These concerns do not mean that Western-style change interventions are necessarily ineffective elsewhere. Rather, it suggests that we need to develop a more contingency-oriented perspective with respect to the participants' cultural values.

ETHICAL ISSUES WITH ORGANISATIONAL CHANGE

LEARNING OBJECTIVE

Discuss four ethical issues in organisational change.

Some organisational change practices also face ethical issues.[52] One ethical concern is the threat to the privacy rights of individuals. The action research model is built on the idea of collecting information from organisational members, yet this requires employees to provide personal information and emotions that they may not want to divulge.[53] A second ethical concern is that some change activities potentially increase management's power by inducing compliance and conformity in organisational members. This power shift occurs because change creates uncertainty and may re-establish management's position in directing the organisation. For instance, action research is a system-wide activity that requires employee participation rather than allowing individuals to get involved voluntarily.

A third concern is that some organisational change interventions undermine the individual's self-esteem. The unfreezing process requires participants to disconfirm their existing beliefs, sometimes including their own competence at certain tasks or interpersonal relations. Some specific change practices involve direct exposure to personal critique by co-workers, as well as public disclosure of one's personal limitations and faults. A fourth ethical concern is the change management consultant's role in the change process. Ideally, consultants should occupy 'marginal' positions with the clients they are serving. This means that they must be sufficiently detached from the organisation to maintain objectivity and avoid having the client become too dependent on them. However, some consultants tend to increase, rather than decrease, clients' dependence, for financial gain. Others have difficulty maintaining neutrality because they often come to the situation with their own biases and agendas.

Organisational change is a complex process with a variety of approaches and issues. Many corporate leaders have promised more change than they were able to deliver because they underestimated the time and challenges involved with this process. Yet the dilemma is that most organisations operate in hyper-fast environments that demand continuous and rapid adaptation. As the opening vignette about Medibank Private showed, organisations survive and gain competitive advantage by mastering the complex dynamics of moving people through the continuous process of change.

PERSONAL CHANGE FOR THE ROAD AHEAD

In the last section of this textbook, the attention shifts from organisational change to a few practical ideas on personal change and development in organisations. Whether you are just starting your career or are already well along the trail, the following principles should help you improve both your prospects and your long-term career satisfaction. These points do not cover everything you need to remember about developing your career. Rather, they highlight some of the key strategies that will help you along the road ahead.

UNDERSTAND YOUR NEEDS AND VALUES

While working as a Navy diver, Dan Porzio prepared for his next career in financial planning. But he was far from happy in his new field, so he took a job selling mobile phones. Still unhappy, Porzio moved into the investment industry, where he worked for three years. During that time he visited a career counsellor and discovered why he lacked interest in his work. 'I thought those other jobs were ones that I wanted to do but I found out I was doing things that didn't jive with my character,' Porzio explains. With that knowledge in hand, Porzio found a job that fitted his personality, as captain of the *Annabelle Lee* riverboat in Richmond, Virginia.[54]

Dan Porzio is following the first piece of advice regarding personal growth and development: understand your needs and values. How do you know what path is most fulfilling for you? One piece of advice is to follow Porzio's direction by completing self-assessments of your vocational interests and recounting enjoyable experiences to a career counsellor. Holland's occupational choice model presented in Chapter 2 helps to align your personality and interests with the work environment. It may also be useful to get feedback from others regarding activities that they notice you like or dislike. This applies the Johari Window model described in Chapter 3, whereby you learn more about yourself through information presented by close associates.

UNDERSTAND YOUR COMPETENCIES

Knowing yourself also involves knowing what you are capable of doing.[55] Although we might visualise our future as an Albert Einstein or a prime minister, we need to take our potential abilities into account. The more the work we perform is aligned with our personal competencies, the more we develop a 'can-do' attitude that fuels our feelings of empowerment. Self-assessments, performance results and constructive feedback from friends can help us to identify our capabilities. Also, keep in mind that competencies extend beyond technical skills; employers are also looking for generic competencies, such as communication, problem solving and emotional intelligence.

SET CAREER GOALS

Goal setting is a powerful way to motivate and achieve results, and this applies as much to careers as to any other activity. Career goals are benchmarks against which we evaluate our progress and identify strategies to develop our competencies. Career consultant Barbara Moses emphasises that career goal setting is a fundamental element in becoming a 'career activist'. It involves writing your own script rather than waiting for someone to write it for you, being vigilant by identifying and preparing for opportunities, and becoming an independent agent by separating your self-identity from your job title, your organisation or what other people think you should be.[56]

MAINTAIN NETWORKS

Networking makes a difference in personal career growth. This observation is supported by several research studies and from evidence in executive placement firms. One large placement firm reported that 64 per cent of the 7435 clients in its executive career transition program found new employment through networking. As one successful job hunter advises: 'Be prepared, know your story, and network, network, network.'[57] Some networks are more effective than others, however. Specifically, job seekers tend to be more successful with large non-redundant networks. Networks that extend beyond your current sphere of work are also critical. The reason is that careers change much more today than in the past, so you need to establish connections to other fields where you may someday find yourself.[58]

GET A MENTOR

Thus far, the discussion has emphasised self-leadership in personal development. We need to set our own goals, motivate ourselves for career advancement, and visualise where we want to go. But personal development in organisational settings also benefits from the help of others. Mentoring is the process of learning the ropes of organisational life from a senior person within the company. Mentors give protégés more visible and meaningful work opportunities, and they also provide ongoing career guidance. You might think of them as a career coach, because they provide ongoing advice and feedback.[59]

ORGANISATIONAL BEHAVIOUR: THE JOURNEY CONTINUES

Nearly 100 years ago industrialist Andrew Carnegie said: 'Take away my people, but leave my factories, and soon grass will grow on the factory floors. Take away my factories, but leave my people, and soon we will have a new and better factory.' Carnegie's statement reflects the message woven throughout this textbook: that organisations are not buildings or machinery or financial assets. Rather, they are the people in them. Organisations are human entities—full of life, sometimes fragile, always exciting.

CHAPTER SUMMARY

Lewin's force field analysis model states that all systems have driving and restraining forces. Change occurs through the process of unfreezing, changing and refreezing. Unfreezing produces disequilibrium between the driving and restraining forces. Refreezing realigns the organisation's systems and structures with the desired behaviours.

Restraining forces are manifested as employee resistance to change. The main reasons why people resist change are direct costs, saving face, fear of the unknown, breaking routines, incongruent organisational systems and incongruent team dynamics. Resistance to change may be minimised by keeping employees informed about what to expect from the change effort (communicating), by teaching employees valuable skills for the desired future (learning), by involving them in the change process, by helping them cope with the stress of change, by negotiating trade-offs with those who will clearly lose from the change effort, and by using coercion (sparingly and as a last resort).

Organisational change also requires driving forces. This means that employees need to have an urgency for change by becoming aware of the environmental conditions that demand change in the organisation. The change process also requires refreezing the new behaviours by realigning organisational systems and team dynamics with the desired changes.

Every successful change requires a clear, well-articulated vision of the desired future state. Change agents rely on transformational leadership to develop a vision, communicate that vision and build commitment to the vision of a desirable future state. The change process also often applies a diffusion process in which change begins as a pilot project and eventually spreads to other areas of the organisation.

Action research is a highly participative, open-systems approach to change management that combines an action-orientation (changing attitudes and behaviour) with research orientation (testing theory). It is a data-based, problem-oriented process that diagnoses the need for change, introduces the intervention, and then evaluates and stabilises the desired changes.

Appreciative inquiry embraces the positive organisational behaviour philosophy by focusing participants on the positive and the possible. It tries to break out of the problem-solving mentality that dominates organisational change through the action research model. The four stages of appreciative inquiry include discovery, dreaming, designing and delivering. A third approach, called parallel learning structures, relies on social structures developed alongside the formal hierarchy with the purpose of increasing the organisation's learning. They are highly participative arrangements, composed of people from most levels of the organisation who follow the action research model to produce meaningful organisational change.

One significant concern is that organisational change theories developed with a Western cultural orientation potentially conflict with cultural values in some other countries. Also, organisational change practices can raise one or more ethical concerns, including increasing management's power over employees, threatening individual privacy rights, undermining individual self-esteem, and making clients dependent on the change consultant.

Five strategies that assist personal development in organisational settings are: understand your needs and values, understand your competencies, set career goals, maintain networks and find a mentor.

KEY TERMS

action research p. 512
appreciative inquiry p. 514
change agent p. 511

force field analysis p. 502
future search p. 508
parallel learning structures p. 516

refreezing p. 503
unfreezing p. 503

DISCUSSION QUESTIONS

1. The chances are that the university or college you are attending is currently undergoing some sort of change to align more closely with its environment. Discuss the external forces that are driving these changes. What internal drivers for change also exist?

2. Use Lewin's force field analysis to describe the dynamics of organisational change at Nissan Motor Company.

3. Employee resistance is a *symptom*, not a *problem*, in the change process. What are some of the real problems that may underlie employee resistance?

4. Senior management of a large multinational corporation is planning to restructure the organisation. Currently, the organisation is decentralised around geographical areas so that the executive responsible for each area has considerable autonomy over manufacturing and sales. The new structure will transfer power to the executives responsible for different product groups; the executives responsible for each geographic area will no longer be responsible for manufacturing in their area but will retain control over sales activities. Describe two types of resistance that senior management might encounter from this organisational change.

5. Web Circuits is a Malaysian-based custom manufacturer for high-technology companies. Senior management wants to introduce lean management practices to reduce production costs and remain competitive. A consultant has recommended that the company start with a pilot project in one department and,

when successful, diffuse these practices to other areas of the organisation. Discuss the advantages of this recommendation and identify three ways (other than the pilot project's success) to make diffusion of the change effort more successful.

6. Suppose that you are general manager of branch services at the Bank of Mullewa, which has bank branches throughout Western and South Australia. You notice that several branches have consistently low customer service ratings even though there are no apparent differences in resources or staff characteristics. Describe an appreciative inquiry process in one of these branches that might help to overcome these problems.

7. This chapter suggests that some organisational change activities face ethical concerns. Yet several consultants actively use these processes because they believe they benefit the organisation and do less damage to employees than it seems on the surface. For example, some activities try to open up the employee's hidden area (see Johari Window in Chapter 3) so that there is better mutual understanding with co-workers. Discuss this argument and identify where you think organisational change interventions should limit this process.

8. Career activism is a concept that is gaining interest because it emphasises managing your own development in organisations. What concepts introduced throughout this book are compatible with the career activist concept? In what ways might a person be a career activist?

SKILL BUILDER	**17.1**	THE EXCELLENT EMPLOYEE
CASE STUDY		*Mary Gander, Winona State University*

Emily, who has the reputation of being an excellent worker, is a machine operator in a furniture manufacturing plant that has been growing at a rate of 15–20 per cent each year for the past decade. New additions have been built onto the plant, new plants opened in the region, workers were hired, and the number of products was increased. However, there has been no significant change in the overall approach to operations, plant layout and ways of managing workers, or in the design processes. Plant operations and organisational culture are rooted in traditional Western management practices and logic, based largely on the notion of mass production and economies of scale. Over the past four years, the company has been growing in the number and variety of products produced and in market penetration. However, profitability has been flattening and showing signs of decline. As a result, in developing strategic plans management is beginning to focus on production operations (internal focus) rather than mainly on new market strategies, new products and new market segments (external focus). Management hopes to get manufacturing costs down, to improve consistency of quality and to meet delivery times better, while decreasing inventory and increasing flexibility.

One of several new programs initiated by management in the effort to improve flexibility and lower costs was the cross-training of workers. However, when a representative from Human Resources explained this program to Emily's supervisor, Jim, he reluctantly agreed to cross-train most of his workers, but *not* Emily.

Jim explained to the HR person that Emily works on a machine that is very complex and not easy to operate effectively. She has to 'babysit' it much of the time. Jim has tried many workers on it, and tried to train them, but Emily is the only one who can consistently get product through the machine that is within specification and still meet production schedules. When anyone else tries to operate the machine, which performs a key function in the manufacturing process, there ends up being a big bottleneck or excessive waste is produced, which creates a lot of trouble for Jim.

Jim goes on to explain that Emily knows this sophisticated and complicated machine inside and out, and has been running it for five years. She likes the challenge and says it makes the day go faster. She is meticulous in her work, a very skilled employee who really cares about the quality of her work. Jim told the HR person that he wished all of his workers were like Emily. In spite of the difficulty of operating the machine, Emily runs it so well that product piles up at the next workstation downstream in the production process, as they can't keep up with her!

Jim was adamant about keeping Emily on this machine and not cross-training her. The HR person was frustrated. He could see Jim's point, but he had to follow executive orders: 'Get these people cross-trained.'

Around the same period of time, a university student was doing a field study in the section of the plant where Emily worked and Emily was one of the workers he interviewed. Emily told the student that, in spite of the fact that the plant had some problems with employee morale and excessive employee turnover, she really liked working there. She liked the piece-rate pay system very much and hoped that she did not have to participate in the recent 'Program of the Month' which involved operators learning each other's jobs. She told the student that it would just create more waste if other employees tried to run her machine. She explained that other employees had tried to learn how to operate the machine but couldn't do it as well as she could.

Emily seemed to take a special liking to the student and began to open up to him. She told him that her machine didn't need to be so difficult and touchy to operate, and that with a couple of minor design changes, and better maintenance, virtually anyone could run it. She had tried to explain this to her supervisor a couple of years ago but he had told her to 'do her work and leave operations to the manufacturing engineers'. She also said that, if the workers upstream in the process took a little more care to keep the raw material in slightly tighter specifications, it would go through her machine more easily and trouble-free, but that they were too focused on working fast and making more piece-rate pay. She expressed a lack of respect for the managers who couldn't see this and even joked about how 'managers didn't know anything'.

QUESTIONS

1. Identify the sources of resistance to change in this short case.

2. Discuss whether this resistance is justified or could be overcome.

3. Recommend ways to minimise resistance to change in this incident or in future incidents.

STRATEGIC CHANGE INCIDENTS

17.2 SKILL BUILDER

TEAM EXERCISE

PURPOSE

This exercise is designed to help you to identify strategies to facilitate organisational change in various situations.

INSTRUCTIONS

Step 1: The instructor will place students into teams, and each team will be assigned one of the scenarios presented below.

Step 2: Each team will diagnose its assigned scenario to determine the most appropriate set of change management practices. Where appropriate, these practices should (a) create an urgency to change, (b) minimise resistance to change, and (c) refreeze the situation to support the change initiative. Each of the scenarios is based on real events.

Step 3: Each team will present and defend its change management strategy. Class discussion regarding the appropriateness and feasibility of each strategy will occur after all teams assigned the same scenario have presented. The instructor will then describe what the organisations actually did in these situations.

SCENARIO 1: GREENER TELCO

The board of directors at a large telephone company want its executives to make the organisation more environmentally friendly by encouraging employees to reduce waste in the workplace. There are also expectations by government and other stakeholders for the company to take this action and be publicly successful. Consequently, the managing director wants to significantly reduce the use of paper, refuse and other waste throughout the company's many widespread offices. Unfortunately, a survey indicates that employees do not value environmental objectives and do not know how to 'reduce, reuse, recycle'. As the executive responsible for this change, you have been asked to develop a strategy that might bring about meaningful behavioural change towards these environmental goals. What would you do?

SCENARIO 2: GO FORWARD AIRLINE

A major airline had experienced a decade of rough turbulence, including two bouts of bankruptcy protection, ten managing directors, and morale so low that employees had ripped company logos off their uniforms out of embarrassment. Service was terrible and the aeroplanes rarely arrived or left the terminal on time. This was costing the airline significant amounts of money in passenger layovers. Managers were paralysed by anxiety and many had been with the firm so long that they didn't know how to set strategic goals that worked. One-fifth of all flights were losing money and the company overall was near financial collapse (just three months to defaulting on payroll obligations). The newly hired managing director and you must get employees to improve operational efficiency and customer service quickly. What actions would you take to bring about these changes in time?

SKILL BUILDER | 17.3   TOLERANCE OF CHANGE SCALE

SELF-ASSESSMENT

STUDENT CD

PURPOSE

This exercise is designed to help you understand how people differ in their tolerance of change.

INSTRUCTIONS

Read each of the statements below and circle the response that best fits your personal belief. Then use the scoring key in Appendix B of this book to calculate your results. This self-assessment is completed alone so students rate themselves honestly without concerns of social comparison. However, class discussion will focus on the meaning of the concept measured by this scale and its implications for managing change in organisational settings.

TOLERANCE OF CHANGE SCALE

To what extent does each statement describe you? Indicate your level of agreement by marking the appropriate response on the right.	Strongly agree	Moderately agree	Slightly agree	Neutral	Slightly disagree	Moderately disagree	Strongly disagree
1. An expert who doesn't come up with a definite answer probably doesn't know too much.	❑	❑	❑	❑	❑	❑	❑
2. I would like to live in a foreign country for a while.	❑	❑	❑	❑	❑	❑	❑
3. There is really no such thing as a problem that can't be solved.	❑	❑	❑	❑	❑	❑	❑
4. People who fit their lives into a schedule probably miss most of the joy of living.	❑	❑	❑	❑	❑	❑	❑
5. A good job is one where it is always clear what is to be done and how it is to be done.	❑	❑	❑	❑	❑	❑	❑
6. It is more fun to tackle a complicated problem than to solve a simple one.	❑	❑	❑	❑	❑	❑	❑
7. In the long run, it is possible to get more done by tackling small, simple problems rather than large, complicated ones.	❑	❑	❑	❑	❑	❑	❑
8. Often the most interesting and stimulating people are those who don't mind being different and original.	❑	❑	❑	❑	❑	❑	❑
9. What we are used to is always preferable to what is unfamiliar.	❑	❑	❑	❑	❑	❑	❑
10. People who insist on a yes or no answer just don't know how complicated things really are.	❑	❑	❑	❑	❑	❑	❑
11. A person who leads an even, regular life in which few surprises or unexpected happenings arise really has a lot to be grateful for.	❑	❑	❑	❑	❑	❑	❑
12. Many of our most important decisions are based on insufficient information.	❑	❑	❑	❑	❑	❑	❑
13. I like parties where I know most of the people more than ones where all or most of the people are complete strangers.	❑	❑	❑	❑	❑	❑	❑
14. Teachers or supervisors who hand out vague assignments give one a chance to show initiative and originality.	❑	❑	❑	❑	❑	❑	❑
15. The sooner everyone acquires similar values and ideals, the better.	❑	❑	❑	❑	❑	❑	❑
16. A good teacher is one who makes you wonder about your way of looking at things.	❑	❑	❑	❑	❑	❑	❑

Source: Adapted from S. Budner, 'Intolerance of Ambiguity as a Personality Variable', *Journal of Personality* 30 (1962), pp. 29–50.

NOTES

1   'Leadership: Different Organisations, Common Themes', *ceoforum.com.au*, February 2003; S. Dabkowski, 'Staff Turn Medibank Private Around', *The Age* (Melbourne), 6 November 2003, 2; J. Bajkowski, 'Users Give Board Execs a Reality Lesson', *Computerworld*, 14 June 2005; S. Dabkowski, 'Healthy Diagnosis Deems Medibank Might Be Fit to Float', *The Age* (Melbourne), 3 October 2005, 1; A. Tandukar, 'Listen, Learn, Lead', *Business Review Weekly*, 2 June 2005, 66.

2   K. Lewin, *Field Theory in Social Science* (New York: Harper & Row, 1951).

3   M. Riley, 'High-revving Nasser Undone by a Blind Spot', *Sydney Morning Herald*, 3 November 2001; J. McCracken, 'Nasser Out; Ford In', *Detroit Free Press*, 30 October 2001; M. Truby, 'Can Ford Chief Ride out Storm?', *Detroit News*, 24 June 2001; M. Truby, 'Ford Revolution Spawns Turmoil', *Detroit News*, 29 April 2001.

4   C. O. Longenecker, D. J. Dwyer and T. C. Stansfield, 'Barriers and Gateways to Workforce Productivity', *Industrial Management*, March–April 1998, 21–8; J. Seifman, 'Middle Managers—the Meat in the Corporate Sandwich', *China Staff*, June 2002, 7. The recent Australian survey is reported in *Bosses Want Change but Workers Want More of the Same!* (Sydney: Talent2, 29 June 2005).

5   'The Wrong People Doing the Right Job: Reforming the FBI', *The Economist*, 17 April 2004, 371; National Commission on Terrorist Attacks upon the United States, *The 9/11 Commission Report* (Washington, DC: US Government Printing Office, July 2004); D. Eggen, 'FBI Fails to Transform Itself, Panel Says', *Washington Post*, 7 June 2005, A04; C. Ragavan and C. S. Hook, 'Fixing the FBI', *US News & World Report*, 28 March 2005, 18–24, 26, 29–30; The Commission on the Intelligence Capabilities of the United States Regarding Weapons of Mass Destruction, *Report to the President of the United States* (Washington, DC: 31 March 2005).

6   E. B. Dent and S. G. Goldberg, 'Challenging "Resistance to Change"', *Journal of Applied Behavioral Science* 35 (March 1999), 25–41.

7   D. A. Nadler, 'The Effective Management of Organizational Change', in *Handbook of Organizational Behavior*, ed. J. W. Lorsch (Englewood Cliffs, NJ: Prentice Hall, 1987), 358–69; R. Maurer, *Beyond the Wall of Resistance: Unconventional Strategies to Build Support for Change* (Austin, TX: Bard Books, 1996); P. Strebel, 'Why Do Employees Resist Change?', *Harvard Business Review* (May–June 1996), 86–92; D. A. Nadler, *Champions of Change* (San Francisco, CA: Jossey-Bass, 1998).

8   'Making Change Work for You—Not against You', *Agency Sales Magazine* 28 (June 1998), 24–7..

9   D. Miller, 'What Happens after Success: The Perils of Excellence', *Journal of Management Studies* 31 (1994), 325–58.

10 'Leadership: Different Organisations, Common Themes'.

11 T. G. Cummings, 'The Role and Limits of Change Leadership', in *The Leader's Change Handbook*, eds J. A. Conger, G. M. Spreitzer and E. E. Lawler III (San Francisco: Jossey-Bass, 1999), 301–20; J. P. Kotter and D. S. Cohen, *The Heart of Change* (Boston: Harvard Business School Press, 2002), 15–36. The Aristocrat Leisure incident is cited in B. Andrews, 'Winning Hand', *Business Review Weekly*, 14 April 2005, 72.

12 I. J. Bozon and P. N. Child, 'Refining Shell's Position in Europe', *McKinsey Quarterly*, no. 2 (2003), 42–51.

13 L. D. Goodstein and H. R. Butz, 'Customer Value: The Linchpin of Organizational Change', *Organizational Dynamics* 27 (June 1998), 21–35.

14 D. Darlin, 'Growing Tomorrow', *Business 2.0*, May 2005, 126.

15 L. Grossman and S. Song, 'Stevie's Little Wonder', *Time*, 19 September 2005, 63; S. Levy, 'Honey, I Shrunk the iPod. A Lot', *Newsweek*, 19 September 2005, 58.

16 F. Smith et al., '25 True Leaders', *Australian Financial Review*, 12 August 2005, 62.

17 J. P. Kotter and L. A. Schlesinger, 'Choosing Strategies for Change', *Harvard Business Review* (March–April 1979), 106–14.

18 B. Nanus and S. M. Dobbs, *Leaders Who Make a Difference* (San Francisco: Jossey-Bass, 1999); Kotter and Cohen, *The Heart of Change*, 83–98.

19 M. J. Marquardt, *Optimizing the Power of Action Learning: Solving Problems and Building Leaders in Real Time* (Palo Alto, CA: Davies-Black, 2004).

20 K. T. Dirks, L. L. Cummings and J. L. Pierce, 'Psychological Ownership in Organizations: Conditions under which Individuals Promote and Resist Change', *Research in Organizational Change and Development* 9 (1996), 1–23.

21 B. B. Bunker and B. T. Alban, *Large Group Interventions: Engaging the Whole System for Rapid Change* (San Francisco, CA: Jossey-Bass, 1996); M. Weisbord and S. Janoff, *Future Search: An Action Guide to Finding Common Ground in Organizations and Communities* (San Francisco: Berrett-Koehler, 2000). For a description of Trist and Emery's first search conference, see M. R. Weisbord, 'Inventing the Search Conference: Bristol Siddeley Aircraft Engines, 1960', in *Discovering Common Ground*, ed. M. R. Weisbord (San Francisco: Berret-Koehler, 1992), 19–33.

22 For criticism of a recent future search conference for lacking innovative or realistic ideas, see: A. Oels, 'Investigating the Emotional Roller-Coaster Ride: A Case-Study-Based Assessment of the Future Search Conference Design', *Systems Research and Behavioral Science* 19 (July–August 2002), 347–55; M. F. D. Polanyi, 'Communicative Action in Practice: Future Search and the Pursuit of an Open, Critical and Non-Coercive Large-Group Process', *Systems Research and Behavioral Science* 19 (July 2002), 357–66.

23 R. Larson, 'Forester Defends "Feel-Good" Meeting', *Washington Times*, 28 November 1997, A9; R. E. Purser and S. Cabana, *The Self-Managing Organization* (New York: Free Press, 1998); P. Botsman, 'Government by the People', *Courier-Mail* (Brisbane), 23 July 2002, 11; C. Rance, 'In Bendigo, the People Have Spoken', *The Age* (Melbourne), 30 April 2005, 24; P. Wex, 'Search for City's Future', *Cairns Post*, 20 December 2005, 16.

24 M. McHugh, 'The Stress Factor: Another Item for the Change Management Agenda?', *Journal of Organizational Change Management* 10 (1997), 345–62; D. Buchanan, T. Claydon and M. Doyle, 'Organisation Development and Change: The Legacy of the Nineties', *Human Resource Management Journal* 9 (1999), 20–37.

25 D. Nicolini and M. B. Meznar, 'The Social Construction of Organizational Learning: Conceptual and Practical Issues in the Field', *Human Relations* 48 (1995), 727–46.

26 D. Helfand, 'School Is Down but Looking Up', *Los Angeles Times*, 14 October 2004, B1; 'Mrs Bush Remarks on Helping America's Youth in Sun Valley, California', White House news release (Sun Valley, CA, 27 April 2005), http://www.whitehouse.gov/news/releases/2005/04/20050427-5.html

27 Kotter and Cohen, *The Heart of Change*, 161–77.

28 R. H. Miles, 'Leading Corporate Transformation: Are You up to the Task?', in *The Leader's Change Handbook*, eds J. A. Conger, G. M. Spreitzer and E. E. Lawler III (San Francisco: Jossey-Bass, 1999), 221–67; E. E. Lawler III, 'Pay Can Be a Change Agent', *Compensation & Benefits Management* 16 (Summer 2000), 23–6.

29 R. E. Quinn, *Building the Bridge as You Walk on It: A Guide for Leading Change* (San Francisco: Jossey-Bass, 2004), chapter 11.

30 J. P. Kotter, 'Leading Change: Why Transformation Efforts Fail', *Harvard Business Review* (March–April 1995), 59–67; J. P. Kotter, 'Leading Change: The Eight Steps to Transformation', in *The Leader's Change Handbook*, eds J. A. Conger, G. M. Spreitzer and E. E. Lawler III (San Francisco: Jossey-Bass, 1999), 221–67.

31 R. Caldwell, 'Models of Change Agency: A Fourfold Classification', *British Journal of Management* 14 (June 2003), 131–42.

32 M. Beer, R. A. Eisenstat and B. Spector, *The Critical Path to Corporate Renewal* (Boston: Harvard Business School Press, 1990).

33 R. E. Walton, 'Successful Strategies for Diffusing Work Innovations', *Journal of Contemporary Business* (Spring 1977), 1–22; R. E. Walton, *Innovating to Compete: Lessons for Diffusing and Managing Change in the Workplace* (San Francisco: Jossey-Bass, 1987); Beer, Eisenstat and Spector, *The Critical Path to Corporate Renewal*, chapter 5.

34 E. M. Rogers, *Diffusion of Innovations*, 4th edn (New York: Free Press, 1995).

35 P. Reason and H. Bradbury, *Handbook of Action Research* (London: Sage, 2001); D. Coghlan and T. Brannick, 'Kurt Lewin: The "Practical Theorist" for the 21st Century', *Irish Journal of Management* 24, no. 2 (2003), 31–7; C. Huxham and S. Vangen, 'Researching Organizational Practice through Action Research: Case Studies and Design Choices', *Organizational Research Methods* 6 (July 2003), 383–403.

36 V. J. Marsick and M. A. Gephart, 'Action Research: Building the Capacity for Learning and Change', *Human Resource Planning* 26 (2003), 14–18.

37 L. Dickens and K. Watkins, 'Action Research: Rethinking Lewin', *Management Learning* 30 (June 1999), 127–40; J. Heron and P. Reason, 'The Practice of Co-Operative Inquiry: Research "with" Rather Than "on" People', in *Handbook of Action Research*, eds P. Reason and H. Bradbury (Thousand Oaks, CA: Sage, 2001), 179–88.

38 D. A. Nadler, 'Organizational Frame Bending: Types of Change in the Complex Organization', in *Corporate Transformation: Revitalizing Organizations for a Competitive World*, eds R. H. Kilmann, T. J. Covin and Associates (San Francisco: Jossey-Bass, 1988), 66–83; K. E. Weick and R. E. Quinn, 'Organizational Change and Development', *Annual Review of Psychology* (1999), 361–86.

39 T. M. Egan and C. M. Lancaster, 'Comparing Appreciative Inquiry to Action Research: OD Practitioner Perspectives', *Organization Development Journal* 23, no. 2 (Summer 2005), 29–49.

40 F. Luthans, 'The Need for and Meaning of Positive Organizational Behavior', *Journal of Organizational Behavior* 23 (2002), 695–706; N. Turner, J. Barling and A. Zacharatos, 'Positive Psychology at Work', in *Handbook of Positive Psychology*, eds C. R. Snyder and S. Lopez (Oxford, UK: Oxford University Press, 2002), 715–30; K. Cameron, J. E. Dutton and R. E. Quinn (eds), *Positive Organizational Scholarship: Foundation of a New Discipline* (San Francisco: Berrett Koehler Publishers, 2003); J. I. Krueger and D. C. Funder, 'Towards a Balanced Social Psychology: Causes, Consequences, and Cures for the Problem-Seeking Approach to Social Behavior and Cognition', *Behavioral and Brain Sciences* 27, no. 3 (June 2004), 313–27.

41 D. Whitney and D. L. Cooperrider, 'The Appreciative Inquiry Summit: Overview and Applications', *Employment Relations Today* 25 (Summer 1998), 17–28; J. M. Watkins and B. J. Mohr, *Appreciative Inquiry: Change at the Speed of Imagination* (San Francisco: Jossey-Bass, 2001).

42 Canadian Tire, *Team Values Development Process* (PowerPoint File), (Toronto: Canadian Tire, 24 September 2001); Canadian Tire, *Leadership Guide* (Toronto: Canadian Tire, 2002).

43 F. J. Barrett and D. L. Cooperrider, 'Generative Metaphor Intervention: A New Approach for Working with Systems Divided by Conflict and Caught in Defensive Perception', *Journal of Applied Behavioral Science* 26 (1990), 219–39; Whitney and Cooperrider, 'The Appreciative Inquiry Summit: Overview and Applications'; Watkins and Mohr, *Appreciative Inquiry: Change at the Speed of Imagination*, 15–21.

44 T. Narayan, 'Wipro Inducts "Appreciative Inquiry" for Better Team Work', *Financial Express* (India), 2 December 2002; A. Prayag, 'The Power of Goodness for Corporate Development', *Business Line* (*The Hindu*) (Mumbai, India), 19 May 2004, 5.

45 T. F. Yaeger, P. F. Sorensen and U. Bengtsson, 'Assessment of the State of Appreciative Inquiry: Past, Present, and Future', *Research in Organizational Change and Development* 15 (2004), 297–319; G. R. Bushe and A. F. Kassam, 'When Is Appreciative Inquiry Transformational? A Meta-Case Analysis', *Journal of Applied Behavioral Science* 41, no. 2 (June 2005), 161–81.

46 G. R. Bushe, 'Five Theories of Change Embedded in Appreciative Inquiry', in *18th Annual World Congress of Organization Development* (Dublin, Ireland, 14–18 July 1998).

47 G. R. Bushe and A. B. Shani, *Parallel Learning Structures* (Reading, Mass.: Addison-Wesley, 1991); E. M. Van Aken, D. J. Monetta and D. S. Sink, 'Affinity Groups: The Missing Link in Employee Involvement', *Organization Dynamics* 22 (Spring 1994), 38–54.

48 D. J. Knight, 'Strategy in Practice: Making It Happen', *Strategy & Leadership* 26 (July–August 1998), 29–33; R. T. Pascale, 'Grassroots Leadership—Royal Dutch/Shell', *Fast Company*, no. 14 (April–May 1998), 110–20; R. T. Pascale, 'Leading from a Different Place', in *The Leader's Change Handbook*, eds J. A. Conger, G. M. Spreitzer and E. E. Lawler III (San Francisco: Jossey-Bass, 1999), 301–20; R. Pascale, M. Millemann and L. Gioja, *Surfing on the Edge of Chaos* (London: Texere, 2000).

49 C.-M. Lau, 'A Culture-Based Perspective of Organization Development Implementation', *Research in Organizational Change and Development* 9 (1996), 49–79.

50 T. C. Head and P. F. Sorenson, 'Cultural Values and Organizational Development: A Seven-Country Study', *Leadership and Organization Development Journal* 14 (1993), 3–7; R. J. Marshak, 'Lewin Meets Confucius: A Review of the OD Model of Change', *Journal of Applied Behavioral Science* 29 (1993), 395–415; C.-M. Lau and H. Y. Ngo, 'Organization Development and Firm Performance: A Comparison of Multinational and Local Firms', *Journal of International Business Studies* 32, no. 1 (2001), 95–114.

51 For an excellent discussion of conflict management and Asian values, see several articles in K. Leung and D. Tjosvold (eds), *Conflict Management in the Asia Pacific: Assumptions and Approaches in Diverse Cultures* (Singapore: John Wiley & Sons, 1998).

52 M. McKendall, 'The Tyranny of Change: Organizational Development Revisited', *Journal of Business Ethics* 12 (February 1993), 93–104; C. M. D. Deaner, 'A Model of Organization Development Ethics', *Public Administration Quarterly* 17 (1994), 435–46.

53 G. A. Walter, 'Organization Development and Individual Rights', *Journal of Applied Behavioral Science* 20 (1984), 423–39.

54 J. Tupponce, 'Listening to Those Inner Voices', *Richmond Times–Dispatch*, 11 May 2003, S-3.

55 B. Moses, 'Give People Belief in the Future', *Workforce*, June 2000, 134–41.

56 B. Moses, 'Career Activists Take Command', *Globe & Mail*, 20 March 2000, B6.

57 Drake Beam Morin, *1999 DBM Career Transition Study* (Drake Beam Morin, November 2000); F. T. McCarthy, 'Career Evolution', *The Economist*, 29 January 2000.

58 B. Moses, *The Good News About Careers: How You'll Be Working in the Next Decade* (San Francisco: Jossey-Bass, 1999); S. E. Sullivan, 'The Changing Nature of Careers: A Review and Research Agenda', *Journal of Management* 25 (May 1999), 457–84.

59 S.-C. Van Collie, 'Moving up through Mentoring', *Workforce*, March 1998, 36–40; N. Beech and A. Brockbank, 'Power/Knowledge and Psychosocial Dynamics in Mentoring', *Management Learning* 30 (March 1999), 7–24.

INSERT YOUR CD NOW TO VIEW THE FOOTAGE THAT CORRESPONDS TO THESE CASES

VIDEO CASE STUDIES

CHILDCARE HELP

This video program highlights work–life initiatives at both IBM and Abbott Laboratories. IBM offers its employees a variety of work–life balance options, including unpaid leave, maternity leave, telecommuting and on-site childcare facilities. Abbott Laboratories also invests heavily in childcare and other employee work–life benefits because executives know that these benefits have a meaningful payback in terms of employee morale and productivity.

QUESTIONS

1. Executives at both IBM and Abbott Laboratories refer to the payback of these work–life benefits. Explain how this payback tends to occur.

2. This program specifically shows on-site childcare as a work–life initiative. Explain how an organisational leader instigates an organisational change program where work–life balance becomes an accepted value within the organisation.

HOME SWEET HOME, WORK SWEET WORK

'This is just the way I think a company should be run'
(Dr James Goodnight, President/CEO, SAS Institute).

There is no doubt that SAS Institute is a profitable software company, but behind the scenes the employees claim that it is the corporate culture that sets the company apart from the rest of the software industry.

With a rate of employee turnover of only 4.5 per cent per year compared with an industry average of 18 per cent, and an annual savings rate of $75 million on retention, it is evident that SAS Institute is doing something right.

According to employees at SAS Institute, it is the amenities, the end-of-year profit-sharing schemes and bonuses and the year-round generous benefits that keep them happy and feeling just that little bit 'spoilt'. The self-contained nature of the company instils a culture where employees feel that they are constantly rewarded, trusted, supported and encouraged.

SAS Institute prides itself on providing amenities such as a healthcare centre, which employees and their children can go to in times of illness, thus reducing the employees' time away from work. An on-site childcare centre enforces a cultural belief that family is important to the company. In order to reduce stress and foster balanced and happy workers, the company provides self-contained 'break-out' rooms where employees can escape to at any time of the day. There are three gymnasiums, including an aquatics centre, three outdoor playing fields, and kilometres of walking tracks through bushland. Furthermore, a 35-hour working week is encouraged, so that at 5 pm practically all offices are empty. It is the belief that an employee's home and personal life is an integral part of a successful work life that makes this company's culture stand out from the rest.

QUESTIONS

1. What values make up the organisational culture at SAS Institute?

2. Describe three categories of artefacts through which organisational culture is communicated at SAS Institute.

3. Discuss ways in which SAS Institute's organisational culture instils a sense that leisure and relaxation are essential to work life.

Additional cases

CASE 1
Anchor Foods

CASE 2
Arctic Mining Consultants

CASE 3
Big Screen's big failure

CASE 4
High noon at Alpha Mills

CASE 5
Not all call centres are the workhouses of the twenty-first century

CASE 6
Perfect Pizzeria

CASE 7
Strategic change at Computarget

CASE STUDY I

ANCHOR FOODS

By Brenda Scott-Ladd, Murdoch University

Founded in Adelaide in 1854, Anchor Foods is one of Australia's oldest food industry companies. Now based in Fremantle, Western Australia, the company was until recently owned by Goodman Fielder, a publicly listed multinational food manufacturer, the last of a long list of corporate owners dating back to the early 1980s. During this time Anchor could be likened to the 'poor cousin' that no one knew quite what to do with. As the head offices of successive corporate owners raced to keep up with the fast-evolving food retail industry, Anchor was very much left to its own devices. Anchor products are familiar items on Australian supermarket shelves. The best-known products include cordials, vinegars and dried fruits under the Anchor label, flour, sugar and coconut under the Snowflake label, Spencer's herbs, spices, condiments and Asian sauces, and Lion baking products. Although a long-term survivor, the company was losing market share when it changed hands again in September 2002. Perth businessman David Clapin, former CEO of another Perth-based company Kailis and France Foods, bought Anchor foods outright. At the time he was quoted as saying, 'The purchase of the business represents a significant opportunity for a dedicated focus on the manufacture, marketing and distribution of key branded and innovative food products' (Foodnavigator, 2002). The three years of David Clapin's management have seen significant changes. From a company in decline, Anchor has turned around to become a more streamlined, entrepreneurial and innovative organisation.

Prior to Clapin's takeover, declining market share and returns threatened Anchor's survival. The company was in the doldrums. Most of the managers had been with the company for over ten and in some cases twenty years, and collectively they seemed unable to arrest the slide. There was no innovation. Uncertainty and insecurity added to the problems. There were no new products or fresh branding ideas and distribution networks had declined. There were no funds for upgrades to plant and equipment, for marketing or for updating products. Staff protected their own future rather than the company's. Workers held onto information and operated strictly within their roles. Workers compensation claims increased. 'Although some line staff were not aware of how serious the situation was, managers were!' said Lee Ganley, fifteen-year veteran employee and now purchasing and supply manager, recalling the time shortly before the takeover.

THE EMPLOYEES

Change was not immediate after the takeover. David Clapin became managing director, replacing the departing general manager. Other managers continued on and were given the opportunity to prove themselves. Eventually some were replaced. Over the next six to twelve months the company was reorganised into a lateral process structure. Spencer's Gourmet Foods, which had operated as a separate group within the company, was re-integrated. David Clapin wanted key positions held by the right people and was keen to have good people around him. Three new managers were brought in and the new appointments included Simon Orr-Young as the operations manager, a national sales manager and an experienced IT manager.

Barriers between senior and mid-level managers were broken down, creating better relations and providing opportunities for internal promotion that were not there in the past. There was more interaction between levels of management and staff. David Clapin 'spent time talking to people, researching, asking questions and finding out what Anchor Foods could be doing in each product category, and what they needed to know to meet the need. His personal philosophy is to maximise opportunity and to believe in "what, who and how"' (Foodbiz, 2003). Under Clapin's management the values espoused include 'speed, innovation, value, quality and relationships'. The managing director is accessible and informal in his dealings with all staff. He is generally

'hands-off' but readily becomes involved if he feels he needs to. This is very different from the former hierarchical management structure. Lee Ganley pointed out that at first this created some uncertainty, 'particularly in the early days when so much was happening so fast, but the advantage is that managers feel trusted and respected'. The former structure of Anchor Foods is shown on p. 528.

Initially the company focused on survival. Apart from rebuilding its market position, the systems needed to be restructured and integrated. The company focused on its 'core business'. 'In the past we were the sort of company who would produce a specific five-kilogram order for a retailer,' said Ganley. This was not commercially viable. In all, over a thousand products were dropped. Twenty-two product categories were cut back to twelve, with five core categories: herbs and spices, baking needs, vinegar, flour, and cakes and desserts. Communication was improved and new work values were espoused. 'In the early stages, change was communicated by word-of-mouth, and I think sometimes we fell down here,' said Ganley. It took some time to get a structured management plan in place. Now mid-level managers have key result areas measured by key performance indicators and quarterly targets. A monthly newsletter has recently been implemented and more formal channels of communication are now taking shape.

At first, the impact on line employees was minimal. Even so, many were worried about what might happen. Historically, the company was family oriented, turnover was low and many were long-term employees. Simon Orr-Young recalled: 'Everybody was insecure, but this also meant the place was ripe for change. Naturally, people were worried and we could understand this. Also, we knew we had to work with our employees—we needed them as much as they needed their jobs.' Whenever managers encountered resistance, which happened on a number of occasions, they communicated directly with employees. They opted for win–win solutions and were prepared to compromise. 'We recognised we had a reciprocal relationship and the company was keen to keep employees on side,' said Orr-Young. With this in mind, management made time to meet with all staff individually.

One source of contention arose when the company wanted to increase working hours from thirty-eight to forty per week to gain more productivity. 'We wanted to utilise the flexibility of individual workplace agreements rather than the enterprise bargaining agreements (EBAs),' said Orr-Young. This was to emphasise individual responsibility and performance, particularly for the more senior people, such as supervisors, leading hands and some machine operators. 'But,' stressed Orr-Young, 'we made it clear up-front that no employees would be disadvantaged.' While the company wanted to increase hours, they quickly recognised that not everybody was happy with this. To make the change attractive, the extra hours were paid at 'time and a half' rolled into the standard pay rate. Resistant employees were allowed to stay on the old agreement. Moving staff to the forty-hour week also meant a shift to a monthly pay cycle and so personal financial management became an issue for some. The company's response was flexible, and those affected were allowed to remain on fortnightly pay as an interim measure. Another sticking point occurred when the company wanted to introduce medical reviews. 'Prior to the takeover there were no pre-employment medicals and we wanted to bring these in as a safeguard for employees and the company,' said Orr-Young. Another compromise had to be reached to allay staff concerns. Employees could go to their own family doctor for the medical assessment, which was paid for by the company. Benefits to employees were increased and included company superannuation contributions above the legislated requirements and paid maternity leave. Redundancy entitlements were also increased to help allay staff fears, and some mid to senior managers took voluntary redundancy.

TURNAROUND

By mid-2005 every facet of the business had changed. The company now had a dynamic team of relatively young managers. Under Clapin's leadership there had been a steady growth in profit of over 60 per cent which was re-invested in the business. New packing machines and a new production line have been installed. Anchor has grown in size, with a 30 per cent staffing increase. Prior to the takeover, the factory operated four and a half days a week. Production was initially increased by adding a split shift with existing staff on rotating rosters. Now a permanent afternoon shift is staffed mainly by new employees. The company has gained two government grants for technically challenging and commercially viable food innovations. The first successful project was for commercial production of specialty vinegars, which are currently largely imported. The second grant was for the development of flavoured inclusions for the manufacturing sector. Things have changed a lot, said Orr-Young: 'We've become the presenter of new ideas and concepts to marketers—a leader rather than a follower.'

Sources: Foodbiz (2003), National Food Industry Strategy, Department of Agriculture, Fisheries and Forestry, vol 1, 3, http://www.foodbiz.net.au/v1i3_interviews1.asp, accessed 3 October 2005; Food navigator (2002), 'Goodman-ups-anchor', http://www.foodnavigator.com/news/news-ng.asp?id=44985-, accessed 19 September 2005.

This case was written by Brenda Scott-Ladd in conjunction with Lee Ganley (purchasing and supply manager) and Simon Orr-Young (operations manager) of Anchor Foods.

CASE STUDY 2

ARCTIC MINING CONSULTANTS

Tom Parker enjoyed working outdoors. At various times in the past, he has worked as a ranch hand, a high steel rigger, a headstone installer and a prospector. Now forty-three, Parker is a geological field technician and field coordinator with Arctic Mining Consultants. He has specialised knowledge and experience in all non-technical aspects of mineral exploration, including claim staking, line cutting and grid installation, soil sampling, prospecting and trenching. He is responsible for hiring, training and supervising field assistants for all of Arctic Mining Consultants' programs. Field assistants are paid a fairly low daily wage (no matter how long they work, which may be up to twelve hours or more) and are provided meals and accommodation. Many of the programs are operated by a project manager who reports to Parker.

Parker sometimes acts as a project manager, as he did on a job that involved staking fifteen claims near Eagle Lake, British Columbia. He selected John Talbot, Greg Boyce and Brian Millar, all of whom had previously worked with Parker, as the field assistants. To stake a claim, the project team marks a line with flagging tape and blazes along the perimeter of the claim, cutting a claim post every 500 yards (called a 'length'). The fifteen claims would require almost 100 kilometres of line in total. Parker had budgeted seven days (plus mobilisation and demobilisation) to complete the job. This meant that each of the four stakers (Parker, Talbot, Boyce and Millar) would have to complete a little over seven 'lengths' each day. The following is a chronology of the project.

DAY 1

The Arctic Mining Consultants crew assembled in the morning and drove to Eagle Lake, from where they were flown by helicopter to the claim site. On arrival, they set up tents at the edge of the area to be staked, and agreed on a schedule for cooking duties. After supper, they pulled out the maps and discussed the job—how long it would take, the order in which the areas were to be staked, possible helicopter landing spots, and areas that might be more difficult to stake.

Parker pointed out that, with only a week to complete the job, everyone would have to average seven and a half lengths per day. 'I know that is a lot,' he said, 'but you've all staked claims before and I'm confident that each of you

is capable of it. And it's only for a week. If we get the job done in time, there's a $300 bonus for each man.' Two hours later, Parker and his crew had developed what seemed to be a workable plan.

DAY 2

Millar completed six lengths, Boyce six lengths, Talbot eight and Parker eight. Parker was not pleased with Millar's or Boyce's production. However, he didn't make an issue of it, thinking that they would develop their 'rhythm' quickly.

DAY 3

Millar completed five and a half lengths, Boyce four, and Talbot seven. Parker, who was nearly twice as old as the other three, completed eight lengths. He also had enough time remaining to walk over and check the quality of stakes that Millar and Boyce had completed, then walk back to his own area for helicopter pickup back to the tent site.

That night Parker exploded with anger. 'I thought I told you that I wanted seven and a half lengths a day!' he shouted at Boyce and Millar. Boyce said that he was slowed down by unusually thick underbrush in his assigned area. Millar said that he had done his best and would try to pick up the pace. Parker did not mention that he had inspected their work. He explained that, as far as he was concerned, the field assistants were supposed to finish their assigned area for the day, no matter what.

Talbot, who was sharing a tent with Parker, talked to him later. 'I think that you're being a bit hard on them, you know. I know that it has been more by luck than anything else that I've been able to do my quota. Yesterday I only had five lengths done after the first seven hours and there was only an hour before I was supposed to be picked up. Then I hit a patch of really open bush, and was able to do three lengths in seventy minutes. Why don't I take Millar's area tomorrow and he can have mine? Maybe that will help.'

'Conditions are the same in all of the areas,' replied Parker, rejecting Talbot's suggestion. 'Millar just has to try harder.'

DAY 4

Millar did seven lengths and Boyce completed six and a half. When they reported their production that evening, Parker grunted uncommunicatively. Parker and Talbot did eight lengths each.

DAY 5

Millar completed six lengths, Boyce six, Talbot seven and a half, and Parker eight. Once again Parker blew up, but he concentrated his diatribe on Millar. 'Why don't you do what you say you are going to do? You know that you have to do seven and a half lengths a day. We went over that when we first got here, so why don't you do it? If you aren't willing to do the job, you never should have taken it in the first place!'

Millar replied by saying that he was doing his best, that he hadn't even stopped for lunch, and that he didn't know how he could possibly do any better. Parker launched into him again: 'You have got to work harder! If you put enough effort into it, you will get the area done!'

Later Millar commented to Boyce, 'I hate getting dumped on all the time! I'd quit if it didn't mean that I'd have to walk eighty kilometres to the highway. And besides, I need the bonus money. Why doesn't he pick on you? You don't get any more done than me; in fact, you usually get less. Maybe if you did a bit more he wouldn't be so bothered about me.'

'I only work as hard as I have to,' Boyce replied.

DAY 6

Millar raced through breakfast, was the first one to be dropped off by the helicopter, and arranged to be the last one picked up. That evening the production figures were Millar eight and a quarter lengths, Boyce seven, and Talbot and Parker eight each. Parker remained silent when the field assistants reported their performance for the day.

DAY 7

Millar was again the first out and last in. That night, he collapsed in an exhausted heap at the table, too tired to eat. After a few moments, he announced in an abject tone, 'Six lengths. I worked like a dog all day and I only got a lousy six lengths!' Boyce completed five lengths, Talbot seven, and Parker seven and a quarter.

Parker was furious. 'That means we have to do a total of thirty-four lengths tomorrow if we are to finish this job on time!' With his eyes directed at Millar, he added: 'Why is it that you never finish the job? Don't you realise that you are part of a team, and that you are letting the rest of the team down? I've been checking your lines and you're doing too much blazing and wasting too much time making picture-perfect claim posts! If you worked smarter, you'd get a lot more done!'

DAY 8

Parker cooked breakfast in the dark. The helicopter drop-offs began as soon as morning light appeared on the horizon. Parker instructed each assistant to complete eight lengths and, if they finished early, to help the others. Parker said that he would finish the other ten lengths. Helicopter pickups were arranged for one hour before dark.

By noon, after working as hard as he could, Millar had completed only three lengths. 'Why bother,' he thought to himself. 'I'll never be able to do another five lengths before the helicopter comes, and I'll catch the same amount of abuse from Parker for doing six lengths as for seven and a half.' So he sat down and had lunch and a rest. 'Boyce won't finish his eight lengths either, so even if I did finish mine I still wouldn't get the bonus. At least I'll get one more day's pay this way.'

That night Parker was livid when Millar reported that he had completed five and a half lengths. Parker had done ten and a quarter lengths, and Talbot had completed eight. Boyce proudly announced that he finished seven and a half lengths, but sheepishly added that Talbot had helped him with some of it. All that remained were the two and a half lengths that Millar had not completed.

The job was finished the next morning and the crew demobilised. Millar has never worked for Arctic Mining Consultants again, despite being offered work several times by Parker. Boyce sometimes does staking for Arctic, and Talbot works full-time with the company.

BIG SCREEN'S BIG FAILURE

By Fiona McQuarrie, University College of the Fraser Valley

Bill Brosnan stared at the financial statements in front of him and shook his head. The losses from *Conquistadors*, the movie that was supposed to establish Big Screen Studios as a major Hollywood power, were worse than anyone had predicted. In fact, the losses were so huge that Brosnan's predecessor, Buck Knox, had been fired as a result of this colossal failure. Brosnan had wanted to be the head of a big movie production company for as long as he could remember, and was thrilled to have been chosen by the board of directors to be the new president. But he had never expected that the first task in his dream job would be to deal with the fallout from one of the most unsuccessful movies ever.

The driving force behind *Conquistadors* was its director, Mark Frazier. Frazier had made several profitable movies for other studios and had a reputation as being a maverick with a 'vision'. He was a director with clearly formulated ideas of what his movies should look like, and he also had no hesitation in being forceful with producers, studios, actors and technical staff to ensure that his idea came to life as he had envisioned it. For several years, while Frazier had been busy on other projects, he had also been working on a script about two Spanish aristocrats in the sixteenth century who set out for America to find riches and gold and encountered many amazing adventures on their travels. Frazier was something of an amateur historian, which led to his interest in the real-life stories of the Spanish conquistadors and bringing those stories to life for a twenty-first century audience. But he also felt that creating an epic tale like this would establish him as a serious writer and filmmaker in the eyes of Hollywood, some of whose major powers had dismissed his past work as unimaginative or clichéd.

At the time Big Screen Studios approached Frazier to see if he would be interested in working for the company, Big Screen was going through something of a rough patch. Through several years of hard work and mostly successful productions, Buck Knox, the president of Big Screen, had established Big Screen as a studio that produced cost-efficient and profitable films. The studio also had a good reputation for being supportive of the creative side of filmmaking; actors, writers, directors and producers generally felt that Big Screen trusted them enough to give them autonomy in making decisions appropriate for their productions. (Other studios had reputations for keeping an overly tight rein on production budgets and for dictating

choices based on cost rather than artistic considerations.) However, in the last two years Big Screen had invested in several major productions—a musical, a horror film, and the sequel to a wildly successful film adaptation of a comic book—that for various reasons had all performed well below expectations. Knox had also heard through the grapevine that several of the studio's board members were prepared to join together to force him out of the presidency if Big Screen did not come up with a hit soon.

Knox knew that Frazier was being wooed by several other studios for his next project, and decided to contact Frazier to see if he was interested in directing any of the productions Big Screen was considering in the next year or so. After hearing Knox's descriptions of the upcoming productions, Frazier said, 'What I'd really be interested in doing is directing this script I've been writing.' He described the plot of *Conquistadors* to Knox, and Knox was enchanted by the possibilities—two strong male lead characters, a beautiful woman the men encounter in South America whose affections they fight over, battles, sea voyages, and challenging journeys over mountains and through jungles. However, Knox could also see that this movie might be extremely expensive to produce. He expressed this concern to Frazier, and Frazier replied, 'Yes, but it will be an investment that will pay off. I know this movie will work. And I've mentioned it to two other studios and they are interested in it. I would prefer to make it with Big Screen, but if I have to I will go somewhere else to get it made. That is how strongly I believe in it. However, any studio I work with has to trust me. I won't make the film without adequate financial commitment from the studio, I want final approval over casting, and I won't make the film if I don't get final cut.' ('Final cut' means that the director, not the studio, edits the version of the movie that is released to theatres, and that the studio cannot release a version of the movie that the director does not approve of.)

Knox told Frazier that he would get back to him later that week, and asked Frazier not to commit to any other project until then. He spent several days mulling over the possibilities. Like Frazier, he believed that *Conquistadors* could be a huge success. It certainly sounded like it had more potential than anything else Big Screen had in development. However, Knox was still concerned about the potential cost, and the amount of control over the project that Frazier was demanding. Frazier's reputation as a maverick meant that he probably would not compromise on his demands. Knox was also concerned about his own vulnerability if the movie failed. But on the other hand, Big Screen needed a big hit, and it needed one soon. Big Screen would look very bad if it turned down *Conquistadors* and the movie became a gigantic hit for some other studio. Frazier had a respectable track record of producing moneymakers, so even if he was difficult to work with, the end product usually was successful. At the end of the week Knox phoned Frazier and told him that Big Screen was willing to produce *Conquistadors*. Frazier thanked Knox, and added, 'This film is going to redeem me, and it's going to redeem Big Screen as well.'

Pre-production on the film started almost immediately, after Frazier and the studio negotiated a budget of $50 million. This was slightly higher than Knox had anticipated, but he believed it was not an excessive amount if Frazier was to realise the grand vision he had described. Knox further reassured himself by assigning John Connor, one of his trusted vice-presidents, to act as the studio's liaison with Frazier and to be executive producer on the film. Connor was a veteran of many years in the movie production industry and was experienced in working with directors and budgets. Knox trusted Connor to be able to make Frazier contain the costs of the production within the agreed-upon limits.

THE CASTING DILEMMA

The first major problem the film encountered involved casting. The studio gave Frazier final approval over casting as he had requested. Frazier's first signing was Cole Rogan, a famous action star, to be one of the male leads. The studio did not object to this choice; in fact, Knox and Connor felt that Rogan was an asset because he had a reputation as a star that could 'open' a film. (In other words, audiences would come to a movie just because he was in it.) However, Frazier then decided to cast Frank Monaco as the other male lead. Monaco had made only a few films to date, and those were fluffy romantic comedies. Frazier said that Monaco would bring important qualities of vulnerability and innocence to the role, which would be a strong contrast to Rogan's rugged machismo. However, Connor told Knox he saw two major problems with Monaco's casting: Monaco had never proven himself in an epic adventure role, and he was an accomplished enough actor that he would make the rather wooden Rogan look bad. Knox told Connor to suggest to Frazier that Rogan's role be recast. Unfortunately, it turned out that Frazier had signed Rogan to a 'pay or play' deal, meaning that if the studio released Rogan from the project the studio would have to pay him a considerable sum of money. Knox was somewhat bothered

that Frazier had made this deal with Rogan without consulting either him or Connor, but he told Connor to instruct Frazier to release Rogan and recast the role, and the studio would just accept the payment to Rogan as part of the production costs. Although Frazier complained, he did as the studio asked and chose as a replacement Marty Jones, an actor who had had some success in films but mostly in supporting roles. However, Jones was thrilled to be cast in a major role, and Connor felt that he would be capable of convincingly playing the part.

FILMING ON LOCATION

A few weeks after casting was completed, Connor called Knox and asked to see him immediately. 'Buck,' he said when he arrived at Knox's office, 'we have a really big problem.' Connor said that Frazier was insisting that the majority of the production be filmed in the jungles of South America, where most of the action took place, rather than on a studio soundstage or in a more accessible location. Not only that, but Frazier was also insisting that he needed to bring along most of the crew that had worked on his previous films, rather than staffing the production locally. 'Why does he want that? That's going to cost a hell of a lot,' Knox said. 'I know,' Connor said, 'but he says it's the only way that the film is going to work. He says it just won't be the same if the actors are in a studio or in some swamp in the southern US. According to him, the actors and the crew need to be in the real location to truly understand what the conquistadors went through, and audiences won't believe it's a real South American jungle if the film isn't made in one.'

Knox told Connor that Frazier had to provide an amended budget to reflect the increased costs before he would approve the location filming. Connor took the request to Frazier, who complained that the studio was weakening on its promise to support the film adequately, and added that he might be tempted to take the film to another studio if he was not allowed to film on location in South America. After a few weeks he produced an amended budget of $75 million. Knox was horrified that the budget had increased by 50 per cent in a few weeks. He told Connor that he would accept the amended budget only if two conditions were met: one, that Connor would go on the location shoot to ensure that costs stayed within the amended budget, and, two, that if the costs exceeded Frazier's estimates, Frazier would have to pay the excess himself. Frazier again complained that the studio was attempting to compromise his vision, but grudgingly accepted the modified terms.

Frazier, Connor and the cast and crew headed off to the South American jungle for a scheduled two-month shoot. Immediately it became apparent that there was more trouble.

Connor, who reported daily to Knox, told him after two weeks had passed that Frazier was shooting scenes several times over—not because the actors or the crew were making mistakes, or because there was something wrong with the scene, but because the output just didn't meet his artistic standards. This attention to detail meant that the filming schedule was nearly a week behind after only the first week's work. Also, because the filming locations were so remote, the cast and crew were spending nearly four hours of a scheduled seven-hour work day travelling to and from location, leaving only three hours in which they could work at regular pay rates. Work beyond those hours meant they had to be paid overtime, and as Frazier's demanding vision required shooting ten or twelve hours each day, the production was incurring huge overtime costs. As if that wasn't bad enough, the 'rushes' (the finished film produced each day) showed that Monaco and Jones didn't have any chemistry as a pair, and Gia Norman, the European actress Frazier had cast as the love interest, had such a heavy accent that most of her lines couldn't be understood.

SHOWDOWN IN THE JUNGLE

Knox told Connor that he was coming to the location right away to meet with Frazier. After several days of very arduous travel, Knox, Connor and Frazier met in the canvas tent that served as the director's 'office' in the middle of the jungle. Knox didn't waste any time with pleasantries. 'Mark,' he told Frazier, 'there is no way you can bring this film in for the budget you have promised or within the deadline you agreed to. John has told me how this production is being managed, and it's just not acceptable. I've done some calculations, and at the rate you are going this picture is going to cost $85 million and have a running time of four and a half hours. Big Screen is not prepared to support that. We need a film that's a commercially viable length, and we need it at a reasonable cost.'

'It needs to be as long as it is,' replied Frazier, 'because the story has to be told. And if it has to cost this much, it has to cost this much. Otherwise it will look like crap and no one will buy a ticket to see it.'

'Mark,' replied Knox, 'we are prepared to put $5 million more into this picture, and that is it. You have the choice of proceeding under those terms, and keeping John fully appraised of the costs so that he can help you stay within the budget. If you don't agree to that, you can leave the production, and we will hire another director and sue you for breach of contract.'

Frazier looked as though he was ready to walk into the jungle and head back to California that very minute, but the thought of losing his dream project was too much for him. He muttered, 'OK, I'll finish it.'

Knox returned to California, nursing several nasty mosquito bites, and Connor stayed in the jungle and reported to him regularly. Unfortunately, it didn't seem like Frazier was paying much attention to the studio's demands. Connor estimated that the shoot would run three months rather than two, and that the total cost of the shoot would be $70 million. This left only $10 million of the budget for post-production, distribution and marketing, which was almost nothing for an epic adventure. To add to Knox's problems, he got a phone call from Richard Garrison, the chairman of Big Screen's board of directors. Garrison had heard gossip about what was going on with *Conquistadors* and wanted to know what Knox was going to do to curb Frazier's excesses. Knox told Garrison that Frazier was operating under clearly understood requirements, and that Connor was on the set to monitor the costs. Unfortunately, Knox thought, Connor was doing a good job of reporting, but he didn't seem to be doing much to correct the problems he was observing.

Frazier eventually came back to California after three and a half months of shooting, and started editing the several hundred hours of film he had produced. Knox requested that Frazier permit Connor or himself to participate in the editing, but Frazier retorted that permitting that would infringe on his right to 'final cut', and refused to allow anyone associated with the studio to be in the editing room. Knox scheduled a release date for the film in six months' time, and asked the studio's publicity department to start working on an ad campaign for the film, but not much could be done on either of these tasks without at least a rough cut of the finished product.

FRAZIER'S SHIP COMES IN

Three weeks into the editing, Connor called Knox. 'I heard from Mark today,' he said. 'He wants to do some reshoots.'

'Is that a problem?' Knox asked.

'No,' said Connor. 'Most of it is interior stuff that we can do here. But he wants to add a prologue. He says that the story doesn't make sense without more development of how the two lead characters sailed from Spain to South America. He wants to hire a ship.'

'He wants to WHAT?' exclaimed Knox.

'He wants to hire a sailing ship, like the conquistadors travelled on. There's a couple of tall ships that would do, but the one he wants is in drydock in Mexico, and it would cost at least a million to make the ship seaworthy and sail it up to southern California. And that's on top of the cost of bringing the actors and crew back for a minimum of a week. I suggested to him that we try some special effects or a computerised animation for the scenes of the ship on the ocean, and shoot the shipboard scenes in the studio, but he says that won't be the same and it needs to be authentic.'

At this point Knox was ready to drive over to the editing studios and take care of Frazier himself. Instead, he called Garrison and explained the situation. 'I won't commit any more money to this without the board's approval. But we've already invested $80 million in this, so is a few more million that much of a deal if it gets the damn thing finished and gets Frazier out of our hair? If we tell him no, we'll have to basically start all over again, or just dump the whole thing and kiss $80 million goodbye.' At the other end of the line, Garrison sighed and said, 'Do whatever you have to do to get it done.'

Knox told Connor to authorise the reshoots, with a schedule of two months and the expectation that Frazier would have a rough cut of the film ready for the studio executives to view in three months. However, because of the time Frazier had already spent in editing, Knox had to change the release date, which meant changing the publicity campaign as well—and releasing the film at the same time as one of Big Screen's major competitors was releasing an epic adventure that was expected to be a sure-fire hit. However, Knox felt he had no choice. If he didn't enforce some deadline, Frazier might sit in the editing room and tinker with his dream forever.

Connor supervised the reshoots, and reported that they went as well as could be expected. The major problem was that Gia Norman had had plastic surgery on her nose after the first shoot had been completed, and looked considerably different than she had in the jungles of South America. However, creative lighting, makeup and costuming managed to minimise the change in her appearance. By all accounts, the (very expensive) sailing ship looked spectacular in the rushes, and Frazier was satisfied that his vision had been sufficiently dramatised.

ROUGH CUTS AND MORE CUTS

Amazingly, Frazier delivered the rough cut of the film at the agreed-upon time. Knox, Connor, Garrison and the rest of the studio's executives crowded into the screening room to view the realisation of Frazier's dream. Five and a half hours later, they were in shock. No one could deny that the movie looked fantastic, and that it was an epic on a grand scale, but there was no way the studio could release a film of five and a half hours commercially. Plus Frazier had agreed to produce a movie that was at most two and a half hours long. Knox was at his wits' end. He cornered Garrison in the hallway outside the screening room. 'Will you talk to Mark? He won't listen to me, he won't listen to John. But we can't release this. It won't work.' Garrison agreed, and contacted Frazier the next day. He reported back to Knox that Frazier, amazingly, had agreed to cut the film to two hours and fifteen minutes. Knox, heartened by this news,

proceeded with the previously set release date, which by now was a month away, and got the publicity campaign going.

Two days before the scheduled release date, Frazier provided an advance copy of his shortened version of *Conquistadors* for a studio screening. Knox had asked him to provide a copy sooner, but Frazier said that he could not produce anything that quickly. As a consequence, the version of the film that the studio executives were seeing for the first time was the version that had already had thousands of copies duplicated for distribution to movie theatres all across North America. In fact, those copies were on their way by courier to the theatres as the screening started.

At the end of the screening, the studio executives were stunned. Yes, the movie was shorter, but now it made no sense. Characters appeared and disappeared randomly, the plot was impossible to follow, and the dialogue did not make sense at several key points in the small parts of plot that were discernible. The film was a disaster. Several of the executives present voiced the suspicion that Frazier had deliberately edited the movie this way to get revenge on the studio for not 'respecting' his vision and forcing him to reduce the film's length. Others suggested that Frazier was simply a lunatic who never should have been given so much autonomy in the first place.

Knox, Garrison and Connor held a hastily-called meeting the next morning. What could the studio do? Recall the film and force Frazier to produce a more coherent shorter version? Recall the film and release the five-and-a-half-hour version? Or let the shorter version be released as scheduled and hope that it wouldn't be too badly received? Knox argued that the film should be recalled and Frazier should be forced to produce the product he agreed to produce. Connor said that he thought Frazier had been doing his best to do what the studio wanted, based on what Connor saw on the set, and that making Frazier cut the movie so short compromised the vision that Frazier wanted to achieve. He said the studio should release the long version and present it as a 'special cinematic event'. Garrison, as chairman of the board, listened to both sides, and after figuring out the costs of recalling and/or re-editing the film—not to mention the less tangible costs of further worsening the film's reputation—said, 'Gentlemen, we really don't have any choice. *Conquistadors* will be released tomorrow.'

Knox immediately cancelled the critics' screenings of *Conquistadors* scheduled for that afternoon, so that bad reviews would not appear on the day of the film's release. Despite that pre-emptive step and an extensive advertising campaign, *Conquistadors* was a complete and utter flop. On a total outlay of $90 million, the studio recouped less than $9 million. The reviews of the film were terrible, and audiences stayed away in droves. The only place *Conquistadors* was even close to successful was in some parts of Europe, where film critics called the edited version an example of American studios' crass obsession with making money by compromising the work of a genius. The studio attempted to capitalise on this note of hope by releasing the long version of the film for screening at some overseas film festivals and cinema appreciation societies, but the revenues from these screenings were so small that they made no difference to the overall financial results.

Three months after *Conquistadors* was released, Garrison called Knox and told him he was fired. Garrison told Knox that the board appreciated what a difficult production *Conquistadors* had been to manage, but that the costs of the production had been unchecked to a degree that the board no longer had confidence in Knox's ability to operate Big Screen Studios efficiently. Connor was offered a very generous early retirement package, and accepted it. The board then hired Bill Brosnan, a vice-president at another studio, as Knox's replacement.

After reviewing *Conquistadors'* financial records and the notes that Knox had kept throughout the production, Brosnan was determined that a disaster like this would not undermine his career as it had Knox's. But what could he do to ensure that this would not happen?

HIGH NOON AT ALPHA MILLS

By Arif Hassan and Thivagar Velayutham, International Islamic University, Malaysia

Alpha Plantations Sdn Bhd is an oil palm plantation located in Malaysia. It consists of an oil palm estate and one palm oil mill. It is a wholly owned subsidiary of a British multinational company and was founded with the purpose of supplying crude palm oil for its parent company's detergent manufacturing business. Since its formation, most of the managers have been recruited from the United Kingdom, with many British ex-soldiers and policemen joining up.

Mr Ang Siow Lee first joined the Alpha palm oil mill in 1965 at the age of fifteen as a labourer, and rose through the ranks to become the most senior non-managerial staff in Alpha. He is the senior production supervisor at the mill. His immediate superior is the mill manager and he has two junior supervisors to assist him. The mill operates on a three-shift cycle of twenty-five operators in each shift, and each supervisor (including Mr Ang) is in charge of one shift. Mr Ang is responsible for the daily palm oil processing operations. He coordinates the activities of all three shifts with the two supervisors, prepares the daily production reports, deals with short-term human resource planning issues and minor discipline issues, and sets and evaluates short-term performance targets for all three shifts. In addition, he acts as the 'gatekeeper', which means that any mill personnel who wish to see the mill manager must first see Mr Ang, who then tries to solve the problem, which may be anything from house repairs to a request for an advance on wages. Only in rare cases when Mr Ang cannot resolve the issue is the matter brought to the attention of the mill manager. Mr Ang ran a tight ship, and never let anyone forget it. His superb technical competency helped him keep the mill in top shape. He was accustomed to receiving the highest appraisal ratings from the mill manager, who appreciated his firm, methodical and almost militarily efficient way of running the mill.

The palm oil industry in Malaysia faced many challenges in 1999. World oil prices plunged due to an oversupply, and with it palm oil prices hit a fifteen-year low. This cut the profit margins of all palm oil producers and caused Alpha mill to post losses regularly.

Captain Chubb, the 54-year-old former Royal Engineer and mill manager, was at a loss as to how to improve performance. 'We are doing nothing wrong, and have met all our efficiency targets. It's this market that is killing us!' he exasperatedly explained during the annual year-end visit of the directors from London. Soon after, Captain Chubb was given

his marching orders. In early 2000 a new mill manager was appointed who was very different from all his predecessors. Mr Ian Davison, a 32-year-old who hailed from Edinburgh, Scotland, was not a career plantation engineer and had never managed an agricultural product-processing mill before. He was actually an electronics engineer with an ivy-league MBA on the fast track to a top management position. His previous appointment was as factory manager of a detergent factory in Egypt, where he managed to streamline and modernise operations and increase financial performance dramatically. Headquarters in London had high hopes that he would be able to do the same with Alpha mill and return it to profitability. His first action was to analyse operations at Alpha mill and look for ways to reduce production costs and increase profits. He arrived at the following conclusions:

- Current performance standards allowed too much machine breakdown and changeover time. Better standards were achievable with the latest technology.
- Wastage could be reduced and yield improved considerably by installing machinery based on new technology.
- Personnel numbers were too high. They could be reduced with technology and multitasking and unleashing the full potential of the workers.
- Personnel were just 'cruising along'. They were not fully committed to achieving better performance.
- Hygiene needs were not being met.
- The old colonial and hierarchical company culture was not conducive to performance improvement.
- Information was not shared across the mill. Operators knew only about their own little area in the mill and almost nothing about the company as a whole.

Mr Davison proposed to remedy the situation with the following initiatives:

- Empower operators by reorganising the shifts into self-directed production teams where the supervisors would now play the role of 'facilitators' and thereby gain commitment.
- Install new technology and automation.
- Adopt more stringent performance measures.

Mr Davison implemented and executed these initiatives by first organising an excursion to a local picnic spot for the entire factory. After the icebreakers, games and lunch, he held a briefing session on the beach, where he explained the situation Alpha mill was in and the need to make changes. He then unveiled his plan for the first time. The response was enthusiastic, although some operators privately confessed to not understanding some of the terminology their new manager used. At the end of the excursion, when there was some time allocated for feedback, Mr Ang expressed his full support for Mr Davison's plan. 'We in Alpha mill have full confidence in you, our new leader, and we assure you of our 110 per cent support to make your plan a success,' he said at the end of his speech.

When the new machinery had been installed and each shift had been reorganised into self-directed work teams, the plan was put into motion. Whenever the team faced a problem during processing and tried to find a solution using the techniques that had been taught, Mr Ang would step in after some time, issue instructions and take over the process. 'This is a simple problem. No need to waste time over it. Just do it.' His instructions were always followed and the immediate problem was always solved. However, the production team reverted to the old ways of working, and none of the expected benefits of teaming were realised. Given the new tighter performance standards and reduced manpower, the team consistently underperformed. Team meetings were one-way affairs where Mr Ang would tell everyone else what had gone wrong.

Mr Ang's response to this was to push himself harder. He was always the first to arrive and the last to leave. He would spend a lot of time troubleshooting process problems. He pushed his operators even harder, but he felt that he had less of a 'handle' on his operators now that they had direct access to the mill manager and most of their minor needs were seen to by him. Sometimes he became annoyed at his operators' mistakes and would resort to shouting and cursing, which had the immediate effect of moving people in the direction he wanted. This was in contrast to the mere glare that would have sufficed previously.

The continued poor performance of Alpha mill affected Mr Ang's mid-year appraisal rating, which fell down from 'excellent' to merely 'adequate'. During the appraisal interview, an annoyed Mr Davison bluntly told Mr Ang that he needed to understand clearly what the initiatives were all about, and that he had to let the team take some responsibility, make mistakes and learn from them. 'With your knowledge of this mill, you should be able to provide them with all the technical input they need,' he said. He also added, 'It might help if you treated our people with a little more respect. We aren't living in the 1940s anymore, you know.' Mr Ang was thunderstruck by the appraisal but did not raise any objections on the spot. He deferred to the manager's judgement and promised to do

better. He also reiterated his utmost support for Mr Davison and his plan.

After the mid-year appraisal, there was a noticeable change in Mr Ang's demeanour. He became very quiet and began to take a less active role in the daily running of the mill. He was superficially polite to the operators and answered most requests for help with 'Get the team together and discuss it among yourselves. Show the boss that you can solve it for yourselves.' At first the teams were at a loss and mill performance suffered badly, but within two weeks the team had found its feet and performance began to improve. One of Mr Ang's junior supervisors, Mr Raman, was able to coordinate between production teams to ensure that the performance gains were maintained. The effect on Mr Ang was devastating. He became withdrawn and began to drink more than usual. His presence at team meetings became a mere formality and he contributed next to nothing, taking a back seat to other team members. He spoke very little to mill personnel and became a mere shadow of his former self.

Mr Davison was very aware of the changes taking place on the mill floor. He decided that it was time to have Mr Ang removed from his position. He began to plan a reshuffle of the mill's organisation chart: Mr Ang would be promoted to the new position of mill executive, a staff position with a small pay raise. His responsibility would be to advise the mill manager on technical, quality and efficiency problems faced by the mill. He would be assigned to carry out minor improvement projects and performance audits from time to time. Mr Raman would be promoted to senior supervisor and report directly to the mill manager. Mr Ang would no longer have any line authority over the production team. This reorganisation was approved by head office and Mr Davison proceeded to lay the groundwork for the announcements and the necessary paperwork. Little did he foresee what was to follow.

Mr Ang was in the head office one morning when the personnel executive's clerk congratulated him on his imminent promotion. A surprised Mr Ang inquired further and learned of the plans that Mr Davison had in store for him. It was the final straw. He rushed back to Alpha mill just as Mr Davison was about to conduct his noon mill inspection. The confrontation was very loud, acrimonious and in public. It ended with Mr Ang being terminated for insubordination and gross misconduct.

After Mr Ang had left, Mr Davison felt that the obstacle to better commitment and morale was gone and that performance would improve greatly. He was very wrong. Team performance began to deteriorate and no amount of pep talks could improve it. He began to wonder what had gone wrong.

NOT ALL CALL CENTRES ARE THE WORKHOUSES OF THE TWENTY-FIRST CENTURY

By Julia Connell and Zeenobiyah Hannif, University of Newcastle

It has been said that if every call centre employee went on strike, business as we know it would grind to a halt. Such has been the growth of call centres throughout Australia that they were acknowledged as the fastest growing industry throughout the 1990s, with continued expansion expected for the early part of the twenty-first century. Along with this massive growth, significant discrepancies have emerged in wages and conditions, with some call centres receiving extremely negative publicity due to their management practices. Moreover, tales of mundane work and staff surveillance flourish, leaving the call centre business with a serious image problem.

This case study outlines some of the reasons why call centre turnover tends to be high, while citing examples from SalesForce, an organisation that was awarded the title of Hewitt Best Employer in 2004 and 2005 for Australia and New Zealand, beating some of Australia's Top 20 Companies in the process, an achievement that many would have believed impossible for the typical call centre.

BREAKING THE MOULD OF CALL CENTRE MANAGEMENT STRATEGIES

Situated in Carlton in Melbourne, very close to Lygon Street, SalesForce is not a typical call centre. This is evident from the moment you walk through the door. The work environment is filled with vibrant colours, from the brightly coloured streamers and balloons that hang from the ceilings, to the comfortable couches and the rainforest-inspired wall art.

This is a stark contrast to the often macabre media depictions of call centres as the satanic workhouses of the twenty-first century. Research suggests that work organisation in call centres often resembles Tayloristic production line work because of its highly simplified, controlled, repetitive and restrictive nature. The notorious 'sacrificial' HR strategy is often practised in call centres, whereby customer service representatives (CSRs) are recruited, trained and burnt out before another 'batch' are brought in for the process to begin all over again.

Turnover rates in SalesForce, however, are at an all-time low. This can largely be attributed to the workplace culture, which revolves around the three 'Fs': fun, focus and fulfilment. Geoffrey Court, Team Development Manager, says that employees should feel good about work and this requires having an open culture that is not rule-driven. In addition to providing relaxation rooms, hot-desking is avoided to enable employees to personalise their workspaces. The emphasis is placed on common sense as a means of empowering employees, and making sure that they are well prepared, confident and competent, partly due to training and partly due to the open communication policies. Such policies encourage one-on-one communication; for example, any CSR can call a 'chairs-in', whereby their colleagues roll their chairs together to share an idea or problem; as well, the more formal forums encourage two-way interaction with senior management.

Compare this with many call centres, where some of the most frequently heard complaints relate to poor employee–manager relationships, particularly where the primary focus is on minimising costs and maximising productivity through the fulfilment of various statistical measures (including the amount of time taken to answer calls, the length of time spent on each call, precision in terms of adherence to scripting, wrap-up time, and the average rate of call abandonment).

While most call centres search for people with relevant customer service or computer skills, SalesForce selects people based on their attitudes. SalesForce recruiters believe that, while skills and knowledge can be trained, the right attitude is critical. The recruitment process begins with a thirty-minute telephone interview, basically a conversation to get an idea of the candidate's phone manner and personality. If both parties are happy with the phone call, this is then followed by an in-person group interview involving both team leaders and project managers; in this way all parties can determine whether they seem to be suited to each other. SalesForce has found that it tends to attract a variety of people, as outbound selling is a gregarious activity and, unlike some other call centres, SalesForce avoids scripting where possible. CSRs come from all kinds of backgrounds, ranging from mothers with school-age children and students working on a casual basis to actors and musicians who can make work outings highly entertaining when they are encouraged to show off their creativity. Once employed, new recruits spend two days on induction, where they are immersed in the workplace culture. This involves singing the 'Rainbow Song', made famous by Kermit the Frog, and internalising the belief system of the company, which is that they can enjoy themselves at work.

The greatest training focus within SalesForce is on product knowledge, and, depending on the product and the campaign, training can take anywhere between half a day and four weeks to complete. What sets SalesForce apart from other call centres, however, is that it is a registered training organisation and offers employees twenty different training programs, known as STARS (SalesForce Training and Recognition Systems) courses, which range in focus from computer skills, time management and stress management to team leadership. This is in stark contrast to many call centres, where employees can struggle to get access to even the most basic occupational health and safety or customer service training.

Despite the 'fun' environment encouraged at SalesForce, this is an organisation that takes work seriously. With 1400 employees and contracts from leading organisations in Australia, they cannot afford not to. Matching performance with outcomes initially takes the form of what is referred to as 30/60/90 feedback, which is given after 30, 60 and 90 days of employment during the probationary phase of employment.

With 80 per cent of employees on performance-based pay, and the potential for high performers to reap significant rewards, there is a strong incentive to reach key performance indicators. In fact, SalesForce Managing Director Kevin Panozza has claimed that performance-based pay is used as the key motivator in the workplace, allowing some CSRs to earn more than twice the amount they would under the standard award that the ACTU is proposing to introduce for the industry.

Call centre work is often associated with stress and burnout, factors largely attributed to the lack of people management skills within these environments, insufficient breaks, stringent productivity targets and the emotional pressures associated with continuously dealing with customers. SalesForce actively works to counter these issues. Employees are encouraged to take breaks, and debriefing sessions are administered when necessary. Although targets are set, employees are encouraged to feel comfortable in their workspaces and to interact with their work groups and supervisors when in need of support.

SalesForce also recognises and rewards employee performance with certificates, movie tickets, days out and other gift items. The lively team culture is maintained through various events, including project team dinners, fundraising activities, and company-wide gatherings such as the SalesForce 'Away Day', an entertainment-filled day out for all employees, featuring skits, award presentations, and other activities that give all employees the opportunity to get to know each other better.

In addition, SalesForce encourages those employees who want to develop a career path. Opportunities are available in both sales and customer support, whether it be in administration, team leadership, management, teaching, coaching or other backroom functions. These are opportunities not offered in many call centres, particularly those that employ a sacrificial HR strategy. Employees in these situations find that their only means of career progression is out the door. Furthermore, according to Geoffrey Court, getting ahead in SalesForce does not depend on *who you know*, but rather on knowing *who you are*. Their booklet 'Getting Ahead' not only encourages career diversity and empowers employees with the ability to choose their career paths based on their own goals and objectives but also clearly outlines the seven key steps for career progression. A Career Passport is also available, containing a checklist to help employees take tangible steps towards planning and implementing their career choices. Some employees have been with SalesForce for over six years, which seems to indicate that these strategies are working.

PERFECT PIZZERIA

By James G. Hunt and L. Neeley, Texas Tech University

Perfect Pizzeria in Southville, deep in southern Illinois, is the chain's second-largest franchise. The headquarters is located in Phoenix, Arizona. Although the business is prospering, it has employee and managerial problems.

Each operation has one manager, an assistant manager, and from two to five night managers. The managers of each pizzeria work under an area supervisor. There are no systematic criteria for being a manager or becoming a manager trainee. The franchise has no formalised training period for the manager. No college education is required. The managers for whom the case observer worked during a four-year period were relatively young (ages 24 to 27), and only one had completed college. They came from the ranks of night managers or assistant managers. The night managers were chosen for their ability to perform the duties of the regular employees. The assistant managers worked a two-hour shift during the luncheon period five days a week to gain knowledge about bookkeeping and management. Those who became managers remained at that level unless they expressed an interest in investing in the business.

The employees were mostly college students, with a few high school students performing the less challenging jobs. Because Perfect Pizzeria was located in an area with few job opportunities, it had a relatively easy task of filling its employee quotas. All the employees, with the exception of the manager, were employed part-time. Consequently, they earned only the minimum wage.

The Perfect Pizzeria system is devised so that food and beverage costs and profits are set up according to a percentage. If the percentage of food unsold or damaged in any way is very low, the manager gets a bonus. If the percentage is high, the manager does not receive a bonus; rather, he or she receives only the normal salary.

There are many ways in which the percentage can fluctuate. Because the manager cannot be in the store twenty-four hours a day, some employees make up for their low pay cheques by helping themselves to the food. When a friend comes in to order a pizza, extra ingredients are put on the friend's pizza. Occasional nibbles by eighteen to twenty employees throughout the day at the meal table also raise the percentage figure. An occasional bucket of sauce may be spilled or a pizza accidentally burned. Sometimes the wrong size of pizza may be made.

In the event of an employee mistake or a burned pizza by the oven person, the expense is supposed to come from the individual. Because of peer pressure, the night manager seldom writes up a bill for the erring employee. Instead, the establishment takes the loss and the error goes unnoticed until the end of the month when the inventory is taken. That's when the manager finds out that the percentage is high and that there will be no bonus.

In the present instance, the manager took retaliatory measures. Previously, each employee was entitled to a free pizza, salad and all the soft drinks he or she could drink for every six hours of work. The manager raised this figure from six to twelve hours of work. However, the employees had received these six-hour benefits for a long time. Therefore, they simply took advantage of the situation whenever the manager or the assistant manager was not in the building. Although the night managers theoretically had complete control of the operation in the evenings, they did not command the respect that the manager or assistant manager did. This was because night managers received the same pay as the regular employees, could not reprimand other employees, and were basically the same age or sometimes even younger than the other employees.

Thus, apathy grew within the pizzeria. There seemed to be a further separation between the manager and his workers, who started out to be a closely knit group. The manager made no attempt to alleviate the problem, because he felt it would iron itself out. Either the employees that were dissatisfied would quit or they would be content to put up with the new regulations. As it turned out, there was a rash of employee dismissals. The manager had no problem filling the vacancies with new workers, but the loss of key personnel was costly to the business.

With the large turnover, the manager found he had to spend more time in the building, supervising and sometimes taking the place of inexperienced workers. This was in direct violation of the franchise regulation, which stated that a manager must act as a supervisor and at no time take part in the actual food preparation. Employees were now placed under strict supervision with the manager working alongside them. However, the operation no longer worked smoothly because of differences between the remaining experienced workers and the manager concerning the way in which a particular function should be performed.

After a two-month period, the manager was again free to go back to his office and leave his subordinates in charge of the entire operation. During this period, in spite of the differences between the experienced workers and the manager, the unsold or damaged food percentage had returned to the previous low level and the manager received a bonus each month. The manager felt that his problems had been resolved and that conditions would remain the same, since the new personnel had been properly trained.

It didn't take long for the new employees to become influenced by the other employees. Immediately after the manager had returned to his supervisory role, the unsold or damaged food percentage began to rise. This time the manager took a bolder step. He cut out any benefits that the employees had—no free pizzas, salads or drinks. With the job market at an even lower ebb than usual, most employees were forced to stay. The appointment of a new area supervisor made it impossible for the manager to 'work behind the counter', because the supervisor was centrally located in Southville.

The manager tried still another approach to alleviate the rising unsold or damaged food percentage and maintain his bonus. He placed a notice on the bulletin board stating that if the percentage remained at a high level a lie detector test would be given to all employees. All those found guilty of taking or purposely wasting food or drinks would be immediately terminated. This did not have the desired effect on the employees, because they knew that if they were all subjected to the test they would all be found guilty and the manager would have to dismiss all of them. This would leave him in a worse situation than ever.

Even before the following month's percentage was calculated, the manager knew it would be high. He had evidently received information from one of the night managers about the employees' feelings about the notice. What he did not expect was that the percentage would reach an all-time high. That is the state of affairs at the present time.

Source: J. E. Dittrich and R. A. Zawacki, *People and Organizations* (Plano, Texas: Business Publications, 1981), pp. 126–8. Used by permission of McGraw-Hill/Irwin.

STRATEGIC CHANGE AT COMPUTARGET

By Peter Lok, International Graduate School of Business, University of South Australia, Robert Ogulin, Macquarie University, Jo Rhodes, International Graduate School of Business, University of South Australia

CASE STUDY 7

Computarget is a global manufacturer of personal computers, printers and accessories headquartered in the United States. Its Asian sales and distribution organisation, Asdo, is responsible for the distribution of all computer product lines, including (1) printer products (including scanners), (2) personal computers, and (3) accessories (laser toner, ink cartridges, paper and other consumables). Products are sourced from different Compucom manufacturing divisions in Asia, Europe and the United States, as well as from outside suppliers. Asdo deals with roughly 12 000 stock-keeping units (SKUs) over more than thirty product lines and interfaces with over 100 retail and wholesale customers.

Sales of Computarget's products in Asia helped fuel double-digit growth rates for Computarget during the 1990s. The rapid sales growth and customers' requirements for quicker turnaround times for orders placed increasing demands on the information systems needed to manage the information related to sales and distribution of Asdo's products. Asdo relied on a host of software applications, originally developed at a number of different sites within Computarget. Some applications were developed by Computarget's Corporate IT (CIT) department centrally, some by other Computarget operating divisions and subsequently picked up by Asdo; some had been written elsewhere within Computarget but customised by Asdo, and others had been developed directly within Asdo. According to Asdo management, there were about sixty-four different applications that were part of, or interacted with, Asdo's order fulfilment process.

THE IT TRANSFORMATION CHALLENGE

As technology and markets evolved, Asdo wanted to be able to take fuller advantage of new technologies such as the Internet in order to boost order-fulfilment performance. When the existing systems were originally written, such technologies were not on the horizon or were not widely used.

Asdo's information technology (IT) hardware and software applications were part of the globally managed IT architecture and therefore organisationally belonged to the Corporate Information Technology (CIT) group. Hence, Asdo was dependent on the existing software, designed to run on an IBM mainframe computer, and regular updates by CIT, which were 'handed down' to the operating units.

Two paradigm shifts were simultaneously occurring within the industry. The first involved computer hardware. Many companies were shifting from a strict reliance on mainframe computers to the use of client-server platforms using UNIX operating systems and other distributed and open architectures.

The second paradigm shift involved systems software. A number of companies (such as SAP, Oracle, Peoplesoft and others) began specialising in Enterprise Resource Planning (ERP) packages. ERP systems, such as SAP R/3, integrate all facets of the business, including planning, manufacturing, sales and marketing. ERP helps business managers with business activities such as inventory control, order tracking, customer service, finance and human resources. As these commercial packages became more powerful, they began to offer alternatives to continued internal software development.

Due in part to these paradigm shifts, Asdo revised its approach to software development work and began looking for alternative solutions. Along with a number of other Computarget divisions, Asdo evaluated a number of commercial software systems. It also began to rethink how a software development program should be managed.

STRATEGIC DECISION AND LEADERSHIP

In late 2000 the vice-president of Operations Asia, Michael Chang, and the leadership team of Computarget decided that a workable replacement for the existing system could be achieved only by taking a radically different perspective. Michael secured an initial $2 million budget for the project and received the go-ahead from corporate headquarters. Local, regional and global top management support was enlisted for the pursuit of the project. Further support was secured from individual product groups, such as the Printer Division.

Rather than assign the project to the internal IT department, Michael decided a 'change management approach' would be more appropriate. He approached Al Miller and Peter Wang with the challenge of co-leading a change team to implement the program.

Al had previously had responsibility for some of the distribution activities surrounding the 'supplies' segment of Asdo's business. Just as importantly as his product knowledge, he brought with him his engagement style and a desire to get commitment from others. Peter came from the CIT group and contributed distinct technical knowledge as well as a desire for change in the way information and people were managed.

Michael made it clear that the project would be expected to deliver concrete results at six-month intervals. At the same time, he clearly indicated that he was totally committed to the successful implementation of the project. He would make himself available for any presentations and instructed Al and Peter to formulate a solid implementation plan. Due to the urgency of the project, a 'just do it' approach was encouraged by Michael. However, he was also aware that, in order to sustain success in this change program, the emphasis of the four Es (excite, engage, energise and educate) would need to be adopted.

IT GOVERNANCE

Although Michael obtained the funds to implement the new IT system for Computarget, he was also aware of the importance of IT governance in the organisation. With the proliferation of enterprise applications, e-business and Y2K concerns, Computarget was in constant fire-fighting mode between 1995 and 2000. During this period its IT department often made expedient, fast and loose decisions in order to stay abreast of market demand and respond to market opportunities; the emphasis was on speed of implementation rather than on IT and business alignment.

The transition from using IT as a low-value enabler to IT as fundamental to the enterprise's business processes focused the Computarget leadership on IT governance issues. IT governance is the structure of relationships and processes that direct and control the IT infrastructure to achieve the enterprise's goals.

The Computarget board recognised that developing IT governance structures within Computarget would require rethinking some central relationships: between the board and IT management, between IT management and the business units, and between the board and the business units. Without a clearly defined strategy using a recognised IT governance framework (such as CobIT or ITIL) the board risked failing in its duty to demonstrate the real value of IT investment through IT and business alignment strategies.

IMPLEMENTING THE NEW STRATEGY

Al and Peter set about assembling the core team. They particularly looked for people known for their ability to think 'outside the box', and able to think across process boundaries. Several key members came from the traditional IT group, as Al and Peter knew that the team would need technical knowledge. Yet they also felt that the team needed to be interdisciplinary and would ultimately need to look

broadly across a number of functional areas, and across multiple firms within the supply chain. Al and Peter did an initial scoping to determine the level of understanding of the new system among employees and the level of impact on their existing activities. Furthermore, interviews and focus groups were conducted to determine the level of change readiness and resistance. Early detection of the level of technical competency with the new system, and change readiness, could have a significant impact on the success of the implementation. Key change agents were selected from various departments and an initial change management team was formed with seven team members.

Another major decision made by Al and Peter was to pursue strategic partnerships with outside suppliers and users. The team was extended to include twenty full-time Asdo employees, four part-time team members from the printer factory in Shanghai, one full-time and two part-time members from the transportation company, five full-time consultants, and part-time representation from a major distributor. The full-time consultants had the expertise in change management, that is, the ability to engage employees and to involve them in the planning and implementation phases.

In spite of Michael's insistence for quick, measurable results, Al and Peter decided to spend the first two weeks in team engagement, change readiness and commitment activities, rather than immediately jumping into the details. This team-building initiative stemmed from the leaders' recognition that they were attempting to build commitment and involvement and to reduce resistance. Both the Computarget and the Asdo teams agreed on the implementation strategy and the roll-out workshop timetable to manage the implementation of the project.

Al and Peter decided to take a 'hands off' approach to team management during the implementation phase. It was their intention to encourage greater initiatives and ownership during this phase. Initially this was quite frustrating to the team leaders, as well as to team members. Employees who were used to being assigned individual tasks and being measured on their performance against those tasks faced an adjustment period. Ultimately, however, these team members bought into the thinking that better results could be achieved through involvement and collaboration, and considered each issue from all angles, rather than from just their own perspective based on their traditional job function.

THE 'FRESH ENGINEERING' APPROACH

In developing a replacement for the existing system, the implementation team eventually decided on a 'fresh engineering approach'. This technique is a clean-sheet development of processes, without regard for, or consideration of, the existing process steps. Using this fresh-engineered process, a pilot test would be run on a limited number of products and customers. Once satisfied with the pilot test results, the new process would be rolled out to other products and other customers.

The team concluded that fresh re-engineering was the only way they would be able to achieve significant gains. If the old system functions were at first merely replaced on a one-on-one basis, the team felt they would not have the same incentive to go back later and re-engineer the process to achieve the highest level of improvement.

Both technical and behavioural change workshops were conducted for all departments in order to prepare employees to use the new system. Due to the functionality and processes of the new system, minor organisational and job restructuring had to be conducted to get the maximum benefits from the new system. The affected employees were asked to redesign their own jobs to align with the new system. Although there was resistance at this stage, the level of resistance was minor and compromises were obtained as a result. Overall, the 'train the trainer' program for each department and the workshops were received positively.

THE PILOT PROJECT

As previously mentioned, a major customer had been an active participant on the implementation team and the customer was receptive to pilot testing the new system. The implementation team viewed the pilot project as a critical test of the project's potential future success.

The pilot ran for three months and the distributor attributed the following results to the new system implementation: inventory safety stock reduction of 43 per cent, and turn-around-time (TAT) reduction from twenty-eight days to nine days. Based on these numbers, the new system

was judged a major success. Michael and the leadership team agreed to continue to fund the program and asked for a roll-out plan involving other customers and other products.

The one negative factor of the pilot project was that the customer and Asdo both had to deal with two systems simultaneously. The customer was anxious to get the remainder of the products converted to the new system.

ROLL-OUT

Four options were presented as possible ways to implement, or roll-out, the new order-fulfilment system to the remainder of the customers and products:

1. Convert the remainder of the customers to using the new system for selected printer products only, followed by roll-out of other individual products such as personal computers and peripherals. This would require all customers to interface with both the existing system and the implementation system for some period of time.
2. Convert all products to the new system for selected customers only, and then sequentially convert the remainder of the customers to the new system. This would require Asdo to deal with two systems for each product, but customers would be converted in one effort.
3. Convert the remainder of products and customers simultaneously in one remaining 'big bang'.
4. Incrementally add customers, products and capabilities.

THE CHALLENGES AHEAD

Some executives at Computarget headquarters and at other operational units and factories were more supportive of the new order-fulfilment process than others. It remained to be seen how accommodating the new process would be for products where retail spikes were dramatic, and where the sales and distribution of products was complex.

Theory building and systematic research methods

PEOPLE NEED TO MAKE SENSE of their world, so they form theories about the way the world operates. A **theory** is a general set of propositions that describes interrelationships among several concepts. We form theories for the purpose of predicting and explaining the world around us.[1] What does a good theory look like? First, it should be stated as clearly and as simply as possible so that the concepts can be measured and there is no ambiguity regarding the theory's propositions. Second, the elements of the theory must be logically consistent with each other, because we cannot test anything that doesn't make sense. Finally, a good theory provides value to society; it helps people understand their world better than without the theory.[2]

Theory building is a continuous process that typically includes the inductive and deductive stages shown in Exhibit A.1.[3] The inductive stage draws on personal experience to form a preliminary theory, whereas the deductive stage uses the scientific method to test the theory.

The inductive stage of theory building involves observing the world around us, identifying a pattern of relationships, and then forming a theory from these personal observations. For example, you might casually notice that new employees want their supervisor to give direction, whereas this leadership style irritates long-service employees. From these observations, you form a theory about the effectiveness of directive leadership. (See Chapter 14 for a discussion of this leadership style.)

The theory building process

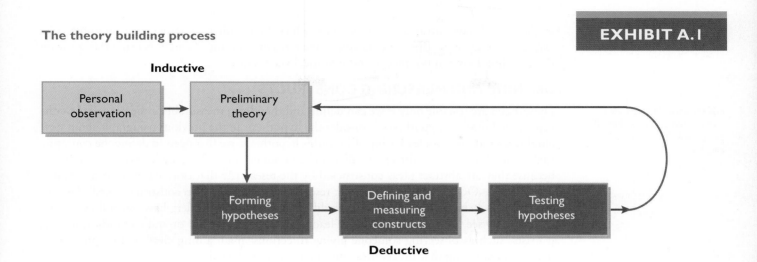

POSITIVISM VERSUS INTERPRETIVISM

Research requires an interpretation of reality, and researchers tend to perceive reality in one of two ways. A common view, called **positivism**, is that reality exists independent of people. It is 'out there' to be discovered and tested. Positivism is the foundation for most quantitative research (statistical analysis). It assumes that we can measure variables and those variables have fixed relationships with other variables. For example, the positivist perspective says that we could study whether a supportive style of leadership reduces stress. If we find evidence of this, then someone else studying leadership and stress would 'discover' the same relationship.

Interpretivism takes a different view of reality. It suggests that reality comes from shared meaning among people in that environment. For example, supportive leadership is a personal interpretation of reality, not something that can be measured across time and people. Interpretivists rely mainly on qualitative data, such as observation and non-directive interviews. They particularly listen to the language people use to understand the common meaning that people have towards various events or phenomena. For example, they might argue that you need to experience and observe supportive leadership to effectively study it. Moreover, you can't really predict relationships because the specific situation shapes reality.[4]

Most OB scholars identify themselves somewhere between the extreme views of positivism and interpretivism. Many believe that inductive research should begin with an interpretivist angle. We should enter a new topic with an open mind and search for shared meaning of people in that situation. In other words, researchers should let the participants define reality rather than let their (the researchers') preconceived notions shape that reality. This process involves gathering qualitative information and letting this information shape their theory.[5] After the theory emerges, researchers shift to a positivist perspective by quantitatively testing relationships in that theory.

THEORY TESTING: THE DEDUCTIVE PROCESS

Once a theory has been formed, we shift into the deductive stage of theory building. This process includes forming hypotheses, defining and measuring constructs, and testing hypotheses (see Exhibit A.1). **Hypotheses** make empirically testable declarations that certain variables and their corresponding measures are related in a specific way proposed by the theory. For instance, to find support for the directive leadership theory described earlier, we need to form and then test a specific hypothesis from that theory. One such hypothesis might be: 'New

positivism A view held in quantitative research in which reality exists independent of the perceptions and interpretations of people.

interpretivism The view held in many qualitative studies that reality comes from shared meaning among people in that environment.

hypotheses Statements making empirically testable declarations that certain variables and their corresponding measures are related in a specific way proposed by the theory.

employees are more satisfied with supervisors who exhibit a directive rather than a non-directive leadership style.' Hypotheses are indispensable tools of scientific research, because they provide the vital link between the theory and empirical verification.

DEFINING AND MEASURING CONSTRUCTS

constructs Abstract ideas constructed by researchers that can be linked to observable information.

Hypotheses are testable only if we can define and then form measurable indicators of the concepts stated in those hypotheses. Consider the hypothesis in the previous paragraph about new employees and directive leadership. To test this hypothesis, we first need to define the concepts, such as 'new employees', 'directive leadership' and 'supervisor'. These are known as **constructs**, because they are abstract ideas constructed by the researcher that can be linked to observable information. Organisational behaviour researchers developed the construct called *directive leadership* to help them understand the different effects that leaders have on followers. We can't directly see, taste or smell directive leadership; instead, we rely on indirect indicators that it exists, such as observing someone giving directions, maintaining clear performance standards, and ensuring that procedures and practices are followed.

As you can see, defining constructs well is very important, because these definitions become the foundation for finding or developing acceptable measures of those constructs. We can't measure directive leadership if we have only a vague idea about what the concept means. The better the definition is, the better our chances are of applying a measure that adequately represents that construct. However, even with a good definition, constructs can be difficult to measure, because the empirical representation must capture several elements in the definition. A measure of directive leadership must be able to identify not only people who give directions but also those who maintain performance standards and ensure that procedures are followed.

TESTING HYPOTHESES

The third step in the deductive process is to collect data for the empirical measures of the variables. Following the directive leadership example, we might conduct a formal survey in which new employees indicate the behaviour of their supervisors and their attitudes towards their supervisor. Alternatively, we might design an experiment in which people work with someone who applies either a directive or a non-directive leadership style. When the data have been collected, we can use various procedures to statistically test our hypotheses.

A major concern in theory building is that some researchers might inadvertently find support for their theory simply because they use the same information used to form the theory during the inductive stage. Consequently, the deductive stage must collect new data that are completely independent of the data used during the inductive stage. For instance, you might decide to test your theory of directive leadership by studying employees in another organisation. Moreover, the inductive process may have relied mainly on personal observation, whereas the deductive process might use survey questionnaires. By studying different samples and using different measurement tools, we minimise the risk of conducting circular research.

USING THE SCIENTIFIC METHOD

scientific method A set of principles and procedures that help researchers to systematically understand previously unexplained events and conditions.

Earlier, it was said that the deductive stage of theory building follows the scientific method. The **scientific method** is a systematic, controlled, empirical and critical investigation of hypothetical propositions about the presumed relationships among natural phenomena.[6] There are several elements to this definition, so let's look at each one. First, scientific research is systematic and controlled, because researchers want to rule out all but one explanation for a set of interrelated events. To rule out alternative explanations, we need to control them in some way, such as by keeping them constant or removing them entirely from the environment.

Second, scientific research is said to be empirical because researchers need to use objective reality—or as close as they can get to it—to test theory. They measure observable elements of the environment, such as what a person says or does, rather than rely on their own subjective opinion to draw conclusions. Moreover, scientific research analyses these data using acceptable principles of mathematics and logic.

Finally, scientific research involves critical investigation. This means that the study's hypotheses, data, methods and results are openly described so that other experts in the field can properly evaluate this research. It also means that scholars are encouraged to critique and build on previous research. Eventually, the scientific method encourages the refinement and eventually the replacement of a particular theory with one that better suits our understanding of the world.

GROUNDED THEORY: AN ALTERNATIVE APPROACH

The scientific method dominates the positivist approach to systematic research, but another approach, called **grounded theory**, dominates research using qualitative methods.[7] Grounded theory is a process of developing knowledge through the constant interplay of data collection, analysis and theory development. It relies mainly on qualitative methods to form categories and variables, to analyse relationships among these concepts, and to form a model based on the observations and analysis. Grounded theory combines the inductive stages of theory development by cycling back and forth between data collection and analysis to converge on a robust explanatory model. This ongoing reciprocal process results in theory that is grounded in the data (thus, the name 'grounded' theory).

Like the scientific method, grounded theory is a systematic and rigorous process of data collection and analysis. It requires specific steps and documentation, and adopts a positivist view by assuming that the results are generalisable to other settings. However, grounded theory also takes an interpretivist view by building categories and variables from the perceived realities of the subjects rather than from an assumed universal truth.[8] It also recognises that personal biases are not easily removed from the research process.

grounded theory A process of developing theory through the constant interplay between data gathering and the development of theoretical concepts.

SELECTED ISSUES IN ORGANISATIONAL BEHAVIOUR RESEARCH

There are many issues to consider in theory building, particularly when we use the deductive process to test hypotheses. Some of the more important issues are sampling, causation and ethical practices in organisational research.

SAMPLING IN ORGANISATIONAL RESEARCH

When trying to find out why things happen in organisations, we typically gather information from a few sources and then draw conclusions about the larger population. If we survey several employees and determine that older employees are more loyal to their company, we would like to generalise this statement to all older employees in our population, not just those whom we surveyed. Scientific inquiry generally requires researchers to engage in **representative sampling**— that is, sampling a population in such a way that we can extrapolate the results of that sample to the larger population.

One factor that influences representativeness is whether the sample is selected in an unbiased way from the larger population. Let's suppose that you want to study organisational commitment among employees in your organisation. A casual procedure might result in sampling too few employees from the head office and too many located elsewhere in the country. If head office employees actually have higher loyalty than employees located elsewhere, the biased sampling would cause the results to underestimate the true level of loyalty among employees in the company. If you repeat the process again next year but somehow overweight employees from the head office, the results might wrongly suggest that employees have

representative sampling The process of sampling a population in such a way that one can extrapolate the results of that sample to the larger population.

increased their organisational commitment over the past year. In reality, the only change may be the direction of sampling bias.

How do we minimise sampling bias? The answer is to randomly select the sample. A randomly drawn sample gives each member of the population an equal probability of being chosen, so there is less likelihood that a subgroup within that population dominates the study's results.

The same principle applies to random assignment of subjects to groups in experimental designs. If we want to test the effects of a team development training program, we need to randomly place some employees in the training group and randomly place others in a group that does not receive training. Without this random selection, each group might have different types of employees, so we wouldn't know whether the training explains the differences between the two groups. Moreover, if employees respond differently to the training program, we couldn't be sure that the training program results are representative of the larger population. Of course, random sampling does not necessarily produce a perfectly representative sample, but we do know that this is the best approach to ensure unbiased selection.

The other factor that influences representativeness is sample size. Whenever we select a portion of the population, there will be some error in our estimate of the population values. The larger the sample, the less error will occur in our estimate. Let's suppose that you want to find out how employees in a 500-person firm feel about smoking in the workplace. If you asked 400 of those employees, the information would provide a very good estimate of how the entire workforce in that organisation feels. If you survey only 100 employees, the estimate might deviate more from the true population. If you ask only ten people, the estimate could be quite different from what all 500 employees feel.

Notice that sample size goes hand in hand with random selection. You must have a sufficiently large sample size for the principle of randomisation to work effectively. In the example of attitudes towards smoking, we would do a poor job of random selection if our sample consisted of only ten employees from the 500-person organisation. The reason is that these ten people probably wouldn't capture the diversity of employees throughout the organisation. In fact, the more diverse the population, the larger the sample size should be, to provide adequate representation through random selection.

CAUSATION IN ORGANISATIONAL RESEARCH

Theories present notions about relationships among constructs. Often, these propositions suggest a causal relationship, namely, that one variable has an effect on another variable. When discussing causation, we refer to variables as being independent or dependent. Independent variables are the presumed causes of dependent variables, which are the presumed effects. In the earlier example of directive leadership, the main independent variable (there might be others) would be the supervisor's directive or non-directive leadership style, because we presume that it causes the dependent variable (satisfaction with supervision).

In laboratory experiments (described later), the independent variable is always manipulated by the experimenter. In the research on directive leadership, we might have subjects (new employees) work with supervisors who exhibit directive or non-directive leadership behaviours. If subjects are more satisfied under the directive leaders, we would be able to infer an association between the independent and dependent variables.

Researchers must satisfy three conditions to provide sufficient evidence of causality between two variables.[9] The first condition of causality is that the variables are empirically associated with each other. An association exists whenever one measure of a variable changes systematically with a measure of another variable. This condition of causality is the easiest to satisfy, because there are several well-known statistical measures of association. A research study might find, for instance, that heterogeneous groups (in which members come from diverse backgrounds) produce more creative solutions to problems. This might be apparent because the measure of creativity (such as number of creative solutions produced within a fixed time) is higher for teams that have a high score on the measure of group heterogeneity. They are statistically associated or correlated with each other.

The second condition of causality is that the independent variable precedes the dependent variable in time. Sometimes, this condition is satisfied through simple logic. In the group heterogeneity example, it doesn't make sense to say that the number of creative solutions caused the group's heterogeneity, because the group's heterogeneity existed before it produced the creative solutions. In other situations, however, the temporal relationship between variables is less clear. One example is the ongoing debate about job satisfaction and organisational commitment. Do companies develop more loyal employees by increasing their job satisfaction, or do changes in organisational loyalty cause changes in job satisfaction? Simple logic does not answer these questions; instead, researchers must use sophisticated longitudinal studies to build up evidence of a temporal relationship between the two variables.

The third requirement for evidence of a causal relationship is that the statistical association between two variables cannot be explained by a third variable. There are many associations that we quickly dismiss as being causally related. For example, there is a statistical association between the number of storks in an area and the birth rate in that area. We know that storks don't bring babies, so something else must cause the association between these two variables. The real explanation is that both storks and birth rates have a higher incidence in rural areas.

In other studies, the third variable effect is less apparent. Many years ago, before polio vaccines were available, a study in the United States reported a surprisingly strong association between consumption of a certain soft drink and the incidence of polio. Was polio caused by drinking this beverage, or did people with polio have an unusual craving for it? Neither. Both polio and consumption of the soft drink were caused by a third variable: climate. There was a higher incidence of polio in the summer months and in warmer climates, and people drink more liquids in these climates.[10] As you can see from this example, researchers have a difficult time supporting causal inferences, because third-variable effects are sometimes difficult to detect.

ETHICS IN ORGANISATIONAL RESEARCH

Organisational behaviour researchers need to abide by the ethical standards of the society in which the research is conducted. One of the most important ethical considerations is the individual subject's freedom to participate in the study. For example, it is inappropriate to force employees to fill out a questionnaire or attend an experimental intervention for research purposes only. Moreover, researchers have an obligation to tell potential subjects about any potential risks inherent in the study so that participants can make an informed choice about whether or not to be involved.

Finally, researchers must be careful to protect the privacy of those who participate in the study. This usually includes letting people know when they are being studied as well as guaranteeing that their individual information will remain confidential (unless publication of identities is otherwise granted). Researchers maintain anonymity through careful security of data. The research results usually aggregate data in numbers large enough that they do not reveal the opinions or characteristics of any specific individual. For example, the average absenteeism of employees in a department would be reported rather than the absence rates of each person. When sharing data with other researchers, it is usually necessary to specially code each case so that individual identities are not known.

RESEARCH DESIGN STRATEGIES

So far, this appendix has described how to build a theory, including the specific elements of empirically testing that theory within the standards of scientific inquiry. But what are the different ways to design a research study so that we get the data necessary to achieve our research objectives? There are many strategies, but they mainly fall under three headings: laboratory experiments, field surveys and observational research.

LABORATORY EXPERIMENTS

A **laboratory experiment** is any research study in which independent variables and variables outside the researcher's main focus of inquiry can be controlled to some extent. Laboratory experiments are usually located outside the everyday work environment, such as a classroom, a simulation lab, or any other artificial setting in which the researcher can manipulate the environment. Organisational behaviour researchers sometimes conduct experiments in the workplace (called *field experiments*) in which the independent variable is manipulated. However, the researcher has less control over the effects of extraneous factors in field experiments than in laboratory situations.

Advantages of laboratory experiments

There are many advantages of laboratory experiments. By definition, this research method offers a high degree of control over extraneous variables that would otherwise confound the relationships being studied. Suppose we wanted to test the effects of directive leadership on the satisfaction of new employees. One concern might be that employees are influenced by how much leadership is provided, not just the type of leadership style. An experimental design would allow us to control how often the supervisor exhibited this style so that this extraneous variable did not confound the results.

A second advantage of lab studies is that the independent and dependent variables can be developed more precisely than in a field setting. For example, the researcher can ensure that supervisors in a lab study apply specific directive or non-directive behaviours, whereas real-life supervisors would use a more complex mixture of leadership behaviours. By using more precise measures, we are more certain that we are measuring the intended construct. Thus, if new employees are more satisfied with supervisors in the directive leadership condition, we are more confident that the independent variable was directive leadership rather than some other leadership style.

A third benefit of laboratory experiments is that the independent variable can be distributed more evenly among participants. In the directive leadership study, we can ensure that approximately half of the subjects have a directive supervisor, whereas the other half have a non-directive supervisor. In natural settings, we might have trouble finding people who have worked with a non-directive leader, and consequently we would be unable to determine the effects of this condition.

Disadvantages of laboratory experiments

With these powerful advantages, you might wonder why laboratory experiments are the least appreciated form of organisational behaviour research.[11] One obvious limitation of this research method is that it lacks realism, and consequently the results might be different in the real world. One argument is that laboratory experiment subjects are less involved than their counterparts in an actual work situation. This is sometimes true, although many lab studies have highly motivated participants. Another criticism is that the extraneous variables controlled in the lab setting might produce a different effect of the independent variable on the dependent variables. This might also be true, but remember that the experimental design controls variables in accordance with the theory and its hypotheses. Consequently, this concern is really a critique of the theory, not the lab study.

Finally, there is the well-known problem that participants are aware that they are being studied and this causes them to act differently from how they normally would. Some participants try to figure out how the researcher wants them to behave and then deliberately try to act that way. Other participants try to upset the experiment by doing just the opposite of what they believe the researcher expects. Still others might act unnaturally simply because they know they are being observed. Fortunately, experimenters are well aware of these potential problems and are usually (although not always) successful at disguising the study's true intent.

FIELD SURVEYS

Field surveys collect and analyse information in a natural environment—an office, a factory or other existing location. The researcher takes a snapshot of reality and tries to determine whether elements of that situation (including the attitudes and behaviours of people in that situation) are associated with each other as hypothesised. Everyone does some sort of field research. You might think that people from some states are better drivers than others, so you 'test' your theory by looking at the way people with out-of-state licence plates drive. Although your methods of data collection might not satisfy scientific standards, this is a form of field research because it takes information from a naturally occurring situation.

field surveys A research design strategy that involves collecting and analysing information in a natural environment, such as an office, a factory or other existing location.

Advantages and disadvantages of field surveys

One advantage of field surveys is that the variables often have a more powerful effect than they would in a laboratory experiment. Consider the effect of peer pressure on the behaviour of members within the team. In a natural environment, team members would form very strong cohesive bonds over time, whereas a researcher would have difficulty replicating this level of cohesiveness and corresponding peer pressure in a lab setting.

Another advantage of field surveys is that the researcher can study many variables simultaneously, thereby permitting a fuller test of more complex theories. Ironically, this is also a disadvantage of field surveys, because it is difficult for the researcher to contain his or her scientific inquiry. There is a tendency to shift from deductive hypothesis testing to more inductive exploratory browsing through the data. If these two activities become mixed together, the researcher can lose sight of the strict covenants of scientific inquiry.

The main weakness with field surveys is that it is very difficult to satisfy the conditions for causal conclusions. One reason is that the data are usually collected at one point in time, so the researcher must rely on logic to decide whether the independent variable really preceded the dependent variable. Contrast this with the lab study in which the researcher can usually be confident that the independent variable was applied before the dependent variable occurred. Increasingly, organisational behaviour studies use longitudinal research to provide a better indicator of temporal relations among variables, but this is still not as precise as the lab setting. Another reason why causal analysis is difficult in field surveys is that extraneous variables are not controlled as they are in lab studies. Without this control, there is a higher chance that a third variable might explain the relationship between the hypothesised independent and dependent variables.

OBSERVATIONAL RESEARCH

In their study of brainstorming and creativity, Robert Sutton and Andrew Hargadon observed twenty-four brainstorming sessions at IDEO, a product design firm in Palo Alto, California. They also attended a dozen 'Monday morning meetings', conducted sixty semi-structured interviews with IDEO executives and designers, held hundreds of informal discussions with these people, and read through several dozen magazine articles about the company.[12]

Sutton and Hargadon's use of observational research and other qualitative methods was quite appropriate for their research objectives, which were to re-examine the effectiveness of brainstorming beyond the number of ideas generated. Observational research generates a wealth of descriptive accounts about the drama of human existence in organisations. It is a useful vehicle for learning about the complex dynamics of people and their activities, such as brainstorming. (The results of Sutton and Hargadon's study are discussed in Chapter 10.)

Participant observation takes the observation method one step further by having the observer take part in the organisation's activities. This experience gives the researcher a fuller understanding of the activities than he or she would gain through just watching others participate in those activities.

In spite of its intuitive appeal, observational research has a number of weaknesses. The main problem is that the observer is subject to the perceptual screening and organising biases that are discussed in Chapter 3 of this textbook. There is a tendency to overlook the routine aspects of organisational life, even though they may prove to be the most important data for research purposes. Instead, observers tend to focus on unusual information, such as activities that deviate from what the observer expects. Because observational research usually records only what the observer notices, valuable information is often lost.

Another concern with the observation method is that the researcher's presence and involvement may influence the people that are being studied. This can be a problem in short-term observations, but in the long term people tend to return to their usual behaviour patterns. With ongoing observations, such as Sutton and Hargadon's study of brainstorming sessions at IDEO, employees eventually forget that they are being studied.

Finally, observation is usually a qualitative process, so it is more difficult to empirically test hypotheses with the data. Instead, observational research provides rich information for the inductive stages of theory building. It helps us to form ideas about the way things work in organisations. We begin to see relationships that lay the foundation for new perspectives and theory. We must not confuse this inductive process of theory building with the deductive process of theory testing.

KEY TERMS

constructs p. 548
field surveys p. 553
grounded theory p. 549
hypotheses p. 547

interpretivism p. 547
laboratory experiment p. 552
positivism p. 547
representative sampling p. 549

scientific method p. 548
theory p. 546

NOTES

1   F. N. Kerlinger, *Foundations of Behavioral Research* (New York: Holt, Rinehart & Winston, 1964), 11.

2   J. B. Miner, *Theories of Organizational Behavior* (Hinsdale, Ill.: Dryden, 1980), 7–9.

3. J. B. Miner, *Theories of Organizational Behavior*, 6–7.

4. J. Mason, *Qualitative Researching* (London: Sage, 1996).

5   A. Strauss and J. Corbin (eds), *Grounded Theory in Practice* (London: Sage Publications, 1997); B. G. Glaser and A. Strauss, *The Discovery of Grounded Theory: Strategies for Qualitative Research* (Chicago: Aldine Publishing Co, 1967).

6   Kerlinger, *Foundations of Behavioral Research*, 13.

7   A. Strauss and J. Corbin (eds), *Grounded Theory in Practice*; B. G. Glaser and A. Strauss, *The Discovery of Grounded Theory: Strategies for Qualitative Research*.

8   W. A. Hall and P. Callery, 'Enhancing the Rigor of Grounded Theory: Incorporating Reflexivity and Relationality', *Qualitative Health Research*, 11 (March 2001), 257–72.

9   P. Lazarsfeld, *Survey Design and Analysis* (New York: The Free Press, 1955).

10 This example is cited in D. W. Organ and T. S. Bateman, *Organizational Behavior*, 4th edn (Homewood, Ill.: Irwin, 1991), 42.

11 D. W. Organ and T. S. Bateman, *Organizational Behavior*, 45.

12 R. I. Sutton and A. Hargadon, 'Brainstorming Groups in Context: Effectiveness in a Product Design Firm', *Administrative Science Quarterly*, 41 (1996), 685–718.

Scoring keys for self-assessment activities

The following pages provide scoring keys for self-assessments that are fully presented in this textbook. Most (although not all) of these self-assessments, as well as the self-assessments that are summarised in this book, are scored on the student CD.

CHAPTER 2

SCORING KEY FOR SELF-MONITORING SCALE

SCORING INSTRUCTIONS: Use the table below to assign numbers to each box you checked. Insert the number for each statement on the appropriate line below the table. For example, if you checked 'Somewhat false' for statement no. 1 ('In social situations, I have the ability…'), you would write a '2' on the line with '(1)' underneath it. After assigning numbers for all thirteen statements, add up your scores to estimate your self-monitoring personality.

For statement items 1, 2, 3, 4, 5, 6, 7, 8, 10, 11, 13		For statement items 9, 12	
Very true	= 6	Very true	= 1
Somewhat true	= 5	Somewhat true	= 2
Slightly more true than false	= 4	Slightly more true than false	= 3
Slightly more false than true	= 3	Slightly more false than true	= 4
Somewhat false	= 2	Somewhat false	= 5
Very false	= 1	Very false	= 6

Sensitive to expressive behaviour of others

$$\underline{\quad}_{(2)} + \underline{\quad}_{(4)} + \underline{\quad}_{(5)} + \underline{\quad}_{(6)} + \underline{\quad}_{(8)} + \underline{\quad}_{(11)} = \underline{\quad}_{(A)}$$

Ability to modify self-presentation

$$\underline{\quad}_{(1)} + \underline{\quad}_{(3)} + \underline{\quad}_{(7)} + \underline{\quad}_{(9)} + \underline{\quad}_{(10)} + \underline{\quad}_{(12)} + \underline{\quad}_{(13)} = \underline{\quad}_{(B)}$$

Self-monitoring total score

$$\underline{\quad}_{(A)} + \underline{\quad}_{(B)} = \underline{\quad}_{Total}$$

INTERPRETING YOUR SCORE: Self-monitoring consists of two dimensions: (a) sensitivity to expressive behaviour of others and (b) ability to modify self-presentation. These two dimensions as well as the total score are defined in the following table, along with the range of scores for high, medium and low levels of each scale.

Self-monitoring dimension and definition	Score interpretation	
Sensitive to expressive behaviour of others: This scale indicates the extent to which you are aware of the feelings and perceptions of others, as expressed by their facial expressions, subtle statements and other behaviours.	High: Medium: Low:	25 to 36 18 to 24 Below 18
Ability to modify self-presentation: This scale indicates the extent to which you are adept at modifying your behaviour in a way that is most appropriate for the situation or social relationship.	High: Medium: Low:	30 to 42 21 to 29 Below 21
Self-monitoring total: Self-monitoring refers to an individual's level of sensitivity to the expressive behaviour of others and the ability to adapt appropriately to these situational cues.	High: Medium: Low:	55 to 78 39 to 54 Below 39

CHAPTER 3

SCORING KEY FOR ASSESSING YOUR PERSONAL NEED FOR STRUCTURE

SCORING INSTRUCTIONS: Use the table below to assign numbers to each box you checked. Insert the number for each statement on the appropriate line below the table. For example, if you checked 'Moderately disagree' for statement no. 3 ('I enjoy being spontaneous'), you would assign a '5' to that statement. After assigning numbers for all twelve statements, add up your scores to estimate your personal need for structure.

For statement items 1, 5, 6, 7, 8, 9, 10, 12		For statement items 2, 3, 4, 11	
Strongly agree	= 6	Strongly agree	= 1
Moderately agree	= 5	Moderately agree	= 2
Slightly agree	= 4	Slightly agree	= 3
Slightly disagree	= 3	Slightly disagree	= 4
Moderately disagree	= 2	Moderately disagree	= 5
Strongly disagree	= 1	Strongly disagree	= 6

INTERPRETING YOUR SCORE: Some people need to 'make sense' of things around them more quickly or completely than do other people. This personal need for perceptual structure relates to selective attention as well as perceptual organisation and interpretation. For instance, people with a strong personal need for closure might form first impressions, fill in missing pieces, and rely on stereotyping more quickly than people who don't mind incomplete perceptual situations.

This scale, called the personal need for structure (PNS) scale, assesses the degree to which people are motivated to structure their world in a simple and unambiguous way. Scores range from 12 to 72, with higher scores indicating a high personal need for structure. PNS norms vary from one group to the next. For instance, a study of Finnish nurses reported a mean PNS score of 34, whereas a study of 236 male and 303 female undergraduate psychology students in the United States had a mean score of 42. The norms in the following table are based on scores from these undergraduate students.

Personal need for structure scale	Interpretation
58 to 72	High need for personal structure
47 to 57	Above-average need for personal structure
38 to 46	Average need for personal structure
27 to 37	Below-average need for personal structure
12 to 26	Low need for personal structure

CHAPTER 4

SCORING KEY FOR COLLEGE OR UNIVERSITY COMMITMENT SCALE

SCORING INSTRUCTIONS: Use the table below to assign numbers to each box you checked. Insert the number for each statement on the appropriate line below the table. For example, if you checked 'Moderately disagree' for statement no. 1 ('I would be very happy…'), you would write a '2' on the line with '(1)' underneath it. After assigning numbers for all twelve statements, add up your scores to estimate your affective and continuance commitment.

For statement items 1, 2, 3, 4, 6, 8, 10, 11, 12		For statement items 5, 7, 9	
Strongly agree	= 7	Strongly agree	= 1
Moderately agree	= 6	Moderately agree	= 2
Slightly agree	= 5	Slightly agree	= 3
Neutral	= 4	Neutral	= 4
Slightly disagree	= 3	Slightly disagree	= 5
Moderately disagree	= 2	Moderately disagree	= 6
Strongly disagree	= 1	Strongly disagree	= 7

Affective commitment

$$\frac{\quad}{(1)} + \frac{\quad}{(3)} + \frac{\quad}{(5)} + \frac{\quad}{(7)} + \frac{\quad}{(9)} + \frac{\quad}{(11)} = \underline{\qquad}$$

Continuance commitment

$$\frac{\quad}{(2)} + \frac{\quad}{(4)} + \frac{\quad}{(6)} + \frac{\quad}{(8)} + \frac{\quad}{(10)} + \frac{\quad}{(12)} = \underline{\qquad}$$

INTERPRETING YOUR AFFECTIVE COMMITMENT SCORE: This scale measures both affective commitment and continuance commitment. Affective commitment refers to a person's emotional attachment to, identification with and involvement in a particular organisation. In this scale, the organisation is the college or university you are attending as a student. How high or low is your affective commitment? The ideal would be to compare your score with the collective results of other students in your class. You can also compare your score with the following results, which are based on a sample of employees.

Affective commitment score	Interpretation
Above 37	High level of affective commitment
32 to 36	Above-average level of affective commitment
28 to 31	Average level of affective commitment
20 to 27	Below-average level of affective commitment
Below 20	Low level of affective commitment

INTERPRETING YOUR CONTINUANCE COMMITMENT SCORE: Continuance commitment occurs when employees believe it is in their own personal interest to remain with the organisation. People with a high continuance commitment have a strong calculative bond with the organisation. In this scale, the organisation is the college or university you are attending as a student. How high or low is your continuance commitment? The ideal would be to compare your score with the collective results of other students in your class. You can also compare your score with the following results, which are based on a sample of employees.

Continuance commitment score	Interpretation
Above 32	High level of continuance commitment
26 to 31	Above-average level of continuance commitment
21 to 25	Average level of continuance commitment
13 to 20	Below-average level of continuance commitment
Below 13	Low level of continuance commitment

CHAPTER 5

SCORING KEY FOR EQUITY SENSITIVITY

SCORING INSTRUCTIONS: To score this scale, called the equity preference questionnaire (EPQ), complete the three steps below:

Step 1: Write your circled numbers for the items indicated below and add them up.

$$\frac{}{(1)} + \frac{}{(2)} + \frac{}{(3)} + \frac{}{(4)} + \frac{}{(5)} + \frac{}{(6)} + \frac{}{(7)} + \frac{}{(10)} = \frac{}{\text{Subtotal A}}$$

Step 2: The remaining items in the equity preference questionnaire need to be reverse-scored. To calculate a reverse score, subtract the direct score from 6. For example, if you circled 4 in one of these items, the reverse score would be 2 (i.e. 6 − 4 = 2). If you circled 1, the reverse score would be 5 (i.e. 6 − 1 = 5). Calculate the *reverse score* for each of the items indicated below and write them in the space provided. Then calculate Subtotal B by adding up these reverse scores.

$$\frac{}{(8)} + \frac{}{(9)} + \frac{}{(11)} + \frac{}{(12)} + \frac{}{(13)} + \frac{}{(14)} + \frac{}{(15)} + \frac{}{(16)} = \frac{}{\text{Subtotal B}}$$

Step 3: Calculate the total score by summing Subtotal A and Subtotal B.

$$\frac{}{\text{(Subtotal A)}} + \frac{}{\text{(Subtotal B)}} = \frac{}{\text{TOTAL}}$$

INTERPRETING YOUR SCORE: The equity preference questionnaire measures the extent to which you are a 'benevolent', an 'equity sensitive' or an 'entitled'. Generally, people who score as follows fall into one of these categories:

EPQ score	Equity preference category
59 to 80	Benevolents: they are tolerant of situations where they are under-rewarded.
38 to 58	Equity sensitives: they want an outcome/input ratio equal to the ratio of the comparison other.
16 to 37	Entitleds: they want to receive proportionately more than others (i.e. like to be over-rewarded).

CHAPTER 6

SCORING KEY FOR THE MONEY ATTITUDE SCALE

SCORING INSTRUCTIONS: This instrument presents three dimensions with a smaller set of items from the original money attitude scale. To calculate your score on each dimension, write the number that you circled in the scale to the corresponding item number in the scoring key below. For example, write the number you circled in the scale's first statement ('I sometimes purchase things…') on the line above 'Item 1'. Then add up the numbers for that dimension. The total score is calculated by adding up all scores an all dimensions.

Money attitude dimension	Calculation	Your score
Money as power/prestige	___ + ___ + ___ + ___ = Item 1 Item 4 Item 7 Item 10	_____
Retention time	___ + ___ + ___ + ___ = Item 2 Item 5 Item 8 Item 11	_____
Money anxiety	___ + ___ + ___ + ___ = Item 3 Item 6 Item 9 Item 12	_____
Money attitude total	Add up all dimension scores =	_____

INTERPRETING YOUR SCORE: The three money attitude scale dimensions measured here, as well as the total score, are defined as follows:

Money as power/prestige:
People with higher scores on this dimension tend to use money to influence and impress others.
Retention time:
People with higher scores on this dimension tend to be careful financial planners.
Money anxiety:
People with higher scores on this dimension tend to view money as a source of anxiety.
Money attitude total:
This is a general estimate of how much respect and attention you give to money.

The following table shows how a sample of Australian MBA students scored on the money attitude scale. The table shows percentiles, that is, the percentage of people with the same or lower score. For example, the table indicates that a score of '12' on the retention scale is quite low, because only 20 per cent of students would have scored at this level or lower (80 per cent scored higher). However, a score of '12' on the prestige scale is quite high, because 80 per cent of students scored at or below this number (only 20 per cent scored higher).

Percentile (% with scores at or below this number)	Prestige score	Retention score	Anxiety score	Total money score
Average score	9.89	14.98	12.78	37.64
Highest score	17	20	18	53
90	13	18	16	44
80	12	17	15	42

continued ▶

Percentile (% with scores at or below this number)	Prestige score	Retention score	Anxiety score	Total money score
70	11	17	14	40
60	10	16	14	39
50	10	15	13	38
40	9	14	12	36
30	8	14	11	34
20	7	12	10	32
10	7	11	8	29
Lowest score	4	8	6	23

CHAPTER 7

SCORING KEY FOR THE CONNOR–DAVIDSON RESILIENCE SCALE

SCORING INSTRUCTIONS: To calculate your score on the Connor–Davidson Resilience Scale, use the following guideline to assign numbers to each box you checked:

0 = Not at all true
1 = Rarely true
2 = Sometimes true
3 = Often true
4 = True nearly all of the time

INTERPRETING YOUR SCORE: Resilience is the capacity of individuals to cope successfully in the face of significant change, adversity or risk. Everyone has some resiliency; it occurs every time we pull through stressful experiences. While everyone needs to recuperate to some extent following a stressful experience, people with high resilience are better able to maintain an equilibrium and, consequently, have lost little ground in the first place. The Connor–Davidson Resilience Scale was recently developed to estimate your level of resilience. Scores range from 0 to 100. Preliminary studies indicate that people with post-traumatic stress disorder score much lower (average score of 48) than primary health care outpatients (average score of 72), who score lower than the general population (average score of 80). The table below allows you to compare your score against the results of 577 people in the general population of the United States.

Resilience score	Interpretation
92 to 100	Top 20 percentile (very high resilience)
86 to 91	21–40 percentile
77 to 85	41–60 percentile (middle of the pack)
65 to 76	61–80 percentile
0 to 64	81–100 percentile (low resilience in general population)

CHAPTER 8

SCORING KEY FOR ASSESSING YOUR CREATIVE PERSONALITY

SCORING INSTRUCTIONS: Assign plus one (+1) point beside the following words if you put a check mark beside them: Capable, Clever, Confident, Egotistical, Humorous, Individualistic, Informal, Insightful, Intelligent, Inventive, Original, Reflective, Resourceful, Self-confident, Sexy, Snobbish, Unconventional, Wide interests.

Assign negative one (−1) point beside the following words if you put a check mark beside them: Affected, Cautious, Commonplace, Conservative, Conventional, Dissatisfied, Honest, Mannerly, Narrow interests, Sincere, Submissive, Suspicious. Words without a check mark receive a zero. Add up the total score, which will range from −12 to +18.

INTERPRETING YOUR SCORE: This instrument estimates your creative potential as a personal characteristic. The scale recognises that creative people are intelligent, persistent and possess an inventive thinking style. Creative personality varies somewhat from one occupational group to the next. The table below provides norms based on undergraduate and graduate university students.

Creative disposition score	Interpretation
Above +9	You have a high creative personality.
+1 to +9	You have an average creative personality.
Below +1	You have a low creative personality.

CHAPTER 9

SCORING KEY FOR THE TEAM ROLES PREFERENCES SCALE

SCORING INSTRUCTIONS: Write the scores circled for each item on the appropriate line below (statement numbers are in brackets), and add up each scale.

Encourager   ____ + ____ + ____ = ____
           (6)   (9)   (11)

Gatekeeper   ____ + ____ + ____ = ____
           (4)   (10)   (13)

Harmoniser   ____ + ____ + ____ = ____
           (3)   (8)   (12)

Initiator   ____ + ____ + ____ = ____
           (1)   (5)   (14)

Summariser   ____ + ____ + ____ = ____
           (2)   (7)   (15)

INTERPRETING YOUR SCORE: The five team roles measured here are different from Belbin's roles. However, these roles are also based on academic writing. The five roles are defined as follows, along with the range of scores for high, medium and low levels of each role. These norms are based on results from a sample of Australian MBA students.

Self-monitoring dimension and definition	Score interpretation	
Encourager: People who score high on this dimension have a strong tendency to praise and support the ideas of other team members, thereby showing warmth and solidarity to the group.	High:	12 and above
	Medium:	9 to 11
	Low:	8 and below
Gatekeeper: People who score high on this dimension have a strong tendency to encourage all team members to participate in the discussion.	High:	12 and above
	Medium:	9 to 11
	Low:	8 and below
Harmoniser: People who score high on this dimension have a strong tendency to mediate intragroup conflicts and reduce tension.	High:	11 and above
	Medium:	9 to 10
	Low:	8 and below
Initiator: People who score high on this dimension have a strong tendency to identify goals for the meeting, including ways to work on those goals.	High:	12 and above
	Medium:	9 to 11
	Low:	8 and below
Summariser: People who score high on this dimension have a strong tendency to keep track of what was said in the meeting (i.e. act as the team's memory).	High:	10 and above
	Medium:	8 to 9
	Low:	7 and below

CHAPTER 10

SCORING KEY FOR THE TEAM PLAYER INVENTORY

SCORING INSTRUCTIONS: To calculate your score on the team player inventory, use the table below to assign numbers to each box that you checked. Then add up the numbers to determine your total score.

For statement items 1, 3, 6, 8, 10		For statement items 2, 4, 5, 7, 9	
Completely agree	= 5	Completely agree	= 1
Agree somewhat	= 4	Agree somewhat	= 2
Neither agree nor disagree	= 3	Neither agree nor disagree	= 3
Disagree somewhat	= 2	Disagree somewhat	= 4
Completely disagree	= 1	Completely disagree	= 5

INTERPRETING YOUR SCORE: The team player inventory estimates the extent to which you are positively predisposed to working on teams. The higher your score, the more you enjoy working in teams and believe that teamwork is beneficial. The following table allows you to compare your score against the norms for this scale. These norms are derived from undergraduate psychology students.

Team player inventory score	Interpretation
40 to 50	You have a strong predisposition or preference for working in teams.
21 to 39	You are generally ambivalent about working in teams.
10 to 20	You have a low predisposition or preference for working in teams.

CHAPTER II

SCORING KEY FOR THE ACTIVE LISTENING SKILLS INVENTORY

SCORING INSTRUCTIONS: Use the table below to score the response you circled for each statement. Write the score for each item on the appropriate line below the table (statement numbers are in brackets), and add up each subscale. For example, if you checked 'A little' for statement no. 1 ('I keep an open mind …'), you would write a '1' on the line with '(1)' underneath it. Then calculate the overall score by summing all subscales.

For statement items 3, 4, 6, 7, 10, 13		For statement items 1, 2, 5, 8, 9, 11, 12, 14, 15	
Not at all	= 3	Not at all	= 0
A little	= 2	A little	= 1
Somewhat	= 1	Somewhat	= 2
Very much	= 0	Very much	= 3

Avoiding interruption (AI) $\underline{\quad}_{(3)} + \underline{\quad}_{(7)} + \underline{\quad}_{(15)} = \underline{\quad}$

Maintaining interest (MI) $\underline{\quad}_{(6)} + \underline{\quad}_{(9)} + \underline{\quad}_{(14)} = \underline{\quad}$

Postponing evaluation (PE) $\underline{\quad}_{(1)} + \underline{\quad}_{(5)} + \underline{\quad}_{(13)} = \underline{\quad}$

Organising information (OI) $\underline{\quad}_{(2)} + \underline{\quad}_{(10)} + \underline{\quad}_{(12)} = \underline{\quad}$

Showing interest (SI) $\underline{\quad}_{(4)} + \underline{\quad}_{(8)} + \underline{\quad}_{(11)} = \underline{\quad}$

Active listening (total score): $\underline{\quad}$

INTERPRETING YOUR SCORE: The five active listening dimensions and the overall active listening scale measured here are defined below, along with the range of scores for high, medium and low levels of each dimension based on a sample of Australian MBA students:

Active listening dimension and definition	Score interpretation	
Avoiding interruption: People with high scores on this dimension have a strong tendency to let the speaker finish his or her statements before responding.	High: Medium: Low:	8 to 9 5 to 7 Below 5
Maintaining interest: People with high scores on this dimension have a strong tendency to remain focused and concentrate on what the speaker is saying even when the conversation is boring or the information is well known.	High: Medium: Low:	6 to 9 3 to 5 Below 3

continued ▶

Self-monitoring dimension and definition	Score interpretation	
Postponing evaluation: People with high scores on this dimension have a strong tendency to keep an open mind and avoid evaluating what the speaker is saying until the speaker has finished.	High: Medium: Low:	7 to 9 4 to 6 Below 4
Organising information: People with high scores on this dimension have a strong tendency to actively organise the speaker's ideas into meaningful categories.	High: Medium: Low:	8 to 9 5 to 7 Below 5
Showing interest: People with high scores on this dimension have a strong tendency to use nonverbal gestures or brief verbal acknowledgements to demonstrate that they are paying attention to the speaker.	High: Medium: Low:	7 to 9 5 to 6 Below 5
Active listening (total): People with high scores on this scale have a strong tendency to actively sense the sender's signals, evaluate them accurately and respond appropriately.	High: Medium: Low:	Above 31 26 to 31 Below 26

Note: The active listening inventory does not explicitly measure two other dimensions of active listening, namely, empathising and providing feedback. Empathising is difficult to measure with behaviours; providing feedback involves similar behaviours as showing interest.

CHAPTER 12

SCORING KEY FOR THE UPWARD INFLUENCE SCALE

SCORING INSTRUCTIONS: To calculate your scores on the upward influence scale, write the number circled for each statement on the appropriate line below (statement numbers are in brackets), and add up each scale.

Assertiveness
$$\underline{\qquad}_{(8)} + \underline{\qquad}_{(15)} + \underline{\qquad}_{(16)} = \underline{\qquad}$$

Exchange
$$\underline{\qquad}_{(2)} + \underline{\qquad}_{(5)} + \underline{\qquad}_{(13)} = \underline{\qquad}$$

Coalition formation
$$\underline{\qquad}_{(1)} + \underline{\qquad}_{(11)} + \underline{\qquad}_{(18)} = \underline{\qquad}$$

Upward appeal
$$\underline{\qquad}_{(4)} + \underline{\qquad}_{(12)} + \underline{\qquad}_{(17)} = \underline{\qquad}$$

Ingratiation
$$\underline{\qquad}_{(3)} + \underline{\qquad}_{(6)} + \underline{\qquad}_{(9)} = \underline{\qquad}$$

Persuasion
$$\underline{\qquad}_{(7)} + \underline{\qquad}_{(10)} + \underline{\qquad}_{(14)} = \underline{\qquad}$$

INTERPRETING YOUR SCORE: Influence refers to any behaviour that attempts to alter someone's attitudes or behaviour. There are several types of influence, including the following six measured by this instrument: assertiveness, exchange, coalition formation, upward appeal, ingratiation and persuasion. This instrument assesses your preference for using each type of influence on your boss or other people at higher levels in the organisation. Each scale has a potential score ranging from 3 to 15 points. Higher scores indicate that the person has a higher preference for that particular tactic. The six upward influence dimensions measured here are defined below, along with the range of scores for high, medium and low levels of each tactic.

Influence tactic and definition	Score interpretation	
Assertiveness: Assertiveness involves actively applying legitimate and coercive power to influence others. This tactic includes persistently reminding others of their obligations, frequently checking their work, confronting them, and using threats of sanctions to force compliance.	High:	8 to 15
	Medium:	5 to 7
	Low:	3 to 4
Exchange: Exchange involves the promise of benefits or resources in exchange for the target person's compliance with your request. This tactic also includes reminding the target of past benefits or favours with the expectation that the target will now make up for that debt. Negotiation is also part of the exchange strategy.	High:	10 to 15
	Medium:	6 to 9
	Low:	3 to 5
Coalition formation: Coalition formation occurs when a group of people with common interests band together to influence others. This tactic pools the power and resources of many people, so the coalition potentially has more influence than if each person operated alone.	High:	11 to 15
	Medium:	7 to 10
	Low:	3 to 6
Upward appeal: Upward appeal occurs when you rely on support from a higher-level person to influence others. In effect, this is a form of coalition in which one or more members is someone with higher authority or expertise.	High:	9 to 15
	Medium:	6 to 8
	Low:	3 to 5
Ingratiation: Flattering your boss in front of others, helping your boss with his or her work, agreeing with your boss's ideas and asking for your boss's advice are all examples of ingratiation. This tactic increases the perceived similarity of the source of ingratiation to the target person.	High:	13 to 15
	Medium:	9 to 12
	Low:	3 to 8
Persuasion: Persuasion refers to using logical and emotional appeals to change others' attitudes. According to several studies, it is also the most common upward influence strategy.	High:	13 to 15
	Medium:	9 to 12
	Low:	3 to 8

CHAPTER 13

SCORING KEY FOR THE DUTCH TEST FOR CONFLICT HANDLING

SCORING INSTRUCTIONS: Write the number circled for each item on the appropriate line below (statement number is under the line), and add up each subscale.

Conflict handling dimension	Calculation	Your score
Yielding	____ + ____ + ____ + ____ = Item 1 Item 6 Item 11 Item 16	____
Compromising	____ + ____ + ____ + ____ = Item 2 Item 7 Item 12 Item 17	____
Forcing	____ + ____ + ____ + ____ = Item 3 Item 8 Item 13 Item 18	____
Problem solving	____ + ____ + ____ + ____ = Item 4 Item 9 Item 14 Item 19	____
Avoiding	____ + ____ + ____ + ____ = Item 5 Item 10 Item 15 Item 20	____

INTERPRETING YOUR SCORE: The five conflict handling dimensions are defined below, along with the range of scores for high, medium and low levels of each dimension:

Conflict handling dimension and definition	Score interpretation	
Yielding: Yielding involves giving in completely to the other side's wishes, or at least cooperating with little or no attention to your own interests. This style involves making unilateral concessions, unconditional promises, and offering help with no expectation of reciprocal help.	High: Medium: Low:	14 to 20 9 to 13 4 to 8
Compromising: Compromising involves looking for a position in which your losses are offset by equally valued gains. It involves matching the other party's concessions, making conditional promises or threats, and actively searching for a middle ground between the interests of the two parties.	High: Medium: Low:	17 to 20 11 to 16 4 to 10
Forcing: Forcing involves trying to win the conflict at the other's expense. It includes 'hard' influence tactics, particularly assertiveness, to get one's own way.	High: Medium: Low:	15 to 20 9 to 14 4 to 8
Problem solving: Problem solving tries to find a mutually beneficial solution for both parties. Information sharing is an important feature of this style because both parties need to identify common ground and potential solutions that satisfy both (or all) of them.	High: Medium: Low:	17 to 20 11 to 16 4 to 10
Avoiding: Avoiding tries to smooth over or avoid conflict situations altogether. It represents a low concern for both self and the other party. In other words, avoiders try to suppress thinking about the conflict.	High: Medium: Low:	13 to 20 8 to 12 4 to 7

CHAPTER 14

SCORING KEY FOR LEADERSHIP DIMENSIONS INSTRUMENT

Transactional leadership

SCORING INSTRUCTIONS: Add up scores for the odd-numbered items (i.e. 1, 3, 5, 7, 9, 11, 13, 15). Maximum score is 40.

INTERPRETING YOUR SCORE: Transactional leadership is 'managing'—helping organisations to achieve their current objectives more efficiently, such as by linking job performance to valued rewards and ensuring that employees have the resources needed to get the job done. The following table shows the range of scores for high, medium and low levels of transactional leadership.

Transactional leadership score	Interpretation
32 to 40	The person you evaluated seems to be a highly transactional leader.
25 to 31	The person you evaluated seems to be a moderately transactional leader.
Below 25	The person you evaluated seems to display few characteristics of a transactional leader.

Transformational leadership

SCORING INSTRUCTIONS: Add up scores for the even-numbered items (i.e. 2, 4, 6, 8, 10, 12, 14, 16). Maximum score is 40. Higher scores indicate that your supervisor has a strong inclination towards transformational leadership.

INTERPRETING YOUR SCORE: Transformational leadership involves changing teams or organisations by creating, communicating and modelling a vision for the organisation or work unit, and inspiring employees to strive for that vision. The following table shows the range of scores for high, medium and low levels of transformational leadership.

Transformational leadership score	Interpretation
32 to 40	The person you evaluated seems to be a highly transformational leader.
25 to 31	The person you evaluated seems to be a moderately transformational leader.
Below 25	The person you evaluated seems to display few characteristics of a transformational leader.

CHAPTER 15

SCORING KEY FOR THE ORGANISATIONAL STRUCTURE PREFERENCE SCALE

SCORING INSTRUCTIONS: Use the table below to assign numbers to each response you circled. Insert the number for each statement on the appropriate line below the table. For example, if you checked 'Not at all' for item no. 1 ('A person's career ladder …'), you would write a '0' on the line with '(1)' underneath it. After assigning numbers for all fifteen statements, add up the scores to estimate your degree of preference for a tall hierarchy, formalisation, and centralisation. Then calculate the overall score by summing all scales.

For statement items 2, 3, 8, 10, 11, 12, 14, 15		For statement items 1, 4, 5, 6, 7, 9, 13	
Not at all	= 3	Not at all	= 0
A little	= 2	A little	= 1
Somewhat	= 1	Somewhat	= 2
Very much	= 0	Very much	= 3

Tall hierarchy (H) $\dfrac{\quad}{(1)} + \dfrac{\quad}{(4)} + \dfrac{\quad}{(10)} + \dfrac{\quad}{(12)} + \dfrac{\quad}{(15)} = \dfrac{\quad}{(H)}$

Formalisation (F) $\dfrac{\quad}{(2)} + \dfrac{\quad}{(6)} + \dfrac{\quad}{(8)} + \dfrac{\quad}{(11)} + \dfrac{\quad}{(13)} = \dfrac{\quad}{(F)}$

Centralisation (C) $\dfrac{\quad}{(3)} + \dfrac{\quad}{(5)} + \dfrac{\quad}{(7)} + \dfrac{\quad}{(9)} + \dfrac{\quad}{(14)} = \dfrac{\quad}{(C)}$

Total score (mechanistic) $\dfrac{\quad}{(H)} + \dfrac{\quad}{(F)} + \dfrac{\quad}{(C)} = \dfrac{\quad}{Total}$

INTERPRETING YOUR SCORE: The three organisational structure dimensions and the overall score are defined below, along with the range of scores for high, medium and low levels of each dimension based on a sample of MBA students:

Organisational structure dimension and definition	Interpretation	
Tall hierarchy: People with high scores on this dimension prefer to work in organisations with several levels of hierarchy and a narrow span of control (few employees per supervisor).	High: Medium: Low:	11 to 15 6 to 10 Below 6
Formalisation: People with high scores on this dimension prefer to work in organisations where jobs are clearly defined with limited discretion.	High: Medium: Low:	12 to 15 9 to 11 Below 9
Centralisation: People with high scores on this dimension prefer to work in organisations where decision making occurs mainly among top management rather than spread out to lower-level staff.	High: Medium: Low:	10 to 15 7 to 9 Below 7
Total score (mechanistic): People with high scores on this dimension prefer to work in mechanistic organisations, whereas those with low scores prefer to work in organic organisational structures. Mechanistic structures are characterised by a narrow span of control and high degree of formalisation and centralisation. Organic structures have a wide span of control, little formalisation and decentralised decision making.	High: Medium: Low:	30 to 45 22 to 29 Below 22

CHAPTER 16

SCORING KEY FOR THE CORPORATE CULTURE PREFERENCE SCALE

SCORING INSTRUCTIONS: In each space below, write in a '1' if you circled the statement and a '0' if you did not. Then add up the scores for each subscale.

Control culture
$$\frac{\quad}{(2a)} + \frac{\quad}{(5a)} + \frac{\quad}{(6b)} + \frac{\quad}{(8b)} + \frac{\quad}{(11b)} + \frac{\quad}{(12a)} = \frac{\quad}{}$$

Performance culture
$$\frac{\quad}{(1b)} + \frac{\quad}{(3b)} + \frac{\quad}{(5b)} + \frac{\quad}{(6a)} + \frac{\quad}{(7a)} + \frac{\quad}{(9b)} = \frac{\quad}{}$$

Relationship culture
$$\frac{\quad}{(1a)} + \frac{\quad}{(3a)} + \frac{\quad}{(4b)} + \frac{\quad}{(8a)} + \frac{\quad}{(10b)} + \frac{\quad}{(12b)} = \frac{\quad}{}$$

Responsive culture
$$\frac{\quad}{(2b)} + \frac{\quad}{(4a)} + \frac{\quad}{(7b)} + \frac{\quad}{(9a)} + \frac{\quad}{(10a)} + \frac{\quad}{(11a)} = \frac{\quad}{}$$

INTERPRETING YOUR SCORE: These corporate cultures may be found in many organisations, but they represent only four of many possible organisational cultures. Also, keep in mind that none of these subscales is inherently good or bad. Each is effective in different situations. The four corporate cultures are defined below, along with the range of scores for high, medium and low levels of each dimension based on a sample of Australian MBA students:

Corporate culture dimension and definition	Score interpretation	
Control culture: This culture values the role of senior executives to lead the organisation. Its goal is to keep everyone aligned and under control.	High: Medium: Low:	3 to 6 1 to 2 0

continued ▶

Corporate culture dimension and definition	Score interpretation		
Performance culture: This culture values individual and organisational performance and strives for effectiveness and efficiency.	High: Medium: Low:	5 to 6 3 to 4 0 to 2	
Relationship culture: This culture values nurturing and well-being. It considers open communication, fairness, teamwork and sharing a vital part of organisational life.	High: Medium: Low:	6 4 to 5 0 to 3	
Responsive culture: This culture values its ability to keep in tune with the external environment, including being competitive and realising new opportunities.	High: Medium: Low:	6 4 to 5 0 to 3	

CHAPTER 17

SCORING KEY FOR THE TOLERANCE OF CHANGE SCALE

SCORING INSTRUCTIONS: Use the table below to assign numbers to each box you checked. For example, if you checked 'Moderately disagree' for statement no. 1 ('An expert who doesn't come up …'), you would write a '2' beside that statement. After assigning numbers for all sixteen statements, add up your scores to estimate your tolerance for change.

For statement items 2, 4, 6, 8, 10, 12, 14, 16		For statement items 1, 3, 5, 7, 9, 11, 13, 15	
Strongly agree	= 7	Strongly agree	= 1
Moderately agree	= 6	Moderately agree	= 2
Slightly agree	= 5	Slightly agree	= 3
Neutral	= 4	Neutral	= 4
Slightly disagree	= 3	Slightly disagree	= 5
Moderately disagree	= 2	Moderately disagree	= 6
Strongly disagree	= 1	Strongly disagree	= 7

INTERPRETING YOUR SCORE: This measurement instrument is formally known as the 'tolerance of ambiguity' scale. Although it was developed forty years ago, the instrument is still used today in research. People with a high tolerance of ambiguity are comfortable with uncertainty, sudden change and new situations. These are characteristics of the hyperfast changes occurring in many organisations today. The table below indicates the range of scores for high, medium and low tolerance for change. These norms are based on results for MBA students in the United States.

Tolerance for change score	Interpretation
81 to 112	You seem to have a high tolerance for change.
63 to 80	You seem to have a moderate level of tolerance for change.
Below 63	You seem to have a low degree of tolerance for change. Instead, you prefer stable work environments.

Glossary

A

ability Includes both the natural aptitudes and learned capabilities required to complete a task successfully.

absorptive capacity The ability to recognise the value of new information, to assimilate it and to apply it to commercial ends.

achievement–nurturing orientation A competitive versus cooperative view of relations with other people.

action learning A variety of experiential learning activities in which employees, usually in teams, are involved in a 'real, complex and stressful problem' with immediate relevance to the company.

action research A data-based, problem-oriented process that diagnoses the need for change, introduces the intervention, and then evaluates and stabilises the desired changes.

adaptive culture An organisational culture in which employees focus on the changing needs of customers and other stakeholders, and support initiatives to keep pace with those changes.

appreciative inquiry An organisational change strategy that directs the group's attention away from its own problems and focuses participants on the group's potential and positive elements.

artefacts The observable symbols and signs of an organisation's culture.

attitudes The cluster of beliefs, assessed feelings and behavioural intentions towards an object.

attribution process The perceptual process of deciding whether an observed behaviour or event is caused largely by internal or external factors.

autonomy The degree to which a job gives employees the freedom, independence and discretion to schedule their work and determine the procedures used in completing it.

B

balanced scorecard (BSC) A reward system that pays bonuses for improved results on a composite of financial, customer, internal process and employee factors.

behaviour modification A theory that explains learning in terms of the antecedents and consequences of behaviour.

bicultural audit Diagnoses cultural relations between companies prior to a merger and determines the extent to which cultural clashes are likely to occur.

Big Five personality dimensions The five abstract dimensions representing most personality traits: conscientiousness, emotional stability, openness to experience, agreeableness and extroversion.

bounded rationality Processing limited and imperfect information and satisficing rather than maximising when choosing between alternatives.

brainstorming A freewheeling, face-to-face meeting where team members aren't allowed to criticise, but are encouraged to speak freely, generate as many ideas as possible, and build on the ideas of others.

C

casual work Any job in which the individual does not have an explicit or implicit contract for long-term employment, or one in which the minimum hours of work can vary in a nonsystematic way.

categorical thinking The mostly unconscious process of organising people and objects into preconceived categories that are stored in our long-term memory.

centralisation The degree to which formal decision authority is held by a small group of people, typically those at the top of the organisational hierarchy.

centrality The degree and nature of interdependence between the power-holder and others.

ceremonies Planned and usually dramatic displays of organisational culture, conducted specifically for the benefit of an audience.

change agent Anyone who possesses enough knowledge and power to guide and facilitate the organisational change effort.

coalition A group that attempts to influence people outside the group by pooling the resources and power of its members.

cognitive dissonance Occurs when people perceive an inconsistency between their beliefs, feelings and behaviour.

collectivism The extent to which people value duty to groups to which they belong as well as group harmony.

communication The process by which information is transmitted and understood between two or more people.

communities of practice Informal groups bound together by shared expertise and a passion for a particular activity or interest

competencies The abilities, values, personality traits and other characteristics of people that lead to superior performance.

conflict The process in which one party perceives that its interests are being opposed or negatively affected by another party.

conflict management Interventions that alter the level and form of conflict in ways that maximise its benefits and minimise its dysfunctional consequences.

constructive conflict Occurs when team members debate their different perceptions about an issue in a way that keeps the conflict focused on the task rather than people.

constructs Abstract ideas constructed by researchers that can be linked to observable information.

contact hypothesis A theory stating that the more we interact with someone, the less we rely on stereotypes to understand that person.

contingency approach The idea that a particular action may have different consequences in different situations.

continuance commitment A bond felt by an employee that motivates him or her to stay only because leaving would be costly.

corporate social responsibility (CSR) An organisation's moral obligation towards its stakeholders.

counterpower The capacity of a person, team or organisation to keep a more powerful person or group in the exchange relationship.

counterproductive work behaviours (CWBs) Voluntary behaviours that are likely to either directly or indirectly harm the organisation.

creativity The development of original ideas that make a socially recognised contribution.

D

decision making A conscious process of making choices from among alternatives with the intention of moving towards some desired state of affairs.

Delphi method A structured team decision-making process of systematically pooling the collective knowledge of experts on a particular subject to make decisions, predict the future or identify opposing views.

distributive justice The perceived fairness in outcomes we receive relative to our contribution and the outcomes and contributions of others.

divergent thinking Reframing a problem in a unique way and generating different approaches to the issue.

divisional structure An organisational structure that groups employees around geographic areas, clients or outputs.

drives Instinctive or innate tendencies to seek certain goals or maintain internal stability.

E

electronic brainstorming Using special computer software, participants share ideas while minimising the team dynamics problems inherent in traditional brainstorming sessions.

emotional contagion The automatic and unconscious tendency to mimic and synchronise one's own nonverbal behaviours with those of other people.

emotional dissonance The conflict between required and true emotions.

emotional intelligence (EI) The ability to monitor our own and others' feelings and emotions, to discriminate between them and to use this information to guide our thinking and actions.

emotional labour The effort, planning and control needed to express organisationally desired emotions during interpersonal transactions.

emotions The feelings experienced towards an object, person or event that create a state of readiness.

empathy A person's ability to understand and be sensitive to the feelings, thoughts and situation of others.

employability An employment relationship in which people are expected to continuously develop their skills in order to remain employed.

employee assistance programs (EAPs) Counselling services that help employees overcome personal or organisational stressors and adopt more effective coping mechanisms.

employee involvement The degree to which employees influence how their work is organised and carried out.

employee share ownership plans (ESOPs) A reward system that encourages employees to buy shares of the company.

empowerment A psychological concept in which people experience more selfdetermination, meaning, competence and impact regarding their role in the organisation.

equity sensitivity A person's outcome/input preferences and reaction to various outcome/input ratios.

equity theory A theory that explains how people develop perceptions of fairness in the distribution and exchange of resources.

ERG theory A motivation theory of three instinctive needs arranged in a hierarchy, in which people progress to the next higher need when a lower one is fulfilled, and regress to a lower need if unable to fulfil a higher one.

escalation of commitment The tendency to repeat an apparently bad decision or to allocate more resources to a failing course of action.

ethical sensitivity A personal characteristic that enables people to recognise the presence of an ethical issue and to determine its relative importance.

ethics The study of moral principles or values that determine whether actions are right or wrong and outcomes are good or bad.

evaluation apprehension When individuals are reluctant to mention ideas that seem silly because they believe (often correctly) that other team members are silently evaluating them.

executive coaching A helping relationship using behavioural methods to assist clients in identifying and achieving goals for their professional performance and personal satisfaction.

Glossary (continued)

exit-voice-loyalty-neglect (EVLN) model The four ways, as indicated in the name, that employees respond to job dissatisfaction.

expectancy theory The motivation theory based on the idea that work effort is directed towards behaviours that people believe will lead to desired outcomes.

extinction Occurs when the target behaviour decreases because no consequence follows it.

extroversion A 'Big Five' personality dimension that characterises people who are outgoing, talkative, sociable and assertive.

F

feedback Any information that people receive about the consequences of their behaviour.

Fiedler's contingency model Developed by Fred Fiedler, the model suggests that leader effectiveness depends on whether the person's natural leadership style is appropriately matched to the situation.

field surveys A research design strategy that involves collecting and analysing information in a natural environment, such as an office, a factory or other existing location.

flaming The act of sending an emotionally charged electronic mail message to others.

force field analysis Kurt Lewin's model of system-wide change that helps change agents diagnose the forces that drive and restrain proposed organisational change.

formalisation The degree to which organisations standardise behaviour through rules, procedures, formal training and related mechanisms.

four-drive theory A motivation theory based on the innate drives to acquire, bond, learn, and defend that incorporates both emotions and rationality.

functional structure An organisational structure that organises employees around specific knowledge or other resources.

fundamental attribution error The tendency to attribute the behaviour of other people more to internal factors than to external factors.

future search System-wide group sessions, usually lasting a few days, in which participants identify trends and identify ways to adapt to those changes.

G

gainsharing plan A reward system in which team members earn bonuses for reducing costs and increasing labour efficiency in their work process.

general adaptation syndrome A model of the stress experience, consisting of three stages: alarm reaction, resistance and exhaustion.

goal setting The process of motivating employees and clarifying their role perceptions by establishing performance objectives.

globalisation Economic, social and cultural connectivity (and interdependence) with people in other parts of the world.

grapevine An unstructured and informal communication network founded on social relationships rather than organisational charts or job descriptions.

grounded theory A process of developing theory through the constant interplay between data gathering and the development of theoretical concepts.

groups People with a unifying relationship.

group polarisation The tendency of teams to make more extreme decisions than individuals working alone.

groupthink The tendency of highly cohesive groups to value consensus at the price of decision quality.

H

halo effect A perceptual error whereby our general impression of a person, usually based on one prominent characteristic, colours our perception of other characteristics of that person.

heterogeneous teams Teams that include members with diverse personal characteristics and backgrounds.

homogeneous teams Teams that include members with common technical expertise, demographics (age, gender), ethnicity, experiences or values.

hypotheses Statements making empirically testable declarations that certain variables and their corresponding measures are related in a specific way proposed by the theory.

I

implicit favourite The decision maker's preferred alternative against which all other choices are judged.

implicit leadership theory A theory stating that people rely on preconceived traits to evaluate others as leaders, and that they tend to inflate the influence of leadership on organisational events.

impression management The practice of actively shaping our public image.

individualism The extent to which people value independence and personal uniqueness.

influence Any behaviour that attempts to alter another person's attitudes or behaviour.

ingratiation Any attempt to increase the extent to which a target person likes us or perceives that he or she is similar to us.

inoculation effect A persuasive communication strategy of warning listeners that others will try to influence them in the future and that they should be wary about the opponent's arguments.

intellectual capital The sum of an organisation's human capital, structural capital and relationship capital.

interpretivism The view held in many qualitative studies that reality comes from shared meaning among people in that environment.

introversion A 'Big Five' personality dimension that characterises people who are quiet, shy and cautious.

intuition The ability to know when a problem or opportunity exists and to select the best course of action without conscious reasoning.

J

jargon Technical language and acronyms as well as recognised words with specialised meanings in specific organisations or groups.

job burnout The process of emotional exhaustion, cynicism and reduced efficacy (lower feelings of personal accomplishment) resulting from prolonged exposure to stress.

job characteristics model A job design model that relates the motivational properties of jobs to specific personal and organisational consequences of those properties

job design The process of assigning tasks to a job, including the interdependency of those tasks with other jobs.

job enlargement Increasing the number of tasks employees perform within their job.

job enrichment Occurs when employees are given more responsibility for scheduling, coordinating and planning their own work.

job evaluation Systematically evaluating the worth of jobs within an organisation by measuring their required skill, effort, responsibility and working conditions.

job rotation The practice of moving employees from one job to another.

job satisfaction A person's attitude regarding their job and work content.

job specialisation The result of division of labour in which each job includes a subset of the tasks required to complete the product or service.

Johari Window The model of personal and interpersonal understanding that encourages disclosure and feedback to increase the open area and reduce the blind, hidden and unknown areas of oneself.

joint optimisation A key requirement in sociotechnical systems theory that a balance must be struck between social and technical systems to maximise an operation's effectiveness.

K

knowledge management Any structured activity that improves an organisation's capacity to acquire, share and use knowledge in ways that improve its survival and success.

L

laboratory experiment Any research study in which independent variables and variables outside the researcher's main focus of inquiry can be controlled to some extent.

leadership Influencing, motivating and enabling others to contribute towards the effectiveness and success of the organisations of which they are members.

leadership substitutes A theory that identifies contingencies that either limit the leader's ability to influence subordinates or make that particular leadership style unnecessary.

learning A relatively permanent change in behaviour that occurs as a result of a person's interaction with the environment.

learning orientation The extent to which an organisation or individual supports knowledge management, particularly opportunities to acquire knowledge through experience and experimentation.

legitimate power The capacity to influence others through formal authority.

locus of control A personality trait referring to the extent to which people believe events are within their control.

M

Machiavellian values The belief that deceit is a natural and acceptable way to influence others.

management by walking around (MBWA) A communication practice in which executives get out of their offices and learn from others in the organisation through face-to-face dialogue.

Maslow's needs hierarchy A motivation theory of needs arranged in a hierarchy, whereby people are motivated to fulfill a higher need as a lower one becomes gratified.

matrix structure A type of departmentalisation that overlays two organisational forms in order to leverage the benefits of both.

mechanistic structure An organisational structure with a narrow span of control and a high degree of formalisation and centralisation.

Glossary (continued)

media richness The datacarrying capacity of a communication medium, including the volume and variety of information it can transmit.

mental imagery Mentally practising a task and visualising its successful completion.

mental models The broad world views or 'theories-in-use' that people rely on to guide their perceptions and behaviours.

mentoring The process of learning the ropes of organisational life from a senior person within the company.

moral intensity The degree to which an issue demands the application of ethical principles.

motivation The forces within a person that affect his or her direction, intensity and persistence of voluntary behaviour.

motivator–hygiene theory Herzberg's theory stating that employees are primarily motivated by growth and esteem needs, not by lower-level needs.

multisource (360-degree) feedback Performance feedback received from a full circle of people around an employee.

Myers–Briggs Type Indicator (MBTI) inventory designed to identify individuals' basic preferences for perceiving and processing information.

N

need for achievement (nAch) A learned need in which people want to accomplish reasonably challenging goals through their own efforts, like to be successful in competitive situations, and desire unambiguous feedback regarding their success.

need for affiliation (nAff) A learned need in which people seek approval from others, conform to their wishes and expectations, and avoid conflict and confrontation.

need for power (nPow) A learned need in which people want to control their environment, including people and material resources, to benefit either themselves (personalised power) or others (socialised power).

needs Deficiencies that energise or trigger behaviours to satisfy those needs.

negative reinforcement Occurs when the removal or avoidance of a consequence increases or maintains the frequency or future probability of a behaviour.

negotiation Occurs whenever two or more conflicting parties attempt to resolve their divergent goals by redefining the terms of their interdependence.

networking Cultivating social relationships with others to accomplish one's goals.

network structure An alliance of several organisations for the purpose of creating a product or serving a client

nominal group technique A structured team decision-making process whereby team members independently write down ideas, describe and clarify them to the group, and then independently rank or vote on them.

norms The informal rules and expectations that groups establish to regulate the behaviour of their members.

O

open systems Organisations that take their sustenance from the environment and, in turn, affect that environment through their output.

organic structure An organisational structure with a wide span of control, little formalisation and decentralised decision making.

organisational behaviour (OB) The study of what people think, feel and do in and around organisations.

organisational citizenship Refers to behaviours that extend beyond the employee's normal job duties.

organisational commitment The employee's emotional attachment to, identification with and involvement in a particular organisation.

organisational culture The basic pattern of shared assumptions, values and beliefs considered to be the correct way of thinking about and acting on problems and opportunities facing the organisation.

organisational learning The knowledge management process in which organisations acquire, share and use knowledge to succeed.

organisational memory The storage and preservation of intellectual capital.

organisational politics Behaviours that others perceive as self-serving tactics for personal gain at the expense of other people and possibly the organisation.

organisational socialisation The process by which individuals learn the values, expected behaviours and social knowledge necessary to assume their roles in the organisation.

organisational strategy The way an organisation positions itself in its setting in relation to its stakeholders, given the organisation's resources, capabilities and mission.

organisational structure The division of labour and the patterns of coordination, communication, work flow and formal power that direct organisational activities.

organisations Groups of people who work interdependently towards some purpose.

P

parallel learning structures Highly participative groups constructed alongside (i.e. parallel to) the formal organisation with the purpose of increasing the organisation's learning and producing meaningful organisational change.

path–goal leadership theory A contingency theory of leadership based on the expectancy theory of motivation that relates several leadership styles to specific employee and situational contingencies.

personality The relatively stable pattern of behaviours and consistent internal states that explain a person's behavioural tendencies.

persuasion Using logical arguments, facts and emotional appeals to encourage people to accept a request or message.

positive reinforcement Occurs when the introduction of a consequence increases or maintains the frequency or future probability of a behaviour.

positivism A view held in quantitative research in which reality exists independent of the perceptions and interpretations of people.

post-decisional justification Justifying choices by unconsciously inflating the quality of the selected option and deflating the quality of the discarded options.

power The capacity of a person, team or organisation to influence others.

power distance The extent to which people accept unequal distribution of power in a society.

prejudice The unfounded negative emotions towards people belonging to a particular stereotyped group.

primacy effect A perceptual error in which we quickly form an opinion of people based on the first information we receive about them.

procedural justice The fairness of the procedures used to decide the distribution of resources.

process losses Resources (including time and energy) expended towards team development and maintenance rather than the task.

production blocking A time constraint in team decision making due to the procedural requirement that only one person may speak at a time.

profit-sharing plan A reward system that pays bonuses to employees based on the previous year's level of corporate profits.

projection bias A perceptual error in which we believe that other people have the same beliefs and behaviours that we do.

prospect theory An effect in which losing a particular amount is more disliked than gaining the same amount.

psychological contract The individual's beliefs about the terms and conditions of a reciprocal exchange agreement between that person and another party.

psychological harassment Repeated and hostile or unwanted conduct, verbal comments, actions or gestures that affect an employee's dignity or psychological or physical integrity and that result in a harmful work environment for the employee.

punishment Occurs when a consequence decreases the frequency or future probability of a behaviour.

R

rational choice paradigm A deeply held view that people should and can make decisions based on pure logic and with all information.

realistic job preview (RJP) Giving job applicants a balance of positive and negative information about the job and work context.

reality shock Occurs when newcomers perceive discrepancies between preemployment expectations and on-the-job reality.

recency effect A perceptual error in which the most recent information dominates our perception of others.

referent power The capacity to influence others based on an identification with and respect for the power-holder.

refreezing The latter part of the change process in which systems and conditions are introduced that reinforce and maintain the desired behaviours.

representative sampling The process of sampling a population in such a way that one can extrapolate the results of that sample to the larger population.

resilience The capability of individuals to cope successfully in the face of significant change, adversity or risk.

rituals The programmed routines of daily organisational life that dramatise the organisation's culture.

role A set of behaviours that people are expected to perform because they hold certain positions in a team and organisation.

role ambiguity A lack of clarity and predictability of the outcomes of one's behaviour.

role conflict Incongruity or incompatibility of expectations associated with the person's role.

S

satisficing Selecting a solution that is satisfactory or 'good enough', rather than optimal or 'the best'

scenario planning A systematic process of thinking about alternative futures and what the organisation should do to anticipate and react to those environments.

Glossary (continued)

scientific management Involves systematically partitioning work into its smallest elements and standardising tasks to achieve maximum efficiency.

scientific method A set of principles and procedures that help researchers to systematically understand previously unexplained events and conditions.

selective attention The process of filtering information received by our senses.

self-actualisation The need for self-fulfilment in reaching one's potential.

self-directed work teams (SDWTs) Cross-functional work groups organised around work processes, that complete an entire piece of work requiring several interdependent tasks, and that have substantial autonomy over the execution of those tasks.

self-fulfilling prophecy Occurs when our expectations about another person cause that person to act in a way that is consistent with those expectations.

self-leadership The process of influencing oneself to establish the self-direction and self-motivation needed to perform a task.

self-monitoring A personality trait referring to an individual's level of sensitivity and ability to adapt to situational cues.

self-reinforcement Occurs whenever someone has control over a reinforcer but delays it until a self-set goal has been completed.

self-serving bias A perceptual error whereby people tend to attribute their favourable outcomes to internal factors and their failures to external factors.

servant leadership The belief that leaders serve followers by understanding their needs and facilitating their work performance.

sexual harassment Unwelcome conduct of a sexual nature that detrimentally affects the work environment or leads to adverse job-related consequences for its victims.

share options A reward system that gives employees the right to purchase company shares at a future date at a predetermined price.

situational leadership theory Developed by Hersey and Blanchard, the model suggests that effective leaders vary their style with the 'readiness' of followers.

skill variety The extent to which employees must use different skills and talents to perform tasks within their job.

social identity theory A model that explains selfperception and social perception in terms of the person's unique characteristics (personal identity) and membership in various social groups (social identity).

social learning theory A theory stating that much learning occurs by observing others and then modelling the behaviours that lead to favourable outcomes and avoiding behaviours that lead to punishing consequences.

social loafing A situation in which people exert less effort (and usually perform at a lower level) when working in groups than when working alone.

socioemotional conflict Any situation where people view their differences as personal attacks rather than attempts to resolve an issue.

sociotechnical systems (STS) theory A theory stating that effective work sites have joint optimisation of their social and technological systems, and that teams should have sufficient autonomy to control key variances in the work process.

span of control The number of people directly reporting to the next level in the organisational hierarchy.

stakeholders Shareholders, customers, suppliers, governments and any other groups with a vested interest in the organisation.

stereotyping The process of assigning traits to people based on their membership in a social category.

stress An individual's adaptive response to a situation that is perceived as challenging or threatening to the person's well-being.

stressors The causes of stress, including any environmental conditions that place a physical or emotional demand on the person.

substitutability The extent to which people who are dependent on a resource have alternatives.

superordinate goals A common objective held by conflicting parties that is more important than their conflicting departmental or individual goals.

T

tacit knowledge Knowledge embedded in our actions and ways of thinking, and transmitted only through observation and experience.

task identity The degree to which a job requires completion of a whole or an identifiable piece of work.

task interdependence The degree to which a task requires employees to share common inputs or outcomes, or requires them to interact in the process of executing their work..

task significance The degree to which the job has a substantial impact on the organisation and/or larger society.

team-based structure A type of departmentalisation with a flat hierarchy and relatively little formalisation, consisting of self-directed work teams responsible for various work processes.

team building Any formal activity intended to improve the development and functioning of a team.

team cohesiveness The degree of attraction people feel towards the team and their motivation to remain members.

team effectiveness The extent to which a team achieves its objectives, achieves the needs and objectives of its members and sustains itself over time.

teams Groups of two or more people who interact with and influence each other, are mutually accountable for achieving common objectives, and perceive themselves as a social entity within an organisation.

theory A general set of propositions that describes interrelationships among several concepts.

third-party conflict resolution Any attempt by a relatively neutral person to help the parties resolve their differences.

transactional leadership Leadership that helps organisations achieve their current objectives more efficiently, such as linking job performance to valued rewards and ensuring that employees have the resources needed to get the job done.

transformational leadership A leadership perspective that explains how leaders change teams or organisations by creating, communicating and modelling a vision for the organisation or work unit, and inspiring employees to strive for that vision.

trust A psychological state comprising the intention to accept vulnerability based on positive expectations of the intent or behaviour of another person.

Type A behaviour pattern A behaviour pattern associated with people having premature coronary heart disease; type As tend to be impatient, lose their temper, talk rapidly and interrupt others.

U

uncertainty avoidance The degree to which people tolerate ambiguity or feel threatened by ambiguity and uncertainty.

unfreezing The first part of the change process whereby the change agent produces disequilibrium between the driving and restraining forces.

upward appeal A type of coalition in which one or more members is someone with higher authority or expertise.

V

valence The anticipated satisfaction or dissatisfaction that an individual feels towards an outcome.

values Stable long-lasting beliefs about what is important in a variety of situations.

values congruence A situation wherein two or more entities have similar value systems

virtual corporations Network structures representing several independent companies that form unique partnership teams to provide customised products or services, usually to specific clients, for a limited time.

virtual teams Teams whose members operate across space, time and organisational boundaries and who are linked through information technologies to achieve organisational goals.

virtual work Work performed away from the traditional physical workplace using information technology

W

win–win orientation The belief that the parties will find a mutually beneficial solution to their disagreement.

win–lose orientation The belief that conflicting parties are drawing from a fixed pie, so the more one party receives, the less the other party will receive.

workaholic A person who is highly involved in work, feels compelled to work and has a low enjoyment of work.

work–life balance The minimisation of conflict between work and non-work demands

Index

Page numbers in **bold** print refer to main entries

7-Eleven, **463**
30/60/90 feedback, 540
360-degree feedback, **151–2**, 177, 216, 358

A

A-B-C model of behaviour modification, **85–6**
Abbott Laboratories, 526
ability, 36, **37–8**
absenteeism, **42**, 87, 180, 183, 202, 213, 370, 372, 418, 504
absorption (uncertainty), 359
absorptive capacity, 20
abstract conceptualisation, 90
abstract ideas, *see* constructs
abuse of others, 40
    see also harassment
accountability, **78**, 83, 158, 182, 266, 301, 458
achievement, 43, 44, 114, **143–4**
achievement-nurturing orientation, **49**
achievement-oriented leadership style, 419, **420**, 423
acquire (drive), 141, **142**, **143**, 144, 145
acting, 113
action learning, **90–1**, 508
action research approach, **512–14**, 516
action scripts, 241
active experimentation, 90
active listening, **338–40**
adaptability/adaptation, 20, 114, 517
adaptive cultures, **481–3**
adjourning (work teams), 275, **276**
Admiral Insurance, 217
advisory teams, 267
affective commitment, 119, 120, 121
affiliation (need), **144**
Africa, **171**, 175, 429, **430**
aggression, 158–9, **213**, 386, 398
Agilent Technologies, **295**, 296, 301, 302
agreeableness, **53**
AirAsia, 359
alarm reactor stage, **203**
Allis, Janine, 111, **454**
Alpha Plantations Consultants case study, **537–8**
Aluminium Elements Corp. case study, **345–7**
ambiguity, 48, 328, 330, 332, 334, 336, 338, 370, 387, 389, **391**, 421, 447, 458, 460
Amcor, 20

AMP, 120, 328
analysability, 463, 464
Anchor Foods case study, **528–9**
Ancol Pty Ltd case study, **24–5**
Ang Siow Lee, **537**, **538**
anger, 158, 211, 240, 330, 397, 403
Animal Logic, 233, 234, 247, 447
antecedents, 85–6
anticipation, 72
anxiety, 53, 212, 217
ANZ Banking Group, 13, **115**
Apple Computer, 237, 250, 506
appreciative inquiry approach, **514–15**
aptitudes and aptitude tests, 37, 52, 115
arbitration, 402, 403, 404
Arctic Mining Consultants case study, **530–1**
Argentina, 206
Aristocratic Leisure, 331–2, 505
Armstrong World Industries, Inc., 399
Arnott, William, **478**
arrogance, 392
Arthur Andersen, 391, **392**, 483
artifacts, 476, **478**, 480, 482, 486, 487, 488
artificial feedback, 188
artistic personality types, 56
ASB Bank, 35, 39
Asdo case study, **543–5**
Asia
    achievement-nurturing orientation &, 49
    conflict minimalisation in, 516
    cultural values in, 46, 47–8, 369
    ethical behaviour &, 51
    individualism and collectivism in, 47
    membership-and seniority-based rewards in, 172
    negotiation teams &, 402
    nonverbal communication in, **336**, 337
    overwork in, 202, 206, **207**
    power distance &, 47–8
    work-related stress in, 202, 206, **207**
    see also China; Hong Kong; Japan
assembly-line technology, 463
assertiveness, 49, **364**, 365, 368, 369, 370, 372, 393, 394
assimilation merging strategy, **486**
associative play, **249**
assumptions, 475, **476**, 478, 488
AT&T, 38
attention, *see* selective attention

attitude object, 107
attitudes, 36, 37, 44, 57, 70, 86, 106, **107–8**, **109**, 110, **116–18**, 235, 366
attribution errors, **79**, 83, **428–9**
attribution process, **78–9**
attribution theory, **78–9**
audience characteristics, 366, 367, **401**
Australia Post, 115
Australian Wheat Board, 49
Austria, 112, 116, **179**, 460
authentic leadership, *see* integrity
autonomy, **181**, 182, 183, 184, 186, 189, 271, 296, **297–9**, 450, 458
Aviva Insurance (Thai) Co. Ltd, 41
avoiding (conflict management), 393, 396, 398,
    see also negative reinforcement
awareness, 71, 72, **77**, 106, 109
    see also self-awareness; social awareness
Axa Australia, 362

B

baby boomers, 9, 11
BakBone Software, **303**
balanced psychological contracts, 121
balanced scorecard, **175–6**
Ballard, Geoffrey, 248
Bank of Nova Scotia, **489**
bargaining zone model of negotiation, **400**
BASF, **450**
Bates, Tony, **11**
Baxter Corp., 182
The Beatles, 248
Becker, John, **191–3**
behaviour modelling, **88–9**, 148
behaviour modification, **85–6**, 177
behavioural consequences of stress, 204, 212, **213–18**
behavioural intentions, 107–8
behavioural perspective of leadership, 414, **417–18**, 424
Belbin's team roles, **280**
beliefs, **107**, 108, 109, 110, 111, 475, 476, 477, 478, 480, 488, 516, *see also* values
Bell Canada, 341
belongingness, 139, 140, 268
benevolence, 43, **44**
Benjamin, Michael, **162**
BHP-Billiton, 177, **242**, 243, **484**, 487

bias, 177, 236, 554
  fundamental attribution errors &, **79**
  projection, **82**, 83
  sampling, 549–50
  selective attention &, **71**, 328
  stereotyping, **77**, 78
bicultural audits, **484**
Big Five personality dimensions, **53–4**, 57
Big Screen Studios case study, **532–6**
Blackberry wireless emailing, 328, 333
blackmail, 364
blame, 369, 429
Blanchard, Ken, 422
blat, 368
blogs, **325**, 327, **328–9**, 332, **341**, 343
Blue Angels, **277**
BMW, 460, 461, 478–9
body language, *see* nonverbal communication
bonds, 141, **142**, **143**, 144, 145, 268, 310,
  326, 330, 343, 426
bonuses, 174, 175, 177
Boost Juice, **111**, 113, **454**
bootlegging, 267
bounded rationality, 238
Boyce, Greg, **530–1**
brain, 72, 78, 84, 109, 139, 142, 236, 240
brainstorming, 295, 303, **309–10**, 553, 554
Branded Product Pty Ltd, **140**
Branson, Richard, **385**, 386, 389, 390
Brazil, 46, **185–6**, 206, 336, 337
breakout space, 295
Brisbane City Council, **397–8**
British Airways, **362**
'Brooks's law', 283
Brosnan, Bill, 532, 536
buddy system, 489, 492, 493
  see also mentoring
Buddy's Snack Company case study, **161–3**
buffering, 335
buffers, 399
Bully Broads case study, **440**
bullying, 205
burnout (job), 111, 113, 211, **212–13**, 214
business ethics, *see* ethics

C
Cadbury Schweppes, **105**, 266
calculus-based trust, **304**, 305, 306
call centre case study, **539–40**

Campbell Soup, 178
Canada, 47, 49, **91**, 116, 178, 205, 206, 211,
  216, 427
CANOE, **53–4**
Canon Inc., 299
Canterbury Emergency Response Unit, **278**,
  279
carbon credits, 3
cardiovascular disease, 212
career breaks, 10
career counselling, 57
career development, 504
career goals, **518**
career satisfaction, 211
carer's leave, 10
Carswell, Neil, **140**
Carter Holt Harvey, 475
case studies, **527–45**
  see also studies at the end of each chapter
casual work, **12**
categorical thinking, **72**, 77
categorisation, 73, **74**, 75
causal relationships, **550–1**, 553
Celebrity CEO Charisma case study, **441**
Celestica Inc., **298**, 299, 461
centralisation, 445, **451–2**, 454, 462–3, 464
centrality, 357, **361**, 363
Centre Street Settlement House case study,
  433–5
CEO fat cats, 156, **157**
ceremonies, 476, **479**, 488
chain of command, 448, 453
challenging goals, **150**
Chang, Michael, 543, 544, 545
change, 6, 37, 428, 453
  resistance to, 502, **503–5**, **506–10**, 529,
    544
  stress &, 208, **507**, **510**
  workforce &, **8–10**, 502
  see also mergers; organisational change;
    takeovers; technological change
change agents, 504, 506, **511–12**, 513, 514,
  544
change diffusion, 511, **512**
Channel Medical centre, 201
characteristics (object), **71–2**
charismatic leadership, 359, 371, 413, 414,
  424–6, 429
Charles Schwab & Co., 446, 479, 484, **485**, 487

Chiat/Day, 361–2
childcare support, **216**
Chile, 47
China, 116, 117, 179, 206, **207**, 427, 445,
  488
Chrysler, **179**, **420**
Chubb, Captain, 537
Circumplex Model of Emotions, **107**
Citibank, **483**
Clapin, David, **528–9**
Clarion Life Insurance Company, 20
Clark, Alison, 153
client-consultant relationship, 513
client structure, 455
closed systems, 18
closing costs, 243
coaching, **152–3**, **161–3**, 414, 431, 449, 450,
  508
coalition formation, **364–5**, 368
Coca-Cola Amatil, 359, 445, 456
Cocoplans, **81**
coercion, **507**, **510**
coercive power, 357, **358–9**, 364, 365, 368,
  371
cognitions, 106, **110**
cognitive awareness, 83
cognitive dissonance, **110–11**
cognitive intelligence (IQ), 115
cognitive model of attitudes, **108**, 109
cohesiveness, *see* team cohesiveness
Coles Myer, **45**, 506
collaboration, 114, 266, 300, 393, 395, 397
collective action, 504
collectivism and individualism, **46–7**, 117,
  273, 284, 300, 396, 398, 483, 490
Colliers International, **477**
co-located teams, 303
Columbia accident, **309**
command-and-confront/control approach,
  138, 300, 301, 403, 451
commissions, 173, 174
commitment, **119–21**, 138, 142, 186, 212,
  269, 368, 370, 387, 422, 426, **428**, 447,
  544, 551
communication
  change resistance &, **507–8**, 529
  conflict &, 386, 387, 388, 389, **392–3**,
    396, **397–8**
  coordination through, **447**, 449

creativity &, 249
cross-cultural differences in, 330, **331**, **336–7**, 393
definition of, 326
disclosure &, 84
emotional intelligence &, 113
employees &, 4, 6, **326–43**
gender differences in, **337–8**
grapevine &, **343**, 488
improving interpersonal, **338–40**
learning &, 85
model of, **326–7**
multidisciplinary anchor &, 16, 17
negotiation &, 402
organisational commitment &, 121
organisational hierarchies &, **340–2**
teams &, 266, 269, **270**, **324–52**, 460
virtual teams &, 301, **302–3**, 304
see also direct communication; informal
    communication; internal
    communication; message; nonverbal
    communication; verbal communication
communication barriers, 326–7, 329, **333–8**
communication channels, 326, **327–33**, 343,
    367, 371, 447
communication flows, 326, 327, 328, 453
communities of practice, 20, 267, 269, 329
company norms, 328
'compassion fatigue', 212
competencies, **37–8**, 84, 113, 114, 184, 185,
    186, 211
competency-based rewards, **173–4**
competency perspective of leadership, **415–17**
competitive advantage, 10, 11, 19, 340, 517
competitiveness, 4, 10, 49, 108, 142, 145
competitors, 462
complaints, 504
complex vs simple environments, **462**
compliance, 368
composite culture, 486
compromise, 394, 396
Computarget case study, **543–5**
computer intranets, *see* intranets
computer-mediated communication, **327–9**
Computershare, 7
concession making, **402**
concrete experience, 90
confidence, *see* self-confidence
conflict avoidance, 40, 144

conflict defined, 386
conflict emotions, **386**, 387, 388, 393
conflict escalation style, **387**, 392
conflict management, 114, 186, 206, 275,
    282, 313, 369, 387, 513
conflict management approaches, **396–9**
conflict management styles, 387, 392, **393–6**,
    398, 399–400
conflict outcomes, 386, **387–9**
conflict perceptions, **386**, 387, 393
conflict process, **386–9**
conflict resolution, 492
    negotiation &, **399–402**
    structural approaches to, **396–9**
    styles of, 387, 392, **393–6**
    third-party, **402–4**
conflict risk, 245, **246**, 273, 276, 283, 334
conflict sources, 386, **389–93**, **396**
conflict stressors, **208–9**
conformity, 43, 44, 279, **307**
confrontation, **144**
congruence, 56
Connor, John, 533–4, 535
Connor-Davidson Resilience Scale, **223–4**
Conquistadors case study, **532–6**
conscientiousness, 40, **53**, 54, 55
consequences of behaviour, 85, 86
consequences of change, 504
conservation, 43, 44
constructive conflict, **308–9**, **387**, **388**, 397,
    478, 481
constructive thought patterns, **187–8**, 189
constructs, 547, **548**
consultants, 361, 399, 512, 517
consumer preferences, 456
consumerism, 206
contact hypothesis, 77
The Container Store case study, **229**
contingencies of organisational design,
    462–4
contingencies of path-goal theory, **420–1**
contingencies of power, **357**, **360–3**
contingencies of reinforcement, **86**
contingency anchor, 16, **17**
contingency approach, **17**
contingency perspective of leadership, 414,
    418–24
contingent (casual) work, **12**
continuance commitment, 119, **120**

continuous improvement process, 271, 272,
    501, 511
continuous reinforcement, 86
control, *see* power; span of control
control system, 480
controlling knowledge, **361**
controlling labour, **361**
controlling tasks, **360–1**
conventional personality types, 57
convergent thinking, 247
conversational overlaps, **337**, 339
Cook, Mimi, **361–2**
cooperativeness, 394
coordinating work activities, **446–9**
coping skills, 204, 210, 211, 212, 213, 217,
    359
core business, 529
core competencies, **461**
core firms, 460–1, 462
core values, 42, 477
corporate blogs, **325**, 341
corporate cults, 45, 483
corporate culture, *see* organisational culture
corporate culture preference scale, **497**
corporate fraud, 178, **355**, 370, **371**, **392**
corporate hierarchies, *see* organisational
    hierarchies
corporate leaders, 363
    communication &, **325**, 328, 334, 340, 508
    organisational change &, 508, 517
    see also leadership
corporate memory, *see* organisational memory
corporate objectives, *see* organisational
    objectives
corporate pressure, 51
corporate social responsibility, 3, 4, 13,
    14–15, 19, 46
corporate structure, *see* organisational structure
corrective feedback, 150, 153
Corrigan, Chris, **385**, 388, 389, 390
corruption, 49, 451
    see also corporate fraud
cost leadership strategy, 464
costs, *see* direct costs
counterpower, 356
counterproductive work behaviours, 39, **40**
countervalues, 477, 478
Court, Geoffrey, 539, 540
co-worker support, 249

Crampton, Tanya, **215**
creative individualism, 490
creative people, **247–9**
creative process model, **246–7**
creative thinking, 478, 481
creativity, 428, 452
  activities that encourage, **249–50**
  definition of, 246
  teams &, 307, **308–11**
  VXF industry &, **233**
  work environment &, **247–9**
credibility, 367
Crimson Tide, 357, **358**
Criterion Group, **458**
critical investigation, 549
critical psychological states, 181, **182**
cross-cultural communication differences, 330, **331**, **336–7**
cross-cultural leadership issues, **429–30**
cross-cultural training, 295
cross-cultural values/issues, **46–9**, **300**, 302, 477
cross-generational conflict, 391
cross-pollination, 250
cultural diversity, 8, **9**, 14, 336
cultural expectations, 429
cultural network management, 487, **488**
cultural norms, 336
cultural sensitivity, 274
cultural values, 43, **46–9**, **112**, 117, 143, 172, **369**, 429, 516, *see also* cross-cultural values/issues
culture
  communication &, 330, **331**, **336–7**, 393
  conflict management &, **390–1**, 393, **396**, 516
  differentiation conflict &, **390–1**
  emotional display norms across, **112**
  job satisfaction across, **116–17**
  leadership issues &, **429–30**
  negotiation &, 402
  nonverbal communication &, 330, **331**, **336–7**
  organisational change &, **516–17**
  psychological contracts across, **122–3**
  self-directed work teams &, **300**
  team diversity &, 274
  value of money &, 172
  virtual teams &, 303
  see also organisational culture

'culture of obedience', 278
customer-driven change, **505–6**
customer-focused culture, 4
customer longevity, 3
customer loyalty, 118
customer needs, 455, 478, 482, 505
customer satisfaction, 3, **118**, **119**, 299, 310, 501
customer service, 105, 267, 512
customer service representatives, **539–40**
customised products/services, 461, 464
cynicism, 212, **213**

D

Dairibord Zimbabwe, 175
Dairy Engineering (NZ) Ltd case study, **125–7**
Daiwa House Industry Co., 174
data analysis, 548, 549, 553
data carrying capacity (medium), 332
data collection, 16, 513, 516, 548, 549, 553
  see also information gathering
Davidson, Diane, 459
Davison, Ian, **537–8**
decentralisation, 445, 446, **451–2**, 453, 459, 462, 463, 464
decision acceptance, 310
decision commitment, 245, **246**
decision knowledge source, 245, **246**
decision making
  accountability for, **78**
  centralised/decentralised, **451–2**, 453, 463, 464
  communication &, 326
  definition of, 234
  delegation of, 451, 458
  emotions &, 235–6, **239–40**, 241
  employee involvement in, **244–6**
  evaluating and choosing alternatives &, 234, 235, **238–41**
  evaluating outcomes of, 234, **241–4**
  goal-directed, 143, **238**
  problem and opportunity identification &, 234, **235–8**
  rational choice paradigm &, **234–5**, **238**, 239
  self-directed work teams &, 296, 297
  teams &, 267, 296, 297, **306–11**
  ubuntu values &, **430**

decision structure, 245, **246**
deculturalisation merger strategy, **486**
deductive theory building stage, **547–8**, 553
deep acting, 113
deep-level diversity, 273
defence mechanisms, 398
defend (drive), 141, **142**, **143**, 144, 145
deference, 364
deficiency needs, 140
delayering, 450
delegating leadership style, 422, 430
delegation, 451, 458
delivery stage, 515
Dell Computer, 13
Deloitte, 12, 215, 363
Delphi method, **310–11**
departmental goals, 397
departmental teams, 267
departmentalisation form, **453–62**
dependence, 356
dependent variables, 550, 551, 552, 553
depersonalisation, *see* cynicism
depression, 211, 212
designing stage, 515
detective theories, **71**
differentiation, **74**, **361**, 464
differentiation conflict, 389, **390–1**, 396, **397**, 398
direct communication, 341, **342**, 398, 447, 448
direct costs, **504**, 510
direct supervision, 447, 449, 452, 454, 460
direction (motivation), 37
directive leadership style, **419**, 420, 421, 423, 431, 548, 550, 552
disclosure, 83, 84
discovery stage, 515
discretion, 357, 358, **361**
discrimination, **75**, 77
display rules, 111
dissensus, 310
distress, 202, **204**, **211–13**
distributive justice, 50, **154–6**, 158
divergent thinking, **247**
diverse vs integrated environments, **462**
diversity awareness, 77, 83, 84
dividends, 175
division of labour, **446**, 449, 463
divisional structure, **455–6**, 458–9

Index (continued)

doctors and medical staff, **201**, 202, 206, **208**, 209
dominant culture, 476, 477, 480, 481
Donnelly Mirrors, 178
downsizing, 208
downward influence, **369**
Dragon Cement, **88**
dreaming stage, 515
drives, 138, **139**, **141–3**, **144–5**, **416**
driving forces, **502**, 503, 505, 507
drum circles, **397**
Dubai (DED), **14**
Duffy, Luke, **355**, 356, 358, 359, 364, 370
Dun & Bradstreet Australasia, **492**
dynamic vs stable environment, **462**

E

Ebbers, Bernie, **371**
effective communication, 326
efficacy reduction, 212, **213**
efficiency-oriented culture, 477
effort, 146, **147–8**
effort-to-performance expectancy, 268, 418
Egypt, 112
Elbow Room Café, **111**
electronic brainstorming, **310**
ELVN model, **117**, 118
email, 302, 303, **327–8**, **329**, 332, 333, 334, 335, 343
emergency response teams, **91**
emoticons, 328
emotional appeals, 366, 426
emotional competencies, 113
emotional conflict, 308
emotional contagion, **330**
emotional display, **112**
emotional dissonance, **112–13**
emotional fatigue, 212
emotional intelligence, **113–16**, 143, 211, 273, **388**, **415**, 416, 418
emotional intelligence competencies model, **113–14**
emotional labour, **111–12**, 113, 115
emotional markers, 71–2, 78, 109, 142, 236, 240
emotional reactions, 106, 236
emotions, 36, 37, 55, 70, 83, 86
  attitude and behaviour &, **109**
  cognitions conflict with, **110**

cognitive dissonance &, **110–11**
communication &, 327, 328
decision making &, **235–8**, **239–40**, 241
definition of, 106
drives &, 142, 143
expectancy theory &, 148
management of, **111–13**
models of, **108**
motivation &, 142, 143, 148
personality &, **111**
types of, **106–7**
workplace &, 105, **106–13**
see also conflict emotions
'emotions as information', 240
empathy, 50, 53, **83**, 114, 337, 338, 339, 342, 392, 415
employability, **12**, 122, 173, 174
employee assistance programs, **217**
employee blogs, 325, 328, 341
employee engagement, **35–6**, 39, 40, 116, 138, 342
employee-friendly workplaces, 3
employee satisfaction, 245, 404, 483
employee share ownership plans, **175**, 176, 177
employee surveys, **341**
employees
  abilities of, 36, **37–8**
  attraction of, 22, **40**, 42, 173
  commitment of, **120–1**, 269, **428**, 502, 507
  communication with, 4, 6, **326–43**
  competencies of, **37**, 249, **517**
  conflict &, 387, 391
  contingencies of path-goal theory &, 420–1
  counterproductive work behaviours of, 39, **40**
  creativity &, **246–50**
  decision making &, **244–6**
  diversity of, **8–10**
  ELVN model &, **117**, 118
  empowerment of, 4, 13, **184–6**, 298, 299, 300, 425, 431, 450, 451, 452, 477, 502, 537
  expectations of, 429, 431
  goal participation &, **150**
  goals of, 172, 246
  influence of, 363, 369
  involvement of, **121**, **244–6**, 267, 309, **507**, **508–10**
  loyalty of, **117**, 118, 119, 120, 121, **228**
  mergers/takeovers &, 486, 487, **528–9**

motivation of, 4, 9–10, 13, 18, 36, **37**, 42, 80, 84, 118, 119, 120, **136–68**, 173, 174, 175, 176, 177, 178, 179, **180–4**, 245, 249, 268, 271, 273, 277, 280, 282, 284, 480, 510, 512
needs and drives of, **138–45**, 269, 326, **517**
organisational change &, 501, 502, **503–5**, **506–10**, 516
organisational citizenship &, **39–40**
organisational politics &, 372
ownership sense &, 483
personal change &, **517–18**
power of, 356, 357, 358–9, 363, 366
resistance to change &, 501, 502, **503–5**, **507**
retention of, 3, 22, 40, 42
role of, 453
role perceptions of, 36, 37, **38–9**
SDWT resistance &, **300**
selection of, 284, **488**, 489, 490–1
situational factors &, 36, 37, **39**
socialising of, **488**, **489–92**
task performance &, **39–40**
turnover of, 3, 9, 35, 40, 42, 45, 46, 105, **117**, 118, 120, 173, 180, 183, 245, 387, 418, 492, 501, 504, 539, 541
work attendance of, 39, **42**
work-non-work stresses &, **208–9**
see also absenteeism; profit-sharing plans; rewards; stress; teams; values; workforce change; workforce expectations; workforce flexibility
employer branding, 40, **41**
employment relationship, **10–12**, 138, 172
empowerment, 4, 13, 171, **184–6**, 298, 299, 300, 425, 431, 450, 451, 452, 463, 477, 502, 517, 537
enabling, 414
enacted values, 43, 46
encounter socialisation stage, 490, **491**
engineering, **76**
Enron, 51
enterprising personality types, 56
enthusiasm, 428
enthusiastic addicts, 211
entrepreneurial spirit, 358, 477
environment, *see* external environment; organisational environment; team environment

environmental change, 359, 478, 481, 482
environmental contingencies, **421**
environmental pressures, 505
environmental stimuli, **70**, 71, 72
equity, 173, 501
equity evaluation, **154–5**
equity principle, 154
equity sensitivity, **156**
equity theory, 153, **154–6**, 159
ERG theory, **141**
Ericsson Canada, 214
errors, *see* attribution errors; mistakes;
    perceptual errors
escalation of commitment, **242–3**
espoused values, 43, 46
establishing client relationship approach, **183**
esteem needs, 139, 140, 142
    see also self-esteem
ethical conduct, 3, 4, 7, **14**, 15, 481, **483**
ethical employment policies, 3
ethical sensitivity, **50**
ethical values and behaviour, **49–52**, 118, 120,
    483
ethics
    definition of, **14**
    organisational change &, **516–17**
    organisational research &, **551**
ethics codes, 51
ethics tests, **51**
Ethiopia, 112
ethnicity/ racial diversity, 8, **9**
European Seal Sands plant, **450**
eustress, 202
evaluating (listening), **339**
evaluation apprehension, **307**, 310, 311
Evercare, 21
exchange, 364, 365, **367–8**, 369
executive coaching, **152–3**
executive dashboards, 151, 153
executives
    influence of, 363
    organisational change &, 501, 502
    power of, 356, 357, 358, 458
    see also leadership; management
exhaustion stage, **203**
exit, **117**
exit-voice-loyalty-neglect (ELVN) model, **117**, 118
expectancy theory, **145–8**, 177, 418–19
expectations, **10–11**, 22, 72, 80, 81, 122, 138,

429, 431, 480
experiental learning, 20, **89–91**, 333
experiments, 548, 549, **552–3**
    see also active experimentation
expert power, 357, **359**, 363, 369, 371
expertise, 454, 456, 458
explicit threats, 364
external attribution, **78**, 79
external environment, **18–19**, 20, 39, 270,
    424, **462–3**, 482, 502, 505
external focus, 482
external influences, 452, 464
external locus of control, 55, 370, 421
extinction, 86
extranets, 328
extroversion, 53, **54**, 111, 189, 211, 416, 417
ExxonMobil, 88
eye contact, 337, 339
e-zines, **341**

F
face saving, 398, 401, **504**, 507, 508, 516
face-to-face interaction, 301, 302, 303, 304,
    310, 327, 328, 329, 332, 337, 367, 401
facial expressions/gestures, 110, 112, 328, 330
family, 209, 213, 215, 217
    see also work-life balance
'fat cat' CEOs, 156, **157**
Fayol, Henri, 449
FBI, **503**
fear, 107, 240, **504**, 508, 511
Federal Signal, 300
FedEx Singapore, 266
feedback, 80, 83, 84, 115
    communication process, 326, 327, 330,
        332, 333, 338, 367
    definition of, 150
    effective, **150–1**
    goal, **150**
    motivation &, 137, 148, 149, **150–3**
    open systems view &, **18**
    self-directed work teams &, 297, 299
    sources of, **151–3**
    span of control &, 450
    virtual teams &, 302
    see also job feedback
feeling types, 54
feelings, 70, 106, 107, 108, 109, 110, 111
    see also emotions

females, *see* women
Fenway Waste Management, **96**
Fiedler's contingency model, **422–3**
field surveys, 552, **553**
'fight-or-flight' response, 142, 202, 213, 218
filtering (message), **334**, 342, 364
financial reward practices, **172–9**
finger dexterity, 37, 38
Finland, 208
Finster Honey Farms, **210**
Fish! principles, 109, **110**
five anchors of organisational behaviour, **15–19**
fixed interval schedule, 87
fixed ratio schedule, 87
flaming, 328
Fletcher, John, **506**
flexibility *see* workforce flexibility
Flight Centre, 447, 480, **489**
"follow the sun" development mode, 302
Fonterra, **6–7**
force field analysis model, **502–5**, 511, 516
forcing (conflict management), 393–4
Ford Motor Company, **503**, 504
forecasting, 359
foreign exchange traders, 39–40
Forest, Buddy & Mark, **161–3**
formal hierarchy, **447–8**
formalisation, **452**, 453, 458, 463, 464
forming, **275–6**
Forward Media, 175
founders actions, **487–8**
Four-D model of appreciative inquiry, **515**
four drive theory, **141–3**, 144, **145–6**
Four Seasons Hotels and Resorts, **112**, 279
framing, 426
France, 47, 112, 116, 427
fraud, 178, **355**, 370, **371**, **392**
Frazier, Mark, **532–5**
freelance contractors, 12
'freeters', 122, **123**
fresh engineering approach, **544–5**
Friedman, Milton, 14–15
FTCA case study, **466–9**
Fuji Xerox, 213
fun, **105**, 109, **110**, 228
functional organisational structure, **453–5**,
    460, 464
fundamental attribution errors, **79**, 429
future search, **508**, **510**

Index (continued)

G

gainsharing plans, 173, **175**, 178, 179
Gangadharan, Rajit, **491**
Ganley, Lee, 528, 529
Garrison, Richard, 534, 535, 536
Gate Gourmet, **362**
Gates, Bill, 335
Gattung, Theresa, **325**
gender
    communication &, **337–8**
    conflict management &, **396**
    influence tactics &, **369**
    leadership style &, **430–1**
    stereotypes of, 75, **76**, 77, 80, **431**
    workforce participation &, 8, **9**
    see also men; women
general adaptation syndrome, **202–3**
General Electric, 503
General Motors, see GM Holden/General
    Motors
Generation-X, 9–10, 11, 138, 173, **491**
Generation-Y, 10, 11, 138, 173, **492**
generational diversity, 8, **9–10**, 122
generational gaps, 391
Gentilin, Dennis, **355**
geographic areas, 447–8, 455, 462
geographic structure, 455, **456**, 457
Germany, 46, 116, 427, 460
gestures, 112, 328, 330, **331**
    see also nonverbal communication
Ghosn, Carlos, 508, **509**
globalisation, **6–8**, 11, 14, 37, 138, 206,
    301–2, 336, 445, 453, 456, 461, 502
GLOBE Project, 8, **429–30**
GM Holden/General Motors, **113**, 115, **265**,
    266, 270, 273, 302, **456–7**, 458
goal commitment, **150**
goal feedback, **150**
goal participation, **150**
goal setting, 4, **149–50**, **153**, 180, 186, **187**,
    217, **312**, 401–2, 420, 426, **518**
goal sharing, 156, 271
goals, 5
    common, 266, 297, 307
    conflict of, 238, 458
    conflict management &, 386, **389–90**,
        396–7
    corporate-wide, **396–7**
    decision making &, 143, **238**

effective, **149–50**
    group, 268, 273, 396
    incompatible, 386, **389–90**
    organisational, 172, 186, 238, 246, 269,
        282, 283, 365, 404, 423, 426, 464, 512
    personal, 271, 280, 396
    problems with, **238**
    superordinate, **396–7**, 426
    team, 266, 271, 276
    see also career goals; challenging goals
Godrej Soaps, **391**
Goldberg, Choo and McKay Associates case
    study, **316–17**
golden handcuffs, 172, 173
Gomersall, John, 171, 179
Google, **10–11**, 325
Gourami Business Challenge (Shell), **274**
governance, **544**
Grant Thornton, 137
grapevine, **343**, 488
Greece, 48
Griffith University Library, **296**, 297
grounded theory, 16, **549**
group affiliations, 268
group dynamics, 4
    see also team dynamics
group membership, 46, 74
group polarisation, **307–8**
groups and teams, **266–8**
groupthink, **307**
growth needs, 140, 181
guanxi, 367–8, 369, **379**
Guild Insurance & Financial Services, 342
guolaosi, 207
gut feelings, 110, **240–1**

H

H.J. Heinz Co., 52
habitual behaviour, 44
Haier Group, **427**, 488
halo effect, **82**
handshake, 337
Hansen, Joe, **220–2**
harassment, **205–6**, 213, 214–15
hard influence tactics, **364–5**, 368, 369, 393
Hargadon, Andrew, 553, 554
harmony, 307, 396, 398, 430, 516
Harvey Norman, 487
Hassell, Jim, 272

Hayden, Fran, **125–6**
HBI plant, **242**
hearing, 70
heart attacks, 212
hedonism, 43
Hellermann Tyton, **311–12**
Hersey, Paul, 422
Herzberg, Frederick, 180
heterogeneous teams, **273–4**, 281, 550–1
Hewitt Associates, 413, 414
Hewlett-Packard Co., 273, 295, 296
hidden knowledge, 22, 387
hierarchies, see organisational hierarchies
high-performance team development,
    294–322
Hilltown case study, **494–6**
H.J. Heinz Co., 52
Holland types, **56–7**, 517
home-based work, 10
    see also virtual work
Home Depot, 117
homogeneous teams, **273–4**, 281
homogenisation, **74**
honesty, 415, 428, 505
Hong Kong, 9, 12, **41**, 47, 48, 49, 206, **208**,
    369, 456
Host Universal, 461
hostile vs munificent environment, **462–3**
hours of work, see work hours
HSBC Bank, **8**
Hsieh Hsuen-Hui, **153**, **154–5**
human capital, 19
human rights, 50
humour, 389
Hungary, 47, 49, 116
hypotheses, **547–8**, 553
hypotheses testing, 547, **548**, 554

I

IBM, 13, 48, 49, 302, 304, 325, **484**, 526
ICICI Bank, **476–7**
ideal values, 475
'ideal worker norm', 206
identification-based trust, **305**, 306
IDEO, 310, 425, 553, 554
Ilham, John, 186
illness, **212**, 213
immigration policies, 9
immune system, 212

impact, 184, 185
implicit favourites, 238, **239**, 241
implicit leadership theory, 414, **428–9**
implicit threats, 364
impression management, 364, 365, **366**, 368
impromptu storytelling, 249
  see also stories and legends
incremental change, 513
incubation, 246–7
independent variables, 550, 551, 552, 553
India, 47, 116, 144, 149, 206, 325, 337, 390, 456, 491
individual behaviour
  MARS model of, **36–9**
  organisations and types of, **39–42**
  see also personal characteristics; personal values; personality
individual differences in stress, 204, **210–11**
individual rewards, **174–7**
individual rights, 50
individualism and collectivism, **46–7**, 117, 273, 284, 300, 396, 398, 483, 490, *see also* cultural values
Indonesia, 42, 47, 49, 206
inductive theory building stage, **546–7**, 548, 549, 553, 554
inequality feelings correction, **155–6**
influence, 114, **363–72**
influence tactics, **363–8**, 369, 370
informal communication, 341, **447**, 448, 449, 452, 453, 459, 463, 464
informal groups, 266, 267, **268**, 269, 276, 365
information
  accessibility of, 186, **364**, 365, 369
  evaluation of, 235–6
  hiding of, **355**, 364, 370, 528
  interpretation of, 72, 75
  organisation of, 339
  power &, **359–60**
  sharing of, 267, 269, 282, 303, 328, 332, 388, 393, 394, 399, 400, 425, 447, 453, 551
  see also knowledge sharing
information control, **364**, 365, 370, 372
  see also knowledge control
information exchange, 326, **327–33**
information flows, 359, 371, 461
information gatekeepers, 359

information gathering, 402, 549
  see also data collection
information load, 335
information overload, 270, 328, 332, **334–5**, 491
information processing, 335, 401
information processing problems, **239**
information technology, 7, 12, 13, 16, 76, 138, 267, 270, 301, 302, 303, 326, **327–9**, 332, 333, **334–5**, 343, 401, 447, 453, 461, 462, 463
Infosys, **413**
ingratiation, **365–6**, 368, 369
initial offer point, 400, 401
initiative, 114, 300
innate drives, 142, 143, 144
innovation, 37, 266, 425, 458, 478
inoculation effect, 367
inputs, 18, 19, 154, 297, 462
inquisition approach, 402, **403–4**
insight, 247
instant messaging, 301, 328, 329, 332, 333, 343
Institute of Biomedical Problems (Moscow) case study, **406–8**
integrated culture, 481
integrated vs diverse environments, **462**
integration merger strategy, **486**
integrator roles, 447
integrity, **415–16**, 417, 428
intellectual capital, 19, 21–2, 40
intelligence, 416
  see also emotional intelligence
intensity (motivation), 37
interactive leadership, 430
interdependence, 7, 266, 267, **271–2**, 296, 297, 300, 303, 356, **391**, 398–9, 449–50, 453, 458
interest (responding), 339
Interface, 15
internal attribution, **78–9**
internal communication, 326, 328, **329**
internal locus of control, 55, 370, 421
Internet, 301
interpersonal conflict management styles, **393–6**
interpersonal processes (team building), **313**
interpersonal relations, 115, 369, 516
interpersonal skills, 359, 431, 460

interpersonal stressors, **204–6**, 212
interpretivism, **547**
interrupting, **337**, 339
intranets, 20, 301, 303, 328
introversion, 54, 111
Intuit, 506
intuition, 54, **240–1**
Invensys PLC, 302
inventive thinking, 248
investigative personality types, 56
Italy, 47, 112

J
Japan, 12, 35, 47, 48, 49, 112, 116, 117, 122, **123**, **174**, 202, 206, **207**, **229**, **336**, 337, 364, 365
jargon, 334
job burnout, 111, 113, 211, **212–13**, 214
job characteristics model, **180–1**
job competition, 173
job description, 357, 448, 452
job design practices, 171, **179–84**, 186
job enlargement, **182–3**, 297
job enrichment, **183–4**, 245, 284, 297, 299
job evaluation, **173**
job feedback, **181**, 183, 186
job interview, 369
job misrepresentation, 492
job performance, **146–8**, 150, 152, 153, 213, 297
job-person matching, **38**
job preview, realistic, **492**
job redesign, 38
job rotation, **182**
job satisfaction, 13, 16, 42, 45, 111, **116–18**, 180, 181, 183, 186, 212, 284, 370, 372, 387, 418, 488, 489, 551
job security, 108, 109, 120, 180, 202, 208, 249, 356, 504
job sharing, 10, 215
job specialisation, **179–80**, **446**, 448, 454, 458, 463, 464
job status-based rewards, **172–3**
Jobs, Steve, **367**, 506
Johari Window, **83–4**, 517
joint optimisation, **299**
joint ventures, 390
judging types, 54
judgment, 107, 241

Index (continued)

Jung, Carl, 54
justice and support, **120**
see also procedural justice

K

kaizen blitz, 298
Kambuku, **171**
karoshi, **207**, 229
Kawamoto, Yoichi, **207**
Kelly, Gail, **417**
Kelly, Simon, 331–2, 505
Kenya, **137**
key variances, **299**
Kiwi Dairy Company, 6
knowledge, 84, 85, 90, 248, 416, 453
see also learning
knowledge acquisition, **20**, 37
knowledge and power, **359–60**
knowledge-based economy, 359
knowledge-based trust, **305**, 306
knowledge bases, 461
knowledge control, **361**
see also information control
knowledge management, **19–22**, 326, 452, 513
knowledge processes, **19–20**
knowledge of results, 181, 182
knowledge sharing, **20**, 266, 302, 341, 456, 458
knowledge specialisation, 449
knowledge transition, 22
knowledge use, **20**
knowledge withholding, 22, 387
knowledge work, 301, 302
Knox, Buck, **532–6**
Koh Ching Hong, **213**
Kolb's experiential learning model, **90**, 91
Korea, 47, 48, 112, 116, 117, 206, 207
Kowloon Shangri-La, **342**
KPMG, 333
KT, 176
Kuwait, 112

L

laboratory experiments, 550, **552–3**
labour control, **361**
labour division, **446**, 449, 463
labour unions, **300**, 360, 361, 452
labour 'waste', 180
Laffey, Alan G., **425–6**
lagging indicators, 88

language barriers, 330, **334**, 336
see also organisational language
LaSorda, Tom, **420**
lateral influence, **369**
Latin America, 391
Lawrence, Paul, 141, 144
Lazarus, Zoe, **360**
leader-member relations, 422
leadership, 4, 14, 46, 53, 79, 144, 218, 236,
358, 363, 372
behavioural theory of, 414, **417–18**, 424
charismatic, 4, 359, 371, **424–6**
competency perspective of, 414, **415–17**
contingency theory of, 414, **418–24**
cross-cultural issues in, **429–30**
effective, 413, 415, 419, 423, 424, 429
Fiedler's contingency model of, **422–3**
gender differences in, **430–1**
implicit leadership theory, 414, **428–9**
organisational change &, **501**, 502, 505,
510, **511–12**
organisational culture &, **487–8**
organisational setting &, **412–41**
organisational strategy &, 464
path-goal theory of, **418–22**
perspectives of, **414–29**
situational leadership theory, **422**
transactional, 420, **424**, 512
transformational, 414, 420, **424–8**, 488,
502, 511
see also corporate leaders; organisational
leadership; team leaders
leadership acceptance, 429
leadership dimensions instrument, **435–6**
leadership emergence, 415
leadership motivation, **416**
leadership stereotypes, **428**
leadership substitutes, **423–4**
leadership teams, 267
leadership traits, **414–17**, **424–6**
leading indicators, 88
lean manufacturing, 298
lean medium, **332**, 333
learned capabilities, 37
learned needs theory, 139, **143–4**
learning, 37
behaviour modification &, **85–7**
change resistance &, **507**, **508**
definition of, 84

drives &, 141, **142**, **143**, 145
experience &, 20, **89–91**, 333
explicit knowledge &, **85**
needs &, 139, **143–4**
observation &, **87–9**
reinforcement &, **85–7**
tacit knowledge &, **85**, 89
see also knowledge management;
organisations
learning behaviour consequences, **89**
learning environment, 477
learning orientation, **90**, 186, 249, 310, 452
leave, 10, **216**, 217
legends, *see* stories and legends
legitimate power, **357–8**, 361, 362, 364, 365,
368, 421, 447
Lenovo Group, 48
Leung Ko May-yee, Margaret, 415, 416
Lewin, Kurt, **502–5**, 511, 512
Lewin's force field analysis model, **502–5**, 511,
516
Lewis, Lynda, **162**
liaison roles, 447
life-balance, *see* work-life balance
life-cycle theory of leadership, *see* situational
leadership theory
life events, 429
Liggett-Stashower Inc., 216
Lighthouse structure, 445
Linsell, Derek, 512
Lionore Australia, 88
Lippert-Johanson Inc. case study, **94–6**
listening, **338–40**, 342, 402, 403, 418
Little, Paul, **385**, 388, 389, 390
Liverpool City Council (UK), 328, **329**
localisation, 112
location (negotiation), **401**
locus of control, **55**, 211, 370, **421**
logic, 89, 107, 109, 110, 142, 234, 235, 238,
240, 241, 366, 387, 398, 551
longitudinal research, 553
Lowe Worldwide, 445, 446
loyalty, 45, **117**, 118, 119, 120, 121, **228**,
488, 492, 551

M

Machiavellianism, 370, 372, **379**
Macintosh computers, **237**, 250, 506
Magical Connections case study, **220–2**

Magna International, 460, 461
Magna Steyr, **179**
Maher, Grahame, 69
Mair, Judith, 481, **482**
Malaysia, 116–17, 137, 177, **451–2**, **537–8**
males, *see* men
management, 6, 450
   direct communication with, **342**
   influence &, 369
   inquisition approach &, 403–4
   power &, 300, 358, 361, 516
   self-directed work team resistance by, **300**
   see also corporate leaders; executives;
      leadership; participative management;
      self-management
management by walking around, **342**
manifest conflict, **386–7**
Manila Diamond Hotel, 397
MARS model, **36–9**, 84, 108, 512
Martin, Josh, **433–5**
Maslow's needs hierarchy, **139–41**, 144, 211
materialism, 49
maternity leave, 216
matrix organisational structure, **456–8**, 464
maturity, 115
Mayo Clinic, **479**
McCallum, Vanessa, 355
McClelland, David, **143–4**
McDonald's Restaurants, 452, 456
McKay, Sanderson and Smith Associates case
   study, **316–17**
McNee, Duncan, 491
meaningfulness, **77**, 83, 84, 181, 182, 184,
   185, 186
mechanistic structures, **452–3**, 462, 464
media leanness, **332**, 333
media richness, **331–3**
mediation, 402, 403, 404, 430
Medibank Private, 270, **501**, 502, 505, 510,
   511, 512, 517
meditation, 217
membership-based rewards, **172**, 173
memory, 72, 213
   see also organisational memory
men
   communication &, **337–8**
   conflict management styles of, **396**
   leadership styles &, **431**
   see also gender

mental imagery, **188**, 189
mental models, **72**, 236, **237**, 241, 248, 275,
   276, 277, 305, 313, 326, 328, 332, 333,
   334, 391, 447, 453, 455, 476, 481, 482,
   490
mental road maps, 447
mentoring, 218, 362, 363, 492, **518**
   see also buddy system; coaching
mergers, **6–7**, **107–8**, 109, 390, **484–7**
   see also takeovers
merit pay, 173
message (communication), 326, 327, 332,
   334–5, **338**, 339, 340, 366–7, 402
metaphors, 426–7, 488
Mexico, 300. 430
Microsoft, 151, 237, 451
Middle East, 336, 337
middle managers, 450
Millar, Brian, **530–1**
Miller, Al, **543–4**
mimicry, 330
mining industry, 40, 175, 177
mistakes, 90, 186, 248, 249, 415, 538, 541
MLC, **41**
Monaro 'skunkworks' group, 265, 266
money, **172**, 179
monopolies, 18
mood, 106, 212, 240
moral intensity, **50**
morale, 105, 117, 144, 171, 501, 509
Morgan, Piers, **157**
morphological analysis, **249–50**
motivating potential score, **195**
motivation
   conflict resolution &, 392–3, 397
   creativity &, 249
   employee, 4, 9–10, 13, 18, 36, **37**, 42, 80,
      84, 118, 119, 120, **136–68**, 173, 174,
      175, 176, 177, 178, 179, **180–4**, 245,
      249, 268, 270, 271, 273, 277, 282,
      283, 284, 480, 510, 512
   employee engagement &, 36
   empowerment &, 186
   expectancy theory of, **145–8**, 177, 418–19
   financial rewards &, 173, 174, 175, 176,
      177, 178, 179
   goal setting and feedback &, **149–53**
   ineffective communication &, **392–3**
   job design practices &, 179, **180–4**

leaders &, **416**
needs and drives &, **138–45**
negotiation &, 401, 402
organisational justice &, **153–9**
self-leadership practices &, **186–9**
SLT &, 422
teleworkers &, 13
workplace, **136–68**
motivator-hygiene theory, **180**
multiculturalism, 49
   see also cultural diversity
multidisciplinary anchor, **15–16**
multiple levels of analysis anchor, 16, **17–18**
multiskilling, 184, 267
multisource feedback, **151–2**, 205
munificent vs hostile environment, **462–3**
mutinies, 357, 358
Myers-Briggs Type Indicator, **54–5**, 240

N

Naidu, Devanda, **205**
NASA, 275, **309**
Nasser, Jacques, 503
National Australia Bank, 40, **340**, **355**, 356,
   359, 364, 372, 480
National Transportation Safety Board, **274–5**
natural grouping approach, 183
natural rewards design, 187, **188**
need for achievement (nAch), **143–4**
need for affiliation (nAff), **144**
need for power (nPow), **144**
need principle, 154
needs, **138–41**, **143–5**, 455, 478, 482, 505
negative reinforcement, **86**
negative self-talk, 188
neglect, **117**, 118, 369
negotiation
   bargaining zone model of, **400**
   change resistance &, **507**, **510**
   definition of, 399
   exchange influence, 367
   introduction to, **399–400**
   resolving conflict through, **399–402**
   situational influences on, **400–1**
negotiators, 400, **401–2**
Nestlé, 451–2, 456
Netherlands, 427
Network Rail, 157
network structure, **460–1**

Index (continued)

networking, **363**, **367–8**, 415, **518**
neuroticism, 53, 211
New Belgium Brewery case study, **32**
New Zealand Dairy Board, 6
New Zealand Dairy Group, 6
News Ltd, **205**
Nigeria, 47
Nilekani, Nandan, **413**, 414, 424
Nirvana Art Gallery case study, **374–7**
Nissan Motor Company, 508, **509**
Nitro, **445**, 446, 447, 452–3, 462
Nohria, Nitin, 141, 144
noise barrier (communication), 326–7, 330, **333–5**
Nokia, 267
nominal group technique, **311**
non-programmed decisions, 235, 246
nonverbal communication, 112, 275, 302, 303, 310, 327, 328, **330–1**, 332, **336–7**, 338, 386, 393, 398
non-work stressors, 204, **208–9**
norming, 275, **276**
norms, 275, **276–9**, 282, 336, 367, 391, 429
see also team norms
Nortel Networks, 13
Norway, 212
novelty, 71

O

obeya, **270**
object characteristics, **71**
observation, 85, **87–9**
observational research, 547, **553–4**
occupational choice model (Holland), **56–7**, 517
occupational stress, **209**
office design, **340–1**, 362, 425, 477, 480
'offshoring, 7
Oliveira, Patricia, 336
OMD, 249
omitting, 335
O'Neill, Catherine, **94–6**
open communication, 249, 313
open systems, 513
open systems anchor, 16, **18–19**
openness to change, 43, 44
openness to experience, 53, **54**
operant conditioning, *see* behaviour modification

opinion, 307
opportunity evaluation, **239**
opportunity identification, 234, **235–8**
optimism, 114, 210, 211, 217, 240
Optus, **35**, 36, 39
oral communication, 327
organic structure, **452–3**, 462, 464
organisational awareness, 114
organisational behaviour defined, **4**
organisational behaviour study, **5–6**
organisational behaviour trends, **6–15**
organisational change, 245, 268, 370, 372, 429
    action research approach to, **512–14**, 516
    appreciative inquiry approach to, **514–15**
    change agents &, **511–12**
    cross-cultural issues in, **516–17**
    diffusion of, **512**
    ethical issues in, **516–17**
    Lewin's forcefield analysis model of, **502–5**, 511, 516
    parallel learning structure approach to, **516**
    personal change &, **517–18**
    unfreezing, changing and refreezing, **505–10**
    see also leadership; mergers
organisational change need diagnosis, 513
organisational charts, 453
organisational citizenship, 39, **40**, 45, 54, 119, 120, 122, 148, 370, 372, 428
organisational commitment, **119–21**, 186, 212, 370, 387, 428, 551
organisational comprehension, 120–1
organisational culture, 3, 4, 20, 43, 81–2, 176, 214, 343, 372, 390, 424
    changing and strengthening, **487–8**
    deciphering through artefacts, **478–80**
    definition of, 476
    elements of, **476–8**
    merging &, **484–7**
    performance &, **480–3**
    socialisation &, **489–93**
organisational design, contingencies of, **462–4**
organisational effectiveness, 426
organisational efficiency, 424, 452
organisational environment, **269–71**, 302
    see also external environment
organisational environment stressors, 204, **208**
organisational expectations, 480
organisational flexibility, 452

organisational goals, 172, 186, 238, 246, 269, 276, 282, 283, 365, 404, 423, 426, 464, 512
organisational hierarchies, **340–2**, 363, 477, see also organisational structure
organisational justice, **153–9**
organisational language, 476, **479**
organisational leadership, 269, **271**, 300, 313, see also leadership
organisational learning, see knowledge management; organisations
organisational loyalty, 488, 492, 551
organisational memory, **21–2**, 488
organisational objectives, 266, 267, 282, 317, 363, 365, 397, 423, 483
organisational politics, 204, 299, **369–72**
organisational processes
    organisational change, **500–26**
    organisational culture, **474–99**
    organisational structure, **444–73**
organisational purpose, 266
organisational research, **546–55**
organisational rewards, **175–6**
organisational socialisation, **488–93**
organisational stages, **490–2**
organisational status, 328
organisational strategy, **464**
organisational structure, 4, 302, 513
    communication &, **340–2**
    contingencies of organisational design &, **462–4**
    definition of, 446
    division of labour and coordination &, **446–9**
    elements of, **449–53**
    forms of departmentalisation, **453–62**
    teams &, 269, **271**, **458–60**
    see also organisational hierarchies
organisational subcultures, **477–8**, 479, 481
organisational successes/failures, 429
organisational system incongruence, **504–5**
organisational values, 43, **44–5**, 186, 206, 372, 427, 477, 486, see also workplace values and ethics
organisations
    definition of, **4–5**
    joining and staying with, 39, **40**, 42
    learning &, 19–20, **84–91**, 513, 516
    perception in, **70–84**
    personality in, **52–7**

power &, **357–60**
size of, 48, 451, 452, 455, **463**
sources of conflict in, **389–93**
types of individual behaviour in, **39–42**
unlearning &, 22, 504, 510
organising bias, 554
Orr-Young, Simon, 528, 529
Outback Steakhouse, Inc., **119**
outcome/input ratio, **154**, **155**, 156
outcome valences, **147**, **148**
outcomes, **146–7**, **148**
outputs, 18, 19, 297, 448–9, 455, 462
outsourcing, 7, 461
overwork, 201, 202, **206**, **207**, **229**
ownership culture, 173, 176, 483
Oxygen Business Solutions, 217, **475**, 480,
    481, 487

P
Pacific National, 385, 386
packaging, 20
Pak 'n Save, **9**
Pakos, John, **201**
Panafric Hotel, **137**, 138
Panozza, Kevin, 540
parallel learning structure approach, **516**
parental leave, 3
Parker, Tom, **530–1**
part-time work, 10
participant observation, **553–4**
participative leadership style, 422, 419, 420,
    429–30, 431
participative management, **244–6**
passive noncompliance, 504
past experience, 143, 146
path-goal theory of leadership, **418–22**
Patrick Corp., **385**, 386, 387, 388, 389–90
'pay for pulse', **172**, 173
peer pressure, 148, 276–7, 307, 359, 541, 553
peer recognition, 137, 150
Pehlic, Hakija, **210**
people-orientated leadership, **418**, 422, 424,
    430, 431
perceiver characteristics, **71–2**
perceiving types, 54
perception
    attribution theory &, **78–9**
    communication &, **334**
    definition of, 70

halo effect &, **82**
improvement of, **83–4**
Johari Window &, **83–4**
primacy effect &, **82**
projection bias &, **82**
recency effect &, **82**
selective attention &, **71–2**
self-fulfilling prophecy &, **80–2**
social identity theory &, **73–4**
see also conflict perceptions; mental models;
    self-perception; stereotypes
perceptions, 36, 106, **334**
perceptions of politics scale, 380
perceptual blinders, **243**
perceptual errors, **79–82**
perceptual organisation and interpretation,
    72–3, 109
perceptual process, **70–3**, 109
perceptual screening bias, *see* bias
perceptual selective attention, 235
Perfect Pizzeria case study, **541–2**
performance
    job satisfaction &, **117–18**
    motivation &, **146–8**
    organisational culture &, **480–3**
performance appraisals, 177
performance-based rewards, **173**, **174–7**, 423
performance expectancy, **146–8**
performance feedback, 188
performance measurement, 284
performance-oriented culture, 476, 477
performance practices (applied)
    empowerment, **184–6**
    financial reward, **172–9**
    job design, **179–84**
    self-leadership, **186–9**
performance-to-outcome expectancy, 419
performing (team), 269–70, 275, **276**, 282
permanent employees, 12
persistence, 37, 247
person-job matching, **38**
person-organisation values congruence, **45**
personal bias, 549
personal change, **517–18**
personal characteristics, **370**, **372**
personal competence, **114**
personal goal setting, **187**, 217
personal identity, 73
personal leave, 216

personal observation, 546
personal power, 370, 371, 424
personal values, 13, 37, **42–3**, 44, 45, 143,
    145, 174, 206, **369**, 475, 478, 486
personalised power, 144
personality, 36, 37, 185
    attitude &, 108
    Big Five dimensions of, **53–4**, 57
    definition of, 52
    emotions &, **111**
    Holland's six types of, **56–7**, 517
    Myers-Briggs Indicator &, **54–5**, 240
    organisational behaviour &, **52–3**
    vocational choice &, **55–7**
personality tests, 52–3, 55, 240
personality traits, 40, 52, **53–5**, **57**, 111, 115,
    174, 189, 211, **415–17**, 424
perspective taking, 83
persuasion, 308, 364, 365, **366–7**, 368, 369,
    402, 414, 447
Peru, 47
Philippines, 116, 206, 337, 397
Philips, 455, 456
physical distance, 330
physical environment stressors, 204, **208**
physical exercise, 217
physical layout, 478, 510
physical setting (negotiation), **401**
physical space, 269, **270**, **340–1**
physical structures, 476, **479–80**
physiological consequences of stress, **212**
physiological needs, 139, 140
physiological stressors, 202, 203, 204, 211, 217
piece-rate systems, 174
Pike Place Fish Market, 109, **110**, **228**
pilot projects, **512**
Pixar Animation Studios, 341
podcasting, 328, 329
politeness, 328, 336, 388
politics, *see* organisational politics
pooled interdependence, 272, 391, 398–9
Portugal, 47, 48
Porzio, Dan, **517**
position power, 422
positive attitude, 109
positive emotions, 109
positive organisational behaviour, 81, **514–15**,
    see also resilience
positive reinforcement, **86**

Index (continued)

positive self-talk, **187–8**
positivism, **547**, 549
post-decisional justification, 241–2
power, 43, 44, 300, 337, 393, 396, 400, 402, 414, 416, 422, 504, 516
  contingencies of, **357**, **360–3**
  definition of, 356
  meaning of, **356**
  model of, **357**
  sources of, **357–60**, 364, 365
  see also expert power; fraud; influence;
    legitimate power; personal power,
    referent power; reward power
power bases, **357–60**, 368, 369
power distance, **47–8**, 49, 358, 364, 369, 404, 429–30
power need, **144**
power sharing, 48
pre-employment socialisation stage, **490–1**
prejudice, **77**
preliminary theory, 547
pressure, *see* stress
Pretoria Portland Cement, **171**, 174, 175, 179, 181, 448
PricewaterhouseCoopers, **304**, **484**
primacy effect, **82**
primary work units, **297**
priority shifts, 140
privacy, 516, 551
problem identification, 234, **235–8**
problem solving, 313, 393, 394, 396, 399–400, 401, *see also* decision making
procedural fairness, 404
procedural justice, 154, **156–9**
procedure clarification, **399**
process losses, 283
Procter & Gamble, 390, **425–6**, 445, 447
product champion, 249
product quality, 299, 427, 478
product/service structure, 455, 456
production blocking, 306, 310, 311
production teams, 267
productivity, 3, 13, 175, 180, 183, 271, 299, 452
profit-sharing plans, 173, **175**, 176
profitability, 176–7
programmed decisions, 235, 246
Project GLOBE, *see* GLOBE Project
projection bias, **82**

promotion-based pay, 173
propensity to trust, **305–6**, 319
prospect theory effect, **243**, 308
psychological consequences of stress, **212–13**
psychological contracts, **121–3**
psychological harassment, **205–6**
public image, 366
punishment, **86**, 305

Q
Qi Gong, 217
qualitative methods, 547, 549, 553, 554
quality action teams, 501
quality control, 427, 478
quantitative methods, 547
quantum change, 513

R
racial/ethnic diversity, 8, **9**
Radical Entertainment, **250**
Raman, Mr, **538**
Ramos, Nadia, **489**, 492
random samples, **550**
rational choice paradigm, **234**, **238**, 239
RBC Financial group, **51**
realistic job preview, **492**
realistic personality types, 56
'reality distortion field', 367
reality shock, **491**
receiver, 326, 327, 332, 333, 334, 338
recency effect, **82**
reciprocal interdependence, 272, 391, 398
reciprocity, 367
recognition, 137, 144, 150, 296
reduced personal efficacy, 212, 213
redundancy, 333, 338
referent power, 357, **359**, 363, 424
reflective observation, 90
refreezing, 503, 505, **510**, 514
Regency Grand Hotel case study, **191–3**
regional balance, 445
regional groups, 447–8, 455, 456
regulations, *see* rules and regulations
reinforcement, 80, **85–7**, 89
  see also self-reinforcement
relational psychological contracts, 121, **122**
relationship building, 337
relationship capital, 19
  see also loyalty; trust

relationship conflict, *see* socioemotional conflict
relationship management, **114–15**
relaxation, 217
relevant goals, 149
renewable energy certificates, 3
representative sampling, **549–50**
research, 513, **546–55**
research design strategies, **551–4**
resilience, 204, **210–11**, **223–4**
resistance (influence tactics), 368
resistance point (negotiation), 400, 402
resistance stage (general adaptation syndrome), **203**
resistance to change, 502, **503–5**, **506–10**, 544
resource allocation, 370, 447
resource increase, 396, **399**
resource scarcity, 370, 372, 389, **391**, 399, 462
resource sharing, 276, 393, 398, 453
resources, 19, 462, 512
  see also inputs
respect, 158, 328, 359, 388, 418, 419, 422, 430, 516, 529, 538, 541
responding, **339–40**
responsibility, 181, 182, 183, 208, 271, 300, 416, 529, *see also* corporate social responsibility
restraining forces, 502, **503–5**, **506–10**
'reward inflation', 87
reward power, 357, **358**, 361, 368
rewards, 4, 6, 88, 118, 144, 145, 148, 150, 159, 171, **172–93**, **269–70**, 271, 277, 279, 283, 296, 302, 424, 479, 486, 487, **488**, 510, 512, 514
Rising Sun Pictures, 233, 234, 247
risk, *see* conflict risk
rituals, 476, **478–9**, 488
Ritz Carlton Hotel, 137, 138
role ambiguity, **206**
role behaviour conflict, **209**
role conflict, **206**
role definition (team building), **312–13**
role establishment, 275
role expectations, 364
role management socialisation stage, 490, **491–2**
role-modelling, 364, 372, 493

role perceptions, 36, 37, **38–9**, 84, 512
role-related stressors, 204, **206**, 212, 214
roles, **279–80**, **312–13**
　see also team roles
routine breaking, **504**
Royal Dutch/Shell, 516
　see also Shell
RSM McGladrey Inc., 216
rules and regulations, 372, 386, 389, 396,
　399, 418, 452, 458
rumours, 343
Russia, 112

S
7-Eleven, **463**
sabbaticals, 217
sabotage, 40, 155, 158
sacrificial HR strategy, 539, 540
safety, 87, **88**, 139, 140
St George Bank, 417
SalesForce case study, **539–40**
sampling, **549–50**
sanctions, 358
SANS Fibres, 266
Sara Lee Bakery, **215**
SARS, **208**
SAS Institute case study, **526**
satellite organisations, 460, 461
satisficing, 238, **239**, 241
Savvides, George, **501**, 502, 505, 510, 511
SC Johnson, 46
scenario planning, 241
Schwartz's values circumplex, **43–4**
scientific management, **180**
scientific method, 16, 54, **548–9**
scoring keys for self-assessment activities,
　556–71
ScotiaBank, **489**, 492
seasonal employment, 12
security, 43, 44
seeing, 70
selective attention, 70, **71–2**, 328
self-actualisation need, 139, **140**, 141, 144,
　145, 211
self-assessment, 114, 517
self-assessment activities scoring keys, **556–71**
self-awareness, **114**, 115
self-confidence, 114, 186, 217, 247, 415, **416**,
　417

self-control, 114
self-determination, 184, 185, 186, 452
self-directed work teams, 267, **296–301**, 414,
　424, 449, 450, 458, 459, 538
self-direction, 43, 44, 46, 186, 423
self-enhancement, 43, 44
self-esteem, 79, 81, 153, 159, 211, 217, 218,
　236, 242, 307, 367, 510, 516–17
self-fulfilling prophecy, **80–2**, 420
self-fulfilment, 140
self-identity, 367, 518
self-image, 74, 142, 153, 268, 305, 370, 393
self-initiative, 300
self-justification, 243
self-leadership practices, **186–9**, 217, 423,
　424, 518
self-management, **114**, 115
self-monitoring, 55, 187, **188**, 189
self-motivation, 186, 422, 423
self-organisation, 461
self-perception, **73**, 75
self-reinforcement, **89**, 187, **189**, 217
self-serving bias, **79**
self-talk, **186–7**, 217
self-transcendence, **43**, 44
selling leadership style, 422
Selye, Hans, **202–3**
Semco Corporation, **185–6**
Semler, Ricardo, **185**, 186
sender, 326, 327, 332, 333, 334
seniority-based rewards, **172**, 173, 174
sense-making process, 480
senses, **70**, 71, 84, 109
sensing, **338–9**
sensing types, 54
separation merger strategy, **486–7**
sequential interdependence, 272, 391, 398,
　399
servant leadership, 418
service, 114
service industries, 12
service teams, 267
7-Eleven, **463**
sex stereotypes, 75, **76**, 77, 80, 431
sexual harassment, **205–6**
share options, 173, **175**, 176, 178
shared leadership, 414
shared values, 13, 42, 43, **120**
Shell, 304, 516

Shell Europe, **505–6**
Shell Gourami Business Challenge, **274**
Sherbo, Kyle, **162–3**
shifting responsibility, 308
'shock events', 42, 117
silence, 330, **337**
silent authority, **364**, 365, 369
Silex Systems Limited, 175
silos of knowledge, 20, 326, 456
simple organisation structure, **453**, 454
simple vs complex environments, **462**
simulated emergencies, **91**
Singapore, 12, 35, 47, 48, 49, 206, 213, 427
situation favourableness, 422–3
situational control, 422, **429**
situational factors, 36, 37, **39**, **51**
situational leadership theory, **422**
skill-based pay, 173
skill shortages, 40
skill variety, **181**, 182, 183
skills, 420, 423, 448, 449, 454
skunkworks, 265, 266, 267
smelling, 70
Smith Barney, **268**
smoothing, 355
social awareness, **114**, 115
social bonding, 310
social capital, 363
social competence, **114**
social control, 480
social esteem, 140
social glue, 480
social identity, 277, 280, 281, 305, 307, 365,
　388–9, 393, 480, 489, 492
social identity theory, **73–4**, 75, **76**, 77, 78,
　141, 142, 156, 268
social interaction, 144, 343
social knowledge, 488
social learning theory, **87–9**, 145, 186, 188
social loafing, **284**
social needs, 140, 141
social networks, 343
social norms, 143
social perception, **73–4**
social personality types, 56
social relationships, 142, 268, 343, 363
social responsibility, 416
　see also corporate social responsibility
social rules of justice, **158**

Index (continued)

social solidarity, 330
social status, *see* status
social support, **218**, 281, 282, 308, 326, 423
socialisation, 43, 487, **488**
socialisation agents, **492–3**
socialisation outcomes stage, 490
socialisation process improvement, **492–3**
socialised power, 144, 370, 416
socioemotional conflict, **387–9**, 392, 394, 402
sociotechnical systems theory, **297–300**, 301
soft influence tactics, **365–8**, 369
solutions, 236
Sony, **145**
South Africa, *see* Pretoria Portland Cement
Spain, 112
span of control, **449–51**, 452
specialised jobs, **179–80**, **446**, 448, 454, 458
specific goals, 149
Speedera Network, **149**
Spencer's Gourmet Foods, 528
Spirit of Tasmania, 38
spirituality, workplace, 211
stability, 487, **488**, 502, 504
stable vs dynamic environment, **462**
stakeholders, 3, 15, **19**, 50, 427, 452, 462, 464, 478, 481, 482, 513
Standard Motor Products, **301**
standardisation, 447, **448–9**, 452, 454, 463, 464
standardised outputs, 448–9
standardised processes, 448
standardised skills, 449
status, 141, 142, 159, **172–3**, 303, 307, 328, 398, 504
stereotypes, 49, **75–8**, 80, 83, 240, 369, 387, 392, 393, 398, **428**, 431
stimulation, 43, 44
stimuli, **70**, 71, 72
stock options, 173, **175**, 176, 178
stories and legends, 249, 476, **478**, 488
storming, 275, **276**, 279
strain-based conflict, **209**
strategic business units, 455
strategic partnerships, 544
strategic vision, **426**, 511
stress, 13, 36, 37, 42, 45, 53, 113, 182, 183, 189, 326, 335
  causes of, **204–9**
  change resistance &, 208, **507**, **510**

consequences of, 204, **211–13**, **217**
definition of, **202**
general adaption syndrome &, **202–3**
individual differences &, 204, **210–11**
informal groups &, 268
SDWTs &, 300
teams &, 300, 460
stress index, 214
stress management, 203, 210, **213–18**, **507**, **510**
stress responses, 202, 203, 210, **212–18**
stressors, **204–9**, 210, 211, 212
stretch goals, 150
strokes, 212
structural capital, 19
structural change, 502
'structure follows strategy', 464
subcontractors, 461, 462
subcultures, **477–8**, 479, 481
subjective expected utility, 235
subjective judgments, 241
subsidiaries, 455
substitutability, 357, **360–1**
subsystems, 18, **19**
Sullivan, Scott, **371**
summarising, 335
Sun Microsystems, 51–2, 272, 325, 326, 328
Sun Valley Middle School, **511**
superordinate goals, **396–7**, 426
supervisors, 447, 448, 449, 450, 452, 453, 454, 460, 492, 512
suppliers, 297
supportive leadership style, **419**, 420, 421, 423
surface acting, 113
Sutton, Robert, 553, 554
Sweden, 183, 299–300
swift trust, 306
Sydney Olympics 2000, **21**, 87
symbols, 426, 427, 479, **480**
Syme, Jim, 388
systematic research anchor, **16**
systemic discrimination, *see* unintentional discrimination
Szygenda, Ralph, **456–7**

T
30/60/90 feedback, 540
360-degree feedback, **151–2**, 177, 216, 358

tactic knowledge, **85**, 89
Taiwan, 47, **153–4**, 202, 207, 427
takeovers, **385**, 386, 387, 388, 390, **528–9**
Talbot, John, **530–1**
talking circles, **398**, 430
target points, 400, 401
task characteristics, 269, **271–2**
task control, **360–1**
task-control stressors, 204, **206**, **208**
task force (project) teams, 267
task identity, **181**, 182, 183, 186
task interdependence, **271–2**, 303, 389, **391**, 396, **398–9**
task-oriented leadership, **418**, 422, 423, 424, 431
task performance, **39–40**
task performance-based rewards, **173**, **174–7**
task-related conflict, *see* constructive conflict
task significance, **181**, 182, 186
task specialisation, 284
  see also specialised jobs
task standardisation, 180
task structure, 421, 422
tasting, 70
Tavistock Institute (UK), 297
Taylor, Frederick Winslow, **180**
team-based organisational structure, **458–60**, 464
team building, **311–13**, 544
team cohesiveness, 269, 275, **280–3**, 297, 303, 307, 310, 311, 312, 330, 387, **388–9**, 421, 553
team composition, 269, 271, **273–4**, 302, **303**
team decision making, 267, 296, 297, **306–11**
team design, **269**, **271–4**, **302–4**
team development, 269, **274–6**, 279, 283, **294–322**, 460
team diversity, **273–4**, 281, 308
team dynamics, **264–92**, 295, 299, 311, **421**, 504, 505, 510
team effectiveness, **269**, 271, 273, 280, 302
team environment, **269–71**, 302, **303**
team leaders, 271, 275–6, 279, 281, 283, 460
team member interaction, 281
team member similarity, 281
team norms, 42, 269, 275, **276–9**, 282, 307, 308, 312, 359, 372, **389**, 423, 489, 490, 508, 514
team objectives, 275

team performance, 269–70, 275, **276**, 282
team problems, **283–4**
team processes
  communication, 266, 269, **270**, **324–52**, 460
  conflict and negotiation, **384–411**
  decision making and creativity, **232–63**
  foundations of team dynamics, **264–92**
  high-performance team development, **294–322**
  leadership in organisational settings, **412–41**
  power and influence in the workplace, **353–82**
team rewards, **175**, **177**, 178
team roles, 269, 275, 276, **279–80**
team size, 269, **272–3**, **281**, 284, 302, **303**, 308
team structure, **308–11**
team subgroups, 273
team success, **281**
team survival, 269
team trust, **304**
team types, 266, **267**, 281
  see also virtual teams
team viability, 269
teams and groups, **266–8**, 453
  see also self-directed work teams; virtual teams
teams defined, **266**
teamwork, 114, 204, 266, 415, 431, 501
technological change, 461
technology, 206, 208, 299, 360, **463–4**
Technology One, **477**
Telecom New Zealand, **325**, 326
telecommunications companies, 35, 36, 38, 39
teleconferences, 303
telework, *see* virtual work
telling leadership style, 422
Telstra, 394, **395**
temporary employment, 12
Teo, Dr Charlie, 448
Teres, John, 334–5
territorial issues, 401
terrorism, 503
text messages, 335
Thai Carbon Black, **244**
Thailand, 35, **38**, **41**, 49, **191–3**, 202, 206, 244
theft, 40, 155, 158
theory, **546**, 550
theory building, **546–8**, 549, 554
theory testing, **547–8**

thinking types, 54
third-party conflict resolution, **402–4**
30/60/90 feedback, 540
thought patterns, constructive, **187–8**, 189
threats, 40, 142, 203, 205, 210, 281, 305, 307, 358, 364, 368, 370, 397, 398, 510
360-degree feedback, **151–2**, 177, 216, 358
time-based conflict, **208–9**
time management, 335
time pressures
  creativity &, 249
  negotiations &, **401**
  team decision-making &, **306–7**
  work-non-work stressor, **208–9**
timing (message), 338
Tokai Rubber Industries Ltd, 174
tolerance of change scale, **523**
Toll Holdings, **385**, 386, 387, 388, 389–90
'town hall meetings', 342
Toyota, 178, **270**, 272, **397**, 447
trade unions, *see* labour unions
tradition, 43, 44
training, 180, 189, 295, 449, 452
trait perspective of leadership, *see* competency perspective of leadership
Tramontano, Paul, **268**
transactional leadership, 420, **424**, 512
transactional psychological contracts, 121–2
transformational leadership, 414, 420, **424–8**, 488, 502, 511
transmission, 326, 327, 332
transparency, 114
Treetop Forest Products case study, **286–8**
trendspotters, **360**
triple-bottom-line, 15
TRLW Automotive, 458–9
Trujillo, Sol, 394, **395**
trust, **120**, 121, 138, 186, 275, 276, **304–6**, 310, 313, 359, 369, 388, 394, 399, 400, 402, 415–16, 418, 422, 428, 492, 510, 529
Turkey, 206
Type A behaviour pattern, **211**
Tyson Foods, 249–50

U
'ubuntu' values, 429, **430**
uncertainty, 48, 370, 391, 528, 529
uncertainty avoidance, **48**, 49
understanding, 326, 333, **397–8**, 398

unfreezing, 503, **505–10**, 516
unintentional discrimination, 75
United Kingdom, 156, **157**, 173, 202, 427, 491
United States, 35, 47, 48, 51, 112, 149, **161–3**, 175, 179, 202, 204, 211, 216
universal theories, 17
universalism, 43, 44
upward appeal, 364, **365**, 368
upward influence, **369**, **378–9**
US Trust, 479, 484, **485**, 487
utilitarianism, **49–50**

V
valences, 146, **147**, **148**, 418
value system, 43, 45
value types, **43–4**
values, 36, 37, **42–9**, 141, 143, 145, 273, 279, **369**, 386, 389, **390–1**, 413, 414, 427, 429, 475, 477, 478, 480, 481, 486, 487, 488, 490, 492, 514, 516, **517**, *see also* cultural values; organisational values; personal values
values and ethics (workplace), **13–15**
values circumplex, Schwartz's, **43–4**
values congruence, **44–6**, 483
Vardalos, Nia, **237**
variability, 463, 464
variable interval schedule, 87
variable ratio schedule, **87**
variables, **550–1**, **552**, 553
Varian Australia, 271, 272
variances, 297, **299**
verbal communication, **327–9**, 330, 332, 336, 398, *see also* language barriers
vicarious learning, 89
Vicelik, Katarina, **187**
video conferencing, 295, 303, 332, 40
violence, *see* workplace violence
Virgin Blue, **385**, 386, 389
Virgin Group, **385**, 386, 387, 388, 390
virtual corporations, **461**
virtual team environment, **302–3**
virtual team processes, 302, **303–4**
virtual team tasks, 302, **303**
virtual teams, **13**, 265, 267, **295**, 296, **301–6**, 391
virtual whiteboards, 295, 301, 303
virtual work, **12–13**, **215**, 502

visibility, 357, **361–2**
vision, 413, 416, 424, **426–8**, 510, 511
vision communication, **426–7**
vision modelling, 426, **427**
visual special effects, **233**, 247
vocational choice, **55–7**, 517
Vodafone, 5, 13, 52, 69
voice, **117**, 118, 157
voice conferencing, 295
voice intonation, 112, 327, 330
voice mail, 335
Volvo, **299–300**

W

W.L. Gore & Associates Inc., **459**
wages and benefits, 529
    financial reward practices &, **172–9**
    organisational justice &, **153–4**, **155**
    see also rewards
Wal-Mart, 15, **477**
walking the talk, 425, **427**
Wang, Peter, 543, 544
The Warehouse, 15
Warner Village Theme Parks, **105**, 109, 111, 113
weblogs, **325**, 327, **328–9**, 332, **341**, 343
Welch, Richard, **360**
wellness programs, 217
West Australian police service, **492**
Western Water, **176**
Westpac Banking Corp, **3–4**, 10, 13, 15, 42, 46, **121**, 216
Weta Digital, 233, 234, 247
Whirlpool, 479
wikis, **341**
Wilkins, Greg, 451
win-lose orientation, **393–4**, 399, 400, 401
win-win orientation, **393**, 400, 401, 529
Wipro Technologies, 84
withdrawal behaviours, 158
W.L. Gore & Associates Inc., **459**
women
    communication &, **337–8**
    conflict management &, 209, **396**
    hostile work environment &, 205
    influence tactics &, **369**
    leadership style &, **430–1**
    networking &, 363
    organisational justice &, **153–4**, **155**

sexual harassment of, 205
social identity &, **76**
stereotyping of, 75, **76**, 77, 80, **431**
time-based conflicts &, 209
value of money to, 172
workforce participation &, 8, **9**
Woodcroft Medical Centre, 201
work activity coordination, **446–9**
work alienation, 113
work attendance, 39, **42**
    see also absenteeism
work avoidance, 40
work behaviour and job satisfaction, **117**
work cycles, 446
work effectiveness, 181
work efficiency and job design, **179–80**, 182
work enthusiasts, 211
work environment, see creativity;
    environmental contingencies; external
    environment; organisational environment;
    physical environment stressors
work hours, 13, **206**, **207**, **215**, 482, 529
work incentives, 180
work-life balance, 6, **10–11**, 13, 22, 46, 214, **215–16**, 278
work-non-work stressors, **208–9**
work overload, 201, 202, **206**, **207**, 208
work-related stress, **200–13**
work sabotage, 40, 155, 158
work teams, see team building; team
    development; team processes; teams and
    groups
workaholism, 204, **211**, 214
workforce change, **8–10**, 502
workforce diversity, 7
workforce expectations, **10–11**, 22, 72, 80
workforce flexibility, 10, **11–12**, 173, 174, 182
workforce stability, 487, **488**
workplace aggression, see aggression
workplace emotions and attitudes, **105–35**
workplace fun, **105**, 109, **110**, 228
workplace motivation, **136–68**
workplace safety, 87, **88**
workplace spirituality, 211
workplace values and ethics, **13–15**, 18, **42–6**
workplace violence, **204**, 205
workspace design, **340–1**
    see also office design

World Wide Web, 237
WorldCom, 370, **371**
written communication, 327

X
Xerox, 13
Xerox PARC, 237

Y
Yamato Transport Company, 246
yielding, 394
Yum Brands Inc., 137

Z
Zang Ruimin, 427, 488